LITERATURE & PHOTOGRAPHY

FRONTISPIECE. William Henry Fox Talbot, 'A Scene in a Library,' from *The Pencil of Nature*, Part 2, Plate 8 (January 1845).

UNIVERSITY OF NEW MEXICO PRESS

ALBUQUERQUE

*L*IT

*P*HOTO

ERATURE

& GRAPHY

INTERACTIONS 1840 - 1990

A Critical Anthology edited by Jane M. Rabb

Library of Congress Cataloging-in-Publication Data

Literature and photography interactions, 1840–1990 : a critical
anthology / edited by Jane M. Rabb. — 1st ed.

p.   cm.

Includes bibliographical references and index.

ISBN 0-8263-1541-0 (cloth). — ISBN 0-8263-1663-8 (pbk.)

1. Literature and photography.   2. Photography in literature.

I. Rabb, Jane M. (Jane Marjorie), 1938–   .

PN56.P46L57   1995

809'.93356—dc20   95-4369
                                                          CIP

For Adam and Rosie, as always

Contents

Preface

The origin and evolution of this critical anthology may help interested readers at the start (or, perhaps more meaningfully, afterwards) better understand its present orientation and structure. My previous book, on the original illustrations for the novels of Charles Dickens, fueled my curiosity about the history of photography and its use in literature. Alan Trachtenberg helped to mobilize this curiosity with his 1979 complaint that "transactions between photography and formal literature" were "important and largely uninvestigated." Over the next decade, preparations for teaching a seminar focusing on some of those "transactions" generated a list for the students of relevant pieces by significant artists. The list burgeoned to such an extent that by the time Beaumont Newhall and others saw it, all agreed it should be more widely shared. The form and contents of the resulting critical anthology have changed many times since. But its purpose has remained constant: to facilitate and even expand the kind of investigation that Trachtenberg urged into the fascinating and varied relationships between serious writers and photographers, in whatever form they worked, from 1840 to 1990.

Who would be interested in such a study? Clearly there was an enthusiastic and varied potential audience including both generalist and specialist readers interested in either or both fields. The former would require scope; the latter depth. How to engage both groups? A dual approach seemed necessary. It was clear that a survey of the largely unmapped territory was needed, doing for English-speaking readers what Erwin Koppen's survey and Diego Mormori's anthology did for German and Italian ones respectively. But areas for deeper mining, such as those revealed in the specialized studies of Ralph Bogardus, Carol Shloss, Jefferson Hunter, and Lorraine York, should be suggested as well. One hundred texts, each with a brief introductory preface and most accompanied by photographs, could reveal to the generalist the variety and quality of the interactions between the two fields, while prefatory notes and a pioneering bibliography of the subject could suggest further directions to the specialist.

Function dictated other aspects of the anthology's structure which evolved through several phases. The work was initially conceived as a collection of primary source materials paired with critical analyses—such as excerpts from Nathaniel Hawthorne's *House of Seven Gables* with the essay by

Alfred Marks, or the piece by Virginia Woolf about Julia Margaret Cameron with Charles Millard's article on Cameron's illustrations for Alfred Tennyson's *Idylls of the King*. But it quickly became evident that there was far more primary source material by important literary figures than anticipated. Much of this material, even by "canonical" authors, has been little known or appreciated, often because it appeared in less formal genres, such as introductions, reviews, diary entries, and letters, rather than in poetry, plays, or novels. Some, to be sure, are not their author's best-known or best works, but they may illuminate them as well as our subject.

Aside from essays by writers better known for their imaginative works, such as E. M. Forster, William Carlos Williams, and Richard Howard, all "secondary" material—even the widely influential writings of Susan Sontag, Walter Benjamin, and Roland Barthes—appears mainly in the introduction and the bibliography. Laurence Senelick's survey of photography and the drama, the first on this important topic and specially commissioned for this anthology, is featured in the appendix.

Given the decision to include only primary sources as selections, the question became one of format. Over time, many were tried—and mostly abandoned. For example, an arrangement by literary or even by photographic genre was considered. Indeed, there are enough essays, short stories, plays, poems, prefaces, memoirs, and "literary" portraits and various kinds of photographs for fine anthologies devoted to each. But such categorization, no matter how welcome its apparent coherence, skewed and obscured the historical evolution of the two fields, separately and in tandem. An arrangement by country worked well for nineteenth-century selections but broke down completely in the more mobile twentieth century; under which country would one place Vladimir Nabokov or Robert Capa? An arrangement by theme—such as the writer as photographer or the photograph as inspiration for a literary work (or vice-versa)—or type, such as the spiritualist or travel photograph, failed as many selections suited more than one topic; under which heading would one put the relevant works by Sir Arthur Conan Doyle? The present largely chronological order won by positive default. It provided the best sense and sweep of the subject's evolution, as well as stimulating juxtapositions along the way, and allowed maximum flexibility for readers, scholars, and especially teachers, to tailor their own groupings with minimum interference by the editor.

Occasionally, however, strict chronological order is honored in the breach. When selections concerning one era were written or published in a much later one or when juxtapositions seemed valid historically and provocative intellectually, pieces are placed accordingly, regardless of publication date. Thus, for example, Brassaï's account of Lewis Carroll is placed in the 1850's, when the Oxford don began to photograph, rather than in 1975, when it was published. Margaret Bourke-White's and Erskine Caldwell's memoirs, published in 1963 and 1980 respectively, both recall the summer of 1936 and are accordingly placed there; similar thinking located the selections by Wright Morris (1982), James Agee (1946), and Gordon Parks (1966), which mainly concern activities in the 1930's and 1940's. The Nabokov poem, first published in Russian in 1927 but not widely known until translated into English for a 1971 volume, or the Hardy poem, probably written in the 1890's but not published until 1917, afforded appealing alternatives; both shuttled back and forth between possible dates before landing in their present slots.

The process of choosing the hundred selections proved fascinating and frustrating throughout. The question of which artists to represent posed a continual challenge. This anthology could easily have been devoted only to artists writing in English, with some international flavor provided by photographers whose work more easily crosses borders and by rare multilingual writers like Nabokov. But it seemed parochial to ignore those foreign writers who either influenced English-speaking ones in either medium or whose work was irresistible in this context, despite the editor's lack of expertise beyond her Anglo-American heritage. (Doubtless other cultures have produced other significant works, less widely known in English-speaking circles and thus not mentioned here.) Similarly, the anthology could have included only relevant texts by notable writers or, if reduced in scale, even by notable photographers; but to eliminate any illuminating piece on either basis would have narrowed its scope and purpose.

Within these elastic guidelines, there were priorities for selections, though never quotas. The artists to be featured were headed by the doubly gifted: those writers who were also avid photographers or those (far fewer) photographers who also wrote about literary artists, works, or issues. Though their avocational work is rarely as successful as the vocational, the engagement of these versatile creators in dual fields merits special attention. Next would come those artists involved in collaborations, some involving pre-existing texts or photographs (both usually by dead artists), others newly conceived. Some joint efforts originated with one or both artists; others with a publisher or, occasionally, an agent. Some collaborations were actively coordinated (Walker Evans and James Agee, John Steinbeck and Robert Capa, Richard Avedon and Truman Capote); some evolved separately in time (Langston Hughes and Roy DeCarava) and place (Richard Avedon and James Baldwin); one was even accomplished by a group of photographers with the writer holding veto power (Paul Laurence Dunbar and the Hampton Institute Camera Club). The motivation, type, and even the process of collaboration, however, appear to have little effect on its ultimate quality.

Next would appear those works generated by professional influence, whether admiration (Paul Strand for Sherwood Anderson), antipathy (Agee and Evans vs. Bourke-White and Caldwell), or a personal relationship, whether affectionate (Nadar and George Sand) or inimical (Cecil Beaton and Evelyn Waugh). Some writers mention photography in many works (Marcel Proust, Vladimir Nabokov, Jerzy Kosinski), just as some photographers often allude to writers (Walker Evans); others utilize the other art rarely (Hilaire Belloc, Villiers de l'Isle-Adam). Finally would come the essays—often nowadays in the guise of prefaces, introductions, and afterwords—by one type of artist about the other, usually a writer about a photographer. These pieces are as varied in motive and content as the works they discuss: some appear objective and disinterested (E. M. Forster, Minor White, Richard Howard); others more subjective, especially those written by friends (George Sand on Nadar, Jack Kerouac on Robert Frank)

1. André Kertész. 'Paris, December 9, 1963.'

or family members (Carl Sandburg on Edward Steichen); and some more obviously commercial (Jean-Paul Sartre on Henri Cartier-Bresson, Lawrence Durrell on Bill Brandt). Whatever their origins, all are informative and interesting on various levels.

But even these priorities remained tacit. Ultimately, the selections were made on the basis of relevance, significance, and interest (only rarely did these criteria compromise quality)—with the hope that the final contents would prove both representative and varied. New names or works compelled continuous reevaluation of the selections, a process which only a deadline foreclosed [Fig. 1]. The availability of material elsewhere was not grounds for exclusion, nor was rarity, however tempting, grounds for inclusion. Some selections have been widely reprinted (those by George Bernard Shaw, Walker Evans, Howard Nemerov, and Duane Michals) or widely quoted (Nathaniel Hawthorne, Henry James); more, however, merit wider circulation and recognition (for example, those by Alexandre Dumas, Villiers de l'Isle-Adam, W. H. Auden, Michael Ondaatje, Michel Tournier). A few have not been published previously, such as the correspondence from Ansel Adams to Mary Austin, between Minor White and Roy DeCarava, and the preface by John Updike. And, of course, most have never appeared in this kind of hospitable context, which may suggest further dimensions to each. Entire pieces or chapters were preferred to scenes and quotes, though exceptions were necessarily made for excerpts from lengthy memoirs, novels, correspondences, and travel accounts. Some obvious candidates were simply too long (Oliver Wendell Holmes, Sr.'s articles, Italo Calvino's short story, and John le Carré's preface for Don McCullin) or too costly to include. Doubtless some readers will miss one favorite artist or object to another's inclusion. These choices are not engraved in stone, but all should contribute to understanding the interaction between the two fields.

A constant dilemma involved *which* of the many possible pieces to use by some of the prolific writers, such as Lewis Carroll, Walt Whitman, Gordon Parks, Jonathan Williams, and Richard Howard, or which pictures by a particularly literate photographer, such as H. P. Robinson, Man Ray, and Henri Cartier-Bresson. Whenever possible, the artist helped decide which text or image best represented him or her. Another challenge was deciding which artist best represented a like-minded group. Who, for example, to select among the many talented portrait photographers of literary figures, or feminist writers, or photographers using language, or poets inspired by a photograph? Whether applying short or longer perspectives, it remains difficult to determine which acclaimed artist of a recent decade (or even the past half century) will prove the most representative or enduring. The introduction pays perhaps disproportionate attention to recent trends, compensating for the fact that this anthology could not represent only selections since 1960. The present contents reflect the editor's best judgment at this moment.

Other concerns surfaced along the way. Some names—Nadar, Alfred Stieglitz, Gertrude Stein, Man Ray, Jean Cocteau, Brassaï, Henri Cartier-Bresson, Manuel Alvarez Bravo—may recur too frequently for some tastes, but the repetition accurately reflects their importance in modern aesthetic history. Sometimes, worthy selections were ultimately incorporated into others or converted to their notes. Thus, for example, Thoreau's musings wound up cited in the Emerson and Carlyle selection while Melville's are mentioned in the Hawthorne. F. Holland Day's essay on William Morris, Maurice Maeterlinck's credo for Stieglitz, Paul Valéry's address on the centenary of Daguerre's announcement, Virginia Woolf's excerpt from *Three Guineas*, Robinson Jeffers's appreciation of Edward Weston, and poems by Philip Larkin and Elizabeth Bishop—all once planned as separate texts—now survive as subordinate materials. Fully one-quarter of the selections have been similarly replaced or reconfigured. As Peter Prescott astutely observed in the introduction to his collection of short stories for Norton, every anthology generates a "shadow" one as well.

Other problems persist. For example, troubling historical gaps occur that cannot in good aesthetic conscience be filled. There was no obvious selection to represent the Civil War period except one of Herman Melville's weaker poems or perhaps a passage from Stephen Crane's *Red Badge of Courage*, clearly but not explicitly influenced by the photographs taken by Mathew Brady and his colleagues. Similarly no suitable piece evoked the First World War. The many possible texts inspired by the 1960's civil rights movement or the Vietnam conflict were eventually pushed out by others of the past quarter century, less topical but perhaps more enduring.

There were some gratifying surprises, however, when the final selections were reviewed. No deliberate effort had been made to represent the preeminent genres in both fields, but an amazing variety of literary and photographic forms resulted. The novel, short story, essay, travel narrative, letter, diary, and poetry are all represented. So are most photographic genres—artistic, documentary, and experimental—including portraits, landscapes, urban scenes, still life, as well as hybrids like photomontages and photograms, and they employ a variety of modes—pictorial, "straight," montage, collage, directorial—as well as other innovative approaches.

There also was no attempt to be geographically diverse or multicultural, but the anthology is both mainly because modern artists, particularly photographers, frequently changed countries and traveled to every continent, sometimes voluntarily, sometimes by necessity. Women and minorities needed no affirmative action to be included here as significant contributors to both fields. Between the time of George Sand and Julia Margaret Cameron and that of Rosellen Brown and Elsa Dorfman, many female artists have achieved recognition in literature and in photography. Minority artists have fared better in our culture as writers than as photographers, but the future will surely produce more than one Gordon Parks and more Asian photographers as internationally admired as Eikoh Hosoe.

Only after the text selections were settled could the photographs be chosen. They accompany most but not all of the texts; occasionally a desired illustration proved unavailable or its conditions of use were prohibitive. Some selections are more fully illustrated than others; a few did not seem to require any. Often the accompanying photograph illustrates an important point made in the selection's preface rather than the text, such as the ones by W. S. Gilbert and Lawrence Durrell. Most regrettably, costs prevented the reproduction of some prints that originally appeared in color, such as those by Leonid Andreyev, Edward Steichen, Gisèle Freund, Marie Cosindas, and John Baldessari; readers are urged to consult the originals in the sources noted.

The title of this critical anthology provoked debate throughout. All agreed it should include the words "Literature" and "Photography" but in which order—and why? That question became a Rorschach test of interests and values. All agreed that a subtitle was needed to indicate the interactive focus and time span. But should the key word be "interactions," "transactions," or "cross-currents"? And what about dates? The starting point was 1839–1989, but 1840–1990 proved not only more accurate in terms of the contents but had the added merit of being easier to say, write, and remember while avoiding any confusion with the recent sesquicentennial volumes. Meanwhile, a table of contents listing one hundred selections involving two artistic fields over a century and a half was obviously visually overwhelming, needing division of some sort. The varied contents with their overlapping themes and forms resisted attempts to categorize and elucidate definitively; each generalization bred too many exceptions. Accordingly the headings adopted—dates at quarter-century intervals—try to lend visual if not conceptual clarity.

Similarly, the introduction and the selections themselves could not be linked or guided by any transcendent concept or ideas beyond the obvious ones: that the historical interactions between literature and photography are varied and interesting and have, at times, been unusually frequent, intense, and productive. This anthology aims to track these interactions and stimulate fresh knowledge and insights, not to promote an overriding theory or interpretation. Such a theory or an interpretation was admittedly sought but not found—hardly surprising given the daunting variety of subjects, artists, forms, periods, and cultures involved. Few enough concepts illuminate the entire history of literature or of photography, never mind encompass or transcend both. In the meantime, viable themes and generalizations recur throughout the introduction—appropriately and humbly entitled "Notes"—which should stimulate conceptually minded readers.

The bibliography, eleven pages at the time of the anthology's conception, grew quickly to its present length. It includes many but not all the works cited throughout the anthology as well as other relevant titles. The painstaking work was largely completed in May of 1992, assured that its pioneer status would give it undeniable value, whatever its deficiencies. The completely unanticipated publication the following month of *Photography and Literature: An International Bibliography of Monographs,* compiled by Eric Lambrechts and Luc Salu, which includes listings in twenty languages of secondary as well as primary source material, deflated that hubris. But serious readers will still need to consult this bibliography, which contrasts in many important respects to theirs. Mine includes more works from English-speaking countries, lists relevant journal and magazine articles as well as books, and cites novels, poems, and plays as well as nonfiction that use, in some significant way, actual or fictional photographs or photographers. My bibliography also follows the traditional library practice of citing in a collaboration whichever artist is listed first, which facilitates finding material—though, until recently, it also often unfairly minimized the photographer's role. Finally, I have tried to check each entry's publication data, which sometimes vary from that supplied in library catalogues and even published bibliographies, by looking at the actual book, article, or dissertation; an asterisk appears before titles not personally reviewed. Readers are urged to contact the editor through the publishers to suggest additional titles or supply further publication information.

Throughout, the paragraphing, spelling, and punctuation of the original texts, however outmoded or idiosyncratic, have been retained whenever possible.

It is hoped is that this anthology will instruct and delight the reader as much as it did the editor and facilitate the study of these two fields, both so central to world civilization.

Cambridge, Massachusetts

Acknowledgments

A critical anthology is necessarily a cooperative rather than a competitive intellectual enterprise. But few can have benefitted from so much continual help from so many knowledgeable and generous people as this one. From the beginning, the endeavor was blessed with a suitable godparent. The late Beaumont Newhall, whose books introduced me to the history of photography, welcomed and sponsored the idea of its publication. Thereafter, Janet Buerger, Eugenia Parry Janis, Elise Katz, Esther Pullman, and Laurence Senelick functioned like guardian angels—often invoked, but as often appearing unsummoned—giving timely assistance and encouragement in countless ways.

Others provided a variety of indispensable services, with patience or expediency, as necessary. Andrew Cahan of Andrew Cahan Booksellers and Fred and Elizabeth Pajerski suggested or located essential books throughout this project. William Barry III and Bill Jay shared their private bibliographical lists. Other important texts were suggested by Timothy Dow Adams, Lillian Bulwa, A. D. Coleman, Amy Conger, Sheryl Conkelton, Jennifer Green, Joseph C. Harris, Laura Hubber, Robert Kiely, Arturo Patten, Thomas Richards, Susan Suleiman, Alan Trachtenberg, and Arthur Trottenberg. Frank Bidart and Lloyd Schwartz, later reinforced by William Alfred, William Corbett, John Hollander, Jane Shore, and Helen Vendler, advised on relevant contemporary poetry; Pearl and Daniel Bell, Margery Gullette, and Peter Prescott shared their knowledge of contemporary fiction, as did Laurence Senelick on Continental literature since 1839. John and Jill Walsh facilitated my use of the Getty Museum's resources, which significantly affected the evolution of this anthology. At a critical juncture, John Szarkowski refined my criteria for selecting the texts.

Such a work depends on the resources of numerous library and museum collections and the cooperation of their staffs, especially the remarkable ones at Harvard, who always did more than their jobs required. My special gratitude goes to the following people for their multiple services: in the Office of the Director of the Harvard University Library, Joan P. Nordell; at the Widener Library, Amy Benson, Charles Berlin, Joe Bourneuf, Kevin J. Donnelly, Michelle Durocher, James Fraser, Jennifer L. Hanlin, Elizabeth Smith, Asuncion Vecchio, and, above all, Barbara Dames, Carolyn Fawcett,

Marion Schoon, and Gerald C. Schwertfeger; at the Fogg Museum, Renata Hejduk and the late Davis Pratt; at the Fine Arts Library, Thomas Batchelder, Jeremy Dawson, Steve Mitchell, Abby Smith, and Cathrine Wolcott; at the Houghton Library, William H. Bond, Elizabeth Falsey, Eleanor M. Garvey, Bonnie Salt, and Richard Wendorf; at the Sackler Museum Photography Department, Michael Nedzweski, Elizabeth Gombosi, and Catherine Weller; at the Harvard Theatre Collection, Brian Benoit, Michael Dumas, Catherine Johnson, and especially Joe Keller; and at the Hilles Library, Suzanne Kemple and Sandra Flores.

Staff members of other American and foreign institutions similarly provided invaluable assistance, for which I am indebted.

In New England: at the Art Institute of Boston, Bonnie Robinson and Christopher James; at the Boston Athenaeum, Sally Pierce and Catharina Slautterback; at the Boston Museum of Fine Arts, Clifford Ackley, John J. Chvostal, Anne Havinga, Shelley Langdale, Karen Quinn, Sue Reed, Barbara Shapiro, and Theodore Stebbins; at the Boston Public Library, John Dorsey, John Ditman, and Alice Kane; at the John Hay Library at Brown University, Jennifer Lee and Patricia Lynch; at the Massachusetts Historical Society, Kathy Griffin, Virginia Smith, and especially Chris Steele; at the Photography Resource Center at Boston University, Dan Younger; at the Thoreau Lyceum, Anne McGrath; at the Mark Twain Memorial, Maura Hagearty and Beverly J. Zell; and at Yale University, Daria Ajue, Suzanne Danos, Rick Hart, Patricia Willis, and especially Dorothea Reading at the Beinecke Rare Book and Manuscript Library; Elizabeth Fairman and Scott Wilcox at the Mellon Center for British Art; and Richard Field, Lisa Hodermarsky, and Lyle Williams at the Yale University Art Gallery.

In New York: for the James Agee Trust, Mary Newman; at the George Arents Research Library at Syracuse University, Carolyn Davis; at Columbia University, at the Rare Book and Manuscript Library, Bernard Crystal and at the Maison Française, Jacqueline Desrez; at the International Museum of Photography at George Eastman House, Katharine Bassney, Barbara Schafter, Becky Simmons, Joseph Struble, David Wooter, and especially Rachel Stuhlman; at the Gilman Paper Company Collection, Maria Umali and especially Pierre Apraxine; at HarperCollins, Inc., Donna Slosky; at *Life* magazine, Marie B. Schumann; Donna Slosky; at Magnum Photos, Inc., Joanne Seador; at the Metropolitan Museum of Art, Maggie Cannon, Malcolm Daniel, Mary Doherty, Maria Morris Hambourg, and especially Jeff Rosenheim; at the J. Pierpont Morgan Library, Susan Walsh and Frederick W. Wilson; at the Museum of Modern Art, Nicole Frideler, Peter Galassi, and Edward Robinson; at the New York Public Library, Nancy Finlay, Edward Kasinec, and Warren Platt; and at the Whitney Museum of American Art, May Castleberry.

In the Middle Atlantic and the Midwest: at the Library of Congress, Verna Curtis, Carol Johnson, Jerry Kearns, and Barbara Natanson; at the National Gallery, Sarah Greenough and Margaret B. Cooley; at the National Portrait Gallery, Ann Shumard; at the Photography Collection, University of Maryland, Baltimore County, Tom Beck; at Princeton University, Charles Greene, Peggy Sherry, and Don Skemer at the Rare Book and

Manuscript Library, and Peter Bunnell and Toby Jurovics at the Minor White Archive; and at the Rutherford Free Library, New Jersey, Miriam Sawyer.

In the South and Southwest: at the Center for Creative Photography at the University of Arizona, Leslie Calmes, Victor La Viola, Marcia Tiede, Trudy Wilner Stack, and especially Amy Rule and Dianne Nilsen; at the Thomas Merton Study Center at Bellarmine College, Louisville, Kentucky, Robert E. Daggy; at the Mississippi Department of Archives and History, H. T. Holmes; at the Museum of Fine Arts in Houston, Anne W. Tucker; at the Harry Ransom Center for Humanities Research at the University of Texas at Austin, Roy Flukinger, Micki McMillan, and especially Andrea Inselmann; and at the Special Collections of the University of Virginia Library, George Riser.

In California: at the Bancroft Library at the University of California, Berkeley, at the Mark Twain Project, Robert H. Hirst, Lawrence Dinnean, Michael B. Frank, Robert Pack Browning, Sonny Gotberg, and Weiming Li, and at the Photograph Services Office, Robert Ogar; at the J. Paul Getty Museum, Gordon Baldwin, Jacklyn Burns, Weston Naef, and especially Andrea Hales; at the Harrison Memorial Library in Carmel, Linda Mills Coppens and Ruth M. Mazza; at the Huntington Library, Sara Hodson, Brita Mack, and Jennifer Watts; at the archives of the State of California Department of Parks and Recreation, Glenn E. Burch and Jan Thompson; and at the University of California at Los Angeles, at the Williams Andrews Clark Library, Dr. Michael Halls, and at the University Research Library, Anne Caiger and Lilace Hatayama.

Overseas: at the BBC Written Archives, Christina Harris; at the Bibliothèque Nationale, Bernard Marbot and Odile Faliu; at the British Library, in the Department of Manuscripts, J. S. Conway, Helen George, and Malcolm Marjorem, and in Reader Admissions, Charlotte Atkinson and Huw Smith; at the Cambridge University Library, Wendy Radford; at the Conan Doyle (Crowborough) Establishment, Malcolm Payne; at the Fox Talbot Museum, Michael Gray; at the Holton Picture Gallery, London, Anna Halvert; at the Israel Museum, Meir Meyer; at the Leeds Russian Archive at the University of Leeds, Richard Davies; at the Marylebone Library, London, Catherine Cooke; at the Maison Balzac, Anne Krimoff; at the Musée d'Orsay, Françoise Heilbrun and Philippe Néagu; at the National Portrait Gallery, London, Terence Pepper; at the Österreichisches Fotoarchiv im Museum Moderner Kunst, Vienna, Monika Faber; at the Österreichisches TheaterMuseum, Vienna, Haris Balic; at the Royal Photographic Society, Bath, Pamela Roberts and Debbie Ireland; at the St. John's College Library, Cambridge, Elizabeth Quarmby; at the Strindberg Museet, Anita Persson; at the Swedish Institute, Lena Daun and Harriet Lindh; at the Theatre Museum in London, Andrew Kirk, at the Trinity College Library, Dublin, Felicity O'Mahony; at the Fachbibliothek für Kunstgeschichte an der Universitätsbibliothek Wien, Vienna, Dr. Viktoria Talos-Lunzer; and at the Victoria and Albert Museum, Mark Haworth-Booth, Pamela King, and Kevin Edge.

Special thanks is also owed those artists, or their family members, who generously contributed time and material to their selections, making them more comprehensive, accurate, and interesting: Richard Avedon; John

Baldessari; Stefan Brecht; Rosellen Brown; Elizabeth Chanler Chatwin; Marie Cosindas; Roy and Sherry Turner DeCarava; Elsa Dorfman; Lee and Maria Friedlander; Allen Ginsberg; Emmet Gowin; Elizabeth Griffin-Bonazzi; Seamus Heaney; Richard Howard; Jill Krementz; Kiki Kosinski; Helen Levitt; Lisa Lyon Lilly; Rollie McKenna; Duane Michals; Hattula Moholy-Nagy; Inge Morath; Michael Ondaatje; Jill Faulkner Summers; Michel Tournier; John Updike; and Jonathan Williams.

The community of scholars truly acted like one throughout this project in many heartwarming ways. Readers will join me in thanking the following experts for their contributions: Ralph Harley on Fox Talbot, D. O. Hill, and Robert Adamson; the late Harry Levin on Honoré de Balzac and Marcel Proust; Denise Bechtel on the early portraits of Walt Whitman; Julia Ballerini, Claude Pichois, and especially Mary Harper on Gérard de Nerval; Digby and Christiane Neave on Alexandre Dumas; Jane Stedman on W. S. Gilbert; Patricia Chute on Leo and Sophia Tolstoy; Cathy Popkin on Anton Chekhov; Elinor Shaffer on Samuel Butler; Barry Jacobs on August Strindberg; Linda Haverty Rugg on Mark Twain; Helmut Gernsheim on Alfred Langdon Coburn; Judith Plotz on Hilaire Belloc; Richard Davies on Leonid Andreyev; Salvatore Nigro on Giovanni Verga; Richard Lancelyn Green on Arthur Conan Doyle; Henry Hatfield and Alfred Hoezel on Thomas Mann; William Koshland on Alfred A. Knopf; Richard Borden on Vladimir Nabokov; Kim Sichel on Brassaï; David Herwaldt on James Agee and Walker Evans; Judith Sensibar on William Faulkner; Paul Mariani on William Carlos Williams; Marsha Bryant on W. H. Auden; Vlada Petric on Lázsló Moholy-Nagy; the late John Hersey on Robert Capa; Peter Bunnell on Minor White; Leo Lensing on the Stockmann portrait of Alexandre Dumas, Günter Grass, and Peter Handke; Bruce Kellner on Carl Van Vechten; Marianne Charlton on Marion Morehouse; Michel Fabre, Werner Sollors, and Lynn Weiss on Richard Wright; Francis Steegmuller on Jean Cocteau; Martin Roberts on Michel Tournier and his French contemporaries; and Belinda Rathbone on John Updike.

Many foreign primary and secondary source materials required translation from French, German, Italian, Russian, or Swedish, which fluent colleagues and friends provided at many stages (and at all hours). Janet Buerger had roughly translated the Champfleury tale, which Laurence Senelick then helped to smooth; Sarah Bingham translated various secondary sources about Victor Hugo and worked with Marina Von Zuylen on the Adèle Hugo diary passages; Marina L. Frederiksen and Mary Harper refined the excerpts from Gérard de Nerval, none of us then aware of their prior English translation in *The Women of Cairo* (1929); Marie-Hélène Gold worked on the difficult Jean-Paul Sartre preface; Russell Alberts, David and Sonia Landes, Francis Steegmuller, and especially June Wilson helped with the allusive Jean Cocteau–Lucien Clergue correspondence, while Marina L. Frederiksen and Francis Steegmuller elucidated Cocteau's relevant poem and preface about Clergue. Norman Shapiro, thanks to Lillian Bulwa, verified my understanding of the Pléaide edition notes on the complex publication history of Villiers de l'Isle-Adam's *L'Eve future*.

Jennifer Charles, Mark Pinson, and especially Ruth Deutsch translated the highlights of Erwin Koppen's survey, *Literatur und Photographie,* as well as the contents of Thomas Mann's "Okkulte Erlebnisse" and "Die Welt ist schön." Ruth and Wolfgang Schocken, Anita Warburg, and the late Gisela Wyzanski provided rough translations of all the Bertolt Brecht quatrains, and Robert Spaethling helped choose and polish the ones included here. Marion Schoon and Leo Lensing translated the titles of various German works listed in the bibliography.

Barbara Lloyd and David Morgenstern translated letters from and texts by Italian scholars concerning Giovanni Verga; they also helped translate some of Verga's letters, as did Piero Boitani, Ruth Feldman, Anastasia Leshinsky, Michele Orlando, and Luciano Rebay. Elene Levin translated part of Alexandre Rodchenko's recollections of Vladimir Mayakovsky; and Pierre Apraxine, Craig Kennedy, John Malmstad, Hugh Olmstead, and William M. Todd interpreted, transliterated, and translated details of other Russian documents about Anton Chekhov and Leo Tolstoy. Barry Jacobs, Robert Selleck, and Brita Stendahl translated some Swedish phrases and data relevant to August Strindberg, and James C. Thomson, Jr., elucidated the romanization of Chinese names. Laurence Senelick, who understands most Continental languages, reviewed—in whole or in part—many of the translations that finally appeared in the anthology.

Still others facilitated this evolution and execution of this complicated work. Vicki Goldberg and Gail Buckland generously shared their long experience preparing complex manuscripts. Elise Katz, Carol Wozick, and Peter Prescott provided guidance and reassurance throughout the arduous permissions process. Adam Shorn and Adam Cohen provided essential computer services, often on an emergency basis. The following people answered countless questions, especially concerning the identity and whereabouts of various experts, materials, and rights holders: Daphne Abeel, Darcy Alexander, Mary Street Alinder, Philip Alleyn, Joyce Backman, Neil Baldwin, Larry Beck for the Sonnabend Gallery, Ralph Bogardus, Dorothy Bohm, Jane Brown for Faber & Faber (USA), Martha Buskirk for *October,* Raymond Corns, Dante Della Terza, Julian Edison, Florence Eichen for Viking Penguin, Norman Evans, George Firmage, Maryesther Fournier, Sally Fox, John Gambell, Ben-Zion Gold, William Goodman, Howard Greenberg and Sarah Morthland for the Howard Greenberg/Photofind Gallery, Wendy Hawkes for Houghton Mifflin, Henry Horenstein, Jeannette Hubber, André Jammes, Felicia Kaplan, Justin Kaplan, Richard S. Kennedy, Hans P. Kraus, Clifford Krainik, John Lambert, Gino Lee, Gérard Lévy, Anne McCauley, Ezra Mark, Richard McAdoo, Alexandra Munroe, John Nathan, Jack Naylor, Richard and Leonée Ormond, Colin Osman, Peter Palmquist, Richard Pfaff, Christopher Phillips, Daniel Pinck, Christopher Pullman, Roger Rosenblatt, Kellye Rosenheim, Claire de Rouen for A. Zwemmer Limited, Mary Ryan for W. W. Norton, William Sharpe, Alma Singer, Kevin Starr, Karen Strassler for the Arion Press, Rose Styron, Jeffrey Thomas, Whitney Tower, Judith Vishniac, Mara Vishniac, William Welling, Robert Whittacker, Jean Youngblood, and André Zarre and Livia B. Feigen for the André Zarre Gallery.

Dr. Katharine Tait and especially Luise Erdmann offered welcome suggestions about the substance as well as the style of the manuscript.

At the University of New Mexico Press, Dana Asbury proved the ideal editor throughout—professionally skillful and personally gracious, encouraging, tactful, good-humored, and patient. Tina Kachele designed the complex manuscript with flexibility and creativity.

My grown children also contributed their impressive talents to this anthology. The dedication attempts to express how much my son's wise counsel about publishing matters and my daughter's enthusiasm about the contemporary interests of her old-fashioned mother have meant.

2. W. S. Gilbert. 'Comic Physiognomist,' from *Men We Meet* series, 1867.

List of Abbreviations

The following abbreviations have been used throughout the notes and bibliography:

BBC	British Broadcasting Corporation, Written Archives Center, Reading, England
Beinecke	Beineke Rare Book and Manuscript Library, Yale University, New Haven, Connecticut
Bodleian	Bodleian Library, Oxford University, Oxford, England
Clark	William Andrews Clark Library, University of California, Los Angeles
CCP	Center for Creative Photography, University of Arizona, Tucson
GEH	International Museum of Photography at the George Eastman House, Rochester, New York
Getty	J. Paul Getty Museum, Malibu, California
John Hay	The John Hay Library, Brown University, Providence, Rhode Island
Houghton	Houghton Library, Harvard University, Cambridge, Massachusetts
HRHRC	Harry Ransom Humanities Research Center, University of Texas at Austin, Texas
Huntington	Henry E. Huntington Library, San Marino, California
JWJ	James Weldon Johnson Collections, Beinecke Rare Book and Manuscript Library, Yale University, New Haven, Connecticut
Lilly	Lilly Library, Indiana University, Bloomington
MHS	Massachusetts Historical Society, Boston
MM	Metropolitan Museum of Art, New York City
Merton Studies Center	Thomas Merton Studies Center, Bellarmine College, Louisville, Kentucky

Henry Miller Archives	Special Collections, University Research Library, University of California, Los Angeles
Minor White Archives	Princeton University, Princeton, New Jersey
MOCA	Museum of Contemporary Art, New York City
MOMA	Museum of Modern Art, New York City
Morgan	Pierpont Morgan Library, New York City
NYPL	New York Public Library, New York City
Princeton	Department of Rare Books and Manuscripts, Princeton University Library, Princeton, New Jersey
RPS	Royal Photographic Society, Bath, England
SUNY/Buffalo	Lockwood Memorial Library, State University of New York at Buffalo
UNM	Department of Special Collections, Zimmerman Library, University of New Mexico, Albuquerque
....	Ellipses used by author or editor of reprinted text.
. . . or	Ellipses added by anthology editor.
*	Editor has not seen the item cited.

Introduction

NOTES TOWARD A HISTORY
OF LITERATURE AND PHOTOGRAPHY

The following remarks may be more useful to the reader unfamiliar with the subject matter as an afterword than as an introduction. To prevent repetition of material found in the selections and the bibliography, examples of the generalizations made here are often provided parenthetically and citations are supplied only for those artists, works, or quotes not included in the selections or readily located in the bibliography.

I

Literature greeted photography warmly when the daguerreotype and the calotype were announced in 1839. Less threatened than painters by the new child of science, writers like Edgar Allan Poe and Walt Whitman in America and John Ruskin in England and others throughout the world heralded the daguerreotype process, although Nathaniel Hawthorne had trouble recalling its name and Herman Melville muttered, "What a devel [*sic*] of an unspellable word."[1] Though, etymologically, photography was defined as writing with light and could similarly be regarded as a system of notation and editing, it was not yet viewed as a "sister" art as painting often was.[2] Aside from working in "black and white" on paper, often in book format, photography appeared to have little in common with formal or even informal literature. Literature was older, firmly established, and more comprehensive; the photograph, despite its readier appeal to people of all ages, nationalities, and backgrounds, and despite its infinite documentary and imaginative possibilities, did not contest its superiority. Both co-existed peaceably in an expanding aesthetic universe.

Especially valued was the ability of Daguerre's process to represent landscapes, objects, and, above all, people more accurately than the eye could see or the mind remember. Few Victorians were more excited about the new portraiture than the young poet Elizabeth Barrett. For one who had suffered the loss of her brother as well as her health, "the wonderful invention of the day" promised a permanent proximity of loved ones. As she wrote enthusiastically to a fellow writer in 1843:

Think of a man sitting down in the sun and leaving his facsimile in all its full completion of outline and shadow, steadfast on a plate, at the end of a minute and a half! The Mesmeric disembodiment of spirits strikes one as a degree less marvelous. And several of these wonderful portraits . . . like engraving—only exquisite and delicate beyond the work of graver—have I seen lately—longing to have such a memorial of every Being dear to me in the world. It is not merely the likeness which is precious in such cases but the association, and the sense of nearness involved in the thing . . . the fact of the very shadow of the person lying there fixed for ever! It is the very sanctification of portraits I think—and it is not at all monstrous in me to say . . . that I would rather have such a memorial of one I dearly loved, than the noblest Artist's work ever produced. I do not say so in respect (or disrespect) to Art, but for Love's sake.[3]

Avid seekers of public recognition, like Walt Whitman and Mark Twain, were quick to take advantage of the daguerreotype and its successors. But soon, the photograph's ubiquity in the public as well as private sphere prompted some reservations. Melville grumbled in *Pierre* (1852) and elsewhere that a portrait of a known figure no longer immortalized genius but "now only dayalized a dunce" and that "true distinction" lay in not publishing one. Gérard de Nerval in 1854 remained disturbed by one unwelcome image of himself, perpetrated by the common practice of engraving daguerreotypes of notables; and in a later decade, Alfred Lord Tennyson complained to Julia Margaret Cameron that "I can't be anonymous by reason of your confounded photographs."[4] But most writers, then as now, seized every opportunity to publicize their images.

Meanwhile, William Fox Talbot, although slower to publicize and share his negative-positive process than Daguerre, more quickly allied photography with literature in other ways besides portraiture: first in his landmark serial publication, *The Pencil of Nature* (1844–46), in which a picture of library books suggested the potential power of combined images and words [Frontispiece], and then in a book, *The Sun Pictures of Scotland* (1845), which represented settings and landmarks mentioned in the celebrated works of Sir Walter Scott [Fig. 3].[5] Talbot's disciples in Scotland, D. O. Hill and Robert Adamson, were also inspired by their country's literary heritage. They photographed fisherfolk, whom Scott had featured in *The Antiquary* (1816) as an enduring archetype of the nation's history and character, as well as tableaux of friends, with suitable costumes and props, acting out passages from other Scott novels or Robert Burns's poems.[6] Publishers like Tauchnitz in Leipzig quickly took the hint, as the technology permitted, inserting photographs in new editions of suitable works like Hawthorne's *Marble Faun* (1860). Indeed, a significant number of the photographically illustrated books of the nineteenth century involved urban landmarks or rural landscapes described in the works of cherished writers, especially past poets. Talbot's pioneering *Sun Pictures* may have helped to define the kind of scenes used and their relationship to a text.[7]

While philosophical thinkers like Ralph Waldo Emerson, Thomas Carlyle, and Henry Thoreau pondered the implications of the new invention in letters, journals, and essays, other writers reacted more pragmatically. Some

writers, especially the French, tested the new invention in exotic locations. Théophile Gautier carried the cumbersome daguerreotype equipment throughout his visit to Spain (1840), as did his old school friend, Nerval, to the Near East (1843), though conditions in both places allowed only its minimal use. Six years later, using an improved paper process, Maxime Du Camp, accompanied by Gustave Flaubert, successfully documented monuments in the Egyptian deserts (1849–50). Alexandre Dumas *père* took along Gustave Le Gray on his long-planned cruise (1861), intending to photograph Greek, Turkish, and other sites famous in history and myth, and Arthur Rimbaud planned to be the first to photograph the Horn of Africa highlands in the early 1880's. Meanwhile, Nadar, encouraged by Charles Baudelaire, George Sand, and Jules Verne, among other writer friends, experimented with cameras and lighting both underground and in the air over Paris.

Some English and American authors were similarly adventurous. John Ruskin, for example, hired servants to help him make daguerreotype records of the Alps as well as distinguished examples of Continental architecture, while Arthur Conan Doyle, then a young doctor, photographed along the west coast of Africa. Meanwhile, early American photographers exploring the West, though not writers, conceived of themselves as "story-tellers" and used "narrative" rather than discrete scenes to give structure and meaning to their experience and values.[8] Whatever the results—and they were often impressive despite unwieldy equipment and daunting environmental conditions—all involved seemed exhilarated by the novelty of their accomplishments. And their audiences relished this enhancement of vicarious experience.

It is not coincidental that literary realism flourished after the invention of photography, earlier in France than elsewhere. As Paul Valéry observed in retrospect, "From the moment that photography appeared, the descriptive genre began to invade Letters . . . . In verse as in prose the decor and exterior aspects of life took an almost excessive place."[9] Indeed, many novelists, such as Champfleury and Émile Zola, may have tried to emulate the camera, with its impersonal, disciplined, detailed, and accurate mirroring of surface reality, in their work. Photography became a metaphor for the veracity and even creativity of many nineteenth-century writers, and the supposedly objective camera became a model for ways of seeing and representing the world; it also may have hastened the inclusion of urban and sexual subjects not formerly considered suitable for elevated literature.

Writers everywhere eventually used aspects of the new invention—popular writers immediately, serious ones selectively. The photographer made his debut as a central character in a few important works, as a romantic figure in Nathaniel Hawthorne's *House of the Seven Gables* (1851) or an obtuse one in Henrik Ibsen's *Wild Duck* (1884). In other narratives, fictional photographs served a variety of functions. For example, they determined the plot of one short story by Anton Chekhov; revealed the present relationship of the lovers in Leo Tolstoy's *Anna Karenina* (1875–77); provided realistic props for a characteristic setting in Mark Twain's *Life on the Mississippi* (1883); supplied fresh metaphors and images throughout the writings of Henry James; prompted speculative authorial asides in Balzac's *Le cousin Pons* (1847); and facilitated Villiers de l'Isle-Adam's satire in *L'Eve future* (1886). Grim Civil War photographs by Mathew Brady and his colleagues intangibly but indisputably affected both the content and style of Stephen Crane's *Red Badge of Courage* (1895).[10]

Most authors then considered their writing complimented when it was called "photographic," a tribute to their credibility, no matter what the genre. Heinrich Heine proudly called a collection of his newspaper essays a "daguerreotyped history book in which each day portrays itself . . . thus both a product of nature and of art"; Whitman boasted that "in these *Leaves [of Grass]* everything is literally photographed, nothing is poeticized, not a stop, not an inch, nothing for beauty's sake . . ."; Strindberg, writing his first novel, *The Red Room* (1879), which established his reputation, promised the work would contain "photographic descriptions of the lives of writers and artists"; and Twain, like Henry Adams, meant to compliment the verbal exactness of their friend William Dean Howells in noting that "everywhere your pen falls it leaves a photograph."[11]

But Howells himself, like many other later nineteenth-century artists who appreciated the camera's objective fidelity to life and used photographs in their work, often used the word "photographic" pejoratively to suggest a limited imagination or ignoble purpose.[12] Henry James displayed the same ambivalence, even while sprinkling terms like "frame" and "point of view" throughout his theoretical prefaces without much acknowledgment to the camera, which so obviously influenced his own vision. Indeed, photography not only influenced the way many writers now perceived their world but, consequently, their style as well as subject matter. All prized verisimilitude, though what was "true" and what was merely accurate was hotly debated. Literature, though better able to provide panoramic sweeps or complex analyses or delicate nuance, increasingly if unconsciously followed the camera's lead in focusing on significant moments or fragments.

Whether or not their writing was considered "photographic," many authors, from the mid-nineteenth century on, became avid amateur photographers. They didn't publicize their avocation, perhaps because they didn't take it very seriously or, if they did, others might regard their versatility as dilettantism; moreover, professional photographers were a socially dubious species as was anyone in "trade." For all these reasons, photographs in their texts, even if affordable, were not always regarded as a special selling point and thus usually bore no attributions—or misleading ones. For example, the first readers of Samuel Butler's *Ex Voto* (1888) learned about the Glasgow firm that printed the photographs and the London outfit from whom copies could be ordered but had to infer that the author himself took the pictures. Contemporary admirers of *The Aran Islands* (1907) never knew that J. M. Synge's photographs of his subject existed since the author considered using them only as the basis for drawings that might serve as illustrations, not as illustrations in their own right.

Indeed, even the most active of these early writer-photographers kept their camera work so private that often their biographers have only recently become aware of them or did little to enlighten readers about their subjects' pictures. Examples of this ignorance or indifference abound. Lewis Carroll's profound involvement with photography for twenty-five years (1855–80) at the height of his career was forgotten until the collector-scholar Helmut Gernsheim chanced on one of his albums nearly a century later. W. S. Gilbert avidly took photographs probably before and especially after his immortal collaborations with Sir Arthur Sullivan, but this interest is mentioned only in passing by his biographer. Jack London's intense interest in photography from 1900 to 1910 is still only cursorily mentioned even in scholarly accounts. Conan Doyle's editors knew before their work about his family snapshots and later obsession with spirit photography but nothing about his pre–Sherlock Holmes essays for the *British Journal of Photography* in the 1880's, not even mentioned in his own memoirs. Photography, though Bret Harte's main recreation while living in London in the mid-1890's, was dismissed by his first important biographer as a "pathetic little hobby."[13]

Even when the photographic interests of major authors have been long known to specialists, the general reader remains ignorant. The involvement of the exiled Victor Hugo family in one photographic project, and that of Strindberg and Rimbaud in many, is still mainly discussed in obscure publications in their native lands. Only in the last decade have comprehensive surveys of the serious photography of Samuel Butler, George Bernard Shaw, Émile Zola, Giovanni Verga, and Leonid Andreyev been published.

Interestingly, these multitalented figures, in common with most of their serious colleagues, resisted using any photographs—whether taken by themselves or anyone else—to illustrate their imaginative work. Perhaps they felt their presence might imply that their words were insufficient or their readers verbally unsophisticated. The ambivalence of Howells and James again proved typical. Howells twice attempted to illustrate the realistic and romantic aspects of texts by using photographs and engravings respectively in *Their Silver Wedding Journey* (1899) and in *London Films* (1905), implying that the camera could capture the letter but not the spirit of certain subjects. James, who elevated the status of illustrative photographs by using them as frontispieces in the collected edition of his fiction, mixed his praise of them with evident wariness, most notably in the preface to *The Golden Bowl* (1909).

Meanwhile, serious photographers throughout the nineteenth century and early in the twentieth, concerned with raising the aesthetic status of the medium, remained at a respectful distance from literature. Only a few camera artists appeared susceptible to the influence of particular writers, such as Maurice Maeterlinck (1862–1949), whose meteoric career was declining even before he won the Nobel Prize for Literature in 1911. The work of "the Belgian Shakespeare," full of allusive, esoteric, often melancholy ponderings about human destiny, offered many artists an appealing alternative to the prevailing realism and naturalism in all Western arts; it affected not only distinguished writers as dissimilar as Oscar Wilde and T. S. Eliot but diversely talented photographers. F. Holland Day was influenced by Maeterlinck's spiritualist thinking and imagery; Alvin Langdon Coburn, who illustrated the American edition of one of Maeterlinck's works, worshipped the writer; Edward Steichen eagerly sought "some of his thoughts" for Alfred Stieglitz's new *Camera Work* (1903), doubtless aware of Stieglitz's esteem for the writer; and André Kertész admired his sophisticated use of simple symbols.[14]

Sometimes a totally different type of artist inspired productive associations between writers and photographers. For example, the French sculptor Rodin, then working on his monumental Balzac figure (1893–98), attracted the presence not only of Steichen but also that of the young German poet Rainer Maria Rilke, who briefly became his personal secretary in 1905. One of Rodin's subjects in the spring of 1906 was Bernard Shaw, who himself photographed the then unknown Rilke and enabled his protégé Coburn to photograph the famous Rodin.[15]

Such memorable contacts between literature and photography, however, remained rare. A few photographers like Julia Margaret Cameron and, later, Coburn worshipfully took portraits of eminent contemporary writers. Others had periodically borrowed subject matter from literary classics, past and present. William Lake Price represented *Don Quixote in His Study* (1855); O. G. Rejlander, a scene from Dickens's *Hard Times* (1860); Henry Peach Robinson, lines from Romantic and Victorian poets in many of his best composite photographs; and Cameron, scenes from canonical English writers since Chaucer for many of her tableaux. Subsequent Pictorialist groups, founded to promote photography as an art, tended to invent their own visual fictions, though Gertrude Käsebier, Clarence White, and other leading Photo-Secessionists also illustrated fiction in magazines and books, which proliferated after 1890 owing to the new halftone printing process.[16] But few embraced Sadakichi Hartman's idea for a "Photographic Illustration Co., capable of issuing conscientious artistic work for the illustration of novels and poems."[17] The explicit truth of images, perhaps, too often jarred with the implicit truth of words. More representative of the tenuous links between photography and literature from 1840 to 1914 may well be F. Holland Day, Alfred Stieglitz's rival as America's leading photographer in the 1890's, who ultimately expressed his passion for literature not as an illustrator but as a book collector and as a publisher of finely designed editions of contemporary English and American writers.

2

The First World War altered this quiescent arrangement on both sides of the Atlantic. With the peace in 1918, all the arts, like their societies, sought renewal. Literature proclaimed traditional forms and content bankrupt; photography, now almost a century old, more loudly insisted that others recognize its aesthetic as well as documentary possibilities. Each got sustenance from the other, thanks to the increased mobility of all artists, especially photographers. Their occupation's unique ability to vault boundaries of place and time served them well. The prewar trans-Atlantic shuttles of Day, Coburn, and Steichen were no longer rare. Typical of this postwar period were the moves of the quartet of talented Hungarian photographers: László Moholy-Nagy worked in Germany before moving to Chicago; Brassaï settled in Paris, as did André Kertész, before unexpectedly moving to New York, and Robert Capa, when not covering battlefields from Spain to Saigon. Photography became not only the most universal but perhaps the most cosmopolitan of Western arts.

Wherever they lived, photographers had increasing contacts with writers. Indeed, a number—Kertész, Moholy-Nagy, and Walker Evans—initially aspired to be writers themselves and were unusually well read. Meanwhile, writers, like the peripatetic Nabokov, who appreciated photographs as links to his multiple pasts and used them throughout his works (whether written in Russian, French, or English), were inevitably more knowledgeable about new visual as well as verbal trends than their more rooted predecessors. Increasing travel and improved communications hastened the pace of cultural cross-currents in the 1920's and 1930's. Accordingly, in Mexico City alone, it was not surprising that D. H. Lawrence sought out Edward Weston, Henri Cartier-Bresson roomed with Langston Hughes, and Tina Modotti met Pablo Neruda, as did Manuel Alvarez Bravo, André Breton, Louis Aragon, and Octavio Paz. Such mobility inevitably made many artists in diverse fields aware of relevant aesthetic innovations, which then rapidly spread; experiments in literature and in photographic portraiture, for example, were sometimes displayed side by side in places like the bookshop salons of Adrienne Monnier and Sylvia Beach in Paris.

This cross-fertilization gratified young artists like Walker Evans, who, though deciding to become a photographer rather than a writer, noted the common qualities in the two media:

Photography seems to be the most literary of the graphic arts. It will have—on occasion and in effect—qualities of eloquence, wit, grace, and economy; style, of course; structure and coherence; paradox and play and oxymoron. If photography tends to be literary, conversely certain writers are noticeably photographic from time to time—for instance James, and Joyce, and particularly Nabokov.[18]

Moreover, the outstanding artists in both fields shared much conceptually. The war had permanently shattered cultural and theoretical as well as human and physical connections. All received aesthetic assumptions, conventions, and productions were stripped, reexamined, and generally found wanting. Old habits had to be discarded, new ideas formed, and new patterns and ties forged, objectively grounded in new social, economic, political, and psychological realities. Weary of prewar technical manipulations, contemporary photographers were now interested in "straight" or "experimental" pictures, particularly of mechanical, natural, or abstract objects rather than humans, landscapes, and tableaux. Weary of the panoramic, the picturesque, and the rhetorical, contemporary writers valued short, often patterned structures that sometimes experimented with representing time or "ordinary" characters and subjects capable of being described with "photographic" objectivity. These modernists in both media, whether interested in shocking, delighting, or instructing, became preoccupied with whatever subjects and techniques would improve "sight" and "insight," with whatever angle or juxtaposition would enable individuals or society to see *more,* as László Moholy-Nagy put it.

Artists became fascinated with the challenge of portraying inner as well as external reality. Virginia Woolf complained that the Edwardian novelists, for all their "realistic" detail, hadn't portrayed life as it was actually lived. Franz Kafka even dared to question photography's veracity, its former unquestioned strength, asserting that the camera was not a mechanical "Know-Thyself" but a "Mistake-Thyself" in portraiture due to its inability to reveal the sitter's hidden life.[19] In evident agreement, even Coburn had abandoned his flattering soft-focus portraits and experimented with vortographs during the war, while afterwards Man Ray, Cecil Beaton, and other photographers, like Woolf, James Joyce, and other writers, tested other novel techniques—often involving various modes of distortion—in their personal as well as their commercial work to capture their subjects' elusive essence.

Despite their shared values, however, neither writers nor photographers appeared eager to unite their talents. By the time Picasso ceded "literary" or narrative elements in the visual arts to photography, its practitioners were not interested.[20] They determined to have their medium viewed as a separate, equal art, independent of others, including literature, and resented losing control too often over the final appearance of their pictures in verbal and visual collaborations. Moreover, the use of narrative of any kind suggested the complex manipulations of Cameron, Robinson, and the Pictorialists, which were regarded now as inauthentic. Some, like Edward

Weston, narrowly equated "pictorial photography" with "illustrative photography," which he then dismissed as a "little byproduct of literature."[21]

Even allusive, subordinate prewar illustrations like those by Coburn for James's collected fiction or by the Hampton Camera Club for Paul Laurence Dunbar's poems did not generate any notable successors,[22] except in Russia, where Vladimir Mayakovsky and Alexander Rodchenko often collaborated in many ways for ideological as well as aesthetic and personal reasons. André Breton's postwar call for books to be illustrated only with photographs was not heeded by his fellow Dadaists or Surrealists; aside from his own collaborations with various photographers, it resulted only in a few, usually esoteric and often erotic, limited editions. Nor did the postwar Stieglitz circle, which included many writers and photographers, illustrate even the works they most admired, such as Edgar Lee Masters's *Spoon River Anthology* (1915) or Sherwood Anderson's *Winesburg, Ohio* (1919), though Evans's trio of pictures for Hart Crane's *Bridge* (1930) might be considered an exception. Their main collaborations proved to be their prose testimonials to Stieglitz on his seventieth birthday (1934). The combination of authors who disdained illustrative help (or mistrusted possible competition) and their publishers who feared the additional expense of including photographs discouraged significant collaborations.

Between the two world wars, then, literature and photography continued to cross paths mainly through friendships and through the portraits that resulted, whether experimental ones by Man Ray or traditional ones (in color now as well as black and white) by Gisèle Freund. The two groups of artists, well informed about each other's work, at least were generous about publicizing it. Jean Cocteau, for example, was the first to praise publicly the photograms of Man Ray; Stieglitz was the first to publish Gertrude Stein; Carl Sandburg wrote the first monograph about a living photographer, Steichen, who later returned the compliment by editing a book of his brother-in-law's portraits. Henry Miller's first novel immortalized Brassaï, his main guide to the Paris underworld, who later helped sustain the writer's reputation in his many memoirs. Meanwhile, the links some modernist photographers (Man Ray, Moholy-Nagy, Beaton) and writers (Cocteau, Brecht) retained with painting, theatre, and film ensured further publicity as well as cross-fertilization of interests for all involved.

Despite the versatility of many of the artists in both media, there were fewer serious writer-photographers in this era. Most of the authors who took up the camera did so mainly to record their journeys on assignment to remote places, either to satisfy public curiosity, like Evelyn Waugh in Abyssinia, Aldous Huxley in Central America, and W. H. Auden in Iceland, or for their own private albums, like Isak Dinesen in Kenya and Vita Sackville-West in Tehran. Waugh's and Auden's experiences proved useful, as Jack London's had been, when both were sent to war zones: Waugh back to Abyssinia after the Italian invasion in 1935 and Auden to China, already at war with Japan in 1938. But both writers, taking pictures for a limited time and purpose, were typically self-effacing as published photographers. Waugh's snapshots in *Waugh in Abyssinia* (1936) can only be deduced by the fact that the rest are attributed to others; Auden never continued his visual experiments after *Letters from Iceland* (1937) or even his conventional pictures after *Journey to a War* (1938).

There were only a few writers of the period whose involvement with the camera proved more enduring. William Faulkner's interest in taking pictures and especially in old cameras, from the 1920's to the mid-1930's, was intense but relatively brief; Eudora Welty ended her short career as a professional photographer in the late 1930's when publishers preferred her short stories to her pictures alone or in combination with her prose. On the other hand, in 1932, Carl Van Vechten gave up a successful career as an arts critic and novelist to devote himself wholly to photography. And later in the decade, young Wright Morris, jailed briefly in fascist Italy in 1933 for "suspect" activities with his first camera, began combining his images with his words in "photo-texts" to document the vanishing structures of his childhood and country.

Writers, however, were increasingly comfortable using photography for subjects, incident, character, or image in their works. The private album picture, usually of a parent or lover, began to be a favorite subject of meditation by many poets after Rilke, Constantine Cavafy, and Thomas Hardy, especially in the face of loss due to war.[23] Sometimes exotic photographic forms were used, such as X-rays in Thomas Mann's *Magic Mountain* (1924) or the photohoroscope in Nabokov's *Invitation to a Beheading* (1938). But some writers still regarded photography with condescension. Though it remained a compliment for Bourke-White to be called a "poetess of the camera," it was usually denigrating to describe an imaginative literary work as "photographic," as E. M. Forster did in his review of Sinclair Lewis. Few authors of the day would have shared Charles Sheeler's opinion that one of his own prints was equal in value to a poem by his close friend William Carlos Williams; and even some photographers might have agreed with Lewis Hine's memorable remark: "If I could tell the story in words, I wouldn't need to lug a camera."[24]

The continuing Depression and ensuing global conflict, however, rendered the purely aesthetic or experimental in all the arts socially frivolous or politically perilous and moved the documentary to the center. Furthermore, the widening scale of events compelled writers and photographers to collaborate. Both images and words were needed to inform, analyze, or protest the latest economic disaster or military outrage, particularly as they affected humans rather than places, objects, or ideas. The new illustrated magazines that arose during this period were, as Szarkowski notes, "predicated on the idea that if one picture was worth a thousand words, ten pictures would make a short story."[25]

Accordingly, writers and photographers teamed up—some on assignment, others on their own initiative—to attempt joint representations of their convulsive world, often to expose inhumane conditions and prompt active reform. John Heartfield worked with Kurt Tucholsky and other German artists to assemble his powerful anti-Nazi photomontages. Erskine Caldwell worked with Bourke-White, and James Agee with Walker Evans, in the South at the height of the Depression. John Swope illustrated John Steinbeck's book on air force training (1942). Some writers and photographers worked alone but used others' images or words: Archibald Mac-

Leish, for example, drew heavily on Farm Security Administration photographs to illustrate his *Land of the Free* (1938), as did Edwin Rosskam when selecting pictures to accompany Richard Wright's text in *Twelve Million Black Voices* (1941). Bertolt Brecht protested fascism and capitalism in quatrains composed in exile from Nazi Germany from 1933 to 1945, later publishing each under the magazine or newspaper photograph that inspired it. Others used their own dual verbal and visual talents, such as Minor White in "Amputations," consisting of poems mourning his dead army buddies, later accompanied by his own photographs. All these passionate undertakings showed that even documentary photographs could be framed or cropped to make their visual "facts" evoke powerful responses from viewers while texts no longer imitated the reputed objective dispassion of the camera.

Meanwhile, though all the arts were invigorated by a sense of mission throughout this war, photography acquired further terrifying associations wherever fighting occurred. As Steinbeck explained:

> The camera is one of the most frightening of modern weapons, particularly to people who have been in warfare, who have been bombed and shelled for at the back of a bombing run is invariably a photograph. In back of ruined towns, and cities, and factories, there is aerial mapping, or spy mapping, usually with a camera. Therefore the camera is a feared instrument, and a man with a camera is suspected and watched wherever he goes. . . . In the minds of most people today the camera is the forerunner of destruction, and it is suspected, and rightly so.[26]

Antoine de Saint-Exupéry, who had temporarily turned his keen vision to mastering aerial reconnaissance photography, might have written movingly about the war experience from this unusual vantage point had he survived his plane crash.[27]

3

With the war's end, the camera, like the pen, soon reverted to more aesthetic uses. Valéry had accurately predicted in 1939, on the one hundredth anniversary of Daguerre's announcement, that:

> Just as water, gas, and electricity are brought into our houses from far off to satisfy our needs in response to a minimal effort, so we shall be supplied with visual or auditory images, which will appear and disappear at a simple movement of the hand, hardly more than a sign.[28]

After 1945, television, like film before it, reduced the public's dependence on still photography and written accounts to satisfy its documentary appetite. Moreover, whatever their experience during the second global conflict, artists and audiences alike were weary of the grim subjects that had so long monopolized the world's attention and demanded release. Audiences and artists alike seemed motivated either by Kafka's persistent desire to forget the worst of the past or by Wright Morris's equally persistent desire to preserve the best.[29] Abroad there was a renewed appreciation of all the arts, especially literature, as the enduring treasures of their recently threatened civilization. Homage was duly paid by photographers. Sites associated with cherished writers, especially of the more glorious English past, were commemorated by Bill Brandt in *Literary Britain* (1951), and photographically illustrated anthologies of old and new poetry classics such as Bryan Holme's *Poet's Camera* (1946) also began to appear.

Writers and photographers then turned to representing postwar realities in new but unexpectedly similar ways. Previous systems and beliefs had once again failed, leading to further economic chaos, military devastation, and spiritual quandary. The only visions an artist could really comprehend and convey were the ones in his or her own mind. Accordingly, literature and photography became more abstract or self-referential. Many photographers, even those with previous writing aspirations like Aaron Siskind and Minor White, turned from their earlier documentaries to abstract, formalist works in which real world references were deliberately excluded as binding. Valéry had long felt that photography, by freeing writers from depending on their imagination to represent external reality, enabled literature to advance along one of its "true paths"—perfecting the expression of abstract thought.[30] Now many writers specialized in often enigmatic private myths that the camera couldn't represent or, like a camera, described people and objects without evident plot, characterization, or omniscient comment. Both fields became increasingly self-conscious, suggestive, and amoral in reaction to the prolonged dominance of documentary and moralistic reality.

Autobiographical work became increasingly common from photographers as well as writers. Along with the publication of Cecil Beaton's voluminous diaries came memoirs by Coburn, Man Ray, Freund, Bourke-White, and others, which illuminated aspects of their relationships with writers. Photographers like Beaton, Steichen, and Richard Avedon, previously acclaimed mainly in books by friends and colleagues, became celebrities as acclaimed writers had often been. And noted writers featured now not only in single pictures but in visual sequences, at home and at work, often taken by photographers like Rollie McKenna or Inge Morath—sometimes friends or spouses of writers—who developed literary portraiture as a professional subspecialty.

Collaborations, though now more often born from creative or commercial rather than documentary need, continued to flourish. Traditionally, the writer or his publisher invited the photographer to illustrate a text. But ambitious photographers, no longer waiting for such requests, initiated some of the most interesting postwar collaborations. Richard Avedon approached both Truman Capote and James Baldwin as did Roy DeCarava Langston Hughes; Lucien Clergue initiated his collaborations with Cocteau; Eikoh Hosoe persuaded Yukio Mishima to model for him; Milton Rogovin secured Pablo Neruda's cooperation; and Paul Strand carefully selected the various writers he worked with on diverse locales abroad. Whatever the origin of such collaborations, postwar artists tried to ensure that words were more than captions and photographs more than illustrations, with neither trying to convey precisely the same thing.

But younger photographers increasingly wanted to be *auteurs* themselves, to invent and present their own stories, not be part of someone else's. While most writers remained content to let their words suggest pictures, many photographers were no longer certain that "one picture was worth a thousand words."[31] Avedon insisted that all pictures are "fictions," creations of the photographer who must round out a portrait study, for example, without the aid of words.[32] But some of his colleagues felt that pictures alone insufficiently represented the complexity of individuals, society, or their own private visions. They wanted their scenes to convey a greater sense of time and space, deeper levels of meaning. They also came to resent the fact that notices in the print media were more influential in establishing a reputation than exhibitions in galleries and museums.[33]

Even photojournalists now wanted to express their own ideas rather than merely reproduce facts. For even visual "facts" could be easily distorted or airbrushed out to suit political and other purposes, as Milan Kundera vividly described:

> In February 1949, Communist leader Klement Gottwald stepped out on the balcony of a Baroque palace in Prague to address the hundreds of thousands of his fellow citizens packed into Old Town Square. It was a crucial moment in Czech history—a fateful moment of the kind that occurs once or twice in a millennium.
>
> Gottwald was flanked by his comrades, with Clementis standing next to him. There were snow flurries, it was cold, and Gottwald was bareheaded. The solicitous Clementis took off his own fur cap and set it on Gottwald's head.
>
> The Party propaganda section put out hundreds of thousands of copies of a photograph of that balcony with Gottwald, a fur cap on his head and comrades at his side, speaking to the nation. On that balcony the history of Communist Czechoslovakia was born. Every child knew the photograph from posters, schoolbooks, and museums.
>
> Four years later Clementis was charged with treason and hanged. The propaganda section immediately airbrushed him out of history and, obviously, out of all the photographs as well. Ever since, Gottwald has stood on that balcony alone. Where Clementis once stood, there is only bare palace wall. All that remains of Clementis is the cap on Gottwald's head.[34]

Creative writers had always slanted their "evidence" by selecting and framing their points of view; photographers now routinely did the same, especially for their "advocacy" pictures. As Steinbeck understood, "Pictures . . . are also opinions . . . [they] set down what the camera operator sees and he sees what he wants to see and what he loves and hates and pities and is proud of."[35] But ultimately, as Wright Morris concluded, "the photograph, after all, is just a photograph. Words will determine its meaning and status."[36]

But what kind of words? The narrative element in both literature and photography, diminished by the prevailing abstraction in both fields, survived mainly in magazine reports and travel books. Photo-essays like those by W. Eugene Smith and Gordon Parks in *Life,* for example, proved more effective than images or words alone in mobilizing American opinion in favor of civil rights and against the Vietnam War and environmental abuse. When Parks, still working for *Life,* began producing autobiographies as well as musical scores and screenplays, he made an effort to keep facts and opinions separate. Richard Wright, recounting his ambivalent experiences in Ghana in *Black Power,* did not. The lines between fact, opinion, and imagination in literature as well as photography continued to blur.

Adding to the ferment were provocative concepts from cultural critics like Walter Benjamin, Roland Barthes, Susan Sontag, and others in the 1960's and 1970's. They challenged the traditional assumptions of all the arts, which, they felt, reflected the imperialist, capitalist, and sexist status quo. To represent their conception of reality, they favored the fragmentary, inconclusive, and digressive rather than the coherent; an understanding of a work as shaped by past and present social and political influences rather than as the "original" inspiration of an individual; an active reader/viewer instead of an omniscient creator; and myriad open-ended interpretations rather than any definitive one. Issues of class, genre, race, and sexual orientation became part of discourse in all the visual arts, especially photography, as they had always been of literary ones.[37] Indeed, photography appeared to be the art form that best reflected postmodernist concerns. Accordingly, photographs, like other revealing cultural artifacts, became "texts," which could and should be "read" on many levels by the general public, not just the sophisticated.

Photographers felt stimulated being in the center of a widespread debate about the nature of aesthetic representation rather than standing wistfully on the sidelines as so often before. Paradoxically, their new central position was partly due to writers, who, as Trachtenberg sadly observed, have always written about photography better than its own practitioners.[38] Moreover, it was a prize-winning poet, Richard Howard, whose translations introduced to the English-speaking public works like Breton's *Nadja* (1928) and Barthes's *Camera Lucida* (1980), the latter becoming one of the central documents in recent photography.

Another paradox was that photographers of the 1970's and 1980's seemed more obviously influenced by the new cultural criticism than writers. Outside academe, the critic Peter Prescott reports, most authors regard most theoretical criticism of any kind as a "joke," irrelevant to their work, while the photographer Harry Callahan plaintively complains about those critics of whatever persuasion, theoretical or not, "who say I don't know what I'm doing. But, son of a bitch, the thing is: *I did it.*"[39] Many artists apparently share Tom Wolfe's distaste for "His Eminence, Art Theory" as well as his fears about the "danger when the explanation of a work of art becomes more important than that work of art."[40] Indeed, the self-referential abstract style and heated tone of current aesthetic theory, perhaps more than its content, often alienated many common readers and viewers as well as artists.

But the most exciting cultural critics, like Barthes, began to analyze narrative as well as images of all kinds, which may have inspired photographers to do the same. Many now began to embrace narrative elements— including content, manipulative techniques, and words—all associated with storytelling, all taboo since the Pictorialists. By inclination and training, the new generation was well equipped to do so. Never had there been so many photographers proficient with words as well as images. Photographers such as Eikoh Hosoe, John Baldessari, and Elsa Dorfman all seriously contemplated becoming writers; Robert Adams earned a doctorate in English, Sally Mann, a master's degree in writing; Danny Lyon, Bruce Charlesworth, and many others often accompanied their pictures with their texts. W. Eugene Smith, Duane Michals, and Barbara Kruger began writing prose and even poetry after earning reputations as fine photographers, while Robert Heinecken tries to write at least an hour daily.[41] When possible, these artists preferred to exhibit their art in books designed by themselves rather than in galleries and museums, which seemed too esoteric and inaccessible to the public. The public—it was clear from the impact of film, television, and advertising—liked images and words linked, especially in stories.

Whatever the format, literary references initially remained outside the photograph, as portfolio or book titles. There had always been occasional groupings that implied literary influence, form, or narrative, like Clarence J. Laughlin's *Visual Poems* and *Poems of the Interior World* (1973), but now titles using the words "Stories" and "Tales" became commonplace. Audiences were never sure what to expect. Baldessari accompanied each scene in his *Ingres and Other Parables* (1971) with an imaginative prose paragraph, but his *Close-Cropped Tales* (1981) contained no words. Viewers of Les Krims's *Deerslayers* (1972) unfamiliar with James Fenimore Cooper's *Deerslayer* (1841), or of Richard Misrach's *Desert Cantos* (1987) unfamiliar with Ezra Pound's *Cantos*, might not realize that they were missing other levels of the photographs' meaning.

Photographers—and writers using photographs—began to pay far more attention to the interpretative possibilities of the traditional title and caption. Previously, titles ran the gamut from minimal to evocative. Walker Evans was always so aware of possible meanings that he often dispensed with titles altogether or assigned his understated pictures a simple place name and date, strategies that both stimulated and discouraged interpretations. More informative titles and ultimately poems had suited Brecht's more political purposes when selecting pictures for his texts, since "a photograph of the Krupp works or GEC yields almost nothing about these institutions."[42] The allusiveness of so many of Alvarez Bravo's titles inspired Paz to write a poem on the subject, but some by younger artists became deliberately oblique. What viewer, for example, could anticipate that the subject of Lyle Bongé's photograph entitled 'Dead Sea Gull near Van Cleave, 1961' was, in fact, a nude girl on a beach or that 'Hokusai's Wave Winding Up,' taken at Marsh Harbour in the Bahamas (1980), depicted an asphalt road?[43]

Similarly, starting in the 1960's, allusive captions—often handwritten—routinely appeared in the portfolios of Diane Arbus and beneath prints by Allen Ginsberg and Elsa Dorfman, sometimes with comments as well as details of time and place, often evoking meanings more usually associated with literature, especially poetry. Walter Benjamin had anticipated these phenomena, realizing that when the camera became sufficiently small, portable, and able to reveal previously secret or private images, extended captions would be needed for the viewer to understand the picture, thus turning "all the relations of life into literature."[44]

Then the building blocks of literature—letters, words, phrases, sentences, and entire narratives—began moving *into* photographs. Letters and words had often been included as elements in scenes (by Dadaists and Surrealists generally, and Man Ray, Cartier-Bresson, Alvarez Bravo, Evans, and Siskind specifically, among others), especially as part of background road and wall signs. But in the 1970's, often to challenge conventional aesthetic and sexist representations of reality, single words turned into phrases (Heinecken); epigrams, and aphorisms (Kruger); associative word chains and narrative paragraphs (Baldessari, Burgin); and even whole pages of text with little or no visual content. For example, the visual artists Barbara Kruger, Sherrie Levine, and Louise Lawler signed their names to a reproduction of an entire eight-page short story by Alberto Moravia, used as a magazine centerfold, and Levine elsewhere appropriated literary passages, just as she had paintings and photographs, but sometimes with no attribution.[45] Such practices hardly made photographs literary. But they did give pictures a new, self-conscious alliance with language and, by extension, with literature.

Most revolutionary was the gradual inclusion of traditional narrative, or "story," as most photographers called it, with or without words. Paz and others had long observed how any kind of narrative could free the photograph, as it did words, from time, giving it "motion as in literature, film, theatre and other verbal modes."[46] But postwar writers largely abandoned the lengthy, carefully crafted, omniscient narrative for shorter autobiographical or experimental fiction, long on idiosyncratic structure and style, short on dramatic content. As the photographer and former English professor Robert Adams regretfully noted:

> Drama and fiction used to be prime reflections of Form, of structure in events . . . the story . . . reminded us of an often painful but nonetheless reassuring order in life. Now sadly, only certain kinds of stories seem to match our experience; they are to our distress the stories that deny any redemptive pattern.[47]

When photographers also wanted to "tell" their own stories, they too often chose to do so through extreme technical manipulations, which tended to question rather than reaffirm any existing order. Some photographic narratives were allusive, as if ratifying Garry Winogrand's statement that "a photo is a literary narrative, ya know what I mean . . . but it's not specific."[48] For example, Ralph Eugene Meatyard, drawing on repetitive structures and names from Gertrude Stein and Flannery O'Connor respectively and perhaps influenced by his many literary friends, compelled the viewer to supply interpretations of his *Lucybelle Crater* series (1974).[49] By contrast, Duane Michals increasingly provided his viewer with verbal guides to his philosophical intentions, first with provocative titles, then with handwritten connectives. Baldessari used age-old literary genres like the allegory, parable, fable, and fairy tale to add space, time, and levels of meaning to his conceptual photographs. In sum, no longer was the imaginative anecdote and its attendant forms the "enemy of photography," as Henri Cartier-Bresson had so long insisted,[50] but a welcome friend after nearly a century's absence.

As many photographers increasingly used materials associated with literature and language, some writers returned the compliment, though sporadically and in more conventional ways. The tradition of the doubly gifted was continued by Richard Wright and Thomas Merton in their last years and by Jonathan Williams, Allen Ginsberg, John Howard Griffin, Julio Cortázar, Bruce Chatwin, Jerzy Kosinski, Yevgeny Yevtushenko, Michael Ondaatje, and Michel Tournier throughout their careers, some more seriously than others. Tournier, for example, not only took pictures and used photographers and photographs in his novels but sponsored a series of television programs on the subject and helped organize the first international festival of photography.

But, perhaps, these artists, or more likely their publishers, recalled the fate of Wright Morris's photo-texts whose format confused readers (and booksellers) and soon went out of print. Except for a few photograph-dependent works like Ondaatje's *Collected Works of Billy the Kid* (1970) and Yevtushenko's *Invisible Threads* (1981), serious imaginative works still were not issued with photographic illustrations. One of Jerzy Kosinski's characters, doubtless echoing the author, offers all the traditional arguments in refusing to permit his publisher to include such illustrations in his books:

> He felt an excessive appeal to the sense of sight was insidious and debilitating, a specious claim to the reproduction of the world as it really was. He resisted the lulling implication that knowledge was above all what was to be seen, and refused the passive luxury of the spectator's chair, the flattening of reality, time arrested in one angle of vision. He suspected that to submit to that vision would be to clog the active play of images that were fluent and mobile within each person, fantasy and emotion that written language alone could quicken.[51]

Even Bruce Chatwin was relieved to learn that the first American edition of *In Patagonia* (1977) would appear without his photographs so that critics here would take the book more "seriously."[52] In certain quarters, attitudes evidently have not shifted much since the Victorian era, when illustrations in a literary work made intellectuals doubt its seriousness or sophistication. But a writer's serious photographs are now increasingly treated with respectful attention; in contrast to the fate of pictures taken by his nineteenth-century predecessors, for example, a book of Chatwin's photographs was recently published only five years after his premature death.

Photographers, especially avid readers like Walker Evans, Siskind, and Laughlin, have always acknowledged their debts in their professional or personal work to favorite writers (Blake, Poe, Baudelaire, Whitman, Joyce, Pound, and William Carlos Williams are mentioned most often). From the 1960's, writers, especially poets—whether or not they themselves used a camera—were often inspired by photographers. Some were inspired by photographs documenting books (Charles Simic, Seamus Heaney), popular magazines (Marianne Moore, Elizabeth Bishop), and newspapers, especially during the civil rights and Vietnam era (Denise Levertov, Kenneth Pitchford). Others addressed specific pictures by known photographers, such as Richard Howard on Nadar's, Jean Cocteau on Lucien Clergue's, and John Logan on Aaron Siskind's. Many more continued to find private photographs a resource for personal verse (Philip Larkin, Ted Hughes, R. W. Thomas, Anne Sexton, Charles Wright, Howard Nemerov, and Robert Creeley, among others). Such personal pictures, which readily prompted memories, required concrete precision to evoke both them and the associated emotion for readers; verse inspired by photographs became a staple cliché of the poetry workshop, according to the veterans Frank Bidart and Lloyd Schwartz.[53]

Countless postwar poets borrowed the language of photography. Some merely needed allusive rather than specific titles, like Edwin Morgan's "Instamatic Poems."[54] But most drew on it for fresh imagery and diction within their verse. Other poets, like Adrienne Rich, did both. Her title *Snapshots of a Daughter-in-Law* (1963) aptly suggests the informal tone and structure of that volume; and the title of one of them, "Photograph of an Unmade Bed" (1969), not only heralds its special diction and imagery but simultaneously honors Imogen Cunningham's playful fulfillment of a Dorothea Lange class assignment.[55] By contrast, Robert Lowell's title "Epilogue" (1976), given to the last poem in his final volume, gives no hint that photographic analogies will be used to structure the argument: that his poetry—like an active camera—has sought to reflect reality with the gracefully illuminated accuracy that characterizes a Vermeer painting; by the end of this poem, as Helen Vendler notes, Lowell calls his work "not by the denigrating name of 'snapshot' but by the honorific name of 'photograph'—a writing with light."[56] This reciprocity between the two fields has been capped by four anthologies since the 1960's, composed partly (Brinnin and Reed's in 1963, Howard's in 1974) or wholly (Barker and Felver's two in 1986) of poets' portraits.

Novelists had long used descriptions of real or fictional photographs for details of plot, character, and setting, and many continued to do so in specific works (Nabokov, Grass, Kosinski). But now a few also drew on the life and work of master photographers. Michael Ondaatje enriched *Coming Through Slaughter* (1976), his fictional biography of a jazz musician, with the few known facts about the photographer E. J. Bellocq; Anne Rice drew on the sensuous life of Jules Lion, a New Orleans mulatto and one of the first American daguerreotypists, in *The Feast of All Saints* (1979); and Richard Powers constructed a complex narrative (1985) around August Sander's famous photograph 'Three Young Farmers on the Way to a Dance.' Perhaps a future author will have his vision of an artist shaped by one of these works, as the photographers Todd Webb and Harry Callahan reportedly formed theirs by reading Somerset Maugham's fictional account of the painter Paul Gauguin in *The Moon and Sixpence* (1919).[57]

Photography has provided further resources for women authors. Pictures have been less effective than words in the feminist struggle, which blends private experience with social protest. But it cannot be coincidental that in the 1970's and 1980's so many acclaimed female writers—Cynthia Ozick, Anne Tyler, Ann Beattie, and Rosellen Brown—made their heroines serious photographers. Since its inception, photography has been an unusually open profession, heedless of gender, age, or background, and it continues to appeal, as Brown suggests, being "both defensive and offensive, protected and aggressive," with flexible hours and creative independence, suitable to caretakers and loners alike.[58]

Personalities—and contacts between them—increased in significance in the past two decades as book publishers were largely taken over by business conglomerates and photographs became valuable commodities in the art marketplace. The celebrity of both writers and photographers became ever more important for the marketing of their works. Not coincidentally, memoirs of veteran photographers began to be reprinted and contemporary ones commissioned. Even photographers like Robert Frank, who mistrusts words, and Don McCullin, who is dyslexic and sometimes finds them "confusing," have nevertheless written personal histories.[59] As all artists became increasingly conscious of their "image," suitable portraits for book jackets and publicity materials became essential, and some photographers further explored that expanding field (Tom Victor, Jill Krementz), thereby contributing to the renown of their subjects—and themselves.

Prefaces, interviews, autobiographical pieces, and portraits gradually abounded in books about literature and photography. Friends and qualified intimates have provided introductions for each other's work since the period George Sand provided one for Nadar (1865), and they continued to do so (Chatwin for Robert Mapplethorpe, Kurt Vonnegut for Krementz, Arthur Miller for Inge Morath, Jonathan Williams for many). What changed, however, was the publisher or agent hiring celebrated writers to provide prefaces for books by celebrated photographers they often didn't know. Lawrence Durrell, for instance, produced two such prefaces, one on Brassaï, an old friend, and a short one on Brandt, whom he admired but never met. John le Carré had not previously met his assigned subject, the war photographer McCullin, but at least he insisted on doing so before writing his penetrating introduction.[60] And both kinds of artists—especially writer-photographers like Eudora Welty and Allen Ginsberg—became the subjects of long interviews that later could be adapted as prefaces to collections of their photographs.

4

As the century ends, literature and photography are closer than ever before, engaged by many shared concerns. Their artists often work together or well understand each other's craft. Fine photographs, like fine books, are now regarded as complex mirrors of society rather than the transparent windows some had thought. In the future, both arts may retreat to old boundaries or create new hybrid forms, but both will have to cope with the new electronics, which, according to Robert Frank, are "eating up" traditional photography and may revolutionize literature as well.[61] In the meantime, the cross-fertilization continues to invigorate both areas.

Publishers, quick to note photography's new commercial respectability, are reissuing landmark works, especially ones involving formal literature, or reprinting works with their original photographs, often omitted since their first appearance. Among recent reprints are all of Wright Morris's formerly shunned photo-texts as well as many other unique collaborations (Auden's with MacNeice and with Isherwood; Wright's with Rosskam; Hughes's with DeCarava; Berry's with Meatyard). Serious picture books of literary sites—such as Shakespeare's Stratford, Yeats's Ireland, Hemingway's Spain—proliferate. The major scholarly monographs on literature and photography (Bogardus, Crispolti, Hunter, Koppen, Shloss, and York) all appeared in the last decade. One hopes that Tom Wolfe is wrong in claiming that aesthetic forms are being—can only be—studied because they are dying or already dead.[62]

Yet the study of the history and practice of photography still has no secure place in our schools and universities. Ironically, photography too often occupies the same humble position in modern academic fine arts departments that literature occupied in classics departments before 1914. The influence of photography is more pervasive than that of literature due to its greater accessibility and ubiquity; these factors may make the study of photography's evolution appear unnecessary while the rapid changes in materials and forms make it difficult. Since its exciting history, artists, and techniques are not generally known, photography and its unexamined achievements are harder to define or link to other arts; and, as Trachtenberg has recently observed, even the record of writers' thoughts on the subject has been neglected in the history of the medium itself.[63] The same scholar's 1979 comments that the important exchanges between photography and formal literature—or any kind of serious literature, for that matter—were largely unstudied, remain only somewhat less valid more than a decade later.[64]

All schools and universities study our literary heritage. But since many more people view images than read words on a daily basis, it seems irresponsible not to teach visual as well as verbal discrimination. Still valid is Walter Lippmann's remark in 1922 that "photographs retain the kind of authority over the imagination today which the printed word had yesterday, and the spoken word before that."[65] As a blend of history, art, and science which has vastly influenced global civilization since 1839, photography should be near the core of academic curricula, not at the periphery [Fig. 4]. The names of Daguerre, Fox Talbot, and Coburn should become as well known to educated people as those of Gutenberg, Milton, and Tennyson. We should not continue to disregard Moholy-Nagy's famous 1928 warning: "Not those ignorant of writing, but of photography will be the illiterates of the future."[66]

1. See Hawthorne's parenthetical inquiry in his letter to Sophia Peabody, December 11, 1839, *The Letters 1813–1843*, ed. William Charcat, vol. 15 of *The Centenary Edition of the Works of Nathaniel Hawthorne* (Columbus: Ohio State University Press, 1989), p. 384, and Melville, letter to Evart A. Duyckinck, February 12, 1851, *The Letters of Herman Melville*, ed. Merrell R. Davis and William H. Gilman (New Haven, Conn.: Yale University Press, 1960), p. 121. See also Trachtenberg's discussion of these words in "Photography: The

4. André Kertész.
'New York City,
April 28, 1969.'

Emergence of a Keyword," in *Photography in Nineteenth Century America,* ed. Martha Sandweiss (Fort Worth, Tex.: Amon Carter Museum; New York: Harry N. Abrams, 1992), p. 1.

2. See John Szarkowski, *Mirrors and Windows: American Photography Since 1960* (New York: MOMA, 1978), p. 14.

3. See Barrett, letter of December 7, 1843, in *Elizabeth Barrett to Miss Mitford: The Unpublished Letters of Elizabeth Barrett to Mary Russell Mitford,* ed. Betty Miller (London: John Murray, 1965), pp. 208–9. One daguerreotype of the poet, taken by Cyrus Macaire in Le Havre in 1858, is mentioned in *The Browning Collections,* comp. Philip Kelley and Betty A. Coley (Waco, Tex.: Armstrong Browning Library at Baylor University et al., 1984), p. 457, F 265, and is often reproduced in books about her.

4. See Melville, *Pierre; or, The Ambiguities* (New York: Harper & Brothers, 1852), Book 17, Ch. 3, pp. 345–47, and letter to Duyckinck, February 12, 1851, in *The Letters,* p. 121: "I respectfully decline being oblivionated by a Daguerretype" [*sic*]; the Nerval selection, n. 6 below; and Tennyson, quoted by Helmut Gernsheim in *Julia Margaret Cameron* (Millerton, N.Y.: Aperture, 1975), p. 35.

5. Graham Smith discusses *Sun Pictures* and the reading that informed it in "William Henry Fox Talbot's Views of Loch Katrine," *Bulletin of the Museum of Art and Archeology, University of Michigan* 7 (1984–85): 48–77. In his *Disciples of Light: Photographs in the Brewster Album* (Malibu, Calif.: J. Paul Getty Museum, 1990), p. 105, Smith notes Talbot's transcription of a passage from Byron's *Childe Harold's Pilgrimage* (1812) beneath one photograph of Lacock Abbey (no. 38), while Robert Lassam, *Fox Talbot, Photographer* (Tisbury, Wilts.: Compton Press; Wimborne, Dorset: Dovecote Press, 1979), p. 10, notes that Thomas Moore, the Irish poet, was a frequent visitor. All note that Talbot won a prize for his Greek verse at Cambridge and became a passionate entymologist, among his

Introduction

many other accomplishments; he may have continued writing poems, according to Andrew Cahan, who was told of a copy of them but didn't see it.

6. See Ralph L. Harley, *The Cultural and Aesthetic Significance of the Newhaven Fisherfolk Photographs by D. O. Hill and Robert Adamson* (Ann Arbor: University Microfilms, 1986), especially pp. 28–96. For mention and/or reproduction of the Hill and Adamson calotypes relevant to Scott and Burns, see David Bruce, *Sun Pictures: The Hill-Adamson Calotypes* (Greenwich, Conn.: New York Graphic Society, 1973), pp. 42, 64–65, 78–79, 102–3, 108–9, 116–19, and 186–87, and Colin Ford, ed., *An Early Victorian Album: The Photographic Masterpieces [1843–1847] of David Octavius Hill and Robert Adams* (New York: Knopf, 1976), pp. 246–48, 251–53, 287, 292–96, and 301–3.

7. See, for example, the discussion of the photographic illustrations for Scott's *Lady of the Lake* (1869) in Betsy Jablow, "Illustrated Texts from Dickens to James," Ph.D. diss., Stanford University, 1978, pp. 58–61.

8. See Sandweiss, "The Narrative Tradition in Western Photography," *Photography in Nineteenth Century America,* ed. Sandweiss, p. 99.

9. Valéry, quoted in Linda Nochlin, *Realism* (Baltimore: Penguin, 1971), p. 44. The controversial term "realism" is intelligently discussed by Jill Kelly, "Photographic Reality and French Literary Realism: Nineteenth-Century Synchronism and Symbiosis," *French Review* 65, no. 2 (December 1991): 195–205, called to the editor's attention by Lillian Bulwa.

10. On the influence of Civil War photographs on Crane's work, see Lincoln Kirstein, "Photographs of America: Walker Evans," in *American Photographs* (New York: MOMA, 1988), p. 191; Szarkowski, *Photography Until Now* (New York: MOMA, 1989), pp. 112 and 117; and Miles Orvell, *The Real Thing: Imitation and Authenticity in American Culture, 1880–1940* (Chapel Hill: University of North Carolina Press, 1989), p. 127.

11. See Heine [1854], quoted in Siegbert S. Prawer, "Heine and the Photographers," in *Paintings on the Move: Heinrich Heine and the Visual Arts,* ed. Suzanne Zantop (Lincoln: University of Nebraska Press, 1989), p. 81, from Heine, *Sämtliche Schriften,* ed. Brieglet Klaus (Munich: Hansser, 1974), vol. 5, p. 239; Whitman, "Notes on the Meaning and Intention of 'Leaves of Grass,'" *Complete Prose Works of Walt Whitman* in *The Complete Writings of Walt Whitman,* ed. Richard Maurice Bucke et al. (New York: G. P. Putnam's Sons, 1902), vol. 9 [may read vol. 6 on the spine], p. 21; Strindberg, quoted in Per Hemmingsson, "Strindberg—the Photographer" (1981), trans. Muriel Larsen, in *August Strindberg Som Fotograf* (1963) (Åhus: Kalejdoskop Forlag, 1989), p. 145; Twain, quoted in letter to Howells, January 21, 1879, in *Mark Twain's Letters,* ed. Albert Bigelow Paine (New York: Harper & Brothers, 1917), vol. 1, p. 346; and Adams, quoted in his selection below.

12. See Ralph Bogardus, "A Literary Realist and the Camera: W. D. Howells and the Uses of Photography," *American Literary Realism: 1870–1910,* 10, no. 3 (Summer 1977): 231–41, and Orvell, *The Real Thing,* pp. 119–25.

13. See George R. Stewart, *Bret Harte: Argonaut and Exile* (Boston : Houghton Mifflin, 1931), p. 316, who condescendingly adds that in 1896–97 Harte "exchanged letters with similarly interested friends over adventures in developing and toning."

14. For Day, see Estelle Jussim, *Slave to Beauty: The Eccentric Life and Controversial Career of F. Holland Day, Photographer, Publisher, Aesthete* (Boston: Godine, 1981), pp. 6, 116, 158, 296 n.12, which refers to his portrait of this literary idol, and 300 n. 20. For Coburn, see Coburn, *Alvin Langdon Coburn Photographer: An Autobiography,* ed. Helmut and Alison Gernsheim (New York: Dover, 1978) [hereafter cited as Coburn, *Autobiography*], pp. 14, 100, and Plate 25; Coburn's portrait of Maeterlinck, taken July 2, 1915, in *More Men of Mark* (London: Duckworth, 1922), Plate 19; and Maeterlinck, *The Intelligence of the Flowers,* trans. Alexander Teixeira de Mattos (New York: Dodd, Mead & Company, 1907), illustrated with four photogravures by Coburn. For Steichen, see *A Life in Photography* (New York: Harmony, 1985), ch. 2, npn and Plate 23; Carl Sandburg, *Steichen the Photographer* (New York: Harcourt Brace, 1929), pp. 27–29; Neil Leonard, "Alfred Stieglitz and Realism," *Art Quarterly* 29 (1966): 283; and see also Sadakichi Hartman [S. H.], "Dawn Flowers (To Maurice Maeterlinck)" [lines suggested by Steichen's "Dawn Flowers"], *Camera Work* 2 (April 1903): 29. For Kertész, see Sandra S. Phillips, David Travis, and Weston J. Naef, *André Kertész of Paris and New York* (Chicago: Art Institute; New York: Metropolitan Museum of Art, 1985), pp. 44 and 268, n. 80.

15. See Sandburg selection, n. 2, below for further references on the contacts of Stieglitz, Steichen, and Coburn with Rodin, and see Shaw's 1906 photograph of Rilke reproduced in *Bernard Shaw on Photography*, ed. Bill Jay and Margaret Moore (Salt Lake City: Peregrine Smith, 1989), following p. 50.

16. Barbara Michaels in "Let's Pretend: Photographic Illustration of Fiction and Poetry around 1900," Logan Prize Essay, Photographic Resource Center, Boston University, 1991, discusses book illustrations by Käsebier, White, and other contemporaries. For examples of some invented self-contained "narratives," see Käsebier's 'The War Widow,' discussed by Szarkowski, *Looking at Photographs* (New York: MOMA, 1973), p. 56, and Michaels, *Gertrude Käsebier: The Photographer and Her Photographs* (New York: Abrams, 1992), pp. 150–52.

17. Sadakichi Hartman, "A Few Reflections on Amateur and Artistic Photography," *Camera Notes* 2 (October 1898): 45, reprinted in *A Photographic Vision: Pictorial Photography, 1889–1923*, ed. Peter C. Bunnell (Salt Lake City: Peregrine Smith, 1980), p. 91, and cited by Michaels, "Let's Pretend," p. 1.

18. Evans, quoted in "Photography," in *Quality*, ed. Louis Kronenberg (New York: Atheneum, 1969), p. 170, reprinted in *Massachusetts Review* 19, no. 4 (Winter 1978): 644, and see also in Leslie Katz, "An Interview with Walker Evans," *Art in America* 59 (March–April 1971): 82–89. See also Stuart Culver, "How Photographs Mean: Literature and the Camera in American Studies," *American Literary History* 1, no. 1 (Spring 1989):190 for critic Clement Greenberg's praise of Evans about his knowledge of modern literature as well as painting.

19. Gustav Janouch, *Conversations with Kafka*, trans. Goronwy Rees (London: Quartet, 1985), p. 144. See also Kafka, *America* (1913), trans. Edwin and Willa Muir (London: George Routledge, 1938), pp. 101 and 103–5, which dramatizes the point; and Franca Schetttino, "Photography in Kafka's *Amerika*: A Case of Transformation in the Narrative Literary Medium," in *The Dove and the Mole: Kafka's Journey into Darkness and Creativity*, ed. Ronard Gottesman and Moshe Lazar (Malibu, Calif.: Undena, 1987), pp. 109–33; and Michel Collomb, "Kafka et la photographie," *Art et Litterature* (Aix-en-Provence: University de Provence, 1988), pp. 151–58.

20. Picasso's declaration that "photography has arrived at a point where it is capable of liberating painting from all literature, from the anecdote, and even from the subject" is quoted by Brassaï, *Picasso & Company* (New York: Doubleday, 1966), pp. 46–47, and widely elsewhere.

21. Weston, "Letter Regarding Pictorialism and the Work of Alfred Stieglitz" (1923), in *Edward Weston on Photography*, ed. Peter Bunnell (Salt Lake City: Peregrine Smith, 1983), p. 33.

22. See Nancy F. McGhee, "Portraits in Black: Illustrated Poems by Paul Laurence Dunbar," *Stony the Road*, ed. Keith L. Schall (Charlottesville: University Press of Virginia, 1977), pp. 70–102.

23. For other examples, see the numerous titles listed in the bibliography under Apollinaire, Max Jacob, C. Day Lewis, and Stephen Spender.

24. Sheeler's remark to Williams is noted in *The J. Paul Getty Journal*, 17 (1989): 162; Hine is quoted in Susan Sontag, *On Photography* (New York: Farrar, Straus & Giroux, 1977), p. 185, and widely elsewhere.

25. Szarkowski, *Looking at Photographs*, p. 154.

26. See Steinbeck, *A Russian Story* (New York: Viking, 1948), p. 5.

27. See Anne Morrow Lindbergh, introduction to Saint-Exupéry, *Wartime Writings of St.-Exupéry* (San Diego: Harcourt Brace Jovanovitch, 1986), pp. xv–xvi, and Joy D. Marie Robinson, *Antoine de Saint-Exupéry* (Boston: Twayne [1984]), pp. 141–42.

28. See Valéry, "The Conquest of Ubiquity," *Aesthetics*, trans. Ralph Manheim (New York: Pantheon/Bollingen, 1964), p. 226.

29. Kafka, quoted in Janouch, *Conversations with Kafka*, p. 31: "We photograph things in order to drive them out of our minds. My stories are a way of shutting my eyes."

30. Valéry, "The Centenary of Photography," in *Occasions*, trans. Roger Shattuck and Frederick Brown in *The Collected Works of Paul Valéry*, ed. Jackson Mathew (London: Routledge & Kegan Paul, 1971), vol. 2, p. 160.

31. "One picture is worth a thousand words" is thought to be a Chinese proverb according to John Bartlett, *Familiar Quotations* (Boston: Little, Brown, 1951), p. 1213. But

Sam Roberts, in "Maybe a Picture can be Worth 1000 Votes too," *New York Times* (July 30, 1990), B 1, credits it to Fred R. Barnard, who amended a previous comment—"a look is worth a thousand words"—in *Printers' Ink* (1921), a newspaper industry journal, but described it as a Chinese proverb so it would be taken more seriously; the comment was immediately credited to Confucius.

32. Avedon, quoted in Rosenberg, "Portraits," introduction to Avedon, *Portraits* (New York: Farrar, Straus & Giroux, 1976), npn.

33. See, for example, Baldessari, "The Best Way to Do Art" and "The Two Artists" in *Ingres and Other Parables* (London: Studio International Publications Ltd., 1972), npn.

34. See Kundera, "Lost Letters," *The Book of Laughter and Forgetting,* trans. Michael Henry Hein (New York: Knopf, 1980), p. 3, called to the editor's attention by William Corbett.

35. See Steinbeck, foreword to *America and Americans* (New York: Viking, 1967), npn.

36. Morris, "Photographs, Images and Words," *Time Pieces: Photographs, Writing, and Memory* (New York: Aperture, 1989), p. 63. See also Morris, "Photography in My Life," *Time Pieces,* pp. 139–40, and John Berger and Jean Mohr, *Another Way of Telling* (New York: Pantheon, [1982]), p. 96, on the necessity for words—in discussion at the least—to add meaning to photographs.

37. Linda Hutcheon, "Photographic Discourse," *The Politics of Postmodernism* (London: Routledge, 1989), p. 46, called to the editor's attention by Robert Kiely.

38. Trachtenberg, ed., *Classic Essays on Photography* (New Haven: Leete's Island Books, [1980]), pp. xii–xiii.

39. Prescott, conversation with the editor, September 3, 1991, and Callahan, quoted in Jonathan Williams, "Homage to F. S.; or, that old-time Ryne Duren—Rex Barney bailout," in *Venus, Jupiter & Mars: The Photographs of Frederick Sommer,* ed. John Weiss (Wilmington: Delaware Art Museum, 1980), p. 51. Indeed, a panel of eminent photographers, including Robert Misrach and David Hockney, participating as panelists at a symposium, "Photography: Object/Idea/Theory," April 23, 1991, at the J. Paul Getty Museum, seemed to reinforce these responses: their expressions while responding to a question about the influence of critical theory on their art ranged from puzzlement to bemused incredulity to indifference.

40. See Wolfe, "Miss Aurora by Astral Projection," *Marie Cosindas: Color Photographs* (Boston: New York Graphic Society, 1978), pp. 14–15, and *Conversations with Tom Wolfe,* ed. Dorothy M. Scura (Jackson: University Press of Mississippi, 1990), p. 123. See also Weeks Hall, quoted in Jonathan Williams, "The Shadow of His Equipage," in *The Magpie's Bagpipe,* ed. Thomas Meyer (San Francisco: North Point Press, 1982), p. 97: "The text of most essays on photographers are a waste of everybody's time. . . . There is nothing, under present conditions, that can be more easily and exactly reproduced than a technically good black-and-white photograph, and it is utter rot to burden those interested in them with irrelevant biographical trivia and pet long-winded theory."

41. See Kate Linker, introduction, *Love for Sale: The Words and Pictures of Barbara Kruger* (New York: Abrams, [1990]), p. 15, and *Heinecken,* ed. James Enyeart ([Carmel, Calif.]: Friends of Photography/Light Gallery, 1980), p. 29; see also, for example, Heinecken, *He/She* (Chicago: n.p., 1980).

42. On Evans and his use of titles, see Jefferson Hunter, *Image and Word: The Interaction of Twentieth-Century Photographs and Texts* (Cambridge: Harvard University Press, 1987), pp. 40 and 74–76; Brecht is quoted in Walter Benjamin, "A Short History of Photography," trans. P. Patton, in Trachtenberg, ed., *Classic Essays,* p. 213.

43. See *The Photographs of Lyle Bongé* (Highlands, N.C.: Jargon Society, [1987]), Figs. 44 and 25.

44. See Benjamin, "A Short History of Photography" in Trachtenberg, ed., *Classic Essays,* p. 215. See also Nancy Newhall, "The Caption: The Mutual Relation of Words and Photographs" (1952), in *From Adams to Stieglitz: Pioneers in Modern Photography* (New York: Aperture, 1989), pp. 135–44.

45. The three artists, using the title "What Do We Own/What Is the Same?" reproduced the pages from Moravia's "The Wardrobe" from *Bought and Sold,* trans. Angus Davidson (New York: Farrar, Straus & Giroux, 1973), pp. 83–89 in the *Franklin Furnace Flue* (December 1980), centerfold. Levine used passages from Moravia and perhaps Barthes and others in "Five Comments," *Blasted Allegories,* ed. Brian Wallis (New York: Museum of Contemporary Art; Cambridge: MIT Press, 1987), pp. 92–93, and the opening pages from

Flaubert's famous short story as "A Simple Heart (After Gustave Flaubert)" in *New Observations* 35 (1985): 15–19.

46. Paz, "The Instant and the Revelation," trans. Eliot Weinberger, preface to Manuel Alvarez Bravo, *Instante Y Revelacion,* ed. Arturo Muñoz (Mexico: Circulo Editorial, 1982), npn.

47. Adams, "Beauty in Photography," *Beauty in Photography: Essays in Defense of Traditional Values* (New York: Aperture, 1981), p. 35.

48. Winogrand, quoted in Helen Gary Bishop, "Looking for Mr. Winogrand," *Aperture* 112 (Fall 1988): 44, called to the editor's attention by Elise Katz.

49. See Meatyard, *The Family Album of Lucybelle Crater,* with texts by Jonathan Greene et al. (N.p.: Jargon Society, 1974), whose title is adapted from the names of the mother and daughter—both called Lucybelle Crater—in O'Connor's story "The Life You Save May Be Your Own," in *A Good Man Is Hard to Find* (New York: Harcourt, Brace, 1955), pp. 53–68; the structural repetition of the pictures was probably influenced by Stein's ideas in "Portraits and Repetition," *Lectures in America* (New York: Random House, 1935), pp. 165–208, noted by Susan Dodge Peters, *The Photographs of Ralph Eugene Meatyard* (Williamstown, Mass.: Williams College Museum of Art, [1977]), p. 11, and discussed by Jonathan Williams and Meatyard in "Three Cogitations," *Lucybelle,* pp. 73–74, and by Anna Hoy in *Fabrications: Staged, Altered and Appropriated Photographs* (New York: Abbeville, 1985), p. 10, who also relates Meatyard's vision "to the Anglo-American tradition of the grotesque, especially the southern version expressed so powerfully by William Faulkner and Carson McCullers." See also specific appreciations of Meatyard by his close writer friends Wendell Berry, Guy Davenport, James Baker Hall, and Jonathan Williams, listed in the bibliography below.

50. Cartier-Bresson, quoted in Andy Grundberg, "Magnum's Postwar Paradox," *Crisis of the Real: Writings on Photography 1974–1989* (New York: Aperture, 1990), p. 192.

51. See Farina's speech in Kosinski, *Passion Play* (New York: St. Martin's Press, 1980), p. 178.

52. According to Elizabeth Chanler Chatwin in conversation with the editor, June 13, 1991.

53. Bidart and Schwartz, in meetings and telephone conversations with the editor throughout January 1991.

54. See Edwin Morgan, "Instamatic Poems" [1971–1973], *Selected Poems* (Manchester: Carcanet Press, 1985), pp. 47–54.

55. See Milton Seltzer, *Dorothea Lange: A Photographer's Life* (New York: Farrar, Straus & Giroux, 1978), p. 305: Lange taught photography briefly in 1957–58; her weekly assignment was to produce a photograph of one's personal environment with no human in it—such as an unmade bed, dishes in the sink, a flight of stairs, etc. One student complained to Cunningham, who, remembering the assignment one morning, arranged some hairpins on her rumpled sheets and photographed them, sending a contact print to Lange. Made as a joke, the image became one of Cunningham's most popular photographs and is reproduced in Judy Dater et al., *Imogen Cunningham: A Portrait* (Boston: New York Graphic Society, 1979), Plate 60, and widely elsewhere.

56. See Vendler, *Harvard Book of Contemporary American Poetry* (Cambridge: Belknap/Harvard University Press, 1985), pp. 12–13. The specific Vermeer painting Lowell probably refers to is the famous 'Woman Reading a Letter,' c. 1666.

57. Szarkowski, introduction to *Harry Callahan* (New York: Aperture/MOMA, 1976), pp. 16–17.

58. Brown, telephone conversation with the editor, June 28, 1991.

59. See Frank, *The Lines of My Hand* (New York: Lustrum Press, 1972), npn: "I don't believe in words, but you can always add something of your own to make it honest"; and see his picture of a clothesline on which is hung a black blanket or towel with <u>WORDS</u> on it, facing the section heading "NOVA SCOTIA Canada"; and McCullin in le Carré, introduction to *Hearts of Darkness* (New York: Knopf, 1981), p. v: "A visual statement has to be very direct and quick. A verbal statement can go on and on and on: it can get very confusing, though it may seem to be much more enlightening."

60. See le Carré, "Introduction," *Hearts of Darkness,* pp. 9–21. See McCullin [with Lewis Chester], *Unreasonable Behavior* (London: Cape, 1990), pp. 226–27; his photograph of le Carré is reproduced on p. 226. See also James Michael Buzard, "Faces, Photos,

Mirrors: Image and Ideology in the Novels of John le Carré," *Works and Days* 7 (Spring 1989): 53–75.

61. Frank, quoted by Sarah Greenough, "Electric Dogs and Impaled Bulls: Robert Frank's Construction *Untitled* and *Mute/Blind,*" paper presented at the symposium "Photography: Object/Idea/Theory," April 22–23, 1991, at the J. Paul Getty Museum.

62. *Conversations with Tom Wolfe,* ed. Scura, p. 123.

63. Trachtenberg, *Photography in Nineteenth Century America,* p. 11.

64. Trachtenberg, ed., *Classic Essays,* p. xiii.

65. Lippmann, *Public Opinion* (1922) (New York: Macmillan, 1950), p. 92.

66. Quoted in "Fotografie ist Lichtgestaltung [Photography Is Construction with Light]," *Bauhaus* 2, no. 1 (1928): 5. Trachtenberg, "Ever the Human Document" in *America and Lewis Hine: Photographs 1904–1940* ([Millerton, N.Y.]: Aperture, [1977]), p. 132, quotes Moholy-Nagy as also saying "a knowledge of photography is just as important as that of the alphabet" and "the illiterates of the future will be ignorant of the use of camera and pen alike."

Part One

1840–1865

1. *Edgar Allan Poe*
"THE DAGUERREOTYPE," 1840

*P*oe (1809–49), known for the often bizarre content and haunting style of his masterful short stories and poems, was fascinated by the scientific advances of his time. In contrast to his young French admirer, Charles Baudelaire,[1] Poe especially valued the photograph, hailing Louis Daguerre's new invention as perhaps the most "extraordinary" achievement of modern science. He understood its mechanical origins and processes far better than most authors did, writing two pieces on improvements in the medium as well as this more general one.[2] Initially drawn to the daguerreotype's magical beauty and accuracy, Poe was equally fascinated by its unforeseen possibilities—not surprising, given his interest in the mysterious. He did not live long enough to see any of these "wildest expectations of the imagination" realized or even Daguerre's unique pictures superseded by the reproducible ones of Fox Talbot. But at various significant moments in the final decade of his tormented life, at the request and expense of others, Poe posed for more daguerreotypes—eight in all—than any other major contemporary writer; he was usually disappointed by the result [Fig. 5].[3]

5. Unknown. 'Edgar Allan Poe,' late October 1848.

"THE DAGUERREOTYPE"

This word is properly spelt Daguerréotype, and pronounced as if written Dagairraioteep. The inventor's name is Daguerre, but the French usage requires an accent on the second e, in the formation of the compound term.[4]

The instrument itself must undoubtedly be regarded as the most important, and perhaps the most extraordinary triumph of modern science. We have not now space to touch upon the *history* of the invention, the earliest idea of which is derived from the camera obscura, and even the minute details of the process of photogeny (from Greek words signifying sun-painting) are too long for our present purpose. We may say in brief, however, that a plate of silver upon copper is prepared, presenting a surface for the action of the light, of the most delicate texture conceivable. A high polish being given this plate by means of a steatitic calcareous stone (called Daguerreolite) and containing equal parts of steatite and carbonate of lime, the fine surface is then iodized by being placed over a vessel containing iodine, until the whole assumes a tint of pale yellow. The plate is then deposited in a camera obscura, and the lens of this instrument directed to the object which it is required to paint. The action of the light does the rest. The length of time requisite for the operation varies according to the hour of the day, and the state of the weather—the general period being from ten to thirty minutes—experience alone suggesting the proper moment of removal. When taken out, the plate does not at first appear to have received a definite impression—some short processes, however, develop it in the most miraculous beauty. All language must fall short of conveying any just idea of the truth, and this will not appear so wonderful when we reflect that the source of vision itself has been, in this instance, the designer. Perhaps, if we imagine the distinctness with which an object is reflected in a positively perfect mirror, we come as near the reality as by any other means. For, in truth, the Daguerreotyped plate is infinitely (we use the term advisedly) is *infinitely* more accurate in its representation than any painting by human hands. If we examine a work of ordinary art, by means of a powerful microscope, all traces of resemblance to nature will disappear—but the closest scrutiny of the photogenic drawing discloses only a more absolute truth, a more perfect identity of aspect with the thing represented. The variations of shade, and the gradations of both linear and aerial perspective are those of truth itself in the supremeness of its perfection.

The results of the invention cannot, even remotely, be seen but all experience, in matters of philosophical discovery, teaches us that, in such discovery, it is the unforeseen upon which we must calculate most largely. It is a theorem almost demonstrated, that the consequences of any new scientific invention will, at the present day exceed, by very much, the wildest expectations of the most imaginative. Among the obvious advantages derivable from the Daguerreotype, we may mention that by its aid, the height of inaccessible elevations may in many cases be immediately ascertained, since it will afford an absolute perspective of objects in such situations, and that the drawing of a correct lunar chart will be at once accomplished, since the rays of this luminary are found to be appreciated by the plate.

1. See the Baudelaire selection below. See also Simon Marsden's photographs, accompanying the kinds of writing Baudelaire most admired, in *Visions of Poe: A Selection of Edgar Allan Poe's Stories and Poems* (New York: Knopf, 1988).

2. See Poe's "Improvements in the Daguerreotype," *Burton's Gentlemen's Magazine* 6 (April–May 1840): 193–94 and 246.

3. See Michael J. Deas, *The Portraits and Daguerreotypes of Edgar Allan Poe* (Charlottesville: University Press of Virginia, 1989), pp. 1–61, especially pp. 87–90 for his discussion of Mathew Brady's unsubstantiated assertion that he photographed Poe.

4. According to Clarence S. Brigham, *Edgar Allan Poe's Contributions to 'Alexander's Weekly Messenger'* (Worcester, Mass.: American Antiquarian Society, 1943), p. 22, Poe's insistence on the French accenting and pronunciation was not followed, even by his own compositors; English speakers everywhere soon anglicized the word.

2. Nadar

[GASPARD-FÉLIX TOURNACHON]

"BALZAC AND THE DAGUERREOTYPE,"
FROM *Quand J'étais photographe*, C. 1899

*H*onoré de Balzac (1799–1850), considered the founder of the realistic novel in France, dramatized the shaping influence of the environment on characters from contemporary life throughout La Comédie Humaine (1842–48). He might have been expected to welcome photography's documentary reinforcement; indeed, within three years of Daguerre's invention, Balzac privately claimed to have anticipated the process with which his own writing was now often compared.[1] He did endure the long daguerreotype sitting at least once, probably in May of 1842, for the noted Bisson brothers (1826–1900), whose new studio was already a popular rendezvous for Paris intellectuals. Nadar (1820–1910), a journalist, not yet France's preeminent portrait photographer with his own studio salon, later purchased the portrait [Fig. 6], which Rodin then used for his famous sculpture of Balzac [Fig. 83].[2] Nadar had long admired the writer, whose modes of literary characterization may have influenced his own conceptions of portraiture.[3] But in his last years, Balzac revealed to Nadar his terror of the camera, which could make the unseen visible. The celebrated novelist believed—as did friends and colleagues like Théophile Gautier and Gérard de Nerval—that everybody was made up of invisible "spectral" layers of skin; he feared that each photograph embodied the transference of one of these layers from the sitter, so that repeated exposures could cause death.[4]

"BALZAC AND THE DAGUERREOTYPE"

People were stunned when they heard that two inventors had perfected a process that could capture an image on a silver plate. It is impossible for us to imagine today the universal confusion that greeted this invention, so accustomed have we become to the fact of photography and so inured are we by now to its vulgarization.

But not so then. There were some who, like stubborn cattle, refused to even believe that it was possible. What an obstinate race of ill-tempered beings we are: resistant by nature to anything that ruffles our ideas or interferes with our habits; naturally suspicious of everything new, we manufacture menace upon menace until, alas, that tragic irony, "the eagerness to kill," rears its awful head. Why, it seems like

only yesterday that one of the learned members of the Institute stood raging in frenzied protest at the first public demonstration of the phonograph. How self-righteously the distinguished professor refused to further dignify with his presence that "ventriloquist hoax," and what a commotion he make stalking out, swearing that the unprincipled charlatan responsible for such a fraud would have to answer to him. . . .

As the "Sublime fills us with rioting confusion," so the unknown sends us spinning, shocking us like a slap in the face.

The appearance of the Daguerreotype—which more properly should be called the Niépcetype—was an event which, therefore, could not fail to excite considerable emotion. Exploding suddenly into existence, it surpassed all possible expectations, undermining beliefs, sweeping theories away. It appeared as it remains, the most brilliant star in the constellation of inventions that have already made of our still unfinished century a Golden Age of Science—for lack of any other virtues to recommend it.

Photographs sprang to life, in fact, with such splendid haste that its rich profusion of blossoms appeared at once, fully formed: the idea rose complete from the human brain, the first induction becoming immediately the finished work. . . .

. . . Niépce and his shrewd colleague were wise to have waited to be born. The Church has always been cool to innovators, if not too warm, and the discovery of 1839 was suspect from the beginning: this mystery smelled strongly of witchcraft and was tainted with heresy—the heavily roasting pot had been dragged onto the fire for much less.

Nothing was lacking for a good witch hunt: sympathetic magic, the conjuring up of spirits, ghosts, Awesome Night—dear to all sorcerers and wizards—reigned supreme in the dark recesses of the camera, a made-to-order temple for the Prince of Darkness. It only required the slightest effort of the imagination to transform our filters into philters.

That public admiration was uncertain at first was to be expected; people were bewildered and frightened. The Human Animal needed time to make up its mind and confront the strange beast.

The uneducated and the ignorant were not the only ones to hesitate before this peril. "The lowliest to the most high," so the common saying goes, trembled before the Daguerreotype. More than a few of our most brilliant intellects shrank back as if some a disease. To choose only from among the very highest: Balzac was one of those who could not rid himself of a certain uneasiness about the Daguerreotype process. . . .

He finally pieced together his own explanation for it. . . . I think I remember seeing this theory developed at great length in a little alcove somewhere in the immense edifice of his work, but I do not have the time to look for it now. I do recall very clearly, however, that he used an exceedingly large number of words to explain it to me on several occasions—he seemed to be quite obsessed with the idea. . . .

According to Balzac's theory, all physical bodies are made up entirely of layers of ghostlike images, an infinite number of leaflike skins laid one on top of the other. Since Balzac believed man was incapable of making something material from an apparition, from something impalpable—that is, creating something from nothing—he concluded that every time someone had his photograph taken, one of the spectral layers was removed from the body and transferred to the photograph. Repeated exposures entailed the unavoidable loss of subsequent ghostly layers, that is, the very essence of life.

Was each precious layer lost forever or was the damage repaired through some more or less instantaneous process of rebirth? I would expect that a man like Balzac, having once set off down such a promising road, was not the sort to go half way, and that he probably arrived at some conclusion on this point, but it was never brought up between us.

As for Balzac's intense fear of the Daguerreotype, was it sincere or affected? I for one believe it was sincere, although Balzac had only to gain from his loss, his ample proportions allowing him to squander his layers without a thought. In any case, it did not prevent him from posing at least for . . . one Daguerreotype. . . .

To suggest that Balzac's fear was something less than real would be to choose one's words very carefully. But, lest we forget, an irrepressible desire to shock has always been the fashionable vice of our brightest minds. These originals, who are still indeed among us today, take such frank delight in making themselves paradoxically ridiculous before our eyes that it would seem to be a mental illness for which we should find a name: *pretentia*. The Romantics coughed languidly at us through their ashen cheeks; the Realists were struck with sudden artless fits of candor; and the Naturalists glared wretchedly with that sordid cast in their eye. Today's generation of decadents and egotists—more tedious by themselves than all the others combined—are afflicted with a shrill screech, the refinement of which only serves to remind us that public madness is not a thing of the past.

Be that as it may, Balzac did not have to look far to find disciples for his new creed. . . . good old [Théophile] Gautier and Gérard de Nerval stepped into line immediately. . . . Both of them, however, without any qualms, were among the first to sit—quite successfully I might add—before our camera.

I could not say for how long this trio of mystics resisted the purely scientific explanation of the Daguerreotype, which was accepted very quickly by the public. As was to be expected, our Pantheon of the day protested vigorously at first, but then quickly accepted the inevitable and spoke of it no more. [from *Quand J'étais Photographe, c.* 1899]

1. See Balzac, entry of May 2, [1842], *Lettres à L'Etrangère* (Paris: Calmann & Lévy, 1906), vol. 2, p. 38, for this claim based on remarks in *Louis Lambert* (1832) in *La Comédie Humaine,* trans. Katherine Prescott Wormely (Boston: Little, Brown, 1896), vol. 13, pp. 138–40. This claim is noted by Harry Levin, *Gates of Horn* (New York: Oxford University Press, 1963), p. 182, and also mentioned by Rosalind Krauss, "Tracing Nadar," *October* 5 (1979): 35. See also Kelly, "Photographic Reality . . . ," *French Review* 65, no. 2 (December 1991): 195 and 199, for comparisons of Balzac's writing with the daguerreotype.

2. This daguerreotype, the only known one of Balzac, is mentioned in the letter cited above and is reproduced in Nigel Gosling, *Nadar* (New York: Knopf, 1976), p. 2; in Krauss, 31; and in two versions—one the reverse of the other—in "Nadar-Balzac: Une Ténébreuse Affaire," *Nadar: Caricatures et Photographies* (Paris: Les Musées de la Ville de Paris, 1990), pp. 20–21, a catalogue for an exhibition at the Maison de Balzac, November 13, 1990–February 17, 1991. For more on Nadar, see the George Sand selection below, and Richard Howard's "Avarice, 1849: A Distraction," in *New York Times Magazine* (July 12, 1993): 3, on his imagined portrait-taking session of Balzac. For more on Rodin's sculpture of Balzac and Edward Steichen's photographs of it, see the Carl Sandburg selection below.

3. See Roger Cardinal, "Nadar and the Photographic Portrait," in *The Portrait in Photography,* ed. Graham Clarke (London: Reaktion Books, 1992), pp. 7–9; see also pp. 11–13.

4. For more on this fear of photography, see also the Champfleury and Nerval selections below; the character José Arcadio Buenda in Gabriel García Márquez, *One Hundred Years of Solitude* (1967), trans. Gregory Rabassa (New York: Harper & Row, 1970), p. 51, who thinks his body is slowly wearing away while his image endures on the metallic plate; and the relevant story by Michel Tournier, "Veronica's Shrouds," in *The Fetishist,* trans. Barbara Wright (New York: Doubleday, 1984), pp. 130–43, especially 138–39. See also Braive, *The Era of the Photograph,* p. 75, who notes that Balzac's *Louis Lambert* does "contain echoes of Swedenborg's theories concerning the transmutation of the ethereal substance (Matter), and particularly those concerning the role of light and the power of the will," and that his only explicit allusion to the daguerreotype in this context appears in *Le cousin Pons* (1847), vol. 19 of *La Comédie Humaine,* p. 150 (near a comment, p. 156, about the apparent absurdity of the theories underlying many significant modern inventions); Lynn R. Wilkinson, "*Le cousin Pons* and the Invention of Ideology," *PMLA* 107, no. 2 (March 1992): 274–89, discusses this work and Balzac's relation to photography.

3. *Champfleury*

[JULES FLEURY HUSSON]

"THE LEGEND OF THE DAGUERREOTYPIST," 1863

Champfleury (1821–89), an art critic and popular novelist of the 1850's, is now remembered as the early leader of French realism, inspired both by Gustave Courbet's revolutionary theories of painting the "vulgar" and by the objective accuracy of the daguerreotype. His influential manifesto, Le Réalisme, *appeared in 1857, the same year as both* Les Fleurs du Mal *by his friend Baudelaire, who had helped launch his career as an art critic, and* Madame Bovary, *which Flaubert reportedly wrote "to annoy Champfleury . . . to show that bourgeois unhappiness and second-rate sentiment can survive good writing."[1] In* Le Réalisme, *Champfleury condemned those who called writers mere "daguerreotypeurs" if they attempted to use as much realism to capture external authenticity as possible.[2] In this story, written just before the daguerreotype was eclipsed by other photographic processes, he dramatizes the irrational fear—shared by sophisticates like Balzac as well as natives of Africa, the Middle East, and the Americas—that each photograph took something away from the subject, whether cell layers or souls.[3] The hero suggests the appearance, though not the distinguished practice, of the contemporary portrait photographer Pierre Petit (1832–1909), as caricatured by another, Étienne Carjat (1828–1906) [Figs. 7–8].[4] Champfleury subsequently became an art historian and administrator, his creativity surpassed by some artists he had championed, like Baudelaire, as well as by others he had demeaned, like Nadar.[5]*

"THE LEGEND OF THE DAGUERREOTYPIST"

The first daguerreotypist to set himself up in Paris was a barber's assistant from the south, named Carcassonne, who, of his former position, retained only his long hair, long cuffs, and a puffy shirt frill which served as a sign; but he assumed the attitudes of a man inspired and a little awesome in the numerous portraits of himself that could be seen under his carriage entrance.

Men who passed in front of the picture frame said to themselves:——I would like to resemble Carcassonne! The young ladies would sigh to themselves:——What a handsome young man is M. Carcassonne!

Finally, there was so much talk in the neighborhood about Carcassonne, about his beauty and his talent as a daguerreotypist, that a man who had just come to town from the provinces, M. Balandard, decided to surprise his wife by bringing her on his return to Chaumont his portrait, done according to this still novel process.

Accordingly one morning the man from the provinces climbed to the studio of Carcassonne, who, having adjusted his shirt frill and tossed back his hair, said:

——We are going to make, Monsieur, an admirable portrait. They won't recognize you.

——But why make a daguerreotype, exclaimed M. Balandard, if no one will recognize me?

——That is a manner of speaking, dear Monsieur ... Please sit down and don't move. I am going to comb your hair, if you will allow me ... Don't move ... They don't cut hair very well in your province, monsieur ... Don't move, I am looking for my scissors ... Snip, snip, snip, done. Look at yourself in this mirror, without moving if you please ... You look ten years younger ... One moment while I put on a touch of pomade ... Don't move.

——What about the portrait? exclaimed M. Balandard impatiently.

——Immediately. But first a little bit of rice powder to wipe off away the *sweat* from your journey, and don't move!

——But why, Monsieur Carcassonne, do you not allow me to move?

——To accustom you from this moment to tolerate the immobility that this operation requires ... Patience, we are going to begin. Don't move!

Then Carcassonne placed opposite M. Balandard a huge daguerreotype camera which looked like a cannon, aimed at the model.

——Don't blink! Hold it! Don't move!

——This position is really intolerable, thought M. Balandard, keeping his eyes wide open.

——Keep your hands still! Chest forward! ... Don't move the rest of your body, said the daguerreotypist, his head inside the machine.

He left the camera returning to M. Balandard.

——There is a lock of hair which is producing the worst effect ... I should have used the curling iron. Please do not get impatient, I am starting. Don't move! One, two, three! Steady! Done!

8. Pierre Petit. 'Self-portrait,' 1850's (with caricature of Petit by Eugene Carjat in the background).

——Finally! cried M. Balandard, getting up, happy to escape the harsh immobility and to admire his features reproduced by the sun.

But the plate, blacker than a negro, did not let him distinguish either his mouth or nose or eyes or ears.

——You moved, cried M. Carcassonne. We have to start again ... Let's go, get into place and don't move.

M. Balandard sat back on his chair and three times the same exasperating black square appeared on the plate.

——You must be perpetual motion itself, monsieur? said the daguerreotypist. But it's nevertheless so easy to stay in place.

The truth was that the former barber's assistant, absolutely ignorant in the art of the daguerreotypist, was randomly using chemical substances unfamiliar to him and the sun was reluctant to help out.

During the fourth attempt at a portrait, M. Balandard felt a peculiar itching on his nose and he had to exert great control over himself not to scratch.

——Ah! ah! exclaimed Carcassonne, this is a better attempt.

And, triumphantly, he showed his client a nose which was delineated in the middle of the black plate.

——You did not move your nose; see how well it can turn out. Have a little courage and we will succeed.

At the sixth portrait, M. Balandard stood up, scratching his ears as if he was being besieged by an army of fleas.

——That's curious, he said, while scratching his ears; they seem smaller to me.

——Bravo! cried Carcassonne, bravo!

This time, the ears of M. Balandard appeared in profile on the plate in all their flatness.

——All is going well, said the daguerreotypist; for the first time, the portrait will come out whole. Don't move!

Then M. Balandard felt as if a legion of ants was in his hair.

——Pay no attention to it, said M. Carcassonne; such is the effect of my pomade, which infiltrates the capillary tissues and activates the root of the hair.

After all that tingling, his hair appeared on the plate in all its majesty.

At the ninth attempt, a strange prickling sensation in the right eye of M. Balandard made him close his left eye. And as a result the right eye showed all by itself on the plate.

——Lord! What torture! exclaimed M. Balandard whose heart was seized by a certain anxiety. What was the meaning of the itches, the tinglings, the pricklings as a result of which the poor man felt like a reduced version of himself. Wasn't it dangerous to be exposed to this mysterious machine which coldly stared at the sitting man with its somber great eye? And what a mournful costume was that of the daguerreotypist who was constantly covering his head with a large black cloth?

If he had had any will power, M. Balandard would have left the studio; but since sitting in the chair opposite the instrument, his will had diminished and he was not able to resist Carcassonne who twenty times forced him to sit down and twenty times more recommenced the portrait with his eternal shout: Don't move.

Meanwhile Carcassonne, by dint of experimenting, began to know what he was doing and managed to get a sort of portrait, very fuzzy but a marvel compared to the first blacknesses.

It is true that to attain these poor results, the daguerreotypist had loaded his plates with extremely violent chemical products.

The sitting had already lasted three hours, and the weakened M. Balandard had just enough strength to mop his dripping brow, when Carcassonne uttered a cry of triumph.

——At last, here is an admirable portrait, the best possible likeness !

To this enthusiasm, an altered voice responded:

——Show me.

——Fine, Monsieur Balandard, but where are you? asked the daguerreotypist.

——Here.

——Where?

——On the chair.

Indeed the sound of the voice did come from the chair where the model had just been sitting; but the man from the provinces was no longer to be seen.

——Monsieur Balandard! cried the daguerreotypist.

——Monsieur Carcassonne!

——Come on, Monsieur Balandard, no more jokes ... Come out of your hiding place.

——Don't you see me, Monsieur Carcassonne? said the voice.

Finally, searching in all the corners of the studio, the awful truth dawned only on the ignorant daguerreotypist who had used such violent acids that the face, body and clothing of the wretched townsman of Chaumont had been devoured by them.

Fifty successive attempts had gradually annihilated the body of the model. There was nothing left of M. Balandard except his voice.

Frightened by the obliteration of a respectable citizen, a crime covered by the legal code, Carcassonne abandoned the dangerous profession of daguerreotypist and returned to his old profession of barber's assistant; but constantly, as an eternal punishment, the ghost of M. Balandard followed him everywhere and ceaselessly begged him to give him back his original form.

And to calm these just recriminations, Carcassonne could only get a moment's peace with a remark which people who get themselves shaved attribute to excessive prudence:

——Don't move!

1. Baudelaire, quoted in Gosling, *Nadar*, p. 184.

2. See *La Réalisme* (Paris: Lévy Frères, 1857), p. 39. See also pp. 91–93, an account of the contest of the daguerreotypists and the artists, which Janet Buerger notes in *French Daguerreotypes* (Chicago: University of Chicago Press, 1989), p. 57, is similar to that of Swift's battle of the Ancients and Moderns in *The Battle of the Books* (1697). Buerger first called Champfleury and his works to the editor's attention.

3. See Nadar selection preface and n. 4 above.

4. Buerger, *French Daguerreotype*, p. 184, n. 9, suggests that the photographer pictured in the illustrations to the tale looks like Petit (who began as a daguerreotypist in 1849 but soon became involved in other photographic activities) as depicted by Carjat, his former apprentice. Other versions of Carjat's widely reproduced caricature appear on the cover of Buerger's *Pierre Petit: Photographer*, exhibition catalogue, September 26, 1980–January 11, 1981 (Rochester, N.Y.: George Eastman House, 1980), and in *Étienne Carjat, 1828–1906: Photographs*, exhibition catalogue, Musée Carnavalet, November 25, 1982–January 23, 1983 (Paris: Les Musées de la Ville de Paris, 1982), p. 10, called to the editor's attention by Laurence Senelick. Both catalogues also reproduce other well-known portraits of writers by Petit (Hugo, Dumas) and Carjat (Baudelaire, Hugo, Rimbaud).

5. Nadar, *Charles Baudelaire Intime: Documents, Notes et Anecdotes* [1911] (Paris: Obsidiane, 1985), pp. 53–54, includes Champfleury's earlier comment that "Pas Serieux, ce Nadar" and Nadar's retaliation; Gosling, p. 185, reproduces Nadar's 1865 portrait of Champfleury.

4. Ralph Waldo Emerson and Thomas Carlyle

FROM *Correspondence*, APRIL 16–JULY 17, 1846

*I*n 1832, Emerson (1803–82), a seminal American thinker, had been widowed for three years and had just resigned from the ministry because of doubts about all orthodoxies. Traveling abroad, he succeeded in meeting Thomas Carlyle (1795–1881), whose distinctive prose articulating German ideas about material phenomena as a reflection of spiritual reality he found deeply appealing. Emerson got Sartor Resartus (1834) and History of the French Revolution (1837) published in America, which secured Carlyle's transatlantic fame. His "transcendental" ideas, rather than his analyses of and remedies for society's evils, were adapted by Emerson as well as by his Concord neighbors, Nathaniel Hawthorne and Henry Thoreau, to their own idealistic purposes. Carlyle and Emerson maintained a long correspondence; beginning in 1846, they also exchanged photographs [Figs. 9–10].[1] Emerson was intrigued by the daguerreotype, which he considered one of history's greatest inventions. He especially appreciated its democratic availability and superior fidelity compared to other representational forms, though acknowledging the limitations of the lengthy process, which rendered subjects' expressions unflatteringly grim; Carlyle, characteristically, noted only its deficiencies.[2] Subsequent meetings revealed more differences between the increasingly autocratic Carlyle and his former American worshipper, whom he now called "moonshiny." Yet they kept exchanging photographs until the older writer's death.[3]

9. Unknown. 'Thomas Carlyle,' April 1846.

FROM *Correspondence*

April 18, 1846

. . . yes, you shall have that sun-shadow, a Daguerreotype likeness, as the sun shall please to paint it: there has often been talk of getting me to that establishment, but I never yet could go. If it be possible, we will have this also ready for the 3d of May. *Provided* you, as you promise, go and do likewise! A strange moment that, when I look upon your dead shadow again; instead of the living face, which remains unchanged within me, enveloped in beautiful clouds, and emerging now and then into strange clearness! Has your head grown greyish? On me are "grey hairs here and there"—and I do "know it." I have lived half a century in this world, fifty years complete on the 4th of December last:

that is a solemn fact for me! Few and evil have been the days of the years of thy servant,—few for any good that was ever done in them [p. 395].

CARLYLE TO EMERSON
April 30, 1846

Here is the *photograph* going off for you by Bookseller Munroe of Boston [Fig. 9]. . . . If your Photograph succeed as well as mine, I shall be almost tragically glad of it. This of me is far beyond all pictures; really very like: I got Laurence the painter to go with me, and he would not let the people off until they had actually made a likeness. My Wife has got another, which she asserts to be much "more amiable-looking," and even liker! O my Friend,

10. Unknown. 'Ralph Waldo Emerson,' May 1846.

it is a strange Phantasmagory of a Fact, this huge tremendous World of ours, Life of ours! [pp. 396–398].

EMERSON TO CARLYLE
May 14, 1846
I daily expect the picture, & wonder—so long as I have wished it, I had never asked it before. I was in Boston the other day & went to the best reputed Daguerreotypist, but though I brought home three transcripts of my face, the house-mates voted them rueful, supremely ridiculous. I must sit again, or . . . I must not sit again, not being of the right complexion which Daguerre & iodine delight in. I am minded to try once more, and if the sun will not take me, I must sit to a good crayon sketcher Mr. Cheney, & send you his draught [p. 398].

EMERSON TO CARLYLE
May 31, 1846
The photograph came safely to my thorough content. I have what I wished. This head is to me out of comparison more satisfying than any picture. I confirm my recollections & I make new observations: it is life to life. Thanks to the Sun! This artist remembers what every other forgets to report, & what I wish to know, the true sculpture of the features, the angles, the special organism, the rooting of the hair, the form & the placing of the head[.] I am accustomed to expect of the English a securing of the essentials in their work, and the sun does that, & you have done it in this portrait, which gives me much to think & feel. I was instantly stirred to an emulation of your love & punctuality, and, last Monday, which was my forty

third birthday, I went to a new Daguerreotypist, who took much pains to make his picture right. I brought home three shadows not agreeable to my own eyes. The machine has a bad effect on me. My wife protests against the imprints as slanderous. My friends say, they look ten years older, and, as I think, with the air of a decayed gentleman touched with his first paralysis. However I got yesterday a trusty vote or two for sending one of them to you, on the ground that I am not likely to get a better. But it now seems probable that it will not get cased & into the hands of Harnden [Package Express Office] in time for the steamer tomorrow. It will then go by that of the 16th [p. 400].

CARLYLE TO EMERSON

June 18, 1846

We expect the Daguerreotype by next Steamer; but you take good care not to prepossess us on its behalf! In fact, I believe, the only satisfactory course will be to get a Sketch done too; if you have any Painter that can manage it tolerably, pray set about that, as the true solution of the business—out of the two together we shall make a likeness for ourselves that will do it. Let the Lady Wife be satisfied with it; *then* we shall pronounce it genuine! [p. 402].

EMERSON TO CARLYLE

July 15, 1846

I sent you the promised Daguerreotype [Fig. 10] with all unwillingness, by the steamer, I think of 16 June [p. 403].

CARLYLE TO EMERSON

July 17, 1846

Since I wrote last to you . . . the photograph, after some days of loitering at the Liverpool Custom-house, came safe to hand. Many thanks to you for this punctuality: this poor Shadow, it is all you could do at present in that matter! But it must not rest there, no. This image is altogether unsatisfactory, illusive, and even in some measure tragical to me! First of all, it is a bad photograph; no eyes discernible, at least one of the eyes not, except in rare favourable lights; then, alas, Time itself and Oblivion must have been busy. I could not at first, nor can I yet with perfect decisiveness, bring out any feature completely recalling to me the old Emerson, that lighted on us from the Blue, at Craigenputtock long ago,—eheu! Here is a genial, smiling energetic face, full of sunny strength, intelligence, integrity, good humour; but it lies imprisoned in baleful shades, as of the valley of Death; seems smiling on me as if in mockery, "Dost know me, friend? I am dead, thou seest, and distant, and forever hidden from thee;—I belong already to the eternities, and thou recognisest me not!" On the whole, it is the strangest feeling I have:—and practically the thing will be that you get us by the earliest opportunity some *living* pictorial sketch, chalk-drawing or the like, from a trustworthy hand; and send *it* hither to represent you. Out of the two I shall compile for myself a likeness by degrees: but as for this present, we cannot put up with it at all; to my Wife and me, and to sundry other parties far and near that have interest in it, there is no satisfaction in this. So there will be nothing for you but compliance, by the first fair chance you have: furthermore I bargain that the *Lady* Emerson have, within reasonable limits, a royal veto in the business (not absolute, if that threaten extinction to the enterprise, but absolute within the limits of possibility); and that she take our case in hand, and graciously consider what can and shall be done. That will answer, I think [pp. 405–6].

---

1. See introduction to Emerson and Carlyle, *The Correspondence of Emerson and Carlyle*, ed. Joseph Slater (New York: Columbia University Press, 1964), especially pp. 50–51 and 60–61.

2. See *The Journals & Miscellaneous Notebooks of Ralph Waldo Emerson*, ed. William H. Gilman et al. (Cambridge: Belknap/Harvard University Press, 1960–82), especially the years 1841–57: vol. 8: pp. 106, 115–16, 138–39, 142, and 429–30; vol. 9: pp. 14, 383, 416–17, and 467; vol. 11: pp. 433–34; vol. 13: pp. 74; vol. 14: pp. 126.

3. See Emerson and Carlyle, *Correspondence*, pp. 50 and nn. 24 and 25, 51, 60–61, 545, 548, 586–87 and n.

5. Walt Whitman

The maturity of Walt Whitman (1819–92), America's most innovative nineteenth-century poet, coincided with photography's evolution from the daguerreotype in 1839 to the portable Kodak in 1880. This review of one of the chain of studios established by the noted daguerreotypist-entrepreneur John Plumbe, together with several other pieces on photography, shows Whitman's initial enthusiasm for the new invention, which proved enduring, especially for portraits.[1] No writer so appreciated photography as a quintessentially American activity, which wed the intellect, senses, and spirit to technology and produced a more honest and detailed "democratic" art, available to all, unlike painting and sculpture. Few were as sensitive to the camera's ability to reproduce overlooked details as well as to shape public perception, whether of events like the Civil War or of individuals.[2] Indeed, as a poet, Whitman wanted to emulate the "Priests of the Sun," whose cameras commemorated aspects of the world without preconceptions.[3] He himself was photographed regularly [Fig. 11][4] in over a hundred portraits by thirty photographers, more than any other major writer of the century. Some of these portraits appeared as frontispieces for editions of Leaves of Grass *(1855–92), the first—an engraving based on a daguerreotype—being used to "identify" the otherwise anonymous poet [Fig. 12].[5] Another portrait even became the subject of one of his poems, "Out from behind This Mask," but a planned volume of them never materialized.[6] Whitman would have relished the later photographic illustrations to some of his works and his evident influence on twentieth-century photographers as well as writers.[7]*

11. Unknown. 'Walt Whitman,' c. 1846–48.

"Visit to Plumbe's Gallery," July 2, 1846

Among the "lions" of the great American metropolis, New York City, is the Picture Gallery at the upper corner of Murray street and Broadway, commonly known as *Plumbe's Daguerreotype establishment.* Puffs, etc., out of the question, this is certainly a great establishment! You will see more *life* there—more variety, more human nature, more artistic beauty, (for what created thing can surpass that masterpiece of physical perfection, the human face?) than in any spot we know of. The crowds continually coming and going—the fashionable belle, the many distinguished men, the idler, the children—these alone are enough to occupy a curious train of attention. But they are not the first thing. To us, the *pictures* address themselves before all else.

What a spectacle! In whatever direction you turn your peering gaze, you see naught but human faces! There they stretch, from floor to ceiling—hundreds of them. Ah! what tales might those pictures tell if their mute lips had the power of speech! How romance then, would be infinitely outdone by *fact*. Here is one now—a handsome female, apparently in a bridal dress. She was then, perhaps, just married. Her husband has brought her to get her likeness; and a fine one he must have had, if this is a correct duplicate of it. Is he *yet* the same tender husband? Another, near by, is the miniature of an aged matron, on whose head many winters have deposited their snowy semblance.—But what a calm serene bearing! How graceful she looks in her old age! . . .

12. Samuel Hollyer. 'Walt Whitman,' 1854. Frontispiece in the first edition
of *Leaves of Grass* (1855), based on a lost daguerreotype by Gilbert Harrison.

. . . Besides these, of course, are hundreds of others. Indeed, it is little else on all sides of you, than a great legion of human faces—human eyes gazing silently but fixedly upon you, and creating the impression of an immense Phantom concourse—speechless and motionless, but yet *realities*. You are indeed in a new world—a peopled world, though mute as the grave. We don't know how it is with others, but we could spend days in that collection, and find enough enjoyment in the thousand human histories, involved in those daguerreotypes.

There is always, to us, a strange fascination, in portraits. We love to dwell long upon them—to infer many things, from the text they preach—to pursue the current of thoughts running riot about them. It is singular what a peculiar influence is possessed by the *eye* of a well-painted miniature or portrait.—It has a sort of magnetism. We have miniatures in our possession, which we have often held, and gazed upon the eyes in them for the half-hour! An electric chain seems to vibrate, as it were, between our brain and him or her preserved there so well by the limner's cunning. Time, space, both are annihilated, and we identify the semblance with the reality.—And even more than that. For the strange fascination of looking at the eyes of a portrait, sometimes goes beyond what comes from the real orbs themselves.

Plumbe's beautiful and multifarious pictures all strike you, (whatever their various peculiarities) with their *naturalness*, and the *life-look* of the eye—that soul of the face! In all his vast collection, many of them thrown haphazard, we notice not one that has a dead eye. Of course this is a surpassing merit. Nor is it unworthy of notice, that the building is fitted up by him in many *ranges of rooms*, each with a daguerrian operator; and not merely as one single room, with one operator, like other places have. The greatest emulation is excited; and persons or parties having portraits taken, retain exclusive possession of one room, during the time.

1. See also Whitman's piece on Brady in the Brooklyn *Evening Star* (February 20, 1846) 2:4, quoted in Alan Trachtenberg, *Reading American Photographs: Images as History, Mathew Brady to Walker Evans* (New York: Hill & Wang, 1989), pp. 60–66, who also, p. 70, quotes from the poet's 1870 letter supporting Brady's attempt to sell his collection of representative Americans to Congress. Joseph J. Rubin, *The Historic Whitman* (University Park: Pennsylvania State University Press, 1973), pp. 255–56 (and 370 n. 2) and pp. 285–86 (and 382 n. 17), quotes from or cites relevant pieces in the Brooklyn *Eagle* (March 12, 1846; August 27, 1853). Denise Bethel, throughout "'Clean and Bright Mirror': Whitman, New York, and the Daguerreotype," *Seaport* 26, no. 1 (Spring 1992): 20–24, reproduces engravings and photographs of other New York daguerreotype studio exteriors and interiors, but none exists of a Plumbe interior, according to Clifford Krainik and William Welling, in conversations with the editor on November 18, 1992; Welling does own a stereoscope photograph of the Plumbe studio exterior, at the intersection of Broadway and Murray.

2. For surveys of Whitman's multifaceted involvement with photography, see Ed Folsom, "Whitman and the Visual Democracy of Photography," *Mickle Street Review* 10 (1988): 51–65; Miles Orvell, *The Real Thing: Imitation and Authenticity in American Culture, 1880–1940* (Chapel Hill: University of North Carolina Press, 1989), pp. 3–29; and Patrick F. Cahill, "Walt Whitman and the Nineteenth Century's Visual Enterprise," Ph.D. diss. (University of California, Santa Cruz, 1992), summarized in *Dissertation Abstracts International* 52, no. 7 (January 1992): 2550A. See also the relevant Boswellian notes by Horace Traubel, Whitman's young admirer as well as later literary advisor, agent, and executor, in *With Walt Whitman in Camden* (Boston: Small, Maynard and Co., 1906; New York: D. Appleton, 1908; New York: Kennerly, 1914; Philadelphia: University of Pennsylvania Press, 1953, ed. Sculley Bradley), vols. 1–4, especially entries for 1888—1: 108 (May 6); 1: 131 (May 10); 1: 283–84 (June 8); 2: 45 (July 27); 2: 107 (August 8); 2: 454 (October 8); 2: 506 (October 19); 3: 23 (November 4); 3: 345–46 (December 20), and 1889—3: 553 (January 17).

3. Whitman, quoted in Rubin, *The Historic Whitman*, p. 282, and cited by Folsom, "Whitman," *Mickle Street Review* 19 (1988): 57.

4. Bethel finds convincing evidence for assigning a later date, c. 1848, for the earliest extant daguerreotype of Whitman in "Notes on an Early Daguerreotype of Walt Whitman," *Walt Whitman Quarterly Review* 9, no. 3 (Winter 1992): 148–53, than the usual c. 1846 one, accepted in her own earlier piece "'Clean and Bright Mirror,'" p. 32.

5. See Trachtenberg, *Reading American Photographs,* pp. 60–70, and Orvell, *The Real Thing,* pp. 8–16, on Whitman's use of recent portraits as frontispieces. On Gabriel Harrison, who took the famous Whitman portrait engraved for the unconventional frontispiece, well suited for the unconventional *Leaves of Grass* (1855), see Bethel, "'Clean and Bright Mirror,'" pp. 22–24, and Whitman [Paumanok], "Letters from New York, November 2, 1850," *National Era* 4, no. 46 (November 14, 1850): 181, which includes praise of him as do other pieces by Whitman cited by Rubin, *The Historic Whitman,* pp. 283 and 381 n. 13, in the *Brooklyn Evening Star* (May 24, 1852) and "An Hour Among the Portraits" (June 7, 1853); and William Innes Homer, "New Light on Thomas Eakins and Walt Whitman in Camden," in *Walt Whitman and the Visual Arts,* ed. Geoffrey M. Sill and Roberta K. Tarbell (New Brunswick, N.J.: Rutgers University Press), pp. 85–93.

6. See Whitman, "Out from behind This Mask (To confront My Portrait, illustrating 'the Wound-Dresser' in *Leaves of Grass*)," *Two Rivulets* (Camden, N.J.: Author's Edition, 1876), pp. 24–25, a poem widely reprinted in later editions of *Leaves of Grass,* those after 1881 with slight subtitle and second line changes. But all versions describe the portrait, which is printed opposite the poem from an engraving of a photograph taken by G[eorge] C. Potter in 1871 in Washington, D.C. No further information about Potter or the location of this negative proved available, but the portrait is reproduced in Henry Saunders's handwritten *100 Whitman Portraits* (Toronto: Henry S. Saunders, 1939), No. 44, a copy of which is at the John Hay Library (MS. 81. 5 codex 30), and in the *Walt Whitman Quarterly Review* 4, nos. 2–3 (Fall-Winter, 1986–87): 17, no. 8; the latter appears with Whitman's comments about the portrait—"the photo has something that he (the engraver) fails to retain," and about Potter—"Not a Leaves of Grass man, but friendly to me"—both on p. 49.

See also Whitman, *Specimen Days* [1882] (Boston: Godine, 1971), pp. 123–88, for many portraits of him (though not the one by Potter mentioned above), and p. 123, for his directions for the planned edition, *Pictures from Life of WW* [sic]. See also Graham Clarke, "'To Emanate a look': Whitman, Photography and the Spectacle of Self," in *American Literary Landscapes: The Fiction and the Fact,* ed. F. A. Bell et al. (New York: St. Martin's, 1988), pp. 78–101.

7. See William Carlos Williams, Introduction (1960) to Whitman, *The Illustrated Leaves of Grass,* ed. Howard Chapnick (New York: Madison Square Press/Grosset & Dunlap, 1971), pp. 9–13; Whitman, *Leaves of Grass,* ill. by Edward Weston (New York: Limited Editions Club, [1942]); and Alan Trachtenberg, "Edward Weston's America: The *Leaves of Grass* Project," in *EW 100: Centennial Essays in Honor of Edward Weston,* ed. Peter C. Bunnell et al. (Carmel, Calif.: The Friends of Photography, 1986), pp. 103–15. For Whitman's influence on photographers, see, for example, the Duane Michals selection below, n. 2, and Lee Friedlander's *American Monument* (New York: Eakins, 1976), npn, which opens with a Whitman quote.

*N*erval (1808–55), like many French romantic writers, was very conscious of his image, photographic and otherwise. In 1843, two years after the first of many mental breakdowns, he decided to visit the Orient (as the French called the Near East as well as Asia). He brought with him daguerreotype equipment both to make his journey more purposeful and his recovery from his illness more publicly evident.[1] He also perhaps was emulating his old friend and colleague Théophile Gautier (1811–72), whose daguerreotypes in Spain in 1840 must have been among the earliest taken in that country.[2] Once at his destination, however, Nerval made only a few pictures because, as he explained to his disapproving father, the necessary chemicals decomposed in the hot climate; none have survived.[3] His account of his journey, Voyage en Orient, *contains two episodes involving daguerreotypists (neither a self-portrait): the first invites Nerval to join him in finding an appealing view to photograph in Cairo; the other is the subject of an amorous adventure in Constantinople.[4] Nerval himself remained ambivalent about the new invention. He admired its documentary aspects but resented its usurpation of travel description by writers like himself and, no doubt, its ability to strip illusions from his cherished Orientalist and other fantasies; moreover, he shared Balzac's fears that the camera stripped away parts of its subjects.[5] In 1854, Nerval complained to a friend about an engraving (on one copy of which he made some agitated, idiosyncratic notations), which was based on a daguerreotype taken of him during a recent illness [Figs. 13–14]. He suggested that the image be regarded only as a posthumous one—a sad irony given his suicide shortly afterwards.[6]*

13. Eugène Gervais.
'Gérard de Nerval,' c. 1854.

FROM *Voyage en Orient*

FROM *Les Femmes du Caire* (THE WOMEN OF CAIRO)

The Hotel Domergue is situated at the end of a cul-de-sac off the main street of the French quarter; it is, after all, a very respectable hotel and very well maintained. The buildings surround a square interior courtyard. . . . A French painter, very pleasant although a bit deaf, and full of talent, although very interested in the daguerreotype, had made his studio in an upper gallery. [from Bk. 1, Ch. 3 ("Le Drogman Abdallah"), vol. 2, p. 271]

. . . the painter of the Hotel Domergue . . . was kind enough to take me into his studio and initiate me into the wonders of his daguerreotype. [from Bk. 1, Ch. 4 ("Inconvénients du Célibat"), vol. 2, p. 276]

. . . . I met at the Castagnol pharmacy the painter from the French hotel, who was having some chloride of gold prepared for his daguerreotype. He proposed that I come with him to find a subject in the city . . . [from Bk. 1, Ch. 5 ("Le Mousky"), vol. 2, pp. 282]

So we rode along, the painter and I, followed by a donkey carrying the daguerreotype, a complicated and fragile machine which had to be set up somewhere in a manner to do us credit. Along the road . . . there was a passageway covered with boards where European commerce displayed its brightest wares. It was a kind of bazaar where the French quarter ends. We turned to the right, then to the left, in the middle of an

increasing crowd; we followed a long, very straight street, which offered to our curiosity at long intervals some mosques, fountains, a monastery of dervishes, and an entire bazaar of hardware and English porcelain. Then, after a thousand turnings, the road became more silent, more dusty, more deserted; the mosques were falling into ruin, the houses collapsing here and there; the noise and the tumult now were heard only in the form of a pack of yelping dogs, relentlessly following our donkeys and following, above all, our frightening black clothes from Europe. Fortunately we passed through a gateway, we changed quarters, and these animals stopped, growling at the furthest boundary of their territory. The whole city is partitioned into fifty-three quarters, each surrounded by large walls, which are divided among Copt, Greek, Turk, Jewish and French people.

The dogs themselves, who swarm in peace in the city without belonging to anyone, recognize these divisions and would not risk going beyond them without danger. A new canine escort soon enough replaced the one which had left us and led us as far as the shacks, situated on the banks of the canal which crosses Cairo and which everyone calls the Calish.

Here we were in a kind of suburb, separated by the canal from the principal quarters of the city; numerous cafés and casinos line the inner bank, while on the other side is a large boulevard enlivened with several dusty palm trees. The water of the canal is green and a little stagnant; but a long row of arbors and trellises, festooned with vines and tropical creepers, serves as a back room to the cafés, presenting the most pleasing glimpses while the smooth water surrounds them with a flattering reflection of the variegated dress of the smokers. The flasks of oil in the chandeliers flare up in the only fires of the day, the crystal smoking pipes sparkle, and the amber liquors float in delicate cups, which negroes serve round in their frames of gold filigree.

After a short stop at one of these cafés, we crossed to the other bank of the Calish and installed on its legs the apparatus by means of which the god of day so agreeably exercises his profession of landscapist. A mosque in ruins with a curiously sculpted minaret, a slender palm tree soaring up from a clump of gum trees—this was, with all the rest, sufficient to compose a tableau worthy of Marilhat [a celebrated orientalist painter]. My companion was in raptures and while the sun worked on his freshly polished plates . . . [I left] him to his work, surrounded by a respectful crowd who believed him to be occupied with magical proceedings . . . [from Bk. 1, Ch. 6 ("Une Aventure au Besestain"), vol. 2, pp. 283–85]

FROM *Les Nuits du Ramazan* (THE NIGHTS OF RAMAZAN)

The painter, seeing that we could not sleep, told a story. It concerned the adventures of an artist friend of his, who had come to Constantinople to make his fortune by means of the daguerreotype camera.

He looked for places where the greatest affluence might be found, and went one day to install his reproductive apparatus under the shady trees near the Sweet Waters.

A child was playing on the grass; the artist was lucky to fix a perfect image on a plate; then in the joy of seeing such a successful attempt, he showed it to the curious, of whom there is never a shortage on these occasions.

The mother approached out of understandable curiosity and was astonished to see her child so clearly reproduced. She believed it was magic.

The artist did not know the Turkish language so that he didn't understand the lady's compliments at first. But a negress who accompanied her gestured to him. The lady climbed into a carriage and returned to Scutari [now Üsküdar].

The painter took under his arm the case of his daguerreotype, an instrument which was not easy to carry, and began to follow the carriage for a couple of miles.

Upon arriving at the first houses in Scutari, he saw the carriage stop in the distance and the lady alight at an isolated house which overlooked the water.

The old woman signaled him not to appear and to wait; when night fell, she showed him into the house.

The artist appeared before the lady, who told him that she had him come in order to use his instrument in taking her portrait in the same manner he had used to reproduce the appearance of her child.

"Madame," replied the artist, or at least he tried to make her understand, "this instrument can only work with the presence of the sun."

"All right, let us wait for the sun," said the woman.

Fortunately for Muslim morality, she was a widow.

The next morning, the artist, taking advantage of a beautiful ray of sun which pierced the grilled window, busied himself reproducing the features of the beautiful lady of the Scutari neighborhood. She was very young, though the mother of a large little boy, because the women of the Orient, as everyone knows, mostly marry when they are around twelve. While he was polishing his plates, a knocking was heard on the outer door.

"Hide yourself!" cried the lady and, assisted by her servant, she hurried the man, with his daguerreotype equipment, into a very narrow closet off the bedroom. There the poor wretch had time to reflect sorrowfully. He didn't know that this lady was a widow and naturally thought that her husband had unexpectedly returned after some trip. He had another hypothesis, no less dangerous: the intervention of the police into this house because the night before someone had noticed the entrance of an infidel. However, he listened hard and as the wooden houses of the Turks do not have very thick walls, was somewhat reassured by hearing only the chattering of feminine voices.

In fact, the lady was simply receiving the visit of one of her friends, but the visits that the women of Constantinople pay one another ordinarily last a whole day, as these idle beauties seek every opportunity to kill the most time possible. To show himself was dangerous; the visitor might be old or ugly; besides, although Muslim women necessarily put up with sharing their spouses, jealousy is not absent from their souls when the matter is a love affair. The unfortunate fellow had found approval.

When evening arrived, the inconvenient friend, after having dined, and, later, taken refreshments and devoted herself a long time, no doubt, to scandalous gossip, finally departed, and the Frenchman was finally allowed to leave his narrow hiding-place.

It was too late to resume the long and difficult work of the portrait. Moreover, the artist had been hungry and thirsty for several hours. The sitting had to be postponed until the next day.

By the third day, he found himself in the position of the sailor who, according to a popular song, was supposed to have been kept a long time at the home of a certain president's wife in the time of Louis XV ... ; he began to get bored.

The conversation of Turkish women is quite monotonous. Moreover, when one does not understand the language, it is difficult to be entertained for a long time in their company. He succeeded in taking the requested portrait and made the lady understand that important matters called him back to Péra. But it was impossible for him to leave the house in broad daylight and once evening came, a magnificent meal prepared by the lady still kept him there as well as his gratitude for such charming hospitality. However, the next day, he vigorously indicated his resolve to leave. Again it was necessary to wait until the evening. But his daguerreotype equipment had been hidden and how could he leave this house without this valuable instrument, as, at this time, it would not be possible to find anything like it in the city? It was his means of earning his livelihood. The women of Scutari are somewhat fierce in their attachments; this particular one made it clear to the artist, who finally had managed to learn some words in her language, that if he tried to leave her hereafter, she would call her neighbors, crying that he had stolen into her house to attack her honor.

Such a troublesome attachment finally exhausted the patience of the young man. He abandoned his daguerreotype equipment and succeeded in escaping through the window while the lady was sleeping.

The sad part of the story is that his friends at Péra, not having seen him for more than three days, had informed the police. They obtained some information about what had occurred at the Sweet Waters of Asia. Some local people had seen the carriage pass, followed at a distance by the artist. Her house was pointed out and the poor Turkish woman would have been killed by the fanatic population for having entertained an infidel, if the police hadn't not secretly removed her. She got off with fifty strokes of the cane and the negress with twenty-five, the law applying only half the punishment to the slave which afflicts a free person. [from Bk. 4, Ch. 1 ("Les Eaux-Douces d'Asie"), vol. 2, pp. 777–79]

1. See Nerval, letters to his father, December 25, 1842, and January 8, 1843, in *Oeuvres Complètes,* ed. Jean Guillaume and Claude Pichois (Paris: Gallimard, 1989), vol. 1, pp. 1387 and 1396.

2. See Gautier, *Voyage en Espagne* [1843], ed. Patrick Berthier (Paris: Gallimard, 1981), ch. 4: pp. 54–55; ch. 6: pp. 91, 94–95; and ch. 10: p. 193, referred to by Helmut Gernsheim, *The History of Photography* (London: Thames & Hudson, 1969), p. 116, called to the editor's attention by Janet Buerger. Gautier, who dedicated *Voyage* to Eugène Piot (1812–91), his traveling companion and later an eminent photographer, was himself a member of early photographic societies, even helping to get photography admitted into the Salon of 1859 (the one Baudelaire acidly reviewed—see his selection below), according to Gernsheim, *History,* p. 244; he also had his *Les Trésors d'Art de La Russie Ancienne et Moderne* (Paris: Gide, 1859) photographically illustrated by Pierre-Ambrose Richebourg, according to Buerger, *French Daguerreotypes,* pp. 3, 61, and 148.

3. Nerval, letters to Gautier [May 2, 1843] and to his father, December 24, 1843, *Oeuvres Complètes,* vol. 1, pp. 1395–96 and 1411 respectively.

4. See Nerval, *Voyage en Orient* in *Oeuvres Complètes,* vol. 2, pp. 271, 276, 282–85, 777–79, and 1630 n. on the identity of the daguerreotypist. These episodes were first published in the *Revue des Deux Mondes* in 1846 and 1847.

5. See Nerval, "Notes et Variantes," in *Oeuvres Complètes,* vol. 2, p. 1405, on his complaints; on his fears see the Balzac selection above and Cardinal, "Nadar and the Photographic Portrait," in *The Portrait in Photography,* ed. Clarke, pp. 13–16, who also discusses Nadar's portraits of Nerval.

6. See Nerval, letter to Georges Bell, May 31, 1854, *Oeuvres,* ed. Albert Béguin and Jean Richer (Paris: Gallimard, 1966), vol. 1, pp. 1131–32, and the discussion of the engraving in Julia Ballerini, *Photography Conscripted: Horace Vernet, Gérard de Nerval and Maxime Du Camp in Egypt* (Ann Arbor, Mich.: University Microfilms, 1987), pp. 179–80 and 359. Ballerini also provides an account, pp. 134–94, of Nerval's relationship to photography and photographers, based partly on that of Ross Chambers in *Gérard de Nerval et La Poétique du Voyage* (Paris: Librairie José Corti, 1969), pp. 307–12. The editor is indebted to Julia Ballerini, Claude Pichois (whose third volume of Nerval's *Oeuvres Complètes,* together with an *Album Nerval,* was published in 1993 by Gallimard, too late to be consulted by the anthology editor), Bernard Marbot, and especially Dr. Mary Harper for their help in identifying and locating the daguerreotype by Legros.

7. Gustave Flaubert and Maxime Du Camp

In 1843, Flaubert (1821–80), who became one of France's great nineteenth-century novelists, met Du Camp (1822–94), who is now more renowned for the photographs he took on one trip than for any of his writings. Becoming close friends, the two young men planned an expedition to the "exotic" Middle East far more carefully than had Nerval.[1] Du Camp secured government support to document monuments and inscriptions there, and he prepared himself with a few lessons in handling cameras and developing prints using new, less cumbersome processes. His teacher was Gustave Le Gray (1820–c. 1882), noted for his aesthetic approach to his pictures as well as his knowledge of the new paper techniques.[2] Du Camp's resulting work, Egypte, Nubie, Palestine et Syrie *(1852), featuring the first published photographs of the region, won him instant acclaim, the Légion d'honneur (1853), and a dedication to one of Charles Baudelaire's poems (1857).[3] But Du Camp never photographed again. Pursuing his literary interests, he founded the* Revue de Paris *(1852), in which Flaubert began publishing* Madame Bovary *(1856), his celebrated novel involving adultery. Fearing censorship, Du Camp began making considerable cuts despite Flaubert's protests; but in 1857 both the* Revue *and the novelist were prosecuted, then acquitted, for outraging public morals and religion. Flaubert continued his reclusive country life while Du Camp led a sociable journalist's existence in Paris. Despite their profound differences, however, they always stayed in touch.*

FROM WRITINGS ABOUT THEIR MIDDLE EAST TRIP

The following selections are taken from two texts: Maxime Du Camp's Literary Recollections *(1882–83) [cited, when needed to avoid confusion, as Du Camp] and* Flaubert in Egypt: A Sensibility on Tour *(1972), trans. and ed. by Francis Steegmuller [cited, when needed, as Flaubert].*

September 7, 1849 [from minutes of the Institute de France, Académie des Inscriptions et Belles-lettres]: "In requesting instructions intended to guide him in the journey he is to undertake, M. Maxime Du Camp told the Academy that he will be equipped with an apparatus (photographic) for the purpose of securing, along his way and with the aid of this marvelous means of reproduction, views of the monuments and copies of the inscriptions. Thanks to the aid of this modern traveling companion, efficient, rapid, and always scrupulously exact, the results of M. du Camp's journey may well be quite special in character and extremely important." [from *Flaubert*, p. 23]

Du Camp: I was anxious to obtain every facility for our journey, so I had applied to the government to provide us with some mission, which should recommend us to the diplomatic and mercantile representatives France maintains in the East.

Need I say that this mission was to be entirely unremunerative? My request was granted. I can scarcely restrain a smile. Gustave Flaubert was entrusted by the Minister of Agriculture and Commerce with the task of collecting information at the different posts and chief halting-places for caravans such as he might consider useful to the Chamber of Commerce. I was more fortunate, and . . . obtained a mission from the Ministère de l'Instruction Publique. [vol. 1, pp. 307]

Du Camp: I had bought a tent, saddles, flasks, boxes of tools, drugs, arms, and I was learning to photograph. I had realized upon my previous travels that I wasted much valuable time trying to draw buildings and scenery I did not care to forget. I drew slowly and not very correctly. Besides, when I re-read the notes I had written upon the spot to describe either a building or a landscape, they often seemed confused,

and I felt that I needed an instrument of precision to record my impressions if I was to reproduce them accurately. I was not about to visit Egypt, Nubia, Palestine, Syria, Armenia, Persia, and many other countries which civilization has traversed in turn, and upon which it has left its traces. I was anxious to collect as much information as possible, and for this reason I put myself to school with a photographer [Le Gray], and began to busy myself with chemicals.

Photography was far from being in those days the art it has since become. There were neither plates, nor collodion, nor rapid process of drying, nor instantaneous photographs. We were still working with moist paper; the process was tedious and lengthy, needing great manual dexterity and more than forty minutes spent upon a negative to obtain a complete picture. The sitter or object had to be posed for at least two minutes, whatever the strength of the chemicals and however powerful the camera, and given the most favourable conditions of light.

Nevertheless, even in this imperfect stage photography marked a distinct advance upon the daguerreotype of the past, which presented objects in an inverse sense, even when the metallic gloss upon the surface allowed of their being distinctly perceived. It was one thing to learn photography, but quite another to convey the apparatus upon the shoulders of men and on the backs of mules and of camels; that was, indeed, a difficult problem. At that date gutta-percha [rubber-like substance] receptacles were unknown. I was compelled to use glass phials or crystal bottles and earthenware vessels, which a blow might shatter at any moment. I had cases prepared as if for the crown jewels, and, in spite of all the dangers incident to frequent transport, I broke nothing, and was the first to bring Europe photographs of the monuments I had visited during my journey in the East. [vol. 1, pp. 296–98]

15. Maxime Du Camp. 'Maison et Jardin dans le quartier frank,' 1852, printed by Louis-Désire Blanquart-Évrard.

Du Camp: We were to leave Paris on the 29th October [1849]. Gustave had accompanied his mother to Nogent-sur-Seine, where she was to stay with a portion of her family, and arrived upon a visit to me on the 26th. I was not aware that he intended to come, but when I returned home that evening my servant told me he had arrived.

At first I did not see him when I entered my study, but presently was aware that he was stretched out at full length upon a black bear skin in front of the bookcase. At first I thought he was asleep, but a sigh which escaped him quickly undeceived me. I never beheld such a state of prostration made all the more remarkable by his tall figure and colossal strength. When I questioned him I could at first only extract groans and complaints.

"I shall never see my mother again; I shall never more look upon my country. This journey is too long; it is too distant; it is tempting Providence. What madness! Why are we going?" . . .

I gave him the night to recover from this state of discouragement, but on the following morning I went to his room before he was up, and said to him—

"You're bound by no engagement. If you think the journey too extensive you ought to give it up, and I will go alone."

The inward struggle was of short duration. "No," he cried. [vol. 1, pp. 308–9]

Flaubert: I had my first sight of the Orient through, or rather in, a glowing light that was like melted silver on the sea. . . . Landing took place amid the most deafening uproar imaginable: negroes, negresses, camels, turbans, cudgelings to right and left, and ear-splitting guttural cries. I gulped down a whole bellyful of colors, like a donkey filling himself with hay. . . . The heat is not at all unbearable, thanks to the sea breeze.

Soliman Pasha, the most powerful man in Egypt . . . received us very graciously. He is to give us orders for all the provincial governors of Egypt and offered us his carriage for the journey to Cairo. . . . In addition, we have M. Galis, chief of the army engineers . . . just to give you an idea of how we are to travel. We have been

given soldiers to hold back the crowd when we want to photograph; I trust you are impressed. As you see, poor old darling, conditions couldn't be better. [from Letter to Madame Flaubert, November 17, 1849, pp. 28–30]

Flaubert: I would never allow anyone to photograph me. Max did it once, but I was in Nubian costume, standing, and seen from a considerable distance in a garden . . . [Fig. 15].

Do you know what the Arabs call me? Since they have great difficulty in pronouncing French names, they invent their own for us Franks . . . Abu-Chanab, which means 'Father of the Moustache.' That word, *abu*, father, is applied to everything connected with the chief detail that is being spoken about. . . . Max's name is a very long one which I don't remember, and which means 'the man who is excessively thin.' Imagine my joy when I learned the honor being paid to that particular part of myself. . . . Max's days are entirely absorbed and consumed by photography. He is doing well, but grows desperate whenever he spoils a picture or finds that a plate has been badly washed. Really, if he doesn't take things easier he'll crack up. But he has been getting some superb results, and in consequence his spirits have been better the last few days. The day before yesterday a kicking mule almost smashed the entire equipment.

. . . We shall leave for Upper Egypt as soon as Max gets the plates (for his photography) that he is expecting from Alexandria. Without that complication we'd have left this very afternoon. It will probably be next Wednesday. [from Letters to Madame Flaubert, nd, p. 56n.; January 5, 1850, pp. 71, 74 ; and February 3, 1850, p. 91]

Du Camp: It is thanks to [the servant's] intelligent help that I was able to bring to successful termination the photographic work that I had undertaken. He distilled the water and washed the utensils, leaving me free to devote myself to the fatiguing business of making negatives. If, some day, my soul is condemned to eternal damnation, it will be in punishment for the rage, the fury, the vexation of all kinds caused me by my photography, an art which at that time was far from being as easy and expeditious as it is today. [from *Le Nil, Egypte et Nubie,* quoted in *Flaubert,* p. 101]

Flaubert: Young Du Camp has gone off to take a picture. He is doing quite well; I think we'll have a nice album. As regards vice, he is calming down; it seems to us that I am inheriting his qualities, for I am growing lewd. [from Letter to Louis Bouilhet, March 13, 1850, p. 130]

Du Camp: There was none of my enthusiasm in Gustave Flaubert. His temperament was calm and self-absorbed. Action and movement were disagreeable to him. Could he have lain on the divan and watched the scenery, the cities and the monuments pass before him like a panorama, he would have liked travelling.

Ever since our first arrival in Cairo I had noticed that he was listless and bored. This voyage, this dream so fondly cherished, and which had once been impossible, it seemed to realize, did not satisfy him. I spoke to him quite plainly—

"If you wish to return to France, my servant can accompany you home."

"No," he replied, "I have come, and I will carry out my intention. Choose our route and I will follow you; it is all the same to me which way we go."

To him one temple seemed precisely like another, the mosques and the points of view exactly similar. I am not sure that when gazing at Elephantine he did not regret the fields of Sotteville nor long for the Seine on the banks of the Nile.

At Philae he sat down in the cool interior of the Temple of Isis to read "Gerfaut," which he had purchased at Cairo.

Sometimes of an evening, when the water murmured gently round our boat, and the constellation of the Southern Cross shone out from the other stars, we would talk . . . his thoughts were occupied by his next novel. "It has taken possession of me," he used to tell me. With the scenery of Africa about him he only dreamt of the Normandy landscape. On the confines of Lower Nubia, when we stood on the summit of Djebel-Aboukir, which overlooks the Second Cataract, while we watched the Nile dash-

ing against the serried black granite rocks, he uttered a cry, "I have found it! Eureka! Eureka! I will call it 'Emma Bovary.'" He repeated the name of Bovary several times as it with a kind of enjoyment, and pronounced the letter *o* in it quite short.[4] Strange to say all the impressions he had received during this journey returned with force when he wrote "Salambô."

Balzac resembled him in this, for he appeared to be observing nothing, and yet he remembered everything. [vol. 1, pp. 337–38]

Flaubert: What is it, oh Lord, this permanent lassitude that I drag about me? It followed me on my travels, and I have brought it home! Deinira's tunic was no less completely welded to Hercules' back than boredom to my life! It eats into it more slowly, that's all [from his Travel Notes, April 12, p. 151].

Du Camp: It was during this brief expedition [a four day march across the desert, April 13–16, 1850] that a painful incident occurred, the only one which saddened our travels, between Flaubert and myself, and we were together forty-eight hours without speaking to each other. The circumstances were as comic as they were weird, for Flaubert yielded to one of those irresistible fancies which took possession of him from time to time . . . . We had started . . . with three skins containing water . . . which was to supply our needs during the expeditions . . . . [The first night] the camel which carried our supply of water . . . broke a leg and fell upon its side, and the skins burst under its weight . . . we had still . . . two days and a half before we could gain Bir-Amber, the only well of drinkable water upon our road . . . .

Suddenly [on the third day], Flaubert said to me—

"Do you recollect the lemon ices we used to eat at Tortoni's?"

I nodded my head affirmatively. He continued—

"Lemon ice is first-rate. Confess, now, that you would not object to a lemon ice at this moment?"

"Yes!" I replied, in rather a rough tone.

Five minutes later he resumed—

"Ah! those lemon ices; all over the glass there is a kind of mist, which looks like a white jelly."

I interrupted—

"Supposing we were to change the subject?"

"It might be as well, but really lemon ice should have its praises sung. You fill the spoon so that there is a little dome of ice which goes into your mouth, and is gently crushed between the tongue and the palate. It melts slowly, coolly, and deliciously caresses the uvula and the gullet, then slips down into the diaphragm, which is not displeased, and is greeted finally by the stomach with joyful laughter, Between you and me, there is a decided lack of lemon-ices in the desert . . . [sic]"

I knew Flaubert well, and that nothing could stop him when he was possessed by one of these moods. I tried not speaking in the hope that my silence would check him. But he began again when he saw that I would not answer, louder than ever—

"Citron ices! Citron ices!"

I felt I could not endure it. Terrible thoughts passed through my brain. I said to myself, "I shall kill him." I pressed against him with my dromedary, and took hold of his arm.

"Where do you mean to ride? In front or behind?"

He replied—

"I will go forward."

I stopped my dromedary, and when our little company had advanced some two hundred yards in front of me I resumed my march. At nightfall I left Flaubert among our men, and made my bed in the sand at a distance of more than two hundred meters from our encampment.

At three o'clock on Sunday morning we started again, still as far apart as on the previous day, and without exchanging a word. About half-past three [in the afternoon] we made Bir-Amber, and we drank. Flaubert threw his arms round me and exclaimed—

"Thank you for not having blown out my brains. In your place I should have done it." [vol. 1, pp. 344–47]

Flaubert: I pay no more attention to my mission than to the King of Prussia. To 'discharge my duties' properly I should have had to give up my journey—it would have been absurd . . . . Can't you see me in every town, informing myself about crops, about production, about consumption? How much oil do you shit here? How many potatoes do you stuff into yourselves?' And in every port: 'How many ships? What tonnage? How many arrivals? How many departures?' And ditto, ditto. *Merde.* Ah, no! [Letter to Bouilhet, June 2, 1850, p. 199]

Du Camp: Gustave Flaubert had travelled through Egypt, Nubia, Palestine, Syria, Rhodes, Asia Minor and Constantinople without interest, but he roused himself when he landed in Greece. Classical associations with which he was thoroughly conversant stirred him with the promise of new emotions. I was delighted to see that this part of our tour interested him, and to hear him speak with pleasure of our future rides together to Epidaurus, Matinea, Orchomenus, and Boesa, with its temple of Apollo Epicurius. His enthusiasm did not diminish. Each evening he took down notes of what he saw in the day, a thing he had never done before, except here and there in Egypt . . . .

I had urged him to write the account of our travels in Greece, which might be told in a brief and interesting manner, and would introduce the author in a credible manner to his readers. My advice was rejected.

Flaubert affirmed that travels were only of use in forming an author's style, and that the incidents of travel might be utilized in a novel, but not in a narrative. In his opinion a book of travels and a newspaper paragraph were much on the same level—they were a low class of literature. He had a soul above both. I did not press the matter, for I well knew that it would be useless to do so, but I wrote and begged him to give the matter his consideration . . . [vol. 1, pp. 371–72; vol. 2, p. 9]

Flaubert: Yes, when I return I shall resume—and for a good long time, I hope—my old quiet life at my round table, between my fireplace and my garden. I shall continue to live like a bear, not giving a damn about my country, about critics, or anyone at all. Those ideas revolt young Du Camp, whose head is full of quite different ones; that is, he has very active plans for his return and intends to throw himself into de-moniacal activity. [from Letter to Bouilhet, June 2, 1850, p. 199]

Du Camp: When I bid Flaubert farewell, my heart was full. [September 18, 1850, vol. 1, p. 351]

1. See Maxime Du Camp, *Literary Recollections* (London: Remington, 1893), vol. 1, pp. 295–96: "Gérard had travelled in the East, and I enjoyed talking with him [but his] tales could not enlighten me greatly, and I tried to acquire more serious information about the East, for the hour of our departure was approaching." Oddly, the subject of photography didn't arise, or wasn't recalled, except perhaps subliminally as Du Camp's very next lines—included in the selection above—refer to his "learning to photograph."

2. Du Camp doesn't name his photography instructor but it was Le Gray, according to André Jammes and Eugenia Parry Janis, *The Art of the French Calotype* (Princeton, N.J.: Princeton University Press, 1983), p. 172, and Elizabeth Anne McCauley, "The Photographic Adventure of Maxime Du Camp," *Perspectives on Photography,* ed. Dave Oliphant and Thomas Zigal (Austin: Humanities Research Center, University of Texas at Aus-tin, 1982), p. 23. See also Ballerini, *Photography Conscripted: Horace Vernet, Gérard de Nerval and Maxime du Camp in Egypt:* pp. 195–273, on this expedition; pp. 134–94, for Nerval's earlier but photographically abortive one; and p. 154, for a reference to his friend Gautier's pioneering photography in Spain in 1840, mentioned in the Nerval selection above. For more on Le Gray, see the Dumas selection below.

3. See Baudelaire's "Le Voyage," trans. Robert Lowell, in *The Flowers of Evil* (1857), ed. Marthiel and Jackson Mathews (New York: New Directions, 1989), pp. 179–85; Lowell dedicated his translation to T. S. Eliot.

4. See Steegmuller, ed., in *Flaubert in Egypt,* pp. 135–36, for a short summary of the debate about Madame Bovary's name, whose source which may well be that of the Cairo hotel keeper, M. Bouvaret, mentioned by Flaubert in his travel notes, p. 38.

8. *Nathaniel Hawthorne*

FROM *The House of the Seven Gables*, 1851

*I*n 1839, Hawthorne (1804–64) wished "there was something in the intellectual world analogous to the Daguerreotype . . . in the visible—something which should print off our deepest and subtlest, and delicatest thoughts and feelings, as minutely and accurately as the above-mentioned instrument paints the various aspects of Nature."[1] After finishing The Scarlet Letter (1850), Hawthorne and his family moved to the Berkshires and tried to embody his wish in The House of the Seven Gables. Incorporating his initial enthusiasm for photography with that of his former Concord neighbors, Emerson and Thoreau (especially the latter's hope that such portraits could reveal "the within outwardness"),[2] Hawthorne made his hero a daguerreotypist and a daguerreotype the "truth detector" that unravels the complex romance.[3] The invention, of which the author and his family by now had some personal experience [Fig. 16], suited his characteristic blend of local and cosmic, science and mystery, reality and illusion.[4] Hawthorne's enthusiasm perhaps abated under the influence of his new neighbor and friend, Herman Melville (1819–91), who disdained the ubiquitous photographic portrait.[5] Yet Hawthorne hardly objected when The Marble Faun (1860), read by travelers to Italy for its combination of romance and guidebook, became the most popular volume in the Tauchnitz Collection of British Authors, his detailed descriptions of Rome reinforced by tipped-in photographs.[6]

. . . The old lady began to talk about the Daguerreotypist, whom, as he seemed to be a well-meaning and orderly young man, and in narrow circumstances, she had permitted to take up his residence in one of the seven gables. But, on seeing more of Mr. Holgrave, she hardly knew what to make of him. He had the strangest companions imaginable;—men with long beards, and dressed in linen blouses, and other such new-fangled and ill-fitting garments;—reformers, temperance-lecturers, and all manner of cross-looking philanthropists;—community-men and comeouters, as Hepzibah believed, who acknowledged no law and ate no solid food, but lived on the scent of other people's cookery, and turned up their noses at the fare. As for the Daguerreotypist, she had read a paragraph in a penny-paper, the other day, accusing him of making a speech, full of wild and disorganizing matter, at a meeting of his banditti-like associates. For her own part, she had reason to believe that he practised animal-magnetism, and, if such things were in fashion now-a-days, should be apt to suspect him of studying the Black Art, up there in his lonesome chamber.

"But, dear Cousin," said Phoebe, "if the young man is so dangerous, why do you let him stay? If he does nothing worse, he may set the house on fire!"

"Why, sometimes," answered Hepzibah, "I have seriously made it a question, whether I ought not to send him away. But, with all his oddities, he is a quiet kind of a person, and has such a way of taking hold of one's mind, that, without exactly liking him, (for I don't know enough of the young man,) I should be sorry to lose sight of him entirely. A woman clings to slight acquaintances, when she lives so much alone as I do."

"But if Mr. Holgrave is a lawless person!" remonstrated Phoebe, a part of whose essence it was, to keep within the limits of law.

"Oh," said Hepzibah carelessly—for, formal as she was, still, in her life's experience, she had gnashed her teeth against human law—"I suppose he has a law of his own!" [Ch. 5, pp. 84–85]

"My name is Phoebe Pyncheon," said the girl, with a manner of some reserve; for she was aware that her new acquaintance could be no other than the Daguerreotypist, of whose lawless propensities the old maid had given her a disagreeable idea. "I did not know that my Cousin Hepzibah's garden was under another person's care."

"Yes," said Holgrave, "I dig, and hoe, and weed, in this black old earth, for the sake of refreshing myself with what little nature and simplicity may be left in it, after men have so long sown and reaped here. I turn up the earth by way of pastime. My sober occupation, so far as I have any, is with a lighter material. In short, I make pictures out of sunshine; and, not to be too much dazzled with my own trade, I have prevailed with Miss Hepzibah to let me lodge in one of these dusky gables. It is like a bandage over one's eyes, to come into it. But would you like to see a specimen of my productions?"

"A daguerreotype likeness, do you mean?" asked Phoebe, with less reserve; for, in spite of prejudice, her own youthfulness sprang forward to meet his. "I don't much like pictures of that sort—they are so hard and stern; besides dodging away from the eye, and trying to escape altogether. They are conscious of looking very unamiable, I suppose, and therefore hate to be seen."

"If you would permit me," said the artist, looking at Phoebe, "I should like to try whether the daguerreotype can bring out disagreeable traits on a perfectly amiable face. But there certainly is truth in what you have said. Most of my likenesses do look unamiable; but the very sufficient reason, I fancy, is, because the originals are so. There is a wonderful insight in heaven's broad and simple sunshine. While we give it credit only for depicting the merest surface, it actually brings out the secret character with a truth that no painter would ever venture upon, even could he detect it. There is at least no flattery in my humble line of art. Now, here is a likeness which I have taken, over and over again, and still with no better result. Yet the original wears, to common eyes, a very different expression. It would gratify me to have your judgement on this character."

He exhibited a daguerreotype miniature, in a morocco case. Phoebe merely glanced at it, and gave it back.

"I know the face," she replied; "for its stern eye has been following me about, all day. It is my Puritan ancestor, who hangs yonder in the parlor. To be sure, you have found some way of copying the portrait without its black velvet cap and gray beard, and have given him a modern coat and satin cravat, instead of his cloak and band. I don't think him improved by your alterations."

"You would have seen other differences, had you looked a little longer," said Holgrave, laughing, yet apparently much struck.—"I can assure you that this is a modern face, and one which you will very probably meet. Now, the remarkable point is, that the original wears, to the world's eye—and, for aught I know, to his most intimate friends—an exceedingly pleasant countenance, indicative of benevolence, openness of heart, sunny good humor, and other praiseworthy qualities of that cast. The sun, as you see, tells quite another story, and will not be coaxed out of it, after half-a-dozen patient attempts on my part. Here we have the man, sly, subtle, hard, imperious, and, withal, cold as ice. Look at that eye! Would you like to be at its mercy? At that mouth! Could it ever smile? And yet, if you could only see the benign smile of the original! It is so much the more unfortunate, as he is a public character of some eminence, and the likeness was intended to be engraved."

"Well; I don't wish to see it any more," observed Phoebe, turning away her eyes. "It is certainly very like the old portrait. But my Cousin Hepzibah has another picture; a miniature. If the original is still in the world, I think he might defy the sun to make him look stern and hard." [Ch. 6, pp. 90–92]

The artist, in a desultory manner, had imparted to Phoebe something of his history. Young as he was, and had his career terminated at the point already attained, there had been enough of incident to fill, very creditably, an autobiographic volume. A romance on the plan of Gil Blas,[7] adapted to American society and manners, would cease to be a romance. The experience of many individuals among us, who think it hardly worth the telling, would equal the vicissitudes of the Spaniard's earlier life; while their ultimate success, or the point whither they tend, may be incomparably higher than any that a novelist would imagine for his hero. Holgrave, as he told Phoebe, somewhat proudly, could not boast of his origin, unless as being exceedingly humble, nor of his education, except that it had been the scantiest possible, and obtained by a few winter-months' attendance at a district-school. Left early to his own guidance, he had begun to be self-dependent while yet a boy; and it was a condition aptly suited to his natural force of will. Though now but twenty-two years old, (lacking some months, which are years, in such a life,) he had already been, first, a country-schoolmaster; next, a salesman in a country-store; and, either at the same time or afterwards, the political-editor of a country-newspaper. He had subsequently travelled New England and the middle states as a peddler, in the employment of a Connecticut manufactory of Cologne water and other essences. In an episodical way, he had studied and practised dentistry, and with very flattering success, especially in many of the factory-towns along our inland-streams. As a supernumerary official, of some kind or other, aboard a packet-ship, he had visited Europe, and found means, before his return, to see Italy, and part of France and Germany. At a later period, he had spent some months in a community of Fourierists. Still more recently, he had been a public lecturer on Mesmerism, for which science (as he assured Phoebe, and, indeed, satisfactorily proved by putting Chanticleer, who happened to be scratching, near by, to sleep) he had very remarkable endowments.

His present phase, as a Daguerreotypist, was of no more importance in his own view, nor likely to be more permanent, than any of the preceding ones. It had been taken up with the careless alacrity of an adventurer, who had his bread to earn; it would be thrown aside as carelessly, whenever he should choose to earn his bread by some other equally digressive means. But what was most remarkable, and perhaps showed a more than common poise in the young man, was the fact, that, amid all these personal vicissitudes, he had never lost his identity. Homeless as he had been—continually changing his whereabout, and therefore responsible neither to public opinion nor to individuals—putting off one exterior, and snatching up another, to be soon shifted for a third—he had never violated the innermost man, but had carried his conscience along with him. It was impossible to know Holgrave, without recognizing this to be the fact. [Ch. 12, pp. 176–77]

The artist hesitated. Notwithstanding what he had just said, and most sincerely, in regard to the self-balancing power with which Phoebe impressed him, it still seemed almost wicked to bring the awful secret of yesterday to her knowledge. It was like dragging a hideous shape of death into the cleanly and cheerful space before a household fire, where it would present all the uglier aspect, amid the decorousness of everything about it. Yet it could not be concealed from her; she must needs know it.

"Phoebe," said he, "do you remember this?"

He put into her hand a daguerreotype; the same that he had shown her at their first interview, in the garden, and which so strikingly brought out the hard and relentless traits of the original.

"What has this to do with Hepzibah and Clifford?" asked Phoebe, with impatient surprise that Holgrave should so trifle with her, at such a moment. "It is Judge Pyncheon! You have shown it to me before!"

"But here is the same face, taken within this half-hour," said the artist, presenting her with another miniature. "I had just finished it, when I heard you at the door."

"This is death!" shuddered Phoebe, turning very pale. "Judge Pyncheon dead!"

"Such as there represented," said Holgrave, "he sits in the next room. The Judge is dead, and Clifford and Hepzibah have vanished! I know no more. All beyond is conjecture. On returning to my solitary chamber, last evening, I noticed no light, either in the parlor, or Hepzibah's room, or Clifford's;—no stir nor footstep about the house. This morning, there was the same deathlike quiet. From my window, I overheard the testimony of a neighbor, that your relatives were seen leaving the house, in the midst of yesterday's storm. A rumor reached me, too, of Judge Pyncheon being missed. A feeling which I cannot describe—an indefinite sense of some catastrophe, or consummation—impelled me to make my way into this part of the house, where I discovered what you see. As a point of evidence that may be useful to Clifford—an also as a memorial valuable to myself; for, Phoebe, there are hereditary reasons that connect me strangely with that man's fate—I used the means at my disposal to preserve this pictorial record of Judge Pyncheon's death."

Even in her agitation, Phoebe could not help remarking the calmness of Holgrave's demeanor. He appeared, it is true, to feel the whole awfulness of the Judge's death, yet had received the fact into his mind without any mixture of surprise, but as an event pre-ordained, happening inevitably, and so fitting itself into past occurrences, that it could almost have been prophesied. [Ch. 20, pp. 302–3]

---

1. Letter to Sophia Peabody, December 11, 1839, *The Letters, 1813–1843*, ed. Thomas Woodson, L. Neal Smith, and Norman Holmes Pearson in *The Centenary Edition of the Works of Nathaniel Hawthorne*, ed. William Charvat et al. (Columbus: Ohio State University Press, 1984), vol. 15, p. 384. The daguerreotype as Hawthorne's standard of truth reappears in a reference to a painting in *The Blithedale Romance* (1852), ch. 21: "the mottled feathers were depicted with the accuracy of a daguerreotype."

See also the author's earliest use of the daguerreotype or similar process in "The Birthmark" (1843) and the result, a variant of a "spirit" photograph: "[Aylmer] proposed to take her portrait by a scientific process of his own invention. It was to be effected by rays of lights striking upon a polished plate of metal. Georgiana assented; but, on looking at the result, as affrighted to find the features of the portrait blurred and indefinable; while the minute figure of a hand appeared where the cheek should have

been." For more about "spirit" photographs, see the Conan Doyle selection below.

2. See Thoreau, *Journal* (February 2, 1841), ed. Bradford Torrey and Francis H. Allen (Boston: Houghton Mifflin, 1906), vol. 1, p. 189; but, after the novelty of the new invention had worn off, his entry for October 13, 1860, vol. 14, pp. 117–18, and even the opening paragraph of "Sounds" in *Walden* (Boston: Ticknor & Fields, 1854), ch. 4, p. 121—as discussed by Jeffrey Saperstein, "Thoreau's *Walden*," *Explicator* 46, no. 4 (Summer, 1988): 17–18—suggests that the heightened receptivity of human vision and imagination, if constantly exercised by alert observation, exceeds the factual or "scientific" vision of any camera.

3. See its analysis in Alfred H. Marks, "Hawthorne's Daguerreotypist: Scientist, Artist, Reformer," in Nathaniel Hawthorne, *The House of the Seven Gables,* ed. Seymour L. Gross (New York: Norton, 1967), pp. 330–47, and see also Carol Shloss, "Nathaniel Hawthorne and Daguerreotypy," in *In Visible Light* (New York: Oxford University Press, 1987), pp. 25–50; Cathy N. Davidson, "Photographs of the Dead: Sherman, Daguerre, Hawthorne,"

South Atlantic Quarterly 89, no. 4 (Fall 1990): 667–701; and Trachtenberg's discussions in *Photography in Nineteenth Century America*, pp. 23–26, and in "Likeness as Identity: Reflections on the Daguerrean Mystique" in *The Portrait in Photography,* ed. Clarke, pp. 180–85.

4. Hawthorne may have been one of the earliest customers at Southworth and Hawes's Boston studio, though the miniature daguerreotype mentioned in his wife's letter of May 1841, cited in Rita Gollin, *Portraits of Nathaniel Hawthorne: An Iconography* (DeKalb: Northern Illinois University Press, 1983), p. 22, appears lost. Gollin, pp. 26–28, also discusses and reproduces the only surviving (badly scratched) daguerreotype of the author, taken in Boston by John Adams Whipple, c. 1848 (and now at the Library of Congress, attributed to Mathew Brady, who might have made a copy of it before 1855), as well as later photographs of the author, including the carte-de-visite made by J. J. Mayall of London, used as a frontispiece to the Tauchnitz edition of *The Marble Faun.* In far better condition than Hawthorne's daguerreotype is the charming one of his children, Una and Julian, reproduced here. Davidson, "Photographs of the Dead," pp. 677 and 686,

quotes Hawthorne's surprise after first seeing himself in a portrait: "I was really a little startled at recognizing myself so apart from myself," and later saying, "There is no such thing as a true portrait. They are all delusions."

5. See Melville, *Pierre; or, The Ambiguities* (New York: Harper & Brothers, 1852), Book 17, ch. 3, pp. 345–47, and letter to Duyckinck, February 12, 1851, in *The Letters of Herman Melville,* ed. Davis and Gilman, p. 121. See also Melville's "On the Photograph of a Corps Commander," *Battle-Pieces,* ed. Hennig Cohen (New York: Thomas Yoseloff, 1963), pp. 103–4 and 248n., called to the editor's attention by John Hollander, who identifies the photograph of Winfield Scott Hancock, engraved on the cover of *Harper's Weekly* 8, no. 387 (May 28, 1864), as the source; *Battle-Pieces* was so otherwise antiwar that Newton Arvin, in *Herman Melville* (New York: William Sloane, 1950), p. 267, dubbed him "the [Mathew] Brady of Civil War verse" after that artist's famous pictures of carnage and ruin. See also Timothy Sweet, *Traces of War: Poetry, Photography, and the Crisis of the Union* (Baltimore: Johns Hopkins University Press, 1990), pp. 169–71, who discusses Melville's perspective in both works.

6. See Ann Wilsher, "The Tauchnitz 'Marble Faun,'" *History of Photography* 4, no. 1 (January 1980): 61–66, and Jablow, "Illustrated Texts from Dickens to James," pp. 63–64. The "Publisher's Advertisement," although appearing three decades after the Tauchnitz editions, introduces a new illustrated two-volume edition of *The Marble Faun* (Boston: Houghton Mifflin, 1890), pp. i–ii, as follows: "So satisfactory is the book [as a souvenir of Rome] that "it early became the custom of visitors to Italy to collect photographs of the statues, paintings, and buildings referred to in the romance, and to interleave the book with them; and this has become so common that dealers in Rome and Florence make it their practice to keep such photographs arranged and ready for the traveller. . . . The publishers of Hawthorne's works have therefore taken the hint from this well-established custom, and have prepared the following edition . . . adding to the text photogravures of fifty subjects. Great care has been taken by the publishers in the choice of photographs, and their selection is not a mere repetition of the dealer's choice . . . no pains have been spared to obtain the best made directly from the objects themselves." See also Timothy Sweet, "Photography and the Museum of Rome in Hawthorne's The Marble Faun," in *Photo-Textualities: Reading Photographs and Literature,* ed. Marsha Bryant (Newark: University of Delaware Press, forthcoming).

7. *Gil Blas* (1715–38) was a widely influential novel by René LeSage.

9. Adèle Hugo

FROM *Le Journal*, NOVEMBER 22, 1852–NOVEMBER 16, 1853

Victor Hugo (1802–85), France's leading representative of Romanticism, applied the movement's belief in the transforming power of the imagination and its use of vivid, sensuous detail to poetry, novels, essays, and plays as well as drawings. Politically right and left at various times—admired yet distrusted by both groups—he went into exile for twenty years after Napoleon III seized power in 1851.[1] Hugo, his wife, Adèle, and their three adult children, Adèle, Charles, and François, settled in the Channel Islands and, among other projects, took up photography. Charles (1826–71), after learning advanced processes in Caen and usually aided by a family intimate, the writer Auguste Vacquerie (1819–95), took many memorable pictures of his father (probably more the stage manager than passive sitter)—"twenty or thirty times a day," Jean Cocteau later snickered.[2] Hugo's family members and even their visitors also appear in various settings and moods, similarly self-conscious, expressive, and intellectual, often holding or reading books [Figs. 17–19].[3] These portraits, as well as island scenes, form the most intensive photographic record of any nineteenth-century writer. Also planned and even advertised, but never published, was a volume about Jersey and the Channel Islands, which was to include Hugo's poems and drawings together with his sons' prose and photographs, according to young Adèle (1830–1915), the family diarist.[4] After 1853, however, the family's preoccupation with photography dwindled, their creative energies engaged in other pursuits.

17. *(left)* Charles Hugo and Auguste Vacquerie. 'Victor Hugo,' c. 1853.

18. *(right)* Charles Hugo and Auguste Vacquerie. 'Madame Adèle Hugo,' c. 1853.

19. *(bottom)* Charles Hugo and Auguste Vacquerie. 'Mademoiselle Adèle Hugo,' c. 1853.

FROM *Le Journal*

NOVEMBER 22, 1852: We're making daguerreotypes. The daguerreotype of my father was made for *Contemplations* and also for *Vengeresses:* the first is calm and has an upward glance; the second is furious. [vol. 1, p. 335]

NOVEMBER 23, 1852: Here is our project: to make daguerreotypes of all Jersey, and to sell them as such. Then once this is done, to run around the world to make in the world what we will have made upon Jersey. [vol. 1, p. 335]

JANUARY 21, 1853: The daguerreotype is all the rage; everyone is taking it up; now we're going to learn photography. This covers the most beautiful projects; this summer we're running around the island; these gentlemen will take all the most beautiful aspects; my father will do the verses, and all that will make a charming work that we will sell some time next year. [vol. 2, p. 23]

APRIL 1853: Letter from Charles Hugo, published in the newspaper, April 10, Sunday, 1853, included in the *Journal*
Caen, April 3, 1853
The Editor:

I had come from Jersey to spend a few days in Caen to take up photographic studies with Mr. Edmond Bacot, whose name is well known among artists who are doing daguerreotypes. These studies are connected to a literary publication which we intend to do during the trips that might develop out of my father's exile.

I was scarcely in Caen a few hours when a police officer, along with another person who, I was told, was an important officer, presented himself in my room at the hotel, to carry on with a detailed interrogation, following orders issued, as it was made clear to me, by the prefect of the province. They checked the furniture, upset my belongings, searched everywhere, even in my bed; they asked me to open my wallet. They naturally didn't find anything they were looking for.

When I wanted to get my passport to return to Jersey, I was informed that the prefect would not sign "that particular report" although it was known otherwise to be perfectly in order. It was only a few days afterwards, and because chance had it that M. Leroy was absent at the moment I presented myself, that I was able to obtain the visa without which I could not re-embark.

I believed myself free of Mr. Leroy's police when, yesterday morning at 8 o'clock, I was awakened by the arrival of two new police officers, bearers of still more rigorous instructions than those of the first. I was for the second time in less than a fortnight denounced as an affiliate of a secret society. The visit of these men lasted an hour and a half and brought no more results than its predecessor. After routine searches among the furnishings of my room, they emerged with my wallet and my notebook of the trip. In my wallet they took and read my confidential letters; they seemed to comment on them in an undertone, then they opened the notebook and spent close to three quarters of an hour examining it. This notebook contained

details of the secret Mr. Bacot uses to produce his beautiful photographic proofs and that its inventor until now refused to give up at any price, and not to anybody, no matter who, even to the society for promotion. Today this secret, that is to say this property, is in the power of Mr. Girard, the head of police operations in Caen. [vol. 2, p. 478]

With [my best wishes] etc,
Charles Hugo.

Newspaper advertisements (not included in the *Journal* but relevant):

[AUGUST 6, 1853: *La Lumière*, no. 32: 126: announces the forthcoming publication of *Jersey and the Channel Islands*, verse and prose, photographs and drawings. The verse by Victor Hugo, the prose by Auguste Vacquerie, Charles Hugo, and François Hugo, photographs by Charles Hugo, and drawings by Victor Hugo.]

[OCTOBER 8, 1853: *La Lumière*, no. 41: 163: announces that the work will be printed in a deluxe and an inexpensive edition.]

NOVEMBER 16, 1853

Auguste Vacquerie

Today I began the work on Jersey.

Charles Hugo

I myself don't know what to do. The subject of Jersey does not at all lend itself to making an interesting book.

Victor Hugo

You are wrong; we can do a very interesting book on Jersey. I even find the subject too rich. Without counting Bastion, Piemont, the Druid monuments, Rullecourt, you still have, or you yourself will have, since it's you, Charles, who is charged with the descriptive part, you shall have to recount all that I am going to tell you. Have you taken some walks near the port?

Charles Hugo and Auguste Vacquerie

No.

Victor Hugo

I take a walk myself each evening at nightfall. Or every evening at twilight, when the sun has set, when the sky is full of clouds, and the stars begin to shine, I walk all alone in front of the harbor. [vol. 2, pp. 347–48]

---

1. "An admirable epoque," sneered Flaubert, noting Du Camp's receipt of the Legion of Honor for his Middle East work, "when one decorates photographers and exiles poets," in a letter to Louise Colet, January 15, 1853, *Correspondance, 1850–59,* in *Oeuvres Complètes* (Paris: Club de l'Honnête Homme, 1974), vol. 13, p. 284. See also Jammes and Janis, "Charles-Victor Hugo," *The Art of the French Calotype,* p. 174.

2. See Cocteau, *Opium: The Diary of a Cure* (1929), trans. Margaret Crosland and Sinclair Road (New York: Grove, [1958]), p. 52.

3. See letter from Madame Hugo to her sister, May 10, 1854, quoted in Vernon M. French, "Auguste Vacquerie: Friend and Follower of Victor Hugo" (Ph.D. diss, University of Texas at Austin, 1952), p. 167, n. 31. Many of the photographs were mounted in albums and presented to friends; one at GEH [17526] includes mainly upper-body portraits, though there are two of the hands of Hugo and his wife; see n. 4 below for a more experimental scene. For further details on the Hugo circle photographs, see the following works, most called to the editor's attention by Françoise Heilbrun and Philippe Néagu: Paul Gruyer, *Victor Hugo Photographe* (Paris: Mendel, 1905); Gillian Greenhill, "The Jersey Years: Photography in the Circle of Victor Hugo," *History of Photography* 4, no. 2 (April 1980): 113–20; Jammes and Janis, *The Art of the French Calotype,* pp. 188–89 (and see pp. 26–27, 44, 57–58, 65–66, 87, p. 120 n. 169, for the evident influence of Hugo's writing on contemporary photography); Philippe Néagu, "Un Projet Photographique du Victor Hugo," *Photographies* 3 (December 1983): 56–61; Fran-

çoise Heilbrun and Néagu, "L'Atelier de Photographie de Jersey," in *Victor Hugo et Les Images* [Colloque de Dijon], ed. Madeleine Blondel and Pierre Georgel (Dijon: Ville de Dijon, 1989), pp. 184–95; and Massin, "Hugo et la photographie," *La Quinzaine Littéraire* 448, nos. 1–15 (October 1985): 18–19. For interesting comparisons between Hugo's drawings and the Jersey photographic scenes, see *Victor Hugo Dessinateur* (Paris: Editions du Minotaure, 1963) and *La Gloire du Victor Hugo,* a catalogue of the exhibit at the Galeries Nationales du Grand Palais, October 1, 1985–January 6, 1986 (Paris: Ministry of Culture, 1985). See also Edward Steichen's photograph, 'Rodin-Le Penseur, Paris,' 1902, which includes the sculptor's marble portrait of Hugo—reproduced in *Camera Work,* no. 11 (July 1905): 35 and no. 14 (April 1906), Special Supplement: 25—mentioned in the Sandburg selection preface below, n. 2, and the text.

4. Perhaps the interesting 1853 photomontage (which shows the author on the so-called rock of exile—the most widely reproduced image of him—in the upper quadrant, with JERSEY on the top left and VICTOR HUGO on the bottom left and an irregular border of appliquéd leaves and flowers) was intended as the cover of this volume; the picture, in the collection of the Musée Victor Hugo in Paris, was reproduced in the exhibition catalogue, *L'Invention d'un Regard* (Paris: Musée D'Orsay, 1989) [October 2–December 3, 1989], p. 53, no. 116. Young Adèle Hugo's unrequited love for an English army officer she met in 1862, which ended tragically in her chronic madness from 1864, is the subject of François Truffaut's film *The Story of Adèle H.* (1975).

Adèle Hugo   45

10. *Brassaï*

"CARROLL THE PHOTOGRAPHER," 1975

Brassaï (1899–1984) [Fig. 95], the worldly photographer of Paris night and street life, might not be expected to admire Charles Lutwidge Dodgson (1832–98), the Oxford math don and clergyman better known under his pseudonym, Lewis Carroll. But Brassaï was delighted to be invited to summarize the photographic achievement of the author of Alice's Adventures in Wonderland (1865), a "sujet qui me passiona."[1] For Carroll had also become recognized as one of England's best amateur photographers, less for his portraits of literary celebrities like Tennyson, the Rossettis, and Ruskin [Fig. 36] than those of young girls—sometimes in costumes, occasionally nude;[2] indeed, one of them, his favorite model, Alice Liddell, had inspired his most famous book [Fig. 21].[3] Less well known are his humorous writings about photography, most done shortly after Carroll himself took up the camera in 1855.[4] For the most amusing one, "Hiawatha's Photographing," a satire on frustrations common to all photographers of families, Carroll used the content and meter of the popular poem "Song of Hiawatha" (1855) by Henry Wadsworth Longfellow (1807–82), then esteemed on both sides of the Atlantic.[5] Ironically, the poem, as Longfellow publicly acknowledged, was itself inspired by an 1851 daguerreotype of the Minnehaha Falls in the Minnesota Territory by Alexander Hesler (1823–95). The Chicago photographer, prompted by his scene's unanticipated celebrity, returned to take another picture of the falls; he reproduced it with four lines from Carroll's poem that assured his own immortality [Fig. 20].[6]

The first signs of a vocation

How was it then that Lewis Carroll took up photography? One of his uncles adored the gadgets of his time, such as the telescope and microscope, and photography was his latest craze. When the young Lewis Carroll saw a camera for the first time, it was more than a shock—it was a revelation. He was so impressed by the sudden appearance of the image as the negative developed that a week later he began writing the first of his pieces inspired by the dark room: "Photography Extraordinary." The title alone is a sign of his enthusiasm. He had a perceptive mind, and saw immediately the most unusual applications of this invention, so he asked himself why they should not be used to record the activity of the brain. He dreamed of a sort of electro-encephalogram worked by photographic means.

"As the invention has not yet been given to the world," he said, "we are only at liberty to relate the results, suppressing all details of chemicals and manipulation."

Then he described an experiment carried out on a young man—a severe case—who was feeble-minded and a cretin.

"The machine being in position, and a mesmeric rapport established between the mind of the patient and the object glass, the young man was asked whether he wished to say anything. He feebly replied *Nothing*. He was then asked what he was thinking of, and the answer, as before, was *Nothing*.... At once commenced .... the operation."

The sensitive paper was applied to the young man's brain. At first the image it left was almost invisible. But as it developed, the impression of thoughts became stronger and stronger with violent contrasts. The text was typical of the excesses of German Romanticism of the early nineteenth century which Lewis Carroll no doubt wanted to ridicule.

A few months after this memorable first encounter with photography, on 22 January 1856, he asked his uncle to buy him a dark room costing £15. His request was granted, and on 18 March he went to London to collect it. At the same time he bought a complete set of equipment, including a tent serving as a portable dark room. He got the latest apparatus and used a new English technique, the collodion or wet-plate process, which was faster and more reliable than the calotype process, and gave greater fidelity of detail. At this time Lewis Carroll was twenty-four and photography had been in existence seventeen years. The collodion process had barely been in existence for five years. The author of "Alice in Wonderland" threw himself into it and discovered his new vocation. He already had the gift and inspiration, and mastery was soon to follow. Indeed it is interesting that it was precisely in 1863 and 1864, the years between the genesis and publication of "Alice in Wonderland" that his most fertile period occurred, the highest point in his career as a photographer, which from now on was to be indissolubly linked to his creative work.

Lewis Carroll as a portrait artist

In the twenty-four years between May 1856 and July 1880, he built up an imposing gallery of portraits of bishops, archbishops and Oxford professors, of artists, writers, actors and actresses. He also took photographs of princes, cardinals and statesmen, not infrequently allowing himself to be guided in his choice by worldly considerations and a certain degree of snobbishness. Among this array from the ranks of the English intelligentsia were the Pre-Raphaelites: Holman Hunt, Millais, Rossetti, John Ruskin; the poets: Tennyson, Browning and MacDonald; the famous physicist Michael Faraday; and the actresses Ellen, Kate and Marion Terry. Lewis Carroll's portraits are less affected than those taken by professionals. He abhorred their use of one or two conventional, stereotyped backgrounds. Nor would he permit touching up. His models were placed in a natural setting in front of a brick or stone wall, garden trees or a staircase. It is true that Adamson's portraits had more strength and those of Mrs. Cameron more depth. But it was not Lewis Carroll's ambition to get right into the heart of his models, but rather to compose a beautiful harmonious picture. Thus while Mrs. Cameron was more attentive to facial expression than to composition, he would leave nothing to chance and his sureness of touch never failed in positioning his subjects, whether there was just one sitter or a whole group. Another difference was Lewis Carroll's dislike of blurred, out of focus pictures of the type so dear to Mrs. Cameron: she was obsessed with close-ups of the face, whereas he preferred full-length portraits, and believed that a whole figure is more expressive than head or bust alone. In this connection, one of the four texts he wrote about photography deserves attention, though it was not published until 1899, after his death. It concerns an old Scots Legend, "The Ladye's History" apparently dating from 1325. It turns out to be about photography: it deals with a "merveillous machine called by men a Chimera (that is, a fabulous and wholly incredible thing)"— this parenthesis also occurs in the text—"where wyth hee took manie pictures." In other words he is clearly writing of a sort of camera, though in a period before the description of the camera obscura by Della Porta, Alberti, Uccello or Leonardo da Vinci. And to complete our astonishment, the word fotograffed occurs (presumably coined in the nineteenth century) in the middle of this strange legend set in fourteenth century Scotland. This is why, in spite of its medieval language, I am tempted to wonder whether this posthumous text is really some sort of pastiche or mystification from the pen of Lewis Carroll. This would be very much in character, knowing his playful nature. Another reason for making one suspect that "The Ladye's History" is an invention of Lewis Carroll's is the way there occurs in the text the same obsession with *full-length* portraits that Lewis Carroll revealed.

"Nevertheless, though he took manie Pictures, yet all fayled yn thys: for some, beginning at the Hedde, reached not toe the Feet; others, taking yn the Feet, yet left out the Hedde." This nightmare is reminiscent of Alice's experience in Wonderland.

The photographer's disappointments
Two other texts reflect his early, unhappy experiences as a photographer. They are satires or parodies, which he himself called skits. One is of the somewhat verbose American Romantic, Longfellow, best known until then for his *Evangeline,* whom Lewis Carroll regarded as "the greatest living master of the language." When in 1855 Longfellow published his "Song of Hiawatha" the creator of "Alice in Wonderland" drew on its Indian hero and transformed him into a photographer, his alter ego.

Thus Hiawatha carries around a heavy, awkward set of equipment; he opens out his camera made of sliding, folding rosewood, pulls joints and pushes the hinges, until he finally obtains the right square or oblong shape:
"Like a complicated figure
In the Second Book of Euclid."
Finally he fixes the camera on a tripod, crouches beneath the dusky cover, stretches out his hand and says
"Be motionless, I beg you!"
The steady increase in the power of lenses, the extraordinary speed of the sensitive materials and all the technical progress which made instant photography possible, even under the worst conditions, all these conspired to take away the magic from photography which, a mere hundred years before, would have still seemed a product of witchcraft. The interminable pose, the forced immobility, the silence, the breath tightly held, the stopping of time itself, all these are part of a quasi-religious ceremony in which the photographer, drawing out from his magic box the effigies of his models can pass as an alchemist, a high priest or a magician: "Mystic, awful was the process" as Lewis Carroll puts it.

But let us return to Hiawatha, embattled with a whole family desperate to be recorded for posterity. Every one of its members suggests an ingenious pose. First came the father, the Governor. He would like velvet curtains as a background hanging over a massive pillar and the corner of a rosewood table. In his left hand he would hold a scroll of something, whilst his right hand would be buried in his waistcoat, just like Napoleon's. He would gaze into the

20. Alexander Hesler.
'Minnehaha Falls,' Minne-
sota Territory, c. 1856.

MINEHAHA FALLS, MIN. TER.

Negative by A. Hesler.

distance with the pensive look of ducks dying in a storm. "Grand, heroic was the notion" comments the author, "yet the picture failed entirely."

Now it is the turn of the Governor's wife:
"She came dressed beyond description,
Dressed in jewels and satin
Far too gorgeous for an empress.
Gracefully she sat down sideways,
With a simper scarcely human,
Holding in her hand a bouquet
Rather larger than a cabbage
All the while that she was sitting,
Still the lady chattered, chattered,
Like a monkey in the forest
'Am I sitting still?' she asked him.
'Is my face enough in profile?
Shall I hold the bouquet higher?
will it come into the picture?'
And the picture failed completely."

As for the son, the "Stunning Cantab", he speaks of "curves of beauty" pervading all his figure, in such a way that the eye, by following them, may centre on a breast-pin. Lewis Carroll's comment:
"He had learnt it all from Ruskin
(Author of the *Stones of Venice*,
Seven Lamps of Architecture,
Modern Painters and some others)."

(This would of course demonstrate that the aesthetics of Ruskin, champion of the Pre-Raphaelites, had influenced certain snobs, even before Proust.) Lewis Carroll adds ironically:
"And perhaps he had not fully
Understood his author's meaning."
But it all makes no difference: the photo is another utter failure.

Then comes the eldest daughter. She makes no suggestions, but simply wonders if her look of "passive beauty" will be faithfully reproduced. And what precisely is the idea of "passive beauty"? A squinting of the left eye and drooping of the right eye, smiling sideways up to the corner of the nostril:
"Hiawatha, when she asked him,
Took no notice of the question,
Looked as if he hadn't heard it;
But, when pointedly appealed to,
Smiled in his peculiar manner,

Coughed and said it didn't matter,
Bit his lip and changed the subject.
Nor in this was he mistaken,
As the picture failed completely."

Now it is the turn of the younger sisters, and finally of the youngest son. His hair is thick and tousled, his face is very red and round, his jacket is dusty and his manner fidgety. His name is Johnny, "Daddy's Darling" as, to his great irritation, he is called by his overbearing sisters. Lewis Carroll notes:
"And, so awful was the picture,
In comparison the others
Seemed, to one's bewildered fancy,
To have partially succeeded."

Finally, Hiawatha takes a snap of the whole family together, and chances on a photo in which all the faces come out good likenesses. Immediately they unite in pouring abuse on it, and say it is the worst picture they could possibly have dreamed of. Hiawatha, they said, had given them such strange, sullen, stupid expressions that anyone who did not know them would take them for most unpleasant people.
"Hiawatha seemed to think so,
Seemed to think it not unlikely."
Their voices screamed out in anger, like dogs and cats howling and wailing in concert;
"But Hiawatha's patience,
His politeness and his patience,
Unaccountably had vanished,
And he left that happy party.
Neither did he leave them slowly,
With the calm deliberation,
The intense deliberation
Of a photographic artist:
But he left them in a hurry
Stating that he would not stand it,
Stating in emphatic language
What he'd be before he'd stand it.
Hurriedly he packed his boxes:
Hurriedly he took his ticket:
Hurriedly the train received him:
Thus departed Hiawatha."

In 1860, three years after the appearance of "Hiawatha's Photographing", he wrote with the same biting humour, "A Photographer's Day Out". Fascinated by the name of Amelia, his favourite, he allowed himself to be drawn by a family in the country, carrying all his equipment himself. Amelia is marvellous, but unfortunately engaged to a young Irishman whose figure was good, but whose character was vulgar and stupid. And how irritating it was to hear him repeat "my Amelia." Having successfully photographed first the father who squinted at the camera, he went on to the mother who "wished to be taken in a favourite Shakespearian character," then the three younger girls, whom he would have like to tie together by the hair, and finally a baby prone to convulsions and requiring seventeen sittings, all of them unsuccessful. He accepts Amelia's suggestion to photograph her at a nearby cottage. Tired and breathless under the weight of the equipment, he climbs a nearby hill to get the best view of the cottage. At last he can uncover the lens. The pose lasts for one minute and forty seconds. Eager to see the result, he covers his head with the hood and develops the picture on the spot. The farmer, who moved a yard during the exposure, has come out as a sort of spider or centipede. The cow has three heads. To complete his misfortunes, just as he is getting the bottle of hypo-sulphite of soda to fix the picture, two repellent country yokels disturb him and order him off this "private property". The plate falls and shatters. He writes: "I remember nothing further, except that I have an indistinct notion that I hit somebody ... all I can tell you is that I am shaken, and sore, and stiff, and bruised...."

Unlike Baudelaire, Lewis Carroll does not use anger, but his lasting humour to chastise, not the new invention itself, but rather the vanity and fatuousness of people demanding the most flattering portraits. His own pictures were natural, without touching up, and thus could only elicit disappointment, bitterness and even rage from his subjects. His "Skits" give us an idea not simply of the difficulties and disappointments of a portraitist of his temper, but also of the attitude to photography of the Victorian middle classes.

The photographs of Alice

However, the problems of the photographer, who had already been treated as an intruder to be sent packing, were transformed into the utmost delight once he focussed on a little girl. Here every picture reveals the unspeakable joys of the time spent in this pleasant intimacy. Indeed this pioneer of English amateur photography is the most remarkable photographer of children in the nineteenth century. He immortalised Alice not only by the extraordinary story but also by his portraits of her, his minor masterpiece. Gernsheim's book contains only one of them. It is the one that appeared, in the form of a medallion, right at the end of the original manuscript [Fig. 20]. The young Muse looks us straight in the eye, her hair arranged like a halo with a parting down the middle. In fact the portrait had been cut out of a larger portrait showing the girl sitting beside a fern and wearing a long white dress with numerous starched pleats. This was to be the first of some ten photos of Alice. The second shows the three Liddell sisters: Lorina, Alice and Edith (who appear in the prefatory poem of "Alice" as Prima, Secunda and Tertia), dressed in white crinolines and sitting on the lawn in front of their beautiful family house in Oxford with its huge glassed-in balcony, its walls covered with ivy and young vines. Another photo reveals the delicate profile of the little girl who is sitting in a garden chair wearing an enormous crinoline. In the fourth photo Alice is seated across the seat of a swing while Lorina stands holding a cricket bat in her hand. Both of them wear little black bonnets topped with white feathers.

The fifth picture shows the three sisters wearing crinolines stretched out on a divan, their hair in disarray. In the sixth photo Lorina and Alice appear as young Chinese girls, dressed in embroidered robes and with their hair mandarin-style. Seated in an armchair "Prima" shelters under a huge parasol held by her sister. The seventh photo: Alice in a white crinoline, sleeping on the lawn. On her dress lies a large black straw hat. The eighth photo is Alice's apotheosis. She sits wearing a sumptuous crinoline with broad sleeves trimmed with flounces, her eyes gazing into the distance, and her hair

21. Lewis Carroll. "Alice in Wonderland," final manuscript page, with a drawing, usually covered by the photograph of Alice here moved aside, c. 1864.

of her own little sister. So the boat wound slowly along, beneath the bright summer day, with its merry crew and its music of voices and laughter, till it passed round one of the many turnings of the stream, and she saw it no more.

Then she thought, (in a dream within the dream, as it were,) how this same little Alice would, in the after-time, be herself a grown woman: and how she would keep, through her riper years, the simple and loving heart of her childhood: and how she would gather around her other little children, and make *their* eyes bright and eager with many a wonderful tale, perhaps even with these very adventures of the little Alice of long-ago: and how she would feel with all their simple sorrows, and find a pleasure in all their simple joys, remembering her own child-life, and the happy summer-days. days.

crowned with a ring of white flowers. The ninth photo shows her as the beggar-maid, and we will return to it later. Finally Alice as a young bride, through the lens of Lewis Carroll. As a rather young Mrs. Reginald Hargreaves she is as ravishing as ever, but her lady's crinoline certainly does not suit her. Her arms are stretched, her hands clasped, her big dreamy eyes are lost in a melancholic emptiness. The deep sadness of the young woman is worrying. ... Was Lewis Carroll in love with her? Did she love him despite the twenty years age difference? Did he plan to marry her? We do not know.

However, around 1865, three years after the genesis of the extraordinary story, a rupture with the Liddell family disturbed their contacts. Was this rupture due to a rejected suit for marriage? It is not known. At all events, Mrs. Liddell made her daughter destroy all her letters from the Rev. Dodgson. Perhaps [Stuart Dodgson] Collingwood [Carroll's nephew and first editor] is alluding to this hopeless love when he speaks of the unknown shadow which darkened Lewis Carroll's life.

A passion for little girls.
According to Collingwood, it is almost certain that Alice was the first "Child girl friend" of Lewis Carroll. He himself confirmed this view. In a letter to her he avowed that he always held her in his memory as the ideal child-friend. The score of girls that followed were "different". However, his own diary, part of which has been published, contradicts this. A number of young girls stirred up in him these same violent emotions, some of them as passionate as his feelings for Alice; and in his diaries he describes them frankly and innocently. On 13 January 1877 he notes: "Went up to town for the day, and took Evelyn with me to the afternoon pantomime at the Adelphi—"Goody Two-Shoes", acted entirely by children. It was a really charming performance. Little Bertie Coote, aged ten, was clown—a wonderfully clever little fellow; and Carrie Coote, about eight, was Columbine, a very pretty graceful little thing. In a few year's time she will be just the child to act "Alice" if it is ever dramatised.

The Harlequin was little girl called Gilchrist, one of the most beautiful children, in face and figure, that I have ever seen. I must get an opportunity of photographing her." For three months he is haunted by the face of the young actress, and on 10 April 1877, he writes in his diary:

"Spent the day in London. Called on Mrs. Gilchrist and spent about half an hour with her and Connie. I was decidedly pleased with Connie, who has a refined and modest manner with just a touch of shyness, and who is about the most gloriously beautiful child (both face and figure) that I ever saw. One would like to do 100 photos of her."

Five days later he writes:

"Devised a plan for getting photos of C. Gilchrist: to be staying in London, to bring her over to Oxford by the early train, and take her back in the evening; this would give me nine hours in Oxford, and cost little more than paying for her and an escort, who would be an encumbrance."

Here is one example among many of the devices he used to get hold of a girl. He would watch out for them in the streets, in the parks, on trains, at archery meetings, at Masonic functions, and most of all at the children's theatre in London. However, faithful to his class, he preferred to choose them from among his colleagues' daughters at Oxford. It was only later, in his period of photographing nudes, that he also used poorer families, who tended to be less strict. The timid mathematics don was capable of daring methods to conquer the nymphet to whose charms he had fallen victim: he used to press his friends to introduce him to the family, and devise all sorts of tricks.

Young Ethel Hatch—who was still alive five years ago in London—told how the author of "Alice in Wonderland" used to carry round with him a small suitcase full of toys, which he would open at the opportune moment. Sometimes he used a copy of "Alice in Wonderland" as bait. Even the room of this Lolita-hunting Blue Beard, and later his enormous glass-house (which he had built at considerable expense so as to shorten the posing time and to make it possible for him to take photographs in any weather and even in bad weather) was a paradise for children. What marvels there were in this studio, and in the four bedrooms, and four sitting rooms where the Rev. Dodgson lived alone. A wide range of dolls, a distorting mirror, practical jokes and tricks. In an enormous cupboard, a whole collection of mechanical toys: bears, rabbits, frogs, clockwork mice which walked, ran and jumped. A bat which the writer himself had made could flap its wings and fly. Other marvels included some twenty music-boxes and a barrel organ from which there emerged strange music when he fed the perforated tapes in upside down. Certain girls were even allowed to enter the mysterious dark room lit by a red lantern and to be present at the moment when the pictures came out. And all this enchantment was to make the young models more willing to be photographed. Before the fateful moment, Lewis Carroll would take them on his knees and kiss and hug them, would tell them incredible stories and draw them funny pictures.

Little girls in disguise
Another means he used to create an enchanting atmosphere was disguise. Lewis Carroll used to dress his little friends up as Turks, Japanese, Chinese, Romans, Bulgarian peasants and many others. In a big trunk he kept costumes from the Drury Lane Theatre. Tennyson's great-niece Agnes Grace Weld is photographed dressed as "Little Red Riding-Hood". Xie Kitchin, a beautiful child, appears as a Chinese woman. Seated on a pile of rich lacquered Chinese boxes, she wears a stiff mandarin's hat and holds a fan in her hand. In another pose, Xie stands in front of the same boxes, barefoot, her long hair tumbling over her shoulders. In another pose again, she is disguised as a young Russian wrapped in a gorgeous white pelisse and wearing a fur hat.

"I ... borrowed some New Zealand articles from the Ashmolean, and took a photograph of her asleep, covered with a native cloak and with anklet etc."

He is speaking of Ella, daughter of an Oxford professor, who later related: "A visit to Mr. Dodgson's rooms to be photographed was always full of surprises. Although he had quaint fancies in the way he dressed his little sitters, he never could bear a dressed-up child."

One day the writer had the idea of photographing her in bed, scared by a ghost. "He tried to get this effect" (hair standing on end, startled expression) "with the aid of my father's electrical machine, but it failed, chiefly I fear because I was too young quite to appreciate the current of electricity that had to be passed through me." She had the naive belief that her body was proof against electricity. Another extraordinary photograph could have been taken from the cinema: *The Elopement*. Its heroine is another Alice, Alice-Jane Donkin. Carrying a bundle in her hand, the girl, who, has already got through the upstairs window, is climbing down the rope-ladder. In her white dress covered with a dark cape, the hood pulled forward over her hair, Alice-Jane seems to be floating in space like a sleep-walker or ghost. What was Lewis Carroll trying to represent in this strange picture? Was it some dream of himself eloping with a young lady who had escaped from her family? The revolt of youth or elopement as an act of rebellion against one's parents? One of Lewis Carroll's favourite costumes was a night-dress. He once wrote to a mother:

"If they have such things as flannel night-gowns, that makes as pretty a dress as you can desire. White does pretty well, but nothing like flannel."

He found the texture and color of flannel more photogenic than white cotton. No doubt he was remembering his own seven sisters, all of them younger than himself—he was the oldest of eleven children. All these sisters slept in flannel night-gowns. This is how he was to photograph Alice Liddell, Irene MacDonald, Mary Millais (daughter of the Pre-Raphaelite painter) and many others.

Photographs of nudes
One day he wrote in his diary:

"I did several pictures of ... little Ella with no other dress than a cloth tied round her, savage-fashion."

This spate of dress and undress, of night-gowns and native loincloths led Lewis Carroll to taking nude photographs. He wrote to one of his friends:

"I *wish* I dared dispense with *all* costume. Naked children are so perfectly pure and lovely."

One day he did dare. However, before doing so, charged Miss Gertrude Thomson, the illustrator of his books, to get some ten or twelve year old children, chosen from young actresses, to pose for her nude so that she could draw them. He particularly emphasised that she should never insist if a child showed any shyness.

"If," he wrote, "I had the loveliest child in the world to draw or photograph, and found she had a modest shrinking (however slight, and however easily overcome) from being taken nude, I would feel it was a solemn duty owed to God to drop the request *altogether*." However, this desire for nudity only involved girls: "I am fond of children" he said wittily "except boys. To me they are not an attractive race of beings."

He wrote that people thought:

"I doted on *all* children. But I am *not* omnivorous like a pig. I pick and choose." In fact he had a strong dislike of little boys. Perhaps he had a bad memory of school, when, shy and stammering, he had been bullied by the other boys. "I confess I do *not* admire naked boys," he wrote. "They always seem to me to need clothes, whereas one hardly sees why the lovely forms of girls should *ever* be covered up."

The first reference to his photographing girls nude was on 21 May 1867. "Mrs. L. brought Beatrice, and I took a photograph of the two and several of Beatrice alone, sans habilement" (*sic*). The "sans habilement" was written in bad French with only one "l", no doubt to throw any indiscreet readers of his diary off the scent. Here is another note from 18 July 1879: "I had warned Mrs. —— that I thought the children so nervous I would not even ask for "bare feet" and was agreeably surprised they were ready for any amount of undress, and seemed delighted at being allowed to run about naked. It was a great privilege to have such a model as —— to take: a *very* pretty face, and a good figure. She was worth any number of my model of yesterday."

It was during this month of July 1879 that Lewis Carroll took the largest number of photographs of girls, sometimes lying on a sofa, sometimes on a blanket in the artist's favourite dress of "*nothing*."

"A kind of photography I have often done lately," he mentioned in his diary. This spate of nudes came near the end of his career as a photographer. He was finally to give it up a few months later, at the end of May 1880 when he was forty-eight. From then on he entrusted the child actresses, and all the new loves he was to know when *Alice* was adapted for the theatre, to the lenses of professional photographers.

The devices and manoeuvres used by this shy Anglican clergyman are astonishingly similar to those of an impenitent seducer. Like Landru, he would draw up a careful list of his "victims" and "conquests." On 25 March 1863, the list already contains a hundred and seven names—a lot more than the figure of twenty confessed to Alice. And rather strangely the girls are not classified according to their surnames, but to their Christian names, all the Beatrices, all the Alices, all the Evelynes together, distinguished only by the date of birth attached to each name.

What was the nature of this strange fascination that drew him to them? This is not the place to go into this question. About a dozen psychoanalysts, most of them English or American have applied themselves to his "case". It should be noted that Lewis Carroll never loved one particular girl—even if he himself thought he did—but rather through her a certain fleeting, transitory state, that brief moment when dawn hovers between night and day. All his young girl-friends were no more than the mediums that revealed this state. Through them the writer kept in touch with the spirit of childhood. The Rev. Dodgson struggled without respite throughout his life against the remorseless process that made them grow up and then snatched them from him, one by one. Each of them could only fulfil her role for a short period of time, while her young body revealed no trace of womanhood. Once her senses were awakened and her breasts began to grow, it was all finished, and the honourable clergyman was once again obliged to set out in search of another... This unending quest, with its quarrels, infatuations, and disillusions, constituted Lewis Carroll's tragic destiny. Late in life he admitted with bitter sadness:

"About nine out of ten, I think, of my child friendships get shipwrecked at the critical point "where the stream and the river meet," and the child-friends, once so affectionate, become uninteresting acquaintances whom I have no wish to set eyes on again."

Destruction of the photographs of nude girls
At all events, to get little girls to undress was a decidedly daring enterprise, particularly if one was an Anglican clergyman in the reign of Victoria. This man who was an innovator in so many areas was one also in this cult of complete nudity of a free morality, without prejudice or constraint. Probably his diary would have told us more on this but unfortunately, inspired by the desire to safeguard his uncle's reputation, Collingwood censored it with the utmost severity. Thus not one of his photographs of nudes survives. In fact they were purged from his twelve albums during his lifetime, and he stipulated that, after his death, they were to be returned to their models or their nearest relatives, or otherwise destroyed.

What a loss! Lewis Carroll found tremendous inspiration in his desire to master this subject which obsessed him to such a degree. When he photographs a clergyman or an Oxford professor, his portrait always has quality and excellent composition, but how cold it is! His tenderness for little girls enabled him to surpass himself, to use all his talent to reveal the beauty of a young face or the delicate frailty of a child's body. In his models' eyes one can still see the state of trance he himself was in at the moment of taking the photo. "They say that we photographers are a blind race at best; that we learn to look at even the prettiest faces as so much light and shade; that we seldom admire, and never love. This is a delusion I long to break through."

Surely this is an admission of the intense emotion he experienced when photographing young girls. No doubt this tension must have reached its height when, after months of waiting, he got a young lady to undress. Probably Lewis Carroll's finest photographs are among the nudes which we can never see.

The fear of growing up
The most striking feature of all the pictures of little girls is their extraordinary seriousness. Apart from little Beatrice Henley, a sweet, bright little thing with long corn-coloured hair, none of the young ladies ever smiles. All share the poet's slightly melancholy expression, his dreamy stare, made harder to bear by the length of the pose. Little Irene MacDonald, barefoot, her hair untidy, in her night-dress holding a comb in one hand and an oval mirror in the other, gazes at the camera with a tragic expression, her eyes open wide at some unknown terror. In the same way, in the most unforgettable and doubtless most revealing picture he ever took, "The Beggar Maid," Alice, standing against a filthy wall, her legs and feet bare, looks at us, her eyes full of enormous sadness. Her dress is torn and hanging in shreds, her flesh bare as though she has just been raped. (There has arisen the misguided custom of only showing the top of this famous photo; but this is a serious mistake, for it distorts its real meaning. In Lewis Carroll's eyes, the bare legs and feet had just as much importance as the face, and perhaps even more so). All the writer's young models seem to be afraid of the future and of the world of grown-ups. They seem to share his own fear and regrets at having to leave childhood behind and to grow and grow, as though they also were experiencing Alice's anguish and terror in "Alice in Wonderland," which might as easily have been called "Alice in Nightmareland."

Through the looking glass
Some people believe that photography was just one of Lewis Carroll's hobbies, but my view is that it was far more important. Indeed, it played a key role in his life. Right from the start he wrote of "Photography Extraordinary" and was one of the first people to take it seriously and to see that it was a technique that deserved to be seriously considered. Furthermore, there

was a natural affinity between his world of strange devices, magic mirrors and changes of size with the world of photography. He immediately felt at home in the half-real zone of the dark-room, in which light rays recreate the intangible illusion of reality. To reveal these images, to capture and materialise them, fixing them for ever, this was a marvel which entranced Lewis Carroll, a marvel which only habit could make uninteresting. The author of "Alice in Wonderland" felt most at home at this point of interchange between a fleeting reality and the realm of shadows taking on life. Through his photography he learned about the extinction of the subject and its resurrection beyond reality: he knew all the paradoxes of photography, how to stop or extend time, how to evoke the presence of what is not there, and remove what is there. Photography had another role in his life, namely, as an escape route for his frustrated love-life. To paraphrase his words, we photographers are nothing but a pack of crooks, thieves and voyeurs. We are to be found everywhere we are not wanted; we betray secrets that were never entrusted to us; we spy shamelessly on things that are not our business; and end up the hoarders of a vast quantity of stolen goods. It was photography that enabled this clergyman tempted by the Devil to purge the wicked "unholy" thoughts that nightly assailed him. It was photography which could act as a substitute for possession. "It was fate" writes Andre Bay, one of his finest translators and admirers, "that made him erect this barrier—photography—between the unattainable young lady and his desire to possess her. He could take her through the camera."

All Lewis Carroll's love life is linked in some way to photography. For him it was the Wonderland, Through the Looking-Glass.

1. See Brassaï, letter to Henry Miller, January 26, 1966, in the Henry Miller Archives.

2. On Carroll's 1857 photographs of Tennyson and some family members, see Dodgson, "A Visit to Tennyson," *Strand Magazine* 21, no. 125 (May 1901): 543–44; *The Letters of Lewis Carroll, 1837–1989*, ed. Morton N. Cohen (New York: Oxford University Press, 1979), vol. 1, pp. 34–35, n. 1; *The Diaries of Lewis Carroll*, ed. Roger L. Green (London: Cassell, 1953), vol. 1, pp. 124–27; and Helmut Gernsheim, *Lewis Carroll Photographer* (New York: Dover, 1969), fol. p. 83, nos. 8, 9, 10, and 13. On his pictures of the Rossettis, see *Letters*, vol. 1, p. 61, n. 3; *Diaries*, vol. 1, pp. 201–5; and William Michael Rossetti, "He Photographs the Rossettis," in *Lewis Carroll: Interviews and Recollections*, ed. Morton N. Cohen (Hampshire & London: Macmillan Press, 1989), pp. 237–39; and Gernsheim, following p. 83, nos. 21, 23, 24. On his photograph of Ruskin, see *Letters*, vol. 1, p. 326; *Diaries*, vol. 2, p. 340, and Stuart Collingwood, *Life and Letters of Lewis Carroll* (New York: Century, 1898), p. 158.

On Carroll's widely discussed photographs of children, see Morton N. Cohen, Introduction to *Lewis Carroll's Photographs of Nude Children* (Philadelphia: Rosenbach Foundation, 1978), pp. 3–32; *The Russian Journal and Other Selections from the Work of Lewis Carroll*, ed. John Francis McDermott (New York: Dover, 1977), p. 112, for Carroll's attempt while in Russia in 1867 to buy a photograph of a child whose father objected; Tournier, "L'Image érotique," *Des clefs et des serrures: images et proses* (Paris: Chêne/Hachette, 1979), pp. 103–8; and Richard Howard, "Move Still, Still So" in *Lining Up* (New York: Atheneum, 1984), pp. 81–88.

3. On Alice Liddell, see Alice Liddell Hargreaves, "The Friendship That Sparked Alice's Adventures" (1932), in *Lewis Carroll*, ed. Cohen, pp. 83–88; and *Dream Child*, a fine 1985 film (available on video) about the elderly Alice's memories of Dodgson. Alice's father, the dean of Christ Church—the Oxford college where Carroll lived much of his life and accomplished most of his enduring visual and verbal work—introduced John Ruskin to photography, according to his recollections in *Praeterita* (1886–87) in *The Works of John Ruskin*, ed. E. T. Cook and Alexander Wedderburn (London: George Allen, 1903–12), vol. 35, pp. 372–73, reprinted in the opening of the Ruskin selection below.

4. Carroll's four main humorous pieces about photography, often reprinted, are most easily accessible in Gernsheim, *Lewis Carroll Photographer*, "Photography Extraordinary," pp. 110–13; "Hiawatha's Photographing," pp. 113–17; "The Ladye's History," pp. 119–20; and "A Photographer's Day Out," pp. 121–25. Other relevant pieces include an unsigned review of the 1860 Photographic Exhibit for *The Illustrated Times* (January 28, 1860): 57, reprinted in *The Rectory Umbrella and Mischmasch* (London: Cassell, 1932), pp. 178–85; and "Four Riddles, 1" (1869) and "Double Acrostics" (1869), reprinted in *The Complete Works of Lewis Carroll*, ed. Alexander Woollcott (New York: Modern Library, 1936), pp. 894 and 924. See also S. F. Spira, "Carroll's Camera," *History of Photography* 8, no. 3 (July–September 1984): 175–77, and Cuthbert Bede [Rev. Edward Bradley], *Photographic Pleasures* [1855] (New York: Amphoto, 1973), the period's other classic humorous work on photography by a pseudonymous clergyman.

5. Carroll, quoted by Gernsheim, *Lewis Carroll,* p. 114, reportedly viewed Longfellow as "the greatest living master of language," and he remains the only American honored with a bust in the Poets' Corner in Westminster Abbey. See also Longfellow, *Hyperion: A Romance,* with photographs by Frances Frith (London: Alfred William Bennett, 1865).

6. Hesler reproduced the scene in "Our Illustrations," *The Photographic & Fine Art Journal* 10, no. 1 (January 1857), facing p. 25. See also Robert Taft, *Photography and the American Scene* [1938], (New York: Dover, 1964), pp. 98 and 471, n. 110; Weston J. Naef, *Era of Exploration* (Boston: New York Graphic Society, 1975), p. 20; and Ann Wilsher, "Photography and Literature: The First Seventy Years," *History of Photography* 2, no. 3 (July 1978): 230.

11. *Henry Peach Robinson*

COMBINATION PRINTS, 1858–68

The visual and verbal gifts of Henry Peach Robinson (1830–1901) made him the leading advocate of art photography in Victorian England. An aspiring painter, whose avid reading and fluent writing were reinforced by numerous jobs with booksellers (the publishers and printers of the time), he switched to photography in 1851. The controversial success and technique of O. G. Rejlander's (1813–75) 'The Two Ways of Life' (1857), a Hogarthian narrative formed from thirty separate negatives, encouraged Robinson to use combination prints, often inspired by literary subjects.[1] *'Fading Away' (1858) [Fig. 22], with lines from Shelley printed on the mat, secured him royal patronage and attracted new friends like Lewis Carroll, Cuthbert Bede, and various Pre-Raphaelite artists.*[2] *The latter's stress on realistic detail influenced some of Robinson's subsequent tableaux, two inspired by Tennyson's Arthurian poems [Fig. 23] and others by verses from Arnold (1867) and Wordsworth [Figs. 24–26].*[3] *Forced by illness due to overwork into retirement as an active photographer in 1864, Robinson nevertheless maintained a studio, lectured widely, wrote eleven books, including his influential* Pictorial Effect in Photography *(1869), and cofounded the Linked Ring (1892) to advance photography as an art. Many of his composition theories and manipulative techniques—well received in his day but later vigorously opposed by Alfred Stieglitz (the first American member of the Linked Ring) and other "straight" photographers—are finding favor again among postmodernist artists, who are often unaware of the source.*

Must then that peerless form,
Which love and admiration cannot view
Without a beating heart, those azure veins
Which steal like streams along a field of snow,
That lovely outline which is fair
As breathing marble, perish!

Percy B. Shelley
"Queen Mab," 1813, Part 1, lines 12–17

22. Henry Peach Robinson. 'Fading Away.' Alternate Version, 1858.
The verses were printed on the mat of the first nearly identical version.

Down she came and found a boat
Beneath a willow left afloat
And round about the prow she wrote
The Lady of Shalott.
And down the river's dim expanse
Like some bold seer in a trance
Seeing all his own mischance
With a glassy countenance
Did she look to Camelot.
And at the closing of the day
She loosed the chain and down she lay

The broad stream bore her far away
The Lady of Shalott.
Lying robed in snowy white
That loosely flew to left and right
Thro' the noises of the night
She floated down to Camelot.
And as the boat head wound along
The willowy hills and fields among
They heard her singing her last song
The Lady of Shalott.

Alfred Lord Tennyson,
"The Lady of Shalott," 1831/1842, Part 4,
Lines 123–144

23. Henry Peach Robinson. 'Lady of Shalott,' 1861.
The verses were printed on the mat of the original
exhibition print.

    . . . when all is ycladde
With pleasaunce, the gound with grasse, the woods
With greene leaves, the bushes with blossoming buds
Youngthes folke now flocken in everywhere
To gather May-buskets and smelling brere:
And home they hasten the postes to dight
And all the kirke pillours care day light
With hawthorne buds, and sweet eglantine.
And girlands of roses, and soppes in wine.

Edmund Spenser, from "May," *The Shepherd's Calendar.* 1579, lines 6–14

24. Henry Peach Robinson. 'Bringing Home the May,' 1862.

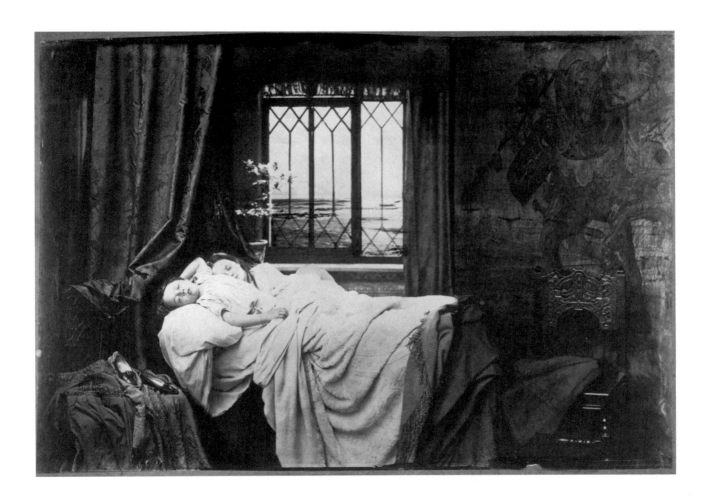

They sleep in sheltered rest
Like helpless birds in the warm nest.

Matthew Arnold, "Tristram and Iseult," 1852, Part 1, lines 327–28

25. Henry Peach Robinson. 'Sleep,' 1865.

Up with me! up with me into the clouds!
  For thy song, Lark, is strong;
Up with me, up with me, into the clouds!
  Singing, singing,
With clouds and sky about thee ringing,
  Lift me, guide me, till I find
That spot which seems so to thy mind!

William Wordsworth, "To a Sky-Lark,"
1805/1807, lines 1–7

26. Henry Peach Robinson and Nelson King Cherrill.
'Watching the Lark, Borrowdale,' 1868.

1. 'The Two Ways of Life' is reproduced in Stephanie
Spencer, *O. G. Rejlander: Photography as Art* (Ann Arbor,
Mich.: UMI Research Press, 1985), Plate 23, as is Rej-
lander's *Hard Times,* which shares the title and theme of
Charles Dickens's 1854 novel. See also Robinson, "The
Poets and Photography," *Photographic News* 8, no. 283
(February 5, 1864): 62–63, and William Lake Price's well-
known 'Don Quixote in his Study' (1855), which may
have influenced Robinson, reproduced in Margaret F.
Harker, *Henry Peach Robinson: Master of Photographic
Art 1830–1901* (Oxford: Blackwell, 1988), p. 25.

2. 'She Never Told Her Love' (1857), a preliminary
study for 'Fading Away,' which quotes some lines from
Shakespeare, is reproduced in Harker, *Robinson,* Plate
45, as is the first version of the scene, with lines from
Shelley inscribed on the mat, Plate 47. For Robinson's
contacts with Bede, Carroll, and the Pre-Raphaelites, see
Spencer, *Rejlander,* pp. 8 and 25, and Harker, *Robinson,*
pp. 31 and 59. For more on Dante Gabriel Rossetti's involvement with photography, see Michael Bartram, *The
Pre-Raphaelite Camera: Aspects of Victorian Photography* (Boston: New York Graphic Society, [1985]), pp. 135–
38; *Pre-Raphaelite Photography,* ed. Graham Ovenden
(New York: St. Martin's, [1984]), pp. 18–27; and Alicia
Craig Faxon, "D. G. Rossetti's Use of Photography," *History of Photography* 16, no. 3 (Autumn, 1992): 254–62.
See also Lindsay Smith, "'The Seed of the Flower': Photography and Pre-Raphaelitism," in *The Pre-Raphaelites
in Context* (San Marino, Calif.: Huntington Library, 1992),
pp. 37–53.

3. The Wordsworth scene, designed by Robinson, was
constructed from a portrait of his young daughter, Maud,
and a landscape by his new business partner, Nelson

King Cherrill, according to Harker, *Robinson,* p. 52. In
addition to the photographs reproduced here, see also
Robinson's earlier prints illustrating the works of Shakespeare (1859–63), Plates 11–14, and his 1858 illustrations
of *The Story of Little Red Riding Hood* (1858), Plates
48–51, which are interesting to compare with Carroll's
single image of the heroine, reproduced in Gernsheim,
Lewis Carroll Photographer, Plate 10, and with John
Baldessari's adaptation of Grimm's *Little Red Cap,* reproduced in Coosje van Bruggen, *John Baldessari* (New York:
Rizzoli, 1990), p. 224. Robinson's and Cameron's interpretations of Elaine with Lancelot's shield, both reproduced in Bartram, *The Pre-Raphaelite Camera,* pp. 164–
65, make another provocative comparison. See also Robinson's late scene from Samuel Richardson's *Pamela* (1882),
reproduced in Harker, *Robinson,* Plate 70.

12. *Charles Baudelaire*

FROM "THE SALON OF 1859," 1859

One might think that Baudelaire (1821–67), as an admirer of Poe, the daguerreotype enthusiast, and as a close friend of Nadar, the eminent portraitist [Fig. 27],[1] *would have been more receptive to photography in this review of the annual Paris art exhibition. The 1859 Salon was the first that included works of the camera, previously excluded on the grounds that they were products of science, not art. But the author of the influential and controversial* Les Fleurs du Mal *(1857) took the occasion to condemn photography as a fine art. Baudelaire had long regarded the camera with condescension, valuing it mainly as an industrial tool, or, at best, a ready servant providing documentary aid to the memory of a creative artist. But with its rising status, he increasingly found it a threat. The camera's mechanical reproduction of external reality well served human desire for exact copies—of people, natural scenes, and exotic places—but posed a grave threat to the imagination. For Baudelaire, as for Poe, the imagination best reflected internal emotions and dreams, which comprised artistic truth. But Baudelaire, unlike Poe, felt photography stifled rather than stimulated the imagination by so easily satisfying its curiosity.*[2] *His review proved one of the opening salvos in the ongoing battle over whether photography is an art.*[3]

The desire to astonish and to be astonished is very proper. "It is a happiness to wonder;" but also "it is a happiness to dream."[4] The whole question, then, if you insist that I confer upon you the title of artist or of connoisseur of the fine arts, is to know by what processes you wish to create or to feel wonder. Because the Beautiful is *always* wonderful, it would be absurd to suppose that what is wonderful is *always* beautiful. Now our public, which is singularly incapable of feeling the happiness of dreaming or of marvelling (a sign of its meanness of soul), wishes to be made to wonder by means which are alien to art, and its obedient artists bow to its taste; they try to strike, to surprise, to stupefy it by means of unworthy tricks, because they know that it is incapable of ecstasy in front of the natural devices of true art.

During this lamentable period, a new industry arose which contributed not a little to confirm stupidity in its faith and to ruin whatever might remain of the divine in the French mind. The idolatrous mob demanded an ideal worthy of itself and appropriate to its nature—that is perfectly understood. In matters of painting and sculpture, the present-day *Credo* of the sophisticated, above all in France (and I do not think that anyone at all would dare to state the contrary), is this: "I believe in Nature, and I believe only in Nature (there are good reasons for that). I believe that Art is, and cannot be other than, the exact reproduction of Nature (a timid and dissident sect would wish to exclude the more repellent objects of nature, such as skeletons or chamber-pots). Thus an industry that could give us a result identical to Nature would be the absolute of art." A revengeful God has given ear to the prayers of this multitude. Daguerre was his Messiah. and now the faithful says to himself: "Since Photography gives us every guarantee of exactitude that we could desire (they really believe that, the mad fools!), then Photography and Art are the same thing." From that moment our squalid society rushed, Narcissus to a man, to gaze at its trivial image on a scrap of metal. A madness, an extraordinary fanaticism took possession of all these new sun-worshippers. Strange abominations took form. By bringing together a group of male and female clowns, got up like butchers and laundry-maids at a carnival, and by begging these *heroes* to be so kind as to hold their chance grimaces for the time necessary for the performance, the operator flattered himself that he was reproducing tragic or elegant scenes from ancient history. Some democratic writer ought to have seen here a cheap method of disseminating a loathing for history and for painting among the people, thus committing a double sacrilege and insulting at one and the same time the divine art of painting and the noble art of the actor. A little later a thousand hungry eyes were bending over the peepholes of the stereoscope, as though they were the attic-windows of the infinite. The love of pornography, which is no less deep-rooted in the natural heart of man than the love of himself, was not to let slip so fine an opportunity of self-satisfaction. And do not imagine that it was only children on their way back from school who took pleasure in these follies; the world was infatuated with them. I was once present when some friends were discreetly concealing some such pictures from a beautiful woman, a woman of high society, not of mine—they were taking upon themselves some feeling of delicacy in her presence; but "No," she cried. "Give them to me! Nothing is too much for me." I swear that I heard that; but who will believe me? "You can see that they are great ladies" said Alexandre Dumas. "There are some still greater!" said Cazotte.[5]

As the photographic industry was the refuge of every would-be painter, every painter too ill-endowed or too lazy to complete his studies, this universal infatuation bore not only the mark of a blindness, an imbecility, but had also the air of a vengeance. I do not believe, or at least I do not wish to believe, in the absolute success of such a brutish conspiracy, in which, as in all others, one finds both fools and knaves; but I am convinced that the ill-applied developments of photography, like all other purely material

developments of progress, have contributed much to the impoverishment of the French artistic genius, which is already so scarce. In vain may our modern Fatuity roar, belch forth all the rumbling wind of its rotund stomach, spew out all the undigested sophisms with which recent philosophy has stuffed it from top to bottom; it is nonetheless obvious that this industry, by invading the territories of art, has become art's most mortal enemy, and that the confusion of their several functions prevents any of them from being properly fulfilled. Poetry and progress are like two ambitious men who hate one another with an instinctive hatred, and when they meet upon the same road, one of them has to give place. If photography is allowed to supplement art in some of its functions, it will soon have supplanted or corrupted it altogether, thanks to the stupidity of the multitude which is its natural ally. It is time, then, for it to return to its true duty, which is to be the servant of the sciences and arts—but the very humble servant, like printing or shorthand, which have neither created nor supplemented literature. Let it hasten to enrich the tourist's album and restore to his eye the precision which his memory may lack; let it adorn the naturalist's library, and enlarge microscopic animals; let it even provide information to corroborate the astronomer's hypotheses; in short, let it be the secretary and clerk of whoever needs an absolute factual exactitude in his profession—up to that point nothing could be better. Let it rescue from oblivion those tumbling ruins, those books, prints and manuscripts which demand a place in the archives of our memory—it will be thanked and applauded. But if it be allowed to encroach upon the domain of the impalpable and the imaginary, upon anything whose value depends solely upon the addition of something of a man's soul, then it will be so much the worse for us!

I know very well that some people will retort, "The disease which you have just been diagnosing is a disease of imbeciles. What man worthy of the name of artist, and what true connoisseur, has ever confused art with industry?" I know it: and yet I will ask them in my turn if they believe in the contagion of good and evil, in the action of the mass on individuals, and in the involuntary, forced obedience of the individual to the mass. It is an incontestable, and irresistible law that the artist should act upon the public, and that the public should react upon the artist; and besides, those terrible witnesses, the facts, are easy to study; the disaster is verifiable. Each day art further diminishes its self-respect by bowing down before external reality; each day the painter becomes more and more given to painting not what he dreams but what he sees. Nevertheless *it is a happiness to dream,* and it used to be a glory to express what one dreamt. But I ask you! does the painter still know this happiness?

Could you find an honest observer to declare that the invasion of photography and the great industrial madness of our times have no part at all in this deplorable result? Are we to suppose that a people whose eyes are growing used to considering the results of a material science as though they were the products of the beautiful, will not in the course of time have singularly diminished its faculties of judging and of feeling what are among the most ethereal and immaterial aspects of creation?

1. For more on Nadar, see the Nadar, Sand, and Dumas selections, and for more on Nadar's relationship with Baudelaire, as well as reproductions of his four memorable portraits of him, see Gosling, *Nadar,* pp. 66–67 and 237; Nadar, *Charles Baudelaire Intime: Documents, Notes et Anecdotes* [1911], (Paris: Obsidiane, 1985); Heilbrun, "One of Nadar's First Portraits of Baudelaire," paper presented at the J. Paul Getty Symposium, "Photography: Object/Idea/Theory," April 22, 1991; and Cardinal, "Nadar and the Photographic Portrait" in *The Portrait in Photography,* ed. Clarke, pp. 16–20.

2. For further discussion of Baudelaire's ideas on photography, see Benjamin, "On Some Motifs in Baudelaire" (1939) in *Illuminations,* ed. Hannah Arendt (New York: Schocken, 1969), pp. 186–88, and Susan Blood, "Baudelaire against Photography: An Allegory of Old Age," *Modern Language Notes* 101, no. 4 (September 1986): 817–37. See also the W. C. Williams selection below for Baudelaire's influence on Walker Evans.

3. Relevant here, however, might be Baudelaire's letters to Nadar in 1856: "I am writing a Salon now, without having seen it. But I have a catalogue. . . ." Then later, "I lied to you a little, but so very little. I did visit the Salon, only once, a visit dedicated to seeking out the novelties . . . ," quoted in Elizabeth G. Holt, *The Art of All Nations, 1850–1873: The Merging Role of Exhibitions and Critics* (Garden City, N.Y.: Anchor Books, 1981), pp. 268–69.

4. [Original editor's note] Quoted from Poe, *Morella.*

5. [Original editor's note] The first remark is taken from Dumas's play *La Tour de Nesle* (Act I, sc. 9); the second from Gérard de Nerval's preface to Cazotte's *Le Diable amoureux.* The somewhat complicated point of the joke is explained by Crépet in his note on this passage (*Curiosités esthétiques,* p. 490).

Part Two
1865–1890

Armandine Lucie-Aurore Dupin Dudevant (1804–76), fleeing conventional married life, adopted the pseudonym of George Sand, wore male dress, smoked cigars, took lovers, including the composer Frederic Chopin and the poet Alfred de Musset, and gradually won acceptance as a leading Romantic figure. Her writings had long been admired by Nadar, the pseudonym of Gaspard-Félix Tournachon (1820–1910), who became the friend and favored portrait photographer of leading mid-century French artists.[1] He also pioneered in taking aerial and underground pictures (from 1858) and conceived the modern photo-interview (1886). Sand, whom Nadar photographed in 1860 [Fig. 28], supported his passionate faith in the future of aerial flight, as did other writers such as Hugo, who wrote about the balloon as a symbol of liberty and democracy, and Baudelaire, who wrote (unused) letters of introduction to fellow English aeronauts, the poet Algernon Swinburne and the painter James McNeill Whistler.[2] To further publicize his views, Nadar established societies, often headquartered in his studio—to which Sand, Alexandre Dumas, and Jules Verne, the noted science fiction writer, belonged—and published a journal.[3] He also made dramatic flights in a specially constructed balloon named "Le Géant," which included room for passengers, a photographic laboratory, and a printing press, and composed Mémoires de Géant (1864) and Le Droit au Vol (1865), for which Sand wrote this preface. During the Prussian siege of Paris in 1870, Nadar's balloons—one named after Sand, another after Hugo—provided the capital's only link with the rest of France as well as the world's first passenger and postal air service.

Truth has two modes of existence, marked by two distinct phases; that in which it is merely demonstrated, and that in which it can be proved.

In the former, it reposes first of all upon the faith which is the instinct of the Good and the Beautiful, then upon reason, and finally upon intellectual certitude.

In the latter it rests upon the experience acquired by the accomplished fact.

Honour to those men whose initiative sets free the first hypothesis, the sovereign induction, from the chaos of dreams, from the thousand gropings of the imagination struggling with the unknown! When great and generous minds have succeeded in well posing the question to be solved, they have already made a grand step: they have opened the way.

Afterwards come the men of application, not less useful, not less admirable, who, by clever and patient experiments, proceed from the hypothesis to the discovery. From that time, Genius becomes a material force; and the idea which was only a promise becomes the real benefit with which the human race enriches itself.

Thus it has been with all our conquests in the domains of Science and of Industry. Every light has its precursory dawn, and he who perceives the one may predict the other. But all do not see the glimmer of the first breaking of a truth, and it is at this earliest stage of undecided brightness that it is disputed, sometimes even repulsed with passion, so formidable is the apparition of those great stars of progress which upset customary notions, destroy to a certain extent the world of the past, and, on the day when their rays burst forth above the horizon, cause man to enter upon new conditions of existence.

Thus it was with steam, with electricity, and with all those surprising inventions which, within the last century, have so essentially modified public and private life in and around us.

In the little work which follows our brief reflections, and also in the "Mémoires du Géant" (a book so innocently dramatic), read the protestations, the persecutions even, called forth by every truth passing through the phases of research and demonstration. It is when it stands most in need of consideration, study, and encouragement, that sarcasm and an impatient desire to crush it, rise up about the dawning truth. "Prove thyself!" is cried out on all sides, "and we will believe in thee."

Truth replies: "Assist me to ripen, to manifest myself. Give me the means for becoming a fact, and for that, know me; deny me not. I am but an idea, a soul, so to speak, and yet you expect to touch me before you have permitted me to take a body! I exist nevertheless; I exist in a sphere a real for the eyes of the understanding as if I were already a palpable fact. Respect me, alas! for if you deny me, you deny yourselves. I am yours, since I bring you that future; and if you affirm that I shall never be, you say that you yourselves desire never to exist."

Among the adepts, the ardent vulgarisers, and the devoted servants of Truth in the stage of demonstration, Nadar, who is neither a *savant* nor a speculator, but, in my opinion, a great logician and a man of firm will, here lays before us his earnest and deliberate Word.

This Word, summed up in the "Right to Fly," possesses a veritable worth and a veritable force. Let it be meditated without prejudice, and every serious mind will acknowledge, that the question of the "Right to Fly" is one of those magnificent questions which cannot remain unsolved from the moment that they are well posed.

1. See Nadar's portraits of Sand, c. 1864, reproduced in Gosling, *Nadar,* pp. 179 and 224 (wearing the same wig as that worn by Nadar, shown on p. 11), and his piece on Sand in *Les Droits de l'Homme* (June 13, 1876), reproduced in Jean Prinet, Antoinette Dilasser, and *Lamberto Vitali, *Nadar: Testi di Nadar* (Turin: Einaudi, 1973). See also Cardinal, "Nadar and the Photographic Portrait" in *The Portrait in Photography,* ed. Clarke, pp. 6–24 on his portraits of some of Sand's literary contemporaries such as Dumas *père* and Baudelaire.

2. See Gosling, *Nadar,* pp. 13–20.

3. Gosling, *Nadar,* p. 13, notes that Verne was the secretary of the earliest aerial group—"The Society for the Encouragement of Aerial Locomotion by means of Heavier-than-Air Machines" (est. c. 1863); Nadar made him, transparently disguised under the anagram "Ardan," the hero of his *De la Terre à la Lune* (1865), published in English as *From the Earth to the Moon,* trans. Louis Mercier and Eleanor C. King (New York: Scribner, Armstrong & Company, 1874), see especially ch. 18. For more on the relationship between Nadar and Verne, see Arthur B. Evans, *Jules Verne Rediscovered: Didacticism and the Scientific Novel* (New York: Greenwood Press, 1988), p. 20. See also Howard's series of relevant poems, collectively entitled "Homage to Nadar," in *Misgivings: Poems* (New York: Athenaeum, 1979), pp. 19–57, and Tournier, "Un Certain Tournachon," *Le Crépuscule des masques* (Paris: Hoëbeke, 1992), pp. 20–29.

14. *Alexandre Dumas père*

FROM "ACROSS HUNGARY," 1866

*D*umas (1802–70) was celebrated for his historical plays and novels like The Three Musketeers (1844), which reflected his own thirst for chivalrous adventure and exotic travel. He welcomed the "new and unexpected pleasures" that resulted from the invention of his friend Daguerre, especially the "cherished resemblances" of loved ones.[1] But his own experiences with photographers proved mixed. Commencing a long-planned cruise in 1860 to destinations famous in history and myth—Greece, Turkey, Palestine, Egypt—Dumas invited along Gustave Le Gray (1820–82), Du Camp's former instructor. Le Gray was known for his technical and aesthetic innovations as well as a wide subject range—land- and sea-scapes, historic monuments, military scenes, and portraits. But when Dumas converted the voyage to a relief mission to help Garibaldi unify Italy, Le Gray disembarked, toured the Middle East, and settled in Cairo; he remained there as an art teacher and photographer, abandoning his family and professional responsibilities in France.[2] In 1865–66, the restless author traveled again to central Europe, where a sitting for a female photographer in Vienna [Fig. 29] prompted this humorous recollection of previous studio ordeals with its unexpectedly serious recommendation.[3] Back in Paris, Dumas resumed his friendship with Nadar, who had taken his portrait in 1857, often dropping by his studio and joining his new Société des Aéronautes (1866).[4] After enduring a final scandal in 1866, involving the threat of publication of compromising photographs of himself with an actress, Dumas seemed exhausted, dying four years later.[5]

FROM "ACROSS HUNGARY"

I have, in leaving Vienna, forgotten to describe a curious enough fact. At Vienna photography is generally practised by women.

I may here mention, again, the horror I have already expressed elsewhere, *à propos* of a portrait of myself, which one of the journals has published; I may also add, that I have a horror of photography, and that this horror extends itself to all photographers. Now, as I am accustomed not to avow love or hatred, except with sentiments founded on reason, here are the reasons for my dislike to photographs and for photographers.

Let us commence with photography.

When—in 1837, if I remember rightly—my friend Daguerre came to show me the first examples of his Daguerreotype, which faithfully represented a street in Paris, with a cage and canary bird in the foreground, and he made an observation that the inside of the cage had not come out correctly, seeing that the bird—not knowing the honour paid him by the science—had moved. I naturally commenced to laugh, that the sun, which had been 6,000 years according to the Bible, 12,000 years according to the zodiac of Denderah, and 36,000 years according to the Chinese, had been engaged in reopening the crops in the field, the peaches upon the stairs, and love in the heart, was now to be forced out of its millenniary idleness to reproduce the different aspects of the world it illuminates. After this first access of hilarity had passed, I applauded the ingenious invention, which I believed only at first applicable to inanimate objects more or less immobile, without suspecting the disastrous consequences of it, and that, violated like Lucrece, by MM. Niepce and Talbot, this honourable matron would deliver, in dying, this fierce, shameless thing called photography, which would itself undertake to reproduce, not only landscapes, monuments, ruins—reproductions for which it had a particular aptitude—but also living persons, men, ugly enough naturally, and whom it does not embellish; women, the consolation of the eye when she is not that of the heart, whom it disfigures; I was not only altogether in error

myself, but, by applauding it, I propagated this deplorable error.

In fact, what are the results of photography? I have already mentioned the merit, that of disfiguring the human race, already ugly enough as it is. Then, of producing a class of false artists, composed in general of those who had not the ability to become painters; they make themselves photographers, calling themselves, some the pupils of Ingres, and others the pupils of Delaroche, as if to be a photographer they needed to be the pupil of one of these; false artists, incapable painters, who with some exceptions, if photography did not exist, could not have been photographers, and would have been trained up to some trade useful to society, instead of the disastrous occupation to which they have abandoned themselves; an occupation that has no other results than that of vulgarising art without extending it.

Formerly, when people gave their portraits, they could not give them profusely; they were so valuable that they gave them only to those persons whom they dearly loved. A portrait in oil by Ingres or Horace Vernet cost three thousand francs; a miniature by Isabey, or by Mme. de Mirbel, cost a thousand francs. In receiving a portrait of a friend or lover, they received a gift doubly precious, the present combining in one the image of the beloved person and a valuable work of art.

Now all that is passed. One gives portraits to those who ask for them as we would alms to a mendicant; and if the portrait is not given to a person to whom we are altogether indifferent, it is made a matter of exchange, and we give one portrait with a stipulation that we receive another. No one ventures to refuse a thing that costs ten sous, and when, if it is refused, it will be bought for twenty from any of the sellers of novelties. All kinds of people, who are the most indifferent to you, include you in their collections; you and your *confrères,* those of the art which you practise, and the science which you profess. You are arranged like a collection of butterflies or moths; only there is the difference that the beautiful butterflies of the Tropics, or specimens of rare and sacred beetles, may cost a hundred francs each, while the greatest contemporaneous men joined in collection are invariably sold at ten sous a piece. It is humiliating.

So much for photography. Let us pass to the photographers. Though you may enjoy little celebrity, your arrival is welcomed—whether you travel in France or abroad—by a deputation of photographers. Informed beforehand by the journals, they come to ask you to sit for your portrait. You have to employ in vain, when you are fact to face with them, those ruses that your imagination suggests to you. You change, like Proteus, to lion, serpent, water, or fire. You plead in vain: "But I am old and I am ugly:" that is always disagreeable to say, even to a photographer. You have vainly to add: "Photography makes me uglier still;" and that is disagreeable for them to hear. Nothing does, however. You object because of the little time you have. You are answered, "Monsieur, it is a thing of a moment." You cry out, "Yes, I know your moments; it is the not the first time I have sat." "Monsieur," resolutely says the photographer, "do not confound me with my confrères; I have invented a completely new process; you will only have to seat yourself, and before you have winked your eye—*crac!*—your portrait will be done." You soon understand all resistance is useless. You make your condition; they are granted you in advance. You have to move when you like, you will rise when you like, and you will leave when you like; and you are finally informed of the floor. "On the third floor, Monsieur, and a very easy staircase." "Go on, it is not too high," you will murmur; you decide; and like M. de Montmorency, who, condemned to be executed at five o'clock in the evening demanded it to be three, so as to die at the same hour as Our Lord Jesus Christ, you demand to be executed at once, and you follow the photographer. You mount to the third floor. This is the first deception that awaits you. "Monsieur," says the photographer to you, pointing out to you a winding staircase, "will you ascend, if you please, this staircase?" "Ah, ah! you told me that I only had to ascend to the third floor." "The saloon is, in fact, on the third floor," says the photographer, smiling a charming smile, "but the atelier is on the fifth; you comprehend, it is to have the best light." You look dolorously at the two tiers, and determine to travel over it all. "At last!" you murmur; and you mount the two other steps. The platform is ready, the chair is on it; it is exactly the same preparation as that for the garrot. Nothing is wanting, not even the *tige de fer* [iron column]. You are directed to the chair, and you sit down with a sigh.

"How do you wish me to place myself?" you ask.

"Just as you will; take a familiar pose. Photography is, you know, the reproduction of nature."

You take your habitual position. The photographer directs his apparatus towards you.

"Pardon, Monsieur," says the photographer; "Will you do me the favour of drawing in your right foot, and placing on the same level your left foot?"

The very pose of Thomas Diafoirus in the *Malade Imaginaire* [Molière's play]. "It will not be graceful," you venture to say.

"It would be still less graceful, I suppose," says the photographer, who is becoming excited, "to have the right foot enormous, and the left imperceptible! They will believe you to be lame, like Byron; and one can be a poet without being club-footed!"

You bow to the compliment, and you draw in your foot, and, by a natural movement, you let your left hand glide down upon your knee.

"Pardon, pardon, Monsieur!" cries the photographer;" it is your left hand now that will become enormous, and your right hand will not be more in proportion. Nature, Monsieur, nature!"

That both your hands may be in proportion, you draw back to you your left hand, and place your right hand in your pocket.

"I warn you, Monsieur," raising himself, after having looked at you through his apparatus, says the scholar of M. Ingres or M. Delaroche, "I warn you that in photography there is nothing so ugly as a hand in the pocket. You have a maimed air; and you do not wish that anyone should think that the man who writes such beautiful things is one-handed."

You draw your hand from your pocket, and you pass your thumb into the slope of your waistcoat. "Is it better thus?"

"It is not bad, although the position is a little forced; but it is no matter; that will do, that will do; only do not stir."

"As much as you wish when you are not in a position as you are now."

"And my head—what shall I do with it?"

"Whatever you wish, only place it naturally."

You let your head fall a little more to the left, then the right.

"Ah!" says the photographer, "This would be good for Alexander the Great; and though you have good right to that title, perhaps the world would see a certain affectation on your part, if you awarded it to yourself."

"But, finally, Monsieur, how do you wish me to hold my head?"

"Straight, parbleu!"

You arrange your head.

"There, that is good, but you could not hold it like that; I will put you the head-rest." And the photographer places round the occiput a circle of iron.

"There, viola!" he says, satisfied at last that the position is natural. "Well, be it so. Nature, Monsieur, nature!"

"And my eyes—what shall I do with them?"

"What you like." And you accordingly look down.

"Oh no, no!" says the photographer; "it is absolutely necessary that you look at some object."

"The ceiling?"

"No, too high."

"The carpet?"

"No, too low."

"But, finally what ought I to look at?"

The photographer places himself before his apparatus, takes the pose of a gunner who is going to put the match to a piece of cannon, and seriously says, "Look at my shoulder."

You look at the shoulder of the photographer.

"Now smile."

"At your shoulder?"

"Yes."

You smile. At the end of a minute, during which your arteries have counted the seconds, the photographer closes his lenses and carries away his negative. At the end of ten minutes he opens the door and tranquilly says to you, "You have moved; it has not come out well. We must begin again."

At Vienna, as I have told you, they are nearly all women who take photographs. On the material side of the operation there are the same inconveniences; but, at least, the ideal side offers compensation. Firstly, the women who take the photographs are naturally pretty; and at Vienna, where, as I have already said, all the women nearly are pretty, the lady photographers ought to be beautiful. They are so. Now see the difference. Firstly, if you are invited by a pretty woman, you are not told on what floor she lives; you know beforehand that the angels, represented here by women, adhere instinctively the nearest possible to the sky. You mount, then, without complaint, three, four, and even five storeys. You pant; it is with emotion. You kiss the hand that is extended to you; that is your recompense. If you do not talk German you talk the universal language—the language of signs. This has the double advantage of being the most expressive, and of making in five minutes the same way as the others in an hour. Then, as your charming photographeress cannot explain by word what she wishes, she takes your hands, and places them where she wishes them to be; she takes your head, and places it where she wishes it to be turned. Now, I do not know that there is anything disagreeable in feeling your head placed in position by two pretty hands. Then a time before, instead of saying, like the photographer, "Look at my shoulder!" she says, "Look at me!" and she does not need to add, "You will smile;" the smile comes upon the lip by itself when one looks at a pretty woman.

As for me, behold my history. On arriving at Vienna, I learnt that I was waited on by a charming photographer, whose name I will mention, to recommend her to all my friends, and to all those to whom my affirmation would become a recommendation—Madame Wilhelmine Stockmann. "Where does she live?" asked I. "Fifth floor, Kohlmark No. 1." And behold, I who could not bear photography, make my first visit to thank a photographer for having asked of me the favour of taking my portrait. Madame Stockmann is not a Viennese, she is a Hungarian. When the Hungarians are pretty, they are very pretty. I posed three, four, five times, as often as my photographer wished, and she made of me three excellent photographs, which, instead of having a sulky expression, reproduced my best smile [Fig. 29]. At the moment of my leaving the atelier, my pretty photographer, in reproaching me for not being a little more serious, had asked me to write my name in her album. Not only did I write my name, but underneath my name these four lines:—

"Si je ne suis point sérieux,
Ce n'est point à vous d'en médire;

La faute en est à vos beaux yeux,
A qui mon c ur tient à souire."

(If I am not at all serious
It is not for you to criticize me;
The fault is in your beautiful eyes,
At which my heart keeps smiling.)

The lines are not good, but they would have been worse if I had failed to make a photograph.

Now let us approach the serious question. The plague of modern society is, that there is not enough employment for women. For the most part, the careers of art and industry open to men, they are closed to women. Why, then, in Paris, should not the women imitate the example that is given them in Vienna? Why, should not the women make photographers? Then, if they would permit me to venture an idea that comes to me whenever I enter the grand "Magasins," like "La grande ville de Paris," "La trois Quartiers," Like "Le grand Saint Louis," I have constantly seen there the women at the counting-house, and the men doing the work of the counter in unfolding and displaying the fabrics. Would it not be more logical that this work was made for women? The women would know more of fabrics, and make much of the value of the qualities of the merchandise. If this system were employed, ten thousand young girls, who are to-day between misery and prostitution, would gain to-morrow three francs per day. The charge of the countinghouse is the work of men; displaying measuring, and cutting the stuffs is the work of women. It is true that the tradesmen to whom I have spoken of this change, all, in approving the social morality, disapprove the prospect of the custom. They pretend that they make it necessary to make the women served by men, and men by women: and perhaps, in fact, they are right. The more motive for the women to be made photographers.

1. Dumas is quoted in "Alexander Dumas on Photography," *Photographic News* (August 10, 1866): 379, which Janet Buerger called to the attention of the editor, who, however, was unable to locate these recollections by the writer for the Society for the Encouragement of Industry, given "about two years ago"; more likely these remarks were made in 1857 during the author's longest visit to England, described by F. W. J. Hemmings, *The King of Romance: Portrait of Alexander Dumas* (London: Hamish Hamilton, 1979), pp. 170–71.

2. See Dumas, *On Board the "Emma," Adventures with Garibaldi's "Thousand" in Sicily* [c. 1861], trans. R. S. Garnett (London: Ernest Benn, 1929), especially pp. 62–63, 89, 99, 114, 146–48, 150–51, 162–63, 165–66, 229, 254, 270, and 274. See also Eugenia Parry Janis, *The Photography of Gustave Le Gray* (Chicago: Art Institute of Chicago and University of Chicago Press, 1987), pp. 125–43, for further details of this voyage including some of Le Gray's photographs and engravings based on them. No portrait of Dumas by Le Gray is known.

3. For further information about Wilhelmine Stockmann, the woman photographer mentioned in the Dumas piece below, see *Geschichte den Fotografie in Österreich* (Bad Ischl: Verein Zur Eranbeitung der Geschichte den Fotografie in Österreich, 1983), vol. 2, p. 184. She apparently founded a Vienna studio, managed from 1865 by her husband, Nikolaus, also a photographer. The portrait reproduced here of Dumas, signed N. Stockmann but probably taken by his wife, was located for the editor by Dr. Viktoria Talos-Lunzer at the suggestion of Leo Lensing. No others seem to exist in any major public collection in Vienna, according to both Dr. Talos-Lunzer in her letter to the editor of February 11, 1993, and Monika Faber in her letter to the editor of January 18, 1993, nor in France, according to Digby and Christiane Neave of Marly-Le-Loire, who have compiled a catalogue of Dumas portraits (though they were unaware of this one) and who discussed the matter with the editor by telephone on September 16, 1992.

4. Nadar's father was Dumas's first publisher, and Nadar and Dumas planned but never executed a collaborative theatre project in the mid-1850's, according to a label at the Nadar exhibition at the MMA, April 1995. See Gosling, *Nadar,* pp. 16 and 118, facing a reproduction of the portrait, which has been variously dated from 1855 to 1859; and Cardinal, "Nadar and the Photographic Portrait," in *The Portrait in Photography,* ed. Clarke, pp. 11–12.

5. See Hemmings, *The King of Romance,* p. 208, on these 1866 photographs of Dumas with the actress Adah Isaacs Menken which brought him further notoriety.

15. W. S. Gilbert

"A TALE OF A DRY PLATE," [c. 1860–70,] 1890

Gilbert (1836–1911) had been a bored clerk, a failed barrister, and probably an active amateur photographer in the 1860s before securing fame with the illustrated Bab Ballads *(collected 1869), some dramatic burlesques and verse plays, and the librettos for the cherished Gilbert and Sullivan operettas, such as* H.M.S. Pinafore *(1878) and* The Pirates of Penzance *(1879). This little-known short story, probably written but not published around the time of his 1865* Bab *ballad mocking the mania for the carte-de-visite and his 1867 caricature of a grateful photographer [Fig. 2], suggests his early photographic interests.[1] In subsequent decades, when the theatre totally consumed his time, Gilbert used his earlier photographic experience in his librettos only occasionally and conventionally, though with characteristic humor. The captain of the* Pinafore *gives Sir Joseph's photograph to his daughter to encourage the lord's suit, and the twins in* Utopia, Limited *(1893) assert that Kodaks do their "best" to capture them accurately: "If evidence you would possess/ of what is maiden bashfulness/ You only need a button press—/And we do all the rest."[2] After breaking with Sullivan, however, Gilbert again took up the camera, which features more significantly in his play* The Fairy's Dilemma *(1904).[3] In his last years, he spent a considerable amount of time photographing, developing, and mounting in albums prints taken of family members, friends, and especially his cherished home, Grym's Dyke [Fig. 30]; Gilbert loved its lavish interiors, landscaped grounds, and man-made pond, in which he drowned tragically while rescuing a guest.[4]*

"A Tale of a Dry Plate"

I am a junior partner in a large mercantile house. Certain irregularities had occurred in our Colombo branch, and I was dispatched by the firm to investigate them, and to place matters on a more satisfactory footing. I need not go into details on this point, as they are irrelevant to my story.

I sailed by the *Kaiser-i-Hind* from Tilbury, accompanied by my valet. At the Liverpool Street terminus an elderly lady in widow's mourning asked me some questions as to the conveyance of luggage from the Tilbury station to the ship; she should have sent her luggage to the docks, but had omitted to do so. As I replied to her questions, I saw that she was accompanied by a very beautiful girl of eighteen. There is no need to beat about the bush—I fell in love with her, there and then. It is a commonplace way of putting it, but I don't know that I could make matters clearer by a more elaborate method of expression. As they and I travelled to Tilbury in the same compartment, we entered into conversation, as people will readily do who know that they are to travel many thousand miles together. I learnt that the lady was a Mrs. Selby, widow of a Colonel Selby, who had died about six months since. Broken in health, and weakened by long weeping, she had been advised to take a sea voyage, in the belief that change of scene and beneficent sea air would do much to restore her to health, if not to happiness. As I happened to have met Colonel Selby on two occasions—once in London and once in a country house—my acquaintance with his widow and daughter rapidly ripened into friendship. We sailed on a fine October afternoon, and by the time we were off the "Start" I had almost established myself on the footing of an old friend.

Pass over the voyage. It lasted five weeks, but it seemed like five days. I lived but in Clara's presence. I scarcely spoke to anyone on board except to Clara and her mother. People see more of each other, if they care to do so, in a

30. W. S. Gilbert. House and Pond at Grym's Dyke, c. 1905.

few weeks' voyage than in a lifetime on shore, and before we reached Colombo I had declared my love to Clara, and she had accepted it. If there is unalloyed happiness on earth, it was given to us as we neared Ceylon.

Unalloyed, save by the thought that we were about to part for a time; for Clara was to go on to Calcutta, where her late father's brother was quartered, whereas I was to remain in Ceylon for three months. We were to return to England at about the same date, and it was arranged that as soon as possible after our arrival we were to be married.

I have some little skill in photography, and I had brought with me a camera and some dry plates, intending to photograph any striking scenes that I might come across during my journey. But the aid of dry plates, photography, and especially travelling photography, is much simplified. The traveller can take a photograph, shut the plate in a light-tight box, and develop it twelve months afterwards if he pleases. There is no need to encumber oneself with chemicals; all the messy portion of the process can be done at home, in the seclusion of one's own dark room. I had not intended to take any photographs on the voyage, for dry plates are extraordinarily sensitive to the action of the faintest ray of light, and it was practically impossible to make my cabin dark enough to allow of my transferring plates from the dark box to the slides without absolutely spoiling them. But I happened to have left two plates in one of the slides, and before we reached our destination I devoted one of these to Clara and one to Mrs. Selby.

We parted tearfully, but not unhappily. We were to meet in three months' time, and our lives were then to be passed together. I believe we were too full of happiness in this prospect to grieve very much over our parting. As the *Kaiser* steamed away for Calcutta, I kept the happiness of our next meeting steadily before me, and it served to keep me in good spirits. The time passed slowly; but it passed. I had received two letters from Clara, written from Calcutta, full of life, and hope, and joy at the prospect before us. She was going to spend a month at Allahabad, and a fortnight at Bom-

bay, and she was then to return to Marseilles by a Messageries ship, the captain of which was an intimate friend of the uncle with whom she had been staying at Calcutta. By this arrangement she would arrive in England about a month before me.

At length my sailing orders came, and on one of the happiest days of my life I set foot on board the good ship *Mirzapore*, which was to convey me to Port Said, on my way home, *viâ* Brindisi. I had written to Mrs. Selby, begging her to bring Clara to meet me in Paris. Her doing so would but shorten our period of separation by some ten or twelve hours, but I knew that these hours were golden to her as well as to me, and I was selfish for both of us. After a stormy voyage, I reached Brindisi in due course; I hurried to the Post Restante, for I had asked her to reply to me there, but there was nothing for me. It was evident that my letter had not reached her; perhaps she had delayed a few days in Paris on her way home. She had a *trousseau* to prepare, and it is a strange article of faith among women that this can be done more effectually in Paris than elsewhere; consequently, nothing was more probable than that she was there at that moment; my letter would probably be forwarded to her, and if so, she would surely be at the station on the arrival of the train from Italy.

As I rushed across Europe I had but one thought in my mind—would Clara be at the Paris terminus to meet me? The towns flew by me when I thought of her, and yet at times the intervals between them seemed interminable. Every stoppage irritated me; yet the two days were not tedious. I could always lose all count of time by allowing my mind to dwell upon the incidents of our voyage together, and especially on the crowning incident that was yet to come. But when the doubting question arose whether or not we should meet in Paris, the train seemed to dawdle as it never dawdled before. At length we reached the terminus. I eagerly scanned the few people on the platform as we entered the station, and my heart sank when I saw she was not there. Then I remembered that on French railways friends of passengers are not, as a rule, allowed on the platform, and my hopes rose again. They were dashed, for there was no Clara for me in the waiting-rooms or at the entrance.

A dim sense of calamity—unknown, and the more terrible for being unknown—took possession of me. I hurried across Paris to the "Nord," reached Calais in due course, crossed to Dover and made my way to London, which I reached late at night. The next day, at nine in the morning, I hurried to Mrs. Selby's house in Oxford Square. I rang the bell, and it was answered by a maid-servant in deep black. I asked for Mrs. Selby, but so inarticulately that the girl did not understand me. I pulled myself together, and repeated the question. The girl stammered awkwardly. Had I not heard? No! I had heard nothing; was anything wrong? The French ship in which Mrs. Selby and Clara had sailed from Bombay had been lost—as it was supposed—in a hurricane between Bombay and Aden, and all souls drowned.

I staggered as from a strong man's blow. I remember nothing until I found myself lying on the sofa in the dining-room, tended by an elderly gentleman, Mrs. Selby's brother and administrator. He, of course, did not know me; still less did he know of my relation towards his dead niece. I told him all, and he treated me with the greatest kindness. He could give me no hope; the ship was then six weeks overdue, and the insurances on her had been duly paid.

Desolate and heart-broken I left him, and went to my mother's house in Devonshire. After three weeks of fever I began to recover strength, but the light of my life was extinct, and an undefinable sense of night was all that remained to me. As soon as I was strong enough to stand, I thought of the photographs I had taken in Singapore. They were all that was left to me of my dead love, and with a feeling of unspeakable awe, I proceeded to raise her presentment as it were from the grave. In the closely darkened room, illuminated only be the dim red light of my developing lamp, I prepared the necessary chemicals with a trembling and uncertain hand. I took the plate from the slide in which it had been enclosed for so many months, and as I looked upon its plain creamy surface, so soon to be sanctified by her image, I almost felt that I was engaged on some unhallowed deed of necromancy. Breathless with excitement, I poured the developer upon it, and as I awaited the result, I could hear my heart thumping against my chest. I had not long to wait. Slowly, but surely and distinctly, the features of my darling came to me from the grave. Notwithstanding the inversion of its tones, it stood plainly before me—herself in every detail. As I watched the gradual perfection of the portrait, I cried like a child. At length the development was complete, and, shaking like a leaf, I took it from its bath to examine it more closely. As I did so the door of the room was suddenly opened, a flood of light was admitted, and the photograph was ruined beyond reparation.

With an inarticulate cry, I seized the intruder in my weakened grasp—it was my valet, who had accompanied me on my voyage out and home. I know not what I said to him, in my furious despair—the words, whatever they were, passed into forgetfulness as they were spoken.

"Sir, sir," said he, "I bring you great news. "Miss Selby—Mrs. Selby. Their boat was picked up by a sailing ship. She encountered adverse winds, and only reached Plymouth yesterday—and—and—Miss Clara is here—and I have come to tell you so!"

1. Jane W. Stedman, who is writing the definitive biography of Gilbert and who called to the editor's attention these examples as well as most of the others cited below in correspondence throughout 1991, feels that many of his short stories, like this one, though not published until 1890, were written in the 1860's or 1870's. See also Gilbert, "To Euphrosyne with My Carte De Visite," *Fun* 2, n.s. (December 23, 1865): 150, reprinted in *The Bab Ballads,* ed. James Ellis (Cambridge: Belknap Press/Harvard University Press, 1970), p. 69, and the caricature, from "Men We Meet," *Fun* 5, n.s. (May 18, 1867): 105, reproduced in the Acknowledgments above [Fig. 2].

2. See Gilbert, *H.M.S. Pinafore,* 1: 72, and *Utopia Limited,* 1: 574, in *The Savoy Operas* (London: Macmillan, 1959); the twins draw on the famous Kodak advertisement, described in the Adams selection below, n. 5.

3. See Gilbert, "The Fairy's Dilemma; An Original Domestic Pantomime" (1904), *Original Plays,* 4th Series (London: Chatto & Windus, 1911), pp. 12–14. In this scene, the Reverend Aloysius Parfitt photographs Judge

Whortle, his fiancée's irascible father, which illustrates the dramatist's favorite theme of reality and illusion while satirizing two of his favorite pretentious targets, parents and court officials. This play was adapted for the theatre from a short story of the same title, which originally appeared, with no photographic episode, in *The Graphic* (Christmas Number, 1900): 5–9. See also the opening scene of an enlarged version of *Ruy Blas* (1866) in which Don César de Bazar becomes a photographer after dissipating his fortune, in the unpublished MS in the British Library (W. S. Gilbert Papers, 15, Add. MS 49303).

4. See entries in Gilbert's journals from 1905 to 1911 in the British Library (W. S. Gilbert Papers, Add. 49323–49329). Hesketh Pearson, *Gilbert: His Life and Strife* (London: Methuen, 1957), reproduces one of Gilbert's photographs, insert facing p. 240; others taken by him of friends are in albums, also in the British Library, and a few others of the Grym's Dyke house and grounds are at the Morgan Library, but the whereabouts of the many other photographs he must have taken are unknown.

ameron (1815–79) considered herself a writer even after taking up photography with characteristic passion at age forty-eight. While a busy wife and the mother of six children and numerous foster children, she published some original poems as well as a translation of the popular neomedieval German ballad Leonora *(1847) (previously attempted by Sir Walter Scott, among others).[1] She also wrote countless daily letters, began a novel, and offered to ghost-write for her friend W. M. Thackeray.[2] Her photographs often reflect her literary friendships and tastes: soft-focus portraits of writers like Browning, Carlyle, Longfellow, George Du Maurier, and especially her neighbor and friend Alfred Tennyson [Fig. 32]; allegorical tableaux, inspired by lines from Shakespeare, Milton, the Romantic poets, and contemporary writers; and painstaking illustrations for Tennyson's popular* Idylls of the King *(1875).[3] Friends like the poet Coventry Patmore favorably reviewed her exhibitions, and strangers like Victor Hugo, to whom she sent examples of her work, asserted that "no-one has ever captured the rays of the sun and used them as you have. I throw myself at your feet."[4] Her great-niece Virginia Woolf (1882–1941), whose mother was one of Cameron's favorite models [Fig. 31], helped maintain her great-aunt's reputation through this essay for the first book on Cameron's work and through her only play,* Freshwater *(1923; 1935); both works, however, seem to value Cameron's eccentricity more than her photography.[5] Yet, perhaps from studying Cameron, Woolf became more sensitive to photographs, judging by her subsequent use of them in* Orlando *(1928), her imaginative biography of Vita Sackville-West, and in* Three Guineas *(1938), her feminist antiwar polemic.[6] Meanwhile, Woolf, though not yet one of England's foremost women of letters, was much sought after as a sitter by photographers.[7]*

Julia Margaret Cameron, the third daughter of James Pattle of the Bengal Civil Service, was born on June 11, 1815. Her father was a gentleman of marked, but doubtful, reputation, who after living a riotous life and earning the title of "the biggest liar in India," finally drank himself to death and was consigned to a cask of rum to await shipment to England. The cask was stood outside the widow's bedroom door. In the middle of the night she heard a violent explosion, rushed out, and found her husband, having burst the lid off his coffin, bolt upright menacing her in death as he had menaced her in life. "The shock sent her off her head then and there, poor thing, and she died raving." It is the father of Miss Ethel Smyth who tells the story *(Impressions that Remained),* and he goes on to say that, after "Jim Blazes" had been nailed down again and shipped off, the sailors drank the liquor in which the body was preserved, "and, by Jove, the rum ran out and got alight and set the ship on fire! And while they were trying to extinguish the flames she ran on a rock, blew up, and drifted ashore just below Hooghly. And what do you think the sailors said? 'That Pattle had been such a scamp that the devil wouldn't let him go out of India!'"

His daughter inherited a strain of that indomitable vitality. If her father was famous for his lies, Mrs. Cameron had a gift of ardent speech and picturesque behaviour which has impressed itself upon the calm pages of Victorian biography. But it was from her mother, presumably, that she inherited her love of beauty and her distaste for the cold and formal conventions of English society. For the sensitive lady whom the sight of her husband's body had killed was a Frenchwoman by birth. She was the daughter of Chevalier Antoine de l'Étang, one of Marie Antoinette's pages, who had been with the Queen in prison till her death, and was only saved by his own youth from the guillotine. With his wife, who had been one of the Queen's ladies, he was exiled to India, and it is at Ghazipur, with the miniature that Marie Antoinette gave him laid upon his breast, that he lies buried.

But the de l'Étangs brought from France a gift of greater value than the miniature of the unhappy Queen. Old Madame de l'Étang was extremely handsome. Her daughter, Mrs. Pattle, was lovely. Six of Mrs. Pattle's seven daughters were even more lovely than she was. "Lady Eastnor is one of the handsomest women I ever saw in any country," wrote Henry Greville of the youngest, Virginia. She underwent the usual fate of early Victorian beauty: was mobbed in the streets, celebrated in odes, and even made the subject of a paper in *Punch* by Thackeray, "On a good-looking lady." It did not matter that the sisters had been brought up by their French grandmother in household lore rather than in book learning. "They were artistic to their finger tips, with an appreciation—almost to be called a culte—for beauty." In India their conquests were many, and when they married and settled in England, they had the art of making round them, whether at Freshwater or at Little Holland House, a society of their own ("Pattledom" it was christened by Sir Henry Taylor), where they could drape and arrange, pull down and build up, and carry on life in a high-handed and adventurous way which painters and writers and even serious men of affairs found much to their liking. "Little Holland House, where Mr. Watts lived, seemed to me a paradise," wrote Ellen Terry, "where only beautiful things were allowed to come. All the women were graceful, and all the men were gifted." There, in the many rooms of the old Dower House, Mrs. Prinsep lodged Watts and Burne Jones, and entertained innumerable friends among lawns and trees which seemed deep in the country, though the traffic of Hyde Park Corner was only two miles distant. Whatever they did, whether in the cause of religion or of friendship, was done enthusiastically.

Was a room too dark for a friend? Mrs. Cameron would have a window built instantly to catch the sun. Was the surplice of the Rev. C. Beanlands only passably clean? Mrs. Prinsep would set up a laundry in her own house and wash the entire linen of the clergy of St. Michael's at her own expense. Then when rela-

31. Julia Margaret Cameron. 'A Beautiful Vision' [Julia Duckworth], 1872.

tions interfered, and begged her to control her extravagance, she nodded her head with its coquettish white curls obediently, heaved a sigh of relief as her counsellors left her, and flew to the writing-table to despatch telegram after telegram to her sisters describing the visit. "Certainly no one could restrain the Pattles but themselves," says Lady Troubridge. Once indeed the gentle Mr. Watts was known to lose his temper. He found two little girls, the granddaughters of Mrs. Prinsep, shouting at each other with their ears stopped so that they could hear no voices but their own. Then he delivered a lecture upon self-will, the vice, he said, which they had inherited from their French ancestress, Madame de l'Étang. "You will grow up imperious women," he told them, "if you are not careful." Had they not into the bargain an ancestor who blew the lid off his coffin?

Certainly Julia Margaret Cameron had grown up an imperious woman; but she was without her sisters' beauty. In the trio where, as they said, Lady Somers was Beauty, and Mrs. Prinsep Dash, Mrs. Cameron was undoubtedly Talent.

"She seemed in herself to epitomize all the qualities of a remarkable family," wrote Mrs. Watts, "presenting them in a doubly distilled form. She doubled the generosity of the most generous of the sisters, and the impulsiveness of the most impulsive. If they were enthusiastic, she was so twice over; if they were persuasive, she was invincible. She had remarkably fine eyes, that flashed like her sayings, and grew soft and tender if she was moved. . . ." But to a child[8] she was a terrifying apparition "short and squat, with none of the Pattle grace and beauty about her, though more than her share of their passionate energy and wilfulness. Dressed in dark clothes, stained with chemicals from her photography (and smelling of them too), with a plump eager face and a voice husky, and a little harsh, yet in some way compelling and even charming," she dashed out of the studio at Dimbola, attached heavy swans' wings to the children's shoulders, and bade them "Stand there" and play the part of the Angels of the Nativity leaning over the ramparts of Heaven.

But the photography and the swans' wings were still in the far future. For many years her energy and her creative powers poured themselves into family life and social duties. She had married, in 1838, a very distinguished man, Charles Hay Cameron, "a Benthamite jurist and philosopher of great learning and ability," who held the place, previously filled by Lord Macaulay, of fourth Member of Council at Calcutta. In the absence of the Governor-General's wife, Mrs. Cameron was at the head of European society in India, and it was this, in Sir Henry Taylor's opinion, that encouraged her in her contempt for the ways of the world when they returned to England. She had little respect, at any rate, for the conventions of Putney. She called her butler peremptorily "Man." Dressed in robes of flowing red velvet, she walked with her friends, stirring a cup of tea as she walked, half-way to the railway station in hot summer weather. There was no eccentricity that she would not have dared on their behalf, no sacrifice that she would not have made to procure a few more minutes of their society. Sir Henry and Lady Taylor suffered the extreme fury of her affection. Indian shawls, turquoise bracelets, inlaid portfolios, ivory elephants, "etc.," showered on their heads. She lavished upon them letters six sheets long "all about ourselves." Rebuffed for a moment, "she told Alice [Lady Taylor] that before the year was out she would love her like a sister," and before the year was out Lady Taylor could hardly imagine what life had been without Mrs. Cameron. The Taylors loved her; Aubrey de Vere loved her; Lady Monteagle loved her; and "even Lord Monteagle, who like eccentricity in no other form, likes her." It was impossible, they found, not to love that "genial, ardent, and generous" woman, who had "a power of loving which I have never seen exceeded, and an equal determination to be loved." If it was impossible to reject her affection, it was even dangerous to reject her shawls. Either she would burn them, she threatened, then and there, or, if the gift were returned, she would sell it, buy with the proceeds a very expensive invalid sofa, and present it to the Putney Hospital for Incurables with an inscription which said, much to the surprise of Lady Taylor, when she chanced upon it, that it was the gift of Lady Taylor herself. It was better, on the whole, to bow the shoulder and submit to the shawl.

Meanwhile she was seeking some more permanent expression of her abundant energies in literature. She translated from the German, wrote poetry, and finished enough of a novel to make Sir Henry Taylor very nervous lest he should be called upon to read the whole of it. Volume after volume was despatched through the penny post. She wrote letters till the postman left, and then she began her postscripts. She sent the gardener after the postman, the gardener's boy after the gardener, the donkey galloping all the way to Yarmouth after the gardener's boy. Sitting at Wandsworth Station she wrote page after page to Alfred Tennyson until "as I was folding your letter came the screams of the train, and then the yells of the porters with the threat that the train would not wait for me," so that she had to thrust the document into strange hands and run down the steps. Every day she wrote to Henry Taylor, and every day he answered her. . . .

. . . But the zenith of Mrs. Cameron's career

was at hand. In 1860 the Camerons bought two or three rose-covered cottages at Freshwater, ran them together, and supplemented them with outhouses to receive the overflow of their hospitality. For at Dimbola—the name was taken from Mr. Cameron's estate in Ceylon—everybody was welcome. "Conventionalities had no place in it." Mrs. Cameron would invite a family met on the steamer to lunch without asking their names, would ask a hatless tourist met on the cliff to come in and choose himself a hat, would adopt an Irish beggar woman and send her child to school with her own children. "What will become of her?" Henry Taylor asked, but comforted himself with the reflection that though Julia Cameron and her sisters "have more of hope than of reason," still "the humanities are stronger in them than the sentimentalities," and they generally brought their eccentric undertakings to a successful end. In fact the Irish beggar child grew up into a beautiful woman, became Mrs. Cameron's parlour-maid, sat for her portrait, was sought in marriage by a rich man's son, filled the position with dignity and competence, and in 1878 enjoyed an income of two thousand four hundred pounds a year. Gradually the cottages took colour and shape under Mrs. Cameron's hands. A little theatre was built where the young people acted. On fine nights they trapesed up to the Tennysons and danced; if it were stormy, and Mrs. Cameron preferred the storm to the calm, she paced the beach and sent for Tennyson to come and pace by her side. The colour of the clothes she wore, the glitter and hospitality of the household she ruled reminded visitors of the East. But if there was an element of "feudal familiarity," there was also a sense of "feudal discipline." Mrs. Cameron was extremely outspoken. She could be highly despotic. "If ever you fall into temptation," she said to a cousin, "down on your knees and think of Aunt Julia." She was caustic and candid of tongue. She chased Tennyson into his tower vociferating "Coward! Coward!" and thus forced him to be vaccinated. She had her hates as well as her loves, and alternated in spirits "between the seventh heaven and the bottomless pit." There were visitors who found her company agitating, so odd and bold were her methods of conversation, while the variety and brilliance of the society she collected round her caused a certain "poor Miss Stephen" to lament: "Is there *nobody* commonplace?" as she saw Jowett's four young men drinking brandy and water, heard Tennyson reciting 'Maud,' while Mr. Cameron wearing a coned hat, a veil, and several coats paced the lawn which his wife in a fit of enthusiasm had created during the night.

In 1865, when she was fifty, her son's gift of a camera gave her at last an outlet for the energies which she had dissipated in poetry and fiction and doing up houses and concocting curries and entertaining her friends. Now she became a photographer. All her sensibility was expressed, and, what was perhaps more to the purpose, controlled in the new born art. The coal-house was turned into a dark room; the fowl-house was turned into a glass-house. Boatmen were turned into King Arthur; village girls into Queen Guenevere. Tennyson was wrapped in rugs: Sir Henry Taylor was crowned with tinsel. The parlour-maid sat for her portrait and the guest had to answer the bell. "I worked fruitlessly but not hopelessly," Mrs. Cameron wrote of this time. Indeed, she was indefatigable. "She used to say that in her photography a hundred negatives were destroyed before she achieved one good result; her object being to overcome realism by diminishing just in the least degree the precision of the focus." Like a tigress where her children were concerned, she was as magnificently uncompromising about her art. Brown stains appeared on her hands, and the smell of chemicals mixed with the scent of the sweet briar in the road outside her house. She cared nothing for the miseries of her sitters nor for their rank. The carpenter and the Crown Prince of Prussia alike must sit as still as stones in the attitudes she chose, in the draperies she arranged, for as long as she wished. She cared nothing for her own labours and failures and exhaustion. "I longed to arrest all the beauty that came before me, and at length the longing was satisfied," she wrote. Painters praised her art; writers marvelled at the character her portraits revealed. She herself blazed up at length into satisfaction with her own creations. "It is a sacred blessing which has attended my photography," she wrote. "It gives pleasure to millions." She lavished her photographs upon her friends and relations, hung them in railway waiting-rooms, and offered them, it is said, to porters in default of small change.

Old Mr. Cameron meanwhile retired more and more frequently to the comparative privacy of his bedroom. He had no taste for society himself, but endured it, as he endured all his wife's vagaries, with philosophy and affec-

tion. "Julia is slicing up Ceylon," he would say, when she embarked on another adventure or extravagance. Her hospitalities and the failure of the coffee crop ("Charles speaks to me of the flower of the coffee plant. I tell him that the eyes of the first grandchild should be more beautiful than any flowers," she said) had brought his affairs into a precarious state. But it was not business anxieties alone that made Mr. Cameron wish to visit Ceylon. The old philosopher became more and more obsessed with the desire to return to the East. There was peace; there was warmth; there were the monkeys and the elephants whom he had once lived among "as a friend and a brother." Suddenly, for the secret had been kept from their friends, the Camerons announced that they were going to visit their sons in Ceylon. Their preparations were made and friends went to say good-bye to them at Southampton. Two coffins preceded them on board packed with glass and china, in case coffins should be unprocurable in the East; the old philosopher with his bright fixed eyes and his beard "dipt in moonlight" held in one hand his ivory staff and in the other Lady Tennyson's parting gift of a pink rose; while Mrs. Cameron, "grave and valiant," vociferated her final injunctions and controlled not only innumerable packages but a cow.

They reached Ceylon safely, and in her gratitude Mrs. Cameron raised a subscription to present the Captain with a harmonium. Their house at Kalutara was so surrounded by trees that rabbits and squirrels and minah birds passed in and out while a beautiful tame stag kept guard at the open door. Marianne North, the traveller, visited them there and found old Mr. Cameron in a state of perfect happiness, reciting poetry, walking up and down the verandah, with his long white hair flowing over his shoulders, and his ivory staff held in his hand. Within doors Mrs. Cameron still photographed. The walls were covered with magnificent pictures which tumbled over the tables and chairs and mixed in picturesque confusion with books and draperies. Mrs. Cameron at once made up her mind that she would photograph her visitor and for three days was in a fever of excitement. "She made me stand with spiky coconut branches running into my head . . . and told me to look perfectly natural," Miss North remarked. The same methods and ideals ruled in Ceylon that had once ruled in Freshwater. A gardener was kept, though there was no garden and the man had never heard of the existence of such a thing, for the excellent reason that Mrs. Cameron thought his back "absolutely superb." And when Miss North incautiously admired a wonderful grass green shawl that Mrs. Cameron was wearing, she seized a pair of scissors, and saying: "Yes, that would just suit you," cut it in half from corner to corner and made her share it. At length, it was time for Miss North to go. But still Mrs. Cameron could not bear that her friends should leave her. As at Putney she had gone with them stirring her tea as she walked, so now at Kalutara she and her whole household must escort her guest down the hill to wait for the coach at midnight. Two years later (in 1879) she died. The birds were fluttering in and out of the open door; the photographs were tumbling over the tables; and, lying before a large open window Mrs. Cameron saw the stars shining, breathed the one word "Beautiful," and so died.

1. See Cameron's translation of Gottfried Bürger's poem in Mike Weaver, *Julia Margaret Cameron, 1815–1879* (London: Herbert Press, 1984), pp. 146–51; her preface and sole review in Helmut Gernsheim, *Julia Margaret Cameron: Her Life and Photographic Work* (Millerton, N.Y.: Aperture, 1975), pp. 184–85; "On receiving a copy of Arthur Clough's Poems at Fresh Water Bay" (1862), written to Clough's widow, who had visited the Isle of Wight before the poet's premature death, in Weaver, *Cameron*, pp. 154–57; and "On a Portrait" (1875) in Gernsheim, *Cameron*, p. 185, and Weaver, *Cameron*, p. 158.

2. Cited in Amanda Hopkinson, *Julia Margaret Cameron* (London: Virago Press, 1986), p. 78. The Thackerays were close friends of Mrs. Cameron's, and after the author's death, his two daughters stayed with her; the eldest, Anne Thackeray Ritchie, received one of Mrs. Cameron's albums, now at the HRHRC. Both have recorded their memories of Cameron, as has Tennyson's son, Hallam: see Anne Thackeray Ritchie: Letter to Walter Senior [Easter, 1865], in *Letters of Anne Thackeray Ritchie*, ed. Hester Ritchie (London: John Murray, 1924), pp. 125–27, reprinted in *Thackeray and His Daughter: The Letters and Journals of Anne Thackeray Ritchie*, ed. Hester Ritchie (London and New York: Harper and Brothers, 1924), pp. 138–40; *Records of Tennyson, Ruskin and Browning* (London: Macmillan; New York: Harper & Brothers, 1892), pp. 43–44; "Mrs. Cameron," in *From Friend to Friend*, ed. Emily Ritchie (London: John Murray, 1919), pp. 1–39; and *Recollections of Anne Thackeray Ritchie*, comp. Hester Thackeray Fuller and Violet Hammersley (Dublin: Euphorion Books, 1951), pp. 109–14, 116–17, 155; Hester Thackeray Fuller, *Three Freshwater Friends: Tennyson, Watts and Mrs. Cameron* (Newport, Isle of Wight: County Press, 1936), pp. 32–34; and

Hallam Tennyson, *Alfred Lord Tennyson, A Memoir by His Son* (London: Macmillan, 1987), vol. 1, pp. 513–14, and vol. 2, pp. 85–86.

3. For reproductions and valuable commentary on these portraits and tableaux, see Anita Ventura Mozley's exhibition catalogue, *Mrs. Cameron's Photographs from the Life* (Palo Alto, Calif.: Stanford University, 1974); Colin Ford, *The Cameron Collection* (London: Van Nostrand Reinhold in association with the National Portrait Gallery, 1975); and Weaver, *Cameron*, passim. For a detailed discussion of Cameron's illustrations for the *Idylls,* see Charles W. Millard, "Julia Margaret Cameron and Tennyson's *Idylls of the King,*" *Harvard Library Bulletin* 21, no. 2 (April 1, 1973): 187–201.

4. See [Coventry Patmore], "Mrs. Cameron's Photographs," *Macmillan's Magazine* 13 (January 1866): 230–31, and the Hugo letter, translated and quoted in Gernsheim, *Cameron,* p. 67.

5. Cameron's many pictures of her favorite niece, Julia, who married Leslie Stephen after the death of her first husband, Herbert Duckworth, are widely reproduced in Gernsheim, Weaver, and elsewhere; Cameron's photograph of Woolf's father is reproduced in Frederic William Maitland, *The Life and Letters of Leslie Stephen* (London: Duckworth; New York: G. Putnam's Sons, 1906), insert facing p. 197. For corrections to Woolf's account of her great-aunt for the Hogarth Press publication of *Victorian Photographs of Famous Men and Fair Women* (London, 1926), see Gernsheim, *Cameron,* pp. 15–57, and the "Editor's Note" in Cameron, *Victorian Photographs of Famous Men and Fair Women* (Boston : Godine, 1973), p. 21. Woolf's study of Cameron inspired her only play, *Freshwater: A Comedy,* ed. Lucio P. Ruotolo (New York: Harvest/Harcourt Brace Jovanovitch, 1976), which was drafted in 1923 and revised when produced as a Bloomsbury private theatrical in 1935.

6. *Orlando* (London: Hogarth Press, 1928) contains a few photographs of Vita Sackville-West, who inspired the book, while those in *Three Guineas* (1938) portray the splendid dress of members of the English ruling class, who are contrasted and linked with victims of the Spanish Civil War as seen in news photographs (pp. 20–21), described but not reproduced by Woolf in a cause and effect argument many readers failed to understand or appreciate. The unattributed photographs in both works were probably taken by Leonard Woolf, who used them similarly in *Quack, Quack!* (London: Hogarth, 1935), as noted by Diane Gillespie, "'Her Kodak Pointed at His Head': Virginia Woolf and Photography," in *Virginia Woolf: Themes and Variations,* eds. Vera Neveroc-Furk and Mark Hussey (New York: Pace University Press, 1993), p. 39. See Julia Duffy and Lloyd Davis, "Demythologizing Facts and Photographs in Virginia Woolf's *Three Guineas,*" in Marsha Bryant, ed., *Photo-Textualities: Reading Photographs and Literature* (Newark: University of Delaware Press, forthcoming). For more contextual details of Woolf's involvement with photography, see Val Williams, "Only Connecting: Julia Margaret Cameron and Bloomsbury," *The Photographic Collector* 4, no. 1 (Spring 1983): 40–49, and "Carefully Creating an Idyll: Vanessa Bell and Snapshot Photography 1907–1946," *Women Photographers* (London: Virago, 1986), pp. 80–83.

7. See portraits of and comments about Woolf by Gisèle Freund, "Virginia Woolf," *The World in My Camera,* trans. June Guicharnaud (New York: Dial Press, 1974), pp. 129–37; Man Ray, *Self-Portrait* (Boston: New York Graphic Society, 1988), p. 153, whose comments refer to pictures reproduced in *Man Ray Photographs,* trans. Carolyn Breakspear (London: Thames and Hudson, 1987), pp. 219–20; Lady Ottoline Morrell, *Lady Ottoline's Album,* ed. Carolyn G. Heilbrun (New York: Knopf, 1976), pp. 72–75, 78–80; Vanessa Bell, *Vanessa Bell's Family Album,* comp. Quentin Bell and Angelica Garnett (London: Jill Norman & Hobhouse, 1981); and Gillespie, "'Her Kodak Pointed at His Head.'" The Harvard University Theatre Collection has about 1400 photographs that belonged to Leonard and Virginia Woolf, including seven albums of snapshots. See also Roger Poole, "A Phenomenological Reading of Certain Photographs," in *Virginia Woolf Miscellanies: Proceedings of the First Annual Conference on Virginia Woolf,* ed. Mark Hussey and Vara Neverow-Turk (New York: Pace University Press, 1992), pp. 172–76.

8. [Woolf's note] Lady Troubridge, *Memories and Reflections,* p. 34.

17. Émile Zola

FROM *The Rush for the Spoil*, 1871

Zola (1840–1902) is best known as the leader of French naturalism, which inspired novelists to portray contemporary life with scientific objectivity, not idealism or artifice. Far more than the realists, he and his many Western adherents stressed the importance of heredity, the impact of industrialism on rural life, and the rise of the self-conscious worker in works like Nana *(1880) and* Germinal *(1885). In 1864, Zola had compared his work to a photograph—"a reproduction that is exact, frank and naive"—but he resented the "stupid reproach" that naturalist writers "wish to be merely photographers."[1] In this sophisticated scene, he shows his amoral heroine amusing herself with the popular carte-de-visite portraits, collected by her stepson-lover, to suggest the decadence of Second Empire life.[2] Around 1888, Zola transferred his keen powers of observation to making photographs. Avidly pursuing his new hobby, he bought several cameras and established darkrooms wherever he lived. Before his accidental death in 1902, Zola took, developed, and printed thousands of pictures in France and also in England (1898–99), where he avoided imprisonment for his advocacy of the accused in the Dreyfus case;[3] his favorite subjects were his wife, his mistress (and their two children), Paris scenes [Fig. 33], and innovations like the railroad, the Eiffel Tower, and the department store. The influence of Zola on the literature of his era is well documented. Less acknowledged is his effect on artists like Alfred Stieglitz, who, after reading his novels in the 1880's in Berlin, began photographing previously unfashionable gritty urban subjects after returning to New York City in the early 1890's.[4]*

FROM *The Rush for the Spoil*

. . . Maxime now instructed Renée. When he went to the Bois with her he told her stories about prostitutes which greatly enlivened her. A new woman could not appear near the lake without his setting forth on a campaign to ascertain the name of her protector, the allowance he made her, and the style in which she lived. He was acquainted with these ladies' homes, and with the particulars of their private life; indeed he was a perfect living catalogue in which all the harlots were numbered, with a complete description of each of them. This gazette of scandal was Renée's delight. On race-days at Longchamps, when she passed by in her carriage, she listened eagerly, albeit retaining her haughtiness as a woman of good society, to the story of how Blanche Muller deceived her embassy attaché with a hair-dresser; or how the little baron had found the count in his drawers in the alcove of a skinny, red-haired notoriety who was called the Crawfish. Each day brought its tattle. When the story was rather too stiff Maxime lowered his voice, but he nevertheless went on to the end. Renée opened her eyes wide, like a child to whom a good trick is related, restrained her laughter, and then stifled it in her embroidered handkerchief, which she gently pressed to her lips. Maxime also brought these women's photographs. He had portraits of actresses in all his pockets and even in his cigar case. At times he had a clearing out and placed these women in the album which was always trailing over the furniture in the drawing-room, and which already contained the portraits of Renée's female friends. There was also some men's photographs in it, Messieurs de Rozan, Simpson, De Chibray, and De Mussy, as well as actors, writers, and deputies who had come to swell the collection no one knew how. It was a strangely mixed society, the prototype of the jumble of ideas and personages that crossed Renée's and Maxime's lives. Whenever it rained, or whenever one was bored, this album proved a great subject of conversation. It always ended by falling under one's hand. The young woman opened it with a sigh for the hundredth time perhaps. By-and-by, how-

33. Émile Zola. 'Parc Monceau, with bust of Guy de Maupassant,' c. 1900.

ever, her curiosity was awakened and the young fellow came and leant behind her. Then long discussions began about the Crawfish's hair, Madam de Meinhold's double chin, Madame de Lauwerens's eyes, and Blanche Muller's bosom; about the Marchioness's nose, which was a trifle on one side, and about the mouth of little Sylvia, who was notorious for her thick lips. They compared the women with each other.

"For myself, if I were a man," said Renée, "I should choose Adeline."

"That's because you don't know Sylvia," answered Maxime, "she has such a funny style. For myself, I prefer Sylvia."

The pages were turned over; at times the Duke de Rozan or Mr. Simpson, or the Count de Chibray appeared, and Maxime added, sneering:

"Besides, your taste is perverted, everyone knows it. Can you see anything more stupid than these gentlemen's faces? Rozan and Chibray look like Gustave, my barber."

Renée shrugged her shoulders, as if to say that this irony did not affect her. She still forgot herself in contemplating the wan, smiling, or stern faces which the album contained; she tarried longer over the portraits of the fast women, and inquisitively studied the exact microscopical details of the photographs, the little wrinkles and the little hairs. One day she even procured a strong magnifying glass, fancying she had perceived a hair on the Crawfish's nose. And, indeed, the glass revealed a slight golden thread which had strayed from the eyebrows down to the middle of the nose. This hair amused them for a long time. For a whole week the ladies who called had to assure themselves in person of the presence of this hair. Thenceforth the magnifying glass served to scrutinize the women's faces. Renée made some astonishing discoveries; she found some unknown wrinkles, rough skins, cavities imperfectly filled up with rice powder. And Maxime ended by hiding the magnifying glass, declaring that one ought not to disgust oneself with the human face like that. The truth was that she scrutinized too closely the thick lips of Sylvia, for whom he had a particular affection. They then invented a new game. They asked this question: "With whom would I willingly spend a night?" and they opened the album, which was entrusted with the duty of replying. This gave rise to some strange couplings. Renée's female friends played at the game during several evenings, and Renée herself was successively married to the Archbishop of Paris, to Baron Gouraud, to M. De Chibray, at which she greatly laughed, and to her husband in person, at which she was greatly distressed. As for Maxime, either by chance, or by the maliciousness of Renée, who opened the album, he always fell upon the Marchioness. But there was never so much laughter as when luck coupled two men or two women together. [Paris: C. Marpa and E. Flammarion, n.d. (1871)]

1. Zola, quoted by Jean Adhémar, "Émile Zola, Photographer," in Van Deren Coke, ed., *One Hundred Years of Photographic History* (Albuquerque: University of New Mexico Press, 1975), p. 4, and Zola, "The Experimental Novel" (1880), quoted in *Documents of Modern Literary Realism,* ed. George J. Becker (Princeton, N.J.: Princeton University Press, 1963), p. 168. As John Lambeth noted, in conversation with the editor on October 25, 1991, Zola had largely stopped writing when he seriously took up photography, which may account for his infrequent references to photography in his works.

2. See Jammes and Janis, *The Art of French Calotype,* pp. 79–80, on this novel, which Eugenia Janis called to the editor's attention.

3. See François Émile-Zola and Massin, *Zola Photographer* (1979), trans. Liliane Emery Tuck (New York: Seaver Books/Henry Holt, 1988), pp. 3–10, for the role of photography in Zola's life and for reproductions of many of his pictures; further photographs are reproduced in *Émile Zola Photographe,* an exhibition catalogue (Chalon-sur-Saone: Musée Nicéphore Nièpce, October 1982). See also Tournier, "Emile Zola Photographe," *Le Crépuscule des masques,* pp. 30–39, and Elinor Shaffer, *Erewhons of the Eye: Samuel Butler as Painter, Photographer and Art Critic* (London: Reaktion Books, 1988), pp. 233–35, who compares Butler's and Zola's photographs.

4. Neil Leonard, "Alfred Stieglitz and Realism," *Art Quarterly* 29 (1966): 278, and Robert E. Haines, *The Inner Eye of Alfred Stieglitz* (Washington, D.C.: University Press of America, 1982), pp. 93 and 101; both note Stieglitz's early interest in literary realism and his special fondness for Zola's novels.

18. *Leo Tolstoy*

FROM *Anna Karenina*, 1875–77

*L*ike many major novelists of the time, Leo Tolstoy (1828–1910), whose epic War and Peace (1866) earned him immortality, occasionally used a fictional photograph to provide a realistic detail of character, setting, or plot—or all of these simultaneously, as here.[1] In this scene from Anna Karenina, *an insightful account of adultery, pictures from a family album deftly and concretely reveal the lovers' newly ambivalent attitudes toward each other after returning from their travels abroad to their disapproving Russian society. Even when Tolstoy later disavowed such worldly writings as the leader of a new, primitive form of Christianity, he himself remained familiar with abundant family photographs, also kept in albums. Most were taken by his wife, Sophia (1844–1919), a serious, sensitive, amateur photographer, who, in 1887, resumed a hobby learned at sixteen, taking, developing, and printing many landscapes and family pictures.[2] These pursuits engaged her own artistic sensibility while distracting her from myriad domestic griefs. The resulting documentation of her husband's last decades—at work [Fig. 34], at rest, and with numerous family members, friends, and admiring colleagues like Chekhov and Gorky at Yasnaya Polyana, Moscow, and the Crimea—added to Tolstoy's legendary stature then and later.[3] Given the Tolstoys' mounting marital discord, the author doubtless viewed some of these photographs—especially their annual anniversary pictures—with the kind of ambivalence he had earlier portrayed so memorably.*

34. Sophia Tolstoy. 'Leo Tolstoy at his desk,' c. 1907.

. . . She got up, and, taking off her hat, took up from the little table an album in which there were photographs of her son at different ages. She wanted to compare them, and began taking them out of the album. She took them all out except one, the latest and best photograph. In it he was in a white smock, sitting astride a chair, with frowning eyes and smiling lips. It was his best, most characteristic expression. With her little supple hands, her white, delicate fingers, that moved with a peculiar intensity to-day, she pulled at a corner of the photograph, but the photograph had caught somewhere, and she could not get it out. There was no paper-knife on the table, and so, pulling out the photograph that was next to her son's (it was a photograph of Vronsky taken at Rome in a round hat with long hair), she used it to push out her son's photograph. "Oh, here is he!" she said, glancing at the portrait of Vronsky, and she suddenly recalled that he was the cause of her present misery. She had not once thought of him all the morning. But now, coming all at once upon that manly, noble face, so familiar and so dear to her, she felt a sudden rush of love for him. [vol. 2, pt. 5, ch. 31, p. 642]

She heard the bell ring before she was ready. When she went into the drawing-room, it was not he, but Yashvin, who met her eyes. Vronsky was looking through the photographs of her son, which she had forgotten on the table, and he made no haste to look round at her.

"We have met already," she said, putting her little hand into the huge hand of Yashvin, whose bashfulness was so queerly out of keeping with his immense frame and coarse face. "We met last year at the races. Give them to me," she said, with a rapid movement snatching from Vronsky the photographs of her son, and glancing significantly at him with flashing eyes. [vol. 2, pt. 5, ch. 31, p. 643]

When Vronsky returned home, Anna was not yet home. . . . That she had gone out without leaving word where she was going, that she had not yet come back, and that all the morning she had been going about somewhere without a word to him—all this, together with the strange look of excitement in her face in the morning, and the recollection of the hostile tone with which she had before Yashvin almost snatched her son's photographs out of his hands, made him serious. He decided he absolutely must speak openly with her. And he waited for her in the drawing room. [vol. 2, pt. 5, ch. 32, p. 645]

1. See Ann Wilsher, "Photography in Literature: The First Seventy Years," *History of Photography* 2, no. 3 (July 1978): 223–34, for a helpful survey of the use of photography by major and minor nineteenth-century writers.

2. For comments on her photographic activities and some reproductions of her works, see *The Diaries of Sophia Tolstoy*, ed. O. A. Golinenko et al., trans. Cathy Porter (New York: Random House, 1985), from p. 84, July 2, 1887, on. For more comprehensive remarks and reproductions, see Sofia Tolstaya and Vladimir G. Chertkov, *Tolstoy in Life* (Tula: Prioskoe, 1988); and Sophia Tolstoy, *Photographies de Sophie Tolstoy*, with an introduction by Serge Tolstoy and text by Pierre Apraxine (Brussels: Mark Bokar, 1991) [seen by the editor in a typescript in English].

3. For further details of this relationship and Sophia's photography, see Yelena V. Barchatova et al., *A Portrait of Tsarist Russia* (New York: Pantheon, 1989), pp. 152 and 156–57. See Tolstaya and Chertkov, *Tolstoy in Life*, p. 69, Plate 79, and p. 253, n. 79, for Sophia's widely reproduced photographs of Tolstoy and Chekhov, and p. 54, for one of Tolstoy and Gorky taken shortly before the latter's arrest and exile as a revolutionary in 1901; the picture was banned in Russia but published abroad as a postcard, according to Braive, *The Era of the Photograph*, p. 298. See also Inge Morath's recent pictures of Yasnaya Polyana in *Russian Journal* (New York: Aperture, 1991), pp. 96–97.

19. Count Philippe-Auguste de Villiers de l'Isle-Adam

"SNAPSHOTS OF WORLD HISTORY" [1878],
FROM *L'Eve future* [*Tomorrow's Eve*], 1880–85

*P*hotography rarely fired the imagination of Villiers (1838–89) or, indeed, most of the French Symbolist writers, except perhaps Rimbaud.[1] The camera registered too accurately the mundane vulgarities and profound evils of their society, from which these artists sought escape. They preferred to evoke—often through musical rhythms, ornate images, and colorful but obscure diction—the "infinite," the "ultimate," and the "ideal" rather than precise reality. Photography probably had little place in Villiers's declining aristocratic family, which provided him with a title, several first names (Jean-Marie-Mathias-Philippe-Auguste), and lofty values, but diminishing funds to support his idiosyncratic lifestyle. But his abiding interest in philosophy, the occult, and in Wagnerian music must have made him receptive to the interests of one of his friends, the poet-inventor Charles Cros, who is credited with conceiving the phonograph before Thomas Edison as well as developing a system of color photography.[2] Cros's photographic experiments in the late 1870's, doubtless informed and may have stimulated this early scene from Villiers's hybrid novel; part philosophical inquiry and part science fiction, the narrative describes the creation of a female android by Edison, who resembles the young Frenchman more than his American original. Through the inventor's meditation on photography, Villiers could safely satirize the chronic discrepancy between human ideals and practices, one of his favorite themes.[3] Interesting also is the forecast of instant photography in the scene's epigraph, supplied by another aristocratic friend who, under the pseudonym Cham, was a photographer as well as a caricaturist and writer.[4]

"Snapshots of World History"

INSTANT PHOTOGRAPHY
A Man Enters: Sir, I'd like to have my pict ...
Photographer, Leaping Forward: Say no more! ... here it is.
　—CHAM

At this point the glance of the engineer fell on that huge magnesium reflector around which the child's voice had been playing a moment before.

—Photography too has come along very late, he continued. Isn't it exasperating to think of all the pictures, portraits, scenes, and landscapes that it could have recorded once, and which are now forever lost to us? Painters use their imaginations; but it's absolute reality that the camera would have brought us. What a difference! . . . Well, there's no help for it; we'll never see again, we'll never *recognize* in their true features the things and the men of former times. Of course it's possible that man will some day be able to recover, either by electricity or by some more subtle means, the undying interstellar reverberations of everything that has occurred on earth; but we'd better not count too much on this discovery, for it's more than probable that the entire solar system will have been vaporized by then in the blazing nebula of the *Zeta* of Hercules, which is drawing us into its orbit with every second that passes. Or at any rate, our planet will have been struck by its satellite, crushed and reduced (for all that its crust is from three to ten leagues thick) to a mere *sack of charcoal*; or else one of our many oscillations on the axis of the planet will have buried us under an enormous layer of ice, as happened in the past. Any one of these things may have happened before we are able to reach into outer space and recapture there the eternal interstellar refraction of things here in the past.

Too bad. For it would have been delightful to possess good photographic prints (taken on the spot) of *Joshua Bidding the Sun Stand Still,* for example. Or why not several different views of *The Earthly Paradise,* taken from the *Gateway of the Flaming Swords;* the *Tree of Knowledge;* the *Serpent;* and so forth? Perhaps a number of shots of *The Deluge, Taken from the Top of Mount Ararat?* (I'll bet that busy Japheth would have carried a camera with him into the Ark, if that marvelous instrument had been available to him.) Later, we would have had photos of *The Seven Plagues of Egypt,* of the *Burning Bush,* and the *Passage of the Red Sea* (with shots before, during, and after the event). There would have been the *Mene, Mene, Tekel, Upharsin* of Belshazzar's Feast, the *Funeral Pyre of Sardanapalus,* the *Standard of Constantinople,* the *Head of Medusa,* the *Minotaur,* etc.; and we would rejoice today in postcards of *Prometheus,* the *Stymphalides,* the *Sybils,* the *Danaids,* the *Furies,* etc., etc.

And all the episodes of the New Testament— what prints they would provide! All the anecdotes of eastern and western history—what a collection! The martyrs, and all the examples of torture, from that of the Seven Maccabees and their mother to those of John of Leyden and Damiens, not forgetting the chief episodes of Christians set against wild beasts in the arenas of Rome, Lyons, and other cities!

One would want, too, all the scenes of torture, from the very beginning of social life down to recent events in the prisons of Holy Inquisition, when the *Monks of Redemption,* equipped with their instruments of iron, spent their leisure time over the years in massacring Moors, heretics, and Jews. And the cruel interrogations that have gone on in the prisons of Germany, Italy, France, the Orient, everywhere, why not those too? The camera, aided by the phonograph (they are near of kin), could reproduce both the sight and the different sounds made by the sufferers, giving a complete, an exact idea of the experience. What an admirable course on instruction for the grade schools, to render healthful the intelligence of modern young people—perhaps even public figures? A splendid magic lantern!

And the portraits of all the great founders of

civilizations, from Nimrod to Napoleon, from Moses to Washington, from Confucius to Mohammed! Pictures of all the famous women, from Semiramis to Catherine the Great, from Thalestris to Joan of Arc, from Zenobia to Christina of Sweden!

And photographs of all the beautiful women, including Venus, Europa, Psyche, Delilah, Rachel, Judith, Cleopatra, Aspasia, Freya, Maneka, Thais, Akedysseril, Roxalana, the Queen of Sheba, Phryne, Circe, Dejanira, Helen, and so on down to the beautiful Pauline Bonaparte! to the Greek veiled by law! to Lady Emma Harte Hamilton!

And of course we'd have all the gods as well, and all the goddesses, down to and including the Goddess Reason, without neglecting Mr. Supreme Being! Life-size, of course!

Well now, isn't it a shame we don't have photographs of that entire crowd? What an album it would make!

Natural history would provide a great field, especially paleontology. There's no doubt in the world that we have a very imperfect notion of the megatherium, for example, that paradoxical pachyderm, and that our notions of the pterodactyl as a gigantic bat, or of the plesiosaurus, monstrous patriarch of the reptiles—are, practically speaking infantile. These strange creatures fought or flew, as their skeletons still bear witness, in the very place where I now stand today, and no more than a few hundred centuries ago, less than no time; less than a quarter or a fifth of the age of this bit of chalk with which I write on the blackboard.

Nature was quick to pass the sponge of her deluges over these awkward sketches, these first nightmares of Life. And yet, what curious prints might have been made of all these creatures! Alas, the vision is lost forever!

The great experimenter heaved a sigh.

—Yes, yes, everything fades, it's true; even discolorations on collodion, even scratches on steel plates. Vanity of vanities, all is vanity, to be sure! One is tempted to smash the camera, blow up the phonograph, and raise one's eyes to the vaults of heaven (which, for that matter, are only a figure of speech) to ask if this gauzy screen of the universe comes to us for free,

or who fuels its great luminary? Who, in a word, pays the rent on this room of ours, insubstantial as it appears, within which the old riddle is constantly being propounded? And where did they dig up these heavy, old-fashioned stage trappings of Time and Space, so trite and patched-up that nobody believes in them anymore?

As for the faithful, I can propose to them a thought which they may well consider naive, paradoxical, superficial—but which is odd. God, we know, is supreme, all powerful, perfectly good; and over the centuries, as everybody knows, He has appeared to numbers of people: to dispute it would be heresy. Yet while all sorts of bad painters and mediocre sculptors have struggled to popularize their notions of His features, to make them *chic,* isn't it painful to think that if He would just allow the slightest, most humble photograph of Himself—or just permit me, Thomas Alva Edison, American engineer, His creature, to make a simple phonographic record of His True Voice (for thunder has lost most of its prestige since Franklin), *the day after that event, there wouldn't be a single atheist left on the earth?*

Thus the great electrician, talking only to himself, toyed playfully with the vague idea—actually a matter of indifference to him—of the vital reflexive spirituality of God.

—But in him who reflects it, the living idea of God appears only to the extent that the faith of the viewer is able to evoke it. Like every other thought, God can exist in the individual only according to the capacity of the individual. No man knows where illusion begins or what reality consists of. Thus, God being the most sublime of conceptions, and all conceptions existing only according to the particular spirit and the *intellectual* eyes of the seer, it follows that the man who dismisses the idea of God from his thoughts does nothing but deliberately decapitate his own mind.

As he pronounced these last words, Edison stopped short in his meditative stroll and looked fixedly out through the great windows into the lunar shadows.

—All right, then, he said suddenly, one challenge for another! Since Life takes such a high hand with us, and answers our questions only with a deep and dubious silence, there's nothing for us to do but see if we can't bring her out of it! . . . In any case, we can already give her a demonstration . . . of what she amounts to in our eyes.

At these words, the eccentric inventor trembled: he had just noted in a ray of moonlight, the dark shadow of a human being, who had moved between him and the light, behind the glass door leading out into the park.

—Who's there? he cried aloud, staring into the dark—and fondling gently in the pocket of his loose dressing-gown of violet silk the butt of a small revolver.

1. See the responses to photography of Villiers's friends Baudelaire and Rimbaud in their selections above and below respectively. See also the occasional work involving photography by Paul Verlaine (1844–96), "Assonances Galantes," in Oeuvres Poétiques Complètes, ed. Jacques Borel (Paris: Gallimard, 1969), pp. 886–87, and Stéphane Mallarmé (1842–98), "Photographies" [1920], written for the photographs of Mme. Méry Laurent, in Oeuvres Complètes, ed. Henri Mondor and G. Jean-Aubry (Paris: Gallimard, 1945), pp. 115–71. See also Villiers, Tomorrow's Eve, trans. Robert Martin Adams (Urbana: University of Illinois, 1986), p. 11, for another reference to the early photography of Nièpce and Daguerre; and Carjat's portraits of Villiers (1865, 1875) in A. W. Raitt, The Life of Villiers de l'Isle-Adam (Oxford: Clarendon Press; New York: Oxford University Press, 1981), fol. p. 238.

2. For more about Cros, see Villiers, Oeuvres Complètes, ed. Alan Raitt and Pierre-Georges Castex, with the collaboration of Jean-Marie Bellefroid (Paris: Gallimard, 1986), vol. 1, pp. 1442–45, and Louis Forestier, Charles Cros (Paris: Minard, 1969), p. 164 as well as 45, 66, and 185. See also an excerpt by Cros, entitled "La Science de l'amour" in André Breton's Anthologie de l'humour noir (Paris: Jean-Jacques Pauvert, 1966), pp. 163–69, called to the editor's attention by Laurence Senelick, which concerns the exchange of photographic portraits; Cros's contain thermometers that register his emotional temperature. See also Raitt, Villiers, p. 354, who notes that when Edison visited Paris in 1889, a copy of L'Eve future was sent to him, but no meeting resulted before Villiers's death the same year.

3. This theme persisted from this novel's conception in 1878 to its final publication in 1885–86 despite other changes. According to Raitt, Life of Villiers, pp. 198–99, 206–7, 290, 303, an incomplete version of L'Eve future was first serialized as L'Eve nouvelle in L'Étoile française (December 14, 1880–February 4, 1881) and revised for its final appearance in La Vie moderne (July 18, 1885–March 27, 1886) and its book publication in May 1886; this chapter was the ninth of the fourteen installments that also appeared in Le Gaulois (September 4–18, 1880). Though the revisions made the novel increasingly less radical theologically and in other ways, the changes in this chapter—to judge by an earlier MS draft reprinted in Oeuvres Complètes, pp. 1493–95, compared to its final versions in La Vie Moderne (July 25, 1885): 496–97 and (August 1, 1885): 510 and in its book form the following year—appear to be mainly stylistic or logical expansions of earlier ideas.

4. Cham was the pseudonym of Count Amédée de Noé, a cartoonist, writer, and photographer who was known for his depictions of street life in all these media, according to Laurence Senelick in a telephone conversation with the editor on January 5, 1993, and biographical dictionaries; further details about this artist or his relationship to Villiers were unavailable.

20. *Arthur Rimbaud*

Rimbaud (1854–91) was the quintessential precocious, rebellious genius who died a painful, premature death. His involvement with photography was characteristically brief but intense. Abandoning a life of brilliant, if sporadic, writing in 1875 to pursue dreams of adventure, Rimbaud restlessly wandered around Europe and the Near East. Finding work in Aden and Harar, later part of Abyssinia (now Ethiopia), he tried to set up as an explorer and trader. One of his earliest plans for making money and preventing boredom involved buying a camera with which to photograph both the Hararis and the strange highlands he hoped to explore for the French Geographical Society.[1] Despite the opposition of his frugal mother, Rimbaud, like Nerval four decades earlier, ordered from Lyon sufficient camera equipment to last for two years. But no expeditions materialized, and the prospective native subjects perhaps feared that the black camera might also "take" their souls.[2] So Rimbaud became involved with other schemes, including gun running and, some suspect, slave trading, all of which ceased with the discovery of his knee tumor; he returned to France for an amputation and soon after died. Though the few photographs that survive are poor [Fig. 35], Rimbaud, like Du Camp before him, embellished the romantic idea of the daring photographer documenting remote, exotic places, no matter what the sordid reality.[3] More significantly, his writing endured, its evocative diction, experimental verse rhythms, and exploitation of the forbidden unconscious influencing both Symbolist and Surrealist artists.[4]

FROM LETTERS FROM ADEN AND HARAR

TO HIS FAMILY,

. . . We are going to send for a camera, and I will send you views of the country and of the people. [from Harar, January 15, 1881, p. 323]

TO HIS FAMILY,

. . . Our photographic and naturalist materials have not yet come, and I think I will have left before they arrive. [from Harar, February 15, 1881, p. 326]

TO HIS FAMILY,

. . . At this moment I am having a camera sent from Lyon. I will take it to Harar, and bring back views of those unfamiliar regions. This will be very profitable. [from Aden, January 18, 1882, p. 341]

TO M. DELAHAYE,5

. . . I am going to compile a work on Harar and the Gallas, which I have explored, and submit it to the Geographical Society. I spent a year in those regions employed by a French trading company.

I have ordered a camera from Lyons which will enable me to include views of these strange districts in my work. [from Aden, January 18, 1882, p. 341]

TO HIS FAMILY,

. . . I wrote to the company's former agent in Aden, Colonel Dubar of Lyon, asking him to send me a complete photographic apparatus, with the object of taking it to Abyssinia, where such a thing is unknown and where it will bring a small fortune in no time at all. [from Harar, September 28, 1882, p. 351]

TO HIS FAMILY,

. . . A letter from Lyon, of October 20th, announces that my photographic equipment is bought. It should be *en route* at the moment [from Aden, November 3, 1882, p. 352].

TO HIS FAMILY,

. . . When I return to Africa, with my photographic equipment, I will send you some interesting things. Here in Aden there is nothing. . . . [from Aden, November 16, 1882, p. 353]

TO HIS MOTHER,

. . . You say I am being robbed. I know very well what a camera alone costs: several hundred francs. But there are chemicals, very numerous and expensive among which are compounds of gold and silver worth up to 250 francs a kilo, [and] there are very expensive lenses, paper, basins, phials and packing materials which increase the sum. I ordered enough supplies to last two years. To my mind, I think I got them inexpensively. I have but one fear, that these things will break *en route* at sea. But if it arrives intact, I will make a large profit, and I will send you some curious things. [from Aden, December 8, 1882, p. 355]

TO HIS FAMILY,

. . . I am leaving again for Harar at the end of the month of March. The forementioned photographic shipment will reach me in a fortnight, and I will be able to use it immediately and repay the cost, which will not be difficult since reproductions of those unknown regions and the unusual types that live here ought to sell in France; and, besides, I will make back an immediate profit, even out here, from the whole. [from Aden, January 6, 1883, p. 357]

TO HIS FAMILY,

. . . The photographic equipment, and all the rest, is in excellent condition. . . . . [from Aden, March 19, 1883, p. 361]

TO HIS FAMILY,

. . . Very soon I will send you another check for 200 francs, because I have to send for mirrors for the photography.

This commission was well done, and if I wish, I will quickly earn back the 2000 francs that this cost me. Here everyone wants his picture taken. They even offer one guinea a photograph. I am not yet well established, or *au courant;* But I will be soon, and I will send you some interesting things.

Enclosed are two [three were sent] photographs of me taken by myself . . . . One of these photographs shows me standing on a terrace of the house, another, standing in a cafe garden [Fig. 35]; another, with my arms crossed in a banana garden. All that has turned white because of the foul water which I use for washing. But I will do better work in the future. This is only to remind you of my face and give you some idea of the scenery here. [from Harar, May 6, 1883, pp. 364–65]

. . . The photography goes well. It was a good idea. I will send you some successful things shortly. [from Harar, May 20, 1883, p. 366]

. . . I am not sending you my photograph; I carefully avoid all unnecessary expenses. Besides I am always badly dressed; one can wear nothing here but very light cotton. [from Aden, January 15, 1885, p. 397]

1. One wonders how much of Rimbaud's urge to pursue photography was due to the influence of Charles Cros, one of Rimbaud's first champions as well as an inventor working on color photography at the time. For his relationship with Rimbaud, see Forestier, *Charles Cros*, pp. 94–101, and see index, p. 52, for other references involving the two friends. See also the Villiers de l'Isle-Adam selection above.

2. Asserted by Enid Starkie, in *Arthur Rimbaud in Abyssinia* (Oxford: Clarendon University Press, 1937), pp. 24–25; see also Duncan Forbes, *Rimbaud in Ethiopia* (Hythe, England: Volturna Press, 1979), pp. 12–40, for further details in a fuller context, and the Nadar and Champfleury selections above about this fear of the camera.

3. Only six of Rimbaud's photographs have survived, including three self-portraits, one of his Greek clerk, and scenes of the Harar marketplace and an Abyssinian hut. Five are in the Musée Rimbaud at Charleville-Mezières, France, and all are reproduced in Henri Matarasso, *Album Rimbaud* (Paris: Gallimard, 1967), pp. 250–55. The only comment on them comes in a letter of July 24, 1885, from Alfred Bardet in Vichy, whose brother Pierre in Lyon had hired Rimbaud to work in his coffee export business: "My brother has forwarded the photographs that you wanted him to send me. I thank you very much for this attention. I got great pleasure seeing something of Harar again. . . . Several of your photographs are a bit blurred, but you can see that there is progress because the others are perfect," quoted in Rimbaud, *Oeuvres Complètes*, ed. Antoine Adam (Paris: Gallimard, 1972), p. 366.

4. See, for example, Rimbaud, *A Season in Hell*, trans. Paul Schmidt, with eight photographs by Robert Mapplethorpe (New York: Limited Editions Club, 1986).

5. Ernest Delahaye, one of his schoolboy friends, had written to him at the request of Paul Verlaine, Rimbaud's sometime friend and fellow poet, who wanted to find out where he was.

21. Anton Chekhov

"THE ALBUM," 1884

his tale by Chekhov (1860–1904), the celebrated author of realistic short stories and more abstract plays, appeared in his first collection, which was published the same year he became a doctor and developed the first symptoms of fatal tuberculosis. Chekhov remained intrigued by both the imaginative and documentary possibilities of photography. Indeed, critics occasionally compared him to a photographer, whose scenes, like those taken by a camera, appeared utterly impartial.[1] Here he uses the photographic album to dramatize the differing public and private realities that characterize many conventional occasions; in another short story, "Vint" (1884), he uses photographs of provincial administrators pasted on cards being played by their clerks, who enjoy this safe way of demeaning their superiors.[2] In 1890, while studying the spartan conditions on the island of Sakhalin, where the czarist government exiled its most dangerous prisoners, Chekhov may have considered accompanying the text of his future book on the subject with photographs. He ordered specific scenes from the local photographer, I. I. Pavalovsky; though doubtless useful as an aide-mémoire, they were not included as illustrations in any of his published accounts about Sakhalin (1891–95).[3] Judging from the size of his personal photography collection, Chekhov always cherished visual records of his family, friends, and theatrical productions.[4]

Kraterov, the titular councillor, as thin and slender as the Admiralty spire, stepped forward and, addressing Zhmyhov, said:

"Your Excellency! Moved and touched to the bottom of our hearts by the way you have ruled us during long years, and by your fatherly care. ..."

"During the course of more than ten years ..." Zakusin prompted.

"During the course of more than ten years, we, your subordinates, on this so memorable for us ... er ... day, beg your Excellency to accept in token of our respect and profound gratitude this album with our portraits in it, and express our hope that for the duration of your distinguished life, that for long, long years to come, to your dying day you may not abandon us. ..."

"With your fatherly guidance in the path of justice and progress ..." added Zakusin, wiping from his brow the perspiration that had suddenly appeared on it; he was evidently longing to speak, and in all probability had a speech ready. "And," he wound up, "may your standard fly for long, long years in the career of genius, industry, and social self-consciousness."

A tear trickled down the wrinkled left cheek of Zhmyhov.

"Gentlemen!" he said in a shaking voice, "I did not expect, I had no idea that you were going to celebrate my modest jubilee. ... I am touched ... Indeed ... very much so. ... I shall not forget this moment to my dying day, and believe me ... believe me, friends, that no one is so desirous of your welfare as I am ... and if there has been anything ... it was for your benefit ..."

Zhmyhov, the actual civil councillor, kissed the titular councillor Kraterov, who had not expected such an honour, and turned pale with delight. Then the chief made a gesture that signified that he could not speak for emotion, and shed tears as though an expensive album had not been presented to him, but on the contrary, taken from him. ... Then when he had a little recovered and said a few mere words

full of feeling and given everyone his hand to shake, he went downstairs amid loud and joyful cheers, got into his carriage and drove off, followed by their blessings. As he sat in his carriage he was aware of a flood of joyous feelings such as he had never known before, and once more he shed tears.

At home new delights awaited him. There his family, his friends, and acquaintances had prepared him such an ovation that it seemed to him that he really had been of very great service to his country, and that if he had never existed his country would perhaps have been in a very bad way. The jubilee dinner was made up of toasts, speeches, and tears. In short, Zhmyhov had never expected that his merits would be so warmly appreciated.

"Gentlemen!" he said before the dessert, "two hours ago I was recompensed for all the sufferings a man has to undergo who is the servant, so to say, not of routine, not of the letter, but of duty! Through the whole duration of my service I have constantly adhered to the principle;—the public, and to-day I received the highest reward! My subordinates presented me with an album ... see! I was touched."

Festive faces bent over the album and began examining it.

"It's a pretty album," said Zhmyhov's daughter Olya, "it must have cost fifty roubles, I do believe. Oh, it's charming! You must give me the album, papa, do you hear? I'll take care of it, it's so pretty."

After dinner Olya carried off the album to her room and shut it up in her table drawer. Next day she took the clerks out of it, flung them on the floor, and put her school friends in their place. The government uniforms made way for white pelerines. Kolya, his Excellency's little son, picked up the clerks and painted their clothes red. Those who had no moustaches he presented with green moustaches and added brown beards to the beardless. When there was nothing left to paint he cut the little men out of the card-board, pricked their eyes with a pin, and began playing soldiers with them. After cutting out the titular councillor Kraterov, he fixed him on a match-box and carried him in the state to his father's study.

"Papa, a monument, look!"

Zhmyhov burst out laughing, lurched for-ward, and, looking tenderly at the child, gave him a warm kiss on the cheek.

"There, you rogue, go and show mamma; let mamma look too."

1. For example, see P. Pertsov, "Iz'iany tvorchestva (Povesti i rasskazy A. Chekova) " [Defective Works (Tales and Short Stories of A. Chekhov)], *Russkoe bogatstyo*, 1 (1893): 43–44: Chekhov takes snapshots of everything "with exactly the same impartiality. His camera does not distinguish between a lovely landscape, the thoughtful face of a young girl, the disheveled figure of an unsuccessful intellectual . . . , an obtuse merchant, or the disgraceful social order. . . ." This citation and translation were provided to the editor by Cathy Popkin.

2. See Chekhov, "Vint," in *The Unknown Chekhov: Stories and Other Writings Hitherto Untranslated,* ed. and trans. Avraham Yarmolinsky (London: Peter Owen, 1954), pp. 61–65, referred to as "The Game of Whist" by Braive, *The Era of the Photograph*, p. 171, and as "Whist" in *The Tales of Chekhov,* trans. Constance Garnett (London: Macmillan, 1917–23), vol. 13, p. 312, who notes that it and "The Album" were included by Chekhov in his *Collected Works* (1899–1902), though not in most subsequent English collections of the short stories.

3. The first English edition of his account, *The Island: A Journey to Sakhalin,* trans. Luba and Michael Terpak (New York: Washington Square Press, 1967), does not mention anything about photographs; the most recent one, *Chekhov, A Journey to Sakhalin,* trans. Brian Reeve (Cambridge, England: Ian Faulkner, 1993), includes unattributed photographs from V. M. Doroshevich, *Sakhalin* (St. Petersburg: Syten, 1903). But Mark Teplinskii, *A. P. Chekhov Na Sakhaline* [A. P. Chekhov on Sakhalin] (Iuzhno-Sakhalinsk: Dal'neostochnoe Knizhnoe Izd-vo,

Sakhalinskoe Otd-nie, 1990), p. 76, discusses Chekhov's order from Pavlovsky, and E. N. Dunaeva, "K Istorii Roboty nad Knigoi: Ostrov Sakhalin" [Towards a History of Work on the Book 'Sakhalin Island'], *Literaturnoe Nasledstovo* (Moscow: Nauka, 1977), vol. 87, pp. 263–93, reproduces them; these sources were provided to the editor by Cathy Popkin and publication data were translated by her and by William M. Todd.

See also earlier discussions in Jean Mitry, *Schriftsteller als Photographen 1860–1919* (Lucerne: C. J. Bücher, 1975), pp. 15–16, 31–42, who attributes the Sakhalin photographs to Chekhov, as does Elsbeth Wolffheim, *Anton Cechov in Selbstzeugnissen und Bilddokumenten* (Reinbek bei Hamburg: Rowohlt, 1982), pp. 75, 78, and 79. Y[elena V.] Barchatova et al., *A Portrait of Tsarist Russia* (New York: Pantheon, 1989), pp. 153–55, states that "Chekhov was another writer who included photography among his skills" but reproduces some of Pavlovsky's photographs without further elaboration or explanation, while Erwin Koppen, *Literatur und Photographie: Über Geschichte und Thematik Einer Medienentdeckung* (Stuttgart: J. B. Metzler, 1987), pp. 208–9, states that it isn't clear whether Chekhov took the pictures himself or commissioned them, but suggests he may not have published them because of czarist censorship.

4. For further information about Chekhov's personal photograph collection and reproductions from it, see Barchatova et al., *Portrait of Tsarist Russia,* pp. 150–60. See also Morath's recent picture of Chekhov's house at Yalta, in *Russian Journal,* p. 103.

22. John Ruskin

FROM *The Works of John Ruskin, 1845–89*

*T*he writings of Ruskin *(1819–1900), the vastly influential critic of Victorian art and society, occupy nearly forty volumes. His initial championing of Turner's paintings and of medieval architecture soon broadened to include all feudal, heroic, and Christian ideals in opposition to science, industrialization, and the competitive greed both inspired. Ruskin initially welcomed photography as a "blessed invention," enchanted by its ability to document nature and architecture, and he urged artists to paint in a similarly fresh and accurate manner. Valuing photographs as aids in his own work, he closely supervised his servants, who had been hired to take daguerreotypes, among their other duties, of the complex buildings he analyzed in his landmark volume,* The Stones of Venice *(1851–53).[1] Later he would claim to have taken the first "sun-portrait" of a Swiss alp [Fig. 37].[2] Yet, over the years, Ruskin remained ambivalent about having portraits taken of himself—even perhaps when he was the Slade Professor of Art at Oxford and the photographer was his colleague Lewis Carroll [Fig. 36].[3] Increasingly embittered by a society that ignored or misinterpreted his idealistic, if often naive, prescriptions, and often unstable mentally, Ruskin came to regard all photography as a literal and figurative* bête noire, *yet another example of a machine undermining the creativity, spirit, and dignity of human labor.[4]*

36. Lewis Carroll. 'John Ruskin,' 1875.

37. John Hobbs. 'Chamoni: La Mer de Glace,' c. 1849.

It must have been during my last days at Oxford that Mr. Liddell, the present Dean of Christ Church,[5] told me of the original experiments of Daguerre. My Parisian friends obtained for me the best examples of his results; and the plates sent to me in Oxford were certainly the first examples of the sun's drawing that were ever seen in Oxford, and, I believe, the first sent to England.

Wholly careless at that time of finished detail, I saw nothing in the Daguerreotype to help, or alarm me; and inquired no more concerning it, until now at Venice I found a French artist producing exquisitely bright small plates, (about four inches square,) which contained, under a lens, the Grand Canal or St. Mark's Place as if a magician had reduced the reality to be carried away into an enchanted land. The little gems of picture cost a napoleon each; but with two hundred francs I bought the Grand Canal from the Salute to the Rialto; and packed it away in thoughtless triumph.

I had no time then to think of the new power, or its meanings; my days were overweighted already. [*Praeterita* (1886–87), vol. 35, pp. 372–73]

I have been lucky enough to get from a poor Frenchman here, said to be in distress, some most beautiful, though very small, Daguerreotypes of the palaces I have been trying to draw; and certainly Daguerreotypes taken by this vivid sunlight are glorious things. It is very nearly the same thing as carrying off the palace itself; every chip of stone and stain is there, and of course there is no mistake about proportions. I am very much delighted with these, and am going to have some more made of pet bits. It is a noble invention—say what they will of it—and any one who has worked and blundered and stammered as I have done for four days, and then sees the thing he has been trying to do so long in vain, done perfectly and faultlessly in half a minute, won't abuse it afterwards. [Letter to father from Venice, October 7, 1845, vol. 3, p. 210, n. 2]

Amongst all the mechanical poison that this terrible 19th century has poured upon men, it has given us at any rate one antidote—the Daguerreotype. It's a most blessed invention; that's what it is. [Letter to father from Padua, October 15, 1845, vol. 3, p. 110, n. 2]

I once intended the illustration to these volumes to be more numerous and elaborate, but the art of photography now enables any reader to obtain as many memoranda of the facts of nature as he needs. . . . [*Modern Painters*, 3 (1846), vol. 5, p. 9]

My drawings are truth to the very letter—too literal, perhaps, so says my father, so says not the Daguerreotype, for it beats me grievously. I have allied myself with it; sith [*sic*] it may no better be, and have brought away some precious records from Florence. It is certainly the most marvellous invention of the century; given us, I think, just in time to save some evidence from the great public of wreckers. As regards art, I wish it had never been discovered, it will make the eye too fastidious to accept mere handling. [Letter to W. H. Harrison, August 12, 1846, vol. 3, p. 210, n. 2]

. . . A power of obtaining veracity in the representation of material and tangible things, which, within certain limits and conditions, is unimpeachable, has now been placed in the hands of all men, almost without labour. I intended to have given a sketch in this place . . . of the probable results of the daguerreotype and calotype within the next few years, in modifying the application of the engravers' art, but I have not had time to complete the experiments necessary to enable me to speak with certainty. [*The Stones of Venice* (1853), vol. 11, p. 199]

All art is great, and good, and true, only so far as it is distinctively the work of *manhood* in its entire and highest sense; that is to say, not the work of limbs and fingers, but of the soul aided, according to her necessities, by the inferior powers; and therefore distinguished in essence from all products of those inferior powers unhelped by the soul. For as a photograph is not a work of art, though it requires certain delicate manipulations of paper and acid, and subtle calculations of time, in order to bring out a good result; so neither would a drawing *like* a photograph, made directly from nature, be a work of art, though it would imply many delicate manipulations of the pencil and subtle manipulations of the pencil and subtle calculations of colour and shade. It is not more art to manipulate a camel's-hair pencil, than to manipulate a china tray and a glass vial. It is no more art to lay on colour delicately, than to lay on acid delicately. It is no more art to use the cornea and retina for the reception of an image, than to use a lens and a piece of silvered paper. But the moment that inner part of the man, or rather that entire and only being of the man, of which cornea and retina, fingers and hands, pencils and colours, are all the mere servant, and instruments; that manhood which has light in itself, though the eyeball is sightless, and can gain in strength when the hand and the foot are hewn off and cast into the fire; the moment this part of the man stands forth with its solemn "Behold, it is I," then the work becomes art indeed, perfect in honour, priceless in value, boundless in power. [*The Stones of Venice* (1853), vol. 11, pp. 201–2]

. . . I have used the help of the daguerreotype without scruple . . . for the present series [about Venetian architecture]; and I much regret that artists in general do not think it worth their while to perpetuate some of the beautiful effects which the daguerreotype alone can seize. [*The Stones of Venice* (1853), vol. 11, p. 312]

Fifteen years ago, I knew everything that the photographs could and could *not* do; —I have long ceased to take the slightest interest in it, my attention being wholly fixed upon the possibility of wresting *luminous* decomposition which literally *paints* with sunlight—no chemist has yet succeeded in doing this. . . . [Letter to Julia Margaret Cameron, February 23, 1863, vol. 37, p. 734]

I tell you (dogmatically, if you like to call it so, knowing it well) a square inch of man's engraving is worth all the photographs that were ever dipped in acid (or left half-washed afterwards, which is saying something). Only it must be man's engraving, not machine's engraving. . . . Believe me, photography can do against line engraving just what Madame Tussaud's wax-work can do against sculpture. That and no more. [*The Cestus of Agalia* (1865), vol. 19, p. 89]

Photographs have an imitable mechanical refinement, and their legal evidence is of great use if you knew how to cross-examine them. They are popularly supposed to be "true," and, at the worst, they are so, in the sense in which an echo is true to a conversation of which it omits the most important syllables and reduplicates the rest. But this truth of mere transcript has nothing to do with Art properly so called; and will never supercede it. [*Cestus of Agalia* (1865), vol. 19, p. 150]

Let me assure you, once for all, that photographs supersede no single quality nor use of fine art, and have so much in common with nature, that they even share her temper of parsimony, and will themselves give you nothing valuable that you do not work for. They supersede no good art, for the definition of art is "Human labour regulated by human design," and this design, or evidence of active intellect in choice and arrangement, is the essential part of the work; which so long as you cannot perceive, you perceive no art whatsoever; which when once you do perceive, you will perceive also to be replaceable by no mechanism. But, farther, photographs will give you nothing you do not work for. They are invaluable for record of some kinds of acts, and for giving transcripts of drawings by great masters; but neither in the photographed scene, nor photographed drawing, will you see any true good, more than in the things themselves, until you have given the appointed price in your own attention and toil. And when once you have paid this price, you will not care for photographs of landscape. They are not true, though they seem so. They are merely spoiled nature. If it is not human design you are looking for, there is more beauty in the next wayside bank than in all the sun-blackened paper you could collect in a lifetime. Go and look at the real landscape, and take care of it; do not think you can get the good of it in a black stain portable in a folio. But if you care for human thought and passion, then learn yourselves to watch the course and fall of the light by whose influence you live, and to share in the joy of human spirits in the heavenly gifts of sunbeam and shade. For I tell you truly, that to a quiet heart, and healthy brain, and industrious hand, there is more delight, and use, in the dappling of one wood-glade with flowers and sunshine, than to the restless, heartless, and idle could be brought by a panorama of a belt of the world, photographed round the equator. [*Lectures on Art, 6: Light* (1870), vol. 20, p. 165]

Anything more beautiful than the photographs of the valley of Chamouni, now in your print-sellers' windows, cannot be conceived. For geographical and geological purposes they are worth anything; for art purposes, worth—a great deal less than zero. [*The Eagles' Nest* (1872), vol. 22, p. 220]

My chemical friends, if you wish ever to know anything rightly concerning the arts, I very urgently advise you to throw away all your vials and washes down the gutter-trap; and if you will ascribe, as you think it so clever to do, in your modern creeds, all virtue to the sun, use that virtue through your own heads and fingers, and apply your solar energies to draw a skillful line or two, for once or twice in your life. You may learn more by trying to engrave . . . the tip of an ear, or the curl of a lock of hair, than by photographing the entire population of the United States of America,—black, white, and neutral-tint. [*Ariadne Florentina* (1872), vol. 22, pp. 376–77]

Photographs are horrid things! [Letter of May 22 (1881) to Faunthorpe, 38: 643]

It must be three or four years now since I was in London . . . and I don't know London any more, nor where I am in it—except the Strand. In which, walking up and down the other day, and meditating over its wonderful displays of etchings and engravings and photographs, all done to perfection such as I had never thought possible in my younger days, it became an extremely searching and troublesome question with me what was to come of all this literally "black art," and how it as to influence the people of our great cities. For the first force of it—clearly in that field every one is doing his sable best: there is no scamped photography nor careless etching; and for second force, there is a quantity of living character in our big towns, especially in their girls, who have an energetic and business-like "know all about it" kind of prettiness which is widely independent of colour, and which, with the parallel business characters, engineering and financial, of the city squiredom, can be vividly set forth by the photograph and the schools of painting developed out of it; then for the third force, there is the tourist curiosity and the scientific naturalism, which go round the world fetching big scenery home for us that we never had dreamed of; cliffs that look like the world split in two, and cataracts that look as if they fell from the moon, besides all kinds of antiquarian and architectural facts, which twenty lives could never have learned in the olden time. What is it all to come to? Are our lives in this kingdom of darkness to be indeed twenty times as wise and long as they were in the light?

The answer—what answer was possible to me—came chiefly in the form of fatigue, and a sorrowful longing for an old Prout washing in with Vandyke brown and British ink, or even a Harding forest scene with all the foliage done in zigzag.[6]

And, indeed, for one thing, all this labour and realistic finishing makes us lose sight of the charm of easily-suggestive lines—nay, of the power of lines, properly so called altogether. . . .

. . . No one has pleaded more for finish than I in past time, or oftener, or perhaps so strongly, asserted the first principle of Leonardo, that a good picture should look like a mirror of the thing itself. But now that everybody can mirror the thing itself—at least the black and white of it—as easily as he takes his hat off, and then engrave the photograph, and steel the copper, and print piles and piles of the thing by steam, all as good as the first half-dozen proofs used to be, I begin to wish a little less to look at. . . . [*The Black Arts: A Reverie in the Strand* (1887), vol. 14, pp. 357–59]

1. See, for example. John Unrau, *Ruskin and St. Mark's* (London: Thames & Hudson, 1984), which includes some of these daguerreotypes taken by Ruskin's servants. For the most complete account and reproductions of Ruskin's photographs, see *I Dagherrotipi Della Collezione Ruskin,* ed. Paolo Constantini and Italo Zannier (Florence: Alinari, 1986), and Michael Bartram, *The Pre-Raphaelite Camera: Aspects of Victorian Photography* (Boston: New York Graphic Society, 1985), pp. 37, 52–53, 74–75, 91, and 93. See also Constantini and Zannler, *Itinerario Fiorentino: Le "mattinate" di John Ruskin nelle fotograffie degli Alinari* (Florence: Alinari, 1986).

2. Throughout his *Works,* ed. Cook and Wedderburn, Ruskin's claims vary. For example, in *Praeterita* (1886–87), vol. 35, p. 352, Ruskin credits one of his daguerreotype assistants, George, with taking "the first image of the Matterhorn, as also of the aiguilles of Chamouni, ever drawn by the sun," though the scenes are usually attributed to one of his servants, John Hobbs [Fig. 37] or Frederick Crawley. But elsewhere he appears to claim the credit for himself: in *Deucalion* (1879), vol. 29, p. 97, he notes that "the first sun-portrait ever taken of the Matterhorn (and as far as I know of any Swiss mountain whatever) was taken by me in the year 1849," and in *The Limestone Alps of Savoy* (1884), vol. 29, p. 569, he asserts that "I took the first photograph (of the Matter-

horn and I believe of any Alp whatever) that had then been made."

3. See an undated letter in the Gernsheim Collection at the HRHRC from Ruskin to an unnamed correspondent wishing to take his picture: " . . . my face is so ugly that I am resolved in future never to show it but where I must; it is quite wasted time to photograph it for I have always to beg that the negative may be negatived finally." Yet he is the subject of several portraits—understandable given his eminence—such as Carroll's photograph of him while Slade Professor of Art at Oxford (1870–78, 1883–85), reproduced here [Fig. 36]; others are reproduced in *John Ruskin and His Circle* (London: Maas Gallery exhibit catalogue, June 11–28, 1991), pp. 24–26.

4. On Ruskin's change of attitude toward photography in general, see R. N. Watson, "Art, Photography and John Ruskin," *British Journal of Photography* 91 (March 10, March 24, April 7, 1944): 82–83, 100–101, and 118–19; and see also the entries under "Photography" in the index to Ruskin, *Works,* vol. 39, pp. 404–5.

5. Dean Liddell was the father of Lewis Carroll's "Alice," mentioned in the Brassaï selection above.

6. Ruskin refers to the English artists Samuel Prout (1783–1852), a landscape and architectural watercolorist, and James Harding (1798–1863), a landscape painter and lithographer.

23. *Samuel Butler*

FROM *The Note-Books,* [1888–93], 1912

utler (1835–1902), now best known as the author of Erewhon *(1872), a utopian novel, and* The Way of All Flesh *(1903), an autobiographical fiction detailing his austere Victorian upbringing, possessed many other talents. In addition to writing in many genres, he composed music and, in the 1860's, became a serious amateur photographer.[1] Butler appreciated photography's ability to document nature quickly, reveal previously restricted information, educate the eye and mind, and strip "High Art" of its pretensions—all inexpensively. He himself specialized in serious photographs of children, abnormal or grotesque figures, and works of art and architecture; ironic shots of slum properties near the beautiful Cambridge colleges; and humorous ones of imagined literary characters, such as Chaucer's beloved "Wife of Bath" from* The Canterbury Tales *[Fig. 38].[2] Butler also used photographs—with drawings or as substitutes for them—to illustrate his own scholarly works such as* Ex Voto *(1888), a study of early Renaissance artists in a northern Italian town, and* The Authoress of the Odyssey *(1897), a controversial pioneering study in classical iconography.[3] The entries relevant to the camera in his published notebooks invariably comment on human vanity and convey the aggressive, often unscrupulous, pleasures of the photographic "hunt" while suggesting how quickly it also absorbed him.[4]*

FROM *The Public Ear*

Those who wish to gain the public ear should bear in mind that people do not generally want to be made less foolish or less wicked. What they want is to be told that they are not foolish and not wicked. Now it is only a fool or a liar or both who can tell them this; the masses therefore cannot be expected to like any but fools or liars or both. So when a lady gets photographed, what she wants is not to be made beautiful but to be told that she is beautiful. [X, p. 163]

FROM *Loving and Hating*

When we really hate a thing it makes us sick, and we use this expression to symbolise the utmost hatred of which our nature is capable; but when we know we hate, our hatred is in reality mild and inoffensive. I, for example, think I hate all those people whose photographs I see in the shop windows, but I am so conscious of this that I am convinced, in reality, nothing would please me better than to be in the shop windows too. . . . I conclude my disapproval is grounded in nothing more serious than a superficial, transient jealousy. [XIII, p. 206]

Unprofessional Sermon iii

Lead us not into temptation. [Matt. 6:13]

For example; I am crossing from Calais to Dover and there is a well-known popular preacher on board, say Archdeacon Farrar.⁵

I have my camera in my hand, and though the sea is rough the sun is brilliant. I see the archdeacon come on board at Calais and seat himself upon the upper deck, looking as though he had just stepped out of a band-box. Can I be expected to resist the temptation of snapping him? Suppose that in the train for an hour before reaching Calais I had said any number of times, "Let us not into temptation," is it likely that the archdeacon would have been made to take some other boat or to stay in Calais, or that I myself, by being delayed on some other temptation, though perhaps smaller? Had I not better snap him and have done with it? Is there

enough chance of good result to make it worth while to try the experiment? The general consensus of opinion is that there is not.

And as for praying for strength to resist the temptation—granted that if, when I saw the archdeacon in the band-box stage, I had immediately prayed for strength I must have been enabled to put the evil thing from me for a time, how long would this have been likely to last when I saw his face grow saintlier and saintlier? I am an excellent sailor myself, but he is not, and when I see him there, his eyes closed and his head thrown back, like a sleeping St. Joseph in a shovel hat, with a basin beside him, can I expect to be saved from snapping him by such a formula as "Deliver us from evil"? Is it in photographer's nature to do so? When David found himself in the cave with Saul he cut off one of Saul's coat-tails; if he had had a camera and there had been enough light he would have photographed him; but would it have been in flesh and blood for him neither to cut off his coat-tail nor to snap him?

There is a photographer in every bush, going about like a roaring lion seeking whom he may devour. [XIII, pp. 213–14]

Snapshotting a Bishop

I must some day write about how I hunted the late Bishop of Carlisle ⁶ with my camera, hoping to shoot him when he was sea-sick crossing from Calais to Dover, and how St. Somebody protected him and said I might shoot him when he was well, but not when he was sea-sick. I should like to do it in the manner of the *Odyssey:*

. . . And the steward went round and laid them all on the sofas and benches and he set a beautiful basin by each, variegated and adorned with flowers, but it contained no water for washing the hands, and Neptune sent great waves that washed over the eyelet-holes of the cabin. But when it was now the middle of the passage and a great roaring arose as of beasts in the Zoological Gardens, and they promised hecatombs to Neptune if he would still the raging of the waves. . . .

At any rate I shot him and have him in my

snapshot book, but he was not sea-sick. [XVI, 1892, p. 254]

The Wife of Bath

There are Canterbury Pilgrims every Sunday in summer who start from close to the old Tabard, only they go by the South-Eastern Railway and come back the same day for five shillings. And, what is more, they are just the same sort of people. If they do not go to Canterbury they go by the *Clacton Belle* to Clacton-on-Sea. There is not a Sunday the whole summer through but you may find all Chaucer's pilgrims, man and woman for man and woman, on board the *Lord of the Isles* or the *Clacton Belle*. Why, I have seen the Wife of Bath on the *Lord of the Isles* myself. She was eating her luncheon off an *Ally Sloper's Half-Holiday,* which was spread out upon her knees [Fig. 38]. Whether it was I who had had too much beer or she I cannot tell, God Knoweth; and whether or no I was caught up into Paradise, again I cannot tell; but I certainly did hear unspeakable words which it is not lawful for a man to utter, and that not above fourteen years ago but the very last Sunday that ever was. The Wife of Bath heard them too, but she never turned a hair. Luckily I had my detective camera with me, so I snapped her there and then. She put her hand up to her mouth at that very moment and rather spoiled herself, but not much. [XVII, 1891, p. 262]

Retouched Photographs

All our education is very much a case of retouching negatives till all the character and individuality is gone.

Count Gattinara di Zubiena sent me this morning what in the innocence of his heart he believes to be a photograph of himself—a smooth, sleek thing like a dummy, and with nothing in it that can conceivably remind me of himself. He did not know that in reality he was sending me a portrait of the photographer, and of his ideas as to what a young Italian Count should look like. I wanted the Count—I did not want a mixture of Count and photographer.

I suppose there would be so little to be done if people would only leave well alone that it is necessary to spoil things in order to enable people to earn an honest living. [from *Further Extracts from the Note-Books*, ed. Bartholomew, 1934, pp. 270–71]

FROM *Apologia*

If I had greatly cared about getting on I think I could have done so. I think I could even now write an anonymous book that would take the public as much as *Erewhon* did. Perhaps I could not, but I think I could. The reason why I do not try is that I like doing other things better. What I most enjoy is running the view of evolution set forth in *Life and Habit*[7] and making things less easy for the hacks of literature and science; or perhaps even more I enjoy taking snapshots and writing music, though aware that I had better not enquire whether this last is any good or not. In fact there is nothing I do that I do not enjoy so keenly that I cannot tear myself away from it, and people who thus indulge themselves cannot have things both ways. I am so intent upon pleasing myself that I have no time to cater for the public. [XXIV, 1890, p. 372]

38. Samuel Butler. 'The Wife of Bath, in the Cabin of the "Lord of the Isles,"' July 19, 1891.

1. See Elinor Shaffer, *Erewhons of the Eye: Samuel Butler as Painter, Photographer and Art Critic* (London: Reaktion Books, 1988), ch. 4, pp. 205–94, for the most complete discussion and reproduction of many Butler photographs. She also noted in conversation with the editor on April 18, 1991, that the remaining unpublished notebooks and letters of Butler doubtless contain further material on photography.

2. See Shaffer, *Erewhons of the Eye,* for a discussion of Butler's 'The Wife of Bath,' p. 220, also reproduced here, and of 'Shylock,' fig. 145, p. 267.

3. See Butler, *Ex Voto: An Account of the Sacro Monte or New Jerusalem at Varallo-Sesia* [1888], rev. ed. (London: Longman, Green, 1890); and note Shaffer's intriguing assertion in *Erewhons of the Eye,* p. 229, that Butler's many photographs of the world of the Sacro Monte, including those not published, form a kind of *"Life of Jesus"* in photographs. See also Butler, *The Authoress of the Odyssey* [1897] (Chicago: University Press of Chicago, 1967).

4. See Bill Jay's relevant discussion of "The Photographer as Aggressor," in *Observations: Essays on Documentary Photography (Untitled 35),* ed. David Featherstone (Carmel, Calif.: Friends of Photography, 1984), pp. 7–23.

5. Frederic William Farrar (1831–1903) was archdeacon of Westminster, 1883–90, Dean of Canterbury, 1895–1903, and a celebrated author, mentioned in the *Dictionary of National Biography,* ed. Sidney Lee, Supplement, 1901–11 (London: Oxford University Press, 1927), pp. 9–12; this information was kindly provided to the editor in a conversation of November 15, 1991, by Richard Pfaff.

6. The late Bishop of Carlisle, also according to Pfaff, was the Rt. Rev. Harvey Goodwin (1818–91), who held that see from 1869 until his death, according to *Handbook of British Chronology,* ed. E. B. Fryde et al. (London: Office of the Royal Historical Society, 1989), 3rd ed., p. 237.

7. In *Life and Habit* (London: Fifield, 1878), Butler favored Lamarck and "creative evolution" over Darwin's "soulless" scientific determinism.

Samuel Butler

119

Part Three
1890–1915

Wells (1866–1946) is now best remembered for his novels, like his autobiographical Tono-Bungay *(1909) and his futuristic science fiction, like* The War of the Worlds *(1898). Yet in his lifetime the author, having surmounted lowly origins, frail childhood health, and uneven education, proved one of the most prolific and popular thinkers of his generation on both sides of the Atlantic; in various forms, his writings energetically criticized society and propagated utopian remedies. Given his faith in scientific progress, Wells was naturally engaged by photography and sometimes used it as a plot device in his novels; more usually, as in this essay, he lamented its willingness and ability to cater to human vanity by falsifying portraits.[1] Though considered more intellectually than aesthetically engaged with the camera, Wells nevertheless wrote a piece, "On Beauty," for Alfred Stieglitz's* Camera Work *(1909).[2] After posing several times for portraits by Alvin Langdon Coburn [Fig. 39], the writer in 1908 invited him to select those of his short stories best suited to photographic interpretation. The resulting collection,* A Door in the Wall *(1911), proved a landmark in the history of the book, given the genuine harmony between the author and the illustrator that, in turn, had inspired the typographer to design a new, uniquely suitable typeface.[3] Wells, meanwhile, also contributed a preface to Coburn's book on* New York *(1910), photographs from which he later hung in his dining room.[4]*

"An album," said my uncle, as he sat and turned over my collection of physiognomy, "is, I think, the best-reading in the world. You get such sidelights on the owner's heredity, George; distant cousins caricature his features and point the moral of his nose, and ancestral faces prophesy his fate. His friends, moreover, figure the secret of his soul. But what a lot we have to learn yet in the art of being photographed, what grotesque and awkward blunders your common sitters make! Why, for instance, do men brush their hair so excessively when they go before the lens? Your cousin here looks like a cheap chess pawn about the head, whereas as I know him his head is a thing like a worn-out paint-brush. Where but in a photograph would you see a parting so straight as this? It is unnatural. You flatten down all a man's character; for nothing shows that more than the feathers and drakes' tails, the artful artlessness, or revolutionary tumult of his hair. Mind you, I am not one of those who would prohibit a man wearing what he conceives to be his best clothes to the photographer's. I like to see the little vanity peeping out—the last moment's folly of a foolish tie, nailed up for a lifetime. Yet all the same, people should understand that the camera takes no note of newness, but much of the cut and fit. And a man should certainly not go and alter his outline into a feminine softness, by pouring oil on his troubled mane and plastering it down with a brush and comb. It is not tidiness, but hypocrisy.

"We have indeed very much to learn in this matter. It is a thing that needs teaching, like deportment or dancing. Plenty of men I have noticed, who would never do it in real life, commit the sin of being over-gentlemanly in an album. Their clothes are even indecently immaculate. They become, not portraits, but fashion-plates. I hate a man who is not rumpled and creased a little, as much as I do a brand new pipe. And, as a sad example of sin on the other hand, on the side of carelessness, I have seen renderings of a very august personage indeed, in a hat—a *hat!* It was tilted, and to add to the atrocity, he was holding a cigar. This I

regard as horrible. Think! your photograph may go into boudoirs. Imagine Gladys opening the album to Ænone: 'Now I will show you *him.*' And there you sit, leering at their radiant sweetness, hat on, and a cigar reeking between your fingers.

"No, George, a man should go very softly to a photographer's, and he should sit before the camera with reverence in his heart and in his attitude, as if he were in the presence of the woman he loved."

He turned to Mrs. Harborough's portrait, looked at it, hesitated, looked again, and passed on.

"I often think we do not take this business of photography in a sufficiently serious spirit. Issuing a photograph is like marriage: you can only undo the mischief with infinite woe, I know of one man who has an error of youth of this kind on his mind—a fancy-dress costume affair, Crusader or Templar—of which he is more ashamed than many men would be of the meanest sins. For sometimes the camera has its mordant moods, and amazes you by its saturnine estimate of your merits. This man was perhaps a little out of harmony with the garments of chivalry, and a trifle complacent and vain at the time. But the photograph of him is so cynical and contemptuous, so merciless in its exposure of his element of foolishness, that we may almost fancy the spook of Carlyle had got mixed up with the chemicals upon the film. Yet it never really dawned upon him until he had distributed this advertisement of his little weakness far and wide, that the camera had called him a fool to his face. I believe he would be glad now to buy them all back at five pounds a copy.

"This of Minnie Hobson is a work of art. Bless me, the girl must be thirty-seven or thirty-eight now, and just look at her! These photographers have got a trick now, if your face is one of the long kind, of raising the camera, bending your head forward, and firing down at you. So our Minnie becomes quite chubby again. Then, this thing has been retouched." My uncle peered into the photograph. "It seems

39. Alvin Langdon Coburn. 'H. G. Wells,' c. 1905.

to me it is pretty nearly all retouching. For instance, if you look at the eye, that high light is not perfectly even; that was touched in on the negative with a pencil. Then about the neck of our Minnie I have observed certain bones, just the slightest indication of her collar-bone, George, but that has disappeared under the retoucher's pencil. Then the infantile smoothness of her cheek, and the beautifully-rounded outline, are produced by the retoucher carefully scraping off the surface of the film where the cheekbone projected with a sharp knife. There are also in real life little lines between the corner of our Minnie's mouth and her nostril. And again, Minnie is one of those people whose dresses never seem to fit, but this fits like a glove. These retouchers are like Midas, and they turn all that comes to their hands to gold; or, like Spring, the flowers come back at their approach. They reverse the work of Ithuriel [angel who sought out Satan], and restore brightness to the fallen. They sit at their little desks, and scratch, scratch, scratch with those delicate pencils of theirs, scratching away age, scratching away care, making the crooked straight, and the rough smooth. They are the fairies of photography, and fill our albums with winsome changelings. Their ministry anticipates in a little way the angels who will take us when we die, releasing us from the worn and haggard body of this death, and showing something of the eternal life and youth that glows within. Or one might say that the spirit of the retoucher is the spirit of Love. It makes plain women beautiful, and common men heroic. Her regal fingers touch for the evil of ungainliness, and behold, we are restored. Her pencil is like the Queen's sword, and it makes knights out of common men.

"When I have my photograph taken," said my uncle, "I always like to think of the retoucher. I idealize her; I fancy her with the sweetest eyes I have ever seen, and an expression infinitely soft and tender. And she looks closely into my face, and her little pencil goes gently and lovingly over my features. Tickle, tickle. In that way, George, I get a really very nice expression indeed." My uncle turned to his own presentment, and mused pleasantly for

a space. Then he looked again at Mrs. Harborough as if inadvertently, and asked her name.

"I like this newer way of taking your photograph, against a mere gray background; just the head of you. One should always beware of the property furniture of the photographer. In the seventies they were great at such aids—a pedestal, a cork rustic stile, wide landscape in the distance, but I think that we are at least getting beyond that now. People in those days must have been afraid to be left alone before a camera, or they wanted it to seem that they were taken unawares, quite against their modesty—did not know what the camera was, and were just looking at it. A very favorite pose for girls was a graceful droop over a sofa, chin on elegant hand. When I was at Dribble-bridge—I was a bright young fellow then—I collected a number of local photographs, ladies chiefly, and the thing was very noticeable when I put them in a row over my mantelshelf. The local 'artist' was intensely fond of that pose. But fancy the local leader finding her cook drooping over the same sofa as herself! Nowadays, I see, you get merely the heads of your girls, with their hair flossed up, intense light from above, and faces in shadow. I think it is infinitely better.

"What horrible things hands become in a photograph! I wonder how it is that the hand in a photograph is always four shades darker than the arm. Every girl who goes to be photographed in evening dress should be solemnly warned to keep her hands out of the picture. They will look as though she has been enamelling the grate, or toying with a bucket of pitch. There is something that sins against my conception of womanly purity in those dark hands."

My uncle shut the album. "Yes, it is a neglected field of education, an important branch of deportment altogether forgotten. Our well-bred ease fails us before the camera: we are lucky if we merely look stiff and self-conscious. I should fancy there would be an opening for some clever woman to teach people how to dress for the occasion and how to sit, what to avoid and how to avoid it. As it is, we go in a state of nervous agitation, obsequiously costumed; our last vestige of self-assertion vanishes before the un-winking Cyclops eye of the instrument, and we cower at the mercy of the thing and its attendant. They make what they will of us, and the retoucher simply edits the review with an eye to the market. So history is falsified before our faces, and we prepare a lie for our grandchildren. We fail to stamp our individualities upon our photographs, and are mere 'dumb, driven cattle' in the matter. We sin against ourselves in this neglect, and act against the spirit of the age. Sooner or later this haphazard treatment of posterity must come to an end." He meditated for a moment. Then as if pursuing a train of thought, "That Mrs. Harborough is a very pretty woman, George. Where did you happen to meet her?"

1. For example, Wells uses a photograph as an important plot device in his novel *Christina Alberta's Father* (London: Cape; New York: Macmillan, 1925), especially pp. 262–68, called to the editor's attention by Bill Jay.

2. See Wells, "On Beauty," *Camera Work* 27 (July 1909): 17.

3. See also Jeffrey A. Wolin, afterword to *The Door in the Wall and Other Stories* (Boston: Godine, 1980), a reprint of the original edition (New York: Mitchell Kennerly, 1911), pp. 155–57, which he terms "the first thoroughly integrated example of a photographically illustrated book"; and Coburn, *Autobiography*, pp. 32, 76, and 78, on their collaboration on the short stories; and p. 39, fig. 14, for a reproduction of a 1909 portrait of Wells by Coburn. The photographer selected a 1905 portrait to include in his *Men of Mark* (London: Duckworth, 1913) as Plate 6, both of which seem more characteristic of the photographer's portraits than the unusual one reproduced here.

4. See Wells's preface to Coburn's *New York* (London: Duckworth, n.d. [1910]), pp. 9–10, and for comments on the work and the aftermath see Coburn, *Autobiography*, pp. 76–78 and 86. For more about Coburn, see the Shaw, Twain, James and Coburn, Belloc, and Pound selections below.

25. Bret Harte

FROM *The Letters of Bret Harte, 1896–97*

*B*ret Harte (1836–1902) lived a paradoxical life. An easterner by birth, he was instrumental in inspiring the legend of the American West in literature as well as "local color" in short stories, using his varied experiences in California (1854–70) as a Wells Fargo guard, miner, printer, journalist, and editor. After a brief period as the most celebrated writer of the Gilded Age, Harte became one of the country's earliest expatriates. He worked as an American consul abroad (1878–85), where his work was increasingly more appreciated than in his native country. It was not surprising that in his last years, having settled in London, Harte became engrossed by photography. Even Mark Twain, his most articulate detractor, had long admired the "photographic exactness" of the style of his former mentor; and Harte always considered the illustrations to his stories as important as the texts.[1] Photography served as his main recreation despite his struggles to master its techniques. In these casual letters to his family members and close friends, Harte's chronic frustration with the camera, developing processes, and results is evident, which perhaps explains why none of his photographs seem to have survived.[2]

FROM *The Letters of Bret Harte*

Note: The recipients of Harte's letters that follow are Nan, his wife, who remained in America; Frank, their son, who was then living in England; May Pemberton, the daughter of his future biographer, T. Edgar Pemberton, with whom Harte collaborated on plays; and Mrs. Boyd, who, with her husband—an illustrator of some of Harte's works—was his closest English friend.

I am here at work, but the air is pure and the place rural and secluded, and I work better than in London. Sometime I may send you some photographs of it—taken by *myself*—when I am a little more proficient in the art. Alas! I have only a cheap instrument and am very bungling. [to Nan Harte, June 30, 1896, from *Letters*, p. 425]

I am quite envious of your photographic success. The little Kodak picture of your sister is wonderfully good, and shames my feeble efforts in the garden at Broadway, except the ones where I "snap-shotted" the 'snap-shooter' herself, and brought down you and the dog with one barrel! Alas, the Mary Anderson de Navarro group turned out a failure, and the sublime patience your father and mother are showing in the most atrocious photographic situations brings tears to my eyes. Your mother, however, has a certain reserved melodramatic look in her eyes, as if she were 'biding her time.' I shall dread coming again to Broadway! [to May Pemberton, undated, 1896, from *Letters*, p. 436]

Thank you so much for the small, indefinite pictures of me and the huge, distinctive one of your father's foot! It may be a foolish, human weakness, but I *should* have liked (as the plates are small) to have had *one* plate *all to myself.* But I am thankful all the same.

Do you keep a set of small plates with *his* foot in the corner—a sort of perpetual reminder—a kind of *ex pede Herculem?* You know *I* don't mind, but it must be disconcerting and *ominous* to the average *young* man whom you take! [to May Pemberton, November 23, 1896, from *Letters*, p. 437]

I send you the photographs I spoke of, and, in a separate parcel, a magnesium light for photographing at night or on a dark day. You must hold the magnesium light, with its reflector, in your hand so as to throw the light on any object (including your father's foot, of course) or any part of the room you wish to show. You light the end of the little magnesium ribbon that projects from the holder, and 'pay it out' by the crank.

I am told that some people light the whole of the ribbon at once, to get a stronger and more protracted light. But as this is always accompanied by the sudden disappearance of the house and the spectators and the operator, and the calling out of the village fire-engine, perhaps you had better not try it. Your parents might object. And for a young lady, it might seen somewhat *ostentatious.* [to May Pemberton, Undated, (1897?), from *Letters*, p. 437]

Besides writing, I have been teaching myself to 'develop' my own photographic plates, and I haven't a stick of clothing or an exposed finger that isn't stained. I sit for hours in a dark-room feeling as if I was a very elderly Faust at some dreadful incantation, and come out of it, blinding at the light, like a Bastille prisoner. And yet I am not successful! I have plates that are wonderful in image and polychromatic in tint, but all 'over' or 'under' developed. I print well enough, but in 'toning,' my prints have a dreadful way of vanishing completely (as perhaps some other things that I have printed will do!) and I am left with a faded scrap of paper. [to Mrs. Boyd, August 15, 1897, from *Letters*, pp. 445–46]

I think something of trying to do the 'developing' of such photographs as I may take here. Mr. Beck has furnished me with a portentous list of the things I need; I have been downstairs to see the 'dark-room'—and the construction doesn't look pleasant! You might draft me some

'Hints to a Young Developer.' [to Frank Harte, March 31, 1897, from *Letters,* p. 447]

I am writing, as usual, and my only *recreation* is photography—my only *trouble* 'developing.' I have been singularly unfortunate, but have at least traced my trouble (by test) to a diabolical 'ruby lamp' which 'fogs' all my plates in 'developing,' as well as in putting them in the camera. And my toning was something weird—I used to get every colour of the rainbow on my prints, and then the whole thing would vanish like a bursting bubble. [to Frank Harte, August 25, 1897, from *Letters,* p. 448]

If you can find the negative of the enclosed, will you print me two or three copies, or, if you haven't time, send the plates to me, and I will do the printing and return the plate if you want it? The 'toning' I will also do, though it is usually something wonderful to contemplate. I also send you a little photo, posed, photographed, developed, printed, and *toned* by me! It is 'Tommy' and a child of the neighborhood (lest you should *not* distinguish them in their high artistic combination!) The *vignette* effect is produced by a bit of cardboard in printing. The 'tone' is all my own—wrong possibly, but beautiful to me! [to Frank Harte, September 23, 1897, from *Letters,* pp. 448–49]

1. See Mark Twain's praise of this quality in an otherwise ambivalent memoir in "Bret Harte," *Mark Twain in Eruption,* ed. Bernard DeVoto (New York: Harper & Brothers, 1940), pp. 262–63, and in Richard O'Connor, *Bret Harte: A Biography* (Boston: Little, Brown, 1966), p. 249.

2. Checking with the major repositories of Harte materials in California, as well as likely sources in London, failed to uncover any photographs included among the letters, papers, and MSS, nor did their administrators know the author ever took any.

*A*cting on Yeats's suggestion that he should return from Paris and write about his native Ireland, the playwright John Millington Synge (1871–1909) went to the Aran Islands in 1898 for the first of five visits. Bringing a camera, or perhaps purchasing one from a fellow visitor, Synge here, as previously in Dublin, Galway, and County Wicklow, took quick, visual notes of ordinary scenes—people working, waiting, marketing, gossiping—everyday activities then considered not picturesque or worth documenting [Fig. 40].[1] He never considered using these vivid but technically imperfect photographs as works of art in their own right but merely as aids for drawings that an artist might use to illustrate his prose account of The Aran Islands, *his first serious work.*[2] *Indeed, Synge's writing alone was sufficiently visual to "teach" Robert Flaherty, who made the notable film* Man of Aran (1932–34), *what to see.*[3] *Synge's photographs of the islanders, like his prose descriptions, were perceptive and made no judgments. But when, in the same year this book appeared, he applied the same amoral perspective to the subject of parricide in his play,* The Playboy of the Western World, *riots broke out at the Abbey Theatre.*

I returned to the middle island this morning, in the steamer to Kilronan, and on here in a curagh that had gone over with salt fish. As I came up from the slip the doorways in the village filled with women and children, and several came down on the roadway to shake hands and bid me a thousand welcomes.

Old Pat Dirane is dead, and several of my friends have gone to America; that is all the news they have to give me after an absence of many months.

When I arrived at the cottage I was welcomed by the old people, and great excitement was made by some little presents I had bought them—a pair of folding scissors for the old woman, a strop for her husband, and some other trifles.

Then the youngest son, Columb, who is still at home, went into the inner room and brought out the alarm clock I sent them last year when I went away.

"I am very fond of this clock," he said, patting it on the back; "it will ring for me any morning when I want to go out fishing. Bedad, there are no two cocks in the island that would be equal to it."

I had some photographs to show them that I took here last year, and while I was sitting on a little stool near the door of the kitchen, showing them to the family, a beautiful young woman I had spoken to a few times last year slipped in, and after a wonderfully simple and cordial speech of welcome, she sat down on the floor beside me to look on also.

The complete absence of shyness or self-consciousness in most of these people gives them a peculiar charm, and when this young and beautiful woman leaned across my knees to look nearer at some photograph that pleased her, I felt more than ever the strange simplicity of the island life.

Last year when I came here everything was new, and the people were a little strange with me, but now I am familiar with them and their way of life, so that their qualities strike me more forcibly than before.

When my photographs of this island [Fig. 40] had been examined with immense delight, and every person in them had been identified—even those who only showed a hand or a leg—I brought out some I had taken in County Wicklow. Most of them were fragments, showing fairs in Rathdrum or Aughrim, men cutting turf on the hills, or other scenes of inland life, yet they gave the greatest delight to these people who are wearied of the sea. [pp. 74–75]

To-day when I went down to the slip I found a pig-jobber from Kilronan with about twenty pigs that were to be shipped for the English market.

When the steamer was getting near, the whole drove was moved down on the slip and the curaghs were carried out close to the sea. Then each beast was caught in its turn and thrown on its side, while its legs were hitched together in a single knot, with a tag of rope remaining, by which it could be carried.

Probably the pain inflicted was not great, yet the animals shut their eyes and shrieked with almost human intonations, till the suggestion of the noise became so intense that the men and woman who were merely looking on grew wild with excitement, and the pigs waiting their turn foamed at the mouth and tore each other with their teeth.

After a while there was a pause. The whole slip was covered with a mass of sobbing animals, with here and there a terrified woman crouching among the bodies, and patting some special favourite to keep it quiet while the curaghs were being launched.

Then the screaming began again while the pigs were carried out and laid in their places, with a waistcoat tied round their feet to keep them from damaging the canvas. They seemed to know where they were going, and looked up at me over the gunnel with an ignoble desperation that made me shudder to think that I had eaten of this whimpering flesh. When the last curagh went out I was left on the slip with a band of woman and children, and one old boar who sat looking out over the sea.

The women were over-excited, and when I

40. J. M. Synge. 'Spinning' [1898].

tried to talk to them they crowded round me and began jeering and shrieking at me because I am not married. A dozen screamed at a time, and so rapidly that I could not understand all they were saying, yet I was able to make out that they were taking advantage of the absence of their husbands to give me the full volume of their contempt. Some little boys who were listening threw themselves down, writhing with laughter among the seaweed, and the young girls grew red with embarrassment and stared down into the surf.

For a moment I was in confusion. I tried to speak to them, but I could not make myself heard, so I sat down on the slip and drew out my wallet of photographs. In an instant I had the whole band clambering round me, in their ordinary mood. [pp. 113–14]

1. See P. J. Pocock, "Synge and the photography of his time," in *The Autobiography of J. M. Synge,* ed. Alan Price (Dublin: Dolmen Press; London: Oxford University Press, 1965), pp. 41–46; this edition also reproduces some of the playwright's Aran photographs, now at the Trinity College Library, as does Price's edition of *The Aran Islands* in *Collected Works,* vol. 2 (London: Oxford University Press, 1966), and Robin Skelton's (Oxford: Oxford University Press, 1979). The most complete collection of Synge's photographs, including some taken elsewhere in Ireland, is reproduced in *My Wallet of Photographs,* ed. Lilo Stephens (Dublin: Dolmen Press, 1971). See also Jean Mitry, *Schriftsteller als Photographen, 1860–1910* (Lucerne and Frankfurt am Main: C. J. Bucher, 1975), who reproduces, pp. 83–92, many of Synge's photographs, but asserts, p. 16, that his Aran photographs were taken between 1892 and 1901 rather than from 1898, as Pocock and others suggest.

2. See Synge, Letter to John Masefield [January 14, 1904], in *The Collected Letters of John Millington Synge,* ed. Ann Saddlemyer (Oxford: Clarendon Press, 1983), vol. 1, p. 73; and see also Jack Yeats's drawings for the first edition of *The Aran Islands* (Dublin: Maunsel; London: Elkin Mathews, 1906), which bear little resemblance to Synge's photographs.

3. Noted in Donna Gerstenberger, *John Millington Synge,* rev. ed. (Boston: Twayne, 1990), p. 8.

27. August Strindberg

I've thought of becoming a photographer! To save my talent as a writer," wrote Strindberg in 1892. Although known for intense, symbolic, psychological dramas like Miss Julie (1888), not his camera work, the Swedish writer (1849–1912) was involved with photography from boyhood and explored various forms and techniques throughout his career.[1] He experimented with documentary calotypes of French peasants (1886); portraits of himself [Fig. 41] and other artists (1886); landscapes (1890); color photography (1890s); photograms of crystal formations (1892); "celestography," involving shots of the sun, moon, and stars (1894–96); and later—long before Stieglitz—cloud formations (1907). He also tried out automatic shutters as well as simpler lenses and worked on double exposures. Believing that only a photograph could reveal and preserve a person's authentic soul, Strindberg, collaborating with Herman Anderson, an old friend who was a professional photographer, took life-size "psychological" portraits of himself and others—at their homes, not in the studio; they used a huge "wunderkamera" with an uncut lens (1906).[2] George Bernard Shaw, viewing these portraits during his 1908 visit to Stockholm, remarked he "had not seen such fine photography, even in London."[3] Despite his intense involvement with both the techniques and aesthetics of photography, Strindberg only rarely used the subject in his imaginative writings—in this short story and, briefly, in two of his plays, Creditors (1890)[4] and The Great Highway (1909).[5]

"PHOTOGRAPHY AND PHILOSOPHY"

There was once a photographer. He photographed like anything, profiles and full faces, three-quarters and full lengths, and he could develop and fix, tone, gold-bath, and print. He was a spanker! But he was never satisfied, for he was a philosopher, a great philosopher and an inventor. He had philosophized the world topsy-turvy. You could see how it was from the plate lying in the developer. There the right-hand side of people was on the left; what was dark became bright, shadows became lights, blue became white, and silver buttons as black as iron. It was topsy-turvy.

He had a companion, who was an ordinary man, full of little peculiarities. For instance, he smoked all day long; he could never learn to shut doors; he put his knife instead of his fork into his mouth; he went into rooms with his hat on; he cut his nails in the middle of the studio floor; and he *would* drink three glasses of beer in the evening. He was full of faults. The philosopher, who for his part was without faults, was irritated by his imperfect brother, and wanted to break with him, but couldn't, because their business kept them together; and as they had to keep together, the involuntary feelings of the philosopher began to turn into unreasoning hatred. It was terrible.

Well, when spring came, they had to take a house for the summer; the companion was sent out to get one. He got one. They moved out one Saturday evening on the steamer. The philosopher sat on the upper deck all the way, drinking punch. He was very corpulent, and was troubled with several complaints, something to do with his liver, for instance; and he had something wrong with his feet, perhaps rheumatism, or what not. Well, when they got to the spot, they landed on the pier.

'Is it here?' asked the philosopher.

'Just a short walk,' answered the companion.

They walked along a path over tree-roots; and it came to an end right in front of a fence. That had to be climbed. Then came a path over stones. The philosopher complained of his feet, but the pain was soon put out of his head by a new fence, which had to be climbed. Then the track disappeared of its own accord; they had to walk on bare boulders and trample their way through undergrowth and brambles.

Inside the third fence stood a bull, who chased the philosopher to the fourth fence, which gave him a sweat-bath and opened his pores. After the sixth fence they saw the cottage. The philosopher went in, and came out on to the veranda.

'Why are there so many trees?' he said. 'They hide the view.'

'Oh, they'll protect us from the sea-wind,' answered his companion.

'And the place looks like a churchyard: why, we're right in the middle of a fir-wood!'

'It's healthy,' said his companion.

Then they went to bathe. But there was no beach in the philosophical sense of the word. There were only pebbles and mud. After the bathe the philosopher wanted to drink a glass of water from the well. It was rusty-brown water with a pungent taste. It wouldn't do. Nothing would do. Meat was unobtainable; fish was the only thing there was.

The philosopher became gloomy and sat down under a gourd to complain. But he had to stay: and his companion went back to town to look after the business during his friend's holiday. Six weeks had gone when the companion returned to his philosopher.

On the pier stood a slim youngster with red cheeks and a brown neck. It was the philosopher, rejuvenated and lusty.

He jumped over six fences, and drove the bull before him.

When they got to the veranda, his companion said:

'You look well: how have you got on?'

'Oh,' said the philosopher, 'splendidly. The fences have taken off my fat, the stones have massaged my feet: the mud has provided me with mud-baths for my rheumatism: the simple diet has cured my liver, and the fire-wood my lungs: and—would you believe it?—the brown well water contained iron, just what I wanted.'

'Yes, my philosopher,' said the companion: 'from the negative you get a print, where shades become lights again. If you would take a print of me and see what faults I haven't got, you wouldn't hate me. Just think: I don't drink spirits, and so I attend to the business properly: I don't steal: I never speak evil of you: I never grumble: I never argue that white is black: I'm never rude to customers: I get up early in the morning: I cut my nails to keep the developer clean: I keep my hat on so as not to drop hairs on to the plates: I smoke tobacco to purify the air of poisonous vapours: I leave doors ajar because I don't want to make a noise in the studio: I drink beer in the evening so as not to take to whisky, and I put my knife into my mouth for fear of pricking myself with the fork.'

'You are indeed a great philosopher,' said the photographer: 'now we'll be friends, and we shall do well.'

1. Strindberg, letter to Ola Hansson, September 13, 1892, in *Strindberg's Letters,* ed. and trans. Michael Robinson (Chicago: University of Chicago Press, 1992), vol. 1, p. 368, and quoted in Per Hemmingsson, "Strindberg—the photographer," p. 157. Hemmingson's book provides the most complete account in English of the writer's photography and reproduces many of his pictures, as do the studies by Göran Soderström and Francesco Carlo Crispolti, cited in the bibliography.

2. This project seems a variant of Strindberg's earlier proposal to publish an autobiography illustrated by photographs, evidently rejected by his publisher, in a letter to Albert Bonnier, November 15, 1886, quoted in *Strindberg's Letters,* ed. Robinson, vol. 1, pp. 217–18, and in Hemmingsson, p. 150. Some other projects are mentioned in *Strindberg's Letters,* vol. 1: to Gustaf Steffan, August 9, 1886, p. 208; to Albert Bonnier, September 20, 1886, pp. 215–16; to Fredrik Vult Von Steijern, August 17, 1890, p. 300; to Per Hasselberg, August 15, 1892, and September 10?, 1892, pp. 366–67.

3. Quoted in Hemmingsson, "August Strindberg," *Creative Camera* (London) 174 (December 1978): 423.

4. See *Creditors* (1890) in *Selected Plays,* trans. Evert Sprinchorn (Minneapolis: University of Minnesota Press, 1986), pp. 294, 296, and 320. See also Barry Jacobs, "Strindberg's *Creditors:* The Doppelgänger Motif and the Avenging Eye," *Annals of Scholarship* 9, no. 3 (1992): 257–78; and Freddie Rokem, "The Camera and the Aesthetics of Repetition: Strindberg's Use of Space and Scenography in *Miss Julie, A Dream Play,* and *The Ghost Sonata,*" *Strindberg's Dramaturgy,* ed. Goran Stockenstrom (Minneapolis: University of Minnesota Press, 1988), pp. 107–28.

5. Hemmingsson, "Strindberg—the photographer," pp. 169–71, after suggesting that Herman Anderson and his brother are the models for the photographer and the philosopher in the tale, and noting that "Strindberg toyed with the idea of a drama about his collaboration with Anderson, who, in an extant draft, is called the Apprentice and Strindberg himself the Builder," also asserts that "The Great Highway," in *Five Plays of Strindberg,* trans. Elizabeth Sprigge (Chicago: Aldine Publishing Company, [1962]), pp. 633–89, especially pp. 667–68, reflects his penitence for his shabby treatment of Anderson, an idea dismissed by Laurence Senelick in his essay in the appendix below.

28. George Bernard Shaw

"EVANS—AN APPRECIATION," 1903

*S*haw (1856–1950), noted as an arts critic before winning fame as a playwright, had long championed artistic and documentary photography, especially when technically unmanipulated.[1] In 1898, when his growing success and marriage to an heiress enabled him to afford luxuries, he bought a camera and became more practically engaged with photography. His favorite and most successful subject was himself, but he was always an unusually cooperative sitter for others as well [Fig. 42].[2] Shaw's most significant writings on the subject coincide with the period of his own best pictures (1901–9). His words, however, remain more highly regarded than his images, whether of himself, friends, or cherished places. His letters of introduction and reviews helped make the reputations of two photographers: Frederick Evans (1853–1943) [Fig. 43], a former bookseller, who became particularly noted for his church interiors; and Alvin Langdon Coburn (1882–1966), who became the favorite portraitist and illustrator of Edwardian authors, such as Henry James, G. K. Chesterton, H. G. Wells, Hilaire Belloc, and John Masefield, to name a few.[3] Surprisingly, Shaw used photographs rarely in his writings and more in earlier than in later ones. But his last published work involved scenes he had taken of his own village, accompanied by simple verses.[4]

Yes: no doubt Evans is a photographer. But then Evans is such a lot of things that it seems invidious to dwell on this particular facet of him. When a man has keen artistic susceptibility, exceptional manipulative dexterity, and plenty of prosaic business capacity, the world offers him a wide range of activities; and Evans, who is thus triply gifted and has a consuming supply of nervous energy to boot, has exploited the range very variously.

I cannot say exactly where I first met Evans. He broke in upon me from several directions simultaneously; and some time passed before I coordinated all the avatars into one and the same man. He was in many respects an oddity. He imposed on me as a man of fragile health, to whom an exciting performance of a Beethoven Symphony was as disastrous as a railway collision to any ordinary Philistine, until I discovered that his condition never prevented him from doing anything he really wanted to do, and that the things he wanted to do and did would have worn out a navy in three weeks. Again, he imposed on me as a poor man, struggling in a modest lodging to make a scanty income in a brutal commercial civilization for which his organization was far too delicate. But a personal examination of the modest lodging revealed the fact that this Franciscan devotee of poverty never seemed to deny himself anything he really cared for. It is true that he had neither a yacht, nor a couple of Panhard cars, nor a liveried domestic staff, nor even, as far as I could ascertain, a Sunday hat. But you could spend a couple of hours easily in the modest lodging looking at treasures, and then stop only from exhaustion.

Among the books were Kelmscott Press books and some of them presentation copies from their maker; and everything else was on the same plane. Not that there was anything of the museum about the place. He did not collect anything except, as one guessed, current coin of the realm to buy what he liked with. Being, as aforesaid, a highly susceptible person artistically, he liked nothing but works of art: besides, he accreted lots of those unpurchasable little things which artists give to sympathetic people who appreciate them. After all, in the republic of art, the best way to pick up pearls is not to be a pig.

But where did the anchorite's money come from? Well, the fact is, Evans, like Richardson, kept a shop; and the shop kept him. It was a book-shop. Not a place where you could buy slate-pencils, and reporter's note-books, and string and sealing-wax and paper-knives, with a garnish of ready-reckoners, prayer-books, birthday Shakespeare, and sixpenny editions of the Waverley novels; but a genuine book-shop and nothing else, in the heart of the ancient city of London, half-way between the Mansion House and St. Paul's. It was jam full of books. The window was completely blocked up with them, so that the interior was dark; you could see nothing for the first second or so after you went in, though you could feel the stands of books you were tumbling over. Evans, lurking in the darkest corner at the back, acquired the habits and aspect of an aziola; the enlargement of his eyes is clearly visible in Mrs. Käsebier's fine portrait of him. Everybody who knows Evans sees in those eyes the outward and visible sign of his restless imagination, and says "You have that in the portraits of William Blake, too"; but I am convinced that he got them by watching for his prey in the darkness of that busy shop.

The shop was an important factor in Evans's artistic career; and I believe it was the artist's instinct of self-preservation that made him keep it. The fact that he gave it up as soon as it had made him independent of it shows that he did not like business for its own sake. But to live by business was only irksome, whilst to live by art would have been to him simply self-murder. The shop was the rampart behind which the artist could do what he liked, and the man (who is as proud as Lucifer) maintain his independence. This must have been what nerved him to succeed in business, just as it has nerved him to do more amazing things still. He has been known to go up to the Dean of an English Cathedral—a dignitary compared to whom the

42. Frederick Evans.
'George Bernard Shaw,'
1896.

President of the United States is the merest worm, and who is not approached by ordinary men save in their Sunday-clothes—Evans, I say, in an outlandish silk collar, blue tie, and crushed soft hat, with a tripod under his arm, has accosted a Dean in his own cathedral and said, pointing to the multitude of chairs that hid the venerable flagged floor of the fane, "I should like all those cleared away." And the Dean has had it done, only to be told then that he must have a certain door kept open during a two hours' exposure for the sake of completing his scale of light.

I took a great interest in the shop, because there was a book of mine which apparently no Englishman wanted, or could ever possibly come to want without being hypnotized and yet it used to keep selling in an unaccountable man-

ner. The explanation was that Evans liked it. And he stood no nonsense from his customers. He sold them what was good for them, not what they asked for. You would see something in the window that tempted you; and you would go in to buy it, and stand blinking and peering about until you found a shop-assistant. "I want," you would perhaps say, "the Manners and tone of Good Society, by a member of the Aristocracy." Suddenly the aziola would pounce, and the shop-assistant vanish. "Ibsen, sir?" Evans would say. "Certainly; here are Ibsen's works, and, by the way, have you read the amazingly clever and thought-making work by Bernard Shaw, The Quintessence of Ibsenism?" and before you are aware of it you had bought it and were proceeding out of the shop reading a specially remarkable passage pointed out by this

43. George Bernard Shaw.
'Frederick Evans,' 1901.

ideal bookseller. But observe, if after a keen observation of you in a short preliminary talk he found you were the wrong sort of man, and asked for the Quintessence of Ibsenism without being up to the Shawian level, he would tell you that the title of the book had been changed, and that it was now called "For Love and My Lady," by Guy de Marmion. In which form you would like it so much that you would come back to Evans and buy all the rest of de Marmion's works.

This method of shopkeeping was so successful that Evans retired from business some years ago in the prime of his vigor; and the sale of the Quintessence of Ibsenism instantly stopped forever. It is now out of print. Evans said, as usual, that he had given up the struggle; that his health was ruined and his resources exhausted. He

then got married; took a small country cottage on the borders of Epping Forest, and is now doing just what he likes on a larger scale than ever. Altogether an amazing chap, is Evans! Who am I that I should "appreciate" him?

I first found out about his photography in one of the modest lodgings of the pre-Epping days (he was always changing them because of the coarse design of the fireplace, or some other crumple in the rose leaf). He had a heap of very interesting drawings, especially by [Aubrey] Beardsley, whom he had discovered long before the rest of the world did; and when I went to look at them I was struck by the beauty of several photographic portraits he had. I asked who did them; and he said he did them himself—another facet suddenly turned on me. At that time the impression produced was much greater than it could be at present; for the question whether photography was a fine art had then hardly been seriously posed; and when Evans suddenly settled it at one blow for me by simply handing me one of his prints in platinotype, he achieved a *coup de théâtre* which would be impossible now that the position of the artist-photographer has been conquered by the victorious rush of the last few years. But nothing that has been done since has put his work in the least out of countenance. In studying it from reproductions a very large allowance must be made for even the very best photogravures. Compared to the originals they are harsh and dry: the tone he produces on rough platinotype paper by skilful printing and carefully aged mercury baths and by delicately chosen mounts, can not be reproduced by an mechanical process. You occasionally hear people say of him that he is "simply" an extraordinary skilful printer in platinotype. This considering that printing is the most difficult process in photography, is a high compliment; but the implication that he excels in printing only will not hold water for a moment. He can not get good prints from bad negatives, nor good negatives from ill-judged exposures, and he does not try to. His decisive gift is, of course, the gift of seeing: his picture-making is done on the screen; and if the negative does not reproduce that picture, it is a failure, because the delicacies he delights in can not be faked: he relies on pure photography, not as a doctrinaire, but as an artist working on that extreme margin of photographic subtlety at which attempts to doctor the negative are worse than useless. He does not reduce, and only occasionally and slightly intensifies; and platinotype leaves him but little of his "control" which enables the gummist so often to make a virtue of a blemish and a merit of a failure. If the negative does not give him what he saw when he set up his camera, he smashes it. Indeed, a moment's examination of the way his finest portraits are modeled by light alone and not by such contour markings or impressionist touches as a retoucher can imitate, or of his cathedral interiors, in which the obscurest detail in the corners seems as delicately penciled by the darkness as the flood of

sunshine through window or open door is penciled by the light, without a trace of halation or over-exposure, will convince any expert that he is consummate at all points, as artist and negative-maker no less than as printer. And he has the "luck" which attends the born photographer. He is also an enthusiastic user of the Dallmeyer-Bergheim lens: but you have only to turn over a few of the portraits he has taken with a landscape-lens to see that if he were limited to an eighteenpenny spectacle-glass and a camera improvised from a soap-box, he would get better results than less apt photographers could achieve with a whole optical laboratory at their disposal.

Evans is, or pretends to be, utterly ignorant of architecture, of optics, of chemistry, of everything except the right thing to photograph and the right moment at which to photograph it. These professions are probably more for edification than for information; but they are excellent doctrine. His latest feat concerns another facet of him: the musical one. He used to play the piano with his fingers. Then came the photographic boom. The English critics, scandalized by the pretensions of the American photographers, and terrified by their performances, began to expatiate on the mechanicalness of camera-work, etc. Even the ablest of the English critics, Mr. D. S. McCall, driven into a corner as much by his own superiority to the follies of his colleagues as by the onslaught of the champions of photography, desperately declared that all artistic drawing was symbolic, a proposition which either exalts the prison tailor who daubs a broad arrow on a convict's jacket above Rembrandt and Velasquez, or else, if steered clear of that crudity, will be found to include ninety-nine-hundredths of the painting and sculpture of all the ages in the clean sweep it makes of photography. Evans abstained from controversy, but promptly gave up using his fingers on the piano and bought a Pianola, with which he presently acquired an extraordinary virtuosity in playing Bach and Beethoven, to the confusion of those who had transferred to that device all the arguments they had hurled in vain at the camera. And that was Evans all over. Heaven knows what he will take to next!

1. See "The Devil's Advocate: Bernard Shaw and Photography," *Bernard Shaw on Photography,* ed. Jay and Moore, pp. 3–46, for an excellent survey of Shaw's long, varied association with photography before introducing his writings on the subject, which began in 1883, and reproducing some of his photographs. See also Melinda Boyd Parsons, "The 'Unmechanicalness' of Photography: Bernard Shaw's Activist Photographic Philosophy," *Colby Library Quarterly* 25, no. 2 (June 1989): 64–73.

2. For Shaw as sitter, see accounts and portrait reproductions in Coburn, *Autobiography,* pp. 13, 24–28, and 40; Coburn, "Bernard Shaw: Photographer," *Photoguide MagazIne* (December 1950): 10–13; F. E. Loewenstein, *Bernard Shaw Through the Camera* (London: B & H White Publications, 1948); Sandburg, *Steichen the Photographer,* pp. 19–21; Steichen, *A Life in Photography,* ch. 4, npn, and Plate 48, originally an autochrome in *Camera Work* (April 1908): 167; Yousuf Karsh, *In Search of Greatness* (New York: Knopf, 1962), pp. 73–76; and Freund, *The World in My Camera,* pp. 100, 124–28, and facing 212.

3. For more on Evans, see a brief account of his photographs inspired by George Meredith, William Wordsworth, and William Morris in Beaumont Newhall, *Frederick H. Evans* (Millerton, N.Y.: Aperture, 1975), npn, in which some are reproduced. Evans extra-illustrated, with thirty-three tipped-in platinum prints, his own copy of Henry James, *A Little Tour in France* (London: William Heineman, 1900), now in a private collection. See also Anne Kelsey Hammond, "Frederick Evans: The Spiritual Harmonies of Architecture," in *British Photography in the Nineteenth Century,* ed. Mike Weaver (Cambridge: Cambridge University Press, 1989), pp. 244–45. For more on Coburn, see Shaw, Preface, "Photographs by Mr. Alvin Langdon Coburn, 1906," in *Shaw on Photography,* ed. Jay and Moore, pp. 102–6; Shaw's widely reproduced portrait of Coburn in *Camera Work* 15 (July 1906): Plate 6; and the Wells selection above as well as the Twain, James and Coburn, Belloc, and Pound selections below.

4. See E. Dean Bevan, comp., *A Concordance to the Plays and Prefaces of Bernard Shaw,* vol. 7 (Detroit: Gale, 1971), pp. 4306–7 in the index under "Photograph," and *Bernard Shaw's Rhyming Picture Guide to Ayot St. Lawrence* (Luton: Leagrave Press, 1950).

29. *Jack London*

*L*ondon (1876–1916) was the most popular American author in
the years preceding the First World War. Like many of his heroes,
he was endowed with prodigious physical as well as intellectual
energy. He often had firsthand experience of the adventures portrayed in
his realistic yet romantic writing, which often involved perilous struggles
for survival in northern wildernesses or tropical seas. The young Stieglitz
was one of the many readers who "devoured each one as it appeared."[1] In
1900, when his first collection of short stories about the Yukon brought
fame, London bought a camera and was taught by his first wife, Bessie, to
develop and print his own pictures.[2] By 1903, he was sufficiently expert to
use his own photographs to illustrate The People of the Abyss (1903), a
sociological study of slums in England's capital.[3] Signing on to cover the
Russo-Japanese War in 1904, London again took his camera—which nearly
ended his career, as told below. Although the last correspondent to reach
Seoul [Fig. 44], he proved the first at the front, sending back accomplished
photographs as well as dispatches to the Hearst papers, which printed some
of them [Fig. 45].[4] Subsequently, after using his photographs to illustrate
another nonfiction work, The Road (1907), London tried to sell his pictures
along with his writings about his long-planned Pacific cruise (1907–9), but
the trouble and expense of using his equipment in wet tropical climates diminished his interest in photography.[5] After 1910, his second wife, Charmion,
became the main photographer in the family; by the time of the author's
premature death, the Londons had amassed more than a hundred photograph albums that copiously documented his colorful rags-to-riches life.[6]

Shimonoseki, Wednesday, February 3.—I journeyed all day from Yokohama to Kobe to catch a steamer for Chemulpo, which last city is on the road to Seoul. I journeyed all day and all night from Kobe to Nagasaki to catch a steamer for Chemulpo. I journeyed back all day from Nagasaki to Moji to catch a steamer for Chemulpo. On Monday morning in Moji, I bought my ticket for Chemulpo, to sail on Monday afternoon. To-day is Wednesday, and I am still trying to catch a steamer for Chemulpo. And thereby hangs a tale of war and disaster, which runs the gamut of the emotions from surprise and anger to sorrow and brotherly love, and which culminates in arrest, felonious guilt and confiscation of property, to say nothing of monetary fines or alternative imprisonment.

For know that Moji is a fortified place, and one is not permitted to photograph "land or water scenery." I did not know it, and I photographed neither land nor water scenery; but I know it now just the same.

Having bought my ticket at the Osaka Shosen Kaisha office, I tucked it into my pocket and stepped out the door. Came four coolies carrying a bale of cotton. Snap went my camera. Five little boys at play—snap again. A line of coolies carrying coal—and again snap, and last snap. For a middle-aged Japanese man, in European clothes and great perturbation, fluttered his hands prohibitively before my camera. Having performed this function, he promptly disappeared.

"Ah, it is not allowed," I thought, and, calling my rickshawman, I strolled along the street.

Later, passing by a two-story frame building, I noticed my middle-aged Japanese standing in the doorway. He smiled and beckoned me to enter. "Some chin-chin and tea," thought I, and obeyed. But alas! it was destined to be too much chin-chin and no tea at all. I was in the police station. The middle-aged Japanese was what the American hobo calls a "fly cop."

Great excitement ensued. Captains, lieutenants and ordinary policemen all talked at once and ran hither and thither. I had run into a hive of blue uniforms, brass buttons and cut-lasses. The populace clustered like flies at doors and windows to gape at the "Russian spy." At first it was all very ludicrous—"capital to while away some of the time ere my steamer departs," was my judgment; but when I was taken to an upper room and the hours began to slip by, I decided that it was serious.

I explained that I was going to Chemulpo. "In a moment," said the interpreter. I showed my ticket, my pass-port, my card, my credentials; and always and invariably came the answer, "in a moment." Also, the interpreter stated that he was very sorry. He stated this many times. He made special trips upstairs to tell me he was very sorry. Every time I told him I was going to Chemulpo he expressed his sorrow, until we came to vie with each other, I in explaining my destination, he in explaining the state and degree of his emotion regarding me and my destination.

And so it went. The hour of tiffin [lunch] had long gone by. I had had an early breakfast. But my appetite waited on his "In a moment" till afternoon was well along. Then came the police examination, replete with searching questions concerning myself, my antecedents, and every member of my family. All of which information was gravely written down. An unappeasable interest in my family was displayed. The remotest relatives were hailed with keen satisfaction and placed upon paper. The exact ascertainment of their antecedents and birthplaces seemed necessary to the point at issue, namely, the snaps I had taken of the four coolies carrying cotton, the five little boys playing and the string of coal coolies.

Next came my movements since my arrival in Japan.

"Why did you go to Kobe?"

"To go to Chemulpo," was my answer. And in this fashion I explained my presence in the various cities of Japan. I made manifest that my only reason for existence was to go the Chemulpo; but their conclusion from my week's wandering was that I had no fixed place of abode. I began to shy. The last time the state of my existence had been so designated it had been followed by a thirty-day imprisonment in a vagrant's cell![7] Chemulpo suddenly grew dim and distant, and began to fade beyond the horizon of my mind.

"What is your rank?" was the initial question of the next stage of the examination.

I was nobody, I explained, a mere citizen of the United States; though I felt like saying that my rank was that of traveler for Chemulpo. I was given to understand that by rank was meant business, profession.

"Traveling to Chemulpo," I said was my business; and when they looked puzzled I meekly added that I was only a correspondent.

Next, the hour and the minute I made the three exposures. Were they of land and water scenery? No, they were of people. What people? Then I told of the four coolies carrying cotton, the five small boys playing and the string of coal coolies. Did I stand with my back to the land? Somebody had informed them that I had taken pictures in Nagasaki (a police lie, and they sprang many such on me). I strenuously denied. Besides it had rained all the time I was in Nagasaki. What other pictures had I taken in Japan? Three—two of Mount Fuji, one of a man selling tea at a railway station. Where were the pictures? In the camera, along with the four coolies carrying cotton, the five small boys playing and the string of coal coolies? Yes.

Now, about those four coolies carrying cotton, the five small boys playing and the string of coal coolies? And then they threshed through the details of the three exposures, up and down, back and forth, and crossways, till I wished that the coal coolies, cotton coolies and small boys had never been born. I have dreamed about them ever since, and I know I shall dream about them until I die.

Why did I take the pictures? Because I wanted to. Why did I want to? For my pleasure. Why for my pleasure?

Pause a moment, gentler reader, and consider. What answer could you give to such a question concerning any act you have ever performed? Why do you do anything? Because you want to; because it is your pleasure. An answer to the question, "Why do you perform an act for your pleasure?" would constitute an

epitome of psychology. Such an answer would go down to the roots of being, for it involves impulse, volition, pain, pleasure, sensation, gray matter, nerve fibers, free will and determinism, and all the vast fields of speculation wherein man has floundered since the day he dropped down out of the trees and began to seek out the meaning of things.

And I, an insignificant traveler on my way to Chemulpo, was asked this question in the Moji police station through the medium of a seventh-rate interpreter. Nay, an answer was insisted upon. Why did I take the pictures because I wanted to, for my pleasure? I wished to take them—why? Because the act of taking them would make me happy. Why would the act of taking them make me happy? Because it would give me pleasure. But why would it give me pleasure? I hold no grudge against the policeman who examined me at Moji, yet I hope that in the life to come he will encounter the shade of Herbert Spencer and be informed just why, precisely, I took the pictures of the four coolies carrying cotton, the five small boys playing and the string of coal coolies.

Now, concerning my family, were my sisters older than I or younger? The change in the line of questioning was refreshing, even though it was perplexing. But ascertained truth is safer than metaphysics, and I answered blithely. Had I a pension from the government? A salary? Had I a medal of service? Of merit? Was it an American camera? Was it instantaneous? Was it mine?

To cut a simple narrative short, I pass on from this sample of the examination I underwent to the next step in the proceedings, which was the development of the film. Guarded by a policeman and accompanied by the interpreter, I was taken through the streets of Moji to a native photographer. I described the location of the three pictures of the film of ten. Observe the simplicity of it. These three pictures he cut out and developed, the seven other exposures, or possible exposures, being returned to me undeveloped. They might have contained the secret of the fortifications of Moji for all the policemen knew; and yet I was permitted to carry them away with me, and I have them now. For the peace of Japan, let me declare that they contain only pictures of Fuji and tea-sellers.

I asked permission to go to my hotel and pack my trunks—in order to be ready to catch the steamer for Chemulpo. Permission was accorded, and my luggage accompanied me back to the police station, where I was again confined in the upper room listening to the "In a moments" of the interpreter and harping my one note that I wanted to go to Chemulpo. In one of the intervals the interpreter remarked, "I know great American correspondent formerly."

"What was his name?" I asked, politely.

"Benjamin Franklin," came the answer; and I swear, possibly because I was thinking of Chemulpo, that my face remained graven as an image.

The arresting officer now demanded that I should pay for developing the incriminating film, and my declining to do so caused him not a little consternation.

"I am very sorry," said the interpreter, and there were tears in his voice; "I inform you cannot go to Chemulpo. You must go to Kokura."

Which last place I learned was a city a few miles in the interior.

"Baggage go?" I asked.

"You pay?" he countered.

I shook my head.

"Baggage go not," he announced.

"And I go not," was my reply.

I was led downstairs into the main office. My luggage followed. The police surveyed it. Everybody began to talk at once. Soon they were shouting. The din was terrific, the gestures terrifying. In the midst of it I asked the interpreter what they had decided to do, and he answered, shouting to make himself heard, that they were talking it over.

Finally rickshaws were impressed, and bag and baggage transferred to the depot. Alighting at the depot at Kokura, more delay was caused by my declining to leave my luggage in the freight office. In the end it was carted along with me to the police station, where it became a spectacle for the officials.

Here I underwent an examination before the Public Procurator of the Kokura District Court. The interpreter began very unhappily, as follows:

"Customs different in Japan from America; therefore you must not tell any lies."

Then was threshed over once again all the details of the four coolies carrying cotton, the five small boys playing and the string of coal coolies; and I was committed to appear for trial next morning.

And next morning, bare-headed, standing, I was tried by three solemn, black-capped judges. The affair was very serious. I had committed a grave offense, and the Public Procurator stated that while I did not merit a prison sentence, I was nevertheless worthy of a fine.

After an hour's retirement the judges achieved a verdict. I was to pay a fine of five yen, and Japan was to get the camera. All of which was eminently distasteful to me, but I managed to extract a grain of satisfaction from the fact that they quite forgot to mulct me of the five yen. There is trouble brewing for somebody because of those five yen. There is the judgment. I am a free man. But how are they to balance accounts?

In the evening at the hotel the manager, a Japanese, handed me a card, upon which was transcribed: Reporter of the "Osaka Asahi Shimbun." I met him in the reading-room, a slender, spectacled, silk-gowned man, who knew not one word of English. The manager acted as interpreter. The reporter was very sorry for my predicament. He expressed the regret of twenty other native correspondents in the vicinity, who in turn, represented the most powerful newspapers in the empire. He had come to offer their best offices: also to interview me.

The law was the law, he said, and the decree of the court could not be set aside; but there were ways of getting around the law. The voice of the newspapers was heard in the land. He and his fellow correspondents would petition the Kokura judges to auction off the camera, he and his associates to attend and bid it in at a nominal figure. Then it would give them the greatest pleasure to present my camera (or the Mikado's, or theirs) to me with their compliments.

I could have thrown my arms about him then and there—not for the camera, but for brotherhood, as he himself expressed it the next moment, because we were brothers in the craft. Then we had tea together and talked over the prospects of war. The nation of Japan he likened to a prancing and impatient horse, the government to the rider, endeavoring to restrain the fiery steed. The people wanted war, the newspapers wanted war, public opinion clamored for war; and war the Government would eventually have to give them.

We parted as brothers part, and without wishing him any ill-luck, I should like to help him out of a hole some day in the United States. And here I remain in my hotel wondering if I'll ever see my camera again and trying to find another steamer for Chemulpo.

P.S.—Just received a dispatch from the United States Minister at Tokio. As an act of courtesy, the Minister of Justice will issue orders to-day to restore my camera!

P.S.—And a steamer sails to-morrow for Chemulpo.

44. Unknown. 'Jack London and Korean official,' 1904.

45. Jack London. 'Captured Russian Cannon,' 1904.

1. Steichen, quoted in Haines, *The Inner Eye of Alfred Stieglitz*, p. 108, n. 16.

2. See, for example, London, letters to Elwyn Hoffman, August 25, November 13, November 22, 1900, and Cornelius Gepfert, November 5, 1900, in *The Letters of Jack London,* ed. Earle Labor et al. (Stanford, Calif.: Stanford University Press, 1988), vol. 1, pp. 210, 219, 220, and 217–18 respectively. Bessie Maddern London's significant role, not mentioned elsewhere, was pointed out by Russ Kingman of the Jack London Research Center in Glen Ellen, California, in a telephone conversation with the editor on June 8, 1992.

3. See London, letters to George P. Brett, September 29, 1902, December 11, 1902, February 16, 1903, and March 20, 1903, in *Letters,* vol. 1, pp. 314, 325, 344, 355, and London, *The People of the Abyss* (New York: Macmillan, 1903), which seems to have reinforced his conflicting beliefs in socialism and revolution.

4. See also, in addition to the selection below, London, letters to Charmion Kittredge, February 3, February 13, May 17, 1904, in *Letters,* pp. 409–10, 412, 429; London, "The Russo-Japanese War: Selected Dispatches," in *Jack London's Tales of Adventures,* ed. Irving Shepard (New York: Hanover House, 1956), pp. 118–30, with the author's photographs between pp. 116 and 117 (reprinted with other dispatches but not accompanied by London's photographs in *Jack London Reports,* ed. King Hendricks and Irving Shepard [New York: Doubleday, 1970], pp. 124–26); a list of all London's newspaper articles concerning this conflict, filed from February 3 to June 26, 1904, in Hensley C. Woodbridge et al., *Jack London: A Bibliography* (New York: Kraus, 1973), pp. 251–54; Eiji Tsujii, "Jack London Items in the Japanese Press of 1904," *Jack London Newsletter* 8 (May–August 1975): 55–58; and Lloyd C. Griscom, *Diplomatically Speaking* (Boston: Little, Brown, 1940), pp. 245–46. The pic-

tures of London during this period may have been taken by his colleagues "Bobbie" Dunn or Robert McLellan, who noted London's rush to the front in a piece for the *San Francisco Examiner* (April 17, 1904): 19, exhibited at the Jack London State Historical Park in Glen Ellen, California.

5. See London, *The Road* (New York: Macmillan, 1907), called to the editor's attention by Andrew Cahan; and London, letters to Ninetta Eames, July 11, August 15, and September 12, 1907; to F. Haydon, October 25, 1908, and to H. C. White Company, September 13, 1910, in *Letters,* vol. 2, pp. 696, 705, 710, 756–57, and 930–31. When London covered the Vera Cruz Expedition in 1914, the pictures accompanying his text were taken by James H. Hare. But the voyage increased the interest in both adventure and photography of one of the young crew members, Martin Johnson (1884–1937), who, with the help of his wife, Osa, later became a renowned hunter and photographer and tried to build a visual "library" of still photographs, slides, and movies of Africa's vanishing wildlife. Rachel Stuhlman first told the editor about this interesting figure.

6. See London, letters to Ralph Kasper, March 19 and April 18, 1913, in *Letters,* vol. 3, pp. 1140 and 1152. Copies of the photographs from 123 large and small London albums—almost all still retained by the family—are in the Jack London Collection at the Huntington Library and at the State of California, Department of Parks and Recreation, Santa Rosa (soon to be moved to Sonoma). The photographs of Charmion Kittredge London are at the Merrill Library, Utah State University.

7. [Original editor's note] A reference to his experiences as a tramp in 1894. He records these in his book *The Road*. He was arrested in Niagara for vagrancy and sentenced to thirty days in the Erie County Penitentiary.

30. *Mark Twain*

FROM WRITINGS, 1866–1906

*L*ong before adopting the pseudonym of Mark Twain, Samuel Langhorne Clemens (1835–1910) recognized the communicative power
of photographs. At only fifteen, as a printer's apprentice, he cleverly held up a compositor's stick containing type for three letters, M, A,
and S, knowing they would spell his first name when reversed in the final
daguerreotype (or "dog-gerytype," as he dubbed it in a later juvenile sketch)
[Fig. 46].[1] Throughout his life, he was involved with all kinds of photographic portraits, whether the one of his future wife, Olivia, with which he
fell in love even before meeting her, or the ones that promoted his own
image, perhaps his greatest artistic creation.[2] The humorist's poses were all
unexpectedly serious [Figs. 47, 49], however, because of his belief that
"there is nothing more damning to go down to posterity than a silly, foolish
smile caught and fixed forever."[3] The creator of Tom Sawyer (1876) and
Huckleberry Finn (1884) often used photographs as illustrations to his
works or bases for them but rarely referred to them in his writings—and
then mainly in his less celebrated nonfiction. They mocked appearance and
reality in portraiture; supplied incident in Innocents Abroad (1869); embellished setting in Life on the Mississippi (1883); reinforced powerful satire in
King Leopold's Soliloquy (1905) [Fig. 48]; and supplied metaphors to describe his creative process.[4] But in his final years Twain appointed a former
professional photographer, Albert Bigelow Paine (1861–1937), as his official
biographer and, later, his literary executor. As the author shrewdly anticipated, photographs of him by Paine, as well as by Alvin Langdon Coburn
and others, would continue to help maintain his legendary status.[5]

FROM WRITINGS

FROM "Letter from Hawaii," JULY 1, 1866
. . . No photograph ever was good, yet, of any-body—hunger and thirst and utter wretched-ness overtake the outlaw who invented it! It transforms into desperadoes the weakest of men; depicts sinless innocence upon the pictured faces of ruffians; gives the wise man the stupid leer of a fool, and the fool an expression of more than earthly wisdom. If a man tries to look serious when he sits for his picture, the photo-graph makes him as solemn as an owl; if he smiles, the photograph smirks repulsively; if he tries to look pleasant, the photograph looks silly; if he makes the fatal mistake of attempt-ing to seem pensive, the camera will surely write him down as an ass. The sun never looks through a photographic instrument that does not print a lie. The piece of glass it prints is well named a "negative"—a contradiction—a misrepresenta-tion—a falsehood. I speak feelingly of this matter, because by turns the instrument has represented me to be a lunatic, a Solomon, a missionary, a burglar and an abject idiot—and I am neither. [from "Scenes in Honolulu–No. 15," July 1, 1866, *Sacramento Daily Union* (Au-gust 1, 1866): 1]

FROM *Innocents Abroad*, 1867/1869
Several times the photographer of the expedi-tion [to the Holy Land] brought out his trans-parent pictures and gave us a handsome magic lantern exhibition. His views were nearly all of foreign scenes, but there were one or two home pictures among them. He advertised that he

would "open his performance in the after cabin at 'two bells' (9 p.m.), and show the passengers where they shall eventually arrive"—which was all very well, but by a funny accident the first picture that flamed out upon the canvas was a view of Greenwood Cemetery! [(Hartford, Conn.; American Publishing Co., 1869), ch. 4, about events in 1867]

FROM LETTER TO OLIVIA L. LANGDON, JANUARY 20–21, 1869
. . . Livy, I am mad at myself for my thoughtlessness—making you run to the daguerrean gallery five times, when I know that it is nothing less than punishment to make you sit up & be stared at by those operators—& I don't *want* them staring at you, & propping up your chin, & profaning your head with the touch of their hands—& so please don't go again, Livy. Never mind the picture, now—wait till you are in New York again. I was too selfish—I thought only of my own gratification & never once of the punishment I was inflicting on you. But bless your heart, Livy, I never *thought* of your going *five* times. Don't you go again, dear—now don't you do it. And just you be the lovely good girl you are, & forgive my stupid thoughtlessness. [*Letters,* vol. 3, p. 54]

FROM LETTER TO JOSEPH H. TWICHELL AND FAMILY, JANUARY 23, 1869
If you could only see the picture! It came last night. She [Olivia] sat six times for a ferrotype—taking 3 weeks to it—& every picture was a slander & I gently said so—very gently—& at last she tried a porcelain type [presto]. When I opened the little velvet case last night, lo! a messenger-angel out of upper Heaven was roosting there! I give you my word of honor that it is a very marvel of beauty—the expression is sweet, & patient, & *so* far-away & dreamy. What respect, what reverent honor it compels! Any man's unconscious move would be to take his hat off in its presence, and if he had not the impulse, I would give it him. [*Letters,* vol. 3, p. 67]

FROM LETTER TO OLIVIA LANGDON, FEBRUARY 27, 1869
I will send Hattie a photograph of the old pattern, & when I sit again, I will send the new one. (I talk of sitting, as complacently as if I were an old hen, & used to it). And this reminds me that I told Mrs. Fairbanks [whom Twain met on the cruise to the Holy Land in 1867; Olivia met her in 1868] you would sit for a large photograph for her, (like mine that hangs in her library,) as a companion to the one I gave her. . . . But you needn't hurry, Livy—in the spring will do. I will take you to the photographer's & "fix" you, to suit myself. [*Letters,* vol. 3, p. 118]

FROM LETTER TO MRS. FAIRBANKS, FEBRUARY 27–28, 1869
I forgot to tell Livy, but I have written her, that I promised you a large photograph to hang up in your library as a companion to mine—but I told her to hold on till I come, & I will "sit" her myself. In fact she ought to hold on till some time when she is in New York, for she has amply proved by sitting five times for a photograph for me that they *can't* take even passable photographs in Elmira. [*Letters,* vol. 3, pp. 132–33]

FROM "NIAGARA"
On the Canada side you drive . . . between long ranks of photographers standing guard behind their cameras, ready to make an ostentatious frontispiece of you and your decaying ambulance, and your solemn crate with a hide on it, which you are expected to regard in the light of a horse, and a diminished and unimportant background of sublime Niagara; and a great many people *have* the incredible effrontery or the native depravity to aid and abet this sort of crime.

Any day, in the hands of these photographers, you may see stately pictures of papa and mamma, Johnny and Bub and Sis, or a couple of country cousins, all smiling vacantly, and all disposed in studied and uncomfortable attitudes in their carriage, and all looming up in their awe-inspiring imbecility before the snubbed and diminished presentment of that majestic presence whose ministering spirits are the rainbows. . . .

There is no actual harm in making Niagara a background whereon to display one's marvelous insignificance in a good strong light, but it requires a sort of superhuman self-complacency to enable one to do it . . . [In *Mark Twain's Sketches, New and Old* (New York: Harper & Brothers, 1875), pp. 71–72]

FROM *A Tramp Abroad*
The success of my last experiment induced me to try an experiment with my photographic apparatus. I got it out and boiled one of my cameras, but the thing was a failure: it made the wood swell up and burst, and I could not see that the lenses were any better than they were before. . . .

NOTE: I leveled my photographic apparatus at it [the Matterhorn] without the loss of an instant, and should have got an elegant picture if my donkey had not interfered. It was my purpose to draw [from?] this photograph all by myself for my book, but was obliged to put the mountain part of it into the hands of the professional artist because I found I could not do landscape well. [(Hartford, Conn.: American Publishing Co., 1880), ch. 38, pp. 437 and 448 note]

FROM "HOUSE BEAUTIFUL," *Life on the Mississippi,* 1883
[According to Twain, the antebellum parlor of the home of each town's wealthiest citizen invariably contained the following, in addition to portraits carved on shells of George Washington and "God Bless Our Home" picked out in needlework.] Opposite, in "gilt frames" of "grandpa and grandma, at thirty and twenty-two, stiff, old-fashioned, high-collared, puff-sleeved, glaring pallidly out from a background of solid Egyptian night . . . spread-open daguerreotypes of dim children, parents, cousins, aunt and friends, in all attitudes but customary ones; no temples portico at back, and manufactured landscape stretching away in the distance—that came in later, with the photograph; all these vague figures lavishly chained and ringed—metal indicated and secured from doubt by stripes and splashes of vivid gold bronze; all of them too much combed, too much fixed up; and all of them uncomfortable in inflexible Sunday-clothes of a pattern which the spectator cannot realize could ever have been in fashion . . . husband sitting, wife standing, with hand on his shoulder—both preserving, all these fading years, some traceable effect of the daguerreotypist's brisk "Now smile, if you please!" [(Boston: James R. Osgood, 1883), ch. 38, pp. 280–81]

FROM *Autobiography* (1892)
What becomes of the multitudinous photographs which one's mind takes of people? Out of the million which my mental camera must have taken of this first and closest friend [Twain's mother], only one clear and strongly defined one of early date remains. It dates back forty-seven years; she was forty years old, then, and I was eight. [from *Autobiography,* ed. Albert Bigelow Paine (Harper & Brothers, 1924), vol. 1, ch. 7, p. 115]

REMARKS ON CHARACTERIZATION
I don't believe an author, good, bad, or indifferent, ever lived, who created a character. It was always drawn from his recollection of someone he had known. Sometimes, like a composite photograph, an author's presentation of a character may possibly be from the blending of more than two or more real characters in his recollection. . . . It is like a star so far away that the eye cannot discern it through the most powerful telescope, yet if a camera is placed in the proper position under the telescope and left for a few hours, a photograph of the star will result. So, it's the same way with the mind; a character one has known some time in life may have become so deeply buried within the recollection that the lens of the first effort will not bring it to view. But by continued application the author will find when he is done, that he has etched a likeness of someone he has known before. [Quoted in Lute Pease, "The Famous Story-Teller Discusses Characters. . . . ," *Portland Oregonian* (August 11, 1895), reprinted in Louis J. Budd, ed., *Critical Essays on Mark Twain, 1867–1910* (Boston: G. K. Hall, 1982), p. 108]

[Editor Albert Bigelow Paine's note:] In spite of all the fine photographs that were made of [Twain], there remained, certainly among those sent to him to be autographed a print of one which, years before, Sarony had made and placed on public sale. It was a good photograph, mechanically and even artistically, but it did not please Mark Twain. Whenever he saw it he recalled Sarony with bitterness and severity. Once he received an inquiry concerning it, and thus feelingly expressed himself.

The alleged portrait has a private history. Sarony was as much of an enthusiast about wild animals as he was about photography; and when DuChaillu brought the first Gorilla to this country in 1819 he came to me in a fever of excitement and asked me if my father was of record and authentic. I said he was; then Sarony, without any abatement of his excitement asked if my grandfather also was of record and authentic. I said he was. Then Sarony, with still rising excitement and with joy added to it, said he had found my great grandfather in the person of the gorilla, and had recognized him at once by his resemblance to me [Fig. 47]. I was deeply hurt but did not reveal this, because I knew Sarony meant no offense for the gorilla had not done him any harm. . . . I went with him to inspect the ancestor, and examined him from several points of view, without being able to detect anything more than a passing resemblance. "Wait," said Sarony with strong confidence, "let me show you." He borrowed my overcoat and put it on the gorilla. The result was surprising. I saw that the gorilla while not looking distinctly like me was exactly what my great grandfather would have looked like if I had one. Sarony photographed the creature in that overcoat, and spread the picture about the world. It has remained spread about the world ever since. It turns up every week in some newspaper somewhere or other. It is not my favorite, but to my exasperation it is everybody else's. Do you think you could get it suppressed for me? I will pay the limit. [*Letters,* ed. Albert

Bigelow Paine (New York: Harper & Brothers, 1917), vol. 2, pp. 785–86]

FROM *King Leopold's Soliloquy,* 1905
(Studies some photographs of mutilated Negroes—throws them down. Sighs.) The kodak has been a sore calamity to us. The most powerful enemy that has confronted us, indeed. In the early years we had no trouble getting the press to "expose" the tales of the mutilations as slanders, lies, inventions of busybody American missionaries and exasperated foreigners who had found the "open door" of the Berlin-Congo charter closed against them when they innocently went out there to trade; and by the press's help we got the Christian nations everywhere to turn an irritated and unbelieving ear to those tales and say hard things about the

tellers of them. Yes, all things went harmoniously and pleasantly in those good days, and I was looked up to as the benefactor of a downtrodden and friendless people. Then all of a sudden came the crash! That is to say, the incorruptible *kodak*—and all the harmony went to hell! The only witness I have encountered in my long experience that I couldn't bribe [Fig. 48]. Every Yankee missionary and every interrupted trader sent home and got one; and now—oh well, the pictures got sneaked around everywhere, in spite of all we can do to ferret them out and suppress them. Ten thousand pulpits and ten thousand presses are saying the good word for me all the time and placidly and convincingly denying the mutilations. Then that trivial little kodak, that a child can carry in its pocket, gets up, uttering never a word, and knocks them dumb! [(Boston: P. R. Warren, 1905/1906), pp. 37–38]

FROM AN AUTOBIOGRAPHICAL DICTATION, DUBLIN, NEW HAMPSHIRE, AUGUST 31, 1906
The pictures which Mr. Paine made on the portico here several weeks ago have been developed and are good [Fig. 49]. For the sake of the moral lesson which they teach I wish to insert a set of them here for future generations to study, with the result, I hope, that they will

48. Unknown. Caricature of a photographer, from *King Leopold's Soliloquy* by Mark Twain, 1906.

"The only witness I couldn't bribe"

reform, if they need it—and I expect they will. I am sending half a dozen of these sets to friends of mine who need reforming, and I have introduced the pictures to them with this formula: This series of photographs registers with scientific precision, stage by stage, the progress of a moral purpose through the mind of the human race's Oldest Friend. [original typescript insert, pp. 1211–17, Mark Twain Project, Bancroft Library; reprinted in *The Autobiography of Mark Twain*, ed. Neider, between pp. 198 and 199]

1. James Preston Waller, "Visions and Revisions of Mark Twain: Samuel L. Clemens in the Camera's Eye, 1851–1885" (Ph.D. diss., Duke University, 1990), pp. 110–15, most fully discusses this daguerreotype portrait and, pp. 116–27, the context of the "*dog*-gerytype" in "'Local' Resolves to Commit Suicide," *Hannibal Journal* (September 16, 1852), reprinted in *Mark Twain: Early Tales and Sketches, 1851–1864*, ed. Edgar M. Brach and Robert H. Hirst (Berkeley: Published for the Iowa Center for Textual Studies by the University of California Press, 1979), vol. 1, pp. 75–76.

2. For the role of photographs in his courtship of Olivia Langdon, see, for example, Twain's letter to her in *Mark Twain's Letters, Volume 2, 1867–68*, ed. Harriet Smith and Richard Bucci, in *The Mark Twain Papers*, ed. Robert H. Hirst et al. (Berkeley: University of California Press, 1990), November 28, 1868, p. 291, while pp. 145–46, n. 3, and 439–40 provide details on the photograph of Olivia that first attracted Twain. See also Twain's letters to Olivia from January 2 to November 25

in *Mark Twain's Letters, Volume 3, 1869*, ed. Victor Fisher and Michael B. Frank, in *The Mark Twain Papers*, ed. Hirst et al., about other photographs of her, all cited in the Index, p. 731, under Olivia L. Langdon, "Portraits and Photographs." Waller, "Visions and Revisions of Mark Twain," pp. 303–7, 349–50, and 376–80, discusses these together with other letters and photographs relating to Olivia in context.

3. Twain's remark, first quoted in Elizabeth Wallace, *Mark Twain and The Happy Island* (Chicago: A. C. McClurg, 1913), p. 34, is discussed by Waller, "Visions and Revisions of Mark Twain," pp. 2–5. Twain's concern about looking foolish may explain his chagrin about the so-called Gorilla portrait of him taken by Napoleon Sarony, evident in his 1905 letter to Mr. Row, reproduced below; Twain's fear resembles that of Ursula in Márquez, *One Hundred Years of Solitude*, p. 51, who doesn't want to survive in a daguerreotype as a "laughingstock for her grandchildren." Twain also calls a photograph "dead and flat" compared to the living subject,

49 (1–8). Albert Bigelow Paine. 'The Development of a Moral Thought,' with handwritten captions by Mark Twain, 1906.

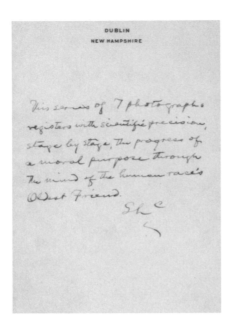

in a letter to Mr. and Mrs. Karl Gerhardt, May 1, 1883, quoted in *Mark Twain: Selected Writings of an American Skeptic,* ed. Victor Doyno (Buffalo, N.Y.: Prometheus Books, 1883), pp. 222–23, and in Waller, p. 566. Waller, pp. 708–96, lists the portraits of Twain in major American collections, many of which he has discussed and reproduced throughout. Linda Haverty Rugg's MS, "Mark Twain's Photographic Autobiography: Illumination and Obfuscation," supplemented her helpful conversations with the editor on January 4–5, 1992.

4. See, for example, Robert H. Hirst and Brandt Rowles, "William E. James's Stereoscopic View of the *Quaker City* Excursion," *Mark Twain Journal* 221 (Spring 1984): 15–33, and Beverly R. David, *Mark Twain and His Illustrators* (Troy, N.Y.: Whitson Publishing Company, 1986), pp. x, 2–8, 15–20. Some of the selections below, as well as additional relevant material, are also quoted and discussed in context by Waller, "Visions and Revisions in Mark Twain": pp. 545–47 *(A Tramp Abroad);* pp. 578 and 584 *(Life on the Mississippi);* pp. 157, 667, and 696 *(The Autobiography of Mark Twain);* and pp. 697–99 *(King Leopold's Soliloquy).* See also Rex Burns, "The Artful Photograph: Mark Twain's Eye," *American Literary Realism* 15, no. 1 (Spring 1982): 62–73.

5. See "Albert Bigelow Paine," *National Cy-*

clopedia of American Biography (New York: James T. White, 1940), vol. 28, p. 113; John Seelye, *Mark Twain in the Movies: A Meditation with Pictures* (New York: Viking Press, 1977), pp. 37–42; and Waller, "Visions and Revisions of Mark Twain," pp. 701–2. Paine, *Mark Twain: A Biography,* 3 vols. (New York: Harper & Brothers, 1912) includes many of his photographs, as does *The Writings of Mark Twain,* Stormfield Edition, 38 vols. (New York: Harper & Brothers, 1929). The original sequence of Paine's seven pictures of Twain, captioned by the writer, are at the Lilly and Bancroft Libraries (1906.18–24); they were first reproduced in Paine, *Mark Twain: A Biography* (New York: Harper & Brothers, 1912), vol. 4, foldout facing p. 1316, and then in Twain, *Autobiography,* ed. Charles Neider (New York: Harper & Brothers, 1959), following p. 164. See also Coburn's autochrome of Twain in bed for Archibald Henderson, *Mark Twain* (New York: Frederick K. Stokes, 1910; London: Duckworth, 1911); his black and white portrait of him in *Men of Mark* (London and New York: Stokes, 1913), Plate 22; and his recollections of him in Coburn, *Autobiography,* pp. 32, 62, 64, and 66, and in Coburn, "Two Visits to Mark Twain," BBC Radio Talk, November 21, 1954, condensed as "Photographing Mark Twain," in *The Listener* 52 (December 2, 1954): 947.

31. Henry Adams and Marian Hooper Adams

FROM LETTERS, 1872–1907

In his preface of his classic study, Mont-Saint Michel and Chartres (1904), Henry Adams (1838–1918) mentions a Kodak camera, the first of many images representing the mechanical, destructive multiplicity of his era as opposed to the more spiritual, creative unity of the Middle Ages.[1] Adams had not always been so condescending about photography. He'd praised the book he gave as an engagement gift to Marian "Clover" Hooper (1843–83) for its "almost photographic truth to nature."[2] He had learned to use a camera for their 1873 honeymoon in Egypt, and was delighted when his pictures—some of which his bride helped print—captured the spirit as well as the appearance of the monuments. A decade later, Clover Adams took up photography, perhaps influenced by her husband and her family's intimate, Oliver Wendell Holmes, Sr. (1809–94), a noted doctor, man of letters, and early stereoscope enthusiast.[3] More serious than her husband in pursuing their shared interest, she bought her own "machine," equipped a darkroom, explored new printing methods, documented her results, and soon won recognition, particularly for her portraits (Fig. 50). But, depressed after her father's death, she soon committed suicide by drinking potassium cyanide, used in developing.[4] For the last of his subsequent restorative trips to the South Seas and the Orient, Adams brought a new Kodak but projected some of his anger and pain onto its limitations, soon regarding all photography as disturbing, even fatal, and becoming "photo-phobic."[5] In 1900, however, he somewhat sheepishly began to take pictures again (Fig. 51), more willing to reconcile photography's role in happier years with its inadvertent one in his personal tragedy.[6]

FROM LETTERS

Note: These excerpts, unless otherwise indicated, are drawn from The Letters of Henry Adams, *ed. J. C. Levenson et al., to various correspondents, who are briefly identified below;* The Letters of Mrs. Henry Adams, 1865–1883, *ed. Ward Thoron; and, after May 1883, the originals at the MHS [on microfilms of the Adams Family papers, Reels 597–98], all addressed to her father.*

HENRY ADAMS, MAY 30 [1872]

I am at present learning to photograph, for we mean to go up the Nile next winter, and I want to carry a photographic apparatus with me. [to Charles Milnes Gaskell, lifelong English friend, MP from Yorkshire in late 1880's, vol. 2, p. 137]

CLOVER ADAMS, JANUARY 24, 1873

Henry has been working like a beaver at photographing . . . and has taken several views which are very good, at least to those who have been to the places. He had much trouble with those at Abu-Simbel, and can't tell until they are printed whether they are a success or not. [p. 71]

CLOVER ADAMS, FEBRUARY 16, 1873

This morning early we floated down to Karnak as Henry wanted to try for some photographs. He worked at it for some hours but was not as successful as he has been at Philae. It is not easy to get views of these great columns twelve feet in diameter, and a photograph gives so little idea of their size. [pp. 75–76]

CLOVER ADAMS, FEBRUARY 19, 1873

Today the river has been so rough that we tied up from noon to sunset as it was not comfortable. We have been printing photographs to pass the time. [p. 76]

HENRY ADAMS, MARCH 4, 1873

I enclose you my photograph of Aboo Simbel, not because it is the best I have taken, but because it is the grandest subject, and none of the professional photographs for sale here have at all caught its spirit. I should not say this if I thought the credit of selecting the point of view belonged to me, but as this in fact belongs to a Mr. Ward, an American friend of ours with bankerial and artistic tastes. . . . I do not hesitate to say that my photograph is worth half a dozen of any I have yet met. [to Gaskell, vol. 2, p. 158]

CLOVER ADAMS, MAY 20, 1883

Am going to take a photo with my new machine this p.m. at Rock Creek. [p. 451]

HENRY ADAMS, JULY 26, 1883

I wish we could send you interesting details of our doings in return, but my wife does nothing except take photographs, while I do nothing except correct proof-sheets. [to Elizabeth Cameron, leading Washington, D.C., hostess and wife of an old friend, the longtime senator from Pennsylvania, vol. 2, p. 507]

HENRY ADAMS, SEPTEMBER 9, 1883

I meant to send you some of my wife's photographs to show you how we all look [Fig. 50], and what we are doing, but I have none just now in a convenient form. [to Gaskell, vol. 2, pp. 511–12]

CLOVER ADAMS, DECEMBER 2, 1883

I photographed Mr. & Mrs. Bancroft [he was a distinguished American historian, 1800–91] on Wednesday. Hers is good technically but not a pleasant likeness. . . . Mr. B. is very good—sitting at this library writing table writing history—a profile view—his hair & beard came out silvery & soft in the picture—I must send you one if I print any more. [Reel 597]

JOHN HAY, DECEMBER 29, 1883

Mrs. Henry Adams has made a remarkable photograph of George Bancroft in his study. He is now eighty-three, and one of these days will be done. I suggest that you get a copy of it and put it in the hand of your engraver—in time. [Hay, Adams's closest friend and an eminent statesman, to the *Century Magazine* editor, Richard W. Gilder, from *Letters and Extracts from a Diary,* sel. Henry Adams (Washington, D.C., 1908), vol. 2, p. 86]

CLOVER ADAMS, DECEMBER 31, 1883

It was science pure and simple which took up all my morning on Sunday & left me asleep in the p.m. A wonderful process of printing from negatives has been perfected lately & the man who owns the patent gave an exhibition of the process at the photograph rooms in the National Museum on Sunday—Mr. C. Richardson [Chemical Expert for Washington D.C.] very kindly smuggled me in—as the only woman—we were 3 hours there tho' the process is really very rapid. I shall buy . . . the right to use his patent for a trifle and will send you a proof. [Reel 597]

HENRY ADAMS, DECEMBER 31 [1883]

When you come, my wife wants you to bring back the children's negatives. She has discovered a new process of printing, and thinks she can do something good. [to Hay, vol. 2, p. 526]

CLOVER ADAMS, JANUARY 6, 1884

Yesterday I was amused to get a letter from R. W. Gilder, the editor of the Century Magazine asking if I would let him have a photo of Mr. Bancroft someone had spoken to him of "with a view to its reproduction in the magazine" & writing Henry to write an article on Papa Bancroft of 7 or 8 pages to go with it. I've just written to decline & telling him Mr. Adams does not fancy the prevailing literary vivisection. . . . The mutual admiration game is about played out or ought to be. [Reel 598]

HENRY ADAMS, JANUARY 6, 1884

We have declined Mr. Gilder's pleasing offer. You know our modesty. . . . As for flaunting our photographs in the 'Century,' we should expect to experience the curse of all our unphotographed friends. [to Hay, vol. 2, p. 527]

CLOVER ADAMS, FEBRUARY 10, 1884

I am going to buy a portrait lens when I can decide which one I want—mine is not made for anything but out of doors work—. . . [Reel 598]

CLOVER ADAMS, FEBRUARY 24, 1884

Printed photos for nearly two hours—seizing a bright sun which is rare of late—then Henry and I drove to Senator [Lucius Q. C.] Lamar's rooms . . . to take his photo. . . . L. brushed his long hair to the regulation smoothness & then I refused to take his likeness until he had rumpled it all up. I took two photos of him & one of Gordon [General Gordon of Georgia] who has a deep hole from Antietam in his left cheek as you'll see next summer. [Reel 598]

HENRY ADAMS, NOVEMBER 23, 1884

Tomorrow my wife will try to take a photograph of your 16th Street front [to Hay, vol. 2, p. 557]

HENRY ADAMS, NOVEMBER 30, 1884

I photographed your house for you last Monday to show your big arch hanging in mid-air; but my wife has been unable . . . to print it . . . [to Hay, vol. 2, p. 558]

Clover Adams committed suicide on December 6, 1885. Over the next five years, Henry Adams took two long trips to Polynesia and the Far East to help recover from his loss.

HENRY ADAMS, JULY 24, 1886

Photographs give no idea of the scale. They show here a gate and there a temple, but they cannot show twenty acres of ground, all ingeniously used to make a single composition. They give no idea of a mountain-flank, with its evergreens a hundred feet high, modeled into a royal, posthumous residence and deified abode. [to Hay, vol. 3, p. 24]

HENRY ADAMS, SEPTEMBER 9, 1886

I, seizing the little priest's camera, mounted to the roof of his porch, and, standing on my head at an angle of impossibility [to photograph a statue of the Buddha], perpetrated a number of libels on Buddha and Buddhism. [to Hay, vol. 3, p. 37]

HENRY ADAMS, AUGUST 26 [1890]
I mean to photograph everything so that you may see it all, but photography is no longer an amusement now that it is all mechanical, and you have fifty pictures in half an hour. [to Mrs. Cameron, vol. 3, p. 271]

HENRY ADAMS, OCTOBER 21, 1890
. . . I mean to enclose some photographs if I can get them . . . but remember that the photograph takes all the fun out of the tropics. Especially it vulgarizes the women, whose charm is chiefly in their size and proportions, their lines, the freedom of their movements, the color of their skin, and their good-natured smiles. . . . The scenery is also spoiled by photographing. The softness of lights and colors, the motion of the palms, the delicacy and tenderness of the mornings and evenings, the moisture of the atmosphere, and all the other qualities which charm one here, are not to be put into a photograph, which simply gives one conventional character to New England and Samoa alike. [to Anna Cabot Mills Lodge, wife of the senator from Massachusetts and a prominent Washington hostess, vol. 3, p. 307]

HENRY ADAMS, OCTOBER 22, 1890
We [John La Farge, the painter, Adams's traveling companion] sit in our native house, receiving visits, watching what goes on among the natives of the village, firing off our Kodaks at everything worth taking; but remember the photograph takes all the color, life and charm out of the tropics, and leaves nothing but a conventional hardness that might as well be Scotch or Yankee for all the truth it has. Women especially suffer, for they pose stiffly, and lose the freedom of movement and the play of feature that most attract us. [to Mrs. Cameron, vol. 3, p. 298]

HENRY ADAMS, OCTOBER 22, 1890
I enclose you a number of photographs of [Polynesian] girls. On the whole the types are fairly characteristic, but you must supply for yourself the color, the movement, the play of muscle and feature, and the whole tropical atmosphere which photographs kill as dead as their own chemicals. [to Hay, vol. 3, p. 304]

HENRY ADAMS, NOVEMBER 3, 1890
I enclose some photographs to illustrate our adventures. They will give you, I know, a false impression of everything . . . [to Mrs. Cameron, vol. 3, p. 318]

HENRY ADAMS, NOVEMBER 13, 1890
I snapped a dozen photographs, but the velocity of the girls' [slide over the water] fall was so great that the Kodak can only give a blur. [to Mrs. Cameron, vol. 3, p. 332]

HENRY ADAMS, DECEMBER 2, 1890
. . . the background of sea, mountain and sky, was lovelier than the best scene-painter in Europe commonly furnishes. I snapped some Kodaks, almost hoping they would fail, for without color such scenes are caricatures. [to Mabel Hooper, his young niece, vol. 3, p. 354]

HENRY ADAMS, JANUARY 24, 1891
In despair of giving even an idea of the refinement that is the soul of the island, I have thrown aside my Kodak and my water-colors, and trust to memory. The photograph is a coarse fraud. and seems to delight only in taking the whole beauty out of the picture. As for my photographs, I could not get them developed here, so I sent my first roll, —a hundred,—down to Sydney, more than two months ago to be developed, and they have not been returned. I doubt they're ever turning up. . . . La Farge has taken the local photographer into his employment, and in that way takes all the studies he wants. [to Mrs. Cameron, vol. 3, p. 388]

HENRY ADAMS, FEBRUARY 13, 1891
La Farge has settled down to painting, varied by his usual mania for collecting [professional] photographs [as studies for his paintings]. I call it a mania because with me it has become a phobia; and he is almost afraid of telling me about his photographs because I detest them so much. . . . I hate photographs abstractly, because they have given me more ideas perversely

and immoveably wrong, than I ever should get by imagination. [to Mrs. Cameron, vol. 3, p. 408]

HENRY ADAMS, MARCH 1, 1891
I tried to photograph the old [chiefess] but I had not heart to risk spoiling [her daughter's] Syrian beauty by distorting it in my camera. [to Mrs. Cameron, vol. 3, p. 421]

HENRY ADAMS, AUGUST 21, 1891
I have not a suggestion of a memory of travel to give you on my return. Even the avaricious La Farge . . . has seen nothing to buy, except of course, the infernal photographs which kill what poetry or art the subject has. [to Hay, vol. 3, p. 533]

HENRY ADAMS, SEPTEMBER 13 AND 18, 1891
. . . Ceylon is a place where vast numbers of travellers come—or at least pass—and these ruined cities are the chief interest of the island; so they are visited by about one Englishman a month, thank Buddha, and praise to

Siva and Vishnu, not even the photograph-fiend is here. . . . La Farge, as usual, was very busy buying photographs for which my hatred has now become a photo-phobia. [to Mrs. Cameron, vol. 3, pp. 543, 547]

HENRY ADAMS, FEBRUARY 26, 1900
If I could describe the dreary indifference with which I feel this life and its humorous uninteresting interests, I should make you dyspeptic for a week. I am trying to take up photography again. . . . I try all sorts of things, one after another, as they occur to me; anything to occupy a day; and there is not a person to play with. [to Mrs. Cameron, vol. 5, p. 99]

HENRY ADAMS, MARCH 12, 1900
To make a small diversion I have taken again to dabbling in photography, not that I want to photograph or care for the results, but just for occupation. I prefer water-color, but the photograph can draw, and I can't. [to Mrs. Cameron, vol. 5, p. 107]

50. Marion Hooper Adams. 'Henry Adams,' 1883.

51. Henry Adams. 'Self-portrait,' 1900.

HENRY ADAMS, APRIL 8, 1902

I know of no form of [self] advertisement as flagrant as the photograph. You see, therefore, how honestly I must wish to avoid it. [to Frances Benjamin Johnston, the first woman press photographer, who had just opened a portrait studio, vol. 5, p. 370]

HENRY ADAMS, MAY 12, 1907

. . . I never had a [formal] photograph taken of me, or a likeness [since 1870], and I never mean to have one; which offers a considerable obstacle to my wish to satisfy your request. [to Robert Underwood Johnson, another reputable local photographer, vol. 6, p. 65]

1. The relevant portion of the preface reads: "The following pages, then, are written for nieces, or for those who are willing, for the time, to be nieces in wish. For convenience of travel in France, where hotels, in out-of-the-way places, are sometimes wanting in space as well as luxury, the nieces shall count as one only. As many more may come as like, but one niece is enough for the uncle to talk to, and one niece is more likely than two to listen. One niece is almost more likely than two to carry a kodak and take interest in it, since she has nothing else, except her uncle, to interest her, and instances occur when she takes interest neither in the uncle nor in the journey. One cannot assume, even in a niece, too emotional a nature, but one may assume a kodak." Adams does not mention the camera again in this work. Of the many available editions, see especially Adams, *Mont-Saint Michel and Chartres* (1904) with photographs by Samuel Chamberlain (New York: Limited Editions Club, 1957). See also Kim Moreland, "The Photo Killeth: Henry Adams on Photography and Painting," *Papers on Language and Literature* 27, no. 3 (Summer 1991): 356–70, which suggested many of the sources used by the editor.

2. Adams gave her *Their Wedding Journey* (1872) by William Dean Howells (1837–1920), reviewing it in the *North American Review* 114 (April 1872): 444, which he edited from 1869 to 1876. He included the following remark, which, most agree, he might not have made at a less sentimental time: "If extreme and almost photographic truth to nature, and remarkable delicacy and lightness of touch can give permanent life to a story, why should this one not be read with curiosity and enjoyment a hundred or two hundred years hence?" Interestingly, Howell's sequel, *Their Silver Wedding Journey* (New York: Harper & Brothers, 1899), 2 vols., included photographs.

HENRY ADAMS, APRIL 2, 1900

Just to divert attention, I fiddle with photographs, and take portraits of everybody [Fig. 51], which are singularly shocking; but it is great fun to develop and print. [to Mrs. Cameron, vol. 5, p. 114]

HENRY ADAMS, APRIL 16, 1900

I've been fussing over photographs a great deal but that is only to pass the time. [to Mrs. Cameron, vol. 5, pp. 119–20]

Henry Adams and Marian Hooper Adams

For more on Howells and photography, see the introductory "Notes . . . ," above, pp. xxxviii–ix.

3. See Moreland, "The Photo Killeth," *PLL:* 358, n. 4. See also Oliver Wendell Holmes, Sr.'s articles, all originally published in the *Atlantic Monthly:* "The Stereoscope and the Stereograph," 3 (June 1859): 733–48; "Sun-Painting and Sun-Sculpture, with a Stereoscopic Trip across the Atlantic," 8 (July 1861): 13–29; and "Doings of the Sunbeam," 12 (July 1863): 1–15; all are included in his essay collection *Soundings from the Atlantic* (Boston: Ticknor and Fields, 1864). Houghton Library has a copy of the first edition of *Mont-Saint Michel and Chartres* (*fAC9 H7375 Zz904 a) inscribed by the author to his old friend, "Mr. Justice Holmes," Dr. Holmes's famous son, who is one of the subjects in one of Marian Adams's photographs in the MHS album, also reproduced in Kaldein, cited in n. 4 below.

4. For more on Clover Adams's photography, see Moreland, "The Photo Killeth," *PLL:* 363–67; Otto Friedrich, *Clover* (New York: Simon & Schuster, 1979), pp. 291–94; and Eugenia Kaledin, *The Education of Mrs. Henry Adams* (Philadelphia: Temple University Press, 1981), pp. 187–98, who reproduces, between 198 and 213, many of her best portraits—of her husband, the statesman John Hay, the architect H. H. Richardson, the jurist Holmes, and other friends. The MHS has two albums of her photographs in addition to an album of scenes she bought on an English trip, c. 1866.

5. See *The Letters of Henry Adams,* ed. J. C. Levenson et al. (Cambridge: Belknap Press/Harvard University Press, 1982), vol. 3, p. 273, n. 4, which notes his purchase of George Eastman's famous box camera, introduced in 1888, advertising: "You press the button, we do the rest."

The purchaser could return the camera and exposed film to Eastman Kodak for developing, thus freeing amateur photographers from the ardors of developing—and any contact with dangerous chemicals—but preventing control over the print. See W. S. Gilbert's spoof of the Kodak camera in the preface to his selection above.

Kaledin, *The Education of Mrs. Henry Adams,* p. 192, notes that Adams had earlier ridiculed Emerson for asserting that "photographs gave more pleasure than paintings," but neglects Adams's full explanation— "(i.e. the photograph of a painting gave him more pleasure than the painting itself)"—in his letter to Oliver Wendell Holmes, Jr., January 4, 1885, *Letters,* ed. Levenson et al., vol. 2, p. 566. See the Emerson-Carlyle selection above, n. 2, for sources of Emerson's writing about photography, none of which states precisely this opinion, though he consistently found photographs more accurate and democratic, though often less expressive, than paintings.

6. Many, if not all, of the photographs taken by Henry Adams, including probably most of those mentioned in the letters below, are at the MHS in albums, with some loose pictures: five albums include views taken by him, mixed in with others purchased from local professional photographers during his travels in 1873 and in the late 1880's; it often is difficult to tell which is which. Another album includes the pictures he took from 1900 on. His continued unwillingness to sit for a formal portrait by other photographers, however, may relate to the fact he apparently had sat for none since 1870, aside from those taken by Clover or friends, according to *Letters,* ed. Levenson et al., vol. 6, p. 713, n. 1, which were doubtless relatively informal, even if posed.

32. Henry James and Alvin Langdon Coburn

HENRY JAMES, FROM PREFACE TO *The Golden Bowl*,
1909, AND ALVIN LANGDON COBURN, FROM
"ILLUSTRATING HENRY JAMES," 1953/1966

The decision of Henry James (1843–1916) to illustrate the collected edition of his fiction (1907–9) with twenty-four frontispieces by Alvin Langdon Coburn was surprising, given his persistent ambivalence about photographs as reflected in this preface as well as throughout his writings.[1] He appreciated their ability to stimulate memory and to record faithfully but disdained them as mechanical, undiscriminating, and inartistic. Yet he appreciated Coburn, a cousin of F. Holland Day, through whom the young man became friends with Edward Steichen and Frederick Evans. Coburn had returned to London in 1904, armed with a list of eminent authors he hoped to photograph for what became Men of Mark *(1913) and* More Men of Mark *(1922). Luckily, the first literary lion captured was Evans's friend George Bernard Shaw, who soon touted Coburn as one of the "most accomplished and sensitive artist-photographers now living" and facilitated his contacts with the writers he sought.[2] James liked Coburn's portrait of him, commissioned for an American magazine in 1905, with its usual flattering, refined soft focus [Fig. 52]; he also admired Coburn's other photographs, especially of architectural details like arches, doors, and domes, which the author realized could reinforce his complex prose yet not compete with it (Figs. 53–58).[3] By choosing Coburn for his collected works, James characteristically affirmed the suitability of photography for illustrations while disavowing it as a serious art in its own right.*

. . . I have so thoroughly "gone into" things, in an expository way, on the ground covered by this collection of my writings, that I should still judge it superficial to have spoken no word for so salient a feature of our Edition as the couple of dozen decorative "illustrations." This series of frontispieces contribute less to ornament, I recognise, than if Mr. Alvin Langdon Coburn's beautiful photographs, which they reproduce, had had to suffer less reduction; but of those that have suffered least the beauty, to my sense, remains great, and I indulge at any rate in this glance at our general intention for the sake of the small page of history thereby added to my already voluminous, yet on the whole so unabashed, memoranda. I should question itself at large—that question of the general acceptability of illustration coming up sooner or later, in these days, for the author of any text putting forward illustrative claims (that is producing an effect of illustration) by its own intrinsic virtue and so finding itself elbowed, on that ground, by another and a competitive process. The essence of any representational work is of course to bristle with immediate images; and I, for one, should have looked much askance at the proposal, on the part of my associates in the whole business, to graft or "grow," at whatever point, a picture by another hand on my own picture—this being always, to my sense, a lawless incident. Which remark reflects heavily, of course, on the "picture-book" quality that contemporary English and American prose appears more and more destined, by the conditions of publication, to consent, however grudgingly, to see imputed to it. But a moment's thought points the moral of the danger.

Anything that relieves responsible prose of the duty of being, while placed before us, good enough, interesting enough and, if the question be of picture, pictorial enough, above all *in itself,* does it the worst of services, and may well inspire in the lover of literature certain lively questions as to the future of that institution. That one should, as an author, reduce one's reader, "artistically" inclined, to such a state of hallucination by the images one has evoked as doesn't permit him to rest till he has noted or recorded them, set up some semblance of them in his own other medium, by his own other art—nothing could better consort than *that,* I naturally allow, with the desire or the pretension to cast a literary spell. Charming, that is, for the projector and creator of figures and scenes that are as nought from the moment they fail to become more or less visible appearances, charming for this manipulator of aspects to see such power as he may possess approved and registered by the springing of such fruit from his seed. His own garden, however, remains one thing, and the garden he has prompted the cultivation of at other hands becomes quite another; which means that the frame of one's own work no more provides place for such a plot than we expect flesh and fish to be served on the same platter. One welcomes illustration, in other words, with pride and joy; but also with the emphatic view that, might one's "literary jealously" be duly deferred to, it would quite stand off and on its own feet that thus, as a separate and independent subject of publication, carrying its text in its spirit, just as that text correspondingly carries the plastic possibility, become a still more glorious tribute. So far my invidious distinction between the writer's "frame" and the draughtsman's; and if in spite of it could still make place for the idea of a contribution of value by Mr. A. L. Coburn to each of these volumes—and a contribution in as different a "medium" as possible—this was just because the proposed photographic studies were to seek the way, which they have happily found, I think, not to keep, or to pretend to keep, anything like dramatic step with their suggestive matter. This would quite have disqualified them, to my rigour; but they were "all right," in the so analytic modern critical phrase, through their discreetly disavowing emulation. Nothing in fact could more have amused the author than the opportunity of a hunt for a series of reproducible subjects—such moreover as might best consort with photography—the reference of which to Novel or Tale should exactly be *not* competitive and obvious, should on the contrary plead its case with some shyness, that of images always confessing themselves mere optical symbols or echoes, expressions of no particular thing in the text, but only of the type or idea of this or that thing. They were to remain at the most small pictures of our "set" stage with the actors left out; and what was above all interesting was that they were first to be constituted.

This involved an amusing search which I would fain more fully commemorate; since it took, to a great degree, and rather unexpectedly and incalculably, the vastly, though but incidentally, instructive form of an enquiry into the street-scenery of London; a field yielding a ripe harvest of treasure from the moment I held up to it, in my fellow artist's company, the light of our fond idea—the idea, that is, of the aspect of things or the combination of objects that might, by a latent virtue in it, speak for its connexion with something in the book, and yet at the same time speak enough for its odd or interesting self. It will be noticed that our series of frontispieces, while doing all justice to our need, largely consists in a "rendering" of certain inanimate characteristics of London streets; the ability of which to suffice to this furnishing forth of my volumes ministered alike to surprise and convenience. Even at the cost of inconsistency of attitude in the matter of the "grafted" image, I should have been tempted, I confess, by the mere pleasure of exploration, abounding as the business at once began to do in those prizes of curiosity for which the London-lover is at any time ready to "back" the prodigious city. It wasn't always that I straightway found, with my fellow searcher, what we were looking for, but that the looking itself so often flooded with light the question of what a "subject," what "character," what a saving sense in things, is and isn't; and that when our quest was rewarded, it was, I make bold to say, rewarded in perfection. On the question, for instance, of the proper preliminary compliment to the first volume of "The Golden Bowl" we easily felt that nothing would so serve as a view of the small shop in which the Bowl is first encountered.

The problem thus was thrilling, for though the small shop was but a shop of the mind, of the author's projected world, in which objects are primarily related to each other, and therefore not "taken from" a particular establishment anywhere, only an image distilled and intensified, as it were, from a drop of the essence of such establishments in general, our need (since the picture was, as I have said, also completely to speak for itself) prescribed a concrete, independent, vivid instance, the instance that should oblige us by the marvel of an accidental rightness. It might so easily be wrong— by the act of being at all. It would have to be in the first place what London and chance and an extreme improbability should have made it, and then it would have to let us truthfully read into it the Princes' and Charlotte's and the Princess's visits. It of course on these terms long evaded us, but all the while really without prejudice to our fond confidence that, as London ends by giving one absolutely everything one asks, so it awaited us somewhere. It awaited us in fact— but I check myself; nothing, I find now, would induce me to say where. Just so, to conclude, it was equally obvious that for the second volume of the same fiction nothing would so nobly serve as some generalised vision of Portland Place. Both our limit and the very extent of our occasion, however, lay in the fact that, unlike wanton designers, we had, not to "create" but simply to recognise—recognise, that is, with the last fineness. The thing was to induce the vision of Portland Place *to* generalise itself. This is precisely, however, the fashion after which the prodigious city, as I have called it, does on occasion meet halfway those forms of intelligence of it that *it* recognises. All of which meant that at a given moment the great featureless Philistine vista would itself perform a miracle, would become interesting, for a splendid atmospheric hour, as only London knows how; and that business would be then to understand. But that record of that lesson takes me too far. [Vol. 23, pp. ix–xiii]

Coburn, from "Illustrating Henry James"

Note: The following text is based on "Illustrating Henry James" from Coburn, Photographer: An Autobiography, *ed. H. & A. Gernsheim, pp. 52–60, with additions (indicated in brackets) from Coburn's BBC Radio Talk, "Henry James and the Camera," broadcast first on July 17, 1953. The two pieces are nearly identical, but the* Autobiography *contains a fuller account of Coburn's work for James in Italy, the BBC transcript more about his London and American scenes, perhaps reflecting the interests of the English audience; the different handling of titles in the two sources has been retained.*

There are some people you cannot help liking the moment you see them, and Henry James was, for me, such a person. My earliest portraits of him had been made for the *Century Magazine* in New York in April 1905. [James was presently returning to England, and so it also happened was I, and he very kindly suggested that I should come and see him at his home in Rye, an invitation which gave me the greatest pleasure.] Henry James met me at the station, and I had a most enjoyable visit, and produced a portrait which evidently satisfied him [Fig. 52], for he subsequently suggested that I should make photographs to be used in all other volumes for the forthcoming collected edition: and thus began our friendship. His home, Lamb House, Rye, appeared as frontispiece to Volume 9, *The Awkward Age*, where it was entitled "Mr. Longdon's" [Fig. 53]. During my second visit to Rye, to photograph the house, James presented me with a charming little two-volume edition of *The American* published in 1883, inscribed with my name and his and dated Lamb House, July 4th, 1906. It was really the third of July, and one can see that he started to make a figure three in the date and then changed his mind and, with a chuckle, made it four instead, for the Fourth of July is American Independence Day and a very appropriate date to be inscribed in a copy of this book!

My first adventure in connection with the James frontispieces was a visit to Paris. I went there at the beginning of October 1906, armed with a detailed document from James explaining exactly what he wanted me to photograph.

He was especially keen to have a *porte cochère* or carriage entrance of one of the aristocratic mansions such as that described in *The American*. His knowledge of the streets of Paris was amazing. He enumerated nine or ten streets I was to traverse, thoroughly saturating my mind with the type of portal required. It was not to be as grand as that of the British Embassy, but I was to see this as being the kind of thing required, only to a lesser degree. The letter continued: "Once you get the type into your head, you will easily recognise specimens by walking in the *old* residential and 'noble' parts of the city . . . Tell a cabman that you want to drive through every street in it, and having got the notion, go back and walk and stare at your ease." This is thoroughness, and shows H. J.'s

52. *(opposite)* Alvin
Langdon Coburn.
'Henry James,' 1906.

53. Alvin Langdon
Coburn. 'Mr. Longdon's,'
[James's home, Lamb
House, Rye], 1906.

54. Alvin Langdon
Coburn. 'Faubourg
St. Germain,' 1906.

way of approaching a problem. The result, entitled "The Faubourg St. Germain" forms the
frontispiece of *The American,* which is the second volume of the collected edition [Fig. 54].

[Another Paris picture was of the Arch de Tri-
omphe [*sic*] which figures in *The Princess Casamassima* and to which James gave the title of
'Splendid Paris, Charming Paris.']

With regard to the Place de la Concorde
H. J. advised:

> Look out there for some combination of ob-
> jects that won't be hackneyed and common-
> place and panoramic; some fountain or statue
> or balustrade or vista or suggestion (of some
> damnable sort or the other) that will serve in
> connection with *The Ambassadors,* perhaps;
> just as some view, rightly arrived at, of Notre-
> Dame would also serve—if sufficiently bedim-
> med and refined and glorified; especially as to
> its Side on the River and Back ditto.

Concerning the seventh volume he wrote:

> I yearn for some aspect of the Théâtre-Français
> for possible use in *The Tragic Muse;* but some-

thing of course of the same transfigured nature; some ingeniously hit-upon angle or presentment of its rather majestic big square mass
and classic colonnade.

In all I made six illustrations during this Paris
visit: "The Court of the Hotel" for *The Rever-
berator;* "By Notre-Dame" for the first volume
of *The Ambassadors;* and lastly "The Luxem-
bourg Gardens" for the second volume of the
same tale. The instructions for this photograph
were:

> There is another passage in the same book
> [*The Ambassadors*] about the hero sitting there
> (in the Luxembourg gardens) against the ped-
> estal of some pleasant old garden-statue to read
> over certain letters with which the story is con-
> cerned. Go into the sad Luxembourg gardens
> to look for my right garden-statue (composing
> with other interesting objects) against which
> my chair was tilted back. Do bring me some-
> thing right, in short, from the Luxembourg.

The instructions ended with the kindly bene-
diction "My blessing on your inspiration and
your weather." I believe he was happy with the
result.

Early in November Henry James came up to London and we gloated together over my prints. Though sixty-three years old, H. J. was like a boy, always displaying unquenchable and contagious enthusiasm over every detail concerning these illustrations. This made it a joy to work with him. That is the splendid thing about an artist, whether his medium of expression be pigments, sounds, or words, or even the Art of life, he does not "grow up," grow stale, or lose freshness of outlook; and Henry James was a true artist in this respect. He never lost the capacity to see things with that freshness of vision, as they are beheld by the very young or the very wise.

My next lengthy pilgrimage in search of frontispieces was to Italy, which yielded four subjects, two in Rome and two in Venice. The Roman pictures were: "Roman Bridge" for the second volume of *Portrait of a Lady,* and "By St. Peter's" for *Daisy Miller.*

I arrived in Venice in the middle of December [and spent Christmas there.] Never before or since have I felt so miserably cold and damp, until I moved into a German pension with enormous stoves and old-fashioned feather beds.

As in the case in Paris, I was provided with most detailed instructions regarding my pictures. The two Venetian illustrations I was to produce were for *The Aspern Papers* and *The Wings of the Dove.*

"Juliana's Court" [Fig. 55] was the very place Henry James had in mind when writing *The Aspern Papers.* The original Juliana, however, had lived in old age in Florence, where she died. She was Claire Claremont, mother of Byron's daughter Allegra, and the Aspern papers of the novel were in fact those of Shelley. The palace which Henry James had taken for his setting was the Palazzo Capello, Rio Marin, which was occupied by friends to whom he gave me a letter of introduction, commending me to their care. He sent me lengthy directions how to find it.

The extremely tortuous and complicated walk—taking Piazza San Marco as a starting point—will show you so much, so many bits and odds and ends, such a revel of Venetian picturesque-

55. Alvin Langdon Coburn. 'Juliana's Court,' 1906.

ness, that I advise your doing it on foot as much as possible . . . It is the old faded pink-faced, battered-looking and quite homely and plain (as things go in Venice) old Palazzino on the right of the small Canal, a little way along, as you enter it by the end of the Canal towards the Station. It has a garden behind it, and I think, though I am not sure, some bit of a garden wall beside it; it doesn't moreover bathe its steps, if I remember right, directly in the Canal, but has a small paved Riva or footway in front of it, and *then* water-steps down from this little quay. As to that, however, the time since I have seen it may muddle me; but I am almost sure. At any rate anyone about will identify for you Ca Capello, which is familiar for Casa C.; *casa,* for your ingenuous young mind, meaning House, being used, save for the greatest palaces, as much as palazzo. You must judge for yourself, face to face with the object, how much, on the spot, it seems to lend itself to a picture. I think it *must,* more or less, or sufficiently; with or without such adjuncts of the rest of the scene (from the bank opposite, from the bank near, or from wherever you can damnably manage it) as may seem to contribute or complete—to be needed, in short, for the interesting effect . . . What figures most is the big old Sala, the large central hall of the principal floor of the house, to which they (my friends) will introduce you, and from which, from the larger, rather bare Venetian perspective of which, and preferably looking towards the garden-end, I very much hope some result. In one way or another, in fine, it seems to me it ought to give something. If it doesn't, even with the help of more or little of the canal-view etc., yield satisfaction, wander about until you find something that looks sufficiently like it, some old second-rate palace on a by-canal, with a Riva in front, and if any such takes you at all, do it at a venture, as a possibly better alternative. But get the Sala at Ca Capello, without fail, if it proves at all manageable or effective.

I was able to photograph Ca Capello in the way H. J. wished.

For the other picture, that of *The Wings,* I had vaguely in mind the Palazzo Barbaro . . . the very old Gothic one. . . . The Barbaro has its water-steps beside it, as it were; that is a little gallery running beside a small stretch of side-canal. But in addition it also has a fine water-steps (I remember) to the front door of its lower apartment. (The side-steps I speak of belong to the apartment with the beautiful range of old *upper* Gothic windows, those attached to the part of the palace concerned in my story). But I don't propose you should attempt here anything but the outside; and you must judge best if you can take the object most effectively from the bridge itself, from the little campo in front of the Academy, from some other like spot further—that is further towards the Salute, or from a gondola (if your gondolier can keep it steady enough) out on the bosom of the Canal.

If none of these positions yield you something you may feel to be effective, try some other palace. . . . And do any other odd and interesting bit you can, that may serve for a sort of symbolised and generalized Venice in case everything else fails; preferring the noble and fine aspect, however, to the merely shabby and familiar (as in the case of those views you already have)—yet especially not choosing the pompous and obvious things that one everywhere sees photos of.

Perhaps the most intimate and personal of all the questing for pictures was the search for and capture of the London scenes, for with most of these I had the personal guidance and collaboration of the author. Henry James knew his London as few men have known it, in all its quaintness. He obviously enjoyed his search, for he wrote of the street scenery of London "yielding a rich harvest of treasures from the moment I held up to it, in my fellow artist's company, the light of our fond idea—the idea, that is, of the aspect of things or combinations of objects that might, by latent virtue in it, speak of its connection with something in the book, and yet at the same time speak enough for its odd or interesting self." H. J. knew so perfectly what we should achieve, for after all it was *his* books we were illustrating, but in spite of this, the photographs were essentially mine! ["The Dome of St. Paul's" for the first volume of *The Princess Casamassima,* I did, in fact, make without his personal presence, but the others we found or "discovered" together.]

The afternoon that we went to St. John's Wood to photograph the little gateway and house which was to serve as the illustration for the second volume of *The Tragic Muse* was an unforgettable experience. It was a lovely afternoon, I remember, and H. J. was in his most festive mood. I was carefree because this time I did not have to hunt for the subject, for I had the most perfect and dependable guide, the creator and author himself. I had not even read *The Tragic Muse,* but I shared his enthusiasm when after considerable searching we came upon exactly the right subject. Where the house is located I do not now recall, it may in fact no longer exist, for so much of London has passed away into the domain of forgotten things; but in the photograph it is preserved, crystallised as a memento of what Henry James had meant it to be.

Now it was tea-time, and pleasantly fatigued by our exertions, now triumphantly rewarded, we looked for a teashop to refresh ourselves, but were only able to find a baker's shop. We descended on this and came out with Bath buns, which we thankfully devoured as we walked down the street. [H.J. told me that as a young lad in his early days in London, he had bought bath buns, much the same as the ones we were eating on this memorable day, at this very same shop in St. John's Wood!

The illustration for *In the Cage* was a grocer's shop containing a post office, and this also required patience and perseverance. . . . Fancy discovering a setting for a story in a post office in a grocer's shop!

"Saltram's Seat," the illustration for *The Coxon Fund* in the fifteenth volume, with its background of tall trees [Fig. 56], was found by us in Hampstead Heath. According to the story, it should have been at Wimbledon, but as H. J. remarked, there was no such a group of trees as his imagination had visualized at Wimbledon! And it was the thing itself which was important rather than the actual location.

We went up to Hampstead Heath in a hansom cab and when we sighted the trees on the horizon, H. J. asked the driver to wait for us while we walked the intervening distance across the heath to our "subject," and I remember how impressed I was when James, to assure our charioteer of our return, left his gold-headed walking-stick in the cab as a hostage!

These little incidents colour one's memory of days which are past, when more important things are perhaps forgotten.

"The Curiosity Shop" for *The Golden Bowl* was one of our most amazing and successful finds [Fig. 57], and James himself commemorates its discovery in his charming preface to that volume.

I think I may be justly proud of his tribute to my illustrations, I had almost said "our illustrations," for in this preface he devotes several pages of his most typical prose to the whole problem of illustrations in general (pictures added to text) and these photographic illustrations in particular.

He confesses that the shop was only "a shop of the mind, of the author's projected world in which objects are primarily related to each other and therefore not 'taken from' a particular establishment anywhere."

56. Alvin Langdon Coburn, 'Saltram's Seat,' 1907.

James has described our search for the shop so perfectly, that it must be read in his words to be fully appreciated. And we actually found it, this little shop of his mind, where the Prince and Charlotte discovered the Golden Bowl. We found it and great was our joy, but even as H. J. refuses to reveal the location of the shop, so I also will remain silent. Let it be but a thing of the mind which the camera by a miracle of chance and the bounty of London was able to record. Probably by now it too has gone, destroyed by bombs or wiped away by the ruthless modernizing of these later days. Even if I might now discover it by renewing my search, I haven't the heart to try. I am content to realise that I am now the only person who would know where to look. The last of the series of my twenty-four illustrations in the second volume of *The Golden Bowl* was "Portland Place" [Fig. 58]. . . . The only way to do full justice to Henry James's tribute to our vision of Portland Place is to quote his own words:

57. Alvin Langdon Coburn. 'The Curiosity Shop,' 1907.

It was equally obvious that for the second volume of the same fiction [*The Golden Bowl*] nothing would so nobly serve as some generalized vision of Portland Place. Both our limit and the very extent of our occasion, however, lay in the fact that unlike wanton designers, we had not to 'create' but simply to recognize—recognize, that is, with the last fineness. The thing was to induce the vision of Portland Place to generalize itself. This is precisely, however, the fashion after which the prodigious city, as I have called it, does on occasion meet halfway those forms of intelligence that *it* recognizes. All of which means that at a given moment the great Philistine vista would itself perform a miracle, would become interesting for a splendid atmospheric hour, as only London knows how, and that our business would be to understand.

[Portland Place has not greatly changed, and from this picture it would be recognized . . . even to this day. . . .

In February of the following year, 1907, I again went to America where three other illustrations were made according to H. J.'s suggestions, and these, together with two other subjects, completed the series of my twenty-four illustrations namely: "The English House" for the first volume of the *Portrait of a Lady*, the real house of the story, and "Some of the Spoils" for *The Spoils of Poynton*. The triumphant culmination of this adventure, from my point of view, was the commemoration by the author himself in the preface to *The Golden Bowl* (the final volume in the series) of our search for and ultimate capture of these pictures.]

Although not literally a photographer, I believe Henry James must have had sensitive plates on his brain on which to record his impressions! He always knew exactly what he wanted, although many of the pictures were but images in his mind and imaginations, and what we did was to browse diligently until we found such a subject. I learned much from my collaboration with this great author, and for this experience I am grateful.

58. Alvin Langdon Coburn. 'Portland Place,' 1907.

Henry James and Alvin Langdon Coburn

1. The most comprehensive and detailed discussion of James's previous experience of photography is provided by Ralph F. Bogardus, *Pictures and Texts: Henry James, A. L. Coburn, and New Ways of Seeing in Literary Culture* (Ann Arbor, Mich.: UMI Research Press, 1984), pp. 51–141 and Stanley Tick, "Positives and Negatives: Henry James vs. Photography," *Nineteenth Century Studies* 7 (1993): 69–101.

2. See Shaw, "Photographs by Mr. Alvin Langdon Coburn, 1906," *Shaw on Photography,* ed. Jay and Moore, pp. 103, and Coburn, *Autobiography,* passim. For more on Coburn's relationships with other authors, see his *Autobiography,* passim, as well as the Wells, Shaw, and Twain selections above and the Belloc and Pound selections below.

3. For more on James's collaboration with Coburn, see Bogardus, *Pictures and Text,* pp. 9–48, 159–202, which includes reproductions of all the frontispieces; Shloss, "Henry James and Alvin Langdon Coburn," in *In Visible Light,* pp. 55–91; Joseph J. Firebaugh, "Coburn: Henry James's Photographer," *American Quarterly* 7 (1955): 215–33; Charles Higgins, "Photographic Aperture: Coburn's Frontispieces to James's New York Edition: The Frame of Prevision," *American Literature* 53, no. 4 (January 1982): 661–75; Jablow, "Illustrated Texts from Dickens to James," pp. 59–181; Michaels, "Let's Pretend: Photographic Illustration of Fiction and Poetry around 1900," pp. 23–24, who notes the sad irony that photographs are omitted from the most recent reprint of James's New York edition (Fairfield, N.J.: Augustus M. Kelley by arrangement with Charles Scribner's Sons, 1976); and Tick, "Positives and Negatives."

*T*he energetic versatility of Hilaire Belloc (1870–1953)—historian, essayist, biographer, novelist, journalist, editor, serious and humorous versifier, and travel writer as well as two-time Liberal Member of Parliament (1906–10)—still obscures his achievements. So do his controversial pro-Catholic, anti-Darwin, anti-socialist, and anti-Semitic attitudes. Somehow, in his frenetic schedule, Belloc found time to write two very different pieces concerning photographs. One was this tenderly elegiac essay, in which he echoed the Wordsworthian view of children as trailing clouds of innocent glory, soon sullied by necessary compromises with the adult world.[1] Lady Ottoline Morrell, an avid picture-taker of her many artist friends, reportedly liked this essay so much that Belloc printed up a special signed copy for her.[2] His other relevant contribution was a lengthy preface to Coburn's first book, London (1909), which, the photographer complained, "completely ignored my pictures!"[3] Yet Coburn included Belloc's portrait in Men of Mark (1913)[4] and was clearly delighted when the writer wanted him to illustrate a new edition of his popular book on the Pyrenees (1909); Belloc even planned a detailed itinerary of sites for the photographer. When the Great War doomed this collaboration, Coburn consoled himself that "a journey in the imagination under the guidance of such a man as Belloc may be a very real experience, almost as real as a physical journey."[5]

In a garden which must, I think, lie somewhat apart and enclosed in one of the valleys of central England, you came across the English grass in summer beneath the shade of a tree; you were running, but your arms were stretched before you in a sort of dance and balance as though you rather belonged to the air and to the growing things about you and above you than to the earth over which you passed; and you were not three years old.

As, in jest, this charming vision was recorded by a camera which some guest had with him, a happy accident (designed, for all we know, by whatever powers arrange such things, an accident of the instrument or of the plate upon which your small, happy, advancing figure was recorded) so chanced that your figure, when the picture was printed, shone all around with light.

I cannot, as I look at it now before me and as I write these words, express, however much I may seek for expression, how great a meaning underlies that accident, nor how full of fate and of reason and of suggested truth that aureole grows as I gaze. Your innocence is beatified by it, and takes on with majesty the glory which lies behind all innocence, but which our eyes can never see. Our happiness seems in that mist of light to be removed and permanent; the common world in which you are moving passes, through this trick of the lens, into a stronger world more apt for such a sight, and one in which I am half persuaded (as I still look upon the picture) blessedness is not a rare adventure, but something native and secure.

Little child, the trick which the camera has played means more and more as I still watch your picture, for there is present in that light not only blessedness, but holiness as well. The lightness of your movement and of your poise (as though you were blown like a blossom along the tops of the grass) is shone through, and your face, especially its ready and wondering laughter, is inspired, as though the Light had filled it from within; so that, looking thus, I look not on, but through. I say that in this portrait which I treasure there is not only blessedness, but holiness as well—holiness which is the cause of blessedness and which contains it, and by which secretly all this world is sustained.

Now there is a third thing in your portrait, little child. That accident of light, light all about you and shining through your face, is not only blessed nor only holy, but it is also sacred, and with that thought there returns to me as I look what always should return to man if he is to find any stuff or profit in his consideration of divine things. In blessedness there is joy for which here we are not made, so that we catch it only in glimpses or in adumbrations. And in holiness, when we perceive it we perceive something far off; it is that from which we came and to which we should return; yet holiness is not a human thing. But things sacred—things devoted to a purpose, things about which there lies an awful necessity of sacrifice, things devoted and necessarily suffering some doom—these are certainly of this world; that, indeed, all men know well at last, and find it part of the business through which their needs must pass. Human memories, since they are only memories; human attachments, since they are offered up and end; great human fears and hopeless human longings—these are sacred things attached to a victim and to a sacrifice; and in this picture of yours with the light so glorifying you all round, no one can doubt who sees it but that the sacredness of human life will be yours also; that is, you must learn how it is offered up to some end and what a sacrifice is there.

I could wish, as I consider this, that the camera had played no such trick, and had not revealed in that haze of awful meaning all that lies beyond the nature of you, child. But it is a truth which is so revealed; and we may not, upon a penalty more terrible than death, neglect any ultimate truth concerning our mortal way.

Your feet, which now do not seem to press upon the lawn across which they run, have to go more miles than you can dream of, through more places than you could bear to hear, and they must be directed to a goal which will not in your very young delight be mentioned before you, or of which, if it is mentioned, you will not understand by name; and your little hands which you bear before you with the little gesture of flying things, will grasp most tightly that which can least remain and will attempt to fashion what can never be completed, and will caress that which will not respond to the caress. Your eyes, which are now so principally filled with innocence that that bright quality drowns all the rest, will look upon so much of deadly suffering and of misuse in men, that they will very early change themselves in kind; and all your face, which now vaguely remembers nothing but the early vision from which childhood proceeds, will grow drawn and self-guarded, and will suffer some agonies, a few despairs, innumerable fatigues, until it has become the face of a woman grown. Nor will this sacred doom about you, which is that of all mankind, cease or grow less or be mitigated in any way; it will increase as surely and as steadily as increase the number of the years, until at last you will lay down the daylight and the knowledge of daylit things as gladly as now you wake from sleep to see them.

For you are sacred, and all those elders about you, whose solemn demeanour now and then startles you into a pretty perplexity which soon calls back their smiles, have hearts only quite different from your quite careless heart, because they have known the things to which, in the manner of victims, they are consecrated.

All that by which we painfully may earn rectitude and a proper balance in the conduct of our short affairs I must believe that you will practise; and I must believe, as I look here into your face, seeing your confident advance (as though you were flying out from your babyhood into young life without any fear), that the virtues which now surround you in a crowd and make a sort of court for you and are your angels every way, will go along with you and will stand by you to the end. Even so, and the more so, you will find (if you read this some years hence) how truly it is written. By contrast with your demeanour, with your immor-

tal hopes, and with your pious efforts the world about you will seem darker and less secure with every passing harvest, and in proportion as you remember the childhood which has led me so to write of you, in proportion as you remember gladness and innocence with its completed joy, in that proportion will you find at least a breaking burden in the weight of this world.

Now you may say to me, little child (not now, but later on), to what purpose is all this complaint, and why should you tell me these things?

It is because in the portrait before me the holiness, the blessedness, and therefore the sacredness are apparent that I am writing as I do. For you must know that there is a false way out and a seeming relief for the rack of human affairs, and that this way is taken by many. Since you are sacred do not take it, but bear the burden. It is the character of whatever is sacred that it does not take that way; but, like a true victim, remains to the end, ready to complete the sacrifice.

The way out is to forget that one is sacred, and this men and women do in many ways. The most of them by way of treason. They betray. They break at first uneasily, later easily, and at last unconsciously, the word which each of us has passed before. He was born in Paradise. All men and all women are conscious of that word, for though their lips cannot frame it here, and though the terms of the pledge are forgotten, the memory of its obligation fills the mind. But there comes a day, and that soon in the lives of many, when to break it once is to be much refreshed and to seem to drop the burden; and in the second and the third time it is done, and the fourth it is done more easily—until at last there is no more need for a man or a woman to break that pledged word again and once again; it is broken for good and for all. This is one most common way in which the sacred quality is lost: the way of treason. Round about such as choose this kind of relief grows a habit and an air of treason. They betray all things at last, and even common friendship is at last no longer theirs. The end of this false issue is despair.

Hilaire Belloc

Another way is to take refuge from ourselves in pleasures, and this is easily done, not by the worse, but by the better sort; for there are some, some few, who would never betray nor break their ancient word, but who, seeing no meaning in a sacrifice nor in a burden, escape from it through pleasure as through a drug, and this pleasure they find in all manner of things, and always that spirit near them which would destroy their sacred mark, persuades them that they are right, and that in such pursuits the sacrifice is evaded. So some will steep themselves in rhyme, some in landscapes, some in pictures, some in the watching of the complexity and change of things, some in music, some in action, some in mere ease. It seems as though the men and women who would thus forget their sacredness are better loved and better warned than those who take the other path, for they never forget certain gracious things which should be proper to the mind, nor do they lose their friends. But that they have taken a wrong path you may easily perceive from this sign: that these pleasures, like any other drug, do not feed or satisfy, but must be increased with every dose, and even so soon pall and are continued not because they are pleasures any longer, but because, dull though they have become, without them there is active pain.

Take neither the one path nor the other, but retain, I beseech you, when the time comes, that quality of sacredness of which I speak, for there is no alternative. Some trouble fell upon our race, and all of us must take upon ourselves the business and the burden. If you will attempt any way out at all it will but lead you to some worse thing. We have not all choices before us, but only one of very few, and each of those few choices is mortal, and all but one is evil.

You should remember this also, dear little child, that at the beginning—oh, only at the very beginning of life—even your reason that God gave may lead you wrong. For with those memories strong upon you of perfect will, of clear intelligence, and of harmonious beauty all about, you will believe the world in which you stand to be the world from which you have

come and to which you are also destined. You have but to treat this world for but a very little while as though it were the thing you think it to find it is not so.

Do you know that that which smells most strongly in this life of immortality, and which a poet has called "the ultimate outpost of eternity," is insecure and perishes? I mean the passionate affection of early youth. If that does not remain, what then do you think can remain? I tell you that nothing which you take to be permanent round about you when you are very young is more than the symbol or clothes of permanence. Another poet has written, speaking of the chalk hills:—

Only a little while remain
The Downs in their solemnity.

Nor is this saying forced. Men and women cannot attach themselves even to the hills where they first played.

Some men, wise but unillumined, and not conscious of that light which I here physically see shining all round and through you in the picture which is before my eyes as I write, have said that to die young and to end the business early was a great blessing. We do not know. But we do know that to die long after and to have gone through the business must be blessed, since blessedness and holiness and sacredness are bound together in one.

But, of these three, be certain that sacredness is your chief business, blessedness after your first childhood you will never know, and holiness you may only see as men see distant mountains lifted beyond a plain; it cannot be your habitation. Sacredness, which is the mark of that purpose whose heir is blessedness, whose end is holiness, will be upon you until you die; maintain it, and let it be your chief concern, for though you neglect it, it will remain and avenge itself.

All this I have seen in your picture as you go across the grass, and it was a accident of the camera that did it. If any one shall say these things do not attach to the portrait of a child, let him ask himself whether they do not attach to the portrait that might be drawn, did human skill suffice, of the life of a woman or a man which springs from the demeanour of childhood; or let him ask himself whether, if a face in old age and that same face in childhood were equally and as by a revelation set down

each in its full truth, and the growth of the one into the other were interpreted by a profound intelligence, what I have said would not be true of all that little passage of ours through the daylight.

1. This essay was called to the editor's attention by Judith Abrams Plotz, who also notes its melancholy affinities to *Dream Children,* ed. and ill. by Elizabeth B. Brownell (Indianapolis: Bowen-Merrill, 1901); this was an album of classic writings about children, illustrated with photographs, whose title was probably inspired by Charles Lamb's "Dream Children: A Reverie," in *The Complete Works and Letters of Charles Lamb* (New York: Modern Library, 1935), pp. 90–93. *Dream Child* is also the title for an elegiac fiction film (1985) about Lewis Carroll as remembered by the elderly Alice Liddell, noted in the Carroll selection, n. 2, above.

2. See Robert Speaight, *The Life of Hilaire Belloc* (London: Hollis & Carter, 1957), p. 291, and see also

Morrell's own vivid snapshots of her many artist friends, though not including Belloc, in *Lady Ottoline's Album,* ed. Heilbrun.

3. See Belloc, preface to Coburn, *London* (London: Duckworth, 1909), pp. 9–21. Coburn understandably preferred the laudatory foreword written by his patron, Shaw, which the publishers rejected, doubtless because it was only three paragraphs; it is quoted in Coburn, *Autobiography,* p. 74, and see also p. 72 for Coburn's memory of his first meeting with the author.

4. See also p. 35, fig. 12, for Coburn's portrait of Belloc, January 20, 1908, first published in *Men of Mark,* Plate 17, and p. 72.

5. See Coburn, *Autobiography,* p. 72.

34. *Leonid Andreyev*

FROM LETTERS TO HIS MOTHER
FROM ABROAD, 1910–14

*I*f I were Tsar, I'd make everyone take up photography," playfully declared Leonid Andreyev (1871–1919), whose vivid reflection of contemporary concerns in his psychological horror stories, polemical articles, and expressionist plays made him one of the most controversial and popular Russian writers of his era.[1] After his brief arrest for prorevolutionary activities (1905) and the death of his wife (1906), he moved with a new bride to the Finnish Gulf (1908), an area popular with artists for its proximity to St. Petersburg and freedom from censorship. Here Andreyev had time to pursue his many interests: yachting, painting, gramophones, and, above all, photography. From the early 1900s, Andreyev had taken hundreds of stereoscopic pictures in black and white; from 1908 to the outbreak of the First World War, he explored color photography, using the new Lumière autochrome process (1907). His favorite subjects continued to be himself (in various costumes as well as nude); family and friends (including the estranged Gorky, and newly met Tolstoy); his unusual custom-built house; and picturesque settings, both at home and abroad. He especially loved Italy, visiting it three times (1910, 1913, and 1914) before the war halted such travel.[2] On Easter 1918, he wrote in his diary, "Should I look at my photographs? Rome? Venice? The Skerries? No."[3] The contrast between those warm, colorful, holiday pictures [Fig. 59] and his misery in postrevolutionary Russia would have been unbearable, for they, along with these lighthearted letters, formed a record of a privileged life now annihilated.[4]

FROM LETTERS TO HIS MOTHER FROM ABROAD

FROM MARSEILLES, DECEMBER 1910

Oh, what an effort it is to travel through all these Europes! All my languages have long since become confused and I now look like a fat Tower of Babel. Yesterday we were thrown off the through-train in the middle of the night, and what became of us nobody knows.

At the moment we are in Marseilles. It's spring. The sea is wonderful. We only look at it from the shore, and even then to avoid any danger I hold on to a lap-post and look with my backside. The town is very beautiful. But we gave Spain a miss—it's too far, and if we keep being thrown off trains you've no idea where we might end up.... I keep saying *merci* the whole time. The expression on my face is French with a slight hint of German.

Don't worry, my little mushroom, about my not writing very often—it's quite impossible on a trip like this. You get very tired from running around all day, in the evening you work out your plans for the next day and then get them all wrong in the morning. On top of that their time here is ahead of ours, so every day is five hours shorter. That's some difference: it's morning now where you are and evening here; and things happen in a different order, the French way: day follows immediately after evening, and night comes after lunch, at two in the afternoon English time. It's called *le smoking*.

...Tomorrow I'm going to spend the whole day taking photos. We'll be staying here for five days or so, we need the rest. . . .

Our trip has generally turned out very successfully, but the most successful part was our sea-journey from Marseilles to Leghorn calling at Corsica on the way. We left Marseilles at eleven in the morning on Sunday, a lovely and sunny but very windy day. At this time of year you can get continuous fog, but we were lucky. Both the sea itself and the mountainous shore that we sailed along until sunset were extremely beautiful. To start with, it's true, there was a heavy swell and lots of people were throwing up all over the place (Anna [his wife] restrained herself, but lay in our cabin groaning all the way to Corsica), but by nightfall the wind had

started blowing from behind us and the swell died down. The waves were huge and I watched them in the moonlight and went wild with delight. I slept well that night and at sunrise the next morning we arrived at Bastia (on Corsica), where we stopped for twenty-four hours. Such beauty and such warmth, with the sun as hot as in spring. We spent the whole day walking about and I felt completely relaxed. Peace and quiet, mountains, cypress....We set sail at eight in the morning—and, Mamochka, you can't imagine anything more beautiful. The sea was like a mirror and light blue, the lovely sun shone warmly on us, the stillness—nothing could ever compare with it. And we went past the most beautiful places: Elba (where Napoleon was locked up), Capraia, Gorgona—and at last out of the sparkling azure sea emerged Italy, pink, hazy, golden, covered in villas and gardens. And to the left, high above the blue haze, rose the snowy peaks of the Alps. I have made quite a few sea-journeys in my time, but never before have I seen anywhere more beautiful than that....We reached Leghorn at about three in the afternoon and went straight on to Florence by train, arriving around eight.

And, brother, isn't Florence just an amazing city. It's so beautiful that it almost beats Rome, come to think of it it's even better. Needless to say we're on our feet the whole time and the soles of my shoes have developed corns....

I honestly have no time to write. First and foremost comes photography—and you know what that means. [pp. 114–15]

FROM ROME, FEBRUARY–MAY 1914

We went out of town to the Via Appia today, but the wind was so strong and there was so much dust from the cars that Nichka sneezed all her innards out and we couldn't see anything, so when it started to rain, we came back and went to a restaurant.... While we were eating, the sun came out and it turned into a warm, pleasant day; we wandered among the ruins of the palatine until six in the evening, taking photos and arguing, enjoying nature and our mutual love. To tell the truth, the shots Anna took

59. Leonid Andreyev. 'Anna Andreyeva in the Roman Campagna,' 1914.

weren't bad at all: if it weren't for her tendency to take nothing but soldiers....

We went out into the Campagna to the Via Appia, taking the train out and walking back into town along the road. Anna [Fig. 61] was lugging a bag with our food, and I had three cameras, a library of guidebooks, various dictionaries and everything else to carry.... When Anichka takes photos she gets very nervous—she moans, suddenly comes over all weak and rolls her eyes so far they end up half way down her back....

We spent the whole evening developing what we had taken during the day—real hard labour; and both of us wail, because nothing turns out the way it should; Anichka's are all over or underexposed, and she rolls her eyes again and makes herself look consumptive.

I went in Anichka's company into the Campagna and for campany (sic!) took with us Savvka [their son] and Minna [his nurse] with a bag. Anichka took the photos, and I must say from the depths of my immortal soul that even I did not expect such brilliant results. What are the Himalayas and Sanatogen by comparison with her! When instead of a lovingly executed, fine portrait of me, which almost gave her consumption, the developed photo showed her *hat*—we thought it was just a trick of nature. But when instead of Minna holding the bag, which was taken for her boyfriend Nikanor, we again saw Anichka's hat—we were surprised. But when instead of a whole horse carrying an unusual load we yet again saw Anichka's hat—we began to get worried, since there was a shot of the whole Campagna still to come. But when instead of a portrait of Savvka, which Anichka had placed all her hopes on, we saw her hat again; when instead of palaces, animals, people and great high mountains we kept on seeing Anichka's *hat*—we lost all patience and begged to be killed, so that we would no longer have to see that damned *hat*.....

And what do you think our investigations revealed? As she was taking the photos and looking into the view-finder, this self-same Anichka lowered her broad-brimmed hat so far that she obscured all her subjects with it; and so the camera—which couldn't care less!—proceeded to photograph her *hat*. [pp. 117–18]

1. Quoted by Ivan Belousov, the poet, translator, and Andreyev's old friend, in Richard Davies, ed., *Leonid Andreyev, Photographs by a Russian Writer: An Undiscovered Portrait of Pre-Revolutionary Russia* (London: Thames & Hudson, 1989), p. 64.

2. Davies, p. 10, estimates the writer took c. 1500 stereoscopic black and white pictures and c. 400 photographs, of which c. 300 are in the Leeds Russian Archives. Some of them, interesting despite their small size and poor reproduction, appear in Andreyev, *Visions*, ed. Olga Andreyev Carlisle (San Diego: Harcourt Brace Jovanovich, 1987).

3. This Easter Day entry, noted by Davies, p. 118, was kindly translated by him over the telephone for the editor on October 15, 1992.

4. For a later perspective on prerevolutionary Russian life and the subsequent role of photographs, see Michael Ignatieff, "Family Photo Albums," *The Russian Album* (New York: Sifton/Viking [1987]), pp. 2–7; and Claudia Roth Pierpont, "Childhoods," *New Yorker* (December 17, 1990): 132, called to the editor's attention by Lillian Bulwa. See also a 1972 portrait of Andreyev's granddaughter, the writer Olga Andreyev Carlisle, in Morath, *Portraits* (New York: Aperture, 1986), p. 75; for other collaborations between Carlisle and Morath, see the Literary Portraits selection, n. 8, below.

35. Alfred Stieglitz and Gertrude Stein

ALFRED STIEGLITZ, "*Camera Work* INTRODUCES GERTRUDE STEIN TO AMERICA" [1912], 1946–47, AND GERTRUDE STEIN, "STIEGLITZ," 1934

Stieglitz (1864–1946) was America's leading champion of photography as a fine art. Through the images he took (in all sorts of weather), the fine publications he edited and founded [Fig. 60], the exhibitions he organized, the innovative galleries he established, and the provocative remarks he made publicly and privately, Stieglitz guided photography's dominant movements—first Pictorialist, then "straight"—in the early twentieth century. While the first to show Continental modernists in America, he also urged native artists to create their own traditions, not ape European ones. His advice was heeded not only by photographers like Paul Strand and painters like Georgia O'Keeffe, who became his wife, but by many writers as well.[1] One of Stieglitz's earliest literary admirers was Gertrude Stein (1874–1946), whose first publications—two pieces on Matisse and Picasso—appeared in his influential quarterly, Camera Work (1912) [Fig. 61].[2] Stein, whose then unconventional household, talented friends, and avant-garde art collection always attracted more interest than her distinctive prose, later expressed her appreciation to Stieglitz; the style of her tribute is somewhat analogous to the photograph in its attempt to capture the subject or the moment in the "continuous present," compelling readers to view it one "frame" at a time, with only minor changes in verbal focus or angle. Keenly aware of the role of photographers in promoting her reputation, Stein welcomed the young Coburn; befriended the recently arrived expatriate Man Ray; accommodated Cecil Beaton during his frequent French visits; and cherished Carl Van Vechten, who became her literary publicist, executor, and posthumous editor.[3]

STIEGLITZ, "*Camera Work* INTRODUCES GERTRUDE STEIN TO AMERICA"

In December 1911—maybe it was January 1912—a huge woman, leading a huge Boston bulldog, came into 291—that 15 foot square room at 291 Fifth Avenue—in which Cézanne, Picasso, Henri Rousseau, Toulouse-Lautrec, Matisse and so much else called "modern" were introduced to America, in the from of a series of integrated exhibitions—or should they not better be called "demonstration"—? For wasn't 291 primarily a public laboratory?

The woman had a portfolio bursting with manuscripts under her arm. It was a funny sight to see this huge woman with this big bulldog and the bursting portfolio in that tiny room.

"Mr. Stieglitz?" the woman inquired.

"Yes, I am Mr. Stieglitz."

"Well, I have some manuscripts here," the woman said. "I have taken them to every publisher in town. Invariably I was told by everyone of these publishers that there was only one man crazy enough in this country, possibly to be interested in anything like these manuscripts. They all mentioned your name. So here I am. Will you look?"

I told the woman that I was not a publisher, but that I did print a magazine, a quarterly called *Camera Work,* which was dedicated to an idea. It was not a money-making affair, quite the contrary. I asked if what I had said was clear to her.

She said, "Yes, I know you are not in business of any kind, neither art nor publishing nor otherwise. But I know that you have been instrumental in introducing Matisse to America as well as Picasso, and here are two manuscripts,—one on Matisse, the other on Picasso,."

I said, "Show them to me."

She handed me the one on Matisse. It was hardly 1500 words long. After having read not more than 30 or 40 words I said, "Show me the one on Picasso." And she showed me the one on Picasso. Again I read 30 or 40 words at the utmost of this manuscript. It appeared to be about 800 words in length.

I said to the woman, "I don't know the meaning of all this. But it sounds good to me. I think I can use both manuscripts. I have had it in mind to publish a number of *Camera Work* showing the evolution of Matisse and of Picasso. But I did not know where to find any literary matter that would go with the pictures of Matisse and Picasso. But somehow or other these manuscripts, even though I don't understand them, seem to fit into the volume I have in mind."

I told the woman that I would print as usual a thousand numbers of *Camera Work*—a Special Number to be dedicated to Matisse and Picasso, and that I would include these two manuscripts. I told her that I could pay whoever had written them no money, but instead would be willing to give the author one hundred copies of the thousand copies printed.

The woman said, "Can't I show you some of the other manuscripts? I have a great many by this author."

I said, "No, these on Matisse and Picasso fit into a purpose. And I am sure that after this Special Number of *Camera Work* will have been published, you will have no trouble in finding publishers for the other manuscripts."

The portly woman said, "I'll leave the manuscripts on Matisse and Picasso with you. I am sure it will be all right. Just go ahead."

I was delighted. Wouldn't the literary people sit up and take notice, as the artists had been forced to sit up and take notice, when Matisse and Picasso, Cézanne, Henri Rousseau, etc. had been introduced by 291 in past years?

The portly woman said, "Don't you want to know the author's name?"

As a matter of fact, I had not noticed that I had failed to ask, "Who is the author?" or to look at the signature at the bottom of the manuscripts.

"And don't you want to know anything about the author?" she asked. "The author is Gertrude Stein, who is an intimate friend of mine. You must know Gertrude Stein."

"How should I know Gertrude Stein," I said.

"Why, she is the sister of Leo Stein. And I know you know Leo Stein."

"My god," I exclaimed, "so that is the woman who was half reclining on a chaise-longue in the Leo Stein Studio in Paris in 1909, wreathed in a sort of semi-Mona Lisa smile as Leo Stein was holding forth for over an hour on art, with Steichen and me as listener."

I laughed and told this woman the story of the séance at Leo Stein's. "Yes," she said, "that's a picture of Leo, and that's Gertrude."

Then the lady introduced herself as Mrs. Knobloch—Mrs. Edward Knobloch, I believe. She began telling me much about Gertrude Stein, Johns Hopkins, William James, etc., etc. It certainly was a most interesting story I listened to. But it did not affect in the least what I had determined to do before I had either heard the name of the author or the particulars about her.

When the Special Number of *Camera Work* appeared in the Spring of 1912, it did create a great stir. A great stir primarily amongst the

literary folks. Stieglitz certainly was cracking a joke this time. A lunch was arranged by some of these literary lights to which I was invited. And wasn't I taken to task at once. "Stieglitz, you can't tell us that there is the slightest value in this gibberish that you have published."

I merely answered, "I have had to listen to similar charges all along the line, about Matisse, Cézanne and Picasso, Marin, Hartley, Weber, Henri Rousseau, and what not. It has ever been the same story when I have introduced a new worker in whatever field."

Thus Gertrude Stein appeared on the scene in America. In due time "Tenderbuttons" was published by somebody. And there was a great hubbub raised about that pamphlet. It had much publicity. *Camera Work* had gone its quiet way. *Camera Work* represented an idea and the Matisse, Picasso, Gertrude Stein issue was nothing more than an integral part of that idea.

If anything is done and something is done then somebody has
to do it.
Or somebody has to have done it.
That is Stieglitz's way.
He has done it.
He remembers very well our first meeting.
But not better than I do.
Oh no not better than I do.
He was the first one that ever printed anything that I had done.
And you can imagine what that meant to me or to any one.
I remember him dark and I felt him having white hair.
He can do both of these things or anything.
Now that sounds as if it were the same thing or not a difficult
thing but it is it just is, it is a difficult thing to do two things as
one, but he just can that is what Stieglitz is and he is important
to every one oh yes he is whether they know it or not oh yes he is.
There are some who are important to everyone whether any one
knows anything of that one or not and Stieglitz is such a one, he
is that one, he is indeed, there is no question but that he is such
a one no question indeed, but that he is one, who is an important
one for everyone, no matter whether they do or whether they
do not know anything about any such thing about any such one
about him.
That is what Stieglitz is.
Any one can recognize him.
Any one does know that there are such ones, all of us do know
That Stieglitz is such a one.
That he is one.
291
I am sorry that I can not go on longer and tell about and more
and more what Stieglitz is, but they never told me what they
were all doing because Stieglitz had said do not bother her she
is in France, but now just in time and I am so glad I find out I
could just say what I know, I like to say what I know, and how
could I know, how could I not know what Stieglitz is.

1. See Haines, *The Inner Eye of Alfred Stieglitz,* for the
most complete discussion of Stieglitz's literary relationships, especially pp. 59–63, 123–24, on Stein; and Richard Thomas, *Literary Admirers of Alfred Stieglitz* (Carbondale: Southern Illinois University Press, 1983), especially
pp. 17–31, on Stein. See also *Intimate Vision: The Photographs of Dorothy Norman,* ed. with an essay by Miles
Barth (San Francisco: Chronicle Books and New York:
International Center of Photography, 1992), for photographs of Sherwood Anderson, 1935, p. 82; Dreiser, 1937,
p. 85; Brecht, 1945, pp. 100–101; Wright, 1946, p. 105;
Mann, n.d., p. 120; Malraux, 1954, p. 123; Spender, n.d.,
p. 125. For more on other writers influenced by Stieglitz,
see the Theodore Dreiser, Sherwood Anderson, W. C.
Williams, Hart Crane, Richard Wright, and Marianne
Moore selections as well as references to D. H. Lawrence
in the Edward Weston selection, to Jean Toomer in the
Langston Hughes selection, and to E. E. Cummings in
the Literary Portraits selection, all below.

2. See Stein, "Henri Matisse" and "Pablo Picasso,"
Camera Work, Special Number (August 1912): 23 and
29, which was the first public appreciation of Picasso.

3. For Coburn's recollections of Stein, see his *Autobiography,* p. 90. For more on Stein's relationship with
Man Ray, Beaton, and Van Vechten, see their selections
below.

*I*n 1900, Dreiser (1871–1945), the midwestern journalist and aspiring novelist who had recently moved to New York, interviewed
Alfred Stieglitz, the aspiring leader of American art photography, and
became the first of many distinguished writers to fall under his spell.[1] He
was amazed that Stieglitz, despite his privileged background, was photographing "homely" as well as beautiful metropolitan subjects. Dreiser could
not have understood that Stieglitz at this time viewed the immigrant poor
as "picturesque"—possessing the energy and purpose lacking in his own
bourgeois circumstances—who could be artistically validated as subjects by
his poetic rendering of them. Stieglitz's interest in such gritty subjects
proved transient. But his example suggested with the force of revelation to
Dreiser that poverty, which the writer knew at first hand, could be a
legitimate subject of serious art, treated with a similar blend of objectivity
and subjectivity. Over time, however, Dreiser perceived that the stark visual
documentation of "the other half," as provided by reformers like Jacob Riis
and Lewis Hine, better suited his concerns than Stieglitz's private aesthetic.
He dramatized his own artistic conversion (as well as the sociopolitical
implications of these grimmer visions of reality) in The "Genius" (1915); the
novel treats the rise and fall of a young painter, Eugene, whose first successful urban subjects resemble those treated by Stieglitz in his earlier photographs [Figs. 62–65].[2]

FROM *The "Genius"*

... The whole city was strange and cold, and if
he had not immediately fallen desperately in
love with it as a spectacle he would have been
unconscionably lonely and unhappy. As it was
the great fresh squares, such as Broadway, Fifth
Avenue and Sixth Avenue; the great spectacles,
such as the Bowery at night, the East River, the
water front, the Battery, all fascinated him with
an unchanging glamor. ...

One of his pet diversions these days and nights
was to walk the streets in rain or fog or snow.
The city appealed to him, wet or white, particularly the public squares. He saw Fifth Avenue
once in a driving snowstorm and under sput-
tering arc lights, and he hurried to his easel
next morning to see if he could not put it down
in black and white [Fig. 62]. It was unsuccessful, or at least he felt so, for after an hour of
trying he threw it aside in disgust. But these
spectacles were drawing him. He was wanting
to do them—wanting to see them shown somewhere in color. Possible success was a solace at
a time when all he could pay for a meal was
fifteen cents and he had no place to go and not
a soul with whom to talk. [Pt. 1, ch. 16,
pp. 108–9]

"I should like to show you several reproductions of pictures of mine," began Eugene in his
most courageous manner. "I have been working on a number with a view to making a show
and I thought that possibly you might be interested in looking at them with a view to displaying
them for me. I have twenty-six all told and—"...

M. Charles [a dealer] looked at them curiously. He was much impressed with the pictures of the East Side Crowd at first, but looking at one of Fifth Avenue in a snow storm, the
battered shabby bus pulled by a team of lean,
unkempt, bony horses, he paused, struck by its
force. He liked the delineation of swirling,
wind-driven snow. The emptiness of this thor-
oughfare, usually so crowded, the buttoned,
huddled, hunched, withdrawn look of those
who traveled it, the exceptional details of piles
of snow sifted on to window sills and ledges

and into doorways and on to the windows of
the bus itself, attracted his attention.

"An effective detail," he said to Eugene, as
one critic might say to another, pointing to a
line of white snow on the window of one side
of the bus. Another dash of snow on a man's
hat rim took his eye also. "I can feel the wind,"
he added.

Eugene smiled.

M. Charles passed on in silence to the steam-
ing tug coming up the East River in the dark
hauling two great freight barges [Fig. 63]. He
was saying to himself that after all Eugene's art
was that of merely seizing upon the obviously
dramatic. It wasn't so much the art of color
composition and life analysis as it was stage
craft. The man before him had the ability to
see the dramatic side of life. Still—

He turned to the last reproduction which
was that of Greeley Square in a drizzling rain
[Fig. 64].[3] Eugene by some mystery of his art
had caught the exact texture of seeping water
on gray stones in the glare of various electric
lights. He had caught the values of various kinds
of lights, those in cabs, those in cable cars,
those in shop windows, those in the street
lamp—relieving by them the black shadows
of the crowds and of the sky. The color work

here was unmistakably good [Part 2, ch. 5, pp. 228–29].

It was some little time before M. Charles condescended to write saying that if it was agreeable he would call. . . .

"Well," he said, pretending to look at the picture on the easel for the first time, "we might as well begin to look at these things. I see you have one here. Very good, I think, quite forceful. What others have you?"

Eugene was afraid this one hadn't appealed to him as much as he hoped it would, and set it aside quickly, picking up the second in the stock which stood against the wall, covered by a green curtain. It was the three engines entering the great freight yard abreast, the smoke of the engines towering straight up like tall, whitish-grey plumes, in the damp, cold air, the sky lowering with blackish-grey clouds, the red and yellow and blue cars standing out in the sodden darkness because of the water [Fig. 65]. You could feel the cold, wet drizzle, the soppy tracks, the weariness of "throwing switches." There was a lone brakeman in the foreground, "throwing" a red brake signal. He was quite black and evidently wet.

"A symphony in grey," said M. Charles succinctly.

They came swiftly after this, without much comment from either, Eugene putting one canvas after another before him, leaving it for a few moments and replacing it with another. His estimate of his own work did not rise very rapidly, for M. Charles was persistently distant, but . . . he saw that Eugene had covered almost every phase of what might be called the dramatic spectacle in the public life of the city and much that did not appear dramatic until he touched it. . . . Everything he touched seemed to have romance and beauty, and yet it was real and mostly grim and shabby.

"I congratulate you, Mr. Whitla," finally ex-

claimed M. Charles, moved by the ability of the man and feeling that caution was no longer necessary. "To me this is wonderful material, much more effective than the reproductions show, dramatic and true. I question whether you will make any money out of it. There is very little sale for American art in this country. It might almost do better in Europe. It *ought* to sell, but that is another matter. The best things do not always sell readily. It takes time. Still I will do what I can. I will give these pictures a two weeks' display early in April without any charge to you whatever." (Eugene started). "I will call them to the attention of those who know. I will speak to those who buy. It is an honor, I assure you, to do this. I consider you an artist in every sense of the word—I might say a great artist. You ought, if you preserve yourself sanely and with caution, to go far, very far. I shall be glad to send for these when the time comes." [Part 2, ch. 6, pp. 230–32]

64. Alfred Stieglitz. 'Savoy Hotel,' New York, 1898.

65. Alfred Stieglitz. 'The Hand of Man' [1902], 1910.

1. Dreiser wrote three magazine articles devoted to or including remarks about Stieglitz: "A Master of Photography," *Success* 2 (June 10, 1899): 47; "The Camera Club of New York," *Ainslee's* (October 4, 1899): 324–35 (especially 328–29); and "A Remarkable Art," *The Great Round World* (May 3, 1902): 430–34 (especially 434). For the most complete discussion of their relationship, see Haines, *The Inner Eye of Alfred Stieglitz,* pp. 75–78, 95, and 122.

2. Dreiser's novel *The "Genius"* (New York: John Lane, 1915) and its relationship to the work of Stieglitz and other photographers is discussed by Shloss in "Theodore Dreiser, Alfred Stieglitz, and Jacob Riis," *In Visible Light,* pp. 129–38, though the Stieglitz photographs she finds

analogous differ somewhat from the ones noted here. See also Ellen Moers, *Two Dreisers* (New York: Viking, 1969), pp. 10–13, who suggests that Dreiser studied Stieglitz's 'Winter on Fifth Avenue, 1892–93,' among other sources, for his representation of the concluding blizzard in *Sister Carrie* (1900)—see *Sister Carrie: An Authoritative Text, Background and Sources Criticism,* ed. Donald Pizer, 2nd ed. (New York: Norton, 1991), ch. 47, p. 363.

3. See also Stieglitz's "Wet Day on the Boulevard, Paris, 1894" and "Reflections, Night, New York, 1896–97," reproduced, among other places, in Dorothy Norman, *Alfred Stieglitz: American Seer* (New York: Random House, 1973), Plates 8 and 14.

Part Four

1915–1940

Verga (1840–1922), a native of Sicily, was Italy's most innovative late nineteenth-century writer. His verismo shaped his best works, in which the harsh daily routines and periodic violence of Sicilian peasants mirror their environment; all is portrayed with terse immediacy through the character's thoughts, speech, and actions rather than omniscient authorial description. Even before fame resulted from Cavalleria Rusticana (1880)—a short story collection known to English readers from the opera it inspired (1890) and the translation by D. H. Lawrence (1928)— Verga took up photography with two other friends, the writers Luigi Capuana (1839–1915) and Federico De Roberto (1861–1927). He soon confessed that far from having "escaped the photographic contagion," it was now his "secret mania."[1] In 1880, Verga gave up his sophisticated mainland life to return to Sicily. He largely ceased writing but, like his mentor and fellow naturalist, Zola, seriously pursued photography.[2] In contrast to the French author's aesthetic urban shots and intimate family scenes, however, Verga's pictures, like his fiction, dispassionately portray the impoverished reality of the villagers and their environment.[3] His documentary use of the camera also contrasts with its symbolic use by his younger fellow Sicilian, the playwright Luigi Pirandello, as yet another instrument of alienation in an increasingly mechanical, urban world.[4] Throughout these letters to his most enduring love, Dina Catellazzi de Sordevolo [Fig. 66], who remained on the mainland, photographs remain a naturally recurring part of Verga's public and private life until his final years, sullied by the Great War and its aftermath.

. . . I thought I saw you in front of the photograph, and I laughed at your impatience. But then it's always you, dear rascal. If only I could have you near by, wrapped up, or in the postal parcel . . . [February 6, 1899, p. 44]

. . . I think about you all the time, and feel near you. I seem to see you in those dear little rooms of yours, of which, however, I am unable to have a photograph because the three I tried to take that day when there was little sunshine, you recall, did not come out at all . . . [November 12, 1900, p. 62]

. . . I have your portraits here in front of me. There are some quite beautiful ones but I prefer above all that first one from Rome, the other one with the painter's smock and beret, and the last one, similar to the framed one which is in your living room. It makes me think of so many things and how many things I say to you. How much those dear eyes and those adored features say to me about you. I love you, I love you so very much, my dear Dina . . . [November 23, 1900, p. 65]

. . . Your two little portraits from Rome are on the reading desk where I write, standing up, in my room. There is another very beautiful one with a hat and a dressing gown with long sleeves—do you have it in mind?—on the mantelpiece; and the one similar to your framed photograph in your drawing room is also in my drawing room. The others, the two with your great hat and the one with the hood, which I call devilish,—well, I don't like them at all. I do not destroy them because they are things of yours, but I will bring them when I return so that you may destroy them with your own hands. I don't like them—don't like them—don't like them. Do you understand? You look nasty there, and you are not my Dina, my Dina whom I love and miss so much, so much . . . [November 29, 1900, p. 67]

. . . If you knew how much and in what ways I thought about you tonight and this morning!

You see? Dear! Dear! Dear one looking at me from this photograph! And you complain that I strew the house with them. Do you also want to know what my family thinks of these photographs? But that I don't know and I don't ask them. I am not sending you the picture with the big hat or the other one of the devil. I will give them to you later with my own hands . . . [December 9, 1900, p. 70]

. . . Love, dear love! How often I have kissed your letter! And its contents inside. How many things I'd like to tell you, and how many things I would like to do! I have in front of me your little portrait that looks at me and I tell it so many things . . . [December 18, 1900, p. 71]

. . . I like both of them. They resemble you but in a very different way. The full figure standing has the nasty look of your holidays. But I also like it in the portfolio together with the one, to me, more humane and merciful. The nasty look with perhaps just a hint of the sardonic flickers in your little eyes and lengthens the mouth lines. Were you angry with me at that moment? But the little figure is slender and elegant and such

66. Giovanni Verga. 'Dina,' c. 1902.

that inspires thanks to God that this beautiful lady is thinking of a miserable mortal like me, although in a nasty moment. Note however that this print has a little white spot on the eye and I want to change it on my return, and maybe will take that little head between my hands to find it—where is it... where is it... [March 3, 1904, pp. 176–77]

. . . I thank you for the photographs. But I don't like the one taken at the dressmaker at all. It's harsh, badly lit. It ages you a hundred years. It is the portrait of your grandmother. It's not my little Dina at all . . . [October 3, 1904, pp. 190–91]

. . . Don't bother sending me the *Illustrazione*. I saw it here at the club. I sent the portrait to our friend Treves [Verga's publisher] on condition of his not placing me in his shop window. But he sent me his portrait and printed my mug anyway. Ah well, by now

when one is in the public eye, we are reduced to the status of prostitutes . . . [May 25, 1906, p. 251]

. . . What pleasure this letter of yours gave me and what pleasure your photograph too! But you know that you really look well, younger, more beautiful, rather elegant in spite of your blemishes? What a joy to see you like this! Coquettish too but I already knew that. Who took that little portrait? And, yes, it is a bit too much in the shade and the lens must certainly not be a Goertz. Thank you, dear little Dina, you did a really loving thing for me . . . [August 26, 1910, p. 357]

. . . As to the photographs that they're requesting from you, I have no more, neither new nor old, and I certainly don't think of having any more taken at my age. For I am very, but very...down, in all senses and ways . . . [May 5, 1916, p. 434]

1. See Andrea Nemiz, *Capuana, Verga, De Roberto: Fotografi* (Palermo: Edikronos, 1982), for the most complete discussion of the subject, and Italo Zannier, *Storia della Fotografia Italiana* (Roma-Bari: Editore Laterza, 1986), pp. 97 and 119–20, whose discussion of Verga and his writer-photographer friends cites the work of Francesco C. Crispoli in *Letteratura e Fotografia: Capuana, Verga, De Roberto, Strindberg, Zola, Carroll* (Rome: R. A. I-Colombo, 1977), which the editor was not able to see. Verga, in his letter to Maria Brusini, October 4, 1887, in *Giovanni Verga: Lettere d'Amore*, ed. Gino Raya (Rome; Tindalo, 1971), p. 469, refers to Capuana, "che e il mio maestro anche di fotografia, e il mio ritrattista ordinario" [who is also my teacher in photography and my usual portraitist]. Verga, as quoted in Giovanni Garra Agosto, *Verga/Fotografo* (Catania: Giuseppe Maimone Editore, 1991), p. 233, at least twice, asked Capuana for photographs to help him with his dramatization of his own work, pp. 13–14, and p. 32, once warned him that his interest in photography was spoiling his "precious capital of time and genius."

2. See comment in letter to Verga, December, 1892, from his brother, Mario, who evidently shared his passion for photography, quoted in Salvatore Nigro, "Verga e l'ospite invisibile," *La Repubblica* (February 21, 1992): 25, made available by the author to the editor, who translates it as follows: "Not a day goes by, one could say, that we don't remark on what would happen if you were here with us, the photographs we could take, the evenings we could spend inside in the dark developing negatives." The unpublished correspondence between the Verga brothers is in a private collection, according to Nigro in a letter to the editor of July 7, 1992, but it does not mention much more about photography; Nigro also notes in a letter of February 9, 1993, that portraits of the Verga brothers by Nadar, whose photographs they greatly admired, have recently been discovered and are in a private collection in Catania. Verga's *Lettere a Paolina*, ed. Gino Raya (Rome: Dermenti, 1980), Letters 169, 180, 181, 189, and 190, also mention his photographic interests.

3. For discussion and reproductions of Verga's photographs, see Mitry's section on "Giovanni Verga" in *Schriftsteller als Photographen*, pp. 18 and 43–54, and especially Agosto, *Verga/Fotografo*.

4. See Pirandello, *Shoot!: The Notebooks of Serafino Gubbio, Cinematograph Operato*, trans. C. K. Scott Moncrieff (New York: E. P. Dutton, 1926), in which the antihero realizes his fears of becoming like a camera in order to survive in an unfeeling, mechanistic world; see especially pp. 319–21 for an interesting scene about the effect of portraits on our perception of the subject over time.

38. Ezra Pound

"VORTOGRAPHS AND PAINTINGS
BY ALVIN LANGDON COBURN," 1917

Pound (1885–1972), the influential but controversial poet, always had a strong interest in all the arts, especially visual ones.[1] As the self-appointed theorist of Anglo-American modernism, the eclectic writer helped found a short-lived London quarterly, Blast (1914–15), to publicize its avant-garde views on contemporary art, including Vorticism; this movement believed that in the center of each art form lay a unique concentration of energy fixed in geometric abstractions, where all motion stopped. While photographing Pound in his usual soft focus manner in 1913, Coburn was drawn to his energetically intellectual sitter and his unconventional ideas of representation.[2] He constructed a Vortoscope, a device with three of the poet's shaving mirrors, which, when attached to a camera, acted like a prism, geometrically fragmenting Pound's appearance in many subsequent portraits [Fig. 67] as well as that of wood and crystal pieces [Fig. 68, 69].[3] Exhibited in 1917 along with some of his paintings, Coburn's pioneering photographic abstractions reduced even the voluble Shaw to silence but prompted a public outcry from another old friend, Frederick Evans.[4] Whether because of these uncharacteristic responses from his close friends or Pound's demeaning treatment of photography in this preface (so at odds with the writer's earlier enthusiasm),[5] Coburn never again experimented with nonrepresentational pictures. Nor did he ever again associate with Pound, who tried to adapt the photographer's Vortoscope to another of his short-lived projects, filmmaking. Indeed, after the First World War, Coburn gradually abandoned serious photography for other pursuits, not taking it up again until after his wife's death in 1957.[6]

"Vortographs and Paintings"

THE VORTOGRAPHS

This note concerns only the vortographs and not the paintings in this exhibition. Mr. Coburn's paintings were done before the invention of the vortescope. He has attached no label to them, but they are roughly speaking, post-impressionist. It should be quite clear that the paintings were not done in agreement with the work of the "Vorticists," and that there is no connection between Mr. Coburn, as painter, and the group known as the vorticist group.

I am concerned here solely with vortography. The tool called the vortescope was invented late in 1916. Mr. Coburn had been long desiring to bring cubism or vorticism into photography. Only with the invention of a suitable instrument was this possible.

In vortography he accepts the fundamental principles of vorticism, and those of vorticist painting in so far as they are applicable to the work of the camera.

The principles of vorticism have been amply set forth by Wyndham Lewis, Ezra Pound and Gaudier-Brzeska. The immediate ancestry is given in two quotations in *Blast:* Pater's "All arts approach the conditions of music"; and Whistler's "We are interested in a painting because it is an arrangement of lines and colours." Cezanne began taking "impressions" of masses. The term "mass" or "form" has been more prominent than the term "line" in recent discussions.

The vorticist principle is that a painting is an expression by means of an arrangement of form and colour in the same way that a piece of music is an expression by means of an arrangement of sound. In painting the form has only two dimensions (though it may suggest or "represent" a third dimension). In sculpture one uses three dimensions.

Or to put it another way: Painting makes use of colour arranged on a surface; Sculpture of masses defined by planes.

In vortography colour is practically excluded. There can be suggestion of colours. There can be a variety in the colour of the paper on which the vortograph is printed. But the medium of the vortographer is practically limited to form (shapes on a surface) and to a light and shade; to the peculiar varieties in lightness and darkness which belong to the technique of the camera.

THE CAMERA IS FREED FROM REALITY

A natural object or objects may perhaps be retained realistically by the vortographer if he chooses, and the vortograph containing such an object or objects will not be injured if the object or objects contribute interest to the pattern, that is to say, if they form an integral and formal part of the whole.

The vortescope is useless to a man who cannot recognise a beautiful arrangement of forms on a surface, when his vortescope has brought them to focus. His selection may be *almost* as creative as a painter's composition. His photographic technique must be assumed. It does not form a part of this discussion, though it is extremely important, and all, or most, of the qualities of the black and white, of light and dark, will depend upon it. These things, however, can be discussed by any intelligent photographer, assuming that such persons exist. There is no need of any special foreword about this part of the technique.

68. Alvin Langdon Coburn. 'Vortograph, no. 3,' 1917.

VORTICISM has reawakened our sense of form, a sense long dead in occidental artists. Any person or animal unable to take pleasure in an arrangement of forms as he or she takes pleasure in an arrangement of musical notes, is thereby the poorer. People are sometimes tone-deaf and colour-blind. Some ears cannot recognise the correct pitch of a note, and some eyes get no pleasure from a beautiful or expressive arrangement of forms.

Until recently people enjoyed pictures chiefly, and often exclusively because the painting reminded them of something else. Numerous contemporaries have passed that state of development.

The modern will enjoy vortograph No. 3, [Fig. 68] not because it reminds him of a shell burst-

69. Alvin Langdon
Coburn. 'Vortograph,
no. 8,' 1917.

ing on a hillside, but because the arrangement of forms pleases him, as a phrase of Chopin might please him. He will enjoy vortograph No. 8, [Fig. 69] not because it reminds him of a falling Zeppelin, but because he likes the shape and arrangement of its blocks of dark and light.

Obviously vortographs will lack certain interests that are to be found in vorticist paintings. They bear the same relation to vorticist painting that academic photography bears to academy painting. Almost any fool can paint an academy picture, and any imbecile can shoot off a Kodak.

Certain definite problems in the aesthetics of form may possibly be worked out with the vortescope. When these problems are solved vorticism will have entered that phase of morbidity into which representative paintings descended after the Renaissance painters had decided upon all the correct proportions of the human body, etc., etc., etc. That date of decline is still afar off. Vorticism and vortography are both at the beginning of their course.

Vortography stands below the other vorticist arts in that it is an art of the eye, not of the eye and hand together. It stands infinitely above photography in that the vortographer combines his forms *at will*. He selects just what actuality he wishes, he excludes the rest. He chooses what forms, lights, masses, he desires, he arranges them *at will* on his screen. He can make summer of London October. The aereën and submarine effects are got in his study. All these vortographs were done in two or three rooms. The dull bit of windowframe (vortograph No. 16) produces "a fine Picasso," or if not a "Picasso" a "Coburn." It is an excellent arrangement of shapes, and more interesting than most of the works of Picabia or of the bad imitators of Lewis.

Art photography has been stuck for twenty years. During that time practically no new effects have been achieved. Art photography is stale and suburban. It has never had any part in aesthetics. Vortography may have, however, very much the same place in the coming aesthetic that the anatomical studies of the Renaissance had in the aesthetics of the academic school. It is at least a subject which a serious man may consider. It is harmony of form, angels, proportions, etc., arranged as we have had a mathematical "harmony" arranged for us in music.

I am not concerned with deciding whether such a mathematical schedule is desirable or would be beneficent. But if it is *possible*, then the vortescope could be extremely useful, and may play a very important part in the discovery of such a system.

Such a system would be of aesthetics and not merely of physics and optics. It would "depend" on the science of optics as much and as little as musical harmony depends on the physiology of the ear.

Impressionism sought its theoretic defence in, if it did not arise from, Berkley's theory of the minimum visible, *i.e.*, of the effect of points of light and colour on the retina.

Pleasure is derivable not only from the stroking or pushing of the retina by light waves of various colour, BUT ALSO by the impact of those waves in certain arranged tracts.

This simple and obvious fact is the basis of the "modern" "art" "revolution."

The eye *likes* certain plainnesses, certain complexities, certain arrangements, certain varieties, certain incitements, certain reliefs and suspensions.

It likes these things irrespective of whether or no they form a replica of known objects.

POSTSCRIPT
BY
ALVIN LANGDON COBURN

In taking this opportunity to thank my anonymous critic for his extremely interesting preface, although I agree in the main with his point of view, I think it only fair to myself to mention one or two matters on which we are of slightly divergent opinion.

In the first place I feel rather hurt at the manner in which he brushes aside my paintings as merely "Post Impressionist." Perhaps to one living exclusively in the rarified atmosphere of Vorticism, they may seem to be unworthy of comment, but I must confess to rather a fondness for their simple homely qualities and their unashamed realism. He then goes on to say that photography is inferior to painting, or words to that effect, and here our opinions most decidedly part company. I affirm that any sort of photograph is superior to any sort of painting aiming at the same result. If these vortographs did not possess distinctive qualities unapproached by any other art method I would not

have considered it worth my while to make them. Design they have in common with other mediums, but where else but in photography will you find such luminosity and such a sense of subtle gradations?

I took up painting as one takes up any other primitive pursuit, because in these days of progress it is amusing to revert to the cumbersome methods of bygone days, that one may return to modernity with a fuller appreciation of its vast possibilities; and so perhaps, after all, my anonymous friend is right in not dwelling unduly on the paintings. Yet still I hope that there may be some who may catch a glimmer of the very great enjoyment their production gave me. They are not, however, the most important part of the present show. People have been painting now for several years, it is no longer a novelty, but this will go down to posterity as the first exhibition of Vortography.

1. See Harriet Zinnes, ed., introduction to *Ezra Pound and the Visual Arts* (New York: New Directions, 1980), pp. xi–xxiv.

2. Coburn's conventional portrait of Pound, October 22, 1913, is reproduced as the frontispiece for the poet's *Lustra* (New York: Knopf, 1917), and in Coburn's *More Men of Mark* (London: Duckworth, 1922), Plate 2. See also Richard Kenin, *Return to Albion: Americans in England* (New York: Holt, Rinehart & Winston, 1979),

pp. 251–59, for a survey of Pound's work with Coburn as well as Man Ray's portrait of Pound (1923), reproduced in *Man Ray Photographs* (London: Thames & Hudson, 1987), p. 250, fig. 341, and his description of Pound in his selection below.

3. The most comprehensive selection of Coburn's Vortographs of Pound and other objects are reproduced and discussed in Frank DiFederico's study, "Alvin Langdon Coburn and the Genesis of Vortographs," *History of*

Photography 11 (October–December 1987): 265–96, together with a list of Coburn's Vortographs at GEH. See also Hunter's discussion of Vortographic portraiture in *Image and Word,* pp. 121–27, and Coburn, *Autobiography,* p. 102, and figs. 27, 54, 55, and 69.

4. See Jay and Moore, Preface to Shaw, *Bernard Shaw on Photography,* ed. Jay and Moore, pp. 28–29; Newhall, *Frederic H. Evans,* npn; and the Evans-Coburn exchange of letters in the *British Journal of Photography* (1917): (February 23): 102; (March 2): 115; (March 9): 126; (March 16): 142–43; and (March 23): 155, partly fueled by Evans's mistaken view that Coburn had written the preface.

5. See Pound's enthusiastic letter about Vortography to his father, September 22, 1916, in Zinnes, ed., *Pound,* p. 293; cf. his snide letter about the coming exhibition ("He and I are to jaw about abstraction in photography and art") to John Quinn, January 24, [1917], p. 281. DiFederico, "Alvin Langdon Coburn," p. 294, suggests that the falling out with Pound was a major factor in Coburn's abandoning photography; cf. Hunter, *Image and Word,* p. 126, who cites Coburn's growing preoccupation with other interests.

6. See Hunter, *Image and Word,* p. 126, who mentions Coburn's absorption with the pianola, astrology, freemasonry, and country life in Wales. Coburn also contributed the charming libretto for *Fairy Gold, A Play for Children and Grown-ups Who Have Not Grown Up* (1938), with music by Sir Granville Bantock.

39. *Thomas Hardy*

"THE PHOTOGRAPH," 1917

*T*he writings of Hardy (1840–1928), especially his pessimistic novels in which characters struggle against indifferent fate, reveal a persistent interest in the literary uses of what he once called the "heliographic science."[1] Though he disparaged "photographic curiousness" and unselective realism, his style can be considered "photographic," with its use of framed settings, voyeuristic characters, decisive pictorial moments, and highly visual diction. Equally characteristic is Hardy's significant use of the photograph in his fiction: as realistic or topical detail, plot device, means of characterization, thematic reinforcement, iconic metaphor, or sometimes all powerfully combined as in his short story "An Imaginative Woman" (1893) or in his bildungsroman, Jude the Obscure (1895).[2] Indeed, a telling scene from this novel—in which Jude discovers that his wife has sold, for the frame's value, the photograph of himself that he gave her on their wedding day—becomes the subject of a much later poem, "The Son's Portrait" (1924/1928).[3] "The Photograph," below, which Hardy felt to be "a man's poem only" yet "possibly among the best I have written," takes up his favorite theme of reality and illusion; but it blurs the line between them by having the speaker animate the pictured subject, thus releasing long-repressed emotion.[4] Though irritated when "kodaked" by curious Dorset tourists, Hardy proved a gracious sitter for serious photographers.[5]

The flame crept up the portrait line by line
As it lay on the coals in the silence of night's profound,
    And over the arm's incline,
And along the marge of the silkwork superfine,
And gnawed at the delicate bosom's defenceless round.

Then I vented a cry of hurt, and averted my eyes;
The spectacle was one that I could not bear,
    To my deep and sad surprise;
But, compelled to heed, I again looked furtivewise
Till the flame had eaten her breasts, and mouth, and hair.

'Thank God, she is out of it now!' I said at last,
In a great relief of heart when the thing was done
    That had set my soul aghast,
And nothing was left of the picture unsheathed from the past
But the ashen ghost of the card it had figured on.

She was a woman long hid amid packs of years,
She might have been living or dead; she was lost to my sight,
    And the deed that had nigh drawn tears
Was done in a casual clearance of life's arrears;
But I felt as if I had put her to death that night! ...

— Well; she knew nothing thereof did she survive,
And suffered nothing if numbered among the dead;
    Yet — yet — if on earth alive
Did she feel a smart, and with vague strange anguish strive?
If in heaven, did she smile at me sadly and shake her head?

1. See, for example, Hardy, *A Laodicean* [1881] (London: Macmillan, 1975), Bk. 5, ch. 4, p. 311. This point, like others in this preface, is indebted to Arlene M. Jackson's "Photography as Style and Metaphor in the Art of Thomas Hardy," *Thomas Hardy Annual* 2 (Atlantic Highlands, N.J.: Humanities Press, 1984), pp. 91–109, except for "The Son's Portrait," which is not mentioned.

2. See Hardy, "An Imaginative Woman," in *Wessex Tales* (London, Macmillan, 1896), pp. 3–31, and *Jude the Obscure*, ed. Norman Page (New York: Norton, 1978): Pt. 1: ch. 11, pp. 60–61; Pt. 2: ch. 1, p. 72; ch. 2, p. 69; Pt. 3: ch. 1, p. 108; ch. 2, p. 111–12; ch. 3, p. 113; ch. 6, p. 129; and Pt. 4, ch. 1, p. 164. See also *A Laodicean*, Bk. 2, ch. 2–3, pp. 201–6; Bk. 5: ch. 4, pp. 310–11; ch. 6, p. 322; ch. 11, p. 353; and ch. 13, pp. 366–67; and *Desperate Remedies* [1871] (London: Macmillan, 1975), ch. 17, pp. 319–21; ch. 18, pp. 324 and 326, discussed in Jennifer M. Green, "Outside the Frame: The Photographer in Victorian Fiction," *Victorian Institute Journal* 19 (1991): 123–28.

3. See *Jude the Obscure*, Pt. 1, ch. 11, p. 85 cf. "The Son's Portrait" (posthumously published, though mentioned by Hardy in 1924) in *Winter Words in Various Moods and Meters* (London: Macmillan, 1928), pp. 60–61.

4. See letter to Ruth Head, August 7, 1921, in *The Collected Letters of Thomas Hardy*, ed. Richard Little Purdy and Michael Millgate (Oxford: Clarendon Press, 1987), vol. 6, p. 96. Jackson, "Photography as Style," p. 101, suggests the poem was originally composed between 1884 and 1890.

5. Quoted in Jackson, "Photography as Style," p. 91. See also Coburn's portrait of Hardy, October 13, 1913, originally published in *More Men of Mark*, Plate 13, and reproduced in Coburn, *Autobiography*, ed. H. and A. Gernsheim, p. 98; and E. O. Hoppe's photograph of Hardy and his wife (1914), reproduced in Michael Millgate, ed., *The Life and Work of Thomas Hardy* (Athens: University of Georgia Press, 1984), fig. 13, following p. 305.

FROM *The Guermantes Way,* 1920,
FROM *Remembrance of Things Past,* 1913–28

With his multivolume Remembrance of Things Past *(1913–27),* Proust *(1871–1922) moved far from the traditional novel with its omniscient authorial perspective and clear, continuous plot. His landmark work filtered past and present experience, whose significance only emerges at the end, through the mind of one sensitive character (who naturally resembles the author). Given the centrality in Proust's writings of time—as experienced duration, not chronology by calendar or clock—and of memory as a nonrational catalyst, it is not surprising to find the author drawing on photographs and related imagery to delineate character, bridge time, elicit emotion, and provoke thought.[1] Here Marcel, the autobiographical central consciousness, is startled by the deterioration of his beloved grandmother, who proves instrumental in his later decision to be a writer. He meditates on the mind as a kind of camera, whose recollected "snapshots" of loved ones, overlaid with feelings and wishes, are not easily reconcilable with unwelcome present realities.[2] Elsewhere in his fiction, Proust generally disparages photography as an instrument of memory for the sensitive viewer compared to unconscious remembrances evoked by the other senses.[3] But few individuals have ever had the time or inclination to cultivate their senses to the degree that Proust did as he sat composing his masterpiece in bed in the quiet of his cork-lined room [Fig. 70].*

. . . My one anxiety was to return to my grandmother; always until then, in this little country town, when I thought of what my grandmother must be doing by herself, I had pictured her as she was when with me, suppressing my own personality but without taking into account the effects of such a suppression; now, I had to free myself, at the first possible moment, in her arms, from the phantom, hitherto unsuspected and suddenly called into being by her voice, of a grandmother really separated from me, resigned, having, what I had never yet thought of her as having, a definite age, who had just received a letter from me in an empty house, as I had once before imagined Mamma in a house by herself, when I had left her to go to Balbec.

Alas, this phantom was just what I did see when, entering the drawing room before my grandmother had been told of my return, I found her there, reading. I was in the room, or rather I was not yet in the room since she was not aware of my presence, and, like a woman whom one surprises at a piece of work which she will lay aside if anyone comes in, she had abandoned herself to a train of thoughts which she had never allowed to be visible by me. Of myself—thanks to that privilege which does not last but which one enjoys during the brief moment of return, the faculty of being a spectator, so to speak, of one's own absence,— there was present only the witness, the observer, with a hat and travelling coat, the stranger who does not belong to the house, the photographer who has called to take a photograph of places which one will never see again. The process that mechanically occurred in my eyes when I caught sight of my grandmother was indeed a photograph. We never see the people who are dear to us save in the animated system, the perpetual motion of our incessant love for them, which before allowing the images that their faces present to reach us catches them in its vortex, flings them back upon the idea that we have always had of them, makes them adhere to it, coincide with it. How, since in the forehead, the cheeks of my grandmother I had been accustomed to read all the most delicate, the most permanent qualities of her mind; how, since every casual glance is an act of necromancy, each face that we love a mirror of the past, how could I have failed to overlook what in her had become dulled and changed, seeing that in the most trivial spectacles of our daily life, our eye, charged with thought, neglects, as would a classical tragedy, every image that does not assist the action of the play and retains only those that may help to make its purpose intelligible. But if, in place of our eye, it should be a purely material object, a photographic plate, that has watched the action, then what we shall see, in the courtyard of the Institute, for example, will be, instead of the dignified emergence of an Academician who is going to hail a cab, his staggering gait, his precautions to avoid tumbling upon his back, the parabola of his fall, as though he were drunk, or the ground frozen over. So is it when some casual sport of chance prevents our intelligent and pious affection from coming forward in time to hide from our eyes what they ought never to behold, when it is forestalled by our eyes, and they, arising first in the field and having it to themselves, set to work mechanically, like films, and shew us, in place of the loved friend who has long ago ceased to exist but whose death our affection has always hitherto kept concealed from us, the new person whom a hundred times daily that affection has clothed with a dear and cheating likeness. And, as a sick man who for long has not looked at his own reflexion, and has kept his memory of the face that he never sees refreshed from the ideal image of himself that he carries in his mind, recoils on catching sight in the glass, in the midst of an arid waste of cheek, of the sloping red structure of a nose as huge as one of the pyramids of Egypt, I, for whom my grandmother was still myself, I who had never seen her save in my own soul, always at the same pace in the past, through the transparent sheets of contiguous, overlapping memories, suddenly in our drawing-room which formed part of a new world, that of time, that in which

70. Man Ray. 'Proust on his Death Bed,' November 1922.

dwell the strangers of whom we say "He's begun to age a good deal," for the first time and for a moment only, since she vanished at once, I saw, sitting on the sofa, beneath the lamp, red-faced, heavy and common, sick, lost in thought, following the lines of a book with eyes that seemed hardly sane, a dejected old woman whom I did not know. [from *Remembrance of Things Past*, vol. 1, pp. 814–15]

1. For other references to photography in Proust's works, see Raoul Chelly, *Repertoire des Thèmes de Marcel Proust* (Paris: Librairie Gallimard [1935]), pp. 253–54 (see "Photographie"); called to the editor's attention by Harry Levin; Victor E. Graham, *The Imagery of Proust* (Oxford: Blackwell, 1966), pp. 150–51; and Terence Kilmartin, comp., "Photography," in *A Reader's Guide to Remembrance of Things Past* (London: Chatto & Windus, 1983). See also discussions of many of them by Stephen C. Infantino in "Proust and Photography: Studies in Single-Lens Reflexivity," Ph.D. diss., University of Southern California, 1986; "Photoghosts," *Romanic Review* 82, no. 4 (November 1991): 500–506; and *Photographic Vision in Proust* (New York: Peter Lang, 1992).

2. For example, see also in Proust, *Remembrance of Things Past*: "Place Named: The Place," *Within a Budding Grove*, vol. 1, pp. 593–94, and "The Heart's Intermission," *Cities of the Plain*, vol. 2, pp. 127–30, for two other moving episodes—one earlier, one later—involving Marcel's grandmother and her photograph, which thus accumulates resonance.

3. See n. 1 above and Susan Sontag's relevant discussion of Proust in *On Photography*, pp. 164–65. See also Arthur Trottenberg, ed., *A Vision of Paris: The Photographs of Eugene Atget/The Words of Marcel Proust* (New York: Macmillan, 1963); Jean-François Chevrier, *Proust et la photographie*, with photographs by Pierre De Fenoyl and Holgar Trüizch (Paris: Éditions de l'Étoile, 1982); and François-Xavier Bouchart, *Marcel Proust: La Figure des Pays* (Paris: Éditions Colona, 1982).

41. F. Holland Day and Amy Lowell

FROM CORRESPONDENCE, MARCH 1921

At the turn of the century, Day (1864–1933) rivaled Alfred Stieg-litz as the leading American photographer and was already important to literary history for several reasons. He initially learned photography to illustrate books in his collection; and his prints often repre-sented themes inspired by English poetry, especially that of Keats [Fig. 71], as well as classical myth and the Bible (featuring himself as the crucified Christ in his most controversial sequence).[1] Day assembled the largest Keats collection in the country, working to establish the first American memorial to the poet in England (1894) and to correct unfavorable misconceptions about his fiancée, Fanny Brawne.[2] Meanwhile, he helped educate Kahlil Gibran (1883–1931), the author of The Prophet *(1923), and from 1895 was in contact with the Hampton Institute, whose camera club members illus-trated the popular dialect poems of Paul Laurence Dunbar (1872–1906).[3] In addition, he founded Copeland and Day, the distinguished but short-lived publishing firm (1893–99) that introduced Americans to the work of such artists as Oscar Wilde, Stephen Crane, D. G. Rossetti, and Aubrey Beards-ley in fine volumes inspired by the design ideals of William Morris.[4] In 1904, however, a studio fire devastated both Day's work and his will. By 1917, suffering real and imagined ailments, he gave up photography as well as all outside routines, retreating to a bed set up in his library with its "Keats corner" [Fig. 72]. In 1921, Amy Lowell, the prima donna of Ameri-can poetry, decided to write a biography of Keats, hoping to draw on Day's collection as well as her own sizable one. The opening of the epistolary duel between these two strong characters as Lowell tried to meet with Day to see his Keats collection suggests the tragicomedy to come.[5]*

2 March *1921*

My dear Mr. Day:

. . . When I see how much unpublished material there is right here within reach in America, I more than ever realize that something ought to be done about it for the sake of a better understanding of Keats. I have, therefore, determined to . . . make a book which shall be a sort of critical biography of the poet, dealing psychologically with his mind, his development. It would be, by no means, the definite and exhaustive sort of work which Sir Sidney Colvin's biography is, but will, I hope, be a little more comprehending and elastic than Sir Sidney's.

One of the things I particularly want to do is to vindicate Fanny Brawne of the hundred-year aspersions that have been cast upon her by unimaginative persons. The more I hear of her, the more I think that she has been a much maligned woman, and the letter you sent me confirms my opinion. I think that there is nothing which one could do that would give Keats greater pleasure than to prove to the world that Fanny Brawne was a really very nice girl and by no means the heartless coquette which Keats, in the agony of his illness permitted himself to think.

I also want to publish, if possible, any unpublished letters of Keats's that I may be able to find. I have three; you tell me you have some; and I think that I shall be able to find others. I should like very much to talk the matter over with you, for I hope greatly for your help and concurrence in my enterprise, and I think you will find that I shall agree sufficiently with your views to make you willing to help me. I hope so, at least, for I have the matter very much at heart, I am leaving this afternoon for another lecture trip and shall not be back until about the 14th of March. When I do come back, I hope you will let me go out to Norwood to see you and talk the thing over and thank you in person for the very material help you have already given me. I tried to telephone you the other day but was told that you could not come to the telephone. So far as I know I could come to see you any day of the week of the 14th except the 14th itself. It would have to be late in the afternoon, as I am not yet sufficiently recovered to do anything early in the day. If you would like to appoint a day of that week when I might see you or preferably telephone when we can canvass various days, I shall be more than grateful.

I have not been able during these few days that I have been at home to go in to the Library to see what you have lent them. This has been a great grief to me, but the doctors forbade me to leave my bed during this short interval of rest. I cannot tell you how anxious I am to have you look favorably upon my idea of the book.

Believe me, with many thanks,

Very sincerely yours,

Amy Lowell

71. F. Holland Day. 'Beauty Is Truth,' c. 1897–99.

Sunday—*13 March 1921*

My dear Miss Lowell

I am surely very deeply interested in such work as that you tell me you have so much at heart. It has been one of my greatest interests during the last five and thirty years, whose passing has seen many new discoveries relating to J. K. & his circle. As to any assistance I might be able to be to your project, I am confident that you would rather I should be perfectly frank at the outset, Therefore let me say that my unpublished material has been kept so with the idea of doing one day what you propose now to do, save that my project embraced no material outside my own collection. The performance of this design has been postponed from time to time for one reason or another, but never abandoned. Had it not been for my invalidism & the impossibility to obtain any adequate supply of hand made paper, the accomplishment would have come this year. With these facts at your command, & were we to "exchange shoes"—to use a graphic New England expression—I wonder whether you would be eager, or even willing, to dispose of material so long "hoarded" for your own use!

I hope the only attitude which I find it possible to take will not appear to you as selfish.

As to the call which you are good enough to propose, let me assure you that nothing would give me greater pleasure, & we may find it possible in the future. Just now, and for some time to come, in all probability, I am denied callers *after* four o'clock. After the warmer weather reaches us, I hope this ban may be broadened. In the meantime any assistance which I feel at liberty to be, can perhaps be accomplished through the services of "*Mr Hays*" the new master of the [U.S.] post.

From what you tell me of your conclusions in regard to F. B. I incline to believe your opinion has perhaps swung somewhat too far in a direction, fathered by your desire, and opposite to that generally and, I believe sincerely, erroneously, held. I found, years ago, two people who remembered F. B. *before she left off mourning*, one of whom had been taught various branches of elementary education by her sister Margaret. The other remembered her well into mature life. The information gained from these as well as from the letters did not show a temperament so filled with intellectuality as one might expect could meet *all* the requirements which might be made upon one who would have proved to be *the* 'mate' for J. K. I do not personally believe that his later judgment was one *wholly* due to his physical disease, but in some measure—tempered at least—by a despair, caused by his sure knowledge of a thinness which existed (or appeared to exist) on the intellectual side of an unusually exubrient personality, which had cast over him a thraldom which he had no slightest wish to break. . . .

In the most gentlemanly manner in the world let me suggest that my name is not *Frederick*—and that my mothers name is not necessary in the address of letters for me. Please once more forgive the manner of writing—of

Yours very sincerely

F. H. Day

P.S.

I discovered the extra copies of the Bust circulars one of which accompanies this letter, for your Collection—if you include such slight things.

MISS LOWELL TO DAY

15 March *1921*

My Dear Mr. Day:

I will not deny that your refusal to allow me permission to use any of your unpublished material is a great blow to me, but I thoroughly sympathize with your desire to publish your own material yourself. The only thing is that this is such a perfect year to bring out anything we know about Keats, and my book, I hope, to have ready by the Autumn. Still you must not suppose that I am so poor a collector as not to realize the pleasure of giving to the world one's belongings one's self, and this does not at all affect my desire to see your most interesting collection, which I hope you may permit me to do at the earliest opportunity.

I do not wish to give you the idea that I think Fanny Brawne was the "perfect mate" for Keats—far from it. She was, for instance, no such charming woman as his sister-in-law, Georgiana Wylie, but that she was quite the heartless and uncomprehending young lady which is usually supposed, I do not think.

Beyond your collection and my own, I have so far run down very little original Keats material. By the way, the original manuscript of the poem, "Hither, Come Hither," which you will remember appeared in the "Ladies Companion" in 1837, is for sale by Gabriel Wells in New York for $600.00 or so. I mention this thing because you may be interested. I am myself over-bought at the moment and cannot think of acquiring it.

I have been very lucky in obtaining from my own collection and elsewhere a good many glimpses into the working of Keats's mind through books which he has read and annotated. This will, I think, from an interesting and, for the most part, unpublished side of my book. The book is not primarily to be a description of any collection whatever, nor is it to be an authoritative biography like Sir Sidney Colvin's nor an exhaustive critical essay like Robert Bridges'. It is to be a sort of mixture of all these things—Keats from the point of view of the new generation; but what I am to call the book I have not yet decided. I should like so much to talk over the whole matter sometime with you who know Keats so well, and possibly when the warmer weather comes you may be willing to allow me to see your treasures and have a little chat with you, and from your larger experience gain perhaps a finer perspective than that I already have.

Please believe that I harbour not the slightest ill will for your decision, although naturally I grieve that things must be so, but understand how truly grateful I am for the help you have already given and the interest you take. It is needless to say that if you would like me to bring over my things for you to see when I do come, it would be the very greatest pleasure for me to do so, since I fear that to ask you here would prove too great a burden upon your strength.

Believe me, with warmest gratitude even if with regret,

Sincerely yours,
Amy Lowell

72. F. Holland Day. 'Keats Corner' (in Day's library, with Keats's death mask to left of column), c. 1894.

MISS LOWELL TO MR. FERRIS GREENSLET

22 March *1921*

Dear Ferris:

Your firm is keeping me good and busy with proof, and the few minutes I have outside that business I am employing to look up unpublished Keats material. Mr. Day does not seem inclined to let me use any of his. He is a silly old hypochondriac, and he tells me that for thirty-five years he has cherished a plan for publishing his material himself, and he still cherishes it, but he is now waiting for the price of hand-made paper to drop, and I do not really think he will ever publish anything. I still have hopes and shall continue to work on them. I have not been able to see him; he is too ill. . . .

1. Estelle Jussim's pioneer study, *Slave to Beauty*, reproduces these and many other Day photographs. Keats's *Ode to a Grecian Urn* (1819) obviously inspired Day's 'Beauty Is Truth' (1896), reproduced here as well as in Jussim, p. 111; the top print earlier appeared as the more simply framed 'The Genius of Greek Art,' with the same lines beneath in plainer lettering; a print is at the GEH (41448). Keats's *Hymn to Apollo* (1817) may possibly have inspired 'Nude Youth with Lyre' (1907), reproduced in Jussim, Plates 43–44, npn. Janet Buerger's unpublished study, "F. Holland Day's Seven Words and the Remnant in Boston," pp. 7 and 29–30, suggests that Day's famous 'Ebony and Ivory' (1897), which portrays a nude black model holding a white ivory figure, reproduced in Jussim, pp. 109 and 224, Plate 11, was inspired by the prologue to D. G. Rossetti's sonnet sequence *The House of Life* (1880), Copeland and Day's first publication (1894); and Buerger suggests that Day's 'Armageddon' (1899), at GEH, was inspired by Alfred Tennyson's poem "Timbuctoo" (1829). The Smithsonian Institution's Archives of American Art (Microfilm 3566) contains a Day photograph of 'Rossettti's Mask' and another of a portrait of the poet Abraham Cowley.

2. For the details of the formation and dispersal of Day's Keats collection and other literary holdings, see Hyder Rollins and Stephen Parrish, *Keats and the Bostonians* (Cambridge: Harvard University Press, 1951), pp. 1–17 and 37–54; Jussim, *Slave to Beauty*, pp. 32–44, 208–13; and the *Catalogue of a Loan Exhibition Commemorating the Anniversary of the Death of John Keats* [1821–1921], February 21–March 14, 1921 (Boston: Boston Public Library, 1921). Day's library remains in his home in Norwood, Mass., now part of the Norwood Historical Society and open to visitors.

3. Gibran never publicly acknowledged Day's support in their lifetimes, but ample evidence is provided in Jean Gibran and Kahlil Gibran, *Kahlil Gibran: His Life and World* (Boston: New York Graphic Society, 1974), pp. 3, 37–38, 40, 49–68, 77, 86–89, 103–5, 112–13, 141–44, 172, 179, 213, 328–29, and 358. For Day's involvement with the Hampton Institute Camera Club, called to the editor's attention by Barbara Michaels in the bibliography appended to "Let's Pretend," p. 3, see the correspondence of February 17, 1905–May 18, 1906 to Day in the Smithsonian Archives of American Art (Microfilm 3565). For more on this group and its best-known Dunbar volumes, see McGhee, "Portraits in Black: Illustrated Poems by Paul Laurence Dunbar," in *Stony the Road*, pp. 70–102.

4. See Joe W. Kraus, *Messrs. Copeland & Day* (Philadelphia: George S. MacManus Co., 1979), for the history of the firm and a bibliography of its publications, and H[olland] D[ay], "William Morris," *The Book Buyer* (November 1895): 545–49, about the versatile artist, whom Day had met in 1890, whose book designs greatly influenced those of Copeland and Day.

5. See Rollins and Parrish, *Keats and the Bostonians*, pp. 21–36, for an engaging summary of the correspondence and its aftermath. See also Amy Lowell's preface to her biography, *John Keats* (Boston: Houghton Mifflin/Riverside, 1925), pp. x–xi, which thanks Day by name but, doubtless at his insistence, not in association with the Brawne letters.

42. *Paul Strand*

*S*trand (1890–1976), who became an eminent practitioner of "straight" photography, first studied with Lewis Hine, who used documentary photography to promote social reform; Hine introduced him to Stieglitz, who encouraged his more aesthetic bent. After seeing works by Picasso, Cézanne, and other modern artists at Stieglitz's 291 gallery, Strand abandoned his earlier pictorial style and experimented with abstraction (1915). After serving in the First World War, he found verbal confirmation of his desire to portray ordinary people and objects in a visually straightforward manner in Spoon River Anthology (1915), the celebrated verse collection by Edgar Lee Masters, and in Winesburg, Ohio (1919), the acclaimed short story collection by Sherwood Anderson (1876–1941); both authors portrayed characters of small midwestern towns in a natural, colloquial style.[1] Perhaps about this time, Strand wrote some poetry himself.[2] Even when he later differed with Stieglitz's increasingly symbolic view of reality, Strand continued to be influenced by the earthier perspectives of Anderson and Masters, regarding some of his own work as visual extensions of their writing.[3] He applied a similarly direct approach to produce objective but empathic portraits of natural subjects, whether of his first wife, Rebecca (1920–26), plants in Maine and the Southwest (1925–28), or sites abroad accompanied by a commissioned text (1950–75).[4]

314 West 83rd Street
New York City
July 20, 1920

My dear Anderson:
Since seeing your water colors at Stieglitz' studio, I have come to know "Winesburg, Ohio," and it has given me a still greater sense of spirit, actively strong and sensitive, penetrating thru the crassness and brutality of the American scene, to a new beauty.

Winesburg came at a time when I needed again, some clear assertion of the spirit which opposes itself fearlessly to the increasing ruthlessness of the material drive. There are moments (perhaps we all have them) when the seeming futility of any expression, comes upon one like a thick fog, in which past and present and future are apparently blotted out. Not long ago, I said to Stieglitz that I thought that of all mediums, photography was the most diabolical, for the reason that one knows beforehand that the thing done, will function to an even lesser degree than any other form of expression—and he agreed.

Nevertheless, one goes on, trying to project itself in terms of a metal image upon paper. And I just want to tell you that you—your work—have given me more faith and new strength. If there is a hope in America, what you are doing is most surely a part of it—. . .

Faithfully yours—
Paul Strand

1. See Masters, *Spoon River Anthology: An Annotated Edition*, ed. John E. Hallwas (Urbana: University of Illinois Press, 1992), especially his poem on the photographer, "Rutherford McDowell," p. 293, which is interesting to compare to a later free verse description by Dave Smith of "The Travelling Photographer: Circa 1880," in *Dream Flights* (Urbana: University of Illinois Press, 1981), pp. 49–54. For more on Anderson, see his selection below.

2. The CCP has eleven poems by Strand [AG94.1], all undated, eight with titles: "A Song to Black," "Spring Song," "Winter," "Wild Flowers," "Portrait," "Question," "Inertia," and "The Avenue."

3. See Sarah Greenough, *Paul Strand: An American Vision* (New York: Aperture/National Gallery of Art, 1990), pp. 41 and 49, for further comments on Anderson's influence on Strand, and p. 122, for Strand's letter to Beaumont and Nancy Newhall, May 2, 1958, which specifically acknowledges the influence of Anderson, as well as of Masters, particularly on *Un Paese*, with text by Cesare Zavattini (Turin: Einaudi, 1955).

4. Strand's collaborations with other writers include: *Time in New England* (1950), ed. and with texts selected by Nancy Newhall (Millerton, N.Y.: Aperture, 1977); *La France de profil*, with text by Claude Roy (Lausanne: La Guilde du Livre, [1952]); *Ti a'Mhurain* (1962), with text by Basil Davidson (New York: Aperture/Grossman, 1968); *Living Egypt*, with text by James Aldridge (New York: Aperture/Horizon Press, 1969); and *Ghana: An African Portrait*, with text by Basil Davidson (Millerton, N.Y.: Aperture, 1975).

43. *Sherwood Anderson*

"ALFRED STIEGLITZ," 1922

*A*nderson (1876–1941) was encouraged to write by Carl Sandburg, a rising poet as well as the brother-in-law of Edward Steichen, the noted photographer and Stieglitz intimate. Like Sandburg, Anderson appreciated ordinary people and commonplace objects. He first attracted wide attention with Winesburg, Ohio (1919), whose inhabitants try, usually without success, to resist or escape the demeaning effects of the machine age. About this time, Anderson, who painted as well as wrote, met Stieglitz, whose photographs offered proof that man could use the machine with integrity to make life more beautiful and meaningful. Stieglitz came to view Anderson as the new American writer, portraying native subjects in an original, straightforward style, as well as the personification of "Strength and Beauty."[1] The older artist also honored the younger one by frequently inviting him to his summer home at Lake George and making him one of his rare portrait subjects (1923); the writer thought the head "turgid" but conceded "that is the man who has done anything good [that] Anderson has ever done" [Fig. 73].[2] Anderson composed this tribute for MSS, a new magazine inspired by Stieglitz (1922), a piece for Stieglitz's "Seven Americans" exhibition catalogue (1925), and a later essay about his significance as well as the dedication to A Story Teller's Story (1924). These writings helped to create and enhance the legend of Stieglitz as "more than father to so many puzzled, wistful children of the arts in this big, noisy, growing and groping America."[3]

"ALFRED STIEGLITZ"

Old man—perpetually young—we salute you,
Young man—who will not grow old—we salute you.

I do not know, cannot know, when the thing happened to Alfred Stieglitz that made him a man beloved of many men. It may have been when he was a young fellow but, as he is an American, it perhaps did not happen with him, within him, until he had come into middle life. At any rate any man going into the presence of Alfred Stieglitz knows that, on a day long ago, something did happen that has sweetened the man's nature, made him a lover of life and a lover of men. It has come about that many men go gladly and freely in and out of this man's presence. Knowing the man you may not agree with his judgments on this, or that piece of work, you may say to yourself that he talks too much, is too much and sometimes too consciously the prophet of the new age, but in a moment, and after you have gone out of his physical presence, something happened within you too.

You are walking in a city street and suddenly you walk more gladly and lightly. Weariness goes out of you. You are in a street lined with buildings, for the most part ugly and meaningless, but something within is now telling you that a breath can blow even this colossal stone and brick ugliness away. Again, and now quite definitely and permanently you know that, although men have blundered terribly in building up the physical world about themselves and although most men have been incurably poisoned by the ugliness created by men, there is at the very heart of humanity a something sweet and sound that has always found and always will find among men, here and there an individual to strive all his life to give voice to man's inner sweetness and health.

As for myself, I have quite definitely come to the conclusion that there is in the world a thing one thinks of as maleness that is represented by such men as Alfred Stieglitz. It has something to do with the craftsman's love of his tools and his materials. In an age when practically all men have turned from that old male love of good work well done and have vainly hoped that beauty might be brought into the world wholesale, as Mr. Ford manufactures automobiles, there has always been, here in America, this one man who believed in no such nonsense, who perhaps often stood utterly alone, without fellows, fighting an old, man's fight for man's old inheritance—the right to his tools, his materials, and the right to make what is sound and sweet in himself articulate through his handling of tools and materials.

There is something definite to be said in this matter, something very important to be said. Whether or not I am clear-headed enough to say it I can't be sure. What I do know is that, in some way, the figure of Alfred Stieglitz stands at the heart of the matter. What I think I believe is that we Americans, in the age that has just passed, have been a very sick people. Let me speak of that for a moment. To me it seems that the outward signs of that impotence that is the natural result of long illness are all about us in America. It is to be seen in the city skyscrapers, in the cowboy plays in our moving picture theatres and in our childish liking of

the type of statesman who boasts, of walking softly and carrying a big stick. True maleness does not boast of its maleness. Only truly strong men can be gentle, tender, patient, and kindly; and sentimental male strutting is perhaps always but an outpouring of poison from the bodies of impotent men. Might it not be that with the coming into general use of machinery men did lose the grip of what is perhaps the most truly important of man's functions in life— the right every man has always before held dearest of all his human possessions, the right in short to stand alone in the presence of his tools and his materials and with those tools and materials to attempt to twist, to bend, to form something that will be that expression of his inner hunger for the truth that is his own and that is beauty. A year ago Mr. Gilbert Cannan made this dark and threatening comment on our modern life. "Befoul the workman's tools and materials long enough," said Mr. Cannan, "and in the end the workman will turn on you and kill you."

I myself think we have gone rather far on the road of befouling. To me it seems that the Ford automobile is about the final and absolute expression of our mechanical age—and is not the Ford car an ugly and ill-smelling thing? And against the Ford car that the vast Ford factories out in Detroit I would like to put for a moment the figure of Alfred Stieglitz as the craftsman of genius, in short the artist. Born into a mechanical age and having lived in an age when practically all American men followed the false gods of cheapness and expediency, he has kept the faith. To me his life is a promise that the craftsmen, who are surely to be reborn into the world, will not have to kill in order to come back into their old inheritance. Against the day of their coming again Alfred Stieglitz has held to the old faith with an iron grip. Through perhaps almost the single strength of this man, something has been kept alive here in America that we had all come near to forgetting.

I have been walking in the streets of New York and thinking of my friend Alfred Stieglitz and suddenly he no longer stands alone. Certain other figures appear and in them I understand in him certain impulses I have not always understood. I have myself come into the years of manhood in an age of Ford factories, and often enough I have run with the pack. Too often in my own work I have not been patient enough. I have stopped halfway, have not gone all the way. Shame comes to me and suddenly memories appear. I remember that when I was a lad in Ohio there were in my town certain fine old workmen come down into our new age out of an older time. In fancy now I see again two such men, and hear them speaking of their work as they stand idling in the evening before one of the stores of my town. The lad, who was myself, is fascinated by their talk and stands behind them, listening. And now suddenly one of the workmen has remembered something he wants to explain to his fellow. They are both wagon-makers and each, in his young manhood, has served his long years of apprenticeship and has gone on his workman's journey. The workman who is talking is trying to explain to his fellow how, in a certain shop where he once worked in the state of Vermont, they made a wagon felloe [outer circle of a wheel].

"You come on," he says and the two old men go away together along the street in the dusk of a summer evening with a boy tagging at their heels. How sharply their figures remain in my mind, the two old lovers filled with a man's love, we moderns have almost forgotten. And now they have gone to one of the two wagon shops in the town, and one of them has lighted a lamp and has opened his chest of tools, How affectionately he handles them, and how bright and clean and sharp the tools are. He begins fitting two pieces of wood together. "At that place I was telling you about we did it like this. Afterward I found out a quicker way but I believe that harder way is the best. It makes a better joint, stands up better in all kinds of weather; that's what I mean," the old workman says—and how sharply his figure comes back to me now as I think of Alfred Stieglitz, the prophet of the old workmen—who by the intensity of his love of tools and materials has made himself such an outstanding American artist.

There is another man in my mind, of the Stieglitz sort. He lives now at Cleveland, Ohio, where he runs a book store, but some twenty years ago he came to America from Germany as a workman, as a church organ builder. On an evening last summer he walked and talked with me, and as he walked and talked his mind went back to his boyhood in a German town. He spoke of the workmen in his father's shop and their treatment of him when he was a lad, learning his trade. When he had grown careless the workman whose assistant he was, did not report the matter to the superintendent but took the blame on himself. Then the old workman and the boy looked into each others' eyes. "I didn't cut up any more monkeyshines after that," said the bookseller of Cleveland.

On Sundays, when he was a lad, my friend at Cleveland walked in the state forest with his father. Other workmen also came with their sons. One of them went to touch one of the trees with his fingers. Soon now that particular tree would be offered for sale and already the workman had put his hand on his materials. He intended to be on hand and to be a bidder when that particular tree was offered for sale. "After my father died," my friend at Cleveland said, "I went to a sale in the forest and bought a tree just because I had once seen my father look long and hungrily at it, and because I knew he would want me to get my hands on it and to work it up."

And this man of Cleveland came to America to be a foreman in one of our church organ factories. He didn't last long. He quit because they used nails instead of wooden pegs in the factory where he was employed. The owner of the factory tried to reason with him but he quit. "Here you have to do things in a hurry, in the American way. What's the difference? No one knows. They can't tell the difference."

But my friend quit. The fact that nails were used instead of wooden pegs seemed to him a quite sufficient explanation of his inability to stay. He thought the nails affected, in a quite poisonous way, the tone of the instruments. He seemed to care about that. "Every time I drove one of the nails it hurt my arm," he said, and there was something that hurt him too when he heard the other workmen driving the nails. The sound hurt him. He winced when he spoke of it, and quite suddenly one saw that the sound of the nails being driven into the materials he loved was to him what the sound of the nails being driven into the cross of Christ might have meant in the ears of a Christian.

It is just the spirit of these men that has always been alive and has always been kept alive in the person of Alfred Stieglitz, the photographer. In a peculiar way he has made himself an outstanding figure in the lives of innumerable American artists. In the beginning of this article I said that something must have happened to him long ago. He saw something we others haven't often seen. To me and to many other men I know his figure has been sharply defined, and as the years pass is becoming more and more sharply defined as the type of the old workman whose love of his tools and his materials has been so passionate that he has emerged out of the workman to become the artist.

And perhaps that he is a photographer is significant too. It may well be the most significant thing of all. For has he not fought all of his life to make machinery the tool and not the master of man? Surely Alfred Stieglitz has seen a vision we may all some day see more and more clearly because of the fight he has made for it.

1. See 1924 letter (and others) from Stieglitz to Anderson, quoted in James Schevill, *Sherwood Anderson: His Life and Work* (Denver: University of Denver Press, 1951), pp. 173–74, and Thomas, "Sherwood Anderson," *Literary Admirers of Alfred Stieglitz,* pp. 65–78. For the most complete discussions of their relationship, see Haines, *The Inner Eye of Alfred Stieglitz,* pp. 2–4, 16–24, 58, 71–75, 95, 98–100, and 120; and Benita Eisler, *O'Keeffe and Stieglitz: An American Romance* (New York: Viking Penguin, 1992), pp. 287–90 and 319–20. See also Anderson's poems and the photographs of Art Sinsabaugh, in *6 Mid-American Chants / 11 Midwest Photographs* (Highlands, N.C.: Jargon Society, 1964).

2. See Anderson's letters to Stieglitz, [May 18 and June 30, 1923], in *Letters of Sherwood Anderson,* ed. Howard Mumford Jones (Boston: Little, Brown, 1953), pp. 97 and 99; Stieglitz's letters to Anderson in *Alfred Stieglitz: Photographs and Writings,* ed. Sarah Greenough and Juan Hamilton (Washington, D.C.: National Gallery of Art, 1983), pp. 208–14; and Georgia O'Keeffe's letters to Anderson in Jack Cowart and Juan Hamilton, *Georgia O'Keeffe: Arts and Letters,* ed. Sarah Greenough (Washington, D.C.: National Gallery of Art, 1987), pp. 172–79, nos. 28–32.

3. In addition to the selection reprinted here, see Anderson's: "A Testament," *MSS* 1 (February 1922): 3–5; "Seven Alive" for *Seven Americans* catalogue, March 9–28, 1925 (New York: Anderson Galleries, 1925), p. 3; "City Plowman," *America and Alfred Stieglitz: A Collective Portrait* (1934), ed. Waldo Frank et al. (Millerton, N.Y.: Aperture, 1975), pp. 146–48; and the dedication to *A Story Teller's Story* (1924), ed. Ray Lewis White (Cleveland: Press of Case Western Reserve University, 1968).

Crane (1899–1932) published only two volumes of poetry before committing suicide, perhaps despairing of disciplining either his life or his imagination. Here, however, he is full of excited optimism the day after meeting Alfred Stieglitz at his gallery in 1923. "That is it. You have captured life," Crane reportedly exclaimed after viewing one of the photographer's apple pictures, which seemed to realize his own aesthetic [Fig. 74].[1] "There never was truer seeing," replied Stieglitz, who was subsequently pleased to help the young poet perceive the ability of an image to immortalize a moment, realize the aesthetic and spiritual possibilities of the new technology, and, above all, use natural objects—like an apple or a cloud—as "equivalents" of subjective emotional states in his writing.[2] Crane often consulted with his new mentor about his verse, and his short poems, like "Sunday Morning Apples" (1926)—perhaps also inspired by Stieglitz's apple scenes—are filled with vivid images, concrete but allusive.[3] His only long verse, The Bridge (1930), however, failed to provide a viable "equivalent" with which to synthesize his mythic vision of America. Though pained by this discrepancy in his most ambitious poem, Crane at least was enthusiastic about its three accompanying photographic illustrations [Fig. 75], which marked the publishing debut of his friend Walker Evans.[4]

LETTER TO ALFRED STIEGLITZ

[New York City]
April 15th, '23

Dear great and good man, Alfred Stieglitz: I don't know whether or not I mentioned to you yesterday that I intend to include my short verbal definition of your work and aims in a fairly comprehensive essay on your work. I had not thought of doing this until you so thoroughly confirmed my conjectures as being the only absolutely correct statement that you had thus far heard concerning your photographs. That moment was a tremendous one in my life because I was able to share all the truth toward which I am working in my own medium, poetry, with another man who had manifestly taken many steps in that same direction in *his* work. Since we seem, then, already so well acquainted I have a request to make of you regarding the kernel of my essay, which I am quoting below as you requested. Until I can get the rest of my essay on your work into form, I would prefer that you keep my statement in strict confidence. I would like to give it a fresh presentation with other amplifications and details concerning what I consider your position as a scientist, philosopher or whatever wonder you are. You know the world better than I do, but we probably would agree on certain reticence and their safeguarding from inaccurate hands. I shall be up to see you probably very soon, and we can talk again. The reason for my not accompanying Mr. Munson this afternoon, however, is that I want to get into certain explanations of your photographs about which, now, I feel a certain proud responsibility.

"The camera has been well proved the instrument of personal perception in a number of living hands, but in the hands of Alfred Stieglitz it becomes the instrument of something more specially vital—apprehension. The eerie speed of the shutter is more adequate than the human eye to remember, catching even the transition of the mist-mote into the cloud, the thought that is jetted from the eye to leave it instantly forever. Speed is at the bottom of it all—the hundredth of a second caught so precisely that the motion is continued from the picture infinitely: the moment made eternal.

"This baffling capture is an end in itself. It even seems to get at the motion and emotion of so-called inanimate life. It is the passivity of the camera coupled with the unbounded respect of this photographer for its mechanical perfectibility which permits nature and all life to mirror itself so intimately and so unexpectedly that we are thrown into ultimate harmonies by looking at these stationary, yet strangely moving pictures.

"If the essences of things were in their mass and bulk we should not need the clairvoyance of Stieglitz's photography to arrest them for examination and appreciation. But they are suspended on the invisible dimension whose vibrance has been denied the human eye at all

74. Alfred Stieglitz. 'Apple and Rain Drops,' 1922.

times save in the intuition of ecstasy. Alfred Stieglitz can say to us today what William Blake said to as baffled a world more than a hundred years ago in his 'To the Christians':

'I give you the end of a golden string:
Only wind it into a ball,—
It will lead you in at Heaven's gate,
Built in Jerusalem's wall.'"

1. Crane's reaction is quoted and discussed in Stieglitz, *Stieglitz,* ed. Greenough and Hamilton, pp. 233 and 235, who say Stieglitz's photograph is the well-known 'Apples and Gable, Lake George, 1922,' as does Haines, in *The Inner Eye of Alfred Stieglitz,* p. 5. But Stieglitz's 'Apple and Rain Drops,' taken the same year, more closely fits the picture of "an apple on a bough, a drop of water glistening on the skin," so described by Crane's editor Brom Weber in "Stieglitz: An Emotional Experience," in Dorothy Norman, ed., *Stieglitz Memorial Portfolio* (New York: Twice A Year Press, 1947), p. 48. For a general overview of Crane's aesthetic relationship to Stieglitz, see also Haines, *The Inner Eye of Alfred Stieglitz,* pp. 4–7, 24–26, and 121, and Thomas, "Hart Crane," *The Literary Admirers of Alfred Stieglitz,* pp. 49–64. See also Greenough, "From the American Earth: Alfred Stieglitz's Photographs of Apples," *Art Journal* 41 (Spring 1981): 46–54, an illuminating study of the myriad meanings of apples to Stieglitz as well as to other contemporary artists, with many relevant photographs, including the two mentioned above.

2. Stieglitz, letter to Crane, April 16, 1923, in the Alfred Stieglitz Archive at the Beinecke, is quoted in Stieglitz, *Stieglitz,* ed. Greenough and Hamilton, p. 233, who also reprint excerpts from Stieglitz's letters to Crane of July 27 and December 10, 1923, pp. 212 and 208 respectively, and reproduce many of Stieglitz's "Equivalents," Plates 57–59. Another letter from Stieglitz to Crane, August 15, 1923, is quoted in Norman, *Stieglitz,* p. 228. What Stieglitz called an "equivalent" Crane termed an "ultimate harmony"; both resemble T. S. Eliot's earlier (1919) "objective correlative."

3. See Crane, "Sunday Morning Apples" (1926), in *The Poems of Hart Crane,* ed. Marc Simon (New York: Liveright, 1986), p. 7. See other letters from Crane to Stieglitz in *The Letters of Hart Crane,* ed. Brom Weber (New York: Hermitage House, 1952), pp. 137–58.

4. Evans provided three photographs [Fig. 77] for *The Bridge* (Paris: Black Sun Press; New York: Liveright, 1930). Evans's portrait of Crane (1929) and his recollections of the poet—"Hart Crane, in his raving way, made a fuss over my things—my first publication, I think, was in the original edition of *The Bridge*"—appear in Leslie Katz, "An Interview with Walker Evans," *Art in America* 59 (March–April 1971): 82 and 86. See also a later edition of *The Bridge* with photographs by Richard Benson (New York: Limited Editions Club, 1981); and Crane, *Porphyro in Akron,* with three photogravures by Andrew Cahan (Columbus, Ohio: Logan Elm Press, 1980).

75. Walker Evans. 'The Bridge,' illustration for *The Bridge* by Hart Crane, 1930.

45. *Arthur Conan Doyle*

FROM *The Wanderings of a Spiritualist, 1922*

Before creating Sherlock Holmes and writing the histories, romances, and Boer War propaganda that led to his knighthood in 1902, Conan Doyle (1859–1930) frequently contributed to the British Journal of Photography, *the world's oldest photographic magazine (1854–).[1] Probably introduced to photography in 1881 by his landlady's nephew, William Burton, a civil engineer and amateur photographer, Doyle contributed articles filled with vivid detail about native and foreign camera excursions to the* Journal, *but these ceased after his marriage (1885) and Burton's departure for Japan (1887). The success of his detective stories for the new* Strand Magazine, *especially his second one, "A Scandal in Bohemia"—which revolves around a photograph that even Holmes never finds—enabled him to give up his medical practice and sell his instruments; he used the proceeds to buy new camera equipment. Oddly, the enthusiastic photographer rarely referred to the subject thereafter in his famous stories, though Sherlock Holmes is unusually knowledgeable about chemistry.[2] After 1916, Doyle mainly photographed family members and friends at home or on his extensive travels around the world [Fig. 76]. He dedicated his energies to spiritualism, including "spirit" photography, in which images—usually of the dead—somehow appeared on prints [Figs. 77, 78]. Doyle avidly defended the credibility of such pictures in extensive popular lectures and writings; he also built up the large collection used in his lectures and displayed in the museum attached to the Psychic Bookshop, which he established in 1925.[3] These activities, combined with his staunch defense of the existence of fairies, impaired his reputation, though not the popularity of his detective stories.*

FROM *The Wanderings of a Spiritualist*

I may count our adventures as actually beginning from the luncheon which was given us in farewell a week or so before our sailing by the spiritualists of England. . . . The secretary said that he could have filled the Albert Hall. It was an impressive example of the solidity of the movement showing itself for the moment round us, but really round the cause. There were peers, doctors, clergymen, officers of both services, and above all, those splendid lower middle class folk, if one talks in our material earth terms, who are the spiritual peers of the nation. Many professional mediums were there also, and I was honoured by their presence, for as I said in my remarks, I consider that in these days of doubt and sorrow, a genuine professional medium is the most useful member of the whole community. Alas! how few they are! Four photographic mediums do I know in all Britain, with about twelve physical phenomena mediums and as many really reliable clairvoyants. [p. 14]

A few days later I followed up the lectures by two exhibitions of psychic pictures and photographs upon a screen. It was certainly an amazing experience for those who imagined that the whole subject was dreamland, and they freely admitted that it staggered them. They might well be surprised, for such a series has never been seen, I believe, before, including as it does choice samples from the very best collections. I showed them the record of miracle after miracle, some of them done under my very eyes, one guaranteed by Russell Wallace, three by Sir William Crookes, one of the Geley series from Paris, two of Dr. Crawford's medium with the ecto-plasm pouring from her, four illustrating the absolutely final Lydia Haig case on the island of Rothesay, several of Mr. Jeffrey's collection and several also of our own society for the Study of Supernormal Pictures, with the fine photograph of the face within a crystal. No wonder that the audience sat spellbound, while the local press declared that no such exhibition had ever been seen before in Australia. It is almost too overwhelming for immediate propaganda purposes. It has a stunning, dazing effect upon the spectators. Only afterwards, I think, when they come to turn it all over in their minds, do they see that the final proof has been laid before them, which no one with the least sense for evidence could reject. But the sense for evidence is not, alas, a universal human quality. [pp. 73–74]

Never before have I experienced such direct visible intervention as occurred during my first photographic lecture at Adelaide. I had shown a slide the effect of which depended upon a single spirit face appearing amid a crowd of others. The slide was damp, and as photos under these circumstances always clear from the edges when placed in the lantern, the whole centre was so thickly fogged that I was compelled to admit that I could not myself see the spirit face. Suddenly, as I turned away, rather abashed by my failure, I heard cries of "There it is," and looking up again I saw this single face shining out from the general darkness with so bright and vivid an effect that I never doubted for a moment that the operator was throwing a spot light upon it, my wife sharing my impression. I thought how extraordinary clever it was that he should pick it out so accurately at the distance. So the matter passed, but next morning Mr. Thomas, the operator, who is not a Spiritualist, came in great excitement to say that a palpable miracle had been wrought, and that in his great experience of thirty years he had never known a photo dry from the centre, nor, as I understood him, become illuminated in such a fashion. Both my wife and I were surprised to learn that he had thrown no ray upon it. Mr. Thomas told us that several experts among the audience had commented upon the strangeness of the incident. I, therefore, asked Mr. Thomas if he would give me a note as to his own impression, so as to furnish an independent account. This is what he wrote:—

Hindmarsh Square, Adelaide

"In Adelaide, on September 28th, I projected a lantern slide containing a group of ladies and gentlemen, and in the centre of the picture, when the slide was reversed, appeared a human face. On the appearance of the picture showing the group the fog incidental to a damp or new slide gradually appeared covering the whole slide, and only after some minutes cleared, and then quite contrary to usual practice did so from a central point just over the face that appeared in the centre, and refused even after that to clear right off to the edge. The general experience is for a slide to clear from the outside edges to a common centre. Your slide cleared only sufficiently in the centre to show the face, and did not, while the slide was on view, clear any more than sufficient to show that face. Thinking that perhaps there might be a scientific explanation to this phenomenon, I hesitated before writing you, and in the meantime I have made several experiments but have not in any one particular experiment obtained the same result. I am very much interested—as are hundreds of others who personally witnessed the phenomenon."

Mr. Thomas, in his account, has missed the self-illuminated appearance of the face, but otherwise he brings out the points. I never gave occasion for the repetition of the phenomenon, for in every case I was careful that the slides were carefully dried beforehand. [pp. 75–77]

A photographer, named Mark Blow, also caused me annoyance by announcing that my photographs were fakes, and that he was prepared to give £25 to any charity if he could not reproduce them. I at once offered the same sum if he could do so, and I met him by appointment at the office of the evening paper, the editor being present of see fair play. I placed my money on the table, but Mr. Blow did not cover it. I then produced a packet of plates from my pocket and suggested that we go straight across to Mr. Blow's studio and produce the photographs. He replied by asking me a long string of questions as to the conditions under which the Crewe photographs were produced, noting down all my answers. I then renewed my proposition. He answered that it was absurd to expect him to produce a spirit photograph since he did not believe in such foolish things. I answered that I did not ask him to produce a spirit photograph, but to fulfil his promise which was to produce a similar result upon the plate under similar conditions. He held out that they should be his own conditions. I pointed out that any school boy could make a half-exposed impression upon a plate, and that the whole test lay in the conditions. As he refused to submit to test conditions the matter fell through, as all such foolish challenges fall through. It was equally foolish on my part to have taken any notice of it. [pp. 164–65]

It was breakfast time on the very morning that I was advertised to lecture before we at last reached our hotel.

Here I received that counter-demonstration which always helped to keep my head within the limits of my hat. This was a peremptory demand from six gentlemen, who modestly described themselves as the leading photographers of the city, to see the negatives of the photographs which I was to throw upon the screen. I was assured at the same time by other photographers that they had no sympathy with such a demand, and that the others were self-advertising busybodies who had no mandate at all for such a request. My experience at Sydney had shown me that such challenges came from people who had no knowledge of psychic conditions, and who did not realise that it is the circumstances under which a photograph is taken, and the witnesses who guarantee such circumstances, which are the real factors that matter, and not the negative which may be so easily misunderstood by those who have not studied the processes by which such things are produced. I therefore refused to allow my photographs to pass into ignorant hands, explaining at the same time that I had no negatives, since the photographs in most cases were not mine at all, so that the negatives would, naturally, be with Dr. Crawford, Dr. Geley, Lady Glenconnor, the representatives of Sir William Crookes, or whoever else had originally taken the photograph. Their challenge thereupon appeared in the Press with a long tirade of abuse attached to it, founded upon the absurd theory that all the photos had been taken by me, and that there was no proof of their truth save in my word. One gets used to being indirectly called a liar, and I can answer arguments with self-restraint which once I would have met with the toe of my boot. However, a little breeze of this sort does no harm, but rather puts ginger into one's work, and my audience were very soon convinced of the absurdity of the position of the six dissenting photographers who had judged that which they had not seen. [pp. 179–80]

Before leaving Brisbane my attention was drawn to the fact that the State photographer, when he took the scene of the opening of the loan, had produced to all appearance a psychic effect. The Brisbane papers recorded it as follows:—

"'It is a remarkable result, and I cannot offer any opinion as to what caused it. It is absolutely mystifying.' Such was the declaration made yesterday by the government photographer, Mr. W. Mobsby, in regard to the unique effect associated with a photograph he took on Thursday last of Sir A. Conan Doyle handed over his subscription to the State Loan organiser. When he arrived, the entrance to the building was thronged by a large crowd, and he had to mount a stepladder, which was being used by the *Daily Mail* photographer, in order to get a good view or the proceedings. Mr. Mobsby took only one picture, just at the moment Sir A. Conan Doyle was mounting the steps at the Government Tourist Bureau to meet the Acting Premier, Mr. J. Fihilly. Mr. Mobsby developed the film himself, and was amazed to find that while all the other figures in the picture were distinct the form of Sir A. Conan Doyle appeared enveloped in mist and could only be dimly seen [Fig. 77]. The photograph was taken on an ordinary film with a No. 3a Kodak, and careful examination does not in any way indicate the cause of the sensational result." I have had so many personal proofs of the intervention of supernormal agencies during the time that I have been engaged upon this task that I am prepared to accept the appearance of this aura as being an assurance of the presence of those great forces for whom I act as a humble interpreter. At the same time, the sceptic is very

77. W. Mobsby [official photographer of Brisbane, Australia]. News photograph of Arthur Conan Doyle, 1921, from *The Wanderings of a Spiritualist* by Doyle, 1922.

welcome to explain it as a flawed film and a coincidence. [pp. 251–53]

At Columbo I was interested to receive a *Westminster Gazette,* which contained an article by their special commissioner upon the Yorkshire fairies. Some correspondent has given the full name of the people concerned, with their address, which means that their little village will be crammed with chars-à-banc, and the peace of their life ruined. It was a rotten thing to do. For the rest, the *Westminster* inquiries seem to have confirmed Gardner and me in every particular, and brought out the further fact that the girls had never before taken a photo in their life. One of them had, it seems, been for a short time in the employ of a photographer, but as she was only a child, and her duties consisted in running on errands, the fact would hardly qualify her, as *Truth* suggests, for making faked negatives which could deceive the greatest experts in London. There may be some loophole in the direction of thought forms, but otherwise the case is as complete as possible. [p. 283]

Early in February I gave a lantern lecture upon psychic phenomena to passengers of both classes. The Red Sea has become quite a favorite stamping ground of mine, but it was much more tolerable now than on that terrible night in August when I discharged arguments and perspiration to a sweltering audience. On this occasion it was a wonderful gathering, a microcosm of the world, with an English peer, and Indian Maharajah, many native gentlemen, whites of every type from four great countries, and a fringe of stewards, stewardesses, and nondescripts of all sorts, including the ship's barber, who is one of the most active men on the ship in an intellectual sense. All went well, and if they were not convinced they were deeply interested, which is the first stage. Somewhere the are great forces which are going to carry on this work, and I never address an audience without the feeling that among them there may be some latent Paul or Luther whom my words may call into activity. [p. 296]

78. William Hope. 'Sir Arthur Conan Doyle, His Widow and Son, Denis,' May 1931.

1. See the editors' introduction to Conan Doyle's *Essays on Photography,* ed. John Michael Gibson and Richard Lancelyn Green (London: Secker & Warburg, [1982]), pp. viii–xxi. See also the illustrations based on his Swiss photographs in D. G. Thomson, "Tobogganing and Ski-Running," *Pearson's Magazine* (December 1897): 696–704, and his faked ones for *The Lost World* (London: Hodder and Stoughton, 1912), discussed in Gibson and Green's introduction to *Essays,* p. xviii, and in John Carr, *The Life of Sir Arthur Conan Doyle* (New York: Harper, 1979), pp. 258–59. The whereabouts of most of Conan Doyle's photographs, including the ones described in these essays, are not known.

2. See Conan Doyle, "A Scandal in Bohemia," *Strand* 2 (July 1891): 61–75. Photography also provides a cover for the villain in "The Red-headed League," *Strand* 2 (August 1891): 190–204; is a hobby of the villain in "The Adventure of the Copper Beeches," *Strand* 2 (June 1892): 613–28; and helps solve the mysterious death in "The Adventure of the Lion's Mane," *Strand* 72 (December 1926): 539–50, all reprinted in *The Complete Sherlock Holmes* (New York: Doubleday, [1960]) and widely elsewhere. See also Allen H. Butler, "A Speculation: Did Holmes Have Photo-Processing Capabilities at the Villa?," *Baker Street Journal* 40, no. 3 (September 1990): 159–60.

3. Conan Doyle's spiritualist efforts increased after the deaths of his son and brother in 1919; his relevant spiritualist works (all published in London by Hodder and Stoughton and in New York by George H. Doran unless otherwise indicated) include: *The Lost World* (1912), pp. 11, 35–37, 160, and 219–21; *The Vital Message* (1919), pp. 156–61; *The Wanderings of a Spiritualist* (1921); *The Case for Spirit Photography* (London: Hutchinson, 1922); *The Coming of the Fairies* (1922; revised ed., London: The Psychic Press, 1928); "Spirit Photography," *The History of Spiritualism* (London: Cassell, 1926), vol. 2, pp. 123–48; "The Combermere Photograph," *Quarterly Transactions of the British College of Psychic Science* 5 (October 1926): 190–92; and see also Geoffrey Crawley, "That Astounding Affair of the Cottingley Fairies," *British Journal of Photography* (December 24, 1982–April 8, 1983). See also a relevant quote from Hawthorne's "The Birthmark" (1843) in the Hawthorne selection, n. 1 above; Thomas Mann's interest in "Phantom" photography, noted in his selection below; and the reference by William Dean Howells, another writer interested in photography, in *The Rise of Silas Lapham* (1885), ch. 1: "[In a family photograph the children] twitched themselves into wavering shadows and might have passed for spirit-photographs of their own little ghosts."

46. Vladimir Mayakovsky

FROM *Pro Eto*, 1923

*I*n 1914, Alexander Rodchenko (1891–1956), then a painter, briefly met Mayakovsky (1893–1930), a writer, and enthusiastically bought a photograph of him.[1] A decade later he himself was taking the definitive portraits of the colorful figure whose talents as a poet, playwright, satirist, propagandist, film actor, and graphic artist made him a hero in the newly collectivist Soviet Union.[2] After meeting again in 1920, the pair soon expressed their shared leftist ideals in many collaborations. First, Rodchenko illustrated Pro Eto (1923), written by Mayakovsky while banished from his married lover, Lili Brik; the final lines of the poem refer to a real photograph of her [Fig. 79], and the accompanying photomontage elaborates the speaker's fantasy about it [Fig. 80].[3] Next, the two produced striking advertising posters; "the whole of Moscow was decorated with our output," recalled Rodchenko.[4] Working with photomontages led to his taking up the camera as a more creative means than painting for documenting Soviet life. Soon other photographs by Rodchenko, usually dramatically angled and boldly patterned—whether in montage or conventional format—illustrated many Mayakovsky poems and covers for the books and magazines he edited.[5] The patronage of the grateful writer, who praised Rodchenko's "exceptional merits as a trailblazer in the field of artistic photomontage," accelerated the influence of his style.[6] After Mayakovsky's suicide, partly due to his disillusionment with the Soviet government, the artist continued illustrating a wide range of publications, scientific as well as literary. Although he returned to painting in the 1940's, Rodchenko also worked on many photographic albums, including an unpublished one, "Ten Years of Soviet Literature," in the years (1947–55) before his death. [7]

FROM *Pro Eto*

Through the World Who's Who
                              he leafs
                                    and thinks aloud:
"XXth century.
              Let's look who's worth reviving.
Mayakovsky ...
              surely not among the brightest.
Decidedly,
          his face is far too plain."
Then from today's worn page
                              I'll holler to the scientist,
Stop turning over pages!
                        Make me live again!

Hope   Put a heart in me,
                    knock thought into my
                                          skull,
pump blood into my veins—
                        give me new birth.
I had no chance of loving,
                        living to the full.
Believe,
        I didn't get
                    my earthly share on earth.
I'm six foot four.
                  Who wants such stature when
for jobs like mine
                  a guinea-pig would suffice.
Caged in a house,
                  I scribbled with a pen
crammed in a room-hole
                      fit perhaps for mice.
I'd take any old job
                    and never ask a bob!
Clean,
      sweep,
            wash,
                  scrub
                        or simply run around.
Why,
    I'd be glad to get a doorman's job
if doormen
          in your days
                      will still be found.
A jolly chap I was;
                    much sense in being jolly
when all we knew
                was misery and rigour.

These days,
            when people bare their teeth,
                              it's solely
to sink 'em in,
            to bite,
                  to snarl
                        or snigger.
Anything may happen—
                  any sort of trouble.
Call me, do,
            for joking helps superbly.
I'll amuse you
            till you actually bubble
with ting-a-linging allegory
                  and hyperbole.
I loved....
            Sure, raking up the past,
                              is not much use.
(Painful?
            Never mind!
At least pain lives when all
                  has ceased)
I did love beasts, though.
                  Have you still got zoos?
Then let me be a keeper for your beasts.
I love the creatures.
                  When I spot a pup—
there's a funny one—
                  all bald—
                        hangs round the baker's—
I feel like I could cough my own liver up:
Here, doggie,
            don't be shy, dear, take this!
Love And then, perhaps,
                  some day
down pathways that I'll
                  sweep
(she too loved beasts),
                  she'll come to see the zoo
smiling the same
                  as on the photo that I keep
they'll bring her back to life—
                  she's nice enough,
                              she'll do.
Your umptieth century
                  will leave them all behind,
trifles
      that stung one's heart
                  in a buzzing swarm,

79. Unknown. 'Lili Brik at the Zoo,' 1922.

И она
— она зверей любила—
тоже ступит в сад.

Vladimir Mayakovsky

and then
          we'll make up
                    for these loveless times
through countless midnights,
                    starry,
                              sweet and warm.
Revive me,
          if for nothing else,
                    because
I,
   poet,
          cast off daily trash
                    to wait for you.
Revive me—
                    never mind under what clause.
Revive me, really,
                    let me live my due,
to love—
          with love no more a sorry servant
of matrimony,
                    lust
                    and daily bread,
but spreading out
                    throughout the universe
                              and further,
forsaking sofas,
                    cursing boudoir and bed.
No more to beg
                    for one day as a dole
and then to age
                    in endless sorrow drowned,
but to see all the globe
                    at the first call
of "Comrade!"
                    turn in glad response around.
No more a martyr
                    to that hole one calls one's hearth,
but to call everybody
                    sister,
                              brother,
to see your closest kin
                    in all the earth,
aye, all the world
                    to be your father and your mother.

1. See Selim O. Khan-Magomedov, *Rodchenko: The Complete Work,* ed. Vieri Quilici (Cambridge: MIT Press, [1986]), p. 22, on this first meeting.

2. See Ibid., pp. 224–25 and 241, for some of the 1924 portraits of Mayakovsky; p. 230, for remarks on them; and pp. 231–33 for some of Rodchenko's portraits of other writers.

3. See *Pro Eto* (usually translated as *About That,* although Elliott [see below] uses *About This,* and Rottenberg uses *It*) in *Longer Poems* in *Selected Works,* trans. Dorian Rottenberg (Moscow: Raduga Publishers, 1986), vol. 2, pp. 91–138, esp. 136–38; Khan-Magomedov, *Rodchenko,* pp. 119–22, for reproductions of the cover and its illustrations, and p. 123, a photograph of Lili Brik holding the published volume; and David Elliott, ed., *Rodchenko and the Arts of Revolutionary Russia* (New York: Pantheon, 1979), pp. 68–71, for alternate illustrations not used, including one, p. 169, never before published. See also Henri Cartier-Bresson, *Photoportraits* (New York: Thames & Hudson, 1985), fig. 52, for a portrait of the much older "Lili," whose surname is listed as "Brik-Maiakovsky," though the pair never married.

4. See Rodchenko, "Working with Mayakovsky" (1939), in Elliott, ed., *Rodchenko,* p. 102; and Khan-Magomedov, *Rodchenko,* pp. 147–52, who reproduces some of these ads.

5. Khan-Magomedov, *Rodchenko,* pp. 138–39, reproduces two photomontages from *Sergeiu Eseninu* (Tiflis: [Zakkriga], 1926); and Elliott, ed., *Rodchenko,* p. 87, reproduces the covers to *Sifilis* (Tiflis: [Zakkriga], 1926), and, p. 192, to *A Conversation with a Tax Inspector About Poetry* (Tiflis: [Zakkriga], 1926). See also Mayakovsky's "Conversations with Comrade Lenin" (1929), trans. Irina Zheleznova, in *Selected Verse* in *Selected Works,* vol. 1, pp. 238–40, which according to Rodchenko, as quoted in Elliott, *Rodchenko,* p. 103, is based on one of two prints that he had reproduced for Mayakovsky that always hung on his wall. Khan-Magomedov, *Rodchenko,* also reproduces: pp. 134–37, some of the magazine covers; pp. 178–83, some of Rodchenko's designs for the USSR exhibition in Paris, 1925, probably commissioned because Mayakovsky was a committee member; and pp. 200–203, pictures of the sets and costumes Rodchenko designed for the second half—set fifty years ahead—of Mayakovsky's play, *The Bedbug* [1929], trans. Katherine Cook-Horujy in *Plays/Articles/Essays,* in *Selected Works,* vol. 3, scene 8, p. 108. In this satire, the Rip Van Winkle-type protagonist finds himself in a world where one "can't even pin up a picture of your girlfriend," and "old postcards" supply information to observers about outmoded activities like dancing.

6. Khan-Magomedov, *Rodchenko,* pp. 121, 133, and 186, quotes Mayakovsky's praise for the photomontages, and, p. 146, his praise for Rodchenko's *The History of the Communist Party in Posters* (1926), one of which is reproduced, p. 167.

7. See Khan-Magomedov, *Rodchenko,* p. 299.

47. Thomas Mann

FROM *The Magic Mountain*, 1924

*J*ust as Goethe (1749–1832) became intrigued by the aesthetic and documentary revelations of the camera obscura, so was his admirer Thomas Mann (1875–1955), by the scientific and spiritual ones of the camera.[1] Mann's unusual interest in photography's less examined forms is evident in his remarks on "phantom" photography in his study of the occult (1924)[2] and in the uses of the X-ray, partly based on research in a hospital, in his best-known novel, The Magic Mountain (1924). In this dense work, the X-ray is significant on many levels: as a sanitarium routine for all patients, which, as in this scene, the central character Hans Castorp and his cousin Joachim must undergo; as a "photographie intime," a token of Castorp's sublimated (yet once consummated) romantic love for Clavdia; and as undeniable evidence of occult phenomena at a séance.[3] Mann did not think highly of conventional photography, to judge by his denigrating use of the photographic reproduction of a painting in an early short story, "Gladius Dei" (1902), and his satire of amateur photography as a pastime of the bored well-to-do in The Magic Mountain.[4] But after his exposure in 1928 to the portraits of E. O. Hoppé and, later, to the studies of August Sander as well as the still lifes of Albert Renger-Patzsch, Mann enthusiastically raised his opinion of photography's aesthetic potential; he even became a willing subject himself.[5] Indeed, some of the most engaging portraits of Mann were taken by his American publisher, Alfred Knopf, himself an avid amateur portrait photographer [Fig. 81].[6]

FROM *The Magic Mountain*

. . . The built-in structure, projecting between the two black-hung windows, divided the room into two unequal parts. Hans Castorp could distinguish physical apparatus. Lenses, switch-boards, towering measuring-instruments, a box like a camera on a rolling stand, glass diaposi-tives in rows set in the walls. Hard to say whether this was a photographic studio, a dark-room, or an inventor's workshop and technological witches' kitchen.

. . . As Hans Castorp took off his waistcoat, Behrens came out of the small recess where he had been standing into the larger one.

. . . I expect, Castorp, you feel a little ner-vous about exposing your inner self to our gaze? Don't be alarmed, we preserve all the ame-nities. Look here, have you seen my picture-gallery? He led Hans Castorp by the arm be-fore the rows of dark plates on the wall, and turned on a light behind them. Hans Castorp saw various members: hands, feet, knee-pans, thigh- and leg-bones, arms, and pelvises. But the rounded living form of these portions of the human body was vague and shadowy, like a pale and misty envelope, within which stood out the clear, sharp nucleus—the skeleton.

"Very interesting," said Hans Castorp.

"Interesting sure enough," responded the Hof-rat. "Useful object-lesson for the young. X-ray anatomy, you know, triumph of the age. . . . The pictures faded. Hans Castorp turned his attention to the preparations for taking Joa-chim's x-ray.

It was done in front of that structure on the

other side of which Hofrat Behrens had been standing when they entered. Joachim had taken his place on a sort of shoe-maker's bench, in front of a board, which he embraced with his arms and pressed his breast against it, while the assistant improved the position, massaging his back with kneading motions, and putting his arms further forward. Then he went behind the camera, and stood just as a photographer would, legs apart and stooped over, to look inside. He expressed his satisfaction and, going back to Joachim, warned him to draw in his breadth and hold it until all was over. Joachim's rounded back expanded and so remained; the assistant, at the switch-board, pulled the handle. Now, for the space of two seconds, fearful powers were in play—streams of thousands, of a hundred thousand of volts, Hans Castorp seemed to recall—which were necessary to pierce through solid matter. They could hardly be confined to their office, they tried to escape through other outlets: there were explosions like pistol-shots, blue sparks on the measuring apparatus; long lightnings crackled along the walls. Somewhere in the room appeared a red light, like a threatening eye, and a phial in Joachim's rear filled with green. Then everything grew quiet, the phenomena disappeared, and Joachim let out his breath with a sigh. It was over.

"Next delinquent," said the Hofrat, and nudged Hans Castorp with his elbow. "Don't pretend you're too tired. You will get a free copy, Castorp; then you can project the secrets of your bosom on the wall for your children and grandchildren to see!"

Joachim had stepped down; the technician changed the plate. Hofrat Behrens personally instructed the novice how to sit and hold himself.

"Put your arms about it," he said. "Embrace the board—pretend it's something else, if you like. Press your breast against it, as though it filled you with rapture. Like that. Draw a deep breath. Hold it!" he commanded. "Now, please!" Hans Castorp waited, blinking, his lungs distended. Behind him the storm broke loose: it crackled, lightened, detonated—and grew still. The lens had looked into his inside.

He got down, dazed and bewildered, notwithstanding he had not been physically sensible of the penetration in the slightest degree.

"Good lad," said the Hofrat. "Now we shall see." The experienced Joachim had already moved over toward the entrance door and taken position at a stand; at his back was the lofty structure of the apparatus, with a bulb half full of water, and distillation tubes; in front of him, breast-high, hung a framed screen on pulleys. On his left, between switch-board and instrumentarium, was a red globe. The Hofrat, bestriding a stool in front of the screen, lighted the light. The ceiling light went out, and only the red glow illumined the scene. Then the master turned this too off, with a quick motion, and thick darkness enveloped the laboratory.

"We must first accustom the eyes," the Hofrat was heard to say, in the darkness. "We must get big pupils, like a cat's, to see what we want to see. You understand, our everyday eyesight would not be good enough for our purposes. We have to banish the bright daylight and its pretty pictures out of our minds."

"Naturally," said Hans Castorp. He stood at the Hofrat's shoulder, and closed his eyes, since the darkness was so profound that it did not matter whether he had them open and shut. "First we must wash our eyes with darkness to see what we want to see. That is plain. I find it quite right and proper, as a matter of fact, that we should collect ourselves a little, beforehand—in silent prayer, as it were. I am standing here with my eyes shut, and have quite a pleasant sleepy feeling. But what is it I smell?"

"Oxygen," said the Hofrat. "What you notice in the air is oxygen. Atmospheric product of our little private thunderstorm you know. Eyes open!" he commanded. "The magicking is about to begin." Hans Castorp hastened to obey.

They heard a switch go on. A motor started up, and sang furiously higher and higher, until another switch controlled and steadied it. The floor shook with an even vibration. The little red light, at right angles to the ceiling, looked threateningly across at them. Somewhere lightening flashed. And with a milky gleam a window of light emerged from the darkness: it was the square hanging screen, before which Hofrat Behrens bestrode his stool, his legs sprawled apart with his fists supported on them, his blunt nose close to the pane, which gave him a view of a man's interior organism. . . . "May I?" [Hans] asked.

. . . "Of course," Joachim replied magnanimously, out of the dark. And to the pulsation of the floor, and the snapping and cracking of the forces at play, Hans Castorp peered through the lighted window, peered into Joachim Ziemssen's empty skeleton. The breastbone and spine fell together in a single dark column. The frontal structure of the ribs was cut across by the paler structure of the back. Above, the collarbones branched off on both sides, and the framework of the shoulder, with the joint and the beginning of Joachim's arm, showed sharp and bare through the soft envelope of flesh. The thoracic cavity was light, but blood-vessels were to be seen some dark spots, a blackish shadow. . . .

. . . But Hans Castorp's attention was taken up by something like a bog, a strange, animal shape, darkly visible behind the middle column, or more on the right side of it—the spectator's right. It expanded and contracted regularly, a little after the fashion of a swimming jelly-fish.

"Look at his heart," and the Hofrat lifted his huge hand again from his thigh and pointed with his forefinger at the pulsating window. Good God, it was the heart, it was Joachim's honour-giving heart, that Hans Castorp saw! . . . He was strongly moved by what he saw—or more precisely, by the fact that he saw it—and felt stirrings of uneasy doubt, as to whether it was really permissible and innocent to stand here in the quaking, crackling darkness and gaze like this; his itch to commit the indiscretion conflicted in his bosom with religious emotion and feelings of concern.

But a few minutes later he himself stood in the pillory, in the midst of the electrical storm, while Joachim, his body closed up again, put on his clothes. Again the Hofrat peered through the milky glass, this time into Hans Castorp's own inside; and from his half-utterances, his broken phrases and bursts of scolding, the young man gathered that what he saw corresponded to his expectations. He was so kind as to permit the patient, at his request, to look at his own hand through the screen. And Hans Castorp saw, precisely what he must have expected, but what it is hardly permitted man to see, and what he had never thought it would be vouchsafed him to see: he looked into his own grave. The process of decay was forestalled by the powers of the light-ray, the flesh in which he walked disintegrated, annihilated, dissolved in vacant mist, and there within it was the finely turned skeleton of his own hand, the seal ring he had inherited from his grandfather hanging loose and black on the joint of his ring-finger— a hard, material object, with which man adorns the body that is fated to melt away beneath it, when it passes on to another flesh that can wear it for yet a little while. With the eyes of his Tienappel ancestress, penetrating, prophetic eyes, he gazed this familiar part of his own body, and for the first time in his life he understood that he would die. [pp. 214–19]

1. Erwin Koppen, *Literatur und Photographie: Über Geschichte und Thematik Einer Medienentdeckung* (Stuttgart: J. B. Metzler, 1987), pp. 24–28.

2. See Mann, "Okkulte Erlebnisse" [Occult Experiences], *Gesammelte Werke* (Frankfurt am Main: S. Fischer, 1960), vol. 10, pp. 135–71, and Mann, entry for February 24, 1920, in *Diaries 1918–1939*, ed. Hermann Kesten, trans. Richard and Clara Winston (New York: Abrams, 1982), p. 86.

3. See Mann, *The Magic Mountain* (1924), trans. H. T. Lowe-Porter (New York: Knopf, 1927), pp. 196, 203–19, 339, 348–49, 389, 436–37, 559–60, and 666, and see also other references on pp. 16, 21, 84, and 255. See also John L. Greenway, "Penetrating Surfaces: X-Rays, Strindberg and *The Ghost Sonata*," *Nineteenth-Century Studies* 5 (1991): 29–46, and William Dean Howell's relevant letter to Mark Twain, May 24, 1906, *Mark Twain–Howells Letters*, ed. Henry Nash Smith and William M. Gibson (Cambridge: Belknap Press/Harvard University Press, 1960), vol. 2, p. 808, in which he recommends a new book, comparing it to "a series of photographs taken with Roentgen rays." Mann would have relished two of

Alvarez Bravo's photographs that incorporated X-rays—'Lucia, 1940s' and 'Flower and Rings, 1940'—reproduced in *Revelaciones: The Art of Manuel Alvarez Bravo* (San Diego: Museum of Photographic Art, 1990), pp. 87 and 119 respectively.

4. See Mann, "Gladius Dei" (1902), *Stories of Three Decades,* trans. H. T. Lowe Porter (New York: Knopf, 1979), pp. 181–93, and *The Magic Mountain,* pp. 627–28.

5. See Mann, "Die Welt ist schön" [The World Is Beautiful] (1928), *Gesammelte Werke* (Frankfurt am Main: S. Fischer, 1960), vol. 10, pp. 901–4, and an excerpt from his letter of January 6, 1930, praising August Sander's *Face of Our Time* (1929) to its publisher, Kurt Wolff, which is quoted in *August Sander: Photographs of an Epoch* (Millerton, N.Y.: Aperture/Philadelphia Museum of Art, 1980), p. 11. Among the many portraits of Mann (who rather enjoyed the sittings, according to Henry Hatfield, in conversation with the editor on November 29, 1991), see the 1936–38 series of him, some with his wife and brother, by Lotte Jacobi, reproduced in *Lotte Jacobi,* ed. Kelly Wise, pp. 106–10; Diana Hulick, "George Platt Lynes: The Portrait Series of Thomas Mann," *History of Photography* 15, no. 3 (Autumn 1991): 211–21; and see Van Vechten's letter to Stein, June 22, 1937, in the Van Vechten selection below.

6. See Alfred A. Knopf, *Sixty Photographs* (New York: Knopf, 1975), which, in addition to Mann, whom he had signed up c. 1918 (according to the publisher's biographer, Peter Prescott, in conversation with the editor, December 2, 1991), includes portraits of six writers mentioned in this anthology: Witter Bynner (see under Adams); Kahlil Gibran (see under Day); John Hersey (see under Capa and Steinbeck); Jean-Paul Sartre; Yukio Mishima; and John Updike. Other Knopf portraits of Mann and other authors he published or knew are at the HRHRC. The cigar shown in the portrait reproduced here [Fig. 83] was doubtless provided by Knopf, who sent them to favored authors on their birthdays and at Christmas, according to his longtime associate William Koshland, in conversation with the editor on October 23, 1992.

*P*hotographs were always important to Nabokov (1899–1977), partly as links between the diverse periods of his life: as a privileged child in Russia, a foreign student at Cambridge, a struggling émigré writer in Berlin and Paris, a teacher and artist in America, and a successful author in Switzerland.[1] Memory for Nabokov was a form of imagination, which photographs—individually and in albums—helped stimulate. In the process of transforming his experiences into art, he often used photographs, as in this early poem, with its already characteristic themes, images and diction originally written in Russian and then, forty years later, translated into English. Photographs proved a reliable means of making and finding connections and patterns in the chaos of life as well as integral devices of plot, setting, and characterization for Nabokov. He used recreated or imagined ones in many forms—snapshots, slides, picture postcards, photohoroscopes—throughout his writings, especially in The Gift (1952), Lolita (1955), and Ada (1969). Most often, such pictures enable the author or his characters to recall the past while permitting an escape from the present, but occasionally they serve to register distaste for the faked in art, as in life.[2] As John Szarkowski has remarked, although Nakobov did not write any extended piece on photography, the "wonderful brief asides scattered through his work . . . are worth whole fascicles of most of the stuff that passes for photographic criticism."[3]

"The Snapshot"

Upon the beach at violet-blue noon,
in a vacational Elysium
a striped bather took
a picture of his happy family.

And very still stood his small naked boy,
and his wife smiled,
in ardent light, in sandy bliss
plunged as in silver.

An by the striped man
directed at the sunny sand
blinked with a click of its black eyelid
the camera's ocellus.

That bit of film imprinted
all it could catch,

the stirless child,
his radiant mother,

and a toy pail and two beach spades,
and some way off a bank of sand,
and I, the accidental spy,
I in the background have been also taken.

Next winter, in an unknown house,
grandmother will be shown an album,
and in that album there will be a snapshot,
and in that snapshot I shall be.

My likeness among strangers,
one of my August days,
my shade they never noticed,
my shade they stole in vain.

Binz, 1927

---

1. See Nabokov, *Speak Memory: An Autobiography Revisited* (New York: G. P. Putnam's, 1967), especially pp. 1, 35, 45, 113, and 141. Indeed, the opening paragraph of his foreword refers to a group photograph in which he was misidentified by the photographer, Gisèle Freund; see her "Apology for an Error: Nabokov," *The World in My Camera,* pp. 218–21.

2. See, for example, the photograph as a device for characterization in *Pale Fire* (New York: G. P. Putnam's, 1962), p. 26; as a device for plot and characterization in *The Gift* (1952), trans. by Michael Scammell and Vladimir Nabokov (New York: G. P. Putnam's, 1963), pp. 39, 49, 53, 65, 87, 114, 120, 141, 151, 164, 180, and 241; as a significant artefact in *Ada, or Ardor: A Family Chronicle* (New York: McGraw-Hill, 1969), ch. 7, pp. 396–409 (here the central characters, after paying a blackmailing former servant for the album, which includes scenes of their youthful lovemaking, review the pictures in it); as an item of fakery in *Invitation to a Beheading,* trans. Dmitri Nabokov (New York: G. P. Putnam's, 1959), pp. 51 and 169–71; as a means of recollection in "From the Gray North" (1967), and in *Poems and Problems* (New York: McGraw-Hill, 1971), p. 149; as an incident and pun in *Transparent Things* (New York: McGraw-Hill, 1972), pp. 13–14; and in all these roles throughout *Lolita*— see *The Annotated Lolita,* ed. Alfred Appel, Jr. (New York: McGraw-Hill, 1970), especially pp. 14–15, 33, 43, 60, 78, 82, 157–58, and 304.

3. Quoted from Szarkowski's letter to the editor, October 2, 1991. See also Walker Evans's comment on Nabokov as a "photographic" writer, quoted in the introductory "Notes . . ." above, p. xliii.

*T*he invention of photography has dealt a mortal blow to the old
modes of expression," wrote Breton (1896–1966) four years before
founding Surrealism (1924).[1] This aesthetic movement, which became
a way of life for some of its adherents, was the first in which the camera had
a significant place.[2] Breton was initially attracted to photography as a link
with automatism ("a true photography of thought"), which fascinated him,
as did dreams, chance encounters, urban street life, and whatever freed
repressed energy, reconciling perception and representation to create a higher
reality.[3] The poet appreciated the way his artist friends like Man Ray and
Manuel Alvarez Bravo, both influenced by his ideas, could manipulate their
photographs to express this new vision.[4] Urging that all books be illustrated
with photographs instead of the customary drawings, Breton followed this
precept in three of his own important works.[5] In the first and best known,
Nadja (1928), photographs mainly document locations of the irrational
events, both authenticating Breton's eccentric narrative and enabling him
to dispense with conventional, realistic ("photographic") description [Fig.
82].[6] The various surrealist magazines Breton established or edited also
featured photographs as well as other forms of graphic art; and he later
made a self-portrait and some collages, using the medium whose artistic
stature he helped to raise.[7]

FROM *Nadja*

Note: The opening section of the book, from which this passage is drawn, sets the stage for the unusual narrative and warns the reader that the process will not be conventional.

Do not expect me to provide an exact account of what I have been permitted to experience in this domain. I shall limit myself here to recalling without effort certain things which, apart from any exertions on my part, have occasionally happened to me, things which, reaching me in unsuspected ways, give me the measure of the particular grace and is grace of which I am the object; I shall discuss these things without pre-established order, and according to the mood of the moment which lets whatever survives survive. My point of departure will be the Hôtel des Grands Hommes, Place du Panthéon, where I lived around 1918, and my first halt the Manoir d'Ango in Varengeville-sur-Mer, where I stayed in August, 1927, still very much the same person—the Manoir d'Ango where I was offered the hospitality, when I wished to be undisturbed, of a hut artificially camouflaged by shrubbery, at the edge of a woods; here, while in other respects occupying myself with whatever I like, I was able to hunt owls as well. (Could it have been otherwise, once I decided to write *Nadja*?) Actually, it is of little importance if an occasional error or omission, a genuine anomaly or lacuna casts a shadow across my narrative, across what, taken as a whole, cannot be substantiated. I must insist, lastly, that such accidents of thought not be reduced to their *unjust* proportion as *faits-divers*, random episodes, so that when I say, for instance, that the statue of Etienne Dolet on its plinth in the Place Maubert in Paris [Fig. 82] has always fascinated me and induced unbearable discomfort, it will not immediately be supposed that I am merely ready for psychoanalysis, a method I respect and whose present aims I consider nothing less than the expulsion of man from himself, and of which I expect other exploits than those of a bouncer. I am convinced, moreover, that as a discipline psychoanalysis is not qualified to deal with such phenomena, since despite its great merits we already do this method too much honor by conceding that it exhausts

Pl. 3. — Si je dis qu'a Paris la statue d'Etienne Dolet, place Maubert, m'a toujours tout ensemble attiré et causé un insupportable malaise...

82. Jacques-André Boiffard. 'La Statue d'Étienne Dolet, Place Maubert,' from *Nadja* by André Breton, 1928.

the problem of dreams or that it does not simply occasion further inhibitions by its very interpretation of inhibitions. Which leads me to my own experience, to what is for me, concerning myself, a virtually continuous subject of meditation and reverie. . . . [pp. 23–24]

Note: More than a third of the way through the book, the title character is finally introduced in these pages.

Last October fourth, toward the end of one of those idle, gloomy afternoons I know so well how to spend, I happened to be in the Rue Lafayette: after stopping a few minutes at the stall outside the *Humanité* bookstore and buying Trotsky's latest work, I continued aimlessly in the direction of the Opera. The offices and workshops were beginning to empty out from top to bottom of the buildings, doors were closing, people on the sidewalk were shaking hands, and already there were more people in the street now. I unconsciously watched their faces, their clothes, their way of walking. No, it was not yet these who would be ready to create the Revolution. I had just crossed an intersection whose name I don't know, in front of a church. Suddenly, perhaps still ten feet away, I saw a young, poorly dressed woman walking toward me, she had noticed me too, or perhaps had been watching me for several moments. She carried her head high, unlike everyone else on the sidewalk. And she looked so delicate she scarcely seemed to touch the ground as she walked. A faint smile may have been wandering across her face. She was curiously made up, as though beginning with her eyes, she had not had time to finish, though the rims of her eyes were dark for a blonde, the rims only, and not the lids (this effect is achieved, and achieved exclusively, by applying the mascara under the lid alone. It is interesting to note, in this regard, that Blanche Derval, as Solange, even when seen at close range, never seemed at all made up. Does this mean that what is only slightly permissible in the street but advisable in the theater is important to me only insofar as it has defied what is forbidden in one case, decreed in the other? Perhaps.) I had never seen such eyes. Without a moment's hesitation, I spoke to this unknown woman, though I must admit that I expected the worst. She smiled, but quite mysteriously and somehow *knowingly*, though I had no reason to think so. She was on her way, she claimed, to a hairdresser on the Boulevard Magenta (I say claimed because she later admitted she was going nowhere). She mentioned the financial difficulties she was having, even insisted on them, but apparently as a way of explaining the wretchedness of her appearance. We stopped at the terrace of a café near the Gare du Nord. I took a better look at her. What was so extraordinary about what was happening in those eyes? What was it they reflected—some obscure distress and at the same time some luminous pride? And also the riddle set by the beginning of a confession which, without asking me anything further, with a

confidence which could (or which could not?) be misplaced, she made me. In Lille, her native city which she had left only two or three years ago, she had known a student she may have loved and who loved her. One fine day she decided to leave him when he least expected it, and this "for fear of getting in his way." This is when she came to Paris, writing him at increasingly longer intervals without ever giving her address. Nearly a year later, however, she ran into him in Paris itself and both of them were extremely surprised. Even as he took her hands, he could not help telling her how changed he found her, and then, still holding these hands, he was surprised to see how well manicured they were (though they are not at all so now). Then she too had mechanically looked at one of the hands holding hers and had not been able to restrain an exclamation upon noticing that the last two fingers were joined together. "But you've hurt yourself!" The young man was obliged to show her his other hand, which revealed the same deformity. She questions me about this for some time and with great feeling: "Is such a thing possible? to live so long with someone, to have every possible chance to observe him, to enjoy discovering his slightest physical and other peculiarities, and to end by knowing him so badly that you haven't ever notice *that*? You think: you think love can do such things? And he was so angry, naturally, the only thing I could do was stop talking, those hands . . . Then he said something I don't understand, there was a word in it I don't understand, he said: 'Ninny! I'm going back to Alsace-Lorraine. At least the women there know how to love.' Why: ninny? Do you know?" Naturally I react quite strongly to the sentence she has just quoted: "It doesn't matter. But I think generalizations about Alsace-Lorraine are vile, certainly the man was a fool, etc. ... and then he left, you haven't seen him since? I'm glad to hear it." She told me her name, the one she had chosen for herself: "Nadja, because in Russian it's the beginning of the word hope, and because it's only the beginning." [pp. 64–66]

Note: In the concluding pages, from which this passage is taken, the narrator reflects on his experiences, including the form of the narrative about them

I have begun by going back to look at several of the places to which this narrative happens to lead; I wanted in fact—with some of the people and some of the objects—to provide a photographic image of them taken at the special angle from which I myself had looked at them. On this occasion, I realized that most of the places more or less resisted my venture, so that, as I see it, the illustrated part of *Nadja* is quite inadequate: Becque surrounded by sinister palings, the management of the Théâtre Moderne on its guard, Porville dead and disillusioning as any French city, the disappearance of almost everything relating to *The Grip of the Octopus* and, above all—for I regarded it as essential, although it has not been otherwise referred to in this book—the impossibility of obtaining permission to photograph an adorable wax-work figure in the Musée Grevin, on the left, between the hall of modern political celebrities and the hall at the rear of which, behind a curtain, is shown "an evening at the theater": it is a woman fastening her garter in the shadows, and is the only statue I know of with eyes, the eyes of provocation, etc. [pp. 151–52]

1. Quoted in "Max Ernst" (1920), in Max Ernst, *Beyond Painting and Other Writings by the Artist and His Friends* (New York: Wittenborn Schultz, 1948), p. 177.

2. See Rosalind Krauss and Jane Livingston, *L'Amour Fou: Photography and Surrealism* (New York: Abbeville, 1985), and Marja Warehime, "Photography, Time, and the Surrealist Sensibility," in Marsha Bryant, ed., *Photo-Textualities: Reading Photographs and Literature* (Newark: University of Delaware Press, forthcoming), for more on photography and the Surrealist movement. See portraits of Breton (and other Surrealist writers) in *Man Ray's Paris Portraits: 1921–39*, ed. Timothy Baum (Washington, D.C.: Middendorf Gallery, [1990]), npn, fig. 21 (1924); Man Ray, *Self-Portrait*, pp. 194 (1934) and 214 (1930); in Freund, *Gisèle Freund Photographer* (New York: Abrams, 1985), p. 120, Plates 115–16 (1939); and in Cartier-Bresson, *Photoportraits*, fig. 278 (Breton, n.d.).

3. Breton, "Max Ernst," p. 177.

4. See Breton's foreword to Man Ray, *La Photographie N'est Pas L'Art* (Paris: GLM, 1937), npn; introduction (1939) to Manuel Alvarez Bravo, *Fifteen Photographs*, trans. Richard Seaver, ed. Lee Friedlander (New York: Double Elephant Press, 1974), npn; and "Souvenir du Mexique," a text with photographs by Alvarez Bravo, in *Minotaure* (Paris) Ser. 3, nos. 12–13 (May 1939): 29–52.

5. See Breton, quoted in *Surrealism and Painting* (1925), trans. Simon Watson Taylor (New York: Harper & Row, 1972), p. 32, and his relevant works: *Nadja* [1928], trans. Richard Howard, with photographs by Jacques-André Boiffard and others (New York: Grove Press, 1960); *Communicating Vessels (Les Vases Communicants)* [1932], trans. Mary Ann Caws and Geoffrey Harris, with photographs (Lincoln: University of Nebraska Press, 1990); and *Mad Love [L'Amour Fou]* (1937), trans. Mary Ann Caws, with photographs by Man Ray, Brassaï, and others (Lincoln: University of Nebraska Press, [1987]). See also other Surrealist collaborations, many involving the Surrealist poet Paul Éluard, such as: *Facile,* with photographs by Man Ray (Paris: GLM, 1935); *Les Jeux de la Poupée,* with illustrations by Hans Bellmer (Paris: Les Éditions Premières, 1949); and *Corps Mémorable* with a cover by Picasso, poem by Jean Cocteau, and photographs by Lucien Clergue (Paris: Pierre Seghers, 1957).

6. See Walter Benjamin's remarks in "Surrealism: The Last Snapshot of the European Intelligentsia," in *Reflections,* trans. Edmund Jephcott (New York: Harcourt Brace Jovanovitch, 1978), p. 183: "In such passages in Breton, the photograph intervenes in a very strange way. It makes the streets, gates, squares of the city into illustrations of a trashy novel, draws off the banal obviousness of this ancient architecture to inject it with the most pristine intensity toward the events described, to which, as in old chambermaids' books, word-for-word quotations with page numbers refer." See also Normand Lalonde, "L'Iconographie photographique de *Nadja*," *French Review* 66, no. 1 (October 1992): 48–58.

7. See *La Révolution Surréaliste* 1–12 (December 1924–December 15, 1929), reprinted (New York: Arno, [1968]); *La Surréalisme au service de la Révolution* 1–6 (July 1930–May 1933), reprinted (Paris: Jean-Michel Place, [1976]; and *Minotaure* 1 (June 1933) to no. 12–13 (May 1939), reprinted (Geneva: Skira, [1981]). Examples of Breton's photographic works are reproduced in Krauss and Livingston, *L'Amour Fou,* p. 8, fig. 3 (1938), and pp. 203–4, figs. 183 (1936) and 184 (1937).

We formed something of a mutual admiration society," wrote Edward Steichen (1879–1973) about Carl Sandburg (1878–1967), who married his sister in 1907 and seemed like a real brother fifty years later.[1] Their intimacy grew with their mutual success. Steichen—a talented painter and gardener as well as photographer—enjoyed a cosmopolitan life abroad and in New York. Initially he was the protégé and overseas talent scout of Alfred Stieglitz and the innovative portraitist of eminent political, financial, and cultural figures.[2] Later he became the chief photographer at Condé Nast (1923–38), supervisor of United States aerial photography in the First World War and of naval photography in the Second, and director of the Museum of Modern Art's influential photography department (1947–62). Sandburg first struggled to earn a living in their native Midwest, trying in his spare time to capture its distinctive subjects and idioms in vigorous free verse; he then made his reputation with Chicago Poems (1916). In addition to poetry, he also produced children's books, adult fiction, a compilation of ballads and folk songs, a memoir, and prize-winning biographies of Abraham Lincoln (1926, 1939).[3] Sandburg made his brother-in-law the subject of the first biographical essay on a living photographer (1929).[4] Steichen later repaid the homage with a book of portraits of Sandburg by himself [Fig. 84] and other leading photographers (1966); elsewhere he placed the writer at the top of his list of major contemporary American artists.[5] Sandburg provided the prologue to the catalogue of Steichen's famous Family of Man exhibition (1955), which moved countless viewers. When it was shown in Moscow, for example, the young Russian poet Yevgeny Yevtushenko "came out a different person" and subsequently began taking photographs to accompany some of his poetry and prose.[6]

. . . One day Steichen was dining at the home of Fritz Thaulow, Norwegian, painter of running water, member of the jury of the Paris Salon. Steichen had made a photograph of Thaulow, who had sent a generous check in payment—as though photographers should be paid no less than distinguished painters for their work and time.

"I'd like to meet that grand master, Rodin," said Steichen.

"You would, would you?" said Thaulow. "I can fix that. We go this afternoon."

And with Mrs. Thaulow—three of them on bicycles—they were soon at Meudon, the country studio of Rodin, ten miles from Paris.

Rose meets them; she is the leading lady of the place; shy of people; sometimes spoken of as a primitive woman, a peasant; she knows the Thaulows and gives them her quiet smile. "Soon the Master will be here."

Over the rim of a hill at twilight comes first a broad black hat, then a silhouetted head with a majestic beard, nose and eyebrows, then the short stocky torso. "God! what a photograph that would make!" Steichen was crying.

And when he told Rodin in a stammered French, "Cher Maître, it is the greatest ambition of my life to make a great photograph of you," the Old Man laughed to Thaulow, "Fritz, you see enthusiasm is not dead yet."

Art was argued then, as now and always; wherever a few were gathered in the name of art there was expression of personal taste, conflict of personal views. What was one man's spinach was another man's poison ivy.

Auguste Rodin, then the most original and talked-of sculptor, had been commissioned to produce a statue of Balzac. He did; the deep-chested writer of a shelf of books trying to gather the whole human procession; the midnight coffee drinker; in a dressing gown; a massive struggling torso. There was hubbub and furore. "He has put the sublime Balzac in a flour sack." The society which had commissioned Rodin to do this work refused to accept it.

Rose cooks dinner. Rose brings wine. Rodin is rested and mellowed after a day's work. Fritz says, "Now, Steichen, bring on your pictures." And the sculptor looks at photographs, gets revelations of a new phase of art. At the evening's end he says to Steichen, "Consider my studio yours. Come whenever you like."

Twice a week, off and on, for six months, Steichen rides his bicycle out to Meudon. Then one day—when he is good and ready—he takes his camera along. He spends ten minutes posing the Old Man. Then he goes away with a plate that after its development has him shouting hallelujah.

A superb head, born to be a clear-lined silhouette, is shaped in a sublime black mass against the luminous white of his Victor Hugo statue, gazed at from the right side and higher up by the somber, contemplative figure of "The Thinker." As a photograph it is a masterpiece of portraiture, an allegory, a document, virile, tender, a marching song without words.

One night at Meudon the Balzac is moved into the open air on a slope overlooking Paris. Moonlight shines down. All night long Steichen works with his camera and "that charlatan, Light." Exposures range from one minute to an hour and a half.

At breakfast an envelope is under Steichen's plate. He opens it to find 1000 francs. "I did not know it would be so much work," says the Old Man.

Three nocturn prints come [Fig. 83]. Life, death, light, night and "Balzac in his dressing gown changed into a stone image enveloped in vapor." . . . Rodin receives the photographs and sends Steichen a bronze of "The Walking Man." She calls Steichen "My son" (mon fils). Thereafter Steichen photographs each new work at the Meudon studio.

Steichen roams the studio one afternoon. His paintings are failures; the world doesn't care about photographs; he is no good, now use; why can't he have the strength, courage, wide human faith, that has produced these bronzed shapes in stone? Rodin finds him in tears.

"What is wrong?" "Oh, I've never done any-

thing in my life and I never will. Everything is wrong and I'm the wrongest of all."

Rodin puts his arms around the young man and says, "Now I know you are a great artist and have the right stuff in you. If I didn't still have such moments I would know I was through (finished)." [pp. 23–26]

1. See Steichen, *Steichen: A Life in Photography* [1963] (New York: Harmony Books, 1985), ch. 6, npn; fig. 94, 'Mr. and Mrs.' (The Sandburgs), 1923; and Sandburg's texts under figs. 91–93. See also Sandburg, "Four Steichen Prints," *Broom* 2 (May 1922): 97, and Penelope Niven, *Carl Sandburg: A Biography* (New York: Scribner's, [1991]), for more about their relationship.

2. See also his literary portraits in his autobiography, *Steichen: A Life*, npn: G. B. Shaw, figs. 47–48; Maurice Maeterlinck, fig. 23; Noël Coward, fig. 142; Thomas Mann, fig. 171; Eugene O'Neill, figs. 135, 182; H. G. Wells, fig. 183; Sinclair Lewis, fig. 185; Willa Cather, fig. 186; Alexander Woollcott, fig. 191; H. L. Mencken, fig. 192; Dorothy Parker, fig. 199; W. B. Yeats, fig. 205; Luigi Pirandello, fig. 206; and his other versions of Rodin's 'Balzac,' figs. 51–53. (It is interesting to compare Stei-chen's experience with Rodin with Coburn's in the latter's *Autobiography*, pp. 38–42.) See also other Steichen photographs of literary interest at MOMA, such as 'Girl Reading Keats,' 1898 [140.61], 'Walden Pond,' 1934 [87.66], and 'Rodin-Le Penseur, Paris,' 1902, which includes the sculptor's marble portrait of Victor Hugo—reproduced in *Camera Work*, no. 11 (July 1905): 35, and in no. 14 (April 1906), Special Steichen Supplement: 25—which is lavishly praised by Sandburg in the excerpt here.

3. See also Sandburg: "The Face of Lincoln," in Frederick Hill Meserve and Carl Sandburg, *The Photographers of Abraham Lincoln* (New York: Harcourt, Brace & Company, 1944), pp. 1–16; and *Poems of the Midwest* (Cleveland: World Publishing Company, 1946), which reprints two of his earlier volumes with photographic illustrations, selected by Elizabeth McCausland, by Al-

exander Gardner, Steichen, Lewis Hine, Berenice Abbott, Dorothea Lange, Gordon Parks, Ben Shahn, and others.

4. For comments on this work, see Paul Rosenberg's "Carl Sandburg and Photography," *New Republic* 61 (January 22, 1930): 251–53, keeping in mind that the writer was an intimate of Stieglitz's who felt that Steichen, his successful former protégé, had "sold out," and Edward Weston, *Daybooks* (Millerton, N.Y.: Aperture, 1973), vol. 2, p. 150.

5. See Steichen, ed., *Sandburg: Photographers View Carl Sandburg* (New York: Harcourt, Brace & World, 1966), and his high estimate of the poet in Steichen, *A Life,* ch. 6, npn. See also the photographs by Steichen in Karl Detzer, *Carl Sandburg: A Study in Personality and Background* (New York: Harcourt, Brace, 1941).

6. See Sandburg, "Prologue," *The Family of Man* (New York: MOMA, 1955), [pp. 4–5]; and Yevtushenko, *Invisible Threads* (London: Secker & Warburg, 1981), pp. 9–10. The Russian writer later met both Steichen and Sandburg in Moscow; see pictures of the trio in Steichen, *Sandburg,* pp. 76–77 and 87. See also Yevtuskeno's *Divided Twins: Alaska and Siberia,* trans. Antonina W. Bouls (New York: Viking Studio, [1988]), and "A Gossamer Thread," in Inge Morath, *Russian Journal* (New York: Aperture, 1991), pp. 11–13. See also Roland Barthes's review of the exhibition, "The Great Family of Man," in *Mythologies* (1957), sel. and trans. Annette Lavers (New York: Noonday, 1988), pp. 100–102.

84. Edward Steichen. 'Carl Sandburg,' 1936.

*B*y the time of this review, Forster (1879–1970) had written all the novels on which his reputation rests, including A Room with a View (1908), Howards End (1910), and A Passage to India (1924). His ambivalence toward photography is evident in all these novels; though functioning differently in each story, photographs are associated—sooner or later—with sudden premature death.[1] Forster's essay on Sinclair Lewis (1885–1951), who won the Nobel Prize the following year for his realistic satires of the American middle class like Main Street (1920) and Babbitt (1922), is particularly interesting for its complex use of photography as a critical metaphor and touchstone.[2] Equating writing with photography, which had begun with the rise of realism and naturalism in literature around the time of Daguerre's invention, had been a compliment more often than not. But by the time Ezra Pound scribbled 'Photography' on the manuscript of T. S. Eliot's Waste Land (1922), the word had acquired pejorative overtones, suggesting a pedestrian and mechanical rather than a creative imitation of reality.[3] To write 'photographically' is used here by Forster to qualify, if not disparage, the achievement of Lewis as well as of H. G. Wells.

'I would like to see Gopher Prairie,' says the heroine of Mr. Sinclair Lewis's *Main Street*, and her husband promptly replies: 'Trust me. Here she is. Brought some snapshots down to show you.' That, in substance, is what Mr. Lewis has done himself. He has brought down some snapshots to show us and posterity. The collection is as vivid and stimulating as any writer who adopts this particular method can offer. Let us examine it; let us consider the method in general. And let us once dismiss the notion that any fool can use a camera. Photography is a great gift, whether or no we rank it as an art. If we have not been to Gopher Prairie we cry: 'So that's it!' on seeing the snap. If we have been we either cry: 'How like it!' or 'How perfectly disgraceful, not the least like it!' and in all three cases our vehemence shows that we are in the presence of something alive.

I have never been to Gopher Prairie, Nautilus, Zenith, or any of their big brothers and sisters, and my exclamations throughout are those of a non-American, and worthless as a comment on the facts. Nevertheless, I persist in exclaiming, for what Mr. Lewis has done for myself and thousands of others is to lodge a piece of a continent in our imagination. America, for many of us, used to mean a very large apron, covered with a pattern of lozenges, edged by a frill, and chastely suspended by a boundary tape round the ample waist of Canada. The frill, like the tape, we visualized slightly; on the New York side it puckered up into skyscrapers, on the farther side it was a blend of cinemas and cowboys, and more or less down the middle of the preposterous garment we discerned a pleat associated with the humour of Mark Twain. But the apron proper, the lozenges of pale pink and pale green—they meant nothing at all: they were only something through which railways went and dividends occasionally came from, and which had been arbitrarily spattered with familiar names, like a lunar landscape. As we murmured 'Syracuse, Cairo, London even, Macon, Memphis, Rochester, Plymouth,' the titles, so charged with meaning in their old settings, cancelled each other out in their new, and

helped to make the apron more unreal. And then Sinclair Lewis strode along, developed his films, and stopped our havering. The lozenges lived. We saw that they were composed of mud, dust, grass, crops, shops, clubs, hotels, railway stations, churches, universities, etc., which were sufficiently like their familiar counterparts to be real, and sufficiently unlike them to be extremely exciting. We saw men and women who were not quite ourselves, but ourselves modified by new surroundings, and we heard them talk a language which we could usually, but not always, understand. We enjoyed at once the thrills of intimacy and discovery, and for that and much else we are grateful, and posterity will echo our gratitude. Whether he has 'got' the Middle West, only the Middle West can say, but he has made thousands of people all over the globe alive to its existence, and anxious for further news. Ought a statue of him, camera in hand, to be erected in every little town? This, again, is a question for the Middle West.

Let us watch the camera at work:

'In the flesh, Mrs. Opal Emerson Mudge fell somewhat short of a prophetic aspect. She was pony-built and plump, with the face of a haughty Pekinese, a button of a nose, and arms so short that, despite her most indignant endeavours, she could not clasp her hands in front of her as she sat on the platform waiting.'

'Angus Duer came by, disdainful as a greyhound, and pushing on white gloves (which are the whitest and the most superciliously white objects on earth) . . .'

'At the counter of the Greek Confectionery Parlour, while they [i.e., the local youths] ate dreadful messes of decayed bananas, acid cherries, whipped cream, and gelatinous ice cream, they screamed to one another: 'Hey, lemme 'lone,' 'Quit dog-gone you, looka what you went and done, you almost spilled my glass swater,' 'Like hell I did,' 'Hey, gol darn your hide, don't you go sticking your coffin-nail in my i-scream.'"

'She saw that his hands were not in keeping with a Hellenic face. They were thick, roughned with needle and hot iron and plough handle. Even in the shop he persisted in his finery. He wore a silk shirt, a topaz scarf, thin tan shoes.'

'The drain pipe was dripping, a dulcet and lively song: drippety-drip-drip-dribble; drippety-drip-drip-drip.'

The method throughout is the photographic. Click, and the picture's ours. A less spontaneous or more fastidious writer would have tinkered at all of the above extracts, and ruined everything. The freshness and vigour would have gone, and nothing been put in their places. For all his knowingness about life, and commercially-travelled airs, Mr. Lewis is a novelist of the instinctive sort, he goes to his point direct. There is detachment, but not of the panoramic type: we are never lifted above the lozenges, Thomas Hardy fashion, to see the townlets seething beneath, never even given as wide a view as Arnold Bennett accords us of his Five Towns. It is rather the detachment of the close observer, of the man who stands half a dozen yards off his subject, or at any rate within easy speaking distance of it, and the absence of superiority and swank (which so pleasantly characterizes the books) is connected with this. Always in the same house or street as his characters, eating their foodstuffs, breathing their air, Mr. Lewis claims no special advantages; though frequently annoyed with them, he is never contemptuous, and though he can be ironic and even denunciatory, he has nothing of the aseptic awfulness of the seer. Neither for good nor evil is he lifted above his theme; he is neither a poet nor a preacher, but a fellow with a camera a few yards away.

Even a fellow with a camera has his favourite subjects, as we can see by looking through the Kodak-albums of our friends. One amateur prefers the family group, another bathing-scenes, another his own house taken from every possible point of view, another cows upon an alp, or kittens held upside down in the arms of a black-faced child. This tendency to choose one subject rather than another indicates the photographer's temperament. Nevertheless, his passion is for photography rather than for selection, a kitten will serve when no cows are present, and, if I interpret Mr. Lewis correctly, we must not lay too much stress on his attitude to life. He has an attitude; he is against dullness, heartiness and intolerance, a trinity of evils most closely entwined; he mistrusts Y.M.C.A. helpfulness and rotarian idealism; while as for a positive creed (if we can accept *Martin Arrowsmith* as an unaided confession of faith) he believes in scientific research. 'So many men, Martin, have been kind and helpful, so few have added to knowledge,' complains the old bacteriologist. One can safely class him with writers termed 'advanced,' with people who prefer truth to comfort, passion to stability, prevention to cure. But the classification lets what is most vital in him escape; his attitude, though it exists, does not dwell in the depths of his being. His likes and dislikes mean less to him than the quickness of his eye, and though he tends to snapshot muscular Christians when they are attacked with cramp, he would sooner snap them amid clouds of angels than not at all. His commentary on society is constant, coherent, sincere; yet the reader's eye follows the author's eye rather than his voice, and when Main Street is quitted it is not its narrowness, but its existence that remains as a permanent possession.

His method of book-building is unaffected and appropriate. In a sense (a very faint sense) his novels are tales of unrest. He takes a character who is not quite at ease in his or her surroundings, contrives episodes that urge this way or that, and a final issue of revolt or acquiescence. In his earlier work both character and episodes are clear-cut; in his later—but let us postpone for a moment the painful problem of a photographer's old age. Carol Endicott, the heroine of his first important book, is a perfect medium, and also a living being. Her walks down Main Street are overwhelming; we see the houses, we see her against them, and when the dinginess breaks and Erik Valborg arises with his gallant clothes and poet's face, we, too, are seduced, and feel that such a world might well be lost for love. Never again is Mr. Lewis to be so poignant or to arrange his simple impressions so nearly in the order of high tragedy; 'I may not have fought the good fight, but I have kept the faith' are Carol's final words, and how completely are they justified by all she has suffered and done! Babbitt follows her—of grosser clay, and a native while she was an exile, but even Babbitt sees that there is something better in life than graft and goodfellowship, though he acquiesces in them at the close. Martin Arrowsmith succeeds where Carol and Babbitt failed, because he is built strongly and prepared to sacrifice a home, but, regarded as a medium, he is identical with them, he can register their doubts and difficulties. And the same is true of Elmer Gantry; his heavy feet are turned to acquiescence from the first, but he, too, has moments of uneasiness, and hypocrisy; religious eroticism and superstition can be focussed through him. And so with Samuel Dodsworth in *Dodsworth*. He reacts this way and that among the main streets of Europe, and many pictures of them can be taken before he decides that they will not do.

Now, in the earlier books this method was a complete success, but with *Elmer Gantry* doubts begin; the theme is interesting, but the snapshots less remarkable. And in *Dodsworth* doubt becomes dismay. Dodsworth is a decent citizen of Zenith who retires early and goes to Europe with his wife. She is cultivated and snobby—a *rechauffée* of the second Mrs. Arrowsmith, but served upon an enormous dish. She talks, talks, flirts, patronizes, talks, and he, humble and observant, gradually realizes her inadequacies, but all the time he talks, talks, talks. The talk is rhetoric, the slang tired, the pictures blurred. The English country church, palace at Venice, restaurant at Paris, journey in an aeroplane, Bernese Oberland, back in New York, the right sort of American tourist, the wrong sort, is there a right sort, is it wrong to think there is a right sort? . . . on the story trundles, unprofitably broadminded and with unlucky thematic parallels to Henry James. The method remains, but something has died. The following quotation will show us what:

'He found that in certain French bathrooms one can have hot water without waiting for a geyser. He found that he needn't have brought two dozen tubes of his favourite (and very smelly) toothpaste from America—one actually could buy toothpaste, corn-plaster, New York Sunday papers, Bromo-Seltzer, Lucky Strikes, safety razor blades, and ice cream almost as easily in Paris as in the United States; and a man he met in Luigi's bar insisted that if one quested earnestly enough he could find B.V.D.'s.'

What has happened? What has changed the Greek Confectionery Parlour at Gopher Prairie, where every decaying banana mattered, to this spiritless general catalogue? The explanation is all too plain: photography is a pursuit for the young. So long as a writer has the freshness of youth on him, he can work the snapshot method, but when it passes he has nothing to fall back upon. It is here that he differs from the artist. The artist has the power of retaining and digesting experiences, which, years later, he may bring forth in a different form; to the end of life he is accompanied by a secret store.

The artist may not be good. He may be very bad. He generally is. And it is not to celebrate him and to decry the photographer that I draw this distinction between them. But it does explain, I think, why quick spontaneous writers (the kind that give me more pleasure than any) are apt, when they lose their spontaneity, to have nothing left, and to be condemned by critics as superficial. They are not superficial, they are merely not artistic; they are members of a different profession, the photographic, and the historian of our future will cease to worry over this, will pick up the earlier and brighter volumes in which their genius is enshrined, and will find there not only that genius, but a record of our age.

Mr. Lewis is not our sole photographer. There is always Mr. H. G. Wells. They have just the same gift of hitting off a person or place in a few quick words; moreover, they share the same indifference to poetry, and pass much the same judgments on conduct. Consequently, one might have expected that their literary careers would be similar, that the authors of *Love and Mr. Lewisham and Main Street* would develop in the same way and at the same rate. They have diverged, and for an instructive reason. Wells is still kicking because photography was only one of his resources. When his early freshness wore off, he could bring into play his restless curiosity about the universe, and thus galvanize his later novels into life. In Mr. Lewis, curiosity about the universe has never been very strong. Only occasionally has he thought of the past, the future, international relationships, science, labour, the salvation or damnation of the globe. The people in the room and the houses across the street are what really interest him, and when the power to reproduce them sharply fails, he has nothing to do except to reproduce them dimly. If this view of his development is correct, the later stages of it are bound to be disappointing. However, there the early books are, done, safe, mankind's for ever; also, the longer one lives, the less important does 'development' appear.

1. This and other meanings can be seen in these three Forster novels. For example, in *A Room with a View* (London: Arnold, 1958), ch. 4, photographs function as a plot device and means of characterization in a key scene involving the newly acquainted principals: Lucy Honeychurch—acting in Florence like the common English tourist the author disdained—buys photographs of some of the famous artworks just before witnessing a murder, which makes her faint; George Emerson, her uncommon future husband, rescues her from the crowd literally (as he will later figuratively) and disposes of the bloodied packet. In *Howards End* (London: Arnold, 1960), the photograph functions more symbolically at the start of the complex narrative: Leonard Bast breaks the photograph of his wife and cuts his fingers on the glass fragments, pp. 51, 53–54, and 57, more seriously than does Margaret Schlegel when she breaks the photograph of Mrs. Wilcox's daughter-in-law, pp. 74 and 76; the two, who have just met, are thus linked further in this figurative, ominous way, preparing the reader for Bast's later death. In *A Passage to India* (London: Arnold, 1978), pp. 50, 107–8, 113, and 163, the photograph of Dr. Aziz's prematurely dead wife functions as a plot device, a means of characterization and a symbol, representing and bridging the culturally antagonistic attitudes and passions dramatized by the novel. Gisèle Freund's portrait of an un- happy-looking Forster (1935), reproduced in her *Freund Photographer*, p. 40, Plate 39, seems appropriate, given these ambivalent attitudes.

2. Ironically, Lewis uses photographs only occasionally in his best-known novels, and then mainly as items in interiors or in newspapers. See, for example, *Main Street* (New York: Harcourt, Brace, 1920), pp. 7, 18, 26, 151, 184, and 435–36; *Babbitt* (New York: Harcourt, Brace, 1922), pp. 91–92, 176, 225, 257, 305, 323, and 398. See also Wright Morris's photographs of shelves of books, largely ones by Lewis, and of the opening page of *Babbitt* in *God's Country and My People* (New York: Harper & Row, 1968), npn. The HRHRC has seven photograph albums from the 1910's and 1920's apparently collected and annotated by Lewis's wife and mother-in-law, called to the editor's attention by Anne McCauley and verified by Andrea Inselmann. See also the portrait of Lewis (1929) by Man Ray in *Man Ray Portraits*, ed. L. Fritz Gruber (N.p.: Editions Prisma, [1967]), npn, and at the Library of Congress (LC USZ62–41464).

3. See T. S. Eliot, *The Waste Land: A Facsimile and Transcript of the Original Draft, Including the Annotations of Ezra Pound*, ed. Valerie Eliot (London: Faber & Faber, 1971), p.11, noted by Lyndall Gordon, 'Prufrock Among the Women,' *Oxford Today* (Trinity Term 1990): 27.

52. *Man Ray*

"AMERICAN AND ENGLISH WRITERS,"
FROM *Self Portrait*, 1963

Man Ray (1890–1976) worked in many artistic mediums—paint-ing, sculpture, collage, and film—but is now best remembered for his camera work. Introduced to photography by Stieglitz, whose shows of European artists greatly influenced him, Man Ray lived in Paris from 1921 to 1939. He soon turned to portrait and commercial pho-tography to support himself while becoming a central figure in the main successive postwar art movements: Dadaism, which wanted to destroy traditional bourgeois values in life as in art, and Surrealism, which wanted to liberate the imagination by fusing material from reality and the Freudian unconscious, especially dreams, to achieve a suprareality. Both movements must have encouraged Man Ray's love of unexpected, often humorous or shocking, juxtapositions.[1] Experimenting with photograms, solarization, granulation, distortion, and other manipulations, he often made evocative abstractions out of mundane objects and female nudes—especially Kiki, later acknowledged as "Queen of Montparnasse," who was his mistress and his favorite model throughout the 1920's. But he never stopped taking more conventional portraits, often of literary figures, whom he recalls here. Some, like Gertrude Stein, became friends.[2] She probably introduced Man Ray to the young Ernest Hemingway [Fig. 85], who later provided a preface for Kiki's Memoirs.[3] Man Ray may have recommended himself to William Carlos Williams [Fig. 86], James Joyce, and Ezra Pound.[4] Still other Ameri-can and English literary subjects, like Virginia Woolf [Fig. 87] may have been referred by Sylvia Beach [Fig. 102], who then often hung their por-traits on the walls of her famous bookstore and literary gathering place, Shakespeare and Company.[5]

Prejudiced as I was in favor of the European school of literature—which accepted me on a broader basis than my English writing visitors, whose interest in me occasionally manifested itself only after I had been recognized as a member of the local avant-garde movement—my contact with American and English writers was a more casual affair. As already explained, it was principally the relation between photographer and sitter. Although I read their work with interest, I could not help comparing it with what seemed to me the more meaty and poetic writing of my French friends. Fortunately, evaluations, criticisms and analyses of prewar English writing have been adequately recorded in print. I can only give a meager account of my actual contact with the physical person—a sort of word portrait that completes my photographs. And this, to be sure, as it occurred at the time of the contact.

My first visit to Gertrude Stein in the rue de Fleurus, shortly after my arrival in France, caused me mixed sensations. Crossing the courtyard, I rang a bell; the door was opened by a small dark woman with long earrings, looking like a gypsy. Inside, I was greeted with a broad warm smile by Gertrude Stein, massive, in a woolen dress and woolen socks with comfortable sandles, which emphasized her bulk. I had brought my camera; it was understood that I was to make some pictures of her in her interior. Miss Stein introduced me to her friend Alice Toklas, whom I had taken for her maid, although, in her print dress trimmed with white lace, she was too carefully groomed. Miss Stein, too, wore a flowered blouse fastened at the neck with a scarf held by a Victorian brooch. Both sat down in chintz-covered armchairs blending with their dresses, while I set up my camera. The room was filled with massive waxed Italian and Spanish furniture on which stood knick-knacks in porcelain, with here and there a small vase containing posies, all of which was discreetly set off by a neutral wainscoting. At one end of the room, between two small windows, hung a large black cross. But above, all around

the room were paintings by Cézanne, Matisse, Braque, and Picasso on a light water-stained wall. At first glance it was difficult to reconcile the effect of these with the more traditional setting below. The intention, no doubt, was to prove that the two different elements could cohabit. If anything, what were considered revolutionary paintings seemed to blend with the older stuff. This was emphasized by the Cézannes and Braques which hung above the ornamental fireplace and had acquired some of its soot. I wished these had kept their original brilliance for my photography.

In another corner hung the portrait of Gertrude Stein by Picasso, a good likeness—I had her sit alongside it for a double portrait. Like many of his more conventional works, it looked unfinished but the hands were beautifully painted. I have no objection to unfinished works, in fact I have an aversion to paintings in which nothing is left to speculation. Certainly, my photographs left nothing to the imagination, that is, my straight photography; I was already trying to overcome this deficiency in my freer work which I pursued on the side. This aroused the interest of a few who closely followed all the newer trends in expression; in general it left others indifferent, those who had no imagination. I must include among these most of my sitters, intent on getting an important-looking image of themselves.

My portraits of Gertrude Stein were the first to appear in print, to give her small circle of readers at the time an idea of how she looked. Perhaps I was impressed by the staidness of her personality but it never occurred to me to try any fantasy or acrobatics with her physiognomy. She might have welcomed the notoriety, as in her writing; and she might have thought more of me as a creative artist. Besides the classics on her walls, she took an interest now and then in some striving young painter—tried to help him, but soon dropped him so that generally he passed into oblivion. It reminds me of a famous gourmet in France who was approached by a manufacturer of margarine to write a phrase extolling the merits of his product. The gourmet wrote: Nothing can replace butter! Gertrude Stein was mature and hardened; nothing that came after her first attachments could equal them. This attitude was carried to the extreme regarding other writers— they were all condemned: Hemingway, Joyce, the Dadaists, the Surrealists, with herself as the pioneer. Her bitterness really showed up when the others got universal attention before she did. In her own circle she always held the floor; if anyone tried to usurp it, that person was shortly called to order. One day at a small gathering, she and two of us were engaged in conversation at one end of the room; in an opposite corner Alice and a woman carried on a lively dialogue. Gertrude stopped short, turned her head in their direction and shouted belligerently for them to lower their voices. It was more than effective—there was a dead silence.

I visited often during the next ten years, she came to my studio for other sittings, and invited me to lunch—Alice's cooking was famous. One of the last sittings, with her hair cropped after an illness, pleased her especially. She looked rather mannish, except for her flowered blouse and the brooch she always wore. In exchange for some prints she did a portrait of me in prose.

By now she had publishers and a public. Requiring photographs for her publicity she ordered a dozen prints which I sent with a modest bill. Soon I received a short note saying that we were all struggling artists, that it was I who had invited her to sit for me, and not she who had solicited me, in short, not to be silly. I did not answer, thinking that she felt I was indebted to her—in any case, I had told her in a previous note, when my pictures of her were reproduced in magazines, that I would do what I could to help her. But I, too, was getting known and had the reputation of being a very expensive photographer, perhaps because I sent out bills more often, when I thought sitters could pay something. It wasn't so much the money I was after—there were plenty of clients who never quibbled and paid enough to make up for those who did not, but I felt more and more that I was being kept from more creative work; I expected a sacrifice from those who were concerned with themselves alone. The flattery and glory that came from portraiture that was often drudgery left me cold. Sometimes, when a prospective client found my price high, I replied ironically that if he or she would like a portrait of myself, it would cost nothing.

Gertrude Stein lived well during her long stay in Paris, whether she already had money from her family, or occasionally sold a painting from her collection—she certainly did not make enough from her writings. When success finally came, she managed her contracts for books and lectures very efficiently—whereas I had started with nothing but my own efforts. I granted that she had made an important contribution to contemporary literature, had been especially helpful to starving European artists, but had profited all she could from her initiative. On one occasion when a collector wished to buy a painting from her, but observed that she was asking more than a work of similar importance brought in the galleries, she replied, Ah, yes, but the latter was not from the Gertrude Stein collection. I read some of her writings, of course—once she read a passage to me, which was more impressive than reading it myself, and I suggested she make recordings. Joyce and the French poet Éluard had made some records to which I listened with pleasure. She never sent me any of her books on publication—I had been rather spoiled by French authors from whom I received many autographed copies—whereas English and American publishers sometimes sent me a subscription blank, if they happened to have my name and address.

Hemingway, a tall young man of athletic build, with his hair low on his forehead, a clear complexion, and a small mustache, was often seen at the bars and cafés in Montparnasse. It was Robert McAlmon, a young American poet and writer I'd met in Greenwich Village, and now married to Bryher, a rich young English girl, who brought him around to me for a portrait. Bob started a publishing affair called Contact Editions for young, unknown writers whom established publishers would not handle. He was getting out Hemingway's book of some

short stories: *In Our Time.* My first portrait gave the man a poetic look, making him very handsome besides. We became friendly; one night he took me to an important boxing match; I wasn't interested in sports myself, but seized the occasion to try out a new hand movie camera I had acquired. I brought an assistant along with another camera, with the idea of getting two different points of view of the fight, and also that one might take up the shooting on a pre-arranged signal after the other's film had run out. Ernest and I were in the fourth or fifth row, while my assistant was in front near the ring, for closeups. When the first round started, the latter raised his camera and had hardly run off a few feet when the manager rushed over and yanked it out of his hands. I discreetly raised my camera and started it rolling. Before I had run off the thirty feet of film there was a dramatic knockout—in the first round. Pandemonium broke out in the hall, Hemingway joining in the shouting and arm-waving. The next day I went to the manager's office to claim my assistant's camera. The manager returned it, first confiscating the film. No pictures were allowed, he said. I returned to my studio, developed the film in my own camera and furnished the illustrated weekly with pictures of a sensational knockout. It was one of my few scoops. I who boasted that I never took a camera out of my studio. I would never be a reporter; it was just another sport—I could never be a Johnny-on-the-spot. Hemingway loved boxing; when he had no one else to spar with, he took on Joan Miró, the Spanish painter, more than a head shorter than himself. When he had no one at all, he'd put a pair of baby boxing gloves on his little boy Bumby's hands, and box with him holding him in his arms. I made other pictures of Hemingway, his wife and the little boy. He was going down to Pamplona for his first bullfight; I lent him my camera, showed him how to use it, and he came back with pictures of the festival and bullfights which were printed up in my studio.

We had a little party one night in my place—a few American and French friends. During the evening he went to the toilet and came out soon, his head covered with blood. He'd pulled what he thought was the chain, but it was the cord of the casement window above, which came down splintering glass on him. He was bandaged up. I put a small felt hat jauntily on his head partly hiding the bandage—the wound wasn't very serious—and took a picture of him [Fig. 85]. There have been other pictures of him wounded, before and after this one, but none which gave him the same look of amusement and indifference to the ups and downs of his career. I can imagine the smile on his face, a little more grim perhaps, just before his death recently. For many years afterwards, our paths got wider and wider apart; in fact, we never met again, he the great adventurer and I the confirmed sedentary one.

When Ezra Pound came into my studio he immediately flopped into an armchair with his legs stretched out, his arms hanging loosely, his black tie flowing, and his pointed red beard raised aggressively, as if to take possession of the place. I knew him as a kindhearted man, always ready to help others, but dominatingly arrogant where literature was concerned. It worked very well with the English-speaking community, but I never heard him mentioned in European circles. Perhaps the basis of his writing was too erudite for other races in that they required an English erudition to be appreciated. However impressive it might have been, I was too ignorant to feel any impact from his work; as for any revolutionary content, I was too steeped in the violent and often gratuitous productions of my French friends, who generally hid their erudition to obtain wider circles of reaction. My immediate contact with Pound was as a photographer—I made his portrait to add to my files, and to the growing collection of English writers on the walls of Sylvia Beach's bookshop: Shakespeare and Company. When he came around again to see the prints he brought his father with him, on a tour through Europe. A pleasant gentleman, who immediately was attracted by one of my paintings on the wall, When he expressed a desire to buy it, Pound discouraged him. It was under heavy glass and would be too inconvenient to carry around. Pound had never looked nor commented upon my work, so I classed him at once among the many other egotists who came to me. I did not regret not selling the painting, as it has since found a place in an important collection, satisfying any egotism that I myself may possess.

James Joyce's *Ulysses* was about to come off the presses; Shakespeare and Company sent the writers to me to have press photos made. Miss Beach also wanted some good portrait prints made for friends. I fixed a fee for this, not much, expecting to receive a copy of this encyclopedic work. I could have asked for it or bought it, but neglected to do both. The book was cheap then; no one could tell whether there would be a demand for it. Anyhow, I went to work on Joyce because his fine Irish face, although marred by thick glasses—he was between two operations on his eyes—interested me. I had read some short pieces by him in the *Little Review,* which had held my attention. I told him so, with the idea of putting him at ease—he seemed to consider the sitting a terrible nuisance. However, he was very patient, until after a couple of shots when he turned his head away from the lights, putting his hand over his eyes and saying that he could no longer face the glare. I snapped this pose, which has become the favorite one, although in certain quarters it was criticized as too artificial, too posed. Later, one evening we sat at the café; Joyce had been drinking and was very gay, singing snatches from operas in a loud voice. I could see where he'd handed down this talent to his son Giorgio, who became an opera singer. Joyce invited me to dinner at his favorite restaurant in Montparnasse, the Trianons, the most expensive, and the wine flowed freely. I talked

about photography and painting, but he stared blankly through his thick glasses and said very little. Every now the than he'd hum a tune between the glasses of wine. The meal was copious and delicious. Reading *Ulysses* later, it seemed to me that here, too, there was a immense background of erudition, of literary knowledge—one would have had to be as well-read as Joyce to appreciate the liberties he had taken with the language, the departures he had made from conventional writing.

William Carlos Williams, the poet, turned up in the studio one day. Except for coming across his well-turned poetry in the little magazines, occasionally, I had lost contact with him since my days in Ridgefield, New Jersey. Now, years later, he had managed to take a vacation from his professional duties as doctor, and

turned up in Paris making the rounds of the American literary group. Someone had directed him to me to be photographed. He was very good-looking; there was no problem and the results were automatically satisfactory [Fig. 86]. He ordered a number of prints which I sent to his hotel, one of the more expensive places on the Left Bank. Judging from this, I included a modest bill and received a check. Two decades later, living in California, I received an invitation from a bookshop where Williams was signing his latest book, an autobiography. We shook hands, my wife was very much impressed with his presence and thrilled with the inscription. There was a reference to our meeting in Paris in the book, commenting on my high prices. Not that it did me any harm, but I was annoyed that he hadn't found something more significant to talk about.

. . . Besides many members of English society, I photographed the writers—T. S. Eliot; Havelock Ellis, his patriarch's head at odds with his baggy tweeds; Aldous Huxley, posed so his bad-eye would not show; Virginia Woolf, whose ascetic face was framed in a severe arrangement of her hair—I had to put some lipstick on her mouth, to which she objected at first, but I explained that it was for technical reasons and would not show in the picture [Fig. 87]. When she left, she forgot to remove the rouge.

87. Man Ray.
'Virginia Woolf,' 1935.

1. See tributes to Man Ray by his literary surrealist friends, Éluard and Breton, in *Man Ray* (Los Angeles: Los Angeles County Museum/Lytton Gallery, 1966), pp. 32–35. See also another tribute, "Lettre ouverte à Man Ray, photographe américain" (1922) by Cocteau, who also illustrated "L'Ange Heurtebise" (1925) with a Man Ray photogram; both are cited in the bibliography below, as is an essay on Man Ray by Tournier, "Un Américain à Paris," *Le Crépuscule des Masques*, pp. 40–48.

2. On Man Ray's relationship with Stein, see their correspondence at the Beinecke, especially his letter of February 12, 1930, and her response, written on it; see also many of his 1920's portraits of Stein, alone and with Alice Toklas, some reproduced, among many other places, in *Perpetual Motif: The Art of Man Ray,* ed. Merry Foresta et al. (New York: Abbeville, 1988), p. 144, fig. 155, and in *Man Ray Photographs* (London: Thames & Hudson, 1987), p. 223, fig. 279. Stein composed a verbal portrait in return for his early photographs called "Man Ray" (1924), reprinted in *Painted Lace and Other Pieces, 1914–1937* (New Haven, Conn.: Yale University Press, 1955), pp. 292–93; and she also mentions him in *The Autobiography of Alice B. Toklas* (New York: Vintage, 1960), pp. 197–98. See also the Stieglitz and Stein selections above.

3. Another of Man Ray's Hemingway portraits, as well as those of Joyce, T. S. Eliot, and Aldous Huxley, are reproduced in the same chapter in *Self Portrait* (Boston: New York Graphic Society/Little, Brown, 1988), pp. 145–53. Still another of Hemingway, haloed by a banjo, 1923, is reproduced in *Man Ray Photographs,* p. 188, fig. 158. See also Hemingway's introduction to *Kiki's Memoirs,* trans. Samuel Putnam (Paris: Edward Titus, 1930), pp. 9–14; Man Ray, who provided four of the photographic illustrations, briefly comments on her *Memoirs* and on his relationship with Kiki in *Self Portrait,* pp. 128–29. Throughout its many editions, Kiki devotes only one short chapter to Man Ray, doubtless because their long intimacy was over by 1929. But in the 1954 edition, she added further material involving Hemingway—with whom she apparently remained in contact—perhaps because his reputation at the time would make her book more respectable and saleable; *Kiki's Memoirs,* like the Paris

edition of D. H. Lawrence's *Lady Chatterley's Lover* (1928), both published by Edward Titus, the husband of Helena Rubenstein who owned an English bookshop, was originally banned by U.S. Customs. See also Billy Klüver and Julie Martin, *Kiki's Paris: Artists and Lovers, 1900–1930* (New York: Abrams, [1989]).

4. See *The Autobiography of William Carlos Williams* (New York: Random House, 1951), p. 199, and Paul Mariani, *William Carlos Williams: A New World Naked* [1983] (New York: Norton, 1991), p. 221, for Williams's distress both with the "sentimental" portrait and the large bill for it. See also the Williams selection below. See also the portraits of James and Nora Joyce, 1926–28, by Man Ray's former assistant, Berenice Abbott, reproduced in Hank O'Neal, *Berenice Abbott, American Photographer* (New York: McGraw-Hill, 1982), pp. 42–45.

5. Other portraits of Woolf are reproduced in *Man Ray Photographs,* pp. 218–19, figs. 272–76; for more about Woolf, see her selection above.

See also Freund's descriptions, as well as her 1937 pictures of Shakespeare and Company and its owner, Sylvia Beach, in *The World in My Camera,* pp. 57–58 and 118, and the Freund selection below.

53. Ansel Adams and Mary Austin

FROM WRITINGS, 1929 AND 1985
(SOME UNPUBLISHED)

Adams (1902–84) remains one of the best-known twentieth-century American photographers due to his dramatic western landscapes, his many books on photographic technique, and his involvement, often as founder, in institutions significant to photography. Trained as a concert pianist and music teacher, Adams was torn between music and photography when he met Albert Bender, a patron of the arts, in 1926. Bender introduced him to many other artists, including the Santa Fe writer Mary Austin (1868–1934), who was nationally acclaimed for her sympathetic understanding of the Indians.[1] *Bender was delighted when the sixty-year-old, whom he termed "the greatest writer in the West," agreed to collaborate with his twenty-five-year-old protégé, "the greatest photographer"; their ideas for a Southwest portfolio evolved into a finely designed book,* Taos Pueblo *(1930).*[2] *Work proceeded smoothly, although Austin never quite overcame her disdain of Adams and he his terror of her. His fears could not have quickly diminished after the writer expressed hostility toward his portrait of her [Fig. 88], taken early in their relationship, when a collaboration was still being considered.*[3] *Yet the artist friends whom Adams met through Austin proved more accepting. Indeed, the husband of the legendary Mabel Dodge Luhan facilitated his photographs for* Taos Pueblo *[Fig. 89], which Austin never saw before writing her prefatory text.*[4] *Near the work's completion, Adams wrote to his wife that "something has clicked inside me and I have an entirely new perspective" about his career, which was now to be photography rather than music.*[5] *Returning to San Francisco, he opened a professional studio. Austin, however, did not live to see Adams's successful career, which she had been instrumental in launching.*[6]

My wife, Virginia, and I traveled to Santa Fe
for an extended visit in 1929 to photograph the
marvelous people and landscape. I loved northern New Mexico, and in the back of my mind
was thinking of moving there. To balance income with expenses, I planned to seek out portrait commissions and what other work came
my way. . . . Mary Austin invited Virginia and
me to stay with her in Santa Fe. We accepted
and our friendship quickly grew. Its natural
progression produced our enthusiastic decision
to collaborate on a book of words and pictures
on a new Mexican subject. As I wrote to Albert [Bender] that spring:

We have finally decided on the subject of the
portfolio. It will be the Pueblo of Taos. Through
Tony Luhan, the Governor of Taos was approached "with velvet"—a council meeting was
held, and the next morning I was granted permission to photograph the Pueblo. It is a stunning thing—the great pile of adobe, five stories
high with the Taos peaks rising in a tremendous way behind. And the Indians are really
majestic, wearing, as they do, their blankets
like Arabs. I think it will be the most effective
subject to work with—and I have every hope
of creating something really fine. With Mary
Austin writing the text...I have a grand task to
come up to it with the pictures. But I am sure I
can do it. Dear Albert—look what you started
when you brought me to Santa Fe! [from Adams,
Autobiography, 1985, p. 90]

Dear Mrs. Austin,

Your portrait is coming along. I will send
you the proffs [*sic*] in a few days. You have undoubtedly wondered about the delay, but I have
already explained it. I do not like to do important work when I am not up to it. [from unpublished letter of January 11, 1929, CCP]

Dear Mrs. Austin,

I have selected several of the best pictures of
you that I secured in Santa Fe, and am working
them up into finished prints . . . . I am anxious
that you be utterly pleased with the prints . . . .

Let me know how many you want; I shall be
glad to make as many as you desire. [from unpublished letter of January 31, 1929]

Dear Mary Austin,

Today I am mailing three pictures of you to
your new address [Fig. 88]. They're fairly well
finished, but not completely so, for I will wait
your final verdict as to the one or ones you
want, together with any suggestions you have
to offer, before going after the final effects . . .

I have tried to keep the pictures as simple as
possible, and have done very little retouching.
The first proofs, however, were so far from
what I had conceived the portrait to be that I
would not send them on to you. I apologize for
the delay. [from unpublished letter of February
10, 1929, CCP]

88. Ansel Adams. 'Mary
Austin, Santa Fe, New
Mexico,' c. 1929.

My Dear Ansel,

. . . I don't know what to say about [the portraits], for I don't know what you can do to them still, but as they are it would be impossible to use them for the purpose for which I have long wanted a good picture.

I dare say you can take away that dreadful smirk, and the drawn look about the mouth, but the carriage of the head, with the face thrust down and forward, and the slumped shoulders are not only not characteristic of me, but contradict the effect is still necessary for me to make on my public.

A photo for publicity must be something other than a likeness; it must convey something of the personal drive, the energetic index, the impact of the whole personality as it affects the public. What I know about that is that is always of an upright and forthgoing quality. Not what people who know me intimately are likely to see.

But wait until I get home and show these to several of my friends. I am too busy now even to think. [from letter of February 23, 1929, Huntington Library]

Dear Mary Austin,

Your letter [is] at hand; I am glad you so definitely express what you think about the pictures—it is seldom that I find anyone who really knows what they want, and your opinions will enable me to work with a closer idea of what is required, in the spring. I am sorry they are not suitable only for the immediate use for which I believe you wanted them.

In April we will try again—I have a new portrait lens which I acquired especially for the trip, and I am sure we shall obtain good results. I do not expect a bulls-eye every time with portraits, although I have had exceeding good luck. [from unpublished letter of February 27, 1929, CCP]

Mabel Dodge Luhan, never a victim of convention, chose to spell her married name differently from her husband Tony Lujan [Fig. 89]. They were both legendary characters in the Southwest fantasy. Mabel's cultural education had been her association with the movers and shakers of her time in Europe and America. She played out her life on a stage, illuminated by her great wealth and the sycophantic bees that flocked to her hive. She did bring great artists into her fold and aided them, but I always felt it was a demonstration of the enticements of the huntress rather than a determined contribution to culture.

Tony, a stolid and burly Taos Indian, had married Mabel after a period of serving as her chauffeur. Tony was a pleasant and theatrical character—his black hair in long braids, his red, black, or white blanket, and his haughty Indian demeanor. He had abandoned his Indian wife for Mabel, and the Pueblo was angered. Mary Austin, always a proponent of human rights, notified Mabel that if she did not do right by Tony's former wife, Mary would bring the weight and wrath of the Bureau of Indian Affairs upon Mabel's head. Mabel provided alimony for life for the displaced wife, and the pueblo returned to peace.

My introduction to Mabel was arranged by Mary. Mabel's home, Los Gallos, was beautiful, and the surrounding country, magnificent. Georgia O'Keeffe, Paul Strand, John Marin, and D. H. Lawrence were among her many guests. All were free to go about their creative business. Some left feeling that they had experienced a new Athens; others found Mabel's strong personality an unbearable strain. My relationships with Mabel and Tony were most agreeable, and *Taos Pueblo* might have been impossible were it not for Mabel's hospitality and Tony's assistance in obtaining the permission of his pueblo to make the photographs. [from Adams, *Autobiography*, 1985, p. 91]

89. Ansel Adams. 'Tony Lujan of Taos Pueblo, New Mexico,' 1930.

1. See Bender's humorous letter to Austin, March 23, 1929, about the impending visit of Adams and his new bride, two years later, in Esther Lanigan Stineman, *Mary Austin: Song of a Maverick* (New Haven and London: Yale University Press, 1989), p. 189. See also Adams (with Mary Street Alinder), *An Autobiography* (Boston: Little, Brown, 1985), pp. 84–87, for Adams's meeting— also arranged by Bender—with Robinson Jeffers, whose poetry he came to appreciate. Adams's own literary specialty was the limerick; some examples are at the CCP [AG 31:2:1:1].

2. Bender, quoted in Nancy Newhall, *The Eloquent Light* (San Francisco: Sierra Club, 1963), vol. 1, p. 45 (and see pp. 51, 54, and 65), and in Augusta Fink, *I-Mary: A Biography of Mary Austin* (Tucson: University of Arizona Press, 1983), p. 233, and see also 239–41, 253, and 256. Adams, *Autobiography,* pp. 89–90, downplays Bender's role in setting up the collaboration; cf. the more objective account in Stineman, *Mary Austin,* pp. 187–89, who also provides a detailed summary of their collaboration, pp. 193–98.

3. See Stineman, *Mary Austin,* pp. 189–90, who reprints most of the unhappy letter from Austin to Adams of February 23, 1929, also reprinted below. The CCP also has many proofs of Adams's portraits of Austin [AG 31:7:4:2]. as well as the entire correspondence between the pair [AG 31:1:1:5], which provides details about other planned but aborted collaborations: one on the Acoma pueblo; another on Spanish arts in New Mexico, for which Adams took around a hundred photographs, whose negatives are at the CCP, and Austin completed a manuscript, now at the Zimmerman Library at the University of New Mexico in Albuquerque. Nothing seems to have resulted from Adams's letter to Austin, May 1,

1930, inviting her to contribute a foreword to a book on Yosemite that he was organizing.

4. Stineman, *Mary Austin,* pp. 183–87, notes Austin's own "photographic" techniques and, pp. 194–96, recounts the pair's exchanges throughout *Taos Pueblo* (San Francisco: Grabhorn Press, 1930; reprinted in facsimile, Boston: New York Graphic Society, 1977). Evident is Austin's condescending treatment of her "illustrator"; Adams's focus on the appearance of the book, hers on its circulation; the greater appreciation accorded his dozen photographs than her prefatory text on the book's publication; and the author's conciliatory remark that "next time . . . I should see your photographs before writing the text." Perhaps in gratitude for the Luhans' help, Adams later contributed photographs, as did Edward Weston, Carl Van Vechten, and others to Mabel Dodge Luhan's *Winter in Taos* (New York: Harcourt Brace, 1935).

5. Quoted from a letter to Virginia Adams [late August 1930] in *Ansel Adams: Letters and Images 1916– 1984,* ed. Mary Street Alinder and Andrea Gray Stillman (Boston: New York Graphic Society/Little, Brown, 1988), pp. 46 and 47, n. 4; and see also Weston J. Naef, afterword to *Taos Pueblo* (1977), npn. The role of Paul Strand's photographs in inspiring Adams's decision and technique is far better known than the stimulus provided by his work with Austin.

6. As Stineman, *Mary Austin,* p. 198, notes, Adams later expressed his appreciation of another Austin work, *The Land of Little Rain* (Boston: Houghton Mifflin, 1903), by illustrating excerpts from its text in a special edition (Boston : Riverside Press/Houghton Mifflin, 1950). See also Adams, "Notes on Mary Austin," *Mary Hunter Austin: A Centennial Booklet* (Independence, Calif.: Mary Austin Home, 1968), p. 7.

54. *Edward Weston*

"LAWRENCE IN MEXICO ..," 1930

*W*eston (1886–1958), now regarded as one of America's greatest photographers, is best known for his studies of natural forms
like peppers, vegetables, rocks, and sand dunes; his intense close-
ups often rendered them erotic abstractions. Yet throughout his career, his
earnings came chiefly from his work as a portrait photographer, first in the
Pictorialist mode, then, after 1915, in the "straight."[1] Working in Mexico
(1923–27), Weston made many of his best-known portraits, including two
of D. H. Lawrence (1885–1930) [Fig. 90]; his controversial works, mostly
banned soon after publication as obscene, might have been expected to
appeal to the photographer, given their shared passionate and sensual involvement with nature.[2] But Weston valued neither Lawrence's books (which
were favorites of Stieglitz) nor even his own portraits of him very highly.[3]
The writer, however, pronounced the photographic likenesses "good" and
offered to help the photographer in any way he could; "Tackle the world,"
added Lawrence. "Its [sic] a rather stupid bull, to be taken by the horns,
not dodged."[4] Not surprisingly, the reclusive Weston ignored this advice.
He much preferred the values of his new neighbor, Robinson Jeffers (1887–
1962); this "great poet plus," despite his far more privileged and cosmopolitan background, shared Weston's passion for the Carmel coast in general
and rocks in particular. Accordingly, the photographer enjoyed making
portraits of this writer; one became the most familiar representation of
Jeffers, another adorned a Time cover (1932).[5] Weston's astute remarks
about Lawrence, like the ones about Jeffers, are taken from entries in his
Daybooks (1923–34), one of the most engaging documents left by any
visual artist.[6]

90. Edward Weston.
'D. H. Lawrence,' 1924.

Edward Weston

With the news of the death of D. H. Lawrence, turned back the leaves of my day-book, kept the second of November, 1924, and read: "D. H. in Mexico, to a Sunday evening shortly after Lawrence, in with Luis Quintanilla [Spanish artist and poet]. My first impression a most agreeable one. He will sit to me Tuesday." With Lawrence came his wife and a Miss Brett, I was given to understand his secretary. And then, Tuesday eve: "The sitting of Lawrence this morning. A tall, slender, rather reserved individual, with reddish beard. He was amiable enough and we parted in a friendly way, but the contact was too brief to penetrate another more than superficially. No way to make a sitting! I should not have attempted it: now I lack sufficient interest to develop my films [Fig. 93]."

Further notes indicate why I did attempt and rush through the sitting on a day when we were both preoccupied. He was leaving for Oaxaca the next day, and I had a luncheon engagement—"in honor (!) of the United States Ambassador to Mexico. God knows his name; I don't —but duty calls. In preparation I trimmed the fringe from by trousers and borrowed a hat from Rafael. Now to buy a collar and I shall be ready!" So read my notes.

I wish I had cancelled my date, and spent the time with Lawrence. But evidently I was considering business before pleasure, and from the condition of my wardrobe, I must have needed business!

My memory carries more than I wrote down about Lawrence: a walk in *el bosque de Chapultepec,* the famous park,—"woods," the Mexicans call it,—Lawrence, Tina and myself,—and certain bits of conversation. His first visit to Mexico not long before had thrilled him, but now he was frankly upset, distressed,—he wished to leave the city for Oaxaca, where he might quietly write. Had Mexico changed, or was Lawrence in a highly neurotic state? Obviously the latter. His resulting book, "The Plumed Serpent," gave evidence. We read the book aloud

during a period of travel through Mexico, a five months trip, which made me see vividly and feel deeply, an itinerary which took us far away from tourist tracks. I recall one place, where the Indians had seen foreigners only once before. So I offer these notes, not as literary criticism, but as my intense reactions, against Lawrence's.

"Despite its entire lack of humor, we were at times convulsed with laughter. * * "

"Besides he makes inaccurate or misleading statements. His chapter on the bull fight is full of absurdities. * * "

"Lawrence tries, it is evident, to bolster up his symbolism by indicating the customs of one locality as representative of all Mexico. I found no market where the Indians 'never asked you to buy,'—they are usually clamorously insistent. Nor do 'the women always hold onto their water jars'—as he points out—'to show their lack of poise.' More often they walk free-handed with regal bearing. Throughout the book, apparently trivial inaccuracies persist, and form a wrong or one-sided impression of Mexico. Lawrence was bewildered, he was frightened, but he over-dramatized his fear. There are fine descriptive passages, intelligent analyses, accurate prophecy, but withal a padding of tiresome allegory * * * a book on Mexico which could have been written only by a neurotic Anglo-Saxon."

Returning to Mexico City we found the artists and writers there, all laughing over "The Plumed Serpent." Covarrubias cartooned Lawrence at his desk, writing, triple outlines around him to indicate shaking with fear!

But overlooking inaccuracies, the book was the emotional reaction of a sick man, one might say of a dying man, so he cannot be criticized by one seeing the land in a less hysterical condition: indeed it may have more value as a piece of writing because of his intensity. And then,—

is there an Anglo-Saxon, even in normal health, who has looked out on the passing Mexican landscape from his Pullman berth at night, without a feeling of awe! Something mysterious there, never to be fully understood by another race. Maybe the old gods *do* still rule!

Of one thing I feel sure: Lawrence had no plastic sense. This reaction I got at once, as I showed him various drawings, photographs, etc., verified later by his remarks in "Plumed Serpent" *re* the great frescoes of Diego Rivera. So I can well imagine his recent venture in painting must be a carrying on of his literary viewpoint in paint. However, I am only surmising.

Lawrence wrote a kindly, sympathetic letter from Oaxaca, thanking me for his proofs, the best he had ever had, offering to help me in every possible way with publishers, giving suggestions for business, admitting that he could not apply them himself. Nor could I!

In Oaxaca, at Hotel Francia, I noted Lawrence's name registered. I decided to call on Padre Ricardo, an English padre with whom he spent some time. But, like a hint to us of that which followed in the religious-civil war, the padre had been arrested and deported to Mexico City the night before by the military. The neighbors spoke in hushed voices, but with flashing eyes; his servant we found in tears. He had been well loved.

I did not meet Lawrence again.

1. See Theodore E. Stebbins, Jr., *Weston's Westons: Portraits and Nudes* (Boston: Museum of Fine Arts, [1989]), especially pp. 10–26, for an overview of Weston's portraits, and *The Daybooks of Edward Weston,* ed. Nancy Newhall (Millerton, N.Y.: Aperture, 1973; 1991), vol. 2, p. 161 (May 19, 1930), for Weston's general assessment of them. See also the Neruda selection below for more about Weston and Tina Modotti, one of his earlier favorite subjects.

2. Weston's focus on nature made him a natural choice to illustrate the Limited Editions Club publication of Whitman's *Leaves of Grass* (New York, 1942). See Richard Ehrlich's introduction to the slightly revised reprint (London: Paddington Press, 1976), pp. iii–viii, and Alan Trachtenberg, "Edward Weston's America: The *Leaves of Grass* Project," in *EW 100: Centennial Essays in Honor of Edward Weston [Untitled 41],* ed. Peter C. Bunnell et al. (Carmel, Calif.: Friends of Photography, 1986), pp. 103–15.

3. According to Haines, *The Inner Eye of Alfred Stieglitz,* pp. 101–3 and 121, Stieglitz wrote to praise Lawrence for his controversial *Studies in Classic American Literature* (1923) and "positively venerated" *Lady Chatterly's Lover* (1928), feeling that it was "one of the grandest that had ever been written, a sort of Bible, on a par with Goethe and Shakespeare." Lawrence approached Stieglitz about possibly exhibiting his paintings, but both had doubts, given the censorship furor that by then inevitably accompanied any of his work, verbal or visual. See also Weston, *Daybooks,* vol. 1, p. 247, who writes on March 2, 1932: "I am not at all proud of the Lawrence portrait. I certainly did a poor technical job that day." See also David Ellis, "Images of D. H. Lawrence: On the Uses of Photographs in Biography," in *The Portrait in Photography,* ed. Clarke, pp. 155–72.

4. See *The Letters of D. H. Lawrence,* ed. James T. Boulton and Lindeth Vasey (Cambridge: Cambridge University Press, 1989), vol. 5: letter to Edward McDonald, November 2, 1924, pp. 175–76 and n. 1, and letter to Weston [December 19, 1924], pp. 185–86.

5. For Weston's portraits of Jeffers, see Stebbins, *Weston's Westons,* pp. 22–23 and Plate 16, which includes reproductions of his 1929 and 1933 portraits; and *Time* 19, no. 11 (April 4, 1932), reproduced in *Edward Weston Omnibus,* ed. Beaumont Newhall and Amy Conger (Salt Lake City: Peregrine Smith Books, 1984), following p. 98, Fig. 15. See also Jeffers's prefatory tribute to Weston in *Edward Weston: Fifty Photographs,* ed. Merle Armitage (New York: Duell Sloan & Pearce, 1947), pp. 7–10; Una Jeffers's tribute in the *Carmel Cymbal* (April 17, 1935): 11; and the Jeffers family snapshots in the HRHRC. See also David Brower, ed. *Not Man Apart: Lines from Robinson Jeffers, Photographs of the Big Sur Coast* (San Francisco: Sierra Club, 1965); Ansel Adams's responses to Jeffers and his poetry in *An Autobiography,* pp. 84–87 and 141; Minor White's 1953 photographs of a dramatic production of Jeffers's poem, "Dear Judas" (1929), in *Mirrors Messages Manifestations* (New York: Aperture, 1969), pp. 84–90; and Kenneth Rexroth, "The Objectivism of Edward Weston, An Attempt at a Functional Definition of the Art of the Camera," MS at the CCP [AG: Edward Weston: 15/29].

6. See Weston, *Daybooks,* ed. Newhall: on Lawrence, see vol. 1: pp. 101–3, 120, 159, 181, and 191; vol. 2: pp. 198, 247, 249, and 269; and on Jeffers, see vol. 2: pp. 113, 116, 123–25, 161–63, 252, 258, 272, and 274.

55. *Henry Miller*

FROM *Tropic of Cancer*, 1934

*M*iller (1891–1980), once legendary for his frank treatment of sex in his largely autobiographical fiction, lived in Paris for a decade (1930–40). There he met Brassaï (1899–1984), another expatriate artist who, inspired by a fellow Hungarian, André Kertész, had become a photographer. He later became Miller's guide through the "secret" world of his Paris de Nuit (1933).[1] Brassaï's trademark scenes of nightclubs and brothels functioned as figurative "illustrations" for Miller's writing, teaching him to see freshly, with "no need to distort or deform, no need to lie or preach."[2] The writer expressed his appreciation by including Brassaï, thinly disguised as "the photographer" [Fig. 91], in his own first published book, Tropic of Cancer (1934); and, after returning to America, he provided introductions to many of Brassaï's postwar works.[3] The two friends—along with Lawrence Durrell (1911–90)—eventually helped legitimize the demi-monde as an artistic rather than a pornographic subject.[4] They stayed in touch, though Brassaï's memoirs about Miller cooled their long friendship. "Et surtout ne lisez pas la biographie que Brassaï a écrit sur moi!" the writer warned a friend, without specifying his objections. "C'est terrible."[5]

91. Brassaï. 'Self-portrait,'
1932. Copyright Gilbert
Brassaï.

FROM *Tropic of Cancer*

Then one day I fell in with a photographer [Fig. 91]; he was making a collection of the slimy joints of Paris for some degenerate in Munich. He wanted to know if I would pose for him with my pants down, and in other ways. I thought of those skinny little runts, who look like bellhops and messenger boys, that one sees on pornographic post-cards in little book-shop windows occasionally, the mysterious phantoms who inhabit the Rue de la Lune and other malodorous quarters of the city. I didn't like very much the idea of advertising my physog in the company of these élite. But, since I was assured that the photographs were for a strictly private collection, and since

it was destined for Munich, I gave my consent. When you're not in your home town you can permit yourself little liberties, particularly for such a worthy motive as earning your daily bread. After all, I hadn't been so squeamish, come to think of it, even in New York. There were nights when I was so damned desperate, back there, that I had to go out right in my own neighborhood and panhandle.

We didn't go to the show places familiar to the tourist, but to the little joints where the atmosphere was more congenial, where we could play a game of cards in the afternoon before getting down to work. He was a good companion, the photographer. He knew the city inside out, the walls particularly; he talked to me about Goethe often, and the days of the Hohenstaufen [old German ruling family], and the massacre of the Jews during the reign of the Black Death. Interesting subjects, and always related in some obscure way to the things he was doing. He had ideas for scenarios too, astounding ideas, but nobody had the courage to execute them. The sight of a horse split-open like a saloon door, would inspire him to talk of Dante or Leonardo da Vinci or Rembrandt; from the slaughterhouse at Villette he would jump into a cab and rush me to the Trocadéro Museum in order to point out a skull or a mummy that had fascinated him. We explored the 5th, the 13th, the 19th and the 20th *arrondissements* thoroughly. Our favorite resting places were lugubrious little spots such as the Place Nationale, Place des Peupliers, Place Contrescarpe, Place Paul-Verlaine. Many of these places were already familiar to me, but all of them I now saw in a different light owing to the rare flavor of his conversation. If to-day I should happen to stroll down the Rue du Château-des-Rentiers, for example, inhaling the fetid stench of the hospital beds with which the 13th *arrondissement* reeks, my nostrils would undoubtedly expand with pleasure, because, compounded with that odor of stale piss and formaldehyde, there would be the odors of our imaginative voyages through the charnel house of Europe which the Black Death had created. [pp. 184–85]

1. See Brassaï, preface to *The Secret Paris of the 30's*, trans. Richard Miller (New York: Pantheon, 1976), npn; cf. the better known and more decorous *Paris de Nuit* [1933] (New York: Pantheon, 1987). For a joint recollection of their first meeting, see Brassaï, *Henry Miller Grandeur Nature* (Paris: Gallimard, 1975), pp. 7–9. Their correspondence is at the Henry Miller Archives.

2. Miller, "The Eye of Paris" (1933), in *The Wisdom of the Heart* (Norfolk, Conn.: New Directions, 1941), pp. 173–74 and 179.

3. See Miller: "L'Oeil de Paris" (1933), *Brassaï* (Paris: Éditions Neuf, 1952), [pp. 1–8]; introduction to Brassaï, *Histoire de Marie* (Paris: Éditions du Point de Jour, 1949), pp. 7–16; and preface to Brassaï, *Picasso and Company* (New York: Doubleday, 1966), pp. ix–xii. See also Brassaï, *Texte d'Henry Miller* (Paris: Éditions Neuf, 1952), and Miller, *Quiet Days in Clichy* (Paris: Olympia Press, 1956), with photographs by Brassaï.

4. See Durrell, introduction to *Brassaï* (New York: MOMA, 1968), pp. 9–15; Brassaï, Miller, Durrell, and Bissière, *Hans Reichel* (Paris: Éditions Jeanne Bucher, [1962]; Krementz's photograph of Miller and Durrell in bed [1974] in *The Writer's Image*, npn; and the Durrell selection below.

5. Miller, quoted in letter to Joseph Delteil, February 19, 1976, in *Correspondance Privée, 1935–1978*, ed. F.-J. Temple (Paris: Pierre Belfond, 1980), p. 168 and n. 7, referring to Brassaï's *Henry Miller Grandeur Nature* (1975), which was followed by his *Henry Miller, Rocher Heureux* (Paris: Gallimard, [1978]). See also Brassaï's earlier pieces on Miller: "Henry Miller in Paris, 1932," *International Henry Miller Letter* (December 1962): 7; "Cour Miller" and "Com Miller, Em Cannes," in Esdras Do Nascimento, *O Mundo de Henry Miller* (Rio de Janeiro: Graffica Record Editoria, 1969), pp. 87–91; and "Inédit. Paris en 1930 Vu," *Photo* 8 (July 1969): 24–33 and 70. For relevant photographs of the pair, see Miller, *My Life and Times* (Chicago: Playboy Press, [1971]), pp. 171–72 and 178, for ones of the two old friends in Brassaï's studio as well as one of Picasso and Brassaï together that Miller had "insisted" on because of their "amazing resemblance." For portraits of Miller only, see the ones by Man Ray (1945) in *Man Ray Photographs*, p. 247, fig. 334; by Freund in *The World in My Camera*, following p. 212 and pp. 238–39; by Cartier-Bresson in *Photoportraits*, p. 218; and see also William Webb's *Henry and Friends—The California Years: 1946–1977* (Santa Barbara, Calif.: Capra Press, 1991), which includes a paragraph about "Brassaï—The Eye of Paris" and a 1973 photograph of him, pp. 92–93. Kim Sichel, in conversation with the editor, August 27, 1992, notes that Brassaï was also friendly with the playwright Samuel Beckett, who lived around the corner in Paris.

56. Langston Hughes

"PICTURES MORE THAN PICTURES: THE WORK OF MANUEL BRAVO AND CARTIER-BRESSON," 1935

Hughes (1902–67) [Fig. 92], whose racially and socially conscious writings during the 1920's Harlem Renaissance made him a major literary figure, enjoyed many personal ties with photographers that also proved professionally productive. Carl Van Vechten, the writer who later became a photographer, continuously promoted Hughes's career after they met in 1924.[1] *Another lifelong friend proved to be Henri Cartier-Bresson, a Mexico City roommate in 1935, who invited Hughes to write this introduction for an exhibition of his pictures and those of another young local artist, Manuel Alvarez Bravo [Fig. 143], doubtless persuading the writer that his sensitivity to form outweighed his ignorance of photography.*[2] *Two decades later, Cartier-Bresson's American publishers agreed to publish some of Roy DeCarava's spirited Harlem photographs if Hughes contributed a text.*[3] *The acclaimed result,* The Sweet Flypaper of Life, *was published in 1955. The same year Hughes agreed to supply the text for a pictorial history of blacks in America being compiled by Michael Meltzer, which, despite many initial rejections by publishers, went through five editions; Hughes later worked with Meltzer on a pictorial history of blacks in American entertainment.*[4] *It is interesting to compare Hughes's connections with photographers with that of his fellow writer Jean Toomer (1894–1967), who, despite his closeness to the supportive Stieglitz circle, never followed up on the success of his first work,* Cane *(1923), an innovative portrayal of southern black life.*[5]

"PICTURES MORE THAN PICTURES: THE WORK OF
MANUEL BRAVO AND CARTIER-BRESSON"

A picture, to be an interesting picture, must be more than a picture, otherwise it is only a reproduction of an object, and not an object of value in itself.

Anyday, one can walk down the street in a big city and see a thousand people. Any photographer can photograph these people—but very few photographers can make their prints not only reproductions of the people taken, but a comment upon them—or mere, a comment upon their lives—or more still, a comment upon the social order that creates these lives.

It is the same with objects as with people. A wall can be merely a wall—but in some of Henri Cartier-Bresson's photographs the walls are painfully human, and live and talk about themselves. There is that vulgar wall behind the man in the brass bed; that great lonesome wall of broken paint and plaster along which some child is wandering; there is a huge sun-bright wall of a prison or an apartment house with a boy who is like a shadow at its base. In other photos there are the tumble-down walls of demolished dwellings in Spain where children are playing in a tumble-down world; in others, the worn-bright gestures of prostitutes against doors that are also walls.

There is the clash of sun and shadow, like modern music, in a Cartier-Bresson picture.

In Bravo, the sun is a quiet veil making the shadows like velvet. The shadows are endlessly deep and full, holding more—and more there—and more. Whereas the sun in a Bravo photo almost always has a sense of humor, one cannot be sure about the shadows.

In a cheap little restaurant where the stools are chained to the counter—the whole open to the street—Bravo's camera shows the stools in the sunshine and a row of Charlie Chaplin feet belonging to the ragged customers dining there. The iron curtain is partly down, and the heads of the customers are in shadow—no one can laugh about the feet!

That is what I mean concerning Bravo.

He photographs the doorways of a casket shop with the adult coffins inside in the shadows. Outside on display in the sun is a child's coffin for such a little death.

He photographs shop windows on fashionable streets, catching through the glass the fine things exhibited therein, and further back things less clear, and behind them all the interior of the shop too deep in shadow for one to see if life is equally fine there.

In one of the most beautiful of Bravo's prints, out of the shadows of a canvas covering dash four motionless wooden horses—part of a merry-go-round—to break your heart.

Manuel Alvarez Bravo, Mexican, and Henri Cartier-Bresson of Paris have succeeded in making pictures that are more than pictures—even when they are less.

Mexico,
March 6, 1935

1. See the letters to Hughes throughout the *Letters of Carl Van Vechten,* ed. Bruce Kellner (New Haven, Conn.: Yale University Press, 1987), which reproduces one of his 1936 portraits of Hughes on p. 78; other relevant photographs and MSS are at the Beinecke. See also the Van Vechten selection below.

2. See Hughes, *I Wonder as I Wander: An Autobiographical Journey* (New York: Hill & Wang, 1956), pp. 293–95, and Hughes's dedication to Cartier-Bresson in *Simple's Uncle Sam* (New York: Hill & Wang, 1965). See also Arnold Rampersad, *The Life of Langston Hughes* (New York: Oxford University Press, 1986), vol. 1, pp. 303–4, 342, 361, and 363; vol. 2, pp. 126, 266, 295, 323, 351, 407; see also p. 294, which reproduces Cartier-Bresson's cover portrait of Hughes for the *Selected Poems of Langston Hughes* (New York: Knopf, 1959). For more on Cartier-Bresson, Alvarez Bravo, and their photographs of this period, see Peter Galassi, *Henri Cartier-Bresson: The Early Work* (New York: Museum of Modern Art, 1987); *Revelaciones: The Art of Manuel Alvarez Bravo* (San Diego: Museum of Photographic Art, 1990), which reproduce the photographs Hughes describes here; and the Sartre and Paz selections below; the Alvarez Bravo, reproduced in the Paz selection, fig. 143, was also probably shown in this 1935 exhibition.

3. See DeCarava and Hughes, *The Sweet Flypaper of Life* [1955] (Washington, D.C.: Howard University Press, 1988), and see the Minor White and DeCarava selection below for further details on this collaboration.

4. See Hughes and Meltzer, *A Pictorial History of the Negro in America* (New York: Crown, 1956, 1963, 1968, 1973, 1983), and *Black Magic: A Pictorial History of the Negro in American Entertainment* (Englewood Cliffs, N.J.: Prentice-Hall, 1967), as well as Rampersad, *The Life of Langston Hughes,* vol. 2, pp. 247–48 and 258.

5. See Cynthia Kerman and Richard Eldridge, *The Lives of Jean Toomer: A Hunger for Wholeness* (Baton Rouge: Louisiana State University Press, [1987]), pp. 130, 141, 213–15, 299, and 342; Haines, *The Inner Eye of Alfred Stieglitz,* pp. 9–10, and 121; Eisler, *O'Keeffe and Stieglitz,* pp. 340–41, 345–46, and 444–50; letters to or about Toomer in Cowart and Hamilton, *Georgia O'Keeffe: Arts and Letters,* ed. Greenough, nos. 66–70, pp. 214–20 and 285, nn. 66–70; Toomer, "The Hill," a tribute to Stieglitz, in Frank, ed., *America and Alfred Stieglitz,* pp. 143–46; and Toomer, "A Double Portrait" and letters and excerpts of letters to O'Keeffe and Stieglitz, January 13, 1924–October 21, 1936, in *A Jean Toomer Reader: Selected Unpublished Writings,* ed. Frederick L. Rusch (New York: Oxford University Press, 1993), pp. 276–82.

57. *Louis Aragon*

"JOHN HEARTFIELD AND
REVOLUTIONARY BEAUTY," 1935

Aragon (1897–1983), a poet, novelist, essayist, journalist, editor, and a leading figure in the Dada movement, was, with André Breton, one of the founders of Surrealism (c. 1919). In this capacity, he was an important influence on Man Ray, Berenice Abbott, Lee Miller, and other young gifted photographers between the world wars.[1] After breaking from the Surrealists in 1931 over his increasingly revolutionary politics, Aragon encouraged artists like John Heartfield (1891–1968), a founding Berlin Dadaist, fellow Communist, and designer.[2] Heartfield's powerful photomontages, whether for jacket designs for his brother's socialist publishing firm, books such as Kurt Tucholsky's Deutschland, Deutschland über Alles *(1929), and leftist journals such as* AIZ, *combined aesthetic principles with political realism and commitment (as had those of Alexander Rodchenko in Moscow).[3] Indeed, the effectiveness of Heartfield's anti-Nazi satires [Figs. 93, 94] compelled their creator to flee Germany (1933) and Prague (1938) for London, where he designed books.[4] Meanwhile, as editor-in-chief (1937–39) of the Communist daily newspaper* Ce Soir, *Aragon supervised the work of the young staff photographers Henri Cartier-Bresson, Robert Capa, and David Seymour, whose association resulted in their postwar founding of the Magnum photo agency. During the Second World War, Aragon began writing poetry, including "Le Paysan de Paris Chante" (1941), a "resistance" piece inspired by photographs of Paris,[5] and afterwards pursued his aesthetic and political activities. Heartfield returned to Germany in 1950, where Bertolt Brecht, a longtime acquaintance who considered his photomontages "classics," invited him to design his theatre productions and nominated him to the German Academy of Arts.[6]*

. . . A negation of dada, an attempt to synthesize the dadaist negation and the poetic heritage of humanity in surrealism—art under the Treaty of Versailles has the disordered appearances of madness. It is not the result of a small group's will, it is the maddened product of a society in which irreconcilable opposing forces are clashing.

Because of this, the lessons of a man moved by events to one of the points of conflict among these rival forces, where a minimum of play was given to the artist and the individual, are all the more precious today. I am speaking of John Heartfield, for whom the entire destiny of art was brought into serious question by the German revolution in the aftermath of the war and whose entire *oeuvre* was destroyed by Hitlerian fascism in 1933.

John Heartfield was one of those who expressed the strongest doubts about painting, especially its technical aspects. He is one of those who recognized the historical evanescence of that kind of oil painting which has only been in existence for a few centuries and seems to us to be painting *per se,* but which can abdicate at any time to a new technique more consistent with contemporary life, with mankind today. As we know, cubism was a reaction on the part of painters to the invention of photography. Photography and cinema made struggling for exact *likeness* childish. Artists drew forth from these new mechanical accomplishments a conception of art which led some to attack naturalism and others to attempt a new definition of reality. With Léger, this led to decorative art; with Mondrian, to abstraction; with Picabia, to the organization of *soirées* on the Riviera.

But near the end of the war, several artists in Germany (Grosz, Heartfield, Ernst), in a spirit very different from the cubists who pasted a newspaper or a matchbox in the middle of a painting in order to give themselves a foothold in reality, came to use in their critique of painting this same photography which had challenged painting to new poetic ends—but relieved of its mimetic function and used for its own expressionistic purpose. Thus was born the *collage,* which was different from the *pasted papers* of cubism, where the thing pasted sometimes mingled with what was painted or drawn, and where the pasted piece could be a photograph as well as a drawing or a figure from a catalogue—in short, a *plastic snapshot* of some sort.

In the face of the decomposition of appearances in modern art, a new and living taste for reality was being reborn under the guise of a simple game. What provided the strength and attraction of the new collage was this sort of verisimilitude borrowed from the figuration of real objects, including even their photographs. The artist was playing with reality's fire. He was becoming once more the master of those appearances in which the technique of oil had little by little lost and drowned him. He was creating modern monsters; he paraded them at will in a bedroom, on Swiss mountains, at the bottom of seas. The dizziness spoken of by Rimbaud overtook him,[7] and the *salon at the bottom of a lake* of A Season in Hell was becoming the prevailing climate of painting.

Beyond this point of expression, beyond this freedom taken by the painter with the real world, what is there? "This happened," said Rimbaud: "Today I know how to salute beauty."[8] What did he mean by that? We can still speak about it at length. The men whom we speak of have met different fates. Max Ernst still prides himself today on not having left that lakeside setting where, with all the imagination one could want, he still endlessly combines the elements of a poetry which is an end in itself. We know what happened to George Grosz. Today we will concentrate more specifically on the fate of John Heartfield, whose show presented by the AEAR at the Maison de la Culture gives us something to dream of and to clench our fists about.

John Heartfield *today knows how to salute beauty.* While he was playing with the fire of appearances, reality blazed around him. In our benighted country, few know that there have been soviets in Germany. Too few know what a magnificent and splendid upheaval of reality were those days of November 1918, when the German people—not the French armies—put an end to the war in Hamburg, in Dresden, in Munich, in Berlin. Ah, if only it had been but a matter of some feeble miracle of a salon at the bottom of a lake when, on their machine-gun cars, the tall blond sailors of the North and Baltic seas were going through the streets with their flags. Then the men in suits from Paris and Potsdam got together; Clemenceau gave back to the social democrat Noske the machine guns which later armed the groups of future Hitlerians. Karl and Rosa fell.[9] The generals rewaxed their mustaches. The social peace bloomed black, red, and gold on the gaping charnel houses of the working class.

John Heartfield wasn't playing anymore. The pieces of photos he had arranged in the past for amazement and pleasure, now under his fingers began to *signify*. The social *forbidden* was quickly substituted for the poetic *forbidden*; or, more exactly, under the pressure of events and in the course of the struggle in which the artist found himself, these two forbiddens merged: there was poetry, but *there was no more poetry that was not also Revolution*. Burning years during which the Revolution—defeated here, triumphant there—rose in the same fashion from the extreme point of art: Mayakovsky in Russia and Heartfield in Germany. And these two poets—one under the dictatorship of the Proletariat and the other under the dictatorship of Capital, beginning from what is most incomprehensible in poetry and from the last form of art-for-the-few, turned out to be the creators of the most striking contemporary examples of what art for the masses, that magnificent and incomprehensible decried thing, can be.

Like Mayakovsky declaiming his poems through loudspeakers for tens of thousands, like Mayakovsky whose voice rolls from the Pacific Ocean to the Black Sea, from the forest of Karelia to the deserts of Central Asia, the thought and art of John Heartfield have known this glory and grandeur to be the knife that penetrates all hearts. It is a known fact that it was from a poster depicting a clenched fist which Heartfield did for the French Communist Party

that the German proletariat took the gesture of the "Red Front." It was this same fist with which the dockworkers of Norway saluted the passage of the *Chelyuskin,* with which Paris accompanied those who died on 9 February,[10] and with which only yesterday at the movies I saw a huge crowd of Mexican strikers frame the swastika-emblazoned image of Hitler. It is one of John Heartfield's constant concerns that the originals of his photomontages be exhibited adjacent to the pages of *A-I-Z,* the illustrated German magazine where they are reproduced, because, he says, it must be shown how these photomontages penetrate the masses.

That is why during the existence of the German "democracy" under the Weimar constitution the German bourgeoisie prosecuted John Heartfield in the courts. And not just once. For a poster, a book cover, for lack of respect to the iron cross or to Emil Ludwig[11] ... When it liquidated "democracy," its fascism did more than just prosecute: twenty years of John Heartfield's work was destroyed by the Nazis.

In exile in Prague, they continued to hunt him down. At the request of the German embassy the Czechoslovakian police closed down the same show which is presently on the walls of the Maison de la Culture and which constitutes everything done by the artist after Hitler's coming to power—this show in which we can recognize classic images like that admirable series of the Leipzig trial which future history books will never be able to do without when retelling the epic of Dimitrov.[12] (Speaking to Soviet writers, Dimitrov was astonished recently to find that literature has neither studied nor used "this formidable capital of revolutionary thought and practice" that is the Leipzig trial.) Among painters, Heartfield is at least one man whom this reproach does not touch and who is the prototype of the anti-fascist artist. Not since *Les Châtiments* and *Napoléon le Petit*[13] has a single poet reached these heights where we find Heartfield, face to face with Hitler. For, in painting as well as in drawing, precedents are lacking—Goya, Wirtz, and Daumier notwithstanding.

John Heartfield *today knows how to salute beauty.* He knows how to create those images

93. John Heartfield. 'The Meaning of Geneva—Where Capital Lives, There Can Be No Peace.' [The speared dove of peace before the League of Nations building.] Cover of *AIZ* (November 27, 1932).

Louis Aragon 283

which are the very beauty of our age, for they represent the cry of the masses—the people's struggle against the brown hangman whose trachea is crammed with gold coins. He knows how to create realistic images of our life and struggle which are poignant and moving for millions of people who themselves are a part of this life and struggle. His art is art in Lenin's sense, because it is a weapon in the revolutionary struggle of the Proletariat.

John Heartfield *today knows how to salute beauty.* Because he speaks for the countless oppressed people throughout the world without lowering for a moment the magnificent tone of his voice, without debasing the majestic poetry of his colossal imagination. *Without diminishing the quality of his work.* Master of a technique of his own invention—a technique which uses for its palette the whole range of impressions from the world of actuality—never imposing a rein on his spirit, blending appearances at will, he has no guide other than dialectical materialism, none but the reality of the historical process which he translates into black and white with the rage of combat.

John Heartfield *today knows how to salute beauty.* And if the visitor who goes through the show of the Maison de la Culture finds the ancient shadow of dada in these photomontages of the last few years—in this Schacht[14] with a gigantic collar, in this cow which is cutting itself up with a knife, in this anti-Semitic dialogue of two birds—let him stop at this dove stuck on a bayonet in front of the Palace of the League of Nations [Fig. 93], or at this Nazi Christmas tree whose branches are distorted to form swastikas [Fig. 94]; he will find not only the heritage of dada but also that of centuries of painting. There are still lifes by Heartfield, such as this scale tipped by the weight of a revolver, or von Papen's wallet,[15] and this scaffolding of Hitlerian cards, which inevitably make me think of Chardin. Here, with only scissors and paste, the artist has surpassed the

O Tannenbaum im deutschen Raum, wie krumm sind deine Ästel

Dem christlichen Tannenbaum wird laut Erlaß des Reichsernährungsministers Darré ab Weihnachten 1934 als artfremdem Eindringling auf deutschem Boden die Fortpflanzung verboten. Erlaubt ist künftighin nur noch der in Walhall gezüchtete braune „Einheitstannenbaum · DRGM".

best endeavors of modern art, with the cubists, who are on that lost pathway of quotidian mystery. Simple objects, like apples for Cézanne in earlier days, and the guitar for Picasso. But here there is also *meaning,* and meaning hasn't disfigured beauty.

John Heartfield today knows how to salute beauty.

94. John Heartfield. 'O Christmas Tree in Germany—How Crooked Are Your Branches!' Cover of *AIZ* (December 27, 1934).

1. See portraits of Aragon in *Man Ray's Paris Portraits: 1921–1939*, ed. Timothy Baum (Washington, D.C.: Middendorf Gallery, [1990]), fig. 8 (1922); Freund, *Freund, Photographer*, p. 122, Plate 117 (1939), and Cartier-Bresson, *Photoportraits*, fig. 229.

2. Aragon was one of many French leftist admirers of Heartfield, who had expressed his enduring anti-war, pro-English sympathies by changing his name from Helmut Herzfeld in 1915. Aragon's lecture here was delivered at a public symposium accompanying an exhibition of all Heartfield's photomontages since 1933, held in Paris on May 2, 1935, to support the courageous art he continued to produce despite personal danger.

3. For example, see Heartfield's book jackets in Peter Pachnicke and Klaus Honnef, eds., *John Heartfield* (New York: Abrams, 1991), for German editions of works by leftist writers such as John Dos Passos, p. 101; Mayakovsky, p. 249; Upton Sinclair, pp. 94, 96, 98–99, 107, 120–21, 275, 293, and 296; and Jack London, exhibited but unidentified under the name of the editor, Franz Jung, p. 328, no. 172, showcase 4; and his jacket for Wright cited below, p. 381, n. 1. See also Tucholsky, *Deutschland, Deutschland über Alles*, trans. Anne Halley, with photographs assembled by Heartfield (Amherst: University of Massachusetts Press, 1972). Tucholsky, in *Gesammelte Werke in 10 Bänden*, ed. Mary Gerold-Tucholsky and Fritz J. Raddetz (Reinbek bei Hamburg: Rowohlt, 1975), vol. 10, p. 24, partly quoted in Pachnicke and Honnef, eds., *John Heartfield*, p. 110, thought highly of Heartfield; writing under one of his pseudonyms, Peter Panther, he declared: "If I wasn't Peter Panther, I'd like to be a dust-jacket in the Malik Press [Heartfield's brother's publishing firm]" and more seriously asserted that he "is really one of the small wonders of the world. . . . I've had one of his photomontages framed and almost all of them are worth hanging onto." This comment, and its source, were called to the editor's attention by Leo Lensing in communications between January 15 and 20, 1993. See also P. V. Brady, "The Writer and the Camera: Kurt Tucholsky's Experiments in Partnership," *Modern Language Review* 74 (1979): 856–70; and H. W. Zehnhoff, "Satirical Techniques of John Heartfield and Kurt Tucholsky in *Deutschland, Deutschland über Alles*," *Word and Image* 4, no. 1 (January–March 1988): 157–62. For more about Rodchenko, see the selection about Mayakovsky (whose sister Aragon married) above.

4. See Heartfield, *The Photomontages of the Nazi Period* (New York: Universe Books, 1977); Pachnicke and Honnef, eds., *John Heartfield*; and David Evans, *John Heartfield: AIZ/VI [Arbeiter-Illustrierte Zeitung Volks Illustrierte] 1930–38*, ed. Anna Lundgren (New York: Kent Gallery, 1992). See also Aragon, "Painting and Reality" (1936), trans. James Johnson Sweeney, in *Photography in the Modern Era: European Documents and Critical Writings, 1913–1940*, ed. Christopher Phillips (New York: Metropolitan Museum of Art/Aperture, [1989]), p. 74, cf. Paul Strand's letter about Aragon's "Painting and Reality," *Art Front* 3 (February 1937): 18.

5. This poem is translated and quoted in Braive, *The Era of the Photograph*, p. 217.

6. On Heartfield's work for Brecht, see Pachnicke and Honnef, eds., *John Heartfield*, pp. 27, 232–35, 250, and 253, and in *Photomontages*, pp. facing title page, pp. 132 and 139, and see also Aragon, "Farewell to Capa," in Cornell Capa and Bhupendra Karia, eds., *Robert Capa, 1913–1955* (New York: Grossman, 1974), p. 121.

The subsequent notes accompany this text in Photography in the Modern Era, *ed. Phillips.*

7. In the 1870's the poet Rimbaud advocated hallucination and the systematic derangement of the senses as methods for achieving the renewal of poetic imagery.

8. The reference is to a line from Rimbaud's "Une Saison en enfer" (1873).

9. Gustav Noske (1868–1946) was the German Minister of the Interior responsible for the bloody suppression of the 1919 Spartacist uprising in Berlin. Karl Liebknecht and Rosa Luxemburg, leaders of the revolutionary Spartacist group, were summarily executed after their arrest during that insurrection.

10. On February 6, 1934, right-wing groups rioted in the heart of Paris, and on February 9 and 12 large counter-rallies were staged by the parties of the left. The events galvanized and unified the left, eventually leading to the formation of the Popular Front.

11. Emil Ludwig (1881–1948) was a prolific German author of popular biographies of great men such as Napoleon. Bismarck and Kaiser Wilhelm II.

12. Georgi Dimitrov (1882–1949), a Bulgarian Communist, was among those accused of responsibility for the Berlin Reichstag fire of 1933. He was put on trial in Leipzig in the fall of that year. His spirited defense of himself and his fellow defendants against the charges brought by Nazi leaders like Goebbels and Göring attracted international attention.

13. In December 1851, following Louis Napoleon's coup d'état, the French poet Victor Hugo went into political exile in Brussels. In 1852 he published *Napoléon le Petit*, a pamphlet excoriating the would-be emperor. In 1853 he brought out a collection of biting, sarcastic poems, *Châtiments*, in response to Louis Napoleon's proclamation of the Second Empire.

14. Hjalmar Schacht (1877–1970), a German financier, was president of the Reichsbank under Hitler, 1933–39.

15. Franz von Papen (1879–1969), a German diplomat and conservative political figure, was chancellor of Germany in the year before Hitler's appointment to that office in 1933.

58. William Faulkner

FROM *Absalom, Absalom!*, 1936

Photographs intrigued the young Faulkner (1897–1962). The southern writer particularly valued their ability to create a legendary identity, to judge by the series of portraits he commissioned in 1928 of himself wearing various uniforms and insignia (not earned) during his brief service in the First World War.[1] He also became an amateur photographer about this time and was fascinated by special cameras.[2] In his early writing, Faulkner's use of fictional pictures continued to reflect his interest in identity and portraits, such as the deceptive photograph that wreaks havoc in the supernatural short story "The Leg" (1925) or the "Rogue's Gallery" of family portraits that Horace Benlow carefully studies in the first version of Sanctuary (1929).[3] The photograph providing a key to the plot in "Evangeline" (1931) was joined by others with various meanings when that unpublished short story evolved into Absalom, Absalom! (1936); their ability to arouse and fuel emotions, especially desire, is compellingly recognized here too, this time by a spinster, Rosa Coldfield.[4] Faulkner's use of fictional photographs diminished in his subsequent works, about the same time that he himself gave up serious photography.[5] But his prose still featured framed, frozen "photographic" moments, variously interpreted by each character. Even before winning the Nobel Prize in 1950, Faulkner was becoming increasingly reticent about being interviewed, perhaps still wishing to control his public image. "No photographs, no recorded documents," he vowed, wanting no "refuse" in history except his printed books."[6] But on occasion, for former colleagues like Carl Van Vechten, he apparently made an exception [Fig. 129].

FROM *Absalom, Absalom!*

Note: Thomas Sutpen (1807–69), a poor white man striving for wealth and respectability, abandons his Haitian wife and son, Charles, on learning that she is part black (1831). His later marriage to the entirely respectable Ellen Coldfield (1818–62) produces two children, Henry (1839–1910) and Judith (1841–84). In 1859, Henry befriends and Judith falls in love with Charles, unaware he is their half-brother. Sutpen forbids the marriage just before he and his sons depart to fight in the Civil War (1861). In 1865, Charles is shot by Henry, now aware of their blood relationship, to prevent the miscegenation rather than the incest that will result from the marriage. In 1909, Rosa (1845–1910), who is Ellen's unmarried sister and younger even than her niece, Judith, here recollects Charles for young Quentin Compson, the son of family friends. In 1910, Quentin, aided by his Harvard roommate from Canada, tries to understand this particularly southern family tragedy.

. . . I had never seen him (I never saw him. I never even saw him dead. I heard a name, I saw a photograph, I helped to make a grave: and that was all) though he had been in my house once, that first New Year's Day when Henry brought him from nephew duty to speak to me on their way back to school and I was not at home. Until then I had not even heard his name, did not know that he existed. Yet on the day when I went out there to stay that summer, it was as though that casual pause at my door had left some seed, some minute virulence in this cellar earth of mine quick not for love perhaps (I did not love him; how could I? I had never even heard his voice, had only Ellen's word for it that there was such a person) and quick not for the spying which you will doubtless call it, which during the past six months between that New Year's and that June gave substance to that shadow with a name emerging from Ellen's vain and garrulous folly, that shape without even a face yet because I had not even seen the photograph then, reflected in the secret and bemused gaze of a young girl: because I who had learned nothing of love, not even parent's love—that fond dear constant violation of privacy, that stultification of the burgeoning and incorrigible I which is the meed and due of all mammalian meat, became not mistress, not beloved, but more than even love; I became all polymath love's androgynous advocate.

There must have been some seed he left, to cause a child's vacant fairy-tale to come alive in that garden. Because I was not spying when I would follow her. I was not spying, though you will say I was. And even if it was spying, it was not jealousy, because I did not love him. (How could I have, when I had never seen him?) And even if I did, not as women love, as Judith loved him, or as we thought she did. If it was love (and I still say, how could it be?) it was the way that mothers love when, punishing the child she strikes not it but through it strikes the neighbor boy whom it has just whipped or been whipped by; caresses not the rewarded child but rather the nameless man or woman who gave the palm-sweated penny. But not as women love. Because I asked nothing of him, you see. And more than that: I gave him nothing, which is the sum of loving. Why, I didn't even miss him. I don't know even now if I was ever aware that I had seen nothing of his face but that photograph, that shadow, that picture in a young girl's bedroom: a picture casual and framed upon a littered dressing table yet bowered and dressed (or so I thought) with all the maiden and invisible lily roses, because even before I saw the photograph I could have recognized, nay, described, the very face. But I never saw it. I do not even know of my own knowledge that Ellen ever saw it, that Judith ever loved it, that Henry slew it: so who will dispute me when I say, Why did I not invent, create it?—And I know this: if I were God I would invent out of this seething turmoil we call progress something (a machine perhaps) which would adorn the barren mirror altars of every plain girl who breathes with such as this—which is so little since we want so little—this pictured face. It would not even need a skull behind it; almost anonymous, it would only need vague inference of some walking flesh and blood desired by someone else even if only in some shadow realm of make-believe.—A picture seen by stealth, by creeping (my childhood taught me that instead of love and it stood me in stead; in fact, if it had taught me love, love could not have stood me so) into the deserted midday room to look at it.

1. Joseph Blotner, in *Faulkner, A Biography* (New York: Random House, 1974), vol. 1, p. 232, describes his half-dozen various poses, three of which are reproduced by Judith Sensibar in "Popular Culture Invades Jefferson: Faulkner's Real and Imagined Photos of Desire," *Faulkner and Popular Culture*, ed. Doreen Fowles and Ann J. Abadie (Jackson: University of Mississippi Press, 1990), pp. 119 and 124–25. Sensibar asserts that these "trick" photographs reinforced his wartime impostures—describing himself as English and fatherless to his fellow trainees, and an active pilot and an officer to his mother—in a later version of this article, "Faulkner's Fictional Photographs: Playing with Difference," in *Out of Bounds: Male Writers and Gender(ed) Criticism,* ed. Laura Claridge and Elizabeth Langland (Amherst: University of Massachusetts Press, 1990), pp. 300–302, and 314, n. 38, as well as in her "William Faulkner: Poet to Novelist: An Imposter Becomes an Artist," in *Psychoanalytic Studies of Biography*, No. 4, ed. George Moraitis and George H. Pollock (Madison, Conn.: International Universities Press, 1987), p. 309, and n. 3.

Certainly such pictures would have reinforced any false impressions he gave his mother, who painted portraits from photographs, using one from this series, according to James Dahl, "A Faulkner Reminiscence: Conversations with Mrs. M. F. Faulkner," *JML* 3, no. 4 (April 1974): 1027 and 1030. But the local photographer, J. R. "Colonel" Cofield—and perhaps the author who "clearly enjoyed the charade"—took the 1928 sitting less seriously, as described in Cofield's "Many Faces, Many Moods," in James W. Webb and A. Wigfall Green, eds., *William Faulkner of Oxford* (Baton Rouge: Louisiana State University Press, 1965), p. 109, and in Carvel Collins, introduction to Jack Cofield, *William Faulkner: The Cofield Collection* (Oxford, Miss.: Yoknapatawpha Press, 1978), p. 56.

2. See Collins, introduction to *The Cofield Collection,* p. x, who notes that in addition to making pictures of and for Faulkner, Cofield developed his film, advised him on camera techniques, and noted that the writer worked hard to perfect his hobby, though without much success.

3. See Faulkner: "The Leg," in *Collected Stories of William Faulkner* (New York: Random House, 1950), pp. 841–42; and *Sanctuary, The Original Text,* ed. Noel Polk (New York: Random House, 1981), pp. 19 (2), 41 (2) 44 (2), 57–59, 63, 143 (2), 145, 146, 149, 167, 205 (2), 210 (1), 220 (2), and 230, cf. the 1931 revised *Sanctuary* in Faulkner, *Novels 1930–1935,* ed. Joseph Blotner and Noel Polk (New York: Library of America, 1985), pp.

227, 294, 325, 333, and 347, in which only the photograph of Horace's stepdaughter that repeatedly stimulates erotic fantasies is meaningfully retained. See also David Madden, "Photographs in the 1929 Version of Sanctuary," *Faulkner and Popular Culture,* ed. Fowles and Abadie, pp. 93–109, and Sensibar, *Out of Bounds,* pp. 307–8.

4. See Faulkner, "Evangeline," in *Uncollected Stories of William Faulkner,* ed. Joseph Blotner (New York: Random House, 1979), pp. 583–609; and *Absalom, Absalom!: The Corrected Text,* ed. Noel Polk (New York: Random House, 1986). In addition to the scene here, pp. 9, 236, and 282 mention the Sutpen family photograph ["strange, contradictory, bizarre, not quite comprehensible," according to Quentin Compson], and pp. 71, 73, 114, 121, and 271 mention the encased photograph, which Rosa assumes must be a picture of her niece, Judith, Charles's fiancée, but which portrays instead Charles's octoroon woman (his wife in "Evangeline") and their son. For further discussion of Rosa's narrative here, see Sensibar, *Out of Bounds,* pp. 302–7. To locate Faulkner's use of photography in his other works, see Jack L. Capps et al., eds., *The Faulkner Concordances* (Ann Arbor, Mich.: UMI Research Press for the Faulkner Concordances Advisory Board, 1977–), 19 vols., in the indices under "Photography" and "Photographs."

5. Cofield, "Many Faces," pp. 109–10, recalls: "In the mid-thirties, Bill was a devout camera fiend. In his rambles in Europe, he had picked up a genuine old Zeiss Camera with one of the finest German mechanisms ever made, [but found it hard to operate and his results poor]. He finally gave it up in disgust, even though cameras always did fascinate him. . . . I never took a shot that he was not at my elbow taking in the complete procedure." The mature Faulkner, perhaps having resolved his problems of identity and desire, focused his picture-taking on his young daughter. Jill Faulkner Summers, in telephone conversations with the editor, January 8 and 9, 1993, recalled that her father, using a Leica, often took pictures of family members, friends, and favorite animals; she has had some of the tiny developed prints enlarged.

6. Faulkner, letter to Malcolm Cowley, February 11, 1949, quoted in Cowley, ed. *The Faulkner-Cowley File: Letters and Memories, 1944–1962* (New York: Viking, 1957), p. 126. Cowley, pp. 66, 71, and 75, also notes that Faulkner thought he was writing for fun, couldn't bear to see his personal affairs discussed in print, and never corrected misstatements about himself, which may, as Sensibar suggests in "Faulkner's Fictional Photographs," p. 314, n. 38, have to do with his earlier verbal and visual

deceptions. There is, however, a portrait by Cartier-Bresson in *Photoportraits,* p. 165. There are also several photographic works about "Faulkner Country," such as those by: Walker Evans, "Faulkner's Mississippi," *Vogue* 112 (October 1, 1948): 144–49, reproduced with other Oxford scenes in *Walker Evans at Work* (New York: Harper & Row, 1982), pp. 170–79; Martin J. Dain, *Faulkner's County: Yoknapatawpha* (New York: Random House, 1964); Alain Desvergnes, *Yoknapatawpha: The Land of William Faulkner,* text by Régis Durand, trans. William Wheeler (Paris: Marval, 1989); Willie Morris and William Eggleston, *Faulkner's Mississippi* (Birmingham, Ala.: Oxmoor House, 1990); and Wright Morris's 'Faulkner Country, Near Oxford, Mississippi,' 1939, in *The Inhabitants* (New York: Scribner's, 1946), npn, and often reproduced in his subsequent books.

59. Erskine Caldwell and Margaret Bourke-White

ERSKINE CALDWELL, FROM *With All My Might*, 1987,
AND MARGARET BOURKE-WHITE, FROM *Portrait of Myself*, 1963

Caldwell's (1903–87) portrayal of rural southerners reduced by poverty to elemental anger, hunger, and lust in books like Tobacco Road *(1932) helped attract audiences during the Depression to works of social protest, thus stimulating the genre.[1] To counter charges of grotesque exaggeration, he planned a factual book on southern sharecroppers, reinforced by incontrovertible evidence provided by Margaret Bourke-White (1904–71). One of the country's most famous and highly paid photographers, she was called the "poetess of the camera" because of her dramatically lit, carefully composed pictures for many large industries and advertisers as well as the Luce publications.[2] Bourke-White became eager to photograph the poor after visiting the Soviet Union (1931) and covering the midwestern drought (1934); the result of her collaboration with Caldwell, aside from their marriage [Fig. 95], was* You Have Seen Their Faces *(1937).[3] The unusual blend of his text, her piteous images, and their invented captions [Fig. 96] won acclaim from most readers; those working at the same time on similar topics, however, were outraged by the book and its success. Walker Evans and James Agee, for example, found Caldwell's solutions simplistic and Bourke-White's manipulations of their subjects insensitive and even immoral; their hostility partly determined the approach of their own study,* Let Us Now Praise Famous Men *(1941).[4] As the Second World War began, Caldwell and Bourke-White collaborated on other timely books, better suited to her talents than his, until their mostly long-distance marriage (1939–42) dissolved.[5] Bourke-White went on to fresh successes; Caldwell never surpassed his earlier ones.[6]*

CALDWELL, FROM *With All My Might*

. . . I had become determined to vindicate my writings about the South and I had formed a clear idea about the kind of book I wanted to prepare. For one thing, it was to be factual study of people in the cotton states living in economic stress and it was my intention to show that my fiction was as realistic as life itself in the contemporary South. And, to be completely authentic, as I was well aware, the book would have to be thoroughly documented with pho-

tographs taken on the scene by a perceptive photographer.

The title of the book had already been selected. It was to be called *You Have Seen Their Faces*.

I asked Maxim Lieber to prepare a list of accomplished photographers who would be desirable collaborators. First of all, a meeting was arranged with Margaret Bourke-White, a spirited young woman with an engaging personality who had published a highly-regarded volume of industrial photographs. In addition, she was well-known for her photographs of Russian industrial and agricultural operations.

Margaret Bourke-White immediately expressed enthusiasm when the purpose of the book was explained and stated without hesitation that she should be the one to take the pictures for the project. At that point, I was not sure that I wanted to collaborate with her since I was not fully convinced that the work I had in mind would be suitable for a female photographer to perform. However, she insisted slightly tearfully on our having an immediate agreement and nothing I said after that daunted her spirits. So as it was, there and then it was decided we would meet in Augusta, Georgia, in the first week of July and travel westward through the Southern states by automobile for six or eight weeks.

Following the meeting with my collaborator, I became concerned about the need to keep complete notes and make typings of other material for use later when the text of the book was being written. And I realized, too, that the secretarial help would be needed to keep accurate accounts of such travel expenses as meals, lodgings, gasoline, and miscellaneous supplies.

The person I thought of at once who would be ideally suitable for the secretarial work was Ruth Carnall. And as I had hoped, when I phoned Ruth to ask if she would be interested in arranging to take a leave of absence from her M-G-M position and join the tour, she shouted with joy and said nothing other than the death of her cherished tawny cat would keep her from meeting Margaret and me in Augusta.

As I had anticipated, the steamy canopy of July heat had settled over the valley of the Savannah River like a suffocating blanket and the only stirring of the humid air was to be found under the ceiling fans in the public rooms of the Richmond Hotel.

The summer heat was familiar to me and, except for occasional cooling showers, it would prevail in state after state for the next two months. And although I had purposely sought to travel in the South during the heat of sum-

mer, which I considered to be the best time of year to observe people in their true workaday way of life, I did begin to wonder what effect it was going to have on Margaret and Ruth.

Ruth arrived at the Richmond Hotel in Augusta after having traveled from Los Angeles at times by train and airplane. Margaret, loaded down with several suitcases and bundles of photographic equipment, arrived in the afternoon of the same day on a train from New York.

I had arrived in Augusta the night before from Maine in my Ford sedan and had limited my impedimenta to a single suitcase and portable typewriter. It was soon evident that the automobile was going to be packed and stacked to the limit with little space left on the back seat for one of the two women. No matter what happened, I had decided I was not going to consent to ride for six or eight weeks in the heat of summer while sitting cramped three abreast on the narrow front seat.

During the first evening we were together, the three of us had a pleasant dinner in the hotel dining room. That was when I had the first opportunity to describe to Margaret and Ruth what we would probably observe during our tour.

I began by saying that in general what we would observe would be people living in various conditions of economic and physical distress. As an extreme example, I cited the plight of chain gang convicts in their black-and-white striped clothing who were physically handicapped by being hobbled at work in steel balls-and-chains. As shocking as such a sight might be, I suggested that what would probably be more common would be our coming into close contact with human beings whose faces and bodies revealed the continuing ravages of hunger, disease, and utter deprivation. I explained that I had such people in mind when I was visualizing a book illustrated with photographs and having the title of *You Have Seen Their Faces*.

After assembling in the hotel lobby the next morning, Margaret took me aside and said in an agitated voice that she had been unable to sleep most of the night for fear she would have to ride on the back seat of the car. Pleading, and almost in tears, she begged me to assure her that she could sit on the front seat. Unprepared to act upon such an unexpected request for favoritism, I could only suggest that she and Ruth should decide which one would sit on which seat.

While the automobile was being loaded with our belongings, and Ruth evidently having perceived that Margaret would claim the privilege of riding on the front seat, it was announced by Ruth that she was going to ride in the rear all the time.

Ruth's unexpected announcement did not end with that statement, however. She elaborated by saying in a jesting yet somewhat caustic manner that her position was that of a hired girl and that untemperamental hired girls knew their place in life and expected to sit at second-table. Ruth's comments ended when she said, looking directly at Margaret, that she had often wondered if it would give her a delightful feeling of superiority to be temperamental.

There was a series of briefly sharp glances between the two young woman after that and we next took our places in the car to start on our travels. I was beginning to realize that I might have prevented the occurrence of unpleasantness by offering to sit on the rear seat myself and let someone else drive the car.

Our travel through the central region of Georgia and Alabama during the first week of our trip was pleasingly productive and without obvious conflict between Margaret and Ruth. In each state, we were in the geographical region of the fall line between the hilly piedmont and the coastal flat-lands. And it was here, among the gullies and sand hills and eroded red-clay hillsides that the most devastating effects of the great American economic depression were seen in the tragic lives of defeated people in the confines of their shacks and shanties [Fig. 96].

The constantly recurring sight of so much dire poverty and untreated illness afflicting children and adults of all ages may have served to reduce to a minimum, at least temporarily, any feeling of animosity existing between the aggressive photographer and the unassuming secretary.

Regardless of what the cause may have been, the result was that Ruth often put her notebook aside and offered to change a flashbulb or move a reflector when Margaret was setting and lighting a scene for a portrait or interior photograph. Moreover, neither did she become impatient or annoyed when Margaret, devoted as she was to time-consuming and meticulous preparations, would spend two or three hours and take dozens of photographs before being satisfied with what she had put on film.

It was not clear to me what may have brought about a sudden change of attitude on the part of both Margaret and Ruth toward each other. It was the kind of situation that I had imagined might happen sooner or later and I had always wondered if there would be anything I could do to prevent a verbal, or perhaps even a physical, clash between two girls.

The inevitable abrupt turn from congeniality to hostility took place in late afternoon at the end of our fourth week of travel soon after we had stopped for the night in a hotel in Jackson, Mississippi. Immediately and loudly objecting to her room in the hotel, which was one of three similar rooms Ruth had arranged for us to occupy as she usually did, Margaret loudly insisted on having a more comfortable room on a higher floor and with a pleasant view from the window.

I came to the doorway of my room when I heard the argument between the two become excessively loud and boisterous. What I saw was that they were facing each other across the hall from their opposite doorways. Later that evening, I wrote in my notebook much of the conversation heard in the hallway.

Margaret: You did this on purpose.

Ruth: Did what on purpose?

Margaret: Put me in this awful room with a view of absolutely nothing. I won't stand for it. It's too awful for words. I simply won't stay in it. I won't—I won't—anything!

Ruth: All the rooms in this hotel are alike. You probably want a hotel room that costs more.

Margaret: I don't care what anything costs!

Ruth: But why do you want something different than what you've got?

Margaret: Because I'm me. That's why. I'm me!

Ruth: I'll never doubt that as long as I live.

Margaret: What do you mean by that?

Ruth: Whatever you want to make of it. Only a blatant egotist would make your kind of demands.

Margaret: That's insulting. Are you going to do something about changing my room?

Ruth: No!

Margaret slammed her door with a crashing sound that echoed up and down the hall. Later, she had dinner brought to her room. When I tried to call her several times during the evening, she would not answer the phone and she was not seen again until the next morning.

I was beginning to wonder during breakfast with Ruth what could be done to dispel the cloud of ill-feeling between Margaret and Ruth so that work on the book could continue without disruption for the next three or four weeks. It was then when unexpectedly Margaret came into the dining room. She was smiling and pleasant when she sat down at our table and patted Ruth's hand in a friendly gesture. Ruth slowly withdrew her hand from the table.

In view of Margaret's display of excessive friendliness and seeing Ruth's reaction to the patting of her hand, I decided at that moment to change our working plans. For the good of all, it seemed to me that instead of staying several days longer in Mississippi it would be wise to drive all the way to Little Rock, Arkansas, for a well-earned rest of several days after having been together continuously for almost a month.

It was my feeling that not only would there be relief from the effects of so much enforced close association, also there would enough time for hairdressers and movies and other amenities to please Margaret and Ruth. As for myself, after finding a barbershop and a convenient pool room, I wanted to have time to review the month's accumulation of notes and to make plans for the remainder of the tour through the rice and cotton plantations of Arkansas and from there through the entire length of Tennessee.

The day-long trip from Jackson to Little Rock was pleasant and uneventful. After having lunch and crossing the Mississippi at Greenville, off and on for several hours the two young women would suddenly begin singing a song they discovered was familiar to both of them.

When we arrived at the Albert Pike Hotel in Little Rock, and saying she wanted to be sure of having a comfortable room with a pleasing view, Margaret went with Ruth to arrange for our accommodations. We had an early dinner that evening at a candle-lighted table in the hotel dining room.

Afterward, good-nights having been said by all, I was walking across the lobby on the way to my room when Margaret grasped my arm and hastily asked me to stop later at her room for a few minutes to talk about a particular type of photograph for our book. Ruth was too far away to hear what was being said, but the expression on her face was revealing enough to indicate that she was not without understanding.

There was only silence when afterward I knocked several times on Margaret's door. It was not locked, though, and when I stepped inside the only illumination in the room was the glow of city lights coming through the open windows. Although there still was no sound to be heard in the room, I soon saw Margaret in bed with the covering tossed aside in the balmy air of the summer evening. With gradually increasing vision in the dim light, I was soon aware that she was partially clothed in a very thin garment. It was dusty rose in color and had an opening from neck to waist that had not been closed with dangling ribbons and bows. Also, one of her shoulders was bare and likewise a portion of her bosom.

"I waited too long," I said, going to the foot of the bed. "I'm sorry to be so late."

"Oh, that's all right," she said with an unexpected softness of voice. "It's still early in the evening."

I went closer as she began smoothing the bed covering over and over again as if engrossed in thought. I was near enough to her than to be able to smell the odor of a sensuous perfume and was becoming increasingly impassioned. Ever since starting on our tour, I had been constantly impressed by Margaret's enticingly lissome figure and her provocative femininity. However, I was not prepared to find myself in a hotel room with her by invitation.

"And now that you're here," Margaret said, "you can sit down so we can talk for a little while."

Even though there was only the dim glow of city lights in the room, I could see more distinctly than ever the bold bareness of her arms and shoulders, the roundness of breasts under the lacy gown. Still far apart, I had the feeling of being drawn closer and closer to her with the desire to put my arms around her. As if to provide ample space for me, she made a subtle movement toward the far side of the bed. I immediately lay down beside her.

"This is what I've wanted to do for a long time," I told her. "And now that I'm here—"

"But you must stay like you are—this time," she said with a direct firmness. "You could take off your shoes and coat to be more comfortable in this warm night. But nothing more—"

"Can't I even take off my necktie?"

She laughed. "Well, yes, if you wish."

It was midnight when, putting on my shoes and then carrying my coat and necktie, I went down the hall to my room. Restless and wide awake for several hours, I finally fell asleep at dawn.

It was not until midmorning that I woke up and went down to the hotel lobby on my way to breakfast. First with a casual glance and then with a closer look, I saw an envelope in my box at the mail desk. I knew at once what to expect. It could be nothing else. It was a note from Ruth. Fearing the worst, I went to a corner of the lobby and sat down before ripping open the envelope and hastily reading Ruth's brief note.

From the first few words, I knew she had left Little Rock to return home to California. And I was certain long before reaching the end of the farewell letter that it had been written with tears in her eyes. And, sure enough, at the bottom of the page there was the still damp and unmistakable impress of a teardrop. [ch. 15, pp. 145–51]

BOURKE-WHITE, FROM *Portrait of Myself*

. . . It was time to figure out what I should do. The drought had been a powerful eye-opener and had shown me that right here in my own country there were worlds about which I knew almost nothing. *Fortune* assignments had given me a magnificent introduction to all sorts of American people. But this time it was not the cross section of industry I wanted. Nor was it the sharp drama of agricultural crisis. It was less the magazine approach and more the book approach I was after. It was based on a great need to understand my fellow Americans better. I felt it should not be an assignment in the ordinary sense but should be as independent of any regular job as my steel mill pictures had been.

What should be the theme, the spine, the unity? I did not consider myself a writer. I felt this book had to be a collaboration between the written word and the image on the celluloid. I needed an author. Yet curiously enough I gave very little thought to what kind of author. I knew it must be someone who was really in earnest about understanding America. But a good writer or a merely competent writer? A novelist or a nonfiction man? A famous author or an obscure one? To all these things I gave no thought. I simply hoped that I would find the right one.

It seemed a miracle that within a week or two I should hear of an author in search of a photographer. He had a book project in mind

96. Margaret Bourke-White. 'Sweetfern, Arkansas,' from *You Have Seen Their Faces*, 1936.

Sweetfern, Arkansas
"Poor people get passed by."

in which he wanted to collaborate with a photographer. I gathered he had paid little attention to the possibility that there might be mediocre or gifted photographers in the world. He just wanted to find the right one—someone with receptivity and an open mind, someone who would be as interested as he was in American people, everyday people.

He was a writer whose work had extraordinary vitality, an almost savage power. He was the author of an exceedingly controversial book which had been adapted into an equally controversial play. Among the thousands who had seen the play or read the book were many who considered the characters exaggerated, the situations overdrawn. The author wanted to do a book with pictures that would show the authenticity of the people and conditions about which he wrote. He wanted to take the camera to Tobacco Road. His name was Erskine Caldwell. . . .

. . . I could hardly believe this large shy man with the enormous wrestler's shoulders and quiet coloring could be the fiery Mr. Caldwell. His eyes were the soft rinsed blue of well-worn jeans. His hair was carrot—a subdued carrot. The backs of his hands were flecked with cinnamon freckles-cinnamon which had stood long on the kitchen shelf. His whole appearance suggested he was holding himself ready to step back at any moment and blend into the background, where he would remain, patient and invisible, until he had heard what he wanted to hear or experienced what he wanted to experience. Later I learned this was just what he had a special gift for doing. His voice matched his appearance. He spoke softly when he spoke at all.

His seeming mildness and gentleness came as a surprise against the turbulence of his writings. Hoping to ease the painful bashfulness I so strongly felt in him, I suggested it was cocktailtime. No, he seldom drank. This astonished me in the face of the Bacchanalian scenes in his books.

I was equally surprised that, humorist though Caldwell was known to be, his tight-locked face suggested a man who rarely laughs. I remember saying to myself, "This is going to be a colorless and completely impersonal type of man to work with." But I didn't care what he was like as long as we worked well together. I knew (and I knew I wasn't supposed to know) that he did not particularly like my photographs. Caldwell's literary agent thought I should hear the worst before I began, and he told me in secret. Well, that didn't bother me. There were a lot of my pictures I didn't like either—the grinning models for example.

Another difficulty, and again I was informed in confidence, was that Mr. Caldwell did not like the idea of working with a woman. As a countermeasure he planned to hedge himself in with a second woman, a sort of literary secretary with whom he had worked in Hollywood. She would take shorthand notes of important conversations and keep identification data. (She was to go out of my life as abruptly as she came into it, and I no longer remember much about her except that we called her Sally.) If Erskine Caldwell had further misgivings about my pictures, or about my being a woman, which I could not change, he did not give voice to them. We set a date to start work on the book: June 11, 1936.

June eleventh was five and a half months away. As meticulously as though we were leaving next week, Erskine Caldwell got the details. We would meet in Augusta, Georgia, early in the morning in the lobby of Augusta's best hotel. We would look over the Tobacco Road country and then circle through all the cotton-growing states in the Deep South. Mr. Caldwell expressed the hope that the delay would not inconvenience me. He had several pieces of writing he wanted to finish before we started in on our book project.

I, too, had things to finish and was thankful for the extra time. . . .

. . . As with any change of direction in one's life, there were a thousand insistent last-minute details. I wanted so much to come to the book project with all the mind and ideas and serenity that I was capable of. A few more days would wind up everything. After all, it was nearly half a year ago that we had set our starting date. Maybe Mr. Caldwell also had extra things to do; I could always ask.

Through his agent, I learned that Mr. Caldwell was already in Georgia, staying at his father's house in the tiny town of Wrens. I phoned Wrens and got Erskine Caldwell on the line. I explained about the new magazine starting and all the circumstances and said, if it was all the same to him, I would like to have one more week. Instead of the eleventh, could we begin, say, the eighteenth? The frozen wordlessness at the end of the line conveyed to me we might never begin at all, I could hardly believe it. Heavens, I had been planning toward this for all these months! Several long telephone conversations between the literary agent in New York and Mr. Caldwell in Georgia verified my fears. It was all off. At least, it was off until some mythical time when it would be "more convenient" for all parties. I was sure that meant off, period.

What had I done, what had I done! To me it seemed not unreasonable that a date made half a year ahead, with a trip to another hemisphere in between, could be just a little bit elastic. To wreck the entire plan because I had requested postponement for a few days! But reasonable or unreasonable, that was not the point. To have our idea die stillborn, that I could not bear. With Erskine Caldwell already down south and just around the corner from Tobacco Road, there was nowhere unobtrusively to corner him for a little heart-to-heart chat. It was plain that I had worn out my welcome on the telephone. All means of communication seemed to have failed me.

I did the only thing I could think of to do. It was a long chance, but I would try. First I must rule out of my mind every thought except of things I absolutely had to do before leaving New York. I went ahead just as I had planned. It took a tight-packed four days. I had kept clothes and cameras packed, and when my chores were done, I jumped on the plane at midnight.

The hot sun was rising as we landed at Augusta, Georgia. I checked into the shiny, newly varnished "best" hotel and found, on inquiry, that Wrens was six miles away. Over my breakfast I composed a letter as quiet in tone as I could make it. I had come in the hope we could reconsider. I so wanted to start our important work with the slate wiped clean so that I could give my entire attention to this project of ours. Everything was in order now. Summer would be without interruption. I hoped he would believe me and see that I was deeply sincere in wanting to do the book and do it as well as it could possibly be done. I added that I would be at the hotel in case he wanted to send me a message.

I tried unsuccessfully to get a Western Union messenger. The one mail delivery a day did not leave until afternoon, and I wanted Mr. Caldwell to get my note early in the day. I finally secured the personal services of a young lad who swept out the post office. The idea of going on his bicycle to deliver the letter in exchange for five dollars seemed fine to him, as it did to me, and I sat on the porch of the hotel watching him pedal furiously away until he disappeared in his own trailing plume of dust.

It was still not quite eight o'clock. They day dragged on. There were dull-looking movies, but I dared not leave the hotel to go to them. Normally I love walking down Main Street in a town where I have never been before, window-shopping and strolling around the drugstore. But today I dared not take my eyes off the telephone operator at the hotel desk. I thought I would never escape this day, which showed no sign of ending. At six o'clock in the evening, a large figure in a loose blue jacket came into the coffee shop, sat down at the counter and ordered hot coffee. While we waited to be served, Erskine Caldwell looked quietly down at his hands. We drank our coffee in wordless communication. When the last drop was drained, Erskine turned to me and smiled.

"That was a big argument, wasn't it?"

I nodded.

"When do you want to leave?"

"Now."

And so we did. [from chs. 9, 10, pp. 112–21]

1. See the edition of *Tobacco Road* (Savannah: Beehive Press, 1974) that includes, according to Caldwell, p. vii, some of "the revealing documentary photographs" from *You Have Seen Their Faces* (New York: Simon & Schuster, 1937); they are fewer in number and gentler—including many young children—than the ones published in the original work.

2. This phrase is quoted and discussed by William Stott, *Documentary Expression and Thirties America* (New York: Oxford University Press, 1976), pp. 216 and 337, n. 10, and by Lorraine York, *"The Other Side of Dailiness": Photography in the Works of Alice Munro, Timothy Findlay, Michael Ondaatje, and Margaret Laurence* (Toronto: ECW Press, 1988), p. 26.

3. See Bourke-White's phototext, *Eyes on Russia* (New York: Simon & Schuster, 1931) and "The Drought: A Post-Mortem in Pictures," *Fortune* 10, no. 4 (October 1934): 76–83, whose anonymous text, ironically, was provided by James Agee. See Caldwell, *Call It Experience: The Years of Learning How to Write* (New York: Duell, Sloan & Pearce, [1951]), pp. 163–66, for a less detailed version of the origins of this collaboration (in which Ruth is called Sally, as she is in Bourke-White's version above) than the one provided here from *With All My Might: An Autobiography* (Atlanta: Peachtree Publishers, 1987), pp. 145–51; Bourke-White's version of this collaboration is from *Portrait of Myself* (New York: Simon & Schuster, 1963), pp. 125–39. More comprehensive, objective versions are provided by Vicki Goldberg, *Margaret Bourke-White: A Biography* (Reading, Mass.: Addison-Wesley, 1987), pp. 161–71, and Jonathan Silverman, *For the World to See: The Life of Margaret Bourke-White* (New York: Viking/Studio, 1983), pp. 78–80.

4. For example, see Bourke-White's "Notes on Photographs" in *You Have Seen Their Faces*, pp. 187–90, which most readers have found insensitive, cf. Agee and Evans, "Near a Church" and "A Note on the Photographs" (which quotes a magazine article on Bourke-White) in *Let Us Now Praise Famous Men* (Boston: Houghton Mifflin, 1988), pp. 39–43 and 450–54; clearly Agee and Evans meant to contrast their procedures with hers. See also Shloss, *In Visible Light*, pp. 180–87, and Stott, *Documentary Expression*, pp. 59–60 and 216–23, for further discussions of *You Have Seen Their Faces*.

5. See their *North of the Danube* (New York: Viking, 1939); *Say, Is This the U.S.A.?* (New York: Duell, Sloan and Pearce, 1941); and, to a lesser extent, *Russia at War* (London: Hutchinson, [1942]). See also Bourke-White, *Portrait,* pp. 169–70 and 174–88, which details their Soviet trip but doesn't mention *Say, Is This the U.S.A.?* or *Russia at War*; and Silverman, pp. 103–4 and 106–113, cf. Caldwell, *Call It Experience,* pp. 176–80, 191–208, and *With All My Might,* pp. 159–69, 165, and 177–92.

6. See, for example, Caldwell's foreword to Mark Morrow, *Images of Southern Writers* (Athens: University of Georgia Press, 1985), p. vii.

60. *Walker Evans*

"JAMES AGEE IN 1936," 1960

*J*ames Agee (1909–55) [Fig. 97] was delighted to secure the photographer Walker Evans (1903–75), who shared his rebellious
views, for his Fortune *assignment on southern tenant farmers. In
deliberate contrast to Caldwell's and Bourke-White's* You Have Seen
Their Faces *(1937), Agee composed his subjective text, disordered in structure and varied in style, with no coherent arguments or pragmatic solutions; Evans's objective, straightforward photographs stressed the beauty,
dignity, and complexity of their subjects, whom they feared exploiting [Fig.
100].[1] Their differing approaches conflicted productively; as Wright Morris
observed, "The words soar into the empyrean, but the photographs, happily, remain earthbound."[2] The idiosyncratic result, however, proved unac-
ceptable to* Fortune *as an article, and its belated appearance as a book
(1941) was disregarded by readers more concerned with war than with the
economy.[3] Agee and Evans then pursued their separate eccentric ways but
remained friends. When Agee died prematurely, Robert Frank recalls Evans
"just sitting on his desk on front of the window and looking down on
Rockefeller Center—you know, where they ice skate?—and he just sat there
and he cried."[4] But at least Evans survived to see* Let Us Now Praise
Famous Men *become, since the 1960's, the most celebrated documentary of
the Depression era while Caldwell's and Bourke-White's study is now considered an ephemeral success.[5]*

"James Agee in 1936"

At the time, Agee was a youthful-looking twenty-seven [Fig. 97]. I think he felt he was elaborately masked, but what you saw right away—alas for conspiracy—was a faint rubbing of Harvard and Exeter, a hint of family gentility, and a trace of romantic idealism. He could be taken for a likable American young man, an above-average product of the Great Democracy from any part of the country. He didn't look much like a poet, an intellectual, an artist, or a Chris-

tian, each of which he was. Nor was there outward sign of his paralyzing, self-lacerating anger. His voice was pronouncedly quiet and low-pitched, though not of "cultivated" tone. It gave the impression of diffidence, but never of weakness. His accent was more or less unplaceable and it was somewhat variable. For instance, in Alabama it veered towards country-southern, and I may say he got away with this to the farm families and to himself.

His clothes were deliberately cheap, not only because he was poor but because he wanted to be able to forget them. He would work a suit into fitting him perfectly by the simple method of not taking it off much. In due time the cloth would mold itself to his frame. Cleaning and pressing would have undone this beautiful process. I exaggerate, but it did seem sometimes that wind, rain, work, and mockery were his tailors. On another score, he felt that wearing good, expensive clothes involved him in some sort of claim to superiority of the social kind. Here he occasionally confused his purpose, and fell over into a knowingly comical inverted dandyism. He got more delight out of factory-seconds sneakers and a sleazy cap than a straight dandy does from waxed calf Peal shoes and a brushed Lock & Co. bowler.

Physically Agee was quite powerful, in the deceptive way of uninsistent large men. In movement he was rather graceless. His hands were large, long, bony, light and uncared for. His gestures were one of the memorable things about him. He seemed to model, fight, and stroke his phrases as he talked. The talk, in the end, was his great distinguishing feature. He talked his prose, Agee prose. It was hardly a twentieth century style; it had Elizabethan colors. Yet it had extraordinarily knowledgeable contemporary content. It rolled just as it reads; but he made it sound natural—something just there in the air like any other part of the world. How he did this no one knows. You would have blinked, gaped, and very likely run from this same talk delivered without his mysterious ability. It wasn't a matter of show, and it wasn't necessarily bottle-inspired. Sheer energy of imagination was what lay behind it. This he matched with physical energy. Many a man or woman has fallen exhausted to sleep at four in the morning bang in the middle of a remarkable Agee performance, and later learned that the man had continued it somewhere else until six. Like many born writers who are floating in the illusory amplitude of their youth, Agee did a great deal of writing in the air. Often you had the impulse to gag him and tie a pen to his hand. That wasn't necessary; he was an ex-ception among talking writers. He wrote—devotedly and incessantly.

Night was his time. In Alabama he worked I don't know how late. Some parts of *Let Us Now Praise Famous Men* read as though they were written on the spot at night. Later, in a small house in Frenchtown, New Jersey, the work, I think, was largely night-written. Literally the result shows this; some of the sections read best at night, far in the night. The first passage of *A Country Letter* (p. 49), is particularly night-permeated.

Agee worked in what looked like a rush and a rage. In Alabama he was possessed with the business, jamming it all into the days and the nights. He must not have slept. He was driven to see all he could of the families' day, starting, of course, at dawn. In one way, conditions there were ideal. He could live inside the subject, with no distractions. Back-country poor life wasn't really far from him, actually. He had some of it in his blood, through relatives in Tennessee. Anyway, he was in flight from New York magazine editorial offices, from Greenwich Village social-intellectual evenings, and especially from the whole world of high-minded, well-bred, money-hued culture, whether authoritarian or libertarian. In Alabama he sweated and scratched with submerged glee. The families understood what he was down there to do. He'd explain it, in such a way that they were interested in *his* work. He wasn't playing. That is why in the end he left out certain completed passages that were entertaining, in an acid way. One of these was a long, gradually hilarious aside on the subject of hens. It was a virtuoso piece heightened with allegory and bemused with the pathetic fallacy.

He won almost everybody in those families—perhaps too much—even though some of the individuals were hardbitten, sore, and shrewd. Probably it was his diffidence that took him into them. That non-assurance was, I think, a hostage to his very Anglican childhood training. His Christianity—if an outsider may try to speak of it—was a punctured and residual remnant, but it was still a naked, root emotion. It was an ex-Church, or non-Church matter, and it was hardly in evidence. All you saw of it was an ingrained courtesy, and uncourtly courtesy that emanated from him towards everyone, perhaps excepting the smugly rich, the pretentiously genteel, and the police. After a while, in a roundabout way, you discovered that, to him, human beings were at least possibly immortal and literally sacred souls.

The days with the families came abruptly to an end. Their real content and meaning has all been shown. The writing they induced is, among other things, the reflection of one resolute, private rebellion. Agee's rebellion was unquenchable, self-damaging, deeply principled, infinitely costly, and ultimately priceless.

1. The question of exploitation, on Agee's mind throughout *Let Us*, obviously bothered Dale Maharidge and Michael Williamson (and some of their subjects) in their follow-up study, *And Their Children After Them: The Legacy of Let Us Now Praise Famous Men: James Agee, Walker Evans, and the Rise and Fall of Cotton in the South* (New York: Pantheon, [1989]). The royalties for the award-winning book have been pledged to a scholarship fund for the University of Alabama, according to the *New York Times* (December 30, 1990): 31. See also Judith Keller, "Evans and Agee, The Great American Roadside (*Fortune* 1934)," *History of Photography* 16, no. 2 (Summer 1992): 170–71, and Joseph J. Wydeven, "Photography and Privacy: The Protests of Wright Morris and James Agee," *Midwest Quarterly* 23 (Autumn 1981): 103–15.

2. See Morris, "Photographs, Images, and Words," in *Time Pieces: Photographs, Writing, and Memory* (New York: Aperture, 1989), p. 62; Morris was early influenced by Evans's work, but his later assessment here is particularly generous, given his awareness of Evans's dislike of his "photo-texts," quoted in Colin Westerbeck, Jr., "American Graphic: The Photography and Fiction of Wright Morris," in *Multiple Views: Logan Grant Essays on Photography 1983–89*, ed. Daniel P. Younger (Albuquerque: University of New Mexico Press, 1991), p. 300. See also Thomas A. Goodman, "Collaboration in Character," 1985, Logan Grant Prize Essay, TS, Photographic Resource Center, Boston University; Orvell, *The Real Thing*, pp. 277–85; and Szarkowski, "Wright Morris the Photographer," in Wright Morris, *Wright Morris: Origin of a Species* (San Francisco: San Francisco Modern Museum of Art, 1992), pp. 13–15, for a discussion of the two artists' differing approaches to their often similar subjects.

3. Notable exceptions, then and later, were Lionel Trilling's brilliant review "Greatness with One Fault in It," *Kenyon Review* 4 (Winter 1942): 99–102, and W. C. Williams's "The Most Overlooked Book of the Past Quarter Century," undated TS (Za 167) at the Beinecke, which the poet's most eminent biographer, Professor Paul Mariani, writing to the editor on November 30, 1991, suggests may have been a newspaper piece, c. 1950. See also Carl Van Vechten's review, September 30, 1938, TSS (ZaCVV.1), also at the Beinecke. For further background about the evolution and reception of this book, see Stott, *Documentary Expression and Thirties America*, pp. 261–314; John Rogers Puckett, *Five Photo-Textual Documentaries from the Great Depression* (Ann Arbor, Mich.: UMI Research Press, 1984), pp. 111–51; J. A. Ward, *American Silences: The Realism of James Agee, Walker Evans, and Edward Hopper* (Baton Rouge: Louisiana State University Press, 1985), pp. 80–82, 115, and 149–67; Shloss, *In Visible Light*, pp. 179–97; Hunter, *Image and Word*, pp. 73–79; and John Hersey. "Agee," Introduction to *Let Us* (Boston: Houghton Mifflin, 1988), pp. v–xxxix.

4. See Agee's poem "(To Walker Evans." [sic], *Let Us*, [p. 5], which greatly embarrassed the more reticent Evans, according to the editors of *Images of the South: Visits with Eudora Welty and Walker Evans* (Memphis: Center for Southern Folklore, 1977), p. 33. See also Agee's letters to Evans, 1936–51, in the HRHRC, called to the editor's attention by David Herwaldt, who infers from them that Evans wanted Agee to write an afterword to *Americans Photographs* (1938), but he declined, given the pressures of preparing *Let Us* and thinking there would be other opportunities to write about his friend's work. Frank's quote is in *Photography Within the Humanities*, ed. Eugenia Parry Janis and Wendy MacNeil (Danbury, N.H.: Addison House, 1977), p. 65.

5. See Miles Orvell, "Walker Evans and James Agee: The Legacy," *History of Photography* 17, no. 2 (Summer 1993): 166–71; and see also the many poems the work inspired: Donald Justice, "Mule Team and Poster" [on a photograph by Walker Evans (Alabama, 1936)], in *The Sunset Maker: Poems/Stories/A Memoir* (New York: Atheneum, 1987), p. 4; Frank Cady, "Let Us Now Praise Famous Men, Hale County, Alabama, Summer 1936," in *Poets in Photography*, ed. Mark Melnicove (South Harpswell, Me.: Dog Ear Press, 1981), p. 58; and Faye Kicknosway, *Who Shall Know Them* (New York: Penguin, 1985), whose "characters are imagined from the photos of Walker Evans."

61. W. H. Auden

FROM *Letters from Iceland* BY
W. H. AUDEN AND LOUIS MACNEICE, 1937

*A*uden (1907–73) remains the best known and most influential of a group of leftist poets at Oxford in the 1930's: C. Day Lewis, Louis MacNeice, and Stephen Spender. All used material in their verse from photographs—the democratic art, as Auden calls it here—both from newspapers and from personal albums, or as a metaphor.[1] All considered photographs, with their ability to witness and record, essential to credible reporting of the decade's upheavals. But Auden, who also wrote commentary for five documentary films (1935–39), was the only one to use a camera himself to document his writings. The first time was during an excursion with Louis MacNeice to Iceland in 1936, which produced an unconventional travel book composed of serious and witty sections—including prose, poetry, and allusive captions. Together with the text, Auden's "bunch of photographs/Some out of focus, some with wrong exposures" reject conventional documentary representation, especially linear narrative, level perspective [Fig. 98], and any distinction between the observer and the subject.[2] He also used his camera, though more conventionally, to illustrate Journey to a War (1938), written with Christopher Isherwood about their visit to China.[3] Auden's subsequent contact with photography, however, was mainly as portrait subject, perhaps, as he wrote in a later poem, because "the camera may/do justice to laughter, but must/degrade sorrow."[4]

The Accordion playing

FROM *Letters from Iceland*

FROM LETTER TO R. H. S. CROSSMAN, ESQ.[5] JULY 8, 1936

A glacier brilliant in the heights of summer
Feeding a putty-coloured river: a field,
A countryside collected in a field
To appreciate or try its strength;
The two flags twitter at the entrance gates.

I walk among them taking photographs;
The children stare and follow, think of questions
To prove the stranger real. Beyond the wire
The ponies graze who never will grow up to question
The justice of their permanent discipline.

Nevertheless let the camera's eye record it:
Groups in confabulation on the grass,
The shuffling couples in their heavy boots,
The young men leaping, the accordion playing [Fig. 102]
Justice or not, it is a world.
[ch. 7, stanzas 1–3 of 17, p. 91]

FROM W. H. A. TO E. M. A.[6] —NO. 2

[After arriving by bus to Myvatn] I lay in the sun watching the hay being made and taking photographs. If I can get them developed in time, and any of them come out, I'll send you some. It's a pity I am so impatient and careless, as any ordinary person could learn all the techniques of photography in a week. It is *the* democratic art, i.e. technical skill is practically eliminated—the more fool-proof cameras become with focusing and exposure gadgets the better— and artistic quality depends only on choice of subject. There is no place for the professional still photographer, and his work is always awful. The only decent photographs are scientific ones and amateur snapshots, only you want a lot of the latter to make an effect. A single still is never very interesting by itself. We started back [to Akureyre] about five, more crowded than ever, and the petrol stoppage much worse. We stopped to fill up and I was very annoyed because I was on the wrong side of the bus to take the farmer's girl working the pump, which would have made a beautiful Eisenstein sort of shot. [ch. 11, p. 137]

1. See, for example, Day Lewis, "The Album," *Word Over All* (London: Cape, 1943), pp. 8–9; MacNeice, "A Hand of Snapshots," in *Visitations* (London: Faber & Faber, 1957), p. 28; and Spender, "War Photography" and "The Bombed Happiness," in *The Still Center* (London: Faber & Faber, 1939), pp. 62–63 and 69–70 respectively, and "On the Photograph of a Friend, Dead," in *The Generous Days* (London: Faber & Faber, 1971), p. 24.

2. Auden, in the opening "Letter to Lord Byron," in *Letters from Iceland* (London: Faber & Faber, 1937), pp. 21 and 173, perpetuates the idea that he was a completely unserious photographer, as does his student Michael Yates in *W. H. Auden: A Tribute,* ed. Stephen Spender (London: Weidenfeld & Nicolson, 1975), p. 63: Auden "would stumble about the lava like some amphibious monster taking the most extraordinary art shots: the backside of a horse followed by the guide Ari's bottom, a boat, distant views or half-hidden faces between our legs. He clicked away regardless, though I think he did at least adjust the focus." A more serious view of Auden's photography, even when ironic or playful, is provided by Marsha Bryant in her pioneering study, "Auden and the 'Arctic Stare': Documentary as Public Collage in *Letters from Iceland,*" *Journal of Modern Literature* (forthcoming), which the author made available to the editor in TS.

3. Hunter, *Image and Word,* p. 157, calls the photographs "amateurish" in Auden and Isherwood, *Journey to a War* (London: Faber & Faber, 1939), but they may be as underestimated as those in *Letters from Iceland.* Of the two reprinted editions by Faber & Faber (London, 1985–86) and Paragon (New York, 1990) of *Letters from Iceland* and *Journey to a War,* the ones by the original English publisher, oddly enough, omit the photographs.

4. See Auden. "I Am Not a Camera," in *Collected Poems,* ed. Edward Mendelson (London: Faber & Faber, 1976), pp. 630–31. For some of the many portraits of Auden, see Freund, *The World in My Camera,* p. 62 (1942); *Lotte Jacobi,* ed. Wise, p. 65 (1945); Cecil Beaton, *Images* (New York: London House and Maxwell, 1963), npn; Rollie McKenna, *A Life in Photography* (New York: Knopf, 1991), pp. 244–45 (1951 and 1969); and Krementz, *The Writer's Image,* npn (1967).

5. Auden, here attending a sports festival, writes to Richard Crossman (1907–74), an attractive Oxford contemporary—an athlete, poet, and his sometime lover—who was a don [tutor] at this time and later became a noted politician.

6. E. M. A. was Erika Mann Auden, Thomas Mann's actively anti-Nazi daughter, whom Auden married in 1935 (though both were homosexual) to secure her a British passport and safety in England.

62. William Carlos Williams

"SERMON WITH A CAMERA," 1938

Williams (1883–1963), the most accomplished literary physician since Chekhov, attempted to create distinctively American poetry, as contrasted with the expatriate verse of T. S. Eliot or Ezra Pound, his former mentor. His poems, which enormously influenced postwar photographers, are generally characterized by vernacular speech, distanced emotion, and detailed observation of common objects or fragments, usually neglected in art, from which to perceive reality freshly and discern universal truths. Williams, whose vision resembled the camera in its intensity and precision, was unusually well versed in photographic matters due to his long and ambivalent relationship with Stieglitz as well as his close friendship with the painter-photographer Charles Sheeler.[1] Not surprisingly, this unusually visual poet appreciated Evans, an unusually literate photographer, as their works reflected similar values.[2] They even shared reservations about the revered Stieglitz, who Williams complained talked him "deaf, dumb and blind" and whom Evans disdained as "too arty."[3] Evans, influenced by the precision and irony of Flaubert and Baudelaire, had wanted to be a writer but had turned instead to photography, the "most literary of the graphic arts," but he always retained a serious interest in writers and writing.[4] Evans's first published photographs were provided for Hart Crane's Bridge *(1930) [Fig. 75].[5] He composed the prints in his* American Photographs *(1938) [Figs. 99, 101]—some of which also appeared in* Let Us Now Praise Famous Men *(1941) [Fig. 100]—to be "read" sequentially like a text. He wrote as well as photographed for* Time *(1943–45) and* Fortune *(1945–65); and his comments on photography are consistently well-written and full of literary references.*

99. Walker Evans.
'Tin Relic,' 1930.

"Sermon with a Camera"

Note: This version of this review is reprinted as "Walker Evans: American Photographs" in A Recognizable Image: William Carlos Williams on Art and Artists, *ed. Bram Dijkstra, pp. 136–39 [and see pp. 49, 53, 260, for his remarks on the manuscript]. It is based on the manuscript at the State University of New York at Buffalo, with additions from an earlier manuscript at the Beinecke; y = deletions made by an overzealous editor when the piece originally appeared in* The New Republic 96 (October 12, 1938): 282–83; * = deletions made by Williams. The original title is retained here.*

This is an 8 x 9 book of 95^6 photographs on glazed paper taken in the eastern part of the U.S. during the past seven years by a man named Walker Evans, a record of what was in that place for Mr. Evans to see and what Mr. Evans saw there in that time.

(This is a good work, a pleasure to the eye and a satisfaction to the intelligence. I'm glad for us that the pictures are of America instead of being just good pictures, because being so particularly of that place makes them universal. Gives them currency.)^y (Permits us to some extent to deal with all places for us.)^{y*}

In a work of art (and I should say that these pictures are works of art)^{y*} place is everything.

Evans's photographs represent, as Lincoln Kirstein says in his notes to the book, a straight puritanical stare—though not entirely without humor. There is much in them strongly reminiscent of the early practitioners of the photographic art. The composition is of secondary importance in these clear statements. Their beauty permits little of that.

The book is in two parts about evenly divided between portraits and architecture, the products and remains of a life that is constantly in process of passing. The range is from *Parked Car, Small Town Main Street*, 1932, to *Tin Relic*, 1931 [Fig. 99] and from *Alabama Cotton Tenant Farmer's Wife*, 1936 [Fig. 100], to *Main Pump*, 1933 [Fig. 101]. They particularize as Atget did for the Paris of his day. By this the eye and consequently the mind is induced to partake of the list that has been prepared—that we may know it.

The total effect is of a social upheaval, not a photographic picnic.

There is pointed reference in Mr. Kirstein's notes to the work of Brady during the War between the States. In Evans's pictures also we are seeing fields of battle after the withdrawal of the forces engaged. The jumbled wreckage, human and material, is not always so grim in the present case but for all the detachment of the approach the effect is often no less poignant.

But that's not all. These are without question works of art having their own identity, their own flavor, their own breath by which they live for us—and without which we shouldn't look at them past Sunday afternoon. They're good and reward repeated examination.

I'm glad that Evans has promenaded his eyes about America in this case rather than France. (Not that, in the long run, it makes a damned bit of difference—Yes it does. It emphasizes the excellence of the French. Why, at best, brought into relief by our own perceptions they gain brilliancy for us. It was absolutely essential for someone to begin what Evans has done so well.

And we shall see our own country and its implications the better for Evans's work and come to realize that the realm of art is here quite as well as elsewhere.)[y] We go about blind and deaf. We fight off convictions that could we possibly get ourselves into the right mind we should welcome for water in the desert (, convictions that are the very calcium and vitamins without which our bones melt under us)[y]. The artist must save us. He's the only one who can. First we have to see. Or first we have to be taught to see. We have to be taught to see here, because here is everywhere, related to everywhere else, and if we don't see, hear, taste, smell and feel in this place—not only will we

never know anything but the world of sense will be by that much diminished everywhere.

(Jealousies relative to the arts are unthinkable. In such pictures as those of Evans the insects of the arts have laid their eggs against a present winter to go on breeding and puncturing the hides of the dull witted forever.)[y]

Evans saw what he saw here, in this place—this was his universal. In this place he saw what is universal. By his photographs he proves it. Atget would like that.

(One of my pet aversions is the belief that you have to go to special places to find excellence in the arts on the principle that you don't find whales in a mill pond. You don't. Neither do you find brains by drinking cheap wine in a

100. Walker Evans. 'Allie Mae Burroughs, Wife of a Sharecropper, Hale County, Alabama' (also known as 'Annie Mae Gudger'), Summer 1936.

101. Walker Evans. 'Maine Pump,' 1933.

ference being that one sees so much more than the other. And relates it so much more acutely to his purpose.

Not that training isn't necessary. But the real thing the runners-away are after, if they know it, is convenience. It's hard to get the best out of an undeveloped milieu. The word "milieu" shows what I mean. We don't use the American equivalent, place, readily enough, so we run to a French one. But it's nothing but convenience and a certain inability that makes the runner-away[7] at his worst. At his best he is the bringer-in of the means of intercommunication in the arts—though he often forgets that and believes himself exalted in direct proportion to his removal from his basis.)[y]

It is the particularization of the universal that is important. It is the unique field of the artist. Evans is an artist.

It is ourselves we see, ourselves lifted from a parochial setting. We see what we have not theretofore realized, ourselves made worthy in our anonymity. What the artist does applies to everything, every day, everywhere to quicken and elucidate, to fortify and enlarge the life about him and make it eloquent—to make it scream, as Evans does at times, gurgle, laugh and speak masterfully when the occasion offers. (By this, by the multiplicity of the approach, the aggregate of many artists in all possible locations, each, with his own materials making the same excellence—men are drawn closer and made to feel their separate greatness.

Evans is that. He belongs.)[y]

So here's a book of photographs about America. It's not the first, perhaps not even the best book of pictures of us, but it's an eloquent one, one of the most fluent I have come across and enjoyed. The pictures are for the most part mild, but in spite of this, though always exquisitely clear in reasoning and in visual quality, they pack a wicked punch. There's nothing oppressively "photographic" here, it isn't a long nose poking into dirty corners for propaganda and for scandal, there are no trick shots, the composition isn't a particular feature—but the pictures talk to us. And they say plenty.

bistro, or knowledge merely by eating tripe from a dish stamped with the coat of arms of Christ College.)[y]

Of only one thing, relative to a work of art, can we be sure: it was bred of a place. It comes from an application of the senses to that place, a music, and that place can be the middle of the African jungle, the Mexican plateau, a Parisian whorehouse, a room where Oxford chippies sip tea together or a downhill street in a Pennsylvania small town.

(Let the abstract artist go hang his coat back of the door where he sits down, the abstractions he thinks he is freeing are as definitely bound to a place as the work of the most representational artist that ever lived, the only dif-

1. For more on Williams and Stieglitz, see n. 2 below. For more on Williams and Sheeler, see Williams: "Charles Sheeler" (1939), in *A Recognizable Image,* pp. 140–45; foreword to *Charles Sheeler: A Retrospective Exhibition* (Los Angeles: Art Galleries, University of California at Los Angeles, 1954), pp. 7–8; and *The Autobiography of William Carlos Williams* (New York: Random House, 1951), pp. 320–22 and 332–34. Sheeler's portrait of Williams, 1926, is reproduced in Mariani, *William Carlos Williams,* following p. 460.

2. In addition to the review reprinted here, see Williams, "The Most Overlooked Book of the Past Quarter Century," about *Let Us Now Praise Famous Men,* TS. (Za 167) at the Beinecke. See also Williams, introduction (1960) to Walt Whitman, *The Illustrated Leaves of Grass,* ed. Howard Chapnick (New York: Madison Square Press/ Grosset & Dunlap, 1971), pp. 9–13.

3. Evans's disparaging remark is quoted by Shloss, *In Visible Light,* p. 188. Williams's feelings about Stieglitz were far more ambivalent. See Williams, "The American Background," in Frank, ed., *America and Alfred Stieglitz,* pp. 17–26; Williams, "What of Alfred Stieglitz?" (October 16, 1946), in *A Recognizable Image,* ed. Dijkstra, pp. 177–79, discussed in Dijkstra's introduction, pp. 30, 34–36; and Williams, *Autobiography,* pp. xiii and 236. For overviews of their complex relationship, see Haines, *The Inner Eye of Alfred Stieglitz,* pp. 7–9 and 123;

Thomas, "William Carlos Williams," in *The Literary Admirers of Alfred Stieglitz,* pp. 33–47; and Dijkstra, "Stieglitz," in *Cubism, Stieglitz, and the Early Poetry of William Carlos Williams* (Princeton, N.J.: Princeton University Press, 1969), pp. 82–107 and 190–91, which persuasively suggests that Williams's widely reprinted poem, "Young Sycamore" (1923), was probably inspired by Stieglitz's photograph, 'Spring Showers' (1902); and Orvell, *The Real Thing,* pp. 248–52.

4. See Evans's quote cited in the introduction above, n. 18. See also his photographs of Faulkner country, mentioned in the Faulkner selection above, n. 6; *Of Time and Place: Walker Evans and William Christenberry* (San Francisco, Calif.: Friends of Photography; Fort Worth, Tex.: Amon Carter Museum/ University of New Mexico Press, 1990); Trachtenberg, "The Artist of the Real," in *The Presence of Walker Evans* (Boston: Institute of Contemporary Art, 1978), p. 20, who compares the influence of Evans and Ezra Pound; and the Kerouac selection below.

5. Evans's recollection of the poet's enthusiasm about his pictures for *The Bridge* [see one, Fig. 76] is quoted in the Crane selection above, n. 4.

6. There are 87 photographs in the book, as Williams wrote in the original published version, not 95.

7. Williams here originally wrote "expatriate" but crossed it out and substituted "runner-away."

"JAMES JOYCE," FROM *The World
in My Camera* [1938–39], 1974

*After fleeing Nazi Germany in 1933, Freund (1912–) began taking
photographs to support herself while earning a doctorate in art
history at the Sorbonne.[1] She later secured help from two celebrated bookshop owners, Sylvia Beach and her intimate friend, Adrienne
Monnier, who lined their walls with photographs of authors.[2] Freund met
and subsequently photographed many important writers living in Paris
through this pair, who were the courageous first publishers of James Joyce's
Ulysses (1922). This novel, then judged obscene in England and America,
revolutionized the form and content of the modern novel, with its distinctive, difficult "stream of consciousness," and also influenced many visual
artists.[3] Freund's pictorial record of the Irish expatriate (1882–1941) proved
timely, given the outbreak of war and Joyce's subsequent death. Her pictures of him alone as well as with his family and publishers [Fig. 102],
though carefully posed, catch the myriad moods of the fragile genius,
heightened in some by her pioneering use of color.[4] Joyce's regard for her
work enabled Freund to photograph many celebrated English writers. Together with her earlier portraits of French authors and later ones of their
American counterparts, they form a priceless cultural record.[5] After seeing
his own and other portraits by Freund exhibited at Monnier's bookshop in
1939, however, Jean-Paul Sartre commented that "we all look as if we'd just
come back from the war," no doubt mindful that another was about to
begin.[6]*

It was in 1934 that I saw James Joyce for the first time. He was dining with his wife in a restaurant near the Gare Montparnasse. I was still a student, and Joyce was one of the literary idols of my generation. I was fascinated as I observed the tall, slim man on whom the waiter was lavishing the kind of attention reserved for celebrities.

During the last ten years of his life, in the thirties, Joyce moved in very different circles from those he had frequented in the twenties. His former friends—Ezra Pound, for example—had left Paris; and the well-known group that had gathered around F. Scott Fitzgerald and Ernest Hemingway was by then merely a legend. In 1936 Adrienne Monnier's Maison des Amis des Livres had published my thesis in book form. I had the same publisher as Joyce! And so it was that we met that same year at one of Adrienne's dinner parties.

I believe that the main topic of conversation was the art of cooking. But I was so impressed I could hardly eat! I remember, however, that as I watched the play of shadow and light on the fine bone structure of Joyce's face, I thought of the portrait I could do of him that very moment.

During the following months I tried to persuade him to pose, but Joyce kept refusing—with the excuse that he was not feeling well, that his eyesight was troubling him, or that he had too much work to do. In the spring of 1938 he had completed *Finnegans Wake*, which was to come out simultaneously in the United States and in England. One of his closest French friends, the critic Louis Gillet, suggested that I write to him, explaining how important good photographs would be for publicizing the book. He advised me to mention my contacts with the French, British, and American press, as well as my photo-essays, which were then being published in magazines known throughout the world. In his reply Joyce said merely that he would like to see my collection of writers' portraits, and asked me to organize a slide showing at his home.

A few days later I arrived at 7 rue Edmond-Valentin, carrying a small projector, a screen, and my box of photographs. I had promised Joyce's wife, Nora, that I would not stay long, for I knew he was not well.

Joyce, half blind, sat so near the screen that he could have touched the faces of his contemporaries: Claudel, Valéry, Gide, Jules Romains, Montherlant, Aragon. During the entire showing, which lasted over an hour, he said not a word. When I turned on the lights again, I heard him heave a deep and dejected sigh. He appeared to be coming out of a dream.

"They're splendid," he said. "When do you want to photograph me? Not in color, of course. I couldn't stand the harsh lights on my eyes."

I was delighted to at least do a black and white portrait of him. We also spoke of a photostory on "James Joyce in Paris." He had very definite ideas on how he wanted to be presented to the world press on the publication of *Finnegans Wake*. He telephoned his friend and personal adviser Eugene Jolas, publisher of the review *transition*, and asked him to come over the next day so that I could take them together, correcting the proofs of the book. He also wanted me to take a series of photographs in Sylvia Beach's bookshop, Shakespeare and Company, with Adrienne—not for old time's sake, but for practical purposes: Joyce knew that English and American readers associated him with Sylvia, who had so courageously published *Ulysses* in 1922, while French readers knew that Adrienne had published the book in its French translation [Fig. 102]. We decided to end the story with pictures of Joyce at home, surrounded by his wife, son, and grandson— the human side of this great writer, which had almost disappeared behind the smokescreen of literary criticism.

The photographs were taken in several sittings during May of 1938. Joyce was patient and very eager to get good results. When they were ready, he seemed delighted and asked me to destroy only five or six of the hundred I had taken. We than selected some twelve pictures

102. Gisèle Freund. 'James Joyce, Sylvia Beach and Adrienne Monnier at Shakespeare and Company' (showing Joyce a portrait of himself taken in 1920), Paris, March 1939.

photographed in color and kept glancing uneasily at my apparatus. His nervousness finally affected me: I began tangling up wires and dropping things; the atmosphere was getting more and more strained. Suddenly, as Joyce groped about looking for the chair I had arranged for him, he hit his head against a lamp, and cried out as if he had been stabbed, clasping his hands to his forehead.

"I'm bleeding. Your damned photos will be the death of me!" he shouted, forgetting in his pain that he had made it a rule never to swear in the presence of a lady.

"Nora, have you got some scissors?" I called out to his wife, in the next room. Gentle, motherly, and soothing, she came in and approached him as one would a frightened child. I pressed the cold steel against the almost imperceptible scratch to prevent swelling, a remedy I recalled from my childhood.

Now that he was calmer, Joyce sat down and, with a magnifying glass, began to examine the page of a book, as he so often did. I snapped a picture of him and went on to finish my roll of film as quickly as possible, before promising the ailing man that I would really never bother him again.

Visibly relieved, he kept me a few minutes more; we talked about *Finnegans Wake*, speculating on the kind of reception it would get from the critics and public. At the end his voice grew weak and tired; he spoke about death—his own death—predicting that *Finnegans Wake* would be his last book.

I assured him that after years of intense work every writer is depressed and exhausted, that he was still young (he was only fifty-six), and that in France the "young" members of the French Academy were at least sixty. He refused to be consoled, and a touch of gloom hung over us as I left.

I hailed a taxi and asked the driver to take me as quickly as possible to the laboratory, where a technician was waiting to develop the film; the best portrait of Joyce had to be sent immediately to *Time* magazine in New York.

My driver was so anxious to do his best that, as he turned a corner, we skidded and hit another

which I distributed to the press. Since everyone wanted the latest photographs of Joyce, I soon had the pleasure of telling him that he could count on worldwide circulation of my story.

For various reasons the publication of *Finnegans Wake* was delayed, and it was not until May 4, 1939, that it appeared simultaneously in New York and London. Early in March, *Time* magazine asked me for a color portrait of the author to use for one of its covers.

Since I had promised Joyce not to trouble him any more, I was reluctant to approach him again. But his friends thought that a *Time* cover would be great publicity for a book as difficult as *Finnegans Wake*. It was Sylvia Beach who hit on an idea. Joyce, the Irishman, was not only intimately involved with his fictional characters, but superstitious as well. And it happened that my husband's name was the same as that of the hero of *Ulysses*.

"Write to him," Sylvia told me, "and sign your married name."

I could only congratulate Sylvia on the move, for Joyce accepted at once.

The sitting took place on March 8. He opened the door himself when I arrived. He had put on a wine-colored velvet jacket and was wearing several jeweled rings on his long sensitive fingers. He seemed altogether miserable at being car. I was thrown forward and covered with bits of broken glass; my camera was smashed.

I arrived home with blood on my face and tears of rage in my eyes, and at once telephoned Joyce.

"Mr. Joyce," I said, weeping, "you cursed my photos; you put some kind of bad Irish spell on them and my taxi crashed. I was almost killed and your photos are ruined. Now are you satisfied?"

I heard Joyce sigh and guessed that I had not been mistaken: he must have cursed me and now felt responsible for the accident. Embarrassed, he made an appointment with me for another sitting the next day.

When I arrived, he was full of remorse and very anxious to make amends. He had put on a black velvet jacket instead of the wine-colored one, and all his rings were different. This time everything went well, and I kept him only a few minutes.

When I reached the laboratory, I was overjoyed to find that the film of the previous day had not suffered from the accident. So I had two series of color portraits.

Joyce was as happy as a child when *Time* came out with his picture on the cover, and he showed it to everyone who came to see him. Better still, he was really amused by the whole story, which he told his friends, concluding: "I had said I would never be photographed in color. Well, I was caught by Mrs. B., not once but twice. She's even cleverer that the Irish." [pp. 116–23]

1. See Freund's dissertation on nineteenth-century French photography, revised and published as *Photography and Society* [1974], trans. Richard Dunn et al. (Boston: Godine, 1980).

2. See also Noel Riley Fitch, *Sylvia Beach and the Lost Generation: A History of Literary Paris in the Twenties and Thirties* (New York: Norton, 1983), pp. 356–57, for Beach's invaluable help to the photographer; Freund, *The World in My Camera,* especially pp. 55–60; Freund, *Freund, Photographer,* pp. 66–71, for more accounts and photographs of both Beach and Monnier; and *Les Années Vingt: Les Écrivains Américains à Paris et Leurs Amis, 1920–1930,* an exhibition catalogue illustrated with halftones from the archives of Sylvia Beach (Paris: Centre Culturel American, [March 11–April 25, 1959]). A later Cartier-Bresson portrait of Sylvia Beach, n.d., still surrounded by pictures and books, is reproduced in *Photoportraits,* p. 68.

3. For Joyce's references to photography in his two major novels, see *Ulysses* (New York: Random House, 1934), p. 65: Bloom's daughter, Millicent, writes she is "getting on swimming in the photo business. Mr. Coughlin took one of me and Mrs. will send when developed"; and *Finnegans Wake* (New York: Viking, 1939), p. 171, line 33: "for the very fourth snap shotted the as yet unremuneranded national apostate, who was cowardly gun and camera shy," and p. 277, line 25: "and it's time that all paid tribute to this massive mortality, the pink of punk perfection as photography in mud." See also Terence Brown, "Joyce's Magic Lantern," *James Joyce Quarterly* 29, no. 4 (Summer 1991): 791–98 and Craig S. Smith and Matthew L. Jockers, "Joyce's *Ulysses,*" *Explicator* 50, no. 4 (Summer 1992): 235–37. The Moholy-Nagy selection below provides a fine example of Joyce's influence on all artists.

4. See Freund, *Freund, Photographer,* pp. 88 and 90, for two color portraits of Joyce; many of her color portraits of other notable writers also are reproduced throughout this book and in Freund, *The World in My Camera,* inserted between pp. 212 and 213. See also Freund and V. B. Carleton, *James Joyce in Paris. His Final Years* (New York: Harcourt, Brace & World, 1965), and Freund, *Three Days with James Joyce* (1982), trans. Peter St. John Ginna (New York: Persea Books, 1985).

5. See Freund: *The World in My Camera,* and *Gisèle Freund, Photographer,* passim.

6. Quoted in Adrienne Monnier, "In the Land of Faces," *Verve,* nos. 5–6 (1939): 119, and in Simone de Beauvoir, preface to *James Joyce in Paris,* p. ix. See also Christian Caujolle, foreword to Freund, *Gisèle Freund, Photographer,* pp. 9–11.

Part Five

1940–1965

*P*arks (1912–) is the most versatile photographer-writer of our time. His "choice of weapons" to combat widespread discrimination against blacks includes images and words, usually together, in a variety of genres. He has been a fashion photographer, photojournalist, piano player, composer of orchestral pieces and ballets performed here and abroad, director of five Hollywood films, as well as a writer of poetry, fiction, and nonfiction, sometimes accompanied by his own pictures.[1] Parks's four autobiographies variously chronicle his life from his segregated Kansas childhood to his present celebrity status. The second, A Choice of Weapons (1966), details Parks's use of the camera to escape from a marginal existence as busboy, piano player, basketball player, and waiter on a Pullman dining car; here he first began studying magazine pictures and meeting photographers, eventually winning an FSA internship under Roy Stryker. The remaining volumes feature Parks's years as a staff photographer for Life magazine. In the early 1950's, he was assigned to Paris, where he met many European and expatriate artists, including Richard Wright [Fig. 114], whose impassioned text for the photo-documentary Twelve Million Black Voices (1941) had greatly influenced him.[2] In the 1960's, Parks often covered the civil rights movement, becoming friends with Malcolm X, whose own Autobiography (1964) remains one of the classics of the era.[3]

Charlie [another Pullman porter] used to read a lot and one day I thumbed through a magazine he had left behind. There was a portfolio of photographs in it that I couldn't forget; they were of migrant workers. Dispossessed, beaten by dust, storms and floods, they roamed the highways in caravans of battered jalopies and wagons between Oklahoma and California scrounging for work. Some were so poor, the captions read, they traveled by foot, pushing their young in baby buggies and carts. And there were photographs of shanties with siding and roofs of cardboard boxes; the inside walls were dressed with newspapers. I thought back to Philip and wondered if I were staring at members of his family. And across two pages was a memorable picture of a father and his two small sons running to their shanty in a dust storm. The names of the photographers too stuck in my mind—Arthur Rothstein, Russell Lee, Carl Mydans, Walker Evans, Ben Shahn, John Vachon, Jack Delano, Dorothea Lange. They all worked for the Farm Security Administration, a government agency set up by Roosevelt to aid submarginal farmers. These stark images of men, women and children, caught in their confusion and poverty, saddened me. I asked Charlie to give me the magazine and I took it home and kept looking at those photographs and the names of the photographers for months.

The following months I read John Steinbeck's *In Dubious Battle* as well as Erskine Caldwell's and Margaret Bourke-White's *You Have Seen Their Faces*. And, for some reason I could not yet explain, I was becoming restless again. The railway or the money I made there wasn't enough any more. [ch. 16, pp. 174–75]

By now I was convinced of the power of a good picture. And I decided to visit the Institute whenever I came to Chicago. That same afternoon I went to a movie and, during a newsreel, I saw Japanese war planes bomb the U.S.S. Panay. The photographer had stayed at his post, shooting the final belch of steam and smoke that rose when the ill-fated gunboat sank into the Yangtze River. The newspapers and radio reported the bombing; but the newsreel, through its grim directness, brought me face to face with the real horror of war. "It's the same thing as the FSA photographers did with poverty," I thought as I saw watching. When the newsreel ended, a voice boomed over the theater intercom system, "And here he is, Norman Alley, the photographer who shot this remarkable film!" Alley stepped out on the stage in a white suit amid the cheers of the audience, bowed, and after it was quiet he talked about his experience. I was enthralled. He had no way of knowing it, but he had just changed my life. I sat through another show; and even before I left the theater I had made up my mind I was going to become a photographer. [ch. 17, p. 178]

I worked hard at my double life, savoring with anticipation the day I could leave the railway forever. I would take it slower, learn my craft well and then strike out. I felt my wife would be with me all the way. My conscience demanded that I hurry before time and a bigger family trapped me. I read every book on art and photography I could afford. I talked to painters, writers and photographers whenever I discovered them on my car.

One day I saw the word *Life* in big red letters on a passenger's camera bag and discovered he was Bernard Hoffman, a photographer for that publication. We talked for a long time. "Come and work with us someday," he said when he got off in Chicago. And I laughed and promised him that I surely would. Then a few weeks later Bob Capa, the famous war photographer, came aboard, hoping to sleep the four hundred miles back to Chicago, only to be kept awake with my constant barrage of questions. And he said, "See you in Europe," when he stepped wearily off the car several hours later. The contact with these men transformed me into a dynamo.

Vogue was one of the magazines well-to-do passengers left on the train. I used to study the luxurious fashion photographs on its pages and the uncommon name of the photographers who took them—Steichen, Blumenfeld, Horst, Beaton, Hoyningen-Huene. How lucky they were, I thought. Day-dreaming once, I printed my name under a Steichen portrait of Katherine Cornell. And my imagination assured me that it looked quite natural there. [ch. 19, pp. 195–96]

Note: The result of a free-lance job photographing fashion models attracted the attention and patronage of Marva Louis, the wife of Joe Louis, the heavyweight boxing champion. Parks quit his railroad job, became a full-time photographer of both high and impoverished Chicago society, and won a Rosenwald Fellowship, which arranged his year's internship at the FSA.

I came to Washington, excited and eager, on a clear cold day in January. I had been singled out for an unusual blessing. I felt a notch above normal things, bursting with a new strength that would be unleashed upon this historic place. The White House, the Capitol and all the great buildings wherein great men had helped shape the destinies of the world—I would borrow from their tradition, feel their presence, touch their stone. I would walk under trees and on paths where Presidents had once walked. My mind hurried the taxi along to the place where I was to stay. It hastened my unpacking and raced ahead of the streetcar that carried me to the red brick building at Fourteenth and Independence avenues where I would meet Stryker and the photographers of the Farm Security Administration. And I walked confidently down the corridor, following the arrows to my destination, sensing history all around me, feeling knowledge behind every door I passed. I was so uplifted that the plainness of the office I finally entered dumbfounded me. The barnlike room with the plain furniture and bulky file cabinets was as ordinary as any other office I had seen but even more so. No photographs were on the walls and there were no photographers around; ordinary dust clung to the windows and the air was no different from that I had breathed back in Kansas. I stood waiting, a little disappointed, wondering what I had really expected. I didn't know, I finally realized.

A tall blonde girl who said her name was Charlotte came forward and greeted me. "Mr. Stryker will be with you in a minute," she said. She had just gotten the words out when he bounced out and extended his hand. "Welcome to Washington. I'm Roy," were his first words.

"Come into the office and let's get acquainted." I will like this man, I thought.

He motioned me to a chair opposite his desk but before he could say anything his telephone rang. "It's Arthur Rothstein phoning from Montana," Charlotte called from the outer office. The name flashed my thoughts back to the night on the dining car when I first saw it beneath the picture of the farmer and his two sons running toward their shack through the dust storm. *"Arthur? This is Roy."*

I'm here, I thought; at last I'm here.

As he talked I observed the chubby face topped with a mane of white hair, the blinking piercingly curious eyes, enlarged under thick bifocal lenses. There was something boyish, something fatherly, something tyrannical, something kind and good about him. He did not seem like anyone I had ever known before.

They talked for about ten minutes. "That was Rothstein." Stryker said, hanging up. "He had bad luck with one of his cameras." The way he said this pulled me in as if I were already accepted; as if I had been there for years. The indoctrination had begun. "Now tell me about yourself and your plans," he said with a trace of playfulness in his voice. I spent a lot of time telling him perhaps more than he bargained for. After I had finished, he asked me bluntly, "What do you know about Washington?"

"Nothing much," I admitted.

"Did you bring your cameras with you?"

"Yes, they're right here in this bag." I took out my battered Speed Graphic and a Rolleiflex and proudly placed them on his desk.

He looked at them approvingly and then asked me for the bag I had taken them from. He then took all my equipment and locked it in a closet behind him. "You won't be needing those for a few days," he said flatly. He lit a cigarette and leaned back in his chair and continued, "I have some very specific things I would like you to do this week. And I would like you to follow my instructions faithfully. Walk around the city. Get to know it. Buy yourself a few things—you have money, I suppose."

"Yes, sir."

"Go to a picture show, the department stores, eat in the restaurants and drugstores. Get to know this place." I thought his orders were a bit trivial, but they were easy enough to follow. "Let me know how you've made out in a couple of days," he said after he had walked me to the door.

"I will," I promised casually. And he smiled oddly as I left.

I walked toward the business section and stopped at a drugstore for breakfast. When I sat down at the counter the white waiter looked at me as though I were crazy. "Get off of that stool," he said angrily. "Don't you know colored people can't eat in here? Go round to the back door if you want something." Everyone in the place was staring at me now. I retreated, too stunned to answer him as I walked out the door.

I found an open hot dog stand. Maybe this place would serve me. I approached the counter warily. "Two hot dogs, please."

"To take out?" the boy in the white uniform snapped.

"Yes, to take out," I snapped back. And I walked down the street, gulping down the sandwiches.

I went to a theater.

"What do you want?"

"A ticket."

"Colored people can't go in here. You should know that."

I remained silent, observing the ticket seller with more surprise than anything else. She looked at me as though I were insane. What is this, I wondered. Was Stryker playing some sort of joke on me? Was this all planned to exasperate me? Such discrimination here in Washington, D.C., the nation's capital? It was hard to believe.

Strangely, I hadn't lost my temper. The experience was turning into a weird game, and I would play it out—follow Roy's instructions to the hilt. I would try a department store now; and I chose the most imposing one in sight, Julius Garfinckel. Its name had confronted me many times in full-page advertisements in fashion magazines. Its owners must have been filled with national pride—their ads were always identified with some sacred Washington monument. Julius Garfinckel. Julius Rosenwald. I lumped them with the names of Harvey Goldstein, and Peter Pollack—Jews who had helped shift the course of my life. I pulled myself together and entered the big store, with nothing particular in mind. The men's hats were on my right so I arbitrarily chose that department. The salesman appeared a little on edge but he sold me a hat. Then leaving I saw an advertisement for camel's hair coats on an upper floor. I had wanted one since the early days at the Minnesota Club. It was possible now. . . .

. . . The game had temporarily ended on the first floor as far as I was concerned. The purchase of the hat had relieved my doubts about discrimination here; the coat was the goal now. The floor was bare of customers. Only four salesmen stood eying me as I stepped from the elevator. None of them offered assistance so I looked at them and asked to be shown a camel's-hair coat.

No one moved. "They're to your left," someone volunteered.

I walked to my left. There were the coats I wanted, several racks of them. But no one attempted to show them to me.

"Could I get some help here?" I asked.

One man sauntered over. "What can I do for you?"

"I asked you for a camel's-hair coat."

"Those aren't your size."

"Then where are my size?"

"Probably around to your right."

"Probably around to my right?" The game was on again. "Then show them to me."

"That's not my department."

"Then whose department is it?"

"Come to think of it, I'm sure we don't have your size in stock."

"But you don't even know my size."

"I'm sorry. We just don't have your size."

"Well, I'll just wait here until you get one my size."

Anger was at last beginning to take over. There was a white couch in the middle of the floor. I walked over and sprawled out leisurely on it, took a newspaper from my pocket and pretended to read. My blackness stretched across the white couch commanded attention. The manager arrived, posthaste, a generous smile upon his face. My ruse had succeeded, I thought.

"I'm the manager of this department. What can I do for you?"

"Oh, am I to have the honor of being waited on by the manager? How nice," I said, smiling with equal graciousness.

"Well, you see, there's a war on. And we're very short of help. General Marshall was in here yesterday and *he* had to wait for a salesman. Now please understand that—"

"But I'm not General Marshall and there's no one here but four salesmen, you and me. But I'll wait here until they're not so busy. I'll wait right here." He sat down in a chair beside me and we talked for a half hour—about weather, war, food, Washington, and even camel's-hair coats. But I was never shown one. Finally, after he ran out of conversation, he left. I continued to sit there under the gaze of the four puzzled salesmen and the few customers who came to the floor. At last the comfort of the couch made me sleepy; and by now the whole thing had become ridiculous. I wouldn't have accepted a coat if they had given me the entire rack. Suddenly I thought of my camera, of Stryker. I got up and hurried out of the store and to his office. He was out to lunch when I got back. But I waited outside his door until he returned.

"I didn't expect you back so soon," he said. "I thought you'd be out seeing the town for a couple of days."

"I've seen enough of it in one morning." I replied sullenly. "I want my cameras."

"What do you intend to do with them?"

"I want to show the rest of the world what your great city of Washington, D.C., is really like. I want—"

"Okay. Okay." The hint of that smile was on his face again. And now I was beginning to understand it. "Come into my office and tell me all about it," he said. He listened patiently. He was sympathetic; but he didn't return my equipment.

"Young man," he finally began, "you're going to face some very hard facts down here. Whatever else it may be, this is a Southern city. Whether you ignore it or tolerate it is up to you. I purposely sent you out this morning so that you can see just what you're up against." He paused for a minute to let this sink in. Then he continued. "You're going to find all kinds of people in Washington and a good cross-section of the types are right here in this building. You'll have to prove yourself to them, especially the lab people. They are damned good technicians— but they are all Southerners. I can't predict what their attitudes will be toward you and I warn you I'm not going to try to influence them one way or the other. It's completely up to you. I do think they will respect good craftsmanship. Once you get over that hurdle I honestly believe you will be accepted as another photographer—not just as a Negro photographer. There is a certain amount of resentment against even the white photographers until they prove themselves. Remember, these people slave in hot darkrooms while they think about the photographers enjoying all the glamour and getting all the glory. Most of them would like to be on the other end."

We were walking about the building now, and as he introduced me to different people his words took on meaning. Some smiled and extended their hands in welcome. Others, especially those in the laboratory, kept working and acknowledged me with cold nods, making their disdain obvious. Any triumph over them would have to be well earned, I told myself. Stryker closed the door when we were back in his office. "Go home," he advised, "and put it on paper."

"Put what on paper?" I asked puzzled.

"Your plan for fighting these things you say you just went through. Think it out constructively. It won't be easy. You can't take a picture of a white salesman, waiter or ticket seller and just say they are prejudiced. That isn't enough. You've got to verbalize the experience first, then find logical ways to express it in pictures. The right words too are important; they should underscore your photographs. Think in terms of images and words. They can be mighty powerful when they are fitted together properly."

I went home that evening and wrote. I wrote of just about every injustice that I had ever experienced. Kansas, Minnesota, Chicago, New York and Washington were all forged together in the heat of the blast.

Images and words images and words images and words—I fell asleep trying to arrange an acceptable marriage of them.

Stryker read what I had written with a troubled face. I watched his eyes move over the lines, his brows furrow from time to time. When he had finished we both sat quietly for a few minutes. "You've had quite a time," he finally said, "but you have to simplify all this material. It would take many years and all the photographers on the staff to fulfill what you have put down here. Come outside; I want to show you something." He took me over the file and opened a drawer marked "Dorothea Lange." "Spend the rest of the day going through this set of pictures. Each day take on another drawer. And go back and write more specifically about your visual approach to things."

For several weeks I went through hundreds of photographs by Lange, Russell Lee, Jack Delano, Carl Mydans, John Vachon, Arthur Rothstein, Ben Shahn, Walker Evans, John Collier and others. The disaster of the thirties was at my fingertips: the gutted cotton fields, the eroded farmland, the crumbling South, the unending lines of dispossessed migrants, the pitiful shacks, the shameful city ghettos, the breadlines and bonus marchers, the gaunt faces of men, women and children caught up in the tragedy; the horrifying spectacles of sky blackened with locusts, and swirling dust and towns flooded with muddy rivers. There were some no doubt who laid these tragedies to God. But research accompanying these stark photographs accused man himself—especially the lords of the land. In their greed and passion for wealth, they had gutted the earth for cotton; overworked the

farms; exploited the tenant farmers and sharecroppers who, broken, took to the highways with their families in search of work. They owned the ghettos as well as the impoverished souls who inhabited them. No, the indictment was against man, not God; the proof was there in those ordinary steel files. It was a raw slice of contemporary America—clear, hideous and beautifully detailed in images and words. I began to get the point. . . . [ch. 21, pp. 220–28]

. . . Using my camera effectively against intolerance was not so easy as I had assumed it would be. One evening, when Stryker and I were in the office alone, I confessed this to him. "Then at least you have learned the most important lesson," he said. He thought for a moment, got up and looked down the corridor, then called me to his side. There was a Negro charwoman mopping the floor. "Go have a talk with her before you go home this evening. See what she has to say about life and things. You might find her interesting."

This was a strange suggestion, but after he had gone I went through the empty building searching for her. I found her in a notary public's office and introduced myself. She was a tall spindly woman with sharp features. Her hair was swept back from graying temples; a sharp intelligence shone in the eyes behind the steel-rimmed glasses. We started off awkwardly, neither of us knowing my reason for starting the conversation. At first it was a meaningless exchange of words. Then, as if a dam had broken within her, she began to spill out her life story. It was a pitiful one. She had struggled alone after her mother had died and her father had been killed by a lynch mob. She had gone through high school, married and become pregnant. Her husband was accidentally shot to death two days before the daughter was born. By the time the daughter was eighteen she had given birth to two illegitimate children, dying two weeks after the second child's birth. What's more, the first child had been stricken with paralysis a year before its mother died. Now this woman was bringing up these grandchildren on a salary hardly suitable for one person.

103. Gordon Parks. 'American Gothic (Ella Watson and American Flag),' 1942.

"Who takes care of them while you are at work?" I asked after a long silence.

"Different neighbors," she said, her heavily veined hands tightened about the mop handle.

"Can I photograph you?" The question had come out of an elaboration of thoughts. I was escaping the humiliation of not being able to help.

"I don't mind," she said.

My first photograph of her was unsubtle. I overdid it and posed her, Grant Wood style, before the American flag, a broom in one hand, a mop in the other, staring straight into the camera [Fig. 103].

Stryker took one look at it the next day and fell speechless.

"Well, how do you like it?" I asked eagerly.

He just smiled and shook his head. "Well?" I insisted.

"Keep working with her. Let's see what happens." He finally replied. I followed her for nearly a month—into her home, her church and wherever she went. "You're learning," Stryker admitted when I laid the photographs out before him late one evening. "You're showing you can involve yourself in other people. This woman has done you a great service. I hope you understand this." I did understand. [ch. 20, pp. 230–31]

1. Parks's other autobiographies include the fictionalized *The Learning Tree* (New York: Harper & Row, 1963); *To Smile in Autumn* (New York: Norton, 1979); and *Voices in the Mirror: An Autobiography* (New York: Doubleday, 1990), which often varies significant episodes from earlier volumes, such as this FSA experience above, pp. 81–84. For Parks's poetry, see *The Poet and the Camera,* with accompanying color photographs (New York: Viking, 1968); *Whispers of Intimate Things* (New York: Viking, 1971); *In Love* (Philadelphia: Lippincott, 1971); and *Moments Without Proper Names* (New York: Viking, 1975).

2. See Wright's *Twelve Million Black Voices,* with photographs selected by Edwin Rosskam (New York: Viking, 1941), commented on in Parks, *To Smile in Autumn,* pp. 75–76. For more on Wright, see his selection below.

3. See Malcolm X (with Alex Haley), *The Autobiography of Malcolm X* (New York: Grove Press, 1965), and Parks, *To Smile in Autumn,* pp. 129–47, on their relationship. See also Parks, foreword to *The Black Photographers' Annual,* vol. 3 (Brooklyn: Black Photographers Annual, 1976), npn, and foreword to Aaron Siskind [1981], *Harlem: Photographs 1932–1940* (Washington, D.C.: Smithsonian, 1990), pp. 4–5.

*N*eruda (1904–73), the pen name of one of the century's most prolific and influential Hispanic writers, was born in Chile; after early recognition as its leading poet, he was given diplomatic assignments all over the world. While consul general in Mexico (1940–43), he befriended Tina Modotti (1896–1942), sharing many of her revolutionary ideals. Modotti, whose uncle was a pioneer photographer, had emigrated from Italy (1918), appeared in some Hollywood films (1920), and met Edward Weston (1921), becoming his model, pupil, and lover [Fig. 104]. The pair lived in Mexico (1923–26), often exhibiting their prints together, though Modotti's sharply focused scenes of ordinary life were infused with greater social consciousness than Weston's.[1] Her increasing involvement with anti-Fascist politics led to her parting from Weston (1926), expulsion from Mexico (1930), and subsequent years in Berlin, Moscow, and war-torn Spain, among other conflicted areas. Modotti had abandoned photography (1931), but resumed it after returning to Mexico with a false passport (1939). When she died prematurely from a heart attack, one of Weston's portraits of her surmounted her bier [Fig. 105]. Neruda was prompted to write this poem both to honor her name and to silence her reactionary critics; its first three stanzas were engraved on her tombstone.[2] Later in his own distinguished life, Neruda often collaborated with photographers eager to represent his surroundings or take his portrait.[3]

104. *(left)* Edward Weston. 'Tina Modotti,' 1921.

105. *(above)* Unknown. News photograph of Tina Modotti's bier, 1942 (with Edward Weston's 1921 portrait mounted on it).

"TINA MODOTTI IS DEAD"

Tina Modotti, sister, you do not sleep, no, you do not sleep.
Perhaps your heart hears the rose of yesterday
growing, the last rose of yesterday, the new rose.
      Rest gently, sister.

The new rose is yours, the new earth is yours:
you have put on a new dress of deep seed
and your soft silence is filled with roots.
      You shall not sleep in vain, sister.

Pure is your gentle name, pure is your fragile life.
Of bee, shadow, fire, snow, silence, foam,
of steel, line, pollen was built your tough,
      your slender structure.

The jackal at the jewel of your sleeping body
still shows the white feather and the bloody soul
as if you, sister, could rise up,
        smiling above the mud.

To my country I take you so that they will not touch you,
to my snow country so that your purity
will be far from the assassin, the jackal, the Judas:
        there you will be at peace.

Do you hear a step, a step-filled step, something
huge from the great plain, from the Don, from the cold?
Do you hear the firm step of a soldier upon the snow?
        Sister, they are your steps.

They will pass one day by your little tomb
before yesterday's roses are withered,
the steps of tomorrow will pass by to see
        where your silence is burning.

A world marches to the place where you were going, sister.
The songs of your mouth advance each day
in the mouths of the glorious people that you loved.
        Your heart was brave.

In the old kitchen of your country, on the dusty
roads, something is said and passes on,
something returns to the flame of your golden people,
        something awakes and sings.

They are your people, sister: those who today speak your name,
we who from everywhere, from the water and the land,
with your name leave unspoken and speak other names.
        Because fire does not die.

1. For more on Modotti's relations with Weston and many of his photographs of her, see Mildred Constantine, *Tina Modotti: A Fragile Life* [1975], rev. ed. (New York: Rizzoli, 1983), new ed. (San Francisco: Chronicle Books, 1993); Modotti, "The Letters from Tina Modotti to Edward Weston," ed. Amy Stark et al., *The Archive* 22 (January 1986): 3–81; and Weston, *Daybooks,* 2 vols., passim.

2. See Neruda, *Memoirs,* trans. Hardie St. Martin (New York: Farrar, Straus & Giroux, [1977]), pp. 255–564; Constantine, *Tina Modotti,* p. 216, reproduces the engraved tombstone. See also Margaret Hooks, *Tina Modotti: Photographer and Revolutionary* (Hammersmith, England; San Francisco: Pandora/HarperCollins, 1993), pp. 40–52, 56–62, 65–73, and 113–30, and Margaret Gibson's poems, *Memoirs of the Future: The Daybooks of Tina Modotti* (Baton Rouge: Louisiana State University Press, 1986). For more on Modotti's influence on Mexican photographers, see the Paz selection below.

3. See Neruda, *Windows That Open Inward: Images of Chile,* ed. Dennis Maloney, trans. Robert Bly et al., with photographs by Milton Rogovin (Buffalo, N.Y.: White Pine Press, 1985), npn; Neruda, *The House at Iria Negra,* trans. Dennis Maloney and Clark M. Zlotchew, with photographs by Rogovin (Fredonia, N.Y.: White Pine Press, 1988); Luis Poirot and Neruda, *Absence and Presence,* trans. Alastair Reed (New York: Norton, [1990]); Neruda, *Una Casa En La Arena,* with photographs by Sergio Larrain (Barcelona: Editorial Lumen, 1966); and Neruda, *Valparaiso* (1965), with photographs by Sergio Larrain (Paris: Éditions Hazan, 1991). See also portraits of Neruda by Cartier-Bresson, *Photoportraits,* p. 143; Freund, *Freund, Photographer,* p. 187, Plate 173 (1944); and Krementz, *The Writer's Image,* npn (1972).

66. Bertolt Brecht

PHOTOGRAMS FROM *Kriegsfibel*, [1933–45,] 1955

*B*recht (1898–1956), one of the dominant twentieth-century dramatists, was always interested in the uses of photography.[1] He
harnessed this interest to his beliefs before but especially after
fleeing Nazi Germany, hostile toward his fervent Marxism and his activist
popular theatre (1933). In exile, first in Scandinavia and then in California,
Brecht continued compiling, as he had from the mid-1920's, huge scrapbooks of photographs from newspapers and magazines, especially Life, and
particularly scenes from the Spanish Civil War to the end of the Second
World War.[2] Afterwards, he returned to East Germany, where, after blunt-
ing bureaucratic objections, he published a collection of sixty-nine of these
photographs [Figs. 106–109]—mainly of Nazi and Allied leaders, urban
destruction, desolate civilians, and enemy dead—as Kriegsfibel [War Primer,
1955]. Feeling that photographs alone, however powerful, insufficiently represented complex realities, Brecht accompanied each of his "photograms,"
as he called them, with a dense, often ironic, formal quatrain.[3] His coordinated images and words in this work, as in his plays, attempted to provoke
the reader to think critically and question all assumptions about society,
especially fascist and capitalist ones. When sales floundered, Brecht offered
to recommend the book personally to likely libraries and other institutions,
arguing that "our mad suppression of all the facts and judgment about the
Hitler years and the war has got to stop."[4] But his plans to supplement this
work with a companion volume entitled Friedensfibel [Primer of Peace]
remained unfinished.

Daß es entdeckt nicht und getötet werde —
Denn in den Lüften rauften sich die Herrn —
Verkroch viel Volk sich angstvoll in die Erde
Und folgte ihren Kämpfen so von fern.

[So they wouldn't be discovered and killed—
Because in the air the men were fighting each other—
Many people hid fearfully in the ground
And followed their fighting from afar.]

Bertolt Brecht

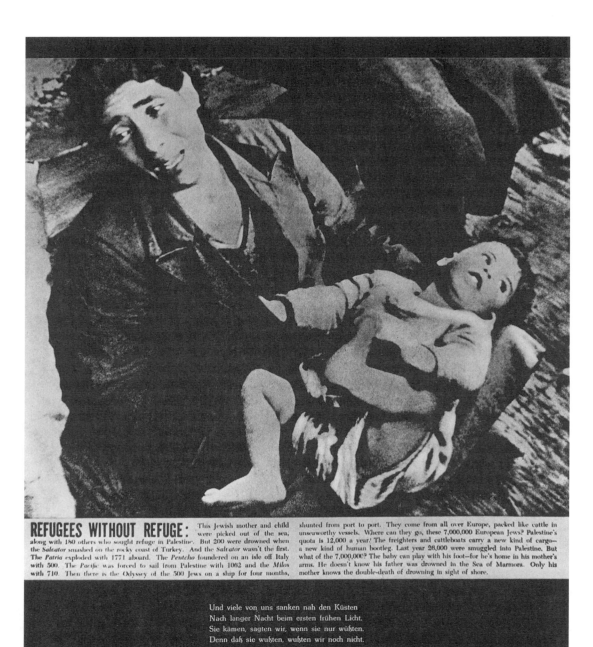

REFUGEES WITHOUT REFUGE: This Jewish mother and child were picked out of the sea, along with 180 others who sought refuge in Palestine. But 200 were drowned when the *Salvator* smashed on the rocky coast of Turkey. And the *Salvator* wasn't the first. The *Patria* exploded with 1771 aboard. The *Pentcho* foundered on an isle off Italy with 500. The *Pacific* was forced to sail from Palestine with 1062 and the *Milos* with 710. Then there is the Odyssey of the 500 Jews on a ship for four months, shunted from port to port. They come from all over Europe, packed like cattle in unseaworthy vessels. Where can they go, these 7,000,000 European Jews? Palestine's quota is 12,000 a year! The freighters and cattleboats carry a new kind of cargo—a new kind of human bootleg. Last year 26,000 were smuggled into Palestine. But what of the 7,000,000? The baby can play with his foot—for he's home in his mother's arms. He doesn't know his father was drowned in the Sea of Marmora. Only his mother knows the double-death of drowning in sight of shore.

Und viele von uns sanken nah den Küsten
Nach langer Nacht beim ersten frühen Licht.
Sie kämen, sagten wir, wenn sie nur wüßten.
Denn daß sie wußten, wußten wir noch nicht.

[And many of us sank near the coast
After the long night at dawn's early light.
They would come, we said, if only they knew
For we did not know yet that they did know.]

Seht diese Hüte von Besiegten! Und
Nicht als man sie vom Kopf uns schlug zuletzt
War unsrer bittern Niederlage Stund.
Sie war, als wir sie folgsam aufgesetzt.

[Look at these hats of the vanquished,
And the bitterness of our final defeat
Was not when they were knocked off our heads.
That was when we dutifully put them on.]

Bertolt Brecht

HITLER: April 20, 1889

Das da hätt einmal fast die Welt regiert.
Die Völker wurden seiner Herr. Jedoch
Ich wollte, daß ihr nicht schon triumphiert:
Der Schoß ist fruchtbar noch, aus dem das kroch.

[That one almost dominated the world once.
The conquered people of the world overcame him.
However, I wish that you wouldn't shout for joy:
The womb from which this thing crawled is still fertile.]

1. See P. V. Brady, "From Cave-Painting to 'Foto-gramm': Brecht, Photography and the *Arbeitsjournal*," *Forum for Modern Language Studies* 14, no. 3 (July 1978): 270–82; Brecht, "Über Photographie," *Gesammelte Werke* (Frankfurt am Main: Werkausgape Editions Suhrkamp, 1967), vol. 18, pp. 270–71; and Jim Car-mody, "Reading Scenic Writing: Barthes, Brecht, and Theatre Photography," *Journal of Dramatic Theory and Criticism* 5, no. 1 (Fall 1990): 25–38.

2. See Brecht, *Arbeitsjournal,* 1938–55, ed. Werner Hecht (Frankfurt am Main: Suhrkamp Verlag, 1973), 2 vols.

3. See Martin Esselin, *Brecht: The Man and His Work* (Garden City, N.Y.: Doubleday, 1960), pp. 103 and 197; Hunter, *Image and Word,* pp. 169–75, and Brecht, quoted in Benjamin, "A Short History of Photography," trans. P. Patton, in Trachtenberg, ed., *Classic Essays in Photography,* p. 213, also noted by Roland Barthes, *Camera Lucida,* trans. Richard Howard (New York: Hill & Wang, 1981), p. 36. See also Charles Simic, "Baby Pictures of Famous Dictators" [1978], in *Selected Poems, 1963–1983* (New York: Braziller, 1985), pp. 124–25.

4. Brecht, quoted from *Letters 1913–1956,* trans. Ralph Manheim and ed. John Willett (New York: Routledge, 1990), p. 691, n. 879.

67. *James Agee*

FROM INTRODUCTION [1946] TO
A Way of Seeing BY HELEN LEVITT, 1965

A gee (1909–55) was obsessed with the role of the camera, which, aside from human consciousness, he deemed "the central instrument of our time."[1] Prizing its ability to register accurately, he emulated it in his writing by recording detail after detail; he often wished to use photographs rather than words.[2] Not surprisingly, Agee found working in film rewarding, whether reviewing (from 1942), writing scripts (from 1937), or making them with the photographer Helen Levitt (from c. 1948). Levitt (1913–) first met Agee in 1938. He happened to stop by while she was seeking Walker Evans's opinion of her portfolio of arresting moments of New York street life [Fig. 110]; she soon became a close friend of both.[3] Agee, like Evans (and also Richard Wright), appreciated the spontaneity and veracity of her photographs, which he called "timeless," the urban equivalent of the subjects in Let Us Now Praise Famous Men.[4] *As Evans put it, "Levitt's work was one of James Agee's great loves; and, in turn, Agee's own magnificent eye was part of her early training."[5] Levitt also cherished his generous character, recalling "there was a lot of Jesus in Jim."[6] Agee gladly wrote this introduction for a planned publication and, when it was deferred, helped Levitt and her collaborators with their innovative films about similar urban subjects; as he confessed to her, poetry, his true vocation, was "too difficult," but film work was "pure pleasure."[7]*

. . . The mind and the spirit are constantly formed by, and as constantly form, the senses, and misuse or neglect the senses only at grave peril to every possibility of wisdom and well-being. The busiest and most abundant of the sense is that of sight. The sense of sight has been served and illuminated by the visual arts for as long, almost, as we have been human. For a little over a hundred years, it has also been served by the camera. Well used, the camera is unique in its power to defile and to destroy that ability. It is clear enough by now to most people that "the camera never lies" is a foolish saying. Yet it is doubtful whether most people realize how extraordinarily slippery a liar the camera is. The camera is just a machine, which records with impressive and as a rule very cruel faithfulness, precisely what is in the eye, mind, spirit, and skill of its operator to make it record. Since relatively few of its operators are notably well endowed in any of these respects, save perhaps in technical skill, the results are, generally, disheartening. It is probably well on the conservative side to estimate that during the past ten to fifteen years the camera has destroyed a thousand pairs of eyes, corrupted ten thousand, and seriously deceived a hundred thousand, for every one pair that it has opened, and taught.

It is in fact hard to get the camera to tell the truth; yet it can be made to, in many ways and on many levels. Some of the best photographs we are ever likely to see are innocent domestic snapshots, city postcards, and news and scientific photographs. If we know how, moreover, we can enjoy and learn a great deal from essentially untrue photographs, such as studio portraits, movie romances, or the national and class types apotheosized in ads for life insurance and feminine hygiene. It is a good deal harder to tell the truth, in this medium, as in all others, at the level of perception and discipline on which an artist works, and the attempt to be "artistic" or, just as bad, to combine "artistry" with something that pays better, has harmed countless photographs for every one it has helped, and is harming more all the time. During the century that the camera has been available, relatively few people have tried to use it at all consistently as an artist might, and of these very few indeed could by any stretch of courtesy be called good artists. Among these few, Helen Levitt is one of a handful who have to be described as good artists, not loosely, or arrogantly, or promotively but simply because no other description will do.

In every other art which draws directly on the actual world, the actual is transformed by the artist's creative intelligence, into a new and different kind of reality: aesthetic reality. In the kind of photography we are talking about here, the actual is not at all transformed; it is reflected and recorded, within the limits of the camera, with all possible accuracy. The artist's task is not to alter the world as the eye sees it into a world of aesthetic reality, but to perceive the aesthetic reality within the actual world, and to make an undisturbed and faithful record of the instant in which this movement of creativeness achieves its most expressive crystallization. Through his eye and through his instrument the artist has, thus, a leverage upon the materials of existence which is unique, opening to him a universe which has never before been so directly or so purely available to artists, and requiring of his creative intelligence and of his skill, perceptions and disciplines no less deep than those required in any other act of aesthetic creation, though very differently deprived, and enriched.

The kind of beauty he records may be so monumentally static, as it is in much of the work of Mathew Brady, Eugène Atget, and Walker Evans, that the undeveloped eye is too casual and wandering to recognize it. Or it may be so filled with movement, so fluid and so transient, as it is in much of the work of Henri Cartier-Bresson and of Miss Levitt, that the undeveloped eye is too slow and too generalized to foresee and to isolate the most illuminating moment. It would be mistaken to suppose that any of the best photography is come at by intellection; it is, like all art, essentially the result of an intuitive process, drawing on all that the artist *is* rather than on anything he thinks, far less theorizes about. But it seems quite natural, though none of the artists can have made any choice in the matter, that the static work is generally the richest in meditativeness, in mentality, in attentiveness to the wonder of materials and of objects, and in complex multiplicity of attitudes of perception, whereas the volatile work is richest in emotion; and that, though both kinds, at their best, are poetic in a very high degree, the static work has a kind of Homeric or Tolstoyan nobility, as in Brady's photographs, or a kind of Joycean denseness, insight and complexity resolved in its bitter purity, as in the work of Evans; whereas the best of the volatile work is nearly always lyrical.

It is remarkable, I think, that so little of this lyrical work has been done; it is perhaps no less remarkable that, like nearly all good photographic art, the little that has been done has been so narrowly distributed and so little appreciated. For it is, after all, the simplest and most direct way of seeing the everyday world, the most nearly related to the elastic, casual and subjective way in which we ordinarily look around us. One would accordingly suppose that, better than any other kind of photography, it could bring pleasure, could illuminate and enhance our ability to see what is before us and to enjoy what we see, and could relate all that we see to the purification and healing of our emotions and of our spirit, which in our time are beguiled with such unprecedented dangerousness towards sickness and atrophy.

I do not at all well understand the reasons for the failure, but a few possibilities may be worth mentioning in passing. For a long time the camera was too slow, large, and conspicuous to work in the fleeting and half-secret world which is most abundant in lyrical qualities. More recently it has become all but impossible, even for those who had it in the first place, to maintain intact and uncomplicated the simple liveliness of soul and of talent without which true lyrical work cannot be done. As small, quick, foolproof cameras became generally available, moreover, the camera has been used so much and so flabbily by so many peo-

ple that it has acted as a sort of contraceptive on the ability to see. And more recently, as the appetite for looking at photographs has grown, and has linked itself with the worship of "facts," and as a prodigious apparatus has been developed for feeding this appetite, the camera has been used professionally, a hundred times to one, in ways which could only condition and freeze the visual standards of a great majority of people at a relatively low grade.

As a further effect of this freezing and standardization, photographers who really have eyes, and who dare to call their eyes their own, and who do not care to modify them towards this standardized, acceptable style, have found it virtually impossible to get their work before most of those who might enjoy it; or to earn, through such work, the food, clothing, shelter, leisure, and equipment which would make the continuance of that work possible. Almost no photographer whose work is preeminently worth looking at has managed to produce more than a small fraction of the work he was capable of, and the work, as a rule, has remained virtually unknown except to a few friends and fellow artists. This is true to a great extent, of course, of artists who work in any field. Yet distinctions, standards, and assumptions exist and have existed for centuries which guarantee a good poet or painter or composer an audience, if generally a small one; and these are not yet formed in relation to photographs. In its broad design, however, this is a familiar predicament, as old as art itself, and as tiresome at least, one may assume, to the artists who suffer the consequences as to the nonartists to whom it is just a weary cliché. I don't propose to discuss who, if anyone, is to blame, being all the less interested in such discussion because I don't think anyone is to blame. I mention it at all only because I presume that the distinction between faithfulness to one's own perceptions and a readiness to modify them for the sake of popularity and self-support is still to be taken seriously among civilized human beings; and because it helps, in its way, to place and evaluate Miss Levitt's work.

At least a dozen of Helen Levitt's photographs seem to me as beautiful, perceptive, satisfying, and enduring as any lyrical work that I know. In their general quality and coherence, moreover, the photographs as a whole body, as a book, seem to me to combine into a unified view of the world, an uninsistent but irrefutable manifesto of a way of seeing, and in a gentle and wholly unpretentious way, a major poetic work. Most of these photographs are about as near the pure spontaneity of true folk art as the artist, aware of himself as such, can come; and an absolute minimum of intellection, of technical finesse, or of any kind of direction or interference on the part of the artist as artist stands between the substance and the emotion and their communication.

It is of absolute importance, of course, that all these photographs are "real" records; that the photographer did not in any way prepare, meddle with, or try to improve on any one of them. But this is not so important of itself as, in so many of them, unretouched reality is shown transcending itself. Some, to be sure, are so perfectly simple, warm and direct in their understanding of a face or of an emotion that they are likely to mean a great deal to anyone who cares much for human beings: it would be hard to imagine anyone who would not be touched by all that is shown—by all that so beautifully took place in the unimagined world— . . . . Readers who particularly like children will find here as much to meditate, and understand, or be mystified by, as anyone, so far as I know, has ever managed to make permanent about children. Sociologically and psychologically, the photographs seem to be only the more rich and illuminating because they are never searching out or exploiting, in their subjects, such purposes—far less the still narrower and more questionable purposes of the journalist, humanitarian, or "documentor." There is in fact a great deal that can be seen here by the purely rational mind and eye, or by a person who is, in a purely rational way, interested in people, in relationships, and in cities.

I would not for a moment want to try to persuade any reader who mistrusts the irrational, to suspend his mistrust, and look further into these pictures. I am nevertheless convinced that the photographs cannot be fully enjoyed, or adequately discussed, on a purely naturalistic or rational basis. Many of them prove, rather, that the actual world constantly brings to the surface its own signals, and mysteries. At its simplest this kind of signaling could be called purely aesthetic. . . . I suspect that only the reader who recognizes this, in his own terms, will thoroughly understand and agree with what I mean by a photograph as a good work of art; or by a lyrical photograph.

The reader who does, is in a position fully to enjoy these photographs. He will realize how constantly the unimagined world is in its own terms an artist, and how deep and deft the creative intelligence must be, to recognize, foresee, and make permanent its best moments. Even in the most benignly open, simple-looking kind of portrait he will see this, and it will add its beauty and vitality: the toes of the baby in 55 and the glasses of the man, and the knobbed, shinning wood of the chair, and the man's knobbed, polished shoes, and the round foreheads and round heads and faces of the man and the baby, all assemble their delicate order like so many syllables in a line of poetry, to enhance the already great charm of the surface content. The rifted asphalt and the burnt match in 3 would lose much of their power if a painter had invented them or that photographer had arranged them; as it is they combine with the drawing to testify to the silent cruelty of nature.

Many people, even some good photographers, talk of the "luck" of photography, as if that were a disparagement. And it is true that luck is constantly at work. It is one of the cardinal creative forces in the universe, one which a photographer has unique equipment for collaborating with. And a photographer often shoots around a subject, especially one that is highly mobile and in continuous and swift development—which seems to me as much his natural business as it is for a poet who is really in the grip of his poem to alter and re-alter the words in his line. It is true that most artists, though they know their own talent and its gifts as luck, work as well as they can against luck, and that in most good works of art, as in little else in creation, luck is either locked out or locked in and semi-domesticated, or put to wholly constructive work; but it is peculiarly a part of the good photographer's adventure to know where luck is most likely to lie in the stream, to hook it, and to bring it in without unfair play and without too much subduing it. Most good photographs, especially the quick and lyrical kind, are battles between the artist and luck, and the happiest victories for the artist are draws. Luck can of course spoil as many photographs as it contributes to, or makes, and can seldom do anything for the photographer who lacks an eye for it, unless he is wholly absorbed in some quite different intention, or is thoroughly naive. . . .

Like most good artists, Miss Levitt is not intellectual and no theorist; she works quite simply, where she feels most thoroughly at home, and that, naturally enough, is where the kind of thing that moves and interests her is likely to occur most naturally and in best abundance. So there was nothing preconceived about the boundaries she has set around her subject matter. Yet it is worth noticing that in much of her feeling for streets, strange details, and spaces, her vocabulary is often suggestive of and sometimes identical with that of the Surrealists. In other words, there seems to be much about modern cities which of itself arouses in artists a sensitiveness, in particular, to the tensions and desolations of creatures in named space. But I think that in Miss Levitt's photographs the general feeling is rather that the surrealism is that of the ordinary metropolitan soil which breeds these remarkable juxtapositions and moments, and that what we call "fantasy" is, instead, reality in its unmasked vigor and grace. It is also worth noticing that nearly all the people in her photographs are poor; that most of them are of the relatively volatile strains; that many are children. It is further worth realizing that there is a logic and good sense about this, so far as her work is concerned. In children and adults alike, of this pastoral stock, there is more spontaneity, more grace, than among human beings of any other kind; and of all city streets, theirs are most populous in warm

weather, and most abundant in variety and in beauty, in strangeness, and in humor.

A great lyrical artist might still possibly find much, among people and buildings of the middle and rich classes, to turn to pure lyrical account. But it seems hardly necessary to point out that flowers grow much more rarely in that soil, perhaps especially in this country at this time, than weeds and cactuses; and that there is much more in that territory to interest the artist who is fascinated by irony, diagnosis, and the terrifying complexities of self-deceit and of evil, than there is for the lyrical artist. I cannot believe it is meaningless that with a few complicated exceptions, our only first-rate contemporary lyrics have gotten their life at the bottom of the human sea: aside from Miss Levitt's work I can think of little outside the best of jazz. Moreover, specialized as her world is, it seems to me that Miss Levitt has worked in it in such a way that it stands for much more than itself; that it is, in fact, a whole and round image of existence. These are pastoral people, persisting like wild vines upon the intricacies of a great city, a phantasmagoria of all that is most contemporary in hardness of material and of appetite. In my opinion they embody with great beauty and fullness not only their own personal and historical selves but also, in fundamental terms, a natural history of the soul, which I presume also to be warm-blooded, and pastoral, and, as a rule, from its first conscious instant onward, as fantastically misplaced in the urgent metropolis of the body, as the body in its world.

So far, I have avoided any attempt to discuss the "meanings" of the photographs, feeling that this is best left as an affair between the pictures themselves and the reader. By less direct means I have tried to furnish the chance reader who may feel that he lacks it, enough suggestions about such pictures as these, that he may go on to their full enjoyment without further interruption by words. But because I realize that we are all so deeply caught in the tyranny of words, even where words are not needed, that they have sometimes to be used as keys to unlock their own handcuffs, I have tried, from here on, to give a more directly suggestive paraphrase. That this paraphrase is extravagant, and that the "story" the pictures tell is arguable, from a rational point of view, and in some ways very sentimental from any point of view, I realize, with regret. The attempt is not rational because so much that is important in the pictures is not rational and because this is liable, I fear, to be insufficiently recognized. I am counting on the absolute reality of the pictures, and on the reader's rational use of eye and mind, to dress the boat; and I make this attempt chiefly because I feel that much of the enjoyment of the pictures depends on an appreciation of the tension which they create, and reveal, between the unimagined world, and the imaginable.

The overall preoccupation in the photographs is, it seems to me, with innocence—not as the word has come to be misunderstood and debased, but in its full, original wildness, fierceness, and instinct for grace and form; much may be suggested to some readers by Yeats's phrase, "the ceremony of innocence." This is the record of an ancient, primitive, transient, and immortal civilization, incomparably superior to our own, as it flourishes, at the proud and eternal crest of its wave, among those satanic incongruities of a twentieth century metropolis which are, for us, definitive expressions and productions of the loss of innocence.

110. Helen Levitt. Untitled (mother and child), New York City, c. 1942.

"... I do not know of any image so completely eloquent as that in the last picture, of all that is most gracious, great, and resplendent of well-being and of loveliness, that living servitude can mean, and bring in blessing. No one could write, paint, act, dance, or embody in music, the woman's sheltering and magnanimous arm, or tilt and voice of smiling head, or bearing and whole demeanor; which are also beyond and above any joy or beauty which a child could possibly experience or embody. She is at once the sweetness of life and the tenderness of death; the soul victorious in the body's world; the salvation and immortality of innocence." [Agee, from the introduction, p. xv]

1. See Agee, quoted in *Let Us,* p. 11; see also relevant references, pp. 13, 149, and metaphors, pp. 87, 108, 198.

2. See Hersey, "Agee," introduction to the 1988 edition of *Let Us,* pp. v–xl, especially pp. xxxiii–iv. See also Shloss, *In Visible Light,* pp. 191–97.

3. See Lawrence Bergreen, *James Agee: A Life* (New York: Dutton, 1984), pp. 232, 249, and 376 (a book Levitt distrusts); *Helen Levitt,* an exhibition catalogue with essays by Sandra S. Phillips and Maria Morris Hambourg (San Francisco: San Francisco Museum of Modern Art, 1991), 16, 36–38, and 54–58; Levitt's many pictures of Agee in *Agee: His Life Remembered,* ed. Ross Spears and Jude Cassidy (New York: Holt, Rinehart & Winston, 1985); and David Madden, ed., *Remembering James Agee* (Baton Rouge: Louisiana State University Press, [1974]).

4. See Agee, *Let Us,* p. 353, and Bergreen, p. 293.

5. Evans, quoted in Roberta Hellman and Marvin Hoshino, *Helen Levitt: Color Photographs* (El Cajon, Calif.: Grossman College, [1980]), npn; in Phillips, "Helen Levitt's New York," *Helen Levitt,* p. 38; and elsewhere. See also Wright's "Recommendation" of Levitt's 1943 MOMA exhibition at the Beinecke [JWJ Misc MS 692 and TS 693.3], which prompted him to propose a collaboration with Levitt which didn't materialize, the photographer recalled in conversation with the editor on February 14, 1992. For more about Wright, see his selection below.

6. Levitt, in conversation with the editor on April 16, 1992.

7. According to Levitt, in conversation with the editor on May 30, 1991, Agee shot some footage and provided commentary for *In the Street* (1952), provided the narrative for *The Quiet One* (1949), and wrote notes for another film, initially called "A Love Story," which was never produced. Agee's remark to Levitt is quoted in *The Collected Short Prose of James Agee,* ed. Robert Fitzgerald (Boston: Houghton Mifflin, 1968), p. 5.

68. László Moholy-Nagy

"JAMES JOYCE," FROM *Vision in Motion*, 1947

*M*oholy-Nagy (1895–1946), a Hungarian Constructivist artist who welcomed industry, technology, and science, greatly influenced many fields, including photography and education. Initially a poet, reviewer, and magazine editor, he became a sculptor, painter, filmmaker, and designer of stage sets, exhibitions, and books as well as a still photographer from 1922 on. Moholy-Nagy's work with both camera and cameraless images together with his exploration with his first wife, Lucia, of the effects of light and unusual vantage points in photograms, photomontages, and photoplastic assemblages helped to persuade the Bauhaus, where he taught (1923–28), to offer formal photography instruction.[1] Believing that experimentation, not tradition, was critical to all arts and that specialization led to fragmentation, he accepted an invitation from some midwestern manufacturers to implement these ideals at a new design school in Chicago. His New Bauhaus (1937–38) folded, but its independent successor, the School of Design (1939), later the Institute of Design (1944), proved viable, partly due to Moholy's energetic inventiveness, enthusiasm, and ability to communicate. One of his radical principles required all students to study, among other arts, both photography and literature for their special lessons in sight and insight, essential to the "New Vision." In a chapter on "Literature," from Vision in Motion (1947), written just before his untimely death, Moholy-Nagy praises (and quotes from) writers—particularly Poe, Thoreau, Whitman, Rimbaud, Dostoevsky, Tolstoy, and, above all, Joyce[2]—who have extended our ability to see in new ways and thus see "more." His experimental attitudes and interdisciplinary approach have become conventions in both photography and literature.

Although the surrealists emphasized such a goal, the new form of communication was not accomplished by them, but more by the dadaists and simultaneously and even more by James Joyce. (This observation is not only valid in literature. It is significant that the revolutionary impulses, and aims crystallized during the first quarter of the XXth century have been diluted everywhere into an often inconsequential estheticism by the young generation.)

Joyce's "Ulysses" was an excellent example of the new literary construction analogous to the cubist collage where different elements, fragments of reality, were fused into a unity of new meanings. Joyce showed that the seemingly inconsistent, illogical elements of the subconscious can give a perfect account of man, the unknown, who is always the same whether the Ulysses of antiquity or today's Leopold Bloom.

"Ulysses" was considered for many years an incomprehensible book, even nonsensical. But viewing the book in the light of the later "Finnegans Wake," it appears as a straight continuation of the 19th century psychological novel. It has a clearly circumscribed content—the story of a day, June 16th, 1904. It has its characters, its direct and symbolic meanings, its place and setting. The book has its own technique of rendering—at some places the technique of the stream of consciousness, of rendering a constant penetration of the subconscious forces along with those of the conscious thoughts drawn from the scientific discourses of Freud and the therapeutic application of psychoanalysis. In spite of its strange richness, "Ulysses" leads the reader with clear logic to a vivid, naturalistic description of the life of an anachronistic city, of the place, events and persons involved, though astonishing elements of the subconscious sometimes enter the field. The inundation of the characters with rude and exalted attributes may at first frighten the inexperienced reader. He may be temporarily misled because of the frightfulness of the subconscious landscape which had not yet been exploited in pre-Joycean literature. However, Joyce handles the subconscious man—a new "ecce homo" with lucid explicitness and one has to submit to the unusual and the shocking without fear as one submits to the knife of the surgeon if recovery is promised.

The peculiarity of Joyce's language is its multiple meaning, achieved through the fusion of the external reality with the subconscious state in the form of the interior monolog—"stream of consciousness"—and the day dreams of an introvert, centripetally condensed. In this way situations—old and new—words and sentences are recast and shifted to unexpected connotations, cunning intricate, pouring out humor and satire. Flashing sparks from the subconscious, mixed with trivialities of routine talk, sharp-tongued gossip illuminate hidden meanings. Puns are of deep significance, touching off liberating explosions. "Ulysses" comes as a breath of fresh air through its nimble, precise definitions of events and persons. . . .

The cunning ambiguity of the Pythian oracle of Delphi was full of contradictory meaning depending upon where the listener put the commas, semicolons and periods. But the quoted passage from Marion Bloom's soliloquy is a stream of the subconscious stringing thoughts like beads without any punctuation to impede the widening and ascending spiral of meaning. But this did not yet make "Ulysses" a revolutionary work. Compared with the writing of the dadaists, who recreated the conscious and subconscious *in integration,* "Ulysses" is still *"naturalism,"* even if of a two-dimensional kind. Joyce demonstrated in it the two levels of our psychophysical existence only in juxtaposition—though with marvelous precision. He telescoped nouns, verbs, adjectives into forceful images, visual and sound projections. He overthrew the old convention of a successive development of ideas. He took elements independent of space or time continuum when he needed them for the characterization of eternal human traits.

Whitman had already tried to show in his poems the finest structure of psychological details, as if they had been seen through a magnifying glass. The French naturalists, the Brothers Goncourt, Zola and later Proust, translated this technique into their prose. Joyce, too, was occupied with the precise formulations of an ultra-naturalism.

In "Ulysses" one has to perceive the whole with its interpenetration of details in order to grasp the dynamic fusion. The whole calls upon one's complete capacities, conscious and subconscious alike. The result is a richness and precision of rendition never before known.

In the new technology there are analogies for such a precision. It is not yet the super-precision of the microscopic section but—at least—that of the close-up. For example, with rubber liquid one can make visible the blood system of the kidney—a most complicated organ, full of minute details, never before seen in renderings of anatomic sections. Now, by injecting latex into the blood vessels and dissolving the tissues in acid after the rubber has set, an exact replica of the kidney can be produced with outside *and* inside visible. With this new technique, as with the new writing technique, *one sees more.*

Another analogy is a colored lantern slide of a cubist painting which is thrown out of focus when projected so that, for example, an unfocussed Picasso still-life of 1922 looks like a Cézanne. The peculiar green-red coloring of the Cézanne apples is repeated exactly in the Picasso apples out of focus. In focus, the same picture may appear to the inexperienced spectator as decomposed into incoherent shapes and color spots, entirely unfamiliar until the unfocussed view is shown which provides an almost macroscopic definition of the apples. The cubist painter, in trying to uncover the essential properties of his subject, worked with an infinitely greater precision than his predecessor. He tried to see more and what he saw he painted more intensely. With Joyce's language one can also see "more."

But what is this "more?"

It has been stated previously that the function of the complementary color in a painting—whether rendered actually, or produced only in the mind of the spectator—is to create a feeling of balance, the satiation of a psychophysical hunger. The way in which this is achieved determines the quality of painting. Joyce groped for a similar law on the large scale of man's total existence and tried to decode the impulses which seek to establish the psychological balance in every situation. Although man in his vanity and illusions is still pressed through heritage and education toward transcendentalism and tries to overcome his crises with metaphysics, Joyce found a rational method to balance such longings for "eternity" with the cyclic recurrence of biological and historical facts, personalities and characters. [pp. 341–44]

---

1. See Moholy-Nagy, *Painting, Photography, Film* (1925), trans. Janet Seligman (Cambridge: MIT Press, [1987]), pp. 27–79, which discusses some of this work and relates it to his ideas about vision generally; so does Van Deren Coke, "Moholy-Nagy," *Avant-Garde Photography in Germany 1919–1939* (New York: Pantheon, [1982]), pp. 9–12.

2. Joyce's cutting and reassembling or splicing of words, so appealing to Moholy-Nagy, still intrigues artists working with photomontages and photocollages. For example, the painter-photographer Jess "loves" *Finnegans Wake*, according to the poet Robert Duncan, quoted in Michael Auping's essay in *Jess's PASTE-UPS (and Assemblies) 1951–1983* (Sarasota, Fla.: Ringling Museum of Art, 1984), pp. 12–13. See also Walker Evans's comment on Joyce as a "photographic" writer, quoted in the introductory "Notes..." above, p. xliii.

69. John Steinbeck and Robert Capa

FROM *A Russian Journal*, 1948

Even in his prize-winning The Grapes of Wrath *(1939), a fictional saga of the migration of Dust Bowl refugees to California, Steinbeck (1902–68) showed a keen awareness of the power of photographs. Indeed, marked parallels have been observed between Steinbeck's graphic prose in his classic work and Dorothea Lange's photographs of similar situations, particularly those in* An American Exodus *(1939), her study of farm labor conditions with Paul Taylor.[1] During the Second World War, Steinbeck's* Bombs Away *(1942), a firsthand documentary for the Air Force on the training of a bomber crew, was enlivened by the photographs of John Swope.[2] Early in the Cold War, Steinbeck met Robert Capa (1913–54), distinguished for his "closer the better" combat photographs, which focused on suffering individuals to shock viewers into ending the horrors of civil and global war. A lively storyteller by nature as well as by profession, Capa had many writer friends, such as William Saroyan, Louis Aragon, Ernest Hemingway, and John Hersey.[3] He and Steinbeck decided to team up to document the life of ordinary people in the Soviet Union [Fig. 111], a subject ignored by public politics. The writer enjoyed working with the colorful photographer, who stole books, cigarettes, and hearts with equal audacity.[4] "He may have had closer friends," mourned Steinbeck after Capa's premature death in Vietnam, but "none who loved him more."[5] The writer's final collaboration with a variety of documentary photographers on* America and Americans *(1966), a patriotic picture book, must have been much less engaging.[6]*

It will be necessary to say first how this story and how this trip started, and what its intention was. In late March, I, and the pronoun is used by special arrangement with John Gunther, was sitting in the bar of the Bedford Hotel on East Fortieth Street. A play I had written four times had melted and run out between my fingers. I sat on the bar stool wondering what to do next. At that moment Robert Capa came into the bar looking a little disconsolate. A poker game he had been nursing for several months had finally passed away. His book had gone to press and he found himself with nothing to do. Willy, the bartender, who is always sympathetic, suggested a Suissesse, a drink which Willy makes better than anybody else in the world. We were depressed, not so much by the news but by the handling of it. For news is no longer news, at least that part of it which draws the most attention. News has become a matter of punditry. A man sitting at a desk in Washington or New York reads the cables and rearranges them to fit his own mental pattern and his by-line. What we often read as news now is not news at all but the opinion of one of half a dozen pundits as to what that news means.

Willy set the two pale green Suissesses in front of us and we began to discuss what there was left in the world that an honest and liberal man could do. In the papers every day there were thousands of words about Russia. What Stalin was thinking about, the plans of the Russian General Staff, the disposition of troops, experiments with atomic weapons and guided missiles, all of this by people who had not been there, and whose sources were not above reproach. And it occurred to us that there were some things that nobody wrote about Russia, and they were the things that interested us most of all. What do the people wear there? What do they serve at dinner? Do they have parties? What food is there? How do they make love, and how do they die? What do they talk about? Do they dance, and sing, and play? Do the children go to school? It seemed to us that it might be a good thing to find out these things, to photograph them, and to write about them.

Russian politics are important just as ours are, but there must be the great other side there, just as there is here. There must be a private life of the Russian people, and that we could not read about because no one wrote about it, and no one photographed it.

Willy mixed another Suissesse, and he agreed with us that he might be interested in such things too, and that this was the kind of thing that he would like to read. And so we decided to try it—to do a simple reporting job backed up with photographs. We would work together. We would avoid politics and the larger issues. We would stay away from the Kremlin, from military men and from military plans. We wanted to get to the Russian people if we could. It must be admitted that we did not know whether we could or not, and when we spoke to friends about it they were quite sure we couldn't.

We made our plans in this way: If we could do it, it would be good, and a good story. And if we couldn't do it, we would have a story too, the story of not being able to do it. With this in mind we called George Cornish at the *Herald Tribune*, had lunch with him, and told him our project. He agreed that it would be a good thing to do and offered to help us in any way.

Together we decided on several things: We should not go in with chips on our shoulders and we should try to be neither critical nor favorable. We would try to do honest reporting, to set down what we saw and heard without editorial comment, without drawing conclusions about things we didn't know sufficiently, and without becoming angry at the delays of bureaucracy. We knew there would be many things we couldn't understand, many things we wouldn't like, many things that would make us uncomfortable. This is always true of a foreign country. But we determined that if there should be criticism, it would be criticism of the thing after seeing it, not before.

In due time our application for visas went to Moscow, and within reasonable time mine came through. I went over to the Russian Consulate in New York, and the Consul General said, "We agree that this is a good thing to do, but why do you have to take a cameraman? We have lots of cameramen in the Soviet Union."

And I replied, "But you have no Capas. If the thing is to be done at all, it must be done as a whole, as a collaboration."

There was some reluctance about letting a cameraman into the Soviet Union, and none about letting me in, and this seemed strange to us, for censorship can control film, but it cannot control the mind of an observer. Here we must explain something that we found to be true during our whole trip. The camera is one of the most frightening of modern weapons, particularly to people who have been in warfare, who have been bombed and shelled, for at the back of a bombing run is invariably a photograph. In back of ruined towns, and cities, and factories, there is aerial mapping, or spy mapping, usually with a camera. Therefore the camera is a feared instrument, and a man with a camera is suspected and watched wherever he goes. And if you do not believe this, try to take your Brownie No. 4 anywhere near Oak Ridge, or the Panama Canal, or near any one of a hundred of our experimental areas. In the minds of most people today the camera is the forerunner of destruction, and it is suspected, and rightly so.

I don't think Capa and I really ever thought that we would be able to do the job we wanted to do. That we were able to do it is as much a surprise to us as to anyone else. We were surprised when our visas came through, and we held a mild celebration with Willy behind the bar when they did. At that point I had an accident and broke my leg and was laid up for two months. But Capa went about assembling his equipment.

There had been no camera coverage of the Soviet Union by an American for many years, so Capa provided the very best of photographic equipment and duplicated all of it in case some of it might be lost. He took the Contax and Rolleiflex that he had used during the war, of course, but he took extras also. He took so many extras, and so much film, and so many lights, that his overweight charge on the overseas airline was something like three hundred dollars.

The moment it became known we were going to the Soviet Union we were bombarded with advice, with admonitions and with warnings, it must be said, mostly from people who had never been there.

An elderly woman told us in accents of dread, "Why, you'll disappear, you'll disappear as soon as you cross the border!"

And we replied, in the interest of accurate reporting, "Do you know anyone who has disappeared?"

"No," she said, "I don't personally know anyone, but plenty of people have disappeared."

And we said, "That might very well be true, we don't know, but can you give us the name of anyone who has disappeared? Do you know anyone who knows anyone who has disappeared?"

And she replied, "Thousands have disappeared."

And a man with knowing eyebrows and a quizzical look, the same man, in fact, who two years before had given the total battle plans for the invasion of Normandy in the Stork Club, said to us, "Well you must stand in pretty good with the Kremlin or they wouldn't let you in. They must have bought you."

We said, "No, not as far as we know, they haven't bought us. We just would like to do a job of reporting."

He raised his eyes and squinted at us. And he believes what he believes, and the man who knew Eisenhower's mind two years ago knows Stalin's mind now.

An elderly gentleman nodded his head at us and said, "They'll torture you, that's what they'll do; they'll just take you into a black prison and they'll torture you. They'll twist your arms and they'll starve you until you're ready to say anything they want you to say."

We asked, "Why? What for? What purpose could it serve?"

"They do that to everybody," he said. "Why I was reading a book the other day—"

A businessman of considerable importance said to us, "Going to Moscow, huh? Take a few bombs and drop them on the Red sons-of-bitches."

We were smothered in advice. We were told

the food to take, otherwise we would starve; what lines of communications to leave open; secret methods of getting our stuff out. And the hardest thing in the world to explain was that all we wanted to do was to report what Russian people were like and what they wore, and how they acted, what the farmers talked about, and what they were doing about rebuilding the destroyed parts of their country. This was the hardest thing in the world to explain. We found that thousands of people were suffering from acute Moscowitis—a state which permits the belief of any absurdity and the shoving away of any facts. Eventually, of course, we found that the Russians are suffering from Washingtonitis, the same disease. We discovered that just as we are growing horns and tails on the Russians, so the Russians are growing horns and tails on us.

A cab driver said, "Them Russians, they bathe together, men and women, without no clothes on."

"Do they?"

"Sure they do," he said. "That ain't moral."

It developed on questioning that he had read an account of a Finnish steam bath. But he was pretty upset at the Russians about it.

After listening to all this information we came to the conclusion that the world of Sir John Mandeville has by no means disappeared, that the world of two-headed men and flying serpents has not disappeared. And, indeed, while we were away the flying saucers appeared, which do nothing to overturn our thesis. And it seems to us now the most dangerous tendency in the world is the desire to believe a rumor rather than to pin down a fact.

We went to the Soviet Union with the finest equipment of rumors that has ever been assembled in one place. And in this piece we insist on one thing: if we set down a rumor, it will be called a rumor.

We had a final Suissesse with Willy at the Bedford bar. Willy had become a full-time partner in our project, and meanwhile his Suissesses got better and better. He gave us advice, some of the best advice we had from anyone. Willy would have liked to come with us. And it might have been a good thing if he had. He made us a super Suissesse, had one himself, and we were finally ready to go.

Willy said, "Behind the bar you learn to listen a lot and not talk very much."

We thought about Willy and his Suissesses a lot during the next few months.

That was the way it started. Capa came back with about four thousand negatives, and I with several hundred pages of notes. We have wondered how to set this trip down and, after much discussion, have decided to write it as it happened, day by day, experience by experience, and sight by sight, without departmentalizing. We shall write what we saw and heard. I know that this is contrary to a large part of modern journalism, but for that very reason it might be a relief.

This is just what happened to us. It is not the Russian story, but simply *a* Russian story. [ch. 1, pp. 3–8]

In one market at Stalingrad there was a photographer with an old bellows camera. He was taking a picture of a stern young army recruit, who sat stiffly on a box. The photographer looked around and saw Capa photographing him and the soldier. He gave Capa a fine professional smile and waved his hat. The young soldier did not move. He gazed fixedly ahead.

· 131 ·

111. Robert Capa. 'Russian photographer,' USSR, 1947, with text by Steinbeck from *A Russian Journal,* 1948.

1. See D. G. Kehl, "Steinbeck's 'String of Pictures' in *The Grapes of Wrath,*" *Image* 17 (March 1974): 1–10, and Shloss, "John Steinbeck and Dorothea Lange: The Surveillance of Dissent," in *In Visible Light,* pp. 211–29.

2. For more about Steinbeck's *Bombs Away: The Story of a Bomber Team* (New York: Viking, 1942), see Jackson J. Benson, *The True Adventures of John Steinbeck, Writer* (New York: Viking, 1984), pp. 504–10. Swope mentions the book, but not Steinbeck, in his 25th reunion report for the Harvard Class of 1930, in the Harvard University Archives; and his posthumous 50th reunion report credits Swope as its author. The collaboration is not mentioned in his *New York Times* obituary (May 15, 1979): B8.

3. For more on Capa's relationships with writers, see Capa and Karia, eds., *Robert Capa, 1913–1954:* Saroyan, "As I Remember Him," pp. 66–67; Aragon, "Farewell to Capata," p. 121; Hersey "The Man Who Invented Himself," pp. 14–18; Hemingway, "He Was a Good Friend," p. 124; and Capa on Hemingway in "A Party for Papa," pp. 65 and 169–71. Also relevant are Capa's pictures of Hemingway and his son, taken in Sun Valley, 1941, in Capa, *Children of War, Children of Peace: Photographs,* ed. Cornell Capa (Boston: Bulfinch, 1991), npn; and Hersey's letter to the editor of May 16, 1991, which

briefly recounts his first meeting with Capa in Algiers in 1943, his help in obtaining and executing a *Life* assignment in Sicily for the photographer, and his decision to write the profile, cited above, when Capa published his autobiography, *Slightly Out of Focus* (New York: Henry Holt, 1947). See also Capa and Irwin Shaw, *Report on Israel* (New York: Simon & Schuster, 1950); and Shloss, "Norman Mailer and Combat Photography," in *In Visible Light,* pp. 233–49.

4. See also Capa, "A Russian Story," in Capa and Karia, eds., *Robert Capa, 1913–1954,* pp. 103–5, and Benson, *Steinbeck,* pp. 598–606, for more on their Russian trip.

5. See Steinbeck, "No One Can Take His Place" (1954), in Capa and Karia, eds., *Robert Capa, 1913–1954,* p. 123, and his introduction to Capa, *Images of War* (New York: Grossman Publishers, 1964), p. 7.

6. The text of Steinbeck, *America and Americans* (New York: Viking, 1966), illustrated with photographs by various *Life, Time,* and other photographers, was clearly a more impersonal, commercial enterprise. See also Benson, *Steinbeck,* p. 754, and Freund's 1961 chance portrait of the author in *The World in My Camera,* p. 242, and comments, pp. 237–38; and in *Freund, Photographer,* p. 157, with similar comments, p. 150.

70. *Wright Morris*

FROM "PHOTOGRAPHY IN MY LIFE," 1982

*M*orris *(1910–) is the most significant American writer-photographer of our century. His serious involvement with photography began in 1935 and accompanied his growth as a writer. In 1939, realizing a powerful relationship could exist between words and images, Morris began using both in his "photo-texts," which documented rural and small town structures and objects, familiar from his Nebraska childhood but fast disappearing. In* The Inhabitants *(1946) and* The Home Place *(1949), he intended each medium to exist independently, joined by the mind of the reader; accordingly his prose never explicitly described the images, and the images evoked rarely included people.[1] While this innovative strategy won some critical praise, most readers were confused or indifferent. Their response compelled Morris to devote himself solely to fiction, which won many awards, and to teaching. In the mid-1960's, prompted by the appreciation of a new generation, Morris concerned himself again with photography in various ways: he reissued some of his old photographs [Fig. 112] with new verbal responses as* God's Country and My People *(1968) [Fig. 113]; he published new pictures in color with an informal narrative in* Love Affair—A Venetian Journal *(1972); he helped mount a retrospective exhibition (1975), which stimulated him to produce a portfolio (1981); and he issued collections of his essays about photography (1982, 1989), including this autobiographical piece, which recounts the evolution of his twin talents and their unique results.[2] Morris's "photo-texts," now being reissued, are currently the object of intense interest.[3]*

In October of 1933 my room on Florianigasse in Vienna looked out on a small garden where the blind came to walk. . . . They walked in pairs, stiffly erect, marching slowly to an unheard music. It shamed me to spy on them . . . , but I was young, each hour seemed precious and I was eager to be one of those on whom nothing was lost. To hold fast to what might escape me, what I needed (I thought) was a camera.

A few weeks previously I had sailed from New York to Antwerp, spent a week in Paris, then came on to Vienna where I planned to spend the winter. . . .

At twenty-three years of age and healthy I was prepared for hard and lean times, but my college years in California had reduced my tolerance for cold. My room was unheated. . . . My first unforeseen expense was for a flannel bathrobe, which I wore as a lining to my raincoat: my second unforeseen expense was a camera. I believe it was called a Zeiss Kolibri. . . . On a grey chill day in an open air market, I found three peasant women, their heads wrapped in babushkas, standing behind the fat plucked geese they were selling. That picture—not quite in focus—is one I still have. Those taken from my window, of the *blindgarten,* have disappeared. Some four months later, in . . . Grossetto, Italy, I would watch one of the prison officials open my camera and expose the film to the light, as he looked for "pictures". . . .

Some fifteen months later I applied the Zeiss Kolibri to the purchase of a Rolleiflex. I was a writer—what need did I have for a camera? For some four or five months I had been obsessed with a childhood, previously of no interest to me: my own. Page after page accumulated as I tried to recover my Nebraska boyhood. Most of these impressions were little more than sketches, verbal pictures of places, of time-stopped moments.

She wiped the table with the dish rag then leaned there, propped on her spread arms. A few leaves rattled in the yard. Some dirty leghorns clucked and waited at the screen. She left the rag on the table and emptied the pan toward the leaky shade. She stood there awhile, her hands pressed into the small of her back. Turning, she looked down the trail bright now with copper leaves at an old man's knees, white in the sun. She watched his brown hands lift Monkey Ward's, tear out a page. She watched him read both sides, very slowly, then tip his head. . . .

As I gathered these impressions it became apparent that I was making images with the characteristics of photographs, such as the eye for detail and the aura of detachment, of impersonal observation. It was clear to me, however, that a writer who wanted a *picture* of something might well *take* it rather than describe it. The pictures I wanted were back in the rural midwest, but I saw similar objects in the alleys and streets of Southern California. With the Rolleiflex camera, on a tripod, I began to search them out. Stoops and doorways, windows and screens, the tubs, tools and utensils of daily living, fences and gates, the patterns formed by light and shadow, verticals and horizontals. My assurance in this matter was puzzling. Except for the image on my mind's eye, I had no example or precedent. I had seen a few of Weston's photographs, but nothing by Dorothea Lange, Walker Evans or the photographers of the Farm Security Administration. Nor did it cross my mind to take pictures of people. I made enlargements of the prints that seemed more interesting than others, and from the deficiencies of what I had done I learned to see the limitations of what I was doing. One limitation was technical. I had yet to learn about the view camera and wide angle lenses. On occasional trips to Los Angeles I saw structures that excited me more than the familiar fragments, but I lacked the equipment to deal with such subjects. My first wife. . . and I were part of, but only moderately aware of, the Depression; she gave piano lessons, I worked part time for the WPA and continued working on a long novel. . . .

In the summer of 1938 my wife accepted a

position to teach at the Westover School in Middlebury, Connecticut. We went east by car, and had our first good look at the pueblo culture of the southwest. . . . Pueblo structures were popular at the time with both photographers and artists, and I ran a fever of excitement on seeing the ruins of Mesa Verde. Adobe walls and textures, patterns of light and shadow, the dominance of the past in all aspects of the present, the palpable sense of time as a presence, made me more fully aware of what I was seeking in the transient ruins of my own culture. I wanted evidence of man in the artifacts that revealed his passing. I was also instinctively drawn to forms that were traditional and impersonal. My need to take up a position fronting these forms, as if they were symbolic facts, I accepted without question. . . .

. . . Where these elements combine in a single photograph I take the greatest pleasure in the resulting image. There are numerous examples. Some structures impress me as icons, with a sense of their own—in the words of Henry James—a mystic meaning proper to themselves to give out. The meeting house in Southbury, Connecticut; the Gano grain elevator in Kansas; the house near McCook, Nebraska; the rear of the Model T Ford, the white house in Wellfleet, are examples of this expressive form. Objects share this quality, singly or in groups, where exposure to human use has shaped them. . . . the drawer of silverware, the bureau drawer at Ed's place, Cahow's barber chair. . . . The simplest snapshot will bear it witness, and we feel this directly, without mediation. In the Pueblo country I was able to sense more of my own inscrutable purpose. The worn and abandoned aroused me. Ten years before I returned to the home place, the farm near Norfolk, Nebraska, I was prepared to appreciate homegrown American ruins and to attempt to salvage what was vanishing. Nothing will compare with the photograph to register what is going, going, but not yet gone. The pathos of this moment, the reluctance of parting, we feel intensely.

After the years in Southern California the green landscape of New England seemed overwhelming. . . . I spent that winter in a cabin on Quassapaug Pond, working on a long novel, and the following summer, back in Wellfleet, I took pictures with my first 4 x 5 view camera. The bellows leaked, but I was able to see the beckoning promise on the ground glass.

In the fall, working on enlargements in a Middlebury farmhouse, I glimpsed the connection between words, my own written words, and the photographs I was taking. Rather than ponder the photograph, then describe my impressions, I found in what I had written the verbal images that enhanced, and enlarged upon, the photograph. The unexpected resonance and play between apparent contraries, and unrelated impressions, was precisely what delighted the imagination. I saw that this was often equally true of the pairings of friends, pets and lovers. In the unanticipated commingling of opposites the element of surprise was life enhancing.

I made a selection of the prints and mounted them with the related text attached. Learning that James Laughlin, of New Directions, was living nearby, I drove over with some examples to show him what I was doing. It did seem to be a new direction. After some reflection he agreed to publish a selection. The introduction I contributed has the tone of a Futurist manifesto, one of many that left the waiting world unchanged.

Laughlin's interest in my photo-text project, along with the results I was getting with my first Schneider-Angulon lens, led me to put my writing aside and to concentrate on *The Inhabitants*. I had in mind a volume of structures and artifacts that would represent the nation as a whole, having seen enough of them in my travels in know how diverse yet characteristic American structures would prove to be. Thoreau's comment is pertinent:

> What of architectural beauty I now see, I know has gradually grown from within outward, out of the necessities and character of the indweller, who is the only builder out of some unconscious truthfulness, and nobleness, without ever a thought for the appearance and whatever additional beauty of this kind is destined to be produced will be preceded by a like uncon-

scious beauty of life . . . it is the life of the inhabitants whose shells they are. . . .

. . . The Midwest and the Southwest, rural and urban, the marvelous houses and barns of New England I had just discovered, but I had seen little of the South except through photographs. Those of Walker Evans, in *American Photographs,* had profoundly confirmed my own responses. I did not see through Evans' eyes, but I was captive of the same materials. The Depression was spectacularly photogenic, and in *Life* magazine I had seen examples of the unmatched power of the camera eye. I also felt the urgency of the true believer about to voyage among the heathen. So many structures (souls) eager and willing to be saved might otherwise be lost! I had watched a barn collapse while I hastened to set up my camera. A strong whiff of missionary zeal fueled my enterprise. My ambitions were large but, fortunately, my means were small, or I might still be lost in the streets of Charleston or the back roads and trails of the Smokies.

In realistic terms, I planned a trip of some eight or ten thousand miles, beginning in the fall of 1940, going south to Georgia, west to Mississippi, north along the river to Nebraska, then southwest through Kansas, New Mexico and Arizona, to California, where I would spend the winter. In early spring I would head east, through Nevada, Utah, Idaho and Wyoming, crossing the plains while the trees were still barren, following the back roads through the farms of Iowa, Indiana and Illinois. I hoped to take as many as a thousand pictures selected from thousands of subjects. I wanted the representative structure that would speak for the numberless variations. I had in mind not one book, but a series, each dealing with a phase of our national life as I had experienced it. Rural, small town, urban and the open road. This first book, *The Inhabitants,* would be a survey of the state of the union in terms of its threatened symbols. How well I visualized it! There was no limit to my confidence, my enthusiasm, and combined with my sense of mission I was a formidable supplicant, able to persuade . . . the head of the Westover School, where my wife was teaching, to contribute $500 to this new direction of photographs and words. A '34 Ford coupe, with a rebuilt motor, the seat wide enough for me to curl up in, was fitted out with recapped tires and a South Wind heater. In October, with a carton of film paces, a 3¼ x 4¼ Graphic View, fitted with the Schneider Angulon lens, I stopped along Route 1, in New Jersey, to wait for a break in the flow of traffic to photograph the gleaming facade of a white church. As so often before, another traveler was about to discover America.

In Washington, D.C., I stopped to see Roy Stryker, of the Farm Security Administration, who had provided employment for a unique assembly of photographers and directed them to an inexhaustible subject. I had fancied I might get a roving assignment from him, or at least wangle a supply of film. He looked at my examples with interest, but without enthusiasm. My conception of words and photographs puzzled him, and he was profoundly bemused by the absence of *people.* People, he said, were what it was all about. I agreed. Having seen thousands of exceptional photographs, those that I showed him did not overwhelm him. I tried to explain that the presence of people in the houses and barns was enhanced by their absence in the photographs. He had heard many things, but nothing so far-fetched as that. A profoundly compassionate man, increasingly aware of the sufferings of millions of Americans, he had little patience for what he felt to be suggestively "arty" in my photographs and texts. His programs hoped to correct social abuses, not serve as an excuse for personal experiment. He was not so blunt, but I understood his meaning. He was also correct in sensing that my purpose was not in the interests of social justice. I wanted the *persona* behind the social abuses, one that would prove to be the same with or without them. We were each right, in terms of what we wanted, and I left his office empty handed. One of Stryker's photographers, who had caught a glimpse of my work, followed me out to the street and spoke to me. He said he liked what he had seen, and that I should not be discouraged. Regrettably, I have forgotten this man's name.

For reasons Stryker would not have approved, I took pictures of the box-like Civil War period houses in the Capitol's slums. I felt, thanks to Stryker, some embarrassment in the pleasure these shabby, dilapidated, lean-to dwellings gave me in the light of the social abuses they revealed. This dilemma, like so many, is part of our complex inscrutable human natures, and will not be resolved by legislation or discussion. The way I see what I photograph is to me life-enhancing. Other ways of seeing are equally valid, but they are not mine. . . .

With my interest in the old, the worn out, the declined, the time-ravaged, the eroded and blighted, the used, abused and abandoned, as well as the structured volumes, the contrasts in texture, the endless gradations from black to white in stone, shingle, clapboard, painted or peeling, such as the rows of wooden and marble stoops in Baltimore after the first extended day of photographing my problem was more practical than esthetic. There seemed to be an inexhaustible bounty of material. I had a finite supply of film. . . .

The over-rich compost of Southern life and history, which I had sampled in the pages of Faulkner, was visible on the surface, in stratified layers, even for a traveler as ignorant as I. Southern atmosphere, as dense and pungent as leaf smoke, to be breathed in and savored like pollen, was in such contrast to my previous experience that I found myself in another country. The surface hospitality, the inflection of the language, the suspicion that there was less just below the surface than on the surface, the provocative sexuality that was a matter of custom, of tradition, not intended to incite more than a flirtation. The warm Southern nights, the music and the black voices seemed as exotic to me as I had found Mexico the previous summer.

Soon enough I discovered I was seen as an intruding alien. The camera, and the camera eye, is justly looked upon with suspicion. I tramped about with this machine, mounted on its tripod, and set it up to conceal myself be-neath the hood, invariably pointed at some house or doorway judged to be of no pictorial interest. Why would I take *that,* except to reveal what was better concealed? I could only have in mind the exposure of whoever lived there, a blot on the peeling Southern escutcheon. As there attention turned from me to my car, with its out-of-state license, the picture seemed clear. I was a Northern snooper out to disfigure the troubled, dilapidated Southern self-image. Black and white both felt it, the black with less malice but a more profound discomfort. My presence testified to their worst suspicions about their own condition. The separate yet commingled cultures of black and white that make the South a unique and a tormented culture were at once unavoidably visible and subject to instant falsification. The impoverished black, the debased poor white, had been well exposed in books and magazines, and such distinctions as might be made were in the eye of the beholder, not the camera.

At the edge of Culpeper, in West [*sic*] Virginia, I found a house and dead tree, equally husk-like, both appearing to date from Lee's surrender, that seemed to speak directly to my troubled state of mind. Was it a portrait, or a caricature? Did it reveal a state of soul or a state of abuse? I could see now one, now the other, by merely blinking my eyes. But in the basking sunshine of a Blue Ridge October I felt the ripeness and warmth of survival more than I felt the chill of inhuman custom. The meaning this structure had to give out was a many layered, many voiced passage of history, too dense and complex to do more than acknowledge, but in this surviving husk it was more life-enhancing than life-defeating;

But that was not all. What I had made, when the shutter clicked, was a photograph. It would be weeks before I saw the negative, and many months would pass before I made a print of what I had seen on the ground glass. Would that image restore my original impressions, or would they be replaced by others? To what extent would this new image, cut off from its surroundings, constitute a new structure? How much of the "reality" had it captured? How much had it ignored? Whether or not it had been my intent, I would end up with something *other* than what was here. It would be a new likeness, a remarkable approximation, a ponderable resemblance, but not a copy. This new image would testify to the photographer's inscrutable presence. I was not appreciative of these distinctions at the time I took the picture, and believed that what I had seen on the ground glass would surely be what I had captured.

I was working on the faith and enthusiasm that what I saw on the ground glass would prove to be the photograph I wanted. Once a week, if possible, I would stop in a town where my film packs of negatives could be developed, and I could be reassured as to what I was doing. Ideally, I would have carried the developing equipment and periodically done the work myself. I had thought of that, and briefly tried it, but my interest in the chemistry side of photography was even less than my talent for it. I had neither the experience nor the confidence to do this crucial work myself. With few, and infrequent, exceptions, the method I had chosen proved to be the right one.

I made my way south along the foothills of the Smokies, the blues of the mountains to the west transparent in the hazy light, deepening to purple as the sun set behind them. The warmth of the season, the golden October light, the harmony that prevailed between man and nature (man and man was another matter) seemed to clarify for me, in an instant, the attachment of the Southerner to where he had come from. A ballad-like sense of peace, if not plenty, seemed as palpable to me as strains of music. I was subject, as my experience had proved, to a lyrical euphoria when exposed to such places. I had felt it repeatedly in Europe, and to the point of dazzlement in Mexico. If something unearthly had occurred, I would have been an eager and willing witness. This mood was both so tangible and so fragile I was reluctant to dispel it. I stayed away from the larger towns and avoided photographing what might arouse comment or suspicion. I confined myself to farmhouses and outbuildings, and to the look of fields and fences in the slanting light. I noted how frequently a coat of whitewash would accent a weathered wall, gate, door or brick chimney. Most of the natives I saw were black, deferential to whites and eager to be helpful. I soon found that their answers to my questions of where I was, and where I hoped to be going, were less concerned with information than with a desire to be cordial. Was this the right road? Yessuh. Was it a good road? Yessuh. If place names were mentioned I might not understand them and this increased my assurance of strangeness. . . .

. . . On a Saturday night in North Carolina, I watched the town fill up with old cars, buggies and wagons that were full of denim-clad poor white country people and their children. . . . They seemed more interesting and intense than the people I had known. . . . To watch them as intently as I cared to, I sat in the car pretending to read a paper. I wouldn't have dreamed of trying to take a picture. I had always felt the camera eye to be intrusive, but never so profoundly as when I contemplated directing it toward such private people. The barefooted children, in hand-me-down clothes, ran about beneath the wagons. How was it that I, a native of the plains, should feel that here I was, at long last, among my own people?

In South Carolina, near the state line, I stopped at the edge of a sun baked bean field. At its center, raised off the ground so high that a small child might walk beneath it, was a large, one-storied clapboard house with a shingled roof and high windows without glass. The windows made deep pockets of shade, and crisp shadows accented the unpainted clapboards. The yard around it was hard and swept clean as a floor, and between me and the house was a covered well with a pulley to raise and lower the galvanized bucket. Not a soul or a dog was in sight; in the high noonday heat I assumed both might be napping.

The patterns of light and shade, the colors of earth and wood, the shimmering flame of light at the edge of the shadows, compelled me to try and get the picture. In all of its weathered and man-shaped details it fulfilled my idea of the beautiful. But I would have to intrude on private property. Stealthily, picking my way along the furrows, extending the legs of the tripod as I approached the house, I set up my camera, stooped beneath the cloth and saw the blurred image on the ground glass. Beads of perspiration seeped into my eyes. I backed away, shirttailed my face, then once more focused on the ground glass. Just to the left of the house, perhaps ten yards behind it, in colors that appeared designed to conceal him, a black giant stood in a posture of resting, his hands clasping a hoe handle. A narrow brimmed hat, tilted forward, shaded his eyes. I pretended not to see him. It made my movements more assured and casual. I was deliberate and open in what I was doing. I moved the tripod, I took several pictures. I felt the passing of time would prove to be to my advantage. On the ground glass I watched him approach me until beads of perspiration burned my eyes. Too late to cut and run, I was paralyzed.

"What you see?" he asked me.

Out from under the cloth I peered up, and up, at the ivory smile in his black face. He was curious. "What you see?" he repeated.

"You want to look?" He did. He crouched low, I hooded him with the cloth, and for a long moment he was silent. Backing away, he shook his head, puzzled. "You don't see it?" He did not. I checked to see if the glass was in focus. It was beautiful. Then it occurred to me it was upside down. "It's upside down," I said, apologetic. That was more mystifying. He had another look at it. What he saw led him to stoop, slapping his knees, then straighten up with a bellow of laughter. Why the image was upside down was something I did not want to go into. . . .

In 1940 the second world war had begun, but we were not yet in it. A slight war fever was palpable among those who might be drafted or felt themselves threatened. In Greenville, South Carolina, I was picked up as a vagrant and charged with being a possible spy. My camera was there beside me and I had obviously been taking pictures. Of what? Of critical installations, surely. The excitement of having captured a spy soon gave rise to a sense of exhil-

aration. The chief of police, a short, fat man with a nervous hysterical manner, leather straps, ammunition belts, pistol in a holster, might have served Mack Sennett as a model for the comical, as opposed to the beefy and brutal, Southern cop.

I was finger-printed and questioned, and all of my gear was inventoried. Then I was taken to the second floor of a jail behind the buildings facing the main street. This was a single large room, with bars at the windows, cots placed around the walls, with a windowless cell, the door heavily barred, in the room's back corner. A local desperado . . . was kept in this cell.

In the room below, as I found out at sunrise, a chain gang of blacks was incarcerated. The racket they made leaving their quarters woke me up. We had a view through the door and the glassless windows over the lower roofs of the town. We could see and hear it come alive in the morning, pause during the heat of the day, become active and noisy approaching the dinner hour, then quiet down in the evening. I shared the room with a motley crew of bums, ne'er do wells and poor whites. They had been drinking and fighting, or merely loafing. Some were loud and bitter for as long as ten minutes. Most were resigned. During part of the day and the long night they were full of talk, tall tales and wild humor. Having me as a new and interested listener meant more than having me as a talker. I did a lot of listening and scratching. Once or twice a day I gave somber speeches to the chief of police as he stood at the door. He liked my performance. While I talked he chewed on a toothpick, dipped one hand to his crotch and gazed reflectively over the roofs of the city, surveying his domain.

On the strength of hoping I was a spy, a plainclothes official, a kindly elderly man with whom I briefly discussed Stark Young and Faulkner, came over from the capital, Columbia. He looked at my papers, heard my story and recommended that I spend at least a week in Charleston, then advised them to release me. I had a long day and night to brood if that advice would ever be taken. On the third or fourth morning, shortly after the chain gang rattled its way down the alley, I had a tin cup of coffee with the chief. He had for me, he said, no hard feelings. He gave me my camera and the keys to my car, and advised me to get the hell out of South Carolina. That advice I took. . . .

I was understandably reluctant to take pictures while in Georgia. I had heard about Georgia, I had read *Tobacco Road,* I had seen the chain gangs in the movies. I kept a low profile. I had recently read The *Heart Is a Lonely Hunter* and heard that Carson McCullers had lived in Columbus. I could believe that. The basking Southern heat, the soft golden light, the way structures and people appeared to be saturated with the scent of a past as dense as leaf smoke, smoldering and drug-like, in which everybody was a willing compliant victim. Walking the dusty streets I envied the writers fortunate enough to come from such places, still sticky with the pollen that clung to them. It seemed to me they need only close their eyes, open their pores and inhale deeply to possess their subjects. The sorghum-like richness of Southern life was both on the surface and fermenting beneath it. Through the dusty lace curtains at my hotel room window I spied on passersby I secretly envied, as Sherwood Anderson spied on his neighbors in Winesberg. They were dream-drugged, these people, and I envied the depth of their addiction.

In the nearby countryside, as I was driving around, I saw the glow of lights that I thought might be a fire. It proved to be a small carnival, with a rocking, clanking ferris wheel, one or two dangerous rides and sideshows of freaks. It had been set up in a field of trampled grass, the air smoking with the savor of barbecued meat. No Chautauqua of my boyhood generated so much excitement and expectation. These countryfolk, with their throngs of small fry, were the crackers I had read about in Erskine Caldwell. I was amazed at the visible kinship linking the cartoon grotesqueries of Li'l Abner or the figures in Faulkner's *Spotted Horses* to the people I saw around me. In the context small occasions provided, larger than life fig-

ures and sentiments materialized. Given a throng of expectant, deprived rural people, a mythic South might emerge from their shared expectations. . . . I largely owed to these few weeks of Southern exposure my feeling that hardship, and hard times, if not destructively brutal or prolonged to the point of negation, are necessary to a density and richness of emotion that seems noticeably absent in happier situations. I did not say to myself that my life had changed, but with the morning light I felt that it had. Missing from my life had been the emotion that finds its fulfillment and release in the ballad. I had discovered the emotion, but how to cultivate it would prove to be the work of a lifetime. A few years later when I had read James Agee's *Let Us Now Praise Famous Men* and had seen Walker Evans' accompanying photographs of the sharecroppers I would fully appreciate the wide range of impressions I had just experienced.

In Pike County, Alabama, I crossed a field of corn stubble to get a clear view of several barns and a house, weathered to the color of dead branches. I moved in closer to get the shingled roof of the house, shimmering with heat. Under the hood of the camera, focusing on the ground glass, I heard an angry, bellowing voice. I uncovered my head and looked around. I saw no one. The voice spoke again—it seemed closer—and the corn stubble crackled as if trampled by cattle. The blast that followed was that of a shotgun behind the barns. In the morning stillness the air seemed to tremble, and so did my legs and hands. I ran for the car, the tripod legs dragging, and some moments later I saw, with the wide, staring eyes, the film of perspiration on my face in the rear view mirror. Could one smell of fear? I thought I could detect it. . . .

I drove south to Mobile, then west along the Gulf Coast, the water as smooth as a pond. Men and boys sat along the shore, fishing, with the lines dangling slack from their long poles. I had not experienced heat that drugged the senses and had about it a lulling, agreeable torpor. To keep from dozing at the wheel I parked and took a nap. Animals and people were both becalmed. I understood the necessity of the siesta. Much later I would understand the need for the bourbon and the mint julep. . . .

In November, driving north from New Orleans, I stopped to see a friend who was then living in Jackson, Mississippi. He took me to meet one of his friends and neighbors, Eudora Welty, and among other things we talked about William Faulkner. Faulkner's town was Oxford, on my route north, but I had no intention of intruding on his privacy. I was encouraged, however, to intrude, if possible, on his old friend Phil Stone. That also seemed unwarranted to me, as a writer who had as of then published nothing, so I spent most of the day in Oxford sitting in the square waiting for history to strike me. It did not. Late in the afternoon I screwed up enough gall, mixed with courage, to appear at the door of Stone's law office. He was there. On admitting my interest in Faulkner, I was taken in tow. Phil Stone was a fluent and accomplished talker, and like most talkers he craved a fresh and good listener, which I proved to be. I was directed to the house down the street, centered in a large lot, which now looms in my mind like a Faulknerian mansion, but unfortunately the details are blurred, and I took no pictures. . . .

I lay awake until daylight seeking a clue to my pleasurable but disordered impressions. In the light of these impressions, Faulkner's fiction seemed both controlled and understated. The soul of the South, as I was privileged to perceive it, seemed to me more complex, and bizarre, than the reports I had read about it. More incredible to me, I found its strangeness wondrous and life-enhancing, rather than merely monstrous and grotesque. I owed these impressions to Phil Stone's remarkable relationship with black people—*his* Negroes, who deliberately chose not to be free. A few were servants in his house, others occupied barns and outbuildings. Something in Phil Stone's nature cultivated and responded to this reversal of historical roles, the master who became the captive of his slaves. I had been greatly impressed by Melville's profound grasp of this dilemma in his novella, *Benito Cereno,* which I saw worked out

with even greater refinement in the way the blacks dominated the Stone household. . . .

. . . I then drove north to where a bank near the road had eroded to leave a raw gully, red as a bleeding wound in the drizzle. I badly wanted this image for *The Inhabitants,* and even as I worked to get the photograph I began to ponder a suitable text.

Perhaps an hour later, raining much harder, I passed a field where a harness-patched plow horse, white as Moby Dick, stood luminous in a piece of over-grazed pasture, his heavy head bowed. I should have stopped to photograph it. That I did not is why I have forever borne it so vividly in mind.

In Arkansas the rain-washed air dried as quickly as a water color. I took pictures of barns, mostly hog farms, the pens black and muddy, the hogs happy, the smell of the ripe manure as rich and juicy as chewed tobacco. I drove a long day, feeling the need of a change. Late at night, near the Missouri line, I parked off the road to sleep. At sunrise I awoke on the rim of the world. The shadow of the car stretched out before me, the light spreading like surf, splashing on objects. It may have been the first time I saw the plains as a metaphor for the sea, a place to be possessed by the imagination. I no more than saw it, I did not feel inspired by the sight to possess it, but coming out of the woods, literally and figuratively, where I had been wandering for more than six weeks, I experienced the prodigal son's elation at the sight of the homeland. I think it amused me. My view of the plains had always been dim. My sentiments on the occasional cross country drives were expressed in my early fiction, where Nebraska was the place one drove all night while your companion slept in the seat. That had been the impression of my friends in the east.

As the sun rose I found much to photograph, anything that stood up so the light would strike it—an almost audible clamor at sunrise—houses and barns. Fences and telephone poles, clusters of trees and dwellings, and like a sail at sea, the occasional gleam of a grain elevator. I saw, but did not fully sense, that these constructions were pathetically temporary on the vast exposed landscape. In this I found their appeal, their life-enhancing poignancy. My instinct was to celebrate the eloquence of structures so plainly dedicated to human use, and to salvage those that were on the edge of dissolution. The plains provided a scenic prop that was free of obstruction, where the sun was sufficient to delineate the object. I took my subjects on the run, as the light fell on them, frequently not at all to their advantage, since I was eager to see what beckoned down the road and was apprehensive about a change in the weather. A rural schoolhouse, near Goodland, Kansas, with its crisp volumes of white contrasted with deep shadows, spoke to me in the same classical terms as the white house in Wellfleet, on the Cape. No need for poignancy here, only visual delight, a clear statement of protestant principle and practice.

The roll and dip of the plains increased as I drove west, reminding me that my boyhood in the flat Platte Valley of Nebraska had given me a mistaken notion of the high plains. They were remarkably sealike, the towns sunbaked and windblown riding the crests of the waves. Near the Colorado border—it might have been Goodland—I found a row of stores, with curtained and blind-drawn windows and slightly tilting false fronts, that would provide me with an inexhaustible image of plains character and experience, mute implacable and yet expectant. Stubbornly and irrationally optimistic.

On the crests of the rise, as I drove south, I caught glimpses of an arrow that pointed at the sky, like a rocket on its pad, the moon its destination. As I moved closer I saw the staggered tiers of a grain elevator approximately in scale with the landscape. The freight train at its base was hardly visible. Only when I saw it enlarged and printed would I have a sense of its proportions. An almost high noon light, filtered through an overcast, revealed the ripple in the sheet metal attached to the structure's surface. This enhanced the reflected shimmer of light. Near the top, appropriately enigmatic, the four letter word G A N O [Figs. 112, 113].

From the edge of the highway, several hundred yards away, I studied the image on the ground glass and took several pictures. My ap-

preciation of what I judge a great image reveals itself in my concern that I might flaw the negative in the taking or in its development. Fortunately, this negative was not flawed, and the print is one I find gratifying. It speaks to me like an icon of the tensions that are overwhelmed by the scale of the landscape and seek release in flight. It can also just be looked at. The photograph, that is, since I am sure the structure itself is long gone. Grain is now stored in huge concrete silos that give a space-age accent to the surrounding plain, and frequently blow up. . . .

In the winter of 1940 Santa Fe was still the town of old adobe houses, hot sun, cool shadows, a bandstand in the square, blankets and silver in the shops and Pueblo Indians crouched under the awning of the Governor's building. Most of the artists and writers had moved on to greener pastures or trickled back to Greenwich Village, but the lobby of the La Fonda Hotel thronged with trend-seeking tourists and self-proclaimed old timers. I listened to their stories. Mabel Dodge Luhan was at home near Taos, where the natives were reduced to Sears & Roebuck blankets. The air was like wine, the light shimmered like tinsel, and I marveled how I had dreamed of living anywhere else. . . .

. . . In a few weeks I had shot more film than I should have, and suffered from a bad case of pueblo country enchantment. I had bought some old pottery, some new blankets, and before the fever maimed me, or abated, I managed to take off. I drove through a starry night to Needles, California, where I had a fine breakfast in the Harvey House in the railroad station, one of the first and last sanctuaries of great coffee. As I drove west out of Needles I felt the resurgence of the old attraction. California, before I set eyes on it, had been for me the sanctuary of my great expectations, and my years at Pomona College had fired the clay of these impressions. . . . In Claremont I drove slowly around the streets and thought the students attractive but extremely youthful. How long had it been since I had been one of them? Not quite five years. In the post office, with its WPA murals painted by . . . a classmate, an old friend was so startled to see me I let myself pass for an imposter. In the mail

But it's not all you see in their kids —
Or maybe you do — maybe Will was what Grandpa had in mind. It was
clear what he should do, and from what I've seen I'd say that he did it —

Donaldson's hitch bar would have to go. So would the split elm and the horse trough full of marbles, the old chain swing. Mr. Cole said the horses would soon go too. Cement paving would wear their hooves to the bone, he said. Willie said, for what did horses have shoes? Mr. Cole spit and said some day the paving would go right out of town. It would go to the east first, and then it would go to the west. He said when Willie had kids he'd bet their kids would ride it for miles. And when their kids had kids they'd ride it clear to Omaha. Willie rolled up his sleeve and felt in the horse trough for marbles. What makes you think, Willie said, that I'm goin' in for kids?

112. Wright Morris. 'Gano Grain Elevator, Western Kansas,' 1941, with text from *The Inhabitants,* 1946.

Wright Morris

THE LAST time I saw my Uncle Dwight I asked him about my mother. It was known I had her eyes and her stubborn will. If she had lived, my life would have been different, no doubt about that. A pioneer woman, the first of the tribe to shoot at the moon. It had seemed to me strange, but was it so unusual? Moon-shooting has long been the custom of the country. Already we are thinking of remoter targets. The Grandfather began it, and I am still at it. Where do we go from here but into orbit? Where else but on the moon did my father spend most of his life?

113. Wright Morris. 'Gano Grain Elevator, Western Kansas,' 1941, with text from *God's Country and My People*, 1968.

Wright Morris

I had received the New Directions volume with the selection of my photographs and texts, along with a brief review from *The New Yorker* in which my name was mentioned. A first on all counts. At the Sugar Bowl cafe I was recognized, and experienced the sensation of being interviewed. Fame, surely. I was treated to a piece of pecan pie. To prolong this occasion I sought out Hal Davis, one of my English teachers, who was very kindly and favorably impressed. In that far time publication was a singular event. Many were called, but few were chosen. I stayed with Hal for two days, smoking his cigarettes and giving him the lowdown on South Carolina hoosegows. The sight of my words in print had stirred banked fires out of my aroused nostalgia, the boy who had arrived, fifteen years before, with his father in the sidecar of a motorcycle. . . . With a stint of writing done, I was both free and eager to turn back to photography. . . .

I headed east in early March, driving northwest from Las Vegas through the mining and ghost towns to Virginia City. Overcast skies, strong winds and freezing cold discouraged much picture taking. I put up in the Comstock Lode Hotel in Virginia City, until a half day of brilliant sunlight gave me the half dozen pictures I was determined to get. One was the pair of weathered houses on a incline, preserved in every detail like the mummies in Guanajuato. The other the abandoned church and Hudson-bracketed house stark against a landscape of desert and sky more in the style of the baroque than American gothic. With these trophies hopefully in the bag I headed northwest for Boise, Idaho, to visit my Aunt Winona, one of my mother's Seventh Day Adventist sisters. A single day with her, and other members of the clan, helped to restore the ties I had with my Nebraska boyhood. Near Pocatello, in a gale-like wind that twice toppled my camera, I managed to get a picture of a cattle shelter in a barren, forbidding landscape. Had the settler found water? There was nothing, anywhere, on which the eye could rest or the body find refuge. In such places I felt the settler's implacable commitment, like a symptom of madness, to self-destruction. He took on the ele-

ments. Anything less would not have gratified his consuming rage.

Blowing snow plagued me across Wyoming, piling up like confetti on the windshield wiper, and I lay awake on the whistling nights fueled by the day's eight or ten cups of coffee. Nebraska too was snow covered, but thawing, and I stopped frequently along the route to photograph houses lapped by waves of dirty snow. The planes and patterns of dormers and gables, in wraps of dirty ermine, were like winter portraits. Just east of Lincoln, on a rise north of the highway, I crossed a field of stubble to take a farmhouse against the blowing winter sky. The roof tilted the snow in such a manner that it reflected a more intense light than the field. The warmth inside the house had helped to thaw a black rim around the roof snow that set it off like a frame, but I would not see these details clearly until they emerged in the darkroom, five or six weeks later.

Through friends I had discovered Brooklyn Heights on the East River. The brownstone houses on Columbia Street had apartments at the rear that overlooked the river and the Brooklyn Bridge. . . . Hart Crane had lived on this street with other writers and poets, and I found a ground floor apartment that had just been repainted, at 196 Columbia Heights. In a few days it had been furnished with a set of springs, boxes for books, and some cushions. Chairs would wait on success. The first order of business was to set up a darkroom. . . . On days when I needed a rest from the darkroom I applied myself to reworking the novel.

In the early fall of 1941, with a portfolio of photographs and texts, I appeared at the Guggenheim Foundation and met Henry Allen Moe. In my allotted time, perhaps fifteen minutes, I tried to compress the facts and the fiction of my commitment to photographs and words. A keen and sympathetic listener, a matchless chain smoker, Mr. Moe gave me warm friendly glances through the veil of smoke between us. Did he feel I might try for a fellowship? He thought I might. I went away in a fever that found some release in the lyrical statement that went along with my application. I have been spared reexposure to my enthusiasm, but I suspect it embraced a passionate desire to salvage the barns, houses and structures of America before they dissolved into thin air. I had no idea, at the time I wrote it, how quickly it would happen.

Shortly after Pearl Harbor I learned of my father's death in Chicago. He had not written me, nor I to him, for several years. When I left for college in California, in 1930, we had gone our separate ways. This story of a father and son who share a varied and adventurous life without the benefits or hazards of communication was more commonplace than unusual, one of the staple ingredients of the American novel and the emerging problems of alienation. This story is told in *Will's Boy*, published in 1981. The impact of my father's death would not assert itself until several years later, when I began to write the story of Will Brady, in *The Works of Love*. The emotions we had seldom shared as father and son preoccupied me to the exclusion of everything else, but I sensed none of this in the dark winter of 1941–42. I served as the building's air raid warden, and spent many evenings on the roof watching the lights of Manhattan blink off during the blackouts. The few that persisted glowed like planets. . . .

In March I learned I had received a Guggenheim Fellowship. This news marked the summit of the great expectations I had been possessed by for several years. The long apprenticeship I had spent as a writer, and the increasing enthusiasm I felt for the prospect of joining photographs and words, prepared me for the elation I felt in this recognition. Like others before me, I pondered how to live to the fullest extent on this huge bounty, a sum of $2,500. Having lived well for years on less than half of that sum in California, that was where we headed.

. . . On this trip I felt the stirrings, however reluctant, of my plains boyhood. My father's death had awakened in me an interest in the past. In Omaha we drove past the places I had lived in as a boy. The houses seemed smaller, the hills and streets less steep, as if they had shrunken in my absence.

From Omaha we drove northwest toward Uncle Harry's farm, near Norfolk, where as a boy I had once spent two weeks of a summer vacation. . . . From the gravel road it looked abandoned. The porch and stoop were lacking from the front of the house, but I recalled that it had never had either. The only door to the house that was used was at the rear. I drove down the shrub-lined driveway to the back and parked the car in the chicken-scratched mounds near the barn. The long yard between the house and the barn, once green as a billiard table, was a thicket of matted grass and half buried croquet wickets. Doors tilted in shed doorways, fences were down, the dead trees of an orchard stood in weeds near the house, every visible object, wagon, implement and structure seemed to be at the end of a losing battle. The peeled branches of long dead trees arched over the house. Never before had I set eyes on such a mockery of my remembrance. If my wife had not been with me, I might have sneaked off. A few mangy bare-bottomed old hens clucked nervously as I walked toward the porch. The screen door, although poked full of holes, was latched. A water pail, floating the handle of the dipper, sat on the table to the left of the door. A draft smelling of pickling beets assailed me from the kitchen. Flies buzzed on both sides of the rusty screen. I called out, but nobody answered. I called again and heard one of the plates shift on the kitchen range. In a moment she appeared, a woman thin as a lath, a faded frock hanging limp from her shoulders. Over the frock a beet-stained apron, the ties dangling. Over her left eye she placed the fingers of one hand. The other stared at me unblinking. It seemed she did not recognize me, but I knew her.

"You don't remember me?" I asked. She didn't seem to. "I'm Will's boy, Wright," I said. It took a moment's time and effort to place me. Her tongue passed slowly over her store teeth.

"You've grown," she said flatly, and unlatched the screen. As she shooed out the flies she noted the car, and its passenger, parked near the barn. "Why don't you folks come in out of the heat?" she said, and waited until I had gone back and fetched my wife. "How's your father?" she said, when I entered the house, but she did not wait for my answer. She had never liked the man who had once sent her three crates of cholera-exposed Leghorn pullets. She had never liked Leghorns. Her idea of a laying and stewing chicken was the Plymouth Rock.

I can no longer distinguish between that actual meeting with Clara, in June, and the fiction I wrote about it that winter in California, the sentiments and nostalgia as palpable as the smell of pickling beets in the kitchen. I know we sat in the parlor, facing Clara in her rocker, and that the two women talked. Only her fan stirred the air in the room. It was of interest to her that I was married, and she inquired about my wife's people. . . .

Some moments before he appeared, my Uncle Harry stopped on the back porch to skim flies off the bucket of water and toss them through the screen. Clara identified who we were, and reminded him that I had once spent some time on the farm. His watery blue eyes gave no sign of recognition. That I was seated in his chair confronted him with a problem only resolved when I surrendered it to him. He silently gazed at the light glare over the fields. We sipped warm water from the amber glasses that were usually stored on the top shelf in the cupboard.

This brief afternoon, during which I said little, listening to the voices of the women, would leave on me an impression from which I would never fully recover, repeatedly returning to the images, and the beet-pickled emotions, of that sultry summer day. In the car was my camera, but I could no more take photographs of what I saw around me than arrange for snapshots of the Second Coming. Images and emotions had saturated my limited responses. I was drugged by feelings that both moved and disturbed me. Had my father's death left in me a core of sorrow that would be responsive to these revisitations?

We drove south from Norfolk to my hometown of Central City, becalmed in the heat and the continuing Depression. Idle farmers sat in the gloom of a tin roofed pool hall. 5¢ cigars were selling for 4¢. I seemed unaware of ties or attachments. Down the road ten miles was Chapman, where my mother was buried, and

I stopped at the barber shop to inquire if anyone might have known my mother or father. My father had once been an agent in Chapman, for the railroad, and my mother had been born on the bluffs just south of the river. As I entered his shop the barber studied my face in his wall mirror. "Don't you tell me," he said, "I'll tell you. You're Will and Grace's boy, aren't you?" I said I was. To my knowledge he had never before set eyes on me. His name was Eddie Cahow. At the turn of the century he had come up from Texas on the Chisholm Trail, but found he liked barbering better than trail riding. In the shop, waiting his turn at the chair, was Mr. Applegate, a farmer who had once courted one of my mother's sisters. For more than forty years he had kept the house she lived in in good repair.

Eddie Cahow was agreeable to my taking pictures inside his shop. I worked fast, fearing that so much of my visible past might disappear before I had caught it. Everything in the shop proved to be of interest. The mirror, with its chalked menu of services and prices, the tonic bottles and brushes on the chiffonier, the case of razors and towels, the postcards sent to Cahow from traveling natives, tucked into the mirror's rim, the barber chair, the sink with its platter for hair massages, the peanut machine, the benches with the plywood seats, the wall of calendar pictures of prize beef and kittens. At the back of the shop, shipped out from Kansas City, was an elegant oak and iron grill that served as a bank, with its teller's window, the top ornamented with cans of flowering plants with trailing vines and tendrils. I took several packs of film, the light being good from the large half-curtained window. Later we followed Mr. Applegate to the top of the bluffs where we saw the house my mother had been born and raised in, with its cupola affording a view of the river valley. Mr. Applegate's sisters, who had kept house for him since he had been spurned by one of my mother's sisters, brought a shoebox out of hiding to show me photographs of my mother's family. The sentiments this one day aroused are still fresh in my mind.

This meeting with Eddie Cahow, his barber shop, and his friends, would lock me into a pact with the bygone that I had begun on the farm near Norfolk. By the time we left, early in the evening, the setting sun burning on the windshield, I was committed to the recovery of a past I had only dimly sensed that I possessed. I was blissfully ignorant of any awareness that this would prove to be the work of a lifetime.

Time has an elusive shimmer in Southern California, both dazzling and insubstantial. . . . I spent my time working on the text for *The Inhabitants* and a novel, *The Man Who Was There,* that grew out of my impressions of the home place and Eddie Cahow's barbershop.

In the summer of 1944 we headed east, for Bryn Mawr, where my wife would teach at the Baldwin School for Girls. Along the way, in the high country of Colorado, we came on the general store in Kokomo—like the house in Culpeper—sitting for its portrait. More pictures were taken in Silver Plume, a mining ghost town, the silence filled with the murmuring purl of water music visible through the cracks in the wooden sidewalk.

Crossing the plains to the east it's all down hill. As the long and empty freight trains clattered by us, with their litany of towns, states and places, the Baltimore and Ohio, the Burlington and Quincy, the Atchison, Topeka & Santa Fe, I began to dream of a series of books that would deal with the migration of Americans, a subject I knew something about. From the farm to the village, the village to the town, the town to the city, the city to the BIG town, and then once more—as I had lived it—back to the open road, irresistibly drawn westward. The farm at Norfolk would be the point of origin, then a small town like Central City, or Chapman, with a barber like Eddie Cahow, than a bigger town, then perhaps New York, and then—but much of that would wait on living, rather than planning. With such landscape in mind I did not feel pressed to make *The Inhabitants* a more inclusive volume, greatly increasing its size, and its production costs. With each mile we moved eastward I recovered the excitement that the stay in California had put on the back burner. Time had slowed, with absence of the seasons and the light glare at the windows, but once we had crossed the Missouri I could once again hear its pulsing, driving, life-enhancing tick. . . .

There was no space in the house for a darkroom, so I turned my attention to writing. On one of my visits to New York I met Maxwell Perkins, of Charles Scribner's Sons. He turned his profile to me, his hearing aid, and occasionally he beamed on me his shy avuncular smile. I liked him immensely. I also sensed that my disorderly novel, *The Man Who Was There,* both pleased and distressed him. He liked novels that were longer, and less experimental. Still palpable to me, in his curtained office, were some of novelist Thomas Wolfe's great and endless expectations. I felt them as a burden. How did one fill such enormous shoes?

A year or more later I appeared in his office with my portfolio of photographs and texts, *The Inhabitants.* He seemed interested, but the format was unwieldy, the relationship between the words and images obscure. I peered around at the walls of his curtained office. High windows gave a view of the Child's restaurant on Fifth Avenue. With his permission, I took a handful of paper clips from his desk and began to clip the mounted photographs with the texts to the office curtains. The stratagem seemed to work. He watched me with an indulgent, bemused smile. I managed to put up more than half the volume, and I promised to take them down on my next visit. Two weeks passed before I returned, but the photographs and texts were where I had left them.

What did he think? He tilted back in his chair, thumbs hooked in his vest, the wide brimmed that pushed back on his head. A familiar and often remarked posture. The smile he gave me needed no elaboration. He said he had no choice, regrettably, but to publish *The Inhabitants.* It would be done inexpensively, so that the host of readers he anticipated could afford the book. I feel that one of the book's signal triumphs was the impression it made on Max Perkins, and his decision that it should be published by Scribner's. There was no precedent for such an undertaking there, and this may have worked to the book's advantage in that I had a voice in all of the production decisions. I wanted the photographs to "bleed" rather than be enclosed by the page. A suitable paper was lacking at the time, but several coats of varnish gave the pages the appearance of glossy prints. The large format of the book pleased me immensely, and I am still staggered to read on the jacket that it sold for $3.75! At such a price Perkins was confident it would sell.

The Inhabitants was "well received," with excellent reviews, but the public did not buy it and the booksellers had no place to *put* it. Only the art book table would accommodate the large format. . . .

In 1946 I applied for a second Guggenheim Fellowship, and I was fortunate enough to receive it. I exchanged my 3¼ x 3¼ view camera for a 4 x 5. In early May of the following spring I drove back to the farm near Norfolk. The Depression ravaged dirt farm of my previous visit was partially concealed and softened by the growth of spring, weeds concealed implements, and gone-to-seed over-ripeness seemed appropriate. I found my Uncle Harry at his ease, smoking a cob pipe, tinkering with an inner tube. Clara was more resigned than bitter. I found her seated in her rocker, her lap full of eggs, chipping at the dung spots with her thumb nail. To my suggestion that I would like to take pictures they expressed no objection. Did they know what I had in mind? They had seen *The Inhabitants*. Feeling the need to justify, rather than explain, I said I wanted to capture what it was like to have lived on a dirt farm for half a century. There was no comment. I recall Clara moving her head from one side to the other, to see the room she sat in. Her shoes were unlaced. The ties of her apron dangled on the floor. I could hear mice stirring in the kitchen's basket of cobs. "I don't know why," she said "but if it's what you want to do, you're free to."

It had never crossed my mind that she would give me leave to the *inside* of her house I was about to reassure her, *You can trust me Clara—* trust me to do what? Wasn't I too greedy to be trusted? Didn't I privately feel I had earned this access? Just a few weeks before I had come on a statement, by Henry James in *The American Scene,* that gave me, I felt, unlimited access.

. . . is to be subject to the superstition that objects and places, coherently grouped, disposed for human use and addressed to it, must have a sense of their own, a mystic meaning proper to themselves to give out: to give out, that is to the participant at once so interested and so detached as to be moved to a report of the matter.

I was hardly detached, but otherwise I was qualified. These objects and places spoke to me profoundly, and I was moved to a report of the matter. My Uncle Harry was indifferent to the nuances of exposure. The young man with his camera had come at a time when the usual reservations were in abeyance. For Clara, the whole farm was a ruin, an accumulation of losses, a disaster that her protestant soul must accept, and here comes this youth, a prodigal relation, who saw in these sorry remains something of value. She could not imagine what, but she could believe it was what he saw. The reservations of a lifetime would struggle in her soul with the dim, unlikely hope that the youth might be right.

At the end of the first day, one of a steady drizzle, I had brought my camera on its tripod in from the porch to make sure it was out of the rain. I stood it up in a dark corner of the kitchen, the lens reflecting the lampglow. Clara gazed at it for a moment with her good eye.

"It's not taking pictures now?" she asked me. I assured her it wasn't. "Just so I'm not in them," she said, and glanced down her flat, faded frock. Would anything convince her there was something of value in what she saw?

I was put in the upstairs bedroom I had had as a boy, almost thirty years before. The window frame was just a few inches off the floor, due to some miscalculation, the folds of the gathered lace curtain as dry and crisp as paper. The storm window, put up several years before, had not been taken down. On the doily of the bureau a satin lined box that had once contained an ivory handled comb, mirror and brush set, now held several corroded rifle cartridges and the partial handle of the missing mirror. Why had she preserved it? We were alike in that we perceived these objects in the light of our emotions and judged this the mystic meaning they had to give out.

At the start my Uncle Harry ignored me. I saw him pass with a hoe, with a pail of water, with another inner tube that needed repairing, indifferent to my presence. I drew him in with questions. Would it rain again? He replied that it usually did. Soon he trailed me around, offered dry suggestions, tested me with his deadpan humor. He still smoked Union Leader, if and when he could find his pipe. When I suggested a picture of himself—the greatest ruin of all—he was compliant. Actually, he had been waiting. In the museum of relics the farm had become he was one of the few that still almost worked. He pointed that out himself.

I had him walk before me, through the door of the barn he had entered and exited for half a century. He had become, like the denims he wore, an implement of labor, one of the discarded farm tools. A personal pride, however, dormant since the Depression, reasserted itself in the way he accepted my appreciative comments. Why not? Had he not endured and survived it all, like the farm itself? Over several days I had remarked that he changed his hats according to the time of day and the occasion. A sporty nautical number in the early morning, at high noon and afternoon one of his wide brimmed straws. In the dusk of evening he preferred an old felt, with a narrow brim, the color and texture of tar paper. All the hats suited him fine. The only piece of apparel we both found out of fashion was new overalls, blue stripes on white, that in no way adapted to his figure or movements and gave off the rasp of a file. He was quick to sense my disapproval and stopped wearing them.

It was Clara's suggestion that I might look in on Ed's place. Ed was a bachelor, related by marriage, who had died several weeks before my arrival. His small farmhouse was directly across the road. The bed had been made, but otherwise, I found the house as a bachelor would have left it. The bric brack of a lifetime, pill boxes, pin cushions, shotgun shells, flashlights,

a watch and chain, a few snapshots. Although the bed had been made, the imprint of this body remained, his feet were almost visible in the shoes beneath it. What I saw on the ground glass evoked in me a commingling of tenderness, pity and sorrow, to the exclusion of more searing emotions. Was there another American emotion to match it? Were not tragic sentiments alien to a free people who were free to choose, and chose more earthly adornments? "Ed passed on last month," Harry had said, as if he had glanced just a bit too late to catch him. What he seemed to see was a movement of the bushes edging the drive.

One evening Clara had shown me a photograph of the Morris family, taken in Ohio in the late 1880s, showing all members of the family, except my father and Harry, forming a line in front of a clapboard house in a fresh fall of snow. Their names had been read aloud to me by Harry—Mitchell and Emerson, Ivy and Mae, Martha and Francena—on and on through a dozen. A crack in time had been made by the click of a shutter, through which I could peer into a world that had vanished. This fact exceeded my grasp, but it excited my emotions. The following day I took the photograph into the open air and pinned it to the clapboards on one side of the house. I saw it clearly on the ground glass before the shutter clicked. Was it in this way I hoped to postpone what was vanishing? A simpler ritual of survival would be hard to imagine. By stopping time I hoped to suspend mortality.

Since I had taken all of the interior shots without artificial lighting I was anxious to get the negatives developed and see what I had done. In Lincoln, while they were being processed, I drove around through the neighboring towns and found many structures on interest. A weathered church near Milford, a railroad station in Panama, a barber pole and barber shop in Weeping Water, in which the photographer can be seen in the mirror. In Central City I woke up the barber, dozing in his chair after lunch. He remembered my father—a railroad man who had turned to raising chickens—but he had no memory of the boy who had sat on the board placed on the chair arms, heard the chirp of the shears and smelled the tonic water doused on his hair. There had been a lot of boys. Looking at me, front and side, brought none of them to mind.

With the negatives in hand I was eager to get back to work in the darkroom. During the three days of driving east I pondered what I should have as a text. Why not such an experience as I had just had, the return of a long prodigal native? Better yet, let him return with his family, a big city girl and two city kids who had never corked the holes in a privy. Let them all respond to the objects and places for which they had few, if any, mystic feelings. The smell of pickling beets, the heat from a cob burning range, the flies to be skimmed off the bucket of water, would have on a city girl an effect more in the line of nausea than nostalgia. More in the line of what this homecoming would need. What would bring them back to such a farm in the first place? The housing shortage in the cities. The need for a place to live. I was so well primed with this story, and it so well suited my emotions, that I postponed the darkroom work and spent the first several weeks writing.

The Home Place, published in 1948, proved to be a radical departure from *The Inhabitants.* The text would be a narration of one day's events, as told by the returning native, and each page of text would face a photograph. The relationship would sometimes be explicit—the object photographed would be mentioned—but in the main photographs would provide the visible ambience for the story, as if we walked about the farm while listening to the narration. The format would be much smaller than *The Inhabitants,* roughly the size of a novel, and the photographs would be cropped. These mutilations removed them, as a group, from the context of artworks, as "images," and presented them as "things" and artifacts. The decision to do the book in this manner permitted no compromise. I wanted to know what such a book would be like, and I found out. The readers I had in mind—it was part of my euphoria— were those who would browse through the book like an album. Most of the readers I found objected to the distraction of the photographs, and those who liked the photographs largely ignored the text. The book was very well received, critically, and continues to find reader-lookers, but it was not bought at the time of publication and confused many reviewers about the author. Was he a writer, who took photographs, or a photographer who did a little writing? The public is ill at ease with the ambidextrous. The writer who does a little painting on the side is not felt to be a "committed" writer. Or painter. My publisher read these reviews, checked the sales figures, and suggested, sensibly, that I stick to my "proper business" as a novelist. I was angered, injured, hit between wind and high water, grievously disappointed—but I listened. Photo-text books were expensive to produce, and on both books Scribner's had lost money. In the volume on which I was then at work, *The World in the Attic,* the second in the series of photo-text books I had planned, I was persuaded to give up the photographs. . . .

At a gathering of photographers—perhaps one of the first—sponsored by Edward Steichen at The Museum of Modern Art, I met Walker Evans, Ben Shahn, Charles Sheeler and numerous others who were full of plans, talk and stimulating controversy. Some of us walked the streets and talked until far into the morning. *The Home Place* had just been published, to high praise from Lewis Mumford, but "straight" photographers were not lacking who saw photo-text as a dangerous corruption. It seemed and was, however, a very good and productive time for the making of photographs, books and talk.

In the early fifties I continued to take photographs and made several trips back to the Midwest, as far as Nebraska. Some photo-text essays appeared in *The New York Times Magazine* during this period but I became increasingly preoccupied with my writing.

1. See Morris, "A Note" introducing "The Inhabitants: An Aspect of American Folkways," *New Directions in Prose and Poetry* (Norfolk, Conn.: New Directions, 1940), pp. 147–48.

2. See Morris: *God's Country and My People* (New York: Harper & Row, 1968); *Love Affair—A Venetian Journal* (New York: Harper & Row, 1972); *Photographs and Words*, ed. and with introduction by James Alinder (Carmel, Calif.: Friends of Photography, 1982), pp. 50–53; *Time Pieces;* and *Wright Morris: Origin of a Species* (San Francisco: San Francisco Museum of Art, 1992).

3. Among the many analyses of Morris's photo-texts, see especially those by Trachtenberg, "The Craft of Vision," *Critique* 4, no. 3 (Winter 1961–62): 41–55, esp. 42–47; Barbara Ann Strelke, "Place and the Power of Imagination," in "Images of Home and Place: Essays, Poems, Photography" (Ph.D. diss., University of New Mexico, 1975), pp. 39–95; A. D. Coleman, "Novel Pictures: The Photofiction of Wright Morris," [1976], in *Light Readings: A Photography Critic's Writings, 1968–1978* (New York: Oxford University Press, 1979), pp. 242–46; Joseph J. Wydeven, "Consciousness Refracted: Photography and the Imagination in the Works of Wright Morris," *Midamerica* 8 (1981): 92–114, and "Images and Icons: The Fiction and Photography of Wright Morris," in Barbara Howard Meldrum, ed., *Under the Sun: Myth and Realism in Western American Literature* (Troy, N.Y.: Whitston, 1985), pp. 176–204; Colin Westerbeck, Jr., "American Graphic: The Photography and Fiction of Wright Morris," in *Multiple Views: Logan Grant Essays on Photography 1983–89*, ed. Daniel P. Younger (Albuquerque: University of New Mexico Press, 1991), pp. 271–302; Philippe Cantie, "Lettre et icone dans l'incipit de *The Inhabitants,*" *Caliban* 29 (1992): 133–44; and Szarkowski, "Wright Morris the Photographer," pp. 9–21, and Sandra S. Phillips, "Words and Pictures," pp. 23–32, in Morris, *Origin of a Species.*

71. *Richard Wright*

FROM *Black Power*, 1954

*W*right (1908–60) addressed the forces acting on the contro-versial central character in Native Son (1940) in his subsequent work, Twelve Million Black Voices: A Folk History of the Negro in the United States (1941). *This text provided a broadly Marxist overview of the typical deprivations of ordinary blacks in urban America; it was accompanied by pictures selected by Edwin Rosskam, largely taken by the Farm Security Administration during the Great Depression.*[1] *Though some of the impact of Wright's passionate, metaphorical account was muted by the outbreak of war two months after its publication, it became an "instant bible" to some artists, such as young Gordon Parks.*[2] *During the Second World War, Wright [Fig. 114], now fully aware of the impact of photographs, became an amateur photographer himself.*[3] *He also thought of collaborat-ing with Helen Levitt, whose pictures of New York children he admired, on a photodocumentary work about Harlem youth, especially delinquents.*[4] *In 1953, while living in Paris, Wright visited the Gold Coast at the invitation of the new prime minister of Ghana, which had recently become indepen-dent. He brought his camera, thinking to accompany his text with his own annotated photographs of memorable individuals and sights [Fig. 115]; but his American publishers, in contrast to his foreign ones, decided against their inclusion.*[5] *Similarly, the photographs he took for his next two books—one on a conference in Bandung, the other on Spain—were excluded from American but not foreign editions.*[6] *As his account of his photographic ex-periences in Ghana here suggests, Wright often felt almost as alienated by the poverty, dirt, nudity, illness, stagnation, and superstition of postcolo-nial African culture as by Western racism, imperialism, and materialism.*

FROM *Black Power*

I took out my camera to photograph the scene and the children let out a warning yell that made every face jerk toward me. At once the women began covering their breasts and the boys rose and ran toward me, yelling:

"Take me! Take me!"

Chances of a natural photograph were impossible, and, not to disappoint the children, I snapped a picture or two of them. I turned to leave and they followed me. I walked faster and they began to run, yelling:

"Take me! Take me!"

I hastily turned a corner, hoping that they'd fall behind; but they came on and on, their ranks swelling as they ran. It was not until I was some five blocks from the compound that they began to fall out, one by one, and return. Didn't their mothers miss them? Wasn't there anyone to look after them? To let tiny children of four and five years of age have that much freedom filled me with wonder. . . . [p. 68]

I paused before a young woman selling tin pans and, by pointing, I indicated that I wanted to buy one. At once a group of women gathered about; it seemed that my buying a pan made them feel that they had the right to examine me at close quarters. The woman to whom I had pointed out the pan seemed baffled; she called hurriedly to a friend. Soon a crowd of no less than fifteen women were ranged about me, chattering excitedly. Finally they called an old man who spoke a little English and he translated. The pan cost seven shillings and I paid, sweating, wondering why the women were evincing such interest. As I started off with the pan under my arm, the old man called me back.

"What is it?" I asked.

The women chattered even more loudly now.

"What you do with pan, Massa? Women wanna know."

I looked at the women and they hid their faces, laughing.

"I'm going to use the pan to boil water. I'm making a chemical solution in which to develop films ..." My voice trailed off, for I could see that he had not understood me.

"They wanna know if you buy it for wife?" the man asked.

"No."

There was another outburst of laughter.

"They wanna know if Massa cook chop in pan?"

"No. I eat in a hotel restaurant," I said.

The women conferred with the man again and he shook his head. Finally he turned to me and asked:

"Massa, women wanna know if Massa make peepee in pan?"

I blinked in bewilderment. The women were howling with laughter now.

I pushed away, hearing their black laughter echoing in my ears as I tried to lose myself in the crowd. I learned afterward that it was considered a disgrace for a man to purchase pots, pans, or food, that it was an open confession that he had no woman to do such things for him, and that no decent, self-respecting African would ever dare be caught buying such a thing as a pan in the public market. In the eyes of those women I'd lost caste, for they'd been

conditioned in a hard masculine school of detribalized thought whose slogans regarding women were: keep 'em ignorant, keep 'em pregnant, and keep 'em ten paces behind you. [pp. 83–84]

As I entered the offices of the United States Information Service to look over the recent newspapers from America, I was stopped by a young lad.

"Dr. Wright, may I speak to you, sar?"

"Certainly. What is it? But I'm no doctor, son."

"I want a camera like that, sar," he said, touching the instrument I held under my arm.

"Well, they are rather expensive, you know."

But I've an idea, sar," he said. "You see, sar, if you gave me a camera like that, I'd take pictures with it here and I'd send you the pictures in Paris and you could sell them, sar."

I blinked, trying to grasp what he was saying.

"I don't understand."

"You see, sar, when you sell my pictures, I wouldn't want you to send me any money until you had sold enough to get your own money back *twice*...."

It was obvious that he had no intention whatsoever of trying to defraud me; he simply did not quite grasp the reality involved in his scheme.

"That's very kind of you," I told him. "But don't you know that they sell these cameras right here in Accra? Have you any money?"

"I could get the money, sar," he told me. "But they wouldn't sell me a camera like *that,* sar."

I finally understood what he meant. He was trying to tell me that he believed that the British would, say, take out some valuable part of the camera before they sold it to him, an African. He was convinced that every move of the British contained some hidden trick to take advantage of him. (Many Africans, I was told, ordered their goods directly from the United Kingdom and paid duty on them, believing that the goods would be of better quality than those sold by foreign merchants in local stores. And an African boy, wanting a bicycle, has been known to beg a Britisher to buy it for him, feeling that the foreign storekeeper would cheat him, but wouldn't dare cheat the Britisher. ... A sodden and pathetic distrust was lodged deep in the African heart.)

"Look, I'd like to help you, but, honestly, I don't know how...."

He seemed to be about twenty-one years of age....

"But I'd pay you back; I'd send the pictures to you. I swear, sar," he begged me.

I sighed. I was angry, but I didn't know with whom; I tried to avoid his pleading eyes. I was not angry with him.

"I'd suggest that you go to a school of photography," I advised him.

He looked crestfallen. He did not accept it. But he nodded and allowed me to pass. I sat down to read, but my mind was trying to fathom how these young boys saw and felt reality. The boy had seemed to feel that he had a claim upon me that I could not accept. I was for him, but not in the direct way he seemed to feel that I ought to be. Did he think that I was naïve enough to make him, a stranger whose merits I did not know, a present of an expensive camera? Obviously, he did. But why? I had never in my life dared ask anybody for a gift so exorbitant.

That evening I discussed this boy's demand with an African who had been educated in the United States.

"That boy thinks that you are his brother— You are of African descent, you see," he told me.

"But you don't give expensive cameras to boys even if they are of your color," I protested.

"You don't understand. The boy was trying to establish a sort of kinship with you. In the Gold Coast, a boy can go and live with his uncle, demand to be fed, clothed, and the uncle cannot refuse him. The uncle has a sacred obligation to comply. Tribal life has bred a curious kind of dependence in the African. Hence, an uncle, if he has four or five nephews, can never accumulate anything. His relatives live on him and there is nothing that he can do about it."

"But what right has the nephew to make such claims?"

"The uncle's sister's blood flows in the nephew's veins.... Look, if an African makes £100,000, do you think he can keep it? No. His family moves in and stays with him until that money is gone. You see, the family here is more of an economic unit than in the West.... Let's say that an African family has gotten hold of a few thousand pounds. They'll hold a family meeting and decide to send Kojo, say, to London to study medicine. Now, they are not giving that money to Kojo; they are *investing* it in him and when he masters his medical subjects, returns home, and starts practicing, the family stops working and goes and lives with Kojo for the rest of their lives. That's their way of collecting their dividends, a kind of intimate coupon clipping, you might say. . . .

"African society is tightly, *tightly* organized.... No one is outside of the bounds and claims of the clan. You may never get rich, but you'll never starve, not as long as someone who is akin to you has something to eat. It's Communism, but without any of the ideas of Marx or Lenin. It has a sacred origin—". [pp. 98–100]

I ran from the balcony; I had to see this at close range. Some ritual whose significance I could not understand was taking place. A thousand questions popped into my mind and no answers could even be imagined. I reached the street just as a young chief, borne aloft on a palanquin decorated in brightly colored silks, came by on the bare black shoulders of his carriers. Above him was the usual vast umbrella being twirled by a panting and sweating boy. Now the brass coffin came again, the black men running as they turned it round and round on their heads, and this time I noticed that in front of the men bearing the brass coffin was a half-nude woman, wearing a skirt made of raffia; she had a huge black fan made from feathers and she was swishing that fan through the air with hurried, frantic motions, as though trying to brush away something invisible. . . .

The parade or procession or whatever it was called was rushing past me so rapidly that I feared that I would not get the photograph I wanted; I lifted my camera and tried to focus and when I did focus I saw a forest of naked black breasts before my eyes through the camera sight. I took the camera from my eyes, too astonished to act; passing me were about fifty women, young and old, nude to the waist, their elongated breasts flopping loosely and grotesquely in the sun. Their faces were painted with streaks of white and sweat ran down their foreheads. They held in each of their hands a short stick—taken from packing boxes—and they were knocking these sticks furiously together, setting up an unearthly clatter, their eyes fixed upon the revolving coffin of brass.... [pp. 129–30]

A mass of shy black children began crowding about. Playfully, without attempting to take a picture, I pointed the lens of the camera at a boy and he shuddered, burst into tears, and ran off screaming.

"What happened to him?" I asked the young electrician.

"Nothing, sar. He's just scared." [p. 143]

We were passing a magnificent woman who sat nursing a fat black baby. The long red rays of the setting sun lit her ebony torso to a soft distinctness. I requested the boy to ask her to let me take a picture. He spoke to her and she nodded her head.

"Penny, Massa," she said, extending her hand.

I fished a shilling out of my pocket and gave it to her. She rose, laughed. I tried to focus my camera and she lunged past me, holding the baby with one hand under its belly, and made a beeline for the mud hut; she was out of sight before I could utter a word. A howl of black laughter echoed through the compound. I stood looking like a blundering fool. She had outwitted me. I laughed too. She had won. [p. 149]

As detached and resistant as I try to be, I find myself sometimes falling heir to the reaction pattern which lingers on here as a kind of legacy of British imperialism. One morning I wanted to take a batch of film to the Photographic Section of the Gold Coast Information Service and I got into a taxi and told the driver:

"Photo section of the Gold Coast Information Service."

"What, Massa?"

"The Photo Section on Boundary Road," I said.

"Yasa, Massa."

He set his car in motion and drove for some time. I noticed that he had taken a route that was not familiar to me.

"Where are you going?" I asked him.

He stopped the car and looked at me, his face flashing a white grin.

"Where Massa wanna go?" he asked me.

"I told you the Photo Section. It's on Boundary Road."

He drove off again; then once more he slowed the car and said to me:

"Massa, tell me where it is...."

"What are you doing?" I demanded. "You drove off like you knew where it was—" Houses have no street numbers in Accra.

"Yasa, Massa," he said, picking up speed. What was wrong with the guy? The taxi sped past buildings that were strange to me; soon I saw the green landscape of the suburbs of Accra.

"Say, boy! Where're you taking me?" I yelled at him, leaning forward.

"Massa, I don't know where it is," He mumbled, slowing the car.

"Then why didn't you *tell* me? Why are you driving about aimlessly?" My voice was so sharp that he winced; that heat and the humidity held me in a grip. I noticed the lazy, relaxed manner in which he sat slouched behind the wheel and I was suddenly angry. "For God's sake, ask somebody on Boundary Road. You know where that is, don't you?

"Yasa, Baas."

He drove on. I sat back and swabbed sweat off my face, chiding myself. I oughtn't to speak to a boy like that.... The car rolled on and I watched for familiar landmarks. I saw none.

"Where are you taking me?" I begged of him.

"I don't know, Massa," he said and stopped the car.

"I want to go to the Photo Section on Boundary Road," I said, talking slowly, making sure that he heard every word.

"Yasa, Massa."

He started the car up again and sped off. The landscape was still strange. But perhaps he's taking a roundabout way to get back into the city? I held myself in. But, no; the city was getting farther and farther away....

"Where are you going?" I asked him.

"I don't know, Massa," he said, slowing the car.

"Ask somebody," I told him.

We went forward slowly and, at the sight of a policeman, he stopped the car and spoke to him in his native tongue. The policeman pointed elaborately and again we were off. I waited, tense, sweating. I looked at my surroundings and saw a huge sign that read:

BRITISH MILITARY COMMAND FOR WEST AFRICA

"Boy, stop!"

The car skidded to a halt, the tires screeching on the concrete pavement.

"Turn this car around!"

He turned the car.

"Now, take me back to my hotel!"

"Massa wanna go back?"

"Yes!"

He started off. I relaxed. I'd get another taxi and start all over again. Jesus.... The British might have thought that I was trying to spy on them if they had found me wandering amidst their military installations. . . . A good five minutes passed and when I looked out of the window of the car I saw the Photo Section of the Gold Coast Information Service as we were speeding past it. I'd found it by accident?

"Stop!" I yelled. "There it is!"

He jammed on his brakes and I went forward against the back of the front seat. I got out and told him to wait. Ten minutes later I emerged and told him to drive me to the Seaview Hotel. At the entrance of the hotel, I got out.

"What do I owe you?"

"Eighteen shillings, Massa," he said, his face averted.

That did it. I got mad. I felt that I was dealing with a shadow.

"Don't be a fool, man! Tell me what I *owe* you!"

He looked at me and grinned shyly.

"Fourteen shillings, Massa."

"Talk sense," I muttered, feeling sweat running on my face.

He waited a long time, scratched his head,

looked at me out of the corners of his eyes, his brows knitted, weighing me.

"Twelve shillings, Massa."

"Are you charging me for taking me out into the country? That was your fault—"

"Ten shillings, Massa." He was still bargaining.

"What was the actual price of my trip? You charge a shilling a mile, three shillings an hour, don't you? Did you drive me nine miles?"

I was determined not to be cheated. He looked at me fully now, grinned again, and said imperturbably:

"What Massa wanna give me?"

"Here are eight shillings," I said; I felt that that was too much, but I was willing to settle for that.

"Thank you, Massa," he said, bowing and smiling.

I stood watching him, wanting to tell him that was no way to act, that he should have been honest with me. He looked at me and burst into a wild laugh, a laugh of triumph. I was on the verge of cursing him, but I controlled myself. Suddenly I too laughed, lifted my arm in the Convention People's Party salute, my elbow resting on my hip, the palm of my hand fronting him.

"FREE—DOOOM!"

He jerked to a surprised attention, gave me a salute in return, shouting:

"FREE—DOOOM!"

I spun on my heels and went to my room. More than once did I find myself slipping into the pattern left here by the British. The Africans had been so trained to a cryptic servility that they made you act a role that you loathed, live a part that sickened you. [pp. 175–78]

I was convinced that the many anthropologists who had studied Ashanti had put down, by and large, the basic truth of their religious customs, and I think that the chief knew this. He was trying to make me believe that the Ashanti had secrets *behind* secrets; and if I pried out those so-called secrets, he could at once allude to still other and more dreadful secrets behind *those* secrets, and so on. But what value have these secrets? Obviously, to his mind, a "secret" possessed the psychological value of intimidating others, of making them think that any move they might make against him, would be met with some countermove of a surprising nature.... In short, in his eyes, you were an enemy until, by his own standards, he had decided that you were not.

At times this denial of plain facts on the part of chiefs became laughable. One chief would tell me a story that was flatly and passionately contradicted on the same day by another chief in a neighboring state. These effacings of reality went so far as to include objective evidence. For instance, with an anthropological volume under my arm showing clear photographs of "blackened stools," one chief defiantly informed me:

"There are *no* such things as blackened stools! There are no such things and there *never* were any! That's a fiction invented by the British to smear us!"

All of this dodging and denying is, of course, aided by the fact that there is no written history. If the Ashanti had a concrete manner of ascertaining what went on yesteryear, they might have escaped the more bizarre aspects of their religion, its more bloodthirsty phases. With a vivid account of what they had done, uncolored by the emotionally charged recital of a "linguist," they might have been able, perhaps, to remember their bare, objective actions and, in remembering them, they would have been made to pause and wonder, would have been able to get beyond the circling coils of abject fear.... [pp. 290–91]

... The woman knelt and placed a small bottle of clear liquid at the head of the coffin.

To one side was a row of men beating drums, blowing horns, and brandishing sticks. Some people were prancing, others dancing, while the onlookers made wild and meaningless grimaces with their faces. I jumped; several muskets had gone off in back of me. I took out my camera and focused. A painted man came running to me.

"You take no picture!" he said, turning hurriedly away.

But another man yelled:

"No; no.... Stay here! We want you take picture!"

I stopped. I explained that I was an American, that I wanted somebody to explain the meaning of the funeral rite to me. I waited while they consulted among themselves. Finally they said that I could take two pictures. But, as I tried to focus my camera, the first wild man who had objected rushed forward, waving that awful knife....

"Take no picture! I kill you!" he screamed.

The others caught him and held him. I stood, undecided.

"You work for British!" the wild man yelled.

'I'm an *American*!" I yelled back.

"You lie! You work for British!"

"I'm an *American*!" I screamed, hoping that the crowd would sympathize with me.

But the crowd looked on with detached curiosity and I knew that they would not have moved a finger if that crazy man had got ever so close to me with that knife. I started backing discreetly off.

I thought hard. People who carry on in this manner over a dead man's body might just as well get the idea into their poetic heads that I was some kind of a ghost, or a prospective sacrificial victim. One flick of one of those monstrous knives would yank me straight into the other world. I managed two more shots with the camera, but my sweaty hands were trembling. The wild man was struggling to get free from his pals.

"He be drunk, Massa," Kojo warningly whispered to me.

"Let's go," I said.

I turned and started toward the car, almost colliding with a tall, handsome woman.

"Take me," she said.

"Hunh?"

"Take me," she said again, putting her hands on her hips.

I got out my camera; I'd take a shot of her just to show this wild and mean-tempered crowd that I was sport, a well-meaning sort of fellow....

"No, no," the woman said, blocking my lens with her hand. "Take me, *me*," she repeated.

I blinked. Then I understood. She was selling and she thought that I would buy.

"Nuts," I said, whirling and making for the car.

The crowd guffawed. The painted men were still rushing in circles about the coffin. I got into the car, slammed the door and locked it. The "take me" woman was smiling invitingly.

"Let's get away from here, Kojo," I said.

A fairly well-dressed man came to the door of the car and tapped on the window glass. Cautiously, I lowered the window an inch.

"You'd better go," he said.

"I'm going," I said. "But what in God's name are they doing?"

"They're trying to frighten away the dead man's spirit," he said.

"Thanks," I said, rolling the window up again, tight.

The motor roared; the car pulled off and I felt better. I lay back and closed my eyes and tried to relax. I don't know if those painted men with their long knives were successful in scaring away the dead man's spirit or not; all I know is that they sure scared the hell out of me.... [pp. 330–31]

---

1. See *Twelve Million Black Voices* [1941] (New York: Thunder's Mouth Press, 1988). See also "Twelve Million Black Voices," *Coronet* 11 (April 1942): 77–92, a condensed version with thirty photos for which Wright wrote verse couplets. John Heartfield designed a cover for the English edition (London: Lindsay Drummond, 1947), reproduced in his *Photomontages of the Nazi Period*, p. 133.

2. See Parks, *To Smile in Autumn*, p. 75, and his 1940's portraits of Wright in the Library of Congress, one of which is reproduced here. See also two 1959 portraits by Freund, one in *The World in My Camera*, p. 230, with comments on pp. 226–27; the other in *Freund, Photographer*, p. 153, with comment on p. 150.

3. Michel Fabre, *Richard Wright: Books and Writers* (Jackson: University Press of Mississippi, 1990), pp. 45 and 16, notes that Wright bought before 1940 the second edition of *How to Make Good Pictures* (Rochester, N.Y.: Eastman Kodak, n.d.) and later purchased Paul Boucher, *Fundamentals of Photography with Laboratory Experiments*, 2nd ed. (New York: Van Nostrand, 1947). An admirer of Stieglitz, whom he met through Dorothy Norman, Wright published in tribute to him a small photograph of a wood in a magazine, according to Fabre in letters of March 25 and April 11, 1992, to the editor, who, however, has been unable to locate it; Wright also contributed to the last two volumes of Norman's *Twice a Year* (nos. 12–13, 1945). See also the letter of March 6, 1944, from Beaumont Newhall to Nancy Newhall in Beaumont Newhall, *Focus: Memoirs of a Life in Photography* (Boston: Bulfinch Press, 1993), p. 118: "Think of what we have meant in human terms alone, to.....Wright....."

4. See Wright's draft and typescript with corrections for "A Recommendation" for Levitt's 1943 exhibition for MOMA, at the Beinecke (JWJ Misc. MS 692 and TS 693); and Fabre, *The Unfinished Quest of Richard Wright*, trans. Isabel Barzun (New York: Morrow, 1973), p. 267. Helen Levitt, in conversation with the editor on January 15, 1992, recalls talking to Wright on the telephone and saying that she was unable to do such a project at that time, though later she made a film, *The Quiet One* (1949), on the very subject Wright suggested, as is noted in her selection above.

5. See Wright's photographs throughout *Black Power: A Record of Reactions in a Land of Pathos* (London: Dennis Dobson, 1954). It is also interesting to compare Wright's experiences with those of other writer-photographers in various parts of Africa: see the Rimbaud, Conan Doyle, and Bruce Chatwin selections and notes. According to the letters of May 5, 1953–July 12, 1954, to his agent and editor in the Harper & Brothers archives at Princeton (CO103, Box 34, Folders 5–6), Wright took over 1,500 photographs, thinking illustrations useful as documentary evidence. He professed neutrality about whether the American publishers used them; unaccountably they did not, instead using one of the Ghanaian prime minister, supplied by the British Information Service. Thirty-four of Wright's photographs, entitled with lines from the text, did appear in the British and Dutch editions (Leiden: Sijthoff, 1954), called to the editor's attention by Fabre in a letter of March 25, 1992. The many Wright photographs at the Beinecke (JWJ/Zan5/ +3/v. 24–26) include some of these published scenes; many more unpublished ones, about fifty of which bear paragraph-long captions about various aspects of Ghanaian life in a similar format to the one reproduced here, and a dozen, accompanied by single-line captions, which are linked to numbered pages; two lists of Gold Coast photographs, with subjects indicated (JWJ/Wright 79 [6]); and one other similar list with yet another set of page numbers, which don't correspond to the Wright MSS at the Beinecke or to any of the published volumes.

6. The foreign editions of *The Color Curtain: A Report on the Bandung Conference* (London: Dobson; The Hague: Van Hoeve, 1956) include some of Wright's photographs, but none appear in the American edition (Cleveland: World Publishers, 1956). Constance Webb, *Richard Wright: A Biography* (New York: G. Putnam's Son, 1968), p. 346, notes that Wright also took "hundreds" of photographs for his next book, *Pagan Spain*

PROVERBS FOR EVERY HOUR.

    The African loves proverbs. He loves to proclaim his pithy sayings to
the world. Hence, drivers of trucks vie with one another in trying to attract
attention to philosophical sentiments. Some slogans painted on trucks read:
GOOD TEACHER. DO GOOD FOR THY NEIGHBOR. SO THEY ARE AND SO THEY MAY BE. On
one God Coast truck I saw a sign that proclaimed: FEAR WOMAN AND LIVE LONG.

115. Richard Wright. 'Proverbs for Every Hour,' with text, c. 1953, unpublished.

(New York: Harper & Brothers, 1956), which are mentioned in Wright's correspondence in the Harper & Brothers archives at Princeton (CO103, Box 34, Folders 6 & 11). Some of these pictures are at the Beinecke (JWJ/Zan S/+3/v. 27), including a dozen with captions and page numbers, probably those included with the final MS, and are mentioned by Fabre, *The Unfinished Quest*, pp. 414 and 608, n. 5. None was included in the American edition, but some apparently were used in two magazine pieces, "Fallas in Valencia," *Illuspress* (January 1959): 5ff, and "Vralt Fastnachtsbrauche," *Illuspress* (May 1959), according to Charles T. Davis and Michel Fabre, *Richard Wright: A Primary Bibliography* (Boston: G. K. Hall, 1982), p. 107.

72. Jean-Paul Sartre

FROM PREFACE TO *D'Une Chine à l'Autre*
BY HENRI CARTIER-BRESSON, 1954

Sartre (1905–80) was a provocative choice to write the preface for Cartier-Bresson's book on China, though he had not yet traveled there. The leading French Existentialist usually popularized his philosophical beliefs in his novels, plays, and literary criticism as well as through leftist political activism. In whatever form he wrote, however, Sartre's insistence on the individual as the source of all meaning in life, not subject to imposed systems of laws and beliefs, particularly suited the postwar generation.[1] No photographer was more of an individual than Cartier-Bresson (1908–), who turned to the camera to better seize the "decisive moment" in settings all over the world, often penetrating beyond the stereotypical to the universal [Fig. 116]. Throughout his various professional turning points, while shifting to and from painting, still photography, film-making, and photojournalism, Cartier-Bresson remained an avid reader; his work was influenced by writers like Aragon, Hughes, and Nabokov almost as much as by visual artists.[2] His portraits include many memorable ones of writers, not only French but ones from around the world, indicative of his cosmopolitan travels and outlook.[3] Cartier-Bresson's photographs, taken during the turbulent transition from Nationalist to Communist rule (1948–49), helped prepare Sartre for his visit to China (1955), a country that subsequently became for him a symbol of worldwide revolutionary hope.

FROM PREFACE TO *D'Une Chine a l'Autre* BY HENRI CARTIER-BRESSON

The origin of the picturesque is war and the refusal to understand the enemy: indeed, our views on Asia first came from irritated missionaries and soldiers. Later arrived the travellers—merchants and tourists—who are the passionless soldiers: pillage is then called "shopping" and rapes are practiced at a high price in specialized shops. But the basic attitude hasn't changed: the natives are killed less often but they are scorned as a group which is a civilized form of massacre; listing *differences* becomes an aristocratic pleasure. "I cut my hair, he braids his; I use a fork; he uses sticks; I write with a quill pen; he traces characters with a brush; I have straight ideas and his are crooked: have you noticed that he hates logical thought, he is happy only if everything goes awry." That is called the game of anomalies: if you find one more, if you discover a new reason not to understand, you will be granted a sensitivity prize in your own country. No wonder that those who reconstruct their fellow beings as if they were a mosaic of irreducible differences, then ask themselves how one can be Chinese.

As a child, I was a victim of the picturesque: everything was done to make the Chinese intimidating. I was told of rotten eggs—they loved them—of men sawed between two planks, of thin and discordant music. In the world that surrounded me, there were things and animals which would be singled out as Chinese: they were small and terrifying, they slipped away between your fingers, they attacked from behind, they suddenly exploded into unexpected din, shadows gliding like fish along the aquarium glass, muffled lanterns, incredible and futile refinements, ingenious tortures and hats with ringing bells. There was also the Chinese soul which, I was told, was simply impenetrable.

"Orientals, you see...". The negroes did not concern me: I'd been taught they were good dogs; with them, we were mammals together. But the Asian scared me; like these crabs from the rice paddies which jump up from between two furrows, like the locusts which descend on the great plain and devastate everything. We are kings of the fish, of the lions, of the rats and of the monkeys; the Chinese is a superior insect, he rules over the insects.

Then came Michaux who first showed the Chinese without a soul or a shell, China without a lotus or Loti.[4]

A quarter of a century later, Cartier-Bresson completes the demystification. There are photographers who push for war because they make stories. They search for a Chinese who has a more Chinese air than the others and ends up finding one. They have him take a typically Chinese pose and surround him with chinoiseries. What have they captured on their film? *A* Chinese? Definitely not: the idea of the Chinese.

The photos of Cartier-Bresson never chatter. They are not ideas; they give us ideas. Without a purpose. Naturally his Chinese are disconcerting: most of them never seem Chinese enough. The smart tourist wonders how they manage to distinguish one another. As for me, after having leafed through the album, I rather wonder how we could possibly confuse them, lumping them altogether under the same heading. The idea of the Chinese becomes more remote and dim: it has become only a convenient phrase. What we have instead are men who resemble each other *as men.* Living, sensual presences who have not yet received their official labels. We have to thank Cartier-Bresson for his gift of nominalism. [pp. 1–2]

116. Henri Cartier-Bresson. Children reading, Shanghai, 1949, from *D'Une Chine à l'Autre*, 1954.

1. Aside from the widely reproduced portrait of Sartre by Cartier-Bresson in *Photoportraits,* p. 249 (1946), see also ones of him, sometimes including his longtime companion, Simone de Beauvoir, by Freund: in *James Joyce in Paris,* p. 42 (1939); *The World in My Camera,* pp. 214, 232, and 234 (1965 and 1969); and *Freund, Photographer,* pp. 137–39; by Strand, reproduced in *Paul Strand: Sixty Years of Photographs* (Millerton, N.Y.: Aperture, 1971), p. 168; by Gjon Mili: reproduced in Mili, *Photography and Recollections* (Boston: New York Graphic Society, [1980]), npn, which includes the introduction that Sartre wrote for a 1946 Paris exhibition of Mili's work; and others in Liliane Sendyk-Siegal, comp., *Sartre: Images d'une vie,* with comments by de Beauvoir (Paris: Gallimard, 1978).

2. See Galassi, *Henri Cartier-Bresson: The Early Work,* pp. 9–50, and the Hughes selection above.

3. See Cartier-Bresson, *Photoportraits,* for many excellent portraits—none dated—of the following literary figures: Ezra Pound, p. 27; Samuel Beckett, p. 33; André Malraux, p. 51; Truman Capote, p. 58; Paul Valéry, p. 72; Paul Éluard, p. 110; René Char, p. 129; Albert Camus, p. 137; Edmund Wilson, p. 142; Pablo Neruda, p. 148; Somerset Maugham, p. 148; Arthur Miller, p. 153; Michel Tournier, p. 159; William Faulkner, p. 165; Robert Lowell, p. 188; Carson McCullers, pp. 194 and 217; Henry Miller, p. 218; Ted Hughes, p. 220; Louis Aragon, p. 229; Jean Anouilh, p. 231; Harold Pinter, p. 239; Aldous Huxley, p. 243; Jean Genêt, p. 255; Katherine Anne Porter, p. 272; and André Breton, p. 278.

4. Henry Michaux (1899–1984) was a poet noted for his travel adventure works, such as *Un Barbare en Asie* (1932); Pierre Loti (1850–1923) wrote novels known for their sentimental romantic adventures in exotic settings.

73. *Minor White and Roy DeCarava*

CORRESPONDENCE, NOVEMBER 1955
(UNPUBLISHED)

*D*eCarava *(1919–), a painter turned photographer who inspired Steichen's encouragement, became the first black artist to win a Guggenheim Fellowship (1952). He specialized in expressive scenes of Harlem life but, finding no market for them, turned for help to Langston Hughes; the writer's addition of a narrative to what became* The Sweet Flypaper of Life *(1955) secured its publication and led to other joint commissions.[1] The award-winning little book attracted the attention of Minor White (1908–76), a major postwar photographer who also was a cofounder and the first editor (1952–75) of* Aperture, *the leading photography magazine. He had long been sensitive to the issues involved with words alone and in combination with images. White's journal, "Memorable Fancies" (1931–50), includes the results of a self-assigned program of poetry writing (1932–37)—after which he decided to become a photographer, not a poet—and three verse cycles relating to his war experiences (1942–45). In 1947, he canceled an exhibition of some of his pictures and verses, which had been criticized for their ambivalent sexual and patriotic content as well as their quality, rather than show the prints without them.[2] White thereafter used his writing talents as a noted teacher, critic, aesthetic theorist, reviewer, and, as here, an editor. DeCarava proposed that their letters be published but, given White's lukewarm response, withdrew the idea.[3] The two remained friendly, however, and their exchange still supplies valuable insights about the nature of verbal and visual collaborations.*

November 11, 1955

As you doubtlessly realize I am very much interested in the kind of production that fuses words and pictures into a third medium. The fusion is fairly easy in TV or on the stage where eye and ear cooperate, but very difficult—as you must know—in book form. There is only a handful of such books in existence: Time in New England by Paul Strand and Nancy Newhall, the two by Wright Morris, Summer's Children by Barbara Morgan, The World of Albert Schweitzer name most of them. I hardly need tell you that "Sweet Flypaper" joins this select little society. Of the lot I believe that Summer's Children is the best fusion to date—and regret that it falls short due to the quality of the individual photographs.

Now where does your charming little book fit into all this? Now kindly remember that I am but little acquainted with you, hence do not know how to best phrase my remarks so that what seems to be criticism is the encouragement that I intend. Or we might say that this is a council of perfection—your photographs are good, but they can be better, and it is towards their being better that I make my remarks.

First of all the text carries the pictures. This is not exactly a surprise considering the relative experience between yourself and Mr. Hughes. As one reads the words with the pictures as intended, the latter falls into place beautifully. And fortunately the text is almost always well balanced to the pictures, to bring this about. Still the pictures in themselves are not as strong as they could be. I know one does not want monumental, landmark photos in this book, but more penetration, pictures that reveal a little more vitality, and pictures that have a greater sense of essence would be very much to the point.

I have argued this point many times with Barbara Morgan; namely that photography is a culminative media and that a large group of good pictures will get over the feeling—they do, but in going through Summer's Children (and now yours) I miss the decisive and incisive image here and there around which the rest could cluster for strength. I find that I do not remember any of the photographs. I will not forget the book; the title and how it is worked into the text is unforgettable. But I want to have a picture to match. I want one that will get inside and that I will live with for a long time. Even though I were to forget it for months on end it should surface now and then and add a moment of warmth.

There is one, top of page 57, "Well that boy is just gun crazy," that might do this. It is too early to say. I can hear you argue—"of course this is a completely personal business," and I am the first to agree. Hence there should be several such pictures in the book so that other kinds of people than myself will find the memorable image that fuses with the title. To do this is not as easy as falling off a log or several logs, but from photographers I want everything.

A particularly unhappy example of failing to fuse words with pictures were the pages on autos. The photo of the street full of cars is ordinary, and the other two show nothing of love for cars. Another example of a weak link between photo and text is on page 74, "Winter coal shoveled in." The photograph really shows a man who is skeptical of another man with a camera. I think you have to watch more carefully what your photography will say to OTHER people. You know what you want them to say so they mean that to you—but do they mean the same to others? To that good old public who has no interest in you as a person or as a photographer?

Well, that is the essence of my remarks. And with your talent and promise I think that the next such book should be much better. I am fascinated to see what you will do with this word and photo fusion on the next try. You are starting early in life down a path that is not well trodden. Paul Strand has been hard at it for a decade or so collaborating first with one and then another writer and each of his books improves. And where he works in a classic, highly restrained style, you are working in an unrestrained style. Your style of photography fits the category, in art history terms, of <u>romantic</u> as compared to Strand's <u>Classicism</u>. The text-word medium is broad, plenty broad and will accommodate both styles with the greatest of ease. Thus I am not asking that you imitate Strand's style—just suggesting that you consider his achievement.

I hope that on the basis of this book that you will get commissions (or opportunities regardless of source) to do more in this medium of word and pictures.

Minor White.

DeCarava, Letter to White

November 21, 1953

Dear Minor,

Thanks very much for the report on The Sweet Flypaper of Life, your words of encouragement and advice. . . . This letter is written only in the desire that you might know me better and is not an attempt to justify in any way either the photographs or the book as a whole. It is intended to supply you with information about myself, Langston Hughes and the circumstances and evolution of the book. The photographs that I made on the Guggenheim Fellowship were never intended to be anything but what they are, a collection of single photographs of Negro people in Harlem. The photographs themselves are the end product and anything that comes after is a by-product and is secondary. Photography, to me is large enough to contain as many approaches and schools as there are people. When I photograph I have one thought uppermost in my mind—to isolate, capture, something, person or time that affects me, that moves me. To do this I must change it, reshape it into an image which express both the object and something of myself. A photographic print is the end in itself, a law unto itself, to be hung on a wall and to be lived with and enjoyed, in the same manner that one lives with and enjoys a lithograph or woodcut. A photograph is a photograph, a picture, an image, an illusion complete within itself, depending neither on words, reproductive processes or anything else for its life, its reason for being. Photography will continue to stagnate unless it accepts its proper place among the visual arts. It must reject its gaudy isolation and fight for Its natural place in the family of art, where each media is an individual yet all are brothers. This is my approach to photography and is intended to supplement rather than negate the many varied and wonderful uses to which photography is put. There is and must be room for the artist as well as the technician in photography as it must be in life itself. The time will come when photography will cast aside its literary crutch and stand on it's own feet as a legitimate medium of expression. for me, photography must be visual, rather than intellectual and ideological. The Sweet Flypaper of Life is a compromise with the economic and cultural realities of our time and place, more so than a compromise of esthetic principles. I wanted my work to be seen by as vast an audience as possible and the book form seems to be the best method available to date, therefore I accept this compromise as a necessary one. To quote Sister Mary Bradley, in The Sweet Flypaper of Life . . . "life, which ain't always so sanitary as we might like it to be." In The Sweet Flypaper of Life the story or narration is pure fiction and was written only from what was seen and felt in the photographs. There was never any attempt or desire on my part to tell Mr. Hughes how or what to write. Although, in the beginning I did offer to give him background material about some of the people and the photographs, but he declined, for which I am very glad, as anything that I might have told him might have only inhibited or hampered him. Langston had over four hundred pictures to work with and he selected those pictures that had a special meaning for him and translated these feelings into the words which grace the pages of our book. The story does not bind itself too tightly and mechanically around the pictures because the words are felt rather than thought, the heart rather than the mind. It is a loose, easy-fitting and simple story about plain, ordinary people in their everyday living. It is the kind of writing which allow the photographs to live and breathe. It was a fortunate day for me when I showed Langston my pictures. He was so excited about the photographs that he personally tried to interest a number of publishers he knew in publishing the photographs alone, in book form. It was only after many nice, glowing rejections, that the publisher, Simon and Schuster, suggested that if Mr. Hughes could write a provocative and interesting text or story to tie the photographs into a marketable package, they would reconsider, but until that time the economic facts of life preclude a book of photographs, no matter how worthy or beautiful. The rest you know ...

Langston had carte blanche to select and write as he saw fit. There is no other writer that I know whom I would have entrusted my work to with as much confidence and trust. I love my work and am very concerned to what uses it is put, to often as not to my financial detriment. It should go without saying, but just to make sure I'll say it anyway ... Langston's writing surpassed my wildest expectations. In order that there be absolutely no misunderstanding I would like to make it clear that nothing in this letter should be interpreted as an apology or justification for either the pictures or the words. The Sweet Flypaper of Life is a wonderful juxtaposition of words and pictures and a fusion of two minds and two art forms into a creative achievement for all concerned, designer, art director, editor and publisher.

It is very kind of you to say that my photographs are good and I'm sure that you mean it but I really don't think they have reached you. Why, I don't know and for me to try and guess would be as unwise as it would be presumptuous.

There is much more that could be said but I think I have written myself out and since there will be other nights and many more thoughts I'd like to close by thanking you again for all that you have said both favorable and unfavorable and which I know were sincere and well intentioned. Your report will certainly be of value in the creation of better photographs and no doubt better photographic books, with or without words.

Sincerely,

Roy DeCarava

WHITE, LETTER TO DeCARAVA

November 30, 1955

Mr. Roy DeCarava
148 West 84th Street
New York 24, New York

Dear Roy:

A wonderful letter, full of warmth and kindness and belief in your own work—and I am grateful for the description of how the text and photos were fused.

It is the faith in your own work, both quiet and strong that gives me the best feeling. With that at the core, criticism, whether harsh, unjust, or the opposite, entirely constructive, will always be of use to you.

The problem that I always face in expressing myself about another's work is how to encourage the personal expression for everything that that is worth and at the same time try to indicate that a greater intensity is desirable; or as I said, that perfection is still ahead.

Steichen told me in a chat about the Family of Man show that "photographers do not get close enough." We are up to their arm pits now but I can only agree with him. Closeness that is spoken of here is, I believe, that which allows the viewer to participate in the action. The action may be across the street, a room, a city or across a mouth—as you well know.

Curious that you should consider the book a compromise, and regret that the photographs have to depend on a "literary crutch", as you call it. I, for one, am greatly intrigued with the combination of words and pictures on a page that fuse into a medium of expression in its own right. It seems clear from the history of the book why you might think in this manner. So I would like to point once again that words and pictures fused is a fabulous medium, rarely tried on a creative level and less often successful. . . .

Sincerely,

Minor White/msw

1. See the Hughes selection above on the publication of *Sweet Flypaper.* See also Rampersad, *The Life of Langston Hughes,* vol. 2, pp. 242–44, 249, 284, 337–38, 370, 416, and 420, for more details on this and later associations between Hughes and DeCarava, including, pp. 319–20, their assignment from Columbia Pictures in 1960–61 to publicize the film adaptation of Lorraine Hansberry's *Raisin in the Sun,* with pieces written by Hughes and photographs by DeCarava, but with no bibliographical data; six relevant and titled TSS, dated November 11, 1960–January 25, 1961, are contained in the Hughes Correspondence (JWJ) at the Beinecke.

2. The lengthy "Memorable Fancies," at the Minor White Archives, Princeton, is being edited by Peter Bunnell for publication. White reprinted some of his verse and prose, often with alterations of phrase and even dates, throughout *Mirrors Messages Manifestations,* especially pp. 32–39, which include some of the "Amputations" and relevant photographs from the canceled 1947 exhibition. See also Bunnell, *Minor White: The Eye That Shapes* (Princeton, N.J.: Art Museum, Princeton Univer-

sity, 1989), which discusses, pp. 2–4, and reproduces, pp. 23–45, some of White's poetry as well as a 1947 photograph entitled '"Metamorphoses" Kafka,' Plate 85. Sherry Turner DeCarava, in conversation with the editor on February 26, 1992, indicated that her husband also has written some unpublished poems.

3. This proposal, apparently raised earlier, is mentioned in a letter from White to DeCarava, January 24, 1956, and in a reply from DeCarava to White, January 26, 1956, both in the Minor White Archives and unpublished. See also White's brief favorable review of *The Sweet Flypaper of Life* in *Image* 4, no. 9 (December 1955): 71, and James S. Peck's longer one in *Aperture* 4, no. 1 (1956): 38, which incorporated some of the specific information that DeCarava wrote to White. For more on DeCarava after 1955, see *Roy DeCarava: Photographs,* ed. James Alinder, with introduction by Sherry Turner DeCarava (Carmel, Calif.: Friends of Photography, [1981]); for more on White after 1955, see Bunnell, *Minor White.*

*K*erouac (1922–69) [Fig. 150] is best known for his quasi-autobio-
graphical On the Road (1957), which portrays young people roaming around America to seek fulfillment away from conventional
society—often with the help of drugs. The book focused attention on the so-
called Beat Generation, with which young poets like Allen Ginsberg were
associated as well as veterans like Henry Miller.[1] At this time, a young Swiss,
Robert Frank, the first European photographer to win a Guggenheim Fellowship, was also exploring the United States. After capturing highways, diners,
jukeboxes, and other centers and symbols of American life [Fig. 117], often
revealing their hollowness, Frank prepared a book, The Americans (1959).
Though its title is a bow to the 1938 work of his sponsor, Walker Evans,
Frank asked Kerouac, whom he had met while working for Life, to write the
preface; the writer's perspective and colloquial style seemed better suited to
his irreverent pictures.[2] The Americans was immediately influential; even
documentary photographers like Eugene Smith, noted for his moral and
technical clarity, appreciated the outsider's perspective, comparing Frank to
Kafka.[3] The photographer later turned to motion pictures. Unable to film
Kerouac's On the Road, Frank used the last act of his unpublished play, "The
Beat Generation," as the basis for Pull My Daisy (1959), for which the author
supplied the voice-over narration.[4]

Just took a trip by car to Florida with Photographer Robert Frank, Swiss born, to get my mother and cats and typewriter and big suitcase full of original manuscripts, and we took this trip on a kind of provisional assignment from *Life* magazine who gave us a couple of hundred bucks which paid for the gas and oil and chow both ways. But I was amazed to see how a photographic artist does the bit, of catching those things about the American Road writers write about. It's pretty amazing to see a guy, while steering at the wheel, suddenly raise his little 300 dollar German camera with one hand and snap something that's on the move in front of him, and through an unwashed windshield at that. Later on, when developed, the unwashed streaks don't harm the light, composition or detail of the picture at all, seem to enhance it. We started off in N.Y. at noon of a pretty Spring day and didn't take any pictures till we had negotiated the dull but useful stretch of the New Jersey Turnpike and come on down to Highway 40 in Delaware where we stopped for a snack in a roadside diner. I didn't see anything in particular to photograph, or "write about," but suddenly Robert was taking his first snap. From the counter where we sat, he had turned and taken a picture of a big car-trailer with piled cars, two tiers, pulling in the gravel driveyard, but through the window and right over a scene of leftovers and dishes where a family had just vacated a booth and got in their car and driven off, and the waitress had not had time yet to clear the dishes. The combination of that, plus the movement outside, and further parked cars, and reflections everywhere in chrome, glass and steel of cars, cars, road, road. I suddenly realized I was taking a trip with a genuine artist and that he was expressing himself in an art-form that was not unlike my own and yet fraught with a thousand difficulties quite unlike those of my own. Contrary to the general belief about photography, you don't need bright sunlight: the best, moodiest pictures are taken in the dim light of almost-dusk, or of rainy days like it was now in Delaware, late afternoon with rain impending in the sky and lights coming on on the road. Outside the diner, seeing nothing as usual, I walked on, but Robert suddenly stopped and took a picture of a solitary pole with a cluster of silver bulbs way up on top, and behind it a lorn American Landscape so unspeakably indescribable, to make a Marcel Proust shudder ... how beautiful to be able to detail a scene like that, on a gray day, and show even the mud, abandoned tin cans and old building blocks laid at the foot of it, and in the distance the road, the old going road with its trucks, cars, poles, roadside houses, trees, signs, crossings ... A truck pulls into the gravel flat, Robert plants himself in front of it and catches the driver in his windshield wild-eyed and grinning mad like an Indian. He catches that glint in his eye ... He takes a picture of a fantastic truck door announcing all the licenses from Arkansas to Washington, Florida to Illinois, with its confusion of double mirrors arranged so the driver can see to the rear around the body of the trailer ... little details writers usually forget about. In darkening day, rain coming on the road, lights already on at 3 pm, mist descending on Highway 40, we see the insect swoop of modern sulphur lamps, the distant haze of forgotten trees, the piled cars being tolled into the Baltimore Harbor Tunnel, all of which Robert snaps casually while driving, one eye to the camera, snap. Thence down into Maryland, lights flashing now in a 4 pm rain, the lonely look of a crossroad stoplight, the zing of telephone wires into the glooming distance where another truck heads obstinately toward some kind of human goal, of zest, or rest. And GULF, the big sign, in the gulf of time ... a not unusual yet somehow always startling sight in all the pure hotdog roadstand and motel whiteness in a nameless district of U.S.A. where red traffic lights always seem to give a sense of rain and green traffic lights a sense of distance, snow, sand ...

Then the colored girl laughing as she collects the dollar toll at the Potomac River Bridge at dusk, the toll being registered in lights on the board. Then over the bridge, the flash and mystery of oncoming car lights (something a writer using words can never quite get), the sense of old wooden jetties however unphotographable far below rotting in the mud and bushes, the old Potomac into Virginia, the scene of old Civil War battles, the crossing into the country known as The Wilderness, all a sadness of steel a mile long now as the waters roll on anyway, mindless of America's mad invention, photographs, words. The glister of rain on the bridge paving, the reds of brakelights, the gray reflections from open holes in the sky with the sun long gone behind rain to the westward hills of Maryland. You're in the South now.

A dreary thing to drive through Richmond Virginia in a drenching midnight downpour.

But in the morning, after a little sleep, America wakes up for you again in the bright morning sun, fresh grass and the hitchhiker flat on his back sleeping in the sun, with his carton suitcase and coat before him, as a car goes by on the road—he knows he'll get there anyway, if at all, why not sleep. His America. And beyond his sleep, the old trees and the long A.C.L. freight balling on by on the main line, and patches of sand in the grass. I sit in the car amazed to see the photographic artist prowling like a cat, or an angry bear, in the grass and roads, shooting whatever he wants to see. How I wished I'd have had a camera of my own, a mad mental camera that could register pictorial shots, of the photographic artist himself prowling about for his ultimate shot—an epic in itself.

We drove down into Rocky Mount North Carolina where, at a livestock auction right outside town, hundreds of out-of-work Southerners of the present recession milled about in the Russia-looking mud staring at things like the merchant's clutter of wares in the back trunk of his fintail new-car ... there he sits, before his tools, drills, toothpaste, pipe tobacco, rings, screwdrivers, fountain pens, gloomy and jut jawed and sad, in the gray Southern day, as livestock moo and moan within and everywhere the cold sense of drizzle and hopelessness. "I

should imagine," said Robert Frank to me that morning over coffee, "though I've never been to Russia, that America is really more like Russia, in feeling and look, than any other country in the world ... the big distances, the faces, the look of families traveling ..." We drove on, down near South Carolina got out of the car to catch a crazy picture of a torn-down roadside eatery that still announced "Dinner is ready, this is It, welcome" and you could see through the building to the fields the other side and around it bulldozers wrecking and working.

In a little town in South Carolina, as we floated by in the car, as I steered for him slowly down Main Street, he leaned from the driver's window and caught three young girls coming home from school. In the sun. Their complaint: "O Jeez."

Further down, the little girl in the front seat with pin curls, her mother doubleparked in front of some Five and Ten.

A car parked near a diner near a junkyard further down, and in the back seat, strung to a necessary leash, a frightened little cat ... the pathos of the road and of Modern America: "What am I doing in all this junk?"

We went off our route a little to visit Myrtle Beach, South Carolina, and got a girl being very pensive leaning on the pinball machine watching her boy's score.

A little down the road to McClellanville South Carolina, scene of beautiful old houses and incredible peace, and the old "Coastal Barber Shop" run by 80 year old Mr. Bryan who proudly declared "I was the first white barber in McClellanville." We asked him where in town we could get a cup of coffee. "Ain't no place, but you go down to the sto and get you a jar of powder coffee and bring it back, I got a nice pot on the stove here and got three cups ..." Mr. Bryan lived on the highway a few miles away, where, "All's I like to do is sit on my porch and watch the cars run." Wanted to make a trade for Robert Frank's 1952 Stationwagon. "Got a nice Thirty Six Ford and another car." "How old is the other car?" "It ain't quite as young but you boys need two cars, don't ya? You goin to get married, ain't ya?" Insists on giving us haircuts. With comb in the hair in the old barber tradition, he gives the photographer a weird haircut and chuckles and reminisces. Barber shop hasn't changed since Photographer Frank was by here about five years ago to photograph the shop from the street door, even the bottles on the shelf are all the same and apparently haven't been moved.

A little ways down a country road, to the colored houses of McClellanville, a Negro funeral, Strawhat Charlie with razor scar looking out the window of his black shiny car, "Yay" ... And the graves, simple mounds covered with clam shells, sometimes one symbolic Coca Cola bottle. Things you can't capture in words, the moody poem of death ...

A little more sleep, and Savannah in the morning. Prowling around we see a brand new garbage truck of the City of Savannah with fantastic propped-up dolls' heads that blink their eyes as the truck lumbers through back alleys and women in their bathrobes come out and supervise ... the dolls, the American flag, the horseshoe in the windshield, the emblems, mirrors, endless pennons and admirable spears, and the boss driver himself, colored, all decked out in boots and cap and a "garbage" knife in his belt. He says "Wait here till we come around the corner and you catch a pitcher of the truck in the SUN" and Robert Frank obliges ... prowling around the back alleys of Savannah in the morning with his all-seeing camera ... the Dos Passos of American photographers.

We investigate bus stations, catch an old boy from the South with floppy Snopes hat waiting at Gate One of the station fingering a roadmap and saying "I don't know where this line go." (*The new Southern Aristocracy!* yell my friends seeing this picture.)

Night, and Florida, the lonely road night of snow white roadsigns at a wilderness crossing showing four endless unreadable nowhere directions, and the oncoming ghost cars. And the roadside gift shoppes of Florida by night, clay pelicans stuck in grass being a simple enough deal but not when photographed at night against the oncoming atom-ball headlights of a northbound car.

A trailer camp ... a swimming pool ... Spanish moss waving from old trees ... and while prowling around to photograph a white pony tethered by the pool we spot four frogs on a stick floating in the cerulean pool ... look closely and judge for yourself whether the frogs are meditating. A Melody Home trailer, the canaries in the window cage, and a little way down the road, the inevitable roadside Florida zoo and the old alligator slumbering like a thousand years and too lazy to shake his horny snout and shake off the peanut shells on his nose and eyes ... mooning in his gravy. Other, grimmer trailer camps, like the one in Yukon Florida, the outboard motorboat on wheels, ready to go, the butane tank, the new lounge chair in the sun, the baby's canvas seat swing, the languorous pretty wife stepping out, cigarette in mouth ... beyond her all wavy grass and swamps ...

Now we're in Florida, we see the lady in the flowery print dress in a downtown Orlando Fla. drugstore looking over the flowery postcards on the rack, for now she's finally made it to Florida it's time to send postcards back to Newark.

Sunday, the road to Daytona Beach, the fraternity boys in the Ford with bare feet up on the dashboard, they love that car so much they even lie on top of it at the beach.

Americans, you can't separate them from their cars even at the most beautiful natural beach in the world, there they are taking lovely sunbaths practically under the oil pans of their perpetually new cars ... The Wild Ones on their motorcycles, with T-shirt, boots, dark glasses, and ivy league slacks, the mad painting job on the motorcycle, and beyond, the confusion of cars by the waves. Another "wild one," not so wild, conversing politely from his motorcycle to a young family sprawled in the sand beside their car ... in the background others leaning on car fenders. Critics of Mr. Frank's photography have asked, "Why do you take so many pictures of cars?" He answers, shrugging, "It's all I see everywhere ... look for yourself."

Look for yourself, the soft day Atlantic waves washing in to the pearly flat hard sand, but everywhere you look, cars, fishtail Cadillacs, one young woman and a baby in the breeze to ten cars, or whole families under swung-across blankets from car to car camping in front of dreary motels.

The great ultimate shot of Mrs. Jones from Dubuque Iowa, come fifteen hundred miles just to turn her back to the very ocean and sit behind the open trunk of her husband's car (a car dealer), bored among blankets and spare tires.

A lesson for any writer ... to follow a photographer and look at what he shoots ... I mean a great photographer and look at what he shoots ... I mean a great photographer, an artist ... and how he does it. The result: Whatever it is, it's America. It's the American Road and it awakens the eye every time.

117. Robert Frank. 'St. Petersburg, Florida,' 1955.

1. See Ginsberg, "Robert Frank to 1985—A Man," *Robert Frank: New York to Nova Scotia,* ed. Anne Wilkes Tucker (Boston: New York Graphic Society, 1986), pp. 74–77, and the photographs of Frank and Kerouac in *Allen Ginsberg Photographs* (Altadena, Calif.: Twelvetrees Press, 1990), npn, and Ginsberg, *Snapshot Poetics: A Photographic Memoir of the Beat Era* (San Francisco: Chronicle Books, 1993), pp. 32–33, 48, and 56. For more about Kerouac and Ginsberg, see the Ginsberg selection below.

2. See Kerouac, introduction to Robert Frank, *The Americans* (New York: Grove, 1959), pp. 5–8, and Frank, essay in *Photography within the Humanities,* ed. Janis and MacNeil, p. 58, and *The Lines of My Hand* [1972] (New York: Pantheon, 1989), npn, about asking Kerouac to write the preface; and Ginsberg, in *Snapshot Poetics,* pp. 14–15, on their similarities. See also Evans, 'Parked Car, Small Town Main Street, 1932,' *American Photographs* [1938] (New York: MOMA, 1988), Part 1, no. 10, which anticipates Frank's photographs of cars. For more about Frank and Ginsberg, see the Ginsberg selection below.

3. See W. Eugene Smith, in *Photography within the Humanities,* ed. Janis and MacNeil, p. 108.

4. See Kerouac, *Pull My Daisy,* with text ad-libbed by Kerouac for film by Frank and Alfred Leslie (New York: Grove, [1961]); and see also Frank, *Zero Mostel Reads a Book* (New York: New York Times Books, 1963).

75. Truman Capote

"COMMENTS," INTRODUCTION TO
Observations BY RICHARD AVEDON, 1959

*T*he southern charm, quick wit, and precocious success of the writer Truman Capote (1924–84) attracted social and artistic celebrities, including Henri Cartier-Bresson, Cecil Beaton, who became a lifelong friend, and Richard Avedon (1923–).[1] Acclaimed for his innovative fashion photography, Avedon wanted to achieve greater variety, veracity, and a wider audience through a book of portraits of artists in many fields; he asked Capote, whose understanding of the complexities of celebrity he admired, to contribute the text.[2] Together with the designer Alexey Brodovitch, Avedon's mentor at Harper's Bazaar, they collaborated beautifully, producing a landmark in book design which did secure more serious attention for the photographer's work.[3] In contrast to Avedon's fashion portraits, his later, harshly lit studies rarely flatter his subjects, whether from high society, the American West, or urban mental hospitals. His 1959 and 1974 close-ups of Capote—first as the beguiling collaborator on Observations, *later as the degenerating author of* In Cold Blood *(1966)—illustrate both approaches [Figs. 118, 119].[4]* Avedon's only subsequent collaboration, Nothing Personal *(1964)*, with his high school classmate James Baldwin (1924–), was more socially conscious but less well integrated conceptually and thus less well received.[5]

Richard Avedon is a man with gifted eyes. An adequate description; to add is sheer flourish. His brown and deceivingly normal eyes, so energetic at seeing the concealed and seizing the spirit, ceasing the flight of a truth, a mood, a face, are the important features: those, and his born-to-be absorption in his craft, photography, without which the unusual eyes, and the nervously sensitive intelligence supplying their power, could not dispel what they distillingly imbibe. For the truth is, though loquacious, an unskimping conversationalist, that sort that zigzags like a bee ambitious to depollen a dozen blossoms simultaneously, Avedon is not, not very, articulate: he finds his proper tongue in silence, and while maneuvering a camera—his voice, the one that speaks with admirable clarity, is the soft sound of the shutter forever freezing a moment focused by his perception.

He was born in New York, and is thirty-six, though one would not think it: a skinny radiant fellow who still hasn't got his full growth, animated as a colt in Maytime, just a lad not long out of college. Except that he never went to college, never, for that matter, finished high school, even though he appears to have been rather a child prodigy, a poet of some talent, and already, from the time he was ten and the owner of a box camera, sincerely embarked on his life's labor: the walls of his room were ceiling to floor papered with pictures torn from magazines, photographs by Muncaczi and Steichen and Man Ray. Such interests, special in a child, suggest that he was not only precocious but unhappy; quite happily he says he was: a veteran at running away from home. When he failed to gain a high-school diploma, his father, sensible man, told him to "Go ahead! Join the army of illiterates." To be contrary, but not altogether disobedient, he instead joined the Merchant Marine. It was under the auspices of this organization that he encountered his first formal photographic training. Later, after the war, he studied at New York's New School for Social Research, where Alexey Brodovitch, then Art Director of the magazine *Harper's Bazaar,* conducted a renowned class in experi-mental photography. A conjunction of worthy teacher with worthy pupil; in 1945, by way of his editorial connection, Brodovitch arranged for the professional debut of his exceptional student. Within the year the novice was established; his work, now regularly appearing in *Harper's Bazaar* and *Life* and *Theatre Arts,* as well as on the walls of exhibitions, was considerably discussed, praised for its inventive freshness, its tart insights, the youthful sense of movement and blood-coursing aliveness he could insert in so still an entity as a photograph: simply, no one had seen anything exactly comparable, and so, since he had staying power, was a hard worker, was, to sum it up, seriously gifted, very naturally he evolved to be, during the next decade, the most generously remunerated, by and large successful American photographer of his generation, and the most, as the excessive number of Avedon imitators bears witness, aesthetically influential.

"My first sitter," so Avedon relates, "was Rachmaninoff. He had an apartment in the building where my grandparents lived. I was about ten, and I used to hide among the garbage cans on his back stairs, stay there hour after hour listening to him practice. One day I thought I must: must ring his bell. I asked could I take his picture with my box camera. In a way, that was the beginning of this book."

Well, then, this book. It was intended to preserve the best of Avedon's already accomplished work, his observations, along with a few of mine. A final selection of photographs seemed impossible, first because Avedon's portfolio was too richly stocked, secondly because he kept burdening the problem of subtraction by incessantly thinking he must: must hurry off to ring the doorbell of latter-day Rachmaninoffs, persons of interest to him who had by far-fetched mishap evaded his ubiquitous lens. Perhaps that implies a connective theme as regards the choice of personalities here included, some private laurel-awarding system based upon esteem for the subjects' ability or beauty; but no, in that sense the selection is arbitrary, on the whole the common thread is only that

118. Richard Avedon. Truman Capote, New York City, 1958, from *Observations*, 1959.

119. Richard Avedon. Truman Capote, New York City, 1974, from *Portraits*, 1976.

these are some of the people Avedon happens to have photographed, and about whom he has, according to his calculations, made valid comment.

However, he does appear to be attracted over and again by the mere condition of a face. It will be noticed, for it isn't avoidable, how often he emphasizes the elderly; and, even among the just middle-aged, unrelentingly tracks down every hard-earned crow's-foot. In consequence there have been occasional accusations of malice. But, "Youth never moves me," Avedon explains. "I seldom see anything very beautiful in a young face. I do, though: in the downward curve of Maugham's lips. In Isak Dinesen's hands. So much has been written there, there is so much to be read, if one could only read. I feel most of the people in this book are earthly saints. Because they are obsessed. Obsessed with work of one sort or another. To dance, to be beautiful, tell stories, solve riddles, perform in the street. Zavattini's mouth and Escudero's eyes, the smile of Marie-Louise Bousquet: they are sermons on bravado."

One afternoon Avedon asked me to his studio, a place ordinarily humming with hot lights and humid models and harried assistants and haranguing telephones; but that afternoon, a winter Sunday, it was a spare and white and peaceful asylum, quiet as the snow-made marks settling like cat's paws on the skylight.

Avedon was in his stocking-feet wading through a shining surf of faces, a few laughing and fairly afire with fun and devil-may-care, others straining to communicate the thunder of their interior selves, their art, their inhuman handsomeness, or faces plainly mankindish, or forsaken, or insane: a surfeit of countenances that collided with one's vision and rather stunned it. Like immense playing cards, the faces were placed in rows that spread and filled the studio's vast floor. It was the finally final collection of photographs for the book; and as we gingerly paraded through this orchard of prunings, warily walked up and down the rows (always, as though the persons underfoot were capable of crying out, careful not to step on a cheek or squash a nose), Avedon said: "Sometimes I think all my pictures are just pictures of me. My concern is, how would you say, well, the human predicament; only what I consider the human predicament may be simply my own." He cupped his chin, his gaze darting from Dr. Oppenheimer to Father Darcy: "I hate cameras. They interfere, they're always in the way. I wish: if I just could work with my eyes alone!" Presently he pointed to three prints of the same photograph, a portrait of Louis Armstrong, and asked which I preferred; to me they were triplets until he demonstrated their differences, indicated how one was a degree darker than the other, while from the third a shadow had been removed. "To get a satisfactory print," he said, his voice tight with that intensity perfectionism induces," one that contains all you intended, is very often more difficult and dangerous than the sitting itself. When I'm photographing, I immediately know when I've got the image I really want. But to get the image out of the camera and into the open is another matter. I mark as many as sixty prints of a picture, would make a hundred if it would mean a fraction's improvement, help show the invisible visible, the inside outside."

We came to the end of the last row, stopped, surveyed the gleaming field of black and white, a harvest fifteen years on the vine. Avedon shrugged. "That's all. That's it. The visual symbols of what I want to tell are in these faces. At least," he added, beginning a genuine frown, the visual symbol of a nature too, in a fortunate sense, vain, too unrequited and questing to ever experience authentic satisfaction, "at least I hope so."

1. Capote worked with Cartier-Bresson on a travel piece for *Harper's Bazaar* (1946), reprinted as "New Orleans," in *Local Color* (New York: Random House, 1950), pp. 3–12, and discussed in John Malcolm Brinnin, *Truman Capote: Dear Heart, Old Buddy* (New York: Delacorte Press/Seymour Lawrence, 1986), pp. 9 and 19–26. Cartier-Bresson's photograph of Capote (1948) is reproduced in Gerald Clarke, *Capote: A Biography* (New York: Simon & Schuster, 1988), following p. 120, fig. 30. See also "Truman Capote at the Sea and in the City," *House Beautiful* 111, no. 4 (April 1969): 93–98, for some color interiors of Capote's homes by Marie Cosindas, each captioned by the author.

Capote provided the introduction to *The Best of Beaton* (London: Weidenfeld & Nicolson, [1968]), pp. 11–14, and is often mentioned in Beaton's later *Diaries*. Clarke, *Capote*, reproduces Beaton's 1948 photograph of Capote, following p. 120, fig. 29, and Tennessee Williams's sarcastic comment about it to Carson McCullers, p. 178; a 1957 picture of both in Japan following p. 312, fig. 47; and mentions, p. 522, Capote's idea for a piece about his relationship with Beaton, entitled *The Siamese Twins Visit Siam,* referring to their 1958 trip to the Orient, though there is no further information about that proposal. See also Capote's "The *Sylvia* Odyssey," *Vogue* 147 (January 15, 1966): 68–75, which features text and "photographs with (handwritten) comments by Capote."

2. Avedon, in telephone conversations with the editor on June 5 and August 20, 1991, maintained he never talked to Patricia Bosworth, whose *Diane Arbus* (New York: Avon, 1985), p. 223, says Avedon regarded Capote as a "cultural icon of the 1950's"; but he didn't disclaim his high regard for the writer at the time.

3. According to Avedon, examples of their close collaboration included Capote's thinking of the title; his insistence on a preface, which drew on a fascinating autobiographical sketch provided by Avedon (who sent it to the editor in June 1991); his suggesting subjects for inclusion like his old friend, Isak Dinesen (but see Clarke, *Capote*, pp. 306–7, for her distress at his text); and his accommodating Brodovitch's request for a capital letter A or T to begin the text accompanying Avedon's photograph of Marianne Moore to reinforce the design of her tricorn hat.

4. Avedon's literary portraits have been reproduced mainly in *Observations,* which, at his insistence, included Capote, p. 149, and in *Portraits,* npn, which included the aging Capote, infuriating the writer; both are reproduced here. See also three portraits (1969, 1980) of Capote in Krementz, *The Writer's Image,* npn.

5. See Avedon and Baldwin, *Nothing Personal* (New York: Atheneum, 1964), npn, which includes portraits of Arthur Miller and the nude Allen Ginsberg (see his remarks on Avedon in his selection below). Baldwin and Avedon were co-editors of their high school magazine, but, according to the photographer, this difficult collaboration—in which each proceeded independently, partly because Baldwin, abroad a lot, was remiss about deadlines—ended their friendship. Other relevant works by both include Avedon's *Alice in Wonderland: The Forming of a Company and the Making of a Play* (New York: Merlin House, 1973), with a text by Doon Arbus, the daughter of his late friend Diane Arbus, and Baldwin's introduction to *The Black Photographers' Annual,* vol. 3, npn [5 pp].

76. Günter Grass

FROM "THE PHOTOGRAPH ALBUM,"
FROM *The Tin Drum,* 1959

According to Grass (1927–), an internationally acclaimed German writer, he "was reared between The Holy Ghost and Hitler's photograph."[1] Though he stopped believing in either figure by the close of the Second World War, he retained faith in the power of the photograph. Grass subsequently devoted his versatile talents as a graphic designer, jazz drummer, sculptor, filmmaker, as well as writer to trying to compel his native land to confront the past that made the Third Reich possible. He understood the power of the photograph to rescue that past from oblivion for nations and individuals alike, without aestheticizing the experience for either. Accordingly, Grass devotes an entire chapter in his first major novel, The Tin Drum *(1959), to the contents of a family photograph album, which also serves to introduce the plot, major characters, and pervasive themes.[2] The analysis of the album by the unstable central character, Oskar, is both credible and unsettling, anticipating Grass's characteristic strategy. The success of* The Tin Drum *freed Grass to take a more active role in German politics, some feel to the detriment of his writing; photography, as an incontrovertible repository of personal history or as totalitarian propaganda, continued to figure in many of his subsequent works.[3] But interactions between words and images were far more conspicuous in the work of some of his Central European contemporaries, such as the more experimental Austrian writer Peter Handke (1942–), who not only used and commented on photography in his writings but sometimes reproduced his own pictures.[4]*

404   1940–1965

I am guarding a treasure. Through all the bad years consisting only of calendar days, I have guarded it, hiding it when I wasn't looking at it; during the trip in the freight car I clutched it to my breast, and when I slept, Oskar slept on his treasure, his photograph album.

What should I do without this family cemetery which makes everything so perfectly clear and evident? It has a hundred and twenty pages. On each page, four or six or sometimes only two photographs are carefully mounted, sometimes symmetrically, sometimes less so, but always in an arrangement governed by the right angle. It is bound in leather. At times my album has been exposed to the wind and weather. The pictures came loose and seemed so helpless that I hastened to paste them back in their accustomed places.

What novel—or what else in the world—can have the epic scope of a photograph album? May our Father in Heaven, the untiring amateur who each Sunday snaps us from above, at an unfortunate angle that makes for hideous foreshortening, and pastes our pictures, properly exposed or not, in his album, guide me safely through this album of mine; may he deter me from dwelling too long on my favorites and discourage Oskar's penchant for the tortuous and labyrinthine; for I am only too eager to get on from the photographs to the originals.

So much for that. Shall we take a look? Uniforms of all sorts, the styles and the haircuts change, Mama gets fatter and Jan gets flabbier, some of these people I don't even know, but I can guess who they are. I wonder who took this one, the art was on the downgrade. Yes, gradually the art photo of 1900 degenerates into the utilitarian photo of our day. Take this monument of my grandfather Koljaiczek and this passport photo of my friend Klepp. One need only hold them side by side, the sepia print of my grandfather and this glossy passport photo that seems to cry out for a rubber stamp, to see what progress has brought us to in photography. And all the paraphernalia this quick photography takes. Actually I should find fault with myself even more than with Klepp,

for I am the owner of the album and should have maintained certain standards. If there is a hell in wait for us, I know what one of the more fiendish torments will be: they will shut up the naked soul in a room with the framed photographs of his day: Quick, turn on the pathos: O man amid snapshots, passport photos. O man beneath the glare of flash bulbs, O man standing erect by the leaning tower of Pisa. O photomaton man who must expose his right ear if he is to be worthy of a passport! And—off with the pathos. Maybe this hell will be tolerable because the worst pictures of all are not taken but only dreamed or, if they are taken, never developed. [pp. 49–50]

I am losing myself amid snapshots of "Strength through Joy" tourists and records of tender boy-scout eroticism. Let me skip a few pages and come to myself, to my first photographic likeness.

I was a handsome child. The picture was taken on Pentecost, 1925. I was eight months old, two months younger than Stephan Bronski, who is shown on the next page in the same format, exuding an indescribable commonplaceness. My postcard has a wavy scalloped edge; the reverse side has lines for the address and was probably printed in a large edition for family consumption. Within the wide rectangle the photograph itself has the shape of an oversymmetrical egg. Naked and symbolizing the yolk, I am lying on my belly on a white fur, which must have been the gift of a benevolent polar bear to an Eastern European photographer specializing in baby pictures. For my first likeness, as for so many photos of the period, they selected the inimitable warm brownish tint which I should call "human" in contrast to the inhumanly glossy black-and-white photographs of our day. Some sort of hazy greenery, probably artificial, provides a dark background, relieved only by a few spots of light. Whereas my sleek healthy body lies flat and complacent on the fur, basking in polar well-being, my billiard-ball skull strains upward and peers with glistening eyes at the beholder of my nakedness.

A baby picture, you may say, like all other baby pictures. Consider the hands, if you please. You will have to admit that my earliest likeness differs conspicuously from all the innumerable records of cunning little existences you may have seen in photograph albums the world over. You see me with clenched fists. You don't see any little sausage fingers playing with tufts of fur in self-forgetful response to some obscure haptic urge. My little claws hover in earnest concentration on a level with my head, ready to descend, to strike. To strike what? The drum!

It is still absent, the photo shows no sign of that drum which, beneath the light bulbs of my Creation, had been promised me for my third birthday; yet how simple it would be for anyone experienced in photo-montage to insert a toy drum of the appropriate size. There would be no need to change my position in any way. Only the ridiculous stuffed animal, to which I am not paying the slightest attention, would have to be removed. It is a disturbing element in this otherwise harmonious composition commemorating the astute, clear-sighted age when the first milk teeth are trying to pierce through.

After a while, they stopped putting me on polar-bear skins. I was probably about a year and a half old when they pushed me, ensconced in a high-wheeled baby carriage, close to a board fence covered by a layer of snow which faithfully follows its contours and convinces me that the picture was taken in January, 1926. When I consider it at length, the crude construction of the fence, the smell of tar it gives off, connect me with the suburb of Hochstriess, whose extensive barracks had formerly housed the Mackensen Hussars and in my time the Free City police. But since I remember no one who lived out there, I can only conclude that the picture was taken one day when my parents were paying a visit to some people whom we never, or only seldom, saw in the ensuing period.

Despite the wintry season, Mama and Matzerath, who flank the baby carriage, are without overcoats. Mama has on a long-sleeved embroidered Russian blouse: one cannot help imagining that the Tsar's family is having its picture taken in deepest, wintriest Russia, that Rasputin is holding the camera, that I am the Tsarevich, and that behind the fence Mensheviks and Bolsheviks are tinkering with homemade bombs and plotting the downfall of my autocratic family. But the illusion is shattered by Matzerath's correct, Central European, and, as we shall see, prophetic shopkeeper's exterior. We were in the quiet suburb of Hochstriess, my parents had left the house of our host just for a moment—why bother to put coats on?—just time enough to let their host snap them with little Oskar, who obliged with his cunningest look, and a moment later they would be deliciously warming themselves over coffee, cake, and whipped cream.

There are still a dozen or more snapshots aged one, two, and two and a half, lying, sitting, crawling, and running. They aren't bad; but all in all, they merely lead up to the full-length portrait they had taken of me in honor of my third birthday.

Here I've got it. I've got my drum. It is hanging in front of my tummy, brand-new with its serrated red and white fields. With a solemnly resolute expression, I hold the sticks crossed over the top of it. I have on a striped pull-over and resplendent patent leather shoes. My hair is standing up like a brush ready for action and in each of my blue eyes is reflected the determination to wield a power that would have no need of vassals or henchmen. It was in this picture that I first arrived at a decision which I have had no reason to alter. It was then that I declared, resolved, and determined that I would never under any circumstances be a politician, much less a grocer, that I would stop right there, remain as I was—and so I did; for many years I not only stayed the same size but clung to the same attire.

Little people and big people, Little Claus and Great Claus, Tiny Tim and Carolus Magnus, David and Goliath, Jack the Giant Killer and, of course, the giant; I remained the three-year old, the gnome, the Tom Thumb, the pigmy, the Lilliputian, the midget, whom no one could persuade to grow. I did so in order to be exempted from the big and little catechism and in order not, once grown to five-foot-eight adulthood, to be driven by this man who face to face with his shaving mirror called himself my father, into a business, the grocery business, which as Matzerath saw it, would, when Oskar turned twenty-one, become his grownup world. To avoid playing the cash register I clung to my drum and from my third birthday on refused to grow by so much a finger's breadth. I remained the precocious three-year-old, towered over by grownups but superior to all grownups, who refused to measure his shadow with theirs, who was complete both inside and outside, while they, to the very brink of the grave, were condemned to worry their heads about "develop-ment," who had only to confirm what they were compelled to gain by hard and often painful experience, and who had no need to change his shoe and trouser size year after year just to prove that something was growing.

However, and here Oskar must confess to development of a sort, something did grow—and not always to my best advantage—ultimately taking on Messianic proportions; but what grownup in my day had eyes and ears for Oskar, the eternal three-year-old drummer? [pp. 58–60]

1. See Grass, "Kleckenburg," *Poems of Günter Grass,* trans. Michael Hamburger and Christopher Middleton (Harmondsworth: Penguin, 1969), p. 80.

2. See Grass, "The Photograph Album," *The Tin Drum* (1959), trans. Ralph Manheim (New York: Harcourt Brace Jovanovich, 1962), pp. 49–61 and see also p. 422.

3. For further examples in the works of Grass (except as noted, all translated by Ralph Manheim and published in New York by Harcourt Brace Jovanovich), see: *Cat and Mouse* (1963), pp. 24, 27, 86, 131, 143–44, 176, 186, and 188; *Flood* (1955) in *Four Plays* (1967), pp. 1, 15, 17, and 21; *Dog Years* (1969), p. 222; *The Plebeians Rehearse the Uprising* (1966), pp. 41, 44, and 52; *Inmarypraise* (1973), trans. Christopher Middleton, with photographs by Maria Rama (1974); *From the Diary of a Snail* (1973), pp. 8, 14, 16; and see also Theodor Wieser, ed., *Günter Grass: Porträt und Poesie* (Neuwind: Luchterhand, 1968), which contains reproductions of twenty-seven family pictures of the writer as well as some of his graphic designs.

4. For example, see Handke, *The Weight of the World,* trans. Ralph Manheim (New York: Farrar, Straus & Giroux, 1984), pp. 7, 20, 41, 81, 83, 91, 97, 140–41, 158, 168, 209, 217, and 231, and *Als das Wünschen noch gehalfen hat* [When Wishing Still Helped] (Frankfurt am Main: Suhrkamp, 1971), which includes photographs throughout—the first in color, the rest in black and white, both called to the editor's attention by Leo Lensing in communications of January 15–20, 1993; unfortunately the English translation, *Nonsense and Happiness,* trans. Ralph Manheim (New York: Urizen, 1984), does not include any photographs.

77. Cecil Beaton
and Evelyn Waugh

CECIL BEATON, FROM *Diaries* [1929, 1949], 1961, AND EVELYN WAUGH, "FOOTLIGHTS AND CHANDELIERS," 1961

Beaton (1904–80), using his charm and upper-class connections, made himself into a versatile, self-taught artist [Fig. 120]. He became a leading fashion photographer for Condé Nast and other publications; a designer of sets and costumes for ballets and theatre productions like My Fair Lady (1956); a celebrity portrait photographer, patronized by the royal family; and a prolific writer of published diaries and memoirs. He befriended many authors, particularly Gertrude Stein and Truman Capote; but none of these relationships endured for as long and with such hostility as that with his former schoolmate Evelyn Waugh (1903–66).[1] The satirist, whose aesthetics were as conservative as his political and religious beliefs, never esteemed photography. A talented draftsman, he regarded the camera, at best, as a "humble assistant to the arts," able to reveal things imperfectly seen by or even invisible to the human eye, at worst a justification of the "sloth" of artists no longer concerned with verisimilitude.[2] Nor did he admire photojournalists, after meeting mostly intrusive or dishonest ones during his two newspaper assignments to Abyssinia (now Ethiopia).[3] His own experience taking photographs to illustrate Ninety-Two Days (1934), an account of his unsatisfying South American journey [Fig. 121], did little to modify his opinions.[4] In his first, successful novel, Decline and Fall (1928), Waugh had satirized Beaton as "little" Davy Lennox, a homosexual society photographer and occasional decorator, who is vain, mercenary, and outrageous in aesthetic taste and practices; his views of Beaton changed little over the intervening decades.[5] "Evelyn Waugh is my enemy," the artist finally concluded.[6]

BEATON, FROM *Diaries*, 1929

. . . Perhaps this experience confirmed a lesson I had been taught the very first day I had been in school: that however terrified one may be, one must never show one's quaking fears. If it is possible to put up an authoritative front or assume an aggressive attitude in turn, then the bully himself will be the first to collapse.

I was not a particularly puny boy, but I was an excellent bait for bullies, for I failed to conceal an inner fear that marked me out as a prospective victim. On the very first morning that Reggie and I set off to the day-school, Heath Mount, Hampstead, I tried not to disclose to my younger brother my dread of the Dickensian cruelty we were probably about to face. But, as we walked along Hampstead Heath with our emerald green caps and satchels, my stomach was queasy at the prospect of having my knuckles slashed with a sharp ruler by some sadistic master, or my backside swiped until it bled.

It was with relief, on that cold autumn morning, that I heard the whistle blow for the eleven o'clock break. Half the morning, at any rate, had passed without disaster. The masters I now knew were not sadistic. Now the entire school was let out to rampage over the asphalt playground. The older boys formed their own posses of interest, others were playing the hearty games continued from last term. All the new boys seemed rather lost and did not know where to go; but none looked more ill at ease than myself. Suddenly, out of nowhere, the bullies arrived. They had recognized their quarry in me. Growling like wire-haired terriers, they were large and solid, with hairy stockings and rough tweeds. Their leader was a boy half the size of the others, wearing Barrie-esque green tweed knickerbockers. Recognising from a distance that I was the most obvious lamb for the slaughter, the leader, having darted silently towards me at great speed, halted a few inches in front of me with a menacing wild stare, while the bigger boys circled me and growled louder. He then stood on his toes and slowly thrust his face with a diabolical stare, closer and closer to mine, ever closer until the eyes converged into one enormous Cyclops nightmare. It was a clever inauguration to the terrors that followed, and my introduction to Evelyn Waugh.

But the 'breaking-down' process, the preliminary to the bullying proper, had not yet been completed. After the Cyclops eye had several times been retracted only to be brought back again in its symbolic horror, Waugh then stood baring his teeth at me. By the time the physical onslaught began, fright had mercifully made me only half conscious. That the tortures were devilish in their invention I can be fairly certain, since they were conducted under such expert leadership. Exactly what torments were endured I have forgotten; however, twenty years later, during the war, when I found myself in China in some military mess, a huge grey-haired major, middle-aged and respectable, came up and said, 'Well, Beaton, I haven't seen you since the days at Heath Mount when Evelyn Waugh and I were beaten for bending your arms back to front.' [from *The Wandering Years, Diaries, 1922–1939*, pp. 172–74]

Beaton, from *Diaries*, 1949

Evelyn has arrived for a few days. Diana [Duff Cooper] admires him immoderately. She is a true friend of his, though I cannot imagine how she, the most straightforward, unpretentious person, put up with Evelyn's snobbery. When I criticize Evelyn—whom I find intolerable—Diana defends him, but admits she can't bear his 'showing off,' being so boringly pompous, and pretending to be deaf.

Of course I am prejudiced. That wise old marvel, [E.] Morgan Forster, wrote somewhere that even in later life one can never forgive the boys who tormented one at school. During my first morning at Heath Mount day school in Hampstead the bullies, led by a tiny, but fierce Evelyn Waugh, at once spotted their quarry in me during the morning 'break' as, terrified, I crept around the outer periphery of the asphalt playground.

It had been a relief that the first two hours of school were not as appalling as I had imagined they would be with cruel masters cracking rulers on one's outstretched fingers, or birching one's naked buttock. But my worst anxieties were realized almost immediately after the 'elevens' bell rang, and with a shriek all the boys, no longer under the supervision of a beak, rushed out to play games of their own devising. Evelyn was already an experienced bully and his expert eyes had seen in me, from a distance of thirty yards, a mother's pretty and excessively timid darling who was an easy victim for ridicule and torture. My arms were turned back to front and my face spattered with spit from the pea-shooters.

Heath Mount's literary master was a young man from Cardiff, Aubrey C. Ensor. He was amused by Evelyn Waugh and by me, and it was in my mother's house that he tasted for the first time fish in aspic. When he visited the Waugh household he expected to find Evelyn's father some sort of human monster, since his son had given such bad accounts of him. When the ten-year-old Evelyn suggested walking Mr. Ensor home along the Spaniards, the man who taught us English remarked that he was agreeably surprised to find old Arthur Waugh such a delightful person. Evelyn, who even in front of Mr. Ensor patronizingly called him 'man' contradicted. 'Oh no, man, he's terrible—he likes Kipling!'

Having survived the rigorous bullying that continued at this school, by the time I arrived at St. Cyprian's boarding school in Eastbourne I had learnt that bullies are often the most easily deflated when they meet with opposition. In sheer self-protection I learnt to overcome my shyness, and at the first sign of aggressiveness to show fight in return. When, several years later, I came across Evelyn, I took the initiative and taunted him. He respected that. I find it unattractive when schoolboys suddenly assume the manner of very grown-up British men. I was amazed at the rich fruit-cake *basso profundo* in which he now spoke, and the elderly pomposity that he had prematurely acquired. It seemed to me the most ludicrous affection.

After Evelyn's novels had brought him fame, he lived in a large house in the West country, with his coat of arms carved in the pediment over the front door. The Waugh parents went to stay for a weekend. Evelyn showed them the rooms they were to occupy. 'This is your room, Father.' Evelyn pointed, 'and this is your wife's. And I hope you won't mind sharing the bathroom between the two rooms.' Mr. Waugh Senior replied: 'Since the woman to whom you refer as my wife and I have shared the same bathroom since we were married, it will be no hardship to do so again this weekend.'

There was another reason for my dislike—and it was mutual. Both Evelyn and I now moved in more exalted spheres than when we lived in Hampstead and Highgate. In our own way we were both snobs, and no snob welcomes another who has risen with him. My particular snobbery was more in the nature of wanting to become part of the world of the 'culturi'. I was magnetized towards the Sitwells, Gerald Berners, Lady Ottoline Morrell, Viola and Iris Tree, Raymond Mortimer, and certain of the Bloomsbury set. Evelyn was attracted by the foibles of those who lived in large, aristocratic houses. He cultivated the Lygons at Madresfield, got elected to the 'best' clubs (where he taunted newer members or visitors), and fostered a fascination, though in many ways despising it, for the highest echelons of the Army and military etiquette. He drank port and put on weight, and attempted to behave in the manner of an Edwardian aristocrat. He was very conscious of what a gentleman should or should not do: no gentleman looks out of a window, no gentleman wears a brown suit. In fact, Evelyn's abiding complex and the source of much of his misery was that he was not a six-foot tall, extremely handsome and rich duke.

We seemed to have certain friends in common and, since we met quite often, it was expedient to put the old hatchet away. Its burial was only temporary. However, for a time a truce was enjoyed. Evelyn seemed to find me amusing, laughed full-bellied at my jokes, while I found his observations about people and general perspicacity quite wonderful. His novels were written in a prose of which I was never tired. Ostensibly we were friends, Evelyn sent me inscribed messages of good will on the front pages of his latest works. But I was always aware that I must not let him find a chink in my armour.

As fellow guests of Duff and Diana at Chantilly, we played a subtle game of cat and mouse. I flattered Evelyn by taking him around the precincts and photographing him in every conceivable posture. (The most significant snap was of Evelyn scowling, with outsize cigar, as he leant on a gate marked '*Défense d'entrer.*') Then, to show how versatile I was, I bade him sit still while I made a crayon sketch of him. I knew that Evelyn, sitting back, pot-belly proffered, was peering with incredibly bright popping eyes and vivisectionist's knowledge, awaiting like a tiger the opportunity to tear me to shreds. But I was never off guard. When he saw the result of the sitting he exclaimed: 'Oh, that's cheating! Anyone can do a passable drawing with a read pencil.'

Evelyn has a talent for making a complimentary word sound suspicious. A mutual friend, Bridget Parsons, gave a cocktail party at which the sudden rush of guests appeared to be overwhelming. Clean glasses ran out. Bridget asked one or two of us if we would take the 'dirties' into the kitchen where they would be washed.

As I passed, Evelyn, standing warming his rump in the fireplace, remarked to the man enjoying the pleasure of his company: 'What on earth is he doing with those glasses?' I shouted into his ear trumpet: 'A buttling job.' Evelyn sneered: 'How extraordinarily *kind*!' After Evelyn had been to a small dinner at my house, he referred to me for some time as 'an extremely *hospitable* person'. Somehow he managed to convey that my chief role in life was to entertain people, and most certainly for some sinister, ulterior motive.

I wonder if Evelyn ever really likes anybody? I believe his second marriage to be an exceedingly happy one, but I cannot imagine his ever loving anyone. Diana says she loves him though she is fully conscious of the unkind and cruel things he does to people. Once the two of them were motoring together through Marlborough. At some traffic lights they came to a stop, and an anguished pedestrian put his head through the car window and said: 'I've got a train to catch. Can you tell me the way to the railway station?' Evelyn gave him elaborate instructions.

The man ran up the hill in a much sweat. Diana put her foot on the accelerator. 'How clever of you to know where the station is.' 'I don't,' said Evelyn. 'I always give people the wrong directions.'

I have heard Diana and Evelyn being appallingly rude to one another—really vilely, squalidly rude—and yet Diana is deeply touched by him. Today, however, Evelyn did get Diana's goat. He had the impertinence to criticize the breakfast tray: he said it 'wasn't fully furnished'! Diana, even several hours later, was still exploding with wrath. 'There was I, trying to get the trays ready for everybody—with Marguerite in bed ill having her you-know-whats. I was doing my best in my nightgown, bare feet and bald pate. Well, I let him have it. I said: "Really, Evelyn, it's too much to put on such an act!" and I gave him the full benefit of everything that I'd been bottling up about his pretentiousness. It really rankled with him—but it'll do him good!' [from *The Strenuous Years: Diaries, 1948–1955*, pp. 68–71]

WAUGH, "FOOTLIGHTS AND CHANDELIERS"

A parlour-game question: what middle-aged Englishman displays the following attributes: 'Our foremost arbiter of taste' (*New Statesman*), 'One of the unassailables of our time' (*Daily Mail*), "The Horace Walpole of our time' (New York *Evening Sun*)? Give it up? Then how about this: 'The Bryon of the camera' (*Life*)? Of course. The answer is Mr. Cecil Beaton, who has published a selection from his diaries, interspersed with reminiscence, covering the years 1922–39.

It is a fairly attractive production, interspersed with the author's line-drawings and a number of plates which seem to be arrayed without relevance to the text. It tells the story of the early years of a man unashamedly on the make. Mr. Beaton reveals himself as a young man consumed by worldly ambition, not for power nor for creation; he simply wanted to get himself known and accepted. As a child he was stage-struck; as an adolescent society-struck.

There was no great difference between the footlights and the chandeliers. Both revealed worlds of make-believe where everyone looked his best and talked cleverly. Mr. Beaton recounts as many painful and humiliating mishaps as Mr. Pooter, of whose diary these pages sometimes remind us, but he climbed steadily to the head of his profession as a portrait photographer until, as a fit climax to this book, he received the command of the Queen Mother, then the Queen, to make the charming series of studies of her at Buckingham Palace—a sitting which his beguiling personality prolonged from twenty minutes to three hours.

In later life he has earned renown as a theatrical designer. He did little in that line before the war. He got the Americans to buy his drawings. But his rise to popularity and prosperity was essentially as a photographer. He had the knack, so grossly lacking in his juniors, of mak-

121. Evelyn Waugh. 'Self-portrait,' 1933. Frontispiece to *Ninety-Two Days*, 1934.

ing his subjects look attractive and elegant. His camera carried him into the presence of the famous and the beautiful and, once there, he often established himself in warm friendship. There was between the wars a society, cosmopolitan, sympathetic to the arts, well-mannered, amusing, above all ornamental even in rather bizarre ways, which for want of a better description the newspapers called 'High Bohemia.' There Mr. Beaton shone. The record of these 'wandering years' ought to be enchanting. Perhaps it will enchant others; alas, not me. There was a gift lacking at his christening. Sir Arthur Bryant writes: 'Cecil Beaton is not only an artist—he can write.' The

publisher gives no date for this opinion. Mr. Beaton is tireless in self-education. He may lately have learned a new art. I can only say that, judging from this book, most of which is twenty years old, he can't write for toffee. Neither in verbal expression nor in literary construction does he show any but the feeblest talent.

The work is heterogeneous. There are passages from the diaries in which he recorded (not, surely, for publication?) his early, naïve aspirations and despairs. There is a theme, lately popularized by Mr. John Betjeman, of the conflict of an aesthetic son with a philistine father, and of the subsequent remorse. Here and, still more, in the descriptions of family tragedy, I find him highly embarrassing, not because such themes are necessarily improper, but because they require a delicacy and restraint, which Mr. Beaton lacked, to dignify them. Mr. Beaton is aware, and sadly comments on the fact more than once, that despite his ever-widening success and popularity there were certain cold people who regarded him as slightly absurd. He went so far as to take lessons from Mrs. Patrick Campbell in order to acquire a deeper tone of voice. Mr. Noël Coward gave him unsolicited advice about discretion in dress and deportment. Apropos of this propensity of his to attract ridicule, I may, perhaps, be excused for correcting his memory on a small point. It is, I confess with shame, true that a crony and I behaved cruelly to him at our Hampstead private school. He was an extremely pretty little boy. The spectacle of his long eyelashes wet with tears was one to provoke the sadism of youth. His offence was that he was reputed to enjoy his music lessons. The bullying of little Beaton was not, as he suggests, an isolated incident, but repeated many times. Our chief sport was to stick pins into him. And it did not stop, as he suggests, because 'if it is possible to put up an authoritative front or assume an aggressive attitude in turn, then the bully himself will be the first to collapse,' but because my companion in this abomination and I were caught out and soundly beaten for it by a master. This lapse of memory makes me wonder whether his account of his ducking at Wilton is entirely

Cecil Beaton and Evelyn Waugh

accurate. I was not there, but I remember the eyewitness accounts which circulated in London a day or two later. They were more farcical than the account given here.

Mr. Beaton belongs to the last generation to whom it was still possible to travel freely in a world not yet much despoiled by politicians and tourists. He took full advantage of his opportunities and saw many spectacles of beauty. It is in his attempts at descriptive passages that his lack of literary skill is most apparent. When he uses words that are at all recondite—'pristine', 'allegiance', 'novitiate', 'funicular', for example—it is too often apparent that he does not know their meanings. Many of his sentences are stilted. 'Few people have yet stirred themselves; business has not been embarked upon.' Why not: 'Few have yet stirred: business has not begun?' 'The Château itself, begun in the sixteenth century, has seen many subsequent additions in the intervening years.' Either 'subsequent' or 'in the intervening years' is redundant. It is a pity that Mr. Beaton, instead of taking lessons in elocution (most people, anyway, enjoyed his voice), did not engage a literary tutor.

He is at his best when he is writing in a cheeky, slangy way about people. Here I find him highly amusing when he is describing people I don't know—the brawl in Hollywood, for example, or the working habits of Bébé Bérard—but I met a great many of his characters and knew many of them well, and I find his portraits flat; not dull, but two-dimensional. They would be, to me, unrecognizable but of

their names (and he is rather odd sometimes about even these, referring to married women and widows as if they were divorcées—'Mrs. Beatrice Guinness', 'Mrs. Venetia Montagu'). I don't think it is simply a case of having a different vision. I don't think that in his early days he was really interested in people except when they were on the stage. He noticed their clothes and their peculiarities and noted scraps of dialogue, but he seemed unaware of their having an existence apart from him, of having a past or ties of kinship, except so far as they were referred to in newspapers, or a future. He lived in the present moment and the present company without historical sense. He had no curiosity, he tells us, about his own grandparents. He shrank from maturity and remarks with great satisfaction of a friend, aged 33, that he is 'mentally several years younger' than when they last met. Ancient buildings existed for him purely as a picturesque setting, not as monuments to a continuing past. It is perhaps significant that one of the artists to excite his highest rapture was the manipulator of a Greek shadow-show. Nor, despite much lack of reticence, does Mr. Beaton display full candour. He seems sometimes to eavesdrop on himself and report what he has learned. I do not hear the authentic note of self-revelation even in his most shy-making confidences. For these reasons I do not think he qualifies for the title, bestowed on him by the *Sunday Times,* of 'memorialist'. I don't think people of the future will turn to him to elucidate the condition of his age.

1. See especially Beaton: in *Photobiography* (New York: Doubleday, 1951) on Stein, pp. 175–79 and 183–85; on Eliot, pp. 185–86; on Shaw, p. 186; and on Capote, pp. 185–87; and in *Images* (New York: London: House and Maxwell, 1963), npn, for interesting portraits of Eliot, Auden, Capote, Stein, and Mary McCarthy. See also *Self-Portrait with Friends: The Selected Diaries of Cecil Beaton 1926–1974,* ed. Richard Buckle (London: Weidenfeld & Nicolson, 1979), especially on Stein and Toklas, pp. 42–43, 71–72, and 163–65; Dinesen, pp. 295 and 352–54; and Capote, passim; and in *The Restless Years, Diaries: 1955–1963* (London: Weidenfeld & Nicolson, 1976), pp. 83–84, 159–61. Further relevant material is contained in the six volumes of Beaton's complete diaries, listed in the bibliography, and see the Welty selection below.

2. See Waugh, "The Death of Painting" (1955), in *The Essays, Articles and Reviews of Evelyn Waugh,* ed. Donat Gallagher (Boston: Little, Brown, [1984]), pp. 503–7.

3. See Waugh, *Remote People* (London: Duckworth, 1931), pp. 47–48 and 59 (though the author probably took the three unattributed snapshots included in the six photographic illustrations); and *Waugh in Abyssinia* (London: Methuen, 1936), pp. 49, 60–61, 173–74, and 212.

4. In Waugh, *Ninety-Two Days* (London: Duckworth, 1934), p. 9, the list of illustrations states that they are

"from photographs taken by the Author," and pp. 236–37 note how disappointing he found most of his exposures. Waugh's *Tourist in Africa* (London: Chapman & Hall, 1960) is also published with photographic illustrations, but none is by the author.

5. See Waugh, *Decline and Fall* (London: Methuen, 1928), pp. 171, 191–92, and 199. For example, little Davy Lennox, who for three years had never been known to give any one a "complimentary sitting," took two eloquent photographs of the back of [Margot Beste-Chetwynde's] head [as Beaton had of Margot, Lady Astor] and one of the reflection of her hands in a bowl of ink." See also Waugh in *A Little Learning: The First Volume of an Autobiography* (London: Chapman & Hall, 1964), p. 90, on young Beaton as a "very pretty little boy" whose "tears on his long eyelashes used to provoke the sadism of my youth," and Christopher Sykeson, *Evelyn Waugh: A Biography* (Harmondsworth: Penguin, 1978), pp. 129 and 382, on their continuing enmity in adulthood.

6. Beaton, quoted in Hugo Vickers, *Cecil Beaton* (Boston: Little, Brown, 1985), p. 14.

78. *Lawrence Durrell*

PREFACE TO *Perspective of Nudes*
BY BILL BRANDT, 1961

*B*randt (1904–83), raised by his English parents in Hamburg and on the Continent, began his photographic career with a portrait of Ezra Pound (1928) when both met in Vienna. Pound gave him an introduction to Man Ray, in whose experimental studio Brandt worked for a few months (1929–30) before moving to London as a photojournalist (1931). His carefully composed pictures of his adopted country led to a commission by a French publisher for a companion volume—similar in mood and chiaroscuro lighting—to Brassaï's Paris de Nuit (1933), which was entitled A Night in London (1938); both became landmarks in the history of the photographic book.[1] But it was Brandt's later work that attracted the notice of Brassaï [Fig. 94] and his friend Lawrence Durrell (1911–90), a poet, novelist, and travel writer whose sensuous books, such as The Black Book (1938) and The Alexandria Quartet (1957–60), are set in the Mediterranean littoral where he lived and worked.[2] "What a genius Brandt is!" Durrell exclaimed after seeing Brandt's 1945 scenes of Haworth [Fig. 122], where the Brontë sisters lived, and other sites associated with writers that later appeared in Literary Britain (1951), for which he generously tried—and failed—to find a publisher.[3] Durrell never met Brandt and thus was not included in his series of densely shadowed portraits of writers and artists in evocative settings, largely done in the late 1940's.[4] But a decade later, Durrell readily supplied this brief but enthusiastic preface for Brandt's new book of nudes, many taken in wide and deep focus, with his usual mysterious blend of intimacy and detachment.[5]

122. Bill Brandt. 'Withens' (also known as 'Wuthering Heights'), c. 1944.

Withens
(Wuthering Heights).

Lawrence Durrell

PREFACE TO *Perspective of Nudes* BY BILL BRANDT

"Celui-lá, c'est un maître!"

We were sitting in front of an olive wood fire, Brassaï, the child and I, talking photographs. All around us, spread on the floor, were Brassaï illustrations to a book on Paris. But the remark he made was about an English photographer who is easily his peer—Bill Brandt.

Nor is the mention of Brassaï here inapposite, for if he is the European maître Brandt is incontestably the English. And so different are their styles that it is worth comparing the two approaches to photography, for they complement one another by their very difference.

Brandt uses the camera as an extension of the eye—the eye of a poet; he is to photography what a sculptor is to a block of marble. His pictures read into things, try to get at the hidden presence which swells in the inanimate object. Whether his subject is live or not—whether woman or child or human hand or stone—he detaches it from its context by some small twist of perception and lodges it securely in the world of Platonic forms. Brassaï is the poet of the human condition; his best pictures are snatched from real life, and reflect the poignance and beauty and despair of the human condition. Even when he goes after a tree or a park bench it is the human connotation which sticks out; his work is touching by its humanity.

But Brandt broods over the nature of things and makes a quiet poetic transcript of them; his work is a prolonged meditation on the mystery of forms. In his best pictures one comes up against the gnomic quality which resides in poetry and sculpture; one forgets the human connotation as if one were reading a poem—even though, as I say, the subject is a human being.

These pictures express the extraordinary merits of his work far better than words can; the play of form and tone sail up out of the prints to startle and confuse one by their authority. If Brassaï finds his style best in his illustrations to the Paris of a Henry Miller or Carco, then Brandt's work should fittingly illustrate Rilke's "Duinese Elegies".[6]

There is nobody of his stature in England today.

---

1. See Brandt: *The English at Home* (London: Batsford, 1936); *A Night in London* (New York: Charles Scribner's Sons, 1938); and *London in the Thirties* (New York: Pantheon, 1984). These photographs have been compared to the contemporary writings of George Orwell by Mark Haworth-Booth in his introduction to Brandt, *Shadow of Light* (New York: DaCapo, 1977), p. 18. Lambrechts and Salu, *Photography and Literature*, p. 34, no. 472, credit Brandt with the unattributed photographs in Orwell's *Road to Wigan Pier* (London: Gollancz, 1937), inserted between pp. 105 and 136; cf. Haworth-Booth, who, in conversation with the editor on September 8, 1992, recalls Orwell saying a Fleet Street photographer took them.

2. See Durrell's introduction to *Brassaï*, pp. 9–15, and the frequent mention of his name throughout Brassaï's *Henry Miller Grandeur Nature* (1975), which also reproduces the photographer's 1932 portrait of him [Plate 3], and *Henry Miller, Rocher Heureux* (1978).

3. See Haworth-Booth's afterword to *Literary Britain* (London: Victoria and Albert Museum, [1984]), npn, for details about Brandt's photographs of literary sites and their reception by Durrell and others. Others are reproduced, though without any reference to literature, in Brandt's self-selected survey, *Shadow of Light*, pp. 103–

18. See also Haworth-Booth's introduction to Brandt's *Behind the Camera* ([New York:] Aperture, [1985]), p. 52, for mention of Durrell's efforts to persuade Faber & Faber, his own future publisher, to publish Brandt's literary sites, and Brandt's selections in *The Land: Twentieth Century Landscape Photographs*, ed. Haworth-Booth (London: Gordon Fraser Gallery, 1975; New York: Da Capo Press, 1976).

4. See Brandt, *Portraits*, which includes his 1928 portrait of Pound (fig. 1); his 1940's portraits of MacNeice (fig. 2), Dylan Thomas (fig. 3), Day-Lewis (fig. 6), Spender (fig. 14), Forster (fig. 20), Elizabeth Bowen (fig. 28), Waugh (fig. 29), and Robert Graves (fig. 64); and his c. 1961–81 portraits of Harold Pinter (figs. 52 and 104), John le Carré (fig. 72), Ted Hughes (fig. 88), and other younger writers.

5. See also Tournier, "Le Lyrisme obscur de Bill Brandt," *Le Crépuscule des masques*, pp. 49–56, and Durrell, foreword to Dorothy Bohm, *Egypt* (London: Thames & Hudson, 1989), pp. 6–8.

6. Rilke's *Duinese Elegies* (1912–21), a cycle of ten poems on human life and fate, named after Duino, the castle owned by his patron, the Princess Marie Von Thurn und Taxis, in which he was staying when he began writing them.

V an Vechten (1880–1964), a successful music, drama, and dance critic as well as novelist, used his conversational prose to promote his iconoclastic tastes, such as Gertrude Stein's writing, Igor Stravinsky's music, Harlem's jazz and blues, and Nijinsky's dances. By 1932, however, partly thanks to an inheritance, he ceased writing and was looking for a new occupation. An avid collector of prints of movie stars in childhood and an amateur photographer in adolescence, Van Vechten appreciated the new, lightweight Leica camera brought from Europe by a friend; soon after buying one himself, he installed a darkroom in his apartment to process his prints. Thus he began his enduring and absorbing occupation as a portrait photographer, using unretouched black and white as well as color to capture the memorable "exact second."[1] As one contemporary observed about the results, "What is literature's loss is photography's gain."[2] Drawing on his wide range of talented friends, Van Vechten took some of the definitive portraits of the era, like those of Stein and her companion, Alice B. Toklas [Fig. 123], with whom he playfully corresponded between visits over many decades.[3] Van Vechten increasingly regarded all such portraits as historic documents as well as self-expression; to preserve his independence, he accepted no commissions, never sold his work, and rarely charged periodicals wanting to reproduce them. Van Vechten established collections of his prints, together with manuscripts and books, at various public institutions and persuaded influential friends to do the same; his promotion of materials concerning black artists remains especially noteworthy.[4]

FROM *Letters*

Note: This excerpt is composed of letters from The Letters of Carl Van Vechten, *edited by Bruce Kellner, except for two to Gertrude Stein from* The Letters of Gertrude Stein and Carl Van Vechten, 1913–1946, 2 vols, *edited by Edward Burns [cited as Burns], and one unpublished one from the Beinecke. { } have been used to indicate brackets in the texts put there by Kellner or Burns; conventional brackets [ ] those used by the anthology editor. Also cited are the portraits of the recipients of the letters below or the artists referred to in them; most are reproduced in alphabetical order in* Portraits: The Photography of Carl Van Vechten, *comp. Saul Mauriber, npn, or in Keith Davis,* The Passionate Observer: Photographs of Carl Van Vechten; *often the portraits of the same subject are not the same in both books.*

Dear Mabel,

. . . I am getting some very wonderful reactions to Parties [his latest book] from a *very* new audience. Stieglitz, Henry McBride [painter], [Charles] Demuth [painter], find it a creative masterpiece & a step in advance for me— "wholly lacking in the photography" which sometimes lurks in my novels, if you know what they mean. Gertrude [Stein], too, thus construes it. [to Mabel Dodge Luhan, December 30, 1930, p. 118; see Luhan in Mauriber]

Dear Hunter,

. . . Anyway, as happens so often with me— every seven years or so—I seem to be entering into a new period, and will probably engage in some new activity . . . I suppose in the end I shall give up writing! [to Hunter Stagg (August 8, 1931), p. 123]

Dear Max,

. . . I practiced photography with lights last night & blew *all* the fuses out, but I'll be ready for you soon. George Lynes [photographer] took me today listening to a sea-shell through spectacles, and I took him. [to Max Ewing, February 18, 1932, p. 125]

Dear Gertrude,

. . . I do nothing but take photographs now— hundreds and hundreds of photographs. You will soon see. Stieglitz has promised me an exhibition. [to Gertrude Stein, February 28, 1932, Burns, vol. 1, p. 252]

[To Donald Angus],

. . . [film actress] Anna May's film is perfectly blank. No one can imagine what happened— except it was April 1. . . . I am very melancholy & about to kill myself on account of Anna May's film. I am convinced the lousy bastards exposed it to the light. What shall I tell Anna May? How can I get that angel to come again? [to Donald Angus, (c. May 1932), p. 125; Kellner n. 6., adds this was the first subject CVV developed and printed himself; this failure prompted him to install full equipment in his apartment].

Dear Dreiser,

It was delightful of you to think of me in relation to the American Spectator, but I have not written a line (beyond that or this contained in letters) for six months and do not propose to do so *until I feel a very strong urge.* In the meantime (and how!) I have become the slave of photography which I have taken up very seriously and it has become very important to me to have you sit for me as soon as you can conveniently. I was therefore very pleased to learn that you had agreed to do so. If possible, it would be better to telephone me (Circle 7–3399, *not* in the book) as I am obliged to arrange for an electrician to assist me, several days in advance. [to Theodore Dreiser, October 18, 1932, p. 128; see Mauriber, and Davis, Plate 19, p. 60]

Dearest Babykins,

. . . The O'Neills came to dinner and loved it and are mad about the photographs. Gene says they are the only photographs he has ever had taken he recognizes. He wants me to do the title page of his book [*Days Without End*]. And he may have a frame at the [Theatre] Guild. [to Fania Marinoff, his actress wife, September 15, 1933, p. 133; see Fania in Mauriber, and in Davis, Plate 254, p. 66, and see O'Neill in Mauriber, and in Davis, Plate 20, p. 61]

Dear Carl,

. . . If I wore a hat I would take if off before your photographs . {. . .} They are damn swell. A joy. You are certainly a photographer. There are but few. [from Alfred Stieglitz to Van Vechten, September 1933, p. 133, n. 3]

Dear Stieglitz,

Your letter naturally pleased me *very much* & also scared me a little—for is not praise from you almost an accolade & am I not in danger of believing I have become a maestro?—It is very hard, but I have hit myself & told me that I'm not good enough even yet! . . . But please you & O'Keeffe come & be photographed when you come back to N.Y.! You would be the pinnacle of the collection!—best buttered dolphins to you both. [to Alfred Stieglitz, September 27, 1933, p. 133; see Stieglitz in Mauriber, and O'Keeffe in Mauriber, and in Davis, Plate 30, p. 73, used in *Life* (February 14, 1938): 28, lower right]

Dear Gertrude,

. . . But you must come over. I Must photograph you both. . . . You've seen very few pictures taken by me. When you do, I think you'll be a little surprised. How I am aching to take you! [to Gertrude Stein, October 23, (1933), Burns, vol. 1, pp. 281–82]

Dear Mr. Ross,

It is true that I made an elaborate series of portraits of Gertrude Stein this summer [Fig. 123], but they are not yet even printed and of course nothing could be done with them until she has seen them. Moreover, I never permit my work to appear in newspapers and those particular pictures I am reserving for a rather grand destiny. However, if you know any magazines that want any, the best plan is to refer them to me and I daresay something can be arranged. [to Mr. Ross, August 21, 1934, unpublished TS, Beinecke; see Stein in Mauriber, and in Davis, Plate 26, p. 69]

123. Carl Van Vechten. Gertrude Stein, Carl Van Vechten, and Alice B. Toklas, January 4, 1935.

Dear James,

I feel more and more obligated as your handsome books continue to come to me and I continue to have none to send to you! You see I have given myself so wholeheartedly to photography (in which I can be my own publisher, printer, and binder!) that I have almost forgotten that I ever was a writer, although perhaps some day this consciousness may return to me! At any rate, for the moment, I have no books of my own to send you. If it would amuse you I could substitute volumes by Gertrude Stein or it might be that you would like one of my photographs of Radio City or Pompeii. What I would rather do than anything else is to make some portraits of you and I hope you will give me that privilege before long. In any case, feel free to command me. [to James Branch Cabell, October 1, 1934, p. 140]

Dear Frances,

. . . What I am always looking for is a new and spectacular background {for photographs} and a cotton print at five cents a yard often makes a very good one (I usually get two yards). Or maybe you might see a banner or a poster. If you brought home a trunkfull of such pretties and dumped them in my lap it wouldn't displease me. [to Frances Williams, (Spring 1935), p. 146]

Dear Grand Duchess,

I've told Miss Cather repeatedly she may come any time of day, even at dawn. . . . I suggested dinner and photographs as a comfortable and painless method. Please tell her she may set her own hour, but that I'd like to take her while America is still Royalist. . . . I'll bring some duplicate examples of Pat [Alfred A. Knopf, Jr.] to you one day. I am experimenting again with framing & may have an idea you'd like to try later. [to Blanche Knopf, (c. January 1936), pp. 148–49; see Cather in Mauriber, and in Davis, Plate 27, p. 70, and see Alfred Knopf in Mauriber]

Dear Baby Woojums,

At LONG LAST, Bennett [Cerf, the publisher] let me read the manuscript . . . and it seems to me that Everybody's Autobiography is one of your finest works. . . . Bennett wants me to illustrate it with photographs. Of course I have hundreds which are suitable, but you may not like the idea at all and if you don't PLEASE SAY SO. . . . I have taken many interesting photographs lately, Thomas Mann, Thomas Wolfe, and Scott Fitzgerald [Fig. 124], among others. [to Gertrude Stein, June 22, 1937, pp. 152–53; see Mann in Mauriber and Davis, Plate 37, p. 82; see Wolfe in Mauriber, and in Davis, Plate 41, p. 87]

{To Gertrude Stein},

Why, my wonderful Baby Woojums, how did I ever give you that idea? [GS construed CVV's proposal to illustrate *Everybody's Autobiography* to mean he would distribute original prints with each copy.] I must have written some very clumsy English. It would be marvellous if we could do it, but I would have to print night and day for eight or nine months, and I would have to print over 40,000 photographs and it would cost thousands and thousands! . . . I didn't feel sure of exactly what you meant till your letter came and then I couldn't cable you as you asked me to because I didn't want to cable I wasn't going to print 40,000 pictures and I didn't know what else to cable and tell Mama Woojums if we all lived in the same town none of these things would happen. [to Gertrude Stein, August 1, (1937), pp. 155–56 and n. 1]

Dear Mr. Knollenberg,

Some time ago we discussed briefly the possibility of my giving the Yale University Library my Negro books and papers. If you still want them I've decided to go ahead with this idea. It isn't a vast collection . . . but it makes up for that, perhaps, in personality and association items. The material includes: books, many firsts, by Negroes and by whites *about* Negroes, inscribed to me, manuscripts, clippings, files of magazines, a vast quantity of pamphlets and minor items, music, including most of the best collections of Spirituals, phonographs [*sic*] records, including almost complete sets of the famous Blues singers Bessie and Clara Smith, scrapbooks, photographs of famous Negroes

124. Carl Van Vechten.
'F. Scott Fitzgerald,' 1937.

by me (a vast collection) and by others, and a very valuable, important, and personal collection of letters from many of the more important Negroes of the day. . . . I would suggest that we name the collection The James Weldon Johnson Memorial Collection of Negro Arts and Letters, founded by Carl Van Vechten. I think this name would be of material assistance to you in assembling future material from others. [to Bernhard Knollenberg, May 29, 1941, pp. 177–78]

Dear Miss Seymour,

. . . You said you need a few biographical facts. {. . .} I have always been interested in photographs and photography, other people's as well as my own. Some of my photographs were made in the early nineties, others around 1908–9. . . . I really settled down to photographs intensively in 1932 and I think it was my original intention to photograph everybody and everything in the world! My first interest in photography is documentary, but I see no harm in being honest and as artistic as possible at the same time. My backgrounds, which are a feature in my work, I borrowed from Matisse, but only one person I know has been clever enough to mention this. [to May (Davenport) Seymour, (October 19, 1942), p. 187]

Dear Langston,

What letters *you* write! Maybe I do too. Sometimes I wonder if OUR letters won't be the pride of the Collection. I haven't gotten around to sending yours to me yet, but will this winter! . . . Roi Ottley [a black historian] came to be photographed Saturday and definitely we are getting the manuscript [for *New World: A-Coming: inside Black America*]. When he saw your new beautiful boxes [CVV presented material to the Johnson Memorial Collection in matching hinged cases bound in blue buckram with red leather labels stamped in gold], he almost swooned and exclaimed, 'The Schomburg Collection doesn't keep things like this." Of course, nobody else does, and even Yale wouldn't, if I didn't do it myself. The material turned into this Collection is in a condition thanks to my energy and foresight which not many other Collections can boast. It is hard work and endless, but I think it is worth it. I have a DEFINITE FEELING that in LESS than five years Yale will have a chair of Negro life and culture and whoever sits in that chair will have the best source material in the country to guide him. [to Langston Hughes, August 16, 1943, pp. 195 and 194 n. 3; see Hughes in Mauriber]

Dearest Nadejda,

. . . As for my writing, I don't like to write and I do not think I have anything very important to contribute to human knowledge. Photography is as hard work as writing, but more agreeable to me and here I can contribute a great deal, by documenting the present age in several fields for important collections. I have no doubt whatever I am doing something useful here, but the creation of nostalgia is at best a luxury that is quite unnecessary to indulge. [to Anna Marble Pollock, January 22, (1944), p. 200]

Dear George,
The picture I sent you of Scott Fitzgerald was made in 1937 when he was 41, about three years before he died. His face by that time reflected some of the things he thought about himself (vide The Crackup) and also drink had taken its toll on his handsome features. For the twenties he was downright beautiful, but certainly not fragile. He was a husky sophisticated beauty if not downright rough, except when he was drunk when he thought nothing of spoiling the face of a waiter or any passerby in any nightclub where he spent most of his later youth. He sometimes got his own face mussed up too. [to George George, July 9, (1945), pp. 216–17; see another Fitzgerald portrait in Mauriber]

Dear James,
. . . I was considerably shaken, as you were, over Ellen {Glascow}'s death, which after all was expected and now comes Gertrude Stein's for which I was totally unprepared. Aside from these greater blows, I have been a pallbearer on five occasions since January 1. . . . I am completely and fully occupied {. . .} by photography (and making up Collections of my photographs of celebrated people for various public institutions.) [to James Branch Cabell, August 3, 1946, p. 224]

Dearest Donald,
. . . I like Paris BETTER . . . the SUN is out and I spent yesterday afternoon with Jean Cocteau and Jean Marais [starring in Cocteau's film, *Orphée*, at a Montmartre cinema studio] and had a grand time, photographing at my leisure. Marais was making a scene at a Mirror, and Cocteau was photographed against the rooftops, also with Chinese boys, quite a scoop. I

have a lot in black and white and color. They were both sweet. [to Donald Angus, October 15, 1949, p. 240; see Cocteau in Mauriber, and in Davis, Plate 45, p. 91]

Dear Wallace,
Thank you for your very kind letter. . . . As you perhaps know, I devote myself pretty completely to photography nowadays and would like very much to photograph you, if you would be so good as to let me know IN ADVANCE some time when you will be in New York and what hours you might have free. [to Wallace Stevens, June 30, 1955, p. 256; n. 6 says CVV never photographed the poet]

Dear Mr. Prentiss,
. . . My only objection to your review of Miss Sprigge's quite awful book [*Gertrude Stein: Her Life and Work,* 1957] is that you mention Noel Coward as her photographer instead of ME. I regard this simply in the light of bad taste! [to Prentiss Taylor, May 29, 1957, p. 269]

Dear Sandy,
. . . It has indeed been too long since I have seen you . . . but I have been caught up in the meshes of fate. That fascinating witch, the Baroness [Karen Blixen, the Danish writer better known under her pseudonym, Isak Dinesen], has been partly responsible because I turn up everywhere there has been a chance to see her. She comes here for MORE photographs tomorrow. There are certain aspects I have missed. I prefer her with her hair showing and in BROWN. Also I think gloves improve her scandalously thin arms. [to Sandy Campbell, April 12, 1959, p. 274; see Dinesen in Mauriber]

Dear Chester,
{...} It is a great relief to know some one who can write about other things occasionally besides the Negro "problem." {. . .} Long ago (perhaps nearly 40 years) I said to James Weldon Johnson, The Negro "problem" will be settled by the artists. It is coming nearer to be every year; the writers, the painters, the actors and singers have done the most. The writers the

125. Carl Van Vechten.
'William Faulkner,' 1954.

tures who constantly reiterate the Negro is inferior. [to Chester Himes, January 30, 1961, p. 279; see Himes in Mauriber]

Dear Mr. Meriwether,
I had met Mr. Faulkner several times before. . . . We had even talked about photographs but they never got beyond that stage until that night in 1954. We were giving a small party and a young lady [asked if she could bring a friend]. . . . When the bell rang I . . . was surprised to see [her] clinging to the arm of William Faulkner. During the course of the evening I asked him if he would mind being photographed. He seemed to be pleased with the idea. It was easy to do so because my assistant was there: we had everything set up (camera and lights). So we excused ourselves and went into the studio and remained there until I had taken ten or twelve pictures [Fig. 125]. I have never seen Mr. Faulkner since . . . [to James B. Meriwether, May 24, 1962, p. 284; see another portrait of Faulkner in Mauriber]

Dear Mr. Maas,
I'd be delighted to see you and your friend. . . . [But] I seriously object to being dubbed a "neglected" novelist. I gave up novel writing in for various excellent reasons, one of which was that I had become more interested in photography, a field in which I have achieved notable success. Moreover my books are read in English courses in many colleges. I have recently become a member of the Institute of Arts and Letters, a young professor is writing a book about me and two well-known painters are painting my portrait. . . . I cannot even be called forgotten. But if you want to write about me under another heading, call me . . . and I will arrange to see you both. [to Willard Maas, October 24, 1961, p. 282]

least, because most of them "harp" on the problem {. . .} This sort of thing MUST eventually ring about changes with those dumb crea-

---

1. For accounts of his involvement with photography, see Van Vechten: "The Tin Trunk," *Sacred and Profane Memories* (New York: Knopf, 1932), pp. 1–24; "Portraits of the Artists," *Esquire* 58, no. 6 (December 16, 1962): 170–74, 256–58; an untitled and previously unpublished account of the evolution of his interest in photography (Goodwin Gallery, Westwood, N.J., February 1977), sent to the editor by Bruce Kellner, who suggests it is an early draft for the *Esquire* piece; Letters to Max Ewing, February 18, 1932, and Donald Angus, c. May 1932, in *Let-*

ters of Carl Van Vechten, ed. Kellner (New Haven: Yale University Press, [1987]), p. 125 and nn. 3 and 6; and in William Ingersoll, "The Reminiscences of Carl Van Vechten: A Rudimentary Narrative," Columbia University Oral History, 1960 (corrected carbon copy in the Van Vechten Collection of the Manuscript Division of the NYPL), quoted in *The Dance Photography of Carl Van Vechten,* ed. Paul Padgett (New York: Schirmer Books, 1981), pp. 5–6. See also Kellner, *Carl Van Vechten and the Irreverent Decades* (Norman: University of Oklahoma Press, 1968), pp. 258–62 and 271–72; Kellner, "Carl Van Vechten, Vintage Photographs," introduction to an exhibition catalogue (London: Duke Street Gallery, March 1981); and Keith F. Davis, "A Privileged Eye: The Life and Photographs of Carl Van Vechten," in *The Passionate Observer: Photographs by Carl Van Vechten* (Kansas City, Mo.: Hallmark Cards Inc., 1992), especially pp. 18–32. Davis, pp. 19–20, notes Van Vechten's occasional use of photography in his prior writings, especially in his revised edition of *Peter Whiffle* [1922] (New York: Knopf, 1927).

2. Henry McBride, quoted in *Dance Photography,* ed. Padgett, p. 9.

3. See his *Portraits: The Photography of Carl Van Vechten,* comp. Saul Mauriber (Indianapolis: Bobbs-Merrill, 1978); *The Letters of Gertrude Stein and Carl Van Vechten, 1913–1946,* ed. Edward Burns (New York: Columbia University Press, 1982), 2 vols., esp. the letters from March 1932, after Van Vechten took up photography, some of which are also included in *The Letters of Carl Van Vechten,* ed. Kellner, as well as in the text here below; and the Stieglitz and Stein selection above. Van Vechten himself sat for many portraits, especially in the 1920's, according to Davis, *The Passionate Observer,* p. 19, and some, including ones by Man Ray, Doris Ullmann, and Richard Avedon, are at the Beinecke.

4. *80 Writers* (New Haven: Yale University Press, June 17, 1960), published on Van Vechten's 80th birthday, lists the books and letters he gave to Yale University, where he also established the James Weldon Johnson Memorial Collection of Negro Arts and Letters to preserve his own collection and those of others; see also *Generations in Black and White: Photographs by Carl Van Vechten from the James Weldon Johnson Memorial Collection,* ed. Rudolph P. Byrd (Athens: University of Georgia Press, 1993). He also donated materials to the New York Public Library, the Museum of the City of New York, Fisk University, Howard University, and Wadleigh High School in New York City (later transferred to the University of New Mexico, when the high school closed), among many other institutions. At the Beinecke is a MS draft (ZA/CVV/3), dated May 19, 1949, of a foreword by Van Vechten to a catalogue of a Stieglitz collection being donated by Georgia O'Keeffe to Fisk University, as also to Yale, at his suggestion; see also his tribute to Stieglitz in *Stieglitz Memorial Portfolio, 1864–1946,* ed. Norman, p. 37, and his *"Keep A-Inchin' Along": Selected Writings of Carl Van Vechten about Black Arts and Letters,* ed. Bruce Kellner (Westport, Conn.: Greenwood, 1979).

A photograph of a string of ponies in a sports magazine [Fig. 126], including the owner's (indistinguishable) favorite, Blue Bug, might seem to be an unlikely source of inspiration for most poets. But animals always appealed to Marianne Moore (1887–1972), who often in her verse juxtaposed their qualities with those of humans in a manner suggesting free association rather than pedantic effort. Photographs long interested her since she first saw those of "droll" Alfred Stieglitz in 1915, the most "beautiful" she'd ever seen.[1] Indeed, over the years photographs, especially from magazines and newspapers, had frequently supplied details, if not the inspiration, for several of her poems.[2] Moreover, Moore not only accurately recalled these visual sources but meticulously documented them (in contrast to her friend and fellow poet Elizabeth Bishop [1911–79]).[3] Moore, with the visual precision of the painter that she, like Bishop, had once wanted to be, here associates the spirit of the polo pony with that of other arts and artists such as Arthur Mitchell, one of Balanchine's acclaimed dancers; Odilon Redon, the French post-impressionist noted for his floral paintings; and Li Siau Than, the Chinese acrobat. Moore's poetry—like the thoroughbred horses—usually displayed an agile yet disciplined grace in the service of a "pastime that is work." Such qualities made Moore much sought after as a photographic subject [Fig. 138] as well as a poet.[4]

*Upon seeing Dr. Raworth Williams' Blue Bug
with seven other ponies, photographed by
Thomas McAvoy:* Sports Illustrated [*Fig. 130*].

In this camera shot,
from that fine print in which you hide
(eight-pony portrait from the side),
    you seem to recognize
    a recognizing eye,
      limber Bug.
Only partly said, perhaps, it has been implied
that you seem to be the one to ride.

I don't know how you got your name
    and don't like to inquire.
      Nothing more punitive than the pest
      who says, "I'm trespassing," and
does it just the same.
    I've guessed, I think.
      I like a face that seems a nest,

a "mere container for the eye"—
    triangle-cornered—and
      pitchfork-pronged ears stiffly parallel:
    bug brother to an Arthur
Mitchell dragonfly,
    speeding to left,
      speeding to right; reversible,

like "turns in an ancient Chinese
    melody, a thirteen
      twisted silk-string three-finger
solo."
    There they are, Yellow River-
scroll accuracies
    of your version
      of something similar—polo.

      Restating it:
    pelo, I turn,
on *polos,* a pivot.

    If a little elaborate,
Redon (Odilon) brought it to mind,
    his thought of the eye,
of revolving—combined somehow with
    pastime—
      pastime that is work,
muscular docility,
    also mentality,

as in the acrobat Li Siau Than,
    gibbon-like but limberer,
    defying gravity,
      nether side arched up,
      cup on head not upset—
China's very most ingenious man.

1. See Charles Molesworth, *Marianne Moore: A Literary Life* (New York: Atheneum, 1990), pp. 62 and 126, on Moore and Stieglitz; see also her untitled piece in Norman, ed., *Stieglitz Memorial Portfolio,* p. 35.

2. The photograph by McAvoy, one of *Life*'s first staff photographers, appeared in *Sports Illustrated* 15, no. 20 (November 13, 1961): 72. For other poems using photographs for details and Moore's "Notes" with earlier "misleading editorial amplifications" removed [and volume and page numbers added by this editor] in *The Complete Poems of Marianne Moore* (London: Macmillan/Penguin, 1982): "Camilla Sabina" [1933], pp. 16–18 and 264, which credits a photograph of a wood rat by Spencer R. Atkinson from the *National Geographic* 61, no. 2 (February 1932): 206, and one of a wire cage, not further located, by Alvin E. Worman of Attleboro, Mass.; "The Frigate Pelican" [1934], pp. 25–26 and 265, which credits a photograph and description of a giant tame armadillo by W. Stephen Thomas of New York, but not their location; "When I Buy Pictures" [1935], p. 48 and p. 268, cites a descriptive paragraph and photograph from the *Literary Digest* (January 5, 1918); "Style" [1956], pp. 169–70 and 288, which credits a photograph of champion figure skater, Dick Button, in the *New York Times* (January 2, 1956): 35; "Hometown Piece for Messrs. Alston and Reese" [1956], pp. 182–84 and 290, which cites a photograph of the baseball catcher Roy Campanella at the moment of victory in the *New York Times* (October 5, 1955) [the one on p. 43 rather than the one on the front page is the most likely]; "Saint Nicholas" [1958], pp. 196–97 and 293–94, which cites a photograph of a chameleon and an accompanying letter to the editor by Dr. Doris M. Cochran in

126. Thomas McAvoy. 'Dr. Raworth Williams's Blue Bug with seven other ponies,' 1961.

Dr. Williams keeps a string of eight ponies at his polo field on farm near Dallas.

Life 45, no. 9 (September 15, 1958): 10; "Old Amusement Park" [1966], pp. 210–11 and 295, which cites a Port Authority photograph given to Moore by Brendan Gill.

3. Bishop imperfectly remembered some characteristic *National Geographic* scenes—not present in the issue she specifically dates—which provided a starting point for one of her finest poems, "In the Waiting Room" [1971], in *Geography III* (New York: Farrar, Straus & Giroux, 1976), pp. 159–61. In the poem, the child speaker, waiting for her aunt in a doctor's office on February 5, 1918 [Bishop turned seven three days later], reads a *National Geographic*, dated February 1918, "and carefully studied the photographs: the inside of a volcano,/black, and full of ashes;/ then it was spilling over/in rivulets of fire./Osa and Martin Johnson/dressed in riding breeches,/ laced boots, and pith helmets./A dead man slung on a pole/—'Long Pig,' the caption said./Babies with pointed heads/wound round and round with string/black, naked women with necks/wound round and round with wire/ like the necks of light bulbs./Their breasts were horrifying." These scenes, though the kind typically shown in the magazine, were in fact not included in any of the wartime issues or any other identifiable one; this discrepancy, surprising given the specificity of the dates but certainly allowable under literary license, is also noted and discussed by Hunter, *Image and Word,* pp. 179–80. This verse, which Bishop selected as perhaps her favorite, is reprinted opposite a portrait of her by Tom Victor in Richard Howard, ed., *Preferences* (New York: Viking, [1974]), p. 27 and facing p. 27.

For more on portraits of Bishop, see the McKenna et al. selection, n. 7, below.

4. See photographs of Moore: by Jacobi (1945) in *Lotte Jacobi,* ed. Kelly Wise, p. 71; by McKenna (1951) in *Twentieth Century Poetry: American and British 1900–1970* [1951, ed. John Malcolm Brinnin and Bill Read (New York: McGraw-Hill, 1970), [p. 298], reprinted in McKenna, *A Life in Photography,* pp. 142–43, which gives the background of the portrait; by Avedon (January 4, 1958) in *Observations,* p. 130, reprinted in *Portraits,* npn; by Krementz (1968) in Krementz, *The Writer's Image,* npn; and by Morehouse (1962), discussed and reproduced in the McKenna et al. selection below.

81. Jean Cocteau and Lucien Clergue

FROM *Correspondance, 1955–63*

The documentary yet metaphorical photographs of Clergue (1934–), portraying circus and theatre performers, bullfighting, decomposing animal corpses, mannequins, and nudes, appealed to Pablo Picasso. The artist offered his support and urged Clergue to contact Jean Cocteau (1891–1963), another creator with a genius for fantasy as well as for spotting and publicizing new talent that sparked his own. Cocteau considered himself a poet, whether writing verse, plays, journalism, or criticism, designing household objects, composing music, inventing ballets, drawing, or making films. He had been quick to see the possibilities of photography in many arts, including his own.[1] An early supporter of Berenice Abbott and Man Ray (though alienated from many Dadaists and Surrealists, who disdained his celebrity, apolitical aestheticism, and overt homosexuality), Cocteau was often the subject of photographic portraits over the years, some experimental.[2] Admiring Clergue's work, especially his *Gypsy* photographs [Fig. 127; cf. Fig. 128], in his last years he often collaborated with the photographer and supplied appreciative poems or prose to accompany his pictures in esoteric volumes of poetry and exhibition catalogues.[3] After Cocteau's death, Clergue remained in Arles, as his mentor had long advised. Among other projects, which often involved writers, he began the first annual international photography festival at Arles in 1970, under the auspices of an organization headed by the novelist Michel Tournier.[4] In the same busy decade, he produced a visual doctoral dissertation, guided by the cultural critic Roland Barthes, who provided an introduction for its publication (1980).[5]

November 7, 1955

Cher Monsieur Cocteau,

. . . Picasso, with whom I spent some five hours yesterday afternoon, gave me to understand that [this projected work] was definitely meant for you. As I was preparing to draw the cover . . . and other rough sketches as well, should we have a future publication, he concluded: "There is really no one but Cocteau to write for you the text of this work which is so close to his world. Present yourself to him on my behalf and make it clear to him that I would be happy about such a collaboration. . . ."

It is useless to tell you precisely the pride and profound joy that I would feel—if it happened that I appeared under the cover of Picasso with a commentary by Jean Cocteau. I hope that at least as much as Picasso's recommendation that the work itself will tempt you. . . . I am only twenty-one years old, already on the far side of the sad line of demarcation, yet hardly separated from childhood but obliged without fail to spend my days in an office about as dismal as all others, little cultivated and having little time to find and follow my vision (if indeed there is one) from the corner of a street or in a dark room—that if I should fail to convey my vision to you, the one that I am presenting, I would not know what else to add. Would you be good enough to let me know that this vision did find the way to your heart as it has earned me the friendship of Picasso who was good enough to confirm that I have something to say and that I am on the verge of being heard because you too were good enough to help me.... [pp. 7–8]

L.C.

December 3, 1955

My dear Lucien Clergue

The silence comes from the avalanche of letters and visits under which anything of importance was impossible to find.

The photos are a weightless mass of poetry and I was wondering in what way to respond to you. I am still wondering. My vagueness has a mathematical precision about it.

You have expressed in several lines your wish. Heaven's knows I would hate not to give pleasure to Picasso. [pp. 8–9]

J.C.

[*Clergue and Cocteau met in January 1957 and agreed to collaborate on* Les Corps Memorable *(1957) and* Poesie der Photographie *(1960), both with covers designed by Picasso. They continued their correspondence, which generated still other kinds of collaborations, mainly involving Clergue's photographs of Gypsies, which he had been taking even before meeting Cocteau.*]

April 27, 1956

My very dear Clergue,

I have great joy in telling you that I was inspired for my chapel[6] by certain of your photographs, *having played the role of intense reality* (more real than real). That seemed to me impossible and remains the rarest tour de force that I can owe to you.

J.C.

[P.S.] Your Gypsies have become the people who betrayed St. Peter. [pp. 19–20]

July 17, 1956

Dear Jean Cocteau,

(. . .) To show you my ceaseless activity, I am sending you by separate post this collection of Gypsies—. . . . These "Goyesque drunks" in effect fascinated me and despite the late hour I was able to capture some of their more telling attitudes—. . . .[7] [p. 22]

L.C.

October 8, 1956

Dear Lucien,

. . . Do not worry about the services which I like to give you. You have repaid me well with others and, yesterday once again, for the poster for the Festival of Menton——I was inspired by one of your Gypsies. [p. 27]

J. C.

November 5, 1957

My very dear Jean,

I have just spent three exciting days among the Gypsies. I made myself one of them to the point of reading their paper and writing their letters because most of them are illiterate and know nothing of the world; they do not know who Cocteau or Picasso are, what Sputnik is and what Egypt means. I spoke to everyone of your chapel and of the homage that you rendered them. Many have promised that if they pass by Villefranche they will go and look at it.

Perhaps a new pilgrimage will be born, thanks to you!

I have above all focused on the children who cry and laugh, holding on the breast of their mother, or the handsome young people carelessly lounging around a hay cart or their dreaming horses behind which a caravan appears in profile. I believe, on a single view of the negatives, I can already respond to these images. We will make a beautiful album . . . [p. 40]

Your L.

Cocteau, Postscript to "Clergue"

The gypsy world forms an aristocracy into which acceptance remains extremely difficult. The aristocracy, properly speaking, now opens its doors and even accepts the idea of working, which for an old Spanish family used to represent and still represents a kind of disgrace.

The gypsy aristocracy preserves a tradition of true luxury, which consists in avoiding unworthy marriages and living free from bondage as evidenced in the life of noble ease led by this clan throughout the world.

Each year Saintes-Maries-de-la-Mer is the meeting place of this royal band. They sing, they dance, they form a circle impenetrable except to those of lively blood. It seems likely that Clergue has in his veins that celebrated drop which in the case of Pushkin was black blood.[8]

The lively blood that the knight Lancelot of the Lake inherited from his mother Melusine was neither red nor blue.[9] It irradiates the soul and endows the body with the inimitable rhythm of flamenco. One either possessed this style (which assumes a universe from which vulgarity would be excluded) or one did not possess it. Whoever possessed it possessed it from birth. That is what makes some Gypsies poets and certain poets true Gypsies.

The photographs by Clergue are like those from a family album. [from *Poesie der Photographie* (c. 1958), pp. 44–45]

March 6, 1958

My very dear Lucien,

. . . I am not ignoring the difficulties which [using Gypsies] represents but it is indispensable to the progress of my film [*Testament d'Orphée*]. I must have two young ones—a boy and a girl, and a mother suckling a baby, the rest ad libbed, and a caravan.[10] They will be paid as if they were artists. [p. 50]

Your J. C.

Cocteau, "Black Homage"

Toward the dark where the sky seeks lofty
  refuge
The spray yields up something of its divinity
But the red flare of a judge's robe
Illuminates the spot which is the reverse side
  of beauty.
An arm of a dry-eyed scarecrow waves
Forever in farewell a linen kerchief
O home ... o hunt ... o pack ... far from home
Some feathered gypsies stand upright on their
  perch
That perch for the gypsies represents a yard-
  arm
Withered from storms with sea-weeds in
  mourning
And I know not what Arlesian cock gave
  Clergue
The order to shroud the pearl of his eye.
[from *Poesie der Photographie* (c. 1958), p. 56]

Holiday, 1958

My dear Lucien Clergue,

I have just learned that some wretched journalist types imagine that I have stolen some images from your photographs. Perhaps it is necessary to tell them that you, with extreme

127. Lucien Clergue. 'Manitas de Plata and José Reyes, Saintes-Maries-de-la-Mer,' 1955.

kindness, have furnished me with these examples. I don't apologize except in the case of the guitarist and the little girl, which is exact . . . [Fig. 127][11].

Degas painted directly on photographic enlargements and Utrillo copied postcards of Montmartre. I contented myself with disguising the types from Saintes-Maries, just as I used marvelous sports photographs for the attitudes of my angels.

Nothing is new in the marvelous interactions of artists and nothing, alas, is new in the hope of the mediocre of suppressing some centimeters of our glory.

I embrace you.

J. C.

P.S. I am adding that the photographs which inspired me can not be shown, because the Gypsies enjoy themselves in them counter to all decency. It is that which creates their expressive violence and their superb grimaces.[12] It was curious to translate them into the language of the Gospels. [pp. 50–51]

May 30, 1959

Dear Lucien,

Everyone is bothersome and here come the Gypsies with their atomic caravans and television in the toilets. We must overcome them and die. I love being confronted with their images, the wretched models. They know nothing of the beauty of barter. How our old friend [Michelangelo] of the Sistine [Chapel] would have loved to photograph his workers, perched on the fragile planks. Dali was right to say that Leonardo [Da Vinci] only worked from photographs.[13] [Fig. 128] [p. 69]

Your J.

June 29, 1963

Thank you my very dear Lucien. Your beautiful images fell on my sick bed and are worth more than the cures. "People" have decided that I am in marvellous health. But actually I feel terrible and can't see any progress in this slow decline and deception against the work and the strength within me.

I embrace you and all your family. [pp. 81–82]

J.

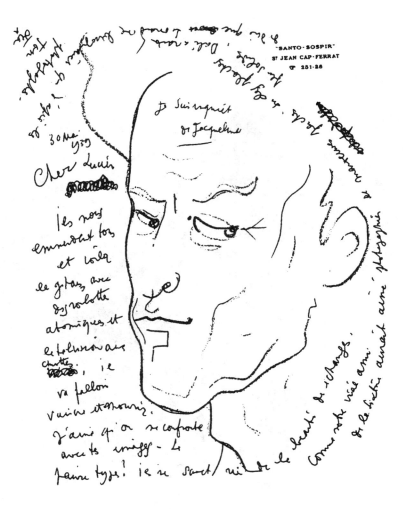

1. See, for example, these relevant works by Cocteau: "The Wedding on the Eiffel Tower" (1921), in *Modern French Theatre: An Anthology of Plays,* ed. and trans. Michael Benedikt and George C. Wallworth (New York: Dutton, 1964), in which the camera functions as both setting and the protagonist; *Le Numéro Barbette* (1926), reissued as *Le No Barbette,* trans. Maria Grossman, ed. Francis Steegmuller, with photographs by Man Ray (Paris: Jacques Damase, 1980), pp. 49–55; and *La Mort et les Statues,* with photographs by Pierre Jahan (Paris: Éditions du Compas, 1946).

2. See Cocteau, "An Open Letter to M. Man Ray, American Photographer" (1922), trans. Robert Wolf, in *Photography in the Modern Era,* ed. Phillips, pp. 1–3. For more on Cocteau's relationship with—and portraits by—Man Ray, see Man Ray, *Self Portrait,* pp. 99, 109, 138, and 143; and *Perpetual Motif: The Art of Man Ray,* ed. Foresta, passim. For Cocteau on Berenice Abbott, see Cocteau, "Les Photographies de Bérénice" (1921), *Oeuvres Complètes de Jean Cocteau* ([Lausanne]: Marguerat, [1947]), vol. 4, p. 158; and see Abbott's photographs of Cocteau reproduced in O'Neal, *Berenice Abbott,* pp. 50–51. Among the many other portraits of the ubiquitous Cocteau, see in Freund, *Freund, Photographer,* p. 116, fig. 112 (1939), and p. 119, fig. 114 (1939); Szarkow-

ski, *Irving Penn* (New York: MOMA, 1984), npn, fig. 12 (1948); Avedon, *Observations,* p. 56 (1958); Inge Morath, *Portraits* (New York: Aperture, 1986), p. 13 (1958); *Lucien Clergue: Eros and Thanatos* (Boston: New York Graphic Society/Eastman House, [1985]), figs. 39 and 40 (1959); and Julie Saul, ed. and comp., *Jean Cocteau: The Mirror and the Mask, A Photo-biography* (Boston: Godine, 1992), pp. 1–2, which includes some of these portraits as well as additional ones by other noted photographers.

3. For Cocteau's adaptations of Clergue's photographs and the use of his resources during his films, see notes 6 and 11 below. See also Cocteau's texts praising the photographer in Clergue, *Numéro Uno* (Paris: Editec, 1963); his text and poem in Clergue, *Toros Mueros* (New York: Brussel & Brussel, 1962); his poem in "Phenixologie Poème-preface anamorphoses à Lucien Clergue excellent photographe," in *Le Testament d'Orphée* (Monaco: Rocher, 1961); and other tributes, many reprinted in *Lucien Clergue/Jean Cocteau* (Lunéville: Musée de Lunéville, 1989), pp. 35, 43–44, 55, 56, 60–61, and 72–73. See also Clergue's work, initially

128. Jean Cocteau. Illustrated letter to Lucien Clergue, May 30, 1959.

secured through Cocteau, in Éluard, *Corps mémorable*; in *Poesie der Photographie* [1957] (Cologne: DuMont Schauberg, 1960), with a cover design by Picasso and texts by Cocteau (two reprinted above); with the poet Federico García Lorca in his *Naissance d'Aphrodite* (Paris: Forces Vives, 1963); with the poet Serge Dieudonne in *Tauromachies No. 1* (Arles: Lucien Clergue, 1965). See also Tournier, "Introduction," *Eros and Thanatos: Lucien Clergue* (Boston: New York Graphic Society, [1985]), pp. 9–11.

4. See the preface to the Tournier selection, and n. 3 above and n. 5 below.

5. See Barthes, "Notes sur un album de photographies de Lucien Clergue," in *Langage de Sables* (Marseille: ACEP, 1980), npn, and the Tournier selection below.

6. According to Marianne Fulton, "Lucien Clergue," in *Lucien Clergue*, p. 21, Cocteau's frescoes in the chapel of Saint-Pierre de Villefranche-sur-Mer have a section dedicated to the Gypsies of Saintes-Maries-de-la-Mer, who gather there annually. Some of the frescoes were inspired by Clergue's photographs—for example, one of a group of raucous Gypsies, entitled 'Gypsies Goyesco, Saintes-Maries-de-la-Mer,' 1955, became a group of Pilate's soldiers, ridiculing St. Peter; it is reproduced in *Lucien Clergue*, p. 21, and in *Correspondance* [p. 94].

7. Clergue is comparing his subjects to those explorations of intense human passions done both early and late in his career by the famous Spanish artist Francisco José de Goya (1746–1828).

8. Alexander Pushkin (1799–1837) is Russia's national poet—of the stature of Shakespeare in England or Goethe in Germany—whose maternal grandfather was the son of a princeling of Abyssinia (now Ethiopia) who, after being taken hostage by the Turks, was abducted from a Constantinople seraglio to the Russian court, where he became a favorite of Peter the Great.

9. Lancelot of the Lake, a central figure in medieval romance, especially the Arthurian legend in both French and English versions, was so named because the Lady of the Lake stole him from his mother, who had briefly turned aside to tend her dying husband, King Ban of Benoyc, leaving her infant on the brink of the water. Lancelot later fell in love with Guinevere, the wife of King Arthur, and his dual loyalties eventually led to the dissolution of the legendary Round Table. Melusine is a well-known fairy in French folklore, but the editor could find no connection between these tales and the many versions of the story of Lancelot or the Arthurian legend. Cocteau is doubtless referring to the lascivious behavior of the Gypsies, on which he comments in the letter dated "Holiday, 1958" above.

10. See Clergue's unattributed photographs of the Gypsies, reproduced in Cocteau, *Le Testament d'Orphée* (Monaco: Rocher, 1961), fol. p. 83. His far better known ones are reproduced in *Lucien Clergue*, figs. 33–37.

11. According to Fulton, "Lucien Clergue," p. 18, Clergue later accompanied the guitarist called Manitas de Plata (meaning "silver hands") as manager and translator on his two trips to the United States and used his music as the sound track for his 1967 film, *Delta de Sel*.

12. See note 6 on the 'Gypsies Goyesco' above.

13. In this letter, Cocteau refers to three artists: Michelangelo Buonarroti (1475–1564), who painted the Sistine Chapel at the Vatican, among other accomplishments, and Leonardo da Vinci (1432–1519), the two best known artists of the Italian Renaissance, and Salvador Dali (1904–89), a Spanish painter associated with many twentieth-century avant-garde movements, including Surrealism. The Gypsies are seen more favorably in the two pieces that Cocteau wrote for *Poesie der Photographie* (1960), reprinted above, probably about the same time.

82. Yukio Mishima

FROM PREFACE TO *Barakei [Ordeal by Roses]*
BY EIKOH HOSOE, 1963

*A*fter his semiautobiographical Confessions of a Mask *(1959),*
Mishima (1925–70) became one of Japan's most celebrated and
controversial writers, familiar with both its classical and avant-
garde values as well as with those of Western culture. Admiring the work of
the photographer Eikoh Hosoe (1933–), the writer asked him to take a
publicity portrait for his next book (1961); impressed by Hosoe's attempt to
transcend his public facade and produce an "interior" portrait, Mishima
agreed to be the model for a sequence exploring a dream cycle of life,
sexuality, death, and rebirth, unified by the rose.[1] To achieve his unique
portrait, Hosoe posed the author in his own baroque Western-style resi-
dence, converted objects into symbols, and—by using different lenses, com-
plex angles, and high-contrast lighting—emphasized line, flat tones, and
grain rather than conventional lights and shadows [Fig. 129]. Hosoe also
supervised the sequencing of his prints and all design details of both edi-
tions of Barakei *(1963, 1971) with Mishima's approval. The author's absorp-*
tion in the entire experience was not surprising. He habitually engaged
photographers to document significant moments in his life; he was vain
about his physique after years of exercise, given his desire to be viewed as a
"man of the body" as well as an intellectual; and he had long associated
beauty, sexuality, and heroism with death. Barakei *established Hosoe's*
reputation; it also doubtless reinforced the obsession Mishima had with his
own death. His later ritual suicide was preceded by a photographic retro-
spective of himself, which he designed and mounted at a Tokyo department
store; the writer also insisted that any publication of his complete works
include photographs of him.[2]

129. Eikoh Hosoe.
#38 from *Barakei*,
1961.

Yukio Mishima

One day, without warning, Eikoh Hosoe appeared and transported me bodily to a strange world. Even before this, I had seen some of the magical work produced with the camera, but Hosoe's work is not so much simple magic as a kind of mechanical sorcery; it is the use of this civilized precision instrument for purposes utterly opposed to civilization. The world to which I was abducted under the spell of his lens was abnormal, warped, sarcastic, grotesque, savage, and promiscuous ... yet there was a clear undercurrent of lyricism murmuring gently through its unseen conduits.

It was, in a sense, the reverse of the world we live in, where our worship of social appearance and our concern for public morality and hygiene create foul, filthy sewers winding beneath the surface. Unlike ours, the world to which I was escorted was a weird, repellent city—naked, comic, wretched, cruel, and overdecorative into the bargain—yet in its underground channels there flowed, inexhaustibly, a pellucid stream of unsullied feeling.

Yes, it was a strange city to which I was taken ... a city not to be found on the map of any land, a city of awesome silences, where Death and Eros frolicked wantonly in broad daylight on the squares ...

We stayed in that city from the autumn of 1961 until the summer of 1962. This is the record of our stay, as told by Hosoe's camera.

Before that camera, as I soon realized, my own spirit and psychology had become totally redundant. It was an exhilarating experience, a state of affairs I had long dreamed of. Hosoe merely explored via the medium of his camera—much as the novelist uses words and the composer sounds—the various combinations in which the objects to be photographed could be placed, and the light and shadow which made those combinations possible. For him, in short, the objects correspond to words and sounds. The objects are stripped of their various meanings, which are flung into a meaningless arrangement where their meaningless reflection of each other eventually restores a certain order to the light and shadow. It is only by such means that the elements with which he composes can acquire an abstract quality similar to that of words and sounds.

A first requirement for this process, of course, is that the objects photographed should have some meaning of which they can be stripped. This is why it was necessary that the human model should be a novelist of sorts, and that the background should consist of Renaissance paintings and Spanish baroque furniture. These were not, thus, a way of effecting satire or parody, but of achieving the photographer's unique type of abstraction. The use, for example, of Giorgione's *Sleeping Venus* and Botticelli's *Birth of Venus* has a quite different significance from Dali's monomaniacal parody of *Evening Bells*. If the photographer is to create works that will stand for his spirit in the same way as artists in other genres, he must first—having no ready-made, abstract components such as words and sounds—supply other means to abstraction instead.

First of all, thus, the externals of the objects to be photographed must be precisely defined and a state of affairs established where, for instance, the model's eye can be, quite simply, an eye and his back a back. Before Hosoe's camera, I was trained until it meant exactly the same to me whether I stared into the lens or turned my back on it completely. If the flesh of my back and the retina of my eye were both treated simply as externals, what sense could there be to looking?

Yet I was not the only one who was placed in a position where he did not rely on his own eyes. It was the same for Hosoe, too, as the photographer. Quite obviously, as he peered into the viewfinder, he was waiting for some metamorphosis to overtake the objects he saw there. From beginning to end, his operations were aimed at preparing a state of affairs where his own eyes might be successfully betrayed, where a successful reversion to the kind of primary images already seen in his subconscious world would be achieved. Thus the objects to be photographed were decided on, placed—sometimes, literally, bound fast—and, together with the photographer himself, consecrated to the uncertain metamorphosis which was supposed to occur as a result of the ritual situation so assiduously arranged. For myself, I was in an objective world where staring eyes and closed, rejection and affirmation, were reduced to precisely the same significance.

It seems to me that before the photograph can exist as art it must, by its very nature, choose whether it is to be a record or a testimony. Whatever special lens are used, and however the subject is thereby distorted, the camera only knows how to relate things directly. However abstract the composition, therefore, the individual meaning of the objects related inevitably remains as a kind of indispersible precipitate. The photographer's whole job is to filter this off by one of two methods. These alternatives are the record and the testimony.

The masterpieces of press photography belong to the former class. The images which the photographer has filtered from reality, whether particular events or the anguish of human reactions to them, already bear a stamp of authenticity which the photographer is powerless to alter by one jot or tittle; the meaning of the objects, by a process of purification, itself becomes the theme of the work. One might say that the photograph that chooses to record takes the absolute authenticity of the object photographed as its form and the purification of the meaning as its theme. On the other hand, when the photograph chooses to testify, the meaning of the objects related by the camera loses some parts in the process of being filtered off, while other parts are distorted and fitted into a new environment so as to serve as formal elements for the work; as for the theme of the work, it lies solely in the expression of the photographer's subjective judgement. His testimony is everything:

This is true ...

This is a photograph, so it is as you see: there are no lies and no deceptions.

Hosoe's art is, supremely, that of the "testimony." The definition of which just given can be fitted to actual examples in his work.

In the way he treats a single rose, for example.... This particular flower embodies the general concept of the thing called "rose" which most men harbor in their brains, along with various special meanings implicit in the place of origin, the species, the form, and the color. The lens of the camera relates, not just the rose, but its meaning as well. It is, indeed, only this meaning—and not the image—which can be twisted and toyed with in the process of filtering out the testimony. In a documentary photograph, the meaning would itself be the theme of the work, but here the meaning of the rose is transformed and worked into the composition as a formal element. It is here that it can become, for the first time, a rose in the form of a palace building, a rose like an elephant, a womb-rose, a phallic rose ... And yet the elephant and the womb remain, not the theme of the work, but mere formal elements. The theme consists solely of Hosoe's testimony:

This is the true rose ...

This is a photograph, so it is as you see: there are no lies and no deceptions.

One can detect here, elevated to an incomparably higher level, the same pathetic emotional appeal that lies concealed in every fake spiritualist photograph, every pornographic photograph; one comes to suspect that the strange, disturbing emotional appeal of the photographic art consists solely in that same, repeated refrain: this is a true ghost ... this is a photograph, so it is as you see: there are no lies, no deceptions.

This plea, this testimony, I feel, constitute the whole of Hosoe's personal message, It is, surely, only via this same monotonous refrain that any self-revelation is possible to the photographer at all?

Yet his works are vibrant with a frail yet intense tremolo of emotion—the emotion of the testimony that cannot partake of the slightest objective credibility. Why do you not believe, when this is a photograph? Why do you not believe, when this is something that actually occurred before my eyes? Little did the photographers of old, with their box-like contraptions covered with red-lined material, dream that the photograph—that product of the machine civilization, that all-mighty monarch of realism, more realistic than the most realistic painters—would be used for such an ironic testimony! The loneliness of these works stems from this, from the repetition of the same testimony each time in different keys; it is here, I would assert without hesitation, that the po- etry of the photograph lies. The photographer has gazed clearly, with his own eyes, on unheard-of metamorphoses, and has testified to them.

1. For accounts and further details of their collaboration, see Thomas Dugan, "Eikoh Hosoe," *Photography Between Covers: Interviews with Photo-Bookmakers* (Rochester, N.Y.: Light Impressions, [1979]), pp. 103–9; Mark Holborn, *Black Sun: The Eyes of Four: Roots and Innovation in Japanese Photography* (New York: Aperture, 1986), p. 16; Ronald J. Hill, afterword to *Eikoh Hosoe* [*Untitled* 42], ed. David Featherstone (Carmel, Calif.: Friends of Photography, 1986), npn; and Edward Putzar, *Japanese Photography, 1945–1985* (Tucson: Pacific West, 1987), pp. 15–16.

2. See John Nathan, *Mishima: A Biography* (Boston: Little, Brown [1974]), pp. 267–69; and see also pp. 125, 130, 146, and 227; Mishima, "Patriotism" (1960), trans. Geoffrey W. Sargeant, in *Death in Midsummer* (New York: New Directions, 1966), pp. 93–118, which features a photograph (p. 94) of the couple who live and die according to the author's values; and Mishima's posthumously published preface to Hosoe, *Embrace* (Tokyo: Shoshin Hyranshi Publishers House, 1971), npn. See also Mutsuo Takahashi, "The Flag" [For Eikoh Hosoe], *Eikoh Hosoe: Photographs* (Santa Fe: Andrew Smith Gallery/ Muso Press, 1990), npn.

FROM *The Painted Bird*, 1964, AND *Blind Date*, 1977

*P*hotography was the first foreign language of my artistic expression," recalled Kosinski (1933–91); English was the second, mani-
festing itself later in his prolific writings.[1] The young Pole welcomed
the camera—and the private darkroom—which he began using in 1950 as
one of the few sanctioned means of individual creativity behind the Iron
Curtain. While studying sociology and history, Kosinski minored in photographic chemistry, modifying emulsions and making his own. By 1956, he
exhibited his distinctive work locally (provoking suspicion of bourgeois
decadence because his many nudes and abstractions lacked social content)
and even internationally (more often than any other Eastern European
photographer), winning several awards [Figs. 130, 131].[2] Escaping to New
York in 1957, Kosinski devoted more time to writing than to photography.
But he often carried a small camera, taking and developing pictures of
friends, colleagues, or whatever caught his attention while walking, skiing,
or exploring kinky night spots; many of his pictures show his taste for the
unexpected subject or pattern.[3] Photography also influenced Kosinski's
writing. For example, all of his novels, including his first, The Painted Bird
(1965), a jolting account of the Holocaust, are structured episodically, like a
montage of recollected album snapshots. Some of his central characters are
often amateur photographers; and photographs are increasingly used for
significant aspects of plot, character, and imagery.[4] In 1988, Kosinski showed
some of his Eastern European prints in his initial public American exhibition; he planned to take up photography seriously again, but failing health
and spirits first drove him to suicide.[5]

FROM *The Painted Bird*

Portraits and photographs of such great men were displayed in the regimental library, in the field hospital, in the recreation hall, in the mess tents, and in the soldiers' quarters. I had often looked at the faces of these wise and great men. Many of them were dead. Some had short, resounding names and long bushy beards. The last one, however, was still living. His portraits were larger, brighter, more handsome than the rest. It was under his leadership, said Gavrila, that the Red army was defeating the Germans and bringing to the liberated peoples a new way of life which made all equal. There would be no rich and poor, no exploiters and exploited, no persecution of the dark by the fair, no people doomed to gas chambers. Gavrila, like all the officers and men in the regiment, owed all he had to this man: education, rank, home. The library owed all its beautifully printed and bound books to him. I owed the care of the army doctors and my recovery to him. Every Soviet citizen was in debt to this man for everything he possessed and for all his good fortune.

This man's name was Stalin.

In the portraits and photographs he had a kind face and compassionate eyes. He looked like a loving grandfather or uncle, long unseen, wanting to take you into his arms. Gavrila read and told me many stories about Stalin's life. At my age young Stalin, then called Soso, fought for the rights of the underprivileged, resisting the centuries-old exploitation of the helpless poor by the pitiless rich.

I looked at the photographs of Stalin in his youth. He had very black, bushy hair, dark eyes, heavy eyebrows, and later even a black mustache. He looked more of a Gypsy than I did, more Jewish than the Jew killed by the German officer in the black uniform, more Jewish even than the boy found by the peasants on the railroad tracks. Stalin was lucky not to have lived his youth in the villages where I had stayed. If he had been beaten as a child all the time for his dark features, perhaps he would not have had so much time to help others; he might have been too busy just fending off the village boys and dogs.

But Stalin was a Georgian. Gavrila did not tell me if the Germans had planned to incinerate the Georgians. But as I looked at the people that surrounded Stalin in the pictures I had not the slightest doubt that if the Germans had captured them, they would all have gone to the furnaces. They were swarthy, black-haired, with burning dark eyes. pp. 213–215]

FROM *Blind Date*

Lavanter knew he had to leave the East, but he knew also that he would need a profession that could support him in the West, a profession with a universal language. While he was finishing at the university after his army service, Lavanter enrolled in night courses at a school of photography. Before long, he had built his own darkroom and chemical laboratory.

In addition to his classes and darkroom work, he spent hours every week in the school's library examining the catalogues and magazines that described advancements in photographic art and reproduced the work of well-known photographers. Lavanter soon learned that photography by its very nature depended on imitating reality in an imaginative, subjective way, but that usually a photographer's technical style could easily be reproduced.

To counteract imitations of his artistic methods, Lavanter began to evolve his own techniques and a style that could not be readily copied. He used a camera adapted to his experiments, and films and papers coated with either existing emulsions that he modified or emulsions he made himself.

Less than two years after he began the course, he was invited to exhibit his work at national and international salons of photography. His photographs were reproduced in art publications, won prizes and awards, and a one-man

130. Jerzy Kosinski. 'Stalin and Worker,' USSR, 1950.

131. Jerzy Kosinski. 'Worker and Stalin,' Warsaw, 1956.

exhibit of his photographs was organized in the capital. He received offers to work for domestic and foreign manufacturers of photographic products and was invited to exhibit his photographs and to lecture abroad by several Western art societies. Convinced that his work would be the finest form of advertising for the export of domestic photographic products, the authorities granted Lavanter a short-term passport for his trip to the West.

During the last week in the Soviet Union, he walked through fields in the farthest suburb of Moscow and noticed remnants of the frail fence that had surrounded the tents of the traveling state circus. Now, in winter, the circus was gone, and the fence and field were abandoned.

It was snowing. The whirling powder had whitewashed the outlines of the railing. Between flurries, the fence looked like a good subject for a black-and-white photograph. Around him, the air was growing blustery; the winds seemed to have chosen the field as their arena, tumbling over each other, raising clouds of snow and puffing them away. He had difficulty holding the camera steady.

A passer-by, hugging his coat, made his way along the wooden railing, which wound through the field like a frozen snake. Before the man vanished in the white squall, Lavanter took the picture.

The cold and wind bit into him. Lavanter thought that if he died here, his frostbitten body would not be discovered until spring came and the snows melted.

From far away came the sound of a motorcycle plowing through the drifts. Soon a burly state militia officer arrived, stopping his bike next to Lavanter. The officer turned off the engine and removed his goggles.

"Your papers, please," he said in an even voice.

"What have I done?" asked Lavanter.

The officer looked from Lavanter's face to his camera. "A man just reported that he saw someone taking pictures of this field. Is that you?"

Lavanter nodded.

"Then your papers, please." The officer extended his thickly gloved hand.

Without a word, Lavanter took off his glove and reached under his coat. After a moment of digging through layers of sweaters, he produced his student I. D. Card.

The officer glanced at the card, then silently put it in a leather bag hanging from his shoulder. He jerked his chin at Lavanter's camera. "Open your camera, Comrade, and expose the film," he said.

"But why?" asked Lavanter.

"Because of what you photographed," answered the officer patiently.

"I photographed this field," Lavanter said, "The fence that crosses it, and an old man who walked past."

"What else?"

"What else is there, Comrade?" said Lavanter. "There is nothing else. Here, take my camera. Whatever you see through the viewer is what I saw." He held out his camera, but the officer pushed it back to him.

"You are here, on one of the coldest days of the year, in the middle of a storm, just to take pictures of an empty field, a broken fence, and some old man passing by."

"I am!"

"That's a lie!" said the officer.

"It's the truth!" said Lavanter.

"Tell the truth, or I'll arrest you!"

Lavanter tried to sound patient. "I took a picture of an old man against the fence and the fence against the field. That's all."

The officer became very angry. "I won't listen to such crap anymore," he said. "I know you photographed this field." He paused. "But we both know that such a field, any field, could serve as a landing site—" he paused again, this time apparently for effect. "A landing site for, let's say, invading paratroopers. Is that what you photographed? Would a Soviet judge believe that you did not? Now, no more trickery. Take out the film!"

Lavanter obeyed. Sheltering his camera from the snow with his coat, he opened it, pulling the entire roll off its spool and exposing it to the light. The corkscrew of film dangled from his hand. He let it go; in an instant it was carried off by the wind and disappeared in the snow.

Lavanter returned to the field the following

day. It was gray and cold. A man dragged himself along the fence, clutching his coat and, every few steps, tugging his hat lower. Seen through the viewfinder, that man's figure, the fence, and the field already appeared as a finished photo. Lavanter took the picture. [pp. 53–56]

1. See Peter Gambaccini, "*Being There* vs. Seeing There: Jerzy Kosinsky Speaks Out on Words and Pictures," *American Photographer* 4, no. 6 (June 1980): 92.

2. For Kosinski's photographic activities in Poland, see in Czeslaw Czapliński, *Jerzy Kosinski: Twarzi i Maski=The Face and Masks=Visage et Masques* (Lodz: Muzeum Sztuky, 1992), especially: "Excerpts from Documents from 1956," trans. Macief Świerkocki, pp. 35–39; Macief Maciejewski, "The Łódź Years of Jerzy Kosiński," trans. by the author, pp. 24–33, especially 28, 31–32; Marin Janion, "Alone in the Dark Room," trans. Jerzy Jarniewicz, pp. 46–57, especially 46–47; Urszula Czartoryska, "To Replace the Reflection of Reality by an Allusion to Reality," trans. Świerkocki, pp. 59–63; and Jerzy Neugebauer, untitled essay, trans. Jarniewicz, pp. 100–106. See also George Plimpton and Rocco Landesman, "The Art of Fiction: Jerzy Kosinski" (1972), in Plimpton, ed., *Writers at Work* (New York: Penguin, 1981), pp. 313–39, and Geoffrey Movius, "A Conversation with Jerzy Kosinski," *New Boston Review* 1, no. 3 (Winter 1975): 3–6.

3. Ryszard Horowitz, untitled essay in *Jerzy Kosinski*, p. 87, says he was a "keen" but not a "good" photographer, as he himself sensed, "which is why he didn't try to pursue photography professionally in New York." For some of Kosinski's other photographs, see his portrait of Arthur Miller and his wife, the photographer Inge Morath, on the inside back of the dust jacket of their collaboration *In the Country* (New York: Viking/Studio, 1977); his pictures of Vane Ivanovic in *LX: Memoirs of a Jugoslav* (New York: Harcourt Brace Jovanovich, 1977), cover and following p. 244; and two self-portraits and a vineyard scene in John Taylor, "The Haunted Bird: The Death and Life of Jerzy Kozinski," *New York* 24 (July 15, 1991): 24–25 and 36–37. See also the portraits of Kosinski taken by Czapliński throughout *Jerzy Kosinski* (together with the photographer's essay/interview, "The Photographic Fiction of Jerzy Kosinski," pp. 64–71, and Anthony Haden-Guest's interview of Czapliński, "Kosinski's Masque," pp. 83–86); and the portrait by Krementz taken at her request, according to Kiki Kosinski in conversations with the editor on December 4 and 15, 1991, reproduced in "Jill Krementz: Unofficial Photographer-Laureate for the Contemporary Literary Scene," *35-MM Photography* (Spring 1975): 30.

4. Byron L. Sherin, *Jerzy Kosinski: Literary Alarmclock* (Chicago: Cabala Press, [1981]), p. 48, is the only critic to also make this evident observation; the Kosinski novels listed in the bibliography, especially the ones after 1973, are particularly relevant; the author endlessly revised (but the texts reprinted above did not change in the editions consulted by the editor). See also Kosinski: "Exegetics," *Paris Review* 97 (1985): 93–99; "How Photogenic Must a Self Be?" (1988), in Czapliński, *Jerzy Kosinski*, pp. 40–45, which Kiki Kosinski made available to the editor in TS; and his remarks on photography in Gambaccini, *American Photographer* 4, no. 6 (June 1980): 92–93, one of which is reprinted in the exhibition brochure for *Jerzy Kosinsky: Early Photographs, Poland and Russia, 1950–1957* (New York: André Zarre Gallery, October 4–31, 1988), in which three of his photographs are reproduced, and as "Photography as Art," in *Passing By: Selected Essays* (New York: Random House, 1992), p. 65. Thanks to André Zarre and Livia Fagin, the editor was able to see most of the exhibited photographs in storage; the photograph described in the excerpt from *Blind Date* above hangs in the Kosinski living room.

5. According to Kiki Kosinski in conversation with the editor, December 4, 1991.

Part Six

1965–1990

*I*n 1939, Merton (1915–68) registered his boredom with a photography exhibition in his diary. But by 1959 the Trappist monk,
becoming an internationally known writer of philosophy, poetry,
prayers, essays, and autobiography, began taking pictures himself—perhaps
a result of planning a book (never published) about the Shakers with his
friend, the photographer Shirley Burden.[1] His subsequent pictures benefitted
from the advice, encouragement, equipment, and printing service provided
by John Howard Griffin (1920–80), whom Merton met in 1960. Griffin was
a fellow Catholic convert, a trained musician, and (after losing and regain-
ing his eyesight) a gifted photographer as well as writer. Merton particularly admired Black Like Me (1961), his riveting account of his experience
posing as a black in the South.[2] Griffin visited Merton annually, making a
visual archive of him and facilitating the monk's pictures. Merton tended to
focus on the textures, patterns, and shadows of the trees, woods, barns,
windows, and common objects made symbolic [Figs. 132, 133] that he often
wrote about.[3] In 1967, through mutual literary friends, Merton also met the
photographer Ralph Eugene Meatyard, whose pictures, often featuring surrealistic masked or blurred figures, were the "most haunting and suggestive,
mythical" he'd ever seen.[4] They talked about collaborating, but the monk accidentally died in Asia during a trip he planned to document with his photographs as well as his writing.[5] Illness prevented Griffin from finishing Merton's official biography, but he left many other accounts of their relationship.

Griffin:

I wrote [the Father Abbot] and Thomas Merton that for many years I had been building a private archive of photographs of men and women, famous and unknown, in their typical activities . . . and that I would like very much, without any intention of publishing to do this with Thomas Merton. Permission was given. . . . When I arrived for the photographic session I was gratified to see that Thomas Merton had made no special preparation. He wore his habit, a blue denim jacket and a knitted black wool cap. A slight stubble of whiskers marked his chin. He suggested that we go up to the hermitage and I quickly agreed. . . . the morning sun, reflecting from the stone floor and walls, filled the room with a soft brilliance ideal for photography. . . . I began to shoot frames to accustom him to the sight and sound of the camera. We talked easily. No problems about his assuming any pose. He was perfectly natural. He was rare in this, utterly unconcerned about his "image". . . . [But] I had other problems. His face concealed nothing. It changed every moment, swiftly, with changes in his thoughts or moods. How to catch all of that? How to capture what was truly characteristic. . . .

We talked photography. He knew nothing about it, but he was fascinated by what I was doing. He was amused when I told him of the tendency of very intelligent men to freeze up and become unnatural the moment the lens was pointed at them. [from *Follow the Ecstasy,* pp. 4–5]

Merton:

. . . Nothing resembles reality less than the photograph. Nothing resembles substance less than its shadow. To convey the meaning of something substantial you have to use not a shadow but a sign, not the limitation but the image. The image is a new and different reality, and of course it does not convey and impression of some object, but the mind of the subject: and that is something else again.

Man is the image of God, not His shadow. At present, we have decided that God is dead, and

that we were his shadow. . . . Take a picture of that, Jack! [from *Conjectures of a Guilty Bystander* (New York: Doubleday, 1966), pp. 133–34 {pre-1964 journal passages}]

Griffin:

As I photographed more and more, Tom began to inch toward me and my cameras. Finally he came and asked about them. I explained that one was a Leica, and the other an Alpa, the same instrument that David Douglas Duncan had used in his reproduction of Picasso's paintings in *Picasso's Picassos.*

I handed it to him, watched him handle it as though it were a precious jewel.

"Wouldn't you like to use it today?" I asked.

It was like placing a concert grand at the disposal of a gifted musician who had never played on anything but an upright. Tom began to shoot as freely as I had been and always afterward he referred to that "Picasso camera." [from *Follow the Ecstasy,* p. 10]

Merton:

The contact sheets of the photos never came. Or rather I never got them. I don't quite know what happens to mail here but curious things do happen, and I hope the contact sheets were not lost, thrown away or whatever. Were they sent? Were you waiting for some kind of reaction? If they were not sent, then forget it. I just wanted to check, though. I am of course eager to see the pix, and see how my own on the Picasso camera came out!!! ... [from Letter to Griffin, November 16, 1966, *Road to Joy,* p. 134]

Merton:

Many thanks for the prints. . . . I liked the one I took of Jacques [Maritain, French philosopher and Catholic convert]—a lucky accident as usual. I thought that it was a bit fussy with light and dark. Should have played around with the aperture if I'd known how.

By the way I don't remember if I ever answered you about the idea of sending prints of my roots or etc. to that academy in California. Really John I don't think it would be all right.

132. Thomas Merton. 'The Soul's Hook' (called by Merton "the only known photograph of God"), c. 1960's.

at leaves and trees and the reflections of water through the ground-glass viewfinder. It was fascinating to see a man who knew little or nothing of photography, working with great speed and energy toward doing something with photography that he had never seen done before. The camera became in his hands, almost immediately, an instrument of contemplation, at least potentially, and it remained that for him until his death, which explains why he became not only a gifted, but a uniquely original photographer. He himself later contradistinguished between his "documentary" photography of places, people and events, and his "serious" work [Fig. 132]. He was never terribly interested in the former, he was profoundly immersed in the latter. In the last two years of his life . . . he continued his photographing, borrowing cameras where and when he could. He photographed natural forms: the roots of trees, leaves, branches. [from *Follow the Ecstasy*, pp. 10–11]

I'm no pro, and there are lots of good pros who are not in that gallery. Just because I happened to press the shutter release accidentally, when the thing was pointing at an interesting object . . . No, honestly, I see no reason why an occasional picture taker like myself, who doesn't even know how to develop a film, can be considered a photographer. So I'll pass. I can't in conscience exhibit in an "academy" or a "hall of fame" or whatever it is, for all your generosity! Thanks anyhow ... [from Letter to Griffin, January 10, 1967, *Road to Joy*, pp. 134–35]

Merton:

John, I wonder if this is a reasonable request: if not, forget it. I know your [son] Gregory is a great man with a camera and in the dark room. Would he want to earn a little pocket money processing some stuff for me? There used to be a brother here who did very nice work but he has gone to Chile to our monastery there. The present brother is also the dentist and optometrist besides being photographer and even if he were interested in my roots, which he supremely isn't—he would not be able to do the work. So he just sends it in to the drugstore and that is fatal. Could Gregory give it a little of his time for a handsome emolument . . . . (Suppose we pay him whatever it is the brother pays the drugstore, that's openly fair, no)? ... [from Letter to Griffin, August 24, 1967, *Road to Joy*, p. 136]

Griffin:

A passion for photography of a special kind had been building in Tom. It was not for ordinary photography. He had no interest whatsoever in ordinary photography, the passion was simply for another means for expressing his vision: the challenge to capture on film something of the solitude and silence and essences that preoccupied him.

As always in my association with him, this interest began to bend the day to its needs. By afternoon, when we went out into the woods and sat at the edge of a lake, Tom talked mostly with the camera at his eye, looking at the world,

Griffin:

Gregory accepted with enthusiasm. The films began to come in all sizes, all formats, depending on what camera Tom had borrowed. They ranged from superb negatives made with a Rolleiflex to miserable ones made on dollar cameras, where little of the detail Tom wanted had been captured because of the cheap lenses. [from *Follow the Ecstasy*, p. 11]

Merton:
Five rolls are on their way to Gregory, separately. I know nothing of such mysteries as ASA speeds. Never use a meter. So I presume everything I did was "standard." Most of it is closeup stuff of roots at f, 11 or f, 22, and mostly around 100 of a sec. If that tells you anything. Much of it may look incomprehensible, it is so close and so abstract. But then again a lot of it may just simply be lousy. I have no idea how it is going to be as I haven't used this camera before. I am immensely grateful to know the negatives will be in the hands of someone who knows. My blessings to Gregory. [from Letter to Griffin, September 2, 1967, *Road to Joy*, p. 137]

Griffin:
Then I wrote and suggested that he would never have much satisfaction until he got himself a good camera that he could learn to know intimately and handle consistently. [from *Follow the Ecstasy*, p. 11]

Merton:
Still have not had a coherent moment to check with authority on the gift of camera, and really I am hesitating about it because I just can't get that involved in another "career." Maybe it would be better if I thought about it for a while: there is the question of my utterly abstract "poverty" to be considered too ... ! Can I think about it for a while? [from Letter to Griffin, September 29, 1967, *Road to Joy*, p. 138]

Just time for a brief note, to enclose this check for Greg, before I go down to concelebrate for this feast. Thanks for your *Reader* which has got here safely and is most handsome. The photographs are utterly powerful, some of them overwhelming. I do hope you go on with the project of a whole book of them. It will be a great one. And the *Reader* itself is so rich. [from Letter to Griffin, December 8, 1967, *Road to Joy*, p. 139]

That reminds me, diffidently I am reminded of your generous offer of a camera that is likely to stay in one piece for a year or two yet. I think that with the demise of this one, I ought to seriously consider your offer. It is justifiable for me to have a camera, I think, since I do occasionally sell a picture and it is not just diddling. (One must be a producer.) That being the case, let's discuss it. What do you suggest? Any time I've used a Nikon I like it. Don't especially like Kodaks or Leicas. I have liked the Rolleiflex for focusing and composition. What do you suggest? You know the kind of thing I most like to do. Obviously I am not covering the Kentucky Derby etc. But I do like a chance at fast funny out of the way stuff too. The possibility of it in case. But as I see it I am going to be on roots, sides of barns, tall weeds, mud-puddles, and junkpiles until Kingdom come. A built-in exposure meter might be a help. [from Letter to Griffin, January 5, 1968, *Road to Joy*, p. 140]

Griffin:
From my point of view, he was showing great gifts and I regretted every negative that was rendered useless because of a poor camera he had used. I felt that something was being lost of jeopardized—an authentic part of his vision. So we finally solved it by my simply sending him the proper equipment [a 35mm Nikon with a 50mm and 100mm lens] "on perpetual loan." [from *Follow the Ecstasy*, p. 12]

Merton:
Your letter about the camera was one of the most exciting things that ever happened. THE most exciting was the arrival of the camera itself. It is superb. I haven't had a chance to take it out, though we have some nice afternoons. . . . So far I have only read the instructions, procured film and become acquainted with the different gadgets. What a thing to have around! I will take reverent care of it, and any time you want it ... I will take good care to see that it goes straight back to you if anything happens to me.... [from Letter to Griffin, March 27, 1968, *Road to Joy*, p. 140]

It is fabulous. What a joy of a thing to work with. I am sending the two first two rolls and hoping that they are ok, that I haven't done something all wrong: but the camera is the most eager and helpful of beings, all full of happy suggestions: "Try this! Do it that way" Reminding me of things I have overlooked, and cooperating in the creation of new worlds. So simply. This is a Zen camera. As for the F. 100, I tell you I'm going to blow my mind with it! It is fantastic, at least in the viewfinder. I'll wait and see what the contacts look like ... [from Letter to Griffin, March 29, 1968, *Road to Joy*, p. 141]

Griffin:
From then on, photography overwhelmed our other interests. A constant stream of film poured into our darkroom to be processed. . . . We corresponded constantly about his work; we would send him contact sheets, he would mark a few, ask for enlargements, we would sent the enlargements, then discuss them by letter.

When I went to Gethsemani, we would get together to discuss other thing—civil rights, the church and civil rights. But after the briefest time, we would abandon that and discuss his pictures, his contact sheets, and end up with our cameras on a photographic jaunt into the woods, or through the cloister.

On my last visit, shortly before his departure for Asia, I went particularly to have a session with him concerning my book *The Church and The Black Man*. We talked about this for a few minutes and fell into a depression about some of the things that were happening. . . . We got gloomier and gloomier . . . Tom was . . . slumped down in a chair, looking at his hands. . . . "We're not going to solve this. It's beyond human solution now. It's in God's hands," he said. "Do you feel like going out and photographing?"

The gloom was instantly replaced. We got into the rented car I had brought and drove up to the hermitage. He grabbed his camera and film and directed me toward an old whiskey plant nearby.

We photographed everything: the peeling paint on window faces of abandoned buildings, plants, weed, rusting railroad cars, a stack of wood-

chips. he would see something in the distance, wander away to photograph it from all angles and then return . . . I marveled at his vigor and enthusiasm.

A sudden downpour drove us back to the abbey . . . . We said good-bye and I watched him through the rain-pocked windows of the car as he hurried into the hermitage, his jean-clad stocky figure bent almost double over the camera to protect it from the rain. [from *Follow the Ecstasy*, pp. 12–13]

Merton:
Last evening, the plane was late taking off and we did not leave Tokyo until after dark. . . . Finally, after we passed over South Vietnam—where there were three big, silent, distant fires—we came down over the vast dim lights of Bangkok. We got out of the plane into tropical heat, a clammy night no worse than Louisville in July. Fascist faces of the passport men, a line of six officials in uniform to stamp a passport once, faces like the officers in Batista's Cuba, and the same pale uniforms. Tired, crafty, venal faces, without compassion, full, in some cases, of self-hate. Men worn out by a dirty system. A conniving one made no move to look at any bag of mine in the customs. He waved me on when I declared fifteen rolls of pan-x film—as if I were a good child. And I was grateful. [from entry of October 17, 1968, *Asian Journal*, p. 10]

The situation of the tourist becomes ludicrous and impossible in a place like Calcutta. How does one take pictures of these streets with the faces, the eyes, of such people, and the cows roaming among them on the sidewalks and buzzards by the score circling over the main streets in the "best" section? [from entry of October 19, 1968, *Asian Journal*, pp. 25–26]

. . . I met today . . . a ten-year-old boy, a lively an intelligent kid living up on the mountain here in a rather poor cottage with an older lama, another boy lama, and a Tibetan family with a huge black goat that was all ready to bite a few chunks out of Harold and me. The boy was charming and I took some pictures of him as he was petulantly rolling down his sleeves to be more ceremonious. He went into his cell and sat cross-legged on his seat and received us with poise and formality. I took his picture there too but it was probably too dark to come out. [from entry of November 3, 1968, *Asian Journal*, p. 97]

The first thing I did after tea was to go to the 18th-century observatory, Jantar Mantar, with its endless abstract shapes and patterns. In a few minutes I had run out of film . . . [later] sent my films to John Howard Griffin for processing, including a roll of Jantar Mantar—a fascinating place! [from entry of November 11, 1968, *Asian Journal*, p. 126]

As soon as it was a little light outside the window I got into my clothes and went out, up the hill to the temple on top with all its prayer flags and incense. The children meanwhile were chanting down at the Tibetan school—joyous, lusty chanting that fitted in with the mountains. And there was Kanchenjunga, dim in the dawn and in haze, not colored by the sun but dovelike in its bluegray—a lovely sight but hard to photograph. [from entry of November 13, 1968, *Asian Journal*, pp. 135–36]

At the Tibetan Refugee Center there was a young nun with shaved head and a sweet smile who, I learned, went to work in the local carpet factory. She posed for a picture with three others who looked like old men. [from entry of November 14, 1968, *Asian Journal*, p. 138]

Griffin:
During the months he was away on the trip to Asia, he sent films to be processed and letters . . . "I suppose I'll need copies of all these Asian photographs as a kind of documentation of the trip." I sensed he did not have the enthusiasm for this "documentation" in photography that he had for the more personal "serious" photography. [from *Follow the Ecstasy*, pp. 13–14]

Merton:
There is another side of Kanchenjunga and of every mountain—the side that has never been photographed and turned into post cards. That is the only side worth seeing. . . .

Later: I took three more photos of the mountain. An act of reconciliation? No, a camera cannot reconcile one with anything. Nor can it see a real mountain. The camera does not know what it takes; it captures materials with which you reconstruct, not so much what you saw as what you thought you saw. Hence the best photography is aware, mindful, of illusion and uses illusion, permitting and encouraging it—especially unconscious and powerful illusions that are not normally admitted on the scene. [from entry of November 19, 1968, *Asian Journal*, p. 153]

Have I failed in my solemn duty as tourist by not taking a photo of a woman of Ghoom, sitting by the roadside, delousing the head of her eight-year-old son? [from entry of November 24, 1968, *Asian Journal*, pp. 167–68]

. . . Contact prints had come from John Griffin of the photos I had taken at Dharamsala. The one of the Dalai Lama is especially good, also the one of Kham tul Rimpoche, and the little tulki in his cell was very visible. [from entry of November 1968, *Asian Journal*, p. 171]

I hope my camera caught some of the enchanted beauty of this landscape! Ceylon is incomparable! [from entry of November 30, 1968, *Asian Journal*, p. 218]

I visited Polonnaruwa on Monday . . . heavy rain in Kandy, and on all the valleys and paddy land and jungle and teak and rubber as we go down to the eastern plains. . . . By Dambulla the rain has almost stopped. The nobility and formality of an ancient mustachioed guide who presents himself under a bo tree. We start up the long sweep of black rock, the vicar general lagging behind, complaining that he dislikes "paganism," telling me I will get much better photos somewhere else, and saying they are all out to cheat me. [from entry of December 4, 1968, *Asian Journal*, p. 231]

I am now preparing to leave Singapore, the city of transistors, tape recorders, cameras, perfumes, silk shirts, fine liquors . . . carrying away only a stock of 35mm. Plus X film. [from entry of December 6, 1968, *Asian Journal,* p. 237]

I find that I was secretly enraged and humiliated by the fact of having overweight luggage yesterday. Today . . . I went all though my baggage, ruthlessly separating out things to be somehow disposed of . . . I sent contact prints to John Griffin with a few marked for enlargement. Took nine rolls of Pan X to the Borneo Studio on Silom Road, hoping they will not be ruined. [from entry of December 7, 1968, *Asian Journal,* p. 248]

Griffin:

On December 11 we received news of Merton's death in Bangkok on the tenth. I returned to Gethsemani on the day of the funeral, December 17, and closed my photographic archives with some shots the next morning of the red clay mount of his grave beneath a large cypress tree in the monastic graveyard.

. . . On learning that his camera would be returned with his effects, I wrote and pleaded that the camera not be opened by customs or anyone else. There might be exposed film in it.

Weeks later the camera and extra lens arrived . . . I was overwhelmed to see how im-

maculately Tom had cared for the equipment—the body and lenses were spotless. . . . I glanced at the frame counter and saw that 18 shots had been taken of the roll in the camera body. [After developing them] . . . I selected one of the last images at random . . . and . . . looked through Tom's eyes on a scene viewed from some high place, downward past an edge of building and a foreground of shore across a broad body of water from which reflected sunlight glinted back into the viewer's eyes—a kind of universal all-embracing view of men and boats and water, seen from the perspective of height and distance [Fig. 133].

Merton:

I dreamt I was lost in a great city and was walking 'toward the center' without quite knowing where I was going. Suddenly I came to a dead end, but on a height, looking at a great bay, the arm of the harbor. . . .

I think sometimes that I may soon die, though I am not yet old (forty seven [in 1962]). I don't know exactly what kind of conviction this thought carries with it or what I mean by it. Death is always a possibility for everyone . . . so if I have a habitual awareness that I may die, and that, if this is God's will, then I am glad. [*Conjectures of a Guilty Bystander,* pp. 170–71, noted and partly quoted in *Follow the Ecstasy,* pp. 14–15]

1. See Michael Mott, *The Seven Mountains of Thomas Merton* (Boston: Houghton Mifflin, 1984), pp. 343–44, which draws on journals not available to the public until 1993, and Merton's letter to another writer-photographer friend, Edward Rice, October 26, 1963, in *The Road to Joy: The Letters of Thomas Merton to New and Old Friends,* ed. Robert E. Daggy (New York: Farrar, Straus & Giroux, 1989), p. 286. Burden provided the cover for Merton's *Selected Poems* (New York: New Directions, 1959), and Merton wrote the introduction for Burden's photographic study of the order's daily life, *God Is My Life:The Story of Our Lady of Gethsemani* (New York: Reynal, 1960), [3 pp]. See also Burden, *Chairs* (New York: Aperture, 1985) and *Presences* (Millerton, N.Y.: Aperture, 1981), which include some of his writing as well as his photographs.

2. See Mott, *Seven Mountains,* pp. 344, 391, 409, 461, 481, 505, 516, 569, 625, n. 285, and 626, n. 330. For more on Griffin, see his *Time to Be Human* (New York: Macmillan, 1977) and Jeff H. Campbell, *John Howard Griffin* (Austin, Tex.: Steck-Vaughn, 1970). For more on the Merton-Griffin relationship, see *The Road to Joy,* ed. Daggy, pp. 131–41, and the following works by Griffin: "In Search of Thomas Merton," in Merton et al., *The Thomas Merton Studies Center* (Santa Barbara: Unicorn Press, 1971), pp. 17–24; *A Hidden Wholeness: The Visual World of Thomas Merton.* with photographs by Merton and Griffin (Boston: Houghton Mifflin, 1970); and Yves R. Simon, *Jacques Maritain: Homage in Words and Pictures* (Albany, N.Y.: Magi Books, 1974), pp. 33–38; *The Hermitage Journals: A Diary Kept While Working on the Biography of Thomas Merton,* ed. Conger

133. Thomas Merton. 'Bangkok Harbor,' printed by John Howard Griffin, 1968.

Beasley, Jr. (Kansas City, Mo.: Andrews and McMeel, 1981), p. 6; and *Follow the Ecstasy: Thomas Merton, The Hermitage Years, 1965–1968* (Fort Worth: JHG Editions/ Latitudes Press, 1983), pp. 3–15. The Merton-Griffin correspondence is at the Merton Studies Center; most of Merton's important letters to Griffin are included in *Road to Joy,* according to its editor, Robert Daggy; Griffin's widow plans to bring out Griffin's unpublished letters.

3. See Mott, *Seven Mountains,* pp. 400 (and 626, n. 330), 409, 481 (and 617–18, n. 29), who notes that one "thorn" pattern photograph appears on the cover of the book of Merton's essays, *Raids on the Unspeakable* (New York: New Directions, 1966). See also Daggy, introduction to Merton, *Day of a Stranger* (Salt Lake City: Gibbs M. Smith, 1981), pp. 10, 21–24; *The Asian Journal of Thomas Merton* [1973], ed. Naomi Burton et al. (New York: New Directions, 1975), which includes many of his photographs as does Deba Prasad Patnaik, ed., *Geography of Holiness: The Photography of Thomas Merton* (New York: Pilgrim Press, 1980); and Merton, *Woods, Shore, Desert: A Notebook, May, 1968* (Santa Fe: Mu-

seum of New Mexico Press, 1987), called to the editor's attention by Robert Kiely; and a work by his longtime writer-photographer friend Edward Rice, *The Man in the Sycamore Tree: The Good Times and Hard Life of Thomas Merton, An Entertainment* (Garden City, N.Y.: Image Books, 1972).

4. See Mott, pp. 476 and 698, n. 25, and 503. See also Meatyard, *Father Louie: Photographs of Thomas Merton* ([New York]: Timken Publishers, [1991]), and Christopher Meatyard, "Merton's 'Zen Camera' and Contemplative Photography," *Kentucky Review* 7, no. 2 (Summer 1987): 122–44. The introduction above contains further references to Meatyard and his and Merton's mutual literary friends—Wendell Berry, Guy Davenport, James Baker Hall, Denise Levertov, and Jonathan Williams, among others—whose relevant works are listed in the bibliography. Mott, *Seven Mountains,* p. 476, mentions other photographers of Merton.

5. See Meatyard, letter to Merton, August 12, 1967, p. 65, and Merton, letter to Meatyard, August 15, 1967, p. 67, in Meatyard, *Father Louie.*

85. *Seamus Heaney*

*P*hotographs have played an important role in the evolution of the sensuous yet precise poetry of Heaney (1939–), acclaimed far beyond his native Ireland. His early poems included "Ancestral Photograph," a meditation on his great-uncle and father which largely drew on his childhood farm experiences.[1] Photographs soon played a more critical role in his maturing work. The archaeologist P. V. Glob used them to illustrate The Bog People (1969), a riveting account of his discovery in a Danish bog of well-preserved Iron Age bodies, perhaps victims of ritual sacrifice; Heaney read it over the Christmas holidays upon publication. "Entranced immediately by the Tollund Man's head" [Fig. 134], he then found that "the unforgettable photographs of those victims blended in my mind with photographs of atrocities, past and present, in the long rites of Irish political and religious struggles"; they inspired both "images and symbols" to unify his vision of his country's contemporary "Troubles."[2] After "The Tollund Man," Heaney was further inspired to write six more "bog" poems (1975), each variously considering the "archetypal pattern" of human violence with anguished compassion and increased pessimism.[3] A subsequent poem, "The Old Team" (1987), also begins with a photograph— of an Edwardian football team—but ends with a reminder of the deadliest human game, war.[4] Most recently, Heaney, who had previously "shied from the combination of speechless image and wordlogged verse," collaborated with the American photographer Rachel Giese (1936–), whose northern Irish landscapes seemed a suitable accompaniment to some favorite lines from his earlier translation of the medieval Irish saga Buile Suibhne (1983).[5]

134. P. V. Glob. 'The Tollund Man, who died 2000 years ago,' c. 1950.

"THE TOLLUND MAN"

I

Someday I will go to Aarhus[6]
To see his peat-brown head,
The mild pods of his eye-lids,
His pointed skin cap.

In the flat country nearby
Where they dug him out,
His last gruel of winter seeds
Caked in his stomach,

Naked except for
The cap, noose and girdle,
I will stand a long time.
Bridegroom to the goddess,

She tightened her torc on him
And opened her fen,
Those dark juices working
Him to a saint's kept body,

Torve of the turfcutters'
Honeycombed workings.
Now his stained face
Reposes at Aarhus.

II

I could risk blasphemy,
Consecrate the cauldron bog
Our holy ground and pray
Him to make germinate

The scattered, ambushed
Flesh of labourers,
Stockinged corpses
Laid out in the farmyards,[7]

Tell-tale skin and teeth
Flecking the sleepers
Of four young brothers, trailed
For miles along the lines.

III

Something of his sad freedom
As he rode the tumbril
Should come to me, driving,
Saying the names

Tollund, Grauballe, Nebelgard,
Watching the pointing hands
Of country people,
Not knowing their tongue.

Out there in Jutland
In the old man-killing parishes
I will feel lost,
Unhappy and at home.

Seamus Heaney

1. Heaney, "Ancestral Photograph" (1966), in *Poems, 1965–75* (New York: Farrar, Straus & Giroux, 1980), p. 16.

2. The quotes are from Heaney, letter to the editor, May 20, 1991, regarding P. V. Glob's *Bog People: Iron-Age Man Preserved* (1969), trans. Rupert Bruce-Mitford (Ithaca: Cornell University Press, 1988), p. 19, and also from Heaney's "Feeling into Words" (1974), in *Preoccupations: Selected Prose 1968–1978* (London: Faber & Faber, 1980), pp. 56–57. Note also Heaney's intriguing comment about Glob's photograph—"The Tollund Man seemed to me like an ancestor almost, one of my old uncles, one of those moustached archaic faces you used to meet all over the Irish countryside"—quoted in James Randall, "An Interview with Seamus Heaney," *Ploughshares* 5, no. 3 (1979): 18; it is also noted and discussed in Neil Corcoran, *Seamus Heaney* (London: Faber & Faber, 1986), p. 77.

3. It is fascinating to compare Heaney's "bog" poems in *Poems, 1965–75*, with the material in Glob's *Bog People*: for examples, see Heaney: "The Grauballe Man," pp. 191–92, cf. Glob, pp. 37–62; Heaney, "Punishment," pp. 192–99, cf. Glob, pp. 112–14; Heaney, "Strange Fruit," p. 194, cf. Glob, pp. 98–100. The poems stand on their own as works of art but mean more when read along with the Glob study. See Hunter, *Image and Word*, pp. 183–95, for more discussion of Heaney's "bog" poems. The enthusiasm of the poet Ted Hughes for these verses led to his sister Olwyn's publishing a limited edition of *Bog Poems* (London: Rainbow Press, 1975) and perhaps heightened his own responsiveness to photographs, discussed in Elizabeth Maslen, "Counterpoint: Collaborations between Ted Hughes and Three Visual Artists," *Word and Image* 2, no. 1 (January–March 1986): 33–44.

4. See Heaney, "The Old Team," *The Haw Lantern* (London: Faber & Faber, 1987), p. 23.

5. See Heaney, Preface to *Sweeney's Flight*, with photographs by Giese [now named Brown] (London: Faber & Faber, 1992), p. vii: "Over the years there had been a number of different proposals to do a book like this one, using my own poems as a supplement or a stimulus for the pictures; yet even though these proposals came from people whose work I knew and admired, I never felt ready to go ahead with the project. My reluctance had to do with an unease about the problematic relation between image and text. . . . I think I felt that in these cases (to be extreme about it) the photograph was absolute and the text a pretext. This was more of a hesitation than a conviction: all I can say is that I tended to foresee misalliance of some sort between the impersonal, instantaneous thereness of the picture on one side of the page, and the personal, time-stretching pleas of the verse on the other." Heaney thought the Sweeney stanzas more anonymous, like nature itself, and he had long wanted to "skim" favorite lines from the saga, presenting them as lyric poems in their own right; after seeing Giese's pictures, he "was immediately emboldened to snip lyric leaves off the old narrative boughs."

6. Heaney did visit Jutland and the museum at Aarhus in October 1973.

7. This stanza refers to the 1798 slaughter of the rebel "Croppies"—so called because of their short hair; the barley corn, left in their pockets, that reportedly germinated on their graves; the 1845 famine victims; and the sectarian slaying of four young brothers in the 1920's, among other atrocities throughout Irish history.

Tournier (1924–), a prize-winning French author, has been involved in photography more extensively than the "new novelists" such as Alain Robbe-Grillet and Marguerite Duras or the critical theorist Roland Barthes, all of whom are far better known to English-speaking readers.[1] Tournier shares his colleagues' fascination with the cultural meanings of signs and images; but he remains less influential, perhaps because of his adaptations of traditional narrative forms, myths, symbolic characters, and layered meanings to dramatize his ideas about contemporary life and its representation in art.[2] For Tournier, photography—especially taking self-portraits [Fig. 135]—has been an absorbing hobby since childhood, when his favorite toy was a Kodak camera. While becoming a writer, after an abortive career as a philosopher, he initiated and hosted a television series, Chambre Noire (1960–65), about notable photographers; and from 1970, with Lucien Clergue, he was instrumental in setting up the first (and still the only) annual international photography festival, held in Arles.[3] Not surprisingly, Tournier often includes photography in his writing, exploring its uses and abuses in twentieth-century culture.[4] He has devoted two collections of essays to the subject: Des Clefs et des serrures *(1979) on selected photographs; and* Le Crépuscule des masques *(1992) on selected photographers. And in two novels,* The Ogre *(1970) and* The Golden Droplet *(1985), as well as the short story* "Veronica's Shrouds" *(1978), the central characters' obsession with the camera, whether as active photographer or passive subject, irrevocably transforms their lives.[5]*

FROM *The Ogre*

May 1, 1939. When I range about the streets in my old Hotchkiss, I'm never quite happy unless the camera case slung around my neck is properly wedged between my legs. I enjoy being equipped with a huge leather-clad sex whose Cyclopean eye opens like lightning when I command it to look, and closes again inexorably on what it has seen. It is a marvelous organ, seer and remembrancer, a tireless hawk that swoops on its prey to steal from it and bring back to its master that which is profoundest in it and most deceptive—appearance! I am intoxicated by the constant availability of this fine compact object, so mysteriously hollow, swinging on its strap like the censer of all the beauties of the earth. The unused film with which it is secretly lined is an immense blind retina, which will see and be dazzled only once, but will never forget.

I've always liked photography, including developing and printing, and as soon as I came to live at the garage I made a darkroom out of a little room with running water from which the light could easily be excluded. Now I realize how providential this hobby was, and how it lends itself to my present preoccupations. For it is plain that photography is a kind of magic to bring about the possession of what is photographed. Anyone who is afraid of having his or her photograph "taken" is only showing the most elementary common sense. It is a method of consumption usually resorted to for want of a better: needless to say, if beautiful landscapes could be eaten they would be photographed much less.

One cannot avoid a comparison with the painter, who works openly, patiently and patently laying down on the canvas, stroke by stroke, his own feelings and personality. The act of photography, on the other hand, is instantaneous and occult, like the wave of a magic wand transforming a pumpkin into a coach, or a maiden who is awake into one who is asleep. The artist is expansive, generous, centrifugal. The photographer is miserly, greedy, avid and centripetal. In other words I am a born photographer. As I don't possess the despotic powers to procure me actual possession of the children I've decided to get hold of, I make use of the snare of photography. And I hasten to add that this is not at all a second best. Whatever the future has in store for me, I shall always love these images, bright and deep as lakes, into which I dive with abandon on certain lonely evenings. In them is life, smiling, plump, on offer, imprisoned in the magic paper, a last survival of slavery, that lost paradise I have not ceased to mourn. Sorcery makes use of the half-amorous, half-murderous possession of the photographed by the photographer. But for me, though I do not reject the power of magic, the object of the act of photography is something greater and higher. It consists in raising the real object to a new power—the *imaginary power*. A photographic image, which is indisputably an emanation of reality, is at the same time consubstantial with my fantasies and on a level with my imaginary universe. Photography promotes reality to the plane of dream; it metamorphoses a real object into its own myth. The lens is the narrow gate through which the elect, those called to become gods and heroes *possessed*, make their secret entry into my inner Pantheon.

That being so, it is clear I don't need to photograph *all* the children in France and in the world in order to satisfy the need for exhaustiveness that is my torment. For each photograph raises its subject to a degree of abstraction that automatically confers on it a certain generality, so that every child photographed is a thousand children possessed.

So on this fine sunny first of May, having breakfasted gaily and briefly, I set out image-hunting, my camera lovingly stowed in its genital position. My eyes were already nothing but view finders, collecting possible pictures from branches, sidewalks, even from inside the cars I passed. The pedestrians of the first of May, the dogs of the first of May, walked with a Sunday gait along streets made peaceful by the holiday. The world filed in procession past my windshield. The world was a window marvelously dressed by an ingenious window dresser

called the First of May. The cops who spend their May Day regulating the traffic made friendly signs at me with their white sticks.

I left the old Hotchkiss by the river near the Pont Alexandre III. Gray gulls, motionless fisherman, deserted yachts, a few clerks washing their cars at the water's edge—perhaps the happiest moment in the week for them. A waterman worked away furiously at the pump of a barge, and at each effort a yellow ejaculation streamed out at the water line. I jumped into a boat and, at the risk of falling in the river, maneuvered into my view finder the yellow jet, the sharp black outline of the hull, and above, against a patch of blue sky, the little chap jumping up and down to bring all his weight to bear on the arm of the pump. On the quay a boy was amusing himself dazzling passers-by with a mirror. I asked him to flash his beam toward the camera and already imagined the photograph that would emerge: a white explosion surmounted by a shaggy head with a great gap-toothed grin.

On the esplanade in front of the Palais de Tokio there were some boys roller-skating and others playing ball. The skaters never stopped skating. The others never skated instead of playing ball. The two groups never mixed; they seemed separated by an almost biological difference. It made one think of ants, some of which are winged and others not.

I particularly noticed two of the skaters, very dark, brothers probably, and alike in dress as well as in face and physique. They differed only in age and height, as faun and faunlet. They swooped about, making swift arabesques, jumping down several steps at once. I asked them to hold hands and skate around under the huge relief that shows Terpsichore and a nymph dancing against an Arcadian background. I took a photograph of the double couple, the little one of flesh and the big one of stone, so unaware of each other yet so well attuned. Then I told the boys Terpsichore was a Greek goddess, one of the Graces, the patroness of roller skaters. After a while everyone's attention was attracted by a young cyclist who had fixed his front wheel to a roller skate. This surprising invention combined a schoolboy's two essential but in theory incompatible attributes. The front wheel of the bicycle didn't go around but slid with a metallic clatter over the flagstones.

After a moment the others resumed what they were doing, chasing each other, vaulting, leaping, dancing thunderous farandoles. One farandole broke up into a leap down several steps. One of the boys tripped, bounced down the rest of the stairs, and ended up at the bottom a poor little motionless heap. I recognized him as the younger of the two brothers, the faunlet. He turned over slowly, sat up, then bent forward over his right knee. He didn't cry, but his face was crumpled up with pain. I knelt beside him and slipped my hand under his knee, into that damp, tender, trembling hollow; a strange sweetness gripped my insides. His wound, caused no doubt by the edge of one of the marble steps, was magnificently clean and sharp: a flawlessly oval ruby slit, a Cyclops' eye with bordered lids and narrow corners, gouged indeed and blind, but scarcely bleeding—just oozing, as if with its own vitreous humor, a slow albuminous trickle of lymph that ran down the calf into the wrinkled sock. A couple of boys undid his skates while I fixed the necessary attachments to my lens and view finder. The casualty now had to stand up and keep standing up for at least a few seconds. I set him on his feet, but he tottered, lime green. "He'll fall," said one of the others. I wasn't going to have that. I slapped him hard and propped him up against the wall. Then I took one shot—but it would come out flat in that direct light. I needed an oblique angle to catch the purple depths of the socket. I twisted the boy around ninety degrees. On to the gouged Cyclops' eye my camera bent its crystal robot's eye. It was a basic confrontation between wounded flesh, reduced to passivity, suffering, open, unable to do anything but be seen, and the pure, possessive, definitive vision of the weapon I was armed with. Kneeling in front of that small statue of suffering, I finished the film in a kind of drunken happiness beyond my control. Then at last came the moment I awaited with jubilation. I let the camera fall on its strap, slipped my right arm under the boy's knees and my left under his armpits, and stood up with my fragile burden.

I stood up, and my shoulders touched the sky, my head was encircled by archangels singing anthems in my praise. Mystic roses poured forth their sweetest perfume. For the second time in a few months I'd lifted a wounded child in my arms and been enfolded in phoric ecstasy. That alone was enough to prove I'd entered upon a new era.

The children around me could not understand the light transverberating my face. I must step back into time, take up the thread of ordinary events again, pretend to be just one more of the great human family. . . .

I went over to my car and put the faunlet in, with the faun beside him to look after him. I dropped them both at a pharmacy in the Place de l'Alma and drove off singing, caressing between my thighs my image box full of new treasures. I knew in advance their beauty would exceed my expectations. [pp. 103–7]

1. See the works by Barthes, Duras, and Robbe-Grillet listed in the bibliography as well as those by other French writer-photographers, Claude Simon and especially Hervé Guilbert. See also Tournier's portrait by Cartier-Bresson in *Photoportraits,* p. 159.

2. See Roger Shattuck, "Locating Michel Tournier," *The Innocent Eye: On Modern Literature and the Arts* (New York: Farrar, Straus & Giroux, 1984), pp. 205–18, called to the editor's attention by Martin Roberts.

3. See Tournier, *Le Crépuscule des masques* (Paris: Editions Hoëbeke, 1992), [p. 9]; and Fulton, "Lucien Clergue," *Lucien Clergue,* p. 26.

4. See David Bevan, "Tournier's Photographer: A Modern Bluebeard?" *Modern Language Studies* 15, no. 3 (Summer 1985): 66–71; and Emily Apter, "Fore-skin and After-Image: Photographic Fetishism in Tournier's Fiction," *L'Esprit Créateur* 29, no. 1 (Spring 1989): 72–82.

5. See Tournier, *The Ogre,* trans. Barbara Bray (New York: Doubleday, 1972), in addition to pp. 103–7 (the selection above), pp. 9–10, 85–86, 92–93, 100, 108–9, 112, 114, 123–24, and 236; "Veronica's Shrouds" in *The Fetishist,* trans. Barbara Wright (London: Collins, 1983), pp. 94–108—and note that another story from this collection, "Amandine, or The Two Gardens," is subtitled

"An Initiatory Story for Olivia Clergue" [the daughter of Lucien Clergue], p. 29; and *The Golden Droplet,* trans. Barbara Wright (New York: Doubleday, 1987), pp. 4–8, 13–14, 22, 45–46, 49, 71–75, 81–83, 85, 88, 103–4, 112, 118, 133–34, 148, 153–58, and especially 159–68. The scene cited last, as Martin Roberts pointed out in a conversation with the editor on August 27, 1992, and in his discussion in "Mutations of the Spectacle: Vitrines, Arcades, Mannequins," *French Cultural Studies* 2 (1991): 211–49, especially pp. 236–45, is a thinly disguised portrait of the photographer Bernard Faucon (1950–). Faucon's fascination with mannequins is evident in *Les Papiers qui volent,* ed. and trans. Yasuo Koboki (Tokyo: Parco, 1986); it is shared by colleagues such as Clergue (see some from a 1956 series in *Lucien Clergue,* Plates 12–16 [1956]), and Guibert (see series in *Vice: Photographies de l'auteur* [Paris: J. Bertoin, 1991], between pp. 40 and 41).

87. Howard Nemerov

You know, I'm going to be remembered for being Howard Nemerov's sister," the talented photographer Diane Arbus (1923–72) asserted shortly before her death; "how ironic and untrue," commented the differently talented poet (1920–91).[1] Nemerov, whose clear but subtle verse often probed contradictory human nature, had remained close to his intuitive, radical sister. She specialized, he noted with obvious distaste, in portraits of "subjects perverse and queer (freaks, professional transvestites, strong men, tattooed men, the children of the very rich)."[2] But Nemerov "never much cared for photographs" of any kind, especially ones of faces that appeared to be "singularly vulnerable."[3] Indeed, the poet allied the camera with science, memory, and material objects, as opposed to his cherished art, imagination, and human relationships; and he objected to the way it stressed seeing "at the expense" of insight, reducing all observed experience to a "flat" statement.[4] Moreover, influenced by psychoanalytic concepts, Nemerov equated writing with harmless "innocence" and photography with painful "guilt" because of its elements of voyeurism, intrusiveness, and exposure.[5] Given these associations, it is not surprising that Nemerov did not appreciate the work of Arbus or even her less confrontational colleagues. Yet his sister's pictures, he conceded, were "spectacular, shocking, dramatic," and he clearly admired her courage in trying to "run" along the edge, in her art and in her life [Fig. 136].[6]

"To D——, Dead by Her Own Hand"

My dear, I wonder if before the end
You ever thought about a children's game—
I'm sure you must have played it too—in which
You ran along a narrow garden wall
Pretending it to be a mountain ledge
So steep a snowy darkness fell away
On either side to deeps invisible;
And when you felt your balance being lost
You jumped because you feared to fall, and thought
For only an instant: That was when I died.

That was a life ago. And now you've gone,
Who would no longer play the grown-ups' game
Where, balanced on the ledge above the dark,
You go on running and you don't look down,
Nor ever jump because you fear to fall.

1. Quoted in Bosworth, *Diane Arbus*, p. 371, and see the charming photograph of the siblings as children between pp. 210 and 211.

2. See Nemerov, *The Journal of the Fictive Life* (New Brunswick, N.J.: Rutgers University Press, 1965), p. 80. But see also Arbus, "Auguries of Innocence," *Harper's Bazaar* (December 1963): 76–79, for her delicate photographs of children, accompanied by excerpts from William Blake and Lewis Carroll.

3. See Nemerov, *Journal,* p. 80.

4. *Ibid.,* p. 81.

5. *Ibid.,* p. 147; and see pp. 82, 118, and 147–49 for his other observations on photography quoted here. See also his two 1947 poems, "An Old Photograph" and "The Photograph of a Girl," in *The Image and the Law* in *The Collected Poems of Howard Nemerov* (Chicago: University of Chicago Press, 1977), pp. 42–44.

6. The life and work of Arbus was an acknowledged inspiration of a play, "Silence, Cunning Exile," by Stuart Greenman, performed by the American Repertory Theatre in Cambridge, Massachusetts, in the spring of 1993.

88. *Rollie McKenna, Marion Morehouse, Inge Morath, Jill Krementz, and Elsa Dorfman*

LITERARY PORTRAITS WITH TEXTS, 1953–73

*I*n 1866, Alexandre Dumas père *asserted that women made better portrait photographers than men.*[1] *More than a century later, many of the outstanding portraits of literary figures have been taken by women, though gender is their only shared attribute. Most have close personal as well as professional ties to significant writers, some of them photographed once for a particular purpose, others at intervals over many years. Their images helped shape the reputation of their subjects as well as their own and provide a unique cultural archive.*

In 1950, Rollie McKenna (1918–) met John Malcolm Brinnin, then the director of the YMHA Poetry Center in New York, and began taking portraits of poets who gave readings there; prominent among them was Dylan Thomas [Fig. 137], with whose family she became friends.[2] *She was the natural choice to take the photographs of those included in Brinnin's and Bill Read's anthology of modern British and American poets (1963), many of whom have kept in touch with McKenna since; their portraits form part of her "Double Takes" collection of literary figures.*[3]

Marion Morehouse (1906–69) was Edward Steichen's favorite model—before her common-law marriage (1934) to E. E. Cummings (1894–1962), a noted poet and one of Stieglitz's admirers—and one of his devoted photography students afterwards (1949).[4] *Morehouse and Cummings collaborated on* Adventures in Value *(1962), a volume of her photographs containing mainly still lifes and nature subjects, each accompanied by his words.*[5] *The book's sole literary portrait was of Marianne Moore [Fig. 138], an appropriate choice as a family friend, an early member of the Stieglitz circle, and a poet often inspired by photographs.*[6] *At the time of her death, Morehouse was planning a book of portraits of her husband and their friends.*[7]

Inge Morath (1923–) worked with many writers before and after her marriage to the playwright Arthur Miller (with whose Helga, a character in After the Fall *(1964), she is often identified).*[8] *Her photographs inspired, or accompanied, Miller's texts for their collaborations on* Russia *(1969),* China *(1979), and their own rural Connecticut (1977) as well as his preface to her collection of portraits (1986), which included many of writers, largely taken in the 1950's and 1960's [Fig. 139].*[9] *Morath's most recent work,* Russian Journal *(1991), includes some informal portraits of literary friends there—*

Rollie McKenna, Marion Morehouse, Inge Morath, Jill Krementz, and Elsa Dorfman some taken during earlier visits—as well as sites associated with Tolstoy, Chekhov, Pushkin, and Dostoevsky.[10]

Jill Krementz (1940–), a photojournalist who admires writers, perceived that providing portraits for their articles, book jackets, and publicity materials was a neglected area. By the time she married Kurt Vonnegut, a decade after the publication of his finest novel, Slaughterhouse-Five (1969), Krementz had taken more than a thousand literary portraits in brief sittings, using unobtrusive equipment in the writer's chosen setting [Fig. 140], and selected some for publication in a book for which Vonnegut wrote the preface (1980).[11] Krementz's work helped set a new standard for authors' jacket portraits, now taken as seriously as other facets of book production; indeed; their new self-consciousness is one of the targets of David Lodge's satire in The Writing Game (1991).[12]

Elsa Dorfman (1937–), once an aspiring writer, worked after college at Grove Press, where she met Charles Olson, Robert Creeley, Robert Duncan, Allen Ginsberg, and their friends. She arranged the first college poetry readings of the 1960's for them, first as part of her job, later through the Paterson Society she formed on returning to Boston. They became friends and willing subjects when Dorfman took up photography in 1965—supporting herself with writing and editing jobs—and recur throughout Elsa's Housebook: A Woman's Photojournal (1974) [Fig. 141].[13] She collaborated on books with Creeley (1973) and Olson (1980) and, since 1980, has taken annual pictures of Ginsberg for his posters and press releases; they resemble more serious versions of his own informal photographic portraits, with similar handwritten captions.[14] Now operating one of the four existing Polaroid 20 x 24 cameras in her thriving portrait studio, she has twice exhibited with Ginsberg and continues to write engagingly about her experience of photography.[15]

137. Rollie McKenna. Dylan Thomas, directing rehearsal of his new play, "Under Milk Wood," May 10, 1953.

Dylan Thomas's career didn't truly take off until he "hit" the United States. Readings at the Poetry Center and tours throughout the country where—in his own words—he "boomed and fiddled while home was burning," all but devoured him. The money he made, so necessary to support his family, passed through his fingers like water. The praise, so addictive, was fleeting. Still, he wanted to read again to his vastly appreciative American audiences and, above all, to write the final ending to his play for voices, *Under Milk Wood*.

Frenetic reading tours, sycophant-laden parties and late-night bar-hopping exhausted him, and just an hour before rehearsing the actors for the first New York performance of *Under Milk Wood*, Dylan was in particularly bad shape.

On arriving at the Poetry Center, he vomited, declared that he could not possibly go on and collapsed in the green room. After half an hour, he was shaken awake. Pulling himself together, he directed for an astonishing three hours, urging the actors over and over: "Love the words. Love the words!" I was so dumbfounded by his recovery that I almost forgot to shoot.

When the night of May 14, 1953, arrived, the theater was packed. The audience, silent at first, then tittering, finally exploded into laughter on realizing that this was no highbrow affair but a loving, ribald tribute to a village. Dylan took fifteen curtain calls as tears slipped down his face. [from McKenna, *My Life in Photos*, p. 132]

138. Marion Morehouse.
'Marianne Moore,'
c. 1950's.

M   in a vicious world—to love virtue
A   in a craven world—to have courage
R   in a treacherous world—to prove loyal
I   in a wavering world—to stand firm.

A   in a cruel world—to show mercy
N   in a biased world—to act justly
N   in a shameless world—to live nobly
E   in a hateful world—to forgive

M   in a venal world—to be honest
O   in a heartless world—to be human
O   in a killing world—to create
R   in a sick world—to be whole

E   in an epoch of UNself—to be ONEself

[E. E. Cummings]

139. Inge Morath. 'Jean Cocteau,' 1968.

Jean Cocteau was staying in the villa Santo Sospiro in St. Jean Cap Ferrat, the house of his lifelong friend Madam Weissweiler. Our photographic rendezvous was for the evening. It was nearly dark when we got to the house. (The writer Dominique Aubier had come with me to work on a text.) Jean Cocteau emerged as we were halfway down the path; in his hand were some of those big roses that look best when they are almost faded. He plucked the peals and scattered them casually in our way as we approached the entrance door. He was very slender and agile, his long hands fluttering as he showed us around the living room whose white walls were completely covered with his drawings. "I tattooed the house," he said.

There was a large tapestry woven from Cocteau's design on the wall behind the dining room table, and first editions of Cocteau-designed ceramics decorated the mantelpiece. It amused him to point out the drawings and objects as he darted in and out of discrete islands of light, his hands only occasionally coming to rest on his tie. Finally he sat down and half stretched out on the leather upholstered fender around the fireplace, without interrupting his talk which now centered on various aspects of the literary scene of the day. He had the chiseled features of a gothic saint, which were, when he spoke, surprisingly mobile. To look at him was fascinating, like staring into the eyes of something dangerous: Don't make the wrong move or darts from these eyes will condemn you with the impatience of a great intellect. [from Morath, *Portraits*, pp. 92–93]

Eudora Welty is one of my favorite writers. She lives in Jackson, Mississippi, in the same house in which she was born. When I told her I'd like to come and take some pictures she invited me to spend the night. That is how I happened to take the picture of her writing at her desk with her still unmade bed in the foreground. [from Krementz, "Jill Krementz," *Something about the Author Series* (1990), vol. 8, p. 173]

140. Jill Krementz. 'Eudora Welty,' Jackson, Mississippi, 1972.

Allen Ginsberg. April 11, 1973.

141. Elsa Dorfman. 'Allen Ginsberg,' April 11, 1973.

Allen Ginsberg is a person dear to me in reality and important as an idea. About once a week, I'm in a situation that makes me ask myself, 'What would Allen have done?' The most recent time this happened, I was having supper with Francis Russell at his house, when a neighbor, who is a Pentecostal Episcopalian and believer in healing, dropped by. Her name was Harriet and she had just come from a three-hour trip to a hospital visiting and praying with a thirty-five-year-old woman dying of cancer. She herself was about forty-two and ninety pounds overweight.

She was very upset by her brief afternoon with the dying woman and kept on assuring herself that God had heard them. . . . Then, to make light of her religious activities, she added with a laugh that she was a forty-year-old Jesus freak. . . .

In my head I heard Allen. He wouldn't be afraid he'd catch Harriet's depression. Or be embarrassed by the rawness of her unhappiness. He wouldn't let her dismiss herself. Somehow, he'd lead her out of that notion toward some self-respect. Perhaps by saying he was a sort of Jesus freak himself—he'd just spent three months meditating ten hours a day and was building a temple with his own hands. Could she top that? [from *Elsa's Housebook*, pp. 16–17]

Rollie McKenna, Marion Morehouse, Inge Morath, Jill Krementz, and Elsa Dorfman

1. See "Alexander Dumas on Photography," *Photographic News* (1866): 379 and 380, reprinted in the Dumas selection above.

2. See McKenna, *Portrait of Dylan: A Photographer's Memoir* (London: Dent, 1982), and *A Life in Photography* (New York: Knopf, 1991), pp. 125–36.

3. See Brinnin and Read, eds., *The Modern Poets: An American-British Anthology* (New York: McGraw-Hill, 1963, 1970), and McKenna, *A Life*, p. 220; pp. 212, 213, 222, and 239 for other photographs of old and new literary friends, and pp. 243–67 for poets McKenna has photographed periodically over the past four decades, such as Auden, Berryman, Graves, Lowell, Merwin, Merrill, and Sexton, who are among those included in her collection entitled "Double Takes," at the Yale University Art Museum. McKenna, *Life*, pp. 140–41, had far better luck photographing the poet Elizabeth Bishop than did some of her other colleagues, like Morehouse, as described in n. 7 below.

4. See Steichen, *A Life in Photography*, npn, and figs. 104 and 107 of his favorite model. Steichen taught Morehouse to use a camera, and doubtless his contacts, together with those of her notable husband and their many artist friends, helped secure some of her initial assignments for *Harper's Bazaar, Life,* and the publishers Harcourt, Brace, all noted in her engagement books at the Houghton [bMS AM 1892 (95–133) 11/*67M-150A]. No detailed information was available for Cummings's relationship with the elderly Stieglitz beyond his inclusion in his larger circle, but note the several references to photography in his *Complete Poems, 1910–1962,* ed. George James Firmage (London: Granada, 1981), vol. 1: pp. 235, 260, 272, and 378; and vol. 2: pp. 499 and 647.

5. See *Adventures in Value* (New York: Harcourt, Brace & World, 1962); and see also Richard S. Kennedy, *Dreams in the Mirror* (New York: Liveright, 1980), pp. 429, 433, 435, and 449.

6. See the Moore selection above for details about her acquaintance with Stieglitz and her use of photographs in her poetry.

7. As the obituary in the *New York Times* (May 19, 1969): 47, reports, Morehouse's pictures were given to a photographer friend, Maryette Charlton; some of her portraits of Ezra Pound are included in the Cummings collection at the Houghton [bMS AM 1892.11 (92) [1–24]; Box 139, no. 1]. See also a letter from Elizabeth Bishop to "Mrs. Cummings," May 8, 1950, at the Houghton [bMS AM 1823.2. (24)/*67M-150], about a prospective portrait, saying she is "wonderfully unphotogenic & camera-shy" but she "can't think of anyone I'd rather have do it"; McKenna, *A Life,* p. 140, reports that Bishop had torn up Morehouse's portrait of her (and the one by Joseph Breitenbach), though the recurrence of her name throughout Morehouse's engagement books at the Houghton suggests that the friendship was not impaired. The names of Dylan Thomas and Octavio Paz and other eminent writers also appear in these engagement books, though whether for photographic or purely social meetings is unclear.

8. See Miller, *After the Fall* (New York: Viking, 1964), and relevant background in Miller, *Timebends: A Life* (New York: Grove, 1987), pp. 493–99. Among other collaborations, Morath contributed photographs—some in color—to Mary McCarthy, *Venice Observed* (New York: Reynal, [1956]); Edouard Sablier, *From Persia to Iran: An Historical Journey* (New York: Viking, 1960); Claude Roy and Paul Sebag, *Tunisie: De Carthage à Demain* (Paris: Delpire, [1961]); Dominique Aubier, *Guerre à La Tristesse [Festival in Pamplona]* (Paris: Delpire, 1955); and Boris Pasternak, *My Sister, Life, and Other Poems,* ed. Olga Andreyev Carlisle (New York: Harcourt Brace Jovanovich, 1976). See also Carlisle, *Grosse Photographen unserer Zeit: Inge Morath* (Lucerne and Frankfurt: Bucher Verlag, 1975), and "Instantaneous Forever," an essay on Morath's work, in Morath, *Russian Journal* (New York: Aperture, 1991), pp. 119–21.

9. The circumstances of their collaborations were briefly described by Morath in a letter to the editor, November 16, 1991. See Morath and Miller: *In Russia* (New York: Viking/Studio, 1969), which was banned in the USSR together with Miller's plays; *In the Country* (New York: Viking/Studio, [1977]); *Chinese Encounters* (New York: Farrar, Straus & Giroux, 1979); and *Portraits* (New York: Aperture, 1986), which includes ones of Miller (1963), p. 31; Mary McCarthy (1956), p. 33; Anaïs Nin (1959), p. 9; Cocteau (1958), p. 13; William Styron (1967), p. 18; Philip Roth (1965), p. 19; Paz (1959), p. 56, and Olga Carlisle (1972), p. 75. Morath also photographed the production of Miller's play, *The Ride Down Mount Morgan* (1991) and took a portrait of him with Louise Bourgeois, the illustrator of his *Homely Girl, A Life* (New York: Peter Blum, 1992), vol. 1. (Vol. 2 features color photographs from ophthalmological studies of pairs of eyes.) Miller has been much photographed by others as well, including Cartier-Bresson, *Photoportraits*, p. 153, Avedon, *Observations*, p. 41 (1958), and Krementz, *The Writer's Image* (1969), np.

10. See in Morath, *Russian Journal*: Yevtushenko, pp. 10, 55, 109; Brodsky, pp. 30 and 109; other writers, pp. 110–15; Tolstoy's Yasnaya Polyana (1965), pp. 96–97; Dostoevsky's flat (1967), pp. 94–95; Pushkin sites (1967), pp. 98–99; and Chekhov's Yalta house (1989), p. 103. See also 'Mark Twain's House' in Morath and Miller, *In the Country,* npn.

11. See Krementz, *The Writer's Image,* with a preface by Vonnegut, pp. vii–x, and an introduction by Trudy Butner Krisher, pp. xi–xvi. See also Vonnegut, "The People One Knows," in *Palm Sunday: An Autobiographical Collage* (New York: Delacorte, 1981), pp. 122–26, which provides a lengthy list of Krementz's mostly well-known subjects; Vonnegut, *Conversations with Kurt Vonnegut,* ed. William Rodney Allen (Jackson: University Press of Mississippi, [1988]), pp. 212 and 250–51; Krementz, "Jill Krementz," *Something about the Author Autobiography Series* (New York: Gale, 1989), vol. 8, pp. 165–83; and Krementz, comp. and ed., *Happy Birthday Kurt Vonnegut: A Festschrift for Kurt Vonnegut on His 60th Birthday* (New York: Delacorte, 1982). See also one of Jerzy

Kosinski's portraits of Krementz in Dorothy Gelatt, "Jill Krementz: Unofficial Photographer-Laureate for the Contemporary Literary Scene," *35–MM Photography* (Spring 1975): 30, 33, and 89.

12. See Lodge, *The Writing Game: A Comedy* (London: Secker & Warburg, 1991), Act 2, scene 2, p. 80. Krementz now specializes in photographing children.

13. See Dorfman, *Elsa's Housebook: A Woman's Photojournal* (Boston: Godine, 1974), pp. 10–21, 36–38, 41, and 46–48. Ginsberg comments on this work in the text reprinted in his selection below.

14. See Dorfman's photographs in Creeley, *His Idea* (Toronto: Coach House Press, March 2, 1973); her photographs and text in "Three Afternoons with Charles Olson," MS, 1980; and in her charming memoir "Allen, My Camera and Me" in *Best Minds: A Tribute to Allen Ginsberg,* ed. Bill Morgan and Bob Rosenthal (New York: Lospecchio Press, 1986), pp. 88–91. For more on Olson and Creeley, see the Williams selection below.

15. Dorfman and Ginsberg exhibited their photographs together at the Vision Gallery in Boston (1988) and at the Courtland Jessup Gallery in Provincetown (1991, 1992). In addition to the other pieces cited above, see Dorfman, "Names, Dates, Places," *Field of Vision,* no. 13 (Spring 1985): 20–24, and her insightful introduction to *Here We Are, Here We Are*—a forthcoming collection of her portraits taken with the giant Polaroid camera since 1987—which the editor read in TS.

89. Rosellen Brown

"GOOD HOUSEKEEPING: A (VERY) SHORT STORY," 1973

The self-destructive titular character of Colette's "Photographer's Missus" (1944) might have become a photographer in her own right in the 1970's, especially in a number of feminist stories like this powerful one by Rosellen Brown (1939–).[1] The updated heroine, now an artist as well as wife and mother, remains frustrated by domestic routines, but her work provides a responsible escape through its imaginative and practical demands. Brown here, as often in her fiction, pays "terrible homage" to these inevitable moments of parental frustration and professional interruption, based on "the autobiography of her thoughts" if not of her life.[2] She also deftly suggests the defensive, aggressive, obsessive, and sensual qualities of picture takers, also present in the photographer heroines of Cynthia Ozick, Anne Tyler, Sue Miller, and Ann Beattie, as well as in the postwar male photographers portrayed by Italo Calvino and Julio Cortázar.[3] In 1987, Brown collaborated with George Krause, creating brief but compelling narratives to accompany some of his photographs of Italian tombstones in Qui Riposa (1962–), his haunting cemetery series.[4]

"Good Housekeeping"

She put the lens of the camera up so close to the baby's rear that she suddenly thought, what if he craps on the damn thing? But she got the shot, diapered him again, lowered the shade and closed the door. Turned the coffee pot so a wan light barely struck off the half shine under the accumulated sludge on its side. Held it over the toilet bowl tilted so the camera wouldn't reflect in the ring of water. In the laundry mountain looking out. Carrots, parsnips, onions—then she stopped, put the camera down, shaved them all, and flung them into the long pile of their own curled skins. That was beautiful, the fingers of vegetable, the fat translucent globes of the onions like polished stones, absolute geometric definition picked out of the random garbage heap, focus on the foreground.

She was working fast, the way the idea had come to her, before the tide of possibility receded. She laid the camera in the rumpled bedclothes so that the sheets formed great warm humps and valleys, the plaid of the blanket coasting off out of sight on one side. There was a faint impression where one of them had lain— it was more or less on his side—like grass that hasn't risen after someone's nap in the sun. Like photographing a ghost. She pulled her underpants off, sat on the bed, put her legs up the way she did in the doctor's stirrups, laid the camera on the bed—well, she couldn't see into the damn viewfinder but it seemed to be aimed— ah, it was the shutter that came, that sound of passionless satisfaction, its cool little click sucking in the core of her, reaming out the dark with its damp sweat like the seeds of some melon. So long it had been her face, she might as well have its puckered features in good light, for posterity. Some faces gape more meanly, anyway. This was so very objective, it would transcend only fact. She found an unused box of condoms lying half covered by socks. She opened the box, arranged a few randomly, only their rolled edges peeking out, surely recognizable. Then, like a teenager nosing in her parents' drawers, she put them neatly back again and buried the box where she had found it.

And the dirty window, its shadowy design as regular as a litho. The soil in the pots waiting for the seedlings to show, that made a lovely stipple where they had been watered, light on a grainy dark, pearly vermiculite on peat. There was something so neat and purposeful about the shelf of pots. Magnified the soil reminded her of little girls she'd known who wore white blouses with Peter Pan collars and sat with a certain obedient stillness no matter what raged around them; for years and years sat that way. Her pepper seedlings, her tomatoes, under there, primly incubating in the still, protected dark.

The food didn't work, neither the lined-up cans nor the omelet she made just for the occasion, heaping it up into ridges—too much like *Good Housekeeping*. Oh, yes, the drawer in the kitchen table that held a little of everything— keys, bills, warrantees on all things electric, seed catalogues, a display so wanton she smiled. Cigarette papers—the grass to go with them was in her spice bottles marked fenugreek (though it looked more like basil or tarragon, finely ground. Wait till some visitor in her kitchen tried to cook with it. . . .). Straight into the bore of the pencil sharpener, a terrifying snout at 10X. Wallpaper they couldn't hide: symmetrical and graceless, cabbage roses with stars between. The welcome mat, its disordered grass lying all tamped down, caked perfectly with half-moons of mud, as though a horse had wiped his feet.

There was a little pile of feathers she had found in the bathroom—the cat had killed another bird and, proud, left this gift of fine, unmutilated evidence. They were mottled on one side, a combed gray on the other, their barbs unevenly separated as though by movement. No, that wouldn't be understood; some objects implied their function, or at the least, how they got where they were, but the feathers needed the cat and even then . . . are murdered birds a part of every household?

She was thinking of the way the show would be hung. Utterly random, on flat matte. No implicit order, no heavy ironies. In spite of the fact that the chemicals in her darkroom had probably spoiled by now from disuse multiplied by time, no bitterness. In fact there was such beauty in these banalities up close that she felt humbled. Like a lecture from her husband the evidence piled up, orderly, inside the shutter, that she was wrong again. That she was right and wrong. She walked on the balls of her feet, spying into all her likely and unlikely corners, elated.

When the baby woke, screaming and swallowing down huge hunks of air and screaming again, she took the camera coolly into the little hall room, seeing herself from a great distance, doing an assignment on herself doing an assignment. She pulled the shade all the way to the tip and then knelt in front of the crib bars. So much light you could see the baby's uvula quivering like an icicle about to drop. . . . When the baby saw the camera he closed his mouth

and reached out, eyes wide. Eyes like cameras. His mother looked back at herself in them, a black box in her lap with a queer star of light in its middle.

"No!" She stood up, stamping. "No, goddammit. What are you *doing?*"

The baby smiled hopefully and reached through the slats.

She put her head in her hands. Then she reached in and, focusing as well as she could with one hand, the baby slapping at her through the bars, wheezing with laughter, she found one cool bare thigh, the rosy tightness of it, and pinched it with three fingers, kept pinching hard, till she got that angry uvula again, and a good bit of very wet tongue. Through the magnifier it was spiny as some plant, some sponge, maybe, under the sea.

1. See Colette, "The Photographer's Missus" (1944), in *The Tender Shoot and Other Stories,* trans. Antonia White (New York: Farrar, Straus & Cudahy, 1959), pp. 368–404. See also Brown, "A Fragment of Autobiography," *Contemporary Authors Autobiography Series,* Volume 10 (Detroit: Gale Research, [1989]), pp. 29–43. Brown has also used photography in a memorable scene in *The Autobiography of My Mother* (New York: Doubleday, 1976), pp. 183–84.

2. The first quote is from a conversation with the editor, June 28, 1991; the second is from Judith Thurman, "Rosellen Brown," *MS* 13, no. 7 (January 1985): 114.

3. See Tyler, *Earthly Possessions* (New York: Knopf, 1977), esp. pp. 10, 27–30, 56–57, 62–63; Ozick, "Shots," in *Levitation: Five Fictions* (New York: Knopf, 1982), pp. 39–57; Beattie, *Picturing Will* (New York: Random House, 1989); Miller, *Family Pictures* (New York: Harper & Row, 1990); Calvino, "Adventures of a Photographer" (1955) in *Difficult Loves,* trans. William Weaver

et al. (San Diego: Harcourt Brace Jovanovich, 1984), pp. 220–35; and Cortázar, "Blow Up" (1963) in *Blow Up and Other Stories,* trans. Paul Blackburn (New York: Pantheon, 1985), pp. 114–31. See also Constance Pierce, "Calvino on Photography," *Review of Contemporary Fiction* 6, no. 2 (Summer 1986): 130–37, and Leonard A. Cheever and Leslie M. Thompson, "Meaning and Truth in Cortazar's 'Blow-Up,'" *Re: Artes Liberales* 12, no. 1 (Fall 1985): 1–17.

4. Brown, an admirer of Krause's work, was delighted to be paired with him for a show of photographers and writers, entitled "One on One," in which image and text hung side by side. A little booklet of their collaboration, *Qui Riposa: Alternate Lives* (Houston: Philip Burton for George Krause, 1987), was published as part of the exhibition, curated by Donald Barthelme and Janet Landay for the Glassell School of Art, Museum of Fine Arts of Houston. For a comprehensive retrospective of Krause's photography, see Anne W. Tucker and George Krause, *George Krause* (Houston: Rice University Press, 1991).

*T*he photographs of Michals (1932–), obviously indebted to Surrealism and Zen Buddhism, have become increasingly literary. "I consider myself to be a novelist or short story writer," he asserts, comparing his efforts to combine images and sentences to "trying to write War and Peace with a haiku form."[1] From the 1960's on, breaking a tacit photographic taboo from the days of Victorian fictional tableaux, Michals began making implicit narrative explicit: using allusive titles for individual prints, sequences, books, and exhibitions, such as the recent "Poetry and Tales"; often adding handwritten captions and texts in prose or verse—usually free but sometimes rhymed and metrical; and sometimes producing unaccompanied prose. Needing words to "talk" about the invisible, more real to him than the visible, Michals composes his photographs to reflect his thoughts about identity, eroticism, religion, and death. He carefully maps out his stories in his head before shooting; he typically uses natural lighting, his apartment as setting, and friends (and occasionally himself) as models—often nude to enhance his abstract as well as erotic concepts. Sometimes he blurs or superimposes images to suggest the supernatural. Michals's work often reflects the influence of avid reading, such as William Blake's illustrated verse ("my Bible"); Walt Whitman's self-revelations; Lewis Carroll's manipulations of scale and time, as in the sequence here [Fig. 142 (1–9)]; Constantine Cavafy's regretful celebrations of youth; as well as the Old and New Testaments, fairy tales, and myths.[2] Michals's expansion of the narrative potential of photographs with texts (which, like many of his colleagues, the photographer prefers in intimate books rather than in galleries) has been widely influential.[3]

142 (1–9). Duane Michals. *Things Are Queer*, 1975.

3

6

9

1. Quoted in Marco Livingstone, "Certain Words Must Be Said" and "A Meeting with Duane Michals," in *Duane Michals: Photographs/Sequences/Texts 1958–1984* (Oxford: Museum of Modern Art, 1984); and see also Thomas Dugan, "Duane Michals," *Photography Between Covers: Interviews with Photo-Bookmakers* (Rochester, N.Y.: Light Impressions, [1979]), pp. 131–48, and Michals, *Now Becoming Then* (Altadena, Calif.: Twin Palms Press, 1990), especially "A Story About a Story" (1989), npn. Michals, in a conversation with the editor, August 20, 1991, says he now writes more than ever before.

2. On Blake, see Michals, "Real Dreams," in *Real Dreams: Photo Stories* (Danbury, N.H.: Addison House, [1976]), pp. 9–10; and other remarks such as "Wherever you are, William Blake, I love you," quoted in Dugan, p. 113. On Whitman, see Michals's dedication to him in *Nature of Desire* (Pasadena, Calif.: Twelvetrees Press, 1986), npn; "A Testimony of Walt's Death," reproduced in Michals, *Now Becoming Then,* npn; and Michals, "The Room Where Walt Whitman Died, March 26, 1892," which uses the same poem as in the preceding work but a different photograph in an exhibition entitled "Poetry and Tales" at the Sidney Janis Gallery, New York City, October 3–November 2, 1991. On Cavafy, see Michals, *Homage to Cavafy* [Ten Poems by Cavafy, Ten Photographs by Michals] ([Danbury, N.H.]: Addison House, [1978]); "An Imaginary Letter Written by Constantine Cavafy to a Young Friend," in *Nature of Desire,* npn; and see also Cavafy, "The Photograph" (1913), in *Collected Poems,* trans. Edmund Keeley and Philip Sherrard, ed. George Savidis (Princeton, N.J.: Princeton University Press, 1989), p. 367.

Other examples of apparent literary influence on Michals's photographs include the following, all widely reproduced in the books by or about him cited in the bibliography: Carroll in the sequences, *Things Are Queer* (1973) and *Take One and See Mt. Fujiyama* (1975); the Bible in "The Birth of Eve" and *Paradise Regained* (1968), "The Apparitions: Adam and Eve" (1971) and "The Return of the Prodigal Son" (1982); fairy tales in *Things Are Queer* (1973); and myth in "Narcissus" (1974) and the "Old Man Kills the Minotaur" (1976). Most of these influences are also mentioned by Max Kozloff's essay in Michals, *Now Becoming Then,* npn, which has a particularly interesting discussion of *Things Are Queer.*

3. See also Michals's interesting literary portraits, usually done on commercial assignment, of 'The Wonderful Christopher Isherwood in the Taft Hotel,' 'Marguerite Duras on a New York Bus,' and 'Tennessee Williams,' all reproduced (and undated) in *Album: The Portraits of Duane Michals, 1958–1988* ([Pasadena, Calif.]: Twelvetrees Press, [1988]), npn.

91. *Octavio Paz*

"FACING TIME" (FOR MANUEL ALVAREZ BRAVO), 1976

*P*az (1914–), whose evocative poems and lucid essays made him Mexico's leading literary figure, was seventeen when he first saw three photographs by Manuel Alvarez Bravo (1902–), who became the country's leading photographer. The scenes revealed the photographer's ability to use one artistic image to suggest others not shown, as did his captions, which created a "net of visual, mental and even tactile relations reminiscent of the lines of a poem united by rhyme."[1] This rich complexity also impressed Tina Modotti when she met Alvarez Bravo (1927). She suggested that Edward Weston see his portfolio (1929) and left him both her camera and her job when she was expelled from Mexico (1930).[2] Though his work often reflected cosmopolitan influences, like French Surrealism and American realism, Alvarez Bravo focused on native subjects—both pre-Columbian and contemporary Mexican [Fig. 143].[3] Meanwhile Paz, somewhat like his former mentor, Pablo Neruda, led a cosmopolitan life as a diplomat, while exploring Latin American visual symbols in his poetry. Inevitably the two artists met and collaborated on a volume of poems and photographs (1982); "each verbal or visual image contains another implicit, latent image," asserted Paz, showing how well he had learned the photographer's lesson a half century earlier.[4]

484

Octavio Paz

Octavio Paz

"Facing Time" (for manuel alvarez bravo)

Photos:
      time dangling from a verbal thread:
Black mountain / white cloud,
           Girl Selling birds.
Manuel's titles
      are not coincidences:
they are verbal arrows,
        flaming signs.
They eye thinks,
      thought sees,
glances touch,
      words burn:
Two pairs of legs [Fig. 147],

Octavio Paz

                    Scale of scales,
A sparrow, of course!,
                              House of lava.
Instantaneous
            and methodical:
lens of revelations.
From eye to image to language
(there and back)
                    Manuel photographs
(names)
        that imperceptible line
between the image and its name,
sensation and perception:
                              time.

The arrow of the eye
                    dead center
in the target of the moment.
                              Four targets,
four variations on a white cloth:
identical and different,
four faces of the same moment.
The four directions of space:
the eye is the center.
                    Point of view
is the point of convergence.

The face of reality,
                    the face of every day,
is never the same face.
                    Blood eclipse:
the face of the murdered worker,
planet fallen on the pavement.
Hiding their faces
                    behind the sheets of their smiles
The laundresses between the lines,
great clouds hanging from the roofs.
Quiet please!
            Portrait of the eternal,
in a dark room
                    a cluster of sparks
on a downpour of black
                              (the silver comb
electrifies the black straight hair).

Time never stops flowing,
                     time
never stops creating,
                     time never stops
erasing its creations,
                     the spring
of visions never stops.
                     The mouths of the river
speak clouds,
                     human mouths
speak rivers.
                     Reality always has another face,
the face of every day,
                     the one we never see,
the other face of time.

Manuel:
          lend me your wooden horse
to go off to the other side of this side.
Reality is more real in black and white.

1. See Paz, "The Instant and the Revelation," in Paz and Alvarez Bravo, *Instante y Relación,* npn; and Nissan N. Perez, "Visions of the Imaginary, Dreams of the Intangible: The Photographs of Manuel Alvarez Bravo," in *Revelaciones: The Art of Manuel Alvarez Bravo,* pp. 31–34. An addition to 'Two Pairs of Legs,' reproduced here, the catalogue reproduces two other photographs mentioned in the poem: 'The Laundresses Between the Lines,' p. 15, and 'Portrait of the Eternal,' p. 45 (the editor was not able to locate reproductions of the others). The catalogue does not reproduce the 1978 portrait of Paz shown in the exhibition.

2. Inspired by Modotti's example, Alvarez Bravo's wife, after their divorce (1935), also became an outstanding photographer in Mexico. She is especially noted for her portraits, such as the one of Paz reproduced in *Fotografias de Lola Alvarez Bravo* (Mexico City: Fondo de Cultura Economica, 1982), npn, discussed by Amy Conger in *Compañeras de México: Women Photograph Women* (University of California, Riverside: University Art Gallery, 1990), p. 14. See also Morath's portrait of Paz, 1959, in *Portraits,* p. 56.

3. See the Breton selection above for his association with and influence on Alvarez Bravo in the 1930's.

4. Quoted in Paz, "The Instant and the Revelation," npn. See also Sye Vice, "Dreams—Visions—Metaphor: The Images of Manual Alvarez Bravo and Malcolm Lowry," *Malcolm Lowry Review* 15 (Fall 1984): 19–24.

92. *Michael Ondaatje*

FROM *Coming Through Slaughter*, 1976

*P*hotography is important in the life and work of Ondaatje (1943–),
an award-winning writer who was born in Sri Lanka and educated in England before settling in Canada. Though his eclectic style
and exotic subject matter owe little to Canadian traditions, his interest in
the camera—as an occasional photographer and filmmaker—is widely shared
by many contemporary writers there.[1] Ondaatje's fascination with photography's role in the conflicts between artistic permanence and the chaos of
experience, as well as the constructive and destructive aspects of creativity,
is evident in much of his fiction as well as in many of his poems.[2] Coming
Through Slaughter (1976), a fictional biography of a legendary New Orleans
jazz figure, uses the few known facts about a contemporary photographer,
E. J. Bellocq (1873–1949), to create a memorable character; Bellocq's portraits of Storyville prostitutes, discovered after his death—some with their
faces scratched out—were later acquired and reprinted by the photographer
Lee Friedlander [Fig. 144].[3] Running in the Family (1982) is a fictional
memoir in which the photographs become visual testaments to memory
and family continuity.[4] In The Collected Works of Billy the Kid (1981), a
collage of various verse and prose genres, the versatile Ondaatje uses photographs—some historical, some taken by himself—both structurally and meta-
phorically throughout.[5] For his private amusement, Ondaatje enjoys taking
pictures of dogs and people in the midst of activities like getting haircuts or
playing chess [Fig. 145].[6]

FROM *Coming Through Slaughter*

Note: Ondaatje does not present in chronological order his blend of a few historical facts and much fiction about two early twentieth-century New Orleans artists, a musician and a photographer, who probably never knew one another. These excerpts begin with Webb, a detective, hunting for a photograph of Buddy Bolden, a pioneer jazz cornetist, whose playing was never recorded. The detective learns that a picture of Buddy with his band has been taken by E. J. Bellocq, a hydrocephalic semi-dwarf who regularly works as a photographer for a shipbuilding company but in his off hours takes pictures of Chinatown and especially of prostitutes; some of the latter prints bear the photographer's knife slashes. Buddy tries to facilitate Bellocq's picture-taking of prostitutes, partly from compassion, partly because he so admires the results. Buddy's woman, Nora, however, is unmoved when informed by Webb that Bellocq has died in a self-set fire, as she blames the photographer for reinforcing Buddy's own self-destructive impulses, not understanding they are part of his creativity.

I need a picture.
Thought you knew him.
I need it to show around.
Still—*shit* man who has pictures taken.
Bolden did, he mentioned one. Perhaps with the band.
You'll have to ask them. Ask Cornish.

But Cornish didn't have one though he said a picture had been taken, by a crip that Buddy knew who photographed whores. Bellock or something.

Bellocq.

He went down to the station and looked in the files for Bellocq's place. They knew Bellocq. He was often picked up as a suspect. Whenever a whore was chopped they brought him in and questioned him, when had he last seen her? But Bellocq never said anything and they always let him go. [p. 50]

The photographs of Bellocq. HYDROCE-PHALIC. 89 glass plates survive. Look at the pictures. Imagine the misshapen man who moved round the room, his grace as he swivelled round his tripod, the casual shot of the dresser that holds the photograph of the whore's baby that she gave away, the plaster Christ on the wall. Compare Christ's hands holding the metal spikes to the badly sewn appendix scar of the thirty year old naked woman he photographed when she returned to the room—unaware that he had already photographed her baby and her dresser and her crucifix and her rug. She now

offering grotesque poses for an extra dollar and Bellocq grim and quiet saying No, just stand there against the wall there that one, no keep the petticoat on this time. One snap to quickly catch her scorning him and then waiting, waiting for minutes so she would become self-conscious towards him and the camera and her status, embarrassed at just her naked arms and neck and remembers for the first time in a long while the roads she imagined she could take as a child. And he photographed that.

What you see in his pictures is her mind jumping that far back to when she would dare to imagine the future, parading with love or money on a beautiful anonymous cloth arm. Remembering all that as she is photographed by the cripple who is hardly taller than his camera stand. Then he paid her, packed, and she had lost her grace. The picture is just a figure against a wall.

Some of the pictures have knife slashes across the bodies. Along the ribs. Some of them neatly decapitate the head of the naked body with scratches. These exist alongside the genuine scars mentioned before, the appendix scar and others non-surgical. They reflect each other, the eye moves back and forth. The cuts add a three-dimensional quality to each work. Not just physically, though you can almost see the depth of the knife slashes, but also because you think of Bellocq wanting to enter the photographs, to leave his trace on the bodies. When this happened, being too much of a gentleman to make them pose holding or sucking his cock,

144. E. J. Bellocq. Plate 20 from *Storyville Portraits*, c. 1912, printed by Lee Friedlander.

the camera on a timer, when this happened he had to romance them later with a knife. You can see that the care he took defiling the beauty he had forced in them was as precise and clean as his good hands which at night had developed the negatives, floating the sheets in the correct acids and watching the faces and breasts and pubic triangles and sofas emerge. The making and destroying coming from the same source, same lust, same surgery his brain was capable of.

Snap. Lady with dog. Lady on sofa half naked. Snap. Naked Lady. Lady next to dresser. Lady at window. Snap. Lady on balcony sunlight. Holding up her arm for the shade. [pp. 54–55]

The next day Webb knew more about Bellocq. The man worked with a team of photographers for the Foundation Company—a shipbuilding firm. Each of them worked alone and they photographed sections of boats, hulls that had been damaged and so on. Job work. Photographs to help ship designers. Bellocq, with the money he made, kept a room, ate, bought equipment, and paid whores to let him photograph them. What had Bolden seen in all this? He would have had to take time and care. Bellocq seemed paralysed by suspicions. He had let Buddy so *close.*

Webb walked around Bellocq for several days. Bellocq with his stoop, and his clothy hump, bent over the sprawled legs of his tripod. Not even bent over but an extension or he didn't have to bend at all, being 4 foot 11 inches. Bellocq with hair at the back of his head down to his shoulders, the hair at the front cut in a fringe so no wisps would spoil his vision. Bellocq sleeping on trains as he went from town to town to photograph ships, the plates wrapped carefully and riding in his large coat pockets. Something about the man who carries his profession with him always, like a wife, the way Bolden carried his mouthpiece even in exile. This is the way Bellocq moved. E. J. Bellocq in his worn, crumpled suits, but uncrumpled behind the knees.

In the no-smoker carriages his face through the glass, the superimposed picture, windows of passing houses across his mouth and eyes. Looking at the close face Webb understood the head shape, the blood vessels, the quiver to the side of the lip. Face machinery. HYDROCE-PHALIC. His blood and water circulation which was of such a pattern that he knew he would be dead before forty and which made the bending of his knees difficult. To avoid the usual splay or arced walk which was the natural movement for people with this problem, he walked straight and forward. That is he went high on the toe, say of his right leg, which allowed the whole left leg enough space to move forward directly under his body like a pendulum, and so travel past the right leg. Then with the other foot. This also helped Bellocq with his height. However, he did not walk that much. He never shot landscapes, mostly portraits. Webb discovered the minds of certain people through their bodies. Or through the perceptions that distinguished them. This was the stage that

Bellocq's circulation and walk had reached. [pp. 56–57]

There is only one photograph that exists today of Bolden and the band.

As a photograph it is not good or precise, partly because the print was found after the fire. The picture, waterlogged by climbing hoses, stayed in the possession of Willy Cornish for several years.

*

The fire begins with Bellocq positioning his chairs all the way round the room. 17 chairs. Some of which he has borrowed. The chairs being placed this way the room, 20' by 20', looks like it has a balcony running all the way around it. Then he takes the taper, lights it, stands on a chair, and sets fire to the wallpaper half way up to the ceiling, walks along the path of chairs to continue the flame until he has made a full circle of the room. With great difficulty he steps down and comes back to the centre of the room. The noise is great. Planks cracking beneath the wallpaper in this heat as he stands there silent, as still as possible, trying to formally breathe in the remaining oxygen. And then breathing in the smoke. He is covered, surrounded by whiteness, it looks as if a cloud has stuffed itself into the room.

Horror of noise. And then the break when he cannot breathe calm and he vomits out smoke and throws himself against the red furniture, against the chairs on fire and he crashes finally into the wall, only there is no wall any more only a fire curtain and he disappears into and through it as if diving through a wave and emerging red on the other side. In an incredible angle. He has expected the wall to be there and his body has prepared itself and his mind has prepared itself so his shape is constricted against an imaginary force looking as if he has come up against an invisible structure in the air.

Then he falls, dissolving out of his pose. Everything has gone wrong. The wall is not there to catch or hide him. Nothing is here to clasp him into a certainty.

But Bellocq had been there photographing the opium dens, each scene packed with bunks that had been removed from sleeping compartments of abandoned trains, his pictures full of grey light which must have been the yellow shining off the lacquered woodwork. Cocoons of yellow silence and outside the streets which were intricate and convoluted as veins in a hand. Two squares between Basin and Rampart and between Tulane and Canal through which Bellocq had moved, never lost, and taken his photographs. [pp. 65–67]

He left Bellocq outside resting on the top steps carefully removing the camera off its sling. Listen I've got this friend who wants photographs of the girls. Same price as a fuck you know that Buddy. Ok, but I want to tell you about him first. Willya call the others in I don't want to say this more than once. He wasn't sure how to explain it. He wasn't even sure himself what Bellocq wanted to do. Listen this guy's a ship photographer—a burst of laughter—and just for himself, nothing commercial, he wants to get pictures of the girls. I don't know how he wants you to be for the picture, he just wants them. Nothing commercial ok. He's not weird or anything is he? No, he's a little bent in the body, something wrong with his legs. No one wanted to. Please, look I promised him, listen I even said no price this time, it's a favour, see he did a few things for me. You gonna be around Charlie? No I can't he doesn't want me to. Two of them left the room saying they were going back to sleep. Listen he's got a good job, he really does photograph ships and things, stuff for brochures. He's very good, he's not a cop, the idea coming into his mind that second as a possible fear of theirs. He's a kind man. Nobody wanted Bellocq and more went away. I'll give you a free knock anytime Charlie but not this. They went then and Nora shrugged sorry across the room. It's morning Charlie, they were all up late last night at Anderson's. All I could do was get them here. And they were watching the two of you arrive. He looked like something squashed or run over by a horse from up here.

Listen Nora you have to do this for me. Let him take some pictures of you. Just this once to show the others it's ok, I promise you it'll be ok. She had moved into the kitchenette and was looking for a match to light the gas. He came over, dug one out of his picket and lit the row of hissing till they popped up blue, something invisible finding a form. He let her fill the kettle and put it on. Then he put himself against her back and leaned his face into her shoulder. His nose against the shoulder strap of her dress. Come out with me into the hall and meet him. Give him some of this tea. He's a harmless man. He put his head up a bit and watched the blue flame gripping the kettle. He was exhausted. He couldn't hustle for others, he didn't know the needs of others. He was fond of them and wanted them happy and was willing to make them happy and was willing to hear their problems but no more. He didn't know how people like Bellocq thought. He didn't know how to put the pieces of him together. He was too shy to ask Bellocq *why* he wanted these pictures or what kind they would be. Three floors up on North Basin Street he was nuzzling this lady. That's all he knew. His mind went blank against the flesh next to him.

What's he got on you? Nothing. He separated himself from her, picked up a knife and tapped against the small window of the kitchen, looking out. It was cold out, there was steam over the river. He had tried to get Bellocq to wear a coat when he had picked him up, but they had gone on, Bellocq cold and so trying to walk fast. He placed his palm against the glass and left the surface of his nerve pattern there. Rubbed it out. Turning he walked past her quickly through the door into the hall. As he was opening the door she said ok very fast. He turned and saw her leaning in the kitchen doorway with a cup in her hand. Then he opened the door to the stairs.

And then running down the stairs fast, almost crying, down two flights before he saw the figure in the main hall standing against the wallpaper looking up at him—the face pale and embarrassed. He must have heard them laughing in there, must have sat there for ten minutes and taken more than five minutes to walk down.

Yes or no, whatever it is, I'm not walking those stairs again.

I'll carry you up then. So decide. Shouting as he ran down.

Bugger you fuck, you shit those voices carry you know.

I know. But it's ok. Nora will do it. He stood on the first stair looking at Bellocq, at Bellocq's sweating face. It's alright, she said she's gonna do it ok? She'll pose.

I heard them Buddy I *heard* them.

They didn't understand man, it's ok now come on. Come on.

Then he lifted the thin body of his friend and carried him up the three flights of stairs. Going slowly for he did not want to damage the camera or hurt the thin bones in the light body he was carrying. Still, he was tired and shaking and exhausted when he put him down on the top step.

She didn't speak to him about Bellocq. Not till this last night. He asked her about Bellocq and she told him what Webb had said, that Bellocq was dead. Died in a fire. This was about an hour after she found him sleeping in his red shirt with the children. . . .

. . . You didn't feel sorry for him?

I hated him Buddy.

But *why*? he was so harmless. He was just a lonely man. You know he even talked to his photographs he was that lonely. Why do you hate him? You never even saw his pictures, they were beautiful. . . . [pp. 124–27]

1. See, for example, York, *"The Other Side of Dailiness": Photography in the Works of Alice Munro, Timothy Findlay, Michael Ondaatje, and Margaret Laurence,* and "'Violent Stillness': Photography and Postmodernism in Canadian Fiction," *Mosaic* 21 (1988): 193–201; and Deborah Bowen, "Borderline Magic: Janette Turner Hospital and Transfiguration by Photography," *Studies in Canadian Literature* 16, no. 2 (1991): 182–96.

2. See the following poems by Ondaatje which involve photography: "Tink, Summer Rider" and "Four Eyes" in *The Dainty Monster* (Toronto: Coach House Press, 1967), pp. 40 and 46; "Burning Hills," "King Kong Meets Wallace Stevens," and "The Gate in His Head," in *Rat Jelly* (Toronto: Coach House, 1973), pp. 56–57 and 61–62; and "Light" and "Uswetakeiyawa" in *There's a Trick With a Knife I'm Learning to Do* (Toronto: McClelland & Stewart, 1979), pp. 105–7.

3. See *E. J. Bellocq: Storyville Portraits: Photographs from the New Orleans Red-Light District, Circa 1912,* ed. John Szarkowski (New York: MOMA, 1970), which Ondaatje drew on for his imagined characterization. It is interesting to compare Ondaatje's use of Bellocq with Richard Powers's use of the German photographer August Sander in *Three Farmers on Their Way to a Dance* (New York: William Morrow, 1985) and Anne Rice's use

of the daguerreotypist Jules Lion in *The Feast of All Saints* (New York: Simon & Schuster, 1979), called to the editor's attention by Kellye Rosenheim.

4. It is also interesting to compare Ondaatje's use of family photographs in *Running in the Family* (Toronto: New Press, 1982), pp. 161–63, with Maxine Hong Kingston's in *The Woman Warrior* (New York: Knopf, 1976) and *China Men* (New York: Knopf, 1980). Kingston's work from this perspective is discussed by Carol E. Neubauer in "Developing Ties to the Past: Photography and Other Sources of Information in Maxine Hong Kingston's *China Men*," *Melus* 10 (Winter 1983): 17–36, and by Timothy Dow Adams in "Photography and Autobiography in Maxine Hong Kingston's *The Woman Warrior and China Men*," *MS*, 1989, called to the editor's attention by Richard Wendorf. See also Ignatieff's essay "Family Photo Albums," in *The Russian Album*, pp. 2–7.

5. See *The Collected Works of Billy the Kid: Left-Handed Poems* (Toronto: Anansi, 1970), in which the final photograph shows the author as a child, dressed as a cowboy; and see also T. D. MacLulich, "Ondaatje's Mechanical Boy: Portrait of the Artist as Photographer," *Mosaic* 14, no. 2 (Spring 1981): 107–19.

6. According to Ondaatje, in reply to a query from the editor in a letter of September 23, 1992.

145. Michael Ondaatje. 'Final Match of the World Chess Championship,' 1990.

Chatwin (1940–89) is one of the legends of his generation. He acted out others' dreams of exploring unspoiled places far from urban civilization—in Patagonia, Wales, Australia—and wrote about them in chiseled prose within an episodic structure, often resembling composed pictures. Indeed, Chatwin always took a camera on these expeditions. His photographs illustrate some editions of his first book, In Patagonia *(1977), an account of his travels to the southern tip of South America; they add interest and credibility to the adventures he relates, whether about his grandmother's cousin Charley, Butch Cassidy and the Sundance Kid, or anonymous natives.[1] Chatwin's subsequent books were not illustrated, but fictional pictures and photographers appear throughout as salient details of setting, character, and narrative. Memorable examples include the taking of the annual family photograph of Da Silva's descendants in* The Viceroy of Ouidah *(1980); the magic lantern slide show used by recruiters during the Great War in* On the Black Hill *(1983); the sepia portraits in the immigrant guide's album in* The Songlines *(1987); and the intrusive state photographer in* Utz *(1989).[2] Given Chatwin's practical, aesthetic, and psychological understanding of the uses of photographs, as well as his appreciation of the esoteric, Robert Mapplethorpe was astute in inviting his former subject [Fig. 146], and subsequent friend, to write a preface to his three-year photographic study of the champion body-builder Lisa Lyon [Fig. 158].[3] Chatwin did not live to see the publication of his essay collection,* What Am I Doing Here *(1989), whose layout he designed, with two of his color photographs on the front and back of the jacket.[4]*

FROM *In Patagonia*

Around 1900 law and order settled in on the last American frontier. The lawmen bought their own fine bloodstock, solved the problem of outpacing the outlaws, and organized crime hid in the cities. Posses flushed out Brown's Hole; the Pinkertons put mounted rangers in box cars, and Butch [Cassidy] saw his friends die in saloon brawls, picked off by hired gunmen, or disappear behind bars. Some of the gang signed on in the U.S. Armed forces and exported their talents to Cuba and the Philippines. But for him the choices were a stiff sentence—or Argentina.

Word was out among the cowboys that the land of the gaucho offered the lawless freedom of Wyoming in the 1870s. The artist-cowboy Will Rogers wrote: "They wanted North American, riders for foremen over the natives. The natives was too slow." Butch believed he was safe from extradition there, and his last tow hold-ups were to raise funds for the journey. After the Winnemucca raid, the five ringleaders, in a mood of high spirits, had their group portrait taken in Fort Worth and sent a copy to the manager. (The photo is still in the office.) [pp. 46–47]

The Salesian fathers in Punta Arenas had a bigger museum than the one at Río Grande. The prize exhibit was a glass showcase containing the photo of a young, intolerant-looking Italian priest, the cured skin of a sea-otter and an account of how the two came together:

On the September 9th 1889 three Alakalufs of the *canales* came to Father Pistone and offered him the otter skin, now conserved in the museum. While the Father examined it, one Indian swung a machete and dealt him a terrible blow on the left maxilla. The other two immediately set on him. The Father struggled with these examples of *Homo Silvestris* but his wound was grave. After some days in agony, he died. The killers had lived in the Mission for seven months, well-loved and cared for by the Salesians as adopted sons. But atavism, ambition and jealousy drove them to crime. Once they had done the deed, they fled. Some time after they returned, and, in contact with Our Religion, they became civilized and were good Christians. [p. 143]

Life-sized painted plaster effigies of the Indians stood in mahogany showcases. The sculptor had given them ape-like features which contrasted with the glucose serenity of the Madonna from the Mission Chapel on Dawson Island. The saddest exhibit was two copy-book exercises and photos of the bright-looking boys who wrote them:

THE SAVIOUR WAS IN THIS PLACE AND I DID
NOT KNOW IT
IN THE SWEAT OF THY BROW SHALT THOU
EAT BREAD.

So, the Salesians had noticed the significance of Genesis 3:19. The Golden Age ended when men stopped hunting, settled in houses and began the daily grind. [p. 144]

As the journalists were debunking de Rougemont, Charley [Chatwin's grandmother's cousin] sailed back to Punta Arenas. The wildness was not yet burned out in him.

The course of his second career is clouded by time and distance. I have had to reconstruct it from faded sepia photographs, purple carbons, a few relics and memories in the very old. The first impressions are of an energetic pioneer, confident in his new handlebar moustache; hunting elephant seals in South Georgia;

salvaging for Lloyd's; helping a German gold-panner dynamite the Mylodon Cave; or striding round the foundry with his German partner, Herr Lion, inspecting the water turbines or the lathes they imported from Dortmund and Göppingen. Lion was a methodical man, who ran the place while Charley chatted up clients. Panama was not yet cut through and the business was good.

The second set of images are of the British Empire's southern-most Consul, a senior citizen of Punta Arenas and director of its bank. He was making money all right (but never quite enough), stiffening with lumbago and "wearying for news" of home. Old members of the British Club still remember him. And I sat in the tall rooms, painted an under-sea green and hung with sporting prints and lithographs of Edward VII. Listening to the chink of whisky glasses and billiard balls, I could picture him on one of the buttoned wash-leather sofas, stretching out his bad leg and talking of the sea.

Among his letters from these years I found one to my grandfather hoping the *Titanic* disaster hadn't put him off yachting; a note to the Hon. Walter Rothschild about a shipment of Darwin's Rheas; and a report, on consular notepaper, to the employer of a dead Scot: "He has been a disgrace to the name of Britisher ever since he came here . . . He used his basin as a W.C. His room was an insult to any animal and his box contained fifteen empty whisky bottles. I am sorry but the truth is best."

A mood of despair gradually creeps into these letters. None of his schemes ever quite turned out as planned. He drilled for oil in Tierra del Fuego, but the drill broke. The land at Valle Huemeules promised big returns, but there were ship-thieves, pumas, squatters and an unscrupulous land-shark: "We are having the devil of a hitch with our land in the Argentine. The government has given it away to a Jew who has kindly sworn that all my sheep and buildings are his." Rather than lose all, he asked the Brauns and Menéndezes for help and they soon whittled his share down to 15 percent.

In 1913 he brought his son out, fresh from school in England, as part of his scheme for toughening him up. Harry Milward stuck out

147. Bruce Chatwin. 'Charley's House in Punta Arenas,' c. 1975 (unpublished). Printed from original negative by Michael Nedzweski, 1992.

one long snowbound winter at Valle Huemeules, loathed the farm, the farm-manager, and at this point his father. Not surprising with letters that ended: "Now goodbye, my lad, and don't forget that God, although you are so very far from any means of grace, still he is just as near you there as here. Your ever loving father ..." The rest of Harry's career was predictable. He went to the war, joined a fast set, married three times and ended up in England, the secretary of a golf club.

In Charley's album I found photos of the new house under construction, a Victorian parsonage translated to the Strait of Magellan [Fig. 147]. He gave half the plot for St. James's Anglican Church and was its warden and principal benefactor. Proudly he unpacked the font given by Queen Alexandra. Proudly he welcomed the Bishop of the Falklands for the con-

secration. But the church was yet another source of trouble. He accused the vicar of choosing obscure hymns so as to show off his own voice solo. The congregation, he insisted, had a right to *"Abide with Me"* or *"Oft in Danger, Oft in Woe."* The Rev. Cater whispered round that Captain Milward was a secret drinker.

The war caught him off his guard, in a Buenos Aires hospital, having an intestinal operation. But the war was soon upon him. Admiral Craddock's visiting card, still pinned to the green baize board in the British Club, is a reminder that the southernmost Consul was the last civilian to see him alive. Charley dined aboard the *Good Hope* two hours before the British fleet sailed for its disastrous encounter with the Germans off Coronel. In a memorandum he records the Admiral's gallant but weary acceptance of Churchill's orders: "I am gong to look for von

Spee and if I find him, my number is hoisted."

Charley hated the war: "So many people cutting each others' throats and not knowing why." He wasn't going to stoop to war hysteria. Nor would he break with his German partner. "Lion is not one of the war-party," he wrote, "but a dear, good, honest white man." The British community hated him for this and put it round that the Consul was politically unreliable. An anonymous letter appeared in the *Buenos Aires Herald,* referring to "the British Consulate, as its consul is pleased to call it."

Another relic of the war years is a gold watch presented for loyal services by the British Admiralty. After Admiral Sturdee sank von Spee's squadron off the Falklands, the cruiser *Dresden* got away and hid at the western end of the Beagle Channel, camouflaged by trees and provisioned by Germans from Punta Arenas. (British residents noticed the dwindling number of dogs in the town and joked about the doggy flavour of the German crew's sausages.) Charley found out where she was and cabled London. But, instead of acting on his advice, the Navy did the exact opposite.

The reason was simple: the "true Britishers" had convinced the Admiralty that the Consul was a German agent and managed to get him sacked. Only when they realized their mistake did Charley get an apology. The watch was to compensate for the calumnies heaped upon him. It took a long time coming. "I'll be in my grave," he wrote, "before I hear anything about that watch."

The third exhibit from this time is a coloured print by Cecil Aldin, of dogs at a feeding bowl. It conjures up the image of Sir Ernest Shackleton, pacing round Charley's living-room, haranguing the newspaper editor, Mr. Charles Riesco, about the plight of his men trapped on Elephant Island. From the article in the *Magellan Times*—"the deep set grey eyes" "greatness equated by modesty" "the best of our race" etc.—you would never guess what happened:

Charley was pretending to doze off in a wing chair while the explorer waved his revolver about to emphasize important points. The first bullet whizzed past Charley's ear and hit the wall. He got up, disarmed his guest and put the weapon on the mantelpiece. Shackleton was quite shaken, apologized and mumbled about the last bullet in the chamber. Charley sat down again, but Shackleton's flow was inseparable from his gun. The second bullet missed again, but hit the print. The hole is in the lower right margin.

Meanwhile the ex-consul's life had taken a new direction. He had met a young Scotswoman called Isabel, who had got stranded, penniless, in Punta Arenas, after working on an estancia in Santa Cruz. Charley looked after her and paid her fare back to Scotland. He was lonely again once she had gone. They wrote to each other: one of his letters contained a proposal.

Belle came back and they started a family. In 1919 Charley calculated his assets at £30,000, enough to retire on and provide for all his children. He sold the Fundición Milward to a Frenchman, M. Lescornez, and his partner Señor Cortéz, agreeing they should defer payments until business recovered from the post-war slump. The family packed, sailed for England, and bought a country house, "The Elms," near Paignton.

Charley the Sailor home from sea. Charley the Pioneer with the restlessness gone; pottering round his garden; taking prizes at the Taunton Flower Show; growing old with his young wife in the English countryside; teaching the boy or playing with his two daughters, one showing signs of beauty, the other of his forthright personality—I am sad to report that this harmonious and symmetrical picture was not to be.

Panama was now cut through. Punta Arenas was again on the way to nowhere. Wool slumped. There was revolution in Santa Cruz. And the foundry failed.

Encouraged by two or more of the "true Britishers." acting out of spite, the new owners milked the business, ran up debts, signed cheques in the Milward name, and ran.

Charley was ruined.

He kissed the children. He kissed Belle. He said goodbye for ever to the green fields of England. He bought a ticket to Punta Arenas, one way, third class. Friends in the first-class saw him gazing sorrowfully at the sea. They offered to pay the difference, but he had his pride. No deck games for him this voyage. He preferred to bunk with shepherds.

Belle sold "The Elms" and followed, and for six years they picked up the pieces. Photos show a stooping old man in a homburg with huge whiskers and wounded eyes. He would hobble down to the foundry and growl at the men and laugh when they laughed. Belle kept the books; she would carry on for nearly forty years. Without her thrift they would have gone under, and, one by one, they paid off the debts.

I have one last image of Charley, dated around 1928, sitting in the tower with his telescope, straining to catch the last of the steamer that carried the boy to school in England. As she headed up eastward and was swallowed into the night, he said: "I'll never see the lad again." [pp. 170–174]

He was going to die. His eyelids were swollen and so heavy he had to strain to stop them falling and covering his eyes. His nose was thin as a beak and his breath came in thick fetid bursts. His coughs retched through the corridors. The other men moved off when they heard him coming.

He took from his wallet a crumpled photograph of himself, on leave from military service, long ago, in a palm-filled garden in Valparaíso. The boy in the photo was unrecognizable in the man: the cocky smile, the wasp-waisted jacket and Oxford bags, and the sleek black hair shining in the sun.

He had worked twenty years on the estancia and now he was going to die. He remembered Mr. Sandars, the manager, who died and was buried at sea. He did not like Sandars. He was a hard man, a despotic man, but the place had gone down since. It was bad under the Marxists and it was worse under the Junta. He spluttered between coughs.

"The workers," he said, "have had to pay for this Marxist Movement, but I do not think it will last."

I left him to die and went down to Punta Arenas to catch the ship. [p. 195]

1. Chatwin's photographs appear in the first English edition of *In Patagonia* (London: Cape, [1977]) and in a later reprint (London: Picador, 1979) as well as in some translations (Japanese, German, and Israeli), but not the first American edition (New York: Summit Books, 1977) —commented on in the introduction and n. 52 above. See other Chatwin photographs in Peter Levi, *The Light Garden of the Angel King: Journeys in Afghanistan* (London: Collins, 1972), in the forthcoming Insight Guide, *Sagamatha Revisited* (Singapore: APA Publications), and in *Far Journeys*, ed. David King and Francis Wyndham (London: Cape; New York: Viking Penguin, 1993), announced in Ben Brantley, "Portfolio by Bruce Chatwin: 'The Nomadic Eye,'" *New Yorker* (July 5, 1993): 70–73, which reproduces five color examples.

2. See Chatwin, *Viceroy of Ouidah* (New York: Summit, 1980), pp. 10–12, and see 1 and 17; *On the Black Hill* (Harmondsworth, England: Penguin, 1984), pp. 12–13, 248, and 91–92, and see 88, 108, 133, and 241; *The Songlines* (New York: Viking, 1987), pp. 37–38, and see 51 and 87; *Utz* [1988] (New York: Viking, 1989), pp. 56–58, and see 26, 40, 122. See also Chatwin and Paul Theroux, *Return to Patagonia* (Boston: Houghton Mifflin, 1986), pp. 28–29.

3. Mapplethorpe took two portraits of Chatwin in 1979—the serious one here, also reproduced in *Certain People: A Book of Photographs* (Pasadena, Calif.: Twelve-trees Press, 1985), p. 79, and in Mapplethorpe, *Mapplethorpe*, ed. and des. Mark Holborn and Dimitri Levas (New York: Random House, 1992), p. 77, and an unpublished smiling one, now in the possession of Elizabeth Chatwin, which the Mapplethorpe Estate denied permission to reproduce here on the grounds that the photographer must have preferred the one he published. Jane Bown's sober portrait is reproduced in *Portraits* (London: Chatto & Windus, [1987]) on the jacket and p. 39, and Lord Snowdon's of him in hiking gear is reproduced in *Sittings: 1979–1983* (London: Weidenfeld & Nicolson, [1983]), p. 77.

The background information about Chatwin's preface, "An Eye and Some Body," for *Lady Lisa Lyon* (New York: Viking/Studio, 1983), pp. 9–14, was supplied to the editor in conversations with Elizabeth Chatwin on June 12, 1991, and with Lisa Lyon Lilly and Mapplethorpe's agent, Carol Leslie, on June 25 and 26, 1991. For more on Mapplethorpe in general and *Lady Lisa Lyon* in particular, see the Howard selection below.

4. See Chatwin, *What Am I Doing Here* (London: Cape, 1989), especially pp. 9, 28, and 36. The American Edition (New York: Viking, 1989) used only Chatwin's cover photograph, turning it around and changing the colors, Elizabeth Chatwin noted in a letter to the editor, January 24, 1992.

*M*arie Cosindas was one of the first photographers to use Polaroid color film as her principal medium. She organizes each of
her painterly photographs—especially of people—with infinite
attention to detail of dress and setting. Her old-fashioned equipment and
approach obviously appealed to Tom Wolfe (1931–) [Fig. 148], one of the
keenest observers of our culture. An artist who is prouder of his drawing
than of his writing, he shares Cosindas's sensitivity to clothes and interiors.[1] Wolfe also admired her courage in using not only color film, traditionally regarded as less aesthetically serious than black and white, but
instant color film, then regarded by many as downright unprofessional.
Moreover, the photographer's meticulous work refused to pay homage to
what Wolfe calls "His Eminence, Art Theory," with the then dominant
gods "Technical Distortion" and "Mindless Candor"; and it represented
the opposite of the commercialism and pretentiousness of life, especially in
the art world, which he has consistently satirized with his distinctive hyper-
bole. Wolfe has also provided prefaces to collections of the work of Annie
Leibovitz and her Rolling Stone colleagues, whose antic outrageousness is
also grounded in painstaking preparation, and Cosindas has taken distinctive photographs of other literary figures.[2]

The Black Hood

I first met Marie Cosindas one day in 1967 when she came by my apartment to have me pose for a portrait. She was from Boston. To be from Boston in the year 1967 was like being from the planet Uranus. I had never laid eyes on her or spoken to her, but somehow it had been arranged that I was going to pose for a picture in a series she was doing on dandies. Ah, well ... in 1967, I'm afraid, I used to sit still to be photographed for any purpose whatsoever ... so long as it did not involve removing my collar button ... or my vest ... or wearing a funny hat or in any other way appearing informal, casual, relaxed, affable, or fun-loving ...

My doorbell rang, I opened the door, and here was Miss Marie Cosindas. Marie Cosindas was not much over five feet tall. She had wavy brown hair and a voice that soaked up her words like absorbent cotton. She was carrying a duffel bag. She had no light stanchions, no silver lamé umbrellas. She moved very quietly.

The year was 1967, as I say, and this was not the way famous photographers traveled about New York. Photographers had become terribly fashionable, and they went around attended by slender young native bearers known as photographer's assistants. They were natives of the Electric Circus and Max's Kansas City. The photographers had reached that base camp in the ascent of Parnassus known as *glamor*. They all seemed to be thyrotic ectomorphs of the sort portrayed in the Antonioni movie *Blow-Up*. As a matter of fact, the very night before my visit from Marie Cosindas I happened to be in a discotheque when a man known as 1967's Photographer of the Century (there were several each year) arrived to capture the *Zeitgeist* with his camera. First his four photographer's assistants, terribly thin young men whose hair hung down over their collarbones, arranged themselves on either side of the dance floor with silver lamé reflector lamps opened up over their heads. They looked like the corps de ballet for an underfinanced but desperately with-it musi-

cal comedy. Then 1967's Photographer of the Century made his entrance at a dead run, carrying a stroboscopic 35mm camera. He bolted into the tubercular-blue gleam of the room and hurled himself toward the floor, feet first, like a baseball player going into second base. He slid ... an ectomorphic sliver ... sweeping through one and all, flailing away at the film-advance lever of his camera, squeezing off six, eight, ten pictures from about calf level During his furious skid. Stroboscopic lights burst all around. They were like rockets. They bounced off the silver lamé umbrellas. The jiggling dancers froze in midspasm as if struck rigid by a vision of Ahura Mazda. It was electrifying! Unforgettable!

Later on I ran into a magazine editor who told me that the photographs themselves had proven to be totally useless. They were full of bits and pieces of hideously grinning faces, polished like skulls from flash overexposure, floating next to grotesquely foreshortened knees lost in clotted shadows out of which rose tilted walls and heaving streaks and congestions of inexplicable detail, while stray items, arms, legs, shoes, cloven bottoms, anorexic elbows, appeared in an amputated condition about the edges. But so what! For there you had it: the authentic beat of the 1960s, the Photographer's Dance, choreographed as divine frenzy.

The fashionable photographers of the late 1960s tended to be dreadful megalomanias. It was part of the going style. There were only two adjectives that were considered complimentary in 1967: "brilliant" and "outrageous." On the other hand, Marie Cosindas struck me as more like a member of the species that Malcolm Muggeridge [an English man of letters] had isolated the year before: the minimomaniac. Minimomaniacs were far more formidable in the long run. They were generally polite and appeared to be calm, so that one only detested the single-mindedness, the overpowering will, and the intensity—burning inside with an invisible heat, like a microwave oven—too late.

Because I knew that Marie Cosindas had had

an exhibition at the Museum of Modern Art the year before, I felt I should try to look as sublime as possible for the session. I was wearing a suit of which I was particularly proud. It had a navy blue jacket of unfinished worsted with covered pearl-grey buttons that matched a pearl-grey doublebreasted waistcoat and pleated pearl-grey pants. Marie Cosindas studied this rig for a while and then directed me to go put on a white suit with white shoes, white shirt, a blue tie, blue socks, and a blue pocket handkerchief. Now, this is what I mean about her invisible microwave willpower. I couldn't explain it, but any possible protest seemed hopeless. I simply went off and changed clothes.

Her modus operandi had put me into some sort of hypnogogic state. She studied my apartment for what seemed like forever. Then she began rearranging it. Somehow a big orange tub chair wound up against an orange, blue, and magenta painting that went from the floor to the ceiling on one wall. Marie Cosindas instructed me to arrange myself in the chair just so: legs crossed this way, one arm resting over there, the other one cocked over here [Fig. 148].

I didn't realize until a year later that she had also positioned my head next to an orange shape on the painting in such a way that a deflated comic strip balloon, or else the departing Universal Soul of the 1960s, appeared to have just slipped out of my mouth.

From her duffel bag and a little case she produced the most superannuated camera equipment I had ever seen: a tripod that appeared to have been lashed together by the last remaining tool-and-die mold-carver from South Main Street in Springfield, Massachusetts; an ancient Linhof box camera with a black cloth for the photographer to disappear under, the sort of camera that used to turn up in cartoons in magazines like *Judge* during the 1930s, evidently because it seemed hilariously old-fashioned even then; a big stopwatch, the kind you used to see at high school track meets; plus about a dozen filters.

These were not the sort of filters with precision-tooled aluminum rims from the Eimfrischtaden Glass Works that one sees in camera shops, however. No, these were little sheets of what appeared to be clear plastic, many of them tinted reddish-grey. They looked as if they might have cost three or four cents apiece. She fastened them over the lens of the camera with Scotch tape.

The session did not proceed with the tachycardiac beat of the 1960s. Marie Cosindas would disappear under the black cloth for what seemed like five or ten minutes at a time, presumably meditating at her view window. Then she would reappear and release the shutter. Then she would remove a big plate, the film holder, from the back of the box, pull out the film, and start up the stopwatch. The film turned out to be Polaroid, somehow adapted to this outsized box. She peeled back the layers just the way anybody would have done it with an ordinary Polaroid snapshot camera. She would stare at the result for another five or ten minutes and then she would put another filter over the lens and fasten it down with the Scotch tape and then the cycle would begin again, with her disappearing under the black cloth, vanishing for so long that I felt alone in the room, and then taking the back off the camera and peeling away the paper, while a brown goo seeped about the edges, and changing the filter and taping the new one on with Scotch tape—until there were five, ten, twenty Polaroid pictures lying on a table like Bazooka bubble gum cards.

By now the fireproof mask of aplomb with which I tried to make my way through that marvelously crazed decade had disintegrated. I could feel a look of naked bemusement spreading over my face as I stared at the ancient camera eye in front of me. I don't think that Marie Cosindas said fifty words the entire time.

I have no idea how long it had been by the time Marie Cosindas informed me she had finished. She gathered up her heap of twenty or thirty Polaroid pictures and her filters and her stopwatch and her camera and stuffed them all back into her bag and disappeared, and I didn't see her again for ten years.

The Blasphemy

The following year, 1968, a friend who was traveling through Europe sent me a clipping from the German newspaper *Die Welt*. There I was, in color, wearing a white suit and sitting in an orange chair in front of an orange, blue, and magenta painting with as wide-eyed and defenseless a look as I had ever noticed on my own face. A headline under the picture said: *"Marie Cosindas: Porträt Tom Wolfe (1967)."* My friend, who didn't read German, concluded that I must be tremendously famous. There was a long caption under the headline. The odd truth was that it said nothing whatsoever about the estimable Mr. Wolfe. But it did have quite a bit to say about the amazing new American photographer Marie Cosindas. The editors explained that they had chosen her work to inaugurate the use of color pictures in *Die Welt*. This was the first color photograph they had ever run. In this epochal moment they were turning to the most extraordinary color photographer of the day: Marie Cosindas. They compared her to Van Dyck. My status was somewhat like Mother Whistler's in Whistler's portrait of her, the actual title of which is *An Arrangement in Grey and Black*. I was part of an arrangement in orange, white, blue, and magenta.

I didn't feel excessively wounded, however, because by 1968 I had begun to find Marie Cosindas' work as amazing as *Die Welt* did. That was a very common reaction as her work began to appear in exhibitions and magazines. People within the world of art photography, as it was then known, were as startled as everyone else. But why? There was nothing shocking or even bizarre about her subject matter, which consisted mainly of portraits and still lives, and her compositions were highly formal.

When John Szarkowski of the Museum of Modern Art first saw her photographs, he told her: "I don't mean to sound blasphemous—but they look like paintings."

"I know they do," said Marie Cosindas.

This was blasphemy in Szarkowski's eyes, because it was already an article of faith among those who cared about photography as an art form that a photograph should not look like a painting done by other means. Szarkowski himself was making the Museum of Modern Art the center for the search for a uniquely photographic aesthetic, as the phrase went. Nonetheless, it was Szarkowski who gave her an exhibition at the Museum in 1966. It was the first full-scale exhibition she had ever had, although she had appeared in some important group shows. The following year she was given exhibitions at Boston's Museum of Fine Arts, the Art Institute of Chicago, and the Spoleto festival in Italy. Her work began to appear in every sort of publication, from the prestigious Swiss journal of art photography, *Camera,* to *Life* and the Sunday supplements. By 1968 she was one of the best-known photographers in the United States.

The startling effect of her pictures unquestionably had something to do with the fact that, as Szarkowski said, they looked like paintings. *Ellen,* which she had done in 1965, was pure Gustav Klimt: the porcelain flesh, the lush fabric, the arms and wrists folded with a slightly concupiscent vulnerability, all of it laid out as decoration against a flat backdrop. *Bruce Pecheur,* another picture from 1965, showed a figure lifted out of a dark background through the use of highlights on the face and hands and a single article of clothing, a vest, after the fashion of Caravaggio; and *Paula Nude* was a perfect Caravaggio angel. The comparisons were easy and endless.

Marie Cosindas had gone to the Boston Museum School to study painting in the 1950s and had a studio on Newbury Street in the Back Bay section of Boston. Her work tended toward a blurred, spontaneous, and rather abstract use of color, like the Late Impressionists'. One of her paintings survives in the background of the still-life photograph called *Floral with Painting.* Her favorite painters were Bonnard and Vuillard, but it would be difficult to say that either painter influenced what she later did in color photography.

Marie Cosindas was introduced to photography rather casually. Her studio happened to be in the same building as one of Boston's first photography galleries, the Carl Siembab. She gradually became part of a circle of photographers that included Walter Chappell, Paul Caponigro, Nathan Lyons, and Minor White, and then took up photography herself. For several years she had been making her living as a commercial artist, doing advertising illustrations, fabric and footwear designs, plaster reproductions of museum pieces, or anything else that paid steadily. Her father, who was a carpenter, and her mother had emigrated from Greece to the United States about 1920, and she was the eighth of their ten children—the twelve of them living in a small apartment in the South End of Boston. Marie Cosindas had attended Boston's Modern School of Fashion Design with the idea of acquiring a trade. But in 1960 she walked out on her last job—which was designing children's slippers with animal faces on them to go with matching hand puppets—and started work as a freelance photographer, making a living chiefly from portraits. At this point she was working in black and white with conventional film.

In 1961 she went to California to study with Ansel Adams in his studio workshop. Adams, like Walter Chappell and Minor White, was a photographer who worked slowly, deliberately, with the most sophisticated attention to composition, light, and tone. Control of every element of the picture and the process was the key to his technique and became the key to Marie Cosindas' as well. But neither Adams nor any other of the photographers who were ranked as fine artists in the 1960s worked in color.

For one thing, it seemed impossible to control color film. A photographer would see one set of colors in his view window—and another set, from some eccentric skew of the tonal scale, would emerge in the print. But a bigger problem may have been the fine artist's Reverence for the Outmoded.

Artists like to be regarded as visionaries, but I can't think of any group of people who resist change more fiercely and bitterly. Much of the artist's visionary acuity is over his shoulder. As the art historian Alan Gowans has demonstrated, artists did not regard the woodcut, the steel engraving, and the lithograph as "artistic" media until they had been rendered obsolete by photogravure. The more self-consciously artistic movie directors clung to the black-and-white film for years *because* Technicolor had superseded it with mass audiences. Ingmar Bergman did not make his first color movie until 1964 *(All These Women)* and even then had the sets, interiors, and costumes done in black, white, and Greg, so that the color peeked through only in the rather pallid Nordic flesh tones of his actors.

There were gifted photographers who worked in color, notably Ernst Haas, Alfred Eisenstaedt, and Irving Penn, but in the early 1960s they tended to be categorized as "commercial" or "journalistic." It got to the point where certain talented men began to look at their own color work that way. Richard Avedon was the prize example. He was doing spectacular color photography for *Vogue* and *Harper's Bazaar,* high-fashion pictures of tremendous richness, lushness, vividness, vitality, exuberance. But for his *serious* work, as he thought of it, the work he wanted to be remembered by in museums, he turned to black and white. He began standing people up against white no-seam paper and lighting their faces so that every wen, hickey, zit, whitehead, blackhead, goober, acne crater, beard follicle, nose hair, ear bristle, crow's foot, wattle, mold, eye bag, and liver spot stood out like a tumor, and the poor grey souls looked like pustular ruins, sad, spent, demoralized. Ah, Lord, you never get out of this world alive! This was *serious* work.

Marie Cosindas, true to the faith, started working in black and white. Ansel Adams took great pride in his ability to look through the viewfinder of his camera and visualize an entire landscape in black and white. It was an uncanny gift. Grass, sky, flowers, horses, the works—he could see it all in tones or dark and light. With Marie Cosindas the opposite began to happen. Even after the color was gone, she kept seeing it. Even after the print was lying in front of her in all its artistically legitimate black-and-white purity, she saw the missing colors.

Adams saw nothing wonderful about that. "You're shooting in black and white," he told her "but you're thinking in color."

He gave her a tan filter that reduced the colors to black and white when you looked through the viewfinder. She looked through the filter and still saw the colors in her mind. It finally reached the point where she rephotographed in color certain still lives she had done first in black and white, such as the picture with the white vase called *Miniature Floral 1.*

In 1962 Marie Cosindas was one of about a dozen photographers to whom the Polaroid Company offered its new color film, Polacolor, in quantity, asking only that they experiment with it. The film would go on the market in 1963. It was not the happiest experiment in the world. Many of the photographers did not feel comfortable working with color in the first place, and others found the instant development process—which merely involved peeling one sheet of paper off another, the negative off the positive, while the brown emulsion seeped—baffling, messy, gimmicky, and somehow unprofessional. The mysteries of The Darkroom had always been synonymous with professionalism itself among photographers even those who never went near a darkroom any longer and instead sent their film off to photo labs. The one Polacolor flower that came up from the casting of the seed was the work of Marie Cosindas.

She discovered that the instant developing process used with Polaroid film—"the darkroom in my hand," as she referred to it—could solve the problem of the unpredictability in color photography. It was not that Polaroid film was much different from any other when it came to faithful reproduction of the colors one saw through the viewfinder. But since she could develop the Polaroid print immediately, she could modify the color as she went along, on the spot, before each new exposure, until she achieved the tones and shades she wanted. She could place any of twenty-four yellow, magenta, cyan, red, blue, and green filters over the lens. Her favorites, magenta and yellow, made colors warmer, particularly the flesh tones. She varied exposure times and development times. Her favorite light was afternoon daylight on an overcast day from a north window. When she used filters in such soft light, she would let the exposure run to eight seconds. In the print the light would remain soft and yet take on an extraordinary luminosity. She would extend development times from 60 seconds, which was normal for Polaroid color film, to 90 and even 120 seconds, which would make certain tones go deeper, particularly in the backgrounds thereby increasing color contrast. Or she could increase the temperature at which the print was developed by turning up the thermostat in the studio to 80 degrees or more. One of the peculiar properties of Polaroid color film was that the warmer the temperature, the warmer the colors. Another was that the color was continuous. Conventional color film came out in a pattern of minute dots. It tended to have a grainy quality when the images were enlarged. Polaroid color had a smoother quality, like paint. Colors tended to be less harsh and more muted. If Marie Cosindas warmed them up still further through the use of filters or temperature or any of the other techniques, they took on a glow and a creamy richness quite unlike anything that had been seen in color photography up to that time.

What made Marie Cosindas' sessions so long and exacting was her determination to exhaust every conceivable combination of the five variables—exposure time, development time, temperature, lighting, and color filtration—until she achieved the colors she wanted. Her procedure was like a painter's, or as close to a painter's as a photographer was likely to get. When she developed a print, peeled off the negative, put the picture on a table, and studied it, she was like the portrait painter stepping back from the easel and appraising his handiwork before returning to the palette to modify the color. The final print was like a painted portrait also in that it could not be duplicated. The Polaroid negative is destroyed in the process of instant development.

I have a feeling that there was one thing about photography that always bothered Marie Cosindas, especially since she had started out as a painter. It was the unspoken curse of the medium, which went: "Photography is not really creative." Naturally no painter would be so gauche as to say publicly that photography was not an art form. Nevertheless, there was an unuttered axiom: "Painters create, photographers select." Not all the enlightened lip service in the world could change that feeling. The condescension with which the most insignificant painter could look down upon an Ansel Adams, a Steichen, or a Stieglitz was absolutely breathtaking. If sneers gave off heat, Alfred Stieglitz himself would have ended up about the size and shape of a smoked oyster.

I think that was one reason, too, why Marie Cosindas made such a point of first creating her pictures—whether portraits or still lives—as formal arrangements even before looking through the viewfinder. I don't think she has ever photographed anything the way she found it except under duress. That goes for human beings as well as still lives. She told people what to wear, and if they didn't have the right things, she would provide them. She insisted on costuming even the most elegant and stylish women. She preferred photographing people in her own studio in Boston. She spent even more time in assembling the backdrops than in taking the pictures. Certain objects she likes appeared over and over: bunches of baby's breath, patchwork quilts, and rugs draped Vermeer style. Like Pisanello, Hals, Greuze, Goya, and Rembrandt, she usually set the backdrop immediately behind the figure. Often she did this by draping fabrics over an easel.

Even more effort, days of it in some cases, went into the composition of her still lives. Her arrangements took the form of a genre that was becoming respectable in the galleries during the 1960s: the *assemblage*. The reward for respectability was translation into the French: still-life arrangements became *assemblages,* just as journalism, when undertaken by well-known novelists, became *reportage*. Rich, congested, and yet delicate and orderly arrangements were the sort that Marie Cosindas delighted in. It was a look that resonated with memories of her childhood. In the apartment that she and her nine brothers and sisters grew up in, there was a corner with a little built-in cupboard that became her private preserve. She used to spend entire afternoons arranging every toy, knickknack, doll, and souvenir she possessed upon the shelves. This motif turns up in both of her pictures called *Memories*. In her work there is also something of the decoration that was found in the Greek Orthodox churches she attended as a child, Byzantine patterns leaving no space unfilled, pictures glowing with the colors of the Keys to Heaven and the Yellow Mantle of the Revealed Faith.

Such rich and evocative color was unusual in the late 1960s, and not merely in photography. Marie Cosindas' pictures looked like paintings, as John Szarkowski had said, but they did not look like the paintings that were in vogue at that time. For a start, of course, no one—no one in *tout le mode*—did portraits and still lives anymore except in the camp form of Warhol's photo booth strips and Lichtenstein's Ben-Day Dot send ups of early Cubism. But more remarkable was the narrow range of colors in the most fashionable of the new painting genres, Pop and Minimalist. It was important to painters in both genres not to use colors that would seem sentimental, romantic, soft, or evocative in any way. The colors in Pop Art were often strong and bright but they were also deliberately kept slick, harsh, and primary. They were consciously borrowed from the color chart of mass-produced printing, as it was used in packaging, advertisements, and comic books. There was something intentionally cynical about the color. The important thing was to be cool, detached, ironic, and in on the joke. The Minimalists finally translated this attitude into a plainly stated theory. They called for an end to "pretty" colors that played on the viewer's sentimental memories and associations. They attacked their rivals in the field of abstract art—the so-called Color Field painters—on precisely that score. They themselves sought to arrive at colors with no sentimental overtones whatsoever. The results were marvelous: lung blue, ham-gone-high green, poisoned-creosote orange, pharyngitic pink, spinal-tap cyannic, cigarette-in-urinal brown, short-order-fried-chicken grey.

Marie Cosindas' colors, on the other hand,

evoked emotions by the job lot. It was as if she had pulled back a curtain and suddenly brought back into the world of art a sense of color that had not been seen since the turn of the century in the era of the Symbolists, the Vienna Secession, and Art Nouveau.

I think her use of color had all the more impact because it was in photographs. The great god Culturatus still looked the other way where photography was concerned. He gave special dispensation. It was still possible, legal, culturally O.K. to look at such colors if they appeared in the pagan form of the photograph. It was even permissible to enjoy them. Marie Cosindas' work was like forbidden fruit unaccountably made available.

His Eminence, Art Theory

I was curious to see how other photographers would follow up on the techniques Marie Cosindas had introduced. What an Aurora dawn I envisioned! By herself Marie Cosindas had established color photography as an artistic medium. Her show at the Museum of Modern Art in 1966 was only the fourth exhibition of color photographs in the Museum's history. The magazine *Camera* ran color photographs for the first time in order to show her work. I somehow expected to see floods of color, of the richest sort, as younger photographers followed her lead in the 1970s.

I couldn't have been more wrong. I watched—I marveled!—as something quite different occurred. The younger photographers began hoisting up on their shoulders, like seven decades of painters before them, the astounding weight of twentieth-century art theory. Photographers started becoming every bit as literary, metaphysical, academic, and nonvisual as the Minimalists and Conceptualists in painting. What did the merely *visual* matter when there was the great god Theory to be served? Such had been the spirit of fashionable American painting for thirty years. With fascination I saw the same spirit beginning to pervade photography.

The trouble was that all along, ever since the 1880s, photographers had been agitated by their inferiority, in terms of status, to painters. The continual although seldom voiced question was: What will establish us as artists in our own right? The early virtuosos, Stieglitz and Steichen, had deliberately imitated painters, even to the point of using gum bichromate to simulate brush strokes. Stieglitz himself eventually began to look upon this as ersatz stuff. Thereafter he, like Paul Strand and Edward Weston and, later, Aaron Siskind and Harry Callahan, called for pictures that had the unique look of the photograph. Which was what exactly? Well, it was a picture in black and white in which all forms were modeled in light and shade and all colors were expressed in tones of light. It was a picture in which the creator used light instead of paint. A very reassuring notion this was, once it took hold. *Light!* One could even argue that it was more elemental than paint, more godly ... *fons et origo* ... There you had one reason why so many renowned photographers resisted color film. Once you reintroduced color into the picture, the photographer was back where he started: in the colossal shadow of the painters.

But what if they had only been kidding themselves all along? What about their eternal emphasis on composition and control of the materials? What about all those prim pure *still lifes* they did and those *nature studies* and *skyscapes?* ... The Strands and Steichens and Westons and Adamses looked at the world like painters. They yearned to be "creative" like painters ... So went the argument that began to circulate as the so-called Snapshot School began to attract attention in the 1970s. The Snapshot stars professed to have no interest in theory whatsoever. That was good thinking. The most successful painters of the 1960s had taken the same stance. You let your attendant gallery owners, critics, and museum curators enunciate the theories—for which you happen to stand out as the supreme illustration.

The new theory—which Gene Thornton, in a brilliant article in the April 1978 *Art News,* has named "the new formalism"—simply took the theory of modern painting, first outlined about 1905, and substituted the words "camera" or "photograph" where necessary. Braque,

Picasso, Matisse, and others had argued that a painting should no longer be treated as a mirror held up to man or nature. A painting should compel the viewer to see it for what it actually was: an arrangement of colors and forms on a flat surface. This notion that honesty and integrity demanded *flatness* in painting—since such was the nature of the canvas—began as a theory but soon became a holy tenet that regulated fashionable painting for most of the next seventy-five years.

Ever since the Renaissance artists had looked upon the flatness of the painting surface as a limitation to be overcome through professional expertise, using techniques such as perspective and chiaroscuro. Braque, Picasso, and Matisse turned this outlook upside down. They cherished flatness, bowed down to it as the very spirit of the enterprise. They also celebrated the primitives who had, it seemed, known this intuitively all along. African art, Micronesian art, Eskimo art, ancient Egyptian art, plus the work of children, madmen, naïfs and village naturals (Grandma Moses)—now it all seemed to have sprung straight from the head of God, whose name was Flat.

For modern painting's flatness the New Formalists have substituted what they see as its equivalent in photography: the unique attribute of the photograph ... which is ... technical distortion. Technical distortion and its obverse, mindless candor. Suddenly there is magic in such items (to borrow from Gene Thornton's list) as random and eccentric framing, blurred images, keeling horizons, distorted scale, unreal colors (puce water, chartreuse skies), grotesque foreshortening ... and nightclub photo lighting with its flash overexposures and clotted shadows and inexplicable detail and tilted walls and stray items—arms, legs, shoes, cloven bottoms, anorexic elbows—appearing in an amputated condition about the edges ...

Once regarded as technical limitations of the medium, as annoyances to be overcome through professional expertise, they now become like animae, tree spirits, to be treated with reverence and looked to for guidance. The New Formalists began celebrating postcards and their too-blue blues, photo mat portraits, snapshots, newspaper and nightclub photographs. This was photography's Primitive Art—sprung straight from the head of God, whose name was Technical Distortion.

But of course! This was precisely the god whom 1967's Photographer of the Century had called forth during his furious slide. Oh that 1967's Photographer of the Century's year had not run out!—and that he were in our midst today!

He would be entering the world of art in a nightclub photo aura. Today photographers are not merely fashionable but are spoken of as artists. No doubt they will follow the example of the painters of the 1950s and the 1960s. They will acquire the discipline to give up such romantic notions as "personal vision" and put their work at the service of His Eminence, Art Theory. In their studios at this very moment there are photographers who with the bravery of the true modern artist are trying to unlearn half a lifetime of professional technique. They struggle to put the *technical distortion* back into their work, to reestablish contact with the godhead ... a little overexposure here, a little inexplicable detail there, a little tubercular blue here and there, and perhaps a few amputated cloven bottoms if one's prayers are answered ...

Meanwhile Marie Cosindas occupies a curious position. She has a status in American photography somewhat like that of Céline in French literature. Céline opened up the most startling and spectacular *terra incognita*. He brought a whole new vocabulary, the language as it was actually spoken, into serious French literature for the first time. Everyone looked, marveled, clucked, fumed, held his head—and practically no one followed him into that rude terrain. He reigned there alone and is now remembered as one of the giants of the French novel in the twentieth century. In the same way Marie Cosindas has advanced the state of the art in color photography to a plateau that only she has been able to occupy. In the eyes of the new gods, Technical Distortion and Mindless Candor, she is a heretic. She has never rejected the idea of dealing with photography as if she were a painter. She puts a premium on control, composition, and formal arrangement. She uses color of the most sensual and evocative sort and is not interested in turning pictures into a dissertation on the nature of photography. By all these things is His Eminence, Art Theory, mocked. And yet her achievements in the use of color have given her a prominence that is largely immune to fashion, theory, and the general scuffle of the art world. She is very close to having the sort of fireproof reputation enjoyed by Weston and Adams.

Marie Cosindas simply travels on into her fantasy of color, as if by astral projection. Sometimes I think that only supreme fantasists can have peace in this world. In any case they have their way. I have met Marie Cosindas, and I can testify to that.

1. See *Conversations with Tom Wolfe*, p. 14. Wolfe has illustrated many of his own works and exhibited many of his drawings, some of which are reproduced in *In Our Time* (New York: Farrar, Straus & Giroux, 1981).

2. See Wolfe, introduction to *Annie Leibovitz Photographs* (New York: Pantheon/Rolling Stone, 1983), npn, and preface to *Rolling Stone: The Photographs*, ed. Laurie Kratochvil (New York: Simon & Schuster, 1989), npn. See also some of the many portraits of Wolfe in *Irving Penn*, ed. Szarkowski, fig. 135 (1966); McKenna, *A Life in Photography*, p. 213 (1970); and Krementz, *The Writer's Image*, npn (1973). See other relevant photographs by Cosindas: one of Ezra Pound (1967), like the one of Wolfe, in *Color Photographs* (Boston: New York Graphic Society, 1978), no. 50; two unattributed ones of Frank Conroy and William Styron in "Four Americans," *Esquire* 70 (October 1968): 119–29; the interiors in "Truman Capote at the Sea and in the City," *House Beautiful* 111, no. 4 (April 1969): 93–98; and two photogravures of Greece in Friedrich Dürrenmatt, *Oedipus* (New York: Limited Book Club, 1989). Cosindas has also taken pictures in Key West of the playwright Tennessee Williams (whose family albums are at the Harvard Theatre Collection), and of the poet James Merrill working on a film (1990), some of which may be included in a book she is planning; according to the artist in conversation with the editor on January 11, 1993.

*T*he year 1951 was an annus mirabile for Williams (1929–), a
*student at Black Mountain College. First, he was inspired to become
a photographer after studying with two teachers: Harry Callahan (1912–),
whose formalist sequences were admired by many (including another Williams, the poet William Carlos);[1] and Aaron Siskind (1903–91), a former
poet and English instructor, who had turned from urban documentaries to
forms with metaphorical possibilities like seaweed, rocks, trees, urban walls
and pavements, and human feet [Fig. 149].[2] Williams was also inspired to
become a poet by the college rector and teacher Charles Olson, whose verse
was known for its eclectic knowledge and plain diction.[3] During the same
year, Williams also founded the Jargon Society, which became one of the
finest American avant-garde presses. He subsequently not only wrote and
photographed on his own account, but promoted other verbal and visual
artists by publishing their works himself or discussing them in colorful
essays elsewhere.[4] These beneficiaries included young unknowns as well as
the veteran photographers Clarence John Laughlin, whose early writings
and reading of the French symbolists are reflected in his "poetic" approach
to reality and the lengthy captions that accompanied his eclectic scenes,
and Frederick Sommer, whose surreal desert scenes and other abstract pictures seek to discern new meanings through "poetic logic."[5] Working from
his homes in both North Carolina and northern England, Williams has
been appropriately called the "Johnny Appleseed" of contemporary literature and photography.[6]*

I was beginning to write a few words about Aaron Siskind at seventy-five when the phone rang. On the other end was that nonpareil typographer and designer from Taloga, Oklahoma, Alvin Doyle Moore. He said: "I'll tell you something you don't know. Art Sinsabaugh tells me that Siskind had no running water in his darkroom in Chicago.... And I said to Art, 'That just means that if you're really good, you can do it anywhere—even on the ground with a stick.'"

I flew into Kennedy from Heathrow on last December 3rd, just in order to join a distinguished company in toasting Aaron with champagne at midnight: it would be his seventy-fifth birthday. I had not seen him in ten years, not since Chicago. Older, certainly, with a bit of Buddhistic paunch, but much the same man I had come to revere back in 1951 at Black Mountain College.

Then, he was simply introduced to me as a friend of Harry Callahan's from New York; an associate of the painters Kline and De Kooning and the Abstract Expressionists. Over the summer I had much of his counsel in the darkroom as he taught me the rudiments of what to do with a Rollei. And those of us fortunate to be in nether Buncombe County, North Carolina, then (Charles Olson, Dan Rice, Lou Harrison, Joel Oppenheimer, Fielding Dawson, Ben Shahn, Katherine Litz, Francine du Plessix Gray, to name a few) spent many a long evening down at Ma Peak's Tavern, three miles from the college, drinking beer and listening to the lore that Siskind and Callahan commanded between them. Edward Dahlberg once said: "Literature is the way we ripen ourselves by conversation...." The beer joint in Hicksville, U.S.A., should never be underestimated. You would not have done better at the Deux Magots or the Café Flore in Paris that summer. And I somehow doubt that you would have found Brassaï and Cartier-Bresson there amidst the too-many tourists. Besides, in Siskind and Callahan, we had two American pioneers who were photographing Chicago, Martha's Vine-yard, and Harlan County, Kentucky, in ways no one had seen before. Were they not precisely on another Black Mountain poet's wavelength? I am reminded of Robert Creeley's perceptive observation: "There is no such thing as place, except as it exists within a given man."

All my favorite avuncular adjectives trot forth when I think about (i.e., have feelings about) Aaron: kindly, astute, enthusiastic, loyal, masterly. He wears his years more lightly than in the SX-70 snaps I did of him that midnight where he looks like the oldest tragedian of the Yiddish theatre—"Jesus, you think I'm mellow? I'm so mellow I'm rotten!"

As for the exhibition of work from 1976 and 1977 that Light Gallery put on to mark Siskind's birthday, what is there to say except that it was one of the great, ennobling, wondrous things I have ever seen. You could spend hours, days, or years in front of any particular print getting its savor, fathoming how a man's unique feelings can be limned on walls and in stones, from Nantucket to Rome to Lima to Paris. A show so good one can only shrug and hardly bear to look at it. I wrote down *Peru 349, Peru 307, Peru 210, Peru 208, Peru 465; Paris 50; Senagalia 28;* and the set of nine prints from *Cusco*—those are quite enough in my three visits to the gallery in three days. There have been few photographers in the history of the craft with equal gifts, with such pictorial quality from one work to another over the decades. If we go to painting, there is Pierre Bonnard, conspicuously—and Vuillard. And Monet, at Giverny. In America, one thinks of Grant Wood and Richard Diebenkorn; i.e., I think of Wood and Diebenkorn—you're on your own to find the odd pairings.

I've stuck to the adjectives of old-fashioned poetical virtue to write of Aaron Siskind. Except for one or two pieces by Tom Hess, most magazine writing about Siskind has been cold and technocratic. You know the words: *anthropomorphic, animistic, typology, methodology, perceptual ambiguity*—about as welcome as a

149. Aaron Siskind. 'F102,' 1957, cover photograph for *The Magpie's Bagpipe* by Jonathan Williams, 1982.

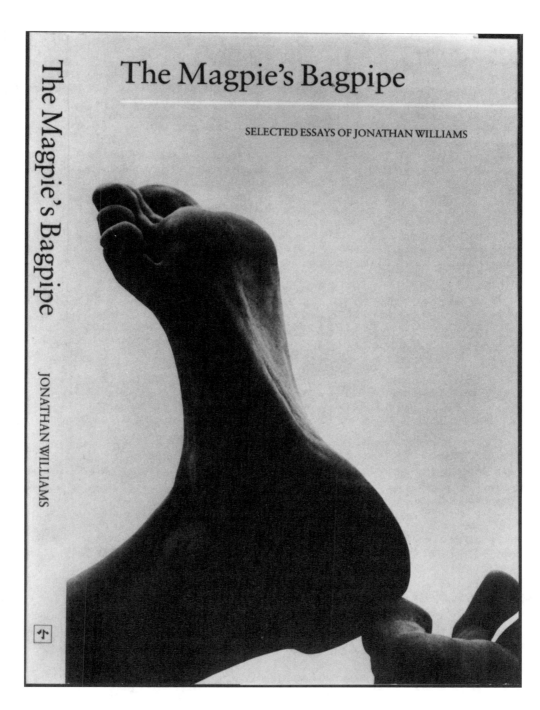

Christmas card from the IRS or another Committee to Reelect Richard Nixon. Recall that Siskind and Franz Kline spoke of "dancing" and of delight. "Is not the aesthetic optimum order with the tensions continuing?" asks Siskind, with precisely the warm linguistic savvy you'd expect.

Seventy-five and better than ever. "Why not?" he asks. "What else have I got to do?" [from "People and Ideas," *Aperture* 82 (1979): 7]

1. "Jesus! Peter Brueghel would have given his left arm (etc.) to have painted the world so clearly, so beautifully," said W. C. Williams about Callahan's work, quoted in Jonathan Williams, "The Eye Sees More Than the Mind Knows," in *The Multiple Image: Photographs by Harry Callahan* (Chicago: Press of the Institute of Design, 1961), npn. See also J[onathan] Williams, foreword to *Harry Callahan: Color 1941–80,* ed. Robert Tow and Ricker Winsor (Providence: Matrix, 1980), npn, and "Letter to Ansel Adams," from "Cloches a Travers Les Feuilles," in *Contemporary Authors Series* (Detroit: Gale Research Publishers, 1990), vol. 12, p. 339.

2. The CCP has some prose, poetry, and translations by Siskind [AG30.18], mostly from the 1920's; some of his writing was published in obscure literary journals, and a few of his poems are included in Carl Chiarenza, *Aaron Siskind: Pleasures and Terrors* (Boston: New York Graphic Society, 1982), especially pp. 7–11, 23, and 200. See also Williams, "Aaron Siskind/Eight Signs," *Black Mountain Review* 5 (Summer 1955): 77–78; *Aaron Siskind, Photographs/John Logan, Poems* (Rochester, N.Y.: Visual Studies Workshop, 1976), and Gordon Parks, foreword to Siskind, *Harlem: Photographs 1932–1940,* pp. 4–5.

3. Olson and the environment he helped create—described by Mary Emma Harris, *The Arts at Black Mountain College* (Cambridge: MIT Press, 1987)—similarly influenced the poets Robert Creeley (1926–) and Denise Levertov (1923–), who were also sensitive to photography. See Creeley, "Harry Callahan—A Note," *Collected Essays* (Berkeley: University of California Press, 1989), p. 384; Creeley, "Questions" and "Mother's Photograph," in *Memory Gardens* (New York: New Directions, 1986), pp. 55 and 59; Levertov, "Looking at Photographs," in *The Poet in the World* (New York: New Directions, 1973), pp. 87–88, and Levertov, "Photo Torn from The Times," p. 23, "In Thai Binh (Peace) Province," p. 25, and "A Letter to Marek about a Photograph," pp. 101–2, in *The Freeing of the Dust* (New York: New Directions, 1975).

4. See James J. Jaffe, comp., *Jonathan Williams: A Bibliographical Checklist of His Writings, 1950–1988* (Haverford, Pa.: Privately printed, [1989]). See also Williams's *Portrait Photographs* (London: Coracle Press, 1979), which includes tipped-in informal color portraits, including many of writers such as Pound (1966), W. C. Williams (1961), Olson (c. 1960), Ginsberg (1973), and Levertov (c. 1959) as well as of the photographers Coburn (1966), Siskind (1960), and Minor White (1962).

5. For more on Laughlin, see *Clarence John Laughlin: The Personal Eye* (Millerton, N.Y.: Aperture/Philadelphia Museum of Art, 1973), which includes Williams's introduction, pp. 5–14; Laughlin's statement, pp. 116–28; his division of all his works into groups—two entitled *Visual Poems* and *Poems of the Inner World,* Groups K & L; and examples of his explanatory captions. See also Williams, "The Eyes of 3 Phantasts: Laughlin, Sommer, Bullock," *Aperture* 9, no. 3 (1961): 98–106; Williams, "Letter to Clarence John Laughlin," from "Cloches a Travers Les Feuilles," *Contemporary Authors Series,* vol. 12, p. 346; and Megan Seielstad, "Clarence John Laughlin and the Third World of Photography," *Louisiana Literature* 4, no. 3 (Fall 1987): 4–26.

For more on Sommer, see his *All Children Are Ambassadors: Photographs and Poetry* (Tucson: Nazraeli Press, 1992); "The Poetic Logic of Art and Aesthetics" [1980], in *Frederick Sommer at Seventy-Five: A Retrospective in Words and Images* (Tucson: CCP, the University of Arizona, 1984), vol. 1; and Williams, "Homage to F. S.; or, that old-time Ryne Duren–Rex Barney bailout," in *Venus, Jupiter and Mars: The Photographs of Frederick Sommer,* pp. 51–52.

6. Buckminster Fuller, quoted in Bob Summer, "Jonathan Appleseed and the Jargon Society," *Publishers Weekly* (March 15, 1985): 26. See also William Corbett, "Praise for Jonathan Williams," *Lillabulero* 14 (Spring 1974): 173–75; Davenport, "Jonathan Williams" (1979), in *The Geography of the Imagination: Forty Essays* (San Francisco: North Point Press, 1981), pp. 180–89; and Webb, "Jonathan Williams—The Johnny Appleseed of Letters" in *Henry and Friends: The California Years, 1946–1977,* pp. 64–65.

FROM "ALLEN GINSBERG'S SACRAMENTAL SNAPSHOTS:
AN INTERVIEW" BY MARK HOLBORN, 1985

*Ginsberg (1926–), one of the most colorful poets of the Beat move-
ment of the late 1950's, is now also securing attention for his photographs. The poet took them over "30 years of epiphanies and moments," whose very transience makes them sacred to him.[1] Less sensational
and shocking than his poetry but often as morally defiant, Ginsberg's
snapshots seem the visual equivalents of diary entries—spontaneous, direct, and technically imperfect. His handwritten captions, perhaps inspired
by those of Diane Arbus, usually do more than identify subjects, settings,
and dates; they often illuminate the style and psychology of both the moment
and the era.[2] Just as his nakedly autobiographical verse documents his
quest for a transcendental consciousness—through drugs, sex, and Eastern
religions—Ginsberg's photographs commemorate his enduring ties with
many of the leading counterculture figures of the past forty years, especially
the writers Jack Kerouac [Fig. 150], William Burroughs, and Gregory Corso
as well as the photographer Robert Frank (1924–).[3] Only recently has Ginsberg taken his photography seriously, as its historic significance becomes
more evident with time. His first published collections (1990, 1993) may
indicate a new direction for the writer as well as a testimony to the "sacramental presence" of certain occasions in his colorful life.[4]*

Jack Kerouac, railroad brakeman's rule-book in pocket, couch pillow airing on fire-escape south view overlooking backyard clotheslines three flights up, my apartment 206 East 7th St. between Avenues B & C, Lower East Side Manhattan. He'd completed On The Road, Visions of Cody, Dr. Sax, had begun Book of Dreams and Pic, was in midst of Subterraneans affair with "Mardou Fox", that novel completed same year along with his romance Maggie Cassady. Burroughs then in residence edited Yage Letters & Queer mss.; Gregory Corso visited that season Probably September 1953.
Allen Ginsberg

MH: The subjects of your photographs, your friends, are legends. . . . How do you feel when people you know are transformed in the public eye by cinema, magazines, or even exhibitions of photographs?

AG: Jack Kerouac wrote about his friends in *The Dharma Bums* as a novel, an epic of his own. Anything that resulted in the media is fall-out from his own original creation. The ordinary magazine myth would not exist without the high artistic creation, without a mutual collaborative artistic creation between friends, that involved mythmaking; which means companions were involved in seeing each other as mythical or sacred in a sacred world primarily; or not so much *mythical* as seeing each other as *real* in a really sacred world. So my motive for taking those snapshots was to make celestial snapshots in a sacred world, recording certain moments in an eternity with a sense of sacramental presence. The sacramental quality comes from an awareness of the transitory nature of the world, an awareness that it's a mortal world, where our brief time together is limited and it's the one and only occasion when we'll be together. This is what makes it sacred, the awareness of the mortality, which comes from a Romantic conception (Keats's) as well as Buddhist understanding (as in the "Shambhala" teachings of Chögyam Trungpa Rinpöche). They are not contradictory origins; and Buddhism was part of the cultural awareness and later practice I shared with Jack Kerouac, Gary Snyder, and Philip Whalen. . . . The very word "sacramental" we used back in the 1940's. We were looking for a "New Vision" and saw each other as sacred people or comrades. In Buddhism the first "mark" or characteristic of life is that of suffering, and the second characteristic is that everything is transitory. The third "mark" is that there's no permanent ego; we're all "empty phantoms" so to speak; the world is "Golden Ash" as Kerouac wrote.

MH: It can be pleasing when photographs start to fade and even fine prints start to turn at the edges. They'll all finally go back to dust. I was always uneasy with the photographic motivation of fixing the so-called "decisive moment" or attempting to create something monumental out of something fleeting.

AG: The poignancy of the photograph comes from looking back to a fleeting moment in a floating world. The transitoriness is what creates the sense of the sacred. . . . It may sound as if I am making too much of such sacramental nature, but we loved one another and saw each other as in our one and only time in eternity, and thus we knew each other to be sacred.

MH: In your exhibition there were two portraits of Robert Frank. Robert Frank occupies a legendary position. *The Americans* is a legendary book. How close is the correspondence between the originality of Kerouac's prose style, his descriptive facility, and Robert Frank's own innovative form and sweeping vision of America?

AG: Frank and Kerouac defined the connection in that book. They found the language. They both started out with their ordinary minds, without changing their ordinary minds and used that ordinariness as a myth, instead of trying to create a myth that didn't exist. So they created a special body of text through what they saw or through the accidents of the camera, but they had already mastered the technical stages. Robert had served a great apprenticeship in photography in Switzerland. He had studied chemistry and cameras very thoroughly. Finally he broke free of it, as Kerouac had broken free of "novelistic" conventions. By adjusting their ears and their eyes they were able to work with spontaneous, natural minds.

MH: There is a sense of space and motion in *The Americans* that echoes *On the Road*.

AG: But Robert is definitely conspicuously European and less sexually romantic than Kerouac, although he is very sympathetic. I know him as a person as well as his photographs, about which I shouldn't presume to speak because I am an amateur and can't pretend to understand all his photography. But I like what he sees, and points out—that's clear, you look through his eyes. . . .

. . . Look at the condition of these negatives and prints. I have 30 years of negatives but I haven't had the means to print them properly. They are like the journals I keep—30 years of epiphanies and moments that I've noticed. So I notice many things, then notice that I notice, and eventually I make a picture of it, as I do with journals, intermittent noticings, which are not really diaristic. I wish I'd had the energy to record all the conversations that I've had with Robert, Kerouac, Corso, or Burroughs. When I have the energy before I go to bed I might make a note, like taking out a camera. I see more than I have the physical capacity to write about. You can't photograph everything. It is good to be able to label a thought, to be able to pull it out of your pocket or off your bookshelf one day.

MH: You have been a subject for Richard Avedon, who is regarded as a very great portrait photographer, but he has also been your subject.

AG: Avedon photographed me when I first went over to his studio in 1964. He got interested in photographing me and Peter Orlovsky naked, among some other pictures. Marvin Israel, who designed some albums for Atlantic Records at the time, used one of the Avedon photographs of my face for the cover of a recording of *Kaddish* that Jerry Wexler put out. Then in the late 1960s my father Louis had a book published and we had a big party in Paterson, New Jersey. Avedon came out with a whole crew and took photographs of every member of our family with American flags eating apple pie. He was interested in my relationship to my family, which was a big European–Jewish–New Jersey family. Avedon got in touch with me this year since it was 20 years since he first photo-

graphed us and he wanted us to come up to his studio so he could do another naked duo photograph. That first photograph he did was used for a cover of *Evergreen Review* and as the frontispiece of a book of letters and love poems that I did with Peter Orlovsky, called *Straight Heart's Delight.*[5] I had my little Olympus XA with me a couple of weeks ago when I went up to his studio; I thought I'd take a picture of him.

Robert Frank has consistently given me help over the last years with my photographs and arranged for Brian Graham, one of his printmaker friends, to make my prints. I was hungry for instruction and thought I would ask Avedon for a little advice. I was always grateful that Avedon saw me as an artist (on his or my own terms) rather than as a public image.

MH: David Hockney worked with his camera to record the surface of daily life and people close to him. Something wonderful happened, not because it was David Hockney, or because Christopher Isherwood was in the corner of the frame; there was something beyond that. A long series of precise descriptions, in themselves no more than essential descriptions, were built up and were culminatively transformed into something more, something that might change the way we look at the world. Do you sense that something as simple as a record of one's life can become something more?

AG: The epigraph of my book of collected poems is "Things are symbols of themselves;" so friends are symbols of themselves. There is a mythology but finally people are just themselves. Being themselves in a general pragmatic state, they don't have to symbolize "hero," they don't have to symbolize anybody but themselves because apparently they are unable to be anything better, whereas everybody else is trying to become a man of distinction or a Yuppie. Robert Frank is unable to be anything better than what he is, so he has to settle for what he is out of sheer helplessness. I have to settle for what I did or do in my writing because I can't do any better, mainly because of incompetence, insights, or such genius facility that whatever is done is sufficient in its rhythm or eye. It's like trying to make out as a heterosexual, which I once tried but didn't succeed. So I am stuck with what I am, queer. It's not "sufficient," as it is, but accepting the insufficiency is realizing the humor of the condition. You just relax. You don't have to know everything to be perfect (the art is in being there)—like Burroughs who allows things to fall their own way. His cut-ups are his way of cutting *out* of his obsessions. Robert Frank leaves a certain amount to chance, like Burroughs with his cut-ups. This allows the phenomenal world to speak for itself, instead of aggressively dominating it, telling the world what it is too insistently. I like Elsa Dorfman's *House Book* photos too—ordinary life around her house—though it includes a lot of romantic poet-face visitors. . . .

MH: What is the connection between your teacher Chogyam Trunpa, Rinpöche, a Tibetan Buddhist, and your photography?

AG: Many of the aesthetic terms I use are his formulations. He practices calligraphy, poetry, tea ceremony, flower arrangement, and photography, as examples of aesthetic perception which involve the three principles of Ground, Path, and Fruition; or heaven, earth, and man; or mind, body, and speech. In aesthetic terms this is equivalent to perception, recognition, and articulation. In Buddhist terms this is equivalent to Body of Law (Dharmakaya); Name and Form (Nirmanakiya); and Body of Intelligence (or bliss) (Sambhogakaya). That last is the intelligence that communicates between emptiness and form, or background and foreground. In all Taoist aesthetics (as in a theory of perception relating to Robert Frank, Jack Kerouac and my own writing, and in Buddhist art), there is open-minded primordial consciousness, which is consciousness without conceptualization, or what we might call "First Thought." From this we get *First Thought, Best Thought,* the title of Trungpa's book of poems (Shambhala Press, Boulder, CO, 1983) to which I wrote an introduction. So there is open mind, or mind without name or form; and there is also a perception of the ordinary, the earth and the immediate sur-roundings. Something is needed to bring the heaven and the earth together, which is the appreciator. The appreciator may manifest a very wry appreciation or a humorous appreciation; or a fart, or a poem, or a haiku; or a photograph. That's Trunpa's aesthetic based on the Nature of the mind and its thought forms. Or it's not *his* aesthetic, but a tradition which links calligraphy, Tibetan poetry, archery, T'ai Chi, and photography. Trungpa's application of the principle to photography was a very literal, simple-minded inclusion of these "three worlds." His photographs would include a piece of the sky, a piece of the ground (tree or building), and something that would be his contribution to this chaos, such as a green pepper hanging from a house post.

The practice gave me the way to be spontaneous. I incorporated the principle into teaching poetry. The phenomenon of mind consciousness consists, say, of separate thought forms that have a beginning, a middle, and an end. The beginning is sensation-perception, in open mind without thought; the middle is recognition or conceptualization; and the end is action or reaction, your own comment. This relates to classical Buddhist psychology. The aesthetic is to model the structure of art from the processes of the mind rather than ignoring the mind and creating a structure that covers up the evidence of the mind.

MH: Is there a relationship between this process and the writing of William Carlos Williams?

AG: Yes. There are those lines of Williams's about "Thursday":

I have had my dream—like others
and it has Come to nothing, so that
I remain now Carelessly
with feet planted on the ground
and look up at the sky—
feeling my clothes about me,
the weight of my body in my shoes,
the rim of my hat, air passing in and out
at my nose—and decide to dream no more.[6]

William Carlos Williams here provides a description of primordial mind, recognition of the condition; and the wry comment that he'll have no more conceptual thoughts. That poem, "Thursday" (like an ordinary day), was written around 1919. . . .

MH: Is there a leap to be made from this process to the practice of making a photograph or seeing a photograph?

AG: Whose photographs? Mine? Robert Frank's? Berenice Abbott's? My photographs appreciate the figure or character or face in the panoramic space of time as in eternity. This is literally the panoramic space of the other side of the apartment; or in the middle of the Metropolitan Museum of Art; or Market Street, San Francisco; or the sky above Kerouac's brow; Phil Whalen in a chair; Neal Cassady on Market Street; Huncke on Times Square; Burroughs in front of a sphinx in the museum, or on the subway; Jack in 1953 on a fire escape; the gang in front of City Lights bookstore; Gregory Corso on Boulevard Pasteur, Tangier, in 1961; Bill Burroughs and Paul Bowles and Gregory and Allen Ansen in the garden of Villa Mouneria in Tangier beneath a clear sky. There are minute particulars, and photographs involve the noticing of their place in history, time, and space, Tangier or Times Square. The particular person, my subject, is aware of this place as I am aware of his place in space and time. We are assuming that the place and time and space are all sacred and vanishing as a moment in eternity, in which *both* characters, the subject and the photographers, are aware of the eternity. A vulgar interpretation would be: "These guys knew they were historic," or "Those guys knew they were mythical." The mythic element comes from the awareness of the eternal, and the eternal comes from awareness of the transitory, which comes in turn with a recognition of suffering. The pain and the realization of the suffering leads to the sacramental compassion for the nature of the fleeting moment. Kerouac wrote a poem expressing this clearly (for me)—*Mexico City Blue's* 54th chorus ends:

On both occasions I had wild
Face looking into lights
On streets where phantoms
Hastened out of sight
Into Memorial Cello Time.[7]

1. Quoted in Ginsberg, "A Commentary of Sacramental Companions," *Allen Ginsberg Photographs* ([Altadena, Calif.]: Twelvetrees Press, 1990), npn; a few of the photographs previously appeared in the "Notes" section of Allen Ginsberg, *Collected Poems, 1947–1980* (New York: Harper & Row, 1984) and later in Ginsberg, *Snapshot Poetics*. See also Ginsberg's unpublished lecture, "Photographic Poetics," March 15, 1988, in the Focus on Photography series sponsored and taped by the Department of Photography, Fogg Art Museum, Harvard University; and his early collaboration with the photographer Alexandra Lawrence in *Ankor Wat* (London: Fulcrum Press, 1968).

2. The connection with Arbus's captions was noted by Elsa Dorfman, in conversation with the editor, July 15, 1991, while discussing her own handwritten captions, which resemble Ginsberg's. For more about Dorfman and Ginsberg, see the selection on McKenna et al. above.

3. See Ginsberg, "Robert Frank to 1985—A Man," in *Robert Frank*, ed. Tucker, p. 81, and the Kerouac and Dorfman selections above. See also Krementz's photograph of Ginsberg, Burroughs, and Jean Genêt at the 1968 Democratic Convention, in *The Writer's Image*, npn.

4. See Michael Schumacher, *Dharma Lion: A Biography of Allen Ginsberg* (New York: St. Martin's Press, 1992), pp. 685–86, in addition to the two Ginsberg photograph collections cited in note 1 above.

5. Gay Sunshine Press, San Francisco, 1980.

6. W. C. Williams, *The Collected Earlier Poems* (New York: New Directions, 1966), p. 202.

7. Kerouac, *Mexico City Blues* (New York: Grove Press, 1959).

pdike (1932–), acclaimed for his polished style and perceptive insights into American domestic life, is also a talented comic draftsman who has studied and written about art.[1] The author used a camera himself—"at the peak of my taking-pics-of-the-kids phrase, a phase I guess most American men go through"[2]—and employed photography in a variety of interesting ways in his writing. For example, he devoted several poems to the subject, accompanying some with family photographs in "Midpoint" (1969).[3] He also featured one professional photographer as the narrator of a tender short story, "The Day of the Dying Rabbit" (1969), and another as the guest of honor at a chic New York party in Bech Is Back (1982), which wittily reflected the rise in the commercial value of photographs and the consequent celebrity status of photographers.[4] In 1986, Updike wrote this foreword to accompany an exhibition catalogue of pictures by fifteen eminent photographers of their own family members [Figs. 151–56], some never before seen publicly; but the project was canceled.[5] Updike recently wrote about the most memorable photograph he'd ever seen—one from Life magazine of a "Dancing Wahine" celebrating Hawaii's statehood in 1959—which to him embodied the "Grandeur. Ephemerality. Eroticism. Poignance" of life itself.[6] He also provided an afterword to a reissue of Edward Steichen's First Picture Book (1930) for young children and an introduction to a book of Magnum photographs.[7]

"All in the Family"

The science and the art of photography have been from the beginning tied to the mystery of time; in fascinated exploration of this mystery we are drawn to the photographs on museum walls, and to those in family albums as well. In just such a way (we think to ourselves), in sunlight indistinguishable from that of tomorrow afternoon, this woman, this child, this Indian chief posed; bodies now forever dissolved were in a certain instant bombarded by photons, were inarguably <u>there</u>. A photograph presents itself not only as a visual representation but as <u>evidence</u>, more convincing than a painting's because of the unimpeachable mechanical means whereby it was made. We do not trust the artist's flattering hand; but we do trust film, and shadows, and light. Yes, trolley tracks once ran down Fifth Avenue, amid all those straw hats, and the Sphinx was buried up to its ears in sand, while gaunt brown guides in dirty caftans squinted toward the mysterious Europeans with their curious black boxes on tripods. And yes, we ourselves once did have this slim smooth shape, with not a gray hair, and our daughter, now herself a mother, was a bald babe in arms. Many of us learn to operate a camera only when we have children, and a record of their growth and change seems suddenly necessary, as once our own seemed to our parents, whose brittle, yellowing snapshots accumulated in shoe boxes and albums out of the same devotional, conservative impulse that collects our color slides in carrousels—priceless evidence, when the moment comes to investigate the baffling death of

152. Emmet Gowin. 'Edith, Danville, Virginia, 1983.'

151. *(opposite)* Dorothea Lange. 'Hands, Maynard and Dan Dixon,' c. 1930.

The very first photographs showed inanimate objects—houses and streets—that remained still for the long length of exposure; the first human figure recorded on film, we learn, was a man whose tiny silhouette was holding still for a shoeshine on a Paris boulevard in 1839. As chemical advances shrank the exposure time from hours to minutes and then seconds, the camera found in the human physiognomy and form the subject it was made for. Even those first stiff daguerreotypes have, in distinction from the always somewhat stylized images of painted portraiture, that helpless individuality, that sharp intimacy peculiar to film. Film is itself <u>exposed</u>, and we expect, when looking at photographs, to encounter nakedness, even though it be that (in this collection) of Paul Strand's wife's extraordinarily close and tenderly open face, or that of Dorothea Lange's husband's veined and weathered hands [Fig. 151].

The painter can imagine or reconstruct, whereas the photographer must have his subject physically present; exposure naturally occurs in the family circle. To the photographer both professional and amateur, to "take" a picture of a spouse or child is an act of love, of possession and of arrest, of rescue from time's flow. This capture, however, can also be felt as unkind: the intimacy and vulnerability of private life are turned public and given an unwelcome permanence; the embarrassed wife and children scream in protest during the slide show, and afterwards try to pull out and throw away the unflattering image. The issue is further complicated when the photographer is an artist, and entitled to an artist's cold eye. One would like to know how, for example, Charis Weston, Nancy Chappell, and Edith Gowin [Fig. 152] felt about the unblinking images of their nude bodies that were produced by their husbands and are here displayed. Perhaps, one must suppose, women burdened with petty vanity or excessive modesty do not marry serious practitioners of the photographic art, and in the spirit of a mutual enterprise submit their bodies to his lens. The family member as model, without the paid compensation models usually get, and with sentimental claims models do not usually (at least until well on their way to becoming

former selves and the strange disappearance of precious days.

That the photograph serves as evidence and souvenir does not mitigate the claim of photography to be an art: all art arises out of an original usefulness, and aesthetic appeal subtly compounds the stimulation of a number of basic appetites. A photograph offers us a glimpse into the abyss of time, and its fascination is tinged, then, with a certain morbidity, and a certain historical prurience. Prurience of the obvious kind, too—the photograph is taken through a kind of peephole, and not many years passed after the technique's invention before it was being used to spy on naked bodies, with an aim of sexual excitation. Like film, skin has a grain, and is sensitive to light; there is an affinity. Stereoptical pornography dates from as early as 1850, and the "art photo" of the nude followed at a distance—the 1880s saw Muybridge's quasi-scientific studies of naked motion and Eakins' sober studio portraits of female nudes masked or with averted faces.

John Updike

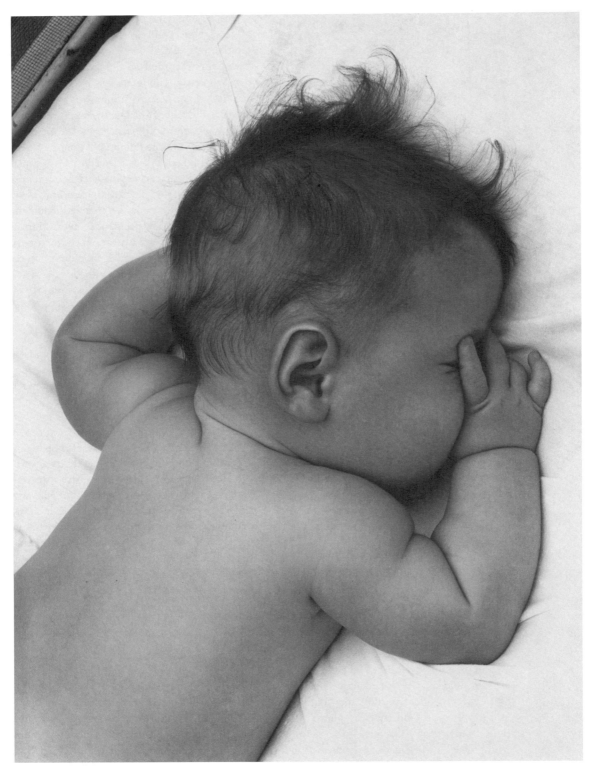

153. Eliot Porter. 'Jonathan,' 1938.

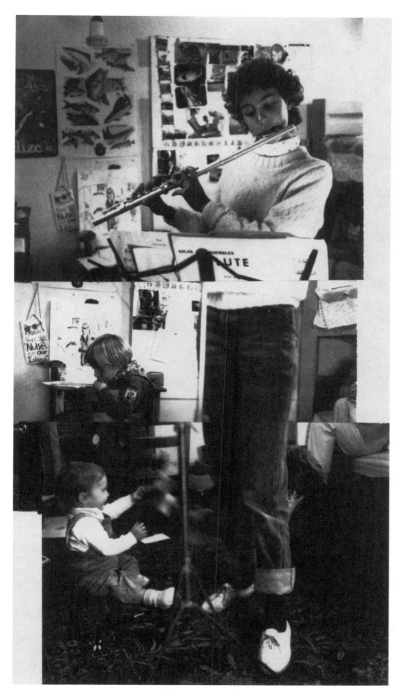

154. Danny Lyon. 'Gabe and Instruments,' November 1984.

wives) exert, is, if not a contradiction in terms, at least a problematical factor in the artistic equation solved variously by our fifteen artists. In these photographs, those of Alfred Stieglitz appear to use family members, particularly his well-endowed niece Georgia Englehard and handsomely bony second wife Georgia O'Keeffe, much as if they were interestingly shaped models, to be posed, captured, and dismissed, whereas Eliot Porter's are warmly infused with family affection and a sense of domestic setting [Fig. 153]—as are, indeed, the paintings of his brother Fairfield. And in the work of Danny Lyon the casual family snapshot has become the form itself, only a wider, quicker, and wittier eye distinguishing his collection from the artlessly snapped souvenirs of a million bourgeois vacations [Fig. 154].

Photography is the first art wherein the tool does most of the work. The musician must understand harmonics, and the painter know something (though, in the cases of Leonardo and Joshua Reynolds, not enough) of his messy medium; but the amateur photographer aims and clicks in happy ignorance of what exactly he triggers within his little black box, and of the mountainous store of chemical and mechanical ingenuities upon which he so easily draws. In truth the aiming and the clicking are, if not everything, a great deal; attempts to combine and distort and otherwise manipulate negatives, whether those of nineteenth-century pseudo-painters Oscar Rejlander or Henry P. Robinson or of today's avant-garde darkroom contortionists, offend (to my mind) the genius of photography. Our aesthetic response is inextricably entwined with the actuality, the there-ness of the subject, thought it was only there for four-hundredths of a second and may look as abstract as Edward Weston's cabbage leaves. The photograph sees for us; it sees faster and sharper than the eye, more steadily and spaciously, but our world is what it sees. In this sense all photography is journalistic, and no useful distinction exists, in the history of the art, between Mathew Brady's plates of Civil War carnage and Julia Cameron's artfully posed portraits of peaceful Victorians. The contempo-

rary parent as photographer (of course it may be the grandparent, or even a child; anyone over five can become, for one lucky shot, a Lartigue) potentially revivals the eminent experts whose family photographs are assembled here.

What is the difference? What makes, we ask ourselves, these photos different from those we and our obedient Nikons take? An energy of combination, perhaps. An exemplary photograph is rarely of one thing only; the focus has been cleverly multiplied. Brett and Neil Weston's bare-chested brawn combined with the structural drama of, respectively, a fallen tree and a half-built boat; Anna Friedlander's intent face combined with the perspective-enlarged bell of her trombone and the profile of the listening dog, who looks blown out of scale by the noise we cannot hear: the capture or concoction of such visual "events" make amusement within

the family generally amusing, and give the domestic picture a detached, ironical frame. Also, we might notice, the natural environment has often a force and presence that set up a counterpoint—the pine trunks that surround Emmeline Stieglitz, the Western terrains behind the Westons. Robert Frank's portraits are notably indirect: his wife, Mary, is seen upstaged by the sweeping shadow she is casting on the wall while she dozes, and then is reduced to a shaggy silhouette while the camera focuses on the quizical face of a statue, and lastly is lost within a surreal composition that rests the ocean exactly on her head and divides her face in half with a shadow that we presume is the photographer's own. Her stare, with one pale eye and one dark one, looks malevolent, or at best impatient; certainly these family portraits are distinguished from our own by the relative absence of smiles.

155. Imogen Cunningham. 'Twins,' 1921 (unpublished).

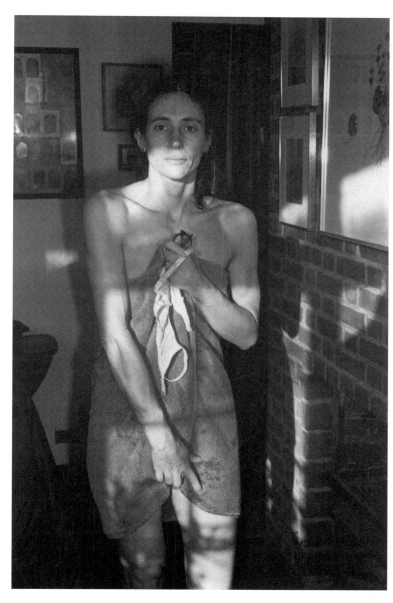

156. Lee Friedlander. 'Maria Friedlander, New City, New York,' 1976.

Something deeper than the amiability of mutual approval and shared happiness is being searched out. These families often appear not only somber but haggard. Childhood, in this photographs, seems often nude but rarely blithe. Imogen Cunningham's children look at their mother with worried expressions [Fig. 155], and little Jazmina MacNeil has tears on her face. But for a happy riot in the Frank household, and an enchanting Impressionist sunburst of smiles from Steichen's first wife and daughter in 1905, the family mood feels ambivalent. And we, the viewer, cannot quite shake our possibly illegitimate curiosity about the subjects themselves, especially when we are invited into the texture and tumult of family life as closely as we are by W. Eugene Smith and Robert Frank. What is happening here? we want to ask them. What do the neighbors think of your all-over tan? What's it like, living with a photographer?

Perhaps we are being unduly sensitive and prone to the medium's morbidity to feel a certain doom moving through this assemblage of vanished moments, of aging women and wary men held up to the light, of first wives yielding to second wives and husbands, of downy toddlerhood turning into haughty adolescence. Always we are aware, in looking at photographs, that something lay beyond the edges, in the dimensions both of space and time. Unlike the older, more humanly shaped arts, which begin with a seed and accumulate their form organically, photography clips its substance out of an actual continuum. A painting includes all that the painter wished to include; Toulouse-Lautrec and Degas were being witty when they transferred to their canvases the fractional forms and interrupted gestures of the new mode of picture-making. Our knowledge that something lurks just beyond the edge of exposure is ominous; a motion picture is more terrifying than a play because a huge anything—a mummy's hand, a knife, a contorted mutilated face—might in the next instant leap onto the screen, whereas all that can enter a stage is another painted, costumed, self-importantly piping, life-sized human being. The violent clipping of, say, the nude mother and daughter that Walter Chappell found (or posed) upon the sand, or the stunning simplification of Harry Callahan's focus upon his infant daughter's pate, achieve out of these parts a sum of implied immensity, a mythic roundness. In the dimension of time, too, a photograph has edges: the glimpses of Eleanor Callahan half-covered by a bedsheet, or Edith Gowin holding her translucent nightgown away from her opaque body, or Maria Friedlander clutching a towel to her with the same hand that holds glasses and a bra [Fig. 156] all invite us to imagine the moments before and after. Is the amorous curve descending or ascending from this point we glimpse, or is that point merely a pose, struck by request? Family life flows through and around these photographs, but the flow is troubled by the unseen presence, the armed and probing invader of the intimate circle, the wit-

ness with camera. He or she is a presence partly sinister, bringing a reminder of time and mortality into the self-forgetful animal cycle of mating and rearing progeny. Because these photographers are artists, the shadows are deeper, the grays more tellingly modulated, the cool that surrounds our islands of warmth more palpable, than in the snapshots we amateurs take in a doting spirit of tribute to those who have consented to share our lives. Not that the customary fond motives and emotions are absent here; but they are present, as it were, in solution, part of a chemistry as complex as that of film itself. Observation, the physicists tell us, is a kind of interaction, which beclouds itself; these beautiful images oscillate indeterminately, fascinatingly between just family and just photography.

Note: The editor was able to see reproductions of many but not all of the originally planned pictures. The following list should help the interested reader locate the specific pictures cited by Updike—some reproduced here, most not—that have been published and other ones of family members by the same photographers.

Harry Callahan: see "Eleanor" (New York: Calloway; Carmel, Calif.: Friends of Photography, 1983), fig. 41 [baby's pate].

Walter Chappell: see Legacy of Light (New York: Knopf, 1987), pp. 158–9 ["Nancy Crocheting," and "Nude Torso between Legs," both in Wingdale, New York, 1962; the ones to be exhibited, perhaps unpublished, were "Meadow and Riversong," Pumice Mine, New Mexico, 1983, and "Nancy Pregnant," Big Sur, California, 1964.

Imogen Cunningham: see in Judy Dater, Imogen Cunningham: A Portrait (Boston: New York Graphic Society, 1979), pp. 13, 22–23, 28, 35, and Plate 58–59. "The Twins" (aka "Ron and Padric") has been exhibited but not previously published.

Robert Frank: see Lines of My Hand (New York: Pantheon, 1989), npn [Mary and Pablo]; Robert Frank: From New York to Nova Scotia, ed. Anne Tucker (Boston: Little, Brown; Houston: Museum of Fine Arts, 1986), p. 29 [Mary and Andrea, New York, 1956] and [pp. 98–99] [Pablo and June Leaf, Frank's second wife]; and in Kerouac, Pull My Daisy (1961), npn [pictures of Pablo as "Little Boy"].

Lee Friedlander: see Like a One-Eyed Cat: Photographs, 1956–1987 (New York: Abrams/Seattle Art Museum, 1989); Maria (Washington, D.C.: Smithsonian Institution Press, 1992); and Peter Galassi, Pleasures and Terrors of Domestic Life (New York: MOMA, 1991) [Daughter, dog and tuba].

Emmet Gowin: see Photographs (Philadelphia: Philadelphia Museum of Art; Boston: Bulfinch Press, 1990), pp. 17–19 and 102–3.

Dorothea Lange: see Photographs of a Lifetime (Millerton, N.Y.: Aperture, 1982), pp. 13, 38–39, 153–58, and Milton Meltzer, Dorothea Lange: A Photographer's Life (New York: Farrar, Straus & Giroux, 1985), pp. 107–9 and 373.

Danny Lyon: see I Like to Eat Right on the Dirt (Clintondale, N.Y.: Black Beauty Books/Filmhaus, 1989) [children].

Wendy MacNeil: see W. Snyder MacNeil: Daughter/ Father. Exhibition catalogue, January 29–March 6, 1988, with an essay by Eugenia Parry Janis (Boston: Photography Resource Center, 1988).

Eliot Porter: see "Jonathan" in Twice a Year 2 (Spring-Summer 1939): frontispiece, between 5–7, and Eliot Porter (Boston: New York Graphic Society in association with the Amon Carter Museum, 1987), pp. 31 [Jonathan, 1938], 40–41 [Stephen, 1948, and Patrick, 1950].

W. Eugene Smith: see William S. Johnson, ed. "Family and Friends, 1945–1958," W. Eugene Smith: Master of the Photographic Essay (Millerton, N.Y.: Aperture, 1981), pp. 125–28; and see also "My Daughter Juanita," Life 35 [2] (September 21, 1953): 165–70.

Edward Steichen: see A Life in Photography, figs. 91–93 [wife].

Alfred Stieglitz: see Sue Davidson Lowe, Stieglitz: A Memoir/Biography (New York: Farrar, Straus & Giroux, 1983), following pp. 232 [young Georgia Englehard]; and Georgia O'Keeffe: A Portrait by Alfred Stieglitz (New York: Metropolitan Museum, [1978]).

Paul Strand: see Belinda Rathbone, "Portrait of a Marriage: Paul Strand's Portraits of Rebecca," J. Paul Getty Museum Journal 17 (1989) 83–98; reprinted in Paul Strand:

Essays on His Life and Work, ed. Maren Stange (New York: Aperture, 1991), pp. 72–86.

Edward Weston: see Weston, *Daybooks,* ed. Newhall, vol. 1, figs. 18 and 21 [Neil] and Stebbins, *Weston's Westons,* Plates 32–70 [Charis Wilson].

1. Updike studied at the Ruskin School of Drawing and Fine Art at Oxford (1954–55). His *Just Looking: Essays on Art* (New York: Knopf, 1989) does not include a piece about photography, but a future volume may well be devoted to the subject and include some of the pieces cited here.

2. Updike, quoted from his letter to the editor, February 28, 1991. A celebrated writer since his college years, Updike has been photographed often, most frequently perhaps by Jill Krementz. See her remarks about Updike in *Something About the Author Autobiography Series,* vol. 8, p. 176, and four of her portraits of him and his family, 1975 and 1979, reproduced in *The Writer's Image,* npn.

3. See Updike, "Midpoint," pp. 3–44 (especially pp. 12–13 and 23–37) and "Camera," p. 54, in *Midpoint and Other Poems* (New York: Knopf, 1969); "Exposure," p. 22, and "Meditation on a News Item," pp. 37–39, in *Telephone Poles and Other Poems* (New York: Knopf, 1963); and "Snapshots" in *The Carpentered Hen and Other Tame Creatures* (New York: Harper & Brothers, 1958), pp. 59–60.

4. See Updike: "The Day of the Dying Rabbit," in *Museums and Women and Other Stories* (New York: Knopf, 1972), pp. 26–40; and "White on White," from *Bech Is Back* (New York: Knopf, 1982), pp. 180–95. Updike has also drawn on photographs for action and imagery in other fictional works: see, for example, "From the Journal of a Leper," in *Problems and Other Stories* (New York: Knopf, 1979), pp. 184 and 187; and in "Bech Panics," in *Bech: A Book* (New York: Knopf, 1970), pp. 99–132.

5. "Just Family: Family Photographs by 15 American Photographers," an exhibition curated by Belinda Rathbone, was to open at the Metropolitan Museum in 1987, with a catalogue published by Knopf; the entire enterprise was canceled when Polaroid withdrew its sponsorship. Rathbone generously provided the editor with a copy of Updike's original text as well as indispensable information about the planned photographs.

6. See Updike, "A State of Ecstasy," *Art and Antiques* 7, no. 1 (January 1990): 74–75.

7. See Updike, "First Things First," *Art and Antiques* (October 1991): 57–60, reprinted as "The Steichens' Book of First Things," an afterword in a reissue of Mary Steichen Calderone, Edward Steichen, and John Updike, *The First Picture Book: Everyday Things for Babies* (New York: Fotofolio/Library Fellows of the Whitney Museum of American Art, 1991), pp. 57–66, a work originally published by Mary Steichen [then Martin] (New York: Harcourt Brace, 1930). See also Updike, Introduction to *Heroes and Anti Heroes, Magnum Images* (New York: Random House, 1991).

John Updike

98. Richard Howard

*H*oward (1929–), a poet, translator, and essayist, is an erudite and versatile man of letters. Interested in all the arts, especially visual ones, he has contributed to bringing literature and photography together in diverse ways. Howard edited and provided commentaries for an anthology of poems chosen by contemporary poets, each photographed by Thomas Victor.[1] His dramatic monologues and dialogues often discuss (with reproductions) nineteenth-century photographs, such as Nadar's of the writers Hugo, Baudelaire, Gautier, and Sand.[2] Another of his poems is set in Julia Margaret Cameron's Freshwater, on the Isle of Wight, and yet another juxtaposes a modern woman talking to her psychiatrist with the elderly Lewis Carroll talking to one of his child subjects.[3] Howard is also one of the most distinguished translators of French literature and in that capacity has introduced to English-speaking audiences such works as Breton's Nadja and Barthes's Camera Lucida, which have profoundly influenced literary critics and photographers.[4] Finally, Howard is a gifted essayist who counts among his best pieces an erudite survey of the nude in photography and finely detailed analyses of photographs by Robert Mapplethorpe (1946–89) [Figs. 157–59], such as the one that follows. His finely detailed work, in whatever genre, always evokes broader aesthetic issues.[5]

FROM "THE MAPPLETHORPE EFFECT"

Figures

In Mapplethorpe's photographs, the world of inorganic form is absent save as it is defined by the organic. What we think of as Leonardo's circle, and Leonardo's square inscribed within it, are evoked by many of the astonishing bodies, astonishingly posed in *Black Book* (1986), and indeed the geometry of these cherished figures is insistently caressed by deliberate and theatrical lighting, by occasional props of flowers—the sheaf of six calla lilies held by *Dennis Speight, 1983* [Fig. 157], alludes to a potential orgasmic flowering, a sort of seminal bouquet—and by the photographers's repeated assertion that it is the bodies of black men which will take the

Richard Howard

158. Robert Mapplethorpe. 'Lisa Lyon with Bow and Arrow,' 1982.

light, and the darkness, with the most resolute formal determination. In most instances, Mapplethorpe's images of the nude male are isolated, solitary. Exceptionally the drama is offered as dialogue (an embrace, an agon between parallel black and white forms); characteristically, the "subject" is a lyric efflorescence within the intervals and analogies of a single body. Moreover this single body itself will not be taken whole but cropped (literally, anatomized) so as to declare its symmetrical relations intramurally, as it were, without reference to classi-

cal canons of wholeness, of completed form— rather, with regard to new proportions, new affinities, among them figures which include the genitals in unabashed exploration of what has always been treated as the body's disgraced member.

In his studies of the bodybuilder Lisa Lyon, it is of course a reversal of stereotypes which Mapplethorpe effects. Precisely the kind of lyric stasis so lovingly studied in male bodies traditionally granted movement and power (in other

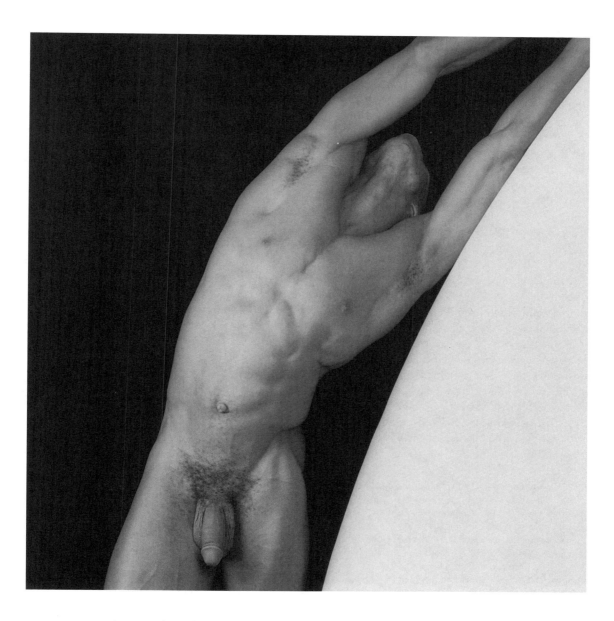

159. Robert Mapplethorpe. 'Thomas,' 1986.

words, a paradoxical anti-phallicism, if we take our lead from the culture's interpretation of the phallic as dominance, as inflexibility, as denial of the other's response) is withheld in the *Lisa Lyon* series: Lyon repeatedly subverts, in images of sleek force and definition [Fig. 158], the conventions of female iconography she is made to criticize, to parody, to transform. "Seeing things like they haven't been seen before"—Mapplethorpe's words hover over all his nude figures, though I am convinced that the major revelation of these studies, the bur-

den of their enormous effort—in which the camera is compelled to acknowledge desire with an avidity not just optic but haptic—is that of the body's implicit *energeia* to rise, to mount, to erect itself into an insurgent principle.

Against what? What is the antagonist of these forms so suavely figured, so cunningly sectioned to reveal new anatomies, inadmissible analogies, what Macbeth calls *understood relations* which bring forth the secret'st man of blood? Perhaps the answer is given most diagrammatically in the photograph *Thomas,* 1986 [Fig. 159]; in darkness, tangent to a great white arc on the right, the frontal nude—garishly lighted so that it has lost its bronze patina so prized by Mapplethorpe—yearns upward, strives, grasps (though the hands are cropped) for ascension while the body *depends,* the very organ of erection limp, the double socle of the thighs ponderous in their (also cropped) downward thrust. In all Mapplethorpe's figures, though, each separate body is its own repertoire of ascensional pulsions, reservoirs of potential elevation against the gravity of its own structure, a headlong architecture of antitheticals.

The unified if never uniform impulse I would discern in Mapplethorpe's flowers, Mapplethorpe's faces, Mapplethorpe's figures is a continuous struggle, the contestation of heft. Solemnity of effigy is the consequence, I suppose, of a certain undecided outcome: flowers spring up against their own weight; engorged with juice, they are never shown attached to the cycle which would make their momentary victory more than just that. Faces are transpicuous with energy, with appetite, yet there is always

the gravity of the features, of the flesh which pulls which *ponderates,* in the sense of bearing down what aspires to rise, to mount to expression, to identity. And figures glow with the potency of their rhythms, their newly revealed analogies of form—yet even as these arresting pelvic landscapes can rise and indeed reach beyond themselves, they are shown always in their dense and onerous potentiality only, the long muscles and the delicate veins finally burdensome, unredeemed—impugning all we used to mean by "phallic." If I reach for such terms as transcendence, redemption, the apparatus of the sacred, it is because I used to think Mapplethorpe's photography was grim with the restrictive occasions of obsession and fetishism; but after a certain meditation, pondering their reasons and their realizations, I discern these pictures—a good share of them—to be emblems of contested mortality, grave with the contradictions of organic life in their aspiration to ecstasy, as crystalline in terms of their own art as the sonatas of Scarlatti or the last paintings of Mondrian, but as problematic, as imprecatory as any representation of the body I know, fond enemy and ally.

1. Howard, *Preferences,* with photographs by Thomas Victor (New York: Viking, 1974). Victor, who, like Rollie McKenna earlier, became a photographer for the YMHA Poetry Center in New York City, was planning a book of literary portraits at his death, according to the obituary in the *New York Times* (February 9, 1989): section 2: 15.

2. See Howard's poems in "Homage to Nadar," in *Misgivings* (New York: Atheneum, 1979), pp. 17–57, and "Homage to Nadar (II)," in *Lining Up* (New York: Atheneum, 1984), pp. 13–39. See also Howard, "Impersonations, II: *Loti Costumed as Osiris,* Photograph by Montastier, 1906 (Musée Carnavalet, Paris)," in *Lining Up,* pp. 57–59; "1891: An Idyll," in *Untitled Subjects* (New York: Atheneum, 1969), pp. 66–70; and "Move Still, Still So," in *Lining Up,* pp. 81–88.

3. See Breton, *Nadja* [1928], trans. Howard (New York: Grove Press, 1960), and Barthes, *Camera Lucida* [1980], trans. Howard (New York: Farrar, Straus & Giroux, 1981).

4. See Howard: "The Nude," *Legacy of Light* (New York: Knopf, 1987), pp. 151–57, and the entire "The Mapplethorpe Effect," introduction to *Robert Mapplethorpe,*

by Richard Marshall (London: Secker & Warburg; New York: Whitney Museum, 1988), pp. 152–59. See also Howard's pieces on younger photographers: his afterword to Alex Kayser, *Heads* (New York: Abbeville, 1985), pp. 122–27, and essay "One Flesh: Photographs by Holly Wright," *Gettysburg Review* 1, no. 3 (September 1988): 569–76.

It is interesting to compare Howard's analysis of Mapplethorpe's photographs with views of his work by other writers. See Susan Sontag, preface to Mapplethorpe, *Certain People: A Book of Portraits* (Pasadena, Calif.: Twelvetrees Press, 1985); Ntozake Shange, "Irrepressibly Bronze, Beautiful and Mine," in Mapplethorpe, *Black Book* (New York: St. Martin's, 1986), npn; Joan Didion, "An Annotation," in Mapplethorpe, *Some Women* (Boston: Bulfinch Press/Little, Brown, 1989), npn. See also Mapplethorpe's illustrations for Arthur Rimbaud, *A Season in Hell* (New York: Limited Editions Club, 1986), and some literary portraits in Mapplethorpe, *Mapplethorpe: Chatwin* (1979) [fig. 150], p. 77; Burroughs (1981), p. 129, and (1980), p. 200; and Mailer (1985), p. 211, and Capote (1981) in Germano Celant, *Mapplethorpe versus Rodin* (Milan: Electa, 1992), p. 52.

FROM "EUDORA WELTY AND PHOTOGRAPHY:
AN INTERVIEW" BY HUNTER COLE
AND SEETHA SRINIVASAN, 1989

Welty (1909–) [Fig. 140] was a serious photographer before becoming a celebrated writer about her native Mississippi. Her interest was stimulated by her father, a photography enthusiast who developed his family pictures and also helped two young men set up the first camera store in Jackson. Welty thought of becoming a professional photographer after completing her formal education in New York City (1931). She got a job as a publicity agent for the W.P.A., photographing throughout Mississippi during the Depression (1933–36), and had two shows in Manhattan (1936–37). But her portfolios, with and without narratives, were rejected for publication, and her idea for a book of cemetery scenes never materialized. More successful selling short stories, Welty then turned her gifts for close observation to writing, though continuing to photograph foreign scenes or literary friends on occasion [Fig. 160]. Though her own pictures were never used in her writing except to help others illustrate or dramatize them, they nevertheless reveal many parallels with her stories: both are selective, focus on single moments—often featuring parades, carnivals, and graveyards—and involve relationships between individuals or small groups who appear typically "Southern."[1] With the growth of scholarly interest in photography and a change in its technical and aesthetic ideals since the 1960's, the "snapshot" qualities of Welty's photographs have been increasingly appreciated.[2]

FROM "EUDORA WELTY AND PHOTOGRAPHY: AN INTERVIEW" BY HUNTER COLE AND SEETHA SRINIVASAN

Was it your father and his love of mechanical instruments that interested you in photography?

I suppose indirectly. The pictures he was taking were mostly of us, but we were hardly conscious of that. I do remember being allowed to handle his camera. He had a nice Eastman camera with a bellows that pulled out a good long way. He made the exposure by pressing a little bulb, as I remember. It took postcard-sized pictures. I learned much later on that he'd had other cameras that produced different-sized photos — I found the negatives he had made. He and my mother used to develop them and print the pictures at night, before we children were born, my mother told me. Domestic scenes, early in their marriage—Mother putting up her hair, Daddy reading. They charm me.

Didn't he encourage some entrepreneur to develop a camera store or a photography shop in Jackson?

He did—when the Schleuters came to Jackson. My father's insurance company, the Lamar Life, was then a little Greek edifice, if you remember, with columns, on Capitol Street, near Mrs. Black's grocery store and the Pythian Castle. On its other side was a vacant lot. The Schleuters came in and asked my father about it and he was interested because he liked photography and because they were two brothers, young and starting out in a strange place. He did encourage them, I don't know in what way. And they started Standard Photo Company, built on the vacant lot, and made a success. They did my pictures all through the years, and advised me and were good friends.

When your pictures were printed, did they give a surprise? A good one or a bad one? You know that various camera lenses have personalities? Did you detect that when you were printing your pictures?

Well, I had only a single lens in those days, you know. I just thought: that was the lens. After I got the Rolleiflex, the only other lens I bought was a portrait attachment, which I didn't use too much because I like showing background, a long perspective, in the kind of portraits I attempt. I wanted to set people in their context. And I think I had a cloud filter; but that's all. I never used lights. I'm not in any sense of the word a professional. I just wanted to get the subject and play with it afterwards; cutting and enlarging and so on, I find my composition. Let it show what was inherent in it.

When you were travelling and taking photographs, you really began to see the state in which you lived. Would you say that your experience with photographs heightened your sense of place?

I think it did. I think the same thing that made me take the pictures made me understand the pictures after I saw them, the same curiosity, interest. I've always been a visual-minded person. Most of us are. I could see a picture composing itself without too much trouble when I started taking landscapes and groups and catching people in action. Practice did make me see what to bring out and define what I was after, I think.

As you reflect on your pictures, what do you see in them now after all these many years?

I see a record. The life in those times. And that's really why I thought *One Time One Place*, in 1970, would make a book. It stands as a record of a time and place.

You have said that a camera is a shy person's protection and that you came from a sheltered life, but you've had the spirit of daring required of an artist. Would you comment on how a shy person such as you took some of these daring photographs?

Well, the daring I meant was referring to my writing instead of photography, but also I think my particular time and place contributed to the frankness, openness of the way the pictures came about. This refers to both the photographer and the subjects of the photographs. I was never questioned, or avoided. There was no self-consciousness on either side. I just spoke to persons on the street and said, "Do you mind if I take this picture?" and they didn't care. There was no sense of violation of anything on either side. I don't think it existed; I know it didn't in my attitude, or in theirs. All of that unself-consciousness is gone now. There is no such relationship between a photographer and a subject possible any longer.

Why it that?

Everybody is just so media-conscious. Maybe it's television. Everybody thinks of pictures as publicity or—I don't know. I wouldn't be interested in doing such a book today, even if it were possible. Because it would assume a different motive and produce a different effect.

What did the pictures teach you about writing fiction? Did they teach you anything?

Nothing consciously, I guess, or specifically. I was writing all this time, but I think perhaps a kindred impulse made me attempt two unrelated things—an inquiring nature, and a wish to respond to what I saw, and to what I felt about things, by something I produced or did.

Did they teach you anything about perception or anything about technique?

I'm sure they taught me about the practice of perception and about technique, but the lessons were not in the abstract. Some perception of the world and some habit of observation shaded into the other, just because in both cases, writing and photography, you were trying to portray what you saw, and truthfully. Portray life, living people, as you saw them. And a camera could catch that fleeting moment, which is what a short story, in all its depth, tries to do.

If it's sensitive enough, it catches the transient moment.

You studied studio art, you painted, you sketched. In these, do you suppose, as perhaps with photography, that you were searching for a way to reach your calling as a writer of fiction?

I don't think so. My way to learn writing was through writing, from the start, and I did write in strict concentration. It may have occurred without my knowing it that the two interests cooperated in their own way, but I wasn't thinking about either writing or photography except through the doing. Technique springs out of the doing; there's something in the heart of a given story that tells me how to do it and do that only. It's *after* the fact of writing a story that I realize what it has taught me.

It was during one of your WPA trips that you discovered you were truly a writer. In Tishomingo County, Mississippi.

Well, I assigned it there because that is the furthest in Mississippi I ever went. I didn't have a blinding moment of revelation. But just when I was working on *Losing Battles,* a novel set in that part of the world, so much came back to me of what I had absorbed. It was so remote from anything I knew in Jackson or had seen in the Delta or on the Coast or in the Black Prairie country, or any of the other parts of Mississippi where I've been. It appealed to me as a stage to put *Losing Battles* on because life there had been so whittled down to the bare bones of existence. No history but the struggle to keep alive. What was life but family? I was trying to describe what the characters' lives were like without benefit of any editorial comment at all, or any interior description. I wanted things shown by speech, by action, and by setting, location. And characters to reveal themselves and each other by conversation—action and conversation. I confined it all within a big family reunion, to a time length of two days and the night between. Plus the essential flashback.

That technique is very much like in photography?

Except that what is shown is selective. Chosen, specific, pertinent, and thus revelatory.

There is no interpretation in a photograph. It's the viewer who interprets it, and what you've described as your technique in Losing Battles *seems very much like a photograph.*

There's a profound difference. The writer interprets before it can begin. Writing fiction, I am interpreting every minute, but always by way of the characters' own words and acts. My usual method of narration is more introspective; I am in the characters' minds all the time. So I was trying to see if I could do without any of it. It proved to be the most difficult novel I think I ever wrote.

As in a story, your photographs have a trace of mystery. In your essay on Chekhov you said that "the very greatest mystery is in unsheathed reality itself." Is this "unsheathed reality" what your photographs were exposing?

That's too abstract for me. No technique was set forth in my mind. I just wanted to capture a moment and use the right light and take advantage of what I saw.

The young girl in your story "A Memory" composes the intractable world by looking at life through a frame she makes with her fingers. In your essay "Place in Fiction" you say, "Place to the writer at work is seen in a frame . . ."

It is.

" . . . not an empty one, a brimming one." Do you recognize the close alliance of photography and fiction writing in your use of a frame?

A frame is fundamental to both, for me. I was conscious of that when I was getting my pictures, at least when I was printing the results. I knew I needed a frame. Well, when I took art from Mrs. Hull [Marie Hull, a painter and teacher in Jackson], she taught us that device: framing with your fingers. Studying drawing and painting made me aware in writing a story of framing your vision, as a way toward capturing it.

When taking a picture, what was your own personal technique in framing an image? Do you recall any?

Using the viewfinder. That's why I liked the Rolleiflex. You see exactly what you are taking, and in the same size.

Have you ever relied upon any of your photographs for a scene or an element in a story you've written?

No. The memory is far better. Personal experience casts its essential light upon it.

.   .   .   .

You said of the pictures in One Time, One Place, *"I did not take these pictures to prove anything." But the photographs do prove something, don't they?*

I think I meant "prove" editorially. *Let Us Now Praise Famous Men*, for instance, was entirely different in motivation from my own photography. I was taking photographs of human beings because they were real life and they were there in front of me and that was the reality. I was the recorder of it. I wasn't trying to exhort the public. When I was in New York during the Depression, it was the same Depression we were feeling here in Mississippi but evident in such another way in the city: lines of people waiting for food and people selling apples and sitting there in Union Square, all reading the daily paper's want ads. It was a different homelessness too from what we see today in New York. These people of the Great Depression kept alive on the determination to get back to work and to make a living again. I photographed them in Union Square and in subways and sleeping in subway stations and huddling together to keep warm, and I felt, then, sort of placed in the editorial position as I took their pictures. Recording the mass of them did constitute a plea on their behalf to the public, their existing plight being so evident in the mass.

Do you think someone, an outsider, for instance, who sees the collection of your black photographs together makes editorial comments?

They might. They might or might not know that poverty in Mississippi, white and black, really didn't have too much to do with the Depression. It was ongoing. Mississippi was long since poor, long devastated. I took the pictures of our poverty because that was reality, and I was recording it. The photographs speak for themselves. The same thing is true of my stories; I didn't announce my view editorially. I tried to show it.

"Unsheathed reality."

It was unsheathed. And when it was published, *One Time, One Place* constituted a statement of that reality. It wasn't needed for me to say, "Look what a bad thing." Or, "Look how these people are facing up to it, meeting it, hoping as well as enduring it."

Will you tell of a proposed book called Black Saturday?

It was essentially the same as what later became *One Time, One Place,* plus a number of my short stories. I was trying to interest a publisher in my stories through the combination. I got a composition ring book and pasted little contact prints in what I fitted up as a sequence to make a kind of story in itself. I used the subject of Saturday because it allowed the most variety possible to show a day among black and white people, what they would be doing, the work and the visit to town and the home and so on. I submitted along with the pictures a set of stories I had written, unrelated specifically to the photos, except that all were the South, and tried to interest book publishers in the combination.

And what was the reaction?

Rejection. It was an amateurish idea.

Did they give a reason?

Well, there were obvious ones to such a combination as I was offering. They said they were sorry. They were understanding and kind, but it was a fact that such a book was unpublishable. They were sympathetic to the stories, but weren't much interested in the photographs—they were not that kind of editors, that was not their department.

Were any of the stories later published?

They were all published. First in magazines, then in *A Curtain of Green* and *The Wide Net,* five or six years later.

And most of the photographs were later published in One Time, One Place.

Yes. I'd like to point out that when a publisher did bring out the book of photographs, thirty years later, it was a literary editor who did it, and saw it through: Albert Erskine, of Random House. He was editor of my last two novels at Random House.

And you didn't publish a story until 1936?

1936 is right. That was the first story I submitted to a magazine, "Death of a Traveling Salesman." A so-called "little magazine" accepted it, called *Manuscript,* published in Athens, Ohio.

It seemed that your taking photographs stopped or seemed considerably slowed down as you began publishing stories. The collection of photographs in the Archives indicates that by about the mid-1940s you had set aside your camera. What happened?

I guess I was still taking pictures. They were for my own pleasure, of my family and friends. The new jobs I had all had to do with journalism, not pictures. And fiction writing was my real work all along. That never let up.

I think the latest photos were in the 1950s.

That's when I lost my camera.

Will you tell about that?

I was on my first trip to Europe, and I carried my Rolleiflex and took pictures all the way through. As I was getting ready to go home, it was May Day and I was in Paris, and I had friends there and had spent the day with them in Meudon, near Versailles I think that is. It was the home of the Mians. He was a sculptor, Aristide Mian. His wife was the American writer Mary Mian. They had three growing daughters. All were on hand, and all kinds of people they knew. So I took pictures of everybody and everything. A record of happiness. Then I left on the train, got off at Gare Montparnasse to take the Metro to my hotel off Boulevard St. Germaine. They'd given me a bunch of lilacs, party food, presents, everything, saying goodbye, and I sat down on the bench in the station holding it all, with my camera beside me. And got up without the camera. I missed it as soon as I got on the subway and took the first train back. Of course it was gone. I never saw it again. Of course what I grieved for most was that roll of film was still in it, the pictures that I had taken. If I could have just got that back, the May Day party, I would have almost given them the camera.

And those people would never be assembled that way again.

Never assembled. Never again.

So that slowed you down in your picture-taking.

I punished myself. I didn't deserve a camera after that. I was so crushed, and by then cameras were much more expensive and of course now they are out of sight.

When the team of Farm Security Administration photographers came on their individual trips through Mississippi, you too were working for a federal agency, the WPA. Did you chance to see Walker Evans or any of them or their work?

Oh, no. What I should have said a while ago is that the difference between my pictures and Walker Evans', among other differences—those people were professionals—is I never posed anybody—that was on principle—and his are all deliberately composed pictures. I let my subjects go on with what they were doing and, by framing or cutting and by selection, found what composition rose from that. So, I think that's a quality that makes them different from those of professionals who were purposefully photographing for an agency, or a cause.

Some of your pictures show people at a sideshow at a carnival. What drew you to photographing oddities like carnival people?

Oh, I love crowds to take pictures in. I photographed everybody. I always did love the fair and circuses. Once or twice to photograph them, I got up early before daylight and went down to see them arrive, watch them set up the tents and the rides down at the fairgrounds. And I remember once happening to eat breakfast with some of the carnival people in the bus station. That was getting close to life!

Some of the people are freaks. Are you familiar with the photographs of Diane Arbus?

Yes, somewhat.

How do you react to photographs of freaks, the kind in her work?

I think that it totally violates human privacy, and by intention. My taking the freak *posters*—not the human beings—was because they were a whole school of naive folk art. And, of course, totally unrelated to what you saw inside the tent. The posters show bystanders being suddenly horrified at a man who could twist himself like a snake. They are all looking with hands drawn back and shrieking, and *they* were all perfectly dressed, probably wearing evening clothes.

. . . .

Could we speak of some of the notable photographers who have taken pictures of writers? You have been in photographs by Jill Krementz, Kay Bell, Thomas Victor, Jerry Bauer, Rollie McKenna, William Eggleston, and others. Do you mind being photographed?

Yes, it's not my nature to be on the other side of the camera. It came about through the circumstance of my being a writer. Many of my stories were in *Harper's Bazaar* and it was through the editors' wish that I was a subject for Cecil Beaton and Louise Dahl-Wolfe, and Irving Penn.

Will you tell about being photographed by Cecil Beaton?

He's the one I was most scared of because I was the most familiar with his work, over the years of seeing it in *Vanity Fair*. I had to go to his apartment in one of the hotels up Fifth Avenue. I didn't know what to wear. I thought I wore the safest thing, "a little black dress." And went up in the elevator and he met me at the door. It seemed to me he was the most shy and reticent and kind person I'd ever seen. And he held a Rolleiflex. It looked just like the one I had lost. And it was hand-held, and he had no lights anywhere. And it was in the winter time, a grey cold day, but he had a great flowering mimosa in the window. Not our mimosa trees, but the South-of-France kind, with little powdery yellow flowers all over it, so it looked very tropical in the window. It was fragrant. My black dress of course was wrong. But he gave me a wicker armchair to stand behind. It looked very "Cecil Beatonish." Everything was very decorative and summery. And I don't remember anything he said except just kindnesses. He offered me some tea or something, and every-

thing was very muted and peaceful. He took the pictures, and we parted. It was like a social visit in a way, but there was not much conversation back and forth.

He stood you over by the window, didn't he?

I've got one of the prints. He sent me one and had autographed it, which I thought was extremely sweet of him.

Will you tell about the photographic session with Louise Dahl-Wolfe, who was a Harper's Bazaar *photographer? A fashion photographer.*

She was interesting. I enjoyed it.

In the photographs of you, it looks as though you are against a rock on the beach.

It's in Central Park. I was to lie back on a rock in Central Park. I had on a tweed suit and a sweater. The session was brisk and very lively, and she was an interesting woman. It was Irving Penn who took me to Central Park too, and we made some funny photographs along with the ones he used.

What kind of funny photographs did he take?

In one of them I was kneeling on the ground by a sign that read "To restrooms and bear den." And one of them was sitting up in a tree, sort of like the one Frank Lyell and I concocted with myself perched in a tree at Annandale while wearing a Spanish shawl, and Frank serenading me from below.

You as a photographer yourself observed how these photographers worked. What specifically did you note about their attitudes and techniques? Anything?

I doubt that I was able. I think I observed rightly that Irving Penn was at an early part of his career. He was venturesome. Whereas, Louise Dahl-Wolfe and Cecil Beaton were majestic figures, whose work everybody knew. What I noticed about all of them was how none of them gave you any directions, laid down any rules. I don't know whether because I was hopeless or whether they just didn't ever do it; they didn't say, "Stand here," and "Put your hand here." They never said, "Smile, please!"

In "Why I Live at the P.O." the narrator tells that the only "eligible" man ever to appear in the town was a photographer who was taking "pose-yourself photos." Could you tell what a "pose-yourself photo" is?

A man that came through little towns and set up a make-shift studio in somebody's parlor and let it be known that he would be taking pictures all day in this place, and a stream of people came. He had backdrops—sepia trees and a stool—then let them pose themselves. That was an itinerant livelihood during the Depression. Itinerants were welcome, bringing excitement like that, when towns were remote and nobody ever went anywhere.

Some of those funny photographs that you and Frank Lyell took are set up like the "tableaux vivants" Julia Margaret Cameron photographed, costume pieces. Hers were a kind of "pose-yourself" photography.

Oh, they were high-minded. I think they belonged to the Rossetti period, taking themselves seriously as art.

You and your friends created some "tableaux vivants." Will you tell about those?

Well, as I say, during the Depression we made our own entertainment and one of our entertainments was to take funny pictures. We dressed up a lot, something to do at night. Even when we had little dinner parties for each other with four or six people, we wore long dresses. And everybody came, you know, we came as somebody, like parties in *Vanity Fair,* people like Lady Abdy, and the Lunts, all the people that Cecil Beaton photographed doing things at parties. We were doing our version of that. We didn't take ourselves seriously. We played charades, word games.

There is one photo of you satirizing Elizabeth Arden and Helena Rubinstein, "Helena Arden," showing you draped in a sheet and applying some very strange cosmetics.

That's right, out of the kitchen. Bon ami.

Was the photography here a parody of "smartness" in the Mencken sense?

No, we were satirizing the advertising game. In the thirties you could laugh at advertising. It was all fun. A lot of it came out of our admiration of the smart world, or longing for the artistic scene we were keeping up with: the theatre, art, and music. We'd all been to New York! The year before, at Columbia.

Didn't you yourself do some freelance fashion photography?

I tried to earn a little money doing that. I took one picture every Sunday for a shop called Oppenheimer's. And the Emporium later. I got my friends and my brother's girlfriends to pose.

In their fashions?

The shops' selections. I would pose them in different places the way they did in *Vanity Fair*—in front if the New Capitol, around the town like that. They were not very god.

And there are some time exposures in which you and a friend are set up as women of fashion.

Right. Helen Lotterhos, Margaret Harmon, and Anne Long. With jars of pampas grass, and rising cigarette smoke. Subtle lighting. These were all fun, you see. And Nothing cost anything. We had jobs, most of us, by day, and thought up our own entertainments in the evening. We'd just come out of college. We were young. We had a good time in the Depression.

What do you recall about photographing Katherine Anne Porter?

I did it every minute. A summer at Yaddo. I went to Yaddo. I'm sure, at her instigation, which you know is in Saratoga Springs, New York. A retreat for artists. She had been there a number of times as a resident. I was reading proofs of my first book. Katherine Anne was supposed to be writing the preface to my book. And my editor used to write me and say jokingly, you're supposed to make her do it. Which, of course, I never mentioned! She was busy writing what was then called *No Safe Harbor*. It was eventually *Ship of Fools*. She had also bought an old run-down clapboard farmhouse, perfectly beautiful, sitting in a meadow outside Saratoga Springs. It was heavenly, in the real country, and she was restoring it. We went out there every day. She bought a car, a Buick, first time she had ever had one, and had just learned to drive. I helped her drive some of the time, if I remember. I would rather help her drive. Anyway, we went forth. So, of course, I took pictures of all the progress of the house and of the daily life of Katherine Anne. All the good pictures I took of her in my life were out there. She found in the walls of this house honey bees' nests that must have been there since it was empty, and she found a whole lot of tiny ladies' slippers and men's shoes from, she thought, Colonial times. And some hoops to be worn with hoop skirts. I was at Yaddo for six weeks or something like that. Katherine Anne and I were already friends, but we became very good friends then. Katherine Anne was a cook. She made French onion soup, an all-day process. I was the grocery girl. I couldn't work in Yaddo. Everybody had a sign on their door saying, "Silence, writer at work." I read my proofs, but I couldn't write in there. Everything was so tense, even exalted. So I walked into Saratoga, and to the races, and took pictures in Saratoga. And I would bring home groceries for Katherine Anne to cook with, and so we had a good time.

Will you comment upon this wonderful photograph of Katherine Anne Porter?

Yes, I was pleased with it because I thought it showed something of her inner spirit, which she didn't usually show in her photographs as a beauty or a performing artist, reading for the public on stage. Of course, those are all radiantly beautiful. But this quiet, unposed one was the inside story; the awareness of the writer I think came through. Its regard is introspective, deeply serious. And I think it's more beautiful. I don't know what she thought of this. I don't know what she thought of any of them. But this one has held up for me, all these years, as a sobering glimpse of the artist's inner life.

Henry Miller was not a friend of yours, but he showed up in Jackson and you and some of your friends took him to see the ruins of Windsor. Is that right? And you took some photographs?

It's a long, stupid story, I think.

Please tell the long and stupid story.

He was not a friend or an acquaintance. He had just come back to America from being an expatriate all these years. And Doubleday, his publisher, thought it would be a wonderful idea for Henry Miller to go all over the country, which he had not seen in, lo, these many years and write his impressions of America. They were going to buy him a glass automobile, so that he could see everything and, in turn, be seen everywhere. He was to write a book to be called *The Air-conditioned Nightmare*. So, John Woodburn, my beloved editor, who was a big tease, thought, "O.K., I'm going to route Henry Miller by Mississippi to see Eudora." With a big laugh. Well, my mother said, "Indeed, he won't enter my house." He was the only person in her life she ever said that about. She was quite firm. But he was going to be here three days. I didn't know exactly what we had that he wanted to see. I did my best, and showed him everything.

I got Hubert Creekmore and Nash Burger, and from time to time a third friend, also a male, to be with us as we drove about in the family car. I took him all around. He was infinitely bored with everything. Nash, who knew a lot about the local history, tried to tell him

160. Eudora Welty. 'Bowen's Court, County Cork, Ireland,' 1950's.

something about the country we were passing through. He didn't even look out. He wore his hat all day. Hubert knew all of Henry Miller's works, but Henry Miller didn't want to start on that. Windsor was one of the places we took him to and Natchez, and the Mississippi River, and the lost town of Rodney—and Vicksburg. And every night we took him to the Rotisserie to eat. If you couldn't have people to dinner at home, as was our case, there was only this one good restaurant to take people to. Sometimes we went to the drive-in part, sometimes to the steak part, sometimes upstairs to the dance part with the band—it was ramshackle. And finally, Henry Miller said, "How does a town like Jackson, Mississippi, rate three good restaurants!"

Well, you had a good story for John Woodburn, didn't you!

Oh, John was crazy about Henry's visit. And, of course we were safe—Henry Miller didn't mention the existence of Jackson in *The Air-Conditioned Nightmare*. And as for the glass automobile—not a sign of that. We had to ride him in the Welty Chevrolet or he couldn't have budged at all.

So much of your writing is set in Mississippi, and you have said that it is from place that much of your fiction arises. Do you see that the photographs you took outside your native state of Mississippi—in Ireland, Wales, Nice, Mexico—show the imprint of place also?

I suppose that what made me take the pictures was some irresistible notion that I might capture some essence of the place I'd just arrived at, new to me and my eyes and my camera. Yes, I was smitten by the identity of place wherever I was, from Mississippi on—I still am. Incidentally, the reason I was in England at the time of the Monk's House picture was to give a paper to a meeting of British teachers of American subjects, and I took for my title "Place in Fiction."

You were a guest of Elizabeth Bowen at Bowen's Court in Ireland. Will you tell about that and about photographs you took there?

Elizabeth Bowen, V. S. Pritchett, Mary Lavin, Katherine Anne Porter—all of them became in time my good friends, and what first drew us together in every case, I believe, was the affinity—the particular affinity—that exists between writers of the short story. Elizabeth Bowen and I had known each other's work for a long time, and we met when I went to Ireland and she invited me to Bowen's Court in County Cork. These pictures came of my first visit to her in the early spring of 1950 and from a summer visit a year or so later [Fig. 160]. I'll add that Elizabeth Bowen responded to place herself with the greatest sensitivity, and did so when she came in turn to visit me in Mississippi.

How did you happen to take a picture of Virginia Woolf's house?

English friends who knew of my veneration for the work of Virginia Woolf drove me to Rodmell to see Monk's House. We stood there, our backs to the River Ouse, and before us the flower-covered house, the windows of the room in which she had written during the last years of her life.

. . . .

Black-and-white and color photography. Which do you prefer?

Well, black-and-white is the only kind I know anything about, but I really do prefer it anyway. I haven't anything against color photography, but I love black-and-white. Just like black-and-white movies. I hate the idea of tinting the old ones.

William Eggleston is a photographer whose work is in color. What do you find most significant about it?

You mean about the color of it?

About his work. Not necessarily the color, but what do you find especially important?

The photographs that make up his book *The Democratic Forest* are presented as a record of the world we have made, of what our present civilization is. And he uses his color very effectively, purposefully. The urban world is such a raucous thing, the color is used to express that. And in contrast he uses color very tenderly in showing the frailty, the vulnerability of what has survived the onrush of urbanization. I don't know what Bill Eggleston would say to that. That's what I see.

You have an interest in signs and billboards, especially the unintentionally ludicrous ones.

Oh, yes, I love those.

And sometimes photographed these. Do you have any recollections of some special ones?

There's the Tiger Rag Gas Station. The Old Miss. Slaughter Pen. There's one sign I saw just recently on the way to Ole Miss, in a town as we passed through, Kosciusko. There was a vacant lot grown up in weeds and a wooden sign on it, very low to the ground saying "Jesus Christ is Lord in Kosciusko." Apparently it's the site of a church that's yet to rise there on the vacant lot. Behind it already is a motel, no connection, I guess, saying "Economy Motel." All signs reveal us.

When you photographed some of the poor people during the Depression, did you feel any responsibility in taking their photographs?

It didn't seem to me I was doing anyone any harm. I wanted to show the life in front of me. I wouldn't have taken a mocking picture; I wasn't taking it to exploit them. I was taking it to reveal them, the situation in which I found them. Some of the people I took said they had never had a picture of themselves in their lives and they wanted me to take it and in that case I tried to get one to them.

When you snapped the shutter, what was the right instant?

You didn't know it until you did it. Or I didn't. And of course, all around every right instant, I've taken others that weren't. I don't mean I took twenty-five shots of one thing like people do with cameras now. I usually just took a few. You shouldn't surround people, you shouldn't dance around people, I think. I didn't put them through any of that.

Retrace you steps when you were traveling as a publicity agent for the WPA. Where did you go and where did you stay and were you traveling alone? What was one of the trips like? Where did you eat?

There was more variety than pattern. It depended on where I was to be sent that day. In Jackson we had an office up in the Tower Building of five people. I worked directly under another publicity agent who knew a lot more than I did. He was a professional newsman, named Louis Johnson. He's dead now. He was senior publicity agent. I was junior publicity agent—which also indicated I was a *girl*. We sometimes traveled together, and he did the news work and I did feature stories, interviews and took some pictures.

What you would do depended on the project. If it were a juvenile court being set up, you would interview the judge on it. We visited a project for the blind of teaching people braille. We'd visit the construction of a farm-to-market road. Mississippi had so few roads then and very little was paved. There were a lot of people who couldn't get to town, farmers who were mired down in bad weather. The WPA went about putting in roads—they'd be tarred sometimes or graveled. We interviewed people living along the road, and the road workers, about the difference it made in their lives. If there was a new air field opening where planes could take off and land, just created out of a farmer's field, we would go and see that. They weren't *airports*. They were just landing fields. I think Meridian and Jackson were the only places that had better than that. I was sent to Meridian with my camera to interview the Key brothers. They had a national reputation of staying up for very long periods of time, testing planes. I'd never been up in an airplane, and I was terrified that I was going to have to do it with the Key brothers. At that time you just leaned out of an airplane and took pictures of the ground below. You sat behind the pilot, with the wind blowing. There was just one passenger seat. But I escaped without being invited. When the tornado devastated Tupelo, the WPA tried to help, and I went up there and photographed Tupelo the day after it'd been struck and nearly demolished. You could expect anything in the way of work.

Did you travel by bus or car?

I mostly went by bus. If it was just going and coming on the same day, I used the family car. I couldn't use it always, since I had brothers in school and my mother needed it.

Did you stay in hotels?

Stayed in hotels. The hotel in my story "The Hitchhiker" was a perfect portrait of some of the hotels I stayed in. Not particular ones, sort of an amalgamation. The good ones had electric fans in summer. That was the only way you could cool off, before air conditioning. No telephone in the room. You had to go to a landing or downstairs to the desk. Very nice people ran them, and kind people.

When you were taking photographs were there ever any angry reactions?

No, I don't remember any. I don't know why there would have been. I remember in Utica photographing the black bootlegger who said, "I'm gone kill you," which was her joke.

With an ice pick.

She had an ice pick. She didn't mean it. She was teasing, like "I'm gonna get you."

You were a young, white, southern woman in black neighborhoods. How were you received when you went to the black districts?

Politely. And I was polite, too. It was before self-consciousness had come into the relationship or suspicion. That's why I say it couldn't be repeated today, anywhere.

Were they curious about you and why you were there?

Perhaps casually. There was usually something to talk about that we both knew, about either what they were doing or about the place. I would say, "I grew up near where you are living now" or ask a question. There were connections.

How did you entice them sometimes to let you take their photograph?

I didn't "entice." My pictures were made in sympathy, not exploitation. If I had felt that way, I would not have taken the pictures. If you are interested in what viewers of these pictures do say about them, I can give you some idea in what they say to me. There's an exhibition of my photographs (mostly black subjects) that the Mississippi Department of Archives and History has been sending for a number of years around the country on requests from galleries and schools. From the letters viewers write to me, I think the photographs are seen as honest and recognizably sympathetic. I have never heard from a hostile viewer, of either race, of

North and South. When I was invited to be present at a showing of my photographs at the Museum of Modern Art in New York, and to give a commentary on each one as it was shown at a slide lecture, I found the audience receptive and openly interested. I recall among those who came up to speak to me afterward a number of blacks, from the North and the South both, who wanted me to know they regarded my photographs as truthful and understanding. I get many letters from people who say they are touched very much by *One Time, One Place*.

Have you any idea of what ever happened to some of the anonymous people whose photographs you took?

I hear from people who recognize themselves or family members. Some of them write and tell me. I don't think of them, of any people, as "anonymous."

. . . .

Some of the persons that Dorothea Lange photographed and those that Walker Evans photographed in Alabama were found not too long ago and shown as they are today. Have you seen any reports of things like that?

No. It would seem to me that was exploiting them. For a second time.

Some of the children whom Walker Evans photographed are resentful.

I don't blame them. I would be too. I'd find that a cause for resentment.

As you said, a lot of the people whose photographs you took had never been in a photograph.

They had so little, and a photograph meant something. And they really were delighted. It didn't matter that it showed them in their patched, torn clothes. They wanted the picture. They were delighted at the evidence of themselves here—a picture was something they could hold. I've had people write to me through the years and say, "I saw my grandfather in your picture of such and such, and could I have a copy of the picture?" When possible I have tried to do that.

Of all a writer's attributes, you have said in "Place in Fiction," place is one of the lesser angels—that feeling wears the crown. These photographs we've talked about convey great feeling. Was this deep feeling the feeling that made you take the pictures?

Why, I'm sure it was. Human feeling for human beings was a response to what I saw.

I think we're talking about passion in the real definition of the word.

I think we are too.

And the passion was there before you snapped the shutter, and you certainly can see it in the photograph.

Well, thank you. That is the finest thing that could be said in their retrospect.

Some believe that it is an artist's works that best express his or her biography. How do you think these pictures you've taken pertain to yours?

Not in any way, I hope, except indirectly. I wasn't trying to say anything about myself in the pictures of people. I was trying to say everything about them, and my taking them was the medium. The photographs are saying what I saw. I was just the instrument, whatever you want to call it.

They're a record not only of what you saw, but they're a record of your feelings.

Yes, but I didn't take them for that. If they do that, it's because I took them with the right feeling, I think, to show what was there and what it meant. I would have thought it was intruding for me to have included myself in what I was doing. Any more than I would in a story. The story has to stand alone.

Here's a hard question.

They're all hard. What?

This will be the last question. You've had a long career. All your work is of great intensity and has from the very first been regarded as superlative. Looking back over the entire body of your artistic work—stories, novels, essays, and photographs—one is astonished by and is in great admiration of your range, your talent, your passion, and your compassion. But rising above all of these is your vision. What do you, that artist, discern as the vision Eudora Welty has expressed in this work?

Well, I think it lies only in the work. It's not for me to say. I think it's what the work shows, comprises altogether. That was a very beautiful question, by the way, which I thank you for, for the form of it. But as in everything, I want the work to exist as the thing that answers every question about its doing. Not me saying what's in the work. In fact, I couldn't Some time, if I have the time left to me I would like to do more, but of course you could never make it full enough. You know, of what is out there and in here.

That's a good answer, too.

Well, it's the truth. I tried to tell the truth.

1. For more on Welty's photography, see Stuart Kidd, "Eudora Welty's Unsuccessful Application to Become a Resettlement Administration Photographer," *Eudora Welty Newsletter* 16, no. 2 (Summer 1992): 6–8; "Eudora Welty: Guy Davenport Celebrates a Writer and Photographer," *Aperture*, no. 81 (1978): 48–59; Charles Mann, "Eudora Welty, Photographer," *History of Photography* 6, no. 2 (April 1982): 145–49; Peggy W. Prenshaw, ed., *Eudora Welty: Critical Essays* (Jackson: University Press of Mississippi, 1979), for essays by Elizabeth A. Meese, "Constructing Time and Place: Eudora Welty in the Thirties," pp. 401–10, and by Barbara McKenzie, "The Eye of Time: The Photographs of Eudora Welty," pp. 389–400, and Ruth D. Weston, "Images of the Depression in the Fiction of Eudora Welty," *Southern Quarterly* 32, no. 1 (Fall 1993): 80–91.

2. Accordingly, increasing numbers of Welty's photographs have been published over the decades: see Welty, "Literature and the Lens," *Vogue* 104 (August 1, 1944): 103–4; Welty, *One Time, One Place, Mississippi in the Depression: A Snapshot Album* (New York: Random House, 1971); *Welty,* sel. and ed. Patti Carr Black (Jackson: Mississippi Department of Archives and History, 1977); Welty, *Twenty Photographs* (Winston-Salem, N.C.: Palemon Press, 1980); *Eudora* (Jackson: Mississippi Department of Archives and History, 1984); Welty, *In Black and White* (Northridge, Calif.: Lord John Press, 1985); and, most comprehensively, Welty, *Eudora Welty: Photographs* (Jackson: University of Mississippi Press, 1989).

100. *John Baldessari*

"BAUDELAIRE MEETS POE," 1980

*L*EARN TO READ. LEARN TO WRITE *proclaimed John Baldessari (1931–) across two pages in a journal.[1] In his own use of the written word in his photography, Baldessari is both a representative and a unique contemporary artist. Like many other postmodernists, the former painter reflects the preoccupations of influential theorists with issues of aesthetic representation; and like them, he uses elements of literature, as well as of many other arts, in his innovative photographic explorations of modes of communication.[2] A longtime teacher and avid reader—perhaps influenced by the poet David Antin, his earliest admirer—Baldessari especially relishes multiple meanings, like those found in the layered narratives of Swift, Hawthorne, and Joyce, the symbolic poems of Poe, Baudelaire, and the "Fugitives" of the American South, as well as the surprising juxtapositions of the Dadaists, Surrealists, and Italian Futurists, among others.[3] His own works, such as 'Baudelaire Meets Poe' (1980) [Fig. 161], can similarly be interpreted on many levels, as his analysis here suggests. Fascinated by language, he often fabricates associative word chains or anecdotes, or more formal structures, often in sequences.[4] Whatever its content (quoted, appropriated, or invented), visual form (Polaroid, Type C prints, movie and TV stills, conventional photographs), genre (parable, fable, allegory, fairy tale), shape (often irregular), and color (each represents an emotion or mood), a Baldessari work inevitably contains allusive but engaging concepts. While providing independent but complimentary photocollage illustrations for Tristram Shandy [1765–67] (1988), Baldessari completely identified with Laurence Sterne, whose radical fiction still challenges artistic conventions with energetic wit.[5] The artist plans further work with literary classics.[6]*

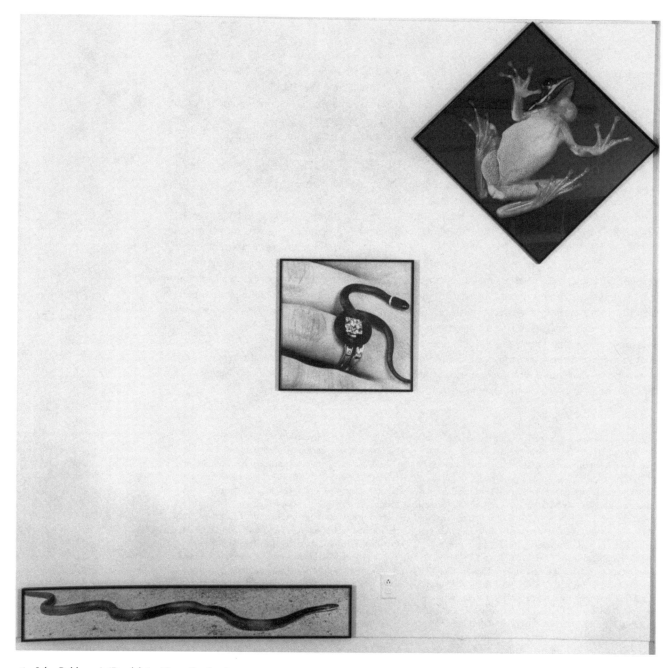

161. John Baldessari. 'Baudelaire Meets Poe,' 1980.

The piece is a visual equivalent of how I believe Baudelaire must have felt at the moment of reading Poe for the first time.

First the snake. Groveling, sneaking along the ground, lowly, slow moving, inertia, held down by gravity. A flat point of view, like Flatland. Maybe how one feels having a writer's block? Not much happening until he encounters Poe. But also redolent of indolent voluptuousness, of poetry chained to the earth. Suggestive of the darker regions of the mind, an atmosphere that is infernal. A sign of the demands of the unconscious. I recall that Baudelaire spoke of his mistress as a ". . . dancing serpent." I could have used a snail, I suppose. But a snake just seems better, nearer to the ground, more endless and richer with poetic overtones. Also this image is in photogravure, but more about that later.

Which gets to the second image. The snake jumps up, curls around, embraces a more specific symbol—a jewel, wraps around it. And a baby snake, a kind of rebirth. Ready to grow. A collision of images, deliberately mixed. High and low. Chosen as Baudelaire says from ". . . forest of images." Juxtaposing such elements seems very much like Baudelaire. Beauty out of evil Baudelaire would say, though I think my point of view is more indefinite, thus back to Poe. At any rate, it stirs the unconscious and the prelogical. Repressed ideas and associations begin to awaken.

The frog stands for an explosion made at the moment of impact of the two minds meeting. In color, larger than the other two images, and bursting out of, travelling out of the plane of the wall. A metamorphosis as well, changing from snake to a frog. Repelling but somehow beautiful, standing for magic. Transubstantiation. The idea reified, made flesh but in a sinister nonsocial fashion.

About the photogravure. It refers to print vs. the color, where the frog is no longer a sign. The frog is the artist freed.

---

1. See Baldessari, "Learn to Read, Learn to Write," *Art Journal* 42, no. 2 (Summer 1982): 134–36.

2. For a brief discussion of the influence on Baldessari of the anthropologist Claude Lévi-Strauss, the philosopher Ludwig Wittgenstein, the linguist Ferdinand de Saussure, and Barthes, see Martha Tucker, "John Baldessari: Pursuing the Unpredictable," in *John Baldessari* (New York: New Museum; Dayton, Ohio: University Art Galleries, Wright State University, [1981]), pp. 11–13.

3. See Robert Pincus-Witten, "Blasted Allegories! The Photography of John Baldessari," in Tucker, *John Baldessari,* pp. 51–61, and Coosje van Bruggen, *John Baldessari* (New York: Rizzoli, [1990]), for these and other authors Baldessari admires, quotes, or variously uses.

4. For examples, see van Bruggan, *Baldessari,* for discussions and reproductions of his: first texts and phototext paintings (1967), pp. 29–44; *Ingres and Other Parables* (London: Studio International, 1971), pp. 69–75; *Word Chain: Sunglasses [Ilene's Story]* (1975), p. 110; *A Sentence of Thirteen Parts (with Twelve Alternate Verbs Ending in FABLE* (Hamburg: Anatol AV und Filmproduktion, 1977), pp. 100–103; *Blasted Allegories* (1978), pp. 108–9 and 112–13; *Baudelaire Meets Poe* (1980), pp. 114–15 and 118; *Fugitive Essays* (1980),

pp. 116–17; his recreations of six Grimm fairy tales, pp. 218–26; and various *Stories* passim.

5. Baldessari provided photocollages for Sterne, *The Life and Opinions of Tristram Shandy, Gentleman* (San Francisco: Arion Press, 1988), 3 vols., discussed in Donna Stein's *Contemporary Illustrated Books: Word and Image, 1967–1988* (New York: Independent Curators, [1990]), p. 60. In a telephone conversation with the editor on October 21, 1990, the artist further explained that he'd first read Sterne in the mid-1960's because it was a friend's favorite, remained intrigued, and praised the work two decades later to other friends. They relayed his opinions to the Arion Press, which had wanted to put out an illustrated edition of *Tristram Shandy* and subsequently commissioned him to be the artist. In preparation, Baldessari read reference books and reread the novel, culling paragraphs that "struck my psyche." He began to feel that Sterne was his *doppelgänger,* a presence in the same room "egging me on"; by the end, he could anticipate what Sterne would write next.

6. Baldessari now plans to illustrate *Don Quixote* and may also join a group of other eminent artists invited to India, each to illustrate a chapter of the *Kamasutra.*

LAURENCE SENELICK, "PHOTOGRAPHY IN THE DRAMA," 1991 (UNPUBLISHED)

*P*hotography's relation to dramatic literature has been richly varied, as this pioneering survey of the subject suggests. Photographic elements—whether shady or strange professionals, inexperienced amateurs, studios as agents of chaos or repression, unwieldy or threatening equipment, real or imagined pictures—have been used onstage in both conventional and unusual ways by dramatists as varied as Dion Boucicault, Henrik Ibsen, August Strindberg, Kurt Weill, Jean Cocteau, and Athol Fugard, among others. Laurence Senelick, Fletcher Professor of Drama at Tufts, brings rare, comprehensive expertise to this subject as a theatre scholar, teacher, author, editor, translator, critic, director, actor, and collector. His most recent publications include* National Theatre in Northern and Eastern Europe 1750–1900 *(Cambridge: Cambridge University Press, 1991);* Gender in Performance *(Hanover, N.H.: University Press of New England, 1992);* Wandering Stars: Russian Emigré Theatre *(Iowa City: University of Iowa Press, 1992);* Cabaret Performance, Volume I, Europe 1890–1920 *(New York, PAJ Press, 1989); and* Cabaret Performance: Volume 2: Europe 1920–40 *(Baltimore: Johns Hopkins University Press, 1992); his writing on photographic subjects has appeared in* History of Photography, Yale Theater, *and* Theatre History Studies.

Lawrence Senelick

An agent in cultural seepage, the drama has usually been swift to put before its audience that latest trends, fads, and social innovations. However, before it can take full advantage of a given phenomenon, the public nature of the stage compels it to wait until the audience is already reasonably familiar with that phenomenon. By the 1850s, the photographer and his apparatus had become sufficiently recognizable to receive theatrical treatment; a majority of playgoers had had a portrait taken or at least been made aware of the process. So, like the popular press, the drama exploited commonly known aspects of the new technology as novel subject matter, most often for comic purposes.

The arcane mysteries of the photographer's methods were less emphasized than were the inconveniences and embarrassments of the sitters. The studio itself was used as a dramatic locale where variegated types had a credible pretext to gather in such standard farce fare as *Your Likeness, One Shilling* by N. Herbert Harington and Edmund Yates (Strand Theatre, London, 1858). The daguerreotype camera with its unwieldy plates and the metal head-clamp of the posing chair appear as comic properties to set in relief the idiosyncracies of those who operate it and those who frequent it.

The uniformity of the daguerreotype process enabled this comic theme to cross cultural and national boundaries, and there is a sameness to the treatment, whether in English afterpieces, French *vaudevilles* or German *Possen*. Typical of the genre is an "original joke-vaudeville" by the Russian farceur Count Vladimir Sollogub: *The Daguerreotype, or I Know All These Faces*[1] (the subtitle quotes a famous line from Griboedov's classic comedy *Woe from Wit*), published in 1856. Here too the photographer's studio simply provides a rendez-vous which allows various characters to be caught in standard imbroglios; but the play does include a number of jokes about photography which seem to have become stock gags by the mid-1850s.

A compartmentalized stage, realistic in its appointments, permits a certain amount of simultaneous action:

The stage is divided into two rooms; one is the reception room, curtained window and an entrance door, decent furniture; on an easel a large blackboard on which are hung daguerreotypes of different sizes. The other room represents the studio, where there are two daguerreotype cameras, square boxes with copper tubes, one large, one smaller; an armchair center; beside it a small table covered by a cloth; behind the armchair an iron stand with a semi-circular head-clamp; a door hung with cloth dividing the two rooms; window, door, etc. [As the curtain rises] AZOTIN is looking into the camera, his head hidden by a black cloth. PUDOVIKOV, wife and children are sitting in a group. AZOTIN walks over to them a few times and corrects the pose, then takes another look. (p. 60)

The daguerreotypist Appolon Merkur'ich Azotin (whose name, Apollo Mercury Nitrite, combines and mocks the scientific and artistic pretensions of photography) complains of being plagued by his demanding but unsophisticated clientele. A large merchant family cannot sit still; a rural landowner wants his dogs in the portraits and, when asked to adopt a natural pose, takes snuff which leads to a fit of sneezing; a garrulous provincial widow brings along three portraits painted of her younger self, with the request that the daguerreotypist "take the waist and nose from this one, the chin from this one . . . but you can leave my own eyes" (p. 77). For all this, the photographer and his place of work remain secondary to a hackneyed romantic intrigue. The only time the actual process of daguerreotypy plays a role in the plot is when a philandering lawyer deliberately jostles an unfixed portrait of his mistress so that the image will disappear before his wife sees it. But this employment of technical knowhow is merely incidental to the events that lead to the denouement.

The joke of the naive or recalcitrant sitter never grew stale in the theatre and achieved its apotheosis in Karl Valentin's cabaret sketch (later filmed) "The Photographer's Studio" ("Im Photoatelier," 1927). The surrealistic and macabre sense of humor of the great Munich clown carries things to an extreme: in the boss's absence, his incompetent apprentices must photograph a nude baby and its idiotic grandmother, a hangman (who wants a head-and-shoulders shot), and a dwarf bride and her giant groom.

> HEINRICH (*crossed the stage and goes into the audience with the camera*). I can't get him in range.
> GROOM. Whassa problem?
> ALFONS. He can't get you clearly in focus, you're too tall, he says we ain't got such long plates.
> HEINRICH (*comes back with the camera*). Do you have to have your head in it.
> GROOM. What kinda question is that? Naturally my head's gotta be in it.
> ALFONS. All you gotta do is take him up to here, than take the head separate, and we'll glue 'em together.[2]

Every accessory of the studio—the camera tripod, a rocking horse, the breakable glass plates—turns, in the hands of these Katzenjammer Kids, into malevolent conveyances of chaos; and when the boss returns, just before the curtain falls, it is to find the studio a shambles, the groom lying on his back, the bride standing with her foot on his stomach as she holds her bouquet aloft, and the apprentice cameraman also stretched out on the floor to achieve his masterpiece. The final tableau is a hilarious caricature of the stilted photographic conventions that preserved and handed on bourgeois ideals.

The satirical treatment of the camera ran concurrent with its use on the stage as the inanimate and insensate detective capable of revealing the truth in murky circumstances. Melodrama offered photography a more central role in dramatic action, most famously in Dion Boucicault's *The Octoroon; or Life in Louisiana* (1859).[3] The comic Yankee character, Salem Scudder, is a former itinerant photographer, inventor a self-developing liquid, who, at the start of Act Two, is taking a portrait of the heroine: his posing her, timing the pose and withdrawing the plate are a reasonably realistic reproduction of the professional procedures. Scudder's complaints echo those of Azotin:

The apparatus can't mistake. When I travelled round with this machine, the homely folks used to sing out, "Hillo, mister, this ain't like me!" "Ma'am," says I, "the apparatus can't mistake." "But, mister, that ain't my nose." "Ma'am your nose drawed it. The machine can't err—you may mistake you phiz but the apparatus don't." "But, sir, it ain't agreeable." "No, ma'am the truth seldom is." (p. 382)

So far the camera and the technique are the usual focal point for laughter at human vanity. But, in Act Four, after a slave boy named Paul has been killed and his friend the Indian Wahnotee is accused and about to be lynched, it is Scudder's camera which, almost unaided, discovers the real culprit.

> PETE. (*who has been looking about the camera.*) 'Top, sar! 'Top a bit! O, laws-a-mussey, see dis! here's a pictur' I found stickin' in that yar telescope machine, sar! look, sar!
> SCUDDER. A photographic plate (*Pete holds his lantern up.*) What's this, eh? two forms! the child—'t is he! dead—and above him—Ah, ah! Jacob M'Closky, 't was you murdered that boy. [. . .] you thought that no witness saw the deed, that no eye was on you—but there was Jacob M'Closky, there was. They eye of the Eternal was on you—the blessed sun in heaven, that, looking down, struck upon this plate the image of the deed. Here you are, in the very attitude of your crime!
> M'CLOSKY. 'T is false!
> SCUDDER. 'T is true! the apparatus can't lie! (p. 303)

In the intervening act, while young Paul was trying to take his own portrait, he was tomahawked by M'Closky, who then stood in front of the lens reading a letter long enough for his image to be imprinted.

Boucicault, a notorious snapper-up of trifles both unconsidered and otherwise, had not invented this scenario, but lifted it from Albany Fonblanque's novel *The Filibuster* (1859). But to equate the camera's veracity to *Nemesis divina* made for a novel and powerful *coup de théâtre*. In fact, Boucicault has it both ways:

photography is not only, by the natural agency of the sun, an implementer of divine justice, it is also, through Scudder's ingenuity, a triumph of modern science. Both the God-fearing and the positivists in the audience had cause to feel proud.

By the early 1860s, the new technology of paper prints and multiple images had co-opted photography as a useful tool of theatrical publicity, at the same time that it was coming to be closely associated with the dissemination of erotic images. The brothers Goncourt reported seeing a graphic nexus made between the two in a topical review, *Oh! La! La! Qu' C'est Bête, Tout Ça* (Théâtre des Variétés, Paris, 1860): one tableau depicted a carte-de-visite photographer shooting pictures of demoiselles in various states of undress.[4] Posing chorus girls in front of a lens added a *soupçon* of voyeurism to the mix, as if the spectator were privy to the intimate sessions in which pornographic pictures were made.

As the novelty wore off and its attributes became routine components of everyday life, photography lent itself to a more metaphoric function. Henrik Ibsen in *The Wild Duck* (*Vildanden*, 1884) provides his realistic picture of a photographer with a symbolic aura. His protagonist Hjalmar Ekdal was based on Edward Larssen, who had taken the earliest photograph of the writer in 1861–62, and whom Ibsen characterized in his notebooks as "a half-baked pessimist, without any initiative, a futile dreamer."[5] Hjalmar, likewise a spoiled and feckless fantasist, is unaware that his wife Gina was once mistress to the industrialist Haakon Werle and that his daughter Hedvig is actually Werle's child. He blithely boasts of Werle's patronage: ". . . I was very keen on settling down to something, and the quicker the better. And both your father and I felt that the idea of photography was best. And Gina thought the same. Besides, there was another reason as well, you see: it just so happened that Gina had taken up retouching" (p. 138). Photography is an appropriate profession for Hjalmar because, like so many of the early butts of caricature, he has pretentions to art and complains of having to "slave away at portraits" (p. 175). He spins reveries about making some new invention in the field. "When I decided to devote myself to photography, you don't suppose it was with the idea of doing nothing but take pictures of anybody who happened to come along. [. . .] I swore that if I was going to dedicate my powers to this calling, I would raise it to the level where it was both an art and a science" (p. 186). This dedication consists of lolling on a sofa, day-dreaming. In his selfish indolence, Hjalmar shirks his professional duties, leaving them to Hedvig even though he knows the close work is deleterious to her eyesight (she has inherited her weak vision from her real father) [Fig. 162]. His wife, who admires him as "no ordinary photographer," carries on most of the actual picture-taking, "the routine jobs" as Hjalmar refers to them, and Act Four begins with her holding a wet plate, promising an unseen customer to have the "first dozen ready for Monday." (p. 199)

Ibsen exploits the irony of the situation for all it's worth. The camera is supposed to record truth, but its manipulator, Hjalmar, is as blind to reality as if he spent his life with his head under the black cloth. He, his wife, and daughter all work at retouching, that is, idealizing reality, removing its blotches and defects. The tiny retouching brush seems a symbol of diligent but idle attempts to disguise the unpleasant truths of life. Art and science are reduced in this garret to irksome routine and vagaries about benefitting humanity by an invention. Next to the central and rather obtrusive symbol of the wild duck itself, photography comes across as a subtler comment on the "life-lie" that propels Ibsen's characters.

August Strindberg, who frequently complained that Ibsen was plagiarizing or mocking him, took Hjalmar Ekdal to be a parody of his own amateur photographing. The only photographer to appear in his prolific dramatic output occurs in his valedictory to the stage, *The Great Highway* (*Stora Landsvägen*, 1909), written three years before his death. The protagonist of this monodrama, the Hunter, while visiting the city of Tophet, is accosted by a poor Photographer who begs that he be allowed to take a portrait. The Hunter grudgingly agrees, with the repeated stipulation that "you don't exhibit me in your

APPENDIX

162. Angus McBean. Scene from *The Wild Duck*, Act 3, by Henrik Ibsen, c. 1960's, printed by Michael Nedzweski, 1992.

show case or put me in a cigarette package or on a soap wrapper. Or if I should turn out to look like a Hottentot or like the latest wholesale murderer, you'll destroy the negative."[6]

Strindberg's own dislike for commercial celebrity is here compounded by his occult beliefs that images might be used for sinister purposes. The photographic establishment is a family business and, as in most of Strindberg's work, families are rotten to the core. The wife, a pushy self-proclaimed artist named Euphrosyne, is responsible for the developing and fixitive baths; the son is a clumsy simpleton who arranges sea-shells for sale; and the daughter, who sells flowers in the shop, is accused of uxoricide. Some biographers claim that this scene is Strindberg's apology for his shabby treatment of his photographic assistant Andersson, but such a sardonic caricature of "art" as an extension of ghastly family life is no consolation prize.

When, at the turn of the century, the professional photographer began to be supplanted by amateurs with Kodaks, this development was also reflected in his disappearance from drama. The first act of Chekhov's *Three Sisters* (*Tri Sestri*, 1901) culminates in a nameday party,

where a young military officer, an enthusiastic dilettante, takes a photo of the guests assembled around the table. The simple process of "You press the button, we do the rest" had entered the middle-class home, even in Russia, and the theatre registered this domestication of photography. It was no longer an arcane ritual, carried on in special precincts, and, as an everyday activity, fit readily into the Moscow Art Theatre's naturalistic depicting of "the way we live now." The photographer's studio makes infrequent appearances in later drama primarily for purposes of nostalgia or farce. Kurt Weill's comic opera *The Tsar Has His Picture Taken* (*Der Zar lässt sich photografieren*, 1928), in which the camera is an infernal machine contrived by anarchists to commit a political assassination, spoofs a number of targets: lurid and over-ingenious detective stories of the *Fantômas* variety, pre-War royalty and its attendant *attentats*, and the elaborate ceremonial of the official photographic portrait, which had now come to seem as obsoletely intricate as an antimacassar.

Surrealism was fascinated by photography, and the portrait photographer made occasional appearances in avant-garde drama, both as a totem of obsolete bourgeois values and an emblem of the artist. In Achille Campanile's proto-absurdist one-act The *Inventor of the Horse* (*L'Inventore del cavallo*, 1925), a loony scientific institute sits for its group portrait: every time the photographer emerges from under his black hood, his hair and beard have grown longer and grayer. The tripod camera is itself a character in Jean Cocteau's musical piece *The Eiffel Tower Wedding Party* (*Les Mariés de la Tour Eiffel*, 1922). It devours a bathing beauty who takes it for a cabaña, a lion and a general (but vomits him up again) and at the play's end, with each number of the photographer's countdown, swallows another set of characters. The photographer, bedevilled by an ostrich which emerged one day when he said "Look at the birdie," serves as Cocteau's own mouthpiece when he says, "Since these mysteries are beyond me, Let's pretend to organize them."[7]

European sophisticates may have found the old traditions of posing for a portrait ludicrous; but in cultures that were still trying to establish identities, the photographer's studio continued to play a major role, a fact which has most clearly been demonstrated in the South African one-act *Sizwe Bansi Is Dead* (1972). The activist white playwright Athol Fugard edited the experiences and improvisations of two black nonprofessional actors, John Kani and Winston Ntshona, and all three are cited as authors (Kani and Ntshona played the various shifting the roles in the original productions). This wry comment on a system which requires black workers to carry passbooks whenever they leave their shantytowns and "homelands" is set in styles's photographic studio in New Brighton township, where a name-board announces his readiness to make portraits for "Reference Books; Passports; Weddings; Engagements; Birthday Parties and Parties."

In a lengthy monologue Styles explains how he left the assembly line at the Ford plant for a trade in which he could be his own "baas"; and thus turned his hobby into a business despite the jeers of his family ("You call that work? Click-click with a camera. Are you mad?"). After contending with equally obnoxious bureau-crats and cockroaches, he set up in a former funeral parlor, where, as he explains, he does more than snap photos for official documents.

This is a strongroom of dreams, The dreamers? My people. The simple people, who you never find mentioned in the history books, who never get statues erected to them, or monuments commemorating their great deeds. People who would be forgotten, and their dreams with them, if it wasn't for Styles. That's what I do, friends. Put down, in my way, on paper the dreams and hopes of my people so that even their children's children will remember a man . . . 'This was our Grandfather' . . . and say his name. Walk into the houses of New Brighton and on the walls you'll find hanging the story of the people the writers of the big books forgot about.[8]

After several anecdotes about portrait sessions of local families, he concludes, "We own nothing except ourselves. This world and its laws, allows us nothing, except ourselves. There is nothing we can leave behind when we die, except the memory of ourselves." The photos help preserve that.

The rest of the play tells the tale of Sizwe Bansi who lost his passbook and consequently cannot apply for work; he happens to stumble over a dead man and is persuaded to take on the corpse's name and passbook. He does this with great reluctance, fearing the loss of his own identity. But gradually Sizwe becomes convinced that identities conferred by society and the government are not the same thing as the self, and, for the sake of his survival and his family's, learns to be Robert Zwelinzima. The final tableau has Styles posing Sizwe for a new passbook photo that will be pasted into the dead man's papers: "'Hold it, Robert. Hold it just like that. Just one more. Now smile, Robert . . . Smile . . . Smile . . .' *Camera flash and blackout.*" In a closed society, photography becomes an instrument of folk memory and a device for subverting the *apartheid* system. What nobler functions could it serve?

Still, the camera's less noble function as a perverter of truth and agent of political suppression has also been exploited in recent drama. In a powerful scene in *The Precious Woman* (1980), a play by the Australian dramatist Louis Nowra, the body of a dying warlord is propped up so that photographs can be made of him. Distribution of these pictures is intended to maintain his government during the Chinese civil war and dishearten the rebels. The photographer, picked up on the street, has not been told of his subject's moribund state.

> CHI YU (to the PHOTOGRAPHER). Have you taken any of Governor Teng before?
> PHOTOGRAPHER. No. Though I did make a bit of money selling pictures of the rebels he had executed in the city square last year. [. . .]
> CHI YU. People buy pictures of executions?
> PHOTOGRAPHER. Landscapes and dead bodies are the favourites. Especially pictures of dead rebels. It's tangible evidence that the rebels are losing.

When the subject's eyes roll about too much, the photographer suggests, "Stand behind me and snap your fingers when I tell you. It works with babies and geriatrics." The macabre charade is kept up even when a shot is required of the once-powerful governor and his wife Su-Ling.

> PHOTOGRAPHER. You want him smiling?
> CHI-YU. No. He must always look stern and uncompromising. [. . .]
> PHOTOGRAPHER. Pinch him while you're standing there . . . instead of a hand on his shoulder, put it behind his back and pinch him on his back. I'll tell you when . . . right . . . I've . . . Now!
> (SU-LING *pinches her husband, who reacts with a painful grimace.*)[9]

The ploys of the studio sitting put in the service of totalitarian government sardonically indict photography for its misrepresentation of the real world.

1. *Daguerrotip". ili Znakomyya vse litsa,* in *Sochineniva grafa V. A.* (St. Petersburg: A. Smirdin Jr., 1856), vol. 4, pp. 59–121. All translations are my own.

2. Karl Valentin, "Im Photoatelier," *Gesammelte Werke* (Munich: R. Piper, 1981), vol. 3, p. 115. All translations are my own. Valentin's burlesque may be contrasted with Carl Sternheim's comedy *The Strongbox* (*Die Kassette,* 1910–11), which provides a full-length portrait of a professional photographer, Alfons Seidenschnur. See Ernst Schürer, "Carl Sternheim's *Die Kassette:* Photography and Art in the 'Heroic Life of the Bourgeoisie,'" in Kathleen Collins, ed. *Shadow and Substance: Essays on the History of Photography* (Bloomfield Hills, Mich.: Amorphous Institute Press, 1990), pp. 229–38.

3. The text I use is that in *Representative American Plays from 1767 to the Present Day,* ed. Arthur Hobson Quinn, 7th ed. rev. (New York: Appleton-Century-Crofts, 1953), pp. 369–98.

4. Edmond and Jules de Goncourt, *Journal* (22 Fév. 1863), ed. Robert Ricatte (Paris: Robert Laffont, 1989), vol. 1, p. 939. See Laurence Senelick, "Eroticism in Nineteenth-century Theatrical Photography," *Theatre History Studies* 11 (1991).

5. Henrik Ibsen, *An Enemy of the People / The Wild Duck / Rosmersholm,* trans. and ed. James Walter McFarlane (New York: Oxford University Press, 1961), p. 430.

6. August Strindberg, *Eight Expressionist Plays,* trans. Arvid Paulson (New York: Bantam Books, 1965), pp. 435–36.

7. Jean Cocteau, *Antigone / Les Mariés de la Tour Eiffel* (Paris: Gallimard, 1928), p. 15

8. Athol Fugard, *Statements* (London: Oxford University Press, 1974).

9. Louis Nowra, *Inside the Island / The Precious Woman* (Sydney: Currency Press, 1985), pp. 130–35.

163. André Kertész. 'Bibliothèque de l'Institut, Paris, 1929.'

This bibliography tries to provide a comprehensive list of relevant works in English as well as some in other languages, but it does not claim to be exhaustive or definitive. It includes many but not all of the works cited in the anthology selections and adds many others, published through 1993, that are valuable or interesting. Listings of alternate editions are often provided to facilitate finding certain works, not as a measure of their relative importance. Works not seen by the editor are indicated by an asterisk.

Adams, Ansel. "Notes on Mary Austin." In *Mary Hunter Austin: A Centennial Booklet*. Independence, Calif.: Mary Austin Home, 1968.

Adams, Ansel, with Mary Street Alinder. *An Autobiography*. Boston: Little, Brown/New York Graphic Society, 1985.

Adams, Ansel, and Mary Austin. *The Land of Little Rain*. See Austin, Mary.

——. *Taos Pueblo*. N.p.: Privately printed, 1930. Reprinted in facsimile, Boston: New York Graphic Society, 1977.

Adams, Henry. *The Letters of Henry Adams*. 6 vols., edited by J. C. Levenson, Ernest Samuels, Charles Vandersee, and Viola Hopkins Winner. Cambridge: Belknap Press/Harvard University Press, 1982–88.

Adams, Marian Hooper. *The Letters of Mrs. Henry Adams, 1865–1883*. Edited by Ward Thoron. Boston: Little, Brown, 1936. Letters written after May 1883 are available on microfilm of Adams Family Papers, 597–98, at MHS, Yale University, and a few other U.S. institutions.

Adams, Robert. "Beauty in Photography" and "Photographing Evil." In *Beauty in Photography: Essays in Defense of Traditional Values*. New York: Aperture, 1981.

Adams, William Howard. *A Proust Souvenir*. With period photographs by Paul Nadar. New York: Vendome Press, 1984.

Adcock, A. St. John. *The Glory That Was Grub Street: Impressions of Contemporary Authors*. With cam-era studies by Emil Otto Hoppé. London: Sampson Low, Marston & Co., 1928.

——. *Gods of Modern Grub Street: Impressions of Contemporary Authors*. With 32 portraits by Emil Otto Hoppé. London: Sampson Low, Marston & Co., 1923.

Adhémar, Jean. "Émile Zola, Photographer." In *One Hundred Years of Photographic History: Essays in Honor of Beaumont Newhall*, edited by Van Deren Coke. Albuquerque: University of New Mexico Press, 1975.

Agee, James. "A Way of Seeing" [1946], excerpt with photographs by Helen Levitt in *Horizon* 7, no. 3 (Summer 1965): 49–59. Reprinted in full as untitled introduction to Helen Levitt, *A Way of Seeing*. New York: Viking, 1965. Reissued by New York: Horizon, 1981, with minor revisions; and by Durham, N.C.: Duke University Press, 1989, with further minor revisions [edition used here].

——. "Note on Photography" [October 1940]. *Cambridge Review* 5 (March 20, 1956): 25 [a comment on preceding portfolio, "Rapid Transit: Eight Photographs" by Walker Evans, pp. 16–24]. Reprinted as introduction to *Many Are Called*, by Walker Evans. Boston: Houghton Mifflin, 1966.

Agee, James, and Walker Evans. *Let Us Now Praise Famous Men*. Boston: Houghton Mifflin, 1941. Reprinted 1960, with added photographs and Evans, "James Agee in 1936"; and 1988, with introduction by John Hersey. [All editions include Agee's poem, "(To Walker Evans.")]

Agosto, Giovanni Garra. *Verga/Fotografo*. With preface by Paolo Mario Sipala and text by Vincenzo Consolo. Catania: Giuseppe Maimone Editore, 1991.

Aiken, Susan. "Isak Dinesen and Photo/Graphic Recollection." *Exposure* 23, no. 4 (Winter 1985): 19–27.

Allen, Richard. *A Souvenir of Newstead Abbey, formerly the Home of Lord Byron*. With photographs. Nottingham: Richard Allen, 1874.

Alvarez Bravo, Lola. *Fotografías de Lola Alvarez Bravo*. Escritores y Artistes de Mexico Series. Mexico City: Fondo de Culture Economica, 1982.

Am Zehnhoff, H. W. "Satire in Word and Image: Satirical Techniques of John Heartfield and Kurt Tucholsky in *Deutschland, Deutschland über Alles*." *Word and Image* (January–March 1988): 157–62.

Ammons, A. R. "Carson's Inlet." In *Water's Edge*, by Harry Callahan. Lyme, Conn.: Callaway, 1980.

Andermann, Andrea, and Alberto Moravia. *Quelques Afriques*. With photographs by Andermann, an introduction by Moravia, and texts by Joseph Conrad, Arthur Rimbaud, André Gide, and others. Paris: Chêne/Hachette, 1982.

*Andersen, Hans Christian. *The Improvisatore; or, Life in Italy*. Translated by Mary Howitt. London: Ward, Lock & Tyler; New York: Harper & Brothers, 1865.

Anderson, Margaret. *My Thirty Years' War*. New York: Covici, Friede, 1930. Reprinted New York: Horizon Press, 1969.

Anderson, Sherwood. "Alfred Stieglitz." *New Republic* 32, no. 412 (October 25, 1922): 215–17. Originally written for *MSS*, no. 4 (December 1922): 15–16. Reprinted, with minor revisions each time, in *Sherwood Anderson's Notebooks*, New York: Boni and Liveright, 1926 [edition used here]; in Dorothy Norman, ed., *Stieglitz Memorial Portfolio, 1864–1946*, New York: Twice A Year Press, 1947; and in *The Sherwood Anderson Reader*, edited by Paul Rosenfeld, Boston: Houghton Mifflin, 1947.

——. "City Plowman." In *America and Alfred Stieglitz: A Collective Portrait*, edited by Waldo Frank et al. New York: Doubleday, Doran, 1934; revised edition, Millerton, N.Y.: Aperture, 1979.

——. *Home Town*. New York: Alliance Book Corporation, 1940.

——. "Seven Alive." In *Seven Americans* [Stieglitz exhibition catalogue]. New York: Anderson Gallery, March 9–28, 1925.

——. *6 Mid-American Chants/11 Midwest Photographs*. See Sinsabaugh, Art.

Andreyev, Leonid. *Photographs of a Russian Writer: An Undiscovered Portrait of Pre-Revolutionary Russia*, edited and with an introduction by Richard Davies. London: Thames & Hudson, 1989.

——. *Visions: Stories and Photographs*. Edited by Olga Andreyev Carlisle. San Diego: Harcourt Brace Jovanovich, 1987.

Les Années Vingt: Les Écrivains Américains à Paris et Leurs Amis, 1920–1930. Illustrated with halftones from the archives of Sylvia Beach. Exhibition catalogue. Paris: Centre Culturel Américain, March 11–April 25, 1959.

Apollinaire, Guillaume. "Photographie" [1912]. In *The Era of the Photograph: A Social History*, by Michel F. Braive, translated by David Britt. London: Thames & Hudson, 1966.

——. *The Poet Assassinated*. Translated by Ron Padgett, and with photographs by Jim Dine. St. Albans, England: Hart-Davis; New York: Holt, Rinehart & Winston, 1968.

Apter, Emily. "Fore-skin and After-Image: Photographic Fetishism in Tournier's Fiction." *L'Esprit Createur* 29, no. 1 (Spring 1989): 72–82.

Aragon, Louis. "Farewell to Capa." In *Robert Capa 1913–1954*, edited by Cornell Capa and Bhupendra Karia. New York: Grossman/Viking, 1974.

——. "John Heartfield et la Beauté Révolutionnaire," *Commune* 20 (April 1935): 985–91. Reprinted as "John Heartfield and Revolutionary Beauty," translated by Fabrice Ziolkowski, in *Photography in the Modern Era: European Documents and Critical Writings, 1913–1940*, edited by Christopher Phillips. New York: Metropolitan Museum of Art/Aperture, 1989.

——. "Painting and Reality," translated by James Johnson Sweeney. *Transition* 25 (Fall 1936): 93–103. Reprinted in *Art Front* 3 (January 1937): 7–11; and as "Untitled Contribution to *The Quarrel over Realism*" in *Photography in the Modern Era: European Documents and Critical Writings, 1913–1940*, edited by Christopher Phillips. New York: Metropolitan Museum of Art/Aperture, 1989.

——. *Le Paysan de Paris*. Translated by Simon Watson Taylor. With lithographs and a photogravure by Henri Cartier-Bresson. N.p.: Limited Edition Club, forthcoming.

——. "Le Paysan de Paris Chante." In *The Era of the Photograph: A Social History*, by Michel F. Braive, translated by David Britt. London: Thames & Hudson, 1966.

Arbus, Diane. "Auguries of Innocence." *Harper's Bazaar* (December 1963): 76–79. [Portraits of children with texts by William Blake and Lewis Carroll.]

Ardagh, John. *Writers' France: A Regional Panorama*. Photographs by Mayotte Magnus. London: Hamish Hamilton, 1989.

Arroute, Jean. "L'Imaginaire de la route américaine." *Revue Française d'Études Américaines* 16, nos. 48–49 (April–July 1991): 321–30 [English summary, p. 338].

Ashbery, John. "City Afternoon" and "Mixed Feelings." In *Self-Portrait in a Convex Mirror*. New York: Viking, 1975. Reissued in a 15-inch round silver-encased edition with portrait by Richard Avedon and prints by Claire De Kooning et al. San Francisco: Arion Press, 1984.

Atwood, Margaret. "This Is a Photograph of Me." In *The Circle Game*. Toronto: Contact Press, 1966. Reprinted in *Selected Poetry of Margaret Atwood*. Toronto: Oxford University Press, 1976.

Auden, W. H. "I Am Not a Camera." In *Collected Poems*, edited by Edward Mendelson. London: Faber & Faber, 1976.

Auden, W. H., and Christopher Isherwood. "Picture Commentary." In *Journey to a War*. London: Faber & Faber; New York: Random House, 1939. Reprinted, without photographs, London: Faber & Faber, 1986; with photographs, New York: Paragon, 1990.

Auden, W. H., and Louis MacNeice. *Letters from Iceland.* London: Faber & Faber; New York: Random House, 1937 [edition used here]. Reprinted, without photographs, London: Faber & Faber, 1985; with photographs, New York: Paragon House, 1990.

"August Strindberg." *Creative Camera* [London] 174 (December 1978): 420–23.

Auster, Paul. *The Invention of Solitude: A Memoir.* New York: Penguin, 1982.

Austin, Mary, and Ansel Adams. *The Land of Little Rain.* With introduction by Carl Van Doren. Boston: Houghton Mifflin/Riverside Press, 1950. Originally published, without photographs, Boston: Houghton Mifflin, 1903.

*Avedon, Richard. *Alice in Wonderland: The Forming of a Company and the Making of a Play.* With text by Doon Arbus. New York: Merlin House, 1973.

———. *Observations.* With comments by Truman Capote. New York: Simon & Schuster, 1959.

———. *Portraits.* New York: Farrar, Straus & Giroux, 1976.

Avedon, Richard, and James Baldwin. *Nothing Personal.* New York: Atheneum, 1964. Reprinted in smaller format, New York: Dell, 1965.

Baer, Morley. *Room and Time Enough: The Land of Mary Austin.* With introduction by Augusta Fink, photographs by Morley Baer, and text by Mary Austin. Flagstaff, Ariz.: Northland Press, 1979.

Baetens, Jan. "Texte et Image dans Le Roman-Photo." *Words & Image* 4, no. 1 (January–March 1988): 170–75.

Bailey, Ronald H., and editors of Alskog. *The Photographic Illusion: Duane Michals.* New York: Crowell; London: Thames & Hudson, 1975.

Baldessari, John. "Baudelaire Meets Poe." Statement written for Michael Sonnabend, Sonnabend Gallery, New York, c. 1980 [version used here]. Reprinted in *Contemporary Photographers,* edited by Colin Naylor. Chicago: St. James Press, 1988.

———. *Ingres and Other Parables.* London: Studio International Publications, 1971.

———. "Learn to Read, Learn to Write." *Art Journal* [New York] 42, no. 2 (Summer 1982): 134–36.

———. *A Sentence of Thirteen Parts (with Twelve Alternate Verbs) Ending in FABLE.* Hamburg: Anatol AV und Filmproduktion, 1977.

Baldwin, James. Introduction to *The Black Photographers Annual,* vol. 3. Brooklyn, N.Y.: Black Photographers Annual, 1976.

Ballerini, Julia. *Photography Conscripted: Horace Vernet, Gérard de Nerval and Maxime Du Camp in Egypt.* Ann Arbor, Mich.: University Microfilms, 1987.

Balzac, Honoré. Entry of May 2, [1842]. In *Lettres à L'Étrangère.* 2 vols. Paris: Calmann & Lévy, 1906.

Banks, Russell. "*Mr. Bennett, Vermont, 1944.*" In *Paul Strand: Essays on His Life and Work,* edited by Maren Stange. New York: Aperture, 1990.

Barchatova, Y[elena] V., et al. *A Portrait of Tsarist Russia: Unknown Photographs from the Soviet Archives.* New York: Pantheon, 1989.

Barish, Evelyn, and Evelyn Hofer. *Emerson in Italy.* With photographs by Evelyn Hofer. New York: Henry Holt, 1989.

Barker, Christopher. *Portraits of Poets.* Edited by Sebastian Barker. Manchester: Carcanet Press, 1986.

Barker, George. "Elegy on Spain." In *Collected Poems, 1930–1955.* London: Faber & Faber, 1957. Reprinted in Valentine Cunningham, *The Spanish Front: Writers on the Civil War.* Oxford: Oxford University Press, 1986.

Barrett, Elizabeth. Letter to Mary Russell Mitford, December 7, 1843. In *Elizabeth Barrett to Miss Mitford: The Unpublished Letters of Elizabeth Barrett to Mary Russell Mitford,* edited by Betty Miller. London: John Murray, 1954. Reprinted in *The Letters of Elizabeth Barrett Browning to Mary Russell Mitford, 1836–1854,* vol. 2, edited by Meredith B. Raymond and Mary Rose Sullivan. Waco, Tex.: Armstrong Browning Library of Baylor University et al., 1983.

Barthes, Roland. *Camera Lucida: Reflections on Photography* [1980]. Translated by Richard Howard. New York: Farrar, Straus & Giroux, 1981.

———. *The Eiffel Tower and Other Mythologies,* translated by Richard Howard. New York: Hill & Wang, 1979. See especially "Shock Photos."

———. *Empire of Signs* [1970]. Translated by Richard Howard. New York: Hill & Wang, 1982.

———. "The Great Family of Man." In *Mythologies* [1957], selected and translated by Annette Lavers. New York: Noonday, 1988.

*———. "Notes sur un album de photographies de Lucien Clergue." In *Langage de Sables.* Marseilles: AGEP, 1980.

———. "On Photography" [1981]. In *The Grain of the Voice: Interviews 1962–1980,* translated by Linda Coverdale. New York: Hill & Wang, 1985; Berkeley: University of California Press, 1991.

———. "The Photographic Message" [1961]. In *Image-Music-Text,* selected and translated by Stephen Heath. New York: Hill & Wang, 1977. Reprinted in *The Barthes Reader,* edited by Susan Sontag, New York: Hill & Wang, 1982; and in *The Responsibility of Forms: Critical Essays on Music, Art and Representation,* translated by Richard Howard, New York: Farrar, Straus & Giroux, 1985.

———. "Photography and Electoral Appeal." In *Mythologies,* selected and translated by Annette Laver. New York: Hill & Wang, 1972.

———. "Rhetoric of the Image" [1964] and "Right in the Eyes" [1977]. In *The Responsibility of Forms* [1964], translated by Richard Howard. New York: Farrar, Straus & Giroux, 1985.

———. *Roland Barthes* [1975]. Translated by Richard Howard. With photographs. New York: Hill & Wang, 1977.

———. *Roland Barthes by Roland Barthes* [1975]. Translated by Richard Howard. New York: Hill & Wang, 1977.

*———. "Sept Photos-Modèles de *Mère Courage*." *Théâtre Populaire* 35 (1959): 17–32.

Barthes, Roland, and André Martin. *La Tour Eiffel.* Paris: CNP/Seuil, 1989.

Bartram, Michael. *Pre-Raphaelite Photography: Aspects of Victorian Photography.* London: Weidenfeld & Nicolson; Boston: New York Graphic Society, 1985.

Bataille, George. *The Story of the Eye, by Lord Auch* [1928]. With illustrations by Hans Bellmer. New York: Urizen Books, 1977.

Baudelaire, Charles. "The Salon of 1859." In *Art in Paris, 1845–1867,* edited and translated by Jonathan Mayne. Oxford: Phaidon Press, 1965. Originally published in *La Review Français* (June 10–July 20, 1859).

———. "The Voyage," translated by Robert Lowell. In *The Flowers of Evil* [1857] by Charles Baudelaire, edited by Marthiel and Jackson Mathews. New York: New Directions, 1989.

Beaton, Cecil. *The Happy Years: Diaries, 1944–1948.* London: Weidenfeld & Nicolson; New York: McGraw-Hill (as *Memoirs of the '40s*); Paris: Coédition Albin Michel-Opera Mundi (as *Les Années Heureuses*), 1972.

———. *The Parting Years: Diaries, 1963–1974.* London: Weidenfeld & Nicolson, 1978.

———. *Photobiography.* London: Oldhams; New York: Doubleday, 1951.

———. *The Restless Years: Diaries, 1955–1963.* London: Weidenfeld & Nicolson, 1976.

———. *Self-Portrait with Friends: The Selected Diaries of Cecil Beaton 1926–1974.* Edited by Richard Buckle. London: Weidenfeld & Nicolson; New York: Times Books, 1979.

———. *The Strenuous Years: Diaries, 1948–1955.* London: Weidenfeld & Nicolson, 1973.

———. *The Wandering Years: Diaries, 1922–1939.* London: Weidenfeld & Nicolson, 1961; Boston: Little, Brown, 1962 [edition used here].

———. *The Years Between: Diaries, 1939–1944.* London: Weidenfeld & Nicolson; New York: Holt, Rinehart & Winston, 1965.

Beaton, Cecil, and Kenneth Tynan. *Persona Grata.* New York: G. Putnam, 1954.

Beattie, Ann. *Picturing Will.* New York: Random House, 1989.

———. "We Are Their Mirrors, They Are Ours." Introduction to *At Twelve: Portraits of Young Women,* by Sally Mann. Millerton, N.Y.: Aperture, 1988.

Beauvoir, Simone de. Preface to *James Joyce in Paris: His Final Years,* by Gisèle Freund and V. B. Carleton. New York: Harcourt, Brace & World, 1965.

Bede, Cuthbert [Edward Bradley]. *Photographic Pleasures: Popularly Portrayed with Pen and Pencil.* London: T. McLean, 1855. Facsimile edition, Garden City, N.Y.: Amphoto, 1973.

Bell, Marvin. "To Heinecken the Photographer" [1975]. In *Heinecken,* edited by James Enyeart. Carmel, Calif.: Friends of Photography/Light Gallery, 1980.

Bell, Vanessa. *Vanessa Bell's Family Album.* Compiled by Quentin Bell and Angelica Garnett. London: Jill Norman & Hobhouse, 1981.

Bellmer, Hans. *Jeux Vagues la Poupée, Les Jeux de la Poupée.* Translated by H. Berggruen and George Hugnet. Illustrated with texts by Paul Éluard. Paris: Éditions de la Revue Messenger, 1939. Reprinted Paris: Les Éditions Premières, 1949.

Belloc, H[ilaire]. "On Her Picture." In *Complete Verse.* London: Gerald Duckworth, 1970.

———. "The Portrait of a Child." In *On Something.* London: Methuen, 1910.

———. Preface to *London,* by Alvin Langdon Coburn. London: Duckworth; New York: Brentano's, 1909.

Benjamin, Walter. "On Some Motifs in Baudelaire." In *Illuminations,* translated by Harry Zohn. New York: Schocken, 1969.

Beny, Roloff. *Merveilles de la Méditerranée.* With texts by Paul Valéry, Jean Cocteau et al. Paris: Arthaud, 1958.

———. *The Thrones of Earth and Heaven.* With foreword by Herbert Read and texts by Freya Stark, Jean Cocteau, Bernard Berenson. Rose Macaulay, and Stephen Spender. London: Thames & Hudson, 1958.

Berger, John. Untitled poem [beginning "When I Open My Wallet"] and "Once Through a Lens." In *And Our Faces, My Heart, Brief as Photos.* New York: Pantheon, 1984. Reprinted New York: Vintage International, 1992.

Berger, John, and Jean Mohr (with the help of Nicolas Philibert). *Another Way of Telling.* New York: Pantheon, 1982.

Bergin, Brooke. "A Wedge in Time: The Poetics of Photography." *Antioch Review* 48, no. 4 (Fall 1990): 509–24.

Berry, Wendell. "Note." In *Ralph Eugene Meatyard,* edited by Jonathan Greene. Lexington, Ky.: Gnomon Press, 1970.

———. "Remembering Gene Meatyard." Foreword to *The Unforeseen Wilderness: Kentucky's Red River Gorge.* With photographs by Ralph Eugene Meatyard. San Francisco: North Point Press, 1991. Reprinted in *Ralph Eugene Meatyard: An American Visionary,* edited by Barbara Tannenbaum. Akron, Ohio: Akron Art Museum; New York: Rizzoli, 1991.

———. *The Unforeseen Wilderness: An Essay on Kentucky's Red River Gorge.* With photographs by Ralph Eugene Meatyard. Lexington: University Press of Kentucky, 1971. Revised and expanded, San Francisco: North Point Press, 1991.

Bethel, Denise. "'Clean and Bright Mirror': Whitman, New York, and the Daguerreotype." *Seaport* 26, no. 1 (Spring 1992): 18–25.

——. "Notes on an Early Daguerreotype of Walt Whitman." *Walt Whitman Quarterly Review* 9, no. 3 (Winter 1992): 148–153.

Betjeman, John. *An Oxford University Chest.* With illustrations by László Moholy-Nagy et al. London: Miles, 1938. Reprinted as *John Betjeman's Oxford.* Oxford: Oxford University Press, 1990.

——. *Victorian and Edwardian London from Old Photographs.* London: Batsford; New York: Viking, 1969.

Betjeman, John, and J. S. Gray. *Victorian and Edwardian Brighton from Old Photographs.* London: B. T. Batsford, 1972.

Betjeman, John, and A. L. Rowse. *Victorian and Edwardian Cornwall from Old Photographs.* London: Fitzhouse, 1990.

Bevan, David G. "Tournier's Photographer: A Modern Bluebeard?" *Modern Language Studies* 15, no. 3 (Summer 1985): 66–71.

Bewick, Eileen. "Photographer of Innocence [Lewis Carroll]." *The Photographic Collector* [London] 1, no. 1 (Spring 1980): 5–12.

Bidart, Frank. "Golden State" [1968–69]. In *Golden State.* New York: Braziller, 1973.

——. "Happy Birthday." In *The Book of the Body.* New York: Farrar, Straus & Giroux, 1976. Reprinted in *In the Western Night: Collected Poems 1965–1990.* New York: Farrar, Straus & Giroux, 1990.

Biddle, Clement. *Airdrie and Fugitive Poems.* Philadelphia: G. Gebbie, 1872.

Bing Xin (or Ping, Hsin) [Xie Wanying]. "The Photograph." In *The Photograph,* translated by Jeff Book. Beijing: Panda Books, 1992.

Bishop, Elizabeth. "In the Waiting Room." *New Yorker* (July 17, 1971): 34. Reprinted in *Geography III.* New York: Farrar, Straus & Giroux, 1976.

Blackmore, R. D. *Lorna Doone.* With photographs by Simon McBride. Letchworth: Webb & Bowen, 1986.

*——. *Lorna Doone: A Romance of Exmoor.* 2 vols., with photographic illustrations by Francis Frith and Charles L. Mitchell. Philadelphia: John C. Winston, 1885.

Blood, Susan. "Baudelaire against Photography: An Allegory of Old Age." *Modern Language Notes* 101, no. 4 (September 1986): 817–37.

Bloom, Barbara. 'Letters to Flaubert.' In "Questioning Documentary," by Brian Wallis. *Aperture* 112, no. 2 (Fall 1988): 68–69.

*Blum-Reid, Sylvie Eve. "Writing Nostalgia: Fiction and Photography." Ph.D. diss., University of Iowa, Iowa City, 1991.

Boewe, Mary. "Dating a Clemens Photograph." *Mark Twain Journal* 23, no. 1 (Spring 1985): 8–9.

Bogardus, Ralph F. "A Literary Realist and the Camera: W. D. Howells and the Uses of Photography." *American Literary Realism, 1870–1910* (1977): 231–41.

——. "The Photographer's Eye: Henry James and *The American Scene.*" *History of Photography* 8 (1984): 179–96.

——. *Pictures and Texts: Henry James, A. L. Coburn, and New Ways of Seeing in Literary Culture.* Ann Arbor, Mich.: UMI Research Press, 1984.

*Borges, José Luis. Foreword to *The Gaucho* by René Burri. Text by José Luis Lanza. Translated by J. R. Wilcock. New York: Crown, 1968.

Bouchart, François-Xavier. *Marcel Proust: La Figure des Pays.* Paris: Éditions Colona, 1982.

Boucicault, Dion. *The Octoroon; or Life in Louisiana* [1859]. In *Plays by Dion Boucicault,* edited by Peter Thomson. Cambridge: Cambridge University Press, 1984.

Boughton, Alice. *Photographing the Famous.* Foreword by James L. Ford. New York: Avondale Press, 1928.

Bourke-White, Margaret. *Portrait of Myself.* New York: Simon & Schuster, 1963.

Bowen, Deborah. "Borderline Magic: Janette Turner Hospital and Transfiguration by Photography." *Studies in Canadian Literature* 16, no. 2 (1991): 182–96.

——. "Camera: The Developed Photographs of Margaret Lawrence and Alice Munro." *Studies in Canadian Literature* 13, no. 1 (1988): 20–23.

*Bowles, Paul. *Paul Bowles Photographs: "How Could I Send a Picture into the Desert?"* Edited by Simon Bischoff in collaboration with the Swiss Foundation for Photography. Zürich; New York: Scalo: D.A.P., 1994.

*——. *Yallah.* Photographs by Peter W. Haeberlin. New York: McDowell, Obolensky. [1957].

Brady, P. V. "From Cave-Painting to 'Fotogramm': Brecht, Photography and the *Arbeitsjournal.*" *Forum for Modern Language Studies* 14, no. 3 (1978): 270–82.

——. "The Writer and the Camera: Kurt Tucholsky's Experiments in Partnership." *Modern Language Review* 74, no. 4 (October 1979): 856–70.

Braive, Michel F. *The Era of the Photograph: A Social History.* Translated by David Britt. London: Thames & Hudson, 1966.

Brandt, Bill, sel. *The Land: Twentieth Century Landscape Photographs.* Edited by Mark Haworth-Booth, with an introduction by Jonathan Williams and poems by Pablo Neruda, Ted Hughes, et al. London: Gordon Fraser Gallery, 1975; New York: Da Capo Press, 1976.

——. *Literary Britain.* With an introduction by John Hayward. London: Cassell, 1951. Reprinted and edited with an afterword by Mark Haworth-Booth. London: Victoria & Albert Museum and Hurstwood Press, 1984; New York: Aperture and Victoria & Albert Museum, 1986.

——. "An Odd Lot: A Gallery of Literary Artists." With commentary by Alan Pryce-Jones. *Lilliput* 25 (November 1949): 49–56.

——. *Portraits.* London: Gordon Fraser Gallery; Austin: University of Texas Press, 1982.

Brantley, Ben. "Portfolio by Bruce Chatwin: 'The Nomadic Eye,' *New Yorker* (July 5, 1993): 70–73.

Brassaï [Gyula Halász]. "Carroll the Photographer," translated by Jeremy Fox, pp. 188–98. In Lewis Carroll, *Lewis Carroll: Photos and Letters to His Child Friends,* edited by Guido Almansi, with notes by Helmut Gernsheim. Parma, Italy: Franco Maria Ricci, 1975.

*——. "Com Miller, Em Cannes." In *Esdras Do Nascimento: O Mundo de Henry Miller,* pp. 87–91. Rio de Janeiro: Gráfica Record Editore, 1969.

——. *Hans Reichel, 1892–1958.* With texts by Brassaï, Henry Miller, Lawrence Durrell, Bissière. [Paris:] Éditions Jeanne Bucher, [1962].

——. *Henry Miller Grandeur Nature.* Paris: Gallimard, 1975.

——. "Henry Miller in Paris, 1932." *International Henry Miller Letter* (December 1962): 7.

——. *Henry Miller, Rocher Heureux.* Paris: Gallimard, 1978.

——. "Inédit. Paris en 1930 Vu." *Photo* 8 (July 1969): 24–33 and 70.

——. "Souvenirs de Mon Enfance." In *Brassaï.* Paris: Editions Neuf, 1952.

Brecht, Bertolt. *Arbeitsjournal, 1938–1955.* 2 vols., edited by Werner Hecht. Frankfurt am Main: Suhrkamp Verlag, 1973.

——. *Kriegsfibel.* East Berlin: Eulenspiegel-Verl, 1955 [edition used here]. Reprinted Frankfurt am Main: Zweitausendeins, 1968, 1977, 1983.

——. "Über Photographie." In *Gesammelte Werke,* vol. 18. Frankfurt am Main: Werkausgape Editions Suhrkamp, 1967.

Breton, André. *La Beauté Convulsive.* Exhibition catalogue. Paris: Éditions du Centre Pompidou, 1991.

——. *Communicating Vessels.* Translated by Mary Ann Caws and Geoffrey Harris. Lincoln: University of Nebraska Press, 1990. Originally published as *Les Vases Communicants.* Paris: Gallimard, 1955.

——. Foreword to *La Photographie N'est Pas l'Art* by Man Ray. Paris: GLM, 1937.

——. Introduction to *Fifteen Photographs* by Manuel Alvarez Bravo. Edited by Lee Friedlander, translated by Richard Seaver. New York: Double Elephant Press, 1974. Originally published as *"Souvenir of Mexico," Minotaure,* nos. 12–13 (1939); reprinted Geneva: Éditions d'Art A. Skira, 1981.

——. *Mad Love.* Translated by Mary Ann Caws, with photographs by Man Ray and Brassaï. Lincoln: University of Nebraska Press, 1987. Originally published as *L'Amour Fou.* Paris: Gallimard, 1937; 1975.

——. *Nadja.* Translated by Richard Howard, with photographs by Jacques-André Boiffard et al. New York: Grove Press; London: Evergreen, 1960. Originally published Paris: Gallimard, 1928; reprinted, with additional photographs, 1964.

Brigman, Anne. *Songs of a Pagan.* Caldwell, Idaho: Caxton Printers, 1949.

Brinnin, John Malcolm, and Bill Read, eds. *The Modern Poets: An American-British Anthology.* With photographs by Rollie McKenna. New York: McGraw-Hill, 1963. Reprinted in text edition, and as *Twentieth Century Poetry: American and British 1900–1970* in trade edition, 1970.

Brodkey, Harold. Preface to *Avedon: Photographs 1947–1977.* New York: Farrar, Straus & Giroux, 1978.

Brodsky, Joseph. Introduction to *Russia: A Portrait,* by Lev Poliakov. New York: Farrar, Straus & Giroux, 1991.

Bronk, William. "My Father Photographed with Friends." *Life Supports: New and Collected Poems.* San Francisco: North Point Press, 1982.

Broodthaers, Marcel. *Broodthaers: Writings, Interviews, Photographs.* Edited by Benjamin H. D. Buchloh, with essays by Ranier Borgemeister et al. and a bibliography by Marie Pascale Gildemyn. Cambridge: MIT Press, 1987 [*October* 42, Special Issue].

Broom: An International Magazine of the Arts, Published by Americans in Italy. Edited by Harold J. Loeb. Rome: November 1921–January 1924.

Brower, David, ed. *Not Man Apart: Lines from Robinson Jeffers.* With photographs of the Big Sur Coast by Ansel Adams and others. San Francisco: Sierra Club, 1965.

Brown, Rosellen. "Good Housekeeping: A (Very) Short Story." In *American Review 18.* New York: Bantam Books, 1973. Reprinted in *Bitches and Sad Ladies,* edited by Pat Rotter. New York: Harper's Magazine Press, 1975 [edition used here].

Brown, Rosellen, and George Kraus. *Qui Riposa.* Houston: Philip Burton for George Kraus, 1987.

Brown, Terence. "Joyce's Magic Lantern." *James Joyce Quarterly* 28, no. 4 (Summer 1991): 791–98.

Brownell, Elizabeth B, ed. *Dream Children.* Indianapolis: Bowen-Merrill, 1901.

Bryant, Marsha. "Auden and the 'Arctic Stare': Documentary as Public Collage in *Letters from Iceland.*" *Journal of Modern Literature* 17, no. 4 (forthcoming). Reprinted in *Photo-Textualities: Reading Photographs and Literature,* edited and with an introduction by Marsha Bryant. Newark: University of Delaware Press, forthcoming.

*——, ed. "Photo-Textualities." Introduction to *Photo-Textualities: Reading Photographs and Literature.* Newark: University of Delaware Press, forthcoming.

Bryant, William Cullen. *Washington Irving: Mr. Bryant's Address on His Life and Genius.* New York: Putnam, 1860.

Buck, Pearl. *China Past and Present.* Photographs by

Henri Cartier-Bresson and other Magnum photographers. New York: John Day, 1972.

——. "Land of the Noble Free." Preface to *American Counterpoint,* by Alexander Alland. New York: John Day, 1943.

——. *Pearl Buck's America.* With photographs from *Life.* N.p.: Bartholomew House, 1971.

——. *The People of Japan.* With photographs by Stuart Fox. New York: Simon & Schuster, 1966.

Buiso, Thomas N. "Looking into Blasket Island Photographs." *Eire* 19, no. 4 (Winter 1984): 16–34.

Bunting, Basil. "Two Photographs." In *First Book of Odes,* No. 21. London: Fulham Press, 1965. Reprinted in *Collected Poems,* Oxford: Oxford University Press, 1978.

Burckhardt, Ruby. *Mobile Homes.* Edited by Kenward Elmslie. Calais, Vt.: Z Press, 1979.

Burden, Shirley. *Chairs.* New York: Aperture, 1985.

——. *God Is My Life.* Introduction by Thomas Merton. New York: Reynal, 1960.

——. *Presences: Photographs with Observations.* With a preface by Thomas Keating. Millerton, N.Y.: Aperture, 1981.

Bürger, G. A. *Leonora.* Translated and with a preface by Julia M[argaret] Cameron, with illustrations by Daniel Maclise, engraved by John Thompson. London: Longman, Brown, Green, and Longmans, 1847. Reprinted: the verse in Mike Weaver, *Julia Margaret Cameron, 1815–1879,* London: Herbert Press, 1984; the preface in Helmut Gernsheim, *Julia Margaret Cameron: Her Life and Photographic Work,* Millerton, N.Y.: Aperture, 1975.

Burgess, Anthony. *Beard's Roman Women.* With photographs by David Robinson. New York: McGraw-Hill, 1976.

Burgin, Victor. *Between.* Oxford: Blackwell and Institute of Contemporary Art; New York: Blackwell, 1986.

Burns, Rex. "The Artful Photograph: Mark Twain's Eye." *American Literary Realism* 15, no. 1 (Spring 1982): 62–73.

*Burns, Robert. *The Life and Works of Robert Burns.* Edited by Robert Chambers, with photographs by George Washington Wilson and James Valentine. London: Chambers, 1884.

*——. *The Poetical Works of Robert Burns.* With 6 photographs by George Washington Wilson. London, 1868.

——. *Tam O'Shanter.* With illustrations by E. H. Miller, photographed by Alexander Gardner. New York: W. J. Widdleton, 1868.

*[Burns, Robert, et al.]. *Scotland: Her Songs and Scenery, as Sung by Her Bards, and Seen in the Camera.* With 10 albumen photographs by Stephen Thompson and 4 by P. Ewing. London: A. W. Bennett, 1868.

Burri, René. *Les Allemands.* Edited by Jean Baudrillard. Paris: Delpire, 1963.

Burroughs, Williams S. Introduction to *New York Inside Out,* by Robert Walker. Toronto: Skyline Press, 1984.

Bush, Martin H. "A Conversation with Gordon Parks." In *The Photographs of Gordon Parks.* Wichita, Kans.: Ulrich Museum of Art, 1983.

Butler, Allen H. "A Speculation: Did Holmes Have Photo-Processing Capability in the Villa?" *Baker Street Journal* 40, no. 3 (September 1990): 159–60.

Butler, Samuel. *The Authoress of the Odyssey.* London and New York: Longmans, Green, 1897. Reprinted as vol. 12 in *The Shrewbury Edition of the Works of Samuel Butler,* edited by Henry Festing Jones and A. T. Bartholomew, London: Cape; New York: E. P. Dutton, 1925; and with a new introduction by David Grene, Chicago: University Press of Chicago, 1967.

——. *Ex Voto: An Account of the Sacro Monte or New Jerusalem at Varallo-Sesia.* London, Trübner, 1888. Revised and expanded edition, New York and London: Longmans, Green, 1890. Reprinted as vol. 9 in *The Shrewbury Edition of the Works of Samuel Butler,* edited by Henry Festing Jones and A. T. Bartholomew. London: Cape; New York: E. P. Dutton, 1924.

——. *Further Extracts from the Note-Books of Samuel Butler.* Edited by A. T. Bartholomew. London: Cape, 1934.

——. *The Note-Books of Samuel Butler.* Edited by Henry Festing Jones. London: A. C. Fifeld, 1912 [edition used here]. Reprinted with slight revisions as vol. 20 of the Shrewbury Edition, edited by Henry Festing Jones and A. T. Bartholomew, London: Cape, New York: E. P. Dutton, 1926.

——. *Samuel Butler: The Way of All Flesh: Photographs, Paintings, Watercolours and Drawings (1835–1902).* Exhibition catalogue, with introduction by E[linor]. S. Shaffer. Bolton, England: Bolton Museum and Art Gallery, 1989.

Buzard, James Michael. "Faces, Photos, Mirrors: Image and Ideology in the Novels of John le Carré." *Works and Days* 7, no. 1 (Spring 1989): 53–75.

Cady, Frank. "Let Us Now Praise Famous Men, Hale County, Alabama, Summer 1936." In *Poets in Photography,* edited by Mark Melnicove. S. Harpswell, Maine: Dog Ear Press, 1981.

*Cahill, Patrick France. "Walt Whitman and the Nineteenth Century's Visual Enterprise." Ph.D. diss., University of California, Santa Cruz. [Summary in *DAI* 52, no. 7 (January 1992), p. 2550A.]

Caldwell, Erskine. Foreword to *Images of Southern Writers,* by Mark Morrow. Athens: University of Georgia Press, 1985.

——. *With All My Might: An Autobiography.* Atlanta: Peachtree Publishers, 1987.

Caldwell, Erskine, and Margaret Bourke-White. *North of the Danube.* New York: Viking, 1939.

——. *Russia at War.* London: Hutchinson [1942].

——. *Say, Is This the U.S.A.,* New York: Duell, Sloan & Pearce, 1941. Reprinted New York: Da Capo Press, 1977.

——. *You Have Seen Their Faces.* New York: Viking, 1937. Reprinted New York: Arno Press/Derbibooks, 1975.

Callis, Jo Ann. *Objects of Reverie: Selected Photographs, 1977–1989.* With poems by Raymond Carver and an essay by Buzz Specter. Des Moines: Des Moines Art Center; Santa Rosa, Calif.: Black Sparrow Press, 1989.

Calvino, Italo. "Adventures of a Photographer" [1955]. In *Difficult Loves,* translated by William Weaver et al. San Diego: Harcourt Brace Jovanovich, 1984.

Cameron, Julia Margaret. "Annals of My Glass House." MS for exhibition catalogue, 1874. Reprinted in *Photographic Journal* 67 or 51 n.s. (July 1927): 296–301; in Helmut Gernsheim, *Julia Margaret Cameron: Her Life and Photographic Work,* Millerton, N.Y.: Aperture, 1975; and in Mike Weaver, *Julia Margaret Cameron, 1815–1879,* London: Herbert Press, 1984.

——. *Illustrations to Alfred Tennyson's Idylls of the King and Other Poems.* London: Henry S. King, Part One, Christmas 1874; Part Two, May 1875. Reprinted in facsimile as *Idylls of the King and Other Poems.* New York: Janet Lehr, 1986.

——. "On a Portrait" [1875]. *Macmillan's Magazine* 33 (February 1876): 372. Reprinted in Helmut Gernsheim, *Julia Margaret Cameron: Her Life and Photographic Work.* Millerton, N.Y.: Aperture, 1975; and in Mike Weaver, *Julia Margaret Cameron, 1815–1879,* London: Herbert Press, 1984.

——. "On Receiving a Copy of Arthur Clough's Poems at Fresh Water Bay." MS, 1862, at the Bodleian (MS Eng. Lett. d178 Fol. 75). Reprinted in Mike Weaver, *Julia Margaret Cameron, 1815–1879.* London: Herbert Press, 1984.

——. *Whisper of the Muse: The Overstone Album and Other Photographs.* With essay by Mike Weaver. Malibu, Calif.: J. Paul Getty Museum, 1986.

Cameron, Julia Margaret, and H. H. H. Cameron. *Alfred, Lord Tennyson and His Friends.* With introduction by H. H. H. Cameron and reminiscences by Anne Thackeray Richie. London: T. Fisher Unwin, 1893.

Campbell, Ian. "The Patrick Photographs of Carlyle." *Carlyle Newsletter* (Edinburgh) 9 (Spring 1988): 22–25.

"Can a Photograph Have the Significance of Art?" *MSS,* no. 4 (December 1922) [entire issue].

Cantie, Philippe. "Lettre et icone dans l'incipit de *The Inhabitants.*" *Caliban* [Toulouse] 29 (1992): 133–44.

Capa, Cornell, and Bhupendra Karia, eds. *Robert Capa, 1913–1954.* New York: Grossman/Viking, 1974. Reprinted in an expanded edition as *Robert Capa,* edited by Anna Farova. New York: Paragraphic/Grossman, 1969. [Both include texts by Aragon, Hersey, Saroyan, Steinbeck, et al., listed in this bibliography.]

Capa, Robert. "A Party for Papa" [Hemingway]. In *Slightly Out of Focus.* New York: Henry Holt, 1947. Reprinted in *Robert Capa, 1913–1954,* edited by Cornell Capa and Bhupendra Karia. New York: Grossman/Viking, 1974.

——. "A Russian Story" [Steinbeck]. In *Robert Capa, 1913–1954,* edited by Cornell Capa and Bhupendra Karia. New York: Grossman/Viking, 1974.

Capa, Robert, and Irwin Shaw. *Report on Israel.* New York: Simon & Schuster, 1950.

Capote, Truman. "Comments." Introduction to *Observations* by Richard Avedon. New York: Simon & Schuster, 1959.

——. *Local Color.* With photographs by Henri Cartier-Bresson, Bill Brandt, Cecil Beaton, et al. New York: Random House, 1950.

——. "New Focus on Familiar Faces." *Life* (October 12, 1959): 136–45.

——. "The *Sylvia* Odyssey." *Vogue* 147 (January 15, 1966): 68–75.

——. "Time, the Timeless, and Beaton's Time Sequences," *Vogue* 152 (November 1, 1968): 172 and 232–33. Reprinted as "Introduction" to *The Best of Beaton* by Cecil Beaton, London: Weidenfeld & Nicolson; New York: Macmillan, [1968]; and as "Cecil Beaton" in *The Dogs Bark: Public People and Private Places,* New York: Random House, 1973.

Capote, Truman, and Henri Cartier-Bresson. "Notes on N.O." *Harper's Bazaar* 80 (October 1946): 268–71 and 361–62. Reprinted as "New Orleans" in *Local Color,* New York: Random House, 1950; without photographs, in *Selected Writings of Truman Capote,* New York: Random House, 1963; and in *The Dogs Bark: Public People and Private Places,* New York: Random House, 1973.

Caputo, Philip, *Delcorso's Gallery.* New York: Holt, Rinehart & Winston, 1983.

*Carjat, Étienne. "Lament of the Photographer." In *Nadar* by Nadar et al. Turin: N.p., 1973.

Carlisle, Olga Andreyev. "Leonid Andreyev, Photographer." In *Leonid Andreyev: Photographs by a Russian Writer,* edited by Richard Davies. London: Thames & Hudson, 1989.

Carlyle, Thomas See under Emerson, Ralph Waldo.

Carmody, Jim. "Reading Scenic Writing: Barthes, Brecht, and Theatre Photography." *Journal of Dramatic Theory and Criticism* 5, no. 1 (Fall 1990): 25–38.

Carroll, Lewis [Charles Dodgson]. *Alice's Adventures Underground,* MS British Library (ms 46700). Reproduced in facsimile editions: London: Genesis Publications in association with Australia and New Zealand Book Company, 1979; London: Pavillion/Michael Joseph, 1985.

——. "Double Acrostics" [1869]. In *Phantasmagoria and Other Poems* (stanzas 8 and 9). London: Macmillan, 1869. Reprinted in *The Complete Works of Lewis Carroll,* edited by Alexander Woollcott. New York: Modern Library, 1936.

——. "Four Riddles, I" [1869]. In *The Complete Works of Lewis Carroll*, edited by Alexander Woollcott. New York: Modern Library, 1936.

——. "Hiawatha's Photography." *The Train* 4 (December 1857): 332–35. Revised in *Phantasmagoria and Other Poems*, London: Macmillan, 1869; revised again in *Rhyme? and Reason?* London: Macmillan, 1883; reprinted in *The Complete Works of Lewis Carroll*, edited by Alexander Woollcott, New York: Modern Library, 1936; and in Helmut Gernsheim, *Lewis Carroll Photographer*, London: Parish, 1949; revised New York: Dover, 1969.

——. "The Ladye's History." In *The Lewis Carroll Picture Book*, by Stuart Collingwood Dodgson. London: T. Fisher Unwin, 1899. Reprinted in Helmut Gernsheim, *Lewis Carroll Photographer*. London: Parish, 1949; revised New York: Dover, 1969.

——. *Lewis Carroll: Photos and Letters to His Child Friends*. Edited by Guido Almansi, with essay by Brassaï, translated by Jeremy Fox, and notes by Helmut Gernsheim. Parma, Italy: Franco Maria Ricci, 1975.

——. *Lewis Carroll Observed: A Collection of Unpublished Photographs, Drawings, Poetry, and New Essays*. Edited by Edward Guiliano. New York: Clarkson N. Potter, 1976.

——. *Lewis Carroll's Photographs of Nude Children*. With introduction by Morton N. Cohen. Philadelphia: Rosenbach Foundation, 1978; New York, 1979.

[——]. (The Lounger.) "Photographic Exhibition." *Illustrated Times* (January 28, 1860): 57. Reprinted in *The Rectory Umbrella and Mischmasch*. London: Cassell, 1932.

——. "A Photographer's Day Out." *South Shields Amateur Magazine* (1860): 12–16. Reprinted in *The Complete Works of Lewis Carroll*, edited by Alexander Woollcott, New York: Modern Library, 1936; and in Helmut Gernsheim, *Lewis Carroll Photographer*, London: Parish, 1949; revised New York: Dover, 1969.

[——]. "Photography Extraordinary." *Comic Times* 13 (November 3, 1855), inserted into author's copy of *Mischmasch* at Houghton (Amory Collection). Reprinted in Stuart Dodgson Collingwood, *The Lewis Carroll Picture Book*, London: T. Fisher Unwin, 1899; in *The Rectory Umbrella and Mischmasch*, London: Cassell, 1932; in *The Complete Works of Lewis Carroll*, edited by Alexander Woollcott, New York: Modern Library, 1936; and in Helmut Gernsheim, *Lewis Carroll Photographer*, London: Parish, 1949, revised New York: Dover, 1969.

[——]. "A Visit to Tennyson," *Strand Magazine* 21, no. 125 (May 1901): 543–44.

Carroll, Paul. "The Photographs in *Nadja*." In *The Luke Poems*. Chicago: Big Table Publishing Company, 1971.

Cartier-Bresson, Henri. *Photoportraits*. London: Thames & Hudson, 1985.

Carver, Raymond. *Carver Country: The World of Raymond Carver*. With photographs by Bob Adelman and an introduction by Tess Gallagher. New York: Scribner's, 1990.

——. "Friendship." In *No Heroics Please*. New York: Vintage, 1992.

——. "My Father's Life," including "Photograph of My Father in His Twenty-Second Year" [reprinted in "Where He Was: Memories of My Father," in *Bill Burke Portraits* (New York: Ecco Press, 1987) and elsewhere]; "Wes Hardin: From a Photograph"; and "Where Is Everyone." In *Fires: Essays, Poems, Stories*. Santa Barbara, Calif.: Capra, 1983; New York: Vintage, 1984.

——. "On an Old Photograph of My Son" and "After-Glow." In *A New Path to the Waterfall*. New York: Atlantic Monthly Press, 1989.

——. "View Finder." *Iowa Review* 9, no. 1 (Winter 1978): 50–52. Reprinted with slight revisions as "Viewfinder" in *What We Talk About When We Talk About Love*. New York: Knopf, 1981.

Cavafy, Constantine P. "The Photograph" [1913]. In *Collected Poems*, translated by Edmund Keeley and Philip Sherrard, edited by George Savidis. Princeton, N.J.: Princeton University Press, 1975, 1989. Reprinted as "Thus" in *The Complete Poems of Cavafy*, translated by Rae Dalven. New York: Harcourt Brace Jovanovich, 1976.

Champfleury, Jules [Fleury-Husson]. "La Légende du Daguerréotype." In *Les Bon Contes Font les Bons Amis*. Paris: Truchy, 1863.

——. *Le Réalisme*. Paris: Michel Lévy, 1857.

Chandler, Raymond. *The Big Sleep*. Illustrated with 40 photographs by Lou Stoumen. San Francisco: Arion Press, 1986.

Charlesworth, Bruce. *Private Enemy–Public Eye: The Work of Bruce Charlesworth*. New York: Aperture, 1989.

Charters, Ann, comp. *Scenes Along the Road: Photographs of the Desolation Angels, 1944–1960*. With 3 poems and comments by Allen Ginsberg. New York: Portents/Gotham Book Mart, 1970.

Chasin, Helen. "Photograph at the Cloisters: April 1972." In *No More Masks!* edited by Florence Howe and Ellen Bass. Garden City, N.Y.: Doubleday/Anchor, 1973.

Chatwin, Bruce. "An Eye and Some Body." Introduction to *Lady, Lisa Lyon*, by Robert Mapplethorpe. New York: Viking/Studio, 1983. Reprinted New York: St. Martin's Press, 1991.

——. *Photographs and Notebooks*, edited by David King and designed by Francis Wyndham. London: Cape; as *Far Journeys: Photographs and Notebooks*, New York: Viking Penguin, 1993. [Five of the color photographs were also reproduced in Ben Brantley, "Portfolio by Bruce Chatwin: 'The Nomadic Eye,'" *New Yorker* (July 5, 1993): 70–73.]

——. *In Patagonia*. London: Cape; without photographs, New York: Summit Books, 1977. Reprinted London: Picador, 1979. *Reprinted in *Where Is a Place: Travels in Patagonia*, by Bruce Chatwin and Paul Theroux, with photographs by Jeff Gnass. San Francisco: Sierra Club, 1992.

———. *On the Black Hill*. London: Cape, 1982; New York: Viking, 1983.

———. *Songlines*. London: Cape; New York: Viking, 1987.

———. *Utz*. London: Cape, 1988; New York: Viking, 1989.

———. *Viceroy of Ouidah*. London, Cape; New York, Summit, 1980.

———. *What Am I Doing Here?* London: Cape; New York: Viking, 1989.

Chekhov, Anton. "The Album." In *The Schoolmaster and Other Stories*, vol. 11, *The Tales of Chekhov*, translated by Constance Garnett. New York: Macmillan, 1921. Reprinted Ecco Press, 1986. Originally published in *Oskoki* 11 (May 5, 1884).

———. "Vint" [also known as "Whist" and "The Game of Whist"]. In *The Unknown Chekhov: Stories and Other Writings Hitherto Untranslated*, edited and translated by Avraham Yarmolinsky. London: Peter Owen, 1954. Originally published in *Oskoki* 11 (September 29, 1884).

Chelly, Raoul. "Photographie." In *Repertoire des Thèmes de Marcel Proust*. Paris: Librairie Gallimard, 1935.

Chesterton, G. K. *London*. Illustrated with 10 photogravures by Alvin Langdon Coburn. London: Privately printed for Alvin Langdon Coburn and Edmund D. Brookes and their friends; *Minneapolis, 1914.

Chevrier, Jean-François. *Proust et la Photographie*. With photographs by Pierre de Fenoyl and Holger Trülzsch. Paris: Éditions de l'Étoile, 1982.

Clattenburg, Ellen Fritz. *The Photographic Work of F. Holland Day*. Exhibition catalogue. Wellesley, Mass.: Wellesley College Art Museum, 1975.

Clarke, Graham. "'To Emanate a Look': Whitman, Photography and the Spectacle of Self." In *American Literary Landscapes: The Fiction and the Fact*, edited by F. A. Bell et al. New York: St. Martin's, 1988.

———. ed. *The Portrait in Photography*. London: Reaktion Books, 1992. [Includes essays on portraits of literary figures by Nadar and Cameron, as well as portraits of D. H. Lawrence by many photographers.]

Clergue, Lucien. See also Cocteau, Jean.

———. *Genèse: 50 Photographies sur des Thèmes d'Amers Choisis par Saint-John Perse*. N.p.: Pierre Belfond, 1973.

———. *Naissance d'Aphrodite*. With poems by Federico García Lorca. Paris: Forces Vives, 1963; as *Aphrodite* in Stuttgart: Ernst Battenberg Verlag, 1963. Reprinted as *Naissance d'Aphrodite/Birth of Aphrodite*, translated by Grace Davis, edited by Jean Petit. New York: Brussel & Brussel, 1966.

———. *Poésie der Photographie*. With cover by Picasso and introduction by Jean Cocteau. Cologne: Du-Mont Schauberg, 1960.

———. *Toros Mueros*. With text by Jean Cocteau, edited by Jean Petit. Paris: Forces Vives, 1963.

———. See under Tournier, Michel.

Coburn, Alvin Langdon. *Alvin Langdon Coburn, Photographer: An Autobiography*. Edited by Helmut Gernsheim and Alison Gernsheim. New York: Frederick A. Praeger; London: Faber & Faber, 1966; expanded New York: Dover, 1978. [Includes many chapters about literary figures, like Henry James, cited below.]

———. "Bernard Shaw, Photographer." *Photoguide Magazine* (December 1950): 10–13.

———. *Fairy Gold, A Play for Children and Grown-ups Who Have Not Grown Up*. With music by Sir Granville Bantock. London: W. Paxton, 1938.

———. "Henry James and the Camera" [also known as "Illustrating Henry James by Photography"]. BBC Radio Talk, recorded April 2, 1953, broadcast July 17, 1953, repeated July 24, 1953. TS.

———. "Illustrating Henry James." In *Alvin Langdon Coburn, Photographer: An Autobiography*, edited by Helmut Gernsheim and Alison Gernsheim. New York: Frederick A. Praeger; London: Faber & Faber, 1966. Reprinted and expanded New York: Dover, 1978 [edition used here].

———. *Men of Mark*. London: Duckworth; New York: Kennerly, 1913.

———. *More Men of Mark*. London: Duckworth, 1922.

———. "Photographing George Meredith." BBC Radio Talk, April 22, 1958, TS. Abridged in *Listener* 56 (May 1, 1958): 731–32.

———. "The Sea Pictures of John Masefield." *Bookman* (March 1914): 300–302.

———. "Two Visits to Mark Twain." BBC Radio Talk, November 21, 1954, TS. Abridged as "Photographing Mark Twain," in *Listener* 52 (December 2, 1954): 947.

*Cocteau. Jean. See also Saul, Julie.

———. *L'Ange Heurtebise*. With photograph by Man Ray. Paris: Stock, 1925. Originally published in *Les Feuilles libres* (May–June, 1925).

———. *Antigone: Les Maries de la Tour Eiffel*. Paris: Gallimard, 1928.

———. "À Clergue Pour Ses Nus" [1956]. In *Corps mémorable*, by Paul Éluard. Paris: Pierre Seghers, 1957; 1969. Reprinted in *Lucien Clergue/Jean Cocteau*. Lunéville: Musée de Lunéville, 1964.

———. "Clergue." In *Poesie der Photographie*, by Lucien Clergue, with cover design by Picasso. Cologne: Dumont Schauberg, 1960. Reprinted in *Correspondance: Jean Cocteau/Lucien Clergue*. Arles: Actes Sud, 1989.

———. *La Mort et les Statues*. Photographs de Pierre Jahan. Paris: Éditions du Compas, 1946. Reprinted Paris: Éditions Seghers, 1977.

———. *Le Numéro Barbette* [also known as *Le No. Bar-*

bette] [1926]. With accompanying photographs by Man Ray, translated by Maria Grossman, edited and with an introduction by Francis Steegmuller. Paris: Jacques Damase, 1980.

———. "An Open Letter to M. Man Ray, American Photographer," translated by Robert Wolf. In *Photography in the Modern Era: European Documents and Critical Writings, 1913–1940,* edited by Christopher Phillips. New York: Metropolitan Museum of Art/ Aperture, 1989. Originally published as "Lettre Ouverte à M. Man Ray, Photographe Américain." *Les Feuilles libres* 26 (April–May 1922): 134–35.

*———. "Phenixologie Poème-preface anamorphoses à Lucien Clergue excellent photographe." In *Le Testament d'Orphée* [with photographs by Clergue]. Monaco: Rocher, 1961. Reprinted in *Correspondance: Jean Cocteau/Lucien Clergue.* Arles: Actes Sud, 1989.

———. "Les Photographies de Bérénice" (1921). In *Oeuvres Complètes de Jean Cocteau.* ([Lausanne]: Marguerat, [1947]), vol. 4.

———. "The Wedding on the Eiffel Tower." In *Modern French Theatre: An Anthology of Plays,* edited and translated by Michael Benedikt and George C. Wallworth. New York: Dutton, 1964. Originally published as *Les Mariés de la Tour Eiffel* [1921]. Paris: Gallimard, 1923.

Cocteau, Jean, and Lucien Clergue. *Correspondance: Jean Cocteau/Lucien Clergue* [1955–63]. Arles: Actes Sud, 1989. [Also includes other previously published prefaces and poems by Cocteau about Clergue, such as "Homage Noir" (1958); "À Lucien Clergue Excellent Photograph"; "Mouchoir d'Adieu" (1960); other illustrated letters from Cocteau to Clergue; and some Cocteau designs based on Clergue's photographs, both shown.]

———. *Numéro Uno.* With text by Jean Cocteau and photographs by Lucien Clergue. Paris: Forces Vives, 1963.

Codignola, Luciano, et al. *Immagini dal Pianeta Strindberg/Images from the Strindberg Planet.* Venice: Edizione "La Biennale di Venezia," 1981.

Cofield, J. R. "Many Faces, Many Moods." In *William Faulkner of Oxford,* edited by James W. Webb and A. Wigfall Green. Baton Rouge: Louisiana State University Press, 1965.

Cofield, Jack. *William Faulkner: The Cofield Collection.* With an introduction by Carvel Collins. Oxford, Miss.: Yoknapatawpha Press, 1978.

Cole, Hunter, and Seetha Srinivasan. "Eudora Welty, Inquiring Photographer." *New York Times Book Review* (October 22, 1989): Section I: 30–33.

———. See also under Welty, Eudora.

Coleman, A. D. "Novel Pictures: The Photofiction of Wright Morris" [1976]. In *Light Readings: A Photography Critic's Writings, 1968–1978.* New York: Oxford University Press, 1979.

*Colette. *La Chatte.* With photographs by Germaine Krull. Paris, 1930.

———. *Paradise Terrestre.* With photographs by D'Izis-Bidermanas. Lausanne: La Guilde du Livre, 1950.

———. "The Photographer's Missus" [1944]. In *The Tender Shoot and Other Stories,* translated by Antonia White. New York: Farrar, Straus & Cudahy, 1959.

Collecott, Diana. "Images at the Crossroads: The H. D. Scrapbook." In *H.D.: Woman and Poet,* edited by Michael King. Orono: National Poetry Foundation, University of Maine, 1986.

Collingwood, Stuart Dodgson. *The Lewis Carroll Picture Book.* London: T. Fisher Unwin, 1899.

Collomb, Michel. "Kafka et la photographie." In *Art et Littérature.* Aix-en-Provence: Université de Provence, 1988.

Conrad, Barnaby. *Hemingway's Spain.* With photographs by Loomis Dean. San Francisco: Chronicle Books, 1989.

Contino, Vittorugo. *Ezra Pound in Italy, From the Pisan Cantos,* edited by Gianfranco Ivancich. With an introduction by Ezra Pound and photographs by Vittorugo Contino. Venice: G. Ivancich, 1970. Reprinted New York: Rizzoli, 1978.

*Cooper, Thompson. *Men of Mark. A Gallery of Contemporary Portraits of Men Distinguished in the Senate, the Church, in Science, Literature and Art, the Army, the Navy, Law, Medicine, etc.* With 146 photographs by Lock and George C. Whitfield with biographical details. 7 vols. London: N.p., 1876–83.

Corbett, William. "Praise for Jonathan Williams." *Lillabulero: The Final Issue* 14 (Spring 1974): 173–74.

———. "Walk Across Boston" and "Snapshot." In *Don't Think: Look.* Cambridge, Mass.: Zoland Books, 1991.

Corso, Gregory. "A Thousand Words." Preface to *Photographs,* by Allen Ginsberg. Altadena, Calif.: Twelvetrees Press, 1990.

Cortázar, Julio. *Around the Day in Eighty Worlds,* translated by Thomas Christensen. San Francisco: North Point Press, 1986.

———. "Blow Up." In *End of the Game and Other Stories,* translated by Paul Blackburn, New York: Pantheon: 1967, and, after the 1966 Antonioni film, reprinted as *Blow Up and Other Stories,* New York: Pantheon, 1985. Originally published as "Las babas del diablo," in *Las Armas Secretas,* Buenos Aires: Editorial Sudamerica, 1959.

———. *Buenos Aires, Buenos Aires.* With photographs by Alicia d'Amico and Sara Facio. Buenos Aires: Editorial Sudamericana, 1968.

*———. Essay in *Paris: Essence of an Image,* by Alecio de Andrade. Geneva: RotoVision, [1981].

———. "Estrictamente No Profesional." In *Humanario,* with photographs by Sara Facio and Alicia d'Amico, and text by Julio Cortázar. Buenos Aires: La Azotea/ Editorial Fotográfica de America Latina, 1976.

———. *Prosa del observatorio.* With the author's photographs of the observatory of Jai Singh in Jaipur, Delhi, 1968.

Barcelona: Editorial Lumen, 1972.

——. *Territorios.* Photographs by Alicia d'Amico. Mexico City: Siglo Ventiuno Editore, 1978.

——. *Ultimo Round.* Mexico: Siglo XXI Editores, 1969.

Costantini, Paolo, and Italo Zannier. *Itinerario Fiorentino: La "Mattinate" di John Ruskin Nelle Fotografie Degli Alinari.* Florence: Alinari, 1986.

Coster, Howard. *Howard Coster's Celebrity Portraits: 101 Photographs of Personalities in Literature and the Arts.* Edited by Terence Pepper. London: National Portrait Gallery; New York: Dover, 1985.

*Cowley, Malcolm. *Exile's Return* [1934]. With photographs by Berenice Abbott. New York: Limited Editions Club, 1981.

Craig, Sandy, and Chris Schwarz. *Down and Out: Orwell's Paris and London Revisited.* With photographs by Chris Schwarz and text by Sandy Craig. Harmondsworth: Penguin, 1984.

Cranch, Christopher P. "The Photograph." In *Ariel and Caliban.* Boston: Houghton Mifflin, 1887.

Crane, Hart. *The Bridge.* With three photographs by Walker Evans. Paris: Black Sun Press; with one photograph, New York: Liveright, 1930.

——. *The Bridge.* With an introduction by Malcolm Cowley and photographs by Richard Benson. New York: Limited Editions Club, 1981.

——. Letters to Alfred Stieglitz, especially April 15–December 5, 1923. In *The Letters of Hart Crane 1916–1932,* edited by Brom Weber. New York: Hermitage House, 1952 [edition used here]. Reprinted Berkeley: University of California Press, 1965. The letter of April 15, 1923, is also included in *Stieglitz Memorial Portfolio, 1864–1946,* edited by Dorothy Norman. New York: Twice a Year Press, 1947.

——. *Porphyro in Akron.* With three photogravures by Andrew Cahan. Columbus, Ohio: Logan Elm Press, 1980.

——. "Sunday Morning Apples." In *White Buildings: Poems,* by Hart Crane. With a foreword by Allen Tate. New York: Boni & Liveright, 1926. Reprinted in *The Poems of Hart Crane,* edited by Marc Simon. New York: Liveright, 1986.

*Creekmur, Corey K. "Lost Objects: Photography, Fiction, and Mourning." In *Photo-Textualities: Reading Photographs and Literature,* edited and with an introduction by Marsha Bryant. Newark: University of Delaware Press, forthcoming.

Creeley, Robert. "Harry Callahan: A Note." *Black Mountain Review* 7 (Autumn 1957): 149–50. Reprinted in *Collected Essays.* Berkeley: University of California Press, 1989.

——. *His Idea.* With photographs by Elsa Dorfman. Toronto: Coach House Press, March 2, 1973.

——. "Questions" and "Mother's Photograph." In *Memory Gardens.* New York: New Directions, 1986.

Crispolti, Francesco Carlo. "Fotografia/Photography." In *Immagini dal Pianeta Strindberg/Images from the Strindberg Planet,* by Lucia Codignola et al., translated by Brenda Balich. Venice: Edizioni "La Biennale di Venezia," 1981.

*——. *Letteratura e Fotografía.* Rome: R.A.I.-Colombo, 1977 [Concerns the writer-photographers Capuana, Verga, De Roberto, Strindberg, Zola, Carroll, etc.]

Crouen, Steve. *Steinbeck Country.* Palo Alto, Calif.: American West, 1977.

Cull, A. Tulloch. *Poems to Pavlova.* With 8 studio photographs of Pavlova. London: Herbert Jenkins, 1913.

Culver, Stuart. "How Photographs Mean: Literature and the Camera in American Studies." *American Literary History* 1, no. 1 (Spring 1989): 190–205.

Cummings, E. E. See under Morehouse, Marion.

Czapliński, Czeslaw. *Jerzy Kosinski: Twarzi i Maski= The Face and Masks=Visage et Masques.* Exhibition catalogue, April 3–May 10, 1992. Lodz: Muzeum Sztuky, 1992. [Book in Polish, English, and French with an essay by Kosinski, photographs of him by Czeslaw Czapliński, and essays about him, his life, and his photographic and literary work, mainly by contemporaries in Poland and abroad.]

Dain, Martin J. *Faulkner's County: Yoknapatawpha.* New York: Random House, 1964.

Daly, Brenda O. "Ann Beattie's Picturing Will: Changing Our Images of 'Good' Mothers and Fathers." In *The Critical Response to Ann Beattie,* edited by Jaye Berman Montresor. Westport, Conn.: Greenwood, 1993.

Dansy, Ken. *Dubliners: After James Joyce.* Brescia: Luigi Micheletti Editore, 1984.

Daudet, Alphonse. *The Nabob* [1877]. With a critical introduction by Professor Trent. London: Heinemann, [19—].

*Daudet, Alphonse, and P. Elséar. *Le Nabab.* Paris, 1880 [a dramatization of the novel].

Davenport, Guy. "Eudora Welty: Guy Davenport Celebrates a Writer and Photographer." *Aperture* 81 (1978): 48–59.

——. Introduction to *An Ear in Bartram's Tree: Selected Poems 1957–1967,* by Jonathan Williams. Chapel Hill: University of North Carolina Press, 1969. Reprinted New York: New Directions, 1972; and as "Jonathan Williams" in *The Geography of the Imagination: Forty Essays,* San Francisco: North Point Press, 1981.

——. Introduction to *Elite/Elate: Selected Poems, 1971–75,* by Jonathan Williams. With a portfolio of photographs by Guy Mendes. Highlands, N.C.: Jargon Society, 1979.

——. "The Invention of Photography in Toledo." *Parenthèse* 1–2, no. 3 (Spring 1976): 141–49. Reprinted with revisions in *Da Vinci's Bicycle: Ten Stories.* Baltimore: Johns Hopkins, 1979.

——. "Ralph Eugene Meatyard: Eight Photographs." *Kentucky Review* 2, no. 1 (February 1968): 33–36. [Photographs in unpaginated insert.]

——. "Reminiscence." In *Ralph Eugene Meatyard,* edited by James Baker Hall. *Aperture* 18, nos. 3 & 4

(1974): 127–131; reissued as a book, Millerton, N.Y. Aperture, 1974. Reprinted as "Ralph Eugene Meatyard," in *Geography of the Imagination*. San Francisco: North Point Press, 1981.

——. "Tom and Gene." Introduction to *Father Louie: Photographs of Thomas Merton*, by Ralph Eugene Meatyard. New York: Timken Publishers, 1991.

David, Michael John. *The Landscape of William Shakespeare*. With photographs by Simon McBride. Exeter: Webb & Bowen; London: Michael Joseph, 1987.

Davidson, Cathy N. "Photographs of the Dead: Sherman, Daguerre, Hawthorne." *South Atlantic Quarterly* 89, no. 4 (Fall 1990): 667–701.

Davies, Hunter. *Beatrix Potter's Lakeland*. With photographs by Cressida Pemberton-Pigott. London: Frederick Warne, 1988.

Davis, Keith. *The Passionate Observer: Photographs by Carl Van Vechten*. Kansas City, Mo.: Hallmark Cards, 1992.

D[ay], F. H[olland]. "William Morris," *Book Buyer* 12, no. 10 (November 1895): 545–49.

Day, F. Holland, and Amy Lowell. Correspondence, January 25, 1921–April 14, 1925. In *Keats and the Bostonians*, edited by Hyder E. Rollins and Stephen M. Parrish. Cambridge: Harvard University Press, 1951.

Deas, Michael J. *The Portraits and Daguerreotypes of Edgar Allan Poe*. Charlottesville: University Press of Virginia, 1989.

DeCarava, Roy. Unpublished letters to Minor White, November 21, 1955, and January 26, 1956. [Originals in the Minor White Archives; a TS of the November 21 letter is at the Beinecke (JWJ Collection, the Hughes Correspondence).]

DeCarava, Roy, and Langston Hughes. *The Sweet Flypaper of Life*. New York: Simon & Schuster, 1955. Reprinted New York: Hill & Wang, 1967; Washington, D.C.: Howard University Press, 1988.

Defoe, Daniel. *A Tour Through the Whole Island of Great Britain*. Edited by Pat Rogers, with photographs by Simon McBride. Exeter: Webb & Bower; London: Michael Joseph, 1989.

De La Mare, Walter. *A Child's Day: A Book of Rhymes*. Two pictures by Carine and Will Cadby. London: Constable; New York: E. P. Dutton, 1920.

Delaney, Frank. *James Joyce's Odyssey*. London: Hodder & Stoughton; New York: Holt, Rinehart and Winston, 1981.

DeLillo, Don. *Mao II*. New York: Viking, 1991.

Delord, Jean. *Barthes et La Photographie*. Paris: Créatis, 1981.

Demachy, Robert. "L'Illustration du livre par les photographs." *La Revue de Photographie* (November 1905): 321–29.

Denby, Edwin. *In Public, In Private*. With photographs by Rudy Burckhardt. N.p.: Dekker Press, 1946.

——. *Mediterranean Cities*. New York: George Wittenborn, 1956.

Dermée, Paul. "Brother Seeing-Eye." Preface to first exhibition catalogue of André Kertész, translated by Nicholas Olivier. Paris: Au Sacre du Printemps Gallery, 1927. Reprinted in *André Kertész: 60 Years of Photographs, 1912–1972*, edited by Nicholas Ducrot, New York: Grossman, 1972; and, untitled, in *Kertész by Kertész: A Self-Portrait*, New York: Abbeville, 1985.

Deschamps, F. *Life in a Book*. Rochester, N.Y.: Visual Studies Workshop, 1986.

Desvergnes, Alain. *Yoknapatawpha: The Land of William Faulkner*. With text by Régis Durand, translated by William Wheeler. Paris: Marval, 1989.

Dickey, James, and William A. Bake. *Wayfarer: A Voice from the Southern Mountains*. Birmingham, Ala.: Oxmoor House, 1988.

Di Federico, Frank. "Alvin Langdon Coburn and the Genesis of Vortographs." *History of Photography* 11 (October–December 1987): 265–96.

Dijkstra, Bram. *The Hieroglyphics of a New Speech: Cubism, Stieglitz, and the Early Poetry of William Carlos Williams*. Princeton, N.J.: Princeton University Press, 1969. Reprinted as *Cubism, Stieglitz, and the Early Poetry of William Carlos Williams*, 1978.

Dinesen, Isak [Karen Blixen]. *Isak Dinesen's Africa: Images of the Wild Continent from the Writer's Life and Words*. With photographs by Arthur Bertrand, Peter Beard, Frank Connor, et al., and introduction by Judith Thurman. San Francisco: Sierra Club Books, 1985.

——. Photographs (January 1914–July 1931) and quotations. In *Longing for Darkness: Kamante's Tales*, collected by Peter Beard. New York: Harcourt Brace Jovanovich, 1975.

Distel, Herbert, and Edgar Lee Masters. *Spoon River Anthology*. Photographs by Herbert Distel. Bern: Bentali, 1990.

Döblin, Alfred. "Faces, Images and Their Truth." Introduction to *The Face of the Time: Sixty Pictures of the German People of the Twentieth Century* [Antlitz der Zeit: 60 Aufnahmen dt. Menschen d. 20 Jh] by August Sander [1929]. Munich: Schirmer Mosel, 1977; 1983.

Dorfman, Elsa. " Allen, My Camera and Me." In *Best Minds: A Tribute to Allen Ginsberg*, edited by Bill Morgan and Bob Rosenthal. New York: Lospeccio Press, 1982.

——. *Elsa's Housebook: A Woman's Photojournal*. Boston: Godine, 1974.

——. "Names, Dates, Places." *Field of Vision*, no. 13 (Spring 1985): 20–24.

——. "Three Afternoons with Charles Olson." MS, 1974.

Dorn, Edward. *The Shoshoneans: The People of the Basin Plateau*. With photographs by Leroy Lucas. New York: William Morrow, 1966.

Dove, Rita, and Tamara Kaida. *The Other Side of the House* [1986]. Tempe, Ariz.: Vari Studios/Pyracantha Press/School of Art, Arizona State University, 1988.

Doyle, Sir Arthur Conan. "The Adventure of the Copper Beeches." *Strand Magazine* 2 (June 1892): 613–28. Reprinted in *The Complete Sherlock Holmes*. New York: Doubleday, 1960; 1970.

——. "The Adventure of the Lion's Mane." *Strand Magazine* 72 (December 1926): 539–50. Reprinted in *The Complete Sherlock Holmes*. New York: Doubleday, 1960; 1970.

——. *The Case for Spirit Photography.* London: Hutchinson; New York: Doran, 1922.

——. "The Combermere Photograph." *Quarterly Transactions of the British College of Psychic Science* 5 (October 1926): 190–92.

——. *The Coming of the Fairies.* London: Hodder & Stoughton, 1922. Revised edition, London: The Psychic Press, 1928.

——. *Essays on Photography.* Edited by John Michael Gibson and Richard Lancelyn Green. London: Secker & Warburg, 1982.

*——. *The Hound of the Baskervilles.* Illustrated with 50 photographs by Michael Kenna. San Francisco: Arion Press, 1985. Reprinted San Francisco: North Point Press, 1986.

——. *The Lost World.* London: Hodder & Stoughton; New York: Doran, 1912.

——. "The Recollections of Captain Wilkie." *Chamber's Journal* 12 (January 26, 1895): 40–42 and 57–59. Reprinted in *McClure's Magazine* 4 (April 1895): 401–7.

——. "The Red-Haired League." *Strand Magazine* 2 (August 1891): 190–204. Reprinted in *The Complete Sherlock Holmes*. New York: Doubleday, 1960; 1970.

——. "A Scandal in Bohemia." *Strand Magazine* 2 (July 1891): 61–75. Reprinted in *The Complete Sherlock Holmes*. New York: Doubleday, 1960; 1970.

——. "Spirit Photography." In *The History of Spiritualism*, vol. 2. London: Cassell; New York: Doran, 1926.

——. *The Vital Message.* London: Hodder & Stoughton; New York: Doran, 1919.

——. *The Wanderings of a Spiritualist.* London: Hodder & Stoughton; New York: Doran, 1921.

Drabble, Margaret. *A Writer's Britain: Landscape in Literature.* With photographs by Jorge Lewinski. London: Thames & Hudson; New York: Knopf, 1979.

Draper, Jo. *Thomas Hardy's England.* Edited by John Fowles and with photographs by J. Stevens-Cox and G. Stevens-Cox. London: Cape; Boston: Little, Brown, 1984.

Dreiser, Theodore. "The Camera Club of New York." *Ainslee's* (October 4, 1899): 324–35. Reprinted in *A Photographic Vision: Pictorial Photography, 1889–1923*, edited by Peter C. Bunnell. Salt Lake City: Peregrine Smith, 1980.

——. *The "Genius."* New York and London: John Lane, 1915.

——. "A Master of Photography." *Success* 2 (June 10, 1899): 47.

——. "A Remarkable Art, The New Pictorial Photography." *Great Round World* (May 3, 1902): 430–34.

Du Camp, Maxime. "Chants de la Matière." In *Les Chants Modernes.* Paris: Lévy, 1855.

——. *Maxime Du Camp's Literary Recollections*, 2 vols. London: Remington, 1893. Originally published as *Souvenirs Littéraires*, 2 vols. Paris: Hachette, 1882–83.

*Duffy, Julia, and Lloyd Davis. "Demythologizing Facts and Photographs in Virginia Woolf's *Three Guineas.*" In *Photo-Textualities: Reading Photographs and Literature*, edited with an introduction by Marsha Bryant. Newark: University of Delaware Press, forthcoming.

Dugan, Thomas. "Eikoh Hosoe" and "Duane Michals." In *Photography Between Covers: Interviews With Photo-Bookmakers.* Rochester, N.Y.: Light Impressions, 1979.

Dumas *pére*, Alexandre. Excerpt from "Across Hungary" in "Alexander Dumas on Photography." *Photographic News* (August 10, 1866): 379–81. Originally published as part of "À Travers la Hongrie" series in *Les Nouvelles*, no. 137 (February 4, 1866): 1–3.

——. *On Board the "Emma," Adventures with Garibaldi's "Thousand" in Sicily* [c. 1861]. Translated and with an introduction by R. S. Garnett. London: Ernest Benn, 1929.

Du Maurier, Daphne. *Enchanted Cornwall: Her Pictorial Memoir.* Edited by Piers Dudgeon. Photographs by Nick Wright. London: M. Joseph and Pilot Productions; New York: Viking Penguin, 1989.

——. "The Little Photographer." In *The Apple Tree: A Short Novel and Some Stories.* London: Gollancz, 1952. Published as *Kiss Me Again, Stranger: A Collection of Eight Stories Long and Short.* New York: Doubleday, 1953.

——. *Vanishing Cornwall.* Photographs by Christian Browning. London: Gollancz, 1981.

Dunaeva, E. N. "K Istorii Raboty Nad Knigoi 'Ostrov Sakhalin'" ["Towards a History of Work on the Book 'Sakhalin Island'"]. *Literaturnoe Nasledstvo* 87 (1977): 263–93. [Includes all the photographs Chekhov ordered of Sakhalin.]

Dunbar, Paul Laurence. *Candle-lightin' Time.* With photographs by the Kiqautan Kamera Klub, Hampton Institute Camera Club, and decorations by Margaret Armstrong. New York: Dodd, Mead & Co., 1901. Reprinted 1908.

——. *Howdy, Honey, Howdy.* With photographs by Leigh Richmond Miner and decorations by Margaret Armstrong. New York: Dodd, Mead & Co., 1905.

——. *Joggin' Erlong.* With photographs by Leigh Richmond Miner and decorations by John Rae. New York: Dodd, Mead & Co., 1906.

——. *Poems of Cabin and Field.* With photographs by

the Hampton Institute Camera Club and decorations by Alice Morse. New York: Dodd, Mead & Co., 1899. Reprinted 1900, 1901, 1904, 1915, and 1918.

——. *When Melindy Sings.* With photographs by the Hampton Institute Camera Club and decorations by Margaret Armstrong. New York: Dodd, Mead & Co., 1903. Reprinted 1904, 1906, and 1913.

——. *L'il Gal.* With photographs by Leigh Richmond Miner and decorations by Margaret Armstrong. New York: Dodd, Mead & Co., 1904

*Duncan, Robert. "An Art of Wandering." *Translations, Salvages: Paste-Ups by Jess.* Dallas: Dallas Museum of Fine Art, 1972.

*——. Introduction to *Jess: Paste-Ups.* Chicago: Museum of Contemporary Art, 1972.

——. "Structure of Rime XXVII." *Paste-Ups by Jess.* San Francisco: San Francisco Museum of Art, 1986.

Duras, Marguerite. Afterword to *Women, Sisters* [1976], by Erica Lennard. New York: Bobbs, Merrill, 1978.

——. *The Lover.* Translated by Barbara Bray. New York: Pantheon Books; London: William Collins, 1985.

——. "The Sound and the Silence." Introduction to *Yves Saint Laurent: Images of Design, 1958–1988,* by Yves Saint Laurent. New York: Knopf, 1988.

Durrell, Lawrence. Foreword to *Egypt,* by Dorothy Bohm. Text by Ian Jeffrey. London: Thames & Hudson, 1989.

——. Introduction to *Brassaï.* New York: Museum of Modern Art, 1968.

——. Preface to *Perspective of Nudes,* by Bill Brandt. London: Bodley Head, 1961; New York: Amphoto, 1962.

Dürrenmatt, Friedrich. *Oedipus.* Translated by Leila Vennewitz. With 2 photogravures by Marie Cosindas. New York: Limited Editions Club, 1989.

*Eco, Umberto. Introduction to *Eugenio Carmi: Una Pittura di Paesaggio.* Milan: Gianpaolo Prearo, 1973.

——. Introduction to *Fotografare l'Arte,* by Pietro Consagra and Ugo Mulas. Milan: Fratelli Fabrri Editori, 1973.

*——. Preface to *Towns.* With photographs by Giulio Confalonieri. Milan: Idea, 1976.

Edel, Leon. "Novel and Camera." In *The Theory of the Novel: New Essays,* edited by John Halperin. New York: Oxford University Press, 1974.

Eigner, Larry, and Harry Callahan. *On My Eyes.* With poems by Larry Eigner, photographs by Harry Callahan, and introduction by Denise Levertov. Highlands, N.C.: Jonathan Williams, 1960.

[Eisenstaedt, Alfred]. "The Lowells of Massachusetts." *Life* 42 (March 18, 1957): 126–37.

*Elder, Paul, comp. *California the Beautiful: Camera Studies by California Artists with Selections in Prose and Verse from Western Writers.* San Francisco: Paul Elder, 1911.

Eliot, George. *Romola.* [1862–63]. 2 vols., illustrated with 69 photographs. Leipzig: Tauchnitz, 1863.

——. *Romola* [1862–63]. 2 vols., illustrated with photogravures. London: Smith, Elder; Boston: Estes & Lauriat, 1890.

Eliot, T. S. *Preludes.* With a photograph by Michael Torosovian. Toronto: Lumière Press, 1987.

Eliot, Valerie [Mrs. T. S.]. "A Photographic Memoir, with a Note by James Olney." *Southern Review* 21, no. 4 (Autumn 1985): 987–98.

Elisofon, Eliot. "Literary South Seas." *Life* 38 (January 24, 1955): [60–77].

Elsken, Ed Van Der. *Love on the Left Bank.* London: André Deutsch, 1956.

Éluard, Paul. *Corps mémorable.* With the cover by Pablo Picasso, a poem by Jean Cocteau, and 12 photographs by Lucien Clergue. Paris: Pierre Seghers, 1957; 1968.

Éluard, Paul, and Man Ray. *Facile.* With poems by Paul Éluard and photographs by Man Ray. Paris: GLM, 1935.

Emerson, Ralph Waldo, and Thomas Carlyle. *The Correspondence of Emerson and Carlyle.* Edited by Joseph Slater. New York: Columbia University Press, 1964.

Émile-Zola, François, and Massin [Claude Menuet]. *Zola Photographer.* Translated by Liliane Emery Tuck. New York: Henry Holt and Company/Seaver Books, 1988. Originally printed as *Zola Photographe.* Paris: Denoël, 1979.

Evans, Walker. See also *Images of the South.*

——. "Faulkner's Mississippi." *Vogue* 112 (October 1, 1948): 144–49. Reprinted (in reduced size), with added photographs, in *Walker Evans at Work.* New York: Harper & Row, 1982.

——. "James Agee, 1936." *Atlantic Monthly* 206 (July 1960): 74–75. Reprinted as foreword to *Let Us Now Praise Famous Men,* by James Agee and Walker Evans, Boston: Houghton Mifflin, 1960 and 1988; and in David Madden, ed., *Remembering James Agee,* Baton Rouge: Louisiana State University Press, 1974.

——. "Photography." *Quality: Its Image in the Arts.* Edited by Louis Kronenberger. New York: Atheneum, 1969. Reprinted in *Massachusetts Review* 19, no. 4 (Winter 1978): 644–46.

——. "Robert Frank." In *U. S. Camera Annual, 1958.* New York: U. S. Camera Publishing Company, 1958. Reprinted in *Robert Frank: New York to Nova Scotia,* edited by Anne Wilkes Tucker. Boston: New York Graphic Society; Houston: Museum of Fine Arts, 1986.

Evans, Walker, and William Christenberry. *Of Time and Place: Walker Evans and William Christenberry.* San Francisco: Friends of Photography; Fort Worth, Tex.: Amon Carter Museum in association with the University of New Mexico, 1990.

Evernden, Neil. "Seeing and Being Seen: A Response to Susan Sontag's Essays on Photography." *Soundings* 68, no. 1 (Spring 1985): 72–87.

*Farrar, F. W., comp. *With the Poets*. With illustrations by Payne Jennings. London: Suttaby, [1865?].

Faulkner, William. *Absalom, Absalom! The Corrected Text* [1936]. Edited by Noel Polk. New York: Random House, 1986.

——. "Evangeline" [1931]. *Uncollected Stories of William Faulkner*. Edited by Joseph Blotner. New York: Random House, 1979.

——. "The Leg" [1925]. In *Collected Stories of William Faulkner*. New York: Random House, 1950.

——. *Sanctuary, The Original Text* [1929]. Edited by Noel Polk. New York: Random House, 1981.

——. *Sanctuary*. In *Novels 1930–1935*, by William Faulkner. Edited by Joseph Blotner and Noel Polk. New York: Library of America, 1985.

Faxon, Alicia Craig. "D. G. Rossetti's Use of Photography." *History of Photography* 16, no. 3 (Autumn 1992): 254–62.

Feldman, Ruth. "Homage to Cartier-Bresson" and "In Memoriam: Young Photographer." In *The Ambition of Ghosts*. University Center, Mich.: Green River Press, 1979.

Felver, Christopher. *The Poet Exposed*. With prologue by Gary Snyder, foreword by Robert Creeley, and afterword by William E. Parker. New York: Alfred Van Der Marck Editions, 1986.

Ferry, David. "Photographs from a Book: Six Poems" and "Graveyard." In *Strangers: A Book of Poems*. Chicago: University of Chicago Press, 1983.

Fields, James Thomas. *Yesterdays with Authors*. 2 vols. With 7 photographs. Boston: Osgood, 1872.

Findley, Timothy. *Can You See Me Yet?: A Play*. Vancouver, B.C.: Talon, 1977.

Firebaugh, Joseph J. "Coburn: Henry James's Photographer." *American Quarterly* 7 (1955): 215–33.

Flaubert, Gustave. Selected letters and writings. In *Flaubert in Egypt: A Sensibility on Tour*, edited by Francis Steegmuller. London: Bodley Head; Boston: Little, Brown, 1972. Reprinted Chicago: Academy Chicago Publishers, 1979; 1989; and London: Michael Haag, 1983 [edition used here].

Flower, Dean. "The View from Prospect House." *Massachusetts Review* 26, nos. 2–3 (Summer–Autumn 1985): 217–32.

Folsom, Ed. "Notes on the Major Walt Whitman Photographers." *Walt Whitman Quarterly Review* 4, nos. 2–3 (Fall–Winter 1986–87): 63–72.

——. "'This Heart's Geography Map': The Photographs of Walt Whitman." *Walt Whitman Quarterly Review* 4, nos. 2–3 (Fall–Winter 1986–87): 1–5.

——. "Whitman and the Visual Democracy of Photography." *Mickel Street Review* 10 (1988): 51–65.

Fonaroff, Schuyler. *The Punjab Frontier: Notes and Photographs from Kipling's India*. College Park: University of Maryland Geographical Publications, 1991.

Fontanella, Lee. "Washington Irving's *Tales of the Alhambra* and Early Photography in Spain." In *The Old and New World Romanticism of Washington Irving*, edited by Stanley Brodwin. New York: Greenwood Press, 1986.

Forster, E. M. "Sinclair Lewis" [1929]. In *Abinger Harvest*. London: Edward Arnold; New York: Harper & Brothers, 1936. Reprinted New York: Harcourt, Brace & World, 1964.

Fowles, John. Essay. In *Land*, by Fay Godwin. London: Heinemann; Boston: Little, Brown, 1985.

——. Introduction to *Open Skies*, by Don McCullin. London: Cape, 1989.

——. *Islands*. With photographs by Fay Godwin. London: Cape; Boston: Little, Brown, 1978.

——. *Lyme Regis Camera*. Wimborne: Dovecote, 1990.

——. *Shipwreck*. With photographs by the Gibsons of Scilly. London: Cape, 1974.

Fowles, John, and Frank Horvat. *The Tree*. Boston: Little, Brown, 1979.

Frank, Robert. "NYC July 29th 1984." In *Best Minds: A Tribute to Allen Ginsberg*, edited by Bill Morgan and Bob Rosenthal. New York: Lospeccio Press, 1982.

Freeman, Judi. *The Dada and Surrealist Word-Image*. Los Angeles: Los Angeles County Museum of Art; Cambridge: MIT Press, 1989.

Freund, Gisèle. *Gisèle Freund, Photographer*. Translated by John Shepley. New York: Abrams, 1985.

——. *Three Days with Joyce*. Translated by Peter St. John Ginna, with preface by Richard Ellman. New York: Persea, 1985. Originally published as *Trois Jours avec Joyce*. Paris: Denoël, 1982.

——. *The World in My Camera*. Translated by June Guicharnaud. New York: Dial Press, 1974. [Includes "James Joyce," used here.] Originally published as *Le Monde et Ma Camera*. Paris: Denoël/Gonthier, 1970.

Freund, Gisèle, and V. B. Carleton. *James Joyce in Paris: His Final Years*. With a preface by Simone de Beauvoir. New York: Harcourt, Brace & World, 1965; London: Cassell, 1966.

*Friswell, J. Hain. *Life Portraits of William Shakespeare*. London: Sampson Low, Son & Marston, 1864.

Frost, Robert. *Seasons*. Selected by Edward Connery Latham, with photographs by Christopher Burkett. New York: Henry Holt, 1992.

Fuentes, Carlos. Introduction to *Gardiens du Temps*, by Flor Garduño. Paris: Arthaud, 1992.

Fuentes, Norberto. *Ernest Hemingway Rediscovered*. Translated by Marianne Sinclair and with photographs by Roberto Herrera Sotlongo. New York: Charles Scribner's, 1988.

Fugard, Athol. *Statements*. London: Oxford University Press, 1974.

*Furness, Walter Roger. *Composite Photography Applied to the Portraits of Shakespeare*. With 14 original composite photographs. Philadelphia: Robert M. Lindsay, 1885. Reprinted in 1903 without photographs.

Furuta, Miyuki. *Why, Mother, Why?* Translated by

Harold P. Wright and with photographs by Eikoh Hosoe. Tokyo: Kodansha International, 1965.

Gatewood, Charles, and William S. Burroughs. *Sidetripping.* With photographs by Charles Gatewood. New York: Strawberry Hill Publishing, 1975.

Gattioni, Christian. "Photographie et écriture." In *Pour La Photographie,* edited by Ciro Bruni. Paris: GERMS, 1983.

Gauss, Kathleen McCarthy. "Surrealism, Symbolism and the Fictional Photograph." In *Photography and Art: Interactions since 1946,* by Andy Grundberg and Kathleen McCarthy Gauss. New York: Abbeville, 1987.

Gautier, Théophile. *Voyage en Espagne de Madrid à Jeroz* [1840]. With photographs by Olivier Garros. Paris: Palatine, 1982.

Gernsheim, Helmut. "G. B. S. and Photography." *Photographic Journal* (January 4, 1951): 31–36.

——. *Incunabula of British Photographic Literature 1839–1875.* London: Scolar Press, 1984.

Gibson, Margaret. *Memoirs of the Future: The Daybooks of Tina Modotti.* Baton Rouge: Louisiana State University Press, 1986.

Gilbert, W. S. [The Comic Physiognomist]. "Men We Meet." *Fun* 5 n.s. (May 18, 1867): 105. Caricature reproduced as the frontispiece in *The Lost Stories of W. S. Gilbert,* edited by Peter Haining, London: Robson, 1985; and in *The Gilbert and Sullivan Birthday Book,* October 1 and 2, edited by Frederick W. Wilson, New York: Cahill, 1983.

——. "A Tale of a Dry Plate." In *Foggerty's Fairy and Other Tales.* London: George Routledge, 1990.

——. "To Euphrosyne with My Carte de Visite." *Fun* 2 n.s. (December 23, 1865): 150. Reprinted in *The Bab Ballads,* edited by James Ellis. Cambridge: Belknap Press/ Harvard University Press, 1970.

Gillespie, Diane. "'Her Kodak Pointed at His Head': Virginia Woolf and Photography." In *Virginia Woolf: Themes and Variations,* edited by Vera Neveroc-Furk and Mark Hussey. New York: Pace University Press, 1993.

Gilman, Sander L. "Heine's Photographs." In *Paintings on the Move: Heinrich Heine and the Visual Arts,* edited by Susanne Zantop. Lincoln: University of Nebraska Press, 1989.

Ginsberg, Allen. *Ankor Wat.* With photographs by Alexandra Lawrence. London: Fulcrum Press, 1968.

——. *Photographs.* With a preface by Gregory Corso. Altadena, Calif.: Twelvetrees Press, 1990.

*——. *Reality Sandwiches: Fotografien.* Edited by Michael Köhler. Berlin: Nishen, 1989.

——. "Robert Frank to 1985—A Man." In *Robert Frank: New York to Nova Scotia,* edited by Anne Wilkes Tucker. Boston: New York Graphic Society; Houston: Museum of Fine Arts, 1986.

——. *Snapshot Poetics: A Photographic Memoir of the Beat Era.* Introduction by Michael Köhler. San Francisco: Chronicle Books, 1993.

Ginsberg, Allen, and Joseph Rachey. "The Right to Depict Children in the Nude." *Aperture* 121 (Fall 1990): 42–45.

Gleason, Herbert W. *Thoreau Country: Photographs and Text Selections from the Works of Henry D. Thoreau.* Edited by Mark Silber, and with an introduction by Paul Brook. San Francisco: Sierra Club Books, 1975. [See other Gleason photographs under Thoreau.]

Goedhart, Gerda. *Bertolt Brecht: Porträts.* Zürich: Verlag Die Arche, 1964.

*Goethe, Johann W. von. *Faust; A Tragedy.* Translated by Theodore Martin, with 14 photographs of paintings by A. Von Kreling. London: Bruckmann, 1877.

*——. *Female Characters of Goethe.* With photographs from the original drawings of William Kaulbach and text by G. H. Lewes. Munich: Bruckmann, 1872.

Goldberg, Vicki, ed. *Photography in Print: Writings from 1816 to the Present.* New York: Touchstone/ Simon & Schuster, 1981. Reprinted without photographs. Albuquerque: University of New Mexico Press, 1989.

Goldin, Amy. "Words in Pictures." In *Narrative Art: Art News Annual XXXVI,* edited by Thomas B. Hess and John Ashbery. New York: Macmillan, 1970.

Goldschmidt, Lucien, and Weston Naef. *The Truthful Lens: A Survey of the Photographically Illustrated Book, 1844–1914.* New York: Grolier Club, 1980.

Goncourt, Edmond, and Jules de Goncourt. Entry for November 22, 1862. In *Journals: Mémoires de la Vie Littéraire,* vol. 1, edited by Robert Ricatte. Paris: Farquelle/Flammarion, 1956.

Gordimer, Nadine, and David Goldblatt. *Lifetimes: Under Apartheid* [text by Gordimer and photographs by Goldblatt]. New York: Viking, 1986.

*——. *On the Mines.* Capetown: C. Struick, 1973.

Gostwick, Joseph. *English Poets; Twelve Essays.* With photographs after paintings by R. Krämer. New York: Appleton, 1875.

*——. *German Poets: A Series of Memoirs and Translations.* With 12 photographs after portrait paintings by Carl Jäger. Munich: Bruckmann; New York: Kirchner, 1875.

Grass, Günter, *Flood* [1954–57]. In *Four Plays,* translated by Ralph Manheim. London: Secker & Warburg; New York: Harcourt Brace Jovanovich, 1968. Reprinted Harmondsworth: Penguin, 1972.

——. "Kleckenburg." In *Poems of Günter Grass,* translated by Michael Hamburger and Christopher Middleton. Harmondsworth: Penguin, 1969.

——. *The Plebians Rehearse the Uprising.* London; Secker & Warburg; New York: Harcourt Brace Jovanovich, 1966. Reprinted Harmondsworth: Penguin, 1972.

——. *The Tin Drum* [1959]. Translated by Ralph Manheim. London: Secker & Warburg; New York: Harcourt Brace Jovanovich, 1962. Reprinted New York: Pantheon, 1974.

Gray, Loren. *Zane Grey: A Photographic Odyssey.* Dallas: Taylor Publishing Company, 1985.

Gray, Thomas. *Poems and Letters.* With 4 landscape photographs. London: Chiswick Press, 1863; 1867.

Green, Jennifer M. "Outside the Frame: The Photographer in Victorian Fiction." *Victorians Institute Journal* 19 (1991): 111–40.

*———. "Signs of the Things Taken: Reading, Writing, and the 19th Century Photograph." Ph.D. diss., University of Pennsylvania, Philadelphia, 1990.

Greene, Jonathan, ed. *Ralph Eugene Meatyard.* Lexington, Ky.: Gnomon Press, 1970.

Greenhill, Gillian. "The Jersey Years: Photography in the Circle of Victor Hugo." *History of Photography* 4 (April 1980): 113–20.

Greenway, John L. "Penetrating Surfaces: X-Rays, Strindberg and *The Ghost Sonata.*" *Nineteenth-Century Studies* 5 (1991): 29–46.

Greve, Janis. "Orphanhood and 'Photo-Portraiture' in Mary McCarthy's *Memories of a Catholic Girlhood.*" In *American Women's Autobiography: Fea(s)ts of Memory.* Edited and with an introduction by Margo Culley. Madison: University of Wisconsin Press, 1992.

Griffin, John Howard. *Follow the Ecstasy: Thomas Merton, The Hermitage Years, 1965–1968.* Fort Worth: JHG Editions/Latitudes Press, 1983.

———. *A Hidden Wholeness: The Visual World of Thomas Merton.* With photographs by Thomas Merton and John Howard Griffin. Boston: Houghton Mifflin, 1970.

———. [Photographic Portraits]. In *The John Howard Griffin Reader,* selected and edited by Bradford Daniel. Boston: Houghton Mifflin, 1968.

———. *A Time to Be Human.* New York: Macmillan; London: Collier Macmillan, 1977.

Griffin, Paul F. "Susan Sontag, Franny Phelan, and the Moral Implications of Photographs." *Midwest Quarterly* 29, no. 2 (Winter 1988): 194–202.

Grusa, Jiří. *Franz Kafka of Prague.* Translated by Eric Mosbacher. London: Secker & Warburg; New York: Schocken, 1983.

Gruyer, Paul. *Victor Hugo, Photographe.* Paris: Charles Mendel, 1905.

Guibert, Hervé. *Dialogue d'Images.* Paris: William Blake, 1992.

———. *L'Image Fantôme.* Paris: Éditions de Minuit, 1981.

———. *Le Seul Visage.* Paris: Éditions de Minuit, 1984.

———. *L'Image de Soi, ou L'Injonction de Son Beau Moment.* Paris: William Blake, 1988.

———. *Vice: Photographies de l'Auteur.* Paris: Éditions Jacques Bertoin, 1991.

*Guilbert, Edmund. *The Home of Washington Irving.* With 6 photographs by Edmund Guilbert. New York: Appleton, 1867.

Gunn, Thom, and Ander Gunn. *Positives.* With verses by Thom Gunn and photographs by Ander Gunn.

Chicago: University of Chicago Press, 1966. Reprinted London: Faber & Faber, 1973.

Gutteridge, Don. "Old Photographs and the Documentary Imperative." *Canadian Literature* (Summer-Fall 1987): 113–14, 253–58.

Haaften, Julia Van. "Original Sun-Pictures: A Check List of the New York Public Library's Holdings of Early Works Illustrated with Photographs, 1844–1900." *Bulletin of the New York Public Library* 80, no. 3 (Spring 1988): 355–415.

Haines, Robert E. *The Inner Eye of Alfred Stieglitz.* Washington, D.C.: University Press of America, 1982. [Stieglitz's Literary Relationships.]

Hall, James Baker. Prose poems about Meatyard in *Ralph Eugene Meatyard,* edited by James Baker Hall. *Aperture* 18, nos. 3 and 4 (1974): 27, 32, 41, 57, 65, 74–75, 93, 109, and 125; reissued as a book, Millerton, N.Y.: Aperture, 1974.

*———. "Review of *The Unforeseen Wilderness* [with text by Wendell Berry and photographs by Ralph Eugene Meatyard]." *Big Rock Candy Mountain* 2, no. 1 (1971).

———. "The Strange New World of Ralph Eugene Meatyard." *Popular Photography* 65, no. 1 (July 1, 1969): 120 and 146.

Halter, Peter. "Distance and Desire: Wright Morris' *The Home Place* as 'Photo-Text.'" *Études de Lettres* 4 (October–December 1990): 65–89.

Hambourg, Maria Morris. Introduction to *Photographers and Authors: Portraits of Twentieth-Century Writers from the Carleton College Collection.* Northfield, Minn.: Carleton College, 1984.

Hamilton, David. *Sisters.* With text by Alain Robbe-Grillet. New York: William Morrow, 1973.

Hammett, Dashiell. *The Maltese Falcon.* Illustrated with 46 period photographs of sites in the novel by Edwin Shea et al. and notes on the photographs by Glenn Todd. San Francisco: Arion Press, 1983.

Handke, Peter. *Als das Wünschen noch Geholfen hat* [When Wishing Still Helped]. Frankfurt am Main: Suhrkamp, 1971. Published without photographs as *Nonsense and Happiness,* translated by Michael Roloff. New York: Urizen, 1976.

———. *The Weight of the World.* Translated by Ralph Manheim. New York: Farrar, Straus & Giroux, 1984.

Hardy, Thomas. *Desperate Remedies* [1871]. With an introduction by C. J. P. Beatty. London: Macmillan, 1975.

———. "An Imaginative Woman" [1893]. In *Wessex Tales.* New York: Harper & Brothers; London, Macmillan, 1896; and in *Life's Little Ironies,* London, Macmillan, 1912.

———. *Jude the Obscure* [1895–96]. *An Authoritative Text, Backgrounds and Sources, Criticism,* edited by Norman Page. New York: Norton, 1978.

———. *A Laodicean* [1881]. With an introduction by Barbara Hardy and notes by Ernest Hardy. London: Macmillan, 1975.

———. "The Photograph." In *Moments of Vision and Miscellaneous Verses.* London: Macmillan, 1917. Reprinted in *The Complete Poems of Thomas Hardy,* edited by James Gibson, London: Macmillan, 1976; and in *The Complete Poetry of Thomas Hardy,* edited by Samuel Hynes, Oxford: Clarendon Press, 1985.

———. "The Son's Portrait" [1924]. In *Winter Words in Various Moods and Meters.* London: Macmillan, 1928. Reprinted in *The Complete Poems of Thomas Hardy,* edited by James Gibson, London: Macmillan, 1976; and in *The Complete Poetry of Thomas Hardy,* edited by Samuel Hynes, Oxford: Clarendon Press, 1985.

Hargreaves, Alice (Liddell). "The Friendship That Sparked *Alice's Adventures.*" In *Lewis Carroll: Interviews and Recollections,* edited by Morton N. Cohen. Hampshire and London: Macmillan Press, 1989.

Hargreaves, Caryl. "Alice's Recollections of Carrollian Days, as told to Her Son, Caryl Hargreaves." *Cornhill Magazine* 73 (July 1922): 1–12. Abridged in Alice Liddell Hargreaves, "The Lewis Carroll That Alice Recalls." *New York Times* 81 (May 1, 1932), Sec. 5: 7 and 15.

Harley, Ralph L. "The Cultural and Aesthetic Significance of the Newhaven Fisherfolk Photographs by D. O. Hill and Robert Adamson." Ph.D. diss., University of New Mexico, Albuquerque, 1984.

———. "The Partnership Motive of D. O. Hill and Robert Adamson." *History of Photography* 10, no. 4 (October–December 1986): 303–12.

Harper, Michael. "The Negatives" and "Photographs." In *Photographs: Negatives: History as Apple Tree.* San Francisco: Scarab Press, 1972. Reprinted as "Photographs: Negatives," in *Song: I Want a Witness.* Pittsburgh: University of Pittsburgh Press, 1972.

———. "Photographs: A Vision of Massacre." *History Is Your Own Heartbeat.* Urbana: University of Illinois Press, 1971.

Harris, Alex, ed. *A World Unsuspected: Portraits of Southern Childhood.* Chapel Hill: University of North Carolina Press for the Center for Documentary Photography at Duke University, 1987.

Harris, Joel Chandler. Preface to *Down South* by Rudolf Eickemeyer, Jr. New York: R. H. Russell, 1900.

Harris, Neil. "Iconography and Intellectual History: The Half-tone Effect." In *New Directions in American Intellectual History,* edited by John Higham and Paul K. Conkin. Baltimore: Johns Hopkins University Press, 1979.

Harte, Bret. Letters from June 30, 1896–September 25, 1897. In *The Letters of Bret Harte,* edited by Geoffrey Bret Harte. Boston: Houghton Mifflin, 1926.

[H]artman, [S]adakichi. "Dawn Flowers (To Maurice Maeterlinck) [lines suggested by Steichen's "Dawn Flowers"]. *Camera Work* 2 (April 1903): 29. Reprinted in *Camera Work Anthology,* edited by Jonathan Green. Millerton, N.Y.: Aperture, 1973.

Hawkins, Bernard. *Hardy's Wessex.* With photographs by Anthony Kersting. London: Macmillan, 1983.

Hawthorne, Nathaniel. *The House of the Seven Gables* [1851]. In *The Centenary Edition of the Works of Nathaniel Hawthorne,* vol. 2, edited by Fredson Bowers. Columbus: Ohio State University Press, 1965.

———. *Transformation, or the Romance of Monte Beni* [also known as *The Marble Faun*]. 2 vols. Leipzig: Tauchnitz, 1860.

Heaney, Seamus. "Ancestral Photograph." In *Death of a Naturalist* 7. London: Faber & Faber; New York: Oxford University Press, 1966. Reprinted in *Poems, 1965–75,* London and Boston: Faber & Faber; New York: Farrar, Straus & Giroux, 1980.

———. *North.* London: Faber & Faber, 1975; New York: Oxford University Press, 1976. [Includes "Bog Queen," "Come to the Bower," "The Grauballe Man," "Kinship," "Punishment," and "Strange Fruit."] Reprinted in *Poems, 1965–75.* London and Boston, Faber & Faber; New York: Farrar, Straus & Giroux, 1980; and in *New Selected Poems,* London: Faber & Faber, and *Selected Poems 1966–1987,* New York: Farrar, Straus & Giroux, 1990.

———. "The Old Team." In *The Haw Lantern.* London: Faber & Faber; New York: Farrar, Straus & Giroux, 1987.

———. *Sweeney's Flight.* Based on the revised text of "Sweeney Astray," with the complete revised text of "Sweeney Astray" and photographs by Rachel Giese. London: Faber & Faber, 1992.

———. "The Tollund Man." In *Wintering Out.* London: Faber & Faber, 1972. Reprinted in *Poems, 1965–75,* London and Boston: Faber & Faber; New York: Farrar, Straus & Giroux, 1980; and in *New Selected Poems,* London: Faber & Faber, and *Selected Poems 1966–1987,* New York: Farrar, Straus & Giroux, 1990.

Heilbrun, Françoise, and Philippe Néagu. "L'Atelier de Photographie de Jersey." In *Victor Hugo et les Images: Colloque de Dijon,* edited by Madeleine Blondel and Pierre Georgel. Dijon: Ville de Dijon, 1989.

Hemenway, Abby Maria, ed. *Poets and Poetry of Vermont.* With 19 photographs. Rutland, Vt.: George A. Tuttle, 1858.

Hemingway, Ernest. "He Was a Good Friend." In *Robert Capa, 1913–1954,* edited by Cornell Capa and Bhupendra Karia. New York: Grossman Publishers, 1974.

———. Introduction to *Kiki of Montmartre,* by [Alice Prin], translated by Samuel Putnam. New York: Edward Titus, 1929. Reprinted in *Kiki's Memoirs,* with photographs by Man Ray, Foujita, et al., Paris: Edward Titus, 1930; in *The Education of a French Model: The Loves, Cares, Cartoons and Caricatures of Alice Prin,* New York: Boar's Head Books, 1950; and in *The Education of a French Model,* New and in *The Education of a French Model,* New York: Bridgehead, 1954; New York: Crest, 1956; New York: Belmont, 1962; and New York: Continental, 1966. Abridged in Billy Klüver and Julie Martin, *Kiki's Paris: Artists and Lovers, 1900–1930,* New York: Abrams, 1989.

*———. *The Old Man and the Sea.* With photogravures by Alfred Eisenstaedt. New York: Limited Editions Club, 1990.

Hemmingsson, Per. "Strindberg—the photographer" [1963, 1981], translated by Muriel Larssen. In *August Strindberg Som Fotograf.* Åhus: Kalejdoskop Forlag, 1989.

Henderson, Archibald. *George Bernard Shaw: His Life and Works.* With photographs by Edward Steichen and Alfred Langdon Coburn. Cincinnati, Ohio: Stewart & Kidd, 1911.

———. *Mark Twain.* With 10 photographs by Alvin Langdon Coburn. New York: Frederick K. Stokes, 1910; London: Duckworth, 1911.

Hendrick, George. "The Fred Hosmer Copy of a Dunshee Ambrotype of Thoreau." *Thoreau Society Booklet.* Concord, Mass.: Thoreau Society, 1981.

Henisch, B. A. and H. K. "Cuthbert Bede." *Image* 18, no. 3 (September 1975): 20–25.

Hersey, John. "Agee." Introduction to *Let Us Now Praise Famous Men,* by James Agee and Walker Evans. Boston: Houghton Mifflin, 1988.

———. "The Man Who Invented Himself." *'47: The Magazine of the Year* 1, no. 7 (September 1947): 68–77. Reprinted with slight abridgment in *Robert Capa 1913–1954,* edited by Cornell Capa and Bhupendra Karia, New York: Grossman, 1974; and as "Robert Capa," in *Life Sketches,* New York: Knopf, 1989.

Heyen, William. "Bread." *Word and Image* 2, no. 1 (January–March 1986): 66–67.

Higgins, Charles M. "Photographic Aperture: Coburn's Frontispieces to James's New York Edition." *American Literature* 53, no. 4 (January 1982): 661–75.

*———. "Through a Camera, Darkly: Early Photography and the American Romantic Imagination from Poe to James." Ph.D. diss., Indiana University, 1988 [summary in *DAI* 50, no. 1 (July 1989): 179A].

Hirst, Robert H., and Brandt Rowles. "William E. James's Stereoscopic Views of the Quaker City Excursion." *Mark Twain Journal* 22, no. 1 (Spring 1984): 15–33.

Holborn, Mark. "Allen Ginsberg's Sacramental Snapshots: An Interview." *Aperture* 101 (Winter 1985): 8–15.

———. "Eikoh Hosoe and Yukio Mishima: The Shadow in the Time Machine." *Artforum* 21 (February 1983): 51–57.

Holland, J. Gill. "Hawthorne and Photography: *The House of the Seven Gables.*" *Nathaniel Hawthorne Journal* 8 (1978): 1–10.

Hollander, John. "*Ave aut Vale.*" In *Harp Lake.* New York: Knopf, 1990.

Holme, Bryan, and Thomas Forman. *Poet's Camera.* With photographs by Bryan Holme and poetry by Thomas Forman. New York: American Studio Books, 1946.

Holmes, Oliver Wendell, Sr. *Soundings from the Atlantic.* Boston: Ticknor and Fields, 1864. Reprinted Boston: J. R. Osgood, 1872, and Boston: Houghton Mifflin, 1880. [Includes Holmes's noted articles on photography and stereographs, all originally published in the *Atlantic Monthly:* "The Stereoscope and the Stereograph 3 (June 1859): 733–48; "Sun-Painting and Sun-Sculpture, with a Stereoscopic Trip across the Atlantic" 8 (July 1861): 13–26; and "Doings of the Sunbeam" 12 (July 1863): 1–15.]

Holroyd, Michael. Preface to *Bernard Shaw on Photography,* edited by Bill Jay and Margaret Moore. Salt Lake City: Peregrine Smith Books, 1989.

Hornung, E. W. *The Camera Fiend.* London: Unwin; New York: Scribner's, 1911.

———. "A Spoilt Negative." *Belgravia* 65 (March 1888): 76–89.

Horvat, Frank. *Goethe in Sicilia.* Palermo: Novocento, 1982.

Hosoe, Eikoh. *Barakei or Ordeal by Roses/Tué Par les Roses/Hinrichtung Mit Rosen.* With photographs by Eikoh Hosoe, and preface and modeling by Yukio Mishima. Tokyo: Shueisha, 1963. Reformatted as *Ordeal by Roses* with afterword by Mark Holborn. New York: Aperture, 1985. Photographs reprinted with excerpts from Mishima's *Confessions of a Mask* (1959) in *Aperture* 79 (1977): 44–63.

*———. *Man and Woman.* With poems by Taro Yamamoto, text by Ed van der Elsken and Tatsuo Fukushima. Tokyo: CamerArt, Inc., 1961.

Hotten, John Camden. *Thackeray the Humourist and Man of Letters.* With a photographic frontispiece by Ernest Edwards. London: Hotten, 1864.

Howard, Richard. Afterword to *Heads,* by Alex Kayser. New York: Abbeville, 1985.

———. "Avarice, 1849: A Distraction." *New York Times Magazine* (July 12, 1993): 3.

———. "1891: An Idyll." In *Untitled Subjects.* New York: Atheneum, 1969.

———. "Homage to Nadar." With photographs by Nadar. In *Misgivings.* New York: Atheneum, 1979. "Nadar," from "Homage to Nadar," reprinted in *Poets on Photography,* edited by Mark Melnicove. South Harpswell, Me.: Dog Ear Press, 1981.

———. "Homage to Nadar (II)." In *Lining Up.* New York: Atheneum, 1984.

———. "Impersonations, II: Loti Costumed as Osiris, Photograph by Montastier, 1906 (Musée Carnavalet, Paris)." In *Lining Up.* New York: Atheneum, 1984.

———. "The Mapplethorpe Effect." Introduction to *Robert Mapplethorpe,* by Richard Marshall. London: Secker & Warburg; New York: Whitney Museum, 1988.

———. "Move Still, Still So." In *Lining Up*. New York: Atheneum, 1984.

———. "The Nude." *Legacy of Light*. New York: Knopf, 1987.

———. "One Flesh: Photographs by Holly Wright." *Gettysburg Review* 1, no. 3 (September 1988): 569–76.

———. *Preferences: 51 American Poets Choose Poems from Their Own Work and from the Past*. With commentary on the choices and an introduction by Richard Howard and photographs of the poets by Thomas Victor. New York: Viking, 1974.

Howells, William Dean. *London Films*. [With photographs and engravings.] New York & London: Harper & Brothers, 1905.

———. *Their Silver Wedding Journey*. [With photographs and engravings.] 2 vols. New York and London: Harper & Brothers, 1899.

Hughes, Langston. "Diego, Lupe and a Leper." In *I Wonder as I Wander: An Autobiographical Journey*. New York: Hill & Wang, 1956.

———. "Pictures More Than Pictures: The Work of Manuel Alvarez Bravo and Cartier-Bresson." [Mexico D.F., El Instituto Nacional de Bellas Artes, 1935]. MS, Beineke [JWJ, Hughes Papers, MS 871]. Translated as *"Fotografias, mas que fotografias," *Todo* [Mexico City] (March 12, 1935).

Hughes, Langston, and Roy DeCarava. MSS, Beinecke (JWJ, Hughes Collection, 489): "Claudia's Language of the Heart: On Location with 'A Raisin in the Sun,'" n.d.; "The Girl with the Tangerine Hair: On Location with 'A Raisin in the Sun,'" November 12, 1960; "When the Stars Arrive: A Day on Location with 'A Raisin in the Sun,'" January 16, 1961; "Cool Zsa-Zsa Gabor: On Location with 'A Raisin in the Sun,'" January 19, 1961; "Movie Making—Mostly Waiting: On Location with 'A Raisin in the Sun,'" January 20, 1961; "Lorraine Hansberry's Hands: A Photographic Study by Roy DeCarava," January 23, 1961; "Caravan to Carry a 'Raisin.' In Chicago Making 'A Raisin in the Sun,'" January 25, 1961.

———. *The Sweet Flypaper of Life*. See DeCarava, Roy.

Hughes, Langston, and Milton Meltzer. *A Pictorial History of the Negro in America*. New York: Crown, 1956. Reprinted 1963, 1968, and as *A Pictorial History of Blackamericans* by Langston Hughes, Milton Meltzer, and C. Eric Lincoln, 1973, 1983.

Hughes, Ted. *Remains of Elmet: A Pennine Sequence*. With photographs by Fay Godwin. London: Faber & Faber, 1979.

———. *River*. With color photographs by Peter Keen. London: Faber & Faber/James & James, 1983; 1985.

———. "Six Young Men." In *The Hawk in the Rain*. London: Faber & Faber, 1957; 1986.

Hugo, Adèle. Entries, November 22, 1852–November 16, 1853. In *Le Journal d'Adèle Hugo*, edited by Frances Vernor Guille. Vols. 1 and 2 [of 3]. Paris: Lettres Modernes, 1968–71.

Hulick, Diana. "George Platt Lynes: The Portrait Series of Thomas Mann." *History of Photography* 15, no. 3 (Autumn 1991): 211–21.

Humpheys, Kathryn Gail. "Counterfeiting Authenticity: Fictional Portraits in the Age of Photography." Ph.D. diss., Cornell University, 1988 [summary in *DAI* 48, no. 12 (June 1988): 3111A].

Hunter, Jefferson. *Images and Word: The Interaction of Twentieth-Century Photographs and Texts*. Cambridge: Harvard University Press, 1987.

Hürlimann, Martin, ed. *Europe in Photographs*. With commentary by Stephen Spender. London: Thames & Hudson, 1951.

Hutcheon, Linda. "Photographic Discourse." In *The Politics of Postmodernism*. London: Routledge, 1989.

Huxley, Aldous. *Beyond the Mexique Bay*. [With photographs by the author.] London: Chatto & Windus, 1934.

———. "The French of Paris" [1953]. Introduction to *Paris in the Fifties*, by Sanford Roth. With photographs by Sanford Roth and text by Beulah Roth. San Francisco: Mercury House, 1988.

*———. Introduction to *Portraits of the Fifties: The Photographs of Sanford Roth*. With text by Beulah Roth. London: Bloomsbury Publishing, 1987.

Ibsen, Henrik. *The Wild Duck* [1884]. In *The Wild Duck/Hedda Gabler*, translated by Michael Meyer. New York: Norton, 1977.

Ignatieff, Michael. "Family Photo Albums." In *The Russian Album*. New York: Sifton/Viking, 1987. Excerpt in *Harper's* 274 (June 1987): 27–28.

Illustrations of Henry Wadsworth Longfellow's "Courtship of Miles Standish." With 8 Brady photographs of drawings by John W. Ehninger. New York: Rudd & Carleton, 1859.

Illustrations to "Les Misérables" of Victor Hugo. With scenes and characters photographed by A. A. Turner, after original designs of G. Brion. New York: Carlton, 1863.

Images of the South: Visits with Eudora Welty and Walker Evans. With introduction by Bill Ferris. Southern Folklore Reports, no. 1. Memphis, Tenn.: Center for Southern Folklore, 1977.

*Infantino, Stephen C. "Photoghosts." *Romantic Review*, 82, no. 4 (November 1991): 500–506.

———. *Photographic Vision in Proust*. New York: Peter Lang, 1992.

———. "Proust and Photography: Studies in Single-Lens Reflexivity." Ph.D. diss., University of Southern California, Los Angeles, 1986.

*Ingersoll, William. "The Reminiscences of Carl Van Vechten: A Rudimentary Narrative," Columbia University Oral History, 1960. [Corrected carbon copy at the NYPL, Manuscript Division.]

Ionesco, Eugène. "The Colonel's Photograph." In *The

Colonel's Photograph, translated by Jean Stewart. New York: Grove, 1969. Originally published as "La Photo du Colonel." *Nouvelle Revue Française* (November 1, 1955).

Ireland, Alexander. *Ralph Waldo Emerson.* With 3 autotype portraits of Emerson. London: Simpkin, Marshall, 1882.

Irving, Washington. *Rip Van Winkle; A Legend of the Kaatskill Mountains.* The Jefferson Edition. With 4 photographs by Napoleon Sarony. New York: G. P. Putnam & Sons, 1870.

Isherwood, Christopher. Introduction to *Images* by Cecil Beaton. New York: London House and Maxwell, 1963.

Izis [Israëlis Bidermanas]. *Paris des Poètes.* With preface by Jacques Prévert. Paris: Nathan, 1977. Originally published as *Paris des Rêves.* With preface by Jean Cocteau. Lausanne: Editions Clairfontaine, 1950. Translated as *Paris Enchanted,* London: Harvill, 1951. [With texts by 45 writers, including Jean Cocteau, Henry Miller, and André Breton.]

Jablow, Betsy L. *Illustrated Texts from Dickens to James.* Ann Arbor, Mich.: University Microfilms, 1978.

Jackson, Arlene M. "Dickens and Photography in *Household Words.*" *History of Photography* 7 (April–June 1983): 147–49.

———. "Photography as Style and Metaphor in the Art of Thomas Hardy." *Thomas Hardy Annual* 2. Atlantic Highlands, N.J.: Humanities Press, 1983.

Jackson, Helen Hunt. *Ramona: A Story.* With introduction and photographs by A. C. Vroman. Boston: Little, Brown, 1930.

Jacob, Max. "Album de Photographs de famille." In *The Era of the Photograph: A Social History,* by Michel F. Braive, translated by David Britt. London: Thames & Hudson, 1966.

Jacobs, Barry. "Strindberg's *Creditors:* The Doppelgänger Motif and the Avenging Eye." *Annals of Scholarship* 9, no. 3 (1992): 257–78.

Jaffe, James J., comp. *Jonathan Williams: A Bibliographical Checklist of His Writings, 1950–88.* Haverford, Pa.: Jaffe, 1989.

Jahan, Pierre. *Un Anniversaire de Jean Cocteau, 1889–1989.* [With photographs by Pierre Jahan et al. and text by Jean Cocteau.] Paris: Marval, 1989.

James, Henry. *The Novels and Tales of Henry James.* The New York Edition. 24 vols., with frontispieces by Alvin Langdon Coburn. New York: Scribner's, 1907–9 [edition used here]. Reprinted with two additional volumes, 1917, 1922; and, without the frontispieces, Fairfield, N.J.: Augustus M. Kelley, Publishers, 1976.

Jammes, André, and Eugenia Parry Janis. *The Art of the French Calotype.* Princeton, N.J.: Princeton University Press, 1983.

Jammes, Marie-Thérèse, and André Jammes. *En Egypte au Temps de Flaubert: 1839–1860, Les Premiers Photographes.* Paris: Grand Palais, 1976.

Translated and abridged as "Egypt in Flaubert's Time: An Exhibition of the First Photographers, 1839–1960. *Aperture* 78 (1977): 62–77.

Janouch, Gustav. *Conversations with Kafka.* Translated by Goronwy Rees. London and New York: Quartetbooks, 1985.

Jay, Bill. "Images in the Eyes of the Dead." *British Journal of Photography* 128 (January 30, 1981): 124–27 and 132–35.

———. "The Photographer in Fiction: An Annotated Bibliography." Author's TS.

Jeffers, Robinson. Untitled introductory piece to *Edward Weston: Fifty Photographs,* edited by Merle Armitage. New York: Duell, Sloan & Pearce, 1947. Reprinted in *Edward Weston Omnibus: A Critical Anthology,* edited by Beaumont Newhall and Amy Conger. Salt Lake City: Peregrine Smith Books, 1984.

Jephson, Rev. J. M. *Shakespeare's Birthplace, Home, and Grave: A Pilgrimage to Stratford-on-Avon in the Autumn of 1863.* With photographic illustrations by Ernest Edwards. London: Lovell Reeve & Co., 1864.

Johnson, William S. *Nineteenth-Century Photography: An Annotated Bibliography, 1839–1879.* Boston: G. K. Hall, 1990.

Johnston, J[ohn], M.D., and J. W. Wallace. *Visits to Walt Whitman in 1890–1891 by Two Lancashire Friends.* With reproductions after photographs by John Johnston and H. B. Binns. London: George Allen & Unwin; New York: Egmont Arens, 1918.

Jussim, Estelle. *Slave to Beauty: The Eccentric Life and Controversial Career of F. Holland Day, Photographer, Publisher, Aesthete.* Boston: Godine, 1982.

Justice, Donald. "Mule Team and Poster" (on a photograph by Walker Evans [Alabama, 1936]). In *The Sunset Maker: Poems/Stories/A Memoir.* New York: Atheneum, 1987.

Kafka, Franz. *Amerika.* Translated by Edwin and Willa Muir. London: George Routledge, 1938.

Kamholtz, Jonathan. "Literature and Photography: The Captioned Vision vs. the Firm, Mechanical Impression." *Centennial Review* 24 (1980): 385–402.

Kane, Henry Bugbee. *Thoreau's Walden: A Photographic Register.* New York: Knopf, 1946.

Karlen, Arno, comp. *A World Through My Windows.* Photographs by Ruth Orkin. [Quotes from Henry James, Gerard Manley Hopkins, Thomas Wolfe, John Dos Passos, Arthur Rimbaud, et al.] New York: Harper & Row, 1978.

Kasten, Barbara. *Constructs.* With an essay by Estelle Jussim. Boston: New York Graphic Society, 1985. [Includes poems by Bishop, Heaney, Hollander, and others.]

Kay-Robinson, Denys. *The Landscape of Thomas Hardy.* With photographs by Simon McBride. Salem, N.H.: Salem House, 1984.

Kehl, D. G. "Steinbeck's 'String of Pictures' in *The Grapes of Wrath.*" *Image* 17 (March 1974): 1–10.

Keller, Judith. "Evans and Agee, 'The Great American Roadside' (*Fortune* 1934)." *History of Photography* 16, no. 2 (Summer 1992): 170–71 [concerns the article in *Fortune* 10, no. 3 (September 1934): 53–63, 172, 174, 177, which included an anonymous text by Agee and accredited photographs by Evans].

Kellner, Bruce. *Carl Van Vechten and the Irreverent Decades.* Norman: University of Oklahoma Press, 1968.

——. Introduction to "Carl Van Vechten, Vintage Photographs." Exhibition catalogue. London: Duke Street Gallery, March 1981.

Kelly, Jill. "Photographic Reality and French Literary Realism: Nineteenth-Century Synchronism and Symbiosis." *French Review* 65, no. 2 (December 1991): 195–205.

Kerouac, Jack. Introduction to *The Americans,* by Robert Frank. New York: Grove, 1959. Reprinted New York: Pantheon, 1986.

——. "On the Road to Florida" (with photographs by Robert Frank) [1958]. *Evergreen Review* 74 (January 1970): 42–47 and 64. Reprinted in *Robert Frank: New York to Nova Scotia,* edited by Anne Wilkes Tucker. Boston: New York Graphic Society/ Little, Brown; Houston: Museum of Fine Arts, 1986 [edition used here].

——. *Pull My Daisy.* With text ad-libbed by Jack Kerouac for film by Robert Frank and Alfred Leslie and an introduction by Jerry Tallmer. New York: Grove, [1961].

Kertész, André. *On Reading.* New York: Grossman, 1971. Reprinted New York: Penguin, 1982, 1986; and as *Lectures,* Paris: Éditions de Chêne, 1975.

Keutel, Walter. "In Pursuit of Invisible Tracks: Photographs of a Dead Author." *New German Critique* 50 (Spring–Summer 1990): 157–72.

Kicknosway, Faye. *Who Shall Know Them.* New York: Viking, 1985.

Kidd, Stuart. "Eudora Welty's Unsuccessful Application to Become a Resettlement Administration Photographer." *Eudora Welty Newsletter* 16, no. 2 (Summer 1992): 6–8.

Kin, Ha. "The First Photograph" and "A Photograph from China." In *Between Silences.* Chicago: University of Chicago Press, 1990.

King, Stephen. See Kruger, Barbara.

Kingston, Maxine Hong. *China Men.* New York: Knopf, 1980.

——. *The Woman Warrior.* New York: Knopf, 1976.

Kipling, Rudyard. "At the End of the Passage." In *Lippincott's Magazine* 46 (August 1890): 246–60. Reprinted in *Life's Handicap: Being Stories of Mine Own People,* London and New York: Macmillan, 1891; in *Mine Own People,* with an introduction by Henry James, New York: Lovell, 1891; and in W. Somerset Maugham, *Maugham's Choice of Kipling's Best,* Garden City, N.Y.: Doubleday, 1953.

Kirstein, Lincoln. "Walt Whitman and Thomas Eakins: A Poet's and a Painter's Camera-Eye." *Aperture* 16, no. 3 (1972): npn.

Knight, Alana, ed. *R[obert]. L[ouis]. S[tevenson]. in the South Seas: An Intimate Photographic Record.* Edinburgh: Mainstream Publishing, 1986.

Knopf, Alfred A. *Sixty Photographs.* New York: Knopf, 1975.

Koppen, Erwin. *Literatur und Photographie: Über Geschichte und Thematik Einer Medienentdeckung* [Literature and Photography: A History and Themes of Media Discovery]. Stuttgart: J. B. Metzler, 1987.

Kosinski, Jerzy. *Being There.* New York: Harcourt Brace Jovanovich, 1971. Reprinted New York: Bantam, 1974.

——. *Blind Date.* Boston: Houghton Mifflin, 1977 [edition used here]. Reprinted New York: Bantam, 1978.

——. *Cockpit.* Boston: Houghton Mifflin, 1975. Reprinted New York: Bantam, 1976.

——. *The Devil Tree.* New York: Harcourt Brace Jovanovich, 1973; New York: Bantam, 1974. Revised and expanded edition, New York: St. Martin's Press, 1981; New York: Bantam, 1981.

——. "Exegetics." *Paris Review* 97 (1985): 93–99.

——. *The Hermit of 69th Street: The Working Papers of Norbert Kosky.* New York: Seaver, 1988. Reprinted New York: Zebra Books, 1991.

——. "How Photogenic Must My Self Be?" [1988]. In *Jerzy Kosinski: Twarzi i Maski=The Face and Masks=Visage et Masques,* with photographs by Czeslaw Czapliński, and essays by Czapliński et al. Exhibition catalogue, April 3–May 10, 1992. Lodz: Muzeum Sztuky, 1992.

——. *Jerzy Kosinski.* See Czapliński, Czeslaw.

——. *The Painted Bird.* Boston: Houghton Mifflin, 1965 (censored edition); 2nd edition, New York: Pocket Books, 1966 (original text restored); 3rd edition, Modern Library, 1970 (newly revised). Reprinted New York: Bantam, 1972; with an introduction by Kosinski, Boston: Houghton Mifflin, 1976 [edition used here].

——. *Passion Play.* New York: St. Martin's Press, 1979. Reprinted. New York: Bantam, 1980.

——. *Pinball.* New York: Bantam, 1982

——. Statement for "Jerzy Kosinsky: Early Photographs, Poland and Russia, 1950–1957." In exhibition brochure, André Zarre Gallery, New York, October 4–31, 1988.

——. *Steps.* New York: Random House, 1968. Reprinted New York, Bantam, 1969.

Kraus, Karl. *Die Letzten Tage der Menschheit: Tragödie in funf Akten mit Vorspiel und Epilog* [The Last Days of Mankind: A Tragedy in Five Acts with Prologue and Epilogue] [1918]. Edited by Christian Wagenknecht, vol. 10 of *Schriften.* Frankfurt am Main: Suhrkamp, 1986.

Krauss, Rosalind. "The Photographic Conditions of Surrealism." In *The Originality of the Avant-Garde* and Other Modernist Myths. Cambridge: MIT Press, 1985.

———. "Tracing Nadar." *October* 5 (Summer 1978): 29–47. Reprinted in *Reading into Photography: Selected Essays, 1959–1980,* edited by Thomas Barrow et al. Albuquerque: University of New Mexico Press, 1982.

Krauss, Rosalind, and Jane Livingston. *L'Amour Fou: Photography and Surrealism.* With an essay by Dawn Ades. Washington, D.C.: Corcoran Gallery and New York: Abbeville Press, 1985.

Krementz, Jill. "Jill Krementz." In *Something About the Author Autobiography Series,* vol. 8, edited by Anne Commire. Detroit: Gale, 1989.

———. *The Writer's Image: Literary Portraits.* With a preface by Kurt Vonnegut. Boston: Godine, 1980.

Kruger, Barbara. *Picture/Readings.* N.p: Barbara Kruger, 1978.

Kruger, Barbara, and Stephen King. *My Pretty Pony.* New York: Library Fellows of the Whitney Museum of American Art, 1988; New York: Knopf, in association with the Whitney Museum of American Art, 1989.

Kumin, Maxine. "A Family Man." In *I Hear My Sisters Saying,* edited by Carol Konek and Dorothy Walters. New York: Crowell, 1976.

———. "Photograph, Maryland Agricultural College Livestock Show, 1924" and "Photograph, U.S. Army Flying School, College Park, Maryland, 1909." In *Nurture: Poems.* New York: Viking, 1989.

Kurlansky, Mervyn, and Jon Naar. *The Faith of Graffiti.* With text by Norman Mailer and photographs by Mervyn Kurlansky and Jon Naar. New York: Praeger/Alskog, 1974; as *Watching My Name Go By,* London: Mathews Miller Dunbar, 1974.

Lalonde, Normand. "L'Iconographie photographique de *Nadja.*" *French Review* 66, no. 1 (October 1992): 48–58.

*Lamb, Charles, and Mary Lamb. *Tales from Shakespeare.* With 12 illustrations in permanent photography from the Boydell Gallery. London: Bickers, 1876.

Lambrecht, Eric, and Luc Salu. *Photography and Literature: An International Bibliography of Monographs.* London: Mansell, 1992.

Lamont, Rosette C. "Murderous Enactments: The Media's Presence in the Drama." *Modern Drama* 28, no. 1 (March 1985): 148–61.

*Landy, J. *Shakespeare's Seven Ages.* With photographs by J. Landy. Cincinnati: Robert Clarke, 1876.

Lanier, Sidney. *Hymns of the Marshes.* With photographic illustrations by Henry Troth. New York: Charles Scribner's, 1907.

Larkin, Philip. "Essential Beauty." In *The Whitsun Weddings.* London: Faber & Faber, 1964. Reprinted in *Collected Poems,* edited by Anthony Thwaite. London: Marvell Press and Faber & Faber; New York: Marvell Press and Farrar, Straus & Giroux, 1988.

———. "Lines on a Young Lady's Photograph Album" [1953]. In *Fantasy Poets, No. 21.* Oxford: Fantasy Press, 1954. Reprinted in *The Less Deceived,* E. Yorkshire: Marvell, 1955; and in *Collected Poems,* edited by Anthony Thwaite, London: Marvell Press and Faber & Faber; New York: Marvell Press and Farrar, Straus & Giroux, 1988.

———. "MCMXIV" [1960], "Sunny Prestatyn" [1962], and "Wild Oats" [1962]. In *The Whitsun Weddings.* London: Faber & Faber, 1964. Reprinted in *Collected Poems,* edited by Anthony Thwaite, London: Marvell Press and Faber & Faber; New York: Marvell Press and Farrar, Straus & Giroux, 1988.

Larrabee, Constance Stuart, and Alan Paton. *Go Well, My Child.* With photographs by Constance Stuart Larrabee with the collaboration of Alan Paton. Washington, D.C.: Smithsonian Institution, 1985.

Lathers, Marie. "Picturing the Ideal Feminine: Photography in Nineteenth-Century Literature." *Yearbook of Interdisciplinary Studies in the Fine Arts* 2 (1990): 357–65.

Laughlin, Clarence John. *Ghosts along the Mississippi: An Essay on the Poetic Interpretation of Louisiana's Plantation Architecture.* New York: Scribner's, 1948.

Lea, Hermann. *Thomas Hardy's Wessex.* London: Macmillan, 1913.

Le Carré, John [David Cornwell]. Introduction to *England's Glory: A Photographic Journey through England's Threatened Landscapes,* by Gareth Huw Davies. With photographs by 24 photographers. London: Weidenfeld & Nicolson, 1987.

———. "McCullin's World." *Sunday Times Magazine* (October 28, 1980). Reprinted as introduction to *Hearts of Darkness* by Don McCullin, New York: Knopf, 1981; and, somewhat abbreviated, as "Essay: Hearts of Darkness," *American Photographer* 6, no. 5 (May 1981): 30–41.

[Leeson], A[delaide] H[anscom]. Illustrations to *The Rubaiyat of Omar Khayyam,* translated by Edward Fitzgerald. New York: Dodge, 1905. [Three different issues: one with plates on tissue; one with plates on paper; one with color illustrations made from Hanscom's photographs.] Variant edition, London: George G. Harrap, 1908.

———. *Sonnets from the Portuguese.* by Elizabeth Barrett Browning. With photographs by Adelaide Hanscom Leeson. New York: Dodge, 1916.

Lensing, Leo. "Literature and Photography: Practical and Theoretical Observations on Their Interaction in Modern Vienna." In *Intertexuality: German Literature and Visual Arts,* edited by Ingeborg Hoesterey and Ulrich Weisstein. Columbia, S.C.: Camden House Press, forthcoming.

———. "Moving Pictures: Photographs and Photographic Meaning in Karl Kraus's *Die Letzten Tage der Menschheit.*" In *Playing for Stakes: German-Language Drama in Social Context (Festschrift for Herbert Lederer),* edited by Anna Kuhn and

Barbara Wright. Oxford, New York and Munich: Berg, 1992.

——. "Peter Altenberg's Fabricated Photographs: Literature and Photography in Fin-de-Siècle Vienna." In *Austrian Studies 1*, edited by Edward Timms and Ritchie Robertson. Edinburgh: Edinburgh University Press, 1990.

Lessing, Doris. Foreword to *The Essential Cat*, by Thomas Wester. London: Souvenir, 1985. [Includes seven poems by Oscar Wilde and others.]

Levertov, Denise. "Looking at Photographs." In *The Poet in the World*. New York: New Directions, 1973.

——. "Photo Torn from The Times," "In Thai Binh (Peace) Province," and "A Letter to Marek about a Photograph." In *The Freeing of the Dust*. New York: New Directions, 1975.

Levi, Peter. *The Light Garden of the Angel King: Journeys in Afghanistan*. With 19 photographic illustrations by Bruce Chatwin. London: Collins, 1972.

Levine, Sherrie. "Five Comments." In *Blasted Allegories*, edited by Brian Wallis. New York: Museum of Contemporary Art and Cambridge: MIT Press, 1987.

——. "A Simple Heart (After Gustave Flaubert)." *New Observations* 35 (1985): 15–19.

Lewis, C. Day. "The Album." In *Word over All*. London: Cape, 1943. Reprinted in *Collected Poems*, London: Cape/Hogarth, 1954; and *Poems of C. Day Lewis, 1925–1972*, edited by Ian Parsons, London: Cape/Hogarth, 1977.

Litchfield, R. B. *Tom Wedgwood, the First Photographer*. London: Duckworth, 1903. [Includes material on the "first" photographer's friendship with Coleridge.]

*Littledale, Henry Anthony. *King Henry's Well, and Pudsey's Leap: Ballads founded on craven Legends*. With 3 interior views. Bolton: Bowland; Manchester: Faulkner, 1856.

The Little Review. Edited by Margaret Anderson, Jane Heap, Ezra Pound, and Francis Picabia. 12 volumes. Chicago: March 1914–May 1929.

Loewenstein, F. E., ed. *Bernard Shaw through the Camera*. London: B. & H. White Publications, 1948.

Logan, John. "Eight Poems on Portraits of the Foot." *The Malahat Review* 2 (April 1967): 65–77. Reprinted in *Spring of the Thief: Poems 1960–62*, New York: Knopf, 1963; in *Aaron Siskind, Photographs / John Logan, Poems*, Rochester, N.Y.: Visual Studies Workshop, 1976; and in *Only the Dreamer Can Change the Dream*, New York: Ecco Press, 1981.

——. "Homage to John Logan" [Three Poems on Aaron Siskind's Rome Work]. *Voyages* 5, nos. 3 and 4 (Spring 1971–72): 10–16. Reprinted in Carl Chiarenza, *Pleasures and Terrors: Aaron Siskind*, Boston: New York Graphic Society, 1982; as "Three Poems on Siskind's Photographs," in *The Anonymous Lover: New Poems*, New York: Liveright, 1973; and as "Three Poems on the Rome Photographs," in

Aaron Siskind, Photographs / John Logan, Poems, Rochester, N.Y.: Visual Studies Workshop, 1976; and in *Only the Dreamer Can Change the Dream*, New York: Ecco Press, 1981.

——. "Lines for Michael in the Picture." In *The Zigzag Walk: Poems, 1963–68*. New York: Dutton, 1969. Reprinted in *Only the Dreamer Can Change the Dream*. New York: Ecco Press, 1981.

——. "On a Photograph by Aaron Siskind." *Chicago Choice* (1961): 68–69. Reprinted in *Spring of the Thief*, New York: Knopf, 1963; in *Aaron Siskind, Photographs / John Logan, Poems*, Rochester, N.Y.: Visual Studies Workshop, 1976; in *Only the Dreamer Can Change the Dream*, New York: Ecco Press, 1981; and in Carl Chiarenza, *Pleasures and Terrors: Aaron Siskind*, Boston: New York Graphic Society, 1982.

——. "A Suite of Six Pieces for Siskind." In *Spring of the Thief: Poems 1960–62*. New York: Knopf, 1963. Reprinted in *Aaron Siskind, Photographs / John Logan, Poems*, Rochester, N.Y.: Visual Studies Workshop, 1976.

London, Jack. "How Jack London Got In and Out of Jail in Japan." *San Francisco Examiner* (February 27, 1904): 2. Reprinted as "A Camera and a Journey," in *In Many Wars by Many War-Correspondents*, edited by George Lynch and Frederick Palmer, Tokyo: Tokyo Printing Company, 1904 [edition used here]; and with original title in *Jack London Reports*, edited by King Hendricks and Irving Shepard, New York: Doubleday, 1970.

——. *The People of the Abyss*. New York and London: Macmillan, 1903. [With photographs by the author.] Reprinted Oakland, Calif.: Star Rover Press, 1982.

——. *The Road*. [With drawings by H. C. Wall and photographs by the author.] New York: Macmillan, 1907.

——. "The Russo-Japanese War: Selected Dispatches." "In *Jack London's Tales of Adventures*, edited by Irving Shepard. [With some of the author's photographs.] New York: Hanover House, 1956.

Longfellow, Henry Wadsworth. *Hyperion: A Romance*. With 24 photographs of the Rhine, Switzerland, and the Tyrol by Frances Frith. London: Alfred William Bennett, 1865. Reprinted Boston: Ticknor & Fields, 1868.

*——. *Nüremberg*. With 28 photographs by Gebbie and Gusson. Philadelphia: Gebbie, 1888.

*——. *The Poetical Works*. The Albion Edition. London: Griffith & Farnon, 1882. Reprinted with photographs by Payne Jennings. London: 1889.

Longford, Elizabeth. *Byron's Greece*. Photographs by Jorge Lewinski. London: Weidenfeld & Nicolson, 1975.

Lowell, Robert. "Old Snapshot from Venice, 1952." In *The Dolphin*. New York: Farrar, Straus & Giroux, 1973.

——. "Suicide," "Marriage," "For Sheridan," and "Epilogue." In *Day by Day*. New York: Farrar Straus & Giroux; London: Faber & Faber, 1977.

Lyon, Danny. *The Bikeriders*. New York: Macmillan; London: Collier-Macmillan, 1968.

——. *I Like to Eat Right on the Dirt: A Child's Journey Back in Space and Time*. Cliftondale, N.Y.: Black Beauty Books, 1989.

——. *The Paper Negative*. Bernalillo, N.M.: Black Beauty, 1980.

Lyons, Joan, ed. *Artist's Book: A Critical Anthology and Source Book*. Rochester, N.Y.: Visual Studies Workshop, 1987.

Maciejewski, Macief. "The Łódź Years of Jerzy Kosinski." In *Jerzy Kosinski: Twarzi i Maski=The Face and Masks=Visage et Masques*. With photographs by Czeslaw Czapliński. Exhibition catalogue, April 3–May 10, 1992. Łódź: Muzeum Sztuky, 1992.

Mack, Richard, and Wynn Bullock. *The Widening Stream*. With poems by Richard Mack and photographs by Wynn Bullock. San Francisco: Peregrine Publications, 1965.

MacLeish, Archibald. Foreword to *The Photographic Eye of Ben Shahn*, edited by Davis Pratt. Cambridge: Harvard University Press, 1975.

——. *Land of the Free*. New York: Harcourt, Brace, 1938. Reprinted New York: DaCapo, 1977.

——. "Old Photograph" and "Photograph Album." In *Collected Poems, 1917–1982*. Boston: Houghton Mifflin, 1985.

——. "Three Photographs: 'Seeing'; 'Family Group'; 'White-Haired.'" In *New and Collected Poems*. Boston: Houghton Mifflin, 1976. Reprinted in *Collected Poems, 1917–1982*. Boston: Houghton Mifflin, 1985.

MacLulich, T. D. "Ondaatje's Mechanical Boy: Portrait of the Artist as Photographer." *Mosaic* 14, no. 2 (Spring 1981): 107–19.

MacNeice, Louis. "A Hand of Snapshots." In *Visitations*. London: Faber & Faber, 1957.

MacNeil, Robert. *Eudora Welty: Seeing Black and White*. Jackson: University Press of Mississippi, 1990.

MacWeeney, Alen, and Sue Allison. *Bloomsbury Reflections*. New York: Norton, 1990.

Madden, David. "The Cruel Radiance of What Is." *Southern Quarterly* 22, no. 2 (Winter 1984): 5–43.

——. "Photographs in the 1929 Version of *Sanctuary*." In *Faulkner and Popular Culture*, edited by Doreen Fowles and Ann J. Abadie. Jackson: University of Mississippi Press, 1990.

Maeterlinck, Maurice. *The Intelligence of the Flowers*. Translated by Alexander Teixeira de Mattos and illustrated with four photogravures by Alvin Langdon Coburn. New York: Dodd, Mead, 1907.

——. Untitled ("Je Crois"). *Camera Work* no. 2 (April 1903): insert. Reprinted and translated as "I Believe" in *Camera Work*, Special Steichen Supplement (April 1906): [1]; in *American Amateur Photographer* 15,

no. 11 (November 1903): 501; in *Camera Work: A Critical Anthology*, edited and with an introduction by Jonathan Green, Millerton, N.Y.: Aperture, 1973, pp. 61–62; and in *Camera Work*, Nendel, Liechtenstein: Kraus Reprint, 1969.

Maharidge, Dale, and Michael Williamson. *And Their Children After Them: The Legacy of Let Us Now Praise Famous Men: James Agee, Walker Evans, and the Rise and Fall of Cotton in the South*. New York: Pantheon, 1989.

Mailer, Norman. *The Bullfight: A Photographic Narrative* [also known as *A Footnote to Death in the Afternoon*]. With photographs by Robert Daley and Peter Buckley, et al. New York: Macmillan, 1967.

——. *Marilyn, A Biography*. With photographs by Avedon, Beaton, et al. New York: Grosset & Dunlap; London: Hodder & Stoughton, 1973.

——. *Of Women and Their Elegance*. With photographs by Milton H. Greene. New York: Simon & Schuster, 1980.

Mallarmé, Stéphane. "Photographies." *Vers de Circonstance*. Paris: Nouvelle Revue Française, 1920. Reprinted in *Oeuvres Complètes*, edited by Henri Mondor and G. Jean-Aubry. Paris: Gallimard, 1945.

Maloney, Dennis, ed. *Windows That Open Inward: Images of Chile*. With photographs by Milton Rogovin [1967] and poems by Pablo Neruda, translated by Robert Bly et al. Buffalo, N.Y.: White Pine Press, 1985.

Mamet, David. "On Paul Ickovic's Photographs." In *Kafka's Grave and Other Stories*. With photographs by Paul Ickovic. New York and Nairobi: Okapi Editions, 1986.

Mancini, Salvatore. *Photographs and Poems*. Aspen, Colo.: Worm Publishers, 1973.

Mann, Charles. "Eudora Welty, Photographer." *History of Photography* 6, no. 2 (April 1982): 145–49.

Mann, Thomas. Excerpt from letter to Kurt Wolff, January 6, 1930. In *August Sander: Photographs of an Epoch*. With a preface by Beaumont Newhall and historical commentary by Robert Kramer. Millerton, N.Y.: Aperture, 1980.

——. "Gladius Dei" [1902]. In *Stories of Three Decades*, translated by H. T. Lowe-Porter. New York: Knopf, 1979.

——. *The Magic Mountain* [1924]. Translated by H. T. Lowe-Porter. New York: Knopf, 1927.

——. "Okkulte Erlebnisse." In *Gesammelte Werke*, vol. 10. Frankfurt am Main: S. Fischer, 1960.

——. "Die Welt ist schön" [The World Is Beautiful]. *Berliner Illustrierte Zeitung* 37, no. 52 (December 23, 1928): 2261–63. Reprinted in *Gesammelte Werke*, vol. 10. Frankfurt am Main: S. Fischer, 1960, 1974, and 1980.

*Marini, Lino. *Il Ghiaccio, Il Granito*. With text by Umberto Eco. Ravenna: Essegi, 1986.

Marks, Alfred H. "Hawthorne's Daguerreotypist: Scientist, Artist, Reformer." In *The House of the Seven*

Gables, by Nathaniel Hawthorne, edited by Seymour L. Gross. New York: Norton, 1967.

Márquez, Gabriel García. Introduction to *The Circle of Life: Rituals from the Human Family Album,* edited by David Cohen and translated by Catherine Brown. San Francisco: Harper San Francisco, 1991.

Marrs, Suzanne. "Eudora Welty's Photography: Images into Fiction." In *Critical Essays on Eudora Welty,* edited by W. Craig Turner and Lee Emling Harding. Boston: G. K. Hall, 1989.

———. "Photography." In *The Welty Collection: A Guide to the Eudora Welty Manuscripts and Documents at the Mississippi Department of Archives and History,* edited by Suzanne Marrs. Jackson: University Press of Mississippi, 1988.

Marsden, Simon. *Visions of Poe: A Selection of Edgar Allan Poe's Stories and Poems.* With photographs and an introduction. New York: Knopf, 1988.

Martin, Reginald. "Reed's *Mumbo Jumbo.*" *Explicator* 44, no. 2 (Winter 1986): 55–56.

Masefield, John. "Liverpool, City of Ships" (with photographs by Alvin Langdon Coburn). *Pall Mall Magazine* 39, no. 167 (March 1907): 272–81.

Maslen, Elizabeth. "Counterpoint: Collaborations between Ted Hughes and Three Visual Artists." *Word and Image* 2, no. 1 (January–March 1986): 33–44.

Massin [Claude Menuet]. "Hugo et la photographie." *La Quinzaine Littéraire* 448, nos. 1–15 (October 1985): 18–19.

Masters, Edgar Lee. "Rutherford McDowell" [1915]. In *Spoon River Anthology: An Annotated Edition,* edited and with an introduction and annotations by John E. Hallwas. Urbana: University of Illinois Press, 1992. [These poems were originally published weekly under the pseudonym of Webster Ford in *Reedy's Mirror from May 29, 1914.]

———. *Spoon River Anthology.* See Distel, Herbert.

Materasso, Henri. *Album Rimbaud.* Paris: Gallimard, 1986.

Matthiessen, Peter. *Men's Lives: The Surfman and Bayman of the South Fork.* New York: Random House, 1986.

Matthiessen, Peter, and Eliot Porter. *The Tree Where Man Was Born,* by Peter Matthiessen/*The African Experience,* by Eliot Porter. New York: E. P. Dutton, 1972.

Mayakovsky, Vladimir. "Conversations with Comrade Lenin" [1929], translated by Irina Zheleznova. In *Selected Verse,* vol. 1, *Selected Works.* 3 vols. Moscow: Raduga Publishers, 1986.

———. *Pro Eto: Ei i Mne* [About This: To Her and Me]. With photomontage illustrations by Alexander Rodchenko. Moscow: Lef Editions, 1923. Reprinted as "It," translated by Dorian Rottenberg. In *Longer Poems,* vol. 2, *Selected Works in Three Volumes,* Moscow: Raduga Publishers, 1986.

*———. *Razgovor s Finispektorom o Poezii* [Conversation with a Tax Collector about Poetry; also known as Talking with the Taxman about Poetry]. With photographs by Alexander Rodchenko. Tiflis: Zakkriga, 1926.

———. *Sergeiu Eseninu* [To Sergei Esenin]. With photomontage illustrations by Alexander Rodchenko. Tiflis: Zakkriga, 1926; and in German as *An Sergei Jessenin,* Moscow: N.p., 1926.

———. *Sifilis* [Syphilis]. With photomontage illustrations by Alexander Rodchenko. Tiflis: Zakkriga, 1926.

Mazur, Gail. "St. Augustine, 1950." *The Pose of Happiness.* Boston: Godine, 1986.

McCarthy, Mary. *The Stones of Florence.* With photographs by Evelyn Hofer and others. New York: Harcourt, Brace, and World, 1959.

———. *Venice Observed.* With photographs by Inge Morath. Paris: Bernier; New York: Reynal, 1956.

McCauley, Elizabeth Anne. "The Photographic Adventure of Maxime Du Camp." In *Perspective on Photography: Essays on the Work of Du Camp, Dancer, Robinson, Stieglitz, Strand, and Smithers at the Humanities Research Center,* edited by Dave Oliphant and Thomas Zigal. Austin: Humanities Research Center, University of Texas, 1982.

McClellan, Katherine Elizabeth. *Henry James in Northampton: Visions and Revisions.* Edited by Dean Flower. Northampton, Mass.: Friends of the Smith College Library, 1971.

McCullin, Don. *Is Anyone Taking Any Notice?* With phrases drawn from the 1970 Nobel lecture by Alexander Solzhenitsyn. Cambridge: MIT Press, 1973.

McDougall, Russell. "'A Portable Kit of Images': Photography in Australian and Canadian Literature in English." *Kunapipi* 9, no. 1 (1987): 110–21.

McGhee, Nancy F. "Portraits in Black: Illustrated Poems by Paul Laurence Dunbar." In *Stony the Road,* edited by Keith L. Schall. Charlottesville: University Press of Virginia, 1977.

McKenna, Rollie. *Artists at Large: Photographs.* Manchester, N.H.: Currier Gallery of Art and Vassar College Art Gallery, 1982.

———. *A Life in Photography.* New York: Knopf, 1991.

———. *Portrait of Dylan: A Photographer's Memoir.* London: J. M. Dent; New York: Stemmer House, 1982.

McKenzie, Barbara. "The Eye of Time: The Photographs of Eudora Welty." In *Eudora Welty: Critical Essays,* edited by Peggy W. Prenshaw. Jackson: University Press of Mississippi, 1979.

———. *Flannery O'Connor's Georgia.* Athens: University of Georgia Press, 1980.

McPhee, John. *Outcroppings.* With photographs by Tom Till and edited by Christopher Merrill. Salt Lake City: Peregrine Smith Books, 1988.

Meatyard, Christopher. "Merton's 'Zen Camera' and Contemplative Photography." *Kentucky Review* 7, no. 2 (Summer 1987): 122–44.

Meatyard, Ralph Eugene. *The Family Album of Lucy-*

belle Crater. With texts by Jonathan Greene, Ronald Johnson, Ralph Eugene Meatyard, Guy Mendes, Thomas Meyer, and Jonathan Williams. N.p.: Jargon Society, 1974.

——. *Father Louie: Photographs of Thomas Merton.* New York: Timken Publishers, 1991. [Includes "Photographing Thomas Merton: A Reminiscence" and "A Eulogy of Thomas Merton," originally published as "Thomas Merton Eulogized: 'Very Much with World,'" *Kentucky Kernel* 60, no. 72 (December 13, 1968): 2.]

Meatyard, Ralph Eugene, and Thomas Merton. Correspondence of August 12, 1967, to November 28, 1968. In Ralph Eugene Meatyard, *Father Louie: Photographs of Thomas Merton.* New York: Timken Press, 1991.

Meese, Elizabeth A. "Constructing Time and Place: Eudora Welty in the Thirties." In *Eudora Welty: Critical Essays,* edited by Peggy W. Prenshaw. Jackson: University Press of Mississippi, 1979.

Mehta, Ashvin. *Gifts of Solitude.* With words by Rabindraneth Tagore. Ahmedabad: Mapin Publishing, 1990.

Meilhac, Henri, and Ludovic Halévy. *Le Photographe.* Paris, 1864.

Melnicove, Mark, ed. *Poets on Photography.* South Harpswell, Me.: Dog Ear Press, 1981.

Melville, Herman. "On the Photograph of a Corps Commander." In *Battle-Pieces and Aspects of the War.* New York: Harper & Brothers, 1866. Reprinted in *Collected Poems,* edited by Howard P. Vincent. Chicago: Packard; New York: Hendricks House, 1947, 1975.

Melvin, Betsy, and Tom Melvin. *Robert Frost Country.* Garden City, N.Y.: Doubleday, 1977.

Mendoza, Tony. *Ernie: A Photographer's Memoir.* Santa Barbara, Calif.: Capra Press, 1985.

——. *Stories.* New York: Atlantic Monthly Press, 1987; distributed by Little, Brown.

Meredith George. *The Works of George Meredith.* The Memorial Edition. With a frontispiece by Alvin Langdon Coburn, several landscapes by Frederick Evans, and other photographs and drawings. London: Constable, 1909–11; New York: Scribner, 1909–12.

Merrill, James. "Some Negatives: X. at the Château." In *The Country of a Thousand Years of Peace and Other Poems.* New York: Atheneum, 1970.

Merton, Thomas. *The Asian Journal of Thomas Merton* [1973]. With photographs by the author and edited by Naomi Burton et al. New York: New Directions, 1975.

——. *Day of a Stranger.* With introduction by Robert E. Daggy. Salt Lake City: Gibbs M. Smith, 1981.

——. *Geography of Holiness: The Photography of Thomas Merton.* Edited by Deba Prasad Patnaik. New York: Pilgrim Press, 1980.

*——. *Gethsemani: A Life of Praise.* With photographs by Art Filmore, Brother Ephrem, and Brother Plus. Trappist, Ky.: Abbey of Gethsemani, 1966.

——. Introduction to *God Is My Life: The Story of Our Lady of Gethsemani,* by Shirley Burden. New York: Reynal, 1960.

——. *The Road to Joy: The Letters of Thomas Merton to New and Old Friends,* selected and edited by Robert E. Daggy. New York: Farrar, Straus & Giroux, 1989.

——. *Woods, Shore, Desert: A Notebook, May, 1968.* With photographs by the author, a foreword by Patrick Hart, and an introduction and notes by Joel Weishaus. Santa Fe: Museum of New Mexico Press, 1987.

Michaels, Barbara L. "Let's Pretend: Photographic Illustration of Fiction and Poetry around 1900." TS, 1991 [Logan Prize Essay, Photographic Resource Center, Boston University].

Michals, Duane. *Album: The Portraits of Duane Michals, 1958–1988.* Pasadena, Calif.: Twelvetrees Press, 1988.

——. *Homage to Cavafy.* Ten poems by Constantine Cavafy and ten photographs by Duane Michals. Danbury, N.H.: Addison House, 1978.

——. *The Journey of the Spirit after Death.* New York: Winter House, 1971.

——. *The Nature of Desire.* Pasadena, Calif.: Twelvetrees Press, 1986.

——. *Now Becoming Then.* With an essay by Max Kozloff. Altadena, Calif.: Twin Palms Press, 1990.

——. *Real Dreams: Photo Stories.* Danbury, N.H.: Addison House, 1976.

——. *Sequences.* New York: Doubleday, 1970.

——. *Sleep and Dreams.* New York: Lustrum, 1984.

——. [Stefan Michals]. *Take One and See Mt. Fujiyama.* New York: Privately published, 1976.

——. *Things Are Queer.* Cologne: Fotogalerie Wilde, 1975. Reprinted in *Duane Michals Photographs/ Sequences/Texts, 1958–1984,* edited by Marco Livingstone. Oxford: Museum of Modern Art, 1984, and often in other works by and about Michals.

Millard, Charles W. "Julia Margaret Cameron and Tennyson's *Idylls of the King.*" *Harvard Library Bulletin* 21 (April 1973): 187–201.

Miller, Arthur. *Homely Girl, A Life.* With illustrations by Louise Bourgeois. New York: Peter Blum, 1992 [vol. 1 features a portrait of Miller and Bourgeois by Inge Morath; vol. 2 features color photographs from ophthalmological studies of pairs of eyes].

——. Introduction to *Portraits,* by Inge Morath. New York: Aperture, 1986.

*——. *Salesman in Beijing.* With photographs by Inge Morath. New York: Viking, 1983.

Miller, Henry. See also Webb, William.

——. "The Eye of Paris" [1933]. Abridged in *Globe* (Minneapolis, Minn.; November 1937) and *The*

Booster (Paris, September 1937). Reprinted in *Max and White Phagocites,* Paris: Obelisk Press, 1938; in *The Wisdom of the Heart,* Norfolk, Conn.: New Directions, 1941; and as "L'Oeil de Paris" in *Brassaï,* Paris: Éditions Neuf, 1952.

———. Introduction to *Histoire de Marie* by Brassaï. Paris: Éditions du Point de Jour, 1949.

———. Preface to *Picasso and Company* by Brassaï, translated by Francis Price. London: Thames & Hudson; New York: Doubleday, 1966. Originally published as *Conversations avec Picasso.* Paris: Gallimard, 1964.

———. *Quiet Days in Clichy.* With photographs by Brassaï. Paris: Olympia Press, 1956. Reprinted 1958.

———. "Stieglitz and John Marin." *Twice a Year,* nos. 8–9 (Spring–Summer 1942): 146–55.

———. *Tropic of Cancer.* With a preface by Anaïs Nin. Paris: Obelisk Press, 1934. Reprinted New York: Grove Press, 1961 [edition used here].

Miller, Sue. *Family Pictures.* New York: Harper & Row, 1990.

Minotaure. 1 (June 1933) to 12–13 (May 1939). Geneva: Skira, 1981.

Mishima, Yukio. Preface to *Barakei* or *Ordeal by Roses/Tué Par les Roses/Hinrichtung Mit Rosen,* by Eikoe Hosoe, translated by John Bester. Photographs by Eikoh Hosoe and modeling by Yukio Mishima. Tokyo: Shueisha, 1963. Reprinted in *Barakei: Ordeal by Roses,* New York: Aperture, 1985; and excerpted with text from Mishima's *Confessions of a Mask* [1959] in *Aperture* 79 (1977): 44–63.

———. Preface to *Embrace* by Eikoh Hosoe. Tokyo: Shashin Hyoronsha, 1971.

Misrach, Richard. *Desert Cantos.* With essay by Reyner Banham. Albuquerque: University of New Mexico Press, 1987.

Mitry, Jean. *Schriftsteller als Photographen, 1860–1910* [Writers as Photographers, 1860–1910]. Lucerne: C. J. Bucher, 1975. [Chapters on the writer-photographers Carroll, Chekhov, Strindberg, Shaw, Synge, Verga, and Zola with some of their photographs.]

Miyoshi, Toyoichino. "Poem." In *Kamaitachi: A Tragi-Comedy,* by Eikoh Hosoe. Tokyo: Gendai Shichosha, 1969.

Moholy-Nagy, László. "James Joyce." In "Literature," from *Vision in Motion.* Chicago: Paul Theobald, 1947.

Moore, Marianne. "Blue Bug." *New Yorker* 38 (May 26, 1962): 40. Reprinted in *The Arctic Ox,* London: Faber & Faber, 1964; in *Tell Me, Tell Me,* New York: Viking, 1966; and in *The Complete Poems of Marianne Moore,* New York: Macmillan/Viking, 1967 [edition used here].

———. *The Complete Poems of Marianne Moore* [1967]. New York: Macmillan/Viking, 1981; London: Macmillan/Penguin, 1982. Includes "Camilla Sabina" [1933]; "The Frigate Pelican" [1934]; "When I Buy Pictures" [1935]; "Style" [1956]; "Hometown Piece

for Messrs. Alston and Reese" [1956]; "Saint Nicholas" [1958]; "Old Amusement Park," [1966], and revised "Notes."

———. Untitled Piece. In *Stieglitz Memorial Portfolio, 1864–1946,* edited by Dorothy Norman. New York: Twice a Year Press, 1947.

Morath, Inge. "Portraits." In *Portraits.* New York: Aperture, 1986.

———. *Russian Journal.* With introduction by Yevgeny Yevtushenko and essays by Andrei Voznesensky and Olga Andreyev Carlisle. New York: Aperture, 1991.

Morath, Inge, and Arthur Miller. *Chinese Encounters.* New York: Farrar, Straus & Giroux, 1979. Excerpted as "In China." *Atlantic* 243 (March 1979): 90–117.

———. *In the Country.* New York: Viking/Studio, 1977.

———. *In Russia.* New York: Viking/Studio, 1969. Excerpted as "In Russia." *Harper's* 239 (September 1969): 37–78.

Moravia. Alberto. "Carlo Naya." Introduction to *Venezia, Archivio Naya,* by Italo Zannier. Venice: Böhm, 1981.

Moravia, Alberto, and Andrea Andermann. See under Andermann.

Morehouse, Marion, and E. E. Cummings. *Adventures in Value.* New York: Harcourt, Brace & World, 1962. [Includes Cummings's poem on Marianne Moore.]

Moreland, Kim. "The Photo Killeth: Henry Adams on Photography and Painting." *Papers on Language and Literature* 27, no. 3 (Summer 1991): 356–70.

Mormorio, Diego, ed. *Gli Scrittore e La Fotographia.* With preface by Leonardo Sciascia. Rome: Riuniti-Albatros, 1988.

Morrell, Lady Ottoline. *Lady Ottoline's Album.* Edited by Carolyn G. Heilbrun. New York: Knopf, 1976.

Morris, Willie, and William Eggleston. *Faulkner's Mississippi.* Text by Willie Morris and photographs by William Eggleston. Birmingham, Ala.: Oxmoor House, 1990.

Morris, Wright. *About Fiction.* New York: Harper & Row, 1975.

———. "Built with More Than Hands." *New York Times* (December 25, 1949): section 6, cover and 12.

———. The Cat's Meow. Los Angeles: Black Sparrow Press, 1975.

———. *A Cloak of Light: Writing My Life.* New York: Harper & Row, 1985.

———. *God's Country and My People.* New York: Harper & Row, 1968. Reprinted Lincoln: University of Nebraska Press, 1981.

———. *The Home Place.* New York. Scribner's, 1949. Reprinted Lincoln: University of Nebraska Press, 1968. Excerpt entitled "Home Town Revisited" in *New York Times* (April 24, 1949): section 6, 24–25.

———. *The Inhabitants.* New York: Scribner's, 1946. Reprinted New York: Da Capo, 1972. Excerpt entitled "The Inhabitants: An Aspect of American

Folkways" with "A Note" by the author in *New Directions in Prose and Poetry,* Norfolk, Conn.: New Directions, 1940, pp. 147–179.

——. "In Our Image." *Massachusetts Review* 19, no. 4 (Winter 1978): 633–43.

——. *Love Affair—A Venetian Journal.* New York: Harper & Row, 1972.

——. "Photographs, Images, and Words." *American Scholar* 48 (Autumn 1979): 457–69. Reprinted in *Discovery and Recognition [Untitled 25],* edited by James Alinder, Carmel, Calif.: Friends of Photography, 1981 [basis of version used here]; and in *Time Pieces: Photographs, Writing, and Memory,* New York: Aperture, 1989.

——. "Photography in My Life." In *Photographs and Words,* edited and with an introduction by James Alinder. Carmel, Calif.: Friends of Photography, 1982. Reprinted with slight abridgment in *Times Pieces: Photographs, Writing, and Memory.* New York: Aperture, 1989.

——. *Solo: An American Dreamer in Europe.* New York: Harper & Row, 1983.

——. *Will's Boy: A Memoir.* New York: Harper & Row, 1981.

——. *Wright Morris: Origin of a Species.* Essays by Sandra Phillips and John Szarkowski. San Francisco: San Francisco Museum of Art, 1992.

Morris, Wright, and Jim Alinder. *Picture America.* Photographs by Jim Alinder and text by Wright Morris. With introduction by Ansel Adams. Boston: Little, Brown, 1982.

Morrison, Toni. Foreword to *The Black Photographers' Annual.* Brooklyn, N.Y.: Black Photographers Annual, 1973.

——. Foreword to *The Harlem Book of the Dead,* by James Van Der Zee and Owen Dodson. With photographs by Van Der Zee, poetry by Dodson, and text by Camille Billops. New York: Morgan & Morgan, 1978.

Morrow, Mark. *Images of the Southern Writer.* Athens: University of Georgia Press, 1985.

Mortimer, Molly. "Bernard Shaw–Photographer." *Contemporary Review* 258, no. 1503 (April 1991): 211–12.

Mossin, Andrew. "Agee and the Photographer's Art." *Aperture* 100 (Fall 1985): 73–75.

Mottram, Ron. "Impulse toward the Visible: Frank Norris and Photographic Representation." *Texas Studies in Literature and Language* 25 (Winter 1983): 574–96.

Movius, Geoffrey. "A Conversation with Jerzy Kosinski." *New Boston Review* 1, no. 3 (Winter 1975): 3–6.

Mozley, Anita Ventura. *Mrs. Cameron's Photographs from the Life.* Exhibition catalogue, January 22–March 10, 1974. Palo Alto, Calif.: Department of Art, Stanford University, 1974.

Munro, Alice. *Lives of Girls and Women.* Toronto: McGraw-Hill, Ryerson, 1971.

Murdoch, Iris. Preface to *Thinking Faces: Photographs 1953–1979,* by Janet Stone. London: Chatto & Windus, 1988.

Nabokov, Vladimir. *Ada, or Ardor: A Family Chronicle.* New York: McGraw-Hill, 1969.

——. *The Annotated Lolita* [1955]. Edited by Alfred Appel, Jr. New York: McGraw-Hill, 1970.

——. *The Gift* [1952]. Translated by Michael Scammell and Vladimir Nabokov. New York: G. P. Putnam's Sons; London: Weidenfeld & Nicolson, 1963.

——. "From the Gray North" [1967]. In *Poems and Problems* (in Russian and English). New York: McGraw-Hill, 1971.

——. "The Snapshot" [1927]. In *Poems and Problems.* (in Russian and English). New York: McGraw-Hill; London: Weidenfeld & Nicolson, 1971. Originally published as "Snimok" in *Rul* [Berlin] (August 28, 1927): 2; reprinted in *The Return of Chorb,* Berlin: Slovo Book Publishing House, 1930.

——. *Speak Memory: An Autobiography Revisited* [1951/1954]. Revised edition. New York: G. P. Putnam's Sons, 1966.

——. "Time and Ebb." *Atlantic Monthly* (January 1945): 81–84. Reprinted in *The Best American Short Stories, 1945,* edited by Martha Foley, Boston: Houghton Mifflin, 1946; and in *Nabokov's Dozen: A Collection of Thirteen Stories,* Garden City, N.Y.: Doubleday, 1958; Freeport, N.Y.: Books for Library Press, 1969.

Nadar [Gaspard-Felix Tournachon]. "Balzac and the Daguerreotype." Translated by Thomas Repensek from *My Life as a Photographer, October* 5 (Summer 1978): 6–10. Originally published in *Quand J'étais Photographe,* Paris: Flammarion, c. 1899, reprinted New York: Arno, 1979.

——. *Charles Baudelaire Intime: Documents, Notes et Anecdotes* [1911]. Paris: Obsidiane, 1985.

——. *Nadar.* 2 vols. Edited by Philippe Néagu and Jean-Jacques Poulet-Allamagny. Paris: Arthur Hubschmid, 1979.

"Nadar-Balzac: Une Ténébreuse Affaire." In *Nadar, Caricatures et Photographies.* Exhibition catalogue. Paris: Maison de Balzac, Fall 1990.

*Napier, George G. *The Homes and Haunts of Alfred Lord Tennyson.* Glasgow: Maclehose, 1892.

——. *The Homes and Haunts of Sir Walter Scott.* Glascow: T. Maclehose, 1892.

*Nathan, Leonard. *Western Reaches: A Collection of Poems.* With a photograph by Edward Weston. San Jose, Calif.: Talisman Press, 1958.

Néagu, Philippe. "Un Projet Photographique du Victor Hugo." *Photographies* 3 (December 1983): 56–61.

Nemerov, Howard. "An Old Photograph" and "The Photograph of a Girl." In *The Image and the Law.* New York: Henry Holt, 1947. Reprinted in *The Collected Poems of Howard Nemerov.* Chicago: University of Chicago Press, 1977.

——. "To D— Dead by Her Own Hand." *Poetry* 120

(July 1972): 219. Reprinted in *Saturday Review* 55 (November 1972): 42; in *Gnomes and Occasions*, Chicago: University of Chicago Press, 1973; in *The Collected Poems of Howard Nemerov*, Chicago: University of Chicago Press, 1977; and in *A Howard Nemerov Reader*, Columbia: University of Missouri Press, 1991.

Nemiz, Andrea. *Capuana, Verga, De Roberto: Fotografi*. With a preface by Leonardo Sciascia. Palermo: Edikronos, 1982.

Neruda, Pablo. *Una Casa en La Arena*. With photographs by Sergio Larrain. Barcelona: Editorial Lumen, 1966.

——. *The House at Iria Negra*. Translated by Dennis Maloney and Clark M. Zlotchew. With photographs by Milton Rogovin. Fredonia, N.Y.: White Pine Press, 1988.

——. "The Islands and Rogovin." In *Windows That Open Inward: Images of Chile*, translated by Robert Bly et al. and edited by Dennis Maloney. With photographs by Milton Rogovin. Buffalo, N.Y.: White Pine Press, 1985.

——. "Tina Modotti Ha Muerto" [Tina Modotti Is Dead] [1942]. In *Residence on Earth/Residencia en la tierra*, translated by Donald D. Walsh. New York: New Directions, 1973. Originally published in *Tercera Residencia 1935–1945*. Buenos Aires: Editorial Losana, 1947.

——. *Valpararais* [1965]. With photographs by Sergio Larrain. Paris: Éditions Hazan, 1991.

Nerval, Gérard de. *Oeuvres Complètes*. 2 vols., edited by Jean Guillaume and Claude Pichois. Paris: Gallimard, 1984; 1989 [edition used here as basis for translation]. [Includes *Voyage en Orient* and correspondence to 1850; the next volume is forthcoming in 1993.] Some excerpts, variously entitled "Scenes de la Vie Egyptienne" or "Scenes de la View Orientale," originally appeared in the *Revue des Deux Mondes* 14–20, n.s. (May 4, 1846–October 15, 1847).

——. *The Women of Cairo: Scenes of Life in the Orient*. 2 vols., with an introduction by Colin Elphinstone. London: G. Routledge, 1929. Reprinted New York: AMS Press, 1982. [A translation of parts of *Voyage en Orient*.]

*Nettles, Bea. *Corners*. With poetry by Grace N. Nettles. Urbana, Ill.: Inky Press, 1988.

——. *The Elsewhere Bird*. With poetry by Grace N. Nettles. Rochester, N.Y.: Privately published, 1974.

——. *The Imaginary Blowtorch*. With poetry by Grace N. Nettles. Rochester, N.Y.: Privately published, 1973.

——. *The Nymph of the Highlands*. With text by Connie Nettles. Rochester, N.Y.: Privately published, 1974.

——. *Of Loss and Love*. With poetry by Grace N. Nettles. Rochester, N.Y.: Privately published, 1975.

Neubauer, Carol E. "Developing Ties to the Past: Photography and Other Sources of Information in Maxine Hong Kingston's *China Men*." *Melus* 10 (Winter 1983): 17–36.

Newby, Eric. *What the Traveller Saw*. With photographs by the author. New York: Viking Studio, 1990.

Newhall, Beaumont. *Focus: Memoirs of a Life in Photography*. Boston: Bulfinch Press, 1993.

Newhall, Nancy. "The Caption: The Mutual Relation of Words and Photographs. "*Aperture* 1, no. 1 (1952): 17–29. Reprinted in *From Adams to Stieglitz: Pioneers in Modern Photography*. New York: Aperture, 1989.

Nigro, Salvatore. "Verga e l'ospite invisibile" [Verga and the invisible guest]. *La Repùbblica* (February 21, 1992): 25.

*Nin, Anaïs. *The Illustrated Delta of Venus*. With photographs by Bob Carlos Clarke. London: Allen, 1978. Reprinted New York: Gallery Books, 1980.

——. *A Photographic Supplement to the Diary of Anaïs Nin*. New York: Harcourt, Brace, 1974.

Norman, Dorothy. *Intimate Vision: The Photographs of Dorothy Norman*. Edited with an essay by Miles Barth. San Francisco: Chronicle Books; New York: International Center of Photography, 1992.

Nye, David E. "'Negative Capability' in Wright Morris's *The Home Place*." *Word and Image* 4 (January–March 1988): 165–69.

Oates, Joyce Carol. "David Hanson's *Colstrip, Montana* Series." *American Art* 6, no. 2 (Spring 1992): 98–101.

O'Brian, Eoin. *The Beckett Country*. London: Black Cat/Faber, 1986.

O'Hara, Frank. "The Day Lady Died." In *The Collected Poems of Frank O'Hara*, edited by Donald Allen. New York: Knopf, 1971. Reprinted New York: Vintage, 1974.

[O'Hara, John]. "Artist from Arles: Lucien Clergue." *New Yorker* (October 28, 1961): 46–47.

Olsen, Tillie, and Julie Olsen Edwards. "Mothers and Daughters." In *Mothers and Daughters: That Special Quality*. New York: Aperture, 1987.

Olster, Stacey. "Photography and Fantasies in the Stories of Ann Beattie." In *Since Flannery O'Connor: Essays on the Contemporary American Short Story*, edited by Loren Logsdon and Charles W. Mayer. Macomb: Western Illinois University Press, 1987.

Ondaatje, Michael. "Burning Hills," "The Gate in His Head," and "King Kong Meets Wallace Stevens." In *Rat Jelly*. Toronto: Coach House, 1973.

——. *The Collected Works of Billy the Kid: Left Handed Poems*. Toronto: Anansi, 1970. Reprinted London: Marion Boyers, 1981; New York, London: Penguin, 1984.

——. *Coming through Slaughter*. Ontario: General Publishing; New York: Norton; London: Marion Boyers, 1976.

——. *The English Patient*. New York: Knopf; Toronto:

McClelland & Stewart; London: Bloomsbury Publishing, 1992.

——. "Four Eyes" and "Tink, Summer Rider." In *The Dainty Monster*. Toronto: Coach House Press, 1967.

——. "Light" and "Uswetakeiyawa." In *There's a Trick With a Knife I'm Learning to Do*. Toronto: McClelland & Stewart, 1979.

——. *Running in the Family*. Toronto: McClelland & Stewart, 1982; London: Gollancz, 1983.

Orlando, Ted. *Scenes of Wonder and Curiosity: The Photographs and Writings of Ted Orlando*. Boston: Godine, 1988.

Orvell, Miles. *The Real Thing: Imitation and Authenticity in American Culture, 1880–1940*. Chapel Hill: University of North Carolina Press, 1989.

——. "Reproduction and 'The Real Thing': The Anxiety of Realism in the Age of Photography." In *The Technological Imagination: Theories and Fiction*, by Teresa deLauretus, edited by Andreas Huyssen and Kathleen Woodward. Madison, Wis.: Coda, 1980.

——. "Walker Evans and James Agee: The Legacy." *History of Photography* 17, no. 2 (Summer 1993): 166–71.

Orwell. George. *The Road to Wigan Pier*. With photographs. London: Victor Gollancz, 1937. Reprinted New York: Harcourt Brace, 1956.

Ozick, Cynthia. "Shots." In *Levitation: Five Fictions*. New York: Knopf, 1982.

Pachnicke, Peter, and Klaus Honnef. *John Heartfield*. Exhibition catalogue. New York: Abrams, 1991.

Padgett, Ron, and Jim Dine. *The Adventures of Mr. and Mrs. Jim and Ron*. London: Cape Goliard, 1970.

*Paine, Wingate. *Mirror of Venus*. Words by Françoise Sagan and Federico Fellini. New York: Ridge Press/Random House, [1966].

Pair, Joyce M. "'Remember Everything': James Dickey, William A. Bake, and DeKalb College." *James Dickey Newsletter* 5, no. 2 (Spring 1989): 2–5.

Palazzoli, Daniela, ed. *Ignota a Me Stesso: Ritratti di Scrittori da Edgar Allan Poe A Jorge Luis Borges*. Text by Leonardo Sciasia. Turin: Bompiani, 1987.

Parks, Gordon. *Born Black*. Philadelphia: Lippincott, 1971.

——. *A Choice of Weapons*. New York: Harper & Row, 1966. Reprinted St. Paul: Minnesota Historical Society Press, 1986.

——. *Flavio*. New York: Norton, 1978.

——. Foreword to *The Black Photographers' Annual, Volume 3*. Brooklyn, N.Y.: Black Photographers Annual, 1976.

——. Foreword to *Harlem Document: Photographs, 1932–1940*, by Aaron Siskind. Providence, R.I.: Matrix, 1981. Reprinted *Harlem: Photographs 1932–1940*. Washington D.C.: Smithsonian, 1990.

——. *In Love*. Philadelphia: Lippincott, 1971.

——. *The Learning Tree*. New York: Harper & Row, 1963.

——. *Moments without Proper Names*. New York: Viking; London: Secker & Warburg, 1975.

——. *The Poet and the Camera*. With an introduction by Stephen Spender. New York: Viking, 1968.

——. *Shannon*. Boston: Little, Brown, 1981.

——. *To Smile in Autumn*. New York: Norton, 1979.

——. *Voices in the Mirror: An Autobiography*. New York: Doubleday, 1990.

——. *Whispers of Intimate Things*. New York: Viking, 1971.

Parsons, Melinda Boyd. "The 'Unmechanicalness' of Photography: Bernard Shaw's Activist Photographic Philosophy." *Colby Library Quarterly* 25, no. 2 (June 1989): 64–73.

Pasternak, Boris. *My Sister, Life, and Other Poems*. Edited by Olga Carlisle, with color photographs by Inge Morath. New York: Harcourt Brace Jovanovich, 1976.

——. "Summer Thunderstorm." In *Poems*, translated by Eugene M. Kayden. Ann Arbor: University of Michigan Press, 1959.

[Patmore, Coventry]. "Mrs. Cameron's Photographs." *Macmillan's Magazine* 13 (January 1866): 230–31.

Paton, Alan. *South Africa in Transition*. With photographs by Dan Weiner. New York: Scribner's, 1956.

Patten, Arturo. *Portraits/Ritratti*. With a preface by Hubert Nyssen and comments by Russell Banks, Michel Tournier, et al. Arles: Actes Sud, 1992.

Paz, Octavio. "Facing Time/Cara al Tiempo" (for Manuel Alvarez Bravo). In *The Collected Poems of Octavio Paz, 1957–1987* [in Spanish and English], edited and translated by Eliot Weinberger, with additional translations by Elizabeth Bishop. New York: New Directions, 1987. Originally published as *"Cara al Tiempo," Plural* (Mexico) 58 (July 1976): 43–45; reprinted in * *Vuelta*, Barcelona: Editorial Seix Barral, 1976.

*——. Preface to *Mexiko* [1968], by Fulvio Roiter. Zurich: Atlantis, 1979.

Paz, Octavio, and Manuel Alvarez Bravo. *Instante y Revelación*. Translated by Eliot Weinberger and edited by Arturo Muñoz. Mexico: Circulo Editorial, 1982. Paz's preface is reprinted in his *Essays on Mexican Art*, trans. Helen Lane. New York: Harcourt Brace, 1993.

Peeler, David P. *Hope Among Us Yet: Social Criticism and Social Solace in Depression America*. Athens: University of Georgia Press, 1987.

Peret, Benjamin, and Louis Aragon. *1929*. With photographs by Man Ray. Paris: N.p, 1929.

Perugini, Kate. "'Edwin Drood,' and the Last Days of Charles Dickens." With illustrations by Alvin Langdon Coburn. In *Pall Mall Magazine* (June 1906): 642–53.

Peterkin, Julia, and Doris Ulmann. *Roll, Jordan, Roll*. New York: Ballou, 1933.

Photographer as Poet. Chicago: Arts Club of Chicago, 1973.

Pierce, Constance. "Calvino on Photography." *Review of Contemporary Fiction* 6, no. 2 (Summer 1986): 130–37.

Pierce, David. *James Joyce's Ireland*. With contemporary photographs by Dan Harper. New Haven, Conn.: Yale University Press, 1992.

Pinsky, Robert. "The Generation Before." In *Sadness and Happiness*. Princeton, N.J.: Princeton University Press, 1975.

Pitavy-Souques, Danièle. "La Friche dans les photographs d'Eudora Welty: Une Réflexion sur la terre américaine dans le sud." *Revue Française d'Études Américaines* 16, nos. 48–49 (April–July 1991): 281–89 [English summary, p. 336].

Pitchford, Kenneth. "Color Photos of the Atrocities [I]" and "Color Photos of the Atrocities—II." In *Color Photos of the Atrocities*. Boston: Atlantic Monthly Press/Little, Brown, 1973.

*Pitts, Terence. *Frederick Evans and George Bernard Shaw*. Tucson: University of Arizona Press, 1979.

Plimpton, George, and Rocco Landesman. "The Art of Fiction: Jerzy Kosinski." *Paris Review*, no. 54 (Summer 1972): 183–207. Reprinted in *Writers at Work*, ed. George Plimpton. New York: Penguin, 1981.

Pocock, P. J. "Synge and the Photography of His Time." In *The Autobiography of J. M. Synge*. Dublin: Dolmen Press; London: Oxford University Press, 1965.

Poe, Edgar Allan. "The Daguerreotype." *Alexander's Weekly Messenger* (January 15, 1840): 2. Reprinted in Clarence S. Brigham, *Edgar Allan Poe's Contributions to 'Alexander's Weekly Messenger,'* Worcester, Mass.: American Antiquarian Society, 1943 [edition used here]; and in Alan Trachtenberg, ed., *Classic Essays in Photography*, New Haven, Conn.: Leete's Island Books, 1980.

——. "Improvements in the Daguerreotype." *Burton's Gentlemen's Magazine* 6 (April 1840): 193–94.

——. *Tales of Mystery and Imagination*. With photographs and drawings by Harry Clarke. London: G. G. Harrop, 1919. Reprinted New York: Brentano's, 1923.

Poirot, Luis, and Pablo Neruda. *Absence and Presence*. Translated by Alastair Reed. New York and London: Norton, 1990.

Pollard, Arthur. *The Landscape of the Brontës*. With photographs by Simon McBride. Exeter: Webb & Bowen, 1986.

Poole, Roger. "A Phenomenological Reading of Certain Photographs." In *Virginia Woolf Miscellanies: Proceedings of the First Annual Conference on Virginia Woolf*, edited by Mark Hussey and Vara Neverow-Turk. New York: Pace University Press, 1992.

Popovkina, T. K. "Sofia Tolstaya's Collection of Photographs." In *Tolstoy in Life*, (in Russian and English), by Sofia Tolstaya and Vladimir G. Chertkov. Tula: Prioskoe, 1988.

Porter, Eliot. *In Wildness Is the Preservation of the World*. From text by Henry David Thoreau. San Francisco: Sierra Club, 1962. Reprinted in new edition, 1989.

Porter, Eliot, Wallace Stegner, and Page Stegner. *American Places*. Edited by John Macrae III. New York: Greenhouse, 1983.

[Pound, Ezra]. "Vortographs and Paintings by Alvin Langdon Coburn." Preface to Camera Club, London. Exhibition catalogue, February 8–28, 1917. Reprinted with minor revisions as "Vortographs" in *Pavannes and Divisions*, New York: Knopf, 1918; in Harriet Zinnes, ed., *Ezra Pound and the Visual Arts*, New York: New Directions, 1980; and in Peter C. Bunnell, ed., *A Photographic Vision: Pictorial Photography, 1889–1923*, Salt Lake City: Peregrine Smith, 1980.

Powers, Richard. *Three Farmers on Their Way to a Dance*. New York: Beachtree Books/William Morris, 1985.

Prawer, Siegbert S. "Heine and the Photographers." In *Paintings on the Move: Heinrich Heine and the Visual Arts*, edited by Suzanne Zantop. Lincoln: University of Nebraska Press, 1989.

Pritchett, V. S. *Dublin: A Portrait*. With photographs by Evelyn Hofer. London: Bodley Head; New York: Harper & Row, 1967.

——. *London Perceived*. With photographs by Evelyn Hofer. London: Chatto & Windus; New York: Harcourt, Brace & World, 1962.

——. *New York Proclaimed*. With photographs by Evelyn Hofer. New York: Harcourt, Brace & World, 1965.

Proust, Marcel. *The Guermantes Way* (1920–21). From *Remembrance of Things Past* [trans. 1922–31]. Translated by C. K. Scott-Moncrieff [1925], New York: Random House, 1934. Originally published as *Le Côté de Guermantes* from *À la Recherche du Temps Perdu*. Paris: Gallimard, 1913–27.

Puckett, John Roger. *Five Photo-Textual Documentaries from the Great Depression*. Ann Arbor, Mich.: UMI Research Press, 1984.

Quartermaine, Peter. "'Living on the Surface': Versions of Real Life in Alice Munro's *Lives of Girls and Women*." *Recherches Anglaises et Nord-Américaines* 20 (1987): 117–26.

Quinn, Edward. *James Joyce's Dublin: With Selected Writings from Joyce's Work*. London: Secker & Warburg, 1974.

Randall, Margaret, ed. *Women Brave in the Face of Danger: Photographs of and Writings by Latin and North American Women*. Trumansberg, N.Y.: Crossing Press, 1985.

*Ranström, Ture. "Photogenie-Photogenique: August Strindberg und die Photographie." In *Der andere Strindberg: Materiallen zu Malerei, Photographie und Theatrepraxis*, edited by Angelika Gundlach with Jörg Scherze. Frankfurt: Insel, 1981.

Ray, Man. "American and English Writers." In *Self*

Portrait. Boston: Little, Brown, 1963. Reprinted Boston: New York Graphic Society/Little, Brown, 1988 [edition used here].

——. *Man Ray: Photographs 1920–1934.* Edited by James Thrall, with portrait by Pablo Picasso and texts by André Breton and Paul Éluard. Paris: Cahiers d'Art; Hartford, Conn,: S. Thrall Soby, 1934. Reprinted in new edition with introduction by A. D. Coleman, New York: 1975, and with introduction by Andreas Haus, Munich: Schirmer/Mosel, 1980.

Read, Bill. *The Days of Dylan Thomas: A Pictorial Biography.* With photographs by Rollie McKenna. New York: McGraw-Hill, 1964.

Reeve, Lovell, ed. *Portraits of Men of Eminence in Literature, Science and Art with Biographical Memoirs.* With photographs from life by Ernst Edwards. London: Lovell Reeve, 1863 (vols. 1–2) and A. W. Bennett, 1865 (vols. 3–6).

Reßler, Konrad. *Bertolt Brecht beim Photographen: Portraitstudien.* Edited by Michael Koetzle, with a preface by Ditmar Albert. Sigen: Affholerbach & Strohmann, 1987.

La Révolution Surréaliste. Vols. 1–12 (December 1924–December 15, 1929). Reprinted New York: Arno, 1968.

Rexroth, Kenneth. "The Objectivism of Edward Weston: An Attempt at a Functional Definition of the Art of the Camera." MS, c. 1932, CCP.

Rice, Anne. *The Feast of All Saints.* New York: Simon & Schuster, 1979.

Rice, Edward. *The Man in the Sycamore Tree: The Good Times and Hard Life of Thomas Merton. An Entertainment.* Garden City, N.Y.: Image Books, 1972.

Rich, Adrienne. "The Photograph of the Unmade Bed" [1969]. In *The Will to Change: Poems 1968–70.* New York: Norton, 1971. Reprinted in *Poets on Photography,* edited by Mark Melnicove. South Harpswell, Me.: Dog Ear Press, 1981.

Rietz, John. "Another Whitman Photograph: The Gurney and Rockwood Sessions Reconsidered." *Walt Whitman Quarterly Review* 9, no. 1 (Summer 1991): 24–25.

Riley, James Whitcomb. *Love-Lyrics.* With photographs by William B. Dyer. Indianapolis: Bobbs-Merrill, 1905.

Rilke, Rainer Maria. "Portrait of My Father as a Young Man" [1907]. In *The Selected Poetry of Rainer Maria Rilke,* edited and translated by Stephen Mitchell, New York: Vintage, 1989; and as "The Cadet Picture of My Father," in *Imitations,* translated by Robert Lowell, New York: Farrar, Straus, 1961.

Rimbaud, Arthur. Letters from Aden and Harar, January 15, 1881–January 15, 1885. In *Oeuvres Complètes,* edited by Antoine Adam. Paris: Gallimard, 1972.

——. *A Season in Hell.* Translated by Paul Schmidt, with 8 photographs by Robert Mapplethorpe. New York: Limited Editions Club, 1986.

[Ritchie, Lady Anne Thackeray]. "From an Island." In *From an Island: A Story and Some Essays.* Leipzig: Tauchnitz, 1877.

Robbe-Grillet, Alain. *Les Demoiselles d'Hamilton.* Photographs by David Hamilton. Paris: Robert Laffont, 1972.

——. Introduction to *Impressions de Turquie* by Henri Cartier-Bresson. Paris: Bureau de Tourisme et d'Information de Turquie, 1968.

——. "Pour Le Roman-Photo." Preface to *Chausse-Trappes* by Edward Lachmann et al. Paris: Éditions de Minuit, 1981.

Roberts, Sam. "One Picture Can Be Worth 100 Votes Too." *New York Times* (July 2, 1990): Section B: 1.

Robinson, H[enry] P[each]. "The Poets and Photography." *Photographic News* 8, no. 283 (February 5, 1864): 62–63.

*Rockwood, George Gardner. *The Classic Grounds of American Authors.* Irving, N.Y.: Rockwood, 1864.

Rodchenko, Alexander. "Working with Mayakovsky." In *Rodchenko and the Arts of Revolutionary Russia,* edited by David Elliott. London: Swemmer/Oxford Modern Museum of Art; New York: Pantheon, 1979. Originally published as *"Rabota s Mayakovkim" [The Work with Mayakovsky]. *V Mire Knig* 6 (1973): 64–66.

——. *Samozveri.* With poems by Sergej Tret'jakov. Moscow: n.p., 1926.

Rogers, Michelle. "Fonction des quatre photographies publiées dans *L'Orion aveugle* de Claude Simon." *French Review* 59, no. 1 (October 1985): 74–83.

Rokem, Freddie. "The Camera and the Aesthetics of Repetition: Strindberg's Use of Space and Scenography." In "*Miss Julie, A Dream Play,* and *The Ghost Sonata,*" *Strindberg's Dramaturgy,* edited by Göran Stockenström. Minneapolis: University of Minnesota Press, 1988.

"Roland Barthes, Une Aventure avec la Photographie." *La Recherche Photographique,* no. 12 (June 1992): 1–92. [Issue devoted to Barthes.]

Rosenfeld, Paul. "Carl Sandburg and Photography." *New Republic* 61 (January 22, 1930): 251–53.

Rossetti, William Michael. "He Photographs the Rossettis." In *Lewis Carroll: Interviews and Recollections,* edited by Morton N. Cohen. Hampshire and London: Macmillan Press, 1989.

Roy, Claude. Introduction to *Marc Riboud: Photographs at Home and Abroad,* translated by I. Mark Paris. New York: Abrams, 1986.

Roy, Claude, and Paul Sebag. *Tunisie: De Carthage à Demain.* Photographs by Inge Morath, André Martin, and Marc Riboud. Paris: Delpire, 1961.

Rubey, Dan. "Reading the Surface of the World: Photography and Perception in Hawthorne's *House of the Seven Gables,* Teshigahara's *Woman in the Dunes,* and Antonioni's *Blow-Up.*" *Selecta* 7 (1986): 123–30.

Rubin, Y. Billy. "Epilogue: Poem Suggested by Mr.

Weston's Picture." In *Edward Weston Omnibus: A Critical Anthology,* edited by Beaumont Newhall and Amy Conger. Salt Lake City: Peregrine Smith Books, 1984.

Rugg, Linda Haverty. "Mark Twain's Photographic Autobiography: Illumination and Obfuscation." Author's TS.

Ruskin, John. *I Dagherrotipi Della Collezione Ruskin.* Edited by Paolo Constantini et al. Florence: Alinari and Venice: Arsenale Editrice, 1986.

———. *The Works of John Ruskin.* Edited by E. T. Cook and Alexander Wedderburn. 39 vols. London: George Allen, 1903–12.

Sackville-West, Vita. *Passenger to Teheran.* London: Hogarth Press, 1926. Reprinted with an introduction by Nigel Nicolson and with photographs, some by the author, Heathfield: Cockbird Press; New York: Moyer Bell, 1990.

Sackville-West, Vita, and Laelia Goehr. *Faces: Profiles of Dogs.* With text by Sackville-West and photographs by Goehr. London: Harvill Press, 1961.

Salu, Luc, and Laurent Roosens. *History of Photography: A Bibliography of Books.* London and New York: Mansell, 1989.

*Samway, Patrick. "Eudora Welty's Eye for the Story." *America* (May 23, 1987): 417–20.

Sand, George [Amandine Aurore Dupin]. Preface to *The Right to Fly,* by Nadar, translated by James Spence Harry. London: Cassell, Petter & Galpin, 1866. Originally published in *Le Droit au Vol,* 3rd ed. Paris: J. Hetzel, 1865.

Sandburg, Carl. "The Face of Lincoln." In *The Photographers of Abraham Lincoln,* by Frederick Hill Meserve and Carl Sandburg. New York: Harcourt, Brace, 1944.

———. "Four Steichen Prints." *Broom* 2 (May 1922): 97.

———. *Poems of the Midwest: Containing Two Complete Volumes: Chicago Poems and Cornhuskers.* With photographic illustrations chosen by Elizabeth McCausland [by Evans, Steichen, Abbott, Hine, Lange, Lee, Parks, Delano, Collier, Shahn, et al.] Cleveland: World, 1946.

———. Prologue to *The Family of Man.* [Exhibition curated by Edward Steichen.] New York: Museum of Modern Art, 1955, 1983. Reprinted New York: Doubleday, 1967.

———. *Steichen the Photographer.* New York: Harcourt, Brace, 1929. Preface abridged in *The Sandburg Range.* New York: Harcourt, Brace, 1957.

Sandweiss, Martha, ed. *Photography in Nineteenth Century America.* With essays by Alan Trachtenberg et al. Fort Worth: Amon Carter Museum; New York: Harry N. Abrams, 1992.

Saperstein, Jeffrey. "Thoreau's *Walden.*" *Explicator* 46, no. 4 (Summer 1988): 17–18.

Saroyan, William. *Look at Us/Let's See/Here We Are/ Look Hard, Speak Soft/I See, You See, We All See/ Stop, Look, Listen/Beholder's Eye/Don't Look Now, But Isn't That You? (Us? U.S.?).* Photographs by Arthur Rothstein. New York: Cowles, 1967.

———. Introduction to *San Francisco: West Coast Metropolis,* by Edwin Rosskam. New York: Alliance Book Corporation; Toronto: Longmans, Green, 1939.

———. "More Capa Inventions." In readers' letters to *'47.* Reprinted as "As I Remember Him" in *Robert Capa, 1913–1954,* edited by Cornell Capa and Bhupendra Karia. New York: Grossman Publishers, 1974.

Sartre, Jean-Paul. Introduction [1946] to *Photographs and Recollections,* by Gjon Mili, translated by Clifton Fadiman [1947]. Boston: New York Graphic Society, 1980.

———. Preface to *D'Une Chine à l'Autre* [From One China to Another] by Henri Cartier-Bresson. Paris: Robert Delpire, 1954 [edition used here]. Reprinted in *Situations, V: Colonialisme et Néo-Colonialisme.* Paris: Gallimard, 1964.

Saul, Julie, ed. and comp. *Jean Cocteau: The Mirror and the Mask.* With an introduction by Julie Saul and an essay by Frances Steegmuller. Boston: Godine, 1992.

Saunders, Henry S. *Whitman Portraits* [variously entitled editions]. Toronto: Horace Saunders, 1922–39.

Scherman, David E., and Rosemary Redlich. *A Chronicle of American Writers from 1607 to 1952 with 173 Photographs of the American Scene That Inspired Them.* New York: Dodd, Mead, 1952.

[Scherman, David E., and Richard Wilcox]. "Literary England." *Life* 14, no. 24 (June 14, 1943): 76–83.

———. *Literary England: Photographs of Places Made Memorable in English Literature.* With a preface by Christopher Morley and text by Richard Wilcox. New York: Random House, 1944.

Schetttino, Franca. "Photography in Kafka's *Amerika:* A Case of Transformation in the Narrative Literary Medium." In *The Dove and the Mole: Kafka's Journey into Darkness and Creativity,* edited by Ronard Gottesman and Moshe Lazar. Malibu, Calif.: Undena, 1987.

*Schulte, Amanda Pogue. *Facts About Poe: Portraits and Daguerreotypes of Edgar Allan Poe . . . with a Sketch of the Life of Poe by James Southall Wilson.* Charlottesville: University of Virginia Records Extension Series, 1926.

Schürer, Ernest. "Carl Sternheim's *Die Kassette:* Photography and Art in the 'Heroic Life of the Bourgeoisie.'" In *Shadow and Substance: Essays on the History of Photography in honor of Heinz K. Henisch,* edited by Kathleen Collins. Bloomfield Hills, Mich.: Amorphous Institute Press, 1990.

Schwartz, Lloyd. "Gisela Brüning." *Pequod* 31 (1990): 138.

———. "Pornography." Author's TS.

———. "Some Notes on My Father." *Green House* 1 (January 1, 1976): 72. Reprinted in *These People.* Middletown, Conn.: Wesleyan University Press, 1981.

*Scott, Sir Walter. *The Lady of the Lake*. With a frontispiece by George Washington Wilson and 13 photographs by Thomas Ogle. London: A. W. Bennett, 1865; 1869.

*——. *The Lady of the Lake*. Author's edition, with photographic illustrations by George Washington Wilson. Edinburgh: Adam and Charles Black, 1871; new. ed., 1874. Reprinted with photographs on both wood covers and 6 photographs, Edinburgh: William Ritchie, 1889.

*——. *The Lay of the Last Minstrel*. With 6 photographs by Russell Sedgfield. London: Provost, 1872.

——. *The Lord of the Isles*. With 3 photographs by Stephen Thompson and 6 by Russell Sedgfield. London: Provost, 1871.

*——. *Marmion: A Tale of Flodden Field*. With 15 photographic illustrations by Thomas Annan. London: A. W. Bennett, 1866.

*——. *The Poetical Works of Sir Walter Scott*. With 12 albumen prints by George Washington Wilson. N.p.: 1881.

Seelye, John. *Mark Twain in the Movies: A Meditation with Pictures*. New York: Viking, 1977.

Sendyk-Siegel, Liliane, comp. *Sartre: Images d'une vie*. With comments by Simone de Beauvoir. Paris: Gallimard, 1978.

Senelick, Laurence. "Eroticism in Early Theatrical Portraits." *Theatre History Studies* 11 (1991): 1–49.

Sennett, Robert. *Photography and Photographers to 1900: An Annotated Bibliography*. New York: Garland, 1985.

Sensibar, Judith. "Faulkner's Fictional Photographs: Playing with Difference." In *Out of Bounds: Male Writers and Gender(ed) Criticism*, edited by Laura Claridge and Elizabeth Langland. Amherst: University of Massachusetts Press, 1990.

——. "Popular Culture Invades Jefferson: Faulkner's Real and Imagined Photos of Desire." In *Faulkner and Popular Culture*, edited by Doreen Fowles and Ann J. Abadie. Jackson: University of Mississippi Press, 1990.

Sexton, Anne. "All My Pretty Ones." In *All My Pretty Ones*. Boston: Houghton Mifflin, 1962. Reprinted in *The Complete Poems of Anne Sexton*. Boston: Houghton Mifflin, 1981.

Shaffer, Elinor. *Erewhons of the Eye: Samuel Butler as Painter, Photographer and Art Critic*. London: Reaktion Books, 1988.

*Shakespeare, William. *The Seven Ages of Man*. Edited by Robert Smirk, with 9 photographs by Stephen Ayling. London: Bocka and S. Ayling, 1864.

The Shakespeare Gallery: A Reproduction in Commemoration of the Tercentenary Anniversary of the Poet's Birth. With 94 photographs after Boydell's engravings. London: L. Booth and S. Ayling, 1864; London and New York: Routledge, 1867.

Shange, Ntozake. "Irrepressibly Bronze, Beautiful & Mine." Preface to *Black Book*, by Robert Mapplethorpe. New York: St. Martin's, 1986.

——. *Photograph: Lovers in Motion*. New York: Samuel French, 1981.

*Sharpe, William. "Cities of Night: Nocturnal Representation and the Makers of the Modern Urban Landscape." [Work in progress.]

Shaw, George Bernard. *Bernard Shaw on Photography*. Edited by Bill Jay and Margaret Moore. Salt Lake City: Peregrine Smith Books, 1989.

——. *Bernard Shaw's Rhyming Picture Guide to Ayot Saint Lawrence*. Luton: Leagrave Press, 1950.

——. "Evans—An Appreciation." In *Camera Work*, no. 4 (October 1903): 13–16. Reprinted in *Photography Journal* (February 1945): 32–33; in *Photography* (December 1961): 27–28, 33; in *The Print*, New York: Time-Life Books, 1970; and in *Bernard Shaw on Photography*, edited by Bill Jay and Margaret Moore, Salt Lake City: Peregrine Smith Books, 1989 [edition used here].

——. Preface to "Photographs by Mr. Alvin Langdon Coburn, 1906." Coburn exhibition, Royal Photographic Society, February 5–March 31, 1906. Reprinted in *Camera Work*, no. 15 (July 1906): 33–35; and in *Bernard Shaw on Photography*, edited by Bill Jay and Margaret Moore, Salt Lake City: Peregrine Smith Books, 1989.

Shelley, Percy. *The Cloud*. With 6 illustrations by Alvin Langdon Coburn. Los Angeles: Privately printed by C. C. Parker, 1912.

Shepard, Sam. *Motel Chronicles*. With photographs by Johnny Dark. San Francisco: City Lights Books, 1982.

*Shloss, Carol. "Double Crossing Frontiers: Literature, Photography, and the Politics of Displacement." In *Photo-Textualities: Reading Photographs and Literature*, edited and with an introduction by Marsha Bryant. Newark: University of Delaware Press, forthcoming.

——. *Visible Light*. New York: Oxford University Press, 1987. [Chapters on Hawthorne, James and Coburn; Agee and Evans; Dreiser; Stieglitz; and Mailer and their relationship to photography.]

Sieff, Jeanloup. *Vers le Ciel d'Or: La Sicile di Guy de Maupassant, 1885*. Palermo: Novecento, 1984.

Simic, Charles. "Baby Pictures of Famous Dictators." *The Iowa Review* (1978): 9. Reprinted in *Classic Ballroom Dances*, New York: Braziller, 1980; in *Poets on Photography*, edited by Mark Melnicove, South Harpswell, Me.: Dog Ear Press, 1981; and in *Selected Poems, 1963–1983*, New York: George Braziller, 1985.

——. "*Shop, Le Bacares*, Pyrénées-Orientales, France, 1950." In *Paul Strand: Essays on His Life and Work*, edited by Maren Stange. New York: Aperture, 1991.

Simon, Claude. *The Georgics*. Translated by Beryl and John Fletcher. London: Calder; New York: Riverrun Press, 1989.

——. *Photographies, 1937–1970*. With a preface by Denis Roche and an essay by Claude Simon. Paris: Maeght, 1992.

Sims, Peter. "Photography 'In Camera.'" *Canadian Literature* (Summer–Fall 1987): 113–14 and 145–66.

Singer, Isaac Bashevis. *A Day of Pleasure*. With photographs by Roman Vishniac. New York: Farrar, Straus & Giroux, 1969.

———. Introduction and commentary to *My Love Affair with Miami Beach*. Photographs by Richard Nagler. New York: Simon & Schuster, 1991.

*Sinsabaugh, Art, and Sherwood Anderson. *6 Mid-American Chants/11 Midwest Photographs* [*Jargon* 45]. With postface by Frederick Eckmann. Highlands, N.C.: Nantahala Foundation and Jonathan Williams, 1964.

Siskind, Aaron, and John Logan. *Aaron Siskind, Photographs/John Logan, Poems*. Rochester, N.Y.: Visual Studies Workshop, 1976.

Sissman, L. E. "Negatives" [1966]. In *Hello Darkness: The Collected Poems of L. E. Sissman*. Boston: Atlantic Monthly Press/Little, Brown, 1978. Reprinted in *Poets on Photography*, edited by Mark Melnicove. South Harpswell, Me.: Dog Ear Press, 1981, p. 54.

Sitwell, Dame Edith. Preface to *Images*, by Cecil Beaton. New York: London House and Maxwell, 1963.

Sitwell, Sacheverell, and Lord Snowdon. *Malta*. London: B. T. Batsford, 1958.

Slote, Bernice, and Lucia Woods. *Willa Cather: A Pictorial Memoir*. With text by Bernice Slote and photographs by Lucia Woods et al. Lincoln: University of Nebraska Press, 1973.

Smadelser, Lokes. "August Strindberg." In *Strindberg*. Exhibition catalogue, Kulterhuset, May 15–October 4, 1981. Stockholm: Liber Forlag, 1981.

Smith, Craig S., and Matthew L. Jockers. "Joyce's *Ulysses*." *Explicator* 50, no. 4 (Summer 1992): 235–37.

Smith, Dave. "The Perspective and Limits of Snapshots." In *Cumberland Station*. Urbana: University of Illinois Press, 1976. Reprinted in *Poets on Photography*, edited by Mark Melnicove. South Harpswell, Me.: Dog Ear Press, 1981.

———. "The Travelling Photographer: Circa 1800." In *Dream Flight*. Urbana: University of Illinois Press, 1981.

Smith, Graham. "William Henry Fox Talbot's View of Loch Katrine." *Bulletin* (Museums of Art and Archeology, University of Michigan) 7 (1984–85): 48–77. Abridged with reduced illustrations as "Views of Scotland" in *Henry Fox Talbot: Selected Texts and Bibliography*, edited by Mike Weaver. Oxford: Clio Press, 1992.

Smith, Henry Holmes. "Short Stories and Other Writings." MSS, CCP [AG 32: 13].

Smith, Lindsay. "'The Seed of the Flower': Photography and Pre-Raphaelitism." *Huntington Library Quarterly* 55 (Winter 1992): 37–53. Reprinted in *The Pre-Raphaelites in Context*. San Marino, Calif.: Huntington Library, 1992.

Smith, Murray. *Dream Time: Photography, 1975–85: Selections from the Writings of D. T. Suzuki (Zen and Swordsmanship) and Lewis Carroll*. Inglewood, Calif.: Tiger Publishing, 1985.

Smith, W. Eugene. "Fiction, Plays, and Writings." MSS, CCP [AG 33: 7–8].

Smith, W. Eugene, with Carole Thomas. *Japan, A Chapter of Image: A Photographic Essay*. Tokyo: Hitachi, 1963. [Includes poetry by Smith under the pseudonym of Walter Trego.]

Snodgrass, W. D. Introduction to *For They Are My Friends*, by Tom Marotta. Photographs by Tom Marotta. New York: Art Reflections, 1976.

———. "Mementos, 1." In *After Experience: Poems and Translations*. New York: Harper & Row, 1968. Reprinted in *Poets on Photography*, edited by Mark Melnicove. South Harpswell, Me.: Dog Ear Press, 1981, p. 26.

Sobelman, Isabelle, and Catherine Montarnal. *En Attendant Beckett*. With photographs by Catherine Montarnal. Paris: Marval, 1987.

*Söderberg, Rolf. *Edvard Munch, August Strindberg: Fotografi som verktyg och experiment/photography as a tool and an experiment*. Translated by Jan Teeland. Stockholm: Alfabeta, 1989.

Soderström, Göran. "Phantasies of a Visual Poet: August Strindberg as a Painter and Photographer." In *August Strindberg*, translated by Patrick Hort. Exhibition catalogue, February 1–April 12, 1987. Zwolle: Uitgeverij and Amsterdam: Riksmuseum Vincent Van Gogh.

Somlyó, György. "Lorand Gaspar—Poet and Photographer." *New Hungarian Quarterly* 29, no. 112 (Winter 1988): 181–82.

*Sommer, Frederick. *All Children Are Ambassadors: Photographs and Poetry*. Tucson: Nazraeli Press, 1992.

———. (with Stephen Aldrich). "The Poetic Logic of Art and Aesthetics" [1972]. In *Frederick Sommer at Seventy-Five: A Retrospective*, edited by Constance W. Glenn and Jane K. Bledsoe. Long Beach, Calif.: Art Museum and Galleries, California State University, 1980. Reprinted in *Frederick Sommer: Images*, vol. 1, Tucson: Center for Creative Photography, the University of Arizona, 1984.

———. "Where Images Come from." In *The Mistress of This World Has No Name: Where Images Come From*. With a preface by Dianne Perry Vanderlip and an essay by Stephen Aldrich. Denver: Denver Art Museum, 1988.

———. *Words and Images*. 2 vols. Tucson, Ariz.: Center for Creative Photography, 1984.

Sontag, Susan. Foreword to *Italy: One Hundred Years of Photography*. With a text by Cesare Colombo. Florence: Alinari, 1988.

———. *On Photography*. Farrar, Straus & Giroux, 1977. Originally published as essays in *New York Review of Books* 20–24 (October 16, 1973–June 23, 1977).

——. Preface to *Certain People: A Book of Portraits*, by Robert Mapplethorpe. Pasadena, Calif.: Twelvetrees Press, 1985.

Sontag, Susan, Vera Lehndorff, and Holger Trulzsch. *Verushka: Trans-Figurations*. London: Thames & Hudson, 1986.

*Soufas, C. Christopher. "Dialectics of Vision: Pictorial vs. Photographic Representation in Lorca's *La Casa de Bernarda Alba*." *Ojancano: Revista de Literatura Espanola* 5 (April 1991): 52–66.

Spender, Stephen. "The Bombed Happiness" and "War Photography." In *The Still Center*. London: Faber & Faber, 1939. Reprinted in Valentine Cunningham, *Spanish Front: Writers on the Civil War*. Oxford: Oxford University Press, 1986.

*——. *Europe in Photographs*. London: Thames & Hudson, 1952.

——. Introduction to *Herbert List: Photographs, 1930–1970*, by Günter Metken. Translated by Ingeborg von Zitzewitz. London: Thames & Hudson, 1981.

——. "On the Photograph of a Friend, Peter Watson." *Poetry* (London and New York) 1–2 (Winter 1956): 3–4. Reprinted as "On the Photograph of a Friend, Dead," in *London Magazine* 11 (February 1971): 22–24; and in *The Generous Days*, London: Faber & Faber; New York: Random House, 1971.

——. "The Photograph." *Collected Poems, 1928–1985*. London: Faber & Faber, 1985.

——. Preface to *A Poet and His Camera*, by Gordon Parks. New York: Studio/Viking, 1968.

Spender, Stephen, and David Hockney. *China Diary*. New York: Abrams, 1982. Reprinted New York: Thames & Hudson, 1993.

*Staunton, Howard, ed. *Memorials of Shakespeare: Comprising the Poet's Will*. With comments by Staunton and 2 photographs by Preston of engraved portraits of Shakespeare. London: Day & Son, 1864.

Stead, Michael. *Literary Landscapes*. Oxford: Lennard Publishing, 1989. [Illustrated excerpts from Fowles, Betjeman, Daphne Du Maurier, and others.]

Steegmuller, Francis. See Saul, Julie.

Stegner, Wallace. Foreword to *Ansel Adams: Images 1923–1974*, by Ansel Adams. Boston: New York Graphic Society, 1974.

——. Preface to *Ansel Adams: Letters and Images 1916–1984*, by Ansel Adams, edited by Mary Street Alinder and Andrea Gray Stillman. Boston: Little, Brown, 1988.

Steichen, Edward, ed. *Sandburg: Photographers View Carl Sandburg*. New York: Harcourt, Brace & World, 1966.

——. *Steichen: A Life in Photography*. Garden City, N.Y.: Doubleday, 1963. Reprinted New York: Harmony Books in association with the Museum of Modern Art, 1985.

Stein, Gertrude. "Man Ray" [1924]. In *Painted Lace and Other Pieces, 1914–1937*, vol. 5, *The Yale Edition of the Unpublished Writings of Gertrude Stein*. With an introduction by Daniel-Henry Kahnweiler. New Haven, Conn.: Yale University Press; London: Cumberlege/Oxford University Press, 1955.

——. "Stieglitz." In *America and Alfred Stieglitz: A Collective Portrait*, edited by Waldo Frank et al. New York: Doubleday, Doran, 1934 [edition used here]. Reprinted Millerton, N.Y.: Aperture, 1979.

——. *Wars I Have Seen*. With portraits by Cecil Beaton. London: B. T. Batsford, 1945.

Stein, Gertrude, and Carl Van Vechten. *The Letters of Gertrude Stein and Carl Van Vechten, 1913–1946*. 2 vols., edited by Edward Burns. New York: Columbia University Press, 1986.

Steinbeck, John. *America and Americans*. With photographs from *Life, Time*, etc. New York: Viking, 1966.

——. *Bombs Away: The Story of a Bomber Team*. With photographs by John Swope. New York: Viking, 1942.

——. *The Forgotten Village*. With 135 photographs from the film of the same name by Rosa Harvan Kline and Alexander Hackenshmid. New York: Viking Press, 1941.

——. Introduction to *Images of War* by Robert Capa. New York: Grossman Publishers, 1964.

——. "Robert Capa: An Appreciation." *Popular Photography* 34–35 (September 1954): 48. Reprinted as "No One Can Take His Place" in *Robert Capa, 1913–1954*, edited by Cornell Capa and Bhupendra Karia. New York: Grossman Publishers, 1974.

Steinbeck, John, and Robert Capa. *A Russian Journal*. New York: Viking, 1948; London: Heinemann, 1949 [edition used here]. Reprinted New York: Paragon, 1989.

Sterne, Laurence. *The Life and Opinions of Tristram Shandy, Gentleman*. 3 vols., with 49 photo-collage illustrations by John Baldessari. San Francisco: Arion Press, 1988.

Sternheim, Carl. *Die Kassette* [1910–11]. In *Gesamtwerk*, vol. 1, edited by Wilhelm Emrich. Neuwind am Rhein: Luchterhand, 1963.

Stevenson, Robert Louis. *A Child's Garden of Verses*. With photo-illustrations by Toni Frissell. New York: U.S. Camera, 1944.

——. *Edinburgh, Picturesque Notes*. With 23 photogravures by Alvin Langdon Coburn. London: Rupert Hart-Davis, 1954.

Stewart, Patrick Leonard. "Charles Sheeler, William Carlos Williams and the Development of the Precisionist Aesthetic, 1917–1931." Ph.D. diss., University of Delaware, Newark, 1981.

Stieglitz, Alfred. *Alfred Stieglitz: Photographs and Writings*. Edited by Sarah Greenough and Juan Hamilton, with preface by J. Carter Brown. Exhibition catalogue. Washington, D.C.: National Gallery of Art, 1983. [Includes letters from Stieglitz to Sherwood Anderson and Hart Crane.]

———. "*Camera Work* Introduces Gertrude Stein to America." *Twice a Year* nos. 14–15 (1946–47): 192–95 [edition used here]. Reprinted in Dorothy Norman, *Alfred Stieglitz: American Seer.* New York: Random House, 1973.

Stillman, William, ed. *Poetic Localities: Photographs of Adirondacks, Cambridge, Crete, Italy, Athens.* New York: Aperture, 1988.

———, ed. *Poetic Localities in Cambridge.* With 11 heliotypes. Boston: Osgood, 1876.

Stott, William. "*Let Us Now Praise Famous Men.*" In *Documentary Expression and Thirties America.* New York: Oxford University Press, 1973.

Strand, Mark. "Fantasia on the Relations Between Poetry and Photography." *Grant Street* 9, no. 2 (Winter 1990): 96–107.

Strand, Paul. *La France de profil.* With text by Claude Roy. Lausanne: La Guilde du Livre, 1952.

———. *Ghana: An African Portrait.* With text by Basil Davidson. Millerton, N.Y.: Aperture, 1975.

———. Letter about Aragon's "Painting and Reality." *Art Front* 3 (February 1937): 18.

———. Letter to Sherwood Anderson, July 20, 1920. In *Paul Strand: An American Vision,* by Sarah Greenough. New York: Aperture/National Gallery of Art, 1990.

———. *Living Egypt.* With text by James Aldridge. London: MacGibbon & Kee; Dresden: VEB Verlag der Kunst; New York: Aperture/Horizon Press, 1969.

———. *Un Paese.* With text by Cesare Zavattini. Turin: Giulio Einaudi, 1955.

———. *Ti a'Mhurain.* With text by Basil Davidson. London: MacGibbon & Kee; Dresden: VEB Verlag der Kunst, 1962. Reprinted New York: Aperture/Grossman, 1968.

———. *Time in New England.* Selected and edited by Nancy Newhall. New York: Oxford University Press, 1950. Reprinted Millerton, N.Y.: Aperture, 1977.

Strelke, Barbara Ann. "Place and the Power of Imagination" [in Wright Morris]. In "Images of Home and Place: Essays, Poems, Photography." Ph.D. diss., University of New Mexico, Albuquerque, 1975.

Strindberg, August. "Photography and Philosophy" [1903]. In *Tales,* translated by L. J. Potts. London: Chatto & Windus, 1930.

Sunshine in the Country: A Book of Rural Poetry. London: Richard Griffin, 1861.

*Svevo, Letizia Fonda Savio and Bruno Meier. *Iconografia Sveviana: Scritti Parole e Immagini Della Vita Privata di Italo Svevo.* Pordenone: Studio Teri, 1981.

La Surréalisme au Service de la Révolution. Vols. 1–6 (July 1930–May 1933). Reprinted Paris: Jean-Michel Place, 1976.

*Sweet, Timothy. "Photography and the Museum of Rome in Hawthorne's Marble Faun." In *Photo-Textualities: Reading Photographs and Literature,* edited and with an introduction by Marsha Bryant. Newark: University of Delaware Press, forthcoming.

———. *Traces of War: Poetry, Photography and the Crisis of the Union.* Baltimore: Johns Hopkins University Press, 1990.

Swigart, Lynn. *Olson's Gloucester.* With photographs by Lynn Swigart, interview with Lynn Swigart by Sherman Paul, and foreword by George Butterick. Baton Rouge and London: Louisiana State Press, 1980.

Synge, John. *The Aran Islands.* Dublin: Maunsel; London: Elkin Mathews, 1907. Reprinted with six photographs by the author in *The Aran Islands,* vol. 2, *Collected Works,* edited by Alan Price, London: Oxford University Press, 1966; and with 14 photographs by the author, in *The Aran Islands,* edited by Robin Skelton, Oxford: Oxford University Press, 1979 [edition used here].

———. *The Autobiography of J. M. Synge.* With 14 photographs by Synge. Dublin: Dolmen Press; London: Oxford University Press, 1965.

———. *My Wallet of Photographs: The Collected Photographs of J. M. Synge,* edited and with an introduction by Lilo Stephens. Dublin: Dolmen Press; New York: Humanities Press, 1971.

Takahashi, Mutsuo. "The Flag" [For Eikoh Hosoe]. In *Eikoh Hosoe: Photographs.* With preface by Peter Bunnell. Santa Fe, N.M.: Andrew Smith Gallery/Muso Press, 1990.

Talbot, William Fox. *The Pencil of Nature.* 6 serial parts. London: Longman, Brown, Green & Longmans, 1844–46. Reprinted as facsimile book, New York: DaCapo, 1969; Hamburg: Calotype Company, 1985; and in facsimile parts, New York: Hans P. Kraus, Jr., and Larry J. Schaaf, 1989; and see in *Henry Fox Talbot: Selected Texts and Bibliography,* edited by Mike Weaver, Oxford: Clio Press, 1992, pp. 75–115.

———. *Sun Pictures of Scotland.* With 23 Calotypes. London: Published by subscription, 1845.

Talese, Gay. *The Bridge.* With photographs by Bruce Davidson. New York: Harper & Row, 1964.

Tanji, Yasutaka, and Wahei Tatematsu. *The Tree.* With photographs by Yasutaka Tanji and essays by Wahei Tatematsu. Tokyo: Graphic-Sha, 1988.

Taylor, John. "The Haunted Bird: The Death and Life of Jerzy Kosinski." *New York* 24 (July 15, 1991): 24–37.

Taylor, Robert N., comp., *Lewis Carroll at Texas: The Warren Weaver Collection and Related Dodgson Materials at the Harry Ransom Humanities Research Center.* Austin: Humanities Research Center, University of Texas, 1985.

Tennyson, Alfred. *The Works of Alfred Tennyson, Poet Laureate.* With 8 photographic illustrations by Payne Jennings. London: R. & A. Suttaby, 1878. Reprinted London: Henry Frowde, 1890.

Teplinskii, Mark. *A. P. Chekhov Na Sakhaline* [Chekhov at Sakhalin]. Iuzhno-Sakhalinsk: Dal'nevostochnoe Knizhnoe Izd-vo, Sakhalinskoe Otd-nie, 1990.

Theroux, Paul. *Picture Palace*. New York: Ballantine, 1978.

Theroux, Paul, and Steve McCurry. *The Imperial Way: Making Tracks from Peshawar to Chittagong*. With photographs by Steve McCurry. London: Hamish Hamilton, 1985.

Thomas, F. Richard. *The Literary Admirers of Alfred Stieglitz*. Carbondale: Southern Illinois University Press, 1983.

Thomas, Lew, ed. *Photography and Language*. San Francisco: Camerawork Press, 1976.

Thomas, R. S. "Album." In *Frequencies*. London: Macmillan, 1978.

Thompson, Stephen. *Venice and the Poets*. London: Provost, 1870.

Thoreau, Henry David. *Cape Cod*. With photographs by William F. Robinson. Boston: Little, Brown, 1985.

———. *The Illustrated Maine Woods*. With photographs from the Gleason Collection, edited by Joseph J. Maldenhauer. Princeton, N.J.: Princeton University Press, 1974.

———. *The Illustrated World of Thoreau*. Edited by Howard Chapnick, with words by Henry David Thoreau, photographs by Ivan Massar, and an afterword by Loren Eiseley. New York: Grosset & Dunlap, 1974.

———. *Thoreau's Cape Cod*. Edited with an introduction by Thea Wheelwright and with early photographs of Herbert Wendell Gleason. Barre, Mass.: Barre Publishers, 1973.

———. *Through the Year with Thoreau*. Sketches of nature from the writings of Henry David Thoreau with 91 corresponding photographic illustrations by Herbert Gleason. Boston: Houghton Mifflin, 1917.

———. *Walden*. With photographs by A. W. Hosmer et al. Boston: Houghton Mifflin/Riverside Press, 1897.

———. *Walden*. With illustrations by Edward Steichen and introduction by Henry Canby. Boston: Merrymount Press for Limited Editions Club, 1936.

———. *Walden or Life in the Woods*. 2 vols. With 7 photographs from negatives of Herbert W. Gleason. Boston: Bibliophile Society, 1909.

Thoreau, Henry, and John Burroughs et al. *In American Fields and Forests*. With photographs by Herbert W. Gleason. Boston: Houghton Mifflin, 1909.

Thurber, James. "Has Photography Gone Too Far?" *New Yorker* 10 (August 11, 1934): 13–14. Reprinted in *Aperture* 2, no. 2 (1954): 13, 16; and in *Photography in Print: Writings from 1816 to the Present*, edited by Vicki Goldberg, New York: Touchstone/ Simon & Schuster, 1981; reprinted Albuquerque: University of New Mexico Press, 1989.

Tick, Stanley. "Positives and Negatives: Henry James vs. Photography." *Nineteenth Century Studies* 7 (1993): 69–101.

Tolstoy, Leo. *Anna Karenina* [1875–77]. 2 vols., translated by Constance Garnett and with an introduc-

tory essay by Thomas Mann. New York: Random House, 1939.

Tolstoy, Sophia. *The Diaries of Sophia Tolstoy*. Edited by O. A. Golinenko et al. and translated by Cathy Porte. New York: Random House; London: Cape, 1985.

———. Photographies de Sophie Tolstoï. With an introduction by Serge Tolstoi and text by Pierre Apraxine. Brussels: Marc Bokar, 1991.

Tolstoy, Sofia (Tolstaya), and Vladimir Chertkov. *Tolstoy in Life*. With an introduction by T. K. Popovkina. Tula: Priokskoe Knizhnoe Izdatelstvo, 1988.

Toomer, Jean. "A Double Portrait" [1946?]. In *A Jean Toomer Reader: Selected Unpublished Writings*, edited by Frederick L. Rusch. New York: Oxford University Press, 1993.

———. "The Hill." In *America and Alfred Stieglitz: A Collective Portrait*, edited by Waldo Frank et al. New York: Doubleday, Doran, 1934. Reprinted New York: Aperture, 1979.

Tournier, Michel. "Arthur Tress." Prelude to *Theater of the Mind*, by Arthur Tress, translated from *L'Oeil* by Evelyne Jesenof. With prelude by Duane Michals and introduction by A. D. Coleman. Dobbs Ferry, N.Y.: Morgan & Morgan, 1976.

———. "Emile Zola photographe." In *Le Vol du Vampire: Notes de Lecture*. Paris: Mercure de France, 1982. Reprinted in *Le Crépuscule des masques*. Paris: Hoëbeke, 1992.

———. *Canada: Journal de Voyage*. With photographs by Edouard Boubat. Ottawa: Les Éditions la Presse, 1977. Reprinted with different photographs and a postscript as *Journal de Voyage au Canada*. Paris: Robert Laffont, 1984.

———. *Des clefs et des serrures: images et proses*. Photographs by Dieter Appelt et al. Paris: Chêne/ Hachette, 1979; Munich, 1980.

———. *Le Crépuscule des masques*. Paris: Hoëbeke, 1992. [Essays and reviews.]

———. *The Golden Droplet*. Translated by Barbara Wright. New York: Doubleday; London, Collins, 1987. Originally published as *La Goutte d'Or*. Paris: Gallimard, 1987.

———. "Herbert List—photographe du silence." In *Herbert List: Photographies 1930–1960*, by Günter Metken. Paris: MAM/Schirmer/Mosel, 1983. Reprinted in *Le Crépuscule des masques*. Paris: Hoëbeke, 1992.

———. "Jean-Philippe Charbonnier: un naturaliste desinvolté." In *Jean-Philippe Charbonnier: 107 Photographies en Noir et Blanc, 1945–1971*. Le Havre: Maison de la Culture du Havre; Paris: Agathe Gaillard, 1972. Reprinted in *Le Crépuscule des masques*. Paris: Hoëbeke, 1992.

———. *L'Imagerie de Michel Tournier*. Selected and with an introduction by Michel Tournier, and edited by Françoise Marquet. Paris: Musée d'Art Modern de la Ville de Paris, December 2, 1987–February 14, 1988.

———. Introduction to *Eros and Thanatos: Lucien Clergue*, by Lucien Clergue. Revised and translated by Barbara Wright. Boston: New York Graphic Society [1985]. Originally published in *Lucien Clergue: Mers, Plages, Sources et Torrents, Arbres.* Paris: Éditions Perceval, 1974.

———. "Mon génial ami, Arthur Tress." In *Rêves,* by Arthur Tress and Michel Tournier. Brussels: Complexe, 1979. Reprinted in *Le Crépuscule des masques,* Paris: Hoëbeke, 1992.

———. *The Ogre.* Translated by Barbara Bray. New York: Doubleday, 1972. Reprinted 1977. Originally published as *Le Roi des Aulnes.* Paris: Gallimard, 1970.

———. "Pouvoir de l'Image et Images du Pouvoir." Preface to *François Mitterrand,* by Konrad R. Müller and Michel Tournier. Paris: Flammarion, 1983.

———. Preface to *Memoirs sans memoire,* by Jacques Henri Lartigue. Paris: Laffont, 1975. Reprinted as "Jacques Lartigue: Le Sage des images," in *La Crépuscule des masques.* Paris: Hoëbeke, 1992.

———. Presentation to *Miroirs: Autoportraits: Photographies by Eduard Boubat.* Paris: Denoël, 1973.

———. "Venise ou la tête coupée." Preface to *Venise, Hier et Demain* by Fulvio Roiter. Paris: Chêne, 1973.

———. "Veronica's Shrouds." In *The Fetishist,* translated by Barbara Wright. New York: Doubleday; London: William Collins, 1984. Originally published as "Les Suaires de Véronique," *Le Coq de Bruyère.* Paris: Gallimard, 1978.

———. *Vues de dos.* With photographs by Edouard Boubat. Paris: Gallimard, 1981.

Trachtenberg, Alan, ed. *Classic Essays on Photography.* New Haven, Conn.: Leete's Island Books, 1980.

———. "The Craft of Vision." *Critique* 4, no. 3 (Winter 1961–62): 41–55, esp. 42–47.

———. "Edward Weston's America: The *Leaves of Grass* Project." In *EW 100: Centennial Essays in Honor of Edward Weston [Untitled* 41], edited by Peter C. Bunnell et al. Carmel, Calif.: Friends of Photography, 1986.

———. *Reading American Photographs: Images as History, Mathew Brady to Walker Evans.* New York: Hill & Wang, 1989.

Transition. Edited by Eugene Jolas. Paris: Shakespeare & Company, April 1927–Spring 1938.

Trassard, Jean-Loup. *Images de la Terre Russe.* With texts and photographs by Jean-Loup Trassard. Paris: Le Temps Qu'il Fait, 1990.

———. *Quailles.* With texts and photographs by Jean-Loup Trassard. Paris: Le Temps Qu'il Fait, 1991.

———. *Territoire.* With texts and photographs by Jean-Loup Trassard. Paris: Le Temps Qu'il Fait, 1989.

Traub, Charles H. *An Angler's Album: Fishing in Photography and Literature.* New York: Rizzoli, 1990.

Traub, Charles H., and Luigi Ballerini. *Italy Observed in Photography and Literature.* Preface by Umberto Eco. New York: Rizzoli, 1988.

Traubel, Horace, ed. *With Walt Whitman in Camden, 1888–89.* Vols. 1–4 [of 6]: 1: Boston: Small, Maynard and Co, 1906; 2: New York: D. Appleton and Co., 1908; 3: New York: Mitchell Kennerly, 1914; 4: edited by Sculley Bradley, Philadelphia: University of Pennsylvania Press, 1953; reprinted Carbondale: Southern Illinois University Press, 1959. First 3 vols. reprinted by New York: Rowman and Littlefield, 1961.

Trilling, Lionel. "Greatness with One Fault in It: A Review of James Agee and Walker Evans, *Let Us Now Praise Famous Men.*" *Kenyon Review* 4, no. 1 (Winter 1942): 99–102.

Trottenberg, Arthur, ed. *A Vision of Paris: The Photographs of Eugene Atget/The Words of Marcel Proust.* New York: Macmillan, 1963; 1980.

Tucholsky, Kurt. *Deutschland, Deutschland über Alles.* Translated by Anne Halley, with photographs assembled by John Heartfield and afterword and notes by Harry Zohn. Amherst: University of Massachusetts Press, 1972. Originally published in Berlin: Neuer Deutscher Verlag, 1929.

Turyn, Anne. *Missives: Dear Pen Pal, Dear John, Lessons and Notes, Flashbulb Memories, Photographs.* New York: Alfred Van Der Marck Editions, 1986.

Twain, Mark [Samuel Langhorne Clemens]. *The Autobiography of Mark Twain* [1924]. Edited by Charles Neider, with photographs by Albert Bigelow Paine. New York: Harper & Brothers, 1959.

———. *King Leopold's Soliloquy: A Defense of His Congo Rule.* With 5 photographs. Boston: P. R. Warren, 1905; 2nd revised edition 1906, pp. 36–37; and distributed as a pamphlet by the Congo Reform Association. Reissued with new photographs, Berlin: South Seas Publishers, 1961, and text included in *Mark Twain on the Damned Human Race,* edited by Janet Smith, New York: Hill & Wang, 1982.

———. Letter from Hawaii, July 1, 1866, published as "Scenes in Honolulu–No. 15" in the *Sacramento Daily Union* (August 1, 1866): 1. Reprinted in *Letters from Hawaii,* edited by A. Grove Day, Honolulu: University Press of Hawaii, 1975 [excerpted for use here]; and excerpted as "Letter to the Editor" of the *Daily Hawaiian Herald,* September 5, 1866, in "Mark Twain on Photographs," *Twainian* 2, no. 1 (January 1940): 6.

———. *Mark Twain's Letters, Volume 2, 1867–68,* edited by Harriet Smith and Richard Bucci, and *Volume 3, 1869,* edited by Victor Fisher and Michael B. Frank. In *The Mark Twain Papers,* edited by Robert H. Hirst et al. Berkeley: University of California Press, 1990, 1992.

———. *Mark Twain's Letters.* Edited by Albert Bigelow Paine. 2 vols. New York: Harper & Brothers, 1917.

Tyler, Anne. *Earthly Possessions.* New York: Knopf, 1977.

Uelsmann, Jerry N. *Jerry N. Uelsmann.* With fables by Russell Edson. New York: Aperture, 1970.

Unrau, John. *Ruskin and St. Mark's*. Photographs by John Hobbs. London: Thames & Hudson, 1984.

Updike, John. "The Day of the Dying Rabbit." *New Yorker* 45 (August 30, 1969): 22–26. Reprinted in *Museums and Women and Other Stories*. New York, Knopf, 1972.

——. "Exposure" and "Meditations on a News Item." In *Telephone Poles and Other Poems*. New York: Knopf, 1963. Reprinted in *Verses*, Greenwich, Conn.: Crest, 1965.

——. "First Things First," *Art and Antiques* (October 1991): 57–60, also published as "The Steichens' Book of First Things," an afterword to a reissue of Mary Steichen Calderone, Edward Steichen, and John Updike, *The First Picture Book: Everyday Things for Babies* (New York: Fotofolio/Library Fellows of the Whitney Museum of American Art, 1991), originally published by Mary Steichen [then Martin] (New York: Harcourt Brace, 1930).

——. Foreword to "Just Family: Family Photographs by 15 American Photographers." TS, 1986; slightly revised as "All in the Family," TS, 1991. Unpublished.

——. Introduction to *Heroes and Anti Heroes, Magnum Images*. New York: Random House and London: Deutsch, 1991.

——. "Midpoint" and "Camera" [1964]. In *Midpoint and Other Poems*. New York: Knopf; London: Deutsch, 1969.

——. "Snapshots." *The Carpentered Hen and Other Tame Creatures*. New York: Harper & Brothers, 1958. Reprinted New York: Knopf, 1982; and in *Verses*, Greenwich, Conn.: Crest, 1965.

——. "A State of Ecstasy." *Art and Antiques* 7, no. 1 (January 1990): 74–75.

Valéry, Paul. "An Appreciation." In *Eternal France* [1930] by Martin Hürlimann. London: Thames & Hudson; Zürich: Atlantis Verlag, 1952. Reprinted in revised and enlarged edition, retitled *France*, 1957; and in new enlarged edition, 1968.

——. "The Centenary of Photography" [January 7, 1939]. In *Occasions*, vol. 2, *The Collected Works of Paul Valéry*, edited by Jackson Mathews and translated by Roger Shattuck and Frederick Brown. Princeton, N.J.: Princeton University Press, 1970; London: Routledge & Kegan Paul, 1971. Reprinted in *Classic Essays in Photography*, edited by Alan Trachtenberg. New Haven, Conn.: Leete's Island Books, 1980.

Van Vechten, Carl. See also Davis, Keith.

——. *The Dance Photography of Carl Van Vechten*. Selected and with an introduction by Paul Padgett. New York: Schirmer Books, 1981.

——. *Generations in Black and White: Photographs by Carl Van Vechten from the James Weldon Johnson Memorial Collection*. Edited by Rudolph P. Byrd. Athens: University of Georgia, 1993.

——. "Keep A-Inchin' Along": Selected Writings of Carl Van Vechten about Black Arts and Letters. Ed-

ited by Bruce Kellner. Westport, Conn.: Greenwood, 1979.

——. *Letters of Carl Van Vechten*. Edited by Bruce Kellner. New Haven, Conn.: Yale University Press, 1987.

——. *Peter Whiffle* [1922]. Revised edition. [Includes some photographic illustrations, including one by the author.] New York: Knopf, 1927.

——. *Portraits: The Photography of Carl Van Vechten*. Compiled by Saul Mauriber. Indianapolis: Bobbs-Merrill, 1978.

——. "Portraits of the Artist." *Esquire* 58, no. 6 (December 1962): 170–74 and 256–58.

——. Untitled [Account of the evolution of Van Vechten's interest in photography]. Westwood, N.J.: Goodwin Gallery, February 1977.

——. Untitled piece. In *Stieglitz Memorial Portfolio, 1864–1946*, edited by Dorothy Norman. New York: Twice a Year Press, 1947.

Van Vechten, Carl, and Gertrude Stein. See Stein, Gertrude.

Varentsova, I[rina] and G. Shcheboleva. *A. P. Chekhov: Dokumenty, Fotografii/Anton Chekhov: Documents, Photographs*. Edited by V. Kuleshov and E. Polotskaia. Moscow: Sov. Rossiia, 1984.

*Vauthier, Simone. "Copie non conforme: Regards sur une nouvelle de Martin Avery." *Fabula* 4 (1984): 59–72.

Veall, Donald, ed. *Literary Walks of Britain*. With photographs by Simon McBride. Exeter: Webb & Bower, 1989.

Verga, Giovanni. *Lettere a Dina*. Edited by Gino Raya. Rome: Editrice Ciranna, 1971. Expanded as *Lettere d'amore*. Rome: Tindalo, 1971 [edition used here as basis for translation]. MSS at the University of Catania, Sicily.

——. *Specchio e Realtà*. Edited by Wladimiro Settimelli. Rome: Editrice Magma, 1976.

——. *Verga/Fotografo*. See Agosto, Giovanni Garra.

Verlaine, Paul. "Assonances Galantes." In *Oeuvres Poétiques Complètes*, edited by Jacques Borel. Paris: Gallimard, 1969; 1983.

Verne, Jules. *From the Earth to the Moon, and A Trip Round It* [1865]. Translated by Louis Mercier and Eleanor C. King. New York: Scribner, Armstrong, 1874.

Vice, Sye. "Dreams—Visions—Metaphor: The Images of Manuel Alvarez Bravo and Malcolm Lowry." *Malcolm Lowry Review* 15 (Fall 1984): 19–24.

Vickers, Hugo. "A Fly in Amber: Beaton as Diarist." In *Cecil Beaton*, edited by David Mellor. London: Barbicon Art Gallery in association with Weidenfeld & Nicolson, 1956.

Vieilledent, Catherine, "La Representation de la terre dans *Let Us Now Praise Famous Men*." *Revue Française d'Études Américaines* 16, nos. 48–49 (April–July 1991): 299–307. [English summary, p. 337.]

——. "Text et Image: La Collaboration de Henry James et Alvin Langdon Coburn." *Revue Française* d'Études Américaines 14, no. 39 (February 14, 1989): 29–45. [English summary, p. 121].

Villiers de l'Isle-Adam, Jean-Marie Mathias Philippe Auguste de. "Snapshots of World History." In Tomorrow's Eve [1886], translated by Robert Martin Adams. Urbana: University of Illinois Press, 1982. Originally published in this final version in L'Eve Future. Paris: Brunhoff, 1886.

Viney, Charles. Sherlock Holmes in London: A Photographic Record of Conan Doyle's Stories. Wellingborough: Equation; Boston: Houghton Mifflin, 1989.

*Virgil. Publii Virgilii Maronis Carmina Omnia Perpetuo. In Collected Works. With 27 photographs after paintings. Paris: Didot, 1858.

Vonnegut, Kurt. "The People One Knows." In Palm Sunday: An Autobiographical Collage. New York: Delacorte, 1981.

——. Preface to The Writer's Image: Literary Portraits, by Jill Krementz. Boston: Godine, 1980.

Walker, Carol Kyros. Walking North with Keats. New Haven, Conn.: Yale University Press, 1992.

Walker, Todd. 8 Shakespeare Sonnets/8 Todd Walker Photographs. Los Angeles: Thumbprint Press, 1965.

*——. A Few Poems by John Donne and Photographs by Todd Walker. N.p.: Thumbprint Press, 1966.

——. A Portfolio of Eighteen Reproductions of Photographs by Todd Walker; in conjunction with and perhaps related to five of the worldly works of sixteenth century poet, John Donne. Tucson, Ariz.: Thumbprint Press, 1968.

Waller, James Preston. "Visions and Revisions of Mark Twain: Samuel L. Clemens in the Camera's Eye, 1851–1885." Ph.D. diss., Duke University, Durham, N.C., 1990.

Walter, James. Shakespeare's Home and Rural Life: With Illustrations of Localities and Scenes Around Stratford-upon-Avon by the Heliotrope Process. London: Longman, Green, Reader, & Dyer, 1874.

Walton, Isaak. The Compleat Angler. Lea & Dove Edition. 2 vols., with 54 photographs, 24 by Peter Emerson. London: Low, Marston, Searle, Riverton, 1888.

Ward, J. A. American Silences: The Realism of James Agee, Walker Evans, and Edward Hopper. Baton Rouge: Louisiana State University Press, 1985.

Ward, Henry Snowden. The Canterbury Pilgrimages. With illustrations by Catherine Weed Ward. London: Adam & Charles Black, 1904; 2nd edition, 1927.

*——. The Land of Lorna Doone. Photographs by Catherine Weed Ward. London: Sampson Low, 1908; 2nd edition, 1925.

Ward, Henry Snowden, and Catherine Weed Ward. The Real Dickens Land. With text by Henry Snowden Ward and photographs by Catherine Weed Ward. London: Chapman & Hall, 1904.

——. Shakespeare's Town and Times. With text by Henry Snowden Ward and photographs by Catherine Weed Ward. London: Dawbarn & Ward, 1896; 2nd edition, 1901; 3rd edition, Sampson Low, 1908.

*Warehime, Marja. "Photography, Time, and the Surrealist Sensibility." In Photo-Textualities: Reading Photographs and Literature, edited and with an introduction by Marsha Bryant. Newark: University of Delaware Press, forthcoming.

*Warren, Robert Penn. All the King's Men. 10 photogravures by Hank O'Neal. [New York]: Limited Editions Club, 1989.

Watson, R. N. "Art, Photography and John Ruskin." British Journal of Photography (March 10, March 24, April 7, 1944): 82–83, 100–101, and 118–19.

*Watt, Stephen. "Photographs in Biographies: Joyce, Voyeurism, and the 'Real' Nora Barnacle." In Photo-Textualities: Reading Photographs and Literature, edited and with an introduction by Marsha Bryant. Newark: University of Delaware Press, forthcoming.

Waugh, Evelyn. "The Death of Painting." In Time and Tide 36 (December 3, 1955): 1586 and 1588. Reprinted in The Saturday Books, No. 16, edited by John Hadfield, London: Hutchinson, 1956; in A Little Order: A Selection from His Journalism, edited by Donat Gallagher, London: Eyre Methuen, 1977; Boston: Little, Brown, 1980; and in The Essays, Articles and Reviews of Evelyn Waugh, edited by Donat Gallagher, London: Methuen, 1983; Boston: Little, Brown, 1984.

——. "Footlights and Chandeliers." Spectator 297 (July 21, 1961): 96–97. Reprinted in The Essays, Articles and Reviews of Evelyn Waugh, edited by Donat Gallagher. London: Methuen, 1983; Boston: Little, Brown, 1984 [edition used here].

——. Ninety-Two Days: The Account of a Tropical Journey Through British Guiana and Part of Brazil. With illustrations from photographs taken by the author. London: Duckworth; New York: Farrar & Rinehart, 1934. Reprinted, without illustrations, London: Methuen, 1991.

——. Remote People. With 8 illustrations [5 probably by Waugh, 3 attributed to others]. London: Duckworth, 1931. Reprinted, without illustrations, New York: Ecco Press, 1990; and as They Were Still Dancing, New York: Farrar & Rinehart, 1932.

——. Waugh in Abyssinia. London: Methuen, 1936.

Weaver, Mike. Alvin Langdon Coburn: Symbolist Photographer, 1882–1966. New York: Aperture, 1986.

——. Julia Margaret Cameron, 1815–1879. London: Herbert Press, 1984.

——. "Talbot's Broom and Swift's Broomstick." History of Photography 15, no. 3 (Autumn 1991): 242–43.

Webb, William. Henry and Friends: The California Years, 1946–1977. With photographs by William Webb. Santa Barbara, Calif.: Capra Press, 1991 [includes "Jonathan Williams—The Johnny Appleseed of Letters" and "Brassaï—The Eye of Paris"].

Weems, Carrie Mae. "Stories and Photographs." *Aperture* 112 (Fall 1988): 61, 64–65.

Wegman, William. *Cinderella*. New York: Hyperion, 1993.

——. *Little Red Riding Hood*. New York: Hyperion, 1993.

Weill, Kurt. *Der Zar Lässt Sich Photographieren/The Tsar Has His Picture Taken* [1928]. Translated by Lionel Salter. Vienna: Universal-Edition, 1985.

Weiner, Dan. *South Africa in Transition*. With text by Alan Paton. New York: Scribner's, 1958.

Weiss, Margaret. "Poets as People." *Saturday Review of Literature* 54 (May 15, 1971): 52–53.

Wells, H. G. "The Art of Being Photographed." *Pall Mall Gazette* 57 (December 1, 1893): 3. Reprinted in *Select Conversations with an Uncle*. London: John Lane; New York: Merriam Company, 1895.

——. *The Country of the Blind*. With frontispiece by Alvin Langdon Coburn. New York: Privately printed, Christmas, 1915.

——. *The Door in the Wall*. With illustrations by Alvin Langdon Coburn. London: Kennerly, 1911. Facsimile edition, with afterword by Jeffrey A. Wolin, Boston: Godine, 1980.

——. Preface to Alvin Langdon Coburn, *New York*. London: Duckworth, 1910; New York: Brentano's, 1911.

Wells, Robert. "Hellenistic Torso." *Word and Image* 2, no. 1 (January–March 1986): 82.

Welty, Eudora. See also *Images of the South*.

——. *In Black and White*. Northridge, Calif.: Lord John Press, 1985.

——. *Eudora*. Edited by Patti Carr Black. Jackson: Mississippi Department of Archives & History, 1984.

——. *Eudora Welty: Photographs*. With introduction, "Eudora Welty and Photography: An Interview," conducted by Hunter Cole and Seetha Srinivasan. Jackson: University of Mississippi Press, 1989.

——. Introduction to *The Democratic Forest* by William Eggleston. New York: Doubleday; London: Secker & Warburg, 1989.

——. "Literature and the Lens." *Vogue* 104 (August 1, 1944): 103–4.

——. *One Time, One Place, Mississippi in the Depression; A Snapshot Album*. New York: Random House, 1971. Text reprinted as "One Time, One Place," in *The Eye of the Story: Selected Essays and Reviews*. New York: Random House, 1978.

——. *Twenty Photographs*. Winston-Salem, N.C.: Palemon Press, 1980.

——. *Welty: An Exhibition at the Mississippi State Historical Museum*. Selected and edited by Patti Carr Black. Jackson: Mississippi Department of Archives and History, 1977.

West, Nancy Martha. "Soft Murder by the Camera Eye: Photographic Fears and the Victorian Writer." Ph.D. dissertation. University of North Carolina, 1992. [Includes discussion of Hawthorne, Hardy, Conan Doyle, and Oliver Wendell Holmes, Sr.]

Westerbeck, Colin, Jr. "American Graphic: The Photography and Fiction of Wright Morris." In *Multiple Views: Logan Grant Essays on Photography 1983–89*, edited by Daniel P. Younger. Albuquerque: University of New Mexico, 1991.

Westling, Louise. "The Loving Observer of *One Time, One Place*." *Mississippi Quarterly* 39, no. 4 (Fall 1986): 587–604.

Weston, Edward. *The Daybooks of Edward Weston*. 2 vols., edited by Nancy Newhall. Volume I originally published in Rochester: George Eastman House, 1961; Volume II in New York: Horizon Press in collaboration with George Eastman House. Reprinted in 2 vols. Millerton, N.Y.; Aperture, 1973; in one volume, 1991.

——. "Lawrence in Mexico.." *The Carmelite* 3, no. 6 (Supplement) (March 19, 1930): ix–xi.

Weston, Ruth D. "Images of the Depression in the Fiction of Eudora Welty." *Southern Quarterly* 32, no. 1 (Fall 1993): 80–91.

*Wexler, Laura Jane. "The Puritan in the Photograph." Ph.D. diss., Columbia University, 1986 [summary in *DAI* 47, no. 10 (April 1987): 3760A].

White, Clarence. *Eben Holden* by Irving Bacheller. Boston: Lothrop Publishing, 1903.

White, Minor. "Amputations" [1945], TS, with photographs, 1947. Minor White Archives.

——. Correspondence with Roy DeCarava about *The Sweet Flypaper of Life*. November 11 and 30, 1955. MSS Minor White Archives.

——. "Memorable Fancies" [1931–50], TS, Minor White Archives.

——. "Minor Testament." TS, Minor White Archives.

——. *Mirrors Messages Manifestations*. Millerton, N.Y.: Aperture, 1969; 1982.

——. Review of *The Sweet Flypaper of Life*, by Roy DeCarava and Langston Hughes. *Image* 4, no. 9 (December 1955): 71.

Whitman, Walt. "An Hour Among the Portraits." *Brooklyn Evening Star* (June 7, 1852).

——. *Leaves of Grass*. 2 vols., with illustrations by Edward Weston. New York: Limited Editions Club, 1942. Reprinted with different introduction as Edward Weston, *Leaves of Grass by Walt Whitman*. New York and London: Paddington Press, 1976.

——. "My Picture Gallery" [1880] and "Pictures" [1846]. In *The Complete Poems*, edited by Francis Murphy. Harmondsworth: Penguin, 1975.

[——]. (O. P. Q.) "Scores and Sights of Broadway—Thursday, February 19." *Brooklyn Evening Star* (February 20, 1846) 2:4.

——. "Out From Behind This Mask (To confront My Portrait, illustrating 'The Wound-Dresser') in *Leaves of Grass*." In *Two Rivulets*, Camden, N.J.: Author's Edition, 1876; and Norwood, Pa.: Norwood Editions, 1979. [Often reprinted in longer form after

1881 in editions of *Leaves of Grass,* with slight changes in the subtitle and in the first four words of the second line.] Originally published in a shorter untitled version in the *New York Daily Tribune* (February 19, 1876): 4.

[———]. (Paumanok.) "Letters from New York, November 2, 1850." *National Era* 4, no. 46 (November 14, 1850): 181. Reprinted in Rollo G. Silver, "Whitman in 1850: Three Uncollected Articles," *American Literature* 19, no. 4 (January 1948): 306–13.

*———. *Song of the Open Road.* 6 photogravures by Aaron Siskind [New York]: Limited Editions Club, 1990.

———. *Specimen Days.* Philadelphia: Rees Welch, 1882. Reprinted Philadelphia: David McKay, 1892; and with introduction by Alfred Kazin. Boston: Godine, 1971.

[———]. "Visit to Plumbe's Gallery." *Brooklyn Daily Eagle* 5, no. 160 (July 2, 1846): 1 [version used here]. Reprinted in *The Gathering of the Forces,* vol. 2, edited by Cleveland Rogers and John Black. New York: G. P. Putnam's, 1920.

———. *Walt Whitman in Camden: A Selection of Prose from Specimen Days.* With a preface by Christopher Morley and 3 photographic illustrations by Arnold Genthe. Camden, N.J.: Haddon Craftsmen, 1938.

*Whittier, John Greenleaf. *Snow Bound; A Winter Idyll.* With 5 photographs and circular photo inserted in upper cover. London: Alfred W. Bennett, 1867.

Wiesel, Elie. Foreword to *A Vanished World,* by Roman Vishniac, translated by Richard Howard. New York: Farrar, Straus & Giroux, 1983; 1986.

Wieser, Theodor, ed. *Günter Grass: Porträt und Poesie.* Neuwind: Luchterhand, 1968.

Wilber, Ann. "The Tauchnitz 'Marble Faun.'" *History of Photography* 4 (January 1980): 61–66.

Wilbur, Richard. Foreword to *A Life in Photography* by Rollie McKenna. New York: Knopf, 1991.

———. Foreword to *New England Reflections, 1882–1907: Photographs by the Howes Brothers,* edited by Alan B. Newman. New York: Pantheon Books, 1981.

Wilkinson, Lynn R. "*Le cousin Pons* and the Invention of Ideology." *PMLA* 107, no. 2 (March 1992): 274–89.

Williams, James Leon. *Gray's Elegy and Its Author.* Boston: Joseph Knight, 1890; Troy, N.Y.: Nims & Knight, 1891.

———. *The Land of Sleepy Hollow and the Home of Washington Irving: A Series of Photogravure Representations, With Descriptive Letterpress.* New York: Knickerbocker Press, 1887.

Williams, Jonathan. "Aaron Siskind at 75." *Aperture* 82 (1979): 7 [version used here]. Reprinted in *The Magpie's Bagpipe.* San Francisco: North Point Press, 1982.

———. "Aaron Siskind/Eight Signs." *Black Mountain Review* 5 (Summer 1955): 77–78.

———. "Afterword: A Digestive Biscuit from the Blue Ridge for Delicate Palates . . ." to *The Photographs of Lyle Bongé.* Highlands, N.C.: Jargon Society, 1982. Reprinted as "O. L Bongé of Biloxi, Mississippi," in *The Magpie's Bagpipe,* edited by Thomas Meyer. San Francisco: North Point Press, 1982.

———. Afterword to *Letter in a Klein Bottle: Photographs by John Menapace.* Highlands, N.C.: Jargon Society, 1984.

———. *Amen/Huzza/Selah.* With the author's photographs. Black Mountain, N.C.: Jargon Society, 1960.

———. "And the Running Blueberry Would Adorn the Parlours of Heaven." Foreword to *Harry Callahan: Color, 1941–1980,* edited by Robert Tow and Ricker Winsor. Providence, R.I.: Matrix, 1980.

———. "An Aubade from Verlaine's Days (for Alfred Stieglitz)." In *Elite/Elate Poems: Selected Poems 1971–75.* N.p.: Jargon Society, 1979.

———. *Blues and Roots/Rue and Bluets: A Garland for Appalachia.* With photographs by Nicholas Dean. New York: Grossman, 1971.

———. "The Camera Non-Obscura." In *The Magpie's Bagpipe,* edited by Thomas Meyer. San Francisco: North Point Press, 1982.

———. "Cloches à Travers les Feuilles." In *Contemporary Authors Autobiography Series,* vol. 12, edited by Joyce Nakamarura. Detroit, Mich.: Gale Research, 1990. [Includes "Letter to Ansel Adams" and "Letter to Clarence John Laughlin."]

———. "'Coming Through Unfettered,' As Ray Says . . . ." Afterword to *Murmurs at Every Turn: The Photographs of Raymond Moore.* London: Travelling Light, 1981.

———. "Do You See What I See?" Foreword to *A Southeast Photography Portfolio,* by Carolyn Demeritt et al. Highlands, N.C.: Appalachian Environmental Arts Center, 1988.

———. *Eight Days in Eire.* Photographs by Mike Harding. Rocky Mount, N.C.: North Carolina Wesleyan Press, 1990.

———. "Elegy for a Photograph of William Carlos Williams." In *Get Hot or Get Out: A Selection of Poems, 1957–81.* Metuchen, N.J.: Scarecrow Press, 1982.

———. *Elite/Elate Poems: Selected Poems, 1971–75.* A Portfolio of Photographs by Guy Mendes. N.p.: Jargon Society, 1979. [Includes "The Photographer Looks at His Prints and Turns Poet (for Ralph Eugene Meatyard: 1925–1972)"; "Quiet Nights"; "In Lucas, Kansas (for Clarence John Laughlin)"; and "G.B.S. 'Le Penseur' (for Alvin Langdon Coburn)."]

———. "Everything's Everywhere." Preface to *The Sleep of Reason: Lyle Bongé's Ultimate Ash-Hauling Mardi Gras Photographs.* Highlands, N.C.: Jargon Society, 1974.

———. "The Eye Sees More Than the Mind Knows." Introduction to *The Multiple Image: Photographs by Harry Callahan.* Chicago: Press of the Institute of Design, 1961.

———. "The Eyes of 3 Phantasts: Laughlin, Sommer, Bullock." *Aperture* 9, no. 3 (1961): 98–106.

———. "Homage to F. S.; or, that old-time Ryne Duren—Rex Barney bailout." In *Venus, Jupiter and Mars: The Photographs of Frederick Sommer*, edited by John Weiss. Wilmington: Delaware Art Museum, 1980.

———. *In a New Light: Writings on Photography 1961–1988*. Forthcoming.

———. "In Dixieland I'll Take My Stan-back & Other Mordacious Gospels." Introduction to *I Shall Save One Land Unvisited: Eleven Southern Photographers*, edited by Jonathan Williams. Frankfort, Ky.: Gnomon Press, 1978.

———. Introduction to *Hot What? Collages, Texts, Photographs*, by Lyle Bongé, Fielding Dawson, and Jonathan Williams. Dublin, Ga.: Mole Press, 1975.

*———. Introduction to *The Photographer's Art*. Kent, Ohio: Kent State University, 1981.

———. Introduction to *Railroad Men: A Book of Photographs and Collected Stories of Simpson Kalisher*. New York: Clarke & Way, 1961.

———. *The Magpie's Bagpipe*. Edited by Thomas Meyer. San Francisco: North Point Press, 1982. [This volume also includes essays on the Abraham Brothers (1981), Wynn Bullock (1976), Susan Sontag (1978), and Frank Sutcliffe (1974).]

———. "Muse-Flash for Ralph Eugene Meatyard." In *Get Hot or Get Out: A Selection of Poems, 1957–81*. Metuchen, N.J.: Scarecrow Press, 1982.

———. "The Photographs of Guy Mendes: 'Eh, La Bas, The F-Stops Here!'" Afterword to *Guy Mendes, Light at Hand: Photographs, 1970–85*. Frankfort, Ky.: Gnomon, 1986.

———. *Portrait Photographs*. London: Coracle Press; Frankfort, Ky.: Gnomon Press, 1979.

———. Preface to *White Trash Cooking*, by Ernest Matthew Micker. With color photographs by William Christenberry. Berkeley: Ten Speed Press, 1986.

———. "Shadow of His Equipage." Introduction to *Clarence John Laughlin: The Personal Eye*. Exhibition catalogue. Millerton, N.Y.: Aperture, 1973; reissued as book, 1975. Reprinted in *The Magpie's Bagpipe*, edited by Thomas Meyer. San Francisco: North Point Press, 1982.

———. "Some Speak of a Return to Nature—I Wonder Where They Could Have Been?" In Bill Brandt, *The Land: Twentieth Century Landscape Photographs*, selected by Bill Brandt, edited by Mark Haworth-Booth. London: Gordon Fraser Gallery, 1975. Reprinted in *The Magpie's Bagpipe*, edited by Thomas Meyer. San Francisco: North Point Press, 1982.

———. *Ten Photographs*. Belper, Derbyshire: Aggie Weston's Editions, 1982.

———. "They All Want to Go and Dress Up." Preface to *The Appalachian Photographs of Doris Ulmann*. Penland, N.C.: Jargon Society, 1971. Reprinted in *The Magpie's Bagpipe*, edited by Thomas Meyer. San Francisco: North Point Press, 1982.

———. *Walks to the Paradise Garden*. With photographs by Roger Manley and Guy Mendes. Forthcoming.

———. "When the Sharp Shinned Hawk Appears . . ." [New Southern Photography: Between Myth and Reality]. *Aperture* 115 (Summer 1989): 64–71.

———. *Who Is Little Enis?* A BroadSide poem with a photograph by Guy Mendes. Highlands, N.C.: Jargon Society, 1974.

Williams, Val. "Only Connecting: Julia Margaret Cameron and Bloomsbury." *Photographic Collector* (London) 4, no. 1 (Spring 1983): 40–49.

Williams, William Carlos. "The American Background." In *America and Alfred Stieglitz: A Collective Portrait*, edited by Waldo Frank. New York: Doubleday, Doran, 1934. Reprinted New York: Aperture, 1979.

———. Introduction to *Charles Sheeler: Paintings, Drawings, Photographs*. New York: Museum of Modern Art, 1939. Reprinted, with earlier emendations indicated, as "Charles Sheeler" in *A Recognizable Image: William Carlos Williams on Art and Artists*, ed. Bram Dijkstra. New York: New Directions, 1978.

———. "The Most Overlooked Book of the Past Quarter Century," MS, [c. 1950's?], Beinecke.

———. "Sermon with a Camera." *New Republic* 96 (October 12, 1938): 282–83. Reprinted with revisions indicated as "Walker Evans: American Photographs," in *A Recognizable Image: William Carlos Williams on Art and Artists*, edited by Bram Dijkstra. New York: New Directions, 1978 [edition used here, with original title].

———. "What of Alfred Stieglitz?" [1946]. In *A Recognizable Image: William Carlos Williams on Art and Artists*, edited by Bram Dijkstra. New York: New Directions, 1978.

———. "Whitman's *Leaves of Grass* and Photography" [1960]. In *A Recognizable Image: William Carlos Williams on Art and Artists*, edited by Bram Dykstra. New York: New Directions, 1978. Reprinted with revisions as an introduction to *The Illustrated Leaves of Grass*, by Walt Whitman, edited by Howard Chapnick. New York: Madison Square Press, 1971.

———. "Young Sycamore," *The Dial* 82, no. 3 (March 1923): 210–11. Reprinted in *Collected Poems, 1921–1931*, New York: Objectivist Press, 1934; *Selected Poems*, New York: New Directions, 1949; and *The Collected Poems of William Carlos Williams*, vol. 1, edited by A. Walton Litz and Christopher MacGowen, New York: New Directions, 1986.

*Wilner, Eleanor, and Trudy Wilner Stack. "Here and Never: Poets on Photography." Authors' MS.

Wilsher, Ann. "Photography and Literature: The First Seventy Years." *History of Photography* 2 (1978): 223–34.

*Wilson, John, and D[avid]. O[ctavius]. Hill. *The Land of Burns: A Series of Landscapes and Portraits*

Illustrative of the Life and Writings of the Scottish Poet. With photographs from paintings by D. O. Hill and texts by John Wilson and Robert Chambers. Glasgow: Blackie & Son, 1846.

Wilson, Sharon R. "Camera Images in Margaret Atwood's Novels." In *Margaret Atwood: Reflections and Reality,* edited by Beatrice Mendez-Egle. Edinburgh: Pan American University, 1987.

Witherall, Elizabeth Hall. "Thoreau and Gleason." In *The Illustrated A Week on the Concord and Merrimack Rivers* by Henry David Thoreau, edited by Carl F. Howde et al. With photographs from the Gleason Collection. Princeton, N.J.: Princeton University Press, 1983.

Witkin, Lee D., and Barbara London. *Photograph Collector's Guide.* Boston: New York Graphic Society, 1979.

Wodehouse, P. G. "About My Friends." Preface to *Son of Bitch,* by Elliott Erwitt. New York: Grossman, 1974.

Wolfe, Tom. Introduction to *Annie Leibovitz Photographs.* New York: Pantheon/Rolling Stone, 1983.

———. "Miss Aurora by Astral Projection." In *Color Photographs,* by Marie Cosindas. Boston: New York Graphic Society, 1978.

———. Preface to *Rollingstone: The Photographs,* edited by Laurie Kratochvil. New York: Simon & Schuster, 1989.

*Wolford, Mary. "Baudelaire, Photography and Clarence John Laughlin." M.A. thesis, Indiana University, Indianapolis, 1983.

Wood, Charles B., III. *The Photograph and the Book,* catalogue 37. With introduction by Eugenia Parry Janis. So. Woodstock, Conn.: Charles B. Wood III, 1976.

———. *The Photograph and the Book—II,* catalogue 41/42. S. Woodstock, Conn.: Charles B. Wood III, 1978.

Woods, Lucia. "Light and Shadow in the Cather World: A Personal Essay." *Great Plains Quarterly* 4, no. 4 (Fall 1984): 245–63.

Woodward, Harry. "In Bold and Fearless Connection: A Study of the Fiction of Flannery O'Connor and the Photography of Diane Arbus." Ph.D. diss., University of Minnesota, Minneapolis, 1978.

Woolf, Douglas. *Spring of the Lamb.* With photographs by Ralph Eugene Meatyard. Highlands, N.C.: Jargon Society, 1972.

Woolf, Virginia. *Freshwater: A Comedy* [1923, 1935], edited by Lucio P. Ruotolo. New York: Harvest/Harcourt Brace Jovanovich, 1985.

———. "Julia Margaret Cameron." In *Victorian Photographs of Famous Men and Fair Women,* by Julia Margaret Cameron. London: Hogarth Press; New York: Harcourt, Brace, 1926 [edition used here]. Reprinted London: Chatto & Windus, 1992, and in a revised and expanded edition, edited by Tristram Powell, Boston: Godine, 1973; London: Chatto, 1992.

———. *Orlando: A Biography.* With 8 photographic illustrations. London: Hogarth Press; New York: Harcourt, Brace, 1928; 1973.

———. *Three Guineas.* With 5 illustrations [probably by Leonard Woolf]. London: Hogarth Press; New York: Harcourt, Brace, 1935.

*Wordsworth, William. *Our English Lakes, Mountains and Waterfalls as Seen by William Wordsworth.* Photographically illustrated by T[homas] Ogle, Russell Sedgfield and J. Eliot with 13 taken especially for this work. London: Alfred Williams Bennett, 1864; new expanded edition, 1868.

Wright, Charles. "Bar Gaimaica, 1959–60" [1981]. In *The World of the Thousand Things: Poems 1980–1990.* New York: Farrar, Straus & Giroux, 1991.

———. "Photographs." In *The Grave of the Right Hand.* Middletown, Conn.: Wesleyan University Press, 1970. Reprinted in *Poets on Photography,* edited by Mark Melnicove. South Harpswell, Me.: Dog Ear Press, 1981.

Wright, James. "Eisenhower's Visit to Franco" [1959]. In *The Branch Will Not Break.* Middletown, Conn.: Wesleyan University Press, 1962. Reprinted in *Poets on Photography,* edited by Mark Melnicove, South Harpswell, Me.: Dog Ear Press, 1981; and in *Collected Poems,* Middletown, Conn.: Wesleyan University Press, 1971.

Wright, Richard. *Black Power: A Record of Reactions in a Land of Pathos.* New York: Harper & Brothers; London: Dennis Dobson, with 34 photographs by the author and slightly different text; Leiden: A. W. Sijthoff, translated by Margrit de Sablonière, with 13 photographs by the author, 1954.

———. *The Color Curtain: A Report on the Bandung Conference.* With photographs by the author. London: Dennis Dobson; The Hague: Van Hoeve; and, without photographs, Cleveland: World Publishers, 1956.

*———. "Fallas in Valencia." *Illuspress* (January 1959): [5ff].

———. "A Recommendation" [of Helen Levitt's Photographs of Children, Museum of Modern Art Exhibition, 1943]. MS and TS at the Beinecke (JWJ Collection, Misc. 692–93).

———. *Twelve Million Black Voices: A Folk History of the Negro in the United States.* Photograph direction by Edwin Rosskam. New York: Viking, 1941. Reprinted London: Lindsay Drummond, 1947; and New York: Thunder's Mouth Press, 1988. Abridged version in *Coronet* 11 (April 1942): 77–92.

*———. "Vralt Fastnachtsbrauche." *Illuspress* (May 1959): 5.

*Wright, William Samuel. *The Loved Haunts of Cowper; or The Photographic Remembrances of Olney and Weston.* Olney: William Samuel Wright, 1867.

Wydeven, Joseph J. "Consciousness Refracted: Photography and the Imagination in the Works of Wright Morris." *Midamerica* 8 (1981): 92–114.

———. "Images and Icons: The Fiction and Photography of Wright Morris." In *Under the Sun: Myth and Realism in Western American Literature*, edited by Barbara Howard Meldrum. Troy, N.Y.: Whitston, 1985.

———. "Focus and Frame in Wright Morris's *The Works of Love*." *Western American Literature* 23 (August 1988): 99–112.

———. "Photography and Privacy: The Protests of Wright Morris and James Agee." *Midwest Quarterly* 23 (Autumn 1981): 103–15.

Wylie, Donovan. *32 Counties*. Photographs of Ireland by Donovan Wylie with new writing by 32 Irish writers. London: Secker & Warburg, 1989.

Yeats, W. B. *Images of Ireland*. With photographs by Alain Le Garsmeur and an essay by Bernard McCabe. Boston: Little, Brown, 1991.

Yevtushenko, Yevgeny. *Divided Twins: Alaska and Siberia*. Translated by Antonina W. Bouls, with photographs by Boyd Norton and Yevgeny Yevtushenko. New York: Viking Studio, 1988; London: Viking, 1989.

———. *Invisible Threads*. New York: Macmillan; London: Secker & Warburg, 1981.

York, Lorraine Mary. *"The Other Side of Dailiness": Photography in the Works of Alice Munro, Timothy Findlay, Michael Ondaatje, and Margaret Laurence*. Toronto: ECW Press, 1988.

———. "'Violent Stillness': Photography and Postmodernism in Canadian Fiction." *Mosaic* 21 no. 3 (1988): 193–201.

*Zannier, Italo, and Paolo Costantini. *Cultura Fotografia in Italia: Antologia Di Testi Sulla Fotografia 1839–1949*. Milan: Touring Club Italiano, 1979.

Zehnhoff, H. W. "Satirical Techniques of John Heartfield and Kurt Tucholsky in *Deutschland, Deutschland über Alles*." *Word and Image* 4, no. 1 (January–March 1988): 157–62.

Zola, Émile. *Émile Zola Photographe*. Chalon-sur-Saône: Musée Nicéphore Niépce, October 1982.

———. *The Rush for the Spoil: A Realistic Novel*. Paris: C. Marpan and E. Flammarion [1896]. Originally published as *La Curée*, Paris, 1871.

Adams, Ansel. From *Ansel Adams: An Autobiography,* Little, Brown and Company. Copyright © 1985 by The Trustees of The Ansel Adams Publishing Rights Trust. All Rights Reserved. Reprinted with permission of The Trustees of the Ansel Adams Publishing Rights Trust. From letters to Mary Austin at the Center for Creative Photography, Tucson, Arizona. Reprinted with permission of The Trustees of The Ansel Adams Publishing Rights Trust.

Adams, Henry. From THE LETTERS OF HENRY ADAMS, Volumes 1–6, edited by J. C. Levenson, Ernest Samuels, Charles Vandersee, and Viola Hopkins Winner. Cambridge, Mass.: The Belknap Press of the Harvard University Press and the Adams Papers, Massachusetts Historical Society. Copyright © 1982, 1988 by the Massachusetts Historical Society. Reprinted by permission of the publishers.

Adams, Marian Hooper. From *The Letters of Mrs. Henry Adams, 1865–1883,* edited by Ward Thoron, Boston: Little, Brown, 1936. Copyright 1936 by Ellen Sturgis Hooper Potter. By permission of Little, Brown and Company. Excerpts from her unpublished letters after May 1883 from the originals on the MHS microfilm of the Adams Family papers, reels 597–98. By permission of the Adams Papers, Massachusetts Historical Society.

Agee, James. From prefatory essay to *A Way of Seeing* by Helen Levitt. Copyright 1989, Duke University Press. Copyright 1965, 1981, 1989 by the James Agee Trust. Reprinted by permission of the publisher and the James Agee Trust.

Anderson, Sherwood. "Alfred Stieglitz" in *The New Republic* (1922). Copyright 1922 by The New Republic Publishing Company. Copyright renewed 1949 by Eleanor Copenhaver Anderson. Reprinted by permission of Harold Ober Associates Incorporated.

Andreyev, Leonid. From *Photographs by a Russian Writer,* edited by Richard Davies. Reprinted by permission of Thames & Hudson Ltd.

Auden, W. H. From W. H. Auden, *Letters From Iceland.* Reprinted by permission of Curtis Brown, Ltd.

Austin, Mary. From letter to Ansel Adams, February 23, 1929. Reprinted by permission of The Huntington Library, San Marino, California.

Baldessari, John. "Baudelaire Meets Poe." Reprinted by permission of John Baldessari and the Sonnabend Gallery, New York City.

Baudelaire, Charles. "The Salon of 1859." Reprinted from *Art in Paris 1845–1862,* translated and edited by Jonathan Mayne. Phaidon Press Limited, Oxford 1965 and 1981. By permission of Phaidon Press Ltd.

Beaton, Cecil. From *The Wandering Years: Diaries, 1922–1939* and from *The Strenuous Years: Diaries, 1948–1955.* Reprinted by permission of the Literary Trustees of Sir Cecil Beaton.

Bourke-White, Margaret. From *Portrait of Myself.* Reprinted by permission of the author's estate and their representatives, Scott Meredith Literary Agency, Inc., 845 Third Avenue, New York, New York 10022.

Brassaï, [Gyula H.] "Carroll The Photographer" from *Lewis Carroll: Photos and Letters to His Child Friends,* Milan: Franco Maria Ricci, 1975, translated from French into English by Jeremy Fox. Reprinted by permission of the publisher.

Brecht, Bertolt. From KRIEGSFIBEL. From "Gesammelte Werke" © Suhrkamp Verlag, Frankfurt am Main. All rights reserved.

Breton, André. From *Nadja* by André Breton, translated by Richard Howard. English translation copyright © 1960, 1988 by Grove Press, Inc. Used by permission of Grove Press, Inc., and Calder Publications Ltd., London.

Brown, Rosellen. "Good Housekeeping," originally in *American Review 18.* Reprinted by permission of HarperCollins.

Caldwell, Erskine. From *With All My Might: An Autobiography* (Atlanta: Peachtree Publishers, 1987). Reprinted by permission of the publisher.

Capote, Truman. "Comments," introduction to *Observations* by Richard Avedon. Copyright © 1959 by Richard Avedon and Truman Capote. Reprinted by permission of Simon & Schuster, Inc.

Carlyle, Thomas. See Emerson, Ralph Waldo.

Chatwin, Bruce. From *In Patagonia.* Copyright © 1977 by Bruce Chatwin. Reprinted by permission of the Estate of Bruce Chatwin, Summit, a division of Simon & Schuster, Inc., and Jonathan Cape.

Chekhov, Anton. "The Album" from *The Schoolmaster and Other Stories,* translated from the Russian by Constance Garnett. Copyright 1921 by Macmillan Publishing Company, renewed 1949 by David Garnett. Reprinted by permission of Chatto & Windus and the Macmillan Publishing Company.

Clergue, Lucien. See Cocteau, Jean.

Coburn, Alvin Langdon. "Illustrating Henry James" from *Alvin Langdon Coburn Photographer: An Autobiography,* edited by Helmut and Alison Gernsheim. Reprinted by permission of Helmut Gernsheim. Excerpts from "Henry James and the Camera," BBC Radio Script. Reprinted by permission of the BBC Written Archives Centre, Cavisham Park, Reading, England.

Cocteau, Jean, and Lucien Clergue. From *Correspondance.* © Actes Sud, 1989. Reprinted by permission of the publisher.

Cole, Hunter, and Srinivasan, Seetha. From "Eudora Welty and Photography: An Interview," Introduction to *Eudora Welty Photographs* (1989). Reprinted by permission of the University Press of Mississippi.

Cummings, E. E. "in a vicious world—top love virtue" (MARIANNE MOORE), in Marion Morehouse, *Adventures in Value* [1962]. Reprinted from *Complete Poems, 1913–1962,* by E. E. Cummings by permission of Liveright Publishing Corporation. Copyright 1923, 1925, 1931, 1935, 1938, 1939, 1940, 1944, 1945, 1946, 1947, 1948, 1949, 1950, 1951, 1952, 1953, 1954, 1955, 1956, 1957, 1958, 1959, 1960, 1961, 1962, 1963, 1968 by the Trustees for the E. E. Cummings Trust. Copyright © 1961, 1963, 1968 by Marion Morehouse Cummings, and by MacGibbon & Kee, an imprint of HarperCollins Publishers Limited.

Day, F. Holland, and Amy Lowell. From *Keats and the Bostonians,* edited by Hyder Rollins and Stephen Parrish. Copyright 1951, by the President and Fellows of Harvard College. Reprinted by permission of the Harvard University Press.

DeCarava, Roy. Unpublished letter to Minor White, TS, November 21, 1955, from the James Weldon Johnson Collection, the Yale Collection of American Literature, the Beinecke Rare Book and Manuscript Library, Yale University. Reprinted by permission of Roy DeCarava and the Beinecke Rare Book and Manuscript Library.

Dorfman, Elsa. From *Elsa's Housebook: A Woman's Photojournal.* © 1992 Elsa Dorfman. Reprinted by permission of the author.

Doyle, Arthur Conan. From *The Wanderings of a Spiritualist* (London: Hodder & Stoughton; New York: George H. Doran, 1922). Reprinted by permission of the copyright owner.

Du Camp, Maxime. See Flaubert, Gustave.

Durrell, Lawrence. Introduction to Bill Brandt, *Perspective of Nudes.* Copyright the Estate of Lawrence Durrell. Reprinted by permission of Curtis Brown, Ltd. on behalf of the Estate of Lawrence Durrell.

Emerson, Ralph Waldo, and Thomas Carlyle. From *The Correspondence of Emerson and Carlyle,* edited by Joseph Slater (New York: Columbia University Press, 1964), and Emerson, *Journals and Miscellaneous Notebooks,* edited by W. H. Gilman et al. (Cambridge: The Belknap Press/ Harvard University Press, 1960–82). Reprinted by permission of the Ralph Waldo Emerson Memorial Association, the Houghton Library, and the Harvard University Press.

Evans, Walker. "James Agee in 1936" from *Let Us Now Praise Famous Men* by James Agee and Walker Evans. Copyright 1939 and 1940 by James Agee. Copyright 1941 by James Agee and Walker Evans. Copyright © 1960 by Walker Evans. Copyright renewed 1969 by Mia Fritsch Agee and Walker Evans. Reprinted by permission of Houghton Mifflin Company.

Faulkner, William. From *Absalom, Absalom!* Copyright 1936 by William Faulkner and renewed 1964 by Jill Faulkner Summers. Reprinted by permission of Random House, Inc. and Curtis Brown, Ltd., London.

Flaubert, Gustave, and Maxime Du Camp. From *Flaubert in Egypt: A Sensibility on Tour,* translated and edited by

Francis Steegmuller; published by Academy Chicago Publishers and reprinted by permission. All rights reserved.

Forster, E. M. "Sinclair Lewis" from *Abinger Harvest*. Reprinted by permission of King's College, Cambridge and The Society of Authors as the literary representatives of the E. M. Forster Estate.

Freund, Gisèle. "James Joyce" from *The World in My Camera* by Gisèle Freund. Copyright © 1974 by Gisèle Freund. Reprinted by permission of Doubleday, a division of Bantam Doubleday Dell Publishing Group, Inc. and the Joan Davies Agency.

Ginsberg, Allen, and Mark Holborn. From "Allen Ginsberg's Sacramental Snapshots: An Interview by Mark Holborn," *Aperture* 101 (Winter 1985): 8–15. Reprinted by permission of Allen Ginsberg and Mark Holborn.

Grass, Günter. From *The Tin Drum* by Günter Grass. © August 1959 by Hermann Luchterhand Verlag GmbH. English translation copyright © 1961, 1962 by Pantheon Books, a division of Random House, Inc. Copyright renewed 1989, 1990 by Random House, Inc. Reprinted by permission of Random House and Martin Secker and Warburg Limited.

Griffin, John Howard. From *Follow the Ecstasy*. Copyright 1983 by The Estate of John Howard Griffin, Elizabeth Griffin-Bonazzi, Executor.

Harte, Bret. From The *Letters of Bret Harte,* edited by Geoffrey Bret Harte. Copyright 1926, © renewed 1954 by Geoffrey Bret Harte. Reprinted by permission of Houghton Mifflin Co. All rights reserved.

Hawthorne, Nathaniel. Reprinted with permission from *The House of the Seven Gables,* Vol. 2 of the Centenary Edition of the works of Nathaniel Hawthorne, edited by Fredson Bowers. Copyright 1965 by the Ohio State University Press.

Heaney, Seamus. "The Tollund Man" from *Poems, 1965–1975* by Seamus Heaney. Copyright © 1972, 1980 by Seamus Heaney. Reprinted by permission of Farrar, Straus & Giroux, Inc. and Faber & Faber Ltd.

Holborn, Mark. See Ginsberg, Allen.

Howard, Richard. "Figures" from "The Mapplethorpe Effect" in *Robert Mapplethorpe,* edited by Richard Marshall. By permission of Richard Howard.

Hughes, Langston. "Pictures More Than Pictures: The Work of Manuel Bravo and Cartier-Bresson," March 6, 1935. Copyright © 1993 Ramona Bass and Arnold Rampersad, Administrators cta Estate of Langston Hughes.

Reprinted by permission of Harold Ober Associates Inc. and the Yale Collection of American Literature, Beinecke Rare Book and Manuscript Library, Yale University.

Kerouac, Jack. "On the Road to Florida." Copyright © 1986 by Jack Kerouac. Reprinted by permission of Sterling Lord Literistic, Inc.

Kosinski, Jerzy. From *The Painted Bird* and *Blind Date* by Jerzy Kosinsky. Reprinted by permission of the Kosinsky Estate.

Krementz, Jill. © From "Jill Krementz" in *Something about the Author Autobiography Series* (New York: Gale Press, 1989), Volume 8, p. 173. Reprinted by permission of Jill Krementz.

Lowell, Amy. See Day, F. Holland.

Mann, Thomas. From *The Magic Mountain* by Thomas Mann, translated by H. T. Lowe-Porter. Copyright 1927 and renewed 1955 by Alfred A. Knopf, Inc. Copyright 1952 by Thomas Mann. Reprinted by permission of Alfred A. Knopf, Inc. and Martin Secker & Warburg Ltd.

Mayakovsky, Vladimir. From *It,* translated by Dorian Rottenberg in *Longer Poems: Selected Works in Three Volumes.* Reprinted by permission of Dorian Rottenberg.

Merton, Thomas. From his prose writings, 1964–68. Reprinted by permission of the Merton Legacy Trust.

Miller, Henry. From *Tropic of Cancer.* Reprinted by permission of Grove Press, Inc.

Mishima, Yukio. From preface to *Kill by Roses* by Eikoh Hosoe. Translated by John Bester. © 1971 Shueisha Inc., Tokyo. Reprinted by permission.

Moholy-Nagy, László. "James Joyce," from "Literature" in *Vision in Motion.* Reprinted by permission of Hattula Moholy-Nagy.

Morris, Wright. From "Photography in My Life" in *Photography & Words* (Carmel: Friends of Photography, 1982), pp. 17–54. Reprinted by permission of Wright Morris and by courtesy of the Friends of Photography.

Nabokov, Vladimir. "The Snapshot." Copyright © 1970 by Article 3C Trust under the will of Vladimir Nabokov. All rights reserved. By arrangement with the Estate of Vladimir Nabokov.

Nadar. From "Balzac and the Daguerreotype" from *My Life as a Photographer* (1900)," trans. Thomas Repensk, *October* 5 (Summer 1978). © By *October.* Reprinted by permission of The MIT Press, Cambridge, Massachusetts.

Nemerov, Howard. "To D—, Dead by Her Own Hand." Reprinted by permission of [the late] Howard Nemerov.

Neruda, Pablo. "Tina Modotti Is Dead," *Residence on Earth.* Copyright © 1973 by Pablo Neruda and Donald D. Walsh. Reprinted by permission of New Directions Publishing Corporation.

Nerval, Gérard de. Translations from *Voyage en Orient* (1851) in *Oeuvres*, volume 2, edited by Albert Béguin and Jean Richer (© Editions Gallimard 1956). By permission of the publisher.

Ondaatje, Michael. From *Coming Through Slaughter.* Copyright © 1976 by Michael Ondaatje. Published by Marian Boyars Publishers Ltd., London, 1976. Reprinted by permission of Marian Boyars Publishers Ltd., and W. W. Norton & Company, Inc.

Parks, Gordon. From *A Choice of Weapons* by Gordon Parks. Copyright © 1965, 1966 by Gordon Parks. Reprinted by permission of HarperCollins Publishers.

Paz, Octavio. "Facing Time" in *The Collected Poems of Octavio Paz, 1957–1987.* Copyright © 1975 by Octavio Paz and Eliot Weinberger. Reprinted by permission of New Directions Publishing Corporation.

Proust, Marcel. From *Remembrance of Things Past* by Marcel Proust. Copyright 1924, 1925, 1927, 1930, 1932 and renewed 1952, 1953, 1955, 1957, 1958, 1960 by Random House, Inc.

Ray, Man. From *Self Portrait* by Man Ray. Copyright © 1963 by Man Ray. By permission of Little, Brown and Company.

Rimbaud, Arthur. From *Oeuvres Complètes,* éd. Antoine Adam, Editions Gallimard, Bibliothèque De La Pléiade, 1972. By permission of the publisher.

Sandburg, Carl. From *Steichen the Photographer.* Reprinted by permission of Harcourt Brace Jovanovich.

Sartre, Jean-Paul. From preface to *D'une Chine à l'autre,* by Henri Cartier-Bresson. Delpire édition—Paris 1954. Reprinted by permission of the publisher.

Senelick, Laurence. Unpublished TS, "Early Photography in the Drama." Copyright L. P. Senelick.

Shaw, Bernard. "Evans—An Appreciation." Reprinted by permission of The Society of Authors on behalf of the Bernard Shaw Estate.

Srinivasan, Seetha. See Cole, Hunter.

Stein, Gertrude. "Stieglitz" in *America and Alfred Stieglitz: A Collective Portrait,* ed. Waldo Frank. Reprinted by permission of Doubleday, a division of Bantam, Doubleday, Dell Publishing Group, Inc.

Steinbeck, John. From *A Russian Journal* by John Steinbeck. Copyright 1948 by John Steinbeck, renewed © 1976 by Elaine Steinbeck, Thom Steinbeck, and John Steinbeck IV. Reprinted by permission of Viking Penguin, a division of Penguin Books USA Inc., and William Heinemann Ltd.

Stieglitz, Alfred. "*Camera Work* Introduces Gertrude Stein," *Twice A Year* 14–15 (1946–1947). Reprinted by permission of Dorothy Norman.

Strand, Paul. Letter to Sherwood Anderson, July 20, 1920. Copyright © Aperture Foundation, Inc., Paul Strand Archive. Reprinted by permission.

Strindberg, August. "Photography and Philosophy" from *Tales,* translated by L. J. Potts. Reprinted by permission of the publishers, Chatto and Windus.

Tournier, Michel. From *The Ogre* by Michel Tournier, translated by Barbara Bray. Translation copyright © 1972 by Doubleday, a division of Bantam Doubleday Dell Publishing Group, Inc. Reprinted by permission of Doubleday, a division of Bantam Doubleday Dell Publishing Group, Inc. and Collins, an imprint of HarperCollins Publishers Limited.

Updike, John. Unpublished TS, "All in the Family." © John Updike. Published by permission of the author.

Van Vechten, Carl. From *Letters of Carl Van Vechten,* edited by Bruce Kellner. Reprinted by permission of Joseph Solomon, Executor of the Estate of Carl Van Vechten. A.l.s. letter of Carl Van Vechten to Mr. Ross, August 21, 1934. Reprinted by permission of Joseph Solomon, Executor of the Estate of Carl Van Vechten and the Yale Collection of American Literature, Beinecke Rare Book and Manuscript Library, Yale University.

Villiers de l'Isle-Adam, Count Philippe-Auguste. From "Snapshots of World History" in *Tomorrow's Eve.* Translated by Ralph Martin Adams. Copyright 1982 by the Board of Trustees of the University of Illinois. Reprinted by permission of the University of Illinois Press.

Waugh, Evelyn. From *The Essays, Articles and Reviews of Evelyn Waugh* edited by Donat Gallagher. Copyright © 1983 by the Estate of Laura Waugh. Introductory material copyright. © 1983 by Donat Gallagher. Reprinted by permission of Little, Brown and Company and Sterling Lord Literistic, Inc.

Welty, Eudora. See Cole, Hunter.

Weston, Edward. "Lawrence in Mexico.." Supplement

to *The Carmelite* 3, no. 6 (March 19, 1930): ix–xi. © 1981 Center for Creative Photography, Arizona Board of Regents.

White, Minor. Unpublished report to Roy DeCarava, TS, November 11, 1955. Copyright © 1992 by The Trustees of Princeton University. All rights reserved. Published by permission of The Minor White Archive, Princeton University.

Williams, Jonathan. "Aaron Siskind at 75," *Aperture* 82 (1979): 7. Reprinted by permission of Jonathan Williams.

Williams, William Carlos. "Walker Evans: American Photographs" from *A Recognizable Image: William Carlos Williams on Art and Artists.* Copyright © 1978 by the Estate of Florence H. Williams. Reprinted by permission of New Directions Publishing Corp.

Wolfe, Tom. "Miss Aurora by Astral Projection" in Marie Cosindas, *Color Photographs* (Boston: New York Graphic Society, 1978), pp. 6–15. Copyright © 1978 by Tom Wolfe. Reprinted by permission of International Creative Management, Inc.

Woolf, Virginia. "Julia Margaret Cameron" in *Victorian Photographs of Famous Men and Fair Women* (Hogarth Press, 1926). Reprinted by permission of the Estate of Virginia Woolf and The Hogarth Press.

Wright, Richard. From *Black Power* (1954). Copyright © 1982 by The Estate of Richard Wright. Reprinted by permission of John Hawkins & Associates, Inc.

Adams, Ansel. 'Mary Austin, Santa Fe, New Mexico,' c. 1929. Proof print, 3 1/4 x 4 1/4 in. (8.0 x 10.5 cm). Courtesy of the Ansel Adams Publishing Rights Trust. © 1992 by The Trustees of the Ansel Adams Publishing Rights Trust. All Rights Reserved.

Adams, Ansel. 'Tony Lujan of Taos Pueblo, New Mexico,' 1930. 12 3/8 x 8 15/16 in. (31.4 x 22.7 cm). Courtesy of the Ansel Adams Publishing Rights Trust. © 1992 by The Trustees of the Ansel Adams Publishing Rights Trust. All Rights Reserved.

Adams, Henry. 'Self-Portrait,' 1900. 4 7/16 x 7 1/2 in. (11.7 x 9.0 cm). Courtesy of the Massachusetts Historical Society.

Adams, Marion Hooper. 'Henry Adams,' 1883. 4 7/16 x 7 3/4 in. (11.7 x 9.7 cm). Courtesy of the Massachusetts Historical Society.

Alvarez Bravo, Manuel. 'Two Pairs of Legs,' 1929. 9 7/16 x 7 1/2 in. (24.0 x 19.0 cm). Courtesy of the Israel Museum. © Manuel Alvarez Bravo.

Andreyev, Leonid. 'Anna Andreyeva in the Roman Campagna,' 1914. Autochrome, 9 1/4 x 8 in. (23.5 x 20.2 cm). Courtesy of Thames & Hudson, London. © Heirs of Vadim and Valentin Andreyev.

Auden, W. H. 'The Accordion playing,' 1936, from W. H. Auden and Louis MacNiece, *Letters from Iceland* (London: Faber & Faber, 1937), facing p. 97. 7 11/16 x 5 1/8 in. (19.5 x 13.0 cm).

Avedon, Richard. Truman Capote, New York City, 1958, from *Observations*, 1959. 8 5/8 x 6 5/8 in. (22.0 x 16.5 cm). Copyright © by Richard Avedon. All rights reserved.

Avedon, Richard. Truman Capote, New York City, 1974, from *Portraits*, 1976. 9 1/4 x 7 5/8 in. (23.5 x 19.4 cm). Copyright © by Richard Avedon. All rights reserved.

Baldessari, John. 'Baudelaire Meets Poe,' 1980. Two black-and-white photographs and one Type-C print; mounted on board. 114 x 114 in. (289.6 x 289.6 cm). Courtesy of the artist and the Sonnabend Gallery, New York.

Beaton, Cecil. 'Self-portrait in Studio,' 1951. 7 7/8 x 7 1/2 in. (20.0 x 19.0 cm). Courtesy of the Gernsheim Collection, Harry Ransom Humanities Research Center, The University of Texas at Austin. Reproduced by permission of Sotheby's London.

Bellocq, E. J. Plate 20 from *Storyville Portraits,* c. 1912, edited by John Szarkowski (New York: Museum of Modern Art, 1970). Printed by Lee Friedlander. 10 x 8 in. (25.4 x 20.3 cm). Collection Lee Friedlander.

Bisson, Louis-Auguste. 'Honoré de Balzac,' c. 1842. Daguerreotype, 5 3/4 x 4 3/4 in. (14.5 x 12.2 cm). Courtesy of the Maison de Balzac, Paris. © Musées de la Ville de Paris by SPADEM.

Boiffard, Jacques-André. 'La Statue d'Étienne Dolet, Place Maubert,' from *Nadja* by André Breton (Paris: Gallimard, 1928), facing p. 26. 4 1/4 x 3 in. (10.8 x 7.7 cm). Reproduced by permission of Madame Henriette Angel.

Bourke-White, Margaret. Margaret Bourke-White and Ernest Caldwell, 1936. 9 1/2 x 6 13/16 in. (24.2 x. 17.6 cm). Courtesy of the Margaret Bourke-White Papers, Special Collections Department, Syracuse University Library. Reproduced by permission of the Margaret Bourke-White Estate.

Bourke-White, Margaret. 'Sweetfern, Arkansas' (with caption), from *You Have Seen Their Faces,* 1936. Page: 11 3/4 x 8 1/8 in. (30.0 x 20.6 cm). Courtesy of the Margaret Bourke-White Papers, Special Collections Department, Syracuse University Library. Reproduced by permission of the Margaret Bourke-White Estate.

Brandt, Bill. 'Withens' (also known as 'Wuthering

Heights'), c. 1944. Gelatin silver print, Image: 9 1/8 x 7 3/4 in. (23.2 x 19.6 cm); Sheet: 9 15/16 x 7 3/4 in. (25.2 x 19.6 cm). The Collection of the J. Paul Getty Museum, Malibu, California [86. XM. 618. 8]. Courtesy Noya Brandt. By permission of the Estate of Bill Brandt.

Brassaï [Gyula Halász]. 'Self-portrait,' 1932, from *Henry Miller Grandeur Nature* (Paris: Gallimard, 1975), [Plate 16], facing p. 1. 5 7/8 x 4 3/4 in. (15.0 x 12 cm). © Gilbert Brassaï.

Butler, Samuel. 'The Wife of Bath, in the Cabin of the "Lord of the Isles,"' July 19, 1891. 3 3/8 x 4 5/16 in. (8.5 x 10.9 cm). Courtesy of the St. John's College Library. By permission of the Master and Fellows of St. John's College, Cambridge.

Cameron, Julia Margaret. 'A Beautiful Vision' [Julia Duckworth], 1872. Albumen print, 12 9/16 x 9 7/8 in. (32.6 x 25.1 cm). Courtesy of the Museum of Fine Arts, Boston. Gift of Mrs. J. D. Cameron Bradley.

Cameron, Julia Margaret. 'The Dirty Monk' [Alfred Tennyson], May 1865. Albumen Print, 10 1/16 x 8 1/4 in. (25.6 x 21 cm). Collection of the J. Paul Getty Museum, Malibu, California [84. XZ. 186.1].

Capa, Robert. 'Russian photographer,' USSR, 1947, from *A Russian Journal* by John Steinbeck, 1948. Page: 9 3/8 x 6 3/4 in. (23.8 x 17.2 cm); Photograph: 6 x 5 3/4 (15.3 x 14.7 cm.). Courtesy of Magnum Photos, Inc. © Robert Capa/Magnum Photos Inc.

Carjat, Etienne. Caricature of Pierre Petit. c. 1850's. Engraving, 7 5/8 x 5 1/2 in. (19.4 x 19.9 cm). Courtesy of the Bibliothèque Nationale, Paris.

Carroll, Lewis [Charles Dodgson]. "Alice in Wonderland," final MS page, no. 90, with drawing usually covered by the photograph but temporarily moved aside, c. 1864. Page size: 9 x 5 1/2 in. (23.1 x 13.9 cm). By permission of the British Library, London.

Carroll, Lewis [Charles Dodgson]. 'John Ruskin,' 1875. 6 3/8 x 4 1/2 in. (16.0 x 11.5 cm). By permission of the Houghton Library, Harvard University.

Cartier-Bresson, Henri. 'Langston Hughes,' n.d. 8 5/8 x 5 13/16 in. (22.0 x 14.7 cm). Courtesy of Magnum Photos, Inc. © Henri Cartier-Bresson/Magnum Photos Inc.

Cartier-Bresson, Henri. Children reading, Shanghai, 1949. 10 x 7 in. (26.2 x 17.7 cm). Courtesy of Magnum Photos, Inc. © Henri Cartier-Bresson/Magnum Photos Inc.

Chatwin, Bruce. 'Charley's House in Punta Arenas,' c. 1975. Printed from original negative by Michael Nedzweski. 9 1/2 x 7 3/4 in. (24.1 x 19.7 cm). Courtesy of

Elizabeth Chatwin. Reproduced by permission of Elizabeth Chatwin.

Clergue, Lucien. 'Manitas de Plata and José Reyes, Saintes-Maries-de-la-Mer,' 1955. Gelatin silver print, 10 5/8 x 10 3/16 in. (27.0 x 26.5 cm). Courtesy of the artist. Reproduced by permission of Lucien Clergue.

Coburn, Alvin Langdon. Caricature of photographer on letterhead of unpublished A.l.s. to John Sweeney, October 17, 1956. 1 3/4 in. x 2 1/4 in. (4.4 x 5.7 cm). By permission of the Houghton Library.

Coburn, Alvin Langdon. 'The Curiosity Shop,' 1907. Frontispiece to *The Golden Bowl*, vol. 23, *The Novels and Tales of Henry James* (New York: Scribner's, 1907–9, 1917, 1922). Photogravure, 5 3/16 x 3 7/16 in. (13.1 x 8.8 cm). Courtesy of Ralph Bogardus and the Department of Special Collections, Zimmerman Library, University of New Mexico.

Coburn, Alvin Langdon. 'Ezra Pound,' 1916. Vortograph, 9 1/4 x 7 1/16 in. (23.6 x 18.0 cm). Reproduced by permission of the International Museum of Photography at George Eastman House.

Coburn, Alvin Langdon. 'Faubourg St. Germain,' 1906. Frontispiece to *The American*, vol. 2, *The Novels and Tales of Henry James* (New York: Scribner's, 1907–9, 1917, 1922). Photogravure, 4 x 3 3/8 in. (10.1 x 8.5 cm). Courtesy of Ralph Bogardus and the Department of Special Collections, Zimmerman Library, University of New Mexico.

Coburn, Alvin Langdon. 'Gertrude Stein,' 1913. 9 1/4 x 7 3/8 in. (23.5 x 18.5 cm). Reproduced by permission of the International Museum of Photography at George Eastman House.

Coburn, Alvin Langdon. 'H. G. Wells,' c. 1905. 9 1/2 x 7 5/16 in. (24.2 x 18.4 cm). Reproduced by permission of the International Museum of Photography at George Eastman House.

Coburn, Alvin Langdon. 'Henry James,' 1906. Frontispiece to *Roderick Hudson*, vol. 1, *The Novels and Tales of Henry James* (New York: Scribner's, 1907–9, 1917, 1922). Photogravure, 5 1/2 x 3 3/4 in. (4.0 x 9.10 cm). Courtesy of Ralph Bogardus and the Department of Special Collections, Zimmerman Library, University of New Mexico.

Coburn, Alvin Langdon. 'Juliana's Court,' 1906. Frontispiece to *The Aspern Papers*, vol. 12, *The Novels and Tales of Henry James* (New York: Scribner's, 1907–9, 1917, 1922). Photogravure, 4 3/ 8 x 3 1/4 in. (10.9 x 8.2 cm). Courtesy of Ralph Bogardus and the Department of Special Collections, Zimmerman Library, University of New Mexico.

Coburn, Alvin Langdon. 'Mr. Longdon's' [James's Lamb House, Rye], 1906. Frontispiece to *The Awkward Age*, vol. 9, *The Novels and Tales of Henry James* (New York: Scribner's, 1907–9, 1917, 1922). Photogravure, 4 3/8 x 3 3/8 in. (11.0 x 8.6 cm). Courtesy of Ralph Bogardus and the Department of Special Collections, Zimmerman Library, University of New Mexico.

Coburn, Alvin Langdon. 'Portland Place,' 1907. Frontispiece to *The Golden Bowl*, vol. 24, *The Novels and Tales of Henry James* (New York: Scribner's, 1907–9, 1917, 1922). Photogravure, 3 7/16 x 4 3/8 in. (8.8 x 11 cm). Courtesy of Ralph Bogardus and the Department of Special Collections, Zimmerman Library, University of New Mexico.

Coburn, Alvin Langdon. 'Saltram's Seat,' 1907. Frontispiece to "The Coxon Fund," vol. 15, *The Novels and Tales of Henry James* (New York: Scribner's, 1907–9, 1917, 1922). Photogravure, 5 1/8 x 3 3/8 in. (13.0 x 8.6 cm). Courtesy of Ralph Bogardus and the Department of Special Collections, Zimmerman Library, University of New Mexico.

Coburn, Alvin Langdon, 'Vortograph, no. 3,' 1917. Vortograph, 9 1/4 x 7 in. (23.5 x 17.8 cm). Reproduced by permission of the International Museum of Photography at George Eastman House.

Coburn, Alvin Langdon, 'Vortograph, no. 8,' 1917. Vortograph, 9 1/8 x 7 1/8 (23.0 x 18.0 cm). Reproduced by permission of the International Museum of Photography at George Eastman House.

Cocteau, Jean. Illustrated letter to Lucien Clergue, May 30, 1959, from *Correspondances* by Jean Cocteau and Lucien Clergue (1989), [p. 88]. 3 1/2 x 2 3/4 in. (8.9 x 7.0 cm). © Actes Sud, 1989.

Cosindas, Marie. 'Tom Wolfe,' 1967. Reproduction from 35 mm. color transparency. Courtesy of the artist. © Marie Cosindas.

Cunningham, Imogen. 'Twins,' 1921. 5 3/4 x 7 1/4 in. (14. 6 x 18.5 cm). Unpublished print. Courtesy of The Imogen Cunningham Trust. © 1978, The Imogen Cunningham Trust.

Day, F. Holland. 'Beauty Is Truth,' c. 1897–99. Platinum print of composite photograph, 9 7/8 x 7 3/4 in. (25.1 x 19.7 cm). Private collection.

Day, F. Holland. 'Keats Corner' (in Day's Library, with Keats's death mask to left of column), c. 1894. 6 1/8 x 4 5/16 in. (15.3 x 11 cm). Private collection.

Dorfman, Elsa. 'Allen Ginsberg,' April 11, 1973 (caption added in 1992). Reproduced in *Elsa's Housebook* (Boston: Godine, 1974), p. 16. 7 3/4 x 7 7/8 in. (19.6 x 20.1 cm). Courtesy of the artist. © 1992 Elsa Dorfman.

Doyle, Arthur Conan. Rudyard Kipling's House in Vermont, "Naulakha," c. November 1894. 5 3/16 x 7 1/4 in. (13.2 x 18.4). Courtesy of the Lancelyn Green Collection.

Du Camp, Maxime (negative), and Louis-Desire Blanquart-Evrard (print). 'Maison et Jardin dans le quartier frank,' from *Egypt, Nubie, Palestine et Syrie* (Paris: Gide and J. Baudry, 1852), Plate III. Salt print, 8 3/8 x 5 3/4 in. (21.3 x 14.6 cm). Collection of the J. Paul Getty Museum, Malibu, California [84. X. 1303. 1. 3].

Evans, Frederick. 'George Bernard Shaw,' 1896. Gelatin silver print, 5 3/4 x 4 5/16 in. (14. 6 x 11.0 cm). Collection of the J. Paul Getty Museum, Malibu, California [84. XM. 444. 77].

Evans, Walker. 'Allie Mae Burroughs, Wife of a Sharecropper, Hale County, Alabama' (also known as 'Annie Mae Gudger'), Summer 1936. Gelatin silver print, Image: 9 17/32 x 7 9/16 in. (24.2 x 19.2 cm); Sheet: 9 25/32 x 7 31/16 in. (24.9 x 20.2 cm). Collection of the J. Paul Getty Museum, Malibu, California [84. XM. 956. 517].

Evans, Walker. 'The Bridge,' illustration for *The Bridge* by Hart Crane, 1930. Photogravure, 2 7/8 x 2 5/16 in. (7.3 x 5.9 cm). Collection of the J. Paul Getty Museum, Malibu, California [84. XB. 1143. 2]. © Estate of Walker Evans.

Evans, Walker. 'James Rufus Agee,' Long Island Beach, 1937. 8 5/8 x 6 3/4 in. (22.0 x 17.3 cm). Courtesy of the Fogg Art Museum, Harvard University, Cambridge, Massachusetts, National Endowment for the Arts Grant. © Estate of Walker Evans.

Evans, Walker. 'Maine Pump,' 1933. Gelatin silver print, 7 7/16 x 5 11/16 in. (18.9 x 14.5 cm). Collection of the J. Paul Getty Museum, Malibu, California [84. XM. 956. 440]. © Estate of Walker Evans.

Evans, Walker. 'Tin Relic,' 1930. Gelatin silver print, Image: 6 1/16 x 7 3/16 in. (15. 4 x 18.3 cm); mount: 11 x 8 1/2 in. (27.9 x 21.6 cm). Collection of the J. Paul Getty Museum, Malibu, California [84. XM. 956. 478]. © Estate of Walker Evans.

Frank, Robert. 'St. Petersburg, Florida,' 1955. Gelatin silver photograph, printed in 1977 by Sid Kaplan and Robert Frank, 8 1/2 x 13 in. (21.6 x 33.0 cm). Courtesy of The Museum of Fine Arts, Houston, museum purchase. © Robert Frank, courtesy Pace/MacGill Gallery, New York.

Freund, Gisèle. 'James Joyce, Sylvia Beach and Adrienne Monnier at Shakespeare and Company' (showing Joyce a portrait of himself taken in 1920), Paris, March 1939. © Gisele Freund/Photo Researchers, Inc.

Friedlander, Lee. 'Diane and Amy Arbus,' New York

City, 1963. 9 1/4 x 6 5/16 in. (23.5 x 16.0 cm). Courtesy of the artist. Collection Lee Friedlander.

Friedlander, Lee. 'Maria Friedlander, New City, New York,' 1976. 9 11/16 x 6 5/16 in. (24.7 x 16.1 cm). Courtesy of the artist. Collection Lee Friedlander.

Gervais, Eugène. 'Gérard de Nerval,' c. 1854. From the exhibition catalogue, *Gérard de Nerval* (Paris: Ville de Paris, Maison de Balzac, 1981), December 18, 1981– March 1, 1982, facing p. ix and described on p. 104. Engraving after daguerreotype by M. Legros (with annotations by Nerval), 6 1/8 x 5 in. (15.5 x 12.7 cm). Courtesy of the Bibliothèque Nationale, Paris. Private collection. Used by permission.

Gilbert, W. S. 'Comic Physiognomist' (Caricature of photographer, with caption "Thank You Very Much") in *Men We Meet* series, Fun 5, no. 105 (May 13, 1867): 105. 2 x 1 1/2 in. (5.0 x 3.7 cm). Courtesy of The Gilbert and Sullivan Collection, The Pierpont Morgan Library, New York.

Gilbert, W. S. House and Pond at Grym's Dyke, c. 1905. 4 5/8 x 6 1/4 in. (11.6 x 16.0 cm). Courtesy of The Gilbert and Sullivan Collection [700730], The Pierpont Morgan Library, New York.

Ginsberg, Allen. 'Jack Kerouac,' 1953 (with handwritten caption). From Allen Ginsberg, *Photographs* (1991). 11 x 7 5/16 in. (28.0 x 18.6 cm). © Allen Ginsberg.

Glob, P. V. 'The Tollund Man, who died 2000 years ago,' c. 1950. From *The Bog People: Iron-Age Man Preserved* by P. V. Glob (Ithaca: Cornell University Press, 1988), p. 19. 6 7/8 x 5 in. (17.5 x 12.7 cm). Reproduced by permission of Gyldendalsk Boghandel.

Gowin, Emmet. 'Edith, Danville, Virginia, 1983.' 6 5/8 x 6 9/16 in. (16.7 x 16.6 cm). Courtesy of Emmet Gowin and the Pace MacGill Gallery, New York.

Heartfield, John. 'The Meaning of Geneva—Where Capital Lives, There Can Be No Peace.' Cover of *AIZ* 2, no. 48 (November 27, 1932). Photomontage, printed as rotogravure, 15 1/8 x 11 in. (38.4 x 27.9 cm). Courtesy of The Metropolitan Museum of Art, Ford Motor Collection, Gift of Ford Motor Company and John C. Wardell, 1987 [1987. 1100. 470]. All rights reserved.

Heartfield, John. 'O Christmas Tree in Germany—How Crooked Are Your Branches!' Cover of *AIZ* 13, no. 52 (December 27, 1934). Photomontage, 10 1/4 x 7 7/8 in. (26.0 x 20.0 cm). Courtesy of The Metropolitan Museum of Art, Ford Motor Collection, Purchase, The Horace W. Goldsmith Foundation Gift, 1987 [1987. 1125. 37]. All rights reserved.

Hesler, Alexander. 'Minnehaha Falls,' Minnesota Territory, c. 1856. Salt print from an albumen negative, 9 x 5 11/16 in (22.7 x 14.5 cm). Courtesy of The Metropolitan Museum of Art.

Hobbs, John. 'Chamoni: La Mer de Glace,' c. 1849. Daguerreotype, 5 1/2 x 7 3/4 in. (14.0 x 19.5 cm). Courtesy of The Ruskin Galleries, Bembridge School, Isle of Wight, England.

Hollyer, Samuel. 'Walt Whitman,' 1854. Frontispiece in the first edition of *Leaves of Grass* (1855), based on a lost daguerreotype by Gilbert Harrison, 7 x 5 in. (17.9 x 12.7 cm). Courtesy of the Special Collections Library, Duke University.

Hope, William. 'Sir Arthur Conan Doyle, His Widow and Son, Denis,' May 1931. 3 5/8 x 2 3/4 in. (9.3 x 7.0 cm). Courtesy of the Lancelyn Green Collection.

Hosoe, Eikoh. #38 from *Barakei*, 1961. Palladium-platinum print, 10 3/16 x 7 1/16 in. (26.5 x. 18.0 cm). Courtesy of the artist and the Howard Greenberg Gallery, New York. © Eikoh Hosoe.

Hugo, Charles, and Auguste Vacquerie, 'Madame Adèle Hugo,' c. 1853. Salt print, 3 9/16 x 2 7/8 in. (9.0 x 7.3 cm), from GEH album [17526]. Reproduced by permission of the International Museum of Photography at George Eastman House.

Hugo, Charles, and Auguste Vacquerie. 'Mademoiselle Adèle Hugo,' c. 1853. Salt print, 3 5/8 x 2 13/16 in. (9.3 x 7.2 cm), from GEH album [17526]. Reproduced by permission of the International Museum of Photography at George Eastman House.

Hugo, Charles and Auguste Vacquerie. 'Victor Hugo,' c. 1853. Salt print, 2 1/8 x 1 9/16 in. (5.4 x 4.0 cm), from GEH album [17526, no. 17523]. Reproduced by permission of the International Museum of Photography at George Eastman House.

Kertész, André. 'Bibliothèque de l'Institut, Paris, 1929' (man reading on library ladder). 9 3/4 x 7 3/4 in. (24.7 x 18.8 cm). © Estate of André Kertész.

Kertész, André. 'New York City, April 28, 1969' (boy reading). 7 x 9 in. (15.8 x 24 cm). © Estate of André Kertész.

Kertész, André. 'Paris, December 9, 1963' (man reading amid piles of books). 6 1/4 x 9 1/2 in (15.8 x 24 cm). © Estate of André Kertész.

Kosinski, Jerzy. 'Stalin and Worker,' USSR, 1950. Gelatin silver print, 6 x 9 in. (15.2 x 23.0 cm). By permission of Katherina von Fraunhofer-Kosinski.

Kosinski, Jerzy. 'Worker and Stalin,' Warsaw, 1956. Gelatin silver print, 10 x 10 in. (15.4 x 15.4 cm). By permission of Katherina von Fraunhofer-Kosinski.

Knopf, Alfred A. 'Thomas Mann' (with a cigar), c. 1938. 8 1/2 x 7 1/2 in. (21.7 x 19 cm). Courtesy of the Harry Ransom Humanities Research Center, The University of Texas at Austin. © Alfred A. Knopf.

Krementz, Jill. 'Eudora Welty,' Jackson, Mississippi, 1972. From *The Writer's Image: Literary Portraits* (1980), npn. 4 3/4 x 6 7/8 in. (12.0 x 17.5 cm). Photograph © Jill Krementz.

Lange, Dorothea. 'Hands, Maynard and Dan Dixon,' c. 1930. 7 5/8 x 9 7/8 in. (19.5 x 25.0 cm). Courtesy of the Dorothea Lange Collection. © 1982, The City of Oakland, California, The Oakland Museum.

LeGros, M. 'Gérard de Nerval,' c. 1853–54. Daguerreotype from the exhibit catalogue *Gérard de Nerval* (Paris: Ville de Paris, Maison de Balzac, 1981), December 18, 1981–March 1, 1982), facing p. ix and described on p. 104. Daguerreotype, 4 1/4 x 3 1/2 in. (10.8 x 7.9 cm). Courtesy of the Bibliothèque Nationale, Paris. Private collection. Used by permission.

Levitt, Helen. Untitled (mother and child), New York City, c. 1942. 11 x 14 in. (17.9 x 35.5 cm). Courtesy of the artist. © Helen Levitt.

London, Jack. 'Captured Russian Cannon,' 1904. 3 1/2 x 5 1/2 in. (9 x 14 cm). Courtesy of the Jack London Collection, California State Park System.

Lyon, Danny. 'Gabe and Instruments,' November 1984. 8 1/4 in. x 4 3/4 at widest (21.0 x 12.0 cm). Courtesy of Magnum Photos, Inc. © Danny Lyon, distributed by Magnum Photos, Inc.

Mapplethorpe, Robert. 'Bruce Chatwin,' 1979. 7 9/16 x 7 9/16 in. (19.2 x 19.2 cm). Courtesy of the Mapplethorpe Foundation. © 1979, The Estate of Robert Mapplethorpe.

Mapplethorpe, Robert. 'Dennis Speight,' 1983. 8 7/8 x 7 in. (22.6 x 17.8 cm). Courtesy of the Mapplethorpe Foundation. © 1983, The Estate of Robert Mapplethorpe.

Mapplethorpe, Robert. 'Lisa Lyon with Bow and Arrow,' 1982. 7 9/16 x 7 1/2 in. (19.2 x 19.0 cm). Courtesy of the Mapplethorpe Foundation. © 1982, The Estate of Robert Mapplethorpe.

Mapplethorpe, Robert. 'Thomas,' 1986. 7 5/8 x 7 5/8 in. (19.2 x 19.3 cm). Courtesy of the Mapplethorpe Foundation. © 1986, The Estate of Robert Mapplethorpe.

McAvoy, Thomas. 'Dr. Raworth Williams's Blue Bug with seven other ponies,' from *Sports Illustrated* 15, no. 21 (November 12, 1961): 72. 3 1/2 x 5 13/16 in. (8.8 x 14.7 cm).

McBean, Angus. Scene from Act 3 of an unidentified production of *The Wild Duck*, by Henrik Ibsen, c. 1960's. Printed from glass negative by Michael Nedzweski. 4 7/16 x 6 3/16 in. (11.3 x 14.7 cm). By permission of the Harvard Theatre Collection, Harvard University.

McKenna, Rollie. Dylan Thomas directing rehearsal of his new play, "Under Milk Wood," May 10, 1953. 8 1/2 x 6 5/16 in. (21.5 x 16.0 cm). Courtesy of the artist. © Rollie McKenna.

Merton, Thomas. 'The Soul's Hook,' c. 1960's (called by Merton "the only known photograph of God") from *Thomas Merton* by James Forest (New York/Ramsey, N.J.: Paulist Press, 1980), p. 89. 3 1/4 x 2 3/8 in. (8.3 x 6.0 cm). By permission of the Merton Legacy Trust.

Merton, Thomas. 'Bangkok Harbor,' 1968. Printed by John Howard Griffin. 13 5/8 x 10 5/8 in. (34.5 x 27.0 cm). Courtesy of the Thomas Merton Study Center. By permission of the Merton Legacy Trust.

[Metcalf, Ralph Hedley.] Woman in bomb shelter, 1941. From *Kriegsfiebel* by Bertolt Brecht (1955), facing p. 42. Total Page: 11 1/2 x 9 7/8 in. (29.6 x 25.0 cm.). Picture: 7 x 8 in. (17.8 x 20.4 cm). © Suhrkamp Verlag, Frankfurt am Main. All rights reserved.

Michals, Duane. *Things Are Queer*, 1975. All the prints are 5 1/ 8 x 7 1/8 in. (13.0 x 18.0 cm). Courtesy of the artist. © Duane Michals.

Mobsby, W. (official photographer, Brisbane, Australia). News photograph of Arthur Conan Doyle, 1921. Reproduced in *The Wanderings of a Spiritualist* by Arthur Conan Doyle (1922), facing p. 252. 3 3/4 x 5 9/16 in. (7.0 x 12.8 cm).

Morath, Inge. 'Jean Cocteau,' 1968. 6 3/8 x 9 7/16 in. (16.2 x 24.0 cm). Courtesy of Magnum Photos, Inc. © Inge Morath/Magnum Photos, Inc.

Morehouse, Marion. 'Marianne Moore,' c. 1950's. 9 5/8 x 6 3/8 in. (24.5 x 16.1 cm). Courtesy of Maryette Charlton. All rights reserved.

Morris, Wright. 'Gano Grain Elevator, Western Kansas,' 1941. Gelatin silver print, 9 1/2 x 7 3/4 in. (24.1 x 19.7 cm). Collection of The Museum of Modern Museum. Purchase. © Wright Morris. [In *The Inhabitants* by Morris (1946), the page measures 11 x 9 in. (17.9 x 22.9 cm); the photograph measures 10 x 8 7/16 (25.4 x 21.4 cm). In *God's Country and My People* by Morris (1968), the page measures 11 1/2 x 9 1/4 in. (29.2 x 23.4 cm); the photograph measures 8 7/8 x 7 5/8 in. (22.5 x 19.4 cm).]

Nadar [Gaspard Félix Tournachon]. 'Charles Baudelaire,' c. 1855. Salt print, 9 7/16 x 6 11/16 in. (24.0 x 17 cm). Courtesy of the Musée D'Orsay, Paris.

Nadar [Gaspard Félix Tournachon]. 'George Sand,' 1861–69. Albumen print, Image: 9 1/2 x 7 7/32 in. (24.1 x 18.4 cm) and Mount: 12 x 8 7/16 in. (30.4 x 21.5 cm). Collection of the J. Paul Getty Museum, Malibu, California [84. XM. 436. 91]

Ondaatje, Michael. 'Final Match of the World Chess Championship,' 1990. 4 1/8 x 6 1/4 in. (10.4 x 15.5 cm). Courtesy of the artist. © Michael Ondaatje.

Paine, Albert Bigelow. 'The Development of a Moral Thought,' with handwritten captions by Mark Twain, 1906. Prints all roughly 6 1/2 x 4 1/2 in. (16.5 x 11.4 cm). Courtesy of the Lilly Library. By permission of the Lilly Library, Indiana University, Bloomington.

Parks, Gordon. 'American Gothic (Ella Watson and American Flag),' 1942. 9 5/8 x 7 in. (24.7 x 19 cm). Courtesy of the Library of Congress.

Parks, Gordon. 'Richard Wright,' c. 1942. Gelatin silver print, 9 1/2 x 7 1/8 in. (24.1 x 18.1 cm). Courtesy of the Library of Congress.

Petit, Pierre. 'Self-portrait,' 1850's (with caricature of Petit by Eugene Carjat in the background). 4 1/4 x 2 7/8 in. (10.5 x 7.5 cm). Courtesy of the Bibliothèque Nationale, Paris.

Porter, Eliot. 'Jonathan,' 1938. Gelatin silver print, 9 11/16 x 7 3/8 in. (24.6 x 18.8 cm). Courtesy of the Eliot Porter Archive, Amon Carter Museum, Fort Worth, Texas.

Ray, Man [Emmanuel Radnitsky]. 'Ernest Hemingway,' 1928. Gelatin silver print, 9 1/16 x 7 3/8 in. (24.2 x 18.7 cm). Courtesy of the John F. Kennedy Library. © 1992 Man Ray Trust-ARS, N.Y./ADAGP, Paris.

Ray, Man [Emmanuel Radnitsky]. 'Proust on his Death Bed,' November 1922. Gelatin silver print, 5 5/16 x 7 13/16 in. (15.l x 19.9 cm). Collection of the J. Paul Getty Museum, Malibu, California [84. XM. 1000. 144]. © 1992 Man Ray Trust-ARS, N.Y./ADAGP, Paris.

Ray, Man [Emmanuel Radnitsky]. 'Virginia Woolf,' 1935. Gelatin silver print, 5 3/8 x 8 in. (20 1/4 x 13 1/2 cm). Courtesy of the Harvard Theatre Collection, Harvard University. © 1992 Man Ray Trust-ARS, N.Y./ADAGP, Paris.

Ray, Man [Emmanuel Radnitsky]. 'William Carlos Williams,' c. 1924–26. Gelatin silver print, 11 3/16 x 8 15/16 in. (28.4 x 22.7 cm). Courtesy of the National Portrait Gallery, Smithsonian Institution. © 1992 Man Ray Trust-ARS, N.Y./ADAGP, Paris.

Rimbaud, Arthur. 'Self-portrait,' Harar, May 1883. 7 x 5 in. (17. 8 x 12.7 cm). Courtesy of the Musée Rimbaud. Reproduced by permission of the Musée Rimbaud, Charleville-Mézières.

Robinson, Henry Peach. 'Bringing Home the May,' 1862. Modern print from nine negatives, 15 1/4 x 39 3/8 in. (38.8 x 100 cm). Courtesy of the Gernsheim Collection, Harry Ransom Humanities Research Center, The University of Texas at Austin.

Robinson, Henry Peach. 'Fading Away.' Alternate Version, 1858. (The verses were printed on the mat of the first—nearly identical—version). Albumen print from five negatives, 9 3/8 x 14 7/8 in. (23.8 x 37.9 cm). Reproduced by permission of the International Museum of Photography at George Eastman House, Rochester, New York.

Robinson, Henry Peach. 'Lady of Shalott,' 1861. (The verses were printed on the mat on the original exhibition print.) Toned albumen print from two negatives, 12 1/2 x 16 5/6 in. (31.8 x. 42.1 cm). Courtesy of the Gernsheim Collection, Harry Ransom Humanities Research Center, The University of Texas at Austin.

Robinson, Henry Peach. 'Sleep,' 1865. Toned albumen print from four negatives, 15 x 21 3/4 in. (38.1 x 55.2 cm). Courtesy of the Gernsheim Collection, Harry Ransom Humanities Research Center, The University of Texas at Austin.

Robinson, Henry Peach, and Nelson King Cherrill. 'Watching the Lark, Borrowdale,' 1868. Albumen print from two negatives, 9 5/6 x 8 1/4 in (24.4 x 20.1 cm). Courtesy of the Gernsheim Collection, Harry Ransom Humanities Research Center, The University of Texas at Austin.

Rodchenko, Alexander. 'Lili and the Zoo Animals,' from *Pro Eto* by Vladimir Mayakovsky (1923). Photomontage on page: 8 11/16 x 5 5/16 in. (22.3 x 13.5 cm). By permission of the Houghton Library, Harvard University.

Sarony, Napoleon. 'Mark Twain' (the "Gorilla" photograph), 1883. 4 13/16 x 4 in. (12.2 x 10.1 cm). Courtesy, The Mark Twain Project, The Bancroft Library, University of California, Berkeley.

Shaw, George Bernard. 'Frederick Evans,' 1901. 9 1/2 x 7 5/8 in. (24 x 19.5 cm). Courtesy of The Royal Photographic Society, Bath.

Siskind, Aaron. 'F102,' 1957. Cover photograph for *The Magpie's Bagpipe,* by Jonathan Williams (1982). 9 x 6 in.

(22.9 x 15.3 cm). By permission of Jonathan Williams and the Estate of Aaron Siskind.

Steichen, Edward. 'Alfred Stieglitz,' 1907 (carrying copy of *Camera Work*). Autochrome, 9 x 6 1/8 in. (22.9 x 15.7 cm). Courtesy of The Metropolitan Museum of Art, The Alfred Stieglitz Collection, 1955. [55. 635. 10].

Steichen, Edward. 'Balzac, Towards the Light, Midnight,' 1908, #58. Gray-green gelatin carbon, 14 3/8 x 19 in. (36.5 x 48.2 cm). Courtesy of The Metropolitan Museum of Art, The Alfred Stieglitz Collection, 1933 [33. 43. 38].

Steichen, Edward. 'Carl Sandburg,' 1936. Montage, gelatin silver print, 13 11/16 x 16 7/8 in (32.3 x 42.7 cm). Collection, The Museum of Modern Art, New York. Gift of the photographer.

Stieglitz, Alfred. 'Apple and Rain Drops,' 1922. Gelatin silver photograph, 4 5/16 x 3 1/2 in. (11 x. 8.9 cm.). Courtesy of the Alfred Stieglitz Collection. © 1992 National Gallery of Art, Washington, D.C.

Stieglitz, Alfred. 'City Across the River,' 1910. Gelatin silver photograph, 4 3/8 x 3 5/8 in. (11.2 x 9.2 cm). Courtesy of The Alfred Stieglitz Collection. © 1992 National Gallery of Art, Washington, D.C.

Stieglitz, Alfred. 'The Hand of Man,' 1902. Photogravure, 1910. 9 1/2 x 12 1/2 in. (24.2 x 31.8 cm.). Courtesy of The Alfred Stieglitz Collection. © 1992 National Gallery of Art, Washington, D.C.

Stieglitz, Alfred. 'Savoy Hotel,' New York, 1898. Platinum photograph tinted with yellow pigment, 5/8 x 4 5/8 in. (9.3 x 11.8 cm). Courtesy of The Alfred Stieglitz Collection. © 1992 National Gallery of Art, Washington, D.C.

Stieglitz, Alfred. 'Sherwood Anderson,' 1923. Palladium photograph, 9 5/8 x 7 5/8 in. (24.4 x 19.3 cm). Courtesy of The Alfred Stieglitz Collection. © 1992 National Gallery of Art, Washington, D.C.

Stieglitz, Alfred. 'Winter, Fifth Avenue,' 1893. Photogravure, 1897, 11 3/16 x 8 3/4 in. (28.4 x 22.2 cm). Courtesy of The Alfred Stieglitz Collection. © 1992 National Gallery of Art, Washington, D.C.

Stockmann, [Wilhemine?] and N[iklaus]. 'Alexandre Dumas,' c. 1865. Carte de Visite, 3 1/2 x 2 1/2 in (8.9 x 6.3 cm). Courtesy of the Österreichisches TheaterMuseum, Vienna.

Strindberg, August. 'Self-portrait,' Gersau, 1886 (with handwritten caption). 6 x 4 1/4 in. (15.1 x 10.9). Courtesy of the Strindbergmuseet. Reproduced by permission of the Strindbergsmuseet, Stockholm.

Synge, J. M. 'Spinning' [1898]. 8 x 11 in. (20.2 x 28 cm). Courtesy of the Trinity College Library, Dublin. By permission of The Board of Trinity College Dublin and the J. M. Synge Trustees.

Talbot, William Henry Fox. 'A Scene in a Library,' from *The Pencil of Nature*, Part 2, Plate 8 (January 1845). Salt print, 5 1/4 x 7 in. (13.5 x 17.5 cm). Courtesy of the Fox Talbot Museum, Lacock.

Talbot, William Henry Fox. 'Sir Walter Scott's Monument,' from *Sun Pictures of Scotland*, October 1844. Salt print, 7 9/16 x 6 5/32 in. (19.2 x 15.7 cm). Collection of the J. Paul Getty Museum, Malibu, California [84. XZ. 573. 2].

Tolstoy, Sophia. 'Leo Tolstoy at his desk,' c. 1907. 9 1/2 x 6 7/8 in. (24 x 17.5 cm). Courtesy of Pierre Apraxine. By permission of the L. A. Tolstoy Museum, Moscow.

Tournier, Michel. 'Autoportrait,' 1992. Color print, 3 1/16 x 3/16 in (9.0 x 13.2 cm.). Courtesy of the artist.

Unknown. Caricature of a photographer. From *King Leopold's Soliloquy* by Mark Twain (1906), p. 37. Figure c. 2 1/2 x 1 1/2 in. (6.3 x 3.8 cm). Courtesy, The Mark Twain Project, The Bancroft Library, University of California, Berkeley.

Unknown. 'Edgar Allan Poe,' late October 1848. Daguerreotype, 4 13/16 x 3 1/2 in. (12.2 x 8.9 cm.). Collection of the J. Paul Getty Museum, Malibu, California [84. XT. 957].

Unknown. Floating helmets, c. 1944–45. From *Kriegsfiebel*, by Bertolt Brecht (1955), facing p. 57. Total page: 11 1/2 x 9 7/8 in. (29.6 x 25.0 cm). Picture: 7 3/4 x 6 1/4 in. (19.7 x 16.0 cm). © Suhrkamp Verlag, Frankfurt am Main. All rights reserved.

Unknown. Hitler speaking, c. 1934. From *Kriegsfiebel*, by Bertolt Brecht (1955), facing p. 69. Total page: 11 1/2 x 9 7/8 in. (29.6 x 25.0 cm). Picture: 9 1/2 x 8 3/16 in. (24.2 x 20. 8 cm.). © Suhrkamp Verlag, Frankfurt am Main. All rights reserved.

Unknown. Jewish mother and baby, 1940. From Brecht, *Kriegsfiebel*, by Bertolt Brecht (1955), facing p. 48. Total page: 11 1/2 x 9 7/8 in. (29.6 x 25.0 cm); picture: 8 5/16 x 9 7/8 in. (21.2 x. 25.0 cm). © Suhrkamp Verlag, Frankfurt am Main. All rights reserved.

Unknown. 'Lili Brik at the Zoo,' 1922, from *Love Is the Heart of Everything: Correspondence between Vladimir*

Mayakovsky and Lili Brik, 1915–1930, edited by Bengst Jangfeldt and translated by Julian Graffy (Edinburgh: Polygon, 1986), insert following p. 150, Fig. 15. 4 x 3 1/4 in. (10.2 x 8 cm).

Unknown. News photograph of Tina Modotti's bier, 1942 (with Edward Weston's 1921 portrait mounted on it). 4 15/16 x 3 1/4 in. (12.5 x 8 cm). Courtesy of Mildred Constantine, author of *Tina Modotti: A Fragile Life,* published by Rizzoli International Publications, Inc., 1983. Used by permission.

Unknown. 'Ralph Waldo Emerson,' May 1846. Daguerreotype, total size: 3 x 4 1/8 in. (7.0 x 10.3 cm). By permission of the Ralph Waldo Emerson Memorial Association and the Houghton Library, Harvard University.

Unknown. 'Samuel Langhorne Clemens with a compositor's stick,' 1850. Daguerreotype, total size, (4 5/8 x 3 3/16 in. (11.8 x 8.1 cm). Courtesy, The Mark Twain Project, The Bancroft Library, University of California, Berkeley.

Unknown. 'Thomas Carlyle,' April 1846. Daguerreotype, total size: 4 3/8 x 3 1/2 in. (11.5 x 8.7 cm). By permission of the Ralph Waldo Emerson Memorial Association and the Houghton Library, Harvard University.

Unknown. 'Una and Julian Hawthorne,' c. 1850. Daguerreotype, Total size: 5 5/16 x 4 7/16 in. (13.7 x 11.4 cm). By permission of the Boston Athenaeum.

Unknown. 'Walt Whitman,' c. 1846–48. Daguerreotype, sight size: 4 7/8 x 3 1/2 in. (12.4 x 8.9 cm); total size: 6 1/2 x 4 1/2 in. (16.5 x 11.5 cm). Courtesy of the Walt Whitman House N. J. D. E. P. E./Division of Parks and Forestry.

Van Vechten, Carl. 'F. Scott Fitzgerald,' 1937. 9 5/8 x 6 3/16 in. (24.4 x 15.7 cm). Courtesy of the Beinecke Rare Book and Manuscript Library, Yale University. By permission of the Estate of Carl Van Vechten, Joseph Solomon, Executor.

Van Vechten, Carl. Gertrude Stein, Carl Van Vechten, and Alice B. Toklas, January 4, 1935. 6 1/4 x 9 5/8 in.

(15.9 x 24.4 cm). Courtesy of the Beinecke Rare Book and Manuscript Library, Yale University. By permission of the Estate of Carl Van Vechten, Joseph Solomon, Executor.

Van Vechten, Carl. 'William Faulkner,' 1954. 9 5/8 x 6 1/8 in. (24.4 x 15.6 cm). Courtesy of the Beinecke Rare Book and Manuscript Library, Yale University. By permission of the Estate of Carl Van Vechten, Joseph Solomon, Executor.

Verga, Giovanni. 'Dina,' c. 1902. From Giovanni Garra Agosto, *Verga/Fotografo* (Giuseppe Maimone Editore, 1991), p. 107 [cat. no. 179]. 6 5/16 x 7 1/2 in. (16.0 x 9.1 cm). By permission of the publishers.

Waugh, Evelyn. 'Self-portrait,' 1933. Frontispiece to Waugh, *Ninety-Two Days* (1934). 5 1/2 x 4 in. (13.8 x 10.1 cm).

Welty, Eudora. 'Bowen's Court, County Cork, Ireland, 1950s.' 4 13/16 x 4 9/16 in. (12.2 x 11.5 cm). Courtesy of the Eudora Welty Collection, Mississippi Department of Archives and History.

Weston, Edward. 'D. H. Lawrence,' 1924. Gelatin silver print, 9 1/2 x 7 7/16 in. (24.1 x 18.9 cm). Courtesy of the Center for Creative Photography. © 1981 Center for Creative Photography, Arizona Board of Regents.

Weston, Edward. 'Tina Modotti,' 1921. 10 x 8 in. (25.5 x 24 cm.). Courtesy of Mildred Constantine, author of *Tina Modotti: A Fragile Life,* published by Rizzoli International Publications, 1983. © 1981 Center for Creative Photography, Arizona Board of Regents.

Wright, Richard. "Proverbs for Every Hour," photograph with text, c. 1953. Unpublished. 8 x 10 in. (20.3 x 25.3 cm). Courtesy of the James Weldon Johnson Memorial Collection, the Beinecke Library. By permission of the Beinecke Rare Book and Manuscript Library, Yale University.

Zola, Émile. 'Parc Monceau, bust of Guy de Maupassant,' c. 1900. Modern print by Jean Adhémer, 2 1/4 x 3 5/16 in. (5.8 cm x 8.4 cm.). Courtesy of the University Art Museum, University of New Mexico, Albuquerque. Gift of Jean Adhémar.

164. Alvin Langdon Coburn. Unpublished caricature
of a photographer, 1956.